Steve. 357 - 5711

455 - 8317

MANAGEMENT CONTROL SYSTEMS

MANAGEMENT CONTROL SYSTEMS

Robert N. Anthony
Ross Graham Walker Professor of Management Control, Emeritus
Graduate School of Business Administration
Harvard University

Vijay Govindarajan
Earl C. Daum 1924 Professor of International Business
The Amos Tuck School of Business Administration
Dartmouth College

NINTH EDITION 1998

Boston, Massachusetts   Burr Ridge, Illinois   Dubuque, Iowa
Madison, Wisconsin   New York, New York   San Francisco, California   St. Louis, Missouri

Irwin/McGraw-Hill

A Division of The **McGraw·Hill** Companies

MANAGEMENT CONTROL SYSTEMS

Copyright © 1998 by The McGraw-Hill Companies, Inc. All rights reserved. Previous editions © 1965, 1972, 1976, 1980, 1984, 1989, 1992, and 1995 by Richard D. Irwin, a Times Mirror Higher Education Group, Inc. company. Printed in the United States of America. Except as permitted under the United States Copyright Act of 1976, no part of this publication may be reproduced or distributed in any form or by any means, or stored in a data base or retrieval system, without the prior written permission of the publisher. The copyright on each case unless otherwise noted is held by the President and Fellows of Harvard College, and they are published herein by express permission. Permission requests to use individual Harvard copyrighted cases should be directed to the Permissions editor, Harvard Business School Publishing, Boston, MA 02163.

Case material of the Harvard Graduate School of Business Administration is made possible by the cooperation of business firms and other organizations which may wish to remain anonymous by having names, quantities, and other identifying details disguised while maintaining basic relationships. Cases are prepared as the basis for class discussion rather than to illustrate either effective or ineffective handling of an administrative situation.

This book is printed on acid-free paper.

2 3 4 5 6 7 8 9 0 DOC/DOC 9 0 9 8   (US edition)

2 3 4 5 6 7 8 9 0 DOC/DOC 9 0 9 8   (International edition)

ISBN 0-256-16878-4

Editorial director: *Michael W. Junior*
Publisher: *Jeffrey J. Shelstad*
Associate editor: *George Werthman*
Editorial assistant: *Martin Quinn*
Marketing manager: *Heather L. Woods*
Project manager: *Alisa Watson*
Production supervisor: *Heather D. Burbridge*
Designer: *Larry J. Cope*
Compositor: *GAC Shepard Poorman*
Typeface: *10/12 Century Schoolbook*
Printer: *R. R. Donnelley & Sons Company*

Library of Congress Cataloging-in-Publication Data

Anthony, Robert Newton (date)
    Management control systems / Robert N. Anthony, Vijay
Govindarajan. — 9th ed.
      p.   cm.
    Includes index.
    ISBN 0-256-16878-4
    1. Industrial management. 2. Industrial management—Case studies.
3. Cost control. I. Govindarajan, Vijay. II. Title. III. Series.
HD31.A589 1998
658.15—dc21   97–21861

INTERNATIONAL EDITION
Copyright © 1998. Exclusive rights by The McGraw-Hill Companies, Inc. for manufacture and export. This book cannot be re-exported from the country to which it is consigned by McGraw-Hill. The International Edition is not available in North America.

When ordering this title use ISBN 0-07-115187-7

http://www.mhcollege.com

About the Authors

Robert N. Anthony is the Ross Graham Walker Professor Emeritus of Management Control at Harvard Business School. Harvard has been his home base, except between 1940 and 1946 when he was in the Navy Supply Corps, and between 1965 and 1968 when he was Assistant Secretary of Defense, Controller.

Professor Anthony is the author or coauthor of 27 books; they have been translated into 14 languages. He has been an Irwin author since 1956 and consulting editor of Irwin's Robert N. Anthony/Willard J. Graham series in Accounting. His *Essentials of Accounting* (Addison-Wesley), now in its sixth edition, is a widely used programmed text.

Professor Anthony has been a director of Carborundum Company and Warnaco, Inc., both Fortune 500 companies, and for 25 years has been a trustee of Colby College, including five years as chairman of the board. He has been a consultant to many companies and government agencies, including General Motors Corporation, American Telephone & Telegraph Company, the General Accounting Office, and the Cost Accounting Standards Board. He has also participated in short educational programs in North America, South America, Europe, Australia, and Asia.

Among Professor Anthony's awards are honorary MA and LHD degrees from Colby College,

election to the Accounting Hall of Fame, the Distinguished Accounting Educator Award from the American Accounting Association, the Accounting Educator of the Year Award from Beta Alpha Psi, the Meritorious Service Award from the Executive Office of the President, the Distinguished Public Service Medal of the

Department of Defense, Comptroller General's Award of the U.S. General Accounting Office, and Distinguished Service Award of the Harvard Business School Association.

Most recently, Professor Anthony has won the Institute of Management Accountants' prestigious R. Lee Brummet award. This award is given to recognize outstanding educators in the field of Management Accounting who have had a significant impact on academia and the business world.

Vijay Govindarajan is the Earl C. Daum 1924 Professor of International Business at the Amos Tuck School of Business Administration at Dartmouth College. Prior to joining the faculty at Tuck, he was on the faculties of The Ohio State University, Harvard Business School, and the Indian Institute of Management (Ahmedabad, India). He has also served as a visiting professor at INSEAD (Fontainebleau, France), the International University of Japan (Urasa, Japan), and Helsinki School of Economics (Helsinki, Finland). Professional credits include Outstanding Teacher of the Year, voted by MBA students during several academic years; Outstanding Faculty, named by *Business Week* in its Guide to Best B-Schools; and a Top Ten Business School Professor in Corporate Executive Education, cited by *Business Week*.

Professor Govindarajan's major teaching and research interests are in the areas of global strategy and organization, strategy implementation, management controls, and strategic cost management. His paper on differentiated controls for differentiated strategies was ranked the number-one-cited journal article in the field of strategic management between 1980 and 1985 in a 1986 survey by Professor Donald Hambrick (Columbia University). Current research examines coordination and control mechanisms within multinational organizations; a paper based on this project received the Glueck Best Research Paper Award from the Academy of Management.

More than 40 articles by Professor Govindarajan have appeared in journals such as *Academy of Management Journal; Academy of Management Review; The Accounting Review; Ac-*

counting Horizons; Accounting, Organizations and Society; Decision Sciences; Issues in Accounting Education; Journal of Cost Management; Journal of Management Accounting Research; Management Accounting; and *Sloan Management Review*. He has published, with Professor John K. Shank, *Strategic Cost Management* (The Free Press, 1993). This book won the Notable Contribution to Management Accounting Literature Award from the Management Accounting Section of the American Accounting Association.

Professor Govindarajan has served as consultant to various organizations, including Abbott Laboratories, AT&T, Champion International, Digital Equipment Corp., Eastman Kodak, B.F. Goodrich, GTE, IBM, Hewlett Packard, Motorola, Price Waterhouse, and Weyerhaeuser.

Professor Govindarajan received his MBA with distinction from the Harvard Business School where he was included in the Dean's Honor List. He also received his doctorate from the Harvard Business School and was awarded the Robert Bowne Prize for the best thesis proposal. Prior to this, Professor Govindarajan received his Chartered Accountancy degree in India. He was awarded the President's Gold Medal for his outstanding performance in obtaining the first rank.

Foreword

The first edition of this book was published 30 years ago. The publisher has asked me to comment on the changes that have been made in this period.

The first edition, written with my colleagues John Dearden and Dick Vancil, consisted of short readings, rather than coherent text material. It had 42 cases, compared with 80 in the eighth edition.

Nevertheless, our approach to the subject was similar to the approach we use now. We focus on management control systems, which are systems intended to help implement strategies. Management control is the middle one of three types of planning and control processes. It is bounded on one side by strategy formulation, which is essentially unsystematic, and on the other side by task control, which can be highly structured. The focus is on management, and the criteria for judging management actions are efficiency and effectiveness. This was the first text with such a focus.

The first edition described what are still the most important ideas: responsibility accounting, expense centers, profit centers, investment centers, transfer pricing, key variables, discretionary expenses, and budgets. We had some material on behavioral considerations, but nowhere near the emphasis that we now give to this subject. We had scarcely anything about differences in management control systems associated with different types of companies (e.g., focus on product differentiation contrasted with a focus on low costs; single business, related businesses, and conglomerates; multinational companies; service companies; financial institutions; nonprofit organizations; governments). Banks and other financial institutions have made tremendous progress in their management control systems in the last 30 years; so have hospitals. By contrast, governments, especially the federal government, have a long way to go. We did not even mention executive compensation as a motivating device, nor the management control of projects. We did not discuss goal congruence as such. In recent editions there is much material on these important topics.

The most important change in substance has been the emphasis on what we now call *strategic planning*, which is chronologically the first step in the management control process. In the first edition, there was a short reading and one case on this topic, reflecting the fact that few companies had formal strategic planning systems.

ix

Beginning in the 1970s, more companies began to use this process, then called *programming* or *long-range planning*. The first attempts were generally unsuccessful. Cases in editions published in the 1970s and early 1980s described these efforts; in general they involved too much paperwork and not enough rigorous thinking about the future. Currently, the process is working well in many companies.

The next most important changes were associated with the development of computers. In the first edition, we had two cases in which the issue was whether the company should acquire a computer. The facts in one of these are interesting: the proposed UNIVAC equipment required 1,400 square feet of space, including air conditioning of 60 tons and 75 KVA of current (compared with 3 square feet, no air conditioning and trivial power requirements for today's desk-top computers); 23 instructions (compared with an unlimited number in desk-top computers today); storage of 1.8 million characters (compared with 120 million); and memory of 10 thousand characters (compared with 1 million or more). The price of the UNIVAC was $488,000 (compared with about $2,000 for an excellent desk-top system). Our first edition had two readings that warned against going overboard on computers: "Can Management Information be Automated?" and "Seven Deadly Dangers in EDP."

We did not foresee the implications of the electronic interchange of information within a company and among companies. Magnetic character recognition was used for checks, a tiny forerunner of the widespread use of bar codes. We did not even imagine that prices of security transactions originating in stock exchanges throughout the world would be available to users everywhere in decision-assisting form in a matter of seconds, and that in some cases they would automatically trigger buy or sell decisions. There were no computer-controlled machines.

We expanded the material on information processing in several succeeding editions, but we now say very little about this topic. We simply assume that all companies have computers.

New, useful techniques and ideas have been developed: satisfactory profits, computer models for companies and specific problems, expert systems, net present value, risk/reward trade-offs, benefit/cost analysis, learning curves, decision trees, sensitivity analysis, linear programming, even nonlinear programming.

But we also described several techniques that at one time were hot topics but that now have disappeared. Human resource accounting—treating employees as assets in the accounts—was much talked about in the 1970s, but was rarely practiced and is now scarcely even mentioned. Many books have been written about zero-based budgeting, a technique now generally believed to be impractical. Similarly for PERT cost and statistically significant analysis of variances.

We also use new terms found in the literature and in practice for old ideas: business units for certain types of profit centers; activity-based costing for job-order costing; cost drivers for bases of allocation; total quality management and value-chain analysis for any organized effort to improve operations; "empowerment" for delegating authority.

There have been two other coauthors. Norton Bedford made significant contributions to concepts. Vijay Govindarajan brings a deep understanding of the relationship between strategy formulation and management control, based on his own practical experience and outstanding research.

Inferences

Many educators and critics of education maintain that the knowledge that students learn in a business school will be obsolete within a few years. The above review suggests that such a conclusion is overly pessimistic. The management control framework that students learned decades ago is still generally valid today. "Life-long learning" is important, but it consists of fitting detailed improvements into the overall framework, which is a lot easier than learning a subject from scratch. Admittedly, a new framework will be developed some day; we developed ours in the 1950s. Faculty must be aware of this possibility, and adopt it if it comes, but until then they need not worry that the framework they now teach will shortly be irrelevant.

Thus, two implications for the future emerge from this review. First, technology will lead to improvements in the effectiveness and efficiency of the management control function in ways not now foreseen. But, second, although the ideas will be articulated more clearly, the framework is unlikely to change; it is grounded on human nature.

Robert N. Anthony
January 1995

Preface

This book provides concepts, text, and cases for a course in management control systems. It is designed to allow students to gain knowledge, insights, and analytical skills related to how a firm's managers go about designing, implementing, and using planning and control systems to implement a firm's strategies. It does not deal extensively with topics such as cost accounting and budgeting procedures, which are discussed in separate accounting courses. The book gives roughly equal emphasis to (1) the techniques of the management control process (e.g., transfer pricing, budget preparation, management compensation), and (2) the behavioral considerations involved in the use of these techniques (e.g., motivation, goal congruence, relative roles of superiors and subordinates).

The book is organized into three main parts. Chapter 1 introduces the overall conceptual framework for the book. Part One (Chapters 2 to 7) describes the environment in which management control takes place (responsibility centers). Part Two (Chapters 8 to 12) describes the sequential steps in the typical management control process (strategic planning, budget preparation, operations, analysis of operations). Part Three (Chapters 13 to 18) describes variations in management control systems (controls for differentiated strategies, service organizations, multinational organizations, and project control).

Changes to Text Material

While retaining the strengths of the eighth edition, we have made a number of changes in both text and case material that we hope will increase their usefulness. In undertaking this revision, we surveyed users of the eighth edition. This revision has benefited from their constructive comments and suggestions.

Several improvements have been made to assist student learning. These include: expanded chapter introductions, more diagrams and exhibits, real-world examples, consistent terminology, expanded chapter summaries, and an up-to-date reference list in each chapter. In particular, we have made the following changes to the text:

(a) We have re-organized the chapters so that Chapter 2 now discusses the strategy formulation process which provides the context for the design of management control systems that is the subject matter of the book;

(b) In Chapter 7, we have re-labeled "residual income" as "economic value added" to be consistent with current practice;

(c) Chapter 11 is new to this edition. In the first part of this chapter, we discuss the *balanced scorecard*, which blends financial information with nonfinancial information, as an aid in strategy implementation. In the second part, we discuss *interactive control*—the use of a subset of management control information in developing new strategies.

We are confident that you will find the text material in this ninth edition well organized, concisely written, laden with current examples, and consistent with the current theory and practice of management control.

Changes in Cases

A key strength of this book is the collection of cases that emphasize actual practice. The cases come from Harvard Business School, The Tuck School at Dartmouth, and from a number of other schools, both in the United States and abroad. The cases not only require the student to analyze situations, but they also give a feel for what actually happens in companies, a feeling that cannot be conveyed adequately in the text. In this sense, the cases can be viewed as extended examples of practice.

The cases are not necessarily intended to illustrate either correct or incorrect handling of management problems. As in most cases of this type, there are no right answers. The educational value of the cases comes from the practice the student receives in analyzing management control problems and in discussing and defending his or her analysis before the class.

We have retained those cases that users have found most helpful in accomplishing the objective of their course. Of the 68 cases in this edition, 47 are retained from the eighth edition. We have 21 (30 percent) new cases in this edition.

The following cases are new to the ninth edition (viz., they were not in the eighth edition):

Case 2–1 T&J's (a re-write of South American Coffee Company)

Case 2–3 DairyPak

Case 3–2 National Tractor and Equipment

Case 4–4 Grand Jean Company

Case 5–1 Profit Center Problems

Case 7–2 Investment Center Problems (B)

Case 7–4 Industrial Products Corporation (an update of Diversified Products Corporation)

Case 8–3 Allied Stationery Products, adapted from Allied Stationery Products (A), (B), and (C)

Case 9–2 Pasy Company (a re-write of Empire Glass Company)

Case 9–3 Boston Creamery (a re-write of Midwest Ice Cream Company)

Case 10–2 Solartronics

Case 11–1 Analog Devices

Case 11–2 Warren Insurance Company

Case 11–3 General Electric Company (B)

Case 12–3 Anita's Apparel

Case 12–4 Wayside Inns, Inc.

Case 12–5 Mary Kay Cosmetics

Case 13–2 Nucor Corporation

Case 13–4 Texas Instruments

Case 13–5 3M Corporation

Case 15–1 Cookie, Inc. (a re-write of Harley Associates, Inc.)

We are confident that instructors will find that this case collection does an excellent job of meeting classroom needs for several reasons:

• Many cases are based on major corporations such as General Electric, Champion International, Xerox, ITT, Skandia, 3M, Texas Instruments,

Hewlett-Packard, General Motors, Johnson & Johnson, Nestlé, Motorola, Mary Kay Cosmetics, Lincoln Electric, Nucor, Citibank, Chemical Bank, Richardson-Merrill, Nordstrom, and Emerson Electric.

- The collection offers a rich diversity of domestic, foreign, and international companies.
- The cases expose students to varied contexts: small organizations, large organizations, manufacturing organizations, service organizations, and nonprofit organizations.
- The collection presents contemporary, interesting situations that students will recognize, enjoy, and learn from.
- We have given significant attention to case length. A major effort has been made to ensure that a majority of the cases are short. We still include a few medium to long cases, "two-day" cases, and "two-part" cases.
- The case collection is flexible in terms of course sequencing, and the cases are comfortably teachable.

We have now included the following cases and their teaching notes in the *Instructor's Manual*. (These cases were part of the eighth edition of the book but are no longer part of the ninth edition of the book.)

Cummins Engine Company
International Telephone and Telegraph
PC&D
American Can Company
Quaker Oats Company
Disctech
Binswanger & Steele
Pullen Lumber Company
Corning Glass Works
Lex Services PLC (A)

Lex Services PLC (B)
Metropolitan Museum of Art
Bulova Watch Company
Eli Lilly and Company
VDW, AG
Siemens Electric Motor Works
Star Industrial Contractors

The above noted cases, included in the *Instructors Manual*, provide additional flexibility for instructors in course sequencing and selecting cases for examinations.

Target Audience

This book is intended for any of the following uses:

- A one-semester or one-quarter course for *graduate* students who have had a course in management accounting and who wish to study management control in greater depth.
- A one-semester or one-quarter course for *undergraduate* juniors or seniors who have already had one or two courses in management accounting.
- *Executive development* programs.
- A *handbook* for general managers, management consultants, computer-based systems designers, and controllers—those who are involved in or are affected by the management control process.

Acknowledgments

We have benefited from the help of many people in the evolution of this book over nine editions. Students, adopters, colleagues, and reviewers have generously supplied an untold number of insightful comments, helpful suggestions, and contributions that have progressively enhanced this book.

The course from which the material in this book was drawn was originally developed at the Harvard Business School by the late Ross G.

Walker. We wish to acknowledge his pioneering work in the development of both the concepts underlying the course and the methods of teaching these concepts. We thank the following members and former members of the Harvard Business School faculty who have contributed much to the development of this book: Francis J. Aguilar, Robert H. Caplan, Charles J. Christenson, Robin Cooper, Russell H. Hassler, Regina E. Herzlinger, Julie H. Hertenstein, Robert A. Howell, Gerard G. Johnson, Robert S. Kaplan, Warren F. McFarlan, Kenneth Merchant, Krishna G. Palepu, John K. Shank, Robert Simons, Richard F. Vancil, and John R. Yeager.

In addition, we wish to acknowledge the assistance provided by Robert H. Deming, James S. Hekiman, John Maureil, Chei-Min Paik, and Jack L. Treynor. We also wish to thank the users who responded to our survey.

Specific comments on the Eighth Edition were provided by Jay Barnes, Boston; Tarakorn Chairatsamekul, Thailand; William Manders, the Netherlands; T.C.V. Narasimha Rao, India; and G. Sethu, India. Many thanks to these users of the book.

Joseph Fisher, Indiana University, contributed the material on agency theory included in Chapter 12. Anant K. Sundaram, The Amos Tuck School of Business Administration, Dartmouth College, contributed the material on exchange rates and performance evaluation included in Chapter 17. Our sincere thanks to Joe Fisher and Anant Sundaram for their fine contributions.

We especially thank Kirk Hendrickson (Tuck 1997) who worked as a research associate on this project. He made significant contributions to all aspects of this book.

Many thanks are due to Sarah Jack who both skillfully edited the text as well as prepared the indexes to the book.

The selection of cases is always vital to a successful management control systems course. In this context our sincere appreciation goes to the supervisors and authors who are responsible for case development. Each has been recognized in the citations to the cases. We are particularly indebted to the companies whose cooperation made the cases possible.

Permission requests to use Harvard copyrighted cases should be directed to the Permissions Manager, Harvard Business School Publishing Division, Boston, MA 02163. Requests to reproduce cases copyrighted by Osceola Institute should be directed to Professor Vijay Govindarajan.

The organization and development of the vast amounts of material necessary to complete this project was no small task. A special note of thanks to Ms. Susan Schwarz, secretary to Professor Govindarajan, who professionally managed thousands of pages of original text and revisions with secretarial and computer skills that were invaluable. We also thank Jeff Shelstead, Alisa Watson, and Marty Quinn at our publisher, McGraw-Hill Higher Education for their help and commitment to our project.

In writing this text, we hope that you will share our enthusiasm both for the rich subject of management control and for the learning approach that we have taken. As always we value your recommendations and thoughts about the book. Your comments regarding coverage and content will be most welcome, as will your calling our attention to specific errors. Please contact: Vijay Govindarajan, Earl C. Daum 1924 Professor of International Business, The Amos Tuck School of Business Administration, Dartmouth College, Hanover, NH 03755; Phone (603) 646-2156; Fax (603) 646-1308; E-mail VG@dartmouth.edu.

April, 1997   **Robert N. Anthony**
Hanover, NH   **Vijay Govindarajan**

Table of Contents

xvii

PART II

The Management Control Process

PART III

Variations in Management Control

1

THE NATURE OF MANAGEMENT CONTROL SYSTEMS

The first section of this introductory chapter describes the meaning of three words in the title of the book: control, management, and systems. The second section distinguishes the management control function, which is our focus, from two other planning and control functions: strategy formulation and task control. The third section contains a road map, providing an overview of the text as well as a brief description of the contents of each chapter.

Basic Concepts

Control

Press the brake pedal, and an automobile slows or stops. Press the accelerator, and the automobile goes faster. Rotate the steering wheel, and the automobile changes its direction. The driver, using these devices, *controls* the speed and direction of the vehicle. If any of these devices were inoperative, the automobile would not do what the driver wanted it to do; that is, it would be out of control. An organization must also be controlled; that is, devices that ensure that it goes where its leaders want it to go must be operative. Control in an organization, however, is much more complicated than the control of an automobile. We shall lead into a discussion of control in organizations by describing the control process in simpler situations.

Examples of a Control System. Any control system has at least four elements:

1. A *detector* or *sensor*, which is a measuring device that identifies what is actually happening in the process being controlled.
2. An *assessor*, which is a device for determining the significance of what is happening. Usually, significance is assessed by comparing the information on what is *actually happening* with some standard or expectation of what *should be happening*.

Exhibit 1–1

*Elements of the
control process*

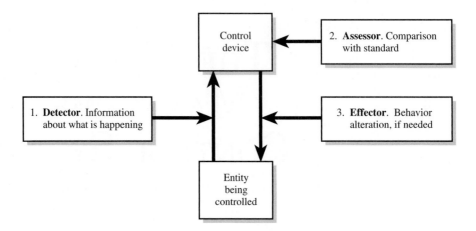

3. An *effector*, which is a device that alters behavior if the assessor indicates the need for doing so. This device is often called "feedback."
4. A *communications network*, which transmits information between the detector and the assessor and between the assessor and the effector.

These basic elements of a control system are diagrammed in Exhibit 1–1. We shall illustrate these with three examples: the thermostat, the regulation of body temperature, and the automobile driver.[1]

Thermostat.   The thermostat is a device for controlling the temperature of a room. Its elements are: (1) a detector, which is a thermometer that measures the current temperature of the room; (2) an assessor, which compares the current temperature with a preset standard of what the temperature should be; (3) an effector, which causes a furnace or other heating device to send heat to the room if the actual temperature is lower than the standard (or which causes an air conditioner to turn on if the temperature is higher than standard), and which causes these appliances to turn off when the temperature reaches the standard level; and (4) a communications network, which transmits information from the thermometer to the assessor and from the assessor to the heating or cooling device.

---

[1]These examples of control systems are arranged in order of increasing complexity. System theorists point out that the universe consists of a hierarchy of systems, in which each higher-level system is more complicated than systems at lower levels. One list of such a hierarchy is: atoms, molecules, crystals, viruses, cells, organs, organisms (e.g., human beings), groups (e.g., teams), organizations, societies, and supranational organizations. See James G. Miller, "Living Systems: Basic Concepts," *Behavior* 10, no. 4 (1965), pp. 192–236. For additional information on systems theory, see Norbert Wiener, *Cybernetics: Or Control and Communication in the Animal and Machine* (New York: John Wiley & Sons, 1948); W. Ross Ashby, *Design for a Brain*, 2nd ed. (New York: John Wiley & Sons, 1960); Michael C. Jackson, *Systems Methodology for the Management Sciences* (Plenum Publishing, 1991).

Body Temperature.   Most mammals are born with a built-in standard of desirable body temperature. In humans, it is 98.6°F. The control of body temperature is achieved as follows: (1) detectors are sensory nerves that are scattered throughout the body; (2) the assessor is the hypothalamus center in the brain, which compares information received from the detectors with the standard of 98.6°F; (3) effectors are muscles and organs for reducing the temperature if it is higher than the standard (panting, sweating, opening of skin pores), or of increasing the temperature if it is below the standard (closing skin pores, shivering); and (4) the communication system of nerves. This control process is called *homeostasis*, which means self-regulating. If the system is functioning properly, it automatically corrects for deviations from the desired state without conscious effort by the human being.

Two important differences make understanding the body temperature control system more difficult than understanding the thermostat. First, the body temperature system is more complicated: sensors are scattered throughout the body, and the actions directed by the hypothalamus involve a variety of muscles and organs. Second, although we know *what* the hypothalamus does, scientists don't really understand *how* this is done.

Automobile Driver.   Assume an automobile driver is on a highway where the speed limit is 65 mph. The driver's control system acts as follows: (1) actual speed is detected by the eye that observes the speedometer (or perhaps the sense of speed is detected by a general perception of movement); (2) the brain assesses this speed in comparison with the driver's desired speed; (3) if the brain judges the speed is too fast, it directs the foot to ease up on the accelerator; and (4) as in the case of body temperature, the detected speed and the action are conveyed by nerves.

This control system has an additional complication over the body temperature system: we cannot state with confidence what, if any, action the brain will direct if the actual speed exceeds 65 mph. Some people obey the speed limit and will ease up on the accelerator; others obey the speed limit at certain times, but not at other times. In this system, control is not automatic; we must know something about the personality of the driver to predict the actual speed of the automobile.

Management

An organization consists of a group of people who work together. The organization has *goals*—that is, it wants to accomplish certain results.[2] In a business organization, earning a satisfactory profit usually is an important goal. The leaders of the organization are its management. There is a hierarchy of managers, with the chief executive officer (CEO) at the top, and business unit, departmental, section

---

[2]Literally, the organization is inanimate and therefore cannot have goals. The goals are the goals of the leader or leaders of the organization.

and other managers below the CEO. Depending on the size and complexity of the organization, there may be several layers in the hierarchy. Except for the chief executive officer, each manager is both a superior and a subordinate. Each supervises people in his or her own organizational unit and is a subordinate of the manager to whom he or she reports. These relationships usually are shown on the organizational chart.

The chief executive officer (or, in some organizations, a team of senior managers) decides on *strategies* that are expected to attain the organization's goals. If the company is organized into business units, business unit managers formulate strategies for their units, subject to the approval of the CEO. The management control process is the process that managers use to assure that the members of the organization implement these strategies.

Contrast with Simpler Control Processes. The control process that managers use has the same elements as those in the control systems described above: detectors, assessors, effectors, and a communications system. Detectors report what is actually happening throughout the organization; assessors compare this information with the desired state, which is the implementation of strategies; effectors take corrective action if there is a significant difference between the actual state and the desired state; and there is a communications system that tells members of the organization what is actually happening and how it compares to the desired state. There are, however, significant differences between the management control process and the processes described in the earlier examples. The more important of these are as follows:

1. Unlike the thermostat or body temperature systems, *the standard is not preset*. Rather, it is a result of a conscious planning process. In this process, management decides what the organization should be doing, and part of the control process is a comparison of actual accomplishments with these plans. Thus, the control process in an organization involves planning. In many situations, planning and control can be viewed as two separate activities. Management control, however, involves both planning and control.

2. Like control of an automobile, but unlike the thermostat and body temperature systems, *management control is not automatic*. Some of the detectors (i.e., instruments for detecting what is happening in the organization) are mechanical, but important information is often detected through the manager's own eyes, ears, and other senses. Although there are routine ways of comparing certain reports of what is actually happening against some standard of what should be happening, managers themselves must judge whether the difference between actual and standard performance is significant enough to warrant action, and, if it is, what action to take. Actions taken to alter the organization's behavior involve human beings; in order to effect change, a manager must interact with another person.

3. Unlike the automobile that involves a single individual (or in some cases the driver and a kibitzer), *management control requires coordination among*

individuals. An organization consists of many separate parts, and management control must ensure that the work of these parts is in harmony with one another. This need does not exist at all in the case of the thermostat, and it exists only to a limited extent in the case of the various organs that control body temperature.

4. *The connection between the observed need for action and the behavior that is required to obtain the desired action is by no means clear-cut.* In the assessor function, a manager may decide that "costs are too high"; but there is no easy or automatic action, or series of actions, that is guaranteed to bring costs down to what the standard says they should be. The term *black box* is used to describe an operation whose exact nature cannot be observed. A management control system is a black box. We cannot know what action a given manager will take when a significant difference between actual and expected performance is assessed, nor what (if any) action others will take in response to the manager's signal. A thermostat is not a black box; we know exactly when it will signal that an action should be taken and what that action will be. In the automobile driver example, the assessor phase also involves judgment, but the effector phase is mechanical.

5. Control in an organization does not come about solely, or even primarily, as a consequence of actions that are taken by an external regulating device like the thermostat. *Much control is self-control;* that is, people act in the way they do, not necessarily because they are given specific instructions by their superior but, rather, because their own judgment tells them what action is appropriate. Automobile drivers who obey the 65 mph speed limit do so, not because the sign commands them to do so, but, rather, because they have consciously decided that it is in their best interest to obey the law.

Systems

A system is a prescribed way of carrying out an activity or set of activities; usually the activities are repeated. The thermostat and the body temperature systems described above are examples. A software program that controls the thousands or millions of steps that the computer takes in carrying out an operation is another example; the computer does precisely what the software instructs it to do. Most systems are less precise than computer programs: their instructions do not cover all eventualities, and the user of the system must make judgments when any of the unforeseen eventualities occur. Nevertheless, a system is characterized by a more or less rhythmic, recurring, coordinated series of steps that are intended to accomplish a specified purpose.

Many management actions are unsystematic. A manager regularly encounters situations for which the rules of the system are not well defined; the manager then uses his or her best judgment in acting. Many interactions between managers or between a manager and a subordinate are of this type. The appropriate response is determined by the manager's skill in dealing with people, not by a rule specified by the system (although the system may suggest the general nature of the appropriate response). *If all systems provided the correct action for all situations, there would be no need for human managers.* This is almost the case with an automated factory; managers are needed only in the event of a system failure.

In this book, we focus primarily on the systematic, i.e., formal, aspects of the management control function. We can describe in considerable depth the nature of the various steps in the system, the information that is collected and used in each step, and the principles that govern the operation of the system; but we cannot, except in general terms, describe appropriate behaviors for the unsystematic aspects of management control. These depend on the skills and personalities of the people involved, their relationships with one another, the environment existing when a particular problem arises, and many other factors. Thus, this book deals primarily with the *formal* part of the management control process. However, it is important to recognize that the way formal control systems are designed affects the informal processes that go on in the organization.

Boundaries of Management Control

Management control is one of several types of planning and control activities that occur in an organization. In this section, we define management control and two other types of planning and control: strategy formulation and task control. Our purpose is to draw boundaries that distinguish management control from the other types. Serious mistakes can be made if principles and generalizations that are applicable to one activity are used in another type for which they are not applicable.

As will be seen, management control fits between strategy formulation and task control in several respects. Strategy formulation is the least systematic of the three, task control is the most systematic, and management control is in between. Strategy formulation focuses on the long run, task control focuses on short-run operating activities, and management control is in between. Strategy formulation uses rough approximations of the future, task control uses current accurate data, and management control is in between. Each activity involves both planning and control; but the emphasis varies with the type of activity. The planning process is much more important in strategy formulation, the control process is much more important in task control, and planning and control are of approximately equal importance in management control.

The relationships of these activities to one another are indicated in Exhibit 1–2. In the following sections we define and describe each of these functions, and compare and contrast them with one another.

Management Control

Management control is the process by which managers influence other members of the organization to implement the organization's strategies.

Several aspects of this definition are amplified below.

Exhibit 1–2

*General
relationships
among planning
and control
functions*

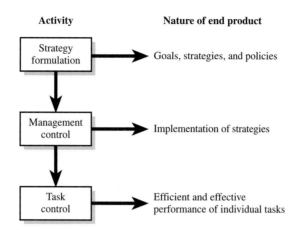

Management Control Activities.   Management control involves a variety of activities. These include: (1) *planning* what the organization should do, (2) *coordinating* the activities of several parts of the organization, (3) *communicating* information, (4) *evaluating* information, (5) *deciding* what, if any, action should be taken, and (6) *influencing* people to change their behavior.

Management control does not necessarily mean that actions should correspond to a plan, such as a budget. The stated plans were based on circumstances that, at the time when they were formulated, were believed to exist, both inside and outside the organization. If the circumstances are now believed to be different from those assumed in the plan, the planned actions may no longer be appropriate. A thermostat responds to the actual temperature in a room. Management control, by contrast, should anticipate what conditions are going to be in the future.

The purpose of management control is to ensure that strategies are carried out so that the organization's objectives are attained. If a manager discovers a better way of operating—one that is more likely to achieve the organization's goals than the actions stated in the plan—then the management control system should not prohibit him or her from operating in that fashion. (In certain circumstances the manager may be required to obtain approval for such a departure.) *Conforming to a budget is not necessarily good, and departure from a budget is not necessarily bad.*

Behavioral Considerations.   Although systematic, the management control process is by no means mechanical. The process involves interactions among individuals; there is no mechanical way of describing these interactions.

Managers have personal goals, and the central control problem is to induce them to act so that when they seek their personal goals, they help to attain the organization's goals. This is called *goal congruence*, which means that the goals of individual members of an organization should be, as far as feasible, consistent with the goals of the organization itself. For reasons that will be explained

8

EXHIBIT 1–3

Framework for strategy implementation

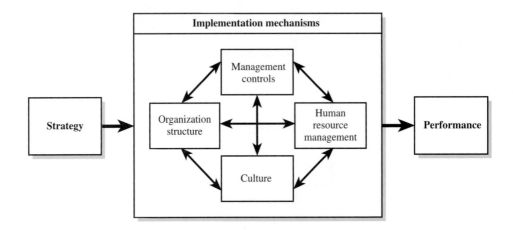

in Chapter 3, perfect goal congruence cannot be achieved. Nevertheless, the system should go as far in this direction as is feasible. The development of optimum compensation plans and other incentives are an important consideration in promoting goal congruence.

Tool for Implementing Strategy.   Management control systems aid management in moving an organization toward its strategic objectives. Thus, *management control focuses primarily on strategy execution.*

Management controls are only one of the tools managers use in implementing desired strategies. As indicated in Exhibit 1–3, strategies get implemented through management controls, organization structure, human resource management, and culture.

Organization structure specifies the roles, reporting relationships, and responsibilities that shape decision making within organizations. Human resource management deals with selection, training, development, evaluation, promotion, and firing of employees. Human resource decisions should be consistent with the chosen strategy and structure so that the required knowledge and skills are developed. Culture refers to the organization's set of common beliefs, attitudes, and norms that explicitly or implicitly guide managerial actions.

In Chapter 3 we describe organization structure, human resource management, and culture as they relate to strategy execution.

Financial and Nonfinancial Emphasis.   *Management control systems encompass both financial and nonfinancial performance measures.* The financial dimension focuses on the monetary "bottom line," which is net income, return on equity, or some similar financial figure. Virtually all organizational subunits also have nonfinancial objectives: product quality, market share, customer satisfaction, on-time delivery, employee morale, and so on.

In Chapter 11 we discuss the *balanced scorecard* as a way of incorporating financial and nonfinancial measures in management control.

Exhibit 1–4

Interactive control

Aid in Developing New Strategies.   As discussed earlier, the primary role of management controls is to help in the execution of chosen strategies. In industries that are subject to very rapid environmental changes, management control information can also provide the basis for thinking about new strategies. This is illustrated in Exhibit 1–4. Simons refers to this as *interactive control*.[3] Interactive control calls to management's attention developments— either troubles (e.g., loss of market share; customer complaints) or opportunities (e.g., opening up of a new market because of removal of certain government regulations)—that become the basis for managers to adapt to a rapidly changing environment by thinking about new strategies. Interactive controls are not a *separate* system, they are an integral part of the management control system. Some management control information helps managers think about new strategies. Interactive control information usually, but not exclusively, tends to be nonfinancial.

We describe interactive control in Chapter 11.

Strategy Formulation

Strategy formulation is the process of deciding on the goals of the organization and the strategies for attaining these goals.[4]

Goals are *timeless*; they exist until they are changed, and they are changed only rarely. In many businesses earning a satisfactory profit (or more specifically, a satisfactory return on investment) is an important goal; in others attaining a large market share is a goal. Nonprofit organizations also have goals; providing the maximum amount of service with the available funding is one such goal. In some organizations the goals are put into writing; but in many they are no more than a general understanding among personnel. In the strategy formulation process, the goals of the organization are

---

[3]Robert Simons, "Control in an Age of Empowerment," *Harvard Business Review*, March– April 1995, pp. 80–88.

[4]In this book we use the word *goals* for the broad overall aims of the organization, and *objectives* for the more specific statements of planned accomplishments in one year or other specified time period. Some people use these two words interchangeably, and others reverse the meanings given above. The words *target* and *aim* are also used as synonyms for either word. If these differences in intended meaning are not made clear, the consequence is confusion.

usually taken as a given; but, occasionally, strategic thinking focuses on the goals themselves.

An organization may select any of innumerable ways to attain its goals. If, for example, the goal is profitability, an organization selects one or more industries, geographical territories, product lines, and niches within product lines. It may decide whether to produce and market the product lines, or to focus on marketing goods produced by other manufacturers; it decides the relative emphasis between advertising and sales promotion in marketing; the emphasis to be given to research and development and the areas on which those efforts are to focus, and on and on. The strategies followed in various organizations differ from one another in many ways.

Strategies are big plans, important plans. They state in a general way the direction in which senior management wants the organization to be heading. A decision by an automobile manufacturer to produce and sell an electric automobile is a strategic decision.

At any given time, an organization operates according to the set of strategies that it has previously adopted. The strategy formulation process involves reexamining some of these strategies, perhaps changing them, or perhaps adopting new strategies. Rarely, if ever, does this examination involve all the organization's strategies. The task of doing so would be much too complicated. Thus, although we call the process *strategy formulation*, it is often more accurately described as *strategy revision*.

The need for reconsidering strategies arises either in response to a perceived threat or to take advantage of a perceived opportunity. Examples of threats are market inroads by competitors, a shift in consumer tastes, or new government regulations. Examples of opportunities are technological innovations, new perceptions of customer behavior, or development of new applications for existing products. A new chief executive officer usually has somewhat different perceptions of both threats and opportunities than his or her predecessor and, for this reason, changes in strategies often occur when a new chief executive officer takes over.[5]

Ideas to address threats or opportunities may originate from anywhere within the organization and at any time. A widely held impression is that ideas originate entirely within the research and development team or within the headquarters staff; although many ideas do come from these departments, they are by no means the exclusive sources. Anyone can have a "bright idea" that, after analysis and discussion, becomes a new strategy. Because there is no way of knowing who will come up with such an idea, complete responsibility for strategy formulation should not be assigned to a particular person or organiza-

---

[5]Examples of companies where changes in the Chief Executive Officers brought about significant shifts in the firm's strategy include General Electric (under Jack Welch), IBM (under Louis V. Gerstner), Asea Brown Boveri (under Percy Barnevik), and American Telephone & Telegraph Company (under Robert Allen).

tional unit. Also, it is important that there be a means of calling worthwhile ideas to the attention of senior management without those ideas being blocked by lower-level organizations.

Distinctions between Strategy Formulation and Management Control.
Strategy formulation is the process of deciding on new strategies; management control is the process of deciding how to implement strategies. From the standpoint of systems design, the most important distinction between strategy formulation and management control is that strategy formulation is essentially unsystematic. Whenever a threat is perceived or when a new idea surfaces, strategy formulation takes place. Since threats or opportunities are not discovered systematically or at regular intervals, strategic decisions are unsystematic (i.e., they can arise at any time).

The nature of analyzing a proposed strategy varies with the type of strategy. Strategic analysis involves much judgment, and the numbers used in the analysis are usually rough estimates. By contrast, the management control process takes place according to a more-or-less fixed timetable, and a series of steps that occur one after the other. Consulting firms have developed what they call "systems" for analyzing an organization's strategies; but these systems are used when the firm happens to be called in, and they are applied to the situation as it exists at that time; they are not systems in the sense of a recurring set of steps followed one after the other every year, or at some other regular interval.

Analysis of a proposed strategy usually involves relatively few people—the sponsor of the idea, headquarters staff, and senior management, possibly assisted by a consultant. (In exceptional cases a serious crisis may lead to a strategy that has repercussions throughout the organization and more people would be involved.) By contrast, the management control process involves managers and their staffs at all levels in the organization.

As mentioned above, strategy formulation almost always involves only part of the organization; it may result in a change in one or a few existing strategies, but many other strategies are unaffected by it. The management control process necessarily involves the whole organization; an important aspect of the process is ensuring that the various parts are coordinated with one another.

Task Control

Task control is the process of assuring that specified tasks are carried out effectively and efficiently.

Task control is *transaction-oriented*—that is, it involves the control of individual tasks. Rules to be followed in carrying out these tasks are prescribed as part of the management control process; unless unforeseen circumstances occur, control of many types of tasks consists of seeing to it that operating activities are carried out according to these rules. Indeed, for some tasks, control can be achieved without the presence of human beings. Numerically controlled machine tools, process control computers, and robots are task control devices. Human beings are used in these tasks only if they are less expensive or more reliable than computers or other control devices. Human beings are likely to be less expensive if the occurrence of unusual events is such that programming a computer with rules for dealing with these events is not worthwhile.

Some types of tasks, in particular tasks performed by professionals—engineers, researchers, lawyers, physicians, and teachers—are not routine; they are not carried out by following a set of rules. Nevertheless, they are repetitive, and there are general guidelines that are useful in performing the tasks.

Many task control activities are *scientific* in that the relationship between cause and effect, the action required to bring an out-of-control condition back to the desired state, or the optimum decision, are known within acceptable limits. Rules for economic order quantity determine the amount and timing of purchase orders. The techniques developed in management science and operations research focus principally on task control. The analogy of the thermostat is valid for task control.

Most of the information in an organization is task control information: the number of items ordered by customers, the pounds of material and units of components used in the manufacture of products, the number of hours employees work, and the amount of cash disbursed.

Systems exist for various types of tasks. There are procurement systems, scheduling systems, order-entry systems, logistics systems, quality control systems, cash management systems, and many others. Task control systems can be extremely complicated.

> **Example.** An entire steel mill may be controlled by electronic devices. Each piece of equipment is controlled by a computer that instructs the equipment to carry out prescribed tasks. The computer senses the environment (e.g., it finds out the temperature of a steel ingot). If the environment is not at the desired state, the computer initiates action to bring it to this state. If the variation cannot be corrected by that computer, the need for corrective action is referred to a computer that controls all the computers in one section of the mill. If necessary, this computer refers the problem to a coordinating computer for the mill as a whole.[6]

The Manufacturing Resource Planning (MRP II) system that is used to control manufacturing operations in many companies requires millions of lines of computer instructions. The switching gear mechanisms used to connect two parties in a telephone conversation cost billions of dollars. Systems for program trading and other types of decisions made by traders in the financial markets involve complicated decision rules and minute-by-minute information about the prices of hundreds of financial instruments.

---

[6]For this and other striking examples, see F. Warren McFarlan and William J. Bruns, Jr., "Information Technology Puts Power in Control Systems," *Harvard Business Review*, September–October 1987, pp. 89–94.

EXHIBIT 1–5 **Examples of Decisions in Planning and Control Functions**

Strategy Formulation	*Management Control*	*Task Control*
Acquire an unrelated business	Introduce new product or brand within product line	Coordinate order entry
Enter a new business	Expand a plant	Schedule production
Add direct mail selling	Determine advertising budget	Book TV commercials
Change debt/equity ratio	Issue new debt	Manage cash flows
Adopt affirmative action policy	Implement minority recruitment program	Maintain personnel records
Devise inventory speculation policy	Decide inventory levels	Reorder an item
Decide magnitude and direction of research	Control of research organization	Run individual research project

---

As the preceding examples suggest, certain activities that once were performed by managers are now automated and, hence, become task control activities. The shift from management control to task control frees some of the manager's time for other management activities (and, in some cases, it eliminates management positions).

Distinctions between Task Control and Management Control. The most important distinction between task control and management control is that many task control systems are *scientific*, whereas management control can never be reduced to a science. By definition, management control involves the behavior of managers, and these behaviors cannot be expressed by equations. Serious errors may be made when principles developed by management scientists for task control situations are applied to management control situations. In management control, managers interact with other managers; in task control, either human beings are not involved at all (as is the case with some automated production processes), or the interaction is between a manager and a nonmanager.

In management control the focus is on organizational units; in task control the focus is on specific tasks performed by these organizational units (e.g., manufacturing Job No. 59268, or ordering 100 units of Part No. 3642).

Management control relates to broad types of activities, and managers decide what is to be done within the general constraints of the strategies. Task control relates to specified tasks, and for most of these tasks, little or no judgment is required as to what is to be done.

Exhibit 1–5 identifies differences among these two functions and that of strategy formulation by giving examples of each.

Relation to Management Accounting

The field of accounting is broadly divided into two parts: financial accounting and management accounting. Financial accounting deals with financial reports prepared for shareholders, investment analysts, and other outside parties; it is governed by generally accepted accounting principles. For nongovernmental organizations, these principles are established by the Financial Accounting Standards Board. Management accounting deals with information prepared for management and others within the organization; its principles are not governed by an authoritative rule-making body—rather, the principles are those that provide useful information to these internal parties.

Management accounting has three subdivisions: full cost accounting, differential accounting, and management control. Full cost accounting measures the full cost of products, processes, services, and other cost objects. Its most important use is as an aid in product pricing and measuring product profitability. It is also used for inventory valuation and for the analysis of certain long-run decisions. Differential accounting estimates what costs would be under alternative courses of action. Management control (also called "responsibility accounting") is the subject matter of this text.

These three types of management accounting are governed by different principles. However, they do not require three separate accounting systems. Much information can be collected in a single system and adapted for use for one of the three accounting purposes outlined above.

Internal Auditing

The topic of internal auditing does not fit neatly into the above structure. It is an important function in any sizable organization, and texts (or sections of auditing texts) discuss it in depth. We mention the topic here because some people confuse this activity with management control. Management control is an activity that is carried out primarily by managers. Internal auditing is a staff activity intended to ensure that information is reported accurately and in accordance with prescribed rules, that fraud and misappropriation of assets is kept to a minimum, and, in some cases, to suggest ways of improving the organization's efficiency and effectiveness.

Road Map for the Reader

This book is organized into three parts. Each part is described briefly in this section.

The Management Control Environment (Part I)

Management control primarily involves the implementation of strategies. As background, therefore, we describe generic types of organization strategies in Chapter 2.

In Chapter 3 we describe some of the characteristics of organizations that affect the management control process, focusing principally on the behavior of members of an organization.

Chapter 4 introduces the idea of responsibility centers. *A responsibility center is an organization unit headed by a manager who is responsible for its activities.* Each responsibility center has inputs and outputs. Inputs are the resources that the responsibility center uses in doing whatever it does. Outputs are the results of its work. Technically, these outputs are *products*, but they are not necessarily products that are sold to outside customers. Services rendered by one responsibility center to another responsibility center are also products. Responsibility centers can be classified according to the degree to which their inputs and outputs are measured in monetary terms.

Chapters 4, 5, 6, and 7 describe different types of responsibility centers and the considerations involved in assigning *financial* responsibility to organization subunits. In Part II of the book (especially in Chapter 11), we deal with incorporating *nonfinancial* measures in management control.

We describe expense centers and revenue centers in Chapter 4. *In an expense center, inputs are measured as monetary costs; but outputs either are not measured at all, or if measured, the measurement is a quantitative, nonmonetary amount.* In an expense center the manager is responsible primarily for expense control. There are two types of expense centers. In an *engineered expense center*, actual costs can be compared with standard costs to obtain a measure of how efficiently the center operated. In a *discretionary expense center*, there is no way of arriving at sound standard costs, and the amounts of expenses vary at the discretion of the manager and of his or her superiors. The efficiency of a discretionary expense center cannot be measured (although the efficiency of some activities within the expense center are measurable).

In a revenue center, revenues are measured in monetary terms, but expenses are not matched with these revenues. Branch sales offices often are revenue centers. A comparison of budgeted and actual revenues indicates the effectiveness of the revenue center.

In a profit center, both revenues and the expenses associated with generating these revenues are measured; the difference between them is profit. Actual profit compared with budgeted profit is a measure of the manager's efficiency and effectiveness. We discuss profit centers in Chapter 5.

If a profit center provides outputs to other responsibility centers, or if it receives inputs from other responsibility centers, prices must be established for these outputs and inputs. These prices are called *transfer prices*, distinguishing them from the market prices charged to outside customers. Developing transfer prices in a way that facilitates management control is discussed in Chapter 6.

In an investment center, both the profit and the investment (i.e., the assets or capital) used in a responsibility center are measured. The return on investment is the broadest measure of the manager's efficiency and effectiveness. Investment centers are discussed in Chapter 7.

The Management Control Process (Part II)

Much of the management control process involves informal communications and interactions between a manager and another manager and between a manager and his or her subordinates. Informal communications occur by means of memoranda, meetings, conversations, and even by facial expressions. They take place within a formal planning and control system. Such a system includes the following activities: (1) strategic planning, (2) budget preparation, (3) program execution, and (4) program evaluation. Each activity leads to the next and recurs in a regular cycle. Collectively, they constitute a closed loop.

Strategic planning, which we discuss in Chapter 8, is the process of deciding on the major programs that the organization will undertake to implement its strategies and the approximate amount of resources that will be devoted to each. The output of the process results in a document called the *strategic plan.* (Some companies refer to this document as the *long-range plan.*) The information in the strategic plan covers a period of several future years, usually three or five. In a profit-oriented company each principal product or product line is a program. In a nonprofit organization the principal types of service that the organization provides are its programs. We will describe other types of programs in Chapter 8.

Strategic planning is the first step in the management control cycle. In a company that uses a calendar year, the planning usually takes place in the spring or summer of the year that precedes the budget year. At that time decisions are made that take account of any changes in strategies that have occurred since the last strategic plan was developed. These decisions are set forth in the strategic plan during the planning period.

We discuss budget preparation in Chapter 9. *An operating budget is the organization's plan for a specified period, usually one year.* The budget represents a fine tuning of the strategic plan, using the most current information. In the budget, revenues and expenses are realigned to correspond to responsibility centers, rather than to programs; thus, the budget shows the expenses that are expected to be incurred by each manager. The process of preparing the budget is essentially one of negotiation between the manager of a responsibility center and his or her superior. The end product of these negotiations is an agreed-upon statement of the expenses that are expected to be incurred during the year (if the responsibility center is an expense center), or the planned profit or expected return on investment (if the responsibility center is a profit center or an investment center).

In Chapters 10, 11, and 12 we discuss performance measurement, performance evaluation, and management compensation.

During the year, managers execute the program or part of a program for which they are responsible; they also report what has happened. Ideally, their reports are structured so that they provide information about both programs and responsibility centers. Reports on responsibility centers may show budgeted and actual information, financial and nonfinancial performance measures, and internal and external information. These reports keep managers at higher levels informed about the status of a program and also help to ensure that the work of the various responsibility centers is coordinated.

Reports also are used as a basis for control. *The process of evaluation is a comparison of actual amounts with the amounts that should have been incurred under the circumstances.* Unless circumstances have changed from those assumed in the budget process, the comparison is between budgeted and actual amounts. If circumstances have changed, the changes are taken into account in the analysis. The analysis leads to praise or constructive criticism of the responsibility center managers.

Chapter 10 deals with analysis and evaluation of financial performance measures.

Chapter 11 expands the focus of performance evaluation to discuss considerations involved in incorporating nonfinancial measures. This chapter discusses the design of a *balanced scorecard* incorporating financial and nonfinancial measures. This chapter also contains a discussion of *interactive controls*—the use of management control information (especially nonfinancial) in developing new strategies.

Chapter 12 describes the considerations involved in designing management incentive compensation plans.

Variations in Management Control (Part III)

The chapters in Part II describe the typical management control process. In Part III we describe variations from the typical pattern. These variations are: controls for different strategies (Chapter 13); modern manufacturing environments (Chapter 14); service organizations (Chapter 15); financial services organizations (Chapter 16); and multinational organizations (Chapter 17).

The final chapter (Chapter 18) describes management control of projects, which is somewhat different from the management control of ongoing operations that has been the focus to this point.

Summary

A system is a prescribed way of carrying out any activity or set of activities. Systems exist for the control of many types of activities. The system used by management to control the activities of an organization is called its management control system. Management control is the process by which managers influence other members of the organization to implement the organization's strategies.

Management control is one of three types of planning and control activities found in organizations. It is facilitated by a formal system that includes a recurring cycle of activities. Another planning and control activity is called strategy formulation. It is the largely unsystematic process of identifying and deciding on new strategies. The third type of planning and control activity is called task control. It is the process of assuring that specified tasks are carried out effectively and efficiently.

The book is divided into three parts. Part I discusses the control environment in an organization. Control is exercised by managers who supervise responsibility centers. Part II describes the management control process. The process consists of a set of regularly recurring activities: strategic planning, budget preparation, execution, and evaluation of performance. Part III describes control systems that depart from the typical pattern.

Suggested Additional Readings

Anthony, Robert N. *The Management Control Function*. Boston: Harvard Business School Press, 1989.

Camillus, John. *Strategic Planning and Management Control*. Lexington, MA: D.C. Heath, 1986.

Dent, Jeremy F. "Global Competition: Challenges for Management Accounting and Control." *Management Accounting Research* 7, no. 2 (June 1996), 247–269.

Emmanuel, Clive R., and David Otley. *Accounting for Management Control*. Wokingham, Berkshire, England: Van Nostrand Reinhold (UK), 1985.

Galbraith, Jay R. *Designing Organizations*. San Francisco: Jossey-Bass Publishers, 1995.

Govindarajan, Vijay. "A Contingency Approach to Strategy Implementation at the Business Unit Level: Integrating Administrative Mechanisms with Strategy." *Academy of Management Journal* 31, no. 4 (1988), pp. 828–53.

Kaplan, Robert, and David Norton. *Balanced Scorecard*. Boston: Harvard Business School Press, 1996.

McKenney, James L. *Waves of Change: Business Evolution Through Information Technology*. Boston: Harvard Business School Press, 1994.

Merchant, Kenneth A. *Rewarding Results*. Boston: Harvard Business School Press, 1989.

Otley, David. "Management Control in Contemporary Organizations: Towards a Wider Framework." *Management Accounting Research* 5, no. 4 (Sept./Dec. 1994), 289–299.

Shank, John K., and Vijay Govindarajan. *Strategic Cost Management*. New York: The Free Press, 1993.

Simons, Robert. *Levers of Control*. Boston: Harvard Business School Press, 1995.

Walther, Thomas, Henry Johansson, John Dunleavy, and Elizabeth Hjelm. *Reinventing the CFO*. New York: McGraw-Hill, 1997.

CASE 1–1
GENERAL ELECTRIC COMPANY

In 1981 General Electric Company was the world's largest diversified industrial corporation. This note is intended to provide a description of some of the systems and procedures designed and used by GE's top managers as they collectively addressed themselves to the ongoing task of conducting the affairs of the company. Following the brief historical section below, this note is divided into three main sections: Organization Structure, Planning Systems, and Operating Systems.

History and Managerial Philosophy

General Electric traced its origins to the establishment of the Edison General Electric Company in 1878. Its original business strategy was developed around the exploitation of the commercial opportunity presented by the harnessing of electricity, the invention of electric lighting, and the electric motor. This led the company into the design, manufacture, and marketing of electric motors and related industrial, farm, and home machinery and appliances, as well as lighting and electricity-generating equipment. As electricity became a ubiquitous part of 20th-century life, the scope of GE's involvement expanded in many directions to include synthetic materials, electronics, nuclear energy, broadcasting, natural resources, and consumer credit.

Already a large company before World War II, GE grew rapidly during the war and continued to grow thereafter. Over the four decades, GE's revenues increased fiftyfold—a compound annual growth rate of 10.5 percent per year. The rate of inflation varied during these years, but in

constant dollars the growth in sales was 5.7 percent per year.

In 1980, GE's revenues were nearly $25 billion, its net earnings exceeded $1.5 billion, and it ranked ninth on *Fortune's* roster of U.S. industrial corporations.

During this period of growth and diversification, GE's management systems were also evolving. The material below is excerpted from "Strategic Management for the 80s," an internal document prepared by GE in 1977 to explain to all GE managers the rationale for creating the new position of Sector executive.

> Adapting the company's management system and structure to internal or external challenges has been a continuous process throughout General Electric's 100 year history. As the company has grown, the complexities brought about by increasing size and diversity have consistently challenged generations of managers to develop new approaches, systems, and organization structures to more effectively meet our goals.
>
> **Decentralization in the 50s.**
> In the 1950s, the company was decentralized to allow for greater organizational flexibility, management opportunity, and entrepreneurship. The company was well positioned for explosive growth during the favorable economic climate of the 1960s.
>
> **Growth in the 60s.**
> Overall company growth was quite dramatic in the 1960s. However, we encountered a phenomenon affecting most large companies at that time called "profitless growth," which means tremendous growth in sales without commensurate growth in earnings. Further, heavy investment in areas which were not yielding profitable growth put us close to our debt/capital limit for an Aaa company. Greater investment selectivity was required along with a system to assist management in allocating financial resources according to the varying potentials and paces of GE's many businesses.
>
> **Strategic Planning for the 70s.**
> As a result, an organization and system change was made, based on strategic planning concepts, to focus our resources on the strategic requirements of our diverse

This case was abridged with permission by Professors Robert N. Anthony and Vijay Govindarajan from Harvard Business School Case 181–111, written under the direction of Professor Richard F. Vancil. Copyright by the President and Fellows of Harvard College.

businesses. Organizationally, we overlaid on our hierarchical structure of Groups, Divisions, and Departments a structure for planning through the identification of unique, stand-alone businesses called Strategic Business Units. In addition, a planning process was designed to surface strategic plans, required of each SBU, for critical review and resource allocation at Corporate level. The profitless growth pattern was reversed, but just as important, SBU management developed a style of management that stresses strategic positioning of businesses and selective allocation of key resources for competitive advantage.

Strategic Management for the 80s.

Judging from the expected challenges of the 1980s, it is timely to move from strategic planning as a process designed for one level—the SBU—to "strategic management" as a management style for all levels of GE managers. The strategic management concept combines planning and management responsibilities at every level where value may be added for the effective implementation of strategic objectives. This value added not only involves the integration of lower-level objectives and strategies, but also requires each level to develop plans for strengthening key internal resources and establishing business development programs unique to the scope of that business level. In short, planning and managing is done at the SBU level for worldwide businesses, at Sector level for multinational industries, and at Corporate level for global/multi-industry strategies.

Commenting on these changes in 1981, one GE executive said:

We don't change our basic structure very often, but when we do, it's a reflection of a basic change in our managerial philosophy. We came out of World War II a finely honed, centralized, functionally organized company. When we decentralized in the early 50s, we did so with a vengeance, almost to the point of acting like a holding company. Setting up the SBUs in 1970 was a recognition that we had gone too far, and that the strategic direction of the company should be directed from the top to some extent. The Sector executives in 1977 helped to move the pendulum a little further in that direction.

Organization Structure

There were five echelons of general managers in the organizational hierarchy: the Chief Executive Office (CEO), Sector executives (6), Group executives (12), Division general managers (54), and Department general managers (181).

Line Management. Exhibit 1 uses the Consumer Product and Services Sector in 1978 to illustrate how the executives at these five levels related to each other for operating management and for strategic management. It shows how the company's operating facilities—production plants, laboratories, warehouses, sales offices, and so forth—which would have required several pages to list, were grouped by product categories or markets under the responsibility of department managers. These, in turn, where the scale of the operations warranted it, were grouped under division general managers. In some instances, several divisions were brought together under a group executive. These operating level designations expressed the management skills and resources required to manage each business or functional component successfully.

Some of these components had the word *business* in their designation. This was the key to their relationship with the strategic planning process, for each such component was the top management level of an SBU. These were viewed as the basic business entities of General Electric. They were set up to assure organization integrity while permitting the SBU general manager to carry out a business strategy effectively and competitively. As such, the SBUs could have stood alone as viable and completely successful independent companies, each within its own defined market or market segment. Depending on the size of its business, an SBU might be located at one of several levels in the hierarchy of the operating structure: a group (as in the case of the Lighting Business Group); a division (as in the case of the Air Conditioning Business Division); a department (as in the case of the Television Business Department, which in 1981 was promoted to Division status); or it could even be an unconsolidated subsidiary (such as GE Credit Corporation). In total, General Electric had 49 SBUs in 1978 (and 39 in 1981).

The general manager of an SBU was responsible for the planning and operation of his or her

Exhibit 1

Partial representation of organization structure

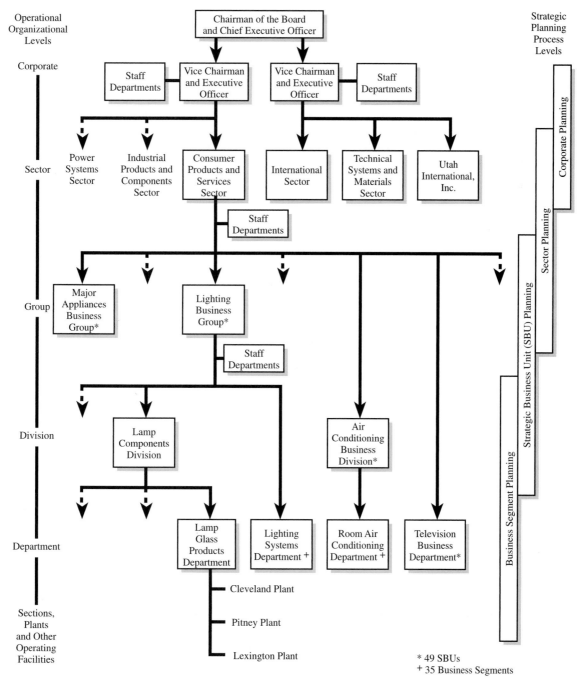

* 49 SBUs
+ 35 Business Segments

business. This involved managing various functions, product areas, and business segments. It was the manager's job to review and approve (within delegated limits) lower-level echelon decisions on investment, organization, manpower, and compensation. The SBU manager was also responsible for developing the SBU's strategic plan, and reviewing and integrating operating, functional, and business segment plans. The formal assignment of authority to managers at the various operational levels (see the left scale in Exhibit 1) did not differ between SBUs and non-SBUs except for the additional responsibilities of the SBU manager in the strategic planning and reporting process.

Above the SBUs were the Sectors. These were macrobusiness/industry areas made up of businesses with common strategic challenges defined by critical market, customer, product, or technology characteristics. Each sector was headed by an executive vice president and sector executive who was assisted by a small staff of functional specialists and strategic planners. As the chief operating executive for the sector, the sector executive managed all SBU managers, reviewed and approved SBU strategies, plans, budgets, investment requests, and key changes in organization and manpower. He was also responsible for the sector's strategic plan. Assisted by his staff, the sector executive was not to replace or replicate the strategic planning and management functions of the units at lower levels, but rather to complement them and "add value" to the management process by identifying and acting upon strategic issues of a sectorwide nature.

One sector executive made the following comment about how this newest echelon of GE management was working out:

> We have made progress in establishing ourselves at the sector management level as it was intended—to provide added value. The job has been made easier because General Electric is well organized and has the management systems and tools already in place. In fact, many of us believe General Electric has one of the best systems going. If one thinks of this organization structure and these

management processes as a giant plumbing system, our job at the sector management level is to plug into the system and serve as a high-pressure pump, and thus generate a more dynamic business operation.

In addition to the operational and strategic management functions, the sector executive also assumed responsibility as the company spokesman for his industry area. The International Sector, in addition to managing affiliates in specific countries, was responsible for integrating resources and capabilities in support of the international strategies of the other sectors.

Functional Staff Departments. Seven major staff organizations were located at GE headquarters in Fairfield, Connecticut. Several of these units had counterparts at lower levels in the line-management hierarchy. For example, each general manager at the department level and higher was supported by a manager of Finance and, in most cases, a manager of Relations, and each SBU manager had a manager for Strategic Planning and other staff officers as necessary to operate in a competitive environment. The existence of other staff offices depended on the nature of the operating unit and the need for staff support at that echelon.

Resource Planning. The role of staff units, in addition to providing functional support to their line manager, was to contribute to strategic planning by identifying resource issues that might have an impact on the operating unit's ability to meet its business objectives. This task was called *resource planning*, and was expected to "add value" in several ways, three examples of which are discussed below.

By reviewing the functional activities of the operating components at their level and below, a staff unit might identify the opportunity to create a new capability with sufficient critical mass to serve the operating units better. (Setting up a research lab at the group level might be feasible even though no single component could afford such a lab.) A second type of staff initiative might identify an existing resource that could gain further economies of scale if it were utilized by other operating components. (A college recruiting program in one division might screen candidates for another division.) Finally, higher-level staff groups had a special responsibility for anticipating future needs for resources, and might identify such needs before the operating components did. (The pervasive effect of electronic microprocessors on many of GE's products was first surfaced in this manner.)

Executive Manpower Staff.   The Executive Manpower Staff was created and centralized because the company had in its managers a rich resource which had to be developed for all its businesses. There was also the need to be able to move people from one part of the organization to another as they developed and grew.

The Executive Manpower Staff had extensive information on the company's managers. It organized the annual manpower review known as Session C that reached down to the lower levels of the organization. All exempt employees were involved. Each filled out a form on his or her background, self-assessment, and plans. The individual's boss then provided an evaluation and assessment. (This was not a performance appraisal, as those were carried out separately.) There was then a feedback session with the subordinate. The boss followed the same procedure with his superior and, in addition, discussed his own people with him. As the process moved on up the pyramid, the focus narrowed to the half-dozen direct reports, but perhaps two dozen individuals farther down the ladder might be discussed. Session C culminated in a review with the executive officers of the manpower resources at the division and SBU management levels.

The Executive Manpower Staff kept on file the annual manpower review reports on all managers from level 15 (section managers) to level 27 (sector executives), a total of about 5,000 managers and individual contributors. It also kept track of 13s and 14s that were rated as promotable and they, too, were in the inventory. This information was filed in computerized form for easy access and retrieval.

It was also the responsibility of the Executive Manpower Staff to prepare slates of candidates for all management positions at the department level and above. Sector executives were usually involved in these decisions, working with a consultant assigned to them from the staff in identifying candidates. Sector executives often had the consultant participate in all types of management activities in the sector which allowed him or her to learn firsthand about people. Then the executive and the consultant would talk about individuals and their relative performance. Because of the strategic management orientation of SBU and sector management, the manpower management process was made easier. Once the strategy had been established, it was easier to assess managers in terms of their capacity to contribute to its accomplishment.

Commenting on the management of executive manpower, one staff consultant stressed the importance of the role played by the sector executive:

> Finding the right people for key management jobs is only part of the task; motivating them is also important. The sector executive that I'm assigned to works hard at motivating his managers, and cannot just appeal to the pocketbook. At this level, compensation, although important, is not the primary motivator. This might seem surprising since the amounts are sizable. They range from between $70,000 and $90,000 in base pay plus about 20 percent to 60 percent in incentive compensation at the department level (level 18 or 19), up to a maximum in 1980 of $1 million in salary and incentive compensation for the chairman of the board. Such levels of compensation are important to preserve our quality pool of managerial talent, but other factors provide the key to good motivation. The sector executive with whom I work participates actively with his staff and with me in reviewing performance screens proposed by all his direct reports and all corporate officers in his SBUs. He also knows how to give people responsibility. He encourages risk taking. But he also gives his managers support when they need it. He uses his staff very well. As a result, the good people under him tend to derive a sense of competence.

Top-Management Boards.   Each manager in GE had a line or staff role, as defined by the organization structure, and also a role as a member of one or more boards or committees. This section focuses on the four boards at the top levels of GE, but committees were widely used at all levels in the company.

Corporate Executive Office. The Corporate Executive Office (CEO) consisted of the Chairman of the Board and the two Vice Chairmen. The CEO was the top line management unit in GE and was not viewed as a committee. The CEO had multiple responsibilities for overall company policy, planning, and operations, and provided direction and leadership across a broad range of complex internal and external challenges. Specifically, the CEO was responsible for the corporate plan, determined corporate objectives and strategies, and reviewed and approved sector strategies, objectives, and budgets. Staff assistance was provided to the chief executive officer (CXO) in his policy making, strategic, and operational roles by a Corporate Policy Board, which he chaired. The vice chairmen managed sector executives and were aided in their sector strategy and investment review roles by a Corporate Operations Board.

Corporate Policy Board. The CPB was the highest internal forum for reviewing company policies and strategies. In a sense, the CPB could be viewed as a CXO staff meeting, providing him the opportunity to hear an open discussion of issues and using his key staff officers as a sounding board. Sector strategies and budgets were presented to the CPB by the sector executive and his staff.

Corporate Operations Board. The COB was co-chaired by the vice chairmen and consisted of selected corporate staff officers. COB meetings for investment reviews and critical-issue resolution were designed to review several sector(s) requests per session.

Sector Executive Board. Each sector executive chaired an SEB that assisted him in reviewing SBU strategies, budgets, and investment requests. SEB members, in addition to key sector staff managers, included two or more members from either corporate or other sector staffs. These outside SEB members were selected by the sector executive with the approval of his vice chairman and the concurrence of the candidate's immediate superior.

Corporate Executive Council. The CEC was composed of the CPB and sector executives and provided a forum for operating and staff executives to meet, review, and discuss corporate and sector operating and planning issues. The CEC meetings were viewed as necessary for high-level operations reviews, and as a valuable opportunity for interchange between the CXO and his operating executives.

One implication of GE's use of several top management committees was that careful advance scheduling for executive time commitments was required.

Planning Systems

General Electric's planning system used the organizational structure in two ways. Operational planning and reporting was carried out routinely, as appropriate, at each organizational level within GE. Strategic planning and related evaluations and reviews, however, were carried out only at the designated strategic levels: corporate, sector, SBU, and, in some instances, business segments. While written plans were prepared at each level, the emphasis was more on dialogue between levels. The plans differed in style and content, reflecting the varied nature of the environment faced by each unique business and the particular approach of its manager. The common threads in strategic plans at each level (see the right scale in Exhibit 1) were that: (1) they performed rigorous environmental analyses and position assessments, identifying major discontinuities; (2) they summarized the objectives and strategies of the components under them; and (3) they specifically addressed priorities and major programs for business development and resource development. Each strategic planning level, thus, was expected to "add value"

Exhibit 2

1981 planning cycle[1]

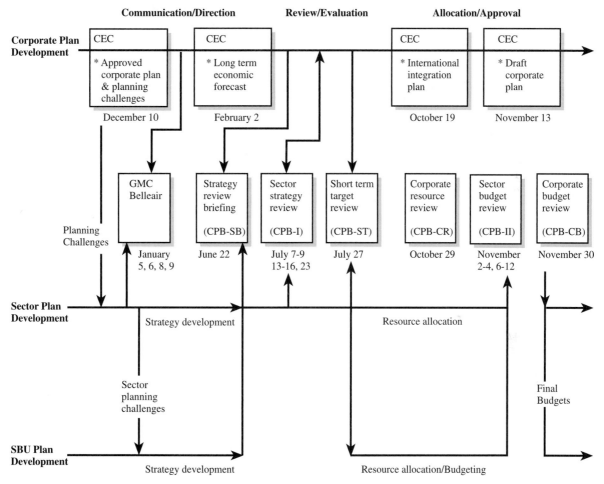

* Subject included on CEC agenda

[1]Reproduction of original company document

to General Electric through its participation in the planning process.

To make the planning system work efficiently and effectively across the broad spectrum of organizational units that made up the entire company, GE followed a formal strategic planning cycle, as shown in the chart in Exhibit 2. The cycle was divided into three parts: Communication/Direction, Review/Evaluation, and Alloca-

tion/Approval. These occurred sequentially as the year progressed, and each is discussed in turn below.

Communication/Direction. For several years prior to the 1981 planning cycle, the GE corporate plan for the coming year was approved at the close of each year. The distribution of this document was restricted to corporate and sector executives and their key staff officers—a group of about 50 individuals. As a part of that document, corporate planning challenges for the subsequent year were passed down to the sector executives who, in turn, provided sector planning challenges to the SBUs. These challenges identified topics which were relevant to most SBUs (e.g., productivity), and which the CEO wished to receive special attention in the forthcoming strategic planning cycle. Early in the year, formal meetings were held with all corporate officers and general managers together (Belleair, General Managers Conference) to review these challenges, along with pertinent background studies, and to consider their implications for strategies and directions.

For 1981, the corporate initiation of the planning cycle was handled somewhat differently. The 1981 corporate plan was distributed to approximately 200 people, including SBU managers and their key staff officers. The challenges approach was expanded to encompass business issues as well as functional issues. For example, the plan defined several "Arenas" that required coordinated strategic efforts by several SBUs. Energy was an *arena* where the CEO saw an opportunity for concerted action by several operating units, and the 1981 plan identified each unit and the role that it should play. As one corporate staff executive explained the rationale for this approach, "It's an attempt to deal with one of our most difficult problems—getting the units in our decentralized structure to work together. Opportunities don't always align themselves with our organization structure. Arenas are intended to bridge the gap between organizational components and to get the components to focus on opportunities that transcend their normal scope."

Review/Evaluation. In June, each SBU submitted its strategic plan to sector and corporate headquarters. The bulk of this document was externally focused, analyzing competitors, assessing market opportunities, and defining major strategic thrusts in terms of new product developments and possible acquisitions. An appendix to the document was the Long-Range Forecast, which presented financial information for the prior five years, the current year, and a forecast of the next five years. The data for the first forecast year was, in effect, the SBU's preliminary proposal for its operating budget and its capital expenditures budget.

Since the establishment of SBUs in 1970, the corporate review and evaluation of strategic plans was accomplished in part through a "portfolio analysis," with each SBU being viewed as a separate business vying for a share of the company's resources with which to pursue growth in its defined market(s). Generally, the sum of the profits proposed by the SBUs was less than the corporate expectation, and the capital requirements were more than corporate believed prudent. The task for corporate management was to close these "gaps." The growth potential of the market and the SBU's current competitive position in that market were considered along with its business strategy, and decisions were then made as to how much of the gaps to assign to each SBU, based on the corporate view of the appropriate overall portfolio of GE's businesses. For example, some SBUs were squeezed for maximum contribution, thus being guided into a harvest strategy, while others were permitted to incur discretionary operating expenses that would result in future growth. This process of assigning the responsibility for the company's profit and capital expenditure requirements was labeled the "resource allocation process."

With the establishment of the Sector management level in 1977, the review of SBUs' strategies was delegated to the sector executives, along with the responsibility for allocating resources among their SBUs. This, however, still produced gaps when the sector proposals reached the CEO. The corporate officers performed the same SBU-level portfolio analysis as before, but aggregated the SBU adjustments and assigned the gaps to each sector, rather than to the individual SBUs. It was then up to the sector executive to decide how to allocate resources among his SBUs. He was free to do it according to criteria different from those utilized at the corporate level, the only requirement being that the sector deliver its budgeted results at the end of the year.

Allocation/Approval.   Resource allocation at GE not only involved two levels of management above the SBUs, it also involved iterative negotiations among all three strategic levels that began in the summer and might continue into the early fall. The initial discussions resulted in tentative allocations of net income requirements and capital budgets from corporate to sectors and from sector to SBUs. The SBU managers then reviewed their situations and could reclaim their case if they felt a serious strategic error was about to be made. Sometimes the sector executive could accommodate the request within his own allocations; other times he might raise the issue at the corporate level. According to one GE executive, "The SBUs don't always win, of course, but it's surprising how often they do."

In the latter part of the year, SBU budgets were presented to sector and corporate levels. They would then be analyzed, discussed, modified, and approved in a series of additional meetings. With the issuance of the corporate plan for the next year, the cycle would start again.

Operating Systems

Once the strategic plans and operating budgets had been agreed upon, as described above, the day-by-day execution of operating activities was the responsibility of the general managers of the operating components (left scale in Exhibit 1). The top management of GE still believed strongly in the concept of decentralization as the best way to run current operations in its diverse set of businesses. Three formal management systems were used to constrain the operating autonomy of GE's managers, as described below under the headings of Reservations of Authority, Monitoring Financial Performance, and Appraising and Rewarding Managerial Performance.

Reservations of Authority.   General Electric had a formal set of corporate policies designed primarily to insure (1) that its managers conformed to corporate standards of conduct in dealing with individuals, organizations, and agencies outside the company, and (2) internal administrative consistency. In the spring of 1981, GE was just completing a review and revision of its formal policies, reducing the total number to about 15 and covering topics such as "Compliance with the Anti-Trust Laws" and "Reimbursing Employees for Business Expenses." The typical policy statement required only two or three pages, but some policies were supplemented by detailed compliance procedures.

One policy that affected every operating general manager covered investments in plant and facilities. The capital budgets that were approved in the planning process had been based on detailed schedules listing each major investment; but the approval of the capital budget represented a strategic commitment to the business, rather than specific approval of the details of each project. Securing authority to expend the funds required that the sponsoring manager prepare an Appropriation Request (A/R) on a prescribed set of forms. Approval authority for A/Rs was limited to $500,000 for a department manager, $1 million for a division manager, $2 million for a group executive, $6 million for a sector executive, and $20 million for the CEO, with larger amounts reserved for the board of directors. The approver of an A/R was to ascertain that the strategic purpose was still valid and then, taking a project perspective, determine that the proposed investment was optimally designed for its intended purpose.

Monitoring Financial Performance.   The current operating performance of GE managers at every level was monitored monthly by a comprehensive integrated set of financial reports.

Exhibit 3   Calculation of Net Income

Net sales billed	xxx
Less: Materials in cost of goods sold	(xxx)
Contributed value from operations	xxx
Less: Direct labor	(xxx)
Other variable costs	(xxx)
LIFO revaluation provision*	(xx)
Contribution margin	xxx
Less: Readiness-to-serve costs	(xxx)
Program expenses	(xx)
Assessments from corporate, sector, group, and division	(xx)
Operating profit	xx
Less: Interest expense/income	(x)
Income taxes	(xx)
Net Income	xx

*Records kept on FIFO basis; adjusted to LIFO for monthly management reports.

The amount of detailed information available at each level was sufficient to permit the manager at that level to review the performance of the operations beneath him or her, and the information was progressively summarized as it moved to higher levels in the management hierarchy.

Profit responsibility in GE was decentralized down to the department level. Each department general manager was responsible for meeting his or her budgeted net income (defined below), and the total of the net income for all the departments in GE was equal to the corporate net income, with only minor adjustments. For a typical department engaged in the manufacture and sale of a line of products, the major categories of expenses in its operating statement are shown in Exhibit 3.

Each expense category could, of course, be broken down in great detail. Three categories, known collectively as "base-costs," require brief explanations. Readiness-to-serve costs were the fixed expenses of the operating components, reflecting its current capacity. These included depreciation and other manufacturing costs and sales and administrative overhead. Program expenses were discretionary expenditures intended to increase future profits through specific programs for developing new products, entering new markets, or improving productivity. Assessments from corporate headquarters were an allocation of corporate overhead based on the department's cost of operations as a proportion of such costs in all departments; the assessment worked out to roughly 1 percent of sales. The amount of assessments from group and division echelons varied, depending on the extent to which they provided common services, such as a common sales force or computer services, to several departments beneath them; such assessments were usually based on usage of the services rather than a proration.

Department general managers were also responsible for the return on investment of their operating unit, and especially for managing the investment in working capital. At the beginning of 1980, a base amount of working capital was established for each department based on its average working capital in 1978. Increases in working capital above that base were funds provided by corporate, and the department was charged interest at the prime rate; decreasing working capital below that amount permitted the department manager to earn interest income at the same rate.

The operating components in GE were relatively free standing, and net income was defined as shown in Exhibit 3 to encourage each general manager to accept responsibility for his or her "piece of the bottom line." Given an approved budget, department general managers had substantial latitude concerning how they achieved their targeted results. Higher-level managers were interested in more than the bottom line, however. They paid particular attention to program expenses, for example, to insure that the net income budget had not been achieved by cutting program expenses, thus, in effect, "eating our seed corn."

Many other aspects of departmental operations were monitored at higher levels, as illustrated by the monthly Review and Estimate of Operations report shown in Exhibit 4. This single piece of paper contained a variety of required data, ratios, and analyses, but also provided space for key measurements which the general manager of the component felt were relevant for his or her operation, such as the sales break-even point or the capacity utilization rate. In the comments section on the reverse of the form, the managers could provide a brief overview and identify particular problems that were receiving current attention. This report was sent up the operating hierarchy until it reached the SBU level. At that point, the same form was used to prepare a consolidated report for the SBU, and those forms were sent up to the sector executive and the CXO.

Appraising and Rewarding Managerial Performance.   Closely related to, but distinguishable from, monitoring performance of each business was the process of evaluating the performance of GE's managers. Because of the diverse nature of the businesses in each sector, the details of this process varied. In general terms, however, each manager developed a set of financial and nonfinancial objectives on which he felt he should be evaluated. These goals, as described below, were called his *performance screen*. He would then review these with his superior, who might suggest revisions and changes. In reaching agreement, they would attach relative weights to each measure.

Financial objectives included several measurements of budgeted performance, such as sales, net income, ROI, cash flow, operating margin, and so on. The weight assigned to each of these elements would vary depending upon the portfolio category of the manager's SBU. Nonfinancial objectives were actions that would provide future benefits to GE, and included items such as "increase market share by—," "maintain cost leadership," "develop a total quality program for the business, encompassing all functions," and so on. Individual weights were assigned to each such element. For an "invest/grow" SBU, the weights on future benefits were usually greater than the weights on current performance; for a "harvest/divest" SBU, the weights on current performance might be several times the weights on future benefits.

Once a year, and more often when appropriate, the performance screens were reviewed by each manager and his boss in order to assess performance. The performance screens, together with Session C manpower reviews and the multiple contacts that took place during the conduct of day-to-day business, provided GE management with a comprehensive evaluation of managerial performance.

The performance evaluation process provided one of several criteria used by management to rank managers for yearly salary reviews and the award of incentive compensation. Salaries were kept competitive with the pertinent markets for managerial talent. Given the size of the organization, however, there was a formal salary scale which limited the discretion that a given organizational unit manager had in assigning salary levels. Yet, at each step in the scale, there was a range within which discretionary increases were permitted.

Incentive compensation was organized in three tiers. There was a pool of incentive compensation funds for managers from levels 15 to 18, another for nonofficers in levels 19 and above, and a third pool for corporate officers. The amount in each pool was determined each year by the Manpower Development and Compensation Committee, based on recommendations coming from the SBUs, and reviewed at sector and corporate level, as well as on general business performance as compared with the market and the economy. Once the pools were determined, sector and SBU management had substantial discretion in assigning amounts to individual managers.

Exhibit 4

Review and estimate of operations

REVIEW AND ESTIMATE OF OPERATIONS

_____ (Component)

Period ended _____   _____ GROUP

(Dollar amounts in thousands)

ACTUAL					OPERATING DATA	ESTIMATE				
Year-To-Date			Current Month			Next Month		Total Year		
Amount	VB%	V%	Amount	VB%		Amount	VB%	Amount	VB%	V%
					Net sales billed					
					Net income					
					Funds flow a)					
					Average investment					
					Contribution margin					
					Base costs					
					Provision for revaluation to LIFO basis					
					Orders received					
			X	X	Unfilled orders (at end of period)					
Actual	Budget	Last Year	Actual	Budget	**Operating Ratios:**	Estimate	Budget	Estimate	Budget	Last Year
					% Net income to net sales billed					
					% Return on investment (average)					
					Investment turnover					
			X	X	Customer receivables - days					
			X	X	Inventories - Number of days output					
		Invest. This Date			**FUNDS FLOW AND INVESTMENT (Generated/Used*)**					Invest. at Dec. 31
		X			Net income/loss*					X
					Customer receivables - total					
					Inventories at component FIFO tax cost					
					Plant and equipment expenditures					
					Depreciation and amortization provision...					
					Progress collections					
					Trade payables					
					All other					
		X			Funds flow					X
		Last Year			**KEY MEASUREMENTS for COMPONENT**					Last Year
					NUMBER OF EMPLOYEES at end of period					
			X	X	Salaried					
			X	X	Hourly					
			X	X	Total					

(a - Equivalent to sum of changes in (1) affiliates' cash and marketable securities, (2) borrowings, and (3) current accounts excluding current year net income/loss.

Casewriter's note: VB% is the percentage variance of actual from budget; V% is the variance of actual from prior year.

Exhibit 4 (*cont'd*)

Review and estimate of operations (continued)

REVIEW AND ESTIMATE OF OPERATIONS

_____
(Component)

Period ended _____   _____ GROUP

(Dollar amounts in thousands)

Year-To-Date			PRICE INDEXES (1974=100.0)	Total Year		
Actual	Budget	Last Year		Estimate	Budget	Last Year
			Selling prices - Orders			
			Sales			
			Direct materials..			
			Employee compensation and benefits............................			

Actual vs. Budget	Actual vs. Last Year	ANALYSIS OF CHANGE IN INCOME **Increase/Decrease* resulting from changes in**	Estimate vs. Budget	Estimate vs. Last Year
		Selling prices		
		Sales volume		
		Product mix		
		Resource prices - Direct material		
		Employee compensation and benefits (variable costs)		
		....		
		Cost improvements - net		
		....		
		Increase/Decrease* in contribution margin		
		Employee compensation and benefits - Resources prices............		
		Employment		
		....		
		....		
		....		
		....		
		Interest expense/(income)		
		General Company, Group and Division assessments		
		Increase*/Decrease in base costs		
		Other income excluding interest income		
		Increase/Decrease* in income before taxes.........................		
		Investment credit, renegotiation, and income taxes		
		Interest of other share owners in net results of affiliates................		
		Increase/Decrease* in net income		

Comments:

_____   _____
General Manager   Date

For corporate officers, recommendations for both salary increases and incentive compensation were reviewed by the Executive Compensation staff under the vice president for executive manpower, which then made recommendations to the chairman and to the Executive Compensation Committee of the board of directors, where the final determination was made.

Questions

1. Describe and evaluate the elements of General Electric's planning and control systems that are designed to facilitate the simultaneous implementation of the variety of strategies being pursued by this widely diversified corporation.

2. What is your assessment of Reginald Jones's tenure (who was the CEO during the 1970s) as the CEO of General Electric?

3. What problems caused General Electric to change its planning and control approach in early 1970 and again in 1977?

4. What should Jack Welch (who succeeded Reginald Jones) try to accomplish during his first six months in office as the CEO?

CASE 1–2
XEROX CORPORATION (A)[1]

Al Senter, after 25 years with Xerox, reached the top of his profession in 1990—Vice President of Finance. A director said, "In many ways Al is the product of the Xerox society, self-confident and outspoken. He is vocal about the proactive role the Xerox financial people must play to make the new company culture work. Al firmly believes in the active participation of the business controllers in decision making." Al remembered the analytical era of the 1970s where accuracy and rigid systems were more important than listening to the customer. The controllers were the numbers people, and there was never enough data or analysis. During this era some good people left the company, and Xerox faced new competitors in the battle for market share. The company, however, changed with the quality cultural revolution of the 1980s. One never satisfied to harvest history, Al had a new agenda which continues and enhances the work started during the previous decade. According to Al,

> The control function must add value to the products by working with line management. We need to actively participate with management in making better decisions. The only way we can do this is to have open communication, top-flight and well-trained people, and to be on the cutting edge of information technology. Finance has to partner with marketing and technology and make clear the value we add. If we can't add value, then we don't belong at Xerox. Our financial team is pretty darn good. We trust each other, and the FEC (Financial Executive Council) is highly respected throughout the company. I keep looking at world-class financial organizations for ideas, and the more I look, the more I appreciate what we have at Xerox. We know, of course, that there are areas where we can improve, and we are addressing them.

Company Background

Xerox, the document company, was a multinational corporation serving the global document-processing and financial services markets. They developed, manufactured, and marketed copiers and duplicators, facsimile products, scanners, workstations, computer software, supplies, and other related equipment in over 130 countries. Their financial services operations included insurance, equipment financing, investments, and investment banking. This case focuses on the document-processing activities of the company.

Xerox was one of the outstanding business success stories in the world. From 1946 to 1973, their annual sales growth exceeded 25 percent, while the annual growth of earnings exceeded 35 percent. This amazing record was due to the dominant position Xerox created in the plain paper copier business. In 1959 the company introduced the revolutionary 914 plain paper copier. This generation of equipment motivated the explosion in the copying business from 20 million copies made annually in 1957 to 9.5 billion copies made annually in 1965.[1] In 1990, the world copy business was over 900 billion copies.

The original patent for the plain paper copier expired in 1970, sending an invitation to potential competitors. In the next decade US firms (IBM and Kodak) and Japanese firms (Canon, Minolta, and others) entered the large and small copy machine industry. Exhibit 1 provides the Xerox corporate financial highlights for the past three decades.

During this rapid growth period, Xerox built its worldwide business network. Joe Wilson,

---

This case was prepared by Lawrence P. Carr, Associate Professor at Babson College. Copyright © by Lawrence Carr.

[1]These data and other pertinent information are contained in the story of the Xerox revitalization. See Gary Jacobson and John Hillkirk, *Xerox: American Samurai* (New York: Macmillan Co., 1986).

EXHIBIT 1 Financial Highlights of Xerox Corporation
(dollars in millions, except per share and employee data)

	1991	1990	1989	1980	1970	1960
Revenue						
Document Processing	13,819	13,583	12,431	8,037	1,690	40
Total Xerox	17,830	17,973	17,229	8,037	1,690	40
Net income						
Document Processing	537	549	488	553	192	3
Total Xerox	454	243	704	565	192	3
Financial position (Total Xerox)						
Current assets	21,766	20,178	18,253	3,515	842	15
Total assets	31,658	31,635	30,088	7,514	1,929	56
Long-term debt	6,247	7,149	7,511	898	382	5
Shareholders' equity	5,140	5,051	5,035	3,630	918	29
Net income per common share	$3.86	$1.66	$6.41	$6.69	$2.33	$0.13
Dividend per common share	$3.00	$3.00	$3.00	$2.80	$0.65	$0.05
Employees at year-end (Document Processing)	100,900	99,000	99,000	117,247	59,267	2,973

the legendary chairman and creator of the name Xerox, decided to grow the company as rapidly as possible.[2] The company sought foreign partners who offered immediate entry into overseas markets. The swift growth, proprietary technology and sales methods (leasing contracts rather than equipment sales), required local people familiar with the culture and market. In 1956 Xerox entered into a 50/50 joint venture with the Rank Organization PLC, forming Rank Xerox Limited. This gave Xerox market access to Europe, Africa, and the Middle East. In 1962 Xerox formed a partnership with Fuji Photo Film Company in Japan to create Fuji Xerox. This gave Xerox access to Japan and Asia. At the same time, separate arrangements were made with the South and Central American countries. Their ownership structure varied based on the country and the local partner.

In the early 70s, Xerox was more concerned with a US government antitrust suit than with

the market entry of domestic and foreign competition. Only at the end of the decade did they recognize the serious competitive problem. The growth, income, and balance sheet strength of Xerox were impressive, attracting more investors who were pleased with the financial performance. Xerox operating managers, however, began to feel the competitive pressure. Between 1970 and 1980, Xerox's market share, as measured by US copier revenues, fell from 96 percent to 45 percent. The Japanese attacked the low- and medium-range of the copier market, while the domestic competitors made inroads in the high-end equipment market. To further frustrate Xerox management, the Japanese firms were selling their equipment at Xerox's manufacturing cost.

David Kearns became chairman in 1982, and was well aware of the significant market share losses. The competition was formidable since they were financially strong, technologically advanced, and enjoyed excellent customer relations. Xerox developed a corporate revitalization plan called "Leadership through Quality." It was built upon the early work in competitive benchmarking and

---

[2]Jacobson and Hillkirk, p. 63.

Exhibit 2   Excerpts from the Xerox Training Literature

The Xerox Quality Strategy— "Leadership through Quality"

- The fundamental principle of this quality strategy is meeting customer requirements.
- The definition of quality is meeting the customer's requirements all of the time.
- The program started with a vision at the top. Senior management drives the program. However, employee involvement is absolutely key. It is the people who do the work, and they know how to do it best. Training and sharing of information are critical to the LTQ implementation.
- Quality is a strategic tool used to improve competitiveness and organizational effectiveness. The focus is on the processes as well as products.
- Quality is a long-term process requiring continuous improvement and management patience.
- Three major components of LTQ are

1. Employee Involvement (EI): Problem-solving process using quality circles, people empowerment, Ishikawa's fish bone chart, and other tools to understand cause and effect of problems.
2. Competitive Benchmarking: Establish standards for comparing internal performance. Implement the best practices learned to improve performance.

3. The Quality Improvement Process: Review and continually improve all internal processes by following a process which focuses on meeting customer requirements.

- Leadership through quality is a fully integrated business process.

Competitive Benchmarking

- The continuous process of measuring Xerox's products, services, and business practices against the toughest competitors or those companies renowned as the leaders.

- The goal is superiority in all areas— quality, product reliability, and cost.

- Benchmarking is a learning experience where the best practices are observed and measured to create targets for future achievement.

- It is part of the total quality leadership program requiring employee involvement and is linked to each operating unit's business plan and strategy.

- It requires the integration of competitive information, practices, and performance into decisionmaking and communication functions at all levels of the business.

---

employee involvement. Exhibit 2 outlines the central features of these programs, which served as the cornerstone of the new Xerox culture. In addition, Xerox senior managers started to improve the cumbersome management process. The corporate reporting and planning process was very long and bureaucratic, with more detail than most managers could absorb. Even worse, the reporting formats were not even consistent between divisions. Xerox improved its management information system and standardized reporting formats to address many of these problems.

Kearns passed the leadership of Xerox to Paul Allaire in 1991, having achieved a company turnaround in the 80s. His strategy changed the culture of Xerox and gave it the competitive muscle to regain market share and made improvements in the company operations. The 1990 annual report reflects some of their success.

> Document Processing achieved the following demonstrable results:
>
> - Customer satisfaction levels increased in every market served by the company.
> - Revenues rose by 9 percent to a record $13.6 billion.
> - Profits increased by 23 percent to $599 million.
> - Return on assets improved by over 2 points to 14.6 percent.
> - $1.1 billion in cash was generated.[3]

Organization

The emphasis was on nine business divisions, supported by three geographic customer operations divisions. These twelve units were organized under three operation families. The primary focus for the management of Xerox was the business management level, which promoted more effective linkages between markets and technologies. These divisions had end-to-end responsibility for satisfying the customer. They were ". . . responsible for Xerox offerings—research and technology, development, manufacturing, marketing, sales, service, administration all work together seamlessly to 'put it together' better and faster for the customers . . ."[4]

The Finance and Control Function

The central focal point for the finance function at Xerox was the Financial Executive Council (FEC). The membership consisted of the senior Corporate Finance staff and the chief financial officers from the major Xerox operating organizations. The FEC evolved in the 1980s in re-

sponse to the senior financial managers' goal of further improving the finance operations and obtaining a greater involvement by the Finance executives. According to Al ". . . they felt financial managers (controllers) could contribute in the formulation of management decisions at the operating units. The move was basically from an accounting policy group to a group which added more value to the management process. In the spirit of Leadership through Quality, the financial practices required streamlining and major revision. The FEC set the course for becoming a world-class financial operation based on their benchmark studies."

Note, the FEC evolved in parallel with the start of the LTQ and Benchmarking activities. The new Xerox LTQ culture demanded an involved and proactive finance group. The key to the value added concept was in helping line managers make more enlightened business decisions. In addition, the FEC was the central developer of the company's financial human resource talent. Executive management recognized the strength and talent of the FEC and regularly used them as a sounding board for policy and strategic considerations.

The FEC actively promoted the building of trust in the Xerox finance community. They typically met once a quarter for 2 days and discussed a wide range of financial and business matters with a structured but informal atmosphere. Many of the members had been on the FEC for 10 years. They knew one another very well, and freely expressed their ideas and opinions. This group engineered the finance and accounting changes in Xerox as the organization and business practices changed drastically in the 1980s. Raghunandan Sachdev ("Sach"), corporate controller and one of the FEC founding members, made the following comment, "It is not clear how the FEC evolved, but Finance needed to stop second-guessing line managers. We had a choice either to become glorified auditors or to get involved in decisions early and become part of the management process. We knew we could add

---

[3]Xerox 1990. Annual Report
[4]*Xerox 2000: Putting It Together*, a company document describing the organizational changes made in 1992.

value to the process and provide managers with valuable analysis and advice. Today the general managers listen to their finance people, use them as sounding boards and have a very close working relationship."

Financial Organization

The 12 business unit controllers in the document processing organization reported directly (solid line) to the general manager of their respective business unit. They had a dotted line relationship to corporate finance for their fiduciary roles, financial reporting, and professional development. The document processing financial organization of Xerox was a modified matrix, multinational organization with the business unit controller having both solid and dotted line reporting responsibility. The Business divisions, with responsibility for product development and manufacturing, managed their business throughout the world. The Customer Operations divisions were organized geographically and managed customer relationships. The management control system concentrated on the responsibility and performance of the twelve business divisions.

There were numerous subunits, such as manufacturing facilities, distribution and service centers, and sales offices, within each business division. Each business unit had its own organization whereby the subunit controller reported directly to his or her general manager and dotted line to the division controller. The following summarizes the global document processing operational organization.

Business Divisions.   As outlined above, the Business divisions were responsible for the overall management of their product business areas worldwide.

US Customer Operations.   US Customer Operations provided sales, service, and customer administration support to the US as contracted with the Business divisions. They purchased document processing and related equipment from the nine business divisions.

Rank Xerox Limited.   They were a 51/49 percent joint venture with the Rank organization when Xerox acquired the majority share in 1969 and operated the company. Rank Xerox marketed and serviced document processing and related equipment in Europe, Africa, and parts of Asia for the Business divisions. The Rank Xerox legal entity also contained manufacturing facilities in Europe. For example, in Holland, they had an extensive sales organization as well as a major production facility that supplied equipment for many other countries including the US. In this case, the Venray plant results legally were consolidated with the Rank Xerox results. For performance purposes, the plant provided product to the Business division. Thus, the plant controller was at the intersection of the performance organization matrix. He reported dotted line to the Rank Xerox CFO and solid line to the plant general manager. The plant general manager reported directly to the Office Document Products Business Division CEO with a dotted line to the Rank Xerox Business Division CEO.

Americas Customer Operations.   This group marketed and serviced document processing products for the Business divisions in Canada, South and Central America, China, and Hong Kong. Some of the South and Central American operations were joint ventures with local companies. In these instances Xerox maintained a majority share and management responsibility.

Fuji Xerox.   This was a 50/50 joint venture with Fuji Film Corporation of Japan. They developed, manufactured, marketed, and serviced Fuji Xerox document processing products in Japan and other territories in the Pacific Rim. They functioned as an independent Japanese corporation, buying and selling to other Xerox divisions.

Development & Manufacturing.   In 1992 the functions of this organization (to develop and manufacture Xerox document processing products, including copiers, duplicators, electronic printers, facsimiles products, scanners, computer software, and supplies) were integrated into the nine business divisions wherever possible. A core Corporate Strategic Services organization provided contracted support to the divisions. In general, if the development or manufacturing facility produced at least 90 percent of their output for a specific business, they were placed in that business group. If these facilities supported multiple business groups, they were placed in the Corporate Strategic Services group.

For external financial reporting purposes, Xerox followed the legal organizational structure. For example, Fuji Xerox was an affiliated company, and Xerox only reported the results of the equity investment in Fuji Xerox. In the Venray example above, they consolidated the factory results with the Rank Xerox results. Xerox incorporated the Rank Xerox (a majority-owned subsidiary) results with the total company through consolidation. For performance measurement, Venray results were reported through their Business divisions. The operational management accounting reports, or performance reporting, focused on Business division results. Management wanted to match accountability and responsibility by operating unit within a business area. Both the financial and management control reporting systems functioned in parallel. A former foreign business unit controller said, "We have to focus on our key objectives and deliver the planned results. This requires we manage our local environment, which may not cooperate with the original plan."

Management Control. The measurement system began with the planning process. Each operating unit within a Business division or Customer Operations division developed its annual and long-range plans. These plans were consolidated into the Business and Customer Operations division plans. This was a common business practice, with reviews and feedback sessions as the planning process cycles through the organization. The overriding principle was that the division general managers were responsible for managing and controlling their environments to deliver the committed results.

With Leadership through Quality (which included competitive benchmarking), management utilized operational measures, such as market share, customer satisfaction, and various quality statistics, as a major part of their measurement scheme. These data augmented the traditional financial-based performance measures, such as return on investment. Competitive benchmarking provided standards of world class performance, and managers were expected to improve, over time, to these levels. Operating units set targets (number of machine installs per machine type, number of customers per territory, on-time delivery rates, service response time levels, customer satisfaction ratings, etc.) for achievement. John McGinty, vice president of control explains, "We learned that activities of a business cause the numbers to happen. Also, we need to get a better notion of time and be able to put an equivalent dollar on time. These quality-related concepts help provide the control framework process of predictive deliverables."

Measurements were a combination of financial and operational targets. Return on assets and a set of operational statistics, based on the critical success factors of the business unit, were the measures. Each operating unit had a set of custom-designed targets. Management linked growth and profit measures to the unit's business economy with operational measures linked to world-class benchmarking performance.

Reporting. Until 1987 the monthly reporting process included a complete financial package. Reports were due on a very tight time schedule, with full reporting to be complete on the fourth work day. Operating activity statistics, added to the schedule in 1987, were readily available at month's end and did not have to wait for the accounting close. The FEC discussed the time and costs versus the information value of global monthly financial results. They determined that monthly financial results in full detail from all the units was not necessary. Units now reported specific, but limited, data (consisting of sales, profits, and key operational statistics) on a monthly basis. For corporate reporting, only a quarterly full financial close of the books was necessary. The value of information had not changed, but there was a significant reduction in the number of indirect people involved in the process. The individual operations continued to produce the data needed to manage their respective business, but with a decrease in corporate reporting requirements.

An informal reporting system had also evolved. Open and honest communication reinforced the controller's dotted line connection to corporate. For example, Sach talked to all of his dotted line associates at least once a week to understand the direction their businesses were taking in the current quarter and the full year. These talks were informative and centered around problems and business risks. The FEC

maintained a standard of "no surprises" and promoted trust among the controllers. The unit controllers knew both the financial and operational matters of their business unit. This was the result of the partnering with line management. The informal network was not a hammer but rather an open discussion of issues. Naturally the informal channel of reporting complemented the formal channel.

Questions

1. Outline the management control system at Xerox. What are the key elements that make the system work?

2. What recent trends at Xerox do you see influencing the management control process?

3. In your opinion, how important are organizational culture and individual personalities in the Xerox control process?

CASE 1–3
STEWART BOX COMPANY

Stewart Box Company was a well-established manufacturer of paperboard cartons and boxes, which were sold primarily as packages for consumer products. The cartons were manufactured in the company's carton factory. The raw material for the carton factory was paperboard, which was manufactured in the company's paperboard mill adjacent to the carton factory. The plant complex also included a 60,000-square foot warehouse where finished orders were stored pending delivery. The company had approximately 425 employees in 1993. Robert Stewart, the president, was also a large stockholder.

The company marketed its products within a radius of about 500 miles from its factory, which was located in a fairly small town. It had sales engineers, who were compensated on the basis of a nominal salary, plus commission. In the marketing organization were six other persons, including three who prepared price quotations for prospective customers according to specifications obtained from the customers. The company had an excellent reputation for product quality and customer service.

The paperboard and carton industry was characterized by strong competition because of the potential overcapacity that existed in most plants. Because of this overcapacity, competition for large orders was particularly keen, and price cutting was common. Stewart met this competition by designing special boxes to customer specifications, by actively catering to its customers' wishes, and by strict adherence to promised delivery dates.

The production process required that the paperboard mill operate continuously on three

This case was prepared by Robert N. Anthony and revised by Vijay Govindarajan. Copyright by the President and Fellows of Harvard College.

shifts for maximum efficiency, but the carton factory operated an average of only one and one-half shifts per day.

A partial organization chart is shown as Exhibit 1. The paperboard mill and the carton factory were profit centers. In the carton factory were 10 production departments, each consisting of a printing press or a group of similar presses and associated equipment, and each was headed by a foreman. There were five service departments, which performed functions such as ink manufacture, quality control, and warehouse storage; each was headed by a supervisor. Each of these 15 departments was an expense center. The 10 production departments were production cost centers, and the 5 service departments were service cost centers.

Accounting System

The company had a job-cost accounting system, using standard costs. The board mill was a single cost center, operating a single paperboard manufacturing machine. A rate per machine-hour was established annually, which combined direct labor and manufacturing overhead costs. Manufactured paperboard was charged to the carton factory at a transfer price that included standard cost plus a standard return on the assets employed in the board mill. The profit component of this charge was subtracted from the inventory amounts as shown on the financial statements (because generally accepted accounting principles do not permit a profit allowance to be included in inventory).

In the carton factory, each order was a job. The job was costed at the standard cost of the materials used on the job, a standard rate per press hour for the time that the job used on presses, and a standard rate per direct labor-hour for other operations. These rates included both

Exhibit 1

Organization chart

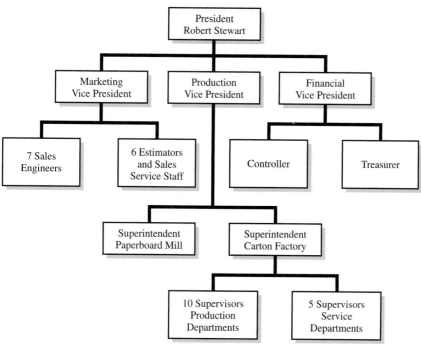

labor and factory overhead costs and were estimated annually. The system also collected actual labor and overhead costs for each responsibility center.

Strategic Planning

The company had a five-year plan, which it revised annually. The management team (president, vice presidents, and superintendents) spent a total of about two days each summer discussing and agreeing on this revision. In 1993, for example, the sales estimates for 1994–98 indicated that the capacity of the warehouse would become inadequate by 1995. This led to an investigation of alternative warehousing arrangements and a decision to build a larger warehouse and to tear down the existing one. The capital required for this warehouse was significant, and it was decided to borrow part of the cost and to finance the remainder from funds generated by operations.

As an aid in deciding on proposed capital acquisitions, the company calculated the net present value and a profitability index whenever the available information was sufficiently reliable to warrant a formal analysis. About 85 percent of the proposals in terms of numbers, but less than 50 percent in terms of dollar magnitude, were in this category. Exhibit 2 is an example of the numerical part of such an analysis. (The accompanying explanation is omitted.) It is for the replacement of a printing press which was so old and worn that maintenance and operating costs were high. The decision was made to acquire this press in 1993, and the $32,000 cost was included in the capital budget for 1994.

Over a period of about five years the company conducted a review of each facet of its operations. For production operations, it usually hired a

Exhibit 2 Analysis of Proposed Printing Press

	Tax Calculation	Present Value Calculation
Annual cash inflows:		
Saving in maintenance costs		$ 3,200
Saving in direct labor costs		9,920
Saving in power		1,600
Saving in supplies		800
Annual pretax cash inflow	$15,520	15,520
Less: Depreciation* 32000 ÷ 10	3,200	
Additional taxable income	12,320	
Additional income tax 34% × 12,320		4,189
Annual aftertax cash inflow		8,131
Present value of cash inflows ($A_{10/10} = 6.145$)		49,961
Investment in press installed		32,000
Net present value		$17,961
Profitability index $49,961/$32,000		1.56

*For simplicity in this illustration, straight-line depreciation is used. The company actually used sum-of-the-years'-digits depreciation for income tax purposes.

consulting firm expert in carton manufacturing methods to conduct this review. For marketing and general administrative functions, it used the management services division of the firm of certified public accountants that audited its financial statements.

Budget Preparation

The controller was responsible for the mechanics of the annual budgeting process. He saw to it that the sales staff prepared sales estimates. These were discussed at length in a meeting attended by Mr. Stewart, the marketing vice president, and the controller. After final sales estimates were agreed upon, the controller communicated these estimates to heads of responsibility centers as a basis for their budget preparation.

Some budget items were stated as a fixed amount per month, others were stated as variable amounts per unit of output, and still others were stated as a fixed amount per month plus a variable amount per unit of output. For the production departments, output was measured in terms of machine-hours or direct labor-hours; and for the service departments, it was measured in terms of an appropriate measure of activity, such as pounds of ink manufactured.

Each responsibility center head discussed his proposed budget first with the controller (who had had long experience in the industry and hence could point out discrepancies or soft spots), and in the case of the carton factory, with its superintendent. Mr. Stewart then discussed the proposed budgets for the board mill and the carton factory with the superintendents of these profit centers. He discussed the marketing budget with the marketing vice president. From these discussions, an approved budget emerged. It consisted of a master budget showing planned revenues and expenses at the estimated sales volume, a variable budget for each responsibility center showing the fixed amount per month and the variable rate per unit of output for each significant item of expense, a purchasing budget, and a cash budget. Standard unit costs and overhead rates were revised if necessary so that they were consistent with the approved budget.

Product Pricing

Pricing was a crucial element in the company's marketing tactics. Prices were prepared by the company's estimators for each bid or order on the basis of sales specifications and the appropriate standard cost elements as shown in tables the company had developed for this purpose. To the calculated amount of total factory costs, there were added allowances for selling and administrative expenses, sales commissions, cash discounts, and a profit margin. These allowances were expressed as percentages, and were based on the budget. A sample price estimate is reproduced as Exhibit 3.[1] The price calculated in the estimate was often adjusted for quotation purposes. It might be lowered to meet competitive conditions, or it might be increased because the design work on the order was judged to be particularly good, or for other reasons. In Exhibit 3, the calculated selling price came to $45.00 per thousand boxes, but the actual quotation was increased to $49.00.

Estimators of several companies met regularly under the auspices of a trade association to price sample boxes according to their own formulas. Based on these meetings, Mr. Stewart concluded that, while most of his competitors were shaving prices below formula, Stewart's quoted prices were higher than the calculated estimate about 65 percent of the time and lower 15 percent of the time. "It all depends on the competition and on your assessment of the whole situation," he once said.

On some occasions, the company departed from its normal pricing practices. This usually happened when orders for cartons were not in sufficient volume to keep the board mill working at capacity. On these occasions the company took orders for paperboard at prices below full cost in order to keep the board mill busy. Such contribution pricing was not used often, however.

Reports

Each month an income statement was prepared (Exhibit 4). It was constructed to focus on the performance of the two profit centers. Also, a spending report was prepared for each of the

---

[1]Many of the abbreviations and terms in this form are peculiar to the company. The purpose of Exhibit 3 is only to illustrate the form used in preparing a price estimate. An understanding of its details is not necessary.

15 expense centers in the carton factory. An example is given in Exhibit 5.

In addition, Mr. Stewart received a variety of other reports on a regular basis. The *internally generated* reports were as follows:

1. Balance sheet, monthly.
2. Selling, general and administrative statement, monthly.
3. Overdue accounts receivable, monthly.
4. Overdue shipments, monthly.
5. Inventory size, monthly.
6. Raw materials shrinkage report, monthly.
7. Cash and securities listing, monthly.
8. Actual sales, weekly, with a monthly comparison of actual and budgeted sales.
9. Carton factory production, monthly. This included operating hours statistics and efficiency percentages.
10. Outstanding orders (backlog) weekly.
11. Machine production report, daily.
12. Quality control report, monthly.

Mr. Stewart examined the reports illustrated in Exhibits 4 and 5 carefully. If there were important departures from plan, he discussed them with the manager responsible. Other reports were prepared primarily for the use of some other executive, and Mr. Stewart received only an information copy. He might or might not glance at these reports in a given month, but he was certain to do so if he suspected that trouble might be brewing in the area covered by the report.

Mr. Stewart also paid close attention to several *external* reports he received regularly from the industry trade association. They showed current economic trends, the probable effects of these trends on different segments of the paperboard carton industry, and sales orders, actual sales, production volume, and other related statistics for all members of the association.

44

Exhibit 3

Price estimate

Preparatory Cost	Production per hours	Rate	Unit	Material Cost		Mfg. Cost	
	F. or E.						
Original Plates	F. or E.						
Electros 9 3/4 × 9 1/4		30.30	28	848	40		
Wood				25	58		
Rule				54	54		
Composing							
Die Making	③	7.76	41.8			324	37
Make-Ready-Ptg.	2×	20.48	30.0			614	40
Make-Ready-C. & C.	11.55	18.00	15.8			284	40
Total Preparatory Cost				928	52	1223	17
Quantity Cost							
Board 65,005 (3 3/4)	171.00 + 25			8892	69		
Board				40	00		
Ink				177	60		
Ink				526	32		
Cases Corrugated	700	.48	1429	685	92		
Cellulose Material							
Board, Storage & Handling		2.99				97	25
Cutting Stock							
Printing		36.32	66				
Cut and Crease						1300	94
Stripping	.933 - 4	.285 +	120			626	56
Cellulose							
Auto Gluing		.899	.466 +	17.98		763	58
Hand Gluing							
Wrapping or Packing		10.405				148	69
Inspection							
Total Quantity Cost				10,322	53	2,937	02
Total Preparatory Cost				928	52	1,223	17
Total Cost to Make				11,251	05	4,160	19
Selling & Administration		45 + 8	(% + $)			1,880	09
Material Forward						11,251	05
Shipping 56 +		11.60 +	260,287			352	86
Freight and Cartage		.64				385	84
Total Cost						18,030	03
Profit		20%				3,606	00
Total Selling Price						21,636	03
Finished Stock Price							
Commission & Discount		4%				865	44
Total Selling Price						22,501	48
Selling Price per M-Calculated						45	00
Selling Price per M-Quoted						49	00

EXHIBIT 4   **Stewart Box Company**
Income Statement ($000 omitted)

	December 1993		12 Months 1993	
	Actual	*Variance**	*Actual*	*Variance**
Board Mill				
External sales	$ 83	$ 19	$ 550	$ 61
Transfers to carton factory	269	26	3,152	208
Total revenues	352	45	3,702	269
Cost of goods sold	270	(26)	2,929	(247)
Gross margin	82	19	773	22
Volume variance		24		54
Other variances		(21)		(22)
Selling and administrative expenses	48	(6)	598	(10)
Board mill profit	34	16	175	44
Carton Factory				
Sales	1066	35	12,749	397
Standard cost of goods sold	787	(29)	9,063	(208)
Gross margin	279	6	3,686	189
Manufacturing variances		26		64
Selling expenses	80	(8)	883	(19)
Administrative expenses	19	2	229	11
Carton factory profit	180	26	2,574	245
Company				
Total factory and mill profits	214	42	2,749	289
Corporate expenses	83	3	731	29
Nonoperating income (loss)	(6)		(19)	3
Income before income tax	125	45	1,999	321
Income tax	43	(14)	680	(104)
Net income	82	31	1,319	217

*( ) = unfavorable

Questions

1. The following questions relate to Exhibit 4 and the December 1993 amounts:
   a. A transfer price was used in connection with two items. What are these two items?
   b. Assuming that inventory levels did not vary in December, what was the actual cost of goods manufactured in the carton factory?
   c. Why is the assumption in question *b* necessary to answer that question?
   d. What is the budgeted amount of corporate expenses?
   e. In December was activity in the board mill above or below the standard volume?

Exhibit 5 Spending Report, Department 14 (two-color Miehle printing presses)

	December 1993		12 Months 1993	
	Actual	*Variance**	*Actual*	*Variance**
Labor—pressmen	$ 9,416	$ (171)	$129,691	$(1,035)
Labor—helpers	3,318	(74)	46,365	(376)
Press supplies	597	192	5,246	234
Repairs	2,355	(966)	13,699	192
Power	774	106	10,190	515
Other controllable overhead	387	83	5,510	738
Total controllable costs	16,847	(830)	210,701	268
Departmental fixed cost	3,882	—	46,579	—
Allocated costs	5,363	—	64,358	—
Total costs	$26,092	—	$321,638	—
Volume variance		(544)		1,619
Total variance		($1,374)		$ 1,887

*( ) = unfavorable

2. The following questions relate to Exhibit 5 and the December amounts:
   a. What was the actual cost of labor—pressmen?
   b. What was the budgeted amount of total controllable cost?
   c. What amount of total controllable cost was applied to products?
   d. Why do no amounts appear in the spending variance column for departmental fixed costs and allocated costs?

3. As his assistant, write a memorandum calling Mr. Stewart's attention to matters you think he should note when he reads Exhibit 4.

4. Do the same with Exhibit 5.

5. What do you regard as the particularly strong points of the system described in this case? What are its weak points? Can you suggest ways of overcoming these weaknesses?

THE MANAGEMENT CONTROL ENVIRONMENT

In Chapter 1 we defined management control as the process by which managers influence other members of the organization to implement the organization's strategies. This process relates to two different types of activities: (1) ongoing operations and (2) projects. In Part I and Part II we limit the discussion to the management control of ongoing operations. The management control of projects (e.g., research and development projects, construction projects, production of motion pictures) is described in Chapter 18.

Chapter 2 describes typical strategies that an organization may adopt. The strategy a company chooses is part of the environment that influences the design of the management control system.

In Chapter 3 we discuss the behavioral characteristics of individuals who work in organizations.

In the next four chapters we discuss responsibility centers, which are the organization units that are central to the management control process. A responsibility center is any organization unit headed by a manager who is responsible for its activities.

Characteristics of a responsibility center relevant to management control are discussed in Chapter 4. All responsibility centers produce outputs (i.e., they do something), and all have inputs (i.e., they use resources). They can be classified on the basis of the measurement of inputs and outputs into four types: revenue centers, expense centers, profit centers, or investment centers.

In a *revenue center* outputs are measured in monetary terms, but inputs are not measured in monetary terms. These responsibility centers usually are part of the marketing organization. We discuss these in Chapter 4.

In an *expense center* the management control system measures inputs in monetary terms (i.e., as costs), but it does not measure outputs in monetary terms. We also discuss expense centers in Chapter 4.

In a *profit center* the system measures both inputs and outputs in monetary terms; that is, inputs are measured as expenses and outputs as revenues. Profit is the difference between expenses and revenues. We discuss profit centers in Chapter 5. Many profit centers transfer products (either goods or services) to other profit centers within the company. The price used in measuring the value of products transferred is called a *transfer price*. Chapter 6 describes transfer pricing.

In an *investment center* the control system measures not only the inputs and outputs in monetary terms but also measures the investment that is employed in the responsibility center. We discuss investment centers in Chapter 7. Chapter 7 describes some of the organizational considerations that are involved in deciding whether a responsibility center should, or should not, be treated as an investment center.

Chapters 4 through 7 outline the management considerations involved in assigning *financial responsibility* to organization subunits. The particular choice of a financial metric would depend upon the behavior expected from subordinates taking into account the organization's strategies. Thus in a cost center, the actions of the responsibility center manager will be directed toward cost control, in a revenue center toward generating revenues, in a profit center toward improving profits, and in an investment center toward enhancing profits in relation to the assets employed. In Chapter 11 we describe the *balanced scorecard* which blends financial measures with nonfinancial measures as a tool for strategy execution.

2

UNDERSTANDING STRATEGIES

Management control systems are tools to implement strategies. Strategies differ between organizations, and controls should be tailored to the requirements of specific strategies. Different strategies require different task priorities, different key success factors, and different skills, perspectives, and behaviors. Thus, a continuing concern in the design of control systems should be whether the behavior induced by the system is the one called for by the strategy.

Strategies are plans to achieve organization goals. Therefore, in this chapter we first describe some typical goals in organizations. Then we discuss strategies at two levels in an organization: the corporate level and the business unit level. Strategies provide the broad context within which one can evaluate the optimality of the elements of the management control systems discussed in Chapters 4 through 12. In Chapter 13 we discuss how to vary the form and structure of control systems in accordance with variations in corporate and business unit strategies.

Goals

Although we often refer to the goals of a corporation, a corporation as such does not have goals. The corporation is an artificial being with no mind or decision-making ability of its own. The goals are arrived at by the chief executive officer (CEO) of the corporation, with the advice of other members of senior management; usually they are ratified by the board of directors. In many well-known corporations, the goals originally set by the founder persist for generations.[1] In the formal management control system of a business, profitability usually is the most important goal, so we discuss it first. Profitability is by no means the only goal, however; we describe other goals in a following section.

---

[1]For example, Henry Ford, Ford Motor Company; Alfred P. Sloan, General Motors; Thomas Watson, IBM; Walt Disney, Walt Disney Company; and George Eastman, Eastman Kodak.

Profitability

In the broadest and conceptually soundest sense, profitability is expressed by an equation that is the product of two ratios:

$$\frac{\text{Revenues} - \text{Expenses}}{\text{Revenues}} * \frac{\text{Revenues}}{\text{Investment}} = \text{Return on investment}$$

An example is:

$$\frac{\$10,000 - \$9,500}{\$10,000} * \frac{\$10,000}{\$4,000} = 12.5\%$$

The first ratio in this equation is the profit margin percentage:

$$(\$10,000 - \$9,500)/\$10,000 = 5\%$$

The second ratio is the investment turnover:

$$\$10,000/\$4,000 = 2.5 \text{ times}$$

The product of these two ratios is the return on investment: $5\% \times 2.5$ times = 12.5%. It can be found directly by dividing profit (i.e., revenues minus expenses) by investment; but this does not draw attention to the two principal components: profit margin and investment turnover.

In the most basic form of this equation, "investment" is the shareholders' investment, which consists of proceeds from issuance of stock, plus retained earnings. One of management's responsibilities is to arrive at the right balance between the two main sources of financing: debt and equity. The shareholders' investment (i.e., equity) is the amount of financing that was not obtained by debt—that is, by borrowing. However, for many purposes, the source of financing is not relevant; "investment" then is the total of debt capital and equity capital.

"Profitability" refers to profits in the long run, rather than in the current year or the current quarter; many current expenditures for advertising, research and development, and other items reduce current profits but increase long-run profits.

Some CEOs focus on only part of the equation. Jack Welch, CEO of General Electric Company, explicitly focused on revenue; he stated that General Electric should not be in any business in which its sales revenues were not the first or second largest of any company in that business. This does not imply that he neglected the other components of the equation; rather, his implication is that if General Electric has the highest market share in its industry, it should be able to make a relatively high return on investment.

Other CEOs focus solely on revenues because they think size of the company itself is a goal; such a focus can lead to problems. If expenses are not low enough, the profit margin will not produce a high enough return on the shareholders' investment. Even if the profit margin is satisfactory, the organization will not earn a satisfactorily high return if the amount of investment is too high.

Some CEOs focus on profit, either as a monetary amount or as a percentage. This focus overlooks the fact that if additional profits are obtained by a greater-than-proportional increase in investment, each dollar of investment has earned less than before.

Maximizing Shareholder Value

In the 1980s and 1990s the term *shareholder value* appeared frequently in the business literature; it was said that the appropriate goal of a for-profit corporation is to maximize shareholder value. Although the meaning of this term isn't always clear from the context, we presume it refers to the market price of the corporation's stock. We believe that achieving *satisfactory profit* better states a corporation's goal than maximizing shareholder value for three principal reasons.[2]

First, "maximizing" implies that there is a way of finding the maximum amount that a company can earn. This is not the case. In deciding between two courses of action, management believes (with some qualifications) that the selected course will add more to profitability than the rejected courses. Management rarely discovers, however, all the alternatives possible and the effect on profitability of each. Profit maximization requires that marginal costs and a demand curve be calculated, and managers usually do not know what these are.[3] If maximization were the goal, managers would spend every working hour (and many sleepless nights) thinking about endless alternatives for increasing profitability; life is generally considered too short to warrant such an effort.

Second, although optimizing shareholder value may be one goal, it is by no means the only goal in most organizations. Certainly a business that does not earn a profit at least equal to its cost of capital is not doing its job. Without achieving this goal, a business cannot discharge any other responsibilities. But economic performance is *not* the *sole* responsibility of a business. Most managers want to behave ethically, and most feel an obligation to other stakeholders in the organization.

Third, shareholder value is usually equated to the market value of the company's stock; but market value is not an accurate measure of what the shareholders' investment is actually worth, except at the moment at which the shares are traded. Today's stock price results from the judgment of the *average* investor; but the average investor tends to think primarily about the company's prospects in the short run, whereas shareholders should want management to make decisions that benefit the corporation in the long run, even at

---

[2]In 1957 Herbert Simon coined the term *satisficing* to describe the appropriate goal, a concept that was an important basis for his award of the Nobel prize for economics. Although later than his original paper on this topic, a convenient source for his analysis is Herbert A. Simon, *The New Science of Management Decision* (Englewood Cliffs, NJ: Prentice Hall, 1977).

[3]Moreover, as Saari has demonstrated, economic models based on profit maximization behave erratically, with slight changes in their assumptions, so they have limited value in solving practical problems. Donald G. Saari, "Erratic Behavior of Economic Models," *Working Paper No. 225,* the Industrial Institute for Economic and Social Research, Stockholm, 1990.

the expense of short-run profitability. Moreover, the average investor is not privy to much of the information that management has concerning the company's long-run prospects.

> **Example.** Henry Ford's operating philosophy was *satisfactory profit,* not *maximum profit.* He wrote, "And let me say right here that I do not believe that we should make such an awful profit on our cars. A reasonable profit is right, but not too much. So it has been my policy to force the price of the car down as fast as production would permit, and give the benefits to the users and laborers—with resulting surprisingly enormous benefits to ourselves."[4]

By rejecting the maximization concept, we do not mean to question the validity of certain obvious principles. A course of action that decreases expenses without affecting another element, such as market share, is sound. So is a course of action that increases expenses with a greater than proportional increase in revenues, such as increased advertising expense in some cases. So is a course of action that increases profit without an increase in shareholder investment, or one that increases profit with a less than proportional increase in shareholder investment, such as an investment in a cost-saving machine. These principles assume, in all cases, that the course of action is ethical and consistent with the corporation's other goals.

Risk

An organization's pursuit of profitability is affected by management's willingness to take risks. The degree of risk taking varies with the personalities of individual managers. Nevertheless, there is an upper limit; some organizations explicitly state that management's primary responsibility is to preserve the company's assets and that the goal of profitability is secondary. The calamitous bankruptcy of hundreds of savings and loan associations in the 1980s is traceable, in large part, to managers who made what appeared to be highly profitable loans without giving adequate recognition to the riskiness of those loans.

Other Goals

In a survey by Posner and Schmidt of 900 American executives, the executives ranked their goals in order of importance: organizational effectiveness ranked first, then high productivity, good organizational leadership, high morale, good organizational reputation, high organizational efficiency, *profit maximization,* organizational growth, organizational stability, value to local community, and service to the public.[5] Clearly, profit, here as profit maximization, is only one of a large number of goals. The same survey asked executives to rank the importance

---

[4]Henry Ford. *My Life and Work* (Garden City, NY: Doubleday, Page & Co., 1922), p. 162.

[5]B. Z. Posner and W. H. Schmidt, "Values and the American Manager: An Update," *California Management Review,* Spring 1984, pp. 202–16.

of various stakeholders to the corporation: customers were ranked first, followed by "myself," subordinates, employees as a whole, bosses, co-workers and colleagues, managers, technical and white-collar employees, founders of the company, craftsmen and skilled workers, *public stockholders,* and elected public officials and government bureaucrats. Again, the fact that public stockholders were ranked 11th out of 12 stakeholders indicates that corporations do not operate solely, or even primarily, for the benefit of their shareholders.

Other studies show that most managements will not condone unethical behavior; they forbid the payment of bribes, even though this would increase profitability; and they support participation in community activities and contributions to educational and charitable organizations, even though these activities increase expenses and, therefore, in the short run, reduce profits.

The Concept of Strategy

Although definitions differ, there is general agreement that a *strategy describes the general direction in which an organization plans to move to attain its goals.*[6] Every well-managed organization has one or more strategies, although they may not be stated explicitly. In the previous section we described the typical goals of an organization. The rest of this chapter will deal with generic types of strategies that can help an organization achieve its goals.

A firm develops its strategies by matching its core competencies with industry opportunities. Exhibit 2–1 lays out schematically the development of a firm's strategies. Kenneth R. Andrews advanced this basic concept. According to Andrews, strategy formulation is a process that senior executives use to evaluate a company's strengths and weaknesses in light of the opportunities and threats present in the environment and then to decide on strategies that fit the company's core competencies with environmental opportunities.[7] Much attention during the past 30 years has focused on developing more rigorous frameworks to conduct environmental analysis (to identify opportunities and threats)[8] and internal analysis (to identify core competencies).[9]

Strategies can be found at two levels: (1) strategies for a whole organization; and (2) strategies for business units within the organization. About 85 percent of *Fortune* 500 industrial firms in the United States have more than one business unit and consequently formulate strategies at both levels.

---

[6]Writings on military strategy go back thousands of years. The military distinguishes between *strategy,* which refers to operations in a particular theater, and *grand strategy,* which relates to worldwide geopolitical goals. As used here, strategy corresponds to *grand strategy* as used in the military.

[7]Kenneth R. Andrews, *The Concept of Corporate Strategy* (Homewood, Ill: Dow Jones-Irwin, 1971).

[8]Michael E. Porter, *Competitive Strategy: Techniques for Analyzing Industries and Competitors* (New York: The Free Press, 1980).

[9]C. K. Prahalad and G. Hamel, "The Core Competence of the Corporation," *Harvard Business Review,* May–June 1990, pp. 79–91.

EXHIBIT 2–1

*Strategy
formulation*

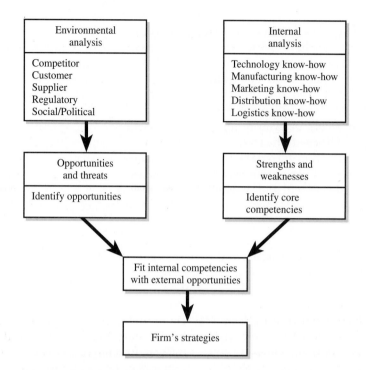

Although strategic choices are different at different hierarchical levels, there is a clear need for consistency in strategies across business unit and corporate levels. Exhibit 2–2 summarizes the strategy concerns at the two organizational levels and the generic strategic options. The remainder of this chapter will elaborate on the ideas summarized in Exhibit 2–2. Given the systems orientation of this book, we will not attempt an exhaustive analysis of the appropriate content of strategies. We rather provide enough appreciation for the strategy formulation process so the reader is able to identify the strategies at various organizational levels as part of an evaluation of the firm's management control system.

Corporate Level Strategy

Corporate strategy is about being in the right mix of businesses. Thus, corporate strategy is concerned more with the question of *where* to compete than with *how* to compete in a particular industry; the latter is a business unit strategy. At the corporate level, the issues are: (1) the definition of businesses in which the firm will participate; and (2) the deployment of resources among those businesses. Corporate-wide strategic analysis results in decisions involving businesses to add, businesses to retain, businesses to emphasize, businesses to de-emphasize, and businesses to divest.

In terms of their corporate level strategy, companies can be classified into one of three categories. A *single industry* firm operates in one line of business.

Exhibit 2–2   Two Levels of Strategy

Strategy Level	Key Strategic Issues	Generic Strategic Options	Primary Organizatonal Levels Involved
Corporate level	Are we in the right mix of industries? What industries or subindustries should we be in?	Single industry. Related diversification. Unrelated diversification.	Corporate office.
Business unit level	What should be the mission of the business unit?	Build. Hold. Harvest. Divest.	Corporate office and business unit general manager.
	How should the business unit compete to realize its mission?	Low cost. Differentiation.	Business unit general manager.

Exxon, which is in the petroleum industry, is an example. A *related diversified* firm operates in several industries, and the business units benefit from a common set of core competencies.[10] *Procter & Gamble* is an example of a related diversified firm; it has business units in diapers (Pampers), detergent (Tide), soap (Ivory), toothpaste (Crest), shampoo (Head & Shoulders), and other branded consumer products. P&G has two core competencies that benefit all of its business units: (a) core skills in several chemical technologies, and (b) marketing and distribution expertise in low-ticket branded consumer products moving through supermarkets. An *unrelated business* firm operates in businesses that are not related to one another; the connection between business units is purely financial. *Textron* is an example. Textron operates in businesses as diverse as writing instruments, helicopters, chain saws, aircraft engine components, forklifts, machine tools, specialty fasteners, and gas turbine engines.

At the corporate level, one of the most significant dimensions along which strategic contexts differ is the extent and type of diversification undertaken by different firms, as depicted in Exhibit 2–3.

Single Industry Firms

One axis in Exhibit 2–3—*extent of diversification*—relates to the number of industries in which the company operates. At one extreme, the company may be totally committed to one industry. Firms that pursue a single industry strategy include *Maytag* (major household appliances), *Wrigley* (chewing gum), *Perdue*

---

[10]Prahalad and Hamel describe the nature of "core competency" on pp. 70–91.

EXHIBIT 2–3

Corporate-level strategies: graphical representation of generic corporate strategies

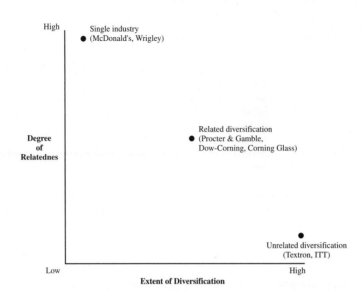

Farms (poultry), and *NuCor* (steel). A single industry firm uses its core competencies to pursue growth within that industry.

> **Example**: NuCor achieved growth of 17% annually over a 27 year period (1970–1997) by focusing exclusively on the steel industry. NuCor used its three core competencies (manufacturing process know-how, technology adoption and implementation know-how, and plant construction know-how) in achieving these results.

Unrelated Diversified Firms

At the other extreme, there are firms, such as Textron, that operate in a number of different industries.

The other axis in Exhibit 2–3—*degree of relatedness*—refers to the nature of linkages across the multiple business units. Here we refer to operating synergies across businesses based on common core competencies and on sharing of common resources. In the case of Textron, except for financial transactions, its business units have little in common. There are few operating synergies across business units within Textron. Textron headquarters functions like a holding company, lending money to business units that are expected to generate high financial returns. We refer to such firms as *unrelated diversified firms* or *conglomerates*. Conglomerates grow primarily through acquisition. Other examples of unrelated diversified firms are Litton and LTV.

Related Diversified Firms

Another group consists of firms that operate in a number of industries and their businesses are connected to each other through operating synergies. We refer to these firms as *related diversified firms*.

Operating synergies consist of two types of linkages across business units: (1) ability to share common resources; and (2) ability to share common core competencies. One way related diversified firms create operating synergies is by having two or more business units share resources such as a common sales force, common manufacturing facilities, and a common procurement function. Such sharing of resources helps the firm reap benefits of economies of scale and economies of scope.

> **Example.** Most of Procter & Gamble's individual products share a common sales-force and a common logistics; most of its products are distributed through super-markets.

Another key characteristic of related diversified firms is that they possess core competencies that benefit many of their business units. They grow by leveraging core competencies developed in one business when they diversify into other businesses.

> **Example.** Dow Corning diversified into several products and markets that use its core competencies in silicon chemistry. Texas Instruments used its competence in electronic technology to diversify into several industrial consumer products. Corning Glass has a diversified set of businesses (cookware, optical wave guides, TV bulbs, and capacitors) but most of its products derive from the company's core competence in specialty glass technology. Other examples of related diversified firms include Procter & Gamble, NEC, Canon, Philip Morris, Du Pont, Emerson Electric, and America Telephone & Telegraph.

Related diversified firms typically grow internally through research and development.

The role of the corporate office in a related diversified firm is twofold: (1) similar to a conglomerate, the chief executive of a related diversified firm must make resource allocation decisions across business units; (2) but, unlike a conglomerate, the chief executive of a related diversified firm must also identify, nurture, deepen, and leverage corporatewide core competencies that benefit multiple business units.

Core Competence and Corporate Diversification

Despite the dismal track record of companies pursuing diversification, many have pursued this strategy since the 1960s. Porter writes:

> I studied the diversification records of 33 large, prestigious U.S. companies over the 1950–1986 period and found that most of them had divested many more

acquisitions than they had kept. The corporate strategies of most companies have dissipated, instead of creating shareholder value.[11]

Research has shown that, on average, related diversified firms perform the best, single industry firms perform next best, and unrelated diversified firms do not perform well over the long term.[12] This is because corporate headquarters, in a related diversified firm, has the ability to transfer core competencies from one business unit to another. C. K. Prahalad and Gary Hamel in their *Harvard Business Review* article, "The Core Competence of the Corporation," (May–June 1990) make a compelling case for corporate diversification based on a company's core competencies. A core competency is what a firm excels at and what adds significant value for customers. Competency-based growth and diversification, therefore, have significant potential for success.

> **Examples.** Honda's key core competency is its ability to design small engines. Honda used this competency initially to enter the motorcycle business. Since then, Honda has leveraged its competency in small engine technology in a variety of businesses such as automobiles, lawn mowers, snow blowers, snowmobiles, and outdoor power tools.
>
> One of Federal Express's core competencies is logistics know-how. It used this competency to create the overnight mail business. Since then, the company has used this competency to enter several new businesses. For instance, Fedex manages all logistics (including internal inventory) for Laura Ashley, a leading cosmetics company.

The business units of a related diversified firm might be worse off if they were split up into separate companies since a related diversified firm can exploit operating synergies across its business units. For instance, if the business units of Honda (motorcycles, automobiles, lawn mowers, etc.) were split up as separate companies, they would then lose the benefit of Honda's expertise in small engine technology.

Unrelated diversified firms, on the other hand, do not possess operating synergies. Most of the failed corporate diversification attempts in the past were of this type. Nevertheless, some unrelated diversified firms (example: General Electric) are highly profitable. Since we continue to see examples of unrelated diversified firms, we discuss this type of corporate strategy.

Implications of Control System Design

Corporate strategy is a continuum with *single industry* strategy at one end of the spectrum and *unrelated diversification* at the other end (*related diversification* is in the middle of the spectrum). Many companies do not fit neatly into one

---

[11]Michael E. Porter, "From Competitive Advantage to Corporate Strategy," *Harvard Business Review,* May–June 1987, p. 28.

[12]Richard P. Rumself, *Strategy, Structure and Economic Performance* (Boston: Division of Research, Harvard Business School, 1974), pp. 128–42.

EXHIBIT 2–4

Corporate-level strategies: summary of three generic strategies

Type of corporate strategy	Single industry firm	Related diversified firm	Unrelated diversified firm
Pictorial representation of strategy	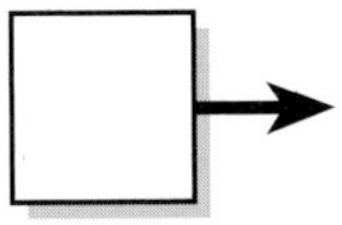	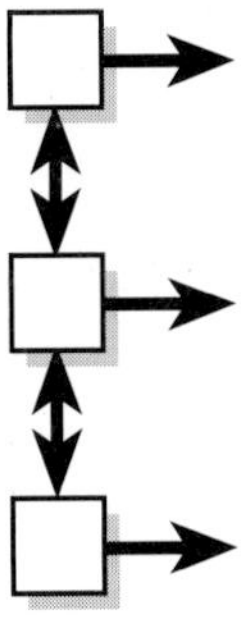	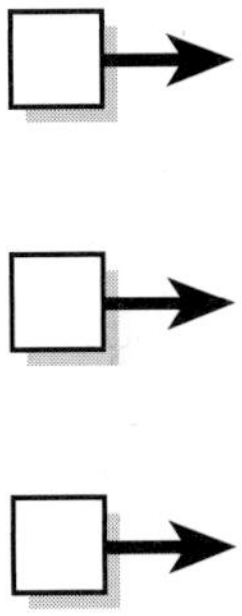
Identifying features	Competes in only one industry	Sharing of core competencies across businesses	Totally autonomous businesses in very different markets
Examples	McDonald's Corporation Perdue Farms Iowa Beef Wrigley Crown, Cork & Seal Maytag Texas Air Ford Motor NuCor	Procter & Gamble Emerson Electric Corning Glass Johnson & Johnson Philip Morris Dow-Corning Du Pont General Foods Gillette Texas Instruments AT&T	ITT Textron LTV Litton Rockwell General Electric

of the three classes. However, most companies can be classified along the continuum. A firm's location on this continuum depends on the extent and type of its diversification. Exhibit 2–4 summarizes the key characteristics of the generic corporate strategies.

The planning and control requirements of companies pursuing different corporate level diversification strategies (i.e., extent and type of diversification) are quite different. The key issue for control systems designers, therefore, is: How should the structure and form of control differ across a NuCor (a single industry firm), a Procter & Gamble (a related diversified firm), or a Textron (an unrelated diversified firm)? In Chapters 4 through 12 we discuss the elements of the management control system. In Chapter 13 we discuss how these control system elements should be designed so they implement a given firm's strategies.

Business Unit Strategies

Competition between diversified firms do not take place at the corporate level. Rather, a business unit in one firm (Procter & Gamble's *Pampers* unit) competes with a business unit in another firm (Kimberly Clark's *Huggies* unit). The corporate office of a diversified firm does not produce profit by itself; revenues are generated and costs are incurred in the business units. Business unit strategies deal with how to create and maintain competitive advantage in each of the industries in which a company has chosen to participate. The *strategy* of a business unit depends on two interrelated aspects: (1) its mission ("what are its overall objectives?") and (2) its competitive advantage ("how should the business unit compete in its industry to accomplish its mission").

Business Unit Mission

In a diversified firm one of the important tasks of senior management is resource deployment, i.e., make decisions regarding the use of the cash generated from some business units to finance growth in other business units. Several planning models have been developed to help corporate level managers of diversified firms to effectively allocate resources.[13] These models suggest that a firm has business units in several categories, identified by their mission; the appropriate strategies for each category differ. Together, the several units make up a portfolio, the components of which differ as to their risk/reward characteristics just as the components of an investment portfolio differ. Both the corporate office and the business unit general manager are involved in identifying the missions of individual business units.

Of the many planning models, two of the most widely used are Boston Consulting Group's two-by-two growth-share matrix (Exhibit 2–5) and General Electric Company/McKinsey & Company's three-by-three industry attractiveness-business strength matrix (Exhibit 2–6). While these models differ in the methodologies they use to develop the most appropriate missions for the various business units, they have the same set of missions from which to choose: *build, hold, harvest,* and *divest.*

Build.   This mission implies an objective of increased market share, even at the expense of short-term earnings and cash flow (Examples: Monsanto's biotechnology, Corning Glass's optical wave guides, Black and Decker's handheld electric tools).

Hold.   This strategic mission is geared to the protection of the business unit's market share and competitive position (Example: IBM's mainframe computers).

---

[13]In a survey of Fortune 1,000 companies, Haspeslagh reported that 75 percent of the companies practiced portfolio planning. P. Haspeslagh, "Portfolio Planning: Uses and Limits," *Harvard Business Review,* January–February 1982, pp. 58–73.

EXHIBIT 2–5 **Business Unit Mission: The BCG Model**

	Cash source	
	High	Low

	High		Low	
High		"Star" **Hold**	"Question mark" **Build**	**High**
Market growth rate				**Cash use**
Low		"Cash cow" **Harvest**	"Dog" **Divest**	**Low**
	High		Low	

Relative market share

Sources: R. A. Kerin, V. Mahajan, and P. R. Varadarajan, *Strategic Market Planning* (Boston: Allyn & Bacon, 1990). B. D. Henderson. *Corporate Strategy* (Cambridge, Mass.: Abt Books, 1979).

Harvest. This mission has the objective of maximizing short-term earnings and cash flow, even at the expense of market share (Examples: American Brands' tobacco products, General Electric's and Sylvania's light bulbs).

Divest. This mission indicates a decision to withdraw from the business either through a process of slow liquidation or outright sale.

While the planning models can aid in the formulation of missions, they are not cookbooks. A business unit's position on a planning grid should not be the sole basis for deciding its mission.

In the Boston Consulting Group (BCG) model, every business unit is placed in one of four categories—**question mark, star, cash cow,** and **dog**—that represent the four cells of a 2×2 matrix, which measures industry growth rate on one axis and relative market share on the other (Exhibit 2–5). BCG views industry growth rate as an indicator of relative industry attractiveness and relative market share as an indicator of the relative competitive position of a business unit within a given industry.

BCG singles out market share as the primary strategy variable because of the importance it places on the notion of *experience curve.* According to BCG, cost per unit decreases predictably with the number of units produced over time (cumulative experience). Since the market share leader will have the greatest accumulated production experience, such a firm should have the lowest costs and highest profits in the industry. The association between market

---

EXHIBIT 2–6   Business Unit Mission: The General Electric Planning Model

---

A

The Portfolio Matrix

Industry attractiveness		Strong	Average	Weak
	High	Winners	Winners	Question marks
	Average	Winners	Average Businesses	Losers
	Low	Profit producers	Losers	Losers

Business strength

B

Recommended Business Strategies

Industry attractiveness		Strong	Average	Weak
	High	Invest/Grow strongly (build)	Invest/Grow selectively (build)	Dominate/ Delay/ Divest
	Average	Invest/Grow selectively (build)	Earn/ Protect (hold)	Harvest/ Divest
	Low	Earn/ Protect (hold)	Harvest/ Divest	Harvest/ Divest

Business strength

Source: R. A. Kerin, V. Mahajan, and P. R. Varadarajan, *Strategic Market Planning* (Boston: Allyn & Bacon, 1990).

share and profitability has also been empirically supported by the Profit Impact of Market Strategy (PIMS) data base.[14]

Although the experience curve is a powerful analytical tool, it has limitations:

1. The concept applies to undifferentiated products where the primary basis of competition is on price. For these products, becoming the low cost player is

---

[14]Robert D. Buzzell, Bradley T. Gale, and Ralph G. M. Sultan, "Market Share—A Key to Profitability," *Harvard Business Review,* January–February 1975, pp. 97–106.

critical. However, market share and low cost are not the only ways to succeed. There are low market share firms (such as Mercedes-Benz in automobiles) that earn high profits by emphasizing product uniqueness rather than low cost.[15]

2. In certain situations improvements in process technology may have a greater impact on the reduction of per-unit cost than cumulative volume per se.

> **Example.** Certain companies in the U.S. steel industry have greatly reduced their per-unit (ton) cost of producing steel and recouped a large portion of worldwide market share by vast investments in technological improvements, not by producing more tons of steel (on a cumulative basis) than their competitors.

3. An aggressive pursuit of reducing cost via accumulated production of standardized items can lead to loss of flexibility in the marketplace.

> **Example.** The classic example of this problem is when, during the 1920s, Henry Ford standardized the car ("I will give you any color provided it is black") and aggressively reduced costs. Ford lost its leadership in the auto industry when General Motors sold the consumers on product variety ("A car for every purse and every purpose"), so much so that in 1927 Ford discontinued the Model T and suffered a 12-month shutdown for retooling.[16]

4. Commitment to the experience curve concept can be a severe disadvantage if new technologies emerge in the industry.

> **Example.** Timex's low cost position in the watch industry, built over several years, was erased overnight when Texas Instruments entered the market with digital watches.

5. Experience is not the only cost driver. Other drivers that affect cost behavior are: scale, scope, technology, and complexity.[17] A firm needs to consider carefully the relevant cost drivers at work to achieve the low cost position.

BCG used the following logic to make strategic prescriptions for each of the four cells in Exhibit 2–5. Business units that fall in the **question mark** quadrant are typically assigned the mission: "build" market share. The logic behind this recommendation is related to the beneficial effects of the experience curve. BCG argued that, by building market share early in the growth phase of an industry, the business unit will enjoy a low-cost position. These units are major users of cash, since cash outlays are needed in the areas of product development, market development, and capacity expansion. These expenditures are aimed at establishing market leadership in the short term, which will depress short-term profits. However, the increased market share is intended to result in

[15]Richard G. Hamermesh, et al, "Strategies for Low Market Share Companies," *Harvard Business Review,* May–June 1978, pp. 95–102.

[16]William J. Abernathy and Kenneth Wayne, "Limits of the Learning Curve," *Harvard Business Review,* September–October 1974, pp. 109–19.

[17]For a discussion on multiple cost drivers, see J. K. Shank and V. Govindarajan, *Strategic Cost Management* (New York: The Free Press, 1993), Chapter 10.

long-term profitability. Some businesses in the question mark quadrant might also be divested if their cash needs to build competitive position are extremely high.

> **Example.** In the early 70s, RCA decided to divest its computer division because of the enormous cash outflows that would have been required to build market share in such a capital-intensive and highly competitive industry.

Business units that fall in the **star** quadrant are typically assigned the mission: "hold" market share. These units already have a high market share in their industry, and the objective is to invest cash to maintain that position. These units generate significant amounts of cash (because of their market leadership), but they also need significant cash outlays to maintain their competitive strength in a growing market. On balance, therefore, these units are self-sufficient and do not require cash from other parts of the organization.

Business units that fall in the **cash cow** quadrant are the primary sources of cash for the firm. Since these units have high relative market share, they probably have the lowest unit costs and consequently the highest profits. On the other hand, since these units operate in low-growth or declining industries, they do not need to reinvest all the cash generated. Therefore, on a net basis, these units generate significant amounts of positive cash flows. Such units are typically assigned the mission: "harvest" for short-term profits and cash flows.

Businesses in the **dog** quadrant have a weak competitive position in unattractive industries. They should be divested unless there is a good possibility of turning them around.

The corporate office should identify cash cows with positive cash flows and redeploy these resources to build market share in question marks.

The General Electric Company/McKinsey & Company grid (Exhibit 2–6) is similar to the BCG grid in helping corporations assign missions across business units. However, its methodology differs from the BCG approach in the following respects:

1. BCG uses industry growth rate as a proxy for industry attractiveness. In the General Electric grid, industry attractiveness is based on weighted judgments about such factors as market size, market growth, entry barriers, technological obsolescence, and the like.

2. BCG uses relative market share as a proxy for the business unit's current competitive position. The General Electric grid, on the other hand, uses multiple factors such as market share, distribution strengths, and engineering strengths to assess the competitive position of the business unit.

Control system designers need to know *what* the mission of a particular business unit is, but *not* necessarily *why* the firm has chosen that particular mission. Since this book focuses on designing control systems for ongoing businesses, it deals with the implementation of the build, hold, and harvest—but not divest—missions. These missions constitute a continuum, with "pure build" at one end and "pure harvest" at the other end. A business unit could be

Exhibit 2–7

Industry structure analysis: Porter's five forces model

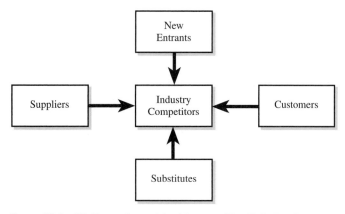

Source: Michael E. Porter, *Competitive Advantage* (New York: Free Press, 1985).

anywhere on this continuum, depending upon the trade-off it is supposed to make between building market share and maximizing short-term profits.

Business Unit Competitive Advantage

Every business unit should develop a competitive advantage in order to accomplish its mission. Three interrelated questions have to be considered in developing the business unit's competitive advantage. First, what is the competitive structure of the industry in which the business unit operates? Second, how should the business unit exploit the industry's competitive structure? Third, what will be the basis of the business unit's competitive advantage? Michael Porter has described two analytical approaches—industry analysis and value chain analysis—as aids in developing a superior and sustainable competitive advantage. Each is described below.

Industry Analysis.   Research has highlighted the important role industry conditions play in the performance of individual firms. Studies have shown that average industry profitability is, by far, the most significant predictor of firm performance.[18] According to Porter, the structure of an industry should be analyzed in terms of the collective strength of five competitive forces (see Exhibit 2–7):[19]

1. *The intensity of rivalry among existing competitors.* Factors affecting direct rivalry are industry growth, product differentiability, number and

---

[18]Birger Wernerfelt and Cynthia A. Montgomery, "Tobin's q and the Importance of Focus in Firm Performance," *American Economic Review,* March 1988, p. 249; Richard Schmalensee, "Do Markets Differ Much?," *American Economic Review,* June 1985, pp. 341–51.

[19]Michael E. Porter, *Competitive Advantage* (New York: The Free Press, 1985).

      diversity of competitors, level of fixed costs, intermittent overcapacity, and exit barriers.

2. *The bargaining power of customers.* Factors affecting buyer power are: number of buyers, buyer's switching costs, buyer's ability to integrate backward, impact of the business unit's product on buyer's total costs, impact of the business unit's product on buyer's product quality/performance, and significance of the business unit's volume to buyers.

3. *The bargaining power of suppliers.* Factors affecting supplier power are number of suppliers, supplier's ability to integrate forward, presence of substitute inputs, and importance of the business unit's volume to suppliers.

4. *Threat from substitutes.* Factors affecting substitute threat are relative price/performance of substitutes, buyer's switching costs, and buyer's propensity to substitute.

5. *The threat of new entry.* Factors affecting entry barriers are capital requirements, access to distribution channels, economies of scale, product differentiation, technological complexity of product or process, expected retaliation from existing firms, and government policy.

We make three observations with regard to the industry analysis:

1. The more powerful the five forces are, the less profitable an industry is likely to be. In industries where average profitability is high (such as soft drinks and pharmaceuticals), the five forces are weak (e.g., in the soft drink industry, entry barriers are high). In industries where the average profitability is low (such as steel and coal), the five forces are strong (e.g., in the steel industry, threat from substitutes is high).

2. Depending upon the relative strength of the five forces, the key strategic issues facing the business unit will differ from one industry to another.

3. Understanding the nature of each force helps the firm to formulate effective strategies. Supplier selection (a strategic issue) is aided by the analysis of the relative power of several supplier groups; the business unit should link with the supplier group for which it has the best competitive advantage. Similarly, analyzing the relative bargaining power of several buyer groups will facilitate selection of target customer segments.

Generic Competitive Advantage.   The five-force analysis is the starting point for developing a competitive advantage since it helps to identify the opportunities and threats in the external environment. With this understanding, Porter claims that the business unit has two generic ways of responding to the opportunities in the external environment and developing a sustainable competitive advantage: low cost and differentiation.

Low Cost.   Cost leadership can be achieved through such approaches as economies of scale in production, experience curve effects, tight cost control, and cost minimization (in such areas as research and development, service, sales

EXHIBIT 2–8

Basis for competitive advantage

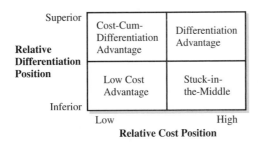

force, or advertising). Some firms following this strategy include: Charles Schwab in discount brokerage, Wal-Mart in discount retailing, Texas Instruments in consumer electronics, Emerson Electric in electric motors, Hyundai in automobiles, Dell in computers, Black and Decker in machine tools, NuCor in steel, Lincoln Electric in arc welding equipment, and BIC in pens.

Differentiation.   The primary focus of this strategy is to differentiate the product offering of the business unit, creating something that is perceived by customers as being unique. Approaches to product differentiation include brand loyalty (Coca-Cola and Pepsi Cola in soft drinks), superior customer service (Nordstrom in retailing), dealer network (Caterpillar Tractors in construction equipment), product design and product features (Hewlett-Packard in electronics), and technology (Motorola in communications). Other examples of firms following a differentiation strategy include: Mercedes in automobiles, Stouffer's in frozen foods, Neiman-Marcus in retailing, Mont Blanc in pens, and Rolex in wristwatches.

Value Chain Analysis.   As noted in the previous section and as depicted in Exhibit 2–8, business units can develop competitive advantage based on low cost, differentiation, or both. The most attractive competitive position is to achieve *cost-cum-differentiation.*

Both intuitively and theoretically, competitive advantage in the marketplace ultimately derives from *providing better customer value for an equivalent cost* or *equivalent customer value for a lower cost.* Competitive advantage cannot be meaningfully examined at the level of the business unit as a whole. The *value chain* disaggregates the firm into its distinct strategic activities. The value chain is the complete set of activities involved in a product, beginning with extraction of raw material and ending with postdelivery support to customers. Exhibit 2–9 depicts such a chain. A company chooses those activities that it will carry out with its own resources and those that it will obtain from outside parties.

Value chain analysis seeks to determine where in the company's operations—from design to distribution—customer value can be enhanced or costs lowered.

For each value added activity, the key questions are:

Exhibit 2–9

Typical value chain for a business

| Product Development | Manu-facturing | Marketing and Sales | Service/Logistics |

Support Activities: Finance, Human Resources, Information Technology

a) Can we reduce costs in this activity, holding value (revenues) constant?

b) Can we increase value (revenue) in this activity, holding costs constant?

c) Can we reduce assets in this activity, holding costs and revenue constant?

d) Most importantly, can we do (a), (b), and (c) simultaneously?

By systematically analyzing costs, revenues, and assets in each activity, the business unit can achieve cost-cum-differentiation advantage.

The value chain framework[20] is a method for breaking down the chain—from basic raw materials to end-use customers—into specific activities in order to understand the behavior of costs and the sources of differentiation. Few if any firms carry out the entire value chain of a product with their own resources. In fact, firms within the same industry vary in the proportion of activities that they carry out with their own resources.

Examples. Chevron in the petroleum industry spans wide segments of the value chain in which it operates, from oil exploration to service stations, but it does not span the entire chain. Fifty percent of the crude oil it refines comes from other producers, and more than one-third of the oil it refines is sold through other retail outlets. More narrowly, a firm such as Maxus Energy is only in the oil exploration and production business. The Limited has "downstream" presence in retail outlets but owns no manufacturing facilities. Reebok is a famous shoe brand, but the firm owns very few retail outlets. Reebok does, however, own its factories. Nike, on the other hand, does only research, design, and marketing; it outsources 100 percent of its athletic footwear manufacturing.

The value chain helps the firm to understand the entire value delivery system, *not* just the portion of the value chain in which it participates. Suppliers and customers, and suppliers' suppliers, and customers' customers have profit margins that are important to identify in understanding a firm's cost/differentiation positioning, since the end-use customers ultimately pay for all the profit margins along the entire value chain. Suppliers not only produce and deliver inputs used in a firm's value activities, but they significantly influence the firm's cost/differentiation position.

---

[20]For a full discussion, see John K. Shank and Vijay Govindarajan, *Strategic Cost Management,* (New York, NY: The Free Press, 1993), Chapters 1, 3, 4, 5; Michael E. Porter, *Competitive Advantage,* (New York, NY: The Free Press, 1985).

Example. Developments by steel "minimills" lowered the operating costs of wire products users who are the customers of the customers of the minimill two stages down the value chain.

Similarly, customers' actions can have a significant impact on the firm's cost/differentiation advantage.

Example. When printing press manufacturers built a new press of "3 meters" width, the profitability of paper mills was affected because paper machine widths must match some multiple of printing press width. Mill profit is affected by customer actions even though the paper mill is two stages upstream from the printer, who is a customer of the press manufacturer!

Summary

Every organization has one or more goals. Profitability is an important goal, but a firm should also adopt goals vis-à-vis employees, suppliers, customers, and community.

Diversified firms undertake strategy formulation at two levels—corporate and business unit. At the corporate level, the key strategic questions is: What set of businesses should the firm be in? The "generic" options for corporate level strategic questions are: (1) a single industry firm, (2) a related diversified firm, or (3) an unrelated diversified firm. A key concept in corporate level strategy is the notion of *core competence*. A core competency is an intellectual asset in which a firm excels.

At the business unit level, the key strategic questions are: (1) what should be the business unit's mission? (The "generic" business unit missions are build, hold, and harvest.) And (2) How should the business unit compete to accomplish its mission? (The "generic" competitive advantages are low cost and differentiation.)

Three tools can help in developing business unit strategies: portfolio matrices, industry structure analysis, and value chain analysis. Portfolio matrices typically position a business unit on a grid where one axis is "market attractiveness" and the other axis is "market share." Such matrices are useful in deciding on the business unit mission.

Industry structure analysis is a tool to systematically assess the opportunities and threats in the external marketplace. This is accomplished by analyzing the collective strength of five competitive forces—existing competitors, buyers, suppliers, substitutes, and new entrants.

The value chain for a business is the linked set of value-creating activities to produce a product, from basic raw material sources for component suppliers to the ultimate end-use product delivered into the final consumers' hands. Each business unit must be understood in the context of the overall chain of value-creating activities of which it is only a part. Value chain analysis is a useful tool in developing competitive advantage based on low cost, or differentiation, or preferably, cost-cum-differentiation.

Control system designers need to be cognizant of the organization's strategies since systems have to support strategies. Chapters 4 through 12 describe the different elements of management control. In Chapter 13 we discuss the planning and control requirements of different corporate and business unit strategies.

Suggested Additional Readings

Andrews, Kenneth R. *The Concept of Corporate Strategy*. Homewood, Ill: Richard D. Irwin, 1980.

Collins, James C., and Jerry I. Porras. "Building Your Company's Vision," *Harvard Business Review,* Sep–Oct 1996, pp. 65–77.

Govindarajan, Vijay, and Anil K. Gupta. "Linking Control Systems to Business Unit Strategy: Impact on Performance." *Accounting Organizations and Society* (1985), pp. 51–66.

Govindarajan, Vijay, and John K. Shank. "Cash Sufficiency: The Missing Link in Strategic Planning." *The Journal of Business Strategy,* Summer 1986, pp. 88–95.

Gupta, Anil K., and Vijay Govindarajan. "Business Unit Strategy, Managerial Characteristics, and Business Unit Effectiveness at Strategy Implementation." *Academy of Management Journal* 27, no. 1 (1984), pp. 25–41.

Hamel, Gary. "Strategy as Revolution." *Harvard Business Review,* July–August 1996, pp. 69–79.

Hax, A. C., and N. S. Majluf. *The Strategy Concept and Process.* Englewood Cliffs, N.J.: Prentice Hall, 1996.

Kerin, Roger A., Vijay Mahajan, and P. Rajan Varadarajan. *Contemporary Perspectives on Strategic Market Planning.* Boston: Allyn & Bacon, 1990.

Oster, Sharon M. *Modern Competitive Analysis.* Oxford University Press, 1990.

Porter, Michael E. *Competitive Strategy.* New York: The Free Press, 1980.

———. *Competitive Advantage.* New York: The Free Press, 1985.

———. "What Is Strategy?" *Harvard Business Review,* Nov–Dec 1996, pp. 61–78.

Prahalad, C. K., and Gary Hamel. *Competing for the Future.* New York: The Free Press, 1995.

Quinn, J. B. *The Intelligent Enterprise.* New York: The Free Press, 1994.

Shank, John K., and Vijay Govindarajan, "Cost Driver Analysis." *Behavioral Accounting Research,* 1993.

———. *Strategic Cost Management.* New York: The Free Press, 1993.

———. "Strategic Cost Analysis of Technology Investments." *Sloan Management Review* 34, 1, Fall 1992, pp. 39–51.

Slyvatski, Adrian. *Value Migration.* Boston: Harvard Business School Press, 1996.

CASE 2–1
T & J's

"I'm completely fed up. How am I supposed to run a profitable plant when I don't have any control over the price of my inputs and none over the volume, price, or mix of my outputs. I'm held hostage by the whims of the purchasing and marketing departments. I didn't go to business school so I could be evaluated on the basis of someone else's performance."

> Lisa Anderson
> Plant Manager—Dayton, Ohio
> October 1993

T&J's, founded in 1910, sold its own brands of coffee throughout the Midwestern and Mid-Atlantic states. The company's stock was closely held by members of the founder's family. The president and the secretary-treasurer were part of the family, and the only members of the management team to have equity stakes.

The home office in Columbus, Ohio, made all operating decisions. The sales policies were centrally managed through the vice president of sales and his two assistants. The president of the company and the vice president of sales jointly assumed responsibility for advertising and promotion. The company's vice president of manufacturing oversaw the roasting, grinding, and packaging of the company's coffees.

The company operated three roasting plants in the Midwest. Each plant had profit and loss responsibility. A plant manager's bonus was a percent of his or her plant's gross margin. Headquarters prepared monthly gross margin statements for each plant (see Exhibit 1). One month of gross margin information for the company is presented in Exhibit 2.

This case was written by Ruthard C. Murphy (T '93) and Anil R. Chitkara (T '94) under the supervision of Professors Vijay Govindarajan and Robert N. Anthony. The case is based on an earlier Note on Coffee prepared by Scott Barrett (T '89) and an earlier case prepared by Russell H. Hassler, Harvard University. Copyright © by Osceola Institute.

At the start of each month, headquarters gave the plant managers production schedules for the current month and a projected schedule for the succeeding month. Deliveries were made as directed by the home office.

Each plant had a small accounting office that recorded all manufacturing costs and prepared payrolls. The home office managed billing, credit, and collection, and prepared all of the company's financial statements.

Plant managers had no discretion with regard to the procurement of green (unprocessed) coffee beans. The following describes how the procurement process supplied the beans—and their cost—to the individual plants.

A special purchasing unit within the company handled the procurement of green coffee beans. The unit was located in New York City, the heart of the green coffee business, because of the need for constant contact with coffee brokers. The purchasing group was largely autonomous. It kept all of its own records and handled all of the financial transactions relating to purchasing, sales to outsiders, and transfers to the three company-operated roasting plants. The unit's manager reported directly to the company's secretary-treasurer.

The purchasing unit's primary function was to obtain the necessary varieties and quantities of green coffee for the roasting plants to blend, roast, pack, and deliver to customers. The purchasing group dealt with over 50 types and grades of coffee beans grown in tropical countries all over the world.

Based on projected sales budgets, the purchasing group entered into future green bean contracts with exporters. These contracts required green coffee delivery three to twelve months out at specific prices. The group also had the option of purchasing on the spot

Exhibit 1 Plant No. 1—Operating Statement for the Month of May

Net sales (shipments at billing prices)		$2,233,860
Less: Cost of sales		
Green coffee—at contract cost		1,120,980
Roasting and grinding		
Labor	$114,660	
Fuel	74,340	
Manufacturing expense	100,860	289,860
Packaging		
Container	253,860	
Packing carton	27,420	
Labor	36,780	
Manufacturing expense	76,320	394,380
Total manufacturing cost		1,805,220
Gross margin		$ 428,640

Exhibit 2 Income Statement for the Month of May

	Plant No. 1	Plants No. 2 and No. 3	Green Coffee (purchasing unit)	Total
Net sales	$2,233,860	$5,964,120	$371,220	$8,569,200
Cost of sales				
Green coffee	1,120,980	2,810,250	333,810	4,265,040
Roasting and grinding	289,860	608,460		898,320
Packaging	394,380	1,406,850		1,801,230
Purchasing department[1]				235,200
	1,805,220	4,825,560		7,199,790
Gross margin	$ 428,640	$1,138,560	$ 37,410	$1,369,410

[1]The operating cost of running the purchasing unit was charged directly to the central office.

market—that is, purchase for immediate delivery. Spot purchases were kept to a minimum. A purchasing agent's knowledge of the market was critical. He or she must judge market trends and make commitments accordingly.

The result of this process was that the green coffee purchasing unit bought a range of coffees in advance for delivery at various dates. At the actual delivery date, the company's sales may not be at the level expected when the original green coffee contract was signed. The difference between actual deliveries and current requirements was handled through either sales or purchases on the spot market. The company would sell to or buy from coffee brokers and sometimes from other roasters.

As an example, commitments for Kona No. 2 (a grade of Hawaiian coffee) might specify the delivery of 22,000 bags (a bag contains 132 lbs. of green coffee) in May. These deliveries would be made under 50 contracts executed at varying prices, 3 to 12 months before the month of delivery. If for some reason demand for the company's products fell in May, the plants' raw material needs could correspondingly fall to 17,000 bags. In this case, the purchasing unit would have to decide between paying for the storage of the surplus 5,000 bags in noncompany facilities, or selling the coffee on the open market. This example has been typical of the company's normal operation.

Generally, the large volume of the company's green coffee purchases permitted it to buy on favorable terms and to realize a normal brokerage and trading profit when selling in smaller lots to small roasting companies. Hence, the usual policy was to make purchase commitments based on maximum potential plant requirements and sell the surplus on the spot market.

In accounting for coffee purchases, a separate cost record was maintained for each contract. This record was charged with payments for coffee purchased, with shipping charges, import expenses, and similar items. With these charges, the purchasing group computed for each contract a net cost per bag. Thus the 50 deliveries of Kona No. 2 cited in the example would come into inventory at 50 different costs. The established policy was to treat each contract on an individual basis.

When green coffee was shipped to a plant, a charge was made for the cost represented by the contracts that covered that particular shipment of coffee. There was no element of profit or loss associated with this transfer. When the company sold green coffee on the open market, the sales were likewise costed on a specific contract basis with a resulting profit or loss on the transaction.

The operating cost of running the purchasing unit was charged to the central office. The cost was recorded as an element in the general corporate overhead.

For the past several years, the plant managers have been dissatisfied with the method of computing gross margin (as evident from the quote at the beginning of the case). Their complaints finally led to the president requesting that the controller study the whole method of reporting the results of plant operations and the purchasing group. As part of evaluating the control system, the controller assembled the data on the coffee industry (see the Appendix to the case).

Questions

1. Evaluate T&J's current control systems for the manufacturing, marketing, and purchasing departments.

2. Considering T&J's competitive strategy, what changes, if any, would you make to the control systems for the three departments?

APPENDIX
NOTE ON COFFEE

The Commodity   Prior to reaching its final form in grocery stores as ground (percolator) or soluble (instant), coffee is referred to by buyers and sellers as "green coffee." This refers to the green beans that are picked from the coffee trees. There are two types of coffee beans, arabica and robusta. Arabica is the coffee favored by American consumers and is grown primarily in South America. Its flavor is not as strong as that of the robusta variety. Robusta coffee's major grower is the Ivory Coast. Not only is its flavor stronger than arabica's, but it is also favored by processors in the production of instant coffee. Thus, with the increased demand for instant coffee, there has been a concomitant growth in relative demand for robusta beans.

The Suppliers   Coffee is generally grown in tropical regions. Brazil has been the largest producer and has supplied between 20 to 30 percent of the world's green coffee. Other large exporting countries include Colombia, Indonesia, the Ivory Coast, and Mexico. Coffee is harvested somewhere in the world during almost every month of the year. For example, Brazil's main harvesting season is April–September; Colombia's is October–March; and the Ivory Coast harvests from November–April.

The Buyers   The United States has been the world's largest single importer of coffee. It buys most of its coffee from Brazil and Colombia. Europe is second, purchasing a little less than half of all coffee exported.

Buyers fall into two categories: roasters and brokers. Roasters include the large food processing companies such as Philip Morris (which acquired General Foods including its Maxwell House business), P&G and Nestlé, as well as regional and local coffee companies. The large players purchase their coffee supplies directly from the growers. Their financial strength has allowed them to generally negotiate favorable terms with the growers. The larger purchasers are also able to inventory coffee stock in order to protect themselves against future price increases.

The smaller coffee processors have normally bought their coffee from brokers. A broker is either a trade firm or a "pure" broker. Trade firms actually purchase the coffee from the country of origin and then sell it to a food processor. Pure brokers never actually take title to the coffee. They merely match buyer and seller in the marketplace. Trade firms generally finance their transactions via secured loans from commercial banks. The banks generally allow a creditworthy company to borrow between 80 and 90 percent of the market value (based on the spot price) of the coffee purchased. The loan is secured with the title to the coffee, which is given to the bank until the trade firm sells the coffee to end users. The trade firm then pays down its loan and takes the remainder of the sale as profit.

It is important to note that the coffee business is a relationship business for buyers whether they are large or small. The development of strong relationships with the growers is important in maintaining a steady supply of coffee. While it is true that coffee is a commodity product and the supply and demand of coffee depends on price, one cannot fly down to Colombia and expect to easily buy a million bags of coffee. Growers want to deal with buyers they can trust and vice versa. The buyer may be from a large food processing company or a small New York City brokerage, but one can be sure that he or she has spent a great deal of time cultivating a relationship. A strong relationship provides two things: information on the coffee market, and an inside track on a grower's crop. This is especially important if a roaster needs a certain type of coffee (e.g., Colombian mild) to maintain a standard blend of ground coffee to keep consumers drinking "to the last drop."

Factors Affecting Price   Weather, specifically frost and drought, is the most important factor affecting production and hence price for western hemisphere coffees. The commodity sections in most major newspapers will often carry stories concerning the effect of weather on harvests. Eastern hemisphere coffee producing countries' crops are most often damaged by insects. The level of coffee inventories in major producing and consuming countries is another important market consideration. Actual or threatened dock strikes may cause a buildup of coffee stocks at a port of exit. Marketing policies of various exporting countries will also affect prices. On the consumer side, high retail prices or concerns about health can reduce consumption, which in turn may exert downward pressure on prices.

The Futures Market   Futures markets for coffee exist in New York, London and Paris. In New York,

coffee futures are traded on the Coffee, Sugar and Cocoa Exchange. There is considerable uncertainty in predicting prices and availability of green coffee beans. Thus, the normal use of the coffee futures market is to set up a hedge to protect one's inventory position against price fluctuations. A hedge is commonly defined as the establishment of a position in the futures market approximately equal to, but in the opposite direction of, a commitment in the cash market (also known as the physical or actual commodity). Only two percent of all futures contracts result in actual delivery of coffee beans. The majority of contracts are closed out by purchasing a contract in the opposite direction or selling one's own contract.

For example, one who owns an inventory of coffee establishes a short position in the futures market. This position will offset a drop in the value of one's inventory due to a decline in coffee prices. The short position obligates the holder to sell coffee at a predetermined price at some future date. If, in the future, coffee prices drop, the short position will increase in value because the holder has locked in a higher sales price. This will offset the decline in value of the actual coffee inventory. It is virtually impossible to set up a perfect hedge position due to imperfections between the physical and futures markets, but the markets do provide protection to the value of one's inventory.

Hedging also allows the coffee merchant to obtain credit from banks. Banks will seldom lend money to the holder of a commodity who has not attempted to properly hedge his or her position.

Coffee Consumption Trends   Per capita coffee consumption has declined precipitously since 1965. Exhibit 3 shows U.S. liquid consumption in several drink categories. While overall coffee consumption has declined, specialty premium and gourmet coffees have bucked this trend and have been selling well. Gourmet coffee sales alone have climbed from approximately $500 million in 1987 to $780 million in 1992. During this period, total coffee sales have moved from $6.3 billion to only $6.8 billion. These specialty brands have attracted new coffee drinkers that are younger and more affluent than the coffee drinkers of 30 years ago. During 1992, gourmet and premium coffees accounted for 19 percent of total consumption. An industry study predicted that by 1994 this share would grow to 30 percent of total retail coffee sales.

EXHIBIT 3   A Generation of Evolving Tastes—U.S. Liquid Consumption Trends (gallons per capita)

	1965	1975	1985	1990
Soft Drinks	17.8	26.3	40.8	47.5
Coffee[1]	**37.8**	**33.0**	**25.8**	**25.2**
Beer	15.9	21.6	23.8	23.4
Milk	24.0	21.8	19.8	19.0
Tea[1]	3.8	7.3	7.3	7.2
Bottled water	—	1.2	5.2	8.8
Juices	6.3	6.8	7.4	6.9
Powdered drinks	—	4.8	6.2	5.3
Wine[2]	1.0	1.7	2.4	2.0
Distilled spirits	1.5	2.0	1.8	1.4
Subtotal	108.1	126.5	140.5	146.7
Imputed water consumption	74.4	56.0	42.0	35.8
Total	182.5	182.5	182.5	182.5

[1]Data are based on 3-year moving averages to counterbalance inventory swings, and to show consumption more realistically.
[2]1985 and 1990 figures include wine coolers.
Source: Beverage Industry—Annual Manual 1992.

Many small firms have stepped in to both create and take advantage of this shift in consumer preference. One of these producers is Seattle-based Starbucks Coffee Company. The company's focus has been on premium and gourmet coffees and customer service. Unlike most producers, Starbucks also controls its retail sales. Starbucks's 126 retail outlets and coffeehouses account for 87 percent of its sales.[1] These outlets are as stylish as the company's coffee. As Starbucks's president explained, "we're not just selling a cup of coffee, we are providing an experience."

Green Mountain Coffee Roasters (Shelburne, Vt.) enjoyed $11 million in sales for 1991. This company had seven retail outlets and over 1,000 restaurant and gourmet food store accounts. GMCR has kept its prices high. GMCR is decidedly a high-tech place. It uses a computerized roaster and a database to help its customers manage their coffee inventories.

[1]Starbucks had sales of approximately $43 million for the six months ending March 29, 1992.

EXHIBIT 4   Selected 1992 Segment Sales and Expense Data[1] ($ in millions)

	Nestlé[3]	Procter & Gamble	Philip Morris
Sales	$9,658	$3,709	$29,048
Cost of sales	4,369	2,373	19,685
Marketing and administration[2]	3,564	1,157	6,594

[1]Since these companies participate in multiple industries, only the segment data for the food or beverage segment (that included the company's coffee business) is provided.
[2]Marketing and administration expenses include research and development costs.
[3]Financial information for Nestlé was converted from Swiss francs into dollars using the average exchange rate for 1992—SF 1.40/$.
Source: 1992 Annual Reports.

While the specialty coffee industry has high hopes for consumer demand, some recent trends in consumer products point to opportunities in the nonspecialty segments. As the conspicuous consumption spree of the roaring 80s subsided, recession has led consumers to be more cost conscious. Accordingly, there has been an increase in demand for lower-priced store brands (private labels). It is not yet clear how this trend will manifest itself in the coffee retail market.

Major Coffee Producers   In 1992, Nestlé was the largest coffee company in the world. In the U.S., the largest coffee producers have been Philip Morris (Maxwell House) and P&G (Folgers). These companies have considerable resources: infrastructure, distribution networks, brand equity, production resources, and marketing expertise. They have largely competed through heavy advertising[2] and aggressive pricing. Not blind to the shifts in coffee consumption, these companies have introduced many new coffee products. Selected financial data on the major competitors is provided in Exhibit 4.

[2]In 1990 Philip Morris and P&G each spent roughly $100 million on coffee advertising.

CASE 2–2
GENERAL MOTORS CORPORATION

In an article in the *NACA Bulletin,* January 1, 1927, Albert Bradley described the pricing policy of General Motors Corporation. At that time, Mr. Bradley was general assistant treasurer; subsequently, he became vice president, executive vice president, and chairman of the board. The following description consists principally of excerpts from Mr. Bradley's article.

General Policy

Return on investment is the basis of the General Motors policy in regard to the pricing of product. The fundamental consideration is the average return over a protracted period of time, not the specific rate of return over any particular year or short period of time. The long-term rate of return on investment represents the official viewpoint as to the highest average rate of return that can be expected consistent with a healthy growth of the business, and may be referred to as the economic return attainable. The adjudged necessary rate of return on capital will vary as between separate lines of industry as a result of differences in their economic situations; and within each industry there will be important differences in return on capital, resulting primarily from the relatively greater efficiency of certain producers.

The fundamental policy in regard to pricing product and expansion of the business also necessitates an official viewpoint as to the normal average rate of plant operation. This relationship between assumed normal average rate of operation and practical annual capacity is known as standard volume.

This case was prepared by R. N. Anthony, Harvard Business School. Copyright © by the President and Fellows of Harvard College. Harvard Business School case 160-005.

The fundamental price policy is completely expressed in the conception of standard volume and economic return attainable. For example, if it is the accepted policy that standard volume represents 80 percent of practical annual capacity, and that an average of 20 percent per annum must be earned on the operating capital, it becomes possible to determine the standard price of a product—that is, that price which with plants operating at 80 percent of capacity will produce an annual return of 20 percent of the investment.

Standard Volume

Costs of production and distribution per unit of product vary with fluctuation in volume, because of the fixed or nonvariable nature of some of the expense items. Productive materials and productive labor may be considered costs that are 100 percent variable, since within reasonable limits the aggregate varies directly with volume, and the cost per unit of product, therefore, remains uniform.

Among the items classified as manufacturing expense or burden there exist varying degrees of fluctuation with volume, owing to their greater or lesser degree of variability. Among the absolutely fixed items are such expenses as depreciation and taxes, which may be referred to as 100 percent fixed since within the limits of plant capacity the aggregate will not change, but the amount per unit of product will vary in inverse ratio to the input.

Another group of items may be classified as 100 percent variable, such as inspection and material handling; the amount per unit of product is unaffected by volume. Between the classes of 100 percent fixed and 100 percent variable is a large group of expense items that are partially variable, such as light, heat, power, and salaries.

In General Motors Corporation, standard burden rates are developed for each burden center, so that there will be included in costs a reasonable average allowance for manufacturing expense. In order to establish this rate, it is first necessary to obtain an expression of the estimated normal average rate of plant operation.

Rate of plant operation is affected by such factors as general business conditions, extent of seasonal fluctuation in sales likely within years of large volume, policy with respect to seasonal accumulation of finished and/or semifinished product for the purpose of leveling the production curve, necessity or desirability of maintaining excess plant capacity for emergency use, and many others. Each of these factors should be carefully considered by a manufacturer in the determination of size of a new plant to be constructed, and before making additions to existing plants, in order that there may be a logical relationship between assumed normal average rate of plant operation and practical annual capacity. The percentage accepted by General Motors Corporation as its policy in regard to the relationship between assumed normal rate of plant operation and practical annual capacity is referred to as standard volume.

Having determined the degree of variability of manufacturing expense, the established total expense at the standard volume rate of operations can be estimated. A *standard burden rate* is then developed, which represents the proper absorption of burden in costs at standard volume. In periods of low volume, the unabsorbed manufacturing expense is charged directly against profits as unabsorbed burden, while, in periods of high volume, the overabsorbed manufacturing expense is credited to profits, as overabsorbed burden.

Return on Investment

Factory costs and commercial expenses for the most part represent outlays by the manufacturer during the accounting period. An exception is depreciation of capital assets, which have a greater

EXHIBIT 1   Allowance for Fixed Investment

Investment in plant and other fixed assets	$15,000,000
Practical annual capacity	50,000 units
Standard volume, percent of practical annual capacity	80%
Standard volume equivalent (50,000 × 80%)	40,000 units
Factory cost per unit at standard volume	$1,000
Annual factory cost of production at standard volume (40,000 × $1,000)	$40,000,000
Standard factor for fixed investment (ratio of investment to annual factory cost of production; $15,000,000 ÷ $40,000,000)	0.375

length of life than the accounting period. To allow for this element of cost, there is included an allowance for depreciation in the burden rates used in compiling costs. Before an enterprise can be considered successful and worthy of continuation or expansion, however, still another element of cost must be reckoned with. This is the cost of capital, including an allowance for profit.

Thus, the calculation of standard prices of products necessitates the establishment of standards of capital requirement as well as expense factors, representative of the normal average operating condition. The standard for capital employed in fixed assets is expressed as a percentage of factory cost, and the standards for working capital are expressed in part as a percentage of sales, and in part as a percentage of factory cost.

The calculation of the standard allowance for fixed investment is illustrated by the example in Exhibit 1.

The amount tied up in working capital items should be directly proportional to the volume of business. For example, raw materials on hand should be in direct proportion to the manufacturing requirements—so many days' supply of this material, so many days' supply of that material, and so on—depending on the condition and location of sources of supply, transportation conditions, etc. Work-in-process should be in direct proportion to the requirements of finished production, since it is dependent on the length of time required for the material to pass from the raw to the finished state, and the amount of labor and other charges to be absorbed in the process. Finished product should be in direct proportion to sales requirements. Accounts receivable should be in direct proportion to sales, being dependent on terms of payment and efficiency of collections.

The Standard Price

These elements are combined to construct the standard price as shown in Exhibit 2. Note that the economic return attainable (20 percent in the illustration) and the standard volume (80 percent as shown in Exhibit 1) are longrun figures and are rarely changed;[1] the other elements of the price are based on current estimates.

Differences among Products

Responsibility for investment must be considered in calculating the standard price of each product as well as in calculating the overall price for all products, since products with identical accounting costs may be responsible for investments that vary greatly. In Exhibit 2, a uniform standard selling price of $1,250 was determined. Let us now suppose that this organization makes and sells two products. A and B, with equal manufacturing costs of $1,000 per unit and equal working capital requirements, and that 20,000 units of each product are produced. However, an analysis of fixed investment indicates that $10

---

[1]A Brookings Institution survey reported that the principal pricing goal of General Motors Corporation in the 1950s was 20 percent of investment after taxes. See Robert F. Lanzillotti, "Pricing Objectives in Large Companies," *American Economic Review,* December 1958.

EXHIBIT 2 Illustration of Method of Determination of Standard Price

	In Relation to	Turnover per Year	Ratio to Sales Annual Basis	Ratio to Factory Cost Annual Basis
Cash	Sales	20 times	0.050	—
Drafts and accounts receivable	Sales	10 times	0.100	—
Raw material and work-in-process	Factory cost	6 times	—	0.16⅔
Finished product	Factory cost	12 times	—	0.08⅓
Gross working capital			0.150	0.250
Fixed investment				0.375
Total investment				0.625
Economic return attainable, 20%			—	—
Multiplying the investment ratio by this, the necessary net profit margin is arrived at			0.030	0.125
Standard allowance for commercial expenses, 7%			0.070	—
Gross margin over factory cost			0.100	0.125
			a	*b*

$$\text{Selling price, as a ratio to factory cost} = \frac{1 + b}{1 - a} = \frac{1 + 0.125}{1 - 0.100} = 1.250$$

$$\text{If standard cost} = \$1,000$$

$$\text{Then standard price} = \$1,000 \times 1.250 = \$1,250$$

million is applicable to product A, while only $5 million of fixed investment is applicable to product B. Each product must earn 20 percent on its investment in order to satisfy the standard condition. Exhibit 3 illustrates the determination of the standard price for product A and product B.

From this analysis of investment, it becomes apparent that product A, which has the heavier fixed investment, should sell for $1,278, while product B should sell for only $1,222, in order to produce a return of 20 percent on the investment. Were both products sold for the composite average

EXHIBIT 3   Variances in Standard Price, Due to Variances in Rate of Capital Turnover

	Product A		Product B		Total Product (A plus B)	
	Ratio to Sales Annual Basis	*Ratio to Factory Cost Annual Basis*	*Ratio to Sales Annual Basis*	*Ratio to Factory Cost Annual Basis*	*Ratio to Sales Annual Basis*	*Ratio to Factory Cost Annual Basis*
Gross working capital	0.150	0.250	0.150	0.250	0.150	0.250
Fixed investment	—	0.500	—	0.250	—	0.375
Total investment	0.150	0.750	0.150	0.500	0.150	0.625
Economic return attainable, 20%	—	—		—	—	—
Multiplying the investment ratio by this, the necessary net profit margin is arrived at	0.030	0.150				
Standard allowance for commercial expenses, 7%			0.030	0.100	0.030	0.125
	0.070	—	0.070	—	0.070	—
Gross margin over factory cost	0.100	0.150	0.100	0.100	0.100	0.125
	a	b	a	b	a	b
Selling price, as a ratio to factory cost $= \dfrac{1+b}{1-a}$	$\dfrac{1.0 + 0.150}{1.0 - 0.100} = 1.278$		$\dfrac{1.0 + 0.100}{1.0 - 0.100} = 1.222$		$\dfrac{1.0 + 0.125}{1.0 - 0.100} = 1.250$	
If standard cost equals	$1,000		$1,000		$1,000	
Then standard price equals	$1,278		$1,222		$1,250	

standard price of $1,250, then product A would not be bearing its share of the investment burden, while product B would be correspondingly over-priced.

Differences in working capital requirements as between different products may also be important due to differences in manufacturing methods, sales terms, merchandising policies, etc. The inventory turnover rate of one line of products sold by a division of General Motors Corporation may be 6 times a year, while inventory applicable to another line of products is turned over 30 times a year. In the second case, the inventory investment required per dollar cost of sales is only one fifth of that required in the case of the product with the slower turnover. Just as there are differences in capital requirements as between different classes

of product, so may the standard requirements for the same class of product require modification from time to time due to permanent changes in manufacturing processes, in location of sources of supply, more efficient scheduling and handling of materials, etc.

The importance of this improvement to the buyer of General Motors products may be appreciated from the following example. The total inventory investment for the 12 months ended September 30, 1926, would have averaged $182,490,000 if the turnover rate of 1923 (the best performance prior to 1925) had not been bettered, or an excess of $74,367,000 over the actual average investment. In other words, General Motors would have been compelled to charge $14,873,000 more for its product during this 12-month period than was actually charged if prices had been established to yield, say, 20 percent on the operating capital required.

Conclusion

The analysis as to the degree of variability of manufacturing and commercial expenses with increases or decreases in volume of output, and the establishment of "standards" for the various investment items, makes it possible not only to develop "Standard Prices," but also to forecast, with much greater accuracy than otherwise would be possible, the capital requirements, profits, and return on capital at the different rates of operation, which may result from seasonal conditions or from changes in the general business situation. Moreover, whenever it is necessary to calculate in advance the final effect on net profits of proposed increases or decreases in price, with their resulting changes in volume of output, consideration of the real economics of the situation is facilitated by the availability of reliable basic data.

It should be emphasized that the basic pricing policy stated in terms of the economic return attainable is a policy, and it does not absolutely dictate the specific price. At times, the actual price may be above, and at other times below, the standard price. The standard price calculation affords a means not only of interpreting actual or proposed prices in relation to the established policy, but at the same time affords a practical demonstration as to whether the policy itself is sound. If the prevailing price of product is found to be at variance with the standard price other than to the extent due to temporary causes, it follows that prices should be adjusted; or else, in the event of conditions being such that prices cannot be brought into line with the standard price, the conclusion is necessarily drawn that the terms of the expressed policy must be modified.[2]

---

²This paragraph is taken from an article by Donaldson Brown, then vice president, finance, General Motors Corporation, in *Management and Administration,* March 1924.

Questions

1. An article in *The Wall Street Journal,* December 10, 1957, gave estimates of cost figures in "an imaginary, car-making division in the Ford–Chevrolet–Plymouth field." Most of the data given below are derived from that article. Using these data, compute the standard price. Working capital ratios are not given; assume that they are the same as those in Exhibit 2.

Investment in plant and other fixed assets	$600,000,000
Required return on investment	30% before income taxes
Practical annual capacity	1,250,000
Standard volume—assume	80%
Factory cost per unit:	
Outside purchases of parts	$ 500*
Parts manufactured inside	$ 600*
Assembly labor	75
Burden	125
Total	$1,300

*Each of these items includes $50 of labor costs.

"Commercial cost," corresponding to the 7 percent in Exhibit 2, is added as a dollar amount, and includes the following:

Inbound and outbound freight	$ 85
Tooling and engineering	50
Sales and advertising	50
Administrative and miscellaneous	50
Warranty (repairs within guarantee)	15
Total	$250

Therefore, the 7 percent commercial allowance in Exhibit 2 should be eliminated, and in its place $250 should be added to the price as computed from the formula.

2. What would happen to profits and return on investment before taxes in a year in which volume was only 60 percent of capacity? What would happen in a year in which volume was 100 percent of capacity? Assume that nonvariable costs included in the $1,550 unit cost above are $350 million (i.e., variable costs are $1,500 − $350 = $1,200). In both situations, assume that cars were sold at the standard price established in Question 1, since the standard price is not changed to reflect annual changes in volume.

3. In the 1975 model year, General Motors gave cash rebates of as high as $300 per car off the list price. In 1972 and 1973 prices had been restricted by price control legislation, which required that selling prices could be increased only if costs had increased. Selling prices thereafter were not controlled, although there was always the possibility that price controls could be reimposed. In 1975, demand for automobiles was sharply lower than in 1974, partly because of a general recession and partly because of concerns about high gasoline prices. Does the cash rebate indicate that General Motors adopted a new pricing policy in 1975, or is it consistent with the policy described in the case?

4. Was this policy good for General Motors? Was it good for America?

Case 2–3
DairyPak

Earle Bensing had some very tough decisions to make in the Summer of 1988. As Vice President for the DairyPak Division of Champion International he faced:

- Declining market share in the growing "branded juice" segment of the domestic paperboard carton market.
- A technologically outmoded manufacturing system in terms of the expanding markets.
- A very limited output capability which had not grown in 10 years.
- A dramatically expanding international market which the corporation had seen as fraught with more problems than opportunities.

The capital spending and strategic positioning decisions he needed to make in 1988 would shape the future of the DairyPak division for many years to come.

I. Liquid Packaging and the Pure-Pak Carton

Millions of Americans, Europeans, Asians and South Americans started their day with milk or juice poured from a paperboard carton. Worldwide, paperboard was still the dominant form of milk and juice packaging in 1988. But the industry had changed dramatically since the "gabled top" Pure-Pak carton rose to prominence in the 1950s.

The Plastic Substitute.   Polyethylene replaced paraffin to coat paperboard in 1961. It didn't take long after that before someone in the oil industry thought of making plastic *cartons* in-

stead of plastic *coating* for paper cartons. Shell Chemical and Hoover International (now Johnson Controls) changed the liquid packaging industry overnight in 1965 when they combined to introduce the plastic resin pellet and the "blow molding" machine to manufacture plastic jugs. The blow molding machine was so easy to use that paper packaging dropped from 82 percent of the milk market in 1971 to 37 percent in 1985.

But the interesting story here was that although plastic captured 100 percent of the *gallon* size carton market, it had not eliminated the other sizes of paper carton as many had predicted it would. Plastic was more economical when resin prices were low. When the price rises, paper looks good. Guessing future levels of ethylene gas prices (the basic driver of polyethylene price) was a notoriously difficult task.

And the dairy owner also had important nonfinancial reasons for staying with the paper carton. First, the dairy did not want to be at the mercy of oil companies. By using dual suppliers—paper and plastic—the dairy created a hedge against volatile input prices. Also, as new uses of the plastic resin were created (industrial and consumer uses of plastic containers), the input price would not go lower since the plastic was just a by-product of ethylene gas. Second, the dairy believed that paper was the best product nutritionally. University studies had shown that paper protected milk vitamins and flavor much better than translucent plastic. Also, recent legislation prohibiting the dumping of plastic in Suffolk County on Long Island had created doubt about the long run viability of plastic.

The Competitors.   Exhibit 1 is a global overview of the paperboard packaging business in 1988. There were five players in the domestic Pure-Pak industry—International Paper, Champion, Potlatch, Westvaco and Weyerhaeuser. All

---

This case was written by Professor John Shank of the Amos Tuck School with the assistance of Mr. David Anthony, T '89. Copyright © by John K. Shank.

Exhibit 1

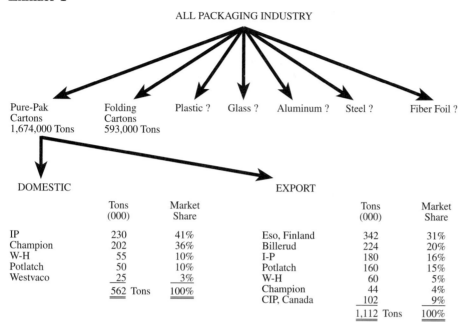

ALL PACKAGING INDUSTRY

Pure-Pak Cartons 1,674,000 Tons — Folding Cartons 593,000 Tons — Plastic? — Glass? — Aluminum? — Steel? — Fiber Foil?

DOMESTIC

	Tons (000)	Market Share
IP	230	41%
Champion	202	36%
W-H	55	10%
Potlatch	50	10%
Westvaco	25	3%
	562 Tons	100%

EXPORT

	Tons (000)	Market Share
Eso, Finland	342	31%
Billerud	224	20%
I-P	180	16%
Potlatch	160	15%
W-H	60	5%
Champion	44	4%
CIP, Canada	102	9%
	1,112 Tons	100%

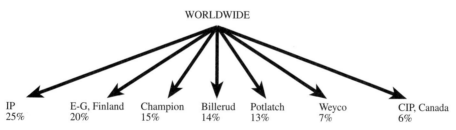

WORLDWIDE

IP	E-G, Finland	Champion	Billerud	Potlatch	Weyco	CIP, Canada
25%	20%	15%	14%	13%	7%	6%

of these companies were vertically integrated producers of the carton all the way back to the wood chip. Also, because of the scale and integration economies of these firms, new vertically integrated entrants were effectively shut out. In fact, because of the scale economies in producing a Pure-Pak carton, it was more likely that a small current player would drop out of the industry—as Georgia Pacific did in 1981 or as Weyco did in the Eastern U.S. in 1982.

International Paper was the industry leader. IP was considered to be the low cost producer, having achieved significant economies with a large and diverse extruding and converting ca-

pacity. IP was also the technological leader, with significant investment in aseptic (germ free) packaging and rotogravure printing (state-of-the-art technology). IP continued to expand capacity, aggressively growing in the nondairy segments by emphasizing their aseptic, hot fill, and other extended life packages, and aggressively pursuing their own off-shore converting operations (e.g., Korea and Japan). Along with these strategies, IP continued to price aggressively. But often IP was considered an unreliable supplier *domestically* because of their willingness to leave a customer when necessary to grow their offshore converting operations.

Exhibit 2   Domestic Competitor Review—1986

Company	Extruders	Folding Carton Capacity (000 annual tons) Liquid Packaging was one use for folding carton stock	Liquid Packaging		Pure-Pak Converting Locations	
			Domestic	Export		
International Paper	4 - Pine Bluff, AR 1 - Raleigh, NC 2 - Mobile, AL 1 - Texarkana, TX	709	230	180	Atlanta, GA Bastrop, LA Framingham, MA Kalamazoo, MI	Kansas City, KA Philadelphia, PA Turlock, CA
Champion	2 - Waynesville, NC	250	202	44	Athens, GA Clinton, IA Ft. Worth, TX	Morristown, NJ Olmsted Falls, OH
Potlatch	2 - Lewiston, ID	300	50	160	Ft. Wayne, IN Pomona, CA Sikeston, MO	
Weyerhaeuser	2 - Longview, WA	193	55	60	Los Angeles, CA Vancouver, WA	
Westvaco	1 - Covington, VA 2 - Laurel, MD	147	25	—	Richmond, VA	

Champion was currently a strong number 2, with more domestic volume than the other three players combined (see Exhibit 1).

Potlatch, Westvaco, and Weyerhaeuser all ranked in a third tier of competition. All three faced difficulties related to quality and inefficient scale. Weyerhaeuser and Potlatch responded by looking increasingly to export markets while trying to maintain selected domestic niches. Westvaco was holding on to its domestic niche. Exhibits 1 and 2 summarize the estimated competitive situation for 1988.

Outside of the U.S. there were three major manufacturers supplying Pure-Pak cartons:

Enso-Gutzeit—Finland—They professed to be the world's top exporter and the world's second largest producer of liquid packaging board—342,000 tons of liquid packaging and fast-food board was supplied during 1987.

Billerud—Sweden—Paperboard production of 224,000 tons in 1988. This corresponded to a world market share of 14 percent. Most of the production

was exported. TetraPak was the largest single customer.

CIP—Montreal, Canada—Three plants (Quebec, Ontario, and Alberta) converted CIP's polycoated stock into cartons for milk and juice. Its plants had a capacity of only 34,000 tons per year.

The Pure-Pak Customers.   There were four groups of customers who formed, filled, and sealed Pure-Pak cartons. Champion's position in these four segments is summarized in Exhibit 3.

Domestic dairies.   In 1976 there were approximately 10,000 dairies across the U.S., processing and distributing milk and juice. Fewer than 1,000 dairies survived in 1988, but dairies were still the largest purchaser of paperboard cartons in the U.S. In 1988, a typical dairy was a large regional packager of many private brands of milk and juice. The dairy's product was usually considered a commodity—no ability to achieve a price premium for the brand name. Industry-wide, dairy profit margins were quite slim. Overall, the profits

---

EXHIBIT 3   Market Segments for Pure-Pak 1987

U.S. Dairies	*Branded Juicers*		*Export*
(Milk and OJ)	*Minute Maid and Citrus Hill*	*Tropicana*	
Historically, Champion has emphasized this segment (about 150,000 tons in 1988)	Relatively Minor Volume (about 2,000 tons)	Zero Volume	32,000 Tons (Coated) 12,000 Tons (uncoated)
Our tons have been shrinking 3% per year since 1980	Flat since 1980	Lost this business for quality reasons in 1981	Champion's "swing" market
Overall market has been shrinking about 3% per year since 1980	Overall market growing at 10%; potential to grow faster (growth in ready-to-serve; greater market penetration in Midwest)		Overall Market growing at more than 10% per year
We have maintained market share (40%) in this declining segment	Are we the "backup" supplier in this segment?		Champion has not been willing to commit here for the long run

came from the very high turnover rates from being the sole supplier in a region. Overall, this segment had declined 3 percent per year over the previous five years, but, by 1988, it had stabilized.

Differentiated juicers.   The second largest segment was the high quality, *differentiated* juice packager—basically Seagrams (Tropicana), Coca Cola (Minute Maid) and Procter and Gamble (Citrus Hill). This segment was created in the 50s by Tropicana. Coca Cola entered in the 1960s using its Minute Maid brand name. Procter and Gamble entered in the 1980s with a new brand name (Citrus Hill). In the five years prior to 1988, chilled juice sales increased more than 82 percent, compared with 17 percent for the whole juice industry. In 1988 it was estimated that *chilled* would outsell *concentrate* for the first time, buoyed by America's craving for convenience. This was the fastest growing segment in liquid packaging in 1988 (approximately 10 percent a year). The segment was extremely competitive as one would guess from the three

key players, giants in consumer products: "An orange juice war is intensifying as major players try to squeeze bigger shares" (*Wall Street Journal,* 4/27/88). The big three juice processors represented over 50% of the ready-to-serve orange juice market—clearly, a great opportunity for the paperboard industry (see Table 1).

The big three customers wanted high impact graphics to market the juice, a technologically advanced carton that retained essential oils, and a carton that would hold the juice over 50 days (versus 14 days for milk). These customers were willing to pay for the differentiated carton.

"Special uses."   The third segment for polyethylene coated board included "ovenable board" (frozen food dishes or microwave dishes) and Pure-Pak cartons used to hold such non-liquid items as nails or mothballs. This market had grown slowly. Overall volume and volume per customer were still low. Overall this was only 4 percent of Champion's volume.

TABLE 1   Differentiated Juice Segment

	1988 Domestic Share Of Market for Ready to Serve Orange Juice	Orange Juice Manufacturers' Use of Paperboard Cartons	
		1980	1987
Tropicana	27.3%	11,000 tons	15,000
Minute Maid	17.7%	7,000	10,000
Citrus Hill	9.1%	0	7,000
Dairies	45.9%	18,000	15,000
Total	100%	36,000	47,000

TABLE 2   The International Market

U.S. Folding Carton Stock Export for Liquid Packaging by Destination (000 tons)

	1985	1986	1987
Far East	214	233	248
Europe	50	56	59
Australia	30	35	36
Africa	30	28	35
Canada	9	17	33
S. America	30	29	29
C. America	13	8	14
Caribbean	3	5	7
Middle East	2	10	6
Other	14	11	14
Total	395	432	481
Uncoated Rolls	94	103	116
Coated Rolls	272	313	336
Converted Cartons	29	16	29

Export.   The fourth group of customers for the Pure-Pak carton was the export market. Worldwide production of Pure-Pak cartons was estimated to be slightly over 1,600,000 tons in 1987 with only 1/3 (562,000) of that used in the United States. The international market had grown by over 16 percent from 1985 to 1988, with consumption increasing by over 100 percent in some countries as shown in Table 2.

II. Champion DairyPak—The Evolution of a "Harvest" Strategy

DairyPak began operation in Cleveland, Ohio with 12 employees in December, 1947, as one of the original licensees of the Pure-Pak technology. By 1950 DairyPak shipped 540 million cartons—over $5 million worth—and the company needed another plant to meet the growing demand. Expansion included converting plants built in Athens, Georgia, in 1951; Clinton, Iowa, in 1952; Fort Worth, Texas, in 1954; and Morristown, New Jersey, in 1958. These five similar converting plants remained intact in 1988 as Champion's milk and juice carton converters.

Since the early 60s through 1988, Champion had produced about 250,000 tons of polyethylene coated board annually. Until 1980, virtually all these tons were converted by the 5 DairyPak plants and sold to dairies. The primary goal of

Champion was to be the low cost producer in a commodity market.

The intrusion of plastic containers in the 1960s dramatically affected the paperboard carton industry and Champion's perspective on DairyPak. Champion watched to see what the dairy industry would do. A consulting study by Booz, Allen Hamilton in 1968 which circulated throughout the industry suggested that by the mid-80s not a single paperboard carton would be sold. Champion's reaction was to watch and wait. While Champion watched and waited, the paper carton did not die, but the Champion infrastructure began to get old and technologically outdated. In fact, since a new machine to produce the raw paperboard was built in 1965, very few capital improvements were implemented or considered until the summer of 1988. Of Champion's 33 converting machines, 29 were installed before 1963.

The Situation in 1988.   In the early 80s, the explosion of the juice market created new

TABLE 3   **Champion's Market Position**

| | Domestic Consumption of Pure-Pak Cartons (000) | | | Champion's Domestic Pure-Pak Cartons | | | |
| | **1980** | **1987** | | **1980** | | **1987** | |
	Tons	*Tons*	*% change*	*Tons*	*% Share*	*Tons*	*% Share*
Dairy	506	374	−26%	200	39	150	40
Non Dairy*	66	120	+82%	30	46	30	25
Total	572	494	−14%	230	40	180	36

Champion's Paperboard Production

	1980 Tons	1987 Tons
Dairy	200	150
Non Dairy*	30	30
Ovenable	0	10
Domestic Coated	9	2
Domestic Uncoated	10	10
Export Coated	11	32
Export Uncoated	0	12
Total	260	246

*Represents juice processors and special end uses of paperboard.

opportunities for the Pure-Pak Carton—opportunities for which Champion was unprepared.

Table 3 shows the changing markets for Champion. This data clearly indicates that Champion had successfully retained share in the declining market segment while losing almost half its share in the fastest growing segment.

The Cost Structure—A Process Flow Perspective.   One way to understand Champion's DairyPak position in 1980 is to study the process flow from wood chips all the way to Pure-Pak cartons.

The trees which become chips were a combination of southern pine and hardwood species. The two chip inputs were mixed with cooking and bleaching chemicals to produce pulp. The Canton Mill had paper processing capacity of 1550 tons per day, but only 1400 tons of pulping capacity.

Therefore 150 tons of processed pulp were purchased on the open market at $700/ton (the in-house pulp cost $278/ton). The paper processing capacity of the mill was divided into 850 tons of envelope paper and 700 tons of paperboard.

The purchased pulp and slush pulp (in-house) were mixed in the paper machine where the pulp was dried to make uncoated paperboard. The paper machine stage added approximately $105 per ton of cost to the pulp.

The uncoated rolls (weighing about one ton each) were then shuttled to the nearby Waynesville, NC extruding plant at a cost of $3 per ton. Polyethylene was applied to both sides of the board at a cost of $94 per ton. From Waynesville, the rolls of coated board traveled either to Champion's five converting plants at an average freight cost of $35 per ton, or were sold to export. Canton also sold some uncoated board each year

EXHIBIT 4   Champion DairyPak System-Selected Segments

| | Paper Mill | | Waynesville Extruding Plant | | | | Converting Plants | |
| | Uncoated Board Sales | | Coated Sales to DairyPak | | Coated Sales to Export | | DairyPak Sales | |
	1980	*1987*	*1980*	*1987*	*1980*	*1987*	*1980*	*1987*
Net Revenue/Ton	$448	$530	$497	$663	$517	$577	$697	$994
Cost/Ton	$365	$471[1]	$444	$540	$444	$540[2]	$671	$992
Profit Before Tax/Ton	$ 83	$ 59	$ 53	$123	$ 67	$ 37	$ 26	$ 2
Tons (000)	10	22	230	180	11	32	230	180

(1) Pulp Cost	$319	424		(2) Mill Cost	$424
Machine Cost	105			Freight to Extruder	3
Freight to Customer	47			Extruder Cost	94
	$471			Freight to Customer	19
					$540

to other converters for other carton applications (see Exhibit 4).

The 5 DairyPak locations paid a fixed transfer price of $680 per ton for the coated board, which included freight. In the first stage of the converting operation, rolls of coated board were spliced together to form a long, continuous web. Next, each particular dairy's name, logo, and design were printed on one side using flexographic printing which was essentially a 1960's technology. The total cost of the conversion operation was $231 per ton, plus $10 per ton for freight to the end customers. Industry averages showed that one ton of board equals 14,400 one-half gallon cartons and the individual carton price was between $.06 and .08 depending on the volume. Average price to a customer for 1/2 gallon cartons was $936 per ton. The half gallon size was not the most profitable item, but represented over 50 percent of sales. This process flow was the same for both milk and juice cartons since Champion did not distinguish the two.

At the juice processor or dairy, the rolls of flat cartons moved along the sealing machines where their polyethylene coating was heated by a gas flame. Each carton was folded and conveyed through "ironing" rolls where it emerged joined together, or "side seamed." Filler machines then formed and sealed the bottom, filled the carton with liquid, and sealed the gabled top. The cycle was complete when dairies and juice processors delivered their product to stores and supermarkets where consumers chose the paper carton over the plastic jug.

A small dairy would usually pay $.08 per 1/2 gallon carton since it could not achieve volume discounts. The milk purchased from dairy farmers would cost $.75 per half gallon. The pasteurizing process would cost $.06 per half gallon and the distribution and shrinkage would add another $.06. The small dairy could sell a half gallon of unbranded milk for an average of $1.04. When a small dairy produced orange juice, the costs were similar except that oranges cost $.80 per half gallon. The price to supermarkets was $1.20 per half gallon, delivered.

Minute Maid, a large branded juice processor had very different economics. The 1/2 gallon carton would usually only cost $.06 because of volume discounts. The oranges themselves would only be $.64 per half gallon, again because of the tremendous volume. Converting, distribution and shrinkage would total $.11. One major cost a branded juice processor added was national

---

TABLE 4   Differences Between Milk and Orange Juice Cartons

	Champion Milk Board	*Ideal Orange Juice Board*
Converting Plant	Faster-Speeds Shorter Runs Lower Print Quality Higher Services Costs	Slower Speeds Longer Runs (*lower* Setup/Ton) Higher Print Quality & Cost More customer support More Sales Time Per Ton Sold
Extruding Plant	Lighter Coat, "Profile" Coating Standard Approach for most customers.	Heavier Coat, "Flat" Coating Differing requirements for different customers—no "standard" approach.
The Paperboard Machine	Production Focus "Get out the tons" *Faster* Speeds (Lower Printability) Not as Strong as O. J. (shorter shelf life)	Higher "Z" Strength Board Twice as much wet strength Resins (vs. milk) *Slower* Speeds (Higher Printability) Stronger than Milk (longer shelf life)
Pulping	The envelope paper machine receives pulp requirements first; Milk board last. Result is more variation for milk board.	Standard pulp mixture that would never change.

---

selling and advertising which averaged 25 percent of the $1.42 wholesale price to supermarkets.

A large New Hampshire supermarket serving a population base of 50,000 sold regional dairy milk for $1.16, Tropicana orange juice for $2.26 (cost of $1.79), Minute Maid for $1.89, and local dairy orange juice for $1.50. This large supermarket sold 1,700 paper half gallons of milk and 7,000 plastic gallons of milk per week. On the orange juice side, 170 half gallons of Tropicana, 170 half gallons of Minute Maid and Citrus Hill together, and 280 half gallons of dairy orange juice were sold each week.

If Champion's accounting system were to separate a 1/2 gallon milk carton from a 1/2 gallon orange juice carton, there would certainly be differences in costs. Table 4 identifies the process differences between the two segments. Costing these process differences is beyond the scope of this case.

Champion Strategy Today. Given the cost structure and changing environment already outlined, Champion still believed that the domestic dairy market would continue to be the principal area of profits, even with the contraction due to plastic. Champion would attempt to

defend its dominant position, but could not expect improvement in current volume unless one of the major competitors (IP, Westvaco, Weyerhaeuser or Potlatch) left the business. For example, in 1982 Weyerhaeuser exited the paperboard carton industry in the East when their paper mill in North Carolina was converted from board to disposable diapers. It was estimated that Champion picked up 30,000 to 40,000 tons a year of Weyerhaeuser's old business through 1988.

Overall, Champion recognized its strengths as:

- Large and efficient board machine
- Efficient and geographically well-located extrusion facility
- 5 competitive and strategically located carton converting plants
- Successful ovenable board converting plant (in the Midwest)
- Very successful position in the dairy market east of the Rockies
- Excellent service reputation among domestic dairies
- Knowledgeable operating people throughout the system

EXHIBIT 5

Champion
Champion International Corporation

To: Canton Mill, Manufacturing Office   Date: May 19, 1988
From: DairyPak Customer Services   Subject: Board Surface Quality

In our constant effort to improve the print quality of our finished product, one fact is obvious: no matter how good the quality of our inks, plates, artwork, machines, and people, we cannot accomplish the high degree of printing excellence we are striving for when our board surface is covered with dimples and pot holes.

The finer the settings on our presses, the more these surface imperfections show up. Please note the enclosed samples. What you see here is the rule, not the exception.

We would greatly appreciate your help in working with whomever necessary to find a way to supply us with a smooth printing surface with which to work. If we may be of assistance, please don't hesitate to call.

As always, your comments and/or suggestions are welcome.

cc: Joe Deal, Jr.
     Robert Ray
     Charlie Ward
     Ed Fritch

But Champion also recognized its weaknesses:

- Limited extrusion capacity
- Lack rotogravure printing
- Champion had been unable to respond efficiently to the diverse needs of the non-dairy segment
- Although tremendous progress had been made, there were still nagging problems with the quality of the board (see Exhibit 5)
- Lack roll wrapping and labeling capability of competitors at the extruding plant
- Reputation of uncertain commitment in export markets

Given the above, the Champion strategy had been and continued to be the low cost producer in the commodity dairy segment, trying to make inroads in the differentiated juice segment, to cautiously upgrade its infrastructure but not to invest in latest printing and roll-wrapping equipment, and to view export and special end-use segments as ancillary (no need for major commitments).

III. The Summer of 1988

Where to compete and how much to invest were the two difficult questions Earle Bensing faced in 1988.

The first proposal he was considering was to renovate the paperboard machine at a total cost of $43,000,000. Phase I of this proposal would cost $16,000,000 to rebuild the "wet end" of the machine and would result in improved internal strength of the board (stronger cartons and improved printability). Phase II would cost another $27,000,000 at the "dry end" of the machine (improved smoothness for better print quality).

A second proposal was to add a third extruder at the Waynesville, NC plant. A "state of the art" extruder cost approximately $17,000,000 and would allow Champion to compete in multilayered polymer coating applications. The newly emerging packages in the juice industry required multiple plastic resins and foils to extend shelf life and to hold difficult liquids. The new extruder would be dedicated to expanding Champion's product line to serve customers with complex co-extrusion needs.

A third proposal Bensing was considering was to add roll wrapping equipment at the Waynesville location. In 1988 coated rolls were shipped overseas unsealed, exposed while they were handled in transit and while laying in a cargo hold. This led to both sanitary and aesthetic problems, since moisture and bacteria could attack the board. State of the art roll wrapping equipment would cost $1,750,000 for the initial capital outlay, 1 operator for the machine at $30,000 a year, and $2.50 per one ton roll in material expense. Champion could not charge customers more for wrapped rolls.

The fourth potential area for investment was adding rotogravure printing. Currently DairyPak used flexography which printed from plates made of rubber. This method was very popular because it was inexpensive. After the initial capital expense of $1.5 million, the plates were about $150 apiece and six were needed for a six color process. The quality was not as good as with offset or rotogravure printing, but high quality printing was never required in the dairy segment of the business.

In rotogravure (or intaglio) printing, the plate cylinder itself was machined and coated to receive the printing image photographically. The portions of the cylinder's surface which would print were etched as microscopic, cup-like cells while the non-printing areas remained untouched. Rotogravure gave an extremely accurate and high quality finish—but it was expensive. The initial capital expense was similar to flexography (approximately $1.5 million) but one cylinder cost $2,500. With a six color process, $15,000 must have been spent for only *one* run. And once that run was complete, those cyl-

TABLE 5 Resource Allocation Options 1988

1. Rebuild the paperboard machine:

| Phase I—Rebuild "wet end" | $16 million |
| Phase II—Rebuild "dry end" | $27 million |

2. Add a third extruder at Waynesville $17 million

3. Add roll wrapping equipment:

Capital Cost		$1.75 million
Operating Costs:	Labor	$30,000/year
	Materials	$2.50/one ton roll

4. Add rotogravure printing as an option for customers:

| Capital Cost | $1.5 million |
| Operating Costs | $15,000 per run |

inders would probably never be used again. These investment opportunities are summarized in Table 5.

Not only did Bensing face investment decisions, he also had to decide who would get the limited amount of board that Champion produced each year. Would it be the dairies, whose total market had been declining 3% a year but who had always been the main customer of DairyPak? Would it be the big juice manufacturers (Coca Cola or Procter & Gamble)—whose market was growing at 10% and who would pay top dollar for board but who demanded a consistent quality that Champion had been unable to produce? Or would it be the export market—which was growing rapidly each year, and where a top price was possible because of a favorable currency situation, but where Champion had never tried to compete aggressively, either as a board supplier or a converter?

The marketing of paperboard cartons to the juice industry offered tremendous potential. Although the New York area made up only 7 percent of U.S. population, New Yorkers consumed 14 percent of the orange juice sold. If the big three's expansion was successful outside New York and New England, quality carton volume could have exploded. This was a great opportunity for Champion, if it had been ready to compete in that market.

The opportunity was definitely there for DairyPak. But did Earle Bensing have the right information to make his decisions? Was there an accurate picture of the costs and value created at the paper machine, the extruding plant and the converting plants? Was there enough information concerning the competitors and the marketplace? Overall, did Mr. Bensing have the financial tools to evaluate the investment and marketing options open to him?

Questions

1. Can you construct a "value chain" of costs and profits from the pulp mill all the way through to the supermarket for milk, for dairy orange juice, and for Minute Maid orange juice? Present all the calculations on the basis of one ton of board.
2. What insights for the business does the "value chain" provide? For example, of the total profit earned per ton of board, how much would be earned by the supermarket, by the processor, and by Champion?
3. When asset data (as shown here) is included, what inferences do you draw about ROA for Champion, the dairy, the juice processor and the retailer?

Assets in the Process Flow

Assets	1988 Market Value (S)	Per Ton of Board
Pulp Mill	400,000,000	$1,600
Paper Machine	300,000,000	1,200
Extruder	42,000,000	190
Converting Plants	141,000,000	830
Juice Processor	55,000,000	2,890
Small Dairy	2,100,000	5,400
Supermarket—space and display cases (dairy section)	103,500	1,800

4. Note that unless a major expansion were undertaken, Champion's output was limited to about 250,000 tons per year of coated board. Which segment(s) do you believe should have been targeted?

BEHAVIOR
IN ORGANIZATIONS

Management control systems influence human behavior. The systems should influence behaviors in a goal congruent manner. We begin this chapter by explaining the concept of goal congruence.

Goal congruence is affected both by informal processes and also by formal systems. Some of the informal factors are external to the organization and some are internal; these are described.

Control is also attained by two types of formal devices. One consists of "rules," broadly defined; the other is a systematic way of planning and controlling.

Different types of organization structures can be used to implement strategies. A discussion of the types of organization structures is essential, since the design of management control systems should fit the organization structure used.

Finally, we describe the function of the controller in the management control process.

Goal Congruence

Senior management wants the organization to attain the organization's goals. However, the members of the organization have their own personal goals, and these are not entirely consistent with the goals of the organization. The actions of individual members of the organization are directed toward achieving their personal goals. The central purpose of a management control system, therefore, is to assure, so far as is feasible, what is called "goal congruence." *Goal congruence in a process means that actions it leads people to take in accordance with their perceived self-interest are also in the best interest of the organization.*

Perfect congruence between individual goals and organizational goals does not exist. One obvious reason is that individual participants usually want as much compensation as they can get; whereas, from the organization's viewpoint, there is an upper limit to salaries beyond which profits would be adversely and unnecessarily affected. As a minimum, however, the management control system should not encourage individuals to act against the best interests of the organization. For example, if the system signals that the emphasis should be only on reducing costs, and if a manager responds by reducing costs at the expense of adequate quality or by reducing costs that he or she controls by causing a more than offsetting increase in costs in other parts of the organization, then the manager has been motivated, but in the wrong direction.

Two questions are important in evaluating any management control practice:

1. What actions does it motivate people to take for their self-interest?
2. Are these actions in the best interest of the organization?

Informal Factors That Influence Goal Congruence

Both formal systems and informal processes influence human behavior in organizations and, therefore, affect the degree to which goal congruence can be achieved. This book is primarily concerned with formal control systems. Nevertheless, the designers of formal systems should consider the informal processes in their design choices because formal mechanisms should be consistent with informal processes in order to effectively implement organization strategies. The system of strategic plans, budgets, and reports is a *formal* control system. Before discussing the formal system, we shall describe *informal* forces. Work ethic, management style, and culture are examples of informal organization processes, some of which are external to the organization, but most of which are internal.

External Factors

External factors are norms of desirable behavior that exist in the society of which the organization is a part. They are often referred to as the *work ethic*. They are manifest in employees' loyalty to the organization, their diligence, their spirit, and their pride in doing a good job (as contrasted with merely putting in time). Some of these attitudes are local: they are specific to the city or region in which the organization does its work. In encouraging companies to locate in their city or state, chambers of commerce or other promotional organizations often claim that their locality has a loyal, diligent work force. Others are industry-specific: the railroad industry has norms that differ from those in the airline industry. Still others are national; some countries have a reputation for excellent work ethics. Currently, for example, Japan, South Korea, Hong Kong, and other East Asian countries have an excellent reputation on this dimension.

Example. Many large Japanese companies go to great lengths to instill loyalty. They have company pep songs. They support baseball teams that compete regionally and nationally. The teams are accompanied by cheerleaders (with cheers specific to the company) and marching bands. These activities are similar to those that instill loyalty in students at an American college or university. Employees dress in the company uniform.

Internal Factors

Culture.   The most important internal factor is the organization's culture, or climate. Organization culture refers to the set of common beliefs, attitudes, norms, relationships, and assumptions that are explicitly or implicitly accepted and evidenced throughout the organization.[1] Similarly, as defined by Kenneth R. Andrews, the term *climate* is used to designate the quality of the internal environment that conditions the quality of cooperation, the development of individuals, the extent of members' dedication or commitment to organizational purpose, and the efficiency with which that purpose is translated into results. Climate is the atmosphere in which individuals help, judge, reward, constrain, and find out about each other. It influences morale—the attitude of the individual toward his or her work and his or her environment.[2]

Cultural norms are extremely important.[3] They explain why either of two organizations may have an excellent formal management control system, but why one has much better actual control than the other. An organization's culture is rarely stated in writing, and attempts to do so almost always result in platitudes.

> **Example.** A young, rapidly growing microcomputer manufacturing company attempted to prepare a statement of its corporate culture. One paragraph in the statement read, "Management by personal communication is part of our way of life. We encourage open, direct, person-to-person communication as part of our daily routine." Notwithstanding the "open communication" buzzword, the statement itself was developed by senior management in strict secrecy, and it was not communicated to the organization until after it had been adopted. Management's deeds were the exact opposite of its words.[4]

A company's culture exists unchanged for many years. Certain practices are rituals; they are carried on almost automatically because "this is the way things are done here." Others are taboos; "we just don't do that here," although no one remembers why. Culture is influenced strongly by the personality and policies of the chief executive officer (and by those of lower-level managers with respect to the part of the organization that they manage). If the organization is unionized, the rules and norms accepted by the union have an important influence on the organization's culture. Attempts to change practices meet resistance, and, the larger and more mature the organization, the greater the resistance is.

---

[1]For a discussion of the concept of corporate culture, see T. E. Deal and A. A. Kennedy, "Culture: A New Look through Old Lenses." *Journal of Applied Behavioral Science* (1983), pp. 498–506.

[2]Kenneth R. Andrews, *The Concept of Corporate Strategy* (Homewood, IL: Dow Jones-Irwin, 1980).

[3]Thomas J. Peters and Robert Waterman, *In Search of Excellence* (New York: Harper & Row, 1982).

[4]Reported by Peter C. Reynolds in "Corporate Culture on the Rocks," *Across the Board,* October 1986, p. 53.

Management Style.   The internal factor that probably has the strongest impact on management control is management style—in particular, the attitude of a manager's superior toward control. Usually the attitude of subordinates reflects in a general way their perception of the attitude of their superiors, modified, of course, by each subordinate's own attitude. The attitude ultimately stems from the attitude of the chief executive officer. This is another way of saying "an institution is the lengthened shadow of a man."[5]

Managers come in all shapes and sizes. Some are charismatic and outgoing; others are less ebullient. Some spend much time looking and talking to people (called "management by walking around"); others rely more heavily on written reports. We know of no way to generalize about the "ideal" manager. The student may form conclusions about the differences between effective and ineffective managers from the cases in this book.

> **Example.** When he [Reginald Jones] was tapped to run General Electric, it was a large, multi-industry company that performed fairly well in a number of mature markets. The company, however, was experiencing a bit of midlife crisis: a price-fixing scandal that sent several executives to jail, coupled with GE's sound defeat in, and subsequent retreat from, the mainframe computer business. Jones provided the salve for those wounds. He instituted formal strategy planning and built up one of the first strategic planning units in a major corporation. Jones was psychologically suited for such an operation: dignified, refined, very bright, able to delegate enormous amounts of authority. GE moved into new areas, but carefully, after much thought, and efficiently. Business was good.
>
> When he retired, Jones and the GE board had the wisdom to select not a man just like him, but one as different as night from day: Jack Welch. Welch nearly eliminated the planning group, shifting planning to line managers. He cut the work force by 20 percent, closed dozens of plants. Not surprisingly, Welch became as well known for his extroverted personality as the introverted Jones had been for his. "He demands action immediately," said one top GE executive.[6]

The Informal Organization.   The lines on an organization chart depict the formal organization—that is, the formal authority and responsibility relationships of the specified managers. The organization chart may show, for example, that the production manager of Division A reports to the general manager. Actually the production manager communicates with several other people in the organization: other managers, support units, and staff people at headquarters—and simply friends and acquaintances. In extreme situations, the production manager may pay inadequate attention to messages received from the general manager. This tends to happen when the production manager is evaluated more on production efficiency than on overall performance. The relationships that constitute the informal organization are important in understanding the realities of the management control process.

---

[5]Ralph Waldo Emerson, *Self Reliance* (1841).

[6]Robert E. Lamb, "CEOs for This Season," *Across the Board,* April 1987, pp. 34–41.

Perception and Communication.   In working toward the goals of the organization, operating managers must know what these goals are and what actions they are supposed to take in order to achieve them. They receive information about what they are supposed to do through various channels. In part, this information is conveyed by budgets and other formal documents; in part, it is conveyed by conversations and other informal means. This information often is not a clear message about what senior management wants done. An organization is complicated, and the actions that should be taken by one part of it to accomplish the overall goals cannot be stated with absolute clarity, even under the best of circumstances.

Moreover, the messages received through various information channels may conflict with one another, or managers may interpret them in different ways. For example, the budget mechanism may convey the impression that managers are supposed to make this year's profits as high as possible, whereas senior management actually doesn't want operating managers to skimp on maintenance or employee training; such actions, although increasing current profits, might reduce future profitability. Operating managers' perceptions of what they are supposed to do are vastly less clear cut than the message that the furnace receives from the thermostat, as exemplified in Chapter 1.

Many erroneous perceptions arise from *functional fixation*—that is, the tendency of people to interpret the meaning of words and phrases according to accustomed definitions, even though these definitions have become obsolete or are not applicable to the current situation. Managers, because of their background in another company or from what they have learned in school, may assume that a term has a different meaning from that intended. Greater emphasis in management control reports on a standard terminology is one way to reduce the impact of functional fixation.

Cooperation and Conflict.   The lines connecting the boxes on an organization chart imply that the way organizational goals are attained is that senior management makes a decision and communicates that decision down through the organizational hierarchy to managers at lower levels of the organization, who then implement it. This implication ignores the personal goals of individuals, and it is not the way an organization actually functions.

In fact, each operating manager reacts to instructions from senior management in accordance with how those instructions affect his or her personal needs. Also, usually more than one manager is involved in carrying out senior management plans, so the interactions among managers also affect how well the plans are implemented. For example, the manager of the maintenance department may be assigned responsibility for ensuring that the maintenance needs of the production departments are satisfied, but the needs of one department may be slighted if there is friction between the maintenance manager and the manager of that department. More importantly, many actions that a manager may want to take in order to achieve personal goals may have an adverse effect on other managers and on overall profitability. For example, managers may argue about which of them is to obtain the use of limited production capacity or other scarce resources, or about potential customers that several managers want to solicit, unless the management control system provides instructions in advance. For these and many other reasons, conflicts exist within organizations, and management control systems should help minimize them.

An organization attempts to maintain an appropriate balance between the forces that create conflict and those that create cooperation. Some conflict is desirable. Conflict results in part from the competition among participants for promotion or other forms of compensation; such competition is, within limits, healthy. A certain amount of cooperation is also obviously essential; but if undue emphasis is placed on developing cooperative attitudes, the most able participants will be denied the opportunity of using their talents fully. The management control system must help to maintain the appropriate balance between conflict and cooperation within the organization.

The Formal Control System

The informal factors discussed above have a great influence on the effectiveness of management control in an organization. The other influence is, of course, the formal systems. These systems can be classified into two types: (1) the management control system, which is our main emphasis in this book and, therefore, not discussed further at this point; and (2) rules, which are described briefly below.

Rules

We use the word *rules* as shorthand for all types of formal instructions and controls. They include standing instructions, practices, job descriptions, standard operating procedures, manuals, and codes of ethics. Unlike the directives or guidance implicit in budget amounts, which change from month to month, these rules are in force indefinitely—that is, they exist until they are modified. Typically, rules are changed infrequently. They relate to matters that range from the most trivial (e.g., paper clips will be issued only on the basis of a signed requisition) to the most important (e.g., capital expenditures of over $5 million must be approved by the board of directors).[7]

Some rules are guides—that is, organization members are permitted, and indeed expected, to depart from them, either under specified circumstances or if in the person's judgment a departure is in the best interests of the organization. For instance, there may be a rule stating the criteria for extending credit to customers, but the credit manager may OK credit to a customer who currently does not meet these criteria if the customer has been especially valuable and may become so again. Departures from the rules may require the approval of higher authority.

---

[7]For a thorough treatment of this topic, see Kenneth A. Merchant, *Control in Business Organizations* (Marshfield, MA: Pitman, 1985).

Some rules should never be broken. A rule that prohibits payment of bribes and a rule that an airline pilot should never take off without permission from the air traffic controller are examples. Some rules are prohibitions against unethical, illegal, or other undesirable actions. Others are positive requirements that certain actions be taken (e.g., fire drills at prescribed intervals). The distinction between prohibitions and positive requirements may not be apparent, and managers should be made aware of the distinction.

Some of the specific types of rules are listed below.

Physical controls. Security guards, locked storerooms, vaults, computer passwords, television surveillance, and other physical controls are part of the control structure. Most of them are associated with task control, rather than with management control.

Manuals. Much judgment is required in deciding which rules should be written and put in a manual; which should be guidelines, rather than fixed rules; what discretion should be allowed; and a variety of other matters. The literature contains only obvious guidance on these matters. Bureaucratic organizations have more detailed manuals than other organizations; large organizations have more than small ones; centralized organizations have more than decentralized ones; and organizations with geographically dispersed units performing similar functions (such as fast-food restaurant chains) have more manuals and rules than single-site organizations.

With the passage of time, some rules become outdated. Manuals and other sets of rules, therefore, need to be reexamined periodically to ensure that they are consistent with the desires of the current senior management. In the pressure of day-to-day activities, the need for reexamination often is overlooked; if so, the manuals are likely to contain rules for situations that no longer exist, or for practices that are obsolete. If these rules are permitted to remain, managers are likely to have an unfavorable impression of the whole manual.

System safeguards. Various safeguards are built into the information processing system to ensure that the information flowing through the system is accurate and to prevent (or at least minimize) fraud and defalcation. They include cross-checks of totals with details, required signatures and other evidence that a transaction has been authorized, separation of duties, frequent counts of cash and other portable assets, and a number of other rules that are described in texts on auditing. They also include checks of the system that are made by internal and external auditors.

Task control systems. In Chapter 1 we defined task control as the process of assuring that specific tasks are carried out efficiently and effectively. Many of these tasks are controlled by rules. If a task is automated, the automated system itself provides the control. Task control systems are outside the scope of this book.

Exhibit 3–1

The formal control process

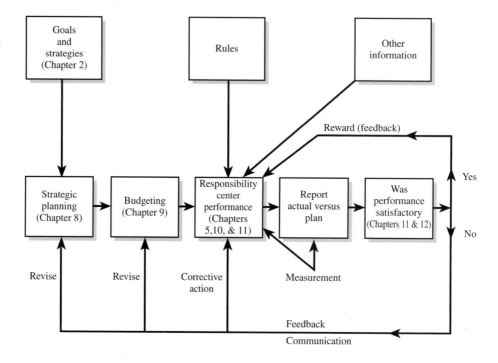

Formal Control Process

Exhibit 3–1 is a sketch of the formal management control process. Its foundation is the organization's goals, and strategies for attaining these goals. A strategic plan is prepared in order to implement these strategies; all available information is used in making this plan. The strategic plan is converted to an annual budget that focuses on the planned revenues and expenses for individual responsibility centers. Responsibility centers also are guided by a large number of rules and other information. They operate, and the results of their operation are measured and reported. Actual results are compared with the plan, to answer the question "was performance satisfactory?" If it was satisfactory, there is feedback to the responsibility center in the form of praise or other reward. If performance was not satisfactory, there is feedback leading to corrective action in the responsibility center and possible revision of the plan. (Like most such diagrams, this sketch is valid only as a generalization. As we shall show in later chapters, the process in practice is less straightforward than this sketch indicates.)

Types of Organizations

The firm's strategy has an important influence on its organization structure.[8] The type of organization structure, in turn, has an influence on the design of management control systems. Although organizations come in all sizes and

---

[8]Alfred D. Chandler, Jr., *Strategy and Structure* (Cambridge, MA: MIT Press, 1962).

shapes, their structures can be grouped into three general categories: (1) a functional structure, in which each manager is responsible for a specified function, such as production or marketing; (2) a business unit structure, in which each business unit manager is responsible for most of the activities of a business unit, which is a semi-independent part of the company; and (3) a matrix structure, in which functional units have dual responsibilities. Abbreviated organization charts for each type are shown in Exhibit 3–2. The discussion here is limited to functional and business unit organizations; matrix organizations are discussed in Chapter 18.

Functional Organizations

The rationale for the functional form of organization is the same as that developed by Frederick Taylor and others for specialization of labor in large-scale production. It involves the notion of a manager who brings specialized knowledge to bear on decisions related to the function. This contrasts with the general-purpose manager, who cannot possibly have as much knowledge about a given function as a specialist in that function. A skilled marketing manager should make better marketing decisions and a skilled production manager should make better production decisions than the decisions made by a manager who is responsible for both marketing and production. Moreover, the skilled specialist should be able to supervise workers in the same function better than the generalist; similarly, skilled higher-level managers should be able to provide better supervision of lower-level managers in the same or similar function. *Thus, an important advantage of a functional structure is efficiency.*

There are five disadvantages of a functional structure. First, in a functional organization, there is no unambiguous way of determining the effectiveness of the separate functional managers because each function contributes jointly to the final output of the organization. If there is a marketing manager and a production manager, there is no unambiguous way of measuring what fraction of the profit was contributed by each. Similarly at lower levels in the organization there is no way of determining how much of the profit was earned by each production department, by the product engineering department, and by the sales office, respectively.

A second disadvantage of the functional organization is that there is no good way of planning the work of the separate functions at lower levels in the organization. In a functional organization, plans for the organization as a whole must be made at the very top because these plans necessarily involve coordination of all the functions that contribute to the final output. Plans for the marketing department must take into account the ability of the production department to produce goods with the specifications and in the quantities that it judges customers will buy, and plans of the production department must take into account the ability of the marketing department to sell goods with the specifications and in the quantities that it is prepared to produce.

Exhibit 3–2

Types of organizations

A. Functional Organization

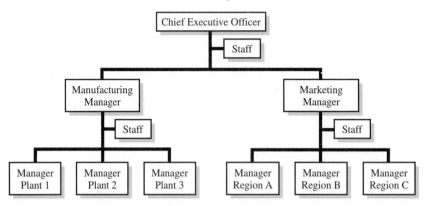

B. Business Unit Organization

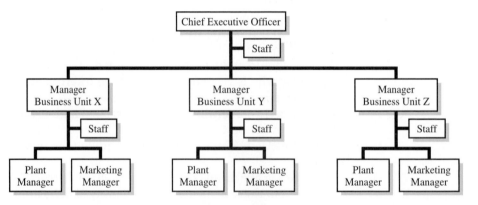

C. Matrix Organization

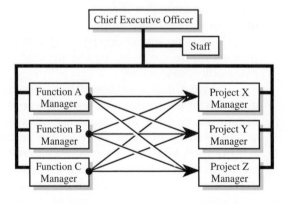

Third, if the organization consists of managers in one function who report to higher-level managers of the same function, who, in turn, report to still higher-level managers of that function, then a dispute between managers of different functions can be resolved only at the very top of the organization, even though it originates at a low level. The marketing department may want to satisfy a customer's need for a certain quantity of product even if it involves overtime work by the manufacturing department, but the manufacturing department may be unwilling to incur the additional costs associated with overtime. Such a dispute can theoretically be resolved only at headquarters, even though it may involve only a branch sales office and one small department of a manufacturing plant. Taking the issue up through several levels in the organization and then communicating the decision down to the level where the dispute originated can be time consuming and frustrating. (As a practical matter, the parties involved may settle such disputes informally, even though this involves crossing organizational lines of authority, but there is no guarantee that this will happen.)

Fourth, functional structures are inadequate when the firm diversifies its products and markets.

> **Example.** When Apple Computer only made Macintosh computers and marketed them through computer dealers, the company could use functional organization effectively to reap the benefits of scale and specialization. However, when Apple diversified into desktops, laptops, and palmtops and distributed its diverse products through multiple channels—direct marketing, direct sales, computer dealers, and mass merchandisers—the company's functional organization was overloaded.[9]

Companies that diversify their products and markets are likely to find a single functional organization suboptimal.

Finally, functional organizations tend to create "silos" across functions, thereby preventing cross-functional coordination in areas such as new product development. This problem can be mitigated by supplementing this organization with lateral cross-functional processes such as cross-functional job rotation and team-based rewards.

> **Examples:** At the Boeing company, in the past design engineers worked independently of the production and operations people who actually built the plane. "Here it is" the designers would say. "Now, go build it." As a result of this approach, Boeing's production people were given overly costly, hard-to-build designs. Under the old, military style of management, if [union member Tony] Russel detected something wrong in his engineering plans, he'd have to go through his supervisor and the problem would move through the chain of command until it eventually reached the engineer. Boeing is now trying to break down their functional hierarchies into design-build teams which are composed of members from all the different functions. The 777 project used these design build teams exclusively. Now, production employees talk directly with engineering.[10]

---

[9]Jay Galbraith, *Designing Organizations* (San Francisco: Jossey-Bass Publishers, 1995), p. 26.
[10]Seth Lubove, "Destroying the old hierarchies," *Forbes,* June 3, 1996, pp. 62–71.

Glaxo Wellcome, the world's largest seller of pharmaceuticals, felt that its scientists did not have enough business sense. As a result, Glaxo Wellcome changed from a functional hierarchical structure to a structure of "therapeutic strategy" teams. These teams consisted of scientists and commercial managers in an attempt to bring the two sides of the business closer together.[11]

Business Units

The business unit form of organization is designed to solve problems inherent in the functional structure. *A business unit, also called a division, is responsible for all the functions involved in producing and marketing a specified product line.* Business unit managers act almost as if their units were separate companies. They are responsible for planning and coordinating the work of the separate functions, and they resolve disputes that arise between these functions. They ensure that the plans of the marketing department are consistent with production capabilities. Their performance is measured by the profitability of the business unit, and this is a satisfactory measure because profit incorporates the activities of both marketing and production.

Examples: Singapore Airlines has created several SBUs, such as its airline leasing group to improve efficiencies in that market and to reduce Singapore Airlines reliance on the sales of its used aircraft.[12]

Nabisco's business units use different distribution systems. Its biscuit unit uses its own trucks and salespeople to deliver directly to retailers' shelves . . . This system is considered to be costly but it is also believed to offer better customer relations and closer control over store inventory and sales.[13]

Business unit managers do not have complete authority. Headquarters reserves the right to make certain decisions. At a minimum, headquarters is responsible for obtaining funds for the company as a whole, and it allocates funds to business units according to its judgment on where the available funds can be put to the best use. Headquarters also approves the business unit budgets, judges the performance of business unit managers, sets their compensation, and if the situation warrants, removes them. Headquarters establishes the "charter" of each business unit—that is, the product lines it is permitted to make and sell or the geographical territory in which it can operate, or both, and occasionally, the customers to which it may sell.

Headquarters also establishes companywide policies. Depending on the wishes of the chief executive officer, these may be few and general, or they may be set forth in several thick volumes of manuals. Headquarters staff offices may

---

[11]Richard Evans, "A giant battles its drug dependency," *Fortune,* August 5, 1996, pp. 88–92.

[12]Mark L. Clifford, "Where will Singapore Air Fly All Those Jets," *Business Week,* August 12, 1996, p. 44.

[13]Lori Bongiorno, "It's put up or shut up time," *Business Week,* July 8, 1996, pp. 100–101.

assist the business units in production and marketing activities and in specialized areas, such as human resources, legal, public relations, controller, and treasury. These headquarters functions are valuable; without them, the business units would be better off being separate companies.

An advantage of the business unit form of organization is that it provides a training ground in general management. The business unit manager should have the entrepreneurial spirit that characterizes the CEO of an independent company.

Another advantage is that because the business unit is closer to the market for its products than the headquarters organization, its manager may make sounder decisions than headquarters can make, and it can react to new threats or opportunities more quickly.

Offsetting these advantages is the possibility that each business unit staff may duplicate some work that in a functional organization is done at headquarters. The business unit manager is presumably a generalist, but his or her subordinates are functional specialists, and they must deal with many of the same problems that specialists in other business units and at headquarters address. The layers of business unit staff may be more expensive than the value gained by divisionalization. Moreover, skilled specialists in certain functions are in short supply, and business units may be unable to attract qualified persons. These problems could be mitigated by supplementing business unit organization with certain centralized functional expertise.

> **Example.** "At Boeing's commercial aircraft group, the design and manufacture of planes is divided into product lines of narrow bodies (737, 757) and wide bodies (747, 767, and eventually the 777). However, the fabrication of major structural components requires very large and expensive computer-controlled machine tools. These would be too expensive to duplicate in each product line. Instead, a central fabrication unit is created and all manufacturing activities requiring scale and skill are placed in it and shared across product lines. This structure is a hybrid of products and functions."[14]

Another disadvantage of the business unit form is that the disputes between functional specialists in a functional organization may be replaced by disputes between business units in a business unit organization. These may involve one business unit infringing on the charter of another unit. There may also be disputes between business unit staffs and headquarters staff.

Although the possibility of holding several managers responsible for pieces of the company's overall profit performance is attractive, the above noted disadvantages may outweigh the benefits of business unit structure. Business units are profit centers or investment centers, and further discussion of the merits and disadvantages of business unit structure in various circumstances is deferred to Chapters 5 and 7, which deal with these responsibility centers.

---

[14]Jay Galbraith, *Designing Organizations* (San Francisco: Jossey-Bass Publishers, 1995), p. 29.

Implications for Systems Design

If ease of control were the only criterion, companies would be organized into business units whenever it was feasible to do so because in a business unit organization, each unit manager is held responsible for the profitability of the unit's product line, and he or she presumably plans, coordinates, and controls the elements that affect its profitability. Control is not the only criterion, however. A functional organization may be more efficient because larger functional units provide the benefits of economies of scale. A business unit organization requires a somewhat broader type of manager than the specialist who manages a function; competent general managers may be difficult to find.

Because of the apparently clear-cut nature of the assignment of profit responsibility in a business unit organization, designers of management control systems sometimes recommend such an organization without giving appropriate weight to the other considerations involved in organization design.[15] Nevertheless, the systems designer must fit the system to the organization, not the other way around. In other words, although the control implications of various organization structures should be discussed with senior management, once management has decided that a given structure is best, all things considered, then the system designer must take that structure as given. Enthusiasts for some control technique may overlook this essential point.

The point also is important in other contexts. For example, many advertising agencies follow the practice of shifting account supervisors from one account to another at fairly frequent intervals and so bring a fresh point of view to the various advertising programs. This practice increases the difficulty of measuring the performance of an account supervisor because the fruits of an advertising campaign may require a long time to ripen. Nevertheless, the systems designer should not insist that the rotation policy be abandoned simply because to do so would make performance measurement easier.

Functions of the Controller

We shall refer to the person who is responsible for designing and operating the management control system as the controller. Actually, in many organizations, the title of this person is chief financial officer.[16]

---

[15]For an excellent discussion of the complex factors that must be considered in making a basic change in organization structure, see Alfred D. Chandler, Jr., *Strategy and Structure* (Cambridge, MA: MIT Press, 1962).

[16]The chief financial officer typically is responsible both for the controllership function (as described here) and also for the treasury function. The title came into common use in the 1970s. At that time, its professional association, the Controllers Institute, became the Financial Executives Institute. The controller and the treasurer report to the chief financial officer. Because we do not discuss the treasurer's function, we use the narrower term, *controller*.

The spelling "comptroller" is also used. This spelling originated with an error made in the 18th century in translating from French to English, but the erroneous spelling has become embedded in dozens of federal and state statutes and in the bylaws of many companies and still persists. "Comptroller" is pronounced the same as "controller"; not *compt'*roller.

The controller usually performs the following functions:

- Designs and operates information and control systems.
- Prepares financial statements and financial reports (including tax returns) to shareholders and other external parties.
- Prepares and analyzes performance reports and assists managers by interpreting these reports, by analyzing program and budget proposals, and by consolidating the plans of various segments into an overall annual budget.[17]
- Supervises internal audit and accounting control procedures to ensure the validity of information, establishes adequate safeguards against theft and defalcation, and performs operational audits.
- Develops personnel in the controller organization and participates in the education of management personnel in matters relating to the controller function.

Prior to the advent of computers, the controller (or chief financial officer) was usually responsible for *processing* the information required by the management control system. Currently, many companies have a chief information officer (CIO) with this responsibility. In some companies the CIO reports to the chief financial officers; in others, the CIO reports to senior management.

Relation to Line Organization

The controllership function is a staff function. Although the controller usually is responsible for the *design and operation* of systems in which control information is collected and reported, the *use* of this information in actual control is the responsibility of line management. The controller also may be responsible for developing and analyzing control measurements and for making recommendations for action to management. Moreover, the controller may police adherence to limitations on spending laid down by the chief executive, control the integrity of the accounting system, and be responsible for safeguarding assets from theft and fraud.

The controller does not make or enforce management decisions, however. The responsibility for control runs from the chief executive officer down through the line organization, which uses information provided by the controller.

The controller does make some decisions. In general, these are decisions that implement policies decided on by line management. For example, a member of the controller organization often decides on the propriety of expenses listed on a travel voucher; line managers usually prefer not to get involved in

---

[17]A survey of chief financial officers of multinational corporations sponsored by KPMG Peat Marwick and Business International found that they have an increasing influence over operations and work more closely with the chief executive officer. KPMG Peat Marwick Main & Co., *The Changing Role of the Modern CFO* (New York, 1989).

Exhibit 3–3

Alternative controller relationships

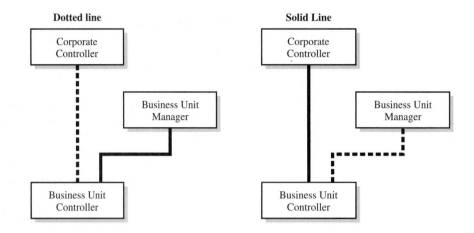

discussions of whether the traveler spent too much on meals or whether the airplane trip should have been made in economy class rather than first class.

The controller plays an important role in the preparation of strategic plans and budgets. Also, the controller organization typically analyzes performance reports, assures that they are accurate, and calls the line manager's attention to items that may indicate the need for action. In these activities, the controller acts almost like a line manager. The difference is that the controller's decision can be overruled by the line manager to whom the subordinate manager is responsible.

The Business Unit Controller

Business unit controllers inevitably have a divided loyalty. On the one hand, they owe some allegiance to the corporate controller, who is presumably responsible for the overall operation of the control system. On the other hand, they owe allegiance to their business unit managers since controllers are responsible for furnishing staff assistance to them. Two possible types of relationships are diagrammed in Exhibit 3–3.

In some companies, the business unit controller reports to the business unit manager, and has what is called a *dotted line* relationship with the corporate controller. Here, the business unit general manager is the controller's immediate boss. This means that the business unit general manager has the ultimate authority in decisions relating to hiring, training, transferring, compensation, promotion, and firing of business unit controllers. However, the business unit general manager usually takes the inputs of the corporate controller before making these decisions. General Electric Company used this approach, as described by the following comment by Bernard R. Doyle:

> Our controllership structure is based on a strong functional reporting line. The business unit controllers report directly to the general managers of their business units, but they have a functional or "dotted line" responsibility to the chief financial officer of the company. The glue that holds it together is that the people in those

business unit functional jobs can be appointed only from a slate of candidates the corporate chief financial officer first approves, and he has the unqualified right to remove these people. But, as importantly, these people are the chief financial officers of their business units. They are team players.[18]

In other companies, business unit controllers report directly to the corporate controller—that is, the corporate controller is their boss, as indicated by a *solid line* on the organization chart. ITT used this approach.[19]

There are problems with each of these relationships. If the business unit controller works primarily for the business unit manager, there is the possibility that he or she will not reveal "fat" in the proposed budget or provide completely objective reports on performance. On the other hand, if the business unit controller works primarily for the corporate controller, the business unit manager may treat him or her as a "spy from the front office," rather than as a trusted aide.

In companies in which the business unit controller's primary loyalty is to the business unit manager, it is expected that business unit controllers will not condone or participate in the transmission of misleading information or the concealment of unfavorable information; their overall ethical responsibilities should not countenance such practices.

> **Example.** In a talk to new business unit controllers, Helmut Maucher, chief executive officer of Nestlé, the world's largest food company, said: "As controller, you report to the business unit manager. The business unit manager has complete responsibility for the unit. However, in rare cases something may happen that means your loyalty to the unit manager is finished and your loyalty to the company takes over. I want a clear line of command, but everything has its limits; and, in that case, you cannot excuse yourself. I want your loyalty in general to be to the business unit manager; but, if he has five girlfriends and drinks too much, you must tell us at headquarters. This is your higher priority of loyalty."

Summary

Senior management wants the organization to attain its goals. Members of the organization have personal goals, and these are not in all respects consistent with the organization's goals. The central purpose of the management control system is to assure goal congruence; that is, the systems should be designed in such a way that actions it leads people to take in their perceived self-interest are also in the best interest of the organization.

Informal factors have an important influence on goal congruence. The most important of these is an organization's culture or climate. There is an informal

---

[18]Jonathan B. Schiff, "Interview with Bernard Doyle of General Electric," *Controllers Quarterly,* v. 6, no. 3, 1990, pp. 2–5.

[19]Vijay Sathe, *Controllership in Divisionalized Firms: Structure, Evaluation, and Development* (New York: American Management Association, 1978), pp. 20–21.

organization alongside the formal organization. An individual's perception and communication of information may be imperfect. Management must ensure a proper balance between the need for cooperation and the need for competition, both of which are desirable within limits. Finally management style has an important influence on control.

In addition to the informal factors, there are rules, guidelines, and procedures that also assist the control process; these make up the formal control system.

Companies can choose from three basic organization structures: functional, business unit, and matrix. The specific choice of organizational form has an influence on the design of the management control system.

The controller is responsible for the design and operation of the control system; but, as a staff officer, he or she does not make management decisions. In companies organized into business units, the proper relationship between the business unit controller and the corporate controller is debatable.

Suggested Additional Readings

Barnard, Chester I. *The Functions of the Executive.* Cambridge, MA: Harvard University Press, 1938.

Chandler, Alfred D., Jr. *The Dynamics of Industrial Capitalism.* Cambridge, MA: Harvard University Press, 1990.

Cyert, Richard M., and James G. March. *A Behavioral Theory of the Firm.* Englewood Cliffs, NJ: Prentice Hall, 1963.

Ferris, K. R., and J. L. Livingstone, eds. *Management Planning and Control: The Behavioral Foundations.* Columbus, OH: Publishing Horizons, Inc., 1989.

Galbraith, Jay R. *Designing Organizations.* San Francisco: Jossey-Bass Publishers, 1995.

Govindarajan, Vijay, and Joseph G. San Miguel. "Contingent Relationship between the Controller and Internal Audit Functions in Large Organizations." *Accounting, Organizations and Society* IX, no. 2, 1984, pp. 179–88.

Kanter, Rosabeth Moss, Barry A. Stein, and Jick Todd. *The Challenge of Organizational Change.* New York: The Free Press, 1992.

Keating, Patrick J., and Stephen P. Jablonsky. *Changing Roles of Financial Management.* New York: Financial Executives Research Foundation, 1990.

Kotter, John P., and James L. Heskitt. *Corporate Culture and Performance.* New York: The Free Press, 1992.

March, James G., and Herbert A. Simon. *Organizations.* New York: John Wiley & Sons, 1993.

Sathe, Vijay. *Controller Involvement in Management.* Englewood Cliffs, NJ: Prentice Hall, 1982.

Staw, Barry M., and L. L. Cummings, eds. *Work in Organizations.* Greenwich, CT: JAI Press, 1990.

Ulrich, David. *Organizational Capability.* New York: John Wiley & Sons, 1994.

Case 3–1
Rendell Company

Fred Bevins, controller of the Rendell Company, was concerned about the organizational status of his divisional controllers. In 1985 and for many years previously, the divisional controllers reported to the general managers of their divisions. Although Mr. Bevins knew this to be the general practice in many other divisionally organized companies, he was not entirely satisfied with it. His interest in making a change was stimulated by a description of organizational responsibilities given him by the controller of the Martex Corporation.

The Rendell Company had seven operating divisions: the smallest had $50 million in annual sales and the largest over $500 million. Each division was responsible for both the manufacturing and the marketing of a distinct product line. Some parts and components were transferred between divisions, but the volume of such interdivisional business was not large.

The company had been in business and profitable for over 50 years. In the late 1970s, although it continued to make profits, its rate of growth slowed considerably. James Hodgkin, later the president, was hired in 1980 by the directors because of their concern about this situation. His first position was controller. He became executive vice president in 1983 and president in 1984. Mr. Bevins joined the company as assistant controller in 1981, when he was 33 years old. He became controller in 1983.

In 1980, the corporate control organization was primarily responsible for (1) financial accounting, (2) internal auditing, and (3) analysis of capital budgeting requests. A budgetary control system was in existence, but the reports prepared under this system were submitted to the top manage-

ment group directly by the operating divisions, with little analysis by the corporate control organization.

Mr. Hodgkin, as controller, thought it essential that the corporate control organization play a more active role in the process of establishing budgets and analyzing performance. He personally took an active role in reviewing budgets and studying divisional performance reports and hired several young analysts to assist him. Mr. Bevins continued to move in the same direction after his promotion to controller. By 1985 the corporate organization was beginning to be well enough staffed so that it could, and did, give careful attention to the information submitted by the divisions.

Divisional controllers reported directly to the divisional general managers, but the corporate controller always was consulted prior to the appointment of a new division controller, and he also was consulted in connection with salary increases for divisional controllers. The corporate controller specified the accounting system to which the divisions were expected to conform and the general procedures they were to follow in connection with budgeting and reporting performance. It was clearly understood, however, that budgets and performance reports coming from a division were the responsibility of that division's general manager, with the divisional controller acting as his staff assistant in the preparation of these documents. For example, the divisional general manager personally discussed his budget with top management prior to its approval, and although the divisional controller usually was present at these meetings to give information on technical points, his role was strictly that of a staff man.

Most of the divisional controllers had worked for Rendell for 10 years or more. Usually they worked up through various positions in the controller organization, either at headquarters, in

This case was prepared by Robert N. Anthony, Harvard Business School. Copyright Harvard Business School case 109-033 by the President and Fellows of Harvard College.

their division, or both. Two of the divisional controllers were in their early 30s, however, and had only a few years' experience in the headquarters controller organization before being made, first, divisional assistant controller and then divisional controller.

Mr. Bevins foresaw increasing difficulties with this relationship as the corporation introduced more modern control techniques. For one thing, he thought the existing relationship between himself and the divisional controllers was not so close that he could urge the development and use of new techniques as rapidly as he wished. More important, he thought that he was not getting adequate information about what was actually happening in the divisions. The divisional controller's primary loyalty was to his division manager, and it was unreasonable to expect that he would give Mr. Bevins frank, unbiased reports. For example, Mr. Bevins was quite sure that some fat was hidden in the divisional expense budgets and that the divisional controllers had a pretty good idea where it was. In short, he thought he would get a much better idea of what was going on in the divisions if reports on divisional activities came directly from controllers working for him, rather than for the divisional manager.

Mr. Bevins, was, therefore, especially interested in the controller organization at the Martex Company as he learned about it from E. F. Ingraham, the Martex controller, when he visited that company.

Until his visit to Martex, Mr. Bevins had not discussed the organization problem with anyone. Shortly thereafter, he gave William Harrigan, his assistant controller, a memorandum describing his visit (see the appendix) and asked for Mr. Harrigan's reaction. Mr. Harrigan had been with Rendell for 25 years and had been a divisional controller before going to headquarters in 1982. Mr. Bevins respected his knowledge of the company and his opinion on organizational matters. Mr. Harrigan was accustomed to speaking frankly with Mr. Bevins. The gist of his comments follows:

I don't think the Martex plan would work with us; in fact, I am not even sure it works at Martex in the way suggested by the job descriptions and organization charts.

Before coming to headquarters, I had five years' experience as a divisional controller. When I took the job, I was told by the corporate controller and by my general manager that my function was to help the general manager every way I could. This is the way I operated. My people got together a lot of the information that was helpful in preparing the divisional budget, but the final product represented the thinking and decisions of my general manager, and he was the person who sold it to top management. I always went with him to the budget meetings, and he often asked me to explain some of the figures. When the monthly reports were prepared, I usually went over them, looking for danger signals, and then took them in to the general manager. He might agree with me, or he might spot other things that needed looking into. In either case, he usually was the one to put the heat on the operating organization, not me.

We did have some problems. The worst, and this happened several times a year, was when someone from the corporate controller's office would telephone and ask questions such as, "Do you think your division could get along all right if we cut $X out of the advertising budget?" Or, "Do you really believe that the cost savings estimate on this equipment is realistic?" Usually, I was in complete agreement with the data in question and defended them as best I could. Once in a while, however, I might privately disagree with the "official" figures, but I tried not to say so.

Questions of this sort really should be asked of the general manager, not of me. I realize that the head office people probably didn't think the question was important enough to warrant bothering the general manager, and in many cases, they were right. The line is a fine one.

The business of the division controller's being an "unbiased source of information" sounds fine when you word it that way, but another way to say it is that he is a front office spy, and that doesn't sound so good. It would indeed make our life easier if we could count on the divisional controllers to give us the real lowdown on what is going on. But if this is to be their position, then we can't expect that the general manager will continue to treat his controller as a trusted assistant. Either the general manager will find somebody else to take over this work unofficially, or it won't get done.

I think we are better off the way we are. Sure, the budgets will have some fat in them, and not all the bad situations will be highlighted in the operating reports, and this makes our job more difficult. But I'd rather have this than the alternative. If we used the Martex method (or, rather, what they claim is their method), we can be sure that the divisional controller will no longer be a member of the management team. They'll isolate him as much as they can, and the control function in the division will suffer.

Questions

1. What is the organizational philosophy of Martex with respect to the controller function? What do you think of it? Should Rendell adopt this philosophy?
2. To whom should the divisional controllers report in the Rendell Company? Why?
3. What should be the relationship between the corporate controller and the divisional controllers? What steps would you take to establish this relationship on a sound footing?
4. Would you recommend any major changes in the basic responsibilities of either the corporate controller or the divisional controller?

APPENDIX
NOTES ON MARTEX CONTROLLER ORGANIZATION

Mr. Ingraham, the corporate controller, reports directly to the president and has reporting to him all division controllers and other accounting, data processing, and analysis groups. The Martex Company's descriptions of responsibility and organization charts are included herein (Exhibits 1, 2, 3, and 4) and indicate the structure and function of the organization.

The controller's organization is charged with the responsibility of establishing cost and profit standards in the corporation and of taking appropriate action to see that these standards are attained. It reviews all research projects and assigns names and numbers to them in order to coordinate research activities in the various divisions and their central research. The organization also handles all matters involving cost and profit estimates.

The present size of divisional controllers' staffs ranges from 3 to 22. Division controllers are not involved in preparing division profit and loss statements; these are prepared by a separate group for all divisions and the corporation.

Line-Staff Relationships

A division manager has no staff of his own, not even a personal assistant. He receives staff assistance from two sources.

First, he has some people assigned to him from the general staff—typically, a controller, an engineer, and a purchasing agent.

All division management and all the corporate staff are located in the corporate headquarters building. However, the assigned staff are located physically with their staff colleagues; for example, a divisional controller and his assistants are located in the controller's section of the building, not near his divisional manager's office.

Second, the division can call on the central staff to the extent that the manager wishes. The divisions are charged for these services on the basis of service rendered. The central staff units are listed in the General Staff Services box of Exhibit 2.

Division Manager-Controller Relationships

The success of the Martex controller organization and its relations with divisional managers appears to be largely the result of managers and controllers having grown up with the arrangement and accepting it long before they arrived at their managerial positions.

Some additional factors that appear to contribute to their successful relationship are the following:

1. A uniform and centralized accounting system.
2. Predetermined financial objectives for each division.
   a. Growth in dollar sales.
   b. A specified rate of profit as a percent of sales.
3. Profit sharing by managers and controllers.

EXHIBIT 1   Position Descriptions from the Martex Management Guidebook

---

Controller

The trend of modern business management is to change the basic concept of the controller's position from that of an administrative function concerned largely with accounting detail to that of an important position in management as it relates to the control of costs and the profitable operation of the business as a whole.

The more our business becomes diversified with operations scattered throughout the United States, the greater is the need for an officer to whom the president delegates authority with respect to those factors affecting costs and profits in the same manner as he may delegate authority to others in strong staff positions.

In our vertical type of organization there is a great need for an appointed officer whose responsibility it is to establish budgetary standards of operations and objective percent of profit on sales targets for each of the operating divisions and domestic subsidiaries. He shall also establish budgetary standards of operation for staff functions in line with divisional and overall company profit objectives. When the standard of operations or profit target is not attained, the controller has the right and the responsibility within his delegated authority to question the failure and recommend changes to accomplish the desired result.

The controller shall work with the various divisions of the company through divisional controllers assigned to each major operating division and staff function. It is not intended that the controller take the initiative away from the division managers, since the responsibility for efficient operations and profits is assumed by the managers. However, the controller and his staff should have the right and the responsibility to expect certain operating results from the division head; and when a difference of opinion occurs as to the reasonableness of the demand for results, the matter should then be referred by either party to the president.

Along with the foregoing, the following responsibilities are an essential part of the position and apply to the corporation and its subsidiaries:

1. The installation and supervision of all accounting records.

2. The preparation, supervision, and interpretation of all divisional and product profit and loss statements, operating statements, and cost reports, including reports of costs and production, research, distribution, and administration.

3. The supervision of taking and costing of all physical inventories.

4. The preparation and interpretation of all operating statistics and reports, including interpretation of charts and graphs, for use by management committees and the board of directors.

5. The preparation, as budget director, in conjunction with staff officers and heads of divisions and subsidiaries, of an annual budget covering all operations for submission to the president prior to the beginning of the fiscal year.

6. The initiation, preparation, and issuance of standard practice regulations and the coordination of systems, including clerical and office methods relating to all operating accounting procedures.

7. Membership of the controller or his designated representative in all division and subsidiary management committees.

He shall be responsible for the selection, training, development and promotion of qualified personnel for his organization and their compensation within established company policy. He shall submit to the president an organization plan for accomplishing desired objectives.

The controller may delegate to members of his organization certain of his responsibilities, but in so doing he does not relinquish his overall responsibility or accountability for results.

Treasurer and Assistant Treasurers

Subject to the rules and regulations of the Finance Committee, the treasurer is the chief financial officer and generally his functions include control of corporate funds and attending to the financial affairs of the corporation and its domestic and foreign subsidiaries wherever located. More specifically the duties and responsibilities are as follows:

Banking: He shall have custody of and be responsible for all money and securities and shall deposit in the name of the corporation in such depositories as are approved by the president all funds coming into his possession for the company account.

Credits and collections: He shall have supervision over all cashiers, cash receipts, and collection records and accounts receivable ledgers. He shall initiate and approve all credit policies and procedures.

EXHIBIT 1   Position Descriptions from the Martex Management Guidebook (*continued*)

Disbursements: He shall authorize disbursements of any kind by signature on checks. This includes direct supervision over accounts payable and payroll departments and indirect supervision over all receiving departments for the purpose of checking on the accuracy of invoices presented for payment. He shall maintain adequate records of authorized appropriations and also determine that all financial transactions covered by minutes of management and executive committees and the board of directors are properly executed and recorded.

General financial reports: He shall prepare and supervise all general accounting records. He shall prepare and interpret all general financial statements, including the preparation of the quarterly and annual reports for mailing to stockholders. This also includes the preparation and approval of the regulations on standard practices required to assure compliance with orders or regulations issued by duly constituted governmental agencies and stock exchanges.

He shall supervise the continuous audit (including internal controls) of all accounts and records and shall supervise the audit and procedures of Certified Public Accountants.

Taxes: He shall supervise the preparation and filing of all tax returns and shall have supervision of all matters relating to taxes and shall refer to the general counsel all such matters requiring interpretation of tax laws and regulations.

Insurance property records: He shall supervise the purchase and placing of insurance of any kind including the insurance required in connection with employee benefits. He shall be responsible for recommending adequate coverage for all ascertainable risks and shall maintain such records as to avoid any possibility that various hazards are not being properly insured. He shall maintain adequate property records and valuations for insurance and other purposes and, if necessary, employ appraisal experts to assist in determining such valuations and records.

Loans: He shall approve all loans and advances made to employees within limits prescribed by the Executive Committee.

Investments: As funds are available beyond normal requirements, he shall recommend suitable investments to the Finance Committees. He shall have custody of securities so acquired and shall use the safekeeping facilities of the banks for that purpose. As securities are added or removed from such vaults or facilities, he shall be accompanied by an authorized officer of the corporation.

Office management: He shall be responsible for the coordination of all office management functions throughout the company and its domestic subsidiaries.

Financial planning: He shall initiate and prepare current and long-range cash forecasts, particularly as such forecasts are needed for financing programs to meet anticipated cash requirements for future growth and expansion. He shall arrange to meet sinking fund requirements for all outstanding debenture bonds and preferred stock and shall anticipate such requirements whenever possible.

He shall have such other powers and shall perform such other duties as may be assigned to him by the board of directors and the president.

The treasurer shall be responsible for the selection, training, development, and promotion of qualified personnel for his organization and their compensation within established company policy. It is expected that since he will have to delegate many of the duties and responsibilities enumerated above, he shall confer with and submit to the president an organization plan and chart.

The treasurer may delegate to members of his organization certain of his responsibilities together with appropriate authority for fulfillment; however, in so doing he does not relinquish his overall responsibility or accountability for results.

The treasurer is a member of the Finance, Retirement, and Inventory Review Committees.

Exhibit 2

Martex organization chart, Division A, January 1, 1985

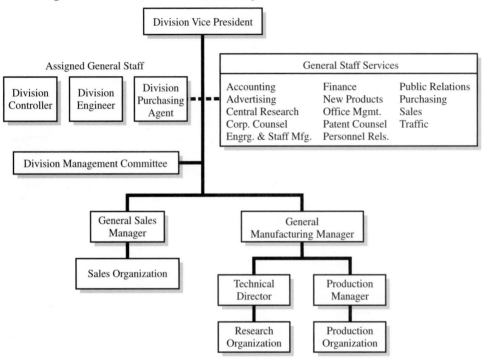

Note: Various levels on the chart do not necessarily indicate relative importance of positions.

EXHIBIT 3

Organization chart of Martex controller's division, January 1, 1985

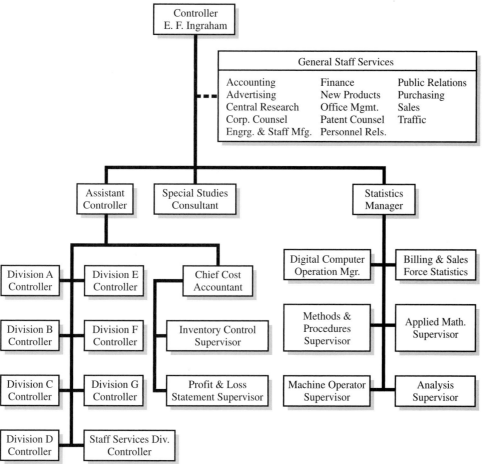

Exhibit 4

Organization chart of Martex treasurer's division, January 1, 1985

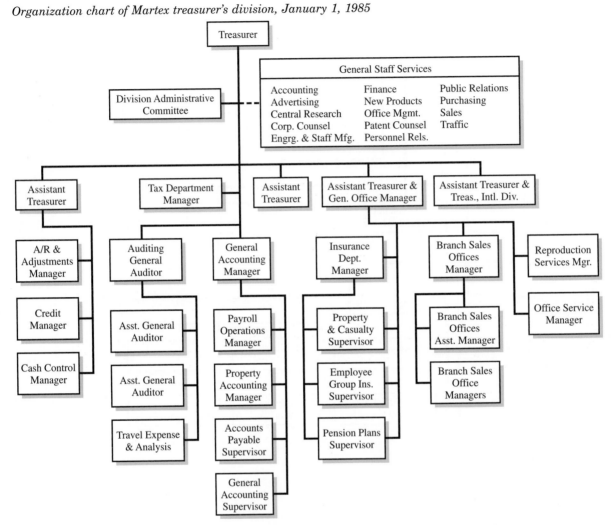

Note: Various levels on the chart do not necessarily indicate relative importance of positions.

Accounting System

The controller's division has complete control of the accounting system. It determines how and what accounts will be kept. The controller's division has developed an accounting system that is the same for all divisions. Mr. Ingraham pointed out that no division had a system perfectly tailored to its needs, but he believes that the disadvantages to the divisions were more than offset by having a system uniform over all divisions and understood by all concerned. Mr. Ingraham indicated it was likely that, if Martex divisions were free to establish their own accounting systems, every division would have a different one within two years, and interpretation by corporate management would be difficult, if possible at all.

The accounting system appears to provide a common basis for all divisional financial reports and analyses, and it aids in maintaining the bond of confidence between division managers and controllers.

Division Objectives

The corporation has established two financial objectives for each division. These are (a) growth in dollar sales, (b) a specified rate of profit as a percent of sales.

These objectives are determined in advance by recommendations of the controller's division with the advice and counsel of divisional managers. The objectives are long range in nature; the target profit rate has been changed only three times since 1965.

The particular percentage of sales selected as the target profit rate is based on several factors, among which are (1) the patentability of products, (2) a desired rate of return on investment, (3) the industry's margin of profit, and (4) the industry's rate of return on investment. These factors and others determine the profit rate finally selected.

Within limits, attainment of these financial objectives represents the primary task required of division general managers by corporate management.

Profit Sharing

Divisional managers receive about 75 percent of their total compensation from profit sharing and stock options. Divisional controllers receive about 25 percent of their compensation from profit sharing—half from a share in divisional profits and the other half from corporate profits.

Division Managers' View of the System

Mr. Ingraham indicated that divisional managers like to have divisional controllers report to the corporate controller because (1) it gives them an unbiased partner armed with relevant information, (2) the controller is in a better position to do the analysis needed for decision making, and (3) when cost reports are issued there is little or no argument about them among affected parties.

Case 3–2
National Tractor and Equipment Company

National Tractor and Equipment Company, Inc., was a manufacturer of a number of products, including a wide line of farm tractors. Tractors were divided into several fairly well-defined types, according to their capacity, and National manufactured tractors of each type. This case deals with one of these types, here referred to as a type X.

Fixed costs represented a relatively large share of total costs at National, and, therefore, achieving a strong sales position was an important means of reducing unit costs and improving profits. Consequently, a major objective of the company was to be the sales leader in each of the several types. If National was not the leader during a particular year, its goal was to surpass whoever was the leader. If National was the leader, its goal was to maintain the size of its lead.

The company had experienced a rather erratic showing in sales of the type X tractors over the previous several years. Though National had been the sales leader in four of the previous six years (1970–75) its lead in 1973 and 1974 had been slim, and in 1975 its chief competitor took over first place. Meanwhile, profits of this division of its business had fluctuated widely. Accordingly, early in 1976, the controller's department made a sales analysis of the type X tractor division.

William Lawrence, who was given the job of making the analysis decided to use the approach the controller had used for other analyses. Usually these analyses started with a comparison of actual costs or actual profit with some benchmark, such as the budget or the figures for some

prior year when performance was satisfactory. The analyst then sought to isolate and quantify the various causes of the difference between actual and the standard applied in that particular case.

In the case of tractors, since management's objective was to surpass the sales leader, unit sales of the leading competitor—here called "competitor A"—seemed to be the most logical standard. Competitor A had sold 13,449 type X tractors in 1975, compared with 10,356 for National—a deficiency of 3,093. (A copy of Mr. Lawrence's analysis as presented to management appears as an appendix to this case.)

Mr. Lawrence began his analysis by looking at the profits and return on assets of the type X tractor division (see Appendix Exhibit 1). Both had improved significantly over the 1973 and 1974 levels. However, in 1975 National dropped from the first-place sales position it had held during 1973 and 1974 and this was of grave concern to management. Furthermore, its market share had decreased from 25.0 percent to 23.5 percent (see Appendix Exhibit 2). Both of its major competitors had increased their market shares, and competitor A had outsold National for the first time in five years.

Mr. Lawrence next prepared the sales portion of the table that appears as Exhibit 3 in the appendix. This exhibit compares sales of type X tractors by National and competitor A for the preceding three years, 1973–1975. The major task, then—and this was the crux of the analysis—was to identify and analyze those factors that accounted for the volume difference in each of the three years.

After he had completed this initial analysis, Mr. Lawrence, representing the controller's department, met with representatives of the sales department and the product development

This case was prepared by J. S. Hekimian under the supervision of R. N. Anthony, Harvard Business School. Copyright © by the President and Fellows of Harvard College. Harvard Business School case 161-010.

department. Together, they discussed the various factors that might have accounted for the volume differences in each of the three years under review. Using their collective judgments and estimates, they broke down the volume difference into as many specific factors as they could agree on. All the remaining factors, they decided, must have accounted for the remaining difference, although they could not agree on the proportions, so they gave the total under other factors.

The first matter that Mr. Lawrence called to the attention of this group was that a major fire in one of competitor A's plants in the latter part of 1974 had severely limited production. He had compiled monthly production estimates for competitor A for 1974 and two prior years. He then had gathered estimates of industry sales during those years and developed certain relationships that seemed to him to hold among estimated monthly sales, actual monthly sales, and actual monthly production for 1972 and 1973 by competitor A. When he applied these relationships to 1974, it seemed evident to him that competitor A had produced significantly fewer type X tractors than it normally would have during the months when its plant was shut down.

Mr. Lawrence then had looked at sales patterns during 1972 and 1973 so that he could make an estimate of how much this lost production had resulted in a shifting of demand from 1974 to 1975; he tried to estimate how many competitor A customers for type X tractors delayed purchase of a new type X tractor from 1974 to 1975 because of the fire. In addition to research with the data available in his office, Mr. Lawrence traveled around the country and talked to distributors and dealers. He became convinced that a large number of potential purchasers of tractors annually had deferred their purchases of new type X tractors. Some of competitor A's dealers had had no type X tractors in stock in the latter part of 1974 because of the fire, and others had had only a limited supply.

On the basis of Mr. Lawrence's analysis and the collective judgments of the other members, the group agreed that the fire caused a shift of 1,500 of competitor A's tractor sales from 1974 to 1975. This shift was recorded as a minus factor in 1975 and a plus factor in 1974.

Sales of type X tractors to government agencies was another factor studied by this group. Since government sales figures were published, the group ascertained that National outsold competitor A by 138 units. Government sales depended almost entirely on price; therefore, this was the type of business a tractor manufacturer could "buy" depending on how badly he wanted it.

Mr. Lawrence had done a considerable amount of research into the advantage that competitor A enjoyed because of its larger owner body.[1] National's owner body had always been smaller than competitor A's, but National had made sizable gains since 1967. There was a tendency for the owner of a tractor to buy the same make when he purchased a new tractor; thus, competitor A enjoyed an advantage. Mr. Lawrence wanted to know *how much* this advantage was. An annual survey made by the trade association of the industry indicated the behavior of a representative sample of buyers of new type X tractors. This survey indicated that owners of competitor A's tractors were more loyal than were National tractor owners (see Table 1). Using these survey results, Mr. Lawrence was able to calculate the advantage to competitor A of its larger owner body. Although only the calculations for 1975 are shown, he applied the same methodology to 1973 and 1974. Members of the group were impressed with this analysis and agreed to accept Mr. Lawrence's figures—a net advantage of 700 units for competitor A in 1975.

The next factor he analyzed was product differences. National did not have so varied a product line as did competitor A. Because of this, National dealers were at a competitive disadvantage for certain models of type X tractors.

---

[1]Owner body is the number of tractors in the hands of owners.

The group was able to agree on the approximate extent of this disadvantage.

The last main heading for variances listed in Exhibit 3 was other factors, which the group thought accounted for the remaining difference between National's sales and competitor A's sales. Mr. Lawrence had prepared a thorough analysis of these factors, too. For example, he had heard that competitor A built a more efficient and more durable type X tractor. He tried to quantify the effect of these variables by use of the data shown in Tables 3 and 4. He also requisitioned five National type X tractors and five competitor A type X tractors, and arranged to have these tractors tested at National's experimental farm to determine their operating characteristics, including power, performance, durability, reliability, and economy. Mr. Lawrence himself actually drove some of these tractors. He also inspected each

tractor and its performance at the end of the testing period.

The group could not agree, however, on the quantitative effect on sales volume of these factors or of the remaining factors listed under other. Therefore, they were represented by one figure. The total variance of all the factors affecting market penetration, of course, equaled the difference in sales between National and competitor A.

Questions

1. Are analyses of this type within the proper scope of a controller's function?

2. Can you suggest a better way of making the analysis?

3. What action, if any, should be taken on the basis of this study?

APPENDIX
AN ANALYSIS OF TYPE X TRACTORS[*]

Profits, Assets, and After-Tax Returns

Exhibit 1 depicts National's profits, assets, and return on assets for the years 1970–75. Profits have ranged from a high of $2.7 million in 1972 to a loss of $200,000 in 1974 and a profit of $2.5 million in 1975. Return on assets employed in 1975 was 20.5 percent after taxes.

Market Penetration versus Competition

Exhibit 2 shows National's penetration of the domestic market for type X tractors for 1970–75, compared with its two major competitors.

National's penetration rose from 24.3 percent in 1970 to a peak of 35.5 percent in 1971. In 1975, National's penetration was 23.5 percent. Competitor A's penetration, which was 27.9 percent in 1970, fell to a

low of 21.8 percent in 1971 and then increased to 30.5 percent in 1975. In four out of the last six years, National outsold competitor A in the type X tractor market. Competitor B's penetration moved from 27.4 percent in 1970 to 23.0 percent in 1971 but declined to 9.9 percent in 1973, rising to 21.2 percent in 1975.

Exhibit 3 sets forth those factors that accounted for differences in market penetration between National and competitor A—its chief competitor in the type X tractor market. The upper portion of the table compares National's and competitor A's sales during the years 1973–75. The lower portion of the table shows the various factors that account for the differences between National's and competitor A's share of the market in each of these years. National's volume was 10,611 units in 1973, compared to competitor A's 10,246. In 1975, National's volume was 10,356 units, representing a market penetration of 23.5 percent, compared with A's volume of 13,449 units and 30.5

---

[*]Prepared by the controller's department.

Exhibit 1

Profits, assets, and after-tax returns

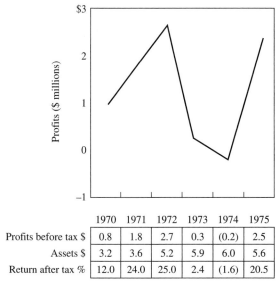

	1970	1971	1972	1973	1974	1975
Profits before tax $	0.8	1.8	2.7	0.3	(0.2)	2.5
Assets $	3.2	3.6	5.2	5.9	6.0	5.6
Return after tax %	12.0	24.0	25.0	2.4	(1.6)	20.5

Exhibit 2

Market penetration versus competition

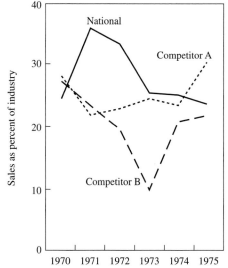

Industry penetration

National %	24.3	35.5	33.0	25.5	25.0	23.5
Competitor A	27.9	21.8	22.8	24.5	23.1	30.5
Competitor B	27.4	23.0	19.6	9.9	20.7	21.2

Volume (000 tractors)

National	10.9	12.8	15.6	10.6	8.4	10.4
Competitor A	12.5	7.9	10.8	10.2	7.8	13.4
Competitor B	12.3	8.3	9.3	4.1	7.0	9.3
Other	9.2	7.1	11.6	16.7	10.5	11.0
Industry total	44.9	36.1	47.3	41.6	33.7	44.1

percent of the market. In 1975, National was outsold by 3,093 units.

Turning to the specific factors that account for this volume difference, we have estimated that the effect of a major fire at one of competitor A's plants in the last half of 1974, which halted production for nearly five months, resulted in a deferral of demand for 1,500 of its type X tractors from 1974 to 1975. This estimate is based on our knowledge of competitor A's output in 1974, compared with other years, and represents our best estimate on what sales might have been without the fire. In 1975, these 1,500 units represented 3.4 percent of market penetration. In 1975, National sold 138 more units to government agencies, equivalent to 0.3 percent of market penetration. We shall examine the effect on our market penetration of differences in the size of our respective owner bodies in subsequent tables.

The product differences result from gaps in our product line that prevent National from entering certain segments of the type X tractor market, thereby providing competitor A with a clear product advantage. For example, competitor A offers a larger variety of attachments and related equipment, which increase the number of different jobs its tractor can perform. We have estimated, for each year, the net market advantage accruing to competitor A because of its broader product line.

Other factors, whose effects cannot be measured quantitatively, are summarized at the bottom of the table, including customer attitudes toward National with respect to operating cost, durability, quality, and similar factors. In 1975, these other factors, in total, represented a net advantage to National of 955 units, or 2.2 percent of market penetration.

Basis for Estimated Advantage to Competitor A of Owner Body

Exhibit 4 shows the estimated number of National and competitor A type X tractors in operation for the years 1967–75.

EXHIBIT 3   Sales of Type X Tractors and Factors Affecting Market Penetration (National versus Competitor A, 1973 to 1975)

	Jan.–Dec. 1973		Jan.–Dec. 1974		Jan.–Dec. 1975	
	Units	Percent of Market*	Units	Percent of Market*	Units	Percent of Market*
Sales:						
National	10,611	25.5%	8,431	25.0%	10,356	23.5%
Competitor A	10,246	24.5	7,828	23.1	13,449	30.5
National over/(under) A	365	1.0%	603	1.9%	(3,093)	(7.0%)
Factors affecting market penetration:						
Effect of major fire at one of competitor A's plants	—	—	1,500	4.5	(1,500)	(3.4)
Sales to government agencies	(3)	—	321	1.0	138	0.3
Competitor A's advantage in size of owner body	(850)	(2.0)	(660)	(1.9)	(700)	(1.6)
Product differences	(269)	(0.6)	(1,071)	(3.2)	(1,986)	(4.5)
Other factors:						
Customer attitudes toward National						
Operating cost						
Durability and quality						
National's price position	1,487	3.6	513	1.5	955	2.2
National's distribution system						
Sales administration						
Other factors						
Total variance	365	1.0%	603	1.9%	(3,093)	(7.0%)

*These percentages were calculated from the rounded numbers given on the preceding page; if calculated from the exact number of units, they would be somewhat different.

In 1967, it is estimated that competitor A had approximately 88,000 type X tractors in operation, while National had approximately 27,000 units in use. By 1975, National units in operation had more than quadrupled to a level of approximately 127,000 units. Competitor A units, on the other hand, had increased by almost 100 percent to a level of 158,000 units. During this period, National units as a percent of competitor A increased from 31 percent in 1967 to 80 percent in 1975. At the same time, our variance, in terms of units, decreased from 60,700 in 1967 to 31,200 in 1975.

Because of the importance of owner loyalty, competitor A's advantage in owner body represents an automatic advantage in market penetration, as indicated in the succeeding pages.

1975 Type X Replacement Patterns

Table 1 indicates the relative loyalty in 1975 of National and competitor A type X tractor owners. In this sample, 48 percent of the National owners who replaced a tractor bought a new National, 27 percent bought an A model, and 25 percent bought some other type X tractor. In contrast, 73 percent of A owners bought a new A, 14 percent bought some type X tractor other than National, and 13 percent of A

EXHIBIT 4

Units in operation

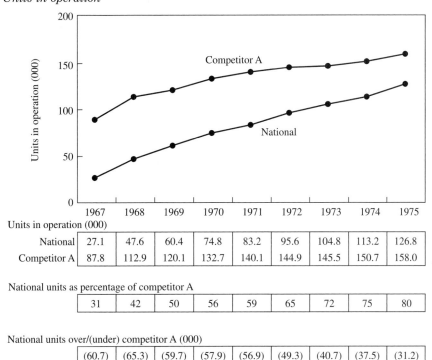

Units in operation (000)	1967	1968	1969	1970	1971	1972	1973	1974	1975
National	27.1	47.6	60.4	74.8	83.2	95.6	104.8	113.2	126.8
Competitor A	87.8	112.9	120.1	132.7	140.1	144.9	145.5	150.7	158.0

National units as percentage of competitor A

31	42	50	56	59	65	72	75	80

National units over/(under) competitor A (000)

(60.7)	(65.3)	(59.7)	(57.9)	(56.9)	(49.3)	(40.7)	(37.5)	(31.2)

owners purchased a National tractor when they re-entered the market.

Effect on Differences in Owner Body on 1975 Tractor Purchases

In Table 2, we have calculated the effect of owner bodies on type X tractor purchases in 1975. We have used actual figures for the size of National and competitor A owner bodies but have assumed that all other factors, including owner loyalty rates, are equal. In this calculation, we have applied National loyalty to both National and competitor A owner bodies. Based on these premises, one would expect National to have a deficiency in market penetration relative to competitor A of 1.6 percent solely as a result of the differences in the size of the two owner bodies, with National market penetration at 27.9 percent and competitor A penetration at 29.5 percent.

Type X Tractor Warranty Expense[1]

Some indication of National's type X tractor quality and durability problem is found in the level of our warranty expense as shown in Table 3. From 1970 to 1973, our warranty expense on the average type X tractor increased from $21.48 to $55.06, an increase of $33.58 per unit. Since 1973 warranty costs have declined to $31.38, a reduction of $23.68. Expense on all components, with the exception of the hydraulic system, has increased over 1970 levels. It seems clear that warranty costs of over $31 per unit are too high and represent an unsatisfactory level of quality as far as the user is concerned.

---

[1]Warranty expense is the amount spent by National for replacements and repairs to tractors in use for which it had accepted responsibility. The company kept detailed records of such costs, broken down not only in the main classifications indicated in Table 4 but also for individual parts within each classification.

TABLE 1*

	Make Purchased			
Make Replaced	*National*	*A*	*Other*	*Total*
National	48%	27%	25%	100%
Competitor A	13	73	14	100
Other	17	20	63	100

* Source: Replacement analysis published annually by trade association.

National N-50 Type X Tractor—Warranty and Design[2] Cost

Table 4 indicates changes in warranty expense and design costs per unit on the N-50 tractor in the 1973, 1974, and 1975 models. In total, during this period, warranty expense has been reduced approximately $33, while design costs have increased $36. Engine warranty expense on this model had declined $40 per unit, while design costs have increased $24. In the case of the transmission, warranty expense has increased $3.30 per unit, despite an increase of $1.77 per unit in design costs.

TABLE 2

	Make Purchased (thousands of units)			
Make Replaced	*National*	*A*	*Other*	*Total Purchased*
National	5.0	2.8	2.6	10.4
Competitor A	3.6	6.4	3.4	13.4
Other	3.7	3.8	12.8	20.3
Total	12.3	13.0	18.8	44.1
Penetration	27.9%	29.5%	42.6%	100.0%
National (under) competitor A:				
Percentage points (1.6)				
Units (0.7)				

[2]Design cost refers to the costs of the tractor itself. These costs are a function of the way in which the tractor is designed. For example, the total standard cost of the 1973 model was $9.78 more than the total standard cost of the 1972 model; the designers had devised a more expensive tractor in 1973. In making the comparisons, wage rates and material costs are held constant.

TABLE 3 Warranty Expense

| | Model Year | | | | | | 1975 (Over)/Under 1970 | |
	1970	*1971*	*1972*	*1973*	*1974*	*1975*	*Per Unit*	*Percent*
Engine	$11.30	$ 7.56	$28.05	$28.40	$22.58	$12.76	$(1.46)	(13%)
Transmission	3.70	3.09	3.90	6.60	6.00	7.19	(3.49)	(94)
Hydraulic system	.80	.46	.74	5.21	1.35	.57	.23	29
Electrical	.65	1.14	1.93	3.88	4.40	3.27	(2.62)	(403)
Other	5.03	4.20	5.20	10.97	8.90	7.59	(2.56)	(51)
Total	21.48	16.45	39.82	55.06	43.23	31.38	(9.90)	(46%)

TABLE 4 Changes by Year

	1973 (Over)/Under 1972 Warranty Design		1974 (Over)/Under 1973 Warranty Design		1975 (Over)/Under 1974 Warranty Design		1975 (Over)/Under 1972 Warranty Design	
Engine	$ 9.80	$(3.74)	$24.00	$(12.99)	$ 6.48	$ (7.62)	40.28	$(24.35)
Transmission	(2.69)	(1.31)	0.59	—	(1.20)	(0.46)	(3.30)	(1.77)
Hydraulic system	(4.48)	(8.90)	3.87	0.94	0.77	(2.97)	0.16	(10.93)
Electrical	(1.93)	—	(.53)	(1.09)	1.13	0.32	(1.33)	(0.77)
Other	(5.70)	4.17	2.00	(.50)	1.33	(1.73)	(2.37)	1.94
Total	(5.00)	(9.78)	29.93	(13.64)	8.51	(12.46)	33.44	(35.88)

RESPONSIBILITY CENTERS: REVENUE AND EXPENSE CENTERS

Management control focuses on the behavior of managers in responsibility centers. This is the first of four chapters dealing with responsibility centers. We describe the nature of responsibility centers in general and the criteria of efficiency and effectiveness that are relevant in measuring the performance of responsibility center managers. We then discuss revenue centers and expense centers, which are two types of responsibility centers. There are two general types of expense centers: engineered expense centers and discretionary expense centers. Discretionary expense centers can be classified further as administrative and support centers, research and development (R&D) centers, and marketing centers; each is discussed. Chapters 4 through 7 discuss the considerations involved in assigning *financial responsibility* (in terms of costs, revenues, profit, and assets) to organization subunits.

In Part II, we discuss how to supplement financial controls with nonfinancial performance measures.

Responsibility Centers

A responsibility center is an organization unit that is headed by a manager who is responsible for its activities. In a sense, a company is a collection of responsibility centers, each of which is represented by a box on the organization chart. These responsibility centers form a hierarchy. At the lowest level in the organization are responsibility centers for sections, work shifts, or other small organization units. At a higher level are departments or business units that consist of several of these smaller units plus staff and management people; these larger units are also responsibility centers. And from the standpoint of senior management and the board of directors, the whole company is a responsibility center, although the term is usually used to refer to units *within* the company.

EXHIBIT 4–1

*Responsibility
center*

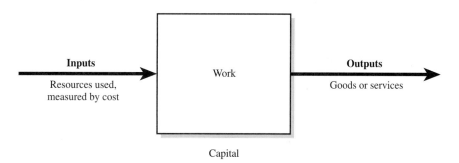

Nature of Responsibility Centers

A responsibility center exists to accomplish one or more purposes; these purposes are its *objectives*. The company as a whole has goals, and senior management has decided on a set of strategies to accomplish these goals. The objectives of responsibility centers are to help implement these strategies. Because the organization is the sum of its responsibility centers, if the strategies are sound, and if each responsibility center meets its objectives, the whole organization should achieve its goals.

Exhibit 4–1 shows the essence of any responsibility center. A responsibility center uses inputs, which are physical quantities of material, hours of various types of labor, and a variety of services. It works with these resources, and it usually requires working capital (e.g., inventory, receivables), equipment, and other assets to do this work. As a result of this work, the responsibility center produces outputs, which are classified either as goods, if they are tangible, or as services, if they are intangible. Every responsibility center has outputs—that is, it does something. In a production plant, the outputs are goods. In staff units, such as human resources, transportation, engineering, accounting, and administration, the outputs are services. For many responsibility centers, especially staff units, outputs are difficult to measure; nevertheless, they exist.

The products (i.e., goods and services) produced by a responsibility center may be furnished either to another responsibility center or to the outside marketplace. In the first case, the products are inputs to the other responsibility center; in the latter case, they are outputs of the whole organization. *Revenues* are the amounts earned from providing these outputs.

Relation between Inputs and Outputs

Management is responsible for obtaining the optimum relationship between inputs and outputs. In some situations, the relationship is causal and direct. In a production department, for example, the inputs of raw material resources become a physical part of the finished goods output. Control focuses on producing the outputs at the time needed, in the desired quantities, according to the correct specifications and quality standards, and with minimum inputs.

In many situations, however, inputs are not directly related to outputs. Advertising expense is an input that is expected to increase sales revenue; but revenue is affected by many factors other than advertising, so the relationship between an additional amount of advertising and the resulting revenue rarely is known. Management's decision on the amount to spend for advertising is based on judgments. For research and development, the relationship between inputs and outputs is even more ambiguous; the value of today's R&D effort may not be known for several years, and the optimum amount that a given company should spend for R&D is indeterminable.

Measuring Inputs and Outputs

The amounts of labor, material, and services used in a responsibility center are physical quantities: hours of labor, quarts of oil, reams of paper, and kilowatt-hours of electricity. In a management control system these amounts are translated into monetary terms. Money provides a common denominator that permits the amount of individual resources to be combined. The monetary amount is ordinarily obtained by multiplying the physical quantity by a price per unit of quantity (e.g., hours of labor times a rate per hour). The resulting amount is called "cost." Thus, the inputs of a responsibility center are ordinarily expressed as costs. *Cost is a monetary measure of the amount of resources used by a responsibility center*.

Note that inputs are resources *used* by the responsibility center. The patients in a hospital or the students in a school are *not* inputs. Rather, inputs are the resources that are used in accomplishing the objectives of *treating* the patients or *educating* the students.

Although the cost of most inputs can be measured, outputs are much more difficult to measure. In a profit-oriented organization, revenue is an important measure of output of the whole organization, but such a measure is rarely a complete expression of outputs; it does not encompass everything that the organization does. For example, this year's revenue does not measure the value of R&D work, employee training, or advertising and sales promotion carried out this year; these inputs produce outputs that will benefit future years. In many responsibility centers, outputs cannot be measured satisfactorily. How can one measure the value of the work done by a public relations department, a quality control department, or a legal staff? In many nonprofit organizations, no good quantitative measure of output exists. A college easily can measure the number of students graduated, but it cannot measure how much education each of them acquired. Many organizations do not attempt to measure the outputs of such responsibility centers. Others use an approximation, or *surrogate*, of the output of some of them, recognizing its limitations.

Efficiency and Effectiveness

The concepts stated above can be used to explain the meaning of *efficiency* and *effectiveness*, which are the two criteria for judging the performance of a responsibility center. The terms are almost always used in a comparative, rather than in an absolute sense. That is, we ordinarily do not say that Responsibility Center A is 80 percent efficient; rather we say that it is more (or less) efficient than its competitor, more (or less) efficient currently than it was in the past, more (or less) efficient compared to its budget, or more (or less) efficient than Responsibility Center B.

Efficiency is the ratio of outputs to inputs, or the amount of output per unit of input. Responsibility Center A is more efficient than Responsibility Center B either (1) if it uses fewer resources than Responsibility Center B, but has the same output; or (2) if it uses the same amount of resources as Responsibility Center B and has a greater output than Responsibility Center B. Note that the first type of measure does not require that output be quantified; it is only necessary to judge that the outputs of the two units are approximately the same. If management is satisfied that Responsibility Centers A and B are both doing a satisfactory job, and if it is a job of comparable magnitude, then the unit with the lower inputs (i.e., the lower costs) is the more efficient. The second type of measure does require some quantitative measure of output; it is, therefore, a more difficult type of measurement in many situations.

In many responsibility centers, a measure of efficiency can be developed that relates actual costs to some standard—that is, to a number that expresses what costs should be incurred for the amount of measured output. Such a measure can be a useful indication of efficiency, but it is never a perfect measure for at least two reasons: (1) recorded costs are not a precisely accurate measure of resources consumed; and (2) standards are, at best, only approximate measures of what resource consumption ideally should have been in the prevailing circumstances.

Effectiveness is the relationship between a responsibility center's outputs and its objectives. The more these outputs contribute to the objectives, the more effective the unit is. Since both objectives and outputs are often difficult to quantify, measures of effectiveness are difficult to come by. Effectiveness, therefore, is often expressed in nonquantitative, judgmental terms, such as "College A is doing a first-rate job, but College B has slipped somewhat in recent years."

An organization unit should be both efficient and effective; it is not a case of choosing one or the other. Ideally, if everyone in an organization is both efficient and effective, that organization should be meeting its goals in an optimum manner. Efficient responsibility centers are those that do whatever they do with the lowest consumption of resources, but if what they do (i.e., their output) is an inadequate contribution to the accomplishment of the organization's goals, they are ineffective. If a credit department handles the paperwork connected with delinquent accounts at a low cost per unit, it is efficient, but if it is unsuccessful in making collections, or if in the process of collecting accounts, it needlessly antagonizes customers, it is ineffective.

In summary, a responsibility center is efficient if it does things right, and it is effective if it does the right things.

The Role of Profits.   One important objective in a profit-oriented organization is to earn profits, and the amount of profits, therefore, is an important measure of effectiveness. Since profit is the difference between revenue, which is a measure of output, and expense, which is a measure of input, profit also is a measure of efficiency. Thus, profit measures both effectiveness and efficiency. When such an overall measure exists, it is unnecessary to determine the relative importance of effectiveness versus efficiency. When such an overall measure does not exist, it is feasible and useful to classify performance measures as relating either to effectiveness or to efficiency. In these situations, there is the problem of balancing the two types of measurements. For example, how do we compare the profligate perfectionist with the frugal manager who obtains less than the optimum output?

Types of Responsibility Centers

There are four types of responsibility centers, classified according to the nature of the monetary inputs or outputs, or both, that are measured: revenue centers, expense centers, profit centers, and investment centers. Their characteristics are shown in Exhibit 4–2. In revenue centers, only outputs are measured in monetary terms; in expense centers, only inputs are measured; in profit centers, both revenues and expenses are measured; and in investment centers, the relationship between profits and investment is measured.

The planning and control systems for responsibility centers differ depending on whether they are revenue centers, expense centers, profit centers, or investment centers. We discuss the appropriate planning and control techniques for revenue centers and expense centers in the remainder of this chapter. Profit centers are discussed in Chapter 5 and investment centers in Chapter 7.

Revenue Centers

In a revenue center, outputs are measured in monetary terms, but no formal attempt is made to relate inputs (i.e., expenses or costs) to outputs. (If expenses were matched with revenues, the unit would be a profit center.) Revenue centers, therefore, are marketing organizations that do not have profit responsibility. Actual sales or orders booked are measured against budgets or quotas.

Each revenue center is also an expense center in that the revenue center manager is held accountable for the expenses incurred directly within the unit. The primary measurement, however, is revenue. Revenue centers are not charged for the cost of the goods that they market. Consequently, they are not profit centers.

The manager of a revenue center does not have knowledge that is needed to make the cost/revenue trade-off required for optimum marketing decisions. Therefore, responsibility for this type of decision cannot be delegated to a revenue center manager. For instance, revenue centers typically do not have authority to set selling prices.

In this book, we do not discuss revenue centers as such. We shall discuss the management of revenue as part of our discussion of profit centers.

EXHIBIT 4–2

*Types of
responsibility
centers*

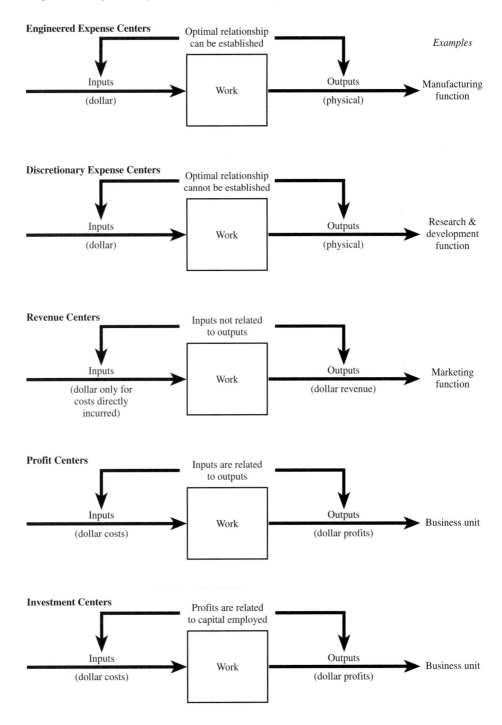

Expense Centers

Expense centers are responsibility centers for which inputs, or expenses, are measured in monetary terms, but for which outputs are not measured in monetary terms. There are two general types: engineered expense centers and discretionary expense centers. They correspond to two types of costs. *Engineered costs* are elements of cost for which the "right" or "proper" amount of costs that should be incurred can be estimated with a reasonable degree of reliability. Costs incurred in a factory for direct labor, direct material, components, supplies, and utilities are examples. *Discretionary costs* (also called *managed costs*) are those for which no such engineered estimate is feasible; the amount of costs incurred depends on management's judgment about the amount that is appropriate under the circumstances. Expense centers in which all, or most, costs are engineered costs are engineered expense centers; expense centers in which most costs are discretionary are discretionary expense centers.

Many expense centers are also cost centers, as this term is used in cost accounting. The distinction is that an expense center is a responsibility center—that is, it has a manager, whereas some cost centers do not have identifiable managers. For example, in a factory, there is usually an "occupancy" cost center, which collects the costs associated with the building, such as heat, air conditioning, light, insurance, and building maintenance. No one manager is responsible for these costs, so this cost center is not an expense center. Similarly, each of the printing presses in a print shop may be cost centers, but only the whole department is an expense center.

Engineered Expense Centers

Engineered expense centers have the following characteristics:

1. Their inputs can be measured in monetary terms.
2. Their outputs can be measured in physical terms.
3. The optimal dollar amount of inputs required to produce one unit of output can be established.

Engineered expense centers usually are found in manufacturing operations. Warehousing, distribution, trucking, and similar units in the marketing organization also may be engineered expense centers, and so may certain responsibility centers within administrative and support departments. Examples are accounts receivable, accounts payable, and payroll sections in the controller department; personnel records and the cafeteria in the human resources department; shareholder records in the corporate secretary department; and the company motor pool. Such units perform repetitive tasks for which standard costs can be developed. (Note that these sections are in departments that are discretionary expense centers.)

In an engineered expense center, the output multiplied by the standard cost of each unit produced represents what the finished product *should* have cost.

When this cost is compared to actual costs, the difference between the two represents the efficiency of the organization unit being measured.

We emphasize that engineered expense centers have other important tasks not measured by costs alone. The effectiveness of these aspects of performance should be controlled. For example, expense center supervisors are responsible for the quality of the products and for the volume of production in addition to their responsibility for cost efficiency. Therefore, the type and amount of production is prescribed and specific quality standards are set so that manufacturing costs are not minimized at the expense of quality. Moreover, managers of engineered expense centers may be responsible for activities, such as training, that are not related to current production; judgments about their performance should include an appraisal of how well they carry out these responsibilities.

There are few, if any, responsibility centers in which all cost items are engineered. Even in highly automated production departments, the amount of indirect labor and of various services used can vary with management's discretion. Thus, the term *engineered expense center* refers to responsibility centers in which engineered costs predominate, but it does not imply that valid engineering estimates can be made for each and every cost item.

Discretionary Expense Centers

The output of discretionary expense centers cannot be measured in monetary terms. They include administrative and support units (e.g., accounting, legal, industrial relations, public relations, human resources), research and development organizations, and most marketing activities.

The term *discretionary* does *not* mean that management's judgments are capricious or haphazard. Management has decided on certain policies that should govern the operation of the company: whether to match, exceed, or spend less than the marketing efforts of its competitors; the level of service that the company provides to its customers; the appropriate amount of spending for R&D, financial planning, public relations; and many other activities. One company may have a small headquarters staff; another company of similar size and in the same industry may have a staff that is 10 times as large. The managements of both companies may be convinced that they made the correct decision on staff size, but there is no objective way of judging which decision was actually better (or whether they were equally good, and the differences reflect other differences about the way the companies operated). Managers are hired and paid to make such decisions.

Management's view about the proper level of discretionary costs is subject to change. Dramatic changes may occur when a new management takes over.

Examples.

1. Percy Barnevik, CEO of Asea Brown Boveri, is known for slashing corporate staff after completing major acquisitions. For instance, the staff in his US subsidiary

(Combustion Engineering) was reduced from 600 people to 100 over 2 years; staff in his German subsidiary was reduced from 1,600 people to 100 in 3 years.[1]

2. Shortly after he became CEO of General Electric Company in 1981, John F. Welch, Jr., cut the corporate staff to 1,000 from 1,700.[2]

3. When Lee Iacocca became CEO of Chrysler in 1980, he almost immediately cut the white-collar ranks by 7,000 people, and a few months later, laid off 8,500 more. These 2 moves cut $500 million in annual costs.[3]

4. In the first 6 months after joining IBM as its chief executive officer, Louis V. Gerstner formed 12 task forces to study growth opportunities, installed a new senior management committee structure, changed the process of evaluating new technology, created a new 11-member executive committee and a 34-member management council, brought in a new chief financial officer and a new senior vice president for human resources and administration, ordered 35,000 layoffs and a $1.75 billion cut in overhead expenses, and changed the basis for management compensation.[4]

After such a drastic change, the level of discretionary expenses generally has a similar pattern from one year to the next.

The difference between budgeted and actual expense is *not* a measure of efficiency in a discretionary expense center. It is simply the difference between the budgeted input and the actual input. It in no way measures the value of the output. If actual expenses do not exceed the budget amount, the manager has "lived within the budget"; however, because by definition the budget does not purport to measure the optimum amount of spending, we cannot say that living within the budget is efficient performance.

In the next section, we discuss the management control systems for discretionary expense centers in general. We then discuss the special considerations involved in designing systems for three of the most common types of discretionary expense centers: administrative and support centers, R&D centers, and marketing centers.

General Control Characteristics

Budget Preparation.   The decisions that management makes about a discretionary expense budget are different from the decisions that it makes about the budget for an engineered expense center. For the latter, management decides whether the proposed operating budget represents the cost of performing task efficiently for the coming period. Management is not so much concerned with the magnitude of the task because this is largely determined

---

[1]William Taylor, "The Logic of Global Business: An Interview with ABB's Percy Barnevik," *Harvard Business Review*, March–April 1991, p. 99.

[2]L. J. Davis, "They Call Him Neutron," *Business Month*, March 1988, p. 27.

[3]From Lee Iacocca, *Iacocca: An Autobiography* (New York: Bantam, 1984), p. 199.

[4]*Business Week*, October 4, 1993, p. 89.

by the actions of other responsibility centers, such as the marketing department's ability to generate sales. In formulating the budget for a discretionary expense center, however, management's principal task is to decide on the magnitude of the job that should be done.

These tasks can be divided generally into two types—continuing and special. *Continuing tasks* are those that continue from year to year—for example, financial statement preparation by the controller's office. *Special tasks* are "one-shot" projects—for example, developing and installing a profit-budgeting system in a newly acquired division.

The technique *management by objectives* is often used in preparing the budget for a discretionary expense center. *Management by objectives is a formal process in which a budgetee proposes to accomplish specific tasks and states a means for measuring whether these tasks have been accomplished.*

There are two different approaches to planning for the discretionary expense centers—incremental budgeting and zero-base review.

Incremental Budgeting. Here, the current level of expenses in a discretionary expense center is taken as a starting point. This amount is adjusted for inflation, for anticipated changes in the workload of continuing tasks, for special tasks, and, if the data are readily available, for the cost of comparable work in similar units.

There are two drawbacks to incremental budgeting. First, because managers of these centers typically want to provide more services, they tend to request additional resources in the budgeting process; and, if they make a sufficiently strong case, these requests will be granted. This tendency is expressed in *Parkinson's Second Law*: Overhead costs tend to increase, period. There is ample evidence that not all of this upward creep in costs is necessary. This problem is especially compounded by the fact that the *current* level of expenditure in the discretionary expense center is taken for granted and is not reexamined during the budget preparation process. Second, when a company faces a crisis or when a new management takes over, overhead costs are sometimes drastically reduced without any adverse consequences.

Despite these limitations, most budgeting in discretionary expense centers is incremental. Time does not permit the more thorough analysis described in the next section.

Zero-Base Review. An alternative approach is to make a thorough analysis of each discretionary expense center on a schedule that will cover all of them over a period of five years or so. The analysis provides a new base. There is a likelihood that expenses will creep up gradually over the next five years, and this is tolerated. At the end of five years, another new base is established.

Such an analysis is often called a *zero-base review*.[5] In contrast with *incremental budgeting* which takes the current level of spending as the starting point, this more intensive review attempts to build up, *de novo*, the resources that actually are needed by the activity. Basic questions are raised: (1) Should the function be performed at all? Does it add value from the standpoint of end-use customers? (2) What should the quality level be? Are we doing too much? (3) Should the function be performed in this way? (4) How much should it cost?

As a part of this approach, it is desirable to compare costs and, if feasible, the output measures of the expense center with information from other sources. Comparisons may be made with averages of similar units within the company, with data published by trade associations and other outside organizations, and even with information obtained by visits to a company in which performance is believed to be outstanding. The latter source, called *benchmarking*, is of course available only if a leading company is willing to cooperate. Despite the natural reluctance to disclose trade secrets to a competitor, such cooperation does exist.

These comparisons may identify activities that appear to be too expensive and, thus, lead to a more thorough examination of them. Such comparisons can be useful, even though there are problems in achieving comparability, finding a "correct" relationship between the cost and output in a discretionary cost situation, and danger in taking an outside average as a standard. All the same, they often lead to the following interesting question: If other organizations get the job done for $X, why can't we?

Zero-base reviews suffer from several potential problems. A zero-base review is time-consuming, and it is also likely to be a traumatic experience for the managers whose operations are being reviewed. This is one reason why such reviews are scheduled once every four or five years, rather than annually. The review establishes a new base for the budget, and the annual budget review attempts to keep costs reasonably in line with this base for the intervening period until the next review is made.

Zero-base review is difficult. Managers will not only do their best to justify their current level of spending but they may also do their best to thwart the entire effort. They consider the annual budget review as a necessary evil, but the zero-base review as something to be put off indefinitely in favor of "more pressing business." If all else fails, they sometimes create enough doubts that the findings are inconclusive, and the status quo prevails.

In the later 1980s and early 1990s, several well-known companies conducted zero-base reviews, usually as a reaction to a downturn in profitability associated with the country's recession. These efforts were often called

---

[5]A zero-base review is to be distinguished from a zero-base budget (ZBB). Zero-base budgeting has been advocated in the literature, was tried in some government agencies and companies in the 1970s, and now has been abandoned. The procedure took more time than was available during the budget preparation process.

downsizing, or, euphemistically, *rightsizing* or *restructuring,* or *process reengineering.*

> **Examples.** Aetna, a large insurance company, began a restructuring program in 1990. It reorganized its three divisions into 15 profit centers, reduced its workforce by more than 10 percent, and incurred $156 million of restructuring charges.[6]
>
> In 1993 Sears, Roebuck & Co. closed 113 retail stores, and eliminated 16,000 full-time and 34,000 part-time jobs, nearly 15 percent of its merchandising employees.[7]
>
> In 1992 General Motors shrank its headquarters office from 13,500 employees to 2,300.[8]
>
> In 1996, Sunbeam's Chairman and Chief Executive Albert J. Dunlap downsized the workforce of the company by half to 6,000 and rationalized manufacturing. The expected annual savings of these reengineering efforts were put at $220 million.[9]

Another tool that is useful in zero-base review is *activity-based* management, a tool more fully discussed in Chapter 8.

Cost Variability.　In discretionary expense centers, costs tend to vary with volume from one year to the next, but they tend *not* to vary with short-run fluctuations in volume within a given year. By contrast, costs in engineered expense centers are expected to vary with short-run changes in volume. The reason for the difference is that, in preparing budgets for discretionary expense centers, management tends to approve a change in budget size that corresponds to changes in budgeted sales volume—that is, additional personnel are budgeted when volume is expected to increase, and layoffs or attrition are planned when volume is expected to decrease. In part, this reflects the fact that volume changes do have an impact throughout the company, even though their actual impact cannot be measured; in part, this results from a management judgment that the company can afford to spend more in prosperous times. Since personnel and personnel-related costs are by far the largest expense item in most discretionary expense centers, the annual budgets for these centers tend to be a constant percentage of budgeted sales volume.

Based on the approved budget, managers of discretionary expense centers hire additional personnel or plan attrition. Having done so, it is uneconomical for them to adjust the work force for short-run fluctuations that occur within the year. Hiring and training personnel for short-run needs is expensive, and temporary layoffs hurt morale. Thus, although costs of discretionary expense centers are sometimes classified as fixed, they are in fact fixed only within a year; they tend to change with changes in volume from one year to the next.

[6]*Financial World,* November 24, 1992, pp. 22–23.

[7]*National Petroleum News,* March 1993, pp. 24–25.

[8]General Motors Corporation, *1992 Annual Report,* p. 4.

[9]"Al Dunlap Revs His Chain Saw," *Business Week,* November 25, 1996, p. 37.

Type of Financial Control.   The financial control exercised in a discretionary expense center is quite different from that in an engineered expense center. The latter attempts to minimize operating costs by setting a standard and reporting actual costs against this standard. The main purpose of a discretionary expense budget, on the other hand, is to allow the manager to control costs by *participating in the planning*. Costs are controlled primarily by deciding what tasks should be undertaken, and what level of effort is appropriate for each. Thus, in a discretionary expense center, financial control is primarily exercised at the planning stage *before* the amounts are incurred.

Measurement of Performance.   The primary job of the manager of a discretionary expense center is to accomplish the desired output. Spending an amount that is "on budget" is satisfactory. Spending more than this amount is cause for concern, and spending less than the budgeted amount may indicate that the planned work is not being done. The financial performance report is not a means for evaluating the efficiency of the manager. This is in contrast with the report in an engineered expense center, which helps higher management to evaluate the manager's efficiency. If these two types of responsibility centers are not carefully distinguished, management may treat the performance report for a discretionary expense center as if it were an indication of efficiency. If this is done, the people responsible for spending may be motivated to spend less than budgeted, and the lower spending will result in less output. In any event, there is little point in trying to increase efficiency by such indirect methods as rewarding executives who spend less than budget.

Control over spending can be exercised by requiring that the manager's approval be obtained before the budget is overrun. Sometimes, a certain percentage of overrun (say, 5 percent) is permitted without additional approval. If the budget really sets forth the best estimate of actual costs, there is a 50 percent probability that it will be overrun, and this is the reason that some latitude is often permitted.

The preceding paragraphs relate to financial control. Total control over discretionary expense centers is achieved primarily by the use of nonfinancial performance measures. For instance, the quality of service provided by many discretionary expense centers can be judged based on the opinion of its users.

Administrative and Support Centers

Administrative centers, which are one type of discretionary expense center, include senior corporate management, business unit management, and managers who are responsible for their staff units. Support centers are units that provide services to other responsibility centers.

Control Problems

The control of administrative expense is especially difficult because of (1) the near impossibility of measuring output, and (2) the frequent lack of congruence between the goals of the staff department and the goals of the company.

Difficulty in Measuring Output.   Some staff activities, such as payroll accounting, are so routinized that they are engineered expense centers. For others, however, the principal output is advice and service; there are no valid means of measuring the value, or even the amount, of this output. If output cannot be measured, it is not possible to set cost standards and measure financial performance against these standards. A budget variance, therefore, cannot be interpreted as representing either efficient or inefficient performance. For instance, if the finance staff were given an allowance to "develop an accounts receivable system," a comparison of actual cost to budgeted cost would not tell management how effectively the job had been done. The job of development and installation might have been poor, regardless of the amount spent.

Lack of Goal Congruence.   Managers of most administrative staff offices want to have an excellent department. Superficially it may appear that an excellent department is best for the company. Actually, a great deal depends on how one defines excellence. For example:

- Line managers want the controller to be able to answer immediately any question involving accounting data. The cost of a system to do this, however, might far exceed the benefits it provides.
- A perfect legal staff will never permit the slightest flaw in any contract they approve. The staff required for complete assurance can be very large, however. The potential loss from minor flaws may be much less than the cost of ensuring perfection.

Thus, although a staff office may want to develop the "ideal" system, program, or function, the ideal may be too costly when compared to the additional profits it generates. At worst, there can be a tendency to "empire build" or to "safeguard one's position," without regard to its value to the company.

The severity of these two problems—the difficulty of measuring output and the lack of goal congruence—is directly related to the size and prosperity of the company. In small and medium-sized businesses, senior management is in close personal contact with staff units and can determine from personal observation what they are doing and whether a unit is worth its cost. Also, in a business with low earnings, discretionary expenses are often kept under tight control. In a large business, senior management cannot possibly know about, much less evaluate, all the staff activities; also, in a profitable company, there is a temptation to approve staff requests for constantly increasing budgets.

The severity of these two problems is also related directly to the organizational level of the staff activity. For example, at the plant level, the administrative staff tends to be controlled carefully by the plant manager who has personal knowledge of what is happening. At the business unit level, the staff has more discretion in the tasks that it performs than at the plant level; at the corporate level, there is even more discretion. In general, the type of staff activity that is performed at the plant and business unit level is closely related to organizational objectives. Discretionary expense centers at the corporate level are the most difficult to judge in relation to objectives.

Support centers often charge other responsibility centers for the services that they provide. For example, the management information services department may charge others for computer services. These responsibility centers are profit centers, as discussed in Chapter 5.

Budget Preparation

The proposed budget for an administrative or support center usually consists of a list of expense items, with the proposed budget being compared with the current year's actual. In some companies, the presentation is more elaborate, consisting of some or all of the following components:

- A section covering the basic costs of the center. This includes the costs of "being in business" plus the costs of all activities that *must* be undertaken and for which no general management decisions are required.
- A section covering the discretionary activities of the center. This includes a description of the objectives and the estimated costs of each such activity. The purpose of this section is to provide information to allow management to make cost-effective decisions.
- A section fully explaining all proposed increases in budget other than those related to inflation.

Clearly, these sections are worthwhile only if the budget is large and if management wishes to decide on the extent of the activities of the center. In other situations, the amount of detail depends on the importance of the expenses and the desires of management. The presentation should be aimed at providing the information needed for an intelligent decision, given the level of the center's activities.

Research and Development Centers

Control Problems

The control of R&D centers, which are also discretionary expense centers, is difficult for the following reasons.

1. Results are difficult to measure quantitatively. As contrasted with administrative activities, R&D usually has at least a semitangible output in patents, new products, or new processes. Nevertheless, the relationship of these outputs to inputs is difficult to measure and appraise. A complete "product" of an R&D group may require several years of effort; consequently, inputs as stated in an annual budget may be unrelated to outputs. Even if an output can be identified, a reliable estimate of its value often cannot be made. Even if the value of the output can be calculated, it is usually not possible for management

to evaluate the efficiency of the R&D effort because of its technical nature. A brilliant effort may come up against an insuperable obstacle, whereas a mediocre effort may, by luck, result in a bonanza.

2. The goal congruence problem in R&D centers is similar to that in administrative centers. The research manager typically wants to build the best research organization that money can buy, even though this is more expensive than the company can afford. A further problem is that research people often may not have sufficient knowledge of (or interest in) the business to determine the optimum direction of the research efforts.

3. Research and development can seldom be controlled effectively on an annual basis. A research project may take years to reach fruition, and the organization must be built up slowly over a long time period. The principal cost is for the work force. Obtaining highly skilled scientific talent is often difficult, and short-term fluctuations in the work force are inefficient. It is not reasonable, therefore, to reduce R&D costs in years when profits are low and increase them in years when profits are high. R&D should be looked at as a long-term investment, not as an activity that varies with short-run corporate profitability.

The R&D Continuum

Activities conducted by R&D organizations lie along a continuum. At one extreme is basic research; the other extreme is product testing. Basic research has two characteristics: first, it is unplanned; management at most can specify the general area that is to be explored; second, there is often a very long time lag before basic research results in successful new product introductions.

> **Example.** In the biotechnology field it took nearly 26 years from the time Watson and Crick defined the structure of the DNA molecule until the first introduction of a product (from 1958 to 1984). It took nearly 24 years from basic research to the successful introduction of a copy machine by Xerox Corporation (from 1936 to 1960).

Financial control systems have little value in managing basic research activities. In some companies, basic research is included as a lump sum in the research program and budget. In others, no specific allowance is made for basic research as such; there is an understanding that scientists and engineers can devote part of their time (perhaps 20 percent, or one day a week) to explorations in whatever direction they find most interesting, subject only to informal agreement with their supervisor.

> **Example.** The discovery of "warm" superconductivity in 1986 was one of the most important breakthroughs of the decade. It was made by two scientists at the IBM research laboratory in Zurich, who were working "on their own time." IBM senior management in Armonk, New York, did not even know that such research was underway.

For product testing projects, on the other hand, the time and financial requirements can be estimated, not as accurately as production activities, but with sufficient accuracy so that a comparison of actual and budget amounts has some validity.

As a project moves along the continuum from basic research, to applied research, to development, to production engineering, to testing, the amount spent per year tends to increase substantially. Thus, if a project ultimately will turn out to be unprofitable, as is the case with 90 percent of projects by some estimates, it should be terminated as soon as possible. The decision to terminate a project is difficult; the project sponsors are likely to report its likelihood of success in the most favorable light. In some cases failure is not discernible until after the product reaches the market.

> **Example.** After 10 years of research and development and many tens of millions of dollars of expense, Polaroid Corporation introduced its instant movie camera, Polavision, with great fanfare at its shareholder meeting in 1977. At that time Dr. Edwin Land, chairman, said, "A new art has been born." Mark Olshaker, author of a 1978 book on Polaroid, wrote, "For the foreseeable future Polavision will be more convenient and economical to use than video tape."[10] But home video cameras quickly came to dominate the market, and by 1981 Polavision was gone; it never made a profit.

R&D Program

There is no scientific way of determining the optimum size of the R&D budget. In many companies, the amount is specified as a percentage of average revenues: *average* rather than *annual* revenue for a specific year, is used because the size of the R&D organization should not fluctuate with short-term swings in revenue. The percentage is arrived at partly by comparison with what competitors are spending (the amounts must be disclosed in published annual reports), partly by what the company is accustomed to spending, and partly by other factors. For example, senior management may authorize a large and rapid increase in the budget if it thinks there has been a significant breakthrough.

The R&D program consists of a number of projects plus, in some companies, a blanket allowance for unplanned work, as mentioned earlier. This program is reviewed annually by senior management, often by a research committee consisting of the chief executive officer, the research director, and the production and marketing managers; the latter are included because they will use the output of successful research projects. This committee makes broad decisions about the magnitude of projects: new projects, projects in which work is to be expanded, projects in which work is to be cut back, and projects that are to be discontinued. These decisions, of course, are highly subjective; they are made within the ceiling established by the overall policy on total research spending. Thus, the research program is determined not by adding the total amount of approved projects, but, rather, by dividing the "research pie" into what seems to be the most worthwhile slices.

---

[10]Mark Olshaker, *The Instant Image* (New York: Stein and Day, 1978), p. 248.

Annual Budgets

If a company has decided on a long-range R&D program and has implemented this program with a system of project approval, the preparation of the annual R&D budget is a fairly simple matter. The annual budget is the calendarization of the expected expenses for the budget period. If the annual budget is in line with the strategic plan and the approved projects (as it should be), the budget approval is routine, and its main function is to assist in cash and personnel planning. Preparation of the budget gives management an opportunity for another look at the R&D program. Management can ask, "In view of what we now know, is this the best way to use our resources next year?" Also, the annual budget ensures that actual costs will not exceed budget without management's knowledge. Significant variances from budget should be approved by management before they are incurred.

Measurement of Performance

Each month or each quarter, actual expenses are compared to budgeted expenses for all responsibility centers and also for projects. These are summarized progressively for managers at higher levels. The purpose of these reports is to assist the managers of responsibility centers to plan their expenses and to assure their superiors that expenses are within approved plans.

In many companies, two types of financial reports are provided to management. The first type compares the latest forecast of total cost with the approved amount for each active project. This report is prepared periodically and given to the executive or group of executives that controls research spending. Its main purpose is to help determine whether changes should be made in approved projects. The second type is a report of actual expenses in each responsibility center compared with the budget amounts. Its main purpose is to help research executives in expense planning and to make sure expense commitments are being met. Neither report of financial information tells management about the effectiveness of the research effort. Progress reports are the formal source for this information. Management makes judgments about effectiveness, partly on the basis of these progress reports but primarily on the basis of face-to-face discussions.

The management control of projects is discussed in more detail in Chapter 18.

Marketing Centers

In many companies, the activities that are grouped under the heading of marketing consist of two quite different types, and the control that is appropriate for one type is different from the control that is appropriate for the other. One set of activities relates to filling orders, and they are called *order-filling* or *logistics* activities. The other type relates to efforts to obtain orders. These are the *true* marketing activities, and are sometimes labeled as such. Alternatively, they may be called *order-getting* activities. Order-filling activities take place *after* an order has been received, and order-getting activities take place *before* an order has been received.

Logistics Activities

Logistics activities are those involved in moving goods from the company to its customers and collecting the amounts due from customers. They include transportation to distribution centers, warehousing, shipping and delivery, billing and the related credit function, and collection of accounts receivable. The responsibility centers that perform these functions are fundamentally similar to expense centers in manufacturing plants. Many are engineered expense centers that can be controlled through standard costs and budgets that are adjusted to reflect the costs at different levels of volume.

Marketing Activities

Marketing activities are those carried on to obtain orders. They include test marketing; establishing, training, and supervising the sales force; advertising; and sales promotion. These activities have important characteristics that affect the management control problem.

The output of a marketing organization can be measured; however, it is difficult to evaluate the effectiveness of the marketing effort because the environment in which it operates cannot be controlled. Economic conditions or competitive actions, over which the marketing department has no control, may be different from that expected when sales budgets were established.

Meeting the budgetary commitment for selling expense is normally a minor part of the evaluation of marketing performance. If a marketing group sells twice as much as its quota, it is unlikely that management will worry if it exceeded its budgeted cost by 10 percent. The impact of sales volume on profits tends to overshadow cost performance. The sales target, not the expense target, is the critical factor in evaluation.

The control techniques that are applicable to logistics activities are generally not applicable to order-getting activities. Failure to appreciate this fact can lead to incorrect decisions. For example, a reasonably good correlation is often found between volume of sales and the level of sales promotion and advertising expense. This may be taken to mean that sales expenses are variable with sales volume. Such a conclusion is fallacious. Budgets that are flexible with changes in sales volume cannot be used to control selling expenses that are incurred *before* the time of sale. Advertising or sales promotion expense budgets should not be adjusted with short-run changes in sales volume. As indicated above, many companies budget marketing expenses as a percentage of budgeted sales, but they do so not because sales volume causes marketing expense, but rather on the theory that the higher the sales volumes, the more the company can afford to spend on advertising.

In summary, a marketing organization has three types of activities and, consequently, three types of activity measures. First, there is the amount of revenue that the activity generates. This is usually measured by comparing actual revenue with budgeted revenue and comparing physical quantities sold with budgeted units. Second, there is the order-filling or logistics activity. Many of these costs are engineered expenses. Third, there are order-getting costs. Order-getting costs *are* discretionary; no one knows what the optimum amounts are. Consequently, the measurement of efficiency and effectiveness for these costs is highly subjective.

Summary

A responsibility center is an organization unit that is headed by a responsible manager. In this chapter, we have described revenue centers and expense centers. Their performance is judged by the criteria of efficiency and effectiveness. In revenue centers, revenues are measured and controlled separately from expenses.

There are two broad types of expense centers: engineered and discretionary. In engineered expense centers, the "right" amount of costs that should be incurred for a given level of output can be estimated. In discretionary expense centers, on the other hand, budgets describe the amounts that can be spent; these are not known to be the optimum amounts, so financial controls do not measure efficiency or effectiveness.

The principal types of discretionary expense centers are administrative and support centers, R&D centers, and marketing centers. Control is most difficult in R&D units, next most difficult in true marketing units (as contrasted with logistic units), and less difficult, but nevertheless more difficult than manufacturing, in administrative and support units.

Suggested Additional Readings

Hammer, Michael, and James Champy. *Reengineering the Corporation*. New York: Harper Collins Publishers, Inc., 1993.

Hammer, Michael, and Steven A. Stanton. *The Reengineering Revolution: A Handbook*. New York: Harper Business Press, 1995.

Horngren, Charles T., George Foster, and Srikank Datar. *Cost Accounting: A Managerial Emphasis*. Englewood Cliffs, NJ: Prentice Hall, 1993.

Institute of Management Accountants. *Statements on Management Accounting*. Statement 4B, "Allocation of Service and Administrative Costs"; Statement 4F, "Allocation of Information Systems Costs"; Statement 4I, "Cost Management for Freight Transportation"; and Statement 4K, "Cost Management for Warehousing." Englewood Cliffs, NJ: Prentice Hall, 1990.

Koning, John W. *The Manager Looks at Research Scientists*. Madison, WI: Science Tech Publishers, 1988.

Kotler, Philip. *Marketing Management: Analysis, Planning, and Control*. Englewood Cliffs, NJ: Prentice Hall, 1996.

Magee, John F., William C. Copacino, and Donald B. Rosenfield. *Modern Logistics Management*. 2nd ed. New York: John Wiley and Sons, 1985.

CASE 4–1
NEW JERSEY INSURANCE COMPANY

On July 16, 1987, John W. Montgomery, a member of the budget committee of the New Jersey Insurance Company, was reading over the current budget report for the law division in preparation for a conference scheduled for the next day with the head of that division. He held such conferences quarterly with each division head. Mr. Montgomery's practice was to think out in advance the questions he wished to ask and the points he thought he should make about each division's performance.

The law division of the New Jersey Insurance Company (NJIC) was responsible for all legal matters relating to the company's operations. Among other things, it advised company management on current and prospective developments in tax and other legislation and on recent court decisions affecting the company. It represented the company in litigation, counseled the departments concerned on the legal implications of policies, such as employee benefit plans, and it examined all major contracts to which the company was a party. It also rendered various legal services with respect to the company's proposed and existing investments.

As shown in Exhibit 1, the head of the law division, William Somersby, reported directly to top management. This relationship ensured that Mr. Somersby would be free to comment on the legal implications of management decisions, much the same as would an outside counsel. The law division was divided into five sections. This case is concerned with only two of these sections, the individual loan section and the corporate loan section. It does not attempt to describe completely the work of these two sections or the professional service rendered by the lawyers.

This case was prepared by J. S. Hekimian under the supervision of Robert N. Anthony, Harvard Business School. Copyright by the President and Fellows of Harvard College. Harvard Business School case 106–049.

Individual Loan Section

The individual loan section was responsible for the legal processing of loans made to individuals and secured by mortgages on real property. The loan instruments were submitted by independent companies situated throughout the country. The company made no loans directly to individual borrowers, although at one time it had made direct loans in the New Jersey area. Most common among the loans submitted by the independent companies were FHA, VA, and conventional loans on homes. These loans usually were made directly by banks or similar financial institutions organized for the purpose. They would batch together a number of loans and sell them to NJIC in a package. The insurance company purchased many thousands of such loans each year.

The investment division of the company was responsible for establishing the terms of these loans, including their amount, interest rate, and maturity. An independent company would submit to the investment division an offer to sell a mortgage loan. It was the function of this division to determine whether or not the property to be mortgaged and the mortgagor were acceptable to NJIC for a mortgage loan. After the proposed loan was approved and its terms worked out, the investment division would forward to the law division the note, mortgage, and related papers which it received from the seller.

The major function of the individual loan section was to perform the legal work necessary on all new loans purchased and on all existing loans. Among other things, it had to check all the loan instruments to make sure they did, in fact, protect the interests of NJIC as required by law and by the investment division. Organizationally, the section was divided into three groups, each headed by an attorney and each responsible for a geographical section of the country—Atlantic Coast, Midwest,

Exhibit 1

Partial organization chart

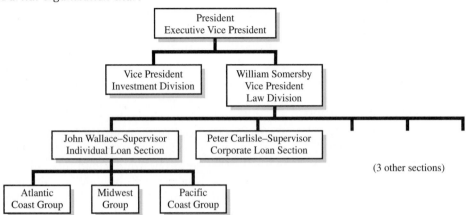

and Pacific Coast. In addition to the three attorneys—there was one who helped out in busy spots and took over a group in case of sickness or vacation and another who was in a training status.

Other than these five attorneys and a supporting secretarial staff, the section was comprised of 26 so-called mortgage examiners. These were persons who had had no formal legal training, but who had been selected carefully and trained by the company to check and approve certain of the loan transactions that came into the section. Because of the repetitive nature of the routine loan transactions, management believed that properly selected and trained individuals could, under the supervision of lawyers, perform this task, which at one time had been performed only by lawyers. Problem cases were referred by the mortgage examiners to the attorneys. John Wallace, head of the individual loan section, estimated that initially it took about three months to train a person to do this type of work. It then took about a year and a half of on-the-job training and experience before the examiner achieved a satisfactory rate of output and two to three years before the average examiner reached optimum performance.

Since the work performed by the mortgage examiners was repetitive, management felt that it

could exercise considerable control over a substantial part of this section. Based on a time study, a work standard of 12 loan transactions per examiner per day had been established some years previously, and this standard later was raised to 15. Records were maintained within the section of the number of loan transactions received each day, the number processed by each examiner, and the backlog.

In evaluating the work of individual examiners, some judgment had to be exercised in applying this standard. For example, in the Atlantic Coast group, an examiner sometimes received a batch of loan transactions in which the mortgaged properties were in a single, large housing subdivision. The legal issues in these transactions tended to be the same. In other parts of the country, however, loans tended to come from scattered localities and, thus, would be quite different from one another in many respects. A supervisor, therefore, in applying the standard would have to be familiar with the type of work an examiner was doing.

Budget Process

Although considerable control could be achieved over the output of individual examiners, control over the entire section was a more difficult problem. Each September, the budget committee of the company issued a memorandum to all division heads, asking them to prepare a budget for the operation of their division during the following year.

The basic intent of the budget process was to get division heads to plan and report in advance the scope of their operations for the following year. Usually, the budgets were prepared by anticipating first the changes in activity levels from the current year and then the cost implications of these changes. Management checked each individual budget for reasonableness, and also checked the total expected cost and revenue to ensure that the overall anticipated profit was satisfactory. The budget was viewed as a device for informing management of the plans a division head had for the coming year so that management could appraise these plans in relation to what other divisional heads had planned and in relation to company policy. The budget was also considered to be a measure of a division head's ability to plan the division's operations and then to operate in accordance with that plan.

On receipt of the budget committee's memorandum in September, division heads began forecasting operations within their divisions for the following year. First, each section head made plans for the section. For example, the individual loan section obtained an estimate of the amount of money that the investment division would have available for individual loans in the following year. Based partially on this estimate and partially on its estimated needs for other activities, the individual loan section developed a budget. This estimate, along with the estimated budgets for the other sections of the law division, was reviewed by Mr. Somersby. The law division then sent its budget to the budget committee for review. Usually, the law division's figures were accepted. Each quarter during the year, actual performance to date was compared with budgeted performance. Heads of divisions were required to explain large deviations from projected estimates.

Although management within the law division could, in theory, vary the size of the staff in the individual loan section, in fact, there was great reluctance to increase or decrease the work force unless a definite trend in volume was apparent. One reason for this was company policy. The company felt a great responsibility toward its employees, and as a matter of policy, would lay off or discharge employees only for serious offenses. This same policy made management reluctant to hire new employees unless there was assurance that the need for them was permanent. Therefore, the law division tended to maintain a staff sufficient to handle a minimum work load, and it supplemented this with overtime.

Another reason for the tendency to maintain a level work force of mortgage examiners was the cost of selecting and training them. Management went to great pains to select outstanding clerks for these jobs. This was followed by a thorough course of study and on-the-job training. Because of this large investment, management wanted to be sure that anyone trained for this job would be needed permanently in the section.

Management within the individual loan section, in attempting to achieve control over the section as a whole and yet in keeping with company policy, had devised several controls. Occasionally, when the work load lessened, supervisors would call the investment division to see if they could get some work that, although perhaps not quite ready to be sent over as a complete batch, could, nevertheless, be sent in parts. Also, since in periods when loan applications were low, foreclosures tended to increase, the mortgage examiners were trained to handle some aspects of foreclosures, and this provided a degree of dovetailing in the work flow. Other than these measures, however, the division preferred to rely on overtime work. The use of outside law firms was out of the question for this type of work because of the far greater cost, even in comparison with overtime wages.

Corporate Loan Section

The corporate loan section was a much different kind of operation. A corporate loan, generally for a much larger amount than an individual loan, was made directly by NJIC to a borrower, such as an industrial or commercial enterprise or a public utility. The loan might be either secured or unsecured. An important advantage to the borrower of this type of loan, compared with a loan evidenced by a bond issue sold to the general public, was that the borrower was not required to furnish a formal prospectus or to file a registration statement with the SEC.

In this type of loan, financial determinations, such as the amount of the loan, interest rate, timing of repayments, restrictive covenants, and so forth were made by the investment division, as was the case with individual loans, but by a different section in that division. Because of the size and complexity of corporate loans, the corporate loan section worked closely with the investment division people, who made these financial determinations. This involved sitting in on the negotiations and rendering advice on all the terms of the transaction. It was the responsibility of the corporate loan section to ensure that the final loan instruments protected the interests of NJIC in the manner intended by the financial people.

On this type of loan, for various reasons, the corporate loan section almost without exception retained well-known outside counsel. One important reason was that an opinion from such an independent law firm contributed to the marketability of the investment in the event of a sale at a later date. Further, in many of these transactions, a number of other investors were involved, and NJIC's law division could not appropriately represent these other investors. If NJIC was the leading investor, it did, however, select the outside counsel to be retained. In addition, it was not possible, without greatly increasing the size of the present staff, for company attorneys to handle all the legal work connected with this type of loan, especially at the time of peak loads. Under this system, any one lawyer had a large number of loan negotiations in process at all times with various outside counsel, and this was beneficial both to the individual and to the company in providing lawyers with a broad base of experience in a variety of situations. The background and experience of company attorneys assured the company of consistency of policy in the negotiation of direct placements.

A substantial part of the work in corporate loans consisted of drafting legal documents. The extent to which company attorneys relied on outside counsel to perform parts of this work depended on the complexity of the transaction (company attorneys tended to do more of the work on more complex transactions) and on how busy company attorneys were. In general, company attorneys handled, as a minimum, enough of the work to be thoroughly familiar with all aspects of the transaction. In many cases, they prepared the first drafts of all legal papers. But in the event that first drafts were left to outside counsel, company attorneys reviewed the work and redrafted it as necessary.

Borrowers were required to pay all expenses incurred in employing outside counsel. However, NJIC made clear to both prospective borrowers and to outside counsel that the counsel were representing NJIC and that their loyalty belonged to NJIC, much the same as for a company attorney. Even though the borrower paid the fee for outside counsel, the head of the corporate loan section, Peter Carlisle, checked closely on the fees charged by outside counsel. Over the years, a thorough tabulation of fees charged for different types of legal work throughout the country had been built up. Mr. Carlisle, simply by referring to this tabulation, could readily determine whether a particular fee was apparently out of line. If there was any substantial deviation, he looked into the case more closely to determine if there was some reasonable explanation; if not, he discussed the matter with the outside counsel and adjusted the fee. Over the years, NJIC had established excellent working relationships with many law firms throughout the country.

The control procedure in this section was substantially different from that in the individual loan section. At the initiation of each transaction, Mr. Carlisle was consulted by the attorney to whom it was referred. Reassignments to equalize the work load of the various attorneys were made as necessary. A degree of control also was achieved through weekly staff conferences with Mr. Carlisle. At this conference, lawyers raised individual problems they had encountered. In addition to keeping Mr. Carlisle informed in detail on what was going on, the conference provided an opportunity for each staff member to draw on the experience of other lawyers, and it served as a vehicle for developing a consistent policy on various matters. Also, the discussion of current negotiations made it more likely that, in case of illness, another lawyer would be prepared to take over the work.

Another control device was the current work assignment report, which each attorney in the section submitted to Mr. Carlisle. Because corporate loan transactions took varying amounts of time to complete, ranging from several weeks to many months, it was found that daily, and in some cases, weekly reports were not feasible. Accordingly, each attorney submitted a report when his work situation suggested to him that a new one was desirable. Each report covered all the time elapsed since the preceding report.

At the top of this report the lawyer briefly indicated his current work status, such as "fully occupied" or "available." Although a detailed format was not prescribed, in general the report described briefly how the lawyer's present jobs were going, what kinds of problems were involved, and what he had completed since his previous report. These reports, in addition to supplementing Mr. Carlisle's knowledge of what was being done in this section, helped tell who was available for more work.

The amount of time a lawyer had to spend on a particular job was not predictable. Major variables were the number and complexity of restrictive covenants in an unsecured note, for example, and the terms and provisions of the security instruments in a secured transaction. The number and complexity of the various covenants in these security instruments did not necessarily vary with the size of the loan, but depended, rather, on the nature, size, and credit standing of the corporate borrower. Many times, a relatively small loan was more complicated than a larger one.

Also, even though the details of a loan had been worked out initially to the satisfaction of the borrower and NJIC, and even though the loan had been in effect for a considerable time, borrowers frequently came back to NJIC to ask for waivers or modifications—that is, they requested changes in the restrictive covenants, the terms, or other conditions or agreements. Such events increased the difficulty of planning in advance how a lawyer was to spend his time.

Unusually heavy work loads in the section were met not only by overtime but also by increasing to the extent feasible the amount of work given to outside counsel. Within limitations, the lawyer responsible for a particular job generally decided how much work would be assigned to outside counsel.

Although the corporate loan section followed the same budget procedure as the individual loan section, one of the variable factors—that is, the extent to which work was delegated to outside counsel—did not affect the budget, since the borrower paid for these services.

Budget Reports

Mr. Montgomery was thoroughly familiar with the background information given above as he began his review of the law division's budget performance for the first half of 1987. The report he had before him consisted of a summary page for the law division (Exhibit 2) and a page for each of the five sections, two of which are shown in Exhibits 3 and 4. The budget figures on the report were one half the budgets for the year.

EXHIBIT 2 Budget Report, Law Division—First Six Months, 1987

Sections	Budget	Actual	Over Budget	Under Budget
Individual loans	$1,330,893	$1,385,154	$54,261	
Corporate loans	$1,176,302	$1,130,073		$46,229
(Three other sections omitted)	—	—	—	—
Total	$5,082,448	$5,107,822	$25,374	
Number of full-time employees	166	160		6

Questions

1. In what ways does Mr. Somersby control the operation of the sections of his division? In what ways does top management control the operation of the law division?

2. What possibilities for improving control, if any, do you think should be explored?

3. As Mr. Montgomery, what comments would you make and what questions would you ask Mr. Somersby about the performance of the two sections of the law division for the first six months of 1987?

EXHIBIT 3 Budget Report, Individual Loan Section—First Six Months, 1987

Costs	Budget	Actual	Over Budget	Under Budget
Employee costs:				
Salaries, full time	$ 924,092	$ 932,201	$ 8,109	
Salaries, part time	—	—	—	
Salaries, overtime	4,500	33,610	29,110	
Borrowed labor	—	5,905	5,905	
Employee lunches	17,055	19,180	2,125	
Insurance retirement, SS, etc.	206,024	208,051	2,027	
Total	1,151,671	1,198,947	47,276	
Direct service costs (Photography, reproduction, etc.):	10,219	12,459	2,240	
Other costs:				
Rent	100,230	100,230		
Office supplies	2,267	3,067	800	
Equipment depreciation and maintenance	11,940	11,940		
Printed forms	3,842	5,367	1,525	
Travel	2,835	3,155	320	
Telephone	7,577	8,690	1,113	
Postage	3,057	3,227	170	
Prorated company services	36,810	37,405	595	
Professional dues	50	100	50	
Miscellaneous	395	567	172	
Total	169,003	173,748	4,745	
Grand total	$1,330,893	$1,385,154	$54,261	
Number of full-time employees	46	46		

EXHIBIT 4   Budget Report, Corporate Loan Section—First Six Months, 1987

Costs	Budget	Actual	Over Budget	Under Budget
Employee costs:				
Salaries, full time	$ 838,720	$ 807,488		$31,232
Salaries, part time	3,000	—		3,000
Salaries, overtime	3,000	—		3,000
Employee lunches	10,325	9,355		970
Insurance retirement, SS, etc.	219,681	211,872		7,809
Total	1,074,726	1,028,715		46,011
Direct service costs (Photography, reproduction, etc.):	4,367	3,720		647
Other costs:				
Rent	61,953	61,953		
Office supplies	1,850	2,955	1,105	
Equipment depreciation and maintenance	7,740	7,740		
Printed forms	445	915	470	
Travel	1,930	1,880		50
Telephone	2,275	2,835	560	
Postage	420	390		30
Prorated company services	20,213	18,357		1,856
Professional dues	200	200		
Miscellaneous	183	413	230	
Total	$ 97,209	$ 97,638	$ 429	
Grand total	$1,176,302	$1,130,073		$46,229
Number of full-time employees	26	24		2

Case 4–2
Whiz Calculator Company

In August Bernard Riesman was elected president of the Whiz Calculator Company. Riesman had been with the company for five years, and for the preceding two years had been vice president of manufacturing. Shortly after taking over his new position, Riesman held a series of conferences with the controller to discuss budgetary control. The new president thought that the existing method of planning and controlling selling costs was unsatisfactory, and he requested the controller to devise a system that would provide better control over these costs.

Whiz Calculator manufactured a complete line of electronic calculators, which it sold through branch offices to wholesalers and retailers, as well as directly to government and industrial users. Most of the products carried the Whiz brand name, which was nationally advertised. The company was one of the largest in the industry.

Under the procedure then being used, selling expenses were budgeted on a "fixed" or "appropriation" basis. Each October, the accounting department sent to branch managers and to other managers in charge of selling departments a detailed record of the actual expenses of their departments for the preceding year and for the current year-to-date. Guided by this record, by estimates of the succeeding year's sales, and by their own judgment, these department heads drew up and submitted estimates of the expenses of their departments for the succeeding year. The estimates made by the branch managers were then sent to the sales manager, who was in charge of all branch sales. He determined whether or not they were reasonable and cleared up any questionable items by correspondence. Upon approval by the sales manager, the esti-

mates of branch expenses were submitted to the manager of marketing, Paula Melmed, who was in charge of all selling, promotional, and warehousing activities.

Melmed discussed these figures and the expense estimates furnished by the other department heads with the managers concerned, and after differences were reconciled, she combined the estimates of all the selling departments into a selling expense budget. This budget was submitted to the budget committee for final approval. For control purposes, the annual budget was divided into 12 equal amounts, and actual expenses were compared each month with the budgeted figures. Exhibit 1 shows the form in which these monthly comparisons were made.

Riesman believed that there were two important weaknesses in this method of setting the selling expense budget. First, it was impossible for anyone to ascertain with any feeling of certainty the reasonableness of the estimates made by the various department heads. Clearly, the expenses of the preceding year did not constitute adequate standards against which these expense estimates could be judged since selling conditions were never the same in two different years. One obvious cause of variation in selling expenses was the variation in the "job to be done," as defined in the sales budget.

Second, selling conditions often changed substantially after the budget was adopted, but there was no provision for making the proper corresponding changes in the selling expense budget. Neither was there a logical basis for relating selling expenses to the actual sales volume obtained or to any other measure of sales effort. Riesman believed that it was reasonable to expect that sales expenses would increase, though not proportionately, if actual sales volume were greater than the forecasted volume;

This case was prepared by Professor Robert N. Anthony and James Reece. Copyright by the President and Fellows of Harvard College. Harvard Business School Case 174–051.

Exhibit 1   Budget Report Currently Used

Month: October	Branch Sales and Expense Performance Branch A				Mgr: N.L. Darden
	This Month				
	Budget†	*Actual*	*Over* Under*	*Percent of Sales*	*Over* Under Year-to-Date*
Net sales	310,000	261,000	49,000	—	70,040*
Manager's salary	2,500	2,500	—	0.96	—
Office salaries	1,450	1,432	18	0.55	1,517
Sales force compensation	15,500	13,050	2,450	5.00	3,502*
Travel expense	3,420	3,127	293	1.20	1,012*
Stationery, office supplies	1,042	890	152	0.34	360
Postage	230	262	32*	0.10	21
Light and heat	134	87	47	0.03	128
Subscriptions and dues	150	112	38	0.04	26
Donations	125	—	125	0.00	130
Advertising expense (local) . . .	2,900	2,700	200	1.03	1,800*
Social security taxes	1,303	1,138	165	0.44	133*
Rental	975	975	—	0.37	—
Depreciation	762	762	—	0.29	—
Other branch expense	2,551	2,426	125	0.93	247*
Total	33,042	29,461	3,581	11.29	4,512*

†One-twelfth of annual budget.

but that, with the existing method of control, it was impossible to determine how large the increase in expenses should be.

As a means of overcoming these weaknesses, the president suggested the possibility of setting selling cost budget standards on a fixed and variable basis, a method similar to the techniques used in the control of manufacturing expenses. The controller agreed that this approach seemed to offer the most feasible solution, and he, therefore, undertook a study of selling expenses to devise a method of setting reasonable standards. Over a period of several years, the accounting department had made many analyses of selling costs, the results of which had been used for allocating costs to products, customers, and territories, and in assisting in the solution of certain special problems, such as determining how large an individual order had to be in order to be profitable. Many of the data accumulated for these purposes were helpful in the controller's current study.

The controller was convinced that the fixed portion of selling expenses—the portion independent of any fluctuation in sales volume—could be established by determining the amount of expenses that had to be incurred at the minimum sales volume at which the company was likely to operate. He, therefore, asked Paula Melmed to suggest a minimum volume figure and the amount of expenses that would have to be incurred at this volume. A staff assistant studied the company's sales records over several business cycles, the long-term outlook for sales, and sales

EXHIBIT 2

Budget for "other branch expense," Branch A

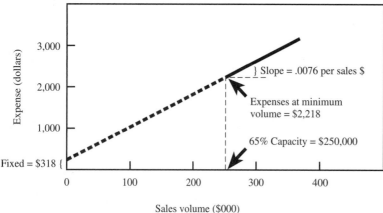

trends of other companies in the industry. From the report prepared by this assistant, Melmed concluded that sales volume would not drop below 65 percent of current factory capacity.

Melmed then attempted to determine the selling expenses that would be incurred at the minimum volume. With the help of her assistant, she worked out a hypothetical selling organization that, in her opinion, would be required to sell merchandise equivalent to 65 percent of factory capacity, complete as to the number of persons needed to staff each branch office and the other selling departments, including the advertising, merchandising, and sales administration departments. Using current salary and commission figures, the assistant calculated the amount required to pay salaries for such an organization. Melmed also estimated the other expenses, such as advertising, branch office upkeep, supplies, and travel, that would be incurred by each branch and staff department at the minimum sales volume.

The controller decided that the variable portion of the selling expense standard should be expressed as a certain amount per sales dollar. He realized that the use of the sales dollar as a measuring stick had certain disadvantages in that it would not reflect such important influ-

ences on costs as order size, selling difficulty of certain territories, changes in buyer psychology, and so on. The sales dollar, however, was the measuring stick most convenient to use, the only figure readily available from the records then being kept, and also a figure that everyone concerned thoroughly understood. The controller believed that a budget that varied with sales would certainly be better than a budget that did not vary at all. He planned to devise a more accurate measure of causes of variation in selling expenses after he had an opportunity to study the nature of these factors over a long period of time.

As a basis for setting the variable expense standards, using linear regression, the controller determined a series of equations that correlated actual annual expenditures for the principal groups of expense items for several preceding years with sales volume. Using these equations, which showed to what extent these items had fluctuated with sales volume in the past, and modifying them in accordance with his own judgment as to future conditions, the controller determined a rate of variation (i.e., slope) for the variable portion of each item of selling expense. The controller thought that, after the new system had been tested in practice, it would be possible to refine these rates, perhaps by the use of a

---

EXHIBIT 3   Budget Report Proposed by Controller

Expense Budget Report	Budget Factors		This Month		Year-to-Date	
					Branch: A Manager: N.L. Darden Month: October	
	Fixed	*Variable*	*Flexible Budget*	*Actual*	*Over*/ Under*	*Over*/ Under*
Net sales			261,000	261,000		
Manager's salary	2,500	—	2,500	2,500	—	†
Office salaries	139	0.0041	1,209	1,432	223*	
Sales force compensation	—	0.0500	13,050	13,050	—	
Travel expense	568	0.0087	2,839	3,127	288*	
Stationery, office supplies	282	0.0026	961	890	71	
Postage	47	0.0006	204	262	58*	
Light and heat	134	—	134	87	47	
Subscriptions and dues	10	0.0005	141	112	29	
Donations	20	0.0003	98	—	98	
Advertising expense (local)	35	0.0100	2,645	2,700	55*	
Social security taxes	177	0.0036	1,117	1,138	21*	
Rental	975	—	975	975	—	
Depreciation	762	—	762	762	—	
Other branch expense	318	0.0076	2,302	2,426	124*	
Total	5,967	0.0880	28,937	29,461	524*	

†The controller had not recalculated budgets for previous months, and figures were therefore not available for this column.

---

technique analogous to the time-study technique that was employed to determine certain expense standards in the factory.

At this point the controller had both a rate of variation and one point (i.e., at 65 percent capacity) on a selling expense graph for each expense item. He, therefore, was able to determine a final equation for each item. Graphically, this was equivalent to drawing a line through the known point with the slope represented by the rate of variation. The height of this line at zero volume represented the fixed portion of the selling expense formula. Exhibit 2 illustrates the procedure, although the actual computations were mathematical rather than graphic.

The selling expense budget for the coming year was determined by adding the new stan-

dards for the various fixed components and the indicated flexible allowances for the year's estimated sales volume. This budget was submitted to the budget committee, which studied the fixed amounts and the variable rates underlying the final figures, making only minor changes before passing final approval.

The controller planned to issue reports each month showing actual expenses for each department compared with budgeted expenses. The variable portion of the budget allowances would be adjusted to correspond to the actual volume of sales obtained during the month. Exhibit 3 shows the budget report that he planned to send to branch managers.

One sales executive privately belittled the controller's proposal. "Anyone in the selling game knows that sometimes customers fall all over each other in their hurry to buy, and other times, no matter what we do, they won't even nibble. It's a waste of time to make fancy formulas for selling cost budgets under conditions like that."

Questions

1. From the information given in Exhibits 1 and 3, determine insofar as you can whether each item of expense is (a) variable with sales volume, (b) partly variable with sales volume, (c) variable with some other factors, or (d) not related to output volume at all.

2. What bearing do your conclusions in question 1 have on the type of budgeting system that is most appropriate?

3. Should the proposed sales expense budgeting system be adopted? Why or why not?

4. What other suggestions do you have regarding the sales expense reporting system for Whiz Calculator?

CASE 4–3
WESTPORT ELECTRIC CORPORATION

On a day in the late autumn of 1987, Peter Ensign, the controller of Westport Electric; Michael Kelly, the manager of the budgeting department (reporting to Ensign); and James King, the supervisor of the administrative staff budget section (reporting to Kelly) were discussing a problem raised by King. In reviewing the proposed 1988 budgets of the various administrative staff offices, King was disturbed by the increases in expenditures that were being proposed. He believed that, in particular, the proposed increases in two offices were not justified. King's main concern, however, was with the entire process of reviewing and approving the administrative staff budgets. The purpose of the meeting was to discuss what should be done about the two budgets in question and to consider what revisions should be made in the approval procedure of administrative staff budgets.

Organization of Westport

Westport Electric is one of the giant US corporations that manufactures and sells electric and electronic products. Sales in 1983 were in excess of $9 billion, and profits after taxes were over $750 million. The operating activities of the corporation are divided into four groups, each headed by a group vice president. These groups are: the Electrical Generating and Transmission Group, the Home Appliance Group, the Military and Space Group, and the Electronics Group. Each of these groups is comprised of a number of relatively independent divisions, each headed by a divisional manager. The division is the basic operating unit of the corporation, and each is a profit center. The divisional

_____
This case was prepared by John Dearden. Copyright by Osceola Institute.

manager is responsible for earning an adequate profit on his investment. There are 25 divisions in the corporation.

At the corporate level there is a research and development staff and six administrative staff offices, each headed by a vice president, as follows: finance, industrial relations, legal, marketing, manufacturing, and public relations. The responsibilities of the administrative staff offices, although they vary depending upon their nature, can be divided into the following categories.

1. *Top management advice.* Each of the staff offices is responsible for providing advice to the top management of the corporation in the area of its specialty. Also, all of the staff vice presidents are members of the Policy Committee, the top decision-making body of the corporation.

2. *Advice to operating divisions and other staff offices.* Each staff office gives advice to operating divisions and, in some instances, to other staff offices. (An example of the latter is the advice the legal staff might give to the finance staff with respect to a contract.) In theory, at least, the operating divisions can accept or reject the advice, as they see fit. In most cases, there is no formal requirement that the operating divisions even seek advice from the central staff. In fact, however, the advice of the staff office usually carries considerable weight and divisional managers rarely ignore it.

3. *Coordination among the divisions.* The staff offices have the responsibility for coordinating their areas of activities among the divisions. The extent of this coordination varies considerably, depending upon the nature of the activity. For example the finance staff has the greatest amount of this coordination to do, because it is necessary to establish and maintain a consistent accounting and budgetary control system. On the other hand, the legal and public relations

Exhibit 1

Organization chart—January 1, 1988

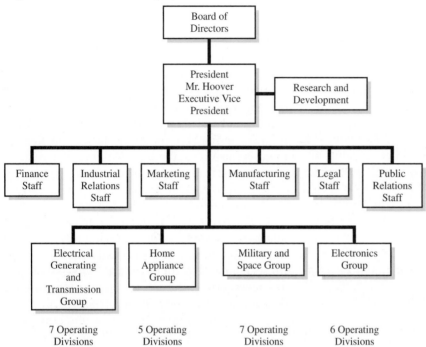

staffs have no direct representation in the activities of the division.

Exhibit 1 is an organizational chart of the Westport Electric Corporation.

The Budgeting Organization

Exhibit 2 provides a partial organization chart of the finance staff. As you can see from the chart, Ensign, the controller, reports to the finance vice president. Reporting to him is Kelly, who is in charge of the budgeting department. Reporting to Kelly is King, who is in charge of the administrative staff budget section.

Approval Procedure

Information submitted. In the early autumn of each year, the budgeting department issues instructions and timetables for the preparation, submission, and approval of the budgets

for the coming year. Since we are concerned in this case with the administrative staff budgets, we will limit our description to the nature of the information submitted by each administrative staff office.

Each staff office completes the following schedule.

Budget by expense classification. This schedule shows the proposed budget, last year's budget, and the current year's expected actual costs, by expense classification (professional salaries, clerical salaries, supplies, consulting services, utilities, and so forth). The purpose of this schedule is to compare the new budget with the current year's budget and the current year's expected actual costs by expense categories.

Budget by activity. This schedule shows the same information as the previous schedule except

EXHIBIT 2

Finance staff—January 1988

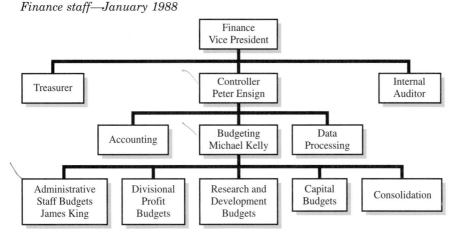

that the information is classified by organizational component. The purpose of this schedule is to show which activities are being increased, which decreased, and which new activities are being proposed.

Explanation of changes.   This schedule is really a letter that accompanies the budget proposal and explains the reasons for the proposed budget. Explanations are divided into the following categories: economic changes (i.e., changes in the general level of wages and materials); increases or decreases in existing activities; new activities added and old activities dropped.

These reports are submitted by each administrative staff office to the budgeting department two weeks before the office is to present its proposed budget.

Presentation of Budget Proposal.   Each administrative staff office budget was approved by the president and the executive vice president in a budget review meeting. The finance vice president sat in on all the budget presentations, but had no official power to approve or disapprove.

On the day scheduled for presentation, the vice president of the administrative staff office whose budget was to be approved would make a

presentation to the president and executive vice president. The presentation would be based on the budget schedules previously submitted, but the explanations justifying the proposals might go into much greater detail. For example, last year the marketing vice president used three-dimensional color slides to describe a new activity that he was proposing to organize.

Attending these meetings were the president, the executive vice president, the administrative staff office vice president and his principal executives, the financial vice president, the controller, the budgeting manager, and the particular budget supervisor involved.

Typically, a budget meeting would proceed as follows: The presentation would be made by the administrative staff vice president. During the presentation, questions would be raised by the president and the executive vice president. These would be answered by the administrative staff vice president or one of his executives. At the end of the presentation, the president and executive vice president would decide whether to approve the budget or whether to curtail some of the proposed activities. Before the final decision, the finance vice president would be asked to comment. In almost every case, he would agree with the decision of the president and executive vice president.

Once approved, the budget became authorization to undertake the budgeted activity for the coming year.

Function of the Budgeting Department.
The functions of the budgeting department with respect to administrative staff budgets has been to prescribe the schedules to be submitted and timetable for their submission and to "keep the presentations honest." In fulfilling the last function, the budgeting department analyzed the proposed budgets and made sure that the facts were correctly stated. For instance, they checked to make sure that the increases due to economic changes were accurate; or if some present activity were to be dropped, they made sure that the cost of this activity was shown as a reduction so that the cost savings could not be used to hide an increase in another activity. The details of the presentation were worked out beforehand between James King and the administrative assistant to the administrative staff vice president involved. When the presentation was made, the budgeting department would be asked to concur with the financial information being presented. The budgeting department, however, took no position on the appropriateness of the proposed budget or the efficiency of the activity. It was this situation that bothered James King.

Budget Evaluation

This was James King's second year as supervisor of the administrative staff budget section. Prior to that, he had been the budget manager in the Electric Stove Division. At the divisional level, the budget analysts exercised considerable influence over the level of efficiency represented in the operating budgets. For example, in the Electric Stove Division, the divisional controller attended every divisional budget meeting and argued long and hard for rejecting any budget that he believed was not sufficiently "tight." Because he had had a considerable amount of experience in the operations of that division, he was

usually successful. King found it hard to reconcile the attitude of the finance vice president (who never seemed to raise any objections to the proposed budgets) with his former boss, the controller of the Electric Stove Division. Consequently, he asked to meet with Ensign and Kelly to see if something could be done to improve the evaluation techniques for administrative staff budgets. Below is an edited version of the meeting between Ensign, Kelly, and King on this problem.

King: All we do about these budgets is to make sure that the accounting figures are correct. We don't do anything about the efficiency represented by the figures, and I know for a fact that it is lousy in at least two cases, and I have my suspicion about some of the others.
Kelly: Tell Peter about Legal.
King: Earlier this year, you remember, we hired a consultant to work with our Data Processing Group. We gave the contract to the legal staff to look over, and it took them three months before they approved it. They had all kinds of nitpicking changes that didn't amount to a hill of beans, but which took up everybody's time.

Shortly after the contract was approved, I had a college friend visiting who's a lawyer in one of the biggest New York firms. We discussed the matter, and he looked over the original contract and the revised one and was astounded at the time that it had taken to get it approved. He said that a simple contract like that would be handled in a day or two by an outside lawyer. Since then, I find that everyone in the organization seems to feel the same way about Legal. They take forever to do a five-minute job, and they never stick their necks out in the slightest.

To add insult to injury, this year the legal staff is asking for a 30 percent increase in their budget to take care of the added cost resulting from the expansion of their work load. The trouble is that, unless we do something, they will get this increase.

Ensign: If everyone feels that the Legal staff is so inefficient, why should Mr. Hoover [the president] approve their budget?

King: I think that Mr. Hoover has neither the time nor the knowledge to evaluate the Legal staff. Any time Mr. Hoover asks for anything from them, he gets superdeluxe treatment. Since none of us are lawyers we have a hard time proving inefficiency, but we know it is there.

Ensign: What is the other budget that you think is out of line?

King: Industrial Relations—especially management training: We are spending more money on senseless training than you can shake a stick at. It's not only costing us money, but it is wasting management's time. For instance, last month we all had to take a course in quality control. It was the most simple-minded course I have ever seen. They gave us a test at the end to see how much progress we made. I gave a copy of the test to my secretary, and she got a 100 percent, without taking the course, or really even knowing what quality control is. Out in the division, the training was even worse. At one time they had a slide film that was supposed to teach us economics in three lessons! The film consisted of "Doc Dollar" explaining to "Jim Foreman" about money markets, capitalism, and so forth. We all felt that it was an insult to our intelligence. In their new budget, Industrial Relations is proposing to increase training by nearly 50 percent, and because the general profit picture is so good, it will probably be approved.

Ensign: If the training program is so bad, why don't we hear more complaints?

King: I will have to admit that I feel more strongly than most of the other people. A lot of managers and supervisors just go along with these programs because to be against management training is like being against motherhood. Also, the personnel evaluation forms that Industrial Relations prescribes have a section on the performance of the individual in these courses. I guess people are afraid to rebel against them because it might hurt their chances of promotion. The point is, at best, they are not worth the money that they cost. No one seems to get much out of them as far as I can see, so we certainly don't want to *increase* the training budget.

The conversation continued for some time. Although he did not express it in exactly these terms, King's other concern was a lack of goal congruence between the activities of the administrative staff office and the earnings for the corporation. It seemed to him that each administrative staff officer, at best, wanted to have the "best" operation in the country and, at worst, was simply interested in building an empire. Even the best operation, however, might cost much more than it was worth in terms of increasing profits. He was also concerned about the ability of the president and the executive vice president to evaluate the efficiency and the effectiveness of the staff offices, or even to decide whether additional activities were really worthwhile. King, therefore, believed it was necessary for someone to evaluate the budget proposals critically, as they did at the divisional level.

The meeting closed with Ensign asking Kelly and King to prepare a proposal that would solve the issue raised in the meeting.

Question

What should Westport Electric do about the evaluation problem raised in the case?

CASE 4–4
GRAND JEAN COMPANY

The Grand Jean Company was founded in the mid-19th century. The firm survived lean years and the 1929 depression largely as the result of the market durability of its dominant product— blue denim jeans. Grand Jean had been a market leader with "wash-and-wear," bell-bottom and flare jeans, and modern casual pants. By 1989 it was one of the world's largest clothing manufacturers. It offered a wide variety of dress and fashion jeans for both men and boys and a complete line of pants for women. It enjoyed a reputation for reasonably priced, quality pants. The company sold 40 million pairs of pants last year.

Production

In each of the last 30 years, Grand Jean sold virtually all its production and often had to begin to ration its pants to buyers as early as four months prior to the close of the production year. The company owned 25 manufacturing plants. The plants' capacity varied, but the average output was about 20,000 pairs of pants per week. With the exception of two or three plants that usually produced only blue-denim jeans, the plants produced various types of pants. The firm augmented its own production capacity by contracting with independent manufacturers. Currently, there were 20 such contractors making all lines of Grand Jean's pants (including blue denim jeans). Last year contractors produced one-third of the total pants sold by Grand Jean.

Tom Wicks, vice president for production operations (see organization chart in Exhibit 1), commented on the firm's use of outside contractors: "The majority of these contractors have been with us for five years or more. Several of

Adapted (with permission) by Professor Joseph G. San Miguel from a case prepared by Professor Charles T. Horngren, *Cost Accounting*, Fifth Edition, Prentice-Hall, Inc. Copyright by Charles T. Horngren and Joseph G. San Miguel.

them have served Grand Jean efficiently and reliably for over 30 years. In our eagerness to get the pants made, we understandably link with some independents who don't know what they are doing and are forced to go out of business after a year or so because their costs are too high. Usually we can tell from an independent's experience and per unit contract price whether or not he's going to survive.

"Contract agreements are made by me and my staff. The ceiling or maximum price we are willing to pay for each type of pants is very well established by now. If a contractor impresses us as being both reliable and capable of making quality pants, we will pay him that ceiling. If we aren't sure, we might bid a little below that ceiling for the first year or two, until the contractor proves himself."

Due to intense domestic and foreign competition, the failure rate in the garment industry was quite high. Hence, new entrepreneurs often stepped in and assumed control of existing facilities.

The Control System

Mr. Wicks continued: "We treat our 25 plants as expense centers. Operations at each plant have been examined thoroughly by industrial and cost engineers. You know, time-and-motion studies and all. I'm quite proud of the standard times and costs we have in place. We have even developed learning curves that tell us how long it will take production of a given type of pants to reach the standard hours allowed per pair after initial start-up or a product switch-over. We know the rate at which total production time per pair reaches standard for every basic style of pants we make. We use this information for budgeting a plant's cost. The marketing staff estimates the quantity of pants of each type it wants produced

Exhibit 1

Grand Jean Company organization chart

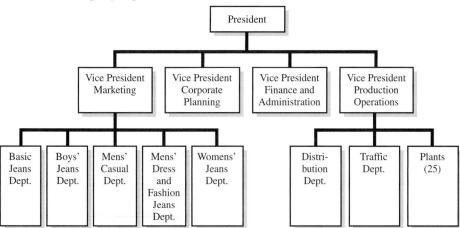

each year. That information is used to divide total production among the plants. If possible, we like to put one plant to work for a whole year on one type of pants. That saves start-up and changeover costs. Since we can sell all we make, we try to keep our plants at peak efficiency. Unfortunately, the marketing folks always manage to complicate production schedules with a lot of midyear changes in pant needs, so this objective is difficult to meet.

"The plant budgeting begins with me and my staff determining what a plant's quota (in pairs of pants) for each month should be for one year ahead of time. We look at the plant's past performance and add a little to this because we expect people to improve around here. These yearly budgets are updated at the end of each month in light of the previous month's production. If a plant manager beats this budget figure, we feel he has done a good job. If he cannot meet the quota, his people have not been working at what the engineers feel is a very reasonable level of speed and efficiency. Or possibly absenteeism or worker turnover, big problems in our plants, have been excessively high. When the quota has not been reached, we want to know why and want the problem corrected as quickly as we can.

"Given the number of pants that a plant actually produces in a month, we can determine the number of standard labor hours allowed for that month. We compare this figure against the actual labor hours to determine how a plant manager performed as an expense center. I phone every plant manager each month to give prompt feedback on either satisfactory or unsatisfactory performance.

"We also look for other things in evaluating a plant manager. Have his community relations been good? Are his employees happy? The owners of this company are very concerned about these factors."

An annual bonus constituted the core of Grand Jean's reward system. Mr. Wicks and his two chief assistants rated each plant manager's performance on a 1-to-5 scale, where 5 was the highest rate. At year-end, Grand Jean's top management determined a bonus base by evaluating the firm's overall performance and profits for the year. The bonus base had been as high as $10,000. The performance rating for each member of Grand Jean's management cadre was multiplied by this bonus base to determine a given manager's bonus. For example, a manager with a 3-point rating would receive a $30,000 bonus.

Grand Jean's management group included many finance and marketing specialists. The casewriter noted that these personnel, who were located at corporate headquarters, were consistently awarded higher ratings by their supervisors than were plant managers. This difference consistently approached a full point.

The five marketing departments listed in Exhibit 1 under the vice president of marketing are treated as revenue centers. Marketing forecasts are used to set sales unit and sales dollar targets. The performance of marketing department managers is measured on the basis of meeting these targets. To meet changing consumer demand, frequent changes in product mix were necessary. The sales force sells all types of jeans within an assigned territory. Their compensation consists of salary plus 8 percent sales commissions. Commissions represent roughly half the average salesperson's compensation. The customers are retail stores and clothing distributors. For marketing department performance assessment, the sales of each line of pants are assigned to the respective marketing department (i.e., basic jeans, etc.). Marketing department managers participated in the company's bonus system.

Evaluation of the System

Mia Packard, a recent business school graduate, gave the casewriter her opinions regarding Grand Jean's production operations and its management control procedures: "Mr. Wicks is one of the nicest executives I've ever met, and a very intelligent businessman. But I really don't approve of the system he uses to evaluate his plant managers. On a recent plant visit as part of my company orientation program, I accidentally discovered that the plant manager was 'hoarding' some of the pants produced over quota. He does this in good months to protect himself against future production deficiencies. That plant manager was really upset that I stumbled onto his pant storehouse. He insisted that other managers did the same thing and begged me not to tell Mr. Wicks. This is odd behavior for a company that usually has to turn away orders near the end of the year! I suspect that most plant managers aren't really pushing for maximum production. If they do increase output, their quotas are going to go up, and yet they won't receive any immediate monetary rewards to compensate for the increase in their responsibilities or requirements. If I were a plant manager, I wouldn't want my production exceeding quota until the end of the year.

"Also, Mr. Wicks worked his way up the ranks of the company. He was a very good plant manager himself and feels that everyone should run a plant the way he did. For example, in Mr. Wick's plant there were 11 workers for every supervisor or member of the office and administrative staff. Since then, Mr. Wicks has elevated this supervision ratio of 11:1 to some sort of sacred index of leadership efficiency. All plant managers aim for it, and, as a result, usually understaff their offices. Because of this, we can't get timely and accurate reports from plants. There simply aren't enough people in the offices out there to generate the information we desperately need when we need it!

"Another thing! Some of the plants have been built within the last five years and have much newer equipment. Yet there is no difference between the standard hours determined in these plants and the older ones. The older sewing machines break down more often, require more maintenance, and probably aren't as easy to work with."

Questions

1. How would you describe the goal(s) of the company as a whole? Is this, or are these, the same as the goal(s) of the company's marketing organization, and the company's 25 managers of manufacturing plants? Explain.

2. Evaluate the current management planning and control system for the manufacturing plants and the marketing departments. What are the strengths and weaknesses?

3. One plant manager recommended that plants be operated as profit centers because it would overcome some of the problems discovered by Mia Packard and the casewriter. This plant manager commented that his "competitor was the nearby independent manufacturer that makes the same pants for Grand Jean as my plant makes. And this outsider might also make pants for Grand Jean's competitors. Because of the competitive market, only the best managed plants survive in this business. Therefore, like the outside company's manager I should have bottom line responsibility and be rewarded accordingly." Do you agree or disagree with the profit center concept for Grand Jean's 25 manufacturing plants? How would this approach affect the plant managers' decisions, performance, etc?

4. If Grand Jean's manufacturing plants were treated as profit centers, three alternatives were suggested for recording revenues for each plant:
   a. Use the selling price recorded by Grand Jean's sales personnel for pants sold to retailers and distributors.
   b. Use full standard manufacturing cost per unit plus a "fair" fixed percentage markup for gross profit.
   c. Use the average contract price Grand Jean paid outside companies for making similar pant types.

   Evaluate these three alternatives. Which one would you recommend? Why is your selection the best one?

Profit Centers

When financial performance in a responsibility center is measured in terms of profit, which is the difference between the revenues and expenses, the responsibility center is called a *profit center*. Profit as a measure of performance is especially useful since it enables senior management to use one comprehensive measure instead of several measures that often point to different directions. In the first part of this chapter, we discuss considerations involved in deciding whether profit centers should be created. We then focus on constituting business units as profit centers, with a reminder that business units and profit centers are not synonymous. Next, we describe how even production and marketing functions can be constituted as profit centers. In the remainder of the chapter, we discuss alternate ways of measuring the *profitability* of a profit center.

General Considerations

A *functional organization* is one in which each of the principal functions of manufacturing and marketing is performed by separate organization units. When such an organization is converted to one in which each major organization unit is responsible for both the manufacturing and the marketing of a product or a family of products, the process is termed *divisionalization*. In general, a company creates business units because it has decided to delegate more authority to operating managers. Some generalizations to keep in mind about organizations are:

- All companies are organized functionally at some level.
- The difference between a functional organization and a business unit organization is a continuum. Between the extremes of the entirely functional structure and the entirely business unit structure are all types of combinations of functional and business unit structures.

- Complete authority for generating profits is never delegated to a segment of the business. The degree of delegation differs among businesses.

Conditions for Delegating Profit Responsibility

Many management decisions involve proposals to increase expenses in the expectation of a greater increase in sales revenue; such decisions are said to involve expense/revenue trade-offs. Additional advertising expense is an example. Another example is increased quality control expense, which can result in more satisfied customers, and hence, increased revenue. Before such a trade-off decision can be delegated safely to a lower-level manager, two conditions should exist.

1. The manager should have the *relevant information* to make expense/revenue trade-offs.
2. There should be some way to measure how effectively the manager is making these trade-offs.

A major consideration in identifying profit centers is to determine the lowest point in an organization where these two conditions prevail. All responsibility centers fit on a continuum ranging between those that clearly should be profit centers to those that clearly should not. Management must decide whether the advantages of giving profit responsibility offset the disadvantages. As with all management control system design choices, there is no clear line of demarcation.

Prevalence of Profit Centers

Although E. I. duPont de Nemours & Company and General Motors Corporation divisionalized in the early 1920s,[1] most companies in the United States remained functionally organized until after the end of World War II. Since that time many major US corporations have divisionalized and have decentralized profit responsibility at the business unit level. Alfred P. Sloan (General Motors) and Ralph J. Cordiner (General Electric) have documented the philosophy of divisionalization and profit decentralization.[2]

A survey by Govindarajan shows the extent to which Fortune 1,000 companies used the profit center concept in the 1990s. Of the 638 usable responses, 93 percent of the companies had two or more profit centers.[3] In many respects,

---

[1]See Alfred D. Chandler, Jr., *Strategy and Structure* (Cambridge, MA: MIT Press, 1962), Chapters 2 and 3.

[2]Alfred P. Sloan, Jr., *My Years with General Motors* (Garden City, NY: Doubleday, 1964); Ralph J. Cordiner, *New Frontiers for Professional Managers* (New York: McGraw-Hill, 1956).

[3]Vijay Govindarajan, "Profit Center Measurement: An Empirical Survey," The Amos Tuck School of Business Administration, Dartmouth College, 1994.

EXHIBIT 5–1A   Use of Profit Centers

	Reece & Cool (1978)	Vancil (1979)	Govindarajan (1994)
Number of questionnaires sent	1,000	684	1,000
Number of responses	620	313	666
Response rate	62%	46%	67%
Number of usable responses	620	291	638
Companies with two or more profit centers	**96%**	**94%**	**93%**

Sources: James S. Reece and William A. Cool, "Measuring Investment Center Performance," *Harvard Business Review*, May–June 1978, pp. 28–49.

Richard F. Vancil, *Decentralization: Management Ambiguity by Design* (Homewood, IL: Dow Jones-Irwin, 1979), p. 169.

Vijay Govindarajan, "Profit Center Measurement: An Empirical Survey," The Amos Tuck School of Business Administration, Dartmouth College, 1994.

EXHIBIT 5–1B   Use of Profit Centers

	Holland[a]	India[b]
Number of usable responses	72	105
Companies with two or more profit centers	64 (89%)	71 (68%)

---

a) Elbert De With, "Performance Measurement and Evaluation in Dutch Companies," Paper presented at the 19th Annual Congress of the European Accounting Association, Bergen 1966.

b) V. Govindarajan and B. Ramamurthy, "Transfer Pricing Policies in Indian Companies: A Survey," *The Chartered Accountant*, Volume XXXII, 5, November 1983, pp. 296–301.

this survey was similar to the one conducted by Vancil[4] as well as the one conducted by Reece and Cool.[5] Because of the more than 15-year gap between the Govindarajan survey and the Vancil and Reece and Cool surveys, we use the relevant findings from the three surveys in Chapters 5, 6, and 7 to identify any significant changes in companies' approaches to profit center measurement during the past 20 years.

As indicated in Exhibit 5–1A, profit centers have been used as an important management control tool throughout the 1970s, 1980s, and 1990s. The survey results from other countries (Exhibit 5–1B) also indicate a heavy reliance on the profit center concept.

---

[4]Richard F. Vancil, *Decentralization: Management Ambiguity by Design* (Homewood, IL: Dow Jones Irwin, 1979), pp. 25, 144–45 and 165–70.

[5]James S. Reece and William A. Cool, "Measuring Investment Center Performance," *Harvard Business Review*, May–June 1978, pp. 28–49.

Examples. Chemical Bank employs the profit center idea and profitability measurements for management control. Profitability measures have helped the bank to drop some unprofitable programs like "Student-Plus" account (a good idea to encourage students to open accounts by offering them lower rates on products and services they used; but these accounts lost money).

There is also an attempt to measure branch profitability more accurately. Historically, if a customer had an account in one branch, that branch got credit for all that customer's business no matter whether the customer used ATMs or services at other branches. The new system allows the bank to know which customers are using which branches and which are using ATMs.

The system also helps the branches to select small target markets. For instance, Chemical, in order to better serve New York's ethnic communities such as Asians, African Americans, and Hispanics, has added an "ethnic market segment" in its system.[6]

The application of the profit center idea helped Novell's chairman and president Robert Frankenberg (who took over from Ray Noorda) to drop several unprofitable businesses such as AppWare and Processor Independent Netware.[7]

Despite the criticism of the use of financial control systems during the past 20 years,[8] corporations have not abandoned such systems. In fact, financial controls continue to be used by corporations as tools to implement strategies. In this and the next two chapters, we examine the considerations involved in appropriately assigning *financial responsibility* to organizational subunits. No doubt, companies are aware of the shortcomings of financial controls, and as we discuss in Chapters 11 and 12, companies actually employ a *balanced scorecard* with a mix of financial and nonfinancial performance measures.

Advantages of Profit Centers

Establishing organization units as profit centers has the following advantages:

- The *speed* of operating decisions may be increased because many decisions do not have to be referred to corporate headquarters.
- The *quality* of many decisions may be improved because they can be made by the managers closest to the point of decision.
- Headquarters management may be *relieved of day-to-day decisions* and can, therefore, concentrate on broader issues.

[6]Robert A. Bennett, "Taking the Measure of Bank Profits," *US Banker*, 104, 4, April 1996, pp. 36–42.

[7]Doyle, T. C., "Novell to Focus on Profit Centers," *Computer Reseller News*, September 5, 1994, p. 202.

[8]Robert Hayes and William Abernathy, "Managing Our Way to Economic Decline," *Harvard Business Review*, July–August 1979; Curran, "Companies That Rob the Future," *Fortune*, July 4, 1988, pp. 84–89; "More than Ever, It's Management for the Short-Term," *Business Week*, November 24, 1986, pp. 92–93; P. Wang, "Claiming Tomorrow's Profits Today," *Forbes*, October 17, 1988, p. 78.

- *Profit consciousness* may be enhanced. Managers who are responsible for profits will be looking constantly for ways to improve them. For example, a manager who is responsible only for marketing activities will be motivated to make sales promotion expenditures that maximize *sales*, whereas a manager who is responsible for profits will be motivated to make sales promotion expenditures that maximize *profits*.

- *Measurement of performance is broadened.* Profitability is a more comprehensive measure of performance than the measurement of either revenues or expenses separately. It measures the effects of management actions on *both* revenues and expenses.

- Managers, subject to fewer corporate restraints, should be freer to use their *imagination and initiative.*

- A profit center provides an excellent *training ground* for general management. Because a profit center is similar to an independent company, its manager is trained in managing all the functional areas. The profit center also provides an excellent means of evaluating the manager's potential for higher management jobs.

- If a company has a strategy of diversification, the profit center structure facilitates use of different *specialists and experts* in different types of businesses. For example, people who are best trained in managing a certain type of business can be assigned to work exclusively in that business if it is a separate business unit.

- Profit centers provide top management with information on the *profitability of the components* of the company.

- Profit centers are subject to pressures to *improve their competitive performance.*

Examples. ABB (Asea Brown Boveri), a European multinational in the power generation, power transmission, and power distribution businesses, is organized in small units with profit and loss responsibility and meaningful autonomy. ABB has 4,500 profit centers. Percy Barnevik, the Chief Executive of ABB, remarked, "We are fervent believers in decentralization. When we structure local operations, we always push to create separate legal entities. Separate companies allow you to create real balance sheets with real responsibility for cash flow and dividends. With real balance sheets, managers inherit results from year to year through changes in equity. Separate companies also create more effective tools to recruit and motivate managers. People can aspire to meaningful career ladders in companies small enough to understand and be committed to."[9]

Japanese companies have started to push responsibility for profit to the lowest possible level in the organization. The Kyocera Corporation, a technology company,

---

[9]William Taylor, "The Logic of Global Business: An Interview with ABB's Percy Barnevik," *Harvard Business Review*, March–April 1991, p. 99.

has divided itself up into 800 small companies (nicknamed amoebas) that are expected to trade both internally and externally. Higashimaru Shoyu, a soy sauce maker, has turned each stage in the production process into a separate profit center, telling the separate parts to buy and sell from each other.[10]

Difficulties with Profit Centers

However, the creation of a profit center may cause difficulties:

• To the extent that decisions are decentralized, top management may *lose some control*. Relying on control reports is not as effective as personal knowledge of an operation. With profit centers, top management must change its approach to control. Instead of personal direction, senior management must rely, to a considerable extent, on management control reports.

• Competent *general managers* may not exist in a functional organization because there may not have been sufficient opportunities for them to develop general management competence.

• Organization units that were once cooperating as functional units may now compete *with one another disadvantageously*. An increase in one manager's profits may decrease those of another. This decrease in cooperation may manifest itself in a manager's unwillingness to refer sales leads to another business unit, even though that unit is better qualified to follow up on the lead, in production decisions that have undesirable cost consequences on other units, or in the hoarding of personnel or equipment that, from the overall company standpoint, would be better off used in another unit.

• *Friction* can increase. There may be arguments over the appropriate transfer price, the assignment of common costs, and the credit for revenues that were generated jointly by the efforts of two or more business units.

• There may be too much emphasis on *short-run profitability* at the expense of long-run profitability. In the desire to report high current profits, the profit center manager may skimp on R&D, training programs, or maintenance. This tendency is especially prevalent when the turnover of profit center managers is relatively high. In these circumstances, managers may have good reason to believe that their actions may not affect profitability until after they have moved to other jobs.

• There is no completely satisfactory system for ensuring that each profit center, by optimizing its own profits, will *optimize company profits*.

• If headquarters management is more capable or has better information than the average profit center manager, the *quality* of some of the decisions may be reduced.

• Divisionalization may cause *additional costs* because it may require additional management, staff personnel, and recordkeeping, and may lead to redundant tasks at each profit center.

---

[10]"In Faint Praise of the Blue Suit," *The Economist*, January 13, 1996, pp. 59–60.

Example. United Airlines recentralized its profit centers that it created in the 1970s because of the complexity of accounting for the different units. In the 80s, United Airlines tried profit centers again which resulted in employee turmoil which resulted in the employee buyout of United.[11]

Business Units as Profit Centers

Business units are usually set up at profit centers. Business unit managers tend to control product development, manufacturing, and marketing resources. They are in a position to influence revenues and costs and as such can be held accountable for the "bottom line." However, as pointed out in the next section, a business unit manager's authority may be constrained; such constraints should be incorporated in designing and operating profit centers.

Constraints on Business Unit Authority

To realize fully the advantages of the profit center concept, the business unit manager would have to be as autonomous as the president of an independent company. As a practical matter, however, such autonomy is not feasible. If a company were divided into completely independent units, the organization would be giving up the advantages of size and synergism. Also, senior management would be abdicating its responsibility in delegating to business unit management all the authority that the board of directors gives to the chief executive. Consequently, business unit structures represent trade-offs between business unit autonomy and corporate constraints. The effectiveness of a business unit organization is largely dependent on how well these trade-offs are made.

Constraints from Other Business Units.   One of the main problems associated with divisionalization occurs when business units must deal with one another. It is useful to think of managing a profit center in terms of control over three types of decisions: (1) the product decision (what goods or services to make and sell); (2) the procurement or sourcing decision (how to obtain or manufacture the goods or services); and (3) the marketing decision (how, where, and for how much are these goods or services to be sold?). If a business unit manager controls all three of these activities, there is usually no difficulty in assigning profit responsibility and measuring performance. In general, the greater the degree of integration within a company, the more difficult it becomes to assign responsibility to a single profit center for all three activities in a given product line; that is, if the production, procurement, and marketing decisions for a single product line are split among two or more business units, separating the contribution of each business unit to the overall success of the product line may be difficult.

---

[11]Joan Feldman, "Divide and Prosper," *Air Transport World*, May 1995, pp. 39–45.

Constraints from Corporate Management.   The constraints imposed by corporate management can be grouped into three types: (1) those resulting from strategic considerations, especially financing decisions; (2) those resulting because uniformity is required; and (3) those resulting from the economies of centralization.

Most companies retain certain decisions, especially financial decisions, at the corporate level, at least for domestic activities. Consequently, one of the major constraints on business units results from corporate control over new investments. Business units must compete with one another for a share of the available funds. Thus, a business unit could find its expansion plans thwarted because another unit has convinced senior management that it has a more attractive program. Corporate management also imposes other constraints. Each business unit has a "charter" that specifies the marketing and/or production activities that it is permitted to undertake, and it must refrain from operating beyond its charter, even though it sees profit opportunities in doing so. Also, the maintenance of the proper corporate image may require constraints on the quality of products or on public relations activities.

Companies impose some constraints on business units because of the necessity for uniformity. One constraint is that business units must conform to corporate accounting and management control systems. This constraint is especially troublesome for units that have been acquired from another company and that have been accustomed to using different systems.

> **Examples.** In 1989 Schering-Plough Corporation completed a seven-year effort to install a companywide accounting and control system. The length of the process was caused principally by difficulties in persuading the business units to adopt the corporate-specified system. In contrast, General Electric Corporation requires only a relatively few numbers be submitted to headquarters with corporate-specified definitions. Nestlé Company permitted business units to report to headquarters in either English, French, German, or Spanish, since most senior managers at headquarters were multilingual.

Some companies require large amounts of planning and reporting information from each profit center. Corporate headquarters may also require uniform pay and other personnel policies, ethical policies, policies on selection of vendors, policies regarding computers and communication equipment, and even the design of the business unit's letterhead.

Certain services are centralized at corporate headquarters because a central organization can provide a particular service to all business units more economically (e.g., data processing, legal services, public relations, training) or because a central service is required (e.g., internal auditing). To some extent, all staff offices provide service to business units, and the business units generally are required to use at least some of these services.

> **Example.** Kinko's Inc., the U.S.'s largest 24-hour photocopying chain, is centralizing much of its operations. Having grown up as a partnership where the partners owned and operated Kinko's stores in different territories, each unit was responsible for its

own purchasing and much of its own financing. Kinko's anticipates savings from more efficient purchasing. They also will see interest expenses drop by $20 million to $30 million by centralizing financing.[12]

In general, corporate constraints do not cause severe problems in decentralization so long as they are dealt with explicitly. Business unit management should understand the necessity for most constraints and should accept them with good grace. The major problems seem to revolve around the optional service activities. Often business units believe (sometimes rightly) that they can obtain a particular service less expensively from an outside source.

Vancil's study includes a thorough discussion of these restrictions on autonomy. The median profit center manager in his survey believed the profit center relied on other units for about one-quarter to one-third of its resources and that the manager had authority to make decisions for about three-quarters of the profit center's costs.

Other Profit Centers

Examples of profit centers, other than business units, are described below.

Functional Units

A multibusiness company is divided into business units that are treated, as far as practical, as independent profit-generating units. Within these business units, subunits may be functionally organized. In such organization units, as well as in companies that are functionally organized, it is sometimes desirable that one or more of the functional units—marketing, manufacturing, and service units—be treated as profit centers. The important point to remember is that no principle states that certain types of units are inherently profit centers and other types are not. The decision on whether a unit should be a profit center is a management option, based on whether the responsibility center manager has enough *influence* (even if not total control) over the activities that affect the bottom line.

Marketing.   A marketing activity can be made into a profit center by charging it with the cost of the products sold. This transfer price provides the marketing manager with the relevant information to make the optimum revenue/cost trade-offs. Since managers of profit centers are measured on profitability, there is a check on how well these decisions are being made. Also, they will be motivated to maximize profits. The profit center should be charged with a transfer price based on *standard* cost, not the actual cost of products sold. Using a standard cost base separates manufacturing cost performance from the marketing performance. The former is affected by changes in the levels of efficiency that are outside of the control of the marketing manager.

---

[12]Nanette Byrnes, "Kinko's goes corporate," *Business Week*, August 19, 1996, p. 58–59.

When should a marketing activity be given profit responsibility? When the marketing manager is in the best position to make the principal cost/revenue trade-offs. This often occurs where different conditions exist in different geographical areas—for example, a *foreign marketing activity*. In such an activity, it may be difficult to control centrally such decisions as how to market a product; how much to spend on sales promotion, when to spend it, and on which media; how to train salespeople or dealers; where and when to establish new dealers.[13]

Manufacturing.   The manufacturing activity is usually an expense center, and the management of such activities is judged on performance versus standard costs and overhead budgets. Problems can occur because standard cost performance does not measure how well all of the responsibilities of the manufacturing manager are being performed. Examples:

- Quality control may be inadequate; products of inferior quality may be shipped to obtain standard cost credit.
- Manufacturing managers may be reluctant to interrupt production schedules in order to produce a rush order to accommodate a customer.
- When a manager is measured against standards, there may be no incentive to manufacture products that are difficult to produce.
- There may be little incentive to improve standards.

As a consequence, where the performance of the manufacturing activities is measured against standard costs, quality control, production scheduling, make-or-buy decisions, and the setting of standards should be controlled separately.

An overall measure of the manufacturing organization can be obtained if the organization is made into a profit center. One way to do this is to give the organization credit for the selling price of the products minus the estimated marketing expenses. Such an arrangement is far from perfect, partly because many factors influencing the volume and mix of sales are outside the control of the manufacturing manager. However, it seems to work better in some cases than the alternative of holding the manufacturing operation responsible only for costs.

Some authors maintain that manufacturing units should not be made into profit centers unless the units sell a large portion of their output to outside customers; they regard units that sell primarily to other business units as *pseudo* profit centers on the grounds that the revenues assigned to them for sales to other units within the company are artificial. Many companies,

---

[13]In a 1989 survey of members of the Controllers Council of the Institute of Management Accountants, 70 percent of the respondents treated marketing activities as revenue centers, rather than as profit centers (*Controllers Update*, February 1990, p. 1).

Exhibit 5–2   **Prevalence of Charging for Administrative Services (percent of firms that charge for administrative services and percent employing the major types of cost assignment methods)**

		Percent by Method		
Administrative Service Category	*Percent of Firms that Charge**	*Usage (actual or estimated)*	*Prorated*	*Other*
1. Finance and accounting	73%	35%	54%	11%
2. Legal	70	35	55	10
3. Electronic data processing	87	63	29	8
4. General marketing services	73	35	56	9
5. Advertising	72	50	41	9
6. Market research services	70	36	54	10
7. Public relations	63	24	62	14
8. Industrial relations	70	32	56	12
9. Personnel	70	35	53	12
10. Real estate	62	37	53	10
11. Operations research department	60	47	42	11
12. Purchasing department	51	40	51	9
13. Top corporate management overhead	63	13	72	15
14. Corporate planning department	61	20	66	14

---

*The total for the denominator includes only respondents who answered "yes" or "no" and excludes missing values and respondents who answered "not applicable."

Source: Richard F. Vancil, *Decentralization: Management Ambiguity by Design* (Homewood, IL: Dow Jones-Irwin, 1979), p. 251.

nevertheless, create profit centers for such units. They believe that, if properly designed, the system can create almost the same motivation that exists in sales to outside customers.

Service and Support Units.   Maintenance units, data processing units, transportation units, engineering units, consulting units, customer service units, and similar support units of an organization can be made into profit centers. These may be headquarters units that service divisions, or they may be similar units within business units. They charge customers for services rendered, and their financial objective is to generate enough business so that their revenues equal expenses. The prevalence of such practices, as reported in the Vancil study, is shown in Exhibit 5–2. (The firms that charge "based on usage" probably treat these units as profit centers.) Usually, the units receiving the services have the alternative of procuring them from an outside vendor if a vendor can offer services of equal quality at a lower price.

Examples. In order to lower costs, Singapore Airlines has created profit centers such as Singapore Airlines Engineering Company and Singapore Airport Terminal Services, which itself has created three profit centers: airport services, catering, and security. Singapore Airlines has set these units up so that Singapore Airlines can use outside vendors for these services if they would like.[14]

Swissair has converted its Engineering and Maintenance Division (EMD) from a cost center to a profit center. This change was done with the following objectives: to make EMD more responsive to the needs of its internal customer, to control EMD's cost structure, and to be competitive for its external customers. In short, Swissair wants EMD to be an independent, entrepreneurial operation and make profits for the company.[15]

Managers of such service units are motivated to control costs; otherwise, customers will go elsewhere. Managers of the receiving units are motivated to make decisions about whether a request for service is worth the cost.

Example. At AT&T the central information resource function, Information Management Services, is a profit center. In 1992 it had revenues of $2 billion and 7,000 professional employees.[16]

Other Organizations

A company having branch operations that are responsible for marketing the company's products in a particular geographical area is often a natural for a profit center type of organization. Even though the branch managers have no manufacturing or procurement responsibilities, profitability is often the best single measure of their performance. Furthermore, the profit measurement is an excellent motivating device. Thus, the individual stores of most retail chains, the individual restaurants in fast-food chains, and the individual hotels in hotel chains are profit centers.

Measuring Profitabil-ity

There are two types of profitability measurements in a profit center, just as there are for the organization as a whole. There is, first, a measure of *management performance*, in which the focus is on how well the manager is doing. This measure is used for planning, coordinating, and controlling the day-to-day activities of the profit center and as a device for providing the proper motivation to the manager. Second, there is a measure of *economic performance*, in which the focus is on how well the profit center is doing as an economic entity. The messages given by these two measures may be quite different. For example, the management performance report of a branch store may show that the profit center manager is doing an excellent job, under the circumstances; but the

---

[14]Joan Feldman, "Divide and Prosper," *Air Transport World*, May 1995, p. 39–45.
[15]Perry Flint, "Cost Center to Profit Center," *Air Transport World* 32, 3, March 1995, p. 20.
[16]"Double Duty CEO," *Financial Executive*, July–August 1992, pp. 15–16.

EXHIBIT 5–3   **Profit Center Income Statement**

		Measure
Revenue	$1,000	
Cost of sales	600	
Variable expenses	180	
Contribution margin	220	1
Fixed expenses incurred in the profit center	90	
Direct profit	130	2
Controllable corporate charges	10	
Controllable profit	120	3
Other corporate allocations	20	
Income before taxes	100	4
Taxes	40	
Net income	$ 60	5

economic performance report may indicate that, because of economic and competitive conditions in its area, the store is a losing proposition and should be closed.

The necessary information for both purposes usually cannot be obtained from a single underlying set of data. Since the management report is used frequently, but the economic report is prepared only on those occasions when economic decisions must be made, considerations relating to management performance measurement have first priority in systems design—that is, the system is designed to measure management performance routinely, and economic information is derived from these reports and from other sources.

Types of Profitability Measures

In order to evaluate the economic performance of a profit center, one must use net income after allocating all costs, including a fair share of the corporate overhead, to the profit center. However, in evaluating the performance of the profit center manager, any of five different measures of profitability can be used: (1) contribution margin, (2) direct profit, (3) controllable profit, (4) income before income taxes, or (5) net income. The nature of these measures is indicated by Exhibit 5–3. Their relative popularity is summarized in Exhibits 5–4A and 5–4B. Each is discussed below.

1. Contribution Margin.   The principal argument for measuring the profit center manager's performance on the basis of contribution margin is that fixed

EXHIBIT 5–4A   **Methods of Measuring Profit**

Types of Expenses Charged to the Profit Center	*Percentage**
Depreciation charge	98%
Fixed expense incurred in the profit center	99
Corporate general and administrative expenses allocated to the profit center	64
Income tax expense	40

*Percentage based on the 593 companies (93%) who reported two or more profit centers in the survey.
Source: Govindarajan, "Profit Center Measurement," p. 1.

EXHIBIT 5–4B   **Methods of Measuring Profit**

	Holland[a]	*India[b]*
Types of Expenses Charged to Profit Centers		
Depreciation charge	96%	98%
Corporate overhead allocated	44%	N.A.
Income tax expense	22%	10%

a) Elbert De With, "Performance Measurement and Evaluation in Dutch Companies,"
   Paper presented at the 19th Annual Congress of the European Accounting Association,
   Bergen 1996.
b) V. Govindarajan and B. Ramamurthy, "Transfer Pricing Policies in Indian Companies:
   A Survey," *The Chartered Accountant*, Volume XXXII, 5, November 1983, pp. 296–301.

expenses are not controllable by the manager, and that the manager, therefore, should focus attention on maximizing the spread between revenue and variable expenses. The problem with this argument is that some fixed expenses are entirely controllable and that almost all fixed expenses are partially controllable. As discussed in Chapter 4, many items of expenses are discretionary; they can be changed at the discretion of the profit center manager. Presumably, senior management wants the profit center to keep these discretionary expenses in line with amounts agreed on in the budget formulation process. A focus on the contribution margin tends to direct attention away from this responsibility. Further, even if an expense, such as administrative salaries, cannot be changed in the short-run, the profit center manager should control the efficiency and productivity of the employees.

2. Direct Profit. This measure shows the amount that the profit center contributes to the general overhead and profit of the corporation. It incorporates all expenses incurred in or directly traced to the profit centers, regardless of whether these items are entirely controllable by the profit center manager. Expenses incurred at headquarters are not allocated to profit centers, however.

A weakness of this measure is that it does not recognize the motivational benefit of charging headquarters costs.

> **Example.** Knight-Ridder, the U.S.'s second largest newspaper publisher, measures each of its newspapers based on operating margin. It sets specific targets for operating margins at each of its newspapers. For 1996 the *Miami Herald* had a target of 18 percent and the *Philadelphia Inquirer* and the *Philadelphia Daily* (which are operated as one unit) had a target of 12 percent.[17]

3. Controllable Profit.   Headquarters expenses can be divided into two categories: controllable and noncontrollable. The former includes headquarters expenses that are controllable, at least to a degree, by the business unit manager (e.g., management information service). Consequently, if these costs are included in the measurement system, the profit will be after the deduction of all expenses that may be *influenced* by the profit center manager.[18] Controllable profits, however, cannot be compared directly with published data, or with trade association data that report the profits of other companies in the industry, because it excludes noncontrollable headquarters expenses.

4. Income before Taxes.   In this measure, all corporate overhead is allocated to profit centers. The basis of allocation reflects the relative amount of expense that is incurred for each profit center.

There are two arguments against such allocations. First, the costs incurred by corporate staff departments, such as finance, accounting, and human resource management, are not controllable by profit center managers. Therefore, they should not be held accountable for what they do not control. Second, it may be difficult to find acceptable methods of allocating the corporate staff services that would properly reflect the relative amount of corporate costs caused by each profit center.

There are, however, arguments for allocating corporate overhead to profit centers in their performance reports:

• Corporate service units have a tendency to empire build, to increase their power base, and to make their units as excellent as possible without regard for their value to the company. If such costs are allocated to profit centers, the possibility that the profit center managers will raise questions about the amount of corporate overhead is greater; this helps to keep the head office spending in check. For instance, companies have been known to sell a corporate aircraft because of complaints from profit center managers about its costs.

• Profit centers' performance will be more realistic and comparable to competitors because competitors pay for similar services.

---

[17]Kambiz Foroohar, "Chip off the old block," *Forbes*, June 17, 1996, pp. 48–49.

[18]This "influenceability" criterion is discussed in John Dearden, "Measuring Profit Center Performance," *Harvard Business Review*, September–October 1987, pp. 84–88. This criterion implies that business unit managers should be held responsible for costs that they can influence, even if they do not have total control over the costs.

• The profit center manager is given the message that the profit center has not earned a profit unless it recovers all costs, including a share of allocated corporate overhead. Thus, profit center managers will be motivated to make optimum long-term marketing decisions (pricing, product mix, and so on) because they must keep in mind that they must recover their share of the corporate overhead. This is desirable, since the company will not otherwise be viable in the long run.

If corporate overheads are allocated to profit centers, budgeted costs, not actual costs, should be allocated. The profit center's performance report then will show an identical amount in the "budget" and "actual" columns for such corporate overhead. This ensures that profit center managers will not complain either about the arbitrariness of allocations or the lack of control over allocated costs since, in their performance reports, no variances would be shown for allocated overheads. The variances would appear in the reports of the responsibility center that incurred the costs.

5. Net Income.   Here, companies measure performance of domestic profit centers at the bottom line, the amount of net income after income tax. There are two principal arguments against using this measure: (1) In many situations, the income after tax is a constant percentage of the pretax income, so there is no advantage in incorporating income taxes; and (2) many decisions that have an impact on income taxes are made at headquarters, and it is believed that profit center managers should not be judged by the consequences of these decisions.

In some companies, however, the effective income tax rate *does* vary among profit centers. For example, foreign subsidiaries or business units with foreign operations may have different effective income tax rates. In other situations, profit centers may influence income taxes by their decisions on acquiring or disposing of equipment, installment credit policies, and other ways in which taxable income differs from income as measured by generally accepted accounting principles. In these situations, it may be desirable to allocate income tax expenses, not only to measure the economic profitability of the profit center but also to motivate the manager to minimize taxes.

Bases of Comparison.   The performance of a profit center is appraised by comparing actual results for one or more of these measures with budgeted amounts. In addition, data on competitors and the industry provide a good cross check on the appropriateness of the budget. Data for individual companies are available in annual and quarterly reports and in Form 10K. (Form 10K data are available from the Securities and Exchange Commission for about 13,000 companies.) Data for industries are published in Dun & Bradstreet, Inc., Key Business Ratios; Standard & Poor's Compustat Services, Inc.; Robert Morris Associates Annual Statement Studies; and annual surveys published in *Fortune, Business Week*, and *Forbes*. Trade associations publish data for the companies in their industries.

Revenues.   Choosing the appropriate revenue recognition method is important. Should revenues be recognized at the time an order is received, at the time an order is shipped, or at the time cash is received?

In addition to that decision, issues relating to common revenues may need to be considered. There are some situations in which two or more profit centers participate in the sales effort that results in a sale; ideally, each should be given appropriate credit for its part in the transaction. For example, the principal contact between the company and a certain customer may be a salesperson from Business Unit A, but the customer may sometimes place orders with the Business Unit A salesperson for products carried by Business Unit B. Although the Unit A salesperson should be motivated to seek such orders, he or she is unlikely to do so if all the revenue resulting from them is credited to Unit B. Similarly, a customer of a bank may carry an account in Branch C, which is credited with the revenue generated by this account, but the customer may prefer to do some banking business with Branch D, because it is more conveniently located or for other reasons. Branch D is unlikely to be eager to provide services to such a customer if all the revenue is credited to Branch C.

Many companies have not given much attention to the solution of these common revenue problems. They take the position that the identification of precise responsibility for revenue generation is too complicated to be practical, and that sales personnel must recognize they are working not only for their own profit center but also for the overall good of the company. Some companies attempt to untangle the responsibility for common sales. They, for example, may credit the business unit that takes an order for a product handled by another unit (Business Units A and D in the above examples) with the equivalent of a brokerage commission or a finder's fee. In the case of a bank, the branch performing a service may be given explicit credit for that service, even though the customer's account is maintained in another branch.

Management Considerations.   Each of the types of profitability measures described in Exhibit 5–3 is used by some companies (with the exception of contribution margin, as is evident from the survey data presented in Exhibit 5–4). Most companies in the United States include some, if not all, of the costs discussed earlier, whether or not they can be influenced by the business unit manager. For example, many U.S. multinational corporations measure the performance of managers of foreign subsidiaries in dollars. Performance, thus, is affected by fluctuations in the value of the dollar relative to the host currency. There are few instances where individual managers can exercise any influence over the value of the dollar.

Most of the confusion in measuring the performance of profit center managers is the result of *not* separating the measurement of the manager from the economic measurement of the profit center. If we consider the measurement of the manager alone, the solution often becomes evident: *Managers should be measured against those items that they can influence.* In the typical company, this probably would be all expenses incurred directly in the profit center. The managers would be measured on an after-tax basis only if they can influence the amount of tax that they pay. Items that they clearly cannot influence, such as currency fluctuation, should be eliminated.

Following the guide of including only those items that the manager can influence does not solve all the problems. Degrees of influence vary. There are always items over which a manager may exercise some influence, but little real control. This is why variance analysis is always important in evaluating management performance. Even with the best variance analysis system, however, judgment will always be necessary. If all items over which the manager has no influence are eliminated (or are reported in such a way that variances do not develop), however, it will make the exercise of this judgment more reliable. This topic is discussed in more depth in Chapter 7.

Summary

A profit center is an organization unit in which both revenues and expenses are measured in monetary terms. Setting up profit centers pushes decision making to lower levels where relevant information in making expense/revenue trade-offs exists. This can speed up decision making, improve the quality of decisions, focus attention on profitability, provide a broader measure of management performance, and other advantages.

Profit centers' autonomy may be constrained by other business units, and also there may be constraints imposed by corporate management. These constraints need to be recognized in operating organization units as profit centers.

Under appropriate circumstances, even the production or marketing functions can be constituted as profit centers. However, considerable judgment is involved in designating a functional unit, such as production or marketing, as a profit center.

Measuring *profit* in a profit center also involves judgments regarding how revenues and expenses should be measured. In terms of revenues, choice of a revenue recognition method is important. In terms of expenses, measurement can range from variable costs incurred in the profit center to fully allocated corporate overhead, including income taxes. Judgments regarding the measurement of revenues and costs should be guided not just by technical accounting considerations, but more importantly by behavioral and motivational considerations. The key is to include those expenses and revenues in profit center managers' reports that the managers can *influence*, even if they cannot totally control them.

Suggested Additional Readings

Alter, Allan E. "The Profit Center Paradox," *Computerworld* 29, 17, April 1995, pp. 101–5.

Dearden, John. "Measuring Profit Center Managers." *Harvard Business Review,* September–October 1987, pp. 84–88.

Govindarajan, Vijay. "Decentralization, Strategy, and Effectiveness of Strategic Business Units in Multi-Business Organizations." *Academy of Management Review* 11, no. 4, 1986, pp. 844–56.

Leibenstein, H. *Inside the Firm: The Inefficiencies of Hierarchy*. Cambridge, MA: Harvard University Press, 1987.

Rayburn, Gale L. *Cost Accounting*. Homewood, IL: Richard D. Irwin, 1991.

Solomons, David. *Divisional Performance: Measurement and Control*. Homewood, IL: Richard D. Irwin, 1965.

Vancil, Richard F. *Decentralization: Management Ambiguity by Design*. Homewood, IL: Dow Jones-Irwin, 1979.

Walsh, Francis J. *Measuring Business-Unit Performance*. Research Bulletin no. 206, New York: The Conference Board, Inc., 1987.

CASE 5–1
PROFIT CENTER PROBLEMS

1. AMAX Automobiles

AMAX Automobiles is a car company with three product lines. Line A is aimed at the luxury segment, line B at the upscale segment, and line C at the mass market segment. Each of the three product lines is sold under a different brand name and utilizes different distribution systems. Lines A, B, and C are currently produced and marketed by Divisions A, B, and C, respectively.

Some components are common to the three divisions. Some of these common components might be sourced externally while others are manufactured inside the company. Also, there exists considerable scope for technology and know-how transfer across the divisions. Specifically, product innovations seem to originate in Division A and then migrate to Divisions B and C. However, process innovations seem to originate in Division C and then migrate to Divisions A and B.

How should AMAX be organized and controlled?

2. Indus Corporation

Indus is a diversified company operating in a number of niche markets that are largely independent of each other, i.e., customer buying decisions in each of these markets are made independently. The company's primary basis for competitive advantage in each of these markets is to be the first mover (and leader) in product innovation.

Case A: The customer is mainly performance rather than price sensitive. Also, there is little production synergy across the various product lines.

Case B: The customer is mainly performance rather than price sensitive. However, there is considerable production synergy across the various product lines.

Case C: The customer is equally sensitive regarding product performance and price. However, there is little production synergy across the various product lines.

Case D: The customer is equally sensitive regarding product performance and price. However, there is considerable production synergy across the various product lines.

In each case, how should Indus be organized and controlled?

Case 5–2
North Country Auto, Inc.

George G. Liddy, part owner of North Country Auto, Inc., was feeling pretty good about the new control systems recently put in place for his five department managers (new and used car sales, service, body, and parts departments). Exhibit 1 describes each department. Mr. Liddy strongly believed in the concept of evaluating each department individually as a profit center. But he also recognized the challenge of getting his managers to "buy in" to the system by working together for the good of the dealership.

Background

North Country Auto, Inc. was a franchised dealer and factory-authorized service center for Ford, Saab, and Volkswagen. Multiple franchises were becoming more common in the 1980s. But the value of multiple franchises did not come without costs. Each of the three manufacturers used a different computerized system for tracking inventory and placing new orders. They also required their dealerships to maintain an adequate service facility with a crew of trained technicians that, in turn, necessitated carrying an inventory of parts to be used in repairs. Exhibit 2 gives balance sheet data with a break out of investment for each product line. North Country also operated a body shop, and in mid-1989, opened a "while-you-wait" oil change service for any make of vehicle.

The dealership was situated in an upstate New York town with a population of about 20,000. It served 2 nearby towns of about 4,000 as well as rural areas covering a 20-mile radius. North Country began operations in 1968, and in 1983, moved 1 mile down the road to its current 6-acre lot, 25,000 square-foot facility. It was

This case was written by Mark C. Rooney (T'90) under the supervision of Professor Joseph Fisher. Copyright © by The Amos Tuck School of Business Administration, Dartmouth College.

owned as a corporation by George Liddy and Andrew Jones, who were both equally active in day-to-day operations. Mr. Liddy purchased an interest in the dealership from a previous partner in 1988. Mr. Jones had been part owner since the start of the business. Whereas Mr. Liddy focused his energies on new and used car sales, Mr. Jones concentrated on managing the parts, service, and body shop departments—commonly referred to as the "back end" of a dealership.

The owners were determined to maintain a profitable back end as a hedge against depressed sales and lower margins in vehicles sales. In an industry characterized by aggressive discounting fueled by a combination of high inventories, a more educated consumer, and a proliferation of new entrants, alternative sources of cash flow were crucial. Industry analysts were estimating that fewer than 50 percent of the dealers in the US would make a profit on new car sales in 1990. Overall net profit margins were expected to fall below 1 percent of sales (*The Wall Street Journal*, December 11, 1989).

George Liddy's Challenge

Before George Liddy bought into the dealership, all the departments operated as part of one business. Department managers were paid salaries and a year-end bonus determined at the owners' discretion based on overall results for the year and a subjective appraisal of each manager.

George Liddy believed this system did not provide proper motivation for the managers. He believed in decentralized profit centers and performance-based compensation as superior models of control. He instructed each of his departmental managers (new, used, service, body, and parts) to run his/her department as if it were an independent business. He knew that the success of the profit center control system was dependent

---

EXHIBIT 1   North Country Auto, Inc.—The Departmental Structure

New Car Sales and Used Car Sales

The new and used car departments each had a sales manager. They shared six salespersons. In addition, these departments shared an office manager and clerks. The managers were paid a flat salary, plus a fixed sum per new or used vehicle sold, and a percentage of their department's gross profit (calculated as sales minus cost of vehicles sold). When the owners and the managers agreed on annual unit volume and margin goals, the dollar weights were set to make each portion approximately one-third of the manager's expected total compensation. The owners claimed that this type of dual incentive bonus structure allowed the managers flexibility in targeting margins and volume. George Liddy maintained, "If the margins are low, the sales manager can try to make it up in volume." The sales force was paid strictly a commission on gross profit. Many dealerships in the area were changing sales compensation to a flat salary plus a partial commission on gross profits generated.

The new car sales manager was responsible for recommending to Liddy new model orders and inventory mix among the three product lines. He also had the authority to approve selling prices and trade-in allowances on customer transactions. Typically, the new car manager was allowed to transfer the trade-in at blue book. However, if the car was obviously of below average quality, the used car department was asked for their estimate of value. The used car manager was responsible for controlling the mix of used car inventory through buying and selling used vehicles at wholesale auto auctions.

Service

The service department occupied over half of the building's usable square footage and was the most labor intensive operation. Service comprised 11 bays with hydraulic lifts, one of which was used for the oil change operation. The department employed a manager, 10 technicians, 3 semiskilled mechanics, 2 counter clerks, and 3 office clerks. The manager was paid a flat salary plus a bonus on the department's gross profit on labor hours billed (computed as labor dollars billed minus total wages of billable technicians and mechanics). Service revenue consisted of labor only. No markup for parts was realized by service department. The bonus portion was planned to be approximately 50 percent of his salary. The technicians, mechanics, and clerks were all paid a flat salary, regardless of actual hours billed. The technicians required specialty training to perform factory-authorized work on each of the specific lines. Sending a technician to school cost about $4,000 over a two-year period. The owners estimated that a new hire could cost as much as $10,000 in nonbillable overruns on warranty jobs, where reimbursement was limited to standard allowable labor hours. Of the 10 techs, 4 were certified for Ford, 3 for Saab, and 3 for Volkswagen. George Liddy and Andrew Jones contemplated reducing the cost of idle time by cross-training, but were averse to risks of turnover among highly skilled labor. Retraining costs could triple when one person quit.

The primary sources of service department revenue were warranty maintenance and repair work, nonwarranty maintenance and repair work, used car reconditioning, and the oil change operation. Warranty work was reimbursed by the factories at their prescribed labor rates, which were typically as much as 20 percent lower than the rates charged directly for nonwarranty work. Lower margins on warranty work were a potential problem for the dealership if they dissuaded the service manager from delivering prompt service to recent buyers. During times of near capacity utilization, the manager would be motivated to schedule higher margin nonwarranty jobs in the place of warranty work.

Parts

The parts department consisted of a manager, three stock keepers, and two clerks. The parts manager was paid a flat salary plus a bonus on department gross profits (computed as total parts sold less cost of parts). The parts manager was responsible for tracking parts inventory for the three lines and minimizing both carrying costs and "obsolescence." The owners defined obsolescence as a part in stock that was not sold in over a year. Mr. Liddy estimated that as many as 25 percent of the parts-on-hand fell into this category. Days supply of parts (inventory turnover) averaged 100 days for the industry. The manager had to be an expert on the return policies, stock requirements, and secondary market of three distinct and unrelated lines of merchandise. It was the parts manager's job to use factory return credits most effectively and identify outside wholesale opportunities so as to minimize large write-downs. Local wholesalers would pay as much as 80 percent of dealer cost for old parts.

Demand for parts was derived almost completely from other departments. Dollar sales volume in parts broke down as follows: 50 percent through service, 30 percent through the body shop, 10 percent wholesale, and 10 percent over-the-counter retail. Similar to service work, parts needed in warranty work were reimbursed at rates as much as 20 percent less than prices charged for nonwarranty work.

EXHIBIT 1   North Country Auto, Inc.—The Departmental Structure (continued)

Body Shop

The body shop consisted of a manager, three technicians, and a clerk. The manager, like the others, was paid a flat salary plus a bonus on departmental profitability. To keep the shop in business in the long run, North Country Auto needed to invest an additional $50,000 in new spray painting equipment. As it was, the body shop was showing a loss after allocation of fixed overhead. Gross margins as high as 60 percent could be attained, but rework and hidden damage beyond estimates tended to drive them down to closer to 40 percent.

Oil Change Operation

The dealership's oil change business operated under the nationally franchised "Qwik Change" logo, using one bay in the service department and one of the semiskilled mechanics. Volume averaged 68 changes per week. The operation was not evaluated as an independent profit center but as a means of filling unused capacity in the service department. The oil change franchise paid for all equipment, reducing the dealership's out-of-pocket investment to $500. After direct labor, direct parts, and the franchise fee, the dealership made about $10.00 on each oil change priced at $21.95. The owners were willing to devote an extra bay to this operation if volume warranted.

EXHIBIT 2   Balance Sheet

North Country Auto, Inc.
Balance Sheet
October 31, 1989
(In thousands)

Assets		Liabilities & equity	
Cash	$ 32	Accounts payable	$ 73
Accounts receivable	228	Notes payable—vehicles	1,294
Saab inventory	253	Long-term debt	344
VW inventory	243		
Ford inventory	773	Total liabilities	1,711
Used cars	231		
Saab parts	75		
VW parts	75		
Ford parts	226		
Body shop materials	6	Stockholders' equity	
Other current assets	89	Common stock	$ 400
		Retained earnings	205
Property & equipment—Net*	85		
($377M gross)			
Total	$2,316	Total	$2,316

*North Country leases both the land and building.

upon the support of his managers. They must understand the rationale for allocating costs to their departments and believe that they have reasonable control over profitability. The managers' bonuses in 1989 were calculated on the basis of departmental *gross* profits. Expenses below the gross profit line were not considered in the bonus calculation. They were only told, in a statement outlining their responsibilities, to exercise "judicious control over discretionary expenses." Implementing a more comprehensive control system tied to actual departmental net profits would require that Liddy break down costs traditionally regarded as general overhead into separate activities associated with specific departments. His strategy with the managers involved a gradual phasing in over the next few years of an "almost" full-cost allocation system, where each department manager would eventually have responsibility for all controllable costs incurred in the department. Fixed expenses, such as interest expense, would be allocated by Liddy for his own decisions, but would not be used in the managers' bonus calculations.

The gradual changeover would allow Liddy, who was new to the dealership, time to become more knowledgeable of the intricacies of North Country Auto's accounting records. He did not want to lose credibility because of perceived arbitrary cost allocations. Exhibit 3 gives a

EXHIBIT 3   Financial Statement

North Country Auto, Inc.
October 31, 1989 (10 months)
(Dollar figures in thousands)

	New	Used	Service	Body	Parts
Sales $6,558		$1,557	$ 672	$231	$ 1,417
Gross profit	502	189	421	145	361
Number of units (vehicles, repairs, or parts)	474	390	9,795	406	40,139
Direct selling (commission & delivery) . . . . $	96	$ 25	n/a	n/a	n/a
Indirect labor	162	74	237	64	156
Department advertising	91	30	19	2	3
Policy work—parts & service (giveaways & rework)	29	12	14	12	1
Supplies & utilities	22	18	19	28	12
Depreciation	3	1	15	5	2
Rent	89	22	67	13	9
Profit before common expenses . . . . $	10	$ 7	$ 50	$ 21	$ 178
Other expenses:					
Interest (on new inventory) . . . . $	110				
Other interest	21				
Owners' salary	65				
Insurance	35				
Net operating profit	$ 35				

Notes to Financial Statements

1. New car sales and gross margins (000s) break down as:

	Sales	Gross profit	# Units
Ford	$3,114	$193	243
Saab	1,502	90	73
VW	1,794	117	158
Financing fees*	148	102	n/a
	$6,558	$502	474

2. Used car sales and margins break down as:

	Sales	Gross profit	# Units
Retail	$1,045	$212	177
Wholesale	423	(59)	213
Financing fees*	89	36	n/a
	$1,557	$189	390

Exhibit 3   Financial Statement (continued)

3. Notes payable for vehicles is a revolving line of credit secured by new car inventory. Payments to the bank are due upon sale of each vehicle financed in inventory. This liability has been reduced over the past 10 months by approximately $1.5 million.

4. Indirect labor consists of department managers, clerks, bookkeepers, and work involving tasks directly related to the activities in a specific department. It does not include sales commissions or billable employees in the back end.

5. Departmental advertising is assigned to departments based on actual ads placed.

6. Policy work consists of dealer concessions made to customers arising from disputes over dealer-installed options on new vehicles, warranty coverage, or cost of repairs. These costs are allocated to the departments in which they occur.

7. Depreciation is allocated by historical cost of leasehold improvements or equipment in each department.

8. Rent is allocated by square footage used by each department, adjusted for the value of the space.

9. Interest expense is treated as a common expense for the purpose of keeping investing and financing costs separate.

10. Insurance consists of both umbrella liability and property damage for the dealership as a whole. Because of the multiple types of coverages included and the bundled pricing, it is not feasible to break out coverage costs by department.

11. Approximately 75 percent of the fixed costs in the used car department related closely to retail vehicle sales and approximately 25 percent to wholesale sales.

12. Total number of parts sold during the year = 40,139 parts; total number of service orders undertaken during the year = 9,795 orders.

13. Using Exhibit 3, North Country determined the following allocations for overhead expenses:

New: $835/vehicle = $396,000/474 vehicles

Used: $665/vehicle = $157,000 × 0.75/177 vehicles

Parts: $32 = $183,000/40,139 parts = 4.55/part × 7 parts
         (2 brake kits, 1 lock assembly, 4 tune-up parts)

Service: $114 = $371,000/9,795 orders × 3 orders
         (lock, brakes, tune-up)

*Finance fees consist of income that the dealer earns on dealer-sourced auto loans. It also includes the dealer's commission on service contracts and extended warranties sold through the dealership.

breakdown of department profitability on an "almost" full-cost basis.

In addition to finding a way to effectively track departmental performance, George Liddy had to devise a sensible system for transfer pricing. Though Mr. Liddy believed that each department at North Country theoretically could operate as an independent business, he acknowledged that a complex interrelationship existed among the profit centers in the course of normal business transactions. A recent new vehicle purchase illustrates the potential problems that could arise.

Alex Walker, manager of the new car sales department, sold a new car for $14,150. This purchase was financed by a cash down payment of $2,000, a trade-in allowance of $4,800, and a bank loan of $7,350. The dealer's cost was $11,420, which included factory price plus sales commission.

The manager of the used car sales department, Amy Robbins, examined the trade-in vehicle. The trade-in had a wholesale guidebook value of $3,500. The guidebook, published monthly, was, at best, a near estimate of liquidation value. Actual values varied daily with the supply-demand balance at auto auctions. These variances could be as much as 25 percent of the book value.

Ms. Robbins believed that she could sell the trade-in quickly at $5,000 and earn a good margin, so she chose to carry it in inventory instead of wholesaling it for a value estimated to be $3,500. Mr. Walker, in turn, used the $3,500 value in calculating his actual profit on the new car sale.

In performing the routine maintenance check on the trade-in, the service department reported that the front wheels would need new brake pads and rotors and that the rear door lock assembly was jammed. The retail estimates for repair would be $300 for the brakes ($125 in parts, $175 in labor) and $75 to fix the lock assembly ($30 in parts, $45 in labor). Cleaning and touch-up (performed by service department as a part of the service order for lock and brake) would cost $75. The service department also recommended that a full tune-up be performed for a retail price of $255 ($80 in parts, $175 in labor).

The repair and tune-up work was completed and capitalized at retail cost into used car inventory at $705. These mechanical repairs would not necessarily increase wholesale value if the car subsequently were sold at the auction. The transfer price for internal work recently had changed from cost to full retail equivalent. The retail markup for labor was 3.5 times the direct hourly rate and about 1.4 times for parts.

George Liddy was concerned that the retail transfer price of the repairs in conjunction with his plan to eventually allocate full costs to each department (as illustrated in Exhibit 3) might encourage the used car sales manager to avoid the possibility of losses in her department by wholesaling trade-in cars that could be resold at a profit for the dealership. This might also hurt the dealership by making its deals less attractive for new car customers.

Knowing how important it was to maintain credibility with each of the departments, Liddy called a meeting with the three department managers. He decided to use the recently completed new car sale to illustrate the effect that transaction would have on departments' profits. In his presentation, Mr. Liddy laid out the transaction and allocation of profits and costs. After this presentation, Mr. Liddy asked for the reactions of his department managers.

Alex Walker was the first to chime in, "I understand that the allowance above book value on the trade-in cannot be accounted for as profit. However, the real issue is how to set the price between me and Amy when we transfer the trade-in. I refuse to be responsible for any loss that might arise if the trade-in vehicle is liquidated at auction for an amount less than the wholesale guidebook value. Her department should be accountable for its valuation errors."

Amy Robbins vehemently disagreed. "My department should not have to subsidize the profits of the new car sales division."

Liddy quickly jumped into this deteriorating argument, "Obviously, we need to carefully consider how to set the price between the new and used car departments and who should be responsible for unexpected losses."

"Another item that concerns me," Robbins went on, "is using full retail price for parts and labor used in the repairs of trade-ins. Given underutilized capacity in service, I do not understand why I am charged full price. It doesn't make sense for the service department to mark up on projects undertaken for new and used car departments within our own dealership. I can't see how we can make profits when one part of our company sells to another."

Robbins added, "When I am unsure of the actual retail value, I tend to wholesale rather than take a risk of a negative margin at retail. However, when I do this, we may be losing as an organization as a whole."

"I agree with Amy on this," stated Walker, "and I have the same problem with dealer-installed options. When I am charged full price for options, I have no incentive to try to sell these items."

"Hold on," said the service department manager. "I make my profit by selling service, and these are the prices I would charge for outside work. To sell service for a lower price inside defeats the purpose of this profit center idea. But I do have a problem with getting full price for parts. The demand for parts is derived almost completely from service, and we are dependent on parts for quick delivery for repairs."

Liddy jumped back in. "Obviously, we are dependent on each other for quality and prompt service. We need to make sure that, as each of you maximizes profits in your departments, you do not negatively affect other departments."

Liddy continued, "I am also concerned about the impact of capitalizing trade-in repairs rather than expensing immediately. We all know that wholesale values drop with each publication of the new guidebook. I am afraid that, when a car is slow to sell, we might be reluctant to sell the car at a loss, even though we should. Car inventory ties up cash, and a key measure of departmental success is our inventory turnover [average industry inventory turnover was 75 days for new cars and 45 days for used cars]. In conclusion, while I think the profit center concept makes good sense for this business, I am concerned about the frictions that are taking place between the departments."

Questions

1. Using the data in the transaction, compute the profitability of this one transaction to the new, used, parts, and service departments. Assume a sales commission of $250 for the trade-in on a selling price of $5,000.
   (Note: Use the following allocations [new, $835; used, $665; parts, $32; service, $114] for overhead expenses while computing the profitability of this one transaction. These overhead allocations are also shown as Note 13 to Exhibit 3.)

2. How should the transfer-pricing system operate for each department (market price, full retail, full cost, variable cost)?

3. If it were found one week later that the trade-in could be wholesaled for only $3,000, which manager should take the loss?

4. North Country incurred a year-to-date loss of about $59,000 *before* allocation of fixed costs on the wholesaling of used cars (see Note 2 to Exhibit 3). Wholesaling of used cars is theoretically supposed to be a break-even operation. Where do you think the problem lies?

5. Should profit centers be evaluated on gross profit or "full cost" profit?

6. What advice do you have for the owners?

Case 5–3
Polysar Limited

As soon as Pierre Choquette received the September report of operations for NASA Rubber (Exhibits 1 and 2), he called Alf Devereux, controller, and Ron Britton, sales manager, into his office to discuss the year-to-date results. Next week, he would make his presentation to the board of directors, and the results for his division for the first nine months of the year were not as good as expected. Pierre knew that the NASA management team had performed well. Sales volume was up and feedstock costs were down, resulting in a gross margin that was better than budget. Why did the bottom line look so bad?

As the three men worked through the numbers, their discussion kept coming back to the fixed costs of the butyl rubber plant. Fixed costs were high. The plant had yet to reach capacity. The European division had taken less output than projected.

Still, Choquette felt that these factors were outside his control. His division had performed well—it just didn't show in the profit results.

Choquette knew that Henderson, his counterpart in Europe, did not face these problems. The European rubber profits would be compared to those of NASA. How would the board react to the numbers he had to work with? He would need to educate them in his presentation, especially concerning the volume variance. He knew that many of the board members would not understand what that number represented or that it was due in part to the actions of Henderson's group.

Pierre Choquette, Alf Devereux, and Ron Britton decided to meet the next day to work on a strategy for the board presentation.

This case was prepared by Robert L. Simons, Harvard Business School. Copyright by the President and Fellows of Harvard College. Harvard Business School case 187–098.

Polysar Limited

In 1986, Polysar Limited was Canada's largest chemical company, with $1.8 billion in annual sales. Based in Sarnia, Ontario, Polysar was the world's largest producer of synthetic rubber and latex and a major producer of basic petrochemicals and fuel products.

Polysar was established in 1942 to meet wartime needs for a synthetic substitute for natural rubber. The supply of natural rubber to the Allied forces had been interrupted by the declaration of war against the United States by Japan in December 1941. During 1942 and 1943, 10 synthetic rubber plants were built by the governments of the United States and Canada, including the Polysar plant in Sarnia.

After the war, the supply of natural rubber was again secure, and the nine US plants were sold to private industry or closed. Polysar remained in operation as a Crown Corporation, wholly owned by the government of Canada. In 1972, by an act of Parliament, the Canada Development Corporation (CDC) was created as a government-owned venture capital company to encourage Canadian business development; at that time, the equity shares of Polysar were transferred to the Canada Development Corporation. In 1986, Polysar remained wholly owned by the CDC; however, in a government sponsored move to privatization, the majority of the shares of the CDC were sold to the Canadian public in the period 1982 to 1985.

Through acquisition and internal growth, Polysar had grown considerably from its original single plant. Polysar now employed 6,650 people, including 3,100 in Canada, 1,050 in the United States, and 2,500 in Europe and elsewhere. The company operated 20 manufacturing plants in Canada, United States, Belgium, France, The Netherlands, and West Germany.

Exhibit 1   Regular Butyl Rubber Statistics and Analyses: NASA Rubber Division

	9 Months Ended September 30, 1986		
Volume (Tonnes)	*Actual (000s)*	*Budget (000s)*	*Deviation (000s)*
Sales	35.8	33.0	2.8
Production	47.5	55.0	−7.5
Transfers:			
To EROW	12.2	19.5	−7.3
From EROW	2.1	1.0	1.1
Fixed Production Costs	*($000s)*	*($000s)*	*($000s)*
Fixed cost—Direct	−21,466	−21,900	434
Allocated cash	−7,036	−7,125	89
Allocated noncash	−15,625	−15,600	−25
Fixed cost to production	−44,127	−44,625	498
Transfers to/from FG inventory	1,120	2,450	−1,330
Transfers to EROW	8,540	13,650	−5,110
Transfers from EROW	−1,302	−620	−682
Fixed cost of sales	−35,769	−29,145	−6,624

Note: As indicated previously, financial data have been disguised and do not represent the true financial results of the company.

Structure

The operations of the company were structured into three groups: basic petrochemicals, rubber, and diversified products (Exhibit 3).

Basic Petrochemicals.   Firman Bentley, 51, was group vice president of Basic Petrochemicals. This business unit produced primary petrochemicals, such as ethylene, as well as intermediate products, such as propylene, butadiene, and styrene monomers. Group sales in 1985 were approximately $800 million, of which $500 million was sold to outside customers, and the remainder was sold as intermediate feedstock to Polysar's downstream operations.

Rubber.   The Rubber Group was headed by Charles Ambridge, 61, group vice president.

Exhibit 2   Regular Butyl Rubber Statement of Net Contribution: NASA Rubber Division

	9 Months Ended September 30, 1986		
	Actual ($000s)	*Budget ($000s)*	*Deviation ($000s)*
Sales revenue—Third party	$65,872	$61,050	$ 4,822
Diversified products group	160	210	−50
Total	66,032	61,260	4,772
Delivery cost	−2,793	−2,600	−193
Net sales revenue	63,239	58,660	4,579
Variable costs:			
Standard	−22,589	−21,450	−1,139
Cost adjustments	54	—	54
Efficiency variance	241	—	241
Total	−22,294	−21,450	−844
Gross margin—$	40,945	37,210	3,735
Fixed costs:			
Standard	−25,060	−23,100	−1,960
Cost adjustments	168	80	88
Spending variance	498	–	498
Volume variance	−11,375	−6,125	−5,250
Total	−35,769	−29,145	−6,624
Gross profit—$	5,176	8,065	−2,889
% of NSR	8.2%	13.7%	5.5%
Period costs:			
Administration, selling, distribution	−4,163	−4,000	−163
Technical service	−222	−210	−12
Other income expense . .	208	50	158
Total	−4,177	−4,160	−17
Business contribution . .	999	3,905	−2,906
Interest on working capital	– 1,875	– 1,900	25
Net contribution	−876	2,005	−2,881

Note: As indicated previously, financial data have been disguised and do not represent the true financial results of the company.

Exhibit 3

Partial organization chart

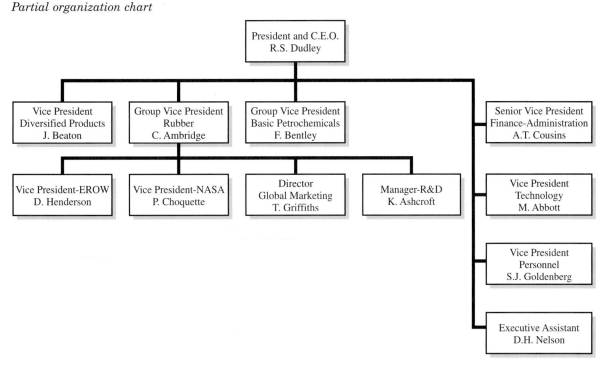

Polysar held 9 percent of the world synthetic rubber market (excluding Communist bloc countries). As the largest group in the company, Rubber Group produced 46 percent of Polysar sales. Major competitors included Goodyear, Bayer, Exxon, and Du Pont.

Rubber products, such as butyl and halobutyl, were sold primarily to manufacturers of automobile tires (six of the world's largest tire companies[1] accounted for 70 percent of the world butyl and halobutyl demand); other uses included belting, footwear, adhesives, hose, seals, plastics modification, and chewing gum.

The rubber group was split into two operating divisions that were managed as profit centers:

NASA (North and South America) and EROW (Europe and rest of world). In addition to the two operating profit centers, the rubber group included a global marketing department and a research division. The costs of these departments were not charged to the two operating profit centers, but instead, were charged against group profits.

Diversified Products.   John Beaton, 48, was vice president of diversified products, a group that consisted of the latex, plastics, and specialty products divisions. This group was composed of high-technology product categories that were expected to double sales within five years. In 1985, the group provided 27 percent of Polysar's sales revenue.

Bentley, Ambridge, and Beaton reported to Robert Dudley, 60, president and chief executive officer.

---

[1]Michelin, Goodyear, Bridgestone, Firestone, Pirelli, and Dunlop.

EXHIBIT 4

Rubber production process

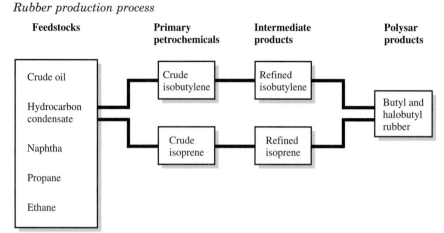

Rubber Group

A key component of Polysar's strategy was to be a leader in high-margin specialty rubbers. The leading products in this category were the butyl and halobutyl rubbers. Attributes of butyl rubber include low permeability to gas and moisture, resistance to steam and weathering, high energy absorption, and chemical resistance. Butyl rubber was traditionally used in inner tubes and general-purpose applications. Halobutyl rubber, a modified derivative, possesses the same attributes as regular butyl, with additional properties that allow bonding to other materials. Thus, halobutyls were used extensively as liners and sidewalls in tubeless tires.

Butyl and halobutyl rubber were manufactured from feedstocks, such as crude oil, naphtha, butane, propane, and ethane (Exhibit 4). Polysar manufactured butyl rubbers at two locations: NASA division's Sarnia plant and EROW division's Antwerp plant.

NASA Butyl Plant

The original Sarnia plant, built in 1942, manufactured regular butyl until 1972. At that time, market studies predicted rapid growth in the demand for high-quality radial tires manufactured with halobutyl. Demand for regular butyl was predicted to remain steady, since poor road conditions in many countries of the world necessitated the use of tires with inner tubes. In 1972, the Sarnia plant was converted to allow production of halobutyls as well as regular butyl.

By the 1980s, demand for halobutyl had increased to the point that Polysar forecast capacity constraints. During 1983 and 1984, the company built a second plant at Sarnia, known as Sarnia 2, to produce regular butyl. The original plant, Sarnia 1, was then dedicated solely to the production of halobutyl.

Sarnia 2, with a capital cost of $550 million, began full operations late in 1984. Its annual nameplate (i.e., design) production capacity for regular butyl was 95,000 tonnes. During 1985, the plant produced 65,000 tonnes.

EROW Butyl Plant

The EROW division's butyl plant was located in Antwerp, Belgium. Built in 1964 as a regular butyl unit, the plant was modified in 1979–80 to allow it to produce halobutyl as well as regular butyl.

The annual nameplate production capacity of the Antwerp plant was 90,000 tonnes. In 1985, as in previous years, the plant operated near or at its nameplate capacity. The Antwerp plant was operated to meet fully the halobutyl demand of EROW customers; the remainder of capacity was used to produce regular butyl.

In 1981, the plant's output was 75 percent regular butyl and 25 percent halobutyl; by 1985, halobutyl represented 50 percent of the plant's production. Since regular butyl demand outpaced the plant's remaining capacity, EROW took its regular butyl shortfall from the Sarnia 2 plant; in 1985, 21,000 tonnes of regular butyl were shipped from NASA to EROW.

Product Scheduling

Although NASA served customers in North and South America and EROW serviced customers in Europe and the rest of the world, regular butyl could be shipped from either the Sarnia 2 or Antwerp plant. NASA shipped approximately one-third of its regular butyl output to EROW. Also, customers in distant locations could receive shipments from either plant due to certain cost or logistical advantages. For example, Antwerp sometimes shipped to Brazil and Sarnia sometimes shipped to the Far East.

A global marketing department worked with regional directors of marketing and regional product managers to coordinate product flows. Three sets of factors influenced these analyses. First, certain customers demanded products from a specific plant, due to slight product differences resulting from the type of feedstock used and the plant configuration. Second, costs varied between Sarnia and Antwerp, due to differences in variable costs (primarily feedstock and energy), shipping, and currency rates. Finally, inventory levels, production interruptions, and planned shutdowns were considered.

In September and October of each year, NASA and EROW division prepared production estimates for the upcoming year. These estimates were based on estimated sales volumes and plant loadings (i.e., capacity utilization). Since

the Antwerp plant operated at capacity, the planning exercise was largely for the benefit of the managers of the Sarnia 2 plant, who needed to know how much regular butyl Antwerp would need from the Sarnia 2 plant.

Product Costing and Transfer Prices

Butyl rubbers were costed using standard rates for variable and fixed costs.

Variable costs included feedstocks, chemicals, and energy. Standard variable cost per tonnes of butyl was calculated by multiplying a standard utilization factor (i.e., the standard quantity of inputs used) by a standard price established for each unit of input. Since feedstock prices varied with worldwide market conditions and represented the largest component of costs, it was impossible to establish standard input prices that remained valid for extended periods. Therefore, the company reset feedstock standard costs each month to a price that reflected market prices. Chemical and energy standard costs were established annually. A purchase price variance (were input prices above or below standard prices?) and an efficiency variance (did production require more or less inputs than standard?) were calculated for variable costs each accounting period.

Fixed costs comprised three categories of cost. Direct costs included direct labor, maintenance, chemicals required to keep the plant bubbling, and fixed utilities. Allocated cash costs included plant management, purchasing department costs, engineering, planning, and accounting. Allocated noncash costs represented primarily depreciation.

Fixed costs were allocated to production based on a plant's "demonstrated capacity" using the following formula:

$$\text{Standard fixed cost per tonne} = \frac{\text{Estimated annual total fixed costs}}{\text{Annual demonstrated plant capacity}}$$

To apply the formula, production estimates were established each fall for the upcoming year. Then, the amount of total fixed costs applicable to this level of production was estimated. The amount of total fixed cost to be allocated to each tonne of output was calculated by dividing total fixed cost by the plant's demonstrated capacity. Exhibit 5 reproduces a section of the controller's guide that defines demonstrated capacity.

Each accounting period, two variances were calculated for fixed costs. The first was a spending variance calculated as the simple difference between actual total fixed costs and estimated total fixed costs. The second variance was a volume variance calculated using the formula:

$$\text{Volume variance} =$$
$$\text{Standard fixed cost per tonne} \times$$
$$\text{Actual tonnes} - \text{Demonstrated capacity}$$

Product transfers between divisions for performance accounting purposes were made at standard full cost, representing, for each tonne, the sum of standard variable cost and standard fixed cost.

Compensation

Employees at Polysar in the past had been paid by fixed salary, with little use of bonuses except at the executive level of the company. In 1984, a bonus system was instituted throughout the company to link pay with performance and strengthen the profit center orientation.

Nonmanagement Employees. The bonus system varied by employee group but was developed with the intention of paying salaries that were approximately 5 percent less than those paid by a reference group of 25 major Canadian manufacturing companies. To augment salaries, annual bonuses were awarded in amounts up to 12 percent of salary, based on corporate and divisional performance. Hourly workers could receive annual bonuses in similar proportions based on performance. All bonuses were based on achieving or exceeding budgeted profit targets. For salaried workers, for example, meeting the 1985 corporate profit objective would result in a 5 percent bonus; an additional $25 million in profits would provide an additional 4 percent bonus. Meeting and exceeding division profit targets could provide an additional 3 percent bonus.

Using periodic accounting information, divisional vice presidents met in quarterly communication meetings with salaried and wage employees to discuss divisional and corporate performance levels.

Management. For managers, the percent of remuneration received through annual bonuses was greater than 12 percent and increased with responsibility levels.

The bonuses of top division management in 1985 were calculated by a formula that awarded 50 percent of bonus potential to meeting or exceeding divisional profit targets and 50 percent to meeting or exceeding corporate profit targets.

Interviews with Rubber Group Vice Presidents[2]

Pierre Choquette. Pierre Choquette, 43, was vice president[3] of the NASA Rubber Division. A professional engineer, Choquette had begun his career with Polysar in plant management. Over the years, he had assumed responsibilities for product management in the United States,

---

[2] Pierre Choquette was interviewed at Harvard Business School in 1985; Doug Henderson was interviewed at Harvard in 1986. Both men were attending the 13-week Advanced Management Program that was developed to strengthen the management skills of individuals with potential to become chief executive officers of their companies. In addition to Choquette and Henderson, Polysar had sent Firman Bentley to the program in 1984.

[3] Due to its relatively large size, Rubber Group was the only group with regional vice presidents. Regional responsibilities of the Basic Petrochemicals Group and the Diversified Products Group were managed by lower-ranking general managers.

EXHIBIT 5 **Controller's Guide**

Polysar	NUMBER:	03:02

	PAGE 1 of 14 PAGES.	

Subject	NEW:	REPLACES
Accounting for Inventories	X	

	ISSUE DATE: Jan. 1/81

ISSUED BY: Director Accounting	Authorized By: Corporate Controller

Purpose

To set out criteria and guidelines for the application of the company's accounting policy for inventories:

> "Inventories are valued at the lower of FIFO (first-in, first-out) cost and net realizable value except for raw materials and supplies which are valued at the lower of FIFO cost and replacement cost."

Specific exclusion

This release does not apply to SWAP transactions.

Definitions

By-products—one or more products of relatively small per unit market value that emerge from the production process of a product or products of greater value.

Cost system—a system to facilitate the classification, recording, analysis and interpretation of data pertaining to the production and distribution of products and services.

Demonstrated capacity is the actual annualized production of a plant which was required to run full out within the last fiscal year for a sufficiently long period to assess production capability after adjusting for abnormally low or high unscheduled shutdowns, scheduled shutdowns, and unusual or annualized items which impacted either favorably or unfavorably on the period's production. The resulting adjusted historical base should be further modified for changes planned to be implemented within the current fiscal year.

    a. Where a plant has been required to run full out within the last fiscal year, production data may be used for a past period after adjusting for changes (debottleneckings/inefficiencies) since that time affecting production.

    b. Where a plant has never been required to run full out, demonstrated capacity could be reasonably considered as "name plate" capacity after adjusting for

        (1.) Known invalid assumptions in arriving at "name plate."
        (2.) Changes to original design affecting "name plate."
        (3.) A reasonable negative allowance for error.

managed a small subsidiary, managed a European plant, and directed European sales.

This business is managed on price and margin. Quality, service, and technology are also important, but it is difficult to differentiate ourselves from other competitors on these dimensions.

When the price of oil took off, this affected our feedstock prices drastically, and Polysar's worldwide business suffered. Now that prices are back down, we are trying to regroup our efforts and bring the business back to long-term health. Polysar will break even in 1985 and show a normal profit again in 1986. Of course, the Rubber Division will, as in the past, be the major producer of profit for the company.

As you know, this is a continuous process industry. The plant is computerized so that we need the same number of people and incur most of the same overhead costs whether the plant is running fast or slow.

The regular butyl plant, Sarnia 2, is running at less than capacity. Although the plant should be able to produce 95,000 tonnes, its demonstrated capacity is 85,000. Last year, we produced 65,000. This leaves us sitting with a lot of unabsorbed fixed costs, especially when you consider depreciation charges.

Still, NASA Rubber has been growing nicely. I think this is in part due to our strong commitment to run the Divisions as profit centers. We have been pushing hard to build both volume and efficiency, and I am pleased that our programs and incentives are paying off.

Our transfers to EROW are still a problem. Since the transfers are at standard cost and are not recorded as revenue, these transfers do nothing for our profit. Also, if they cut back on orders, our profit is hurt through the volume variance. Few of our senior managers truly understand the volume variance and why profit results are so different in the two regions. The accounting is not a problem, but having to continuously explain it to very senior-level managers is. It always comes down to the huge asset that we carry whether the plant is at capacity or not.

We run our businesses on return on net assets, which looks ridiculous for NASA. I worry that, if I am not around to explain it, people will form the wrong conclusion about the health of the business. Also, you sometimes wonder if people ascribe results to factors that are outside your control.

Doug Henderson.   Doug Henderson, 46, vice president of EROW Rubber Division, was also a professional engineer. His career included man-

Exhibit 6   Schedule of Regular Butyl Shipments from NASA to EROW

	Actual Tonnes	Budget Tonnes
1985	21,710	23,500
1984	12,831	13,700
1983	1,432	4,000
1982	792	600
1981	1,069	700

agement responsibilities in plant operations, market research, venture analysis and corporate planning, running a small regional business in Canada, and director of European sales.

The Antwerp plant produces about 45,000 tonnes of halobutyl and 45,000 tonnes of regular butyl each year. In addition, we import approximately 15,000 to 20,000 tonnes of regular butyl from Sarnia each year [Exhibit 6].

We inform Sarnia each fall of our estimated regular butyl needs. These estimates are based on our predictions of butyl and halobutyl sales and how hard we can load our plant. The overall sales estimates are usually within 10 percent, say plus or minus 8,000 tonnes, unless an unexpected crisis occurs.

The EROW business has been extremely successful since I arrived here in 1982. We have increased our share in the high-growth halobutyl market; the plant is running well; and we have kept the operation simple and compact.

Looking at our Statement of Net Contribution (Exhibit 7), our margins are better than NASA's. For one thing, there is a great surplus of feedstock in Europe, and we benefit from lower prices. Also, market dynamics are substantially different.

We pay a lot of attention to plant capacity. For example, we budgeted to produce 250 tonnes per day this year, and we have got it up to 275. We are also working hard to reduce our "off-spec" material as a way of pushing up our yield. If we can produce more, it's free—other than variable cost, it goes right to the bottom line.

Given these factors, Pierre loves it when I tell him jokingly that our success at EROW is attributable to superb management.

EXHIBIT 7 **Regular Butyl Rubber Condensed Statement of Net Contribution: EROW Rubber Division**

	9 Months Ended September 30, 1986 ($000s)
Sales volume—tonnes	47,850
Sales revenue	$94,504
Delivery cost	−4,584
Net sales revenue	89,920
Variable cost:	
Standard	−28,662
Purchase price variance	203
Inventory revaluation	−46
Efficiency variance	32
Total	−28,473
Gross margin	$61,447
Fixed cost to production:	
Depreciation	−4,900
Other	−16,390
	−21,290
Transfers to/from F. G. inventory	−775
Transfers to/from NASA	−7,238
	−29,303
Gross profit	$32,144
Period costs	−7,560
Business contribution	24,584
Interest on W/C	−1,923
Net contribution	$22,661

Notes: 1. Fixed costs are allocated between regular butyl production (above) and halobutyl production (reported separately).

2. Financial data have been disguised and do not represent the true financial results of the company.

Questions

1. Prepare a presentation for the Polysar board of directors to review the performance of the NASA Rubber Division. Pay particular attention to questions that may be raised concerning the accuracy and meaning of the volume variance.

2. What is the best sales and production strategy for EROW Division? NASA Division? Rubber Group in total?

3. What changes, if any, would you recommend be made in the management accounting performance system to improve the reporting and evaluation of Rubber Group performance?

Case 5–4
Abrams Company

Abrams Company manufactured a wide variety of parts for use in automobiles, trucks, buses, and farm equipment. There were three major groups of parts: ignition parts, transmission parts, and engine parts. Abrams' parts were sold both to original equipment manufacturers (OEMs) and to wholesalers. The wholesalers, in turn, resold the parts to retailers who sold them as replacement parts to consumers. The latter market was called the "aftermarket" (AM).

Product and Marketing Divisions

As shown in the partial organization chart in Exhibit 1, Abrams had a "product division" for each of its three part groups. Each of these product divisions was managed by a vice president and general manager who was expected to earn a target return on investment (ROI). Each product division manufactured parts in several plants and sold a major portion of its manufactured parts to OEMs. Each product division had its separate OEM sales department (see Exhibit 1) that worked closely with OEMs to develop new products or change existing products. The remaining manufactured parts were sold by the product division to Abrams' fourth division called the AM Marketing Division (see Exhibit 1) or "AM Division," as it was known to managers. This division was also managed by a vice president and general manager and was solely responsible for marketing Abrams' entire line of parts to AM wholesalers. The AM division operated several company-owned parts distribution warehouses in the US and foreign markets. The AM division was also expected to earn an annual return on investment target.

This case was adapted (with permission) by Professor J. G. San Miguel from a case written by Professor J. S. Reece of the University of Michigan. Copyright © by Joe San Miguel and Jim Reece.

Inside and Outside Sales

In 1992, the four divisions' sales totaled $500 million, which included "inside" sales of $100 million from the three product divisions to the AM division. The $500 million sales were recorded as approximately $130 million for the ignition parts division, $100 million for the transmission parts division, $90 million for the engine parts division, and $180 million for the AM division. After elimination of inside sales, Abrams' outside sales totaled about $400 million. Because of anticipated growth in the parts' aftermarket due to the increase in the number of vehicles being driven and their ages, one of top management's goals for the AM Division was for its sales to reach 50 percent of Abrams' total outside sales.

ROI for the Manufacturing Plants

Continuing the company's ROI strategy, each manufacturing plant within the three product divisions had an annual ROI target to meet. Each product division's OEM sales were traced to the plants that made the parts. The plants maintained finished goods inventories and shipped parts directly to OEM customers. A plant's ROI target was based on budgeted profit (including allocations of division and corporate overhead expenses and an imputed income tax expense) divided by actual beginning-of-the-year net assets (defined as total assets less current liabilities). Exhibit 2 contains an example of the Rochester plant's actual 1992 ROI computation. Actual ROI was actual profit divided by actual beginning-of-the-year net assets.

Top management's stated reason for including allocated overhead expenses and taxes in determining profit was to have the plant profit figure resemble the profit calculation for external financial

Exhibit 1

Partial organization chart

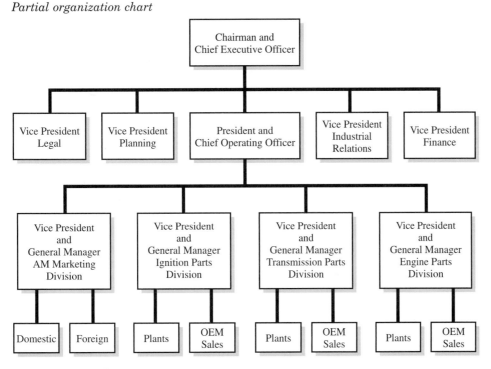

reports to shareholders. The CEO felt this gave a plant manager a clearer perspective of the costs of doing business, the plant's contribution to the corporate bottom line, and added more realism to the plant's results.

The beginning-of-the-year net assets amount was used in the ROI measurement because, in management's view, investment added during a given year resulted in little, if any, incremental profit in that year. The investment would likely increase future profits. Top management felt that such investments might not be proposed if managers were penalized (in the form of higher net assets and lower ROI) in the first year of the new investment. Because the investment base for the year was "frozen" at the beginning-of-the-year level, maximizing profit during the year was equivalent to maximizing ROI. For beginning-of-the-year net assets, cash and receivables were allocated to plants on the basis of sales rev-

enue, while inventories, property, plant, equipment, and current liabilities were traced specifically to each plant. Historical cost less accumulated depreciation (book value) was used to value property, plant, and equipment. The AM division's ROI was measured in the same manner as the plants' ROIs.

Marketing Strategies

The OEM sales department within each of the three product divisions worked with the OEM's engineers to develop innovative and cost-effective new parts to meet the customers' requirements and serviced customer accounts for parts already being supplied to the OEMs. Each of these OEM sales departments was expected to meet an annual sales revenue target. Because the product divisions' customers (OEMs) were different from the AM division's customers, top

EXHIBIT 2   Actual 1992 ROI Computation—Rochester Plant

Abrams Company—Transmission Parts Division
ROCHESTER PLANT
Profit and ROI Statement, December 31, 1992

Sales revenue	$124,866
Cost of goods sold	73,230
Gross margin	51,636
Operating expenses	20,792
Division expenses assigned	11,340
Corporate expenses assigned	3,420
Profit before taxes	16,084
Taxes imputed	4,825
Profit	$ 11,259

Net Assets Assigned as of January 1, 1992

Total Assets:	
Cash and receivables	$ 25,000
Inventories	12,875
Property, plant & equipment at book value	86,560
Total Assets	124,435
Less current liabilities	26,135
Net Assets	$ 98,300
Return on investment	11.5%

management did not feel that the OEM and aftermarket sales organizations should be combined. Even the three product divisions' OEM marketing efforts were not consolidated in one sales organization because each division's OEM marketers tended to work with different people within a given OEM's organization (i.e., ignition, transmission, and engines). Moreover, two of the three product divisions were independent companies before being acquired by Abrams. Thus, there was a long tradition of doing their own OEM marketing.

According to Abrams' executives, the factors critical to success in the OEM market were: the ability to design innovative and dependable parts that met the customer's quality, performance, and weight specifications; meeting delivery schedule requirements so that the OEM could minimize its own parts inventories; and controlling costs. Cost control was important because the market was very price competitive. In the aftermarket business, availability of parts was by far the most important factor to the wholesaler, followed by quality and price.

Incentive Compensation Plan

Approximately 50 Abrams line and staff managers participated in an incentive bonus plan. The dollar amount of the corporate-wide bonus pool was established by a fixed formula linked to corporate earnings per share. Each participant in the bonus plan received a number of standard bonus points. The higher the participant was in the organizational hierarchy, the more standard points he or she received. The total of these points for all participants was divided into the total bonus pool amount to arrive at a standard dollar award per point. Then, this standard rate was multiplied by the participant's number of standard points to arrive at the participant's standard bonus dollars. However, the actual bonus could vary (upward or downward) by as much as 25 percent at the discretion of the participant's superiors.

In the case of a plant manager, the standard award also was adjusted by a formula that related percent of standard award to the plant's profit variance (budget versus actual profit). For example, if the plant's actual profit for the year exceeded its budgeted profit by 4 percent, the plant manager's bonus was raised from 100 percent of standard to 110 percent of standard. In making this bonus adjustment, the plant's actual profit was adjusted for any favorable or unfavorable gross margin variance caused by sales volume to the AM division being higher or lower than budgeted. For example, if a plant's favorable profit variance was attributable to a favorable gross margin volume variance on sales to the AM division, the plant manager's bonus would not be raised above 100 percent of standard. Similarly, the plant manager would not be penalized if the AM division actually purchased less from the plant than the amount that was agreed to by AM division when the plant's annual profit budget was approved by top management.

Management Comments

In general, top management was satisfied with the present management systems and performance measurement scheme. In discussions with the casewriter, however, they mentioned three areas of concern.

First, there always seemed to be a few disputes over transfer prices of parts sold by the product divisions to the AM division. Whenever possible, by corporate policy, internal sales of parts were made at outside OEM market prices. If a part had been sold as an OEM part several years earlier, the original OEM market price was adjusted upward for inflation to arrive at the sales price to the AM division. This procedure caused virtually no disputes. Problems occurred when the part being transferred was strictly an AM division part. That is, it was a part never sold by Abrams in the OEM market and for which there was neither a current OEM outside market price nor a former OEM market price that could be adjusted for inflation. Usually, such transfer price issues were resolved by the two divisions involved, but occasionally the vice president of finance was asked to arbitrate a dispute.

Second, top management felt that the product divisions too often tended to treat the AM division as a captive customer. For example, when the AM division and an outside OEM customer were placing competing demands on a specific manufacturing plant, it appeared that the plant often favored the OEM customer because the OEM customer could take its business elsewhere, whereas the AM division could not purchase parts outside. Top management was not willing to let the AM division sell a competitor's product, feeling this would reflect adversely on the overall image of the company. The AM division was expected to convince the appropriate plant manager to undertake the manufacture of its part needs.

Third, top management felt that both the AM division and the three product divisions carried excessive inventories most of the year. The vice president of planning said, "Thank goodness we have a generous Christmas vacation policy here. At least the inventories get down to a reasonable level at year-end when our production volume is low because of a large number of employee holiday vacations."

Questions

1. Evaluate each of the concerns expressed by top management, and if necessary, make recommendations appropriate to the circumstances described in the case.

2. What is your overall evaluation of Abrams's management control system? Describe any strengths or weaknesses that you identified but did not include in answering the previous question. What changes, if any, would you recommend to top management?

TRANSFER PRICING

Today's organizational thinking is oriented toward decentralization. One of the principal challenges in operating a decentralized system is to devise a satisfactory method of accounting for the transfer of goods and services from one profit center to another in companies that have a significant amount of these transactions. In this chapter we discuss various approaches to arriving at transfer prices for transactions between profit centers and the system of negotiation and arbitration that is essential when transfer prices are used. We also discuss the pricing of services that corporate staff units furnish to profit centers. We discuss international transfer pricing in Chapter 16.

Objectives of Transfer Prices

If two or more profit centers are jointly responsible for product development, manufacturing, and marketing, each should share in the revenue that is generated when the product is finally sold. The transfer price is the mechanism for distributing this revenue. The transfer price is not primarily an accounting tool; rather, it is a behavioral tool that motivates managers to make the right decisions. In particular, the transfer price should be designed so that it accomplishes the following objectives:

- It should provide each segment with the relevant information required to determine the optimum trade-off between *company* costs and revenues.
- It should induce *goal congruent* decisions—that is, the system should be so designed that decisions that improve business unit profits will also improve company profits.
- It should help measure the *economic performance* of the individual profit centers.
- The system should be *simple* to understand and *easy* to administer.

EXHIBIT 6-1   Transfer of Products between Profit Centers

	Vancil (1979)	Govindarajan (1994)
Number of usable responses	291	638
Companies with two or more profit centers	274 (94%)	593 (93%)
Of the companies with two or more profit centers, companies that transfer products between profit centers	249 (91%)	470 (79%)

Sources: Richard F. Vancil, *Decentralization*, p. 169.
Vijay Govindarajan, "Profit Center Measurement," p. 2.

Designing transfer pricing systems is a key management control topic for most corporations; the Govindarajan survey[1] (see Exhibit 6–1) found that 79 percent of companies transfer products between profit centers.

Transfer Pricing Methods

Some writers use the term "transfer price" to refer to the amount used in accounting for *any* transfer of goods and services between responsibility centers. We use a somewhat narrower definition and limit the term *transfer price* to the value placed on a transfer of goods or services in transactions in which at least one of the two parties involved is a *profit center.* Such a price normally includes a profit element, because an independent company would not normally transfer goods or services to another independent company at cost or less. We, therefore, exclude the mechanics for the allocation of costs in a cost accounting system; such costs do not include a profit element. The term *price,* as used here, has the same meaning as it has when it is used in connection with transactions between independent companies.

Fundamental Principle

The fundamental principle is that the transfer price should be similar to the price that would be charged if the product were sold to outside customers or purchased from outside vendors. Application of this principle is complicated by the fact that there is much disagreement in the literature as to how outside selling prices are established. The classical economics literature states that selling prices should be equal to marginal costs, and some authors advocate a transfer price based on marginal cost.[2] This is unrealistic.

---

[1] Vijay Govindarajan, "Profit Center Measurement," p. 2.
[2] Jack Hirschleifer, "On the Economics of Transfer Pricing," *Journal of Business,* July 1956, pp. 172–84.

Few companies follow such a policy in arriving at either selling prices or transfer prices.[3]

Modern economics literature recognizes this fact; but there are few discussions of how to price individual jobs in a job order company (such as a printing shop), how to price "take-or-pay" contracts, or how to negotiate a discount from normal prices when a reduction is in the best interest of both parties. Thus, the transfer pricing literature is actually about pricing in general, modified slightly to take into account factors that are unique to internal transactions.

When profit centers of a company buy from and sell to one another, two decisions must be made periodically for each product that is being produced by one business unit and sold to another.

1. Should the company produce the product inside the company or purchase it from an outside vendor? This is the *sourcing decision*.
2. If produced inside, at what price should the product be transferred between profit centers? This is the *transfer price decision*.

Transfer price systems can range from the very simple to the extremely complex, depending on the nature of the business. We start with the ideal situation and then describe increasingly complex situations.

The Ideal Situation

A transfer price will induce goal congruence if all the conditions listed below exist. Rarely, if ever, will all these conditions exist in practice. The list, therefore, does not set forth criteria that must be met to have a transfer price. Rather, it suggests a way of looking at a situation to see what changes should be made to improve the operation of the transfer price mechanism.

Competent People.   Ideally, managers should be interested in the long-run as well as the short-run performances of their responsibility centers. Staff people involved in negotiation and arbitration of transfer prices also must be competent.

Good Atmosphere.   Managers must regard profitability as measured in their income statement as an important goal and as a significant consideration in the judgment of their performance. They should perceive that the transfer prices are just.

---

[3]A study by the authors of methods of arriving at market prices, with respondents from 501 of the Fortune 1,000 companies, reported that only 17 percent followed such a policy. (Vijay Govindarajan and Robert N. Anthony, "How Firms Use Cost Data in Pricing Decisions," *Management Accounting*, July 1983, pp. 30–34).

Authors sometimes ignore the results of research in their enthusiasm for the classical economics approach. For example, Benke and Edwards interviewed 19 companies and found that *none* of them based transfer prices on variable costs or opportunity costs. They nevertheless recommended a general rule that was based entirely on variable costs and opportunity costs. (Ralph L. Benke, Jr., and James Don Edwards, *Transfer Pricing: Techniques and Uses*, Institute of Management Accountants, 1980.)

A Market Price.   The ideal transfer price is based on a well-established, normal market price for the identical product being transferred—that is, a market price reflecting the same conditions (quantity, delivery time, and the like) as the product to which the transfer price applies. The market price may be adjusted downward to reflect savings accruing to the selling unit from dealing inside the company. For example, there would be no bad debt expense and smaller advertising and selling costs when products are transferred from one business unit to another within the company. Although less than ideal, a market price for a similar, but not identical, product is better than no market price at all.

Freedom to Source.   Alternatives should exist, and managers should be permitted to choose the alternative that is in their own best interest. The buying manager should be free to buy from the outside, and the selling manager should be free to sell outside. In these circumstances, the transfer price policy is simply to give the manager of each profit center the right to deal with either insiders or outsiders, at his or her discretion. The market thus establishes the transfer price. The decision of whether to deal inside or outside also is made by the marketplace. If buyers cannot get a satisfactory price from the inside source, they are free to buy from the outside.

   If the selling profit center can sell all of its products, either to insiders or to outsiders, and as long as the buying center can obtain all of its requirements from either outsiders or insiders, this method is optimum. The market price represents the opportunity cost to the seller of selling the product inside. This is so because, if the product were not sold inside, it would be sold outside. From a company point of view, therefore, the relevant cost of the product is the market price because that is the amount of cash that has been forgone by selling inside. The transfer price represents the opportunity cost to the company.

Full Flow of Information.   Managers must know about the available alternatives and the relevant costs and revenues of each.

Negotiation.   There must be a smoothly working mechanism for negotiating "contracts" between business units.

   If all of the above conditions are present, a transfer price system based on *market prices* would fulfill all of the objectives stated above, with no need for central administration. In the next subsection, we consider situations where one or more of these conditions are not present.

Constraints on Sourcing

Ideally, the buying manager should be given freedom to make sourcing decisions if the profit center is to operate in an entrepreneurial manner. Similarly, the selling manager should be free to sell products in the most advantageous market. However, in real life, freedom to source either might not be feasible or, even if it is feasible, might be constrained by corporate policy. We now consider the situations where profit center managers may not have the freedom to make sourcing decisions and the implications of constraints on sourcing on the appropriate transfer pricing policies.

Limited Markets.   In many companies, markets for the buying or selling profit centers may be limited. There are several reasons for this.

First, the existence of internal capacity might limit the development of external sales. If most of the large companies in an industry are highly integrated, as in the pulp and paper industry, there tends to be little independent production capacity for intermediate products. Thus, these producers can handle only a limited amount of demand from other producers. When internal capacity becomes tight, the market is quickly flooded with demands for the intermediate products. Even though outside capacity exists, it may not be available to the integrated company unless this capacity is used on a regular basis. If the integrated company does not purchase a product on a regular basis, it might have trouble obtaining it from the outside when the capacity is limited.

Second, if a company is the sole producer of a differentiated product, no outside capacity exists.

Third, if a company has made significant investment in facilities, it is unlikely to use outside sources even though outside capacity exists, unless the outside selling price approaches the company's variable cost, which is not usual. For practical purposes, the products produced are captive. Integrated oil companies are good examples of this: the producing unit may be required to send the crude oil to the refining unit, even though the former could potentially sell the crude oil in the open market.

Even in the case of limited markets, the transfer price that best satisfies the requirements of a profit center system is the *competitive* price. Competitive prices will measure the contribution of each profit center to the total company profits. In the case of an integrated oil company, use of the crude oil market prices is the most effective way of evaluating the extracting and refining units as if they were stand-alone businesses. If internal capacity were not available, the company would buy outside at the competitive price. The difference between the competitive price and the inside cost is the money saved by making instead of buying. Moreover, a competitive price measures how well a profit center may be performing against competition.

How does a company find out what the competitive price is, if it does not buy or sell the product in an outside market? Here are some ways.

1. *If published market prices* are available, they can be used to establish transfer prices. However, these should be prices actually paid in the marketplace, and the conditions that exist in the outside market should be consistent with those existing within the company. For example, market prices that are applicable to relatively small purchases (e.g., a "spot" market) would not be valid for measuring what is essentially a long-term commitment.

2. Market prices may be set by *bids*. This generally can be done only if the low bidder has a reasonable chance of obtaining the business. One company accomplishes this by buying about one-half of a particular group of products outside the company and one-half inside the company. The company puts *all* of the products out to bid, but selects one-half to stay inside. The company obtains valid bids, because low bidders can expect to get some of the business. By contrast, if a company requests bids solely to obtain a competitive price and does not award contracts to the low bidder, it will soon find that either no one bids or that the bids are of questionable value.

3. If the *production profit center* sells similar products in *outside markets,* it is often possible to replicate a competitive price on the basis of the outside price. For example, if a manufacturing profit center normally earns a 10 percent profit over standard cost on the products that it sells to outside markets, it can replicate a competitive price by adding 10 percent to the standard cost of its proprietary products.

4. If the *buying profit center* purchases similar products from the *outside* market, it may be possible to replicate competitive prices for its proprietary products. This can be done by calculating the cost of the difference in design and other conditions of sale between the competitive products and the proprietary products.

Excess or Shortage of Industry Capacity.   Suppose the selling profit center cannot sell to the outside market all it can produce—that is, it has excess capacity. The company may not optimize profits if the buying profit center purchased from outside vendors while capacity is available on the inside.

Conversely, suppose the buying profit center cannot obtain the product it requires from the outside, while the selling profit center is selling to the outside. This situation occurs when there is a shortage of capacity in the industry. In this case, the output of the buying profit center is constrained and, again, company profits may not be optimum.

If the amount of intracompany transfers is small or if the situation is temporary, many companies let buyers and sellers work out their own relationships without central intervention. Even if the amount of intracompany transfers is significant, some senior managements still do not intervene, on the theory that the benefits of keeping the profit centers independent offset the loss from suboptimizing company profits.

Some companies allow either the buying or the selling profit center to appeal a sourcing decision to a central person or a committee. For example, a selling profit center could appeal a buying profit center's decision to buy a product from outside when capacity was available inside. In the same way, a buying profit center could appeal a selling profit center's decision to sell outside. The person or group (hereafter called an *arbitration committee*) would, then, make the sourcing decision on the basis of the company's best interests. In every case, the transfer price would be the *competitive price*. In other words, the profit center is appealing only the sourcing decision. It must accept the product at the competitive price.

A word of caution is in order at this point. In some companies, given the option, buying profit centers prefer to deal with an outside source. One reason is service: outside sources may be perceived to provide better service. Another reason may be the internal rivalry that sometimes exists in divisionalized companies. For whatever reason, management should be aware of the strong political overtones that sometimes occur in transfer price negotiations. There is no guarantee that a profit center will voluntarily buy from the inside source when excess capacity exists.

To conclude, even if there are constraints on sourcing, the market price is the best transfer price. *If the market price exists or can be approximated, use it.* However, if there is no way of approximating valid competitive prices, the other option is to develop *cost-based* transfer prices. These are discussed in the next section.

Cost-Based Transfer Prices

If competitive prices are not available, transfer prices may be set up on the basis of cost plus a profit, even though such transfer prices may be complex to calculate and the results less satisfactory than a market-based price. Two decisions must be made in a cost-based transfer price system: (1) How to define cost? and (2) How to calculate the profit markup?

The Cost Basis.   *The usual basis is standard cost.* Actual costs should not be used because production inefficiencies will then be passed on to the buying profit center. If standard costs are used, there is a need to provide an incentive to set tight standards and to improve standards.

Some companies have tried using "efficient producer" costs, but someone has to decide what these costs are, which is difficult.

Under both cost-plus pricing and market-based pricing, companies typically eliminate advertising, financing, or other expenses that the seller does not incur on internal transactions. (This is similar to the practice when two outside companies are arriving at a price. The buyer ordinarily will not pay for cost components that do not apply to the contract.)

The Profit Markup.   In calculating the profit markup, there also are two decisions: (1) On what is the profit markup to be based? and (2) What is the level of profit allowed?

The simplest and most widely used base is a *percentage of costs.* If this base is used, however, no account is taken of capital required. A conceptually better base is a *percentage of investment,* but there may be a major practical problem in calculating the investment applicable to a given product. If the historical cost of the fixed assets is used, new facilities designed to reduce prices could actually increase costs because old assets are undervalued.

The second problem with the profit allowance is the amount of the profit. Senior management's perception of the financial performance of a profit center will be affected by the profit it shows. Consequently, to the extent possible, the profit allowance should be the best approximation of the rate of return that would be earned if the business unit were an independent company, selling to outside customers. The conceptual solution is to base the profit allowance on the investment required to meet the volume needed by the buying profit centers. The investment would be calculated at a "standard" level, with fixed assets and inventories at current replacement costs. This solution is complicated and, therefore, rarely used in practice.

Upstream Fixed Costs and Profits

Transfer pricing can create a significant problem in integrated companies. The profit center that finally sells to the outside customer may not even be aware of the amount of upstream fixed costs and profit included in its internal purchase price. Even if the final profit center were aware of these costs and profit, it might be reluctant to reduce its own profit to optimize company profit. Methods that companies use to mitigate this problem are described below.

Agreement among Business Units. A company could establish a formal mechanism whereby representatives from the buying and selling units meet periodically to decide on outside selling prices and on the sharing of profits for products having significant amounts of upstream fixed costs and profit. This mechanism is workable only if the review process is limited to decisions that involve a significant amount of business to at least one of the profit centers; otherwise, the value of these negotiations may not be worth the effort.

Two-Step Pricing. Another way to handle this problem is to establish a transfer price that includes two charges. First, a charge is made for each unit sold that is equal to the *standard variable cost* of production. Second, a periodic (usually monthly) charge is made that is equal to the *fixed costs* associated with the facilities reserved for the buying unit. One or both of these components should include a profit margin. For example, assume the conditions in Exhibit 6–2.

In this method, the transfer price of $11 per unit is a variable cost so far as Unit Y is concerned. However, the company's variable cost for product A is $5 per unit. Thus, Unit Y does not have the right information to make appropriate short-term marketing decisions. For example, if Unit Y knew the company's variable costs, it could safely take business at less than its normal price under certain conditions.

The two-step pricing method corrects this problem by transferring variable cost on a per unit basis, and transferring fixed cost and profit on a lump sum basis. Under this method, the transfer price for product A would be $5 for each unit that Unit Y purchases plus $20,000 per month for fixed cost, plus $10,000 per month for profit:

$$\frac{\$1,200,000}{12} \times 0.10$$

EXHIBIT 6–2   Two-Step Pricing: Assumed Situation

Business Unit X (manufacturer)	*Product A*
Expected monthly sales to Business Unit Y	5,000 units
Variable cost per unit	$ 5
Monthly fixed costs assigned to product	20,000
Investment in working capital and facilities	1,200,000
Competitive return on investment per year	10%

One way to transfer product A to Business Unit Y is at a price per unit, calculated as follows:

	Transfer Price for Product A
Variable cost per unit	$ 5
Plus fixed cost per unit	4
Plus profit per unit*	2
Transfer price per unit	$ 11

---

*10% of monthly investment per unit = $\dfrac{(\$1,200,000/12) \times 0.10}{5,000}$

If transfers of product A in a certain month are at the expected amount of 5,000 units, then, under the two-step method, Unit Y will pay the variable cost of $25,000 (5,000 units × $5 per unit) plus $30,000 for fixed costs and profit, a total of $55,000. This is the same amount as the amount it would pay Unit X if the transfer price were $11 per unit (5,000 × $11 = $55,000). If transfers in another month were less than 5,000 units, say 4,000 units, Unit Y would pay $50,000 [(4,000 × 5) + $30,000] under the two-step method, compared with the $44,000 it would pay if the transfer price were $11 per unit (4,000 × $11 = $44,000). The difference is its penalty for not using a portion of Unit X's capacity that it has reserved. Conversely, Unit Y would pay less under the two-step method if the transfer were more than 5,000 units in a given month; this represents the savings that Unit X would have because it could produce the additional units without incurring additional fixed costs.

Note that under two-step pricing, the company's variable cost for product A is identical to Unit Y's variable cost for this product, and Unit Y will make the correct short-term marketing decisions. Unit Y also has information on upstream fixed costs and profit relating to product A, and it can use these data for long-term decisions.

The fixed-cost calculation in the two-step pricing method is based on the capacity that is reserved for the production of product A that is sold to Unit Y. The investment represented by this capacity is allocated to product A. The return on investment that Unit X earns on competitive (and, if possible, comparable) products is calculated and multiplied by the investment assigned to the product.

In the example, we calculated the profit allowance as a fixed monthly amount. It would be appropriate under some circumstances to divide the investment into variable (e.g., receivables and inventory) and fixed (e.g., plant) components. Then, a profit allowance based on a return on the variable assets would be added to the standard variable cost for each unit sold.

Following are some points to consider about the two-step pricing method.

- The monthly charge for fixed costs and profit should be negotiated periodically and would depend on the capacity reserved for the buying unit.
- Some questions may be raised about the accuracy of the cost and investment allocation. In some situations, there is no great difficulty in assigning costs and assets to individual products. In any event, approximate accuracy is adequate. The principal problem usually is not the allocation technique; rather, it is the decision about how much capacity is to be reserved for the various products. Moreover, if capacity is reserved for a group of products sold to the same business unit, there is no need to allocate fixed costs and investments to individual products in the group.
- Under this pricing system, the manufacturing unit's profit performance is not affected by the sales volume of the final unit, which solves the problem that arises when other business units' marketing efforts affect the profit performance of a purely manufacturing unit.
- There could be a conflict between the interests of the manufacturing unit and the interests of the company. If capacity is limited, the manufacturing unit could increase its profit by using the capacity to produce parts for outside sale, if it is advantageous to do so. (This weakness is mitigated by stipulating that the marketing unit has first claim on the capacity it has contracted for.)
- This method is similar to the "take or pay" pricing that is frequently used in public utilities, pipelines, coal mining companies, and other long-term contracts.

Profit Sharing.   If the two-step pricing system just described is not feasible, a *profit sharing system* might be used to ensure congruence of business unit interest with company interest. This system operates somewhat as follows.

1. The product is transferred to the marketing unit at standard variable cost.
2. After the product is sold, the business units share the contribution earned, which is the selling price minus the variable manufacturing and marketing costs.

This method of pricing may be appropriate if the demand for the manufactured product is not steady enough to warrant the permanent assignment of facilities, as in the two-step method. In general, this method accomplishes the purpose of making the marketing unit's interest congruent with the company's.

There are several practical problems in implementing such a *profit sharing system*. First, there can be arguments over the way contribution is divided between the two profit centers. Senior management might have to intervene to settle these disputes, which is costly, time consuming, and works against a basic reason for decentralization, namely, autonomy of business unit managers. Second, arbitrarily dividing up the profits between units does not give valid information on the profitability of each segment of the organization. Third, since the contribution is not allocated until after the sale has been made, the manufacturing unit's contribution depends on the marketing unit's ability to sell and on the actual selling price. Manufacturing units may perceive this situation to be unfair.

Two Sets of Prices.   In this method, the manufacturing unit's revenue is credited at the outside sales price, and the buying unit is charged the total standard costs. The difference is charged to a headquarters account and eliminated when the business unit statements are consolidated. This transfer pricing method is sometimes used when there are frequent conflicts between the buying and selling units that cannot be resolved by one of the other methods. Both the buying and selling units benefit under this method.

There are several disadvantages to the system of having two sets of transfer prices, however. The sum of the business unit profits is greater than overall company profits. Senior management must be aware of this situation in approving budgets for the business units and in subsequent evaluation of performance against these budgets. Also, this system creates an illusive feeling that business units are making money, while in fact, the overall company might be losing after taking account of the debits to headquarters. Further, this system might motivate business units to concentrate more on internal transfers (where they are assured of a good markup) at the expense of outside sales. Finally, there is additional bookkeeping involved in first debiting the headquarters account every time a transfer is made and then eliminating this account when business unit statements are consolidated.

The fact that the conflicts between the business units would be lessened under this system could be viewed as a weakness. Sometimes, it is better for headquarters to be aware of the conflicts arising out of transfer prices because such conflicts may signal problems in either the organizational structure or in other management systems. Under the two-sets-of-prices method, these conflicts are smoothed over, thereby not alerting senior management to these problems.

Business Practice

Exhibit 6–3A summarizes the transfer pricing practices of U.S. corporations, based on the Vancil and Govindarajan surveys. For the purposes of comparison, Exhibit 6–3B presents transfer pricing methods practiced in selected countries outside the United States.

Exhibit 6–3A   Transfer Pricing Methods for Goods in U.S. Corporations

	Percentage of Respondents Using the Transfer Pricing Method	
	Vancil (1979)	*Govindarajan (1994)*
Number of respondents	249	470
Cost-based methods		
Variable cost		
At standard	3%	6%
At actual	2	5
Full cost		
At standard	12	13
At actual	13	12
Cost plus markup		
Profit on sales	3	12
Profit on investment	3	5
Other markups	11	n/a
Total	47%	53%
Market price		
Competitor's price	12%	17%
Market-price—catalog	17	9
Market price—bid	2	5
Total	31	31
Negotiated price	22	16
	100%	100%

Note: n/a denotes not applicable.
Sources: Richard F. Vancil, *Decentralization,* p. 180.
Vijay Govindarajan, "Profit Center Measurement," p. 2.

Pricing Corporate Services

In this section we describe some of the problems associated with charging business units for services furnished by corporate staff units. We exclude the cost of central service staff units over which business units have no control (e.g., central accounting, public relations, administration). As described in Chapter 5, if these costs are charged at all, they are allocated, and the allocations do not include a profit component. The allocations are not transfer prices. There remain two types of transfers:

1. For central services that the receiving unit must accept, but for which the amount of the service is at least partially controllable by the unit.

2. For central services that the business unit has the discretion of using or not.

Exhibit 6–3B Transfer Pricing Methods in Different Countries for Domestic Transfer of Goods

	Australia[a]	Canada[b]	Japan[c]	India[d]	United Kingdom[e]
Cost Based					
Variable Cost	—	6%	2%	6%	10%
Full Cost	—	37%	44%	47%	38%
Other	—	3%	0%	0%	1%
Total	65%	46%	46%	53%	49%
Market Price	13%	34%	34%	47%	26%
Negotiated Price	11%	18%	19%	0%	24%
Other	11%	2%	1%	0%	1%
	100%	100%	100%	100%	100%

Sources:

a) M. Joye and P. Blayney, "Cost and Management Accounting Practices in Australian Manufacturing Companies," Accounting Research Centre, The University of Sydney, 1991.

b) R. Tang, "Canadian Transfer Pricing in the 1990s," *Management Accounting,* February 1992.

c) R. Tang, C. Walter, and R. Raymond, "Transfer Pricing—Japanese vs. American Style," *Management Accounting,* January 1979.

d) V. Govindarajan and B. Ramamurthy, "Transfer Pricing Policies in Indian Companies: A Survey," *Chartered Accountant,* November 1983.

e) C. Drury, S. Braund, P. Osborne, and M. Tayles, *A Survey of Management Accounting Practices in U.K. Manufacturing Companies,* London, U.K.: Chartered Association of Certified Accountants, 1993.

Control Over Amount of Service

Business units may be required to use company staffs for services such as management information systems and research and development. In these situations, the business unit manager cannot control the *efficiency* with which these activities are performed; however, the business unit manager can control the *amount* of the service that it receives. There are three schools of thought about such services.

One school holds that a business unit should pay the *standard variable costs* of the discretionary services. If it pays less than this, it will be motivated to use more of the service than is economically justified. For example, if business unit managers were not required to pay at least the variable cost of reports prepared for them by the MIS department, they might request reports or special computer runs that were of little value to them. On the other hand, if business unit managers were required to pay more than the variable cost, they might not elect to use certain services that senior management thought was worthwhile from the company's viewpoint. This possibility is most likely when senior management introduces a new service, such as a new project analysis program. The low price is analogous to the introductory price that companies sometimes use for new products.

Example. For many years, managers of the Corporate Data Processing Services (CDPS) department of the Boise Cascade Corporation did not allocate any of the costs of supporting personal computers (PC), such as purchasing, set-up, and application assistance, to the PC users because they wanted to stimulate PC use. These costs were charged/allocated to all of the other CDPS users, primarily consumers of mainframe computer resources. Even when the PC support costs became so significant that a charge for them was deemed desirable, CDPS managers chose not to charge the full cost. They set the charge at around $100 per month per PC, rather than at their best current-year estimate of $121 per month.[4]

A second school advocates a price equal to the standard variable cost plus a fair share of the standard fixed costs—that is, *the full cost* (but not more than the market price). Proponents argue that, if the business units do not believe the services are worth at least this amount, then there is something wrong with either the quality or the efficiency of the service unit. Full cost represents the company's long-run costs, and this is the amount that should be paid.

A third school advocates a price that is equivalent to the *market price,* or to standard full cost plus a profit margin. The market price would be used if available (e.g., the costs charged by a computer service bureau); if not, the price would be full cost plus a return on investment. The rationale for this position is that the capital employed by the service unit should earn a return just as the capital employed by manufacturing units does. Also, the business units would incur the investment if they provided their own service.

Optional Use of Services

In some cases, management may decide that business units have the option of using or not using central service units. Business units may procure the service from outside, develop their own capability, or simply not use the service at all. This type of arrangement is most often found for such activities as information processing, internal consulting groups, and maintenance work. These service centers are independent; they must stand on their own feet. If the services are not used by the business units, the scope of their activity will be contracted, or they may even be eliminated entirely.

Example. Commodore Business Machines outsourced one of its central service activities—customer service—to Federal Express. James Reeder, Commodore's vice president of Customer Satisfaction, said, "At that time we didn't have the greatest reputation for customer service and satisfaction." But this was Fedex's specialty, handling more than 300,000 calls for service each day. Commodore arranged for Fedex to handle the entire telephone customer service operation from Fedex's hub in Memphis.[5]

---

[4]Kenneth A. Merchant, "Boise Cascade Corporation," University of Southern California case #A911-04.

[5]James Brian Quinn, *Intelligent Enterprise* (New York: The Free Press, 1992), p. 91.

Here, management has the right to outsource a central service that is not competitive.

In this situation, business unit managers control both the *amount and the efficiency* of the central services. Under these conditions, these central groups are profit centers. Their transfer prices should be based on the same considerations as those governing other transfer prices.

Simplicity of the Price Mechanism

The prices charged for corporate services will not accomplish their intended result unless the methods of calculating them are so sufficiently straightforward that business unit managers understand them. Computer experts are accustomed to dealing with complex equations, and the computer itself provides information on the use made of it on a second-by-second basis and at low cost. There is sometimes a tendency, therefore, to charge computer users on the basis of rules that are so complicated that the user cannot understand what the effect on costs would be if he or she decided to use the computer for a given application, or, alternatively, to discontinue a current application. Such rules are counterproductive.

Administration of Transfer Prices

We have so far discussed how to formulate a sound transfer pricing policy. In this section, we discuss how the selected policy should be implemented; specifically, the degree of negotiation allowed in setting the transfer prices, methods of resolving transfer pricing conflicts, and classification of products according to the appropriate method.

Negotiation

In most companies, business units negotiate transfer prices with each other—that is, transfer prices are not set by a central staff group. Perhaps the most important reason for this is the belief that one of the primary functions of line management is to establish selling prices and to arrive at satisfactory purchase prices. If control of pricing is left to the headquarters staff, line management's ability to affect profitability is reduced. Also, many transfer prices require a degree of subjective judgment. Consequently, a negotiated transfer price often is the result of compromises made by both buyer and seller. If headquarters establishes transfer prices, business unit managers can argue that their low profits are due to the arbitrariness of the transfer prices. Another reason for having the business units negotiate their prices is that they usually have the best information on markets and costs, and, consequently, are best able to arrive at reasonable prices.

Example. Business Unit A has an opportunity to supply a large quantity of a certain product to an outside company at a price of $100 per unit. The raw material for this product would be supplied by Business Unit B. Unit B's normal transfer price for this material is $35 per unit, of which $10 is variable cost. Unit A's process cost (excluding raw material) plus normal profit is $85, of which $50 is variable cost. Unit A's total cost plus normal profit, therefore, is $120; at this amount, the selling price of $100 is not attractive. Rejecting the contract would be dysfunctional for the company as a whole because both business units have available capacity. The two units, therefore, would negotiate a lower price for the raw material so that both units would make a contribution to their profit.

If, instead of two business units within a single company, one company had an offer to sell raw material to another company that had a similar sales prospect, the two companies should negotiate in the same fashion. The fact that a transfer price was involved in the first example does not affect how reasonable managers should behave.[6]

Business units must know the ground rules within which these transfer price negotiations are to be conducted. In a few companies, headquarters informs business units that they are free to deal with each other or with outsiders as they see fit, subject only to the qualification that, if there is a tie, the business must be kept inside. If this is done and there are outside sources and outside markets, no further administrative procedures are required. The price is set in the outside marketplace, and if business units cannot agree on a price, they simply buy from or sell to outsiders. In many companies, however, business units are required to deal with one another. If they do not have the threat of doing business with competitors as a bargaining point in the negotiation process, headquarters staff must develop a set of rules that govern both pricing and sourcing of intracompany products.

Because line managers should not spend an undue amount of time on transfer price negotiations, these rules should be specific enough that skill in negotiations is not a significant factor in the determination of the transfer price. Without such rules, the most stubborn manager will negotiate the most favorable prices.

Arbitration and Conflict Resolution

No matter how specific the pricing rules are, there may be instances in which business units will not be able to agree on a price. For this reason, some procedure should be in place for arbitrating transfer price disputes. There can be widely different degrees of formality in transfer price arbitration. At one extreme, the responsibility for arbitrating disputes is assigned to a single executive—for example, the financial vice president or the executive vice president—who talks to business unit managers involved and then announces the

---

[6]David Solomons, in *Divisional Performance: Measurement and Control* (Homewood, Ill.: Richard D. Irwin, 1968, chapter VI), discussed a similar example. He concluded that the transfer pricing system would be dysfunctional because Division A would reject a contract that was in the best interest of the company. He did not mention the possibility of negotiation, and his conclusion was, therefore, incorrect.

price orally. The other extreme is to set up a committee. Usually such a committee will have three responsibilities: (1) to settle transfer price disputes; (2) to review sourcing changes; and (3) to change the transfer price rules when appropriate. The degree of formality employed depends on the extent and type of potential transfer price disputes. In any case, transfer price arbitration should be the responsibility of a high-level headquarters executive or group, since arbitration decisions can have an important effect on business unit profits.

Arbitration can be conducted in a number of ways. With a formal system, both parties submit a written case to the arbitrator. The arbitrator reviews both positions and decides on the price. In establishing a price, the assistance of other staff offices may be obtained. For example, the purchasing department might review the validity of a proposed competitive price quotation, or the industrial engineering department might review the appropriateness of a disputed standard labor cost. As indicated above, in less formal systems, the presentations may be largely oral.

It is important that relatively few disputes be submitted to arbitration. If a large number of disputes are arbitrated, this indicates that the rules are not specific enough, the rules are difficult to apply, or the business unit organization is illogical. In short, this is a symptom that something is wrong. Not only is arbitration time consuming to both line managers and headquarters executives, but also arbitrated prices often satisfy neither the buyer nor the seller. In some companies, an onus is involved in submitting a price dispute to arbitration such that very few are ever submitted. If, as a consequence, legitimate grievances do not surface, the results are undesirable. Preventing disputes from being submitted to arbitration will tend to hide the fact that there are problems with the transfer price system.

Irrespective of the degree of formality of the arbitration, the type of conflict resolution process that is used will also influence the effectiveness of a transfer pricing system. Lawrence and Lorsch pointed out four ways to resolve conflicts: forcing, smoothing, bargaining, and problem solving.[7] The conflict resolution mechanisms range from conflict avoidance through forcing and smoothing to conflict resolution through bargaining and problem solving.

Product Classification

The extent and formality of the sourcing and transfer pricing rules will depend to a great extent on the amount of intracompany transfers and the availability of markets and market prices. The greater the amount of intracompany transfers, and the less the availability of market prices, the more formal and specific the rules must be. If market prices are readily available, sourcing can be controlled by having headquarters review make-or-buy decisions that exceed a specified amount.

---

[7]Paul R. Lawrence and Jay W. Lorsch, *Organization and Environment* (Homewood, IL: Richard D. Irwin, 1967), pp. 73–78.

Some companies divide products into two main classes:

Class I includes all products for which senior management wishes to control the sourcing. These would normally be large volume products, products where no outside source exists, and products where, for quality or secrecy reasons, senior management wishes to maintain control over manufacturing.

Class II are all other products. In general, these are products that can be produced outside the company without any significant disruption to present operations. These are products of relatively small volume, produced with general purpose equipment. Class II products are transferred at market prices.

The sourcing of Class I products can be changed only with the permission of the central management. The sourcing of Class II products is determined by the business units involved. Both the buying and selling units are free to deal either inside or outside the company.

Under this arrangement, management can concentrate on the sourcing and pricing of a relatively small number of high volume products. Rules for transfer prices would be established, using the different methods described in the preceding section as appropriate.

Summary

The delegation of significant amounts of authority is dependent upon the ability to delegate responsibility for profits. Profit responsibility cannot be safely delegated unless two conditions exist:

1. The delegatee has all of the relevant information to make optimum profit decisions.
2. The delegatee's performance is measured on how well he or she has made cost/revenue trade-offs.

Where segments of a company share responsibility for product development, manufacturing, and marketing, a transfer price system is required if these segments are to be delegated profit responsibility. This transfer price system must result in the two conditions described above. In complex organizations it can be a difficult problem to devise a transfer price system that assures the necessary knowledge and motivation for optimum decision making.

Two decisions are involved in designing a transfer pricing system. First is the sourcing decision: Should the company produce the product inside the company or purchase it from an outside vendor? Second is the transfer price decision: At which price should the product be transferred between profit centers?

Ideally, the transfer price should approximate the normal outside market price, with adjustments for costs not incurred in intracompany transfers. Even under conditions where sourcing decisions are constrained, the market price is the best transfer price.

If competitive prices are not available, transfer prices may be set on the basis of cost plus a profit, even though such transfer prices may be complex to calculate and the results less satisfactory than a market-based price. Cost-based transfer can be made at standard cost plus profit margin, or by the use of a two-step pricing system.

The method of negotiating transfer prices should be in place, and there should be an arbitration mechanism for settling transfer price disputes, but these arrangements should not be so complicated that an undue amount of management time is devoted to transfer pricing.

There are probably few instances in complex organizations where a completely satisfactory transfer price system exists. As with many management control design choices, it is necessary to choose the best of perhaps several less than perfect courses of action. The important thing is to be aware of the areas of imperfections and to be sure that administrative procedures are employed to avoid suboptimum decisions.

Appendix
Some Theoretical Considerations

There is a considerable body of literature on theoretical transfer pricing models. Few, if any, of these models are used in actual business situations, however, and for reasons explained below, it is unlikely that they ever will be widely used. Consequently, we have not referred to these models in the body of this chapter. Although they are not directly applicable to real business situations, they are useful in conceptualizing transfer price systems. These models may be divided into three types: (1) models based on classical economic theory, (2) models based on linear programming, and (3) models based on the Shapley value.

Economic Models

The classic economic model was first described by Jack Hirschleifer in the 1956 article referred to in footnote 2 of this chapter. Professor Hirschleifer developed a series of marginal revenue, marginal cost, and demand curves for the transfer of an intermediate product from one business unit to another. He used these curves to establish transfer prices, under various sets of economic assumptions, that would optimize the total profit of the two business units. Using the transfer prices thus developed, the two units would produce the maximum total profit by optimizing their unit profits.

The difficulty with the Hirschleifer model is that it can be used only when a specified set of conditions exist: it must be possible to estimate the demand curve for the intermediate product; the assumed conditions must remain stable; and there can be no alternative uses for facilities used to make the intermediate product. Finally, the model is applicable only to the situation in which the selling unit makes a single intermediate product, which it transfers to a single buying unit, which uses that intermediate product in a single final product. Such conditions exist rarely, if at all, in the real world.

This model (and also the other models) assumes that transfer prices will be imposed by the central staff, and it denies the importance of negotiation among business units. Business unit managers usually have better information than is available to the central staff. *Indeed, if the central staff could determine the optimum production pattern, the question arises: Why is this pattern not imposed directly, rather than attempting to arrive at it indirectly via the transfer price mechanism?*

Linear Programming Model

The linear programming model is based on an opportunity cost approach. This model also incorporates capacity constraints. The model calculates an optimum companywide production pattern, and using this pattern, it calculates a set of values that impute the profit contributions of each of the scarce resources. These are termed *shadow prices,* and one process of calculating them is called "obtaining the dual solution" to the linear program. If the variable costs of the intermediate products are added to their shadow prices, a set of transfer prices results that should motivate business units to produce according to the optimum production pattern for the entire company. This is so because, if these transfer prices are used, each business unit will optimize its profits only by producing in accordance with the patterns developed through the linear program.

If reliable shadow prices could be calculated, this model would be useful in arriving at transfer prices. However, to make the model manageable, even on a computer, many simplifying assumptions must be incorporated in it. It is assumed that the demand curve is known, that it is static, that the cost function is linear, and that alternative uses of production facilities and their profitability can be estimated in advance. As is the case with the economic model, these conditions rarely exist in the real world.

Shapley Value

The theoretical literature has a few articles advocating the use of a number termed the *Shapley value* as the transfer price.[8] The Shapley value was developed in 1953 by L. S. Shapley as a method of dividing the profits of a coalition of companies or individuals among its individual members in proportion to the contribution that each of them made. This is a problem that arises in the theory of games, and the Shapley value generally is considered to provide an equitable solution to that problem.

Whether the same technique is applicable to the transfer price problem is a highly debatable issue. Although the method has been described in the literature for a number of years, few practical applications have been reported. A partial reason for its lack of acceptance is that the computation is lengthy unless there are only a few products involved in the transfer. Another reason is that many of those who have studied the Shapley method do not believe that its underlying assumptions are valid for the transfer pricing problem.

---

[8]For a description and bibliography, see Daniel L. Jensen, "A Class of Mutually Satisfactory Allocations," *The Accounting Review,* October 1977, pp. 842–56.

Suggested Additional Readings

Adler, Ralph W. "Transfer Pricing for World-Class Manufacturing." *Long Range Planning* 29, 1, February 1996, pp. 69–75.

Cassel, Herbert S., and Vincent F. McCormack. "The Transfer Price Dilemma—And a Dual Price Solution." *Journal of Accounting,* September 1987.

Crow, Stephen, and Eugene Sauls. "Setting the Right Transfer Price." *Management Accounting* 76, 6, December 1994, pp. 41–47.

Eccles, Robert G. *The Transfer Price Problem.* Lexington, MA: Lexington Books, 1985.

Govindarajan, Vijay, and Robert N. Anthony. "How Firms Use Cost Data in Pricing Decisions." *Management Accounting,* July 1983, pp. 30–34.

Govindarajan, Vijay. "Profit Center Measurement: An Empirical Study." The Amos Tuck School of Business Administration, Dartmouth College, 1994.

Gupta, Anil K., and Vijay Govindarajan. "Resource Sharing among SBUs: Strategic Antecedents and Administrative Implications." *Academy of Management Journal* 29, 4 (1986), pp. 695–714.

Kovac, Edward J., and Henry P. Troy. "Getting Transfer Prices Right: What Bellcore Did." *Harvard Business Review,* September–October 1989, pp. 148–54.

Maher, Michael W., and Edward Deakin. *Cost Accounting.* Homewood, IL: Richard D. Irwin, 1995.

Solomons, David. *Divisional Performance: Measurement and Control.* Homewood, IL: Richard D. Irwin, 1968, Chap. VI.

Vancil, Richard F. *Decentralization: Management Ambiguity by Design.* Homewood, IL: Dow Jones-Irwin, 1979.

Venkatesan, Ravi. "Strategic Outsourcing: To Make or Not to Make." *Harvard Business Review,* November–December 1992, pp. 98–107.

Watson, David J. H., and John L. Baumier. "Transfer Pricing: A Behavioral Context." *Accounting Review,* July 1985, pp. 466–74.

Case 6–1
Transfer Pricing Problems

1. Division A of Lambda Company manufactures Product X, which is sold to Division B as a component of Product Y. Product Y is sold to Division C, which uses it as a component in Product Z. Product Z is sold to customers outside of the company. The intracompany pricing rule is that products are transferred between divisions at standard cost plus a 10 percent return on inventories and fixed assets. From the information provided below, calculate the transfer price for Products X and Y and the standard cost of Product Z.

Standard Cost per Unit	Product X	Product Y	Product Z
Material purchased outside . .	$2.00	$3.00	$1.00
Direct labor	1.00	1.00	2.00
Variable overhead	1.00	1.00	2.00
Fixed overhead per unit	3.00	4.00	1.00
Standard volume	10,000	10,000	10,000
Inventories (average)	$70,000	$15,000	$30,000
Fixed assets (net)	30,000	45,000	16,000

2. Assume the same facts as stated in Problem 1, except that the transfer price rule is as follows: Goods are transferred among divisions at the standard variable cost per unit transferred plus a monthly charge. This charge is equal to the fixed costs assigned to the product plus a 10 percent return on the average inventories and fixed assets assignable to the product. Calculate the transfer price for Products X and Y and calculate the unit standard cost for Products Y and Z.

3. The present selling price for Product Z is $28.00. Listed below is a series of possible price reductions by competition and the probable im-

pact of these reductions on the volume of sales if Division C does not also reduce its price.

- Possible competitive price: $27.00; $26.00; $25.00; $23.00; $22.00.
- Sales volume if price of Product Z is maintained at $28.00: 9,000; 7,000; 5,000; 2,000; 0.
- Sales volume if price of Product Z is reduced to competitive levels: 10,000; 10,000; 10,000; 10,000; 10,000.

Questions

(a) With transfer price calculated in Problem **1**, is Division C better advised to maintain its price at $28.00 or to follow competition in each of the instances above?

(b) With the transfer prices calculated in Problem **2**, is Division C better advised to maintain its present price of $28.00 or to follow competition in each of the instances above?

(c) Which decisions are to the best economic interests of the company, other things being equal?

(d) Using the transfer prices calculated in problem **1**, is the manager of Division C making a decision contrary to the overall interests of the company? If so, what is the opportunity loss to the company in each of the competitive pricing actions described above?

4. Division C is interested in increasing the sales of Product Z. The present selling price of Product Z is $28.00. A survey is made and sales increases resulting from increases in television advertising are estimated. The results of this survey are provided below. (Note that this particular type of advertising can be purchased only in units of $100,000.)

This case was prepared by Professors John Dearden and Robert N. Anthony. Copyright by Osceola Institute.

	(in thousands)				
Advertising expenditures	$100	$200	$300	$400	$500
Additional volume resulting from additional advertising	10	19	27	34	40

Questions

(a) As manager of Division C, how much television advertising would you use if you purchased Product Y at the transfer price calculated in Problem **1**?

(b) How much television advertising would you use if you purchased Product Y for the transfer price calculated in Problem **2**?

(c) Which is correct from the overall company viewpoint?

(d) How much would the company lose in suboptimum profits from using the first transfer price?

5. Two of the divisions of the Chambers Corporation are the Intermediate Division and the Final Division. The Intermediate Division produces three products: A, B, and C. Normally these products are sold both to outside customers and to the Final Division. The Final Division uses Products A, B, and C in manufacturing Products X, Y, and Z, respectively. In recent weeks, the supply of Products A, B, and C has tightened to such an extent that the Final Division has been operating considerably below capacity because of the lack of these products. Consequently, the Intermediate Division has been told to sell all its products to the Final Division. The financial facts about these products are as follows:

Intermediate Division

	Product A	Product B	Product C
Transfer price	$ 10.00	$ 10.00	$ 15.00
Variable manufacturing cost	3.00	6.00	5.00
Contribution per unit . .	$ 7.00	$ 4.00	$ 10.00
Fixed costs (total)	$50,000	$100,000	$75,000

The Intermediate Division has a monthly capacity of 50,000 units. The processing constraints are such that capacity production can be obtained only by producing at least 10,000 units of each product. The remaining capacity can be used to produce 20,000 units of any combination of the three products. The Intermediate Division cannot exceed the capacity of 50,000 units.

The Final Division has sufficient capacity to produce about 40 percent more than it is now producing because the availability of Products A, B, and C is limiting production. Also, the Final Division can sell all the products that it can produce at the prices indicated above.

Final Division

	Product X	Product Y	Product Z
Selling price	$ 28.00	$ 30.00	$ 30.00
Variable cost:			
Inside purchases	10.00	10.00	15.00
Other variable costs . .	5.00	5.00	8.00
Total variable cost	$ 15.00	$ 15.00	$ 23.00
Contribution per unit . .	$ 13.00	$ 15.00	$ 7.00
Fixed costs (total)	$100,000	$100,000	$200,000

Questions

(a) If you were the manager of the Intermediate Division, what products would you sell to the Final Division? What is the amount of profit that you would earn on these sales?

(b) If you were the manager of the Final Division, what products would you order from the Intermediate Division, assuming that the Intermediate Division must sell all its production to you? What profits would you earn?

(c) What production pattern optimizes total company profit? How does this affect the profits of the Intermediate Division? If you were the executive vice president of

Chambers and prescribed this optimum pattern, what, if anything, would you do about the distribution of profits between the two divisions?

6. How, if at all, would your answers to Problem **5** change if there were no outside markets for Products A, B, or C?

7. The Chambers Company has determined that capacity can be increased in excess of 50,000 units, but these increases require an out-of-pocket cost penalty. These penalties are as follows:

	Cost Penalty		
Volume in Excess of Present Capacity (unit)	*Product A*	*Product B*	*Product C*
1,000	$10,000	$12,000	$10,000
2,000	25,000	24,000	20,000
3,000	50,000	50,000	35,000
4,000	80,000	80,000	50,000

Each of these increases is independent—that is, increases in the production of Product A do not affect the costs of increasing the production of Product B. Changes can be made only in quantities of 100 units, with a maximum increase of 4,000 units for each product. All other conditions are as stated in Problem **5**.

Questions

(*a*) What would be the Intermediate Division's production pattern, assuming that it can charge all penalty costs to the Final Division?

(*b*) The Final Division's optimum production pattern, assuming that it is required to accept the penalty costs?

(*c*) The optimum Company production pattern?

8. How would your answer to Problem **7** differ if the Intermediate Division had no outside markets for Products A, B, and C?

9.[1] Division A of Kappa Company is the only source of supply for an intermediate product that is converted by Division B into a salable final product. A substantial part of A's costs are fixed. For any output up to 1,000 units a day, its total costs are $500 a day. Total costs increase by $100 a day for every additional thousand units made. Division A judges that its own results will be optimized if it sets its price at $0.40 a unit, and it acts accordingly.

Division B incurs additional costs in converting the intermediate product supplied by A into a finished product. These costs are $1,250 for any output up to 1,000 units, and $250 per thousand for outputs in excess of 1,000. On the revenue side, B can increase its revenue only by spending more on sales promotion and by reducing selling prices. Its sales forecast is shown in the table below.

	Sales Forecast
Sales (units)	*Revenue Net of Selling Costs $ (per thousand units)*
1,000	1,750
2,000	1,325
3,000	1,100
4,000	925
5,000	800
6,000	666

Looking at the situation from B's point of view, we can compare its costs and revenues at various levels of output while considering both its own processing costs and what it is charged by A for the intermediates that A will supply. The relevant information is set out in Exhibit 1.

Exhibit 1 makes it clear that the most profitable policy for Division B, in the circumstances,

---

[1]Reproduced with permission from David Solomons, *Divisional Performance: Measurement and Control* (Homewood, IL: Richard D. Irwin, 1965).

Exhibit 1

Division B's Output (units) (1)	B's Own Processing Costs (2) $	A's Charge to B for Intermediates @ $0.40 a Unit (3) $	B's Total Costs (4) = (2) + (3) $	B's Revenue (net of selling costs) per 1,000 Units (5) $	B's Total Revenue (6) = (1) × (5) $	B's Profit (loss) (7) = (6) – (4) $
1,000	1,250	400	1,650	1,750	1,750	100
2,000	1,500	800	2,300	1,325	2,650	350
3,000	1,750	1,200	2,950	1,100	3,300	350
4,000	2,000	1,600	3,600	925	3,700	100
5,000	2,250	2,000	4,250	800	4,000	(250)
6,000	2,500	2,400	4,900	666	4,000	(900)

Exhibit 2

Output (units) (1)	Cost of Producing Intermediates (2) $	Cost of Processing to Completion (3) $	Total Cost (4) = (2) + (3) $	Total Revenue* (5) $	Profit (6) = (5) – (4) $
1,000	500	1,250	1,750	1,750	—
2,000	600	1,500	2,100	2,650	550
3,000	700	1,750	2,450	3,330	850
4,000	800	2,000	2,800	3,700	900
5,000	900	2,250	3,150	4,000	850
6,000	1,000	2,500	3,500	4,000	500

* Taken from column (6) of Exhibit 1.

is to set its output at either 2,000 or 3,000 units a day and to accept a profit of $350 a day. If its output is more than 3,000 or less than 2,000 it will make even less profit.

With Division B taking 3,000 units a day from it, Division A's revenue, at $0.40 a unit, is $1,200, and its total costs are $700. Therefore, A's separate profit is $500 a day. Adding this to B's profit of $350 a day, we get an aggregate profit for the corporation of $850 a day.

Assume now that the company abandons its divisionalized structure, and instead of having two profit centers, A and B, it combines them into a single profit center, with responsibility for both production of the intermediate and processing it to completion. Let us further suppose that, apart from this change of structure, all the other conditions previously present continue to apply. Then the market conditions that formerly faced Division B now confront the single profit center. Its costs are equal to the combined costs of A and B, eliminating, of course, the charge previously made by A to B for the supply of intermediates. The schedule of costs and revenues for the single profit center will then appear as shown in Exhibit 2.

Exhibit 2 shows that the single profit center will operate more profitably than the two divisions together formerly did. By making and selling 4,000 units a day, it can earn a profit of $900 or $50 a day in excess of the best result achieved by the combined activities of Divisions A and B.

The company is seen to have been paying a price for the luxury of divisionalization. By suboptimizing (i.e., by seeking maximum profits for themselves as separate entities), the divisions have caused the corporation to less than optimize its profits as a whole. The reason was, of course, that Division B reacted to the transfer price of $0.40 a unit by restricting both its demand for the intermediate and its own output of the finished product. By making for itself the best of a bad job, it created an unsatisfactory situation for the company. But who can blame it? Assuming that the instructions to its general manager were to maximize the division's separate profit, the manager did just that, given the conditions confronting him or her. The responsibility for the final result really lay with Division A. Yet it is not fair to blame that division, either, for it, too, was only carrying out instructions in seeking to maximize its own profit; and a transfer price of $0.40, while it leads to a less than optimal result for the corporation, does maximize A's own profit.

One further feature of this illustration is worth noting. So far as its own profit was concerned, it was a matter of indifference to Division B whether it sold 2,000 or 3,000 units. We assumed that it decided to sell 3,000. If it had chosen to sell only 2,000, its own profit would have been unaffected, while A's profit would have been diminished by $300. In a situation like this, negotiations about the price between A and B would probably have prevented this further damage to the corporation resulting from suboptimization. But it is unlikely that the divisions, left to themselves, would arrive at an optimal solution from the corporate point of view.

Questions

(a) What is the lowest price that Division A should be willing to accept from Division B for 4,000 units?

(b) What is the highest price at which Division B should be willing to buy 4,000 units from Division A?

(c) If Division A does sell 4,000 units to Division B, what should the transfer price be?

(d) Under what circumstances, if any, would the transfer price be dysfunctional?

Case 6–2
Birch Paper Company

"If I were to price these boxes any lower than $480 a thousand," said James Brunner, manager of Birch Paper Company's Thompson Division, "I'd be countermanding my order of last month for our salesmen to stop shaving their bids and to bid full-cost quotations. I've been trying for weeks to improve the quality of our business, and if I turn around now and accept this job at $430 or $450 or something less than $480, I'll be tearing down this program I've been working so hard to build up. The division can't very well show a profit by putting in bids that don't even cover a fair share of overhead costs, let alone give us a profit."

Birch Paper Company was a medium-sized, partly integrated paper company, producing white and kraft papers and paperboard. A portion of its paperboard output was converted into corrugated boxes by the Thompson Division, which also printed and colored the outside surface of the boxes. Including Thompson, the company had four producing divisions and a timberland division, which supplied part of the company's pulp requirements.

For several years, each division had been judged independently on the basis of its profit and return on investment. Top management had been working to gain effective results from a policy of decentralizing responsibility and authority for all decisions except those relating to overall company policy. The company's top officials believed that in the past few years the concept of decentralization had been applied successfully and that the company's profits and competitive position definitely had improved.

The Northern Division had designed a special display box for one of its papers in conjunction with the Thompson Division, which was equipped to make the box. Thompson's staff for package design and development spent several months perfecting the design, production methods, and materials to be used. Because of the unusual color and shape, these were far from standard. According to an agreement between the two divisions, the Thompson Division was reimbursed by the Northern Division for the cost of its design and development work.

When all the specifications were prepared, the Northern Division asked for bids on the box from the Thompson Division and from two outside companies. Each division manager was normally free to buy from whatever supplier he wished, and even on sales within the company, divisions were expected to meet the going market price if they wanted the business.

During this period, the profit margins of such converters as the Thompson Division were being squeezed. Thompson, as did many other similar converters, bought its paperboard, and its function was to print, cut, and shape it into boxes. Though it bought most of its materials from other Birch divisions, most of Thompson's sales were made to outside customers. If Thompson got the order from Northern, it probably would buy its linerboard and corrugating medium from the Southern Division of Birch. The walls of a corrugated box consist of outside and inside sheets of linerboard sandwiching the fluted corrugating medium. About 70 percent of Thompson's out-of-pocket cost of $400 for the order represented the cost of linerboard and corrugating medium. Though Southern had been running below capacity and had excess inventory, it quoted the market price, which had not noticeably weakened as a result of the oversupply. Its out-of-pocket costs on both liner and corrugating medium were about 60 percent of the selling price.

The Northern Division received bids on the boxes of $480 a thousand from the Thompson

This case was prepared by William Rotch under the supervision of Neil Harlan, Harvard Business School. Copyright by the President and Fellows of Harvard College. Harvard Business School case 158–001.

Division, $430 a thousand from West Paper Company and $432 a thousand from Eire Papers, Ltd. Eire Papers offered to buy from Birch the outside linerboard with the special printing already on it, but would supply its own inside liner and corrugating medium. The outside liner would be supplied by the Southern Division at a price equivalent of $90 a thousand boxes, and it would be printed for $30 a thousand by the Thompson Division. Of the $30, about $25 would be out-of-pocket costs.

Since this situation appeared to be a little unusual, William Kenton, manager of the Northern Division, discussed the wide discrepancy of bids with Birch's commercial vice president. He told the vice president: "We sell in a very competitive market, where higher costs cannot be passed on. How can we be expected to show a decent profit and return on investment if we have to buy our supplies at more than 10 percent over the going market?"

Knowing that Mr. Brunner on occasion in the past few months had been unable to operate the Thompson Division at capacity, it seemed odd to the vice president that Mr. Brunner would add the full 20 percent overhead and profit charge to his out-of-pocket costs. When asked about this, Mr. Brunner's answer was the statement that appears at the beginning of the case. He went on to say that having done the developmental work on the box, and having received no profit on that, he felt entitled to a good markup on the production of the box itself.

The vice president explored further the cost structures of the various divisions. He remembered a comment that the controller had made at a meeting the week before to the effect that costs which were variable for one division could be largely fixed for the company as a whole. He knew that in the absence of specific orders from top management Mr. Kenton would accept the lowest bid, which was that of the West Paper Company for $430. However, it would be possible for top management to order the acceptance of another bid if the situation warranted such action. And though the volume represented by the transactions in question was less than 5 percent of the volume of any of the divisions involved, other transactions would conceivably raise similar problems later.

Questions

1. Which bid should Northern Division accept that is in the best interests of Birch Paper Company?
2. Should Mr. Kenton accept this bid? Why or why not?
3. Should the vice president of Birch Paper Company take any action?
4. In the controversy described, how, if at all, is the transfer price system dysfunctional? Does this problem call for some change, or changes, in the transfer pricing policy of the overall firm? If so, what *specific* changes do you suggest?

Case 6–3
General Appliance Corporation

Organization

The General Appliance Corporation was an integrated manufacturer of all types of home appliances. As shown in Exhibit 1, the company had a decentralized, divisional organization consisting of four product divisions, four manufacturing divisions, and six staff offices. Each division and staff office was headed by a vice president. The staff offices had functional authority over their counterparts in the divisions, but they had no direct line authority over the divisional general managers. The company's organization manual stated: "All divisional personnel are responsible to the division manager. Except in functional areas specifically delegated, staff personnel have no line authority in a division."

The product divisions designed, engineered, assembled, and sold various home appliances. They manufactured very few component parts; rather, they assembled the appliances from parts purchased either from the manufacturing divisions or from outside vendors. The manufacturing divisions made approximately 75 percent of their sales to the product divisions. Parts made by the manufacturing divisions were generally designed by the product divisions; the manufacturing divisions merely produced the parts to specifications provided to them. Although all the manufacturing divisions had engineering departments, these departments did only about 20 percent of the total company engineering.

Transfer Prices

The divisions were expected to deal with one another as though they were independent companies. Parts were to be transferred at prices arrived

at by negotiation between the divisions. These prices generally were based on the actual prices paid to outside suppliers for the same or comparable parts. These outside prices were adjusted to reflect differences in design of the outside part from that of the inside part. Also, if the outside price was based on purchases made at an earlier date, it was adjusted for changes in the general price level since that date. In general, the divisions established prices by negotiation among themselves, but if the divisions could not agree on a price, they could submit the dispute to the finance staff for arbitration.

Source Determination

Although the divisions were instructed to deal with one another as independent companies, in practice this was not always feasible because a product division did not have the power to decide whether to buy from within the company or from outside. Once a manufacturing division began to produce a part, the only way the product division buying this part could change to an outside supplier was to obtain permission of the manufacturing division or, in case of disagreement, appeal to the purchasing staff. The purchasing staff had the authority to settle disputes between the product and manufacturing divisions with respect to whether a manufacturing division should continue to produce a part or whether the product division could buy outside. In nearly every case of dispute, the purchasing staff had decided that the part would continue to be manufactured within the company. When the manufacturing divisions were instructed to continue producing a part, they had to hold the price of the part at the level at which the product division could purchase it from the outside vendor.

In the case of new parts, a product division had the authority to decide on the source of supply.

This case was prepared by John Dearden and Robert N. Anthony, Harvard Business School. Copyright by the President and Fellows of Harvard College. Harvard Business School case 160–003.

EXHIBIT 1

Organization chart

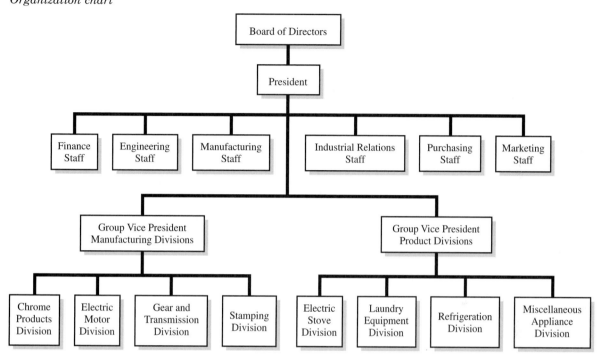

Even for new parts, however, a manufacturing division could appeal to the purchasing staff to reverse the decision if a product division planned to purchase a part from an outside vendor.

Stove Top Problem

The Chrome Products Division sold to the Electric Stove Division a chrome-plated unit that fitted on top of the stove; the unit had to be resistant to corrosion and stain from spilled food. It was also essential that the unit remain bright and new-looking. The Chrome Products Division had been producing this unit since January 1, 1986; prior to that time, it had been produced by an outside vendor.

The unit in question was produced from a steel stamping. Until June 1987, the stamping was processed as follows:

Operations	Processes
1	Machine buffing
2	Nickel plating
3	Machine buffing
4	Chrome plating
5	Machine buffing

About the middle of 1986, the president of General Appliance Corporation became concerned over complaints from customers and dealers about the quality of the company's products. A customer survey appeared to indicate quite definitely that, in the previous year, the company's reputation as a producer of quality products had deteriorated. Although this deterioration was believed to have been caused principally by the poor performance of a new electric motor, which was soon corrected, the president had come to the conclusion that the overall quality of the company's products had been decreasing for the past several years. Furthermore, he believed that it was essential for the company to reestablish itself as a leader in the production of quality products. Accordingly, early in 1987, he called in the manufacturing vice president (i.e., the director of the manufacturing staff office) and told him that for the next six months his most important job was to bring the quality of all products up to a satisfactory level.

In the course of carrying out this assignment, the manufacturing vice president decided that the appearance of the chrome-plated stove top was unsatisfactory. Until then, the bases for rejection or acceptance of this part by the quality control section of the Chrome Products Division were a corrosion test and an appearance test; appearance was largely subjective and, in the final analysis, dependent on the judgment of the quality control person. In order to make the test more objective, three tops were selected and set up as standards for the minimum acceptable quality. Because better than average units were selected, rejects increased to over 80 percent. Personnel from the Chrome Products Division and the manufacturing staff jointly studied the manufacturing process to find a way of making the stove tops conform to the new quality standards. They added copper plating and buffing operations at the beginning of the process and a hand-buffing operation at the end of the manufacturing cycle. The total cost of these added operations was 80 cents a unit. As soon as the new operations were put into effect in June 1987, the rejection rate for poor quality declined to less than 1 percent.

In July 1987, the Chrome Products Division proposed to increase the price of the stove top by 90 cents; 80 cents represented the cost of the added operations, and 10 cents was the profit markup on the added costs. The current price, before the proposed increase, was $10 a unit. This price had been developed as shown in the next column.

Development of Price

Price charged by an outside producer (12/31/85)	$ 9.00
Design changes since 12/31/85	0.50
Changes in raw materials and labor prices since 12/31/85	0.50
Price as of 6/30/87	$10.00

The Electric Stove Division objected to the proposed price increase, and after three weeks of fruitless negotiations, it was decided that the dispute should be submitted to the finance staff for arbitration. The positions of the parties to the dispute are summarized in the following sections.

Chrome Products Division.   In a letter to the vice president for finance, the general manager of the Chrome Products Division stated that he believed that he was entitled to the increased price because:

1. He had been required by the manufacturing staff to add operations at a cost of 80 cents a unit.
2. These operations resulted in improved quality that could benefit only the Electric Stove Division.
3. The present price of $10.00 was based on old quality standards. Had the outside supplier been required to meet these new standards, the price would have been 90 cents higher.

Electric Stove Division.   The general manager of the Electric Stove Division, in appealing the price increase, based his position on the following arguments:

1. There had been no change in engineering specifications. The only change that had taken place was in what was purported to be "acceptable appearance." This was a subjective matter that could not be

measured with any degree of precision. Further, both the particular case and the possible effects of establishing a precedent were objectionable. "If we were to pay for any change in quality standards, not accompanied by a change in engineering specification, we would be opening up a Pandora's box. Every division would request higher prices based on giving us better quality based on some subjective standard. Every request by this division to a manufacturing division to improve quality would be accompanied by a price increase, even though we were requesting only that the quality be brought up to competitive levels."

2. The Electric Stove Division had not requested that quality be improved. In fact, the division had not even been consulted on the change. Thus, the division should not be responsible for paying for a so-called improvement that it neither requested nor approved.

3. Whether there was any improvement in quality from the customer's viewpoint was doubtful, although to the highly trained eye of the quality control personnel there may have been an improvement. The customer would not notice a significant difference between the appearance of the part before and after the change in quality standards.

4. Even if there were an improvement in quality perceptible to the consumer, it was not worth 90 cents. By adding 90 cents to the cost of the stove, features could be added that would be far more marketable than the quality improvement.

5. Any improvement in quality only brought the part up to the quality level that the former outside producer had provided. The cost of the improved quality, therefore, was included in the $10.00 price.

Finance Staff Review.   The finance staff reviewed the dispute. In the course of this review, the engineering department of the manufacturing staff was asked to review the added operations and comment on the acceptability of the proposed cost increases. The quality control department of the manufacturing staff was asked to verify whether quality was actually better as the result of the added operations and whether the new units were of higher quality than the units purchased from the outside vendor 18 months ago. The engineering department stated that the proposed costs were reasonable and represented efficient processing. The quality control department stated that the quality was improved and that the new parts were of superior quality to the parts previously purchased from outside sources.

Thermostatic Control Problem

One of the plants of the Electric Motor Division produced thermostatic control units. The Laundry Equipment Division bought all its requirements for thermostatic control units (about 100,000 a year) from the Electric Motor Division. The Refrigeration Division used a similar unit, and until 1985 it had purchased all its requirements (20,000 a year) from an outside supplier, the Monson Controls Corporation. In 1985, at the request of the Electric Motor Division, the Refrigeration Division purchased 25 percent of its requirements from the Electric Motor Division. In 1986, this percentage was increased to 50 percent, and in 1987 to 75 percent. In July 1987, the Refrigeration Division informed the Monson Controls Corporation that beginning January 1, 1988, it would buy all its thermostatic control units from the Electric Motor Division. The Refrigeration Division made these source changes as a result of Electric Motor Division requests, which were, it said, "in the best interest of the company." The units made outside and inside were comparable in quality, and the price paid to the Electric Motor Division was the same as the price paid to the Monson Controls Corporation. The Laundry Division also paid this same price to the Electric Motor Division.

In 1984, the demand for this kind of thermostatic control unit was high in relation to the industry's production capacity. Between 1985 and 1987, several appliance companies, including the General Appliance Corporation, built or expanded their own facilities to produce this unit so that, by the middle of 1987, the production capacity of the independent companies considerably exceeded the demand. One of the results of this situation was a declining price level. Prices of the Monson Controls Corporation had been as follows:

1984	$3.00
1985	2.70
1986	2.50
1987 (January–June)	2.40

As a result of these price reductions, which the Electric Motor Division had met, the profits of the Electric Motor Division on this product had dropped from a before-tax profit of 15 percent on its investment in 1984 to nearly zero in 1987.

In August 1987, after being told it could no longer supply the Refrigeration Division, the Monson Controls Corporation reduced its price to the Refrigeration Division by 25 cents, retroactive to July 1. The price reduction was not reflected immediately in the intracompany price because the three divisions involved had agreed to use $2.40 for the entire year.

In October 1987, the Electric Motor Division and the Refrigeration Division were negotiating 1988 prices. The Refrigeration Division proposed a price of $2.15, the price paid to the Monson Controls Corporation. The Electric Motor Division, however, refused to reduce its prices below $2.40 to either the Refrigeration Division or the Laundry Equipment Division. After several weeks of negotiations, the disagreement was submitted to the finance staff for settlement.

Electric Motor Division.   The Electric Motor Division based its refusal to accept the last price reduction of the Monson Controls Corporation on the premise that it was made as a last, desperate effort to continue supplying General Appliance Corporation with this part. (Monson Controls Corporation continued to supply General Appliance Corporation with other products, although this control unit had been a major item.) As support for this premise, the Electric Motor Division indicated that at the lower price it would lose money. Since it was as efficient as the Monson Controls Corporation, it concluded that Monson must also be losing money. The price was, therefore, a distress price and not a valid basis for determining an internal price. To support its case further, the Electric Motor Division pointed out the downward trend in the price of this part as evidence of distress pricing practices growing out of the excess capacity in the industry.

The general manager of Electric Motor Division stated that it was going to take all his ability and ingenuity to make a profit even at the $2.40 price. At $2.15, he could never be in a profit position, and if forced to accept a price of $2.15, he would immediately make plans to close the plant and let outside suppliers furnish all the thermostatic control units.

Laundry Equipment Division.   The Laundry Equipment Division based its case for a $2.15 price on the intracompany pricing rules that required products to be transferred between divisions at competitive prices. The general manager pointed out that his annual volume was 100,000 units a year, compared to a total of only 20,000 for the Refrigeration Division. He believed that with his higher volume he could probably obtain an even more favorable price if he were to procure his requirements from outside the corporation.

Refrigeration Division. The Refrigeration Division based its case on the fact that the division not only could, but did, buy the thermostatic control unit from a reliable outside supplier for $2.15. The division was sure that the Monson Controls Corporation had capacity to produce all its requirements and would be happy to do so for $2.15 a unit. Since patronage had been transferred to the Electric Motor Division only as a favor and to benefit the company as a whole, the Refrigeration Division believed it was unjust to make it pay a higher price than it would have paid if the division had not allowed the business to be taken inside the company.

As further evidence to support its case, the Refrigeration Division pointed to an agreement made with the Electric Motor Division at the time it had agreed to purchase all its requirements of the thermostatic control unit from that division. This agreement read, in part: "In the event of a major pricing disparity, it is agreed that further model requirements will be competitively sourced [i.e., sourced to the lowest bidder]."

The Refrigeration Division stated that in light of the major pricing disparity it should be allowed to request quotations from outside suppliers and place the business outside should such a supplier bid lower than the Electric Motor Division.

Finance Staff Review. In the course of arbitrating this transfer price dispute, the finance staff asked the purchasing staff to review the outside market situation for the thermostatic control unit. The purchasing staff replied that there was excess capacity and that, as a result of this, prices were very soft. Eventually, the prices would rise—either when the demand for comparable units increased or when some of the suppliers went out of business. The purchasing staff had no doubt that the Refrigeration Division could purchase all its requirements for the next year or two at $2.15 a unit, or even less. The purchasing staff, however, believed that, if all

the corporation's requirements for this unit were placed with outside suppliers, the price would rise to at least $2.40 because this action would dry up the excess capacity.

Transmission Problem

The Laundry Equipment Division produced automatic washers. Initially, it had purchased its transmissions from two sources—the Gear and Transmission Division and the Thorndike Machining Corporation. The transmission had been developed and engineered by the Thorndike Machining Corporation. In consideration of an agreement to buy one half of its transmissions from the Thorndike Machining Corporation, the General Appliance Corporation had been licensed to produce the transmission. The current agreement ran from 1977 to 1987; at the expiration of the 10 years, General Appliance would have the right to use the design without restrictions.

In early 1985, nearly two years before the end of the agreement, the management of the General Appliance Corporation decided that it would not extend the agreement when it expired, but that it would expand the facilities of the Gear and Transmission Division enough to produce all the company's requirements. Accordingly, in March 1985, the Thorndike Machining Corporation was notified that beginning January 1, 1987, the General Appliance Corporation would manufacture all its own transmissions and, consequently, would not renew the current agreement.

This notification came as a surprise to the Thorndike Machining Corporation. Furthermore, its implications were very unpleasant because the General Appliance Corporation took a major share of the output of an entire plant, and there was little likelihood that the lost business could be replaced. The Thorndike Machining Corporation consequently faced the prospect of an idle plant and a permanent reduction in the level of profits.

In April 1985, the president of the Thorndike Machining Corporation wrote to the president of the General Appliance Corporation, asking that the decision not to extend the current agreement be reconsidered. He submitted a proposed schedule of price reductions that would be made if the current agreement was extended. He stated that these reductions would be possible because (*a*) Thorndike would be better off obtaining a lower price than abandoning the special-purpose machinery used for transmissions and (*b*) it expected increases in productivity. These proposed reductions were as follows:

Present price	$14.00
Price effective 7/1/85	13.50
Price effective 7/1/86	13.00
Price effective 7/1/87	12.50
Price effective 7/1/88	12.00

The letter further stated that the corporation had developed a low-cost transmission suitable for economy washers. This transmission was designed to cost $2 less than the present models and could be made available by January 1, 1988.

On receiving a copy of the letter, the general manager of the Laundry Equipment Division reopened the issue of continuing to buy from the Thorndike Machining Corporation. He had been interested in adding a low-cost automatic washer to the line, and the possibility of a $10 transmission appealed to him. The general manager of the Gear and Transmission Division, however, was interested in expanding his production of transmissions. To satisfy the Laundry Equipment Division he offered to develop a unit that would be comparable in price and performance to the proposed Thorndike Machining Corporation's economy unit. The offer was set forth in a letter signed by the general manager of the Gear and Transmission Division, dated April 22, 1985. The general manager of the Laundry Equipment Division accepted this offer, and no further question was raised about continuing to buy from the Thorndike Machining Corporation.

During the next two months, the engineering department of the Gear and Transmission and the Laundry Equipment Division jointly determined the exact performance features needed for the economy transmission; some of these features were different from those of the proposed Thorndike transmission. In June 1985, the general manager of the Gear and Transmission Division wrote a letter to the general manager of the Laundry Equipment Division, outlining the agreed-on engineering features and including the following price proposal:

Proposed selling price of Thorndike model		$10.00
Probable cost (assuming 11% profit)		9.00
Add:		
Cost of added design features	$0.85	
Increased cost of material and labor since date of quotation	0.75	1.60
Total cost		10.60
Profit		1.06
Adjusted price of G & T Unit		$11.66

The letter went on to say: "Because a price of $11.66 will not give us our objective profit, we propose to sell you this unit for $12. We believe that this is a fair and equitable price, and decidedly to your benefit."

This letter was never acknowledged by the Laundry Equipment Division.

In October 1985, the Gear and Transmission Division submitted a project proposal to the top management of the corporation, requesting money to build facilities to produce the new economy transmission. The project proposal included a profit projection based on a $12 price. The Laundry Equipment Division was quoted in the project proposal as agreeing to the price. There was no objection to this statement from the

Laundry Equipment Division personnel who were asked to comment on the proposed project. The project was approved, and the Gear and Transmission Division proceeded to buy and install the equipment to produce the new transmission.

In the latter part of 1985, the Gear and Transmission Division opened negotiations with the Laundry Equipment Division on the price of the new transmission, proposing $12 plus some minor adjustments for changes in cost levels since the previous year. The Laundry Equipment Division refused to accept the proposed price and countered with an offer of $11.21, developed as shown below.

Development of $11.21 Price

Proposed selling price of Thorndike model		$10.00
Adjustments:		
Cost of added design features	$0.85	
Cost of eliminated design features . . .	(0.50)	
Increased cost of material and labor since date of quotation	0.75	
Net cost change	1.10	
Profit on added cost	0.11	
Total price increase		1.21
Proposed price		$11.21

The Gear and Transmission Division refused even to consider this proposal, and after several days of acrimonious debate, both divisions decided to submit the dispute to the finance staff for arbitration.

Laundry Equipment Division. The Laundry Equipment Division based its case on the following arguments:

1. The division could have purchased a transmission, comparable in performance characteristics to the Gear and Transmission Division's unit, from the

Thorndike Machining Corporation for $11.21.

2. The Gear and Transmission Division had agreed to this price in consideration of being allowed to produce all the transmissions.

3. The intracompany pricing policy was that the supplying divisions should sell at competitive prices.

The general manager of the Laundry Equipment Division stated that it would be unfair to penalize him for keeping the transmission business inside the corporation as a benefit to the Gear and Transmission Division, particularly in the light of the promise made by the general manager of the Gear and Transmission Division.

The general manager also stated that he had not protested the price proposal included in the June 1985 letter because he believed that it was then too early to open negotiations. His cost analysts had not evaluated the proposal, but he assumed that the Gear and Transmission Division was approximately correct in its evaluation of the cost differences from the Thorndike unit. His position was that the difference of 34 cents between the adjusted Thorndike price and the quoted Gear and Transmission price was not worth negotiating until nearer the production date. The Laundry Equipment Division naturally had assumed that the Gear and Transmission Division would live up to its agreement and, therefore, regarded the request for $12 as just a negotiating gimmick.

Gear and Transmission Division. The Gear and Transmission Division based its case on two arguments:

1. The $10 quotation of the Thorndike Machining Corporation was invalid because it represented a final desperate effort to keep a share of the transmission business. A price of this nature should not form a long-term intracompany

pricing base. If the Thorndike Machining Corporation had received the business, it would have eventually raised its price.

2. The Laundry Equipment Division did not object to the Gear and Transmission Division's price proposal until after the facilities to build the transmission were already in place. The $12 price was used in the calculations that showed the profitability of the project, and on which the project approval was based. If the Laundry Equipment Division wished to object, it should have done so when the project was presented to top management. Because facilities were purchased on the assumption of a $12 price, the Laundry Equipment Division should not be allowed to object after the money had been spent.

Finance Staff Review

A review by the finance staff disclosed the following:

1. If the Thorndike Machining quotation of $10 were adjusted for the cost effect of changes in performance characteristics and the increase in general cost levels since the original quotation, the price would be $11.25, or approximately the same as that proposed by the Laundry Equipment Division. The price of $11.66 developed by the Gear and Transmission Division was in error because it failed to allow for a design elimination that would reduce the cost of the Thorndike unit by 50 cents.

2. At $12, the Gear and Transmission Division could expect to earn an aftertax profit of 15 percent on its investment; this was equal to its profit objective. At the $11.25 price, the division would earn about 6 percent after taxes.

3. The purchasing staff stated that, in its opinion, the transmission could be obtained from the Thorndike Machining Corporation at the quoted price level for the foreseeable future.

Questions

1. Be prepared in each of the disputes to play all three of the following roles: general manager of the supplying division, general manager of the buying division, member of the financial staff responsible for arbitrating the dispute. In the case of the general managers, you should not simply repeat the arguments presented in the case; you should also be prepared to give ground where your position is weak, to introduce new (but realistic) arguments to buttress your case, and to deal rationally with your adversary's arguments.

2. What, if any, changes in the company's transfer price policies and procedures would you recommend?

CASE 6–4
STRIDER CHEMICAL COMPANY

On December 9, 1986, the president of Strider Chemical Company, which had sales of around $175 million, announced that on January 1, 1987, the company would be reorganized into separate divisions. Until that time, the company had been organized on a functional basis, with the manufacturing, sales, finance, and research departments each under one person's responsibility. Six divisions were to be set up—four by product group and two by geographical area. Each division was to have its own production, sales, and accounting staff, and a general manager who would be responsible for its operation. The division's operating performance was to be judged by the profit it produced in relation to the investment assigned to it. It was anticipated that the procedure for computing the investment base and the return thereon would have to be carefully worked out if the resultant ratio was to be acceptable to the new division managers as a reasonable measure of their performance.

One of the biggest obstacles to the establishment of the desired monthly profit and loss statement for each division was the pricing of products for transfer from one to another of the various divisions. At the time the divisions were established, the company's president issued a policy statement upon which a pricing procedure was to be used. The president's statement follows.

Statement of Policy

The *maximum,* and usual, price for transfers between profit units is that price which enables the producing unit to earn a return on the investment required, consistent with what it can earn doing business with the *average* of its customers for the product group concerned.

Established prices will be reviewed each six months or when a general change in market prices occurs.

This case was prepared by Robert N. Anthony, Harvard Business School. Copyright by the President and Fellows of Harvard College. Harvard Business School case 166–016.

Discussion

Pricing policy between operating units is particularly important because, to the extent that the price is wrong, the return on one segment of the business is understated, and the return on another is overstated. This not only gives a false measure of how well individuals are performing, but also may make for bad decisions on the business as a whole, which will affect everyone.

Certain elements of expense that may not be found in intracompany relations are:

1. Deductions for cash discounts, freight, royalties, sales taxes, customer allowances, etc.
2. Usual selling expenses and, in many cases, order and billing services.
3. Certain customer services by the research laboratories, such as sales service where this applies.

The producing division that acts as a supplier will establish a price by discounting its *regular* price structure for the elements listed above which apply.

In case the buying division disagrees with the price as computed above, it will explain the basis of its disagreement to the president, who will decide what is to be done.

We are hopeful that this policy will work out equitably, giving each division a fair basis for the business they do. If, in practice, it is found that the policy is not working properly, is complicated in its application or calculation, or is working a hardship, the policy will have to be changed.

Williams Division

The largest of the newly formed divisions, the Williams Division, was strongly affected by the problem of transfer prices since about 23 percent of its sales would be to other divisions.

With only three weeks before the separation into divisions, it was important that a schedule of prices be established quickly for the transfer of products between divisions. The Williams Division's task was complicated by its large number of products. There were several hundred different compounds and materials for which a price had to be fixed. It was, therefore, partly for the sake of expediency that the Williams Division chose to set the prices on the basis of direct manufacturing cost. The figures used in this method were more readily available than those used in setting a price based on the current market price.

A week after the president's policy statement on transfer pricing had been distributed, the Williams Division issued an interpretation of the policy which stated its proposed method for setting prices for the sale of products by the Williams Division to other divisions. The key paragraphs from this statement were as follows:

> The Williams Division will charge the same price to another division as it charges to the average of its existing customers, less an allowance for those expenses incurred with average customers but not with interdivisional customers. These noncomparable expenses to be deducted include Sales Deductions and a part of Selling Expenses. The prices will be calculated in terms of a markup or multiplier factor on Direct Manufacturing Cost. A markup will be recalculated each six months, based on the prior 12 months' experience with regular customers.
>
> The markup for the first six months of 1987 will be 1.41 times Direct Manufacturing Cost as shown in Exhibit 1 which uses actual data for the 12-month period ended October 31, 1986.

By the end of March 1987, the president had received a number of letters from division managers, raising questions about transfer prices. Three of these are summarized as follows:

1. The Williams Division questioned the price which the Johnson Division had established for compound A, a raw material for the Williams Division. The Johnson Division had initially calculated a markup of 1.33, computed in the

EXHIBIT 1   Markup Calculation

	Dollars	Percent
Gross sales to outside customers . . .	$5,126,328	
Less: Amounts not applicable to internal sales:		
Freight, royalties, sales taxes	$ 58,625	
Selling expenses	260,123	
Total deductions	318,748	
Adjusted sales	4,807,580	100%
Direct manufacturing cost	3,404,923	71
Margin	1,402,657	29%

Computation 100 ÷ 71 = 1.41 times

same way the Williams Division computed its markup of 1.41. At a markup of 1.33, however, the Johnson Division would show a net loss since the division had not operated at a profit in the preceding 12 months. It, therefore, raised its markup to 1.41, the same as that used by the Williams Division. At this markup, it would show about the same profit as that of the Williams Division. The Williams Division argued that this markup violated company policy.

2. The International Division questioned the transfer price of several products it purchased from the Williams Division for sale abroad. It said that at these prices the International Division could not meet competitive prices in European markets and still make a profit.

3. The Western Division purchased Chemical B from the Williams Division for resale to its own customers. It submitted data to show that at the computed transfer price the Western Division would be better off to manufacture Chemical B in one of its own plants. Rather than do this, it proposed that the transfer price be cut by 15 percent, which would still leave a margin over direct manufacturing cost for the Williams Division.

As of the end of March, the president had not acted on any of these letters, other than to reply that existing relationships between divisions should be continued until further notice and that after the questions had been decided, adjustments in transfer prices would be made retroactive to January 1.

In view of the numerous questions that had arisen already about the markup, the president was considering the possibility of transferring all products at cost, without any markup.

Questions

1. How should the president respond to the three letters he had received from division managers raising questions about transfer prices?

2. What change, if any, should be made in the transfer price practices of Strider Chemical Company?

Case 6–5
Medoc Company

The Milling Division of the Medoc Company milled flour and manufactured a variety of consumer products from it. Its output was distributed as follows:

1. Approximately 70 percent (by weight) was transferred to the Consumer Products Division and marketed by this division through retail stores. The Consumer Products Division was responsible for these items from the time of packaging; that is, it handled warehousing, shipping, billing, and collections as well as advertising and other sales promotion efforts.
2. Approximately 20 percent was sold by the Milling Division as flour to large industrial users.
3. Approximately 10 percent was flour transferred to the Consumer Products Division and sold by that division to industrial users, but in different industries than those serviced directly by the Milling Division.

Counting each size and pack as one unit, there were several hundred products in the line marketed by the Consumer Products Division. The gross margin percentage on these products was considerably higher than that on flour sold to industrial users.

Wheat was purchased by the Grain Department, which was separate from the Milling Division. The price of wheat fluctuated widely and frequently. Other ingredients and supplies were purchased by the Milling Division.

The Milling Division and Consumer Products Division were 2 of 15 investment centers in the Medoc Company.

Products were transferred from the Milling Division to the Consumer Products Division at a unit price that corresponded to actual cost. There was a variation among products, but on

This case was prepared by Robert N. Anthony, Harvard Business School. Copyright by the President and Fellows of Harvard College. Harvard Business School case 171–284.

the average, this cost included elements in the following approximate proportions:

Flour	30%
Other ingredients and packaging material	25
Labor and variable overhead	20
Nonvariable overhead	25
Total	100%

Also, 75 percent of the Milling Division's investment was charged to the Consumer Products Division in computing the latter's return on investment. This investment consisted of property, plant, equipment, and inventory, all of which was "owned and operated" by the Milling Division.

This transfer price resulted in friction between the Milling Division and the Consumer Products Division, primarily for three reasons.

1. As in many process industries, unit costs were significantly lower when the plant operated at capacity. Indeed, the principal reason for accepting the low-margin industrial business was to permit capacity operations. There was general agreement that acceptance of such business at a low margin, or even at something less than full-cost, was preferable to operating at less than capacity. In recent years, the Milling Division had operated at least 98 percent of capacity.

The Milling Division alleged that the Consumer Products Division was not aggressive enough in seeking this capacity-filling volume. The Milling Division believed that the Consumer Products Division could increase the volume of consumer sales by increasing its marketing efforts and by offering more attractive special deals and that it could do more to obtain industrial business at a price which, although not profitable, nevertheless would result in a smaller loss than what the Milling Division incurred from sales made to the industry it served. This additional volume would benefit the company, even though it reduced the average profit margin of the Consumer Products Division. The Consumer Products Division admitted that there was some validity in this argument, but pointed out that it had little incentive to seek such business when it was charged full cost for every unit it sold.

2. The Consumer Products Division complained that, although it was charged for 75 percent of the investment in the Milling Division, it did not participate in any of the decisions regarding the acquisition of new equipment, inventory levels, etc. It admitted, however, that the people in the Milling Division were technically more competent to make these decisions.

3. The Consumer Products Division complained that since products were charged to it at actual cost, it must automatically pay for production inefficiencies that were the responsibility of the Milling Division.

A careful study had been made of the possibility of relating the transfer price either to a market price or to the price charged by the Milling Division to its industrial customers. Because of differences in product composition, however, this possibility definitely had been ruled out.

The Consumer Products Division currently earned about 20 percent pretax return on investment, and the Milling Division earned about 6 percent.

Top management of the Medoc Company was convinced that, some way or other, the profit performance of the Milling Division and the Consumer Products Division should be measured separately; that is, it ruled out the simple solution of combining the two divisions for profit-reporting purposes.

One proposal for solving the problem was that the transfer price should consist of two elements: (*a*) a standard monthly charge representing the Consumer Products Division's fair share of the nonvariable overhead, plus (*b*) a per-unit charge equivalent to the actual material, labor, and variable overhead costs applied to each unit billed. Investment would no longer be allocated to the Consumer Products Division. Instead, a standard profit would be included in computing the fixed monthly charge.

The monthly nonvariable overhead charge would be set annually. It would consist of two parts:

1. A fraction of the budgeted nonvariable overhead cost of the Milling Division, corresponding to the fraction of products that was estimated would be transferred to the Consumer Products Division (about 80 percent). This amount would be changed only if there were changes in wage rates or other significant noncontrollable items during the year.

2. A return of 10 percent on the same fraction of the Milling Division's investment. This was higher than the return that the Milling Division earned on sales to industrial users. The selection of 10 percent was arbitrary because there was no way of determining a "true" return on products sold by the Consumer Products Division.

Questions

1. What would you recommend given the organizational structure constraints in the case?

2. What would you recommend if there were *no* organizational structure constraints on your options?

MEASURING AND CONTROLLING ASSETS EMPLOYED

In some business units, the focus is on profit as measured by the difference between revenues and expenses, as described in Chapter 5. In other business units, this profit is compared with the assets employed in earning it. We refer to the latter group of responsibility centers as *investment centers* and discuss in this chapter the measurement problems involved in such responsibility centers. In the real world, companies do not use the term *investment center* but rather use the term *profit center* to refer to both the responsibility centers discussed in Chapter 5 and also those in this chapter. We agree that an investment center is a special type of profit center, rather than a separate, parallel category. Our reason for treating investment centers separately is primarily pedagogical; that is, there are so many problems involved in measuring the assets employed in a profit center that the topic warrants a separate chapter.

In this chapter we first discuss each of the principal types of assets that may be employed in an investment center. The sum of these assets is termed the investment base. We then discuss the two methods of relating profit to the investment base: (1) the percentage *return on investment (ROI)* and (2) residual income or *economic value added (EVA)*.[1] We describe the advantages and qualifications relating to the use of each in performance measurement. Finally, we discuss the somewhat different problem of measuring the economic value of an investment center.

---

[1]In previous editions we used the term *residual income* instead of *economic value added*. These two concepts are effectively the same. We will use the term *economic value added* because it is used more commonly now than residual income. EVA is a trademark of Stern Stewart & Co. "Economic Value Added" is an example of how a firm can take a concept that has been described in this and other texts for many years, slap a new name on it, and then register this name as a trademark.

Structure of the Analysis

The purposes of measuring assets employed are analogous to those discussed for profit centers in Chapter 5, namely:

- To provide information that is useful in making decisions about assets employed and to motivate managers to make sound decisions—that is, decisions in the best interests of the company.
- To measure the performance of the business unit as an economic entity.

In examining the several alternative treatments of assets and in comparing ROI and EVA—the two ways of relating profit to assets employed—we are primarily interested in how well the alternatives serve these two purposes.

It should be recognized at the outset that a focus on profits without consideration of the assets employed to generate those profits is an inadequate basis for control. Except in certain types of service organizations, in which the amount of capital is insignificant, an important objective of a profit-oriented company is to earn a satisfactory return on the capital that the company uses. A profit of $1 million in a company that has $10 million of capital does not represent as good a performance as a profit of $1 million in a company that has only $5 million of capital, assuming both companies have a similar risk profile.

Unless the amount of assets employed is taken into account, it is difficult for senior management to compare the profit performance of one business unit with that of other units or of similar outside companies. Comparisons of absolute differences in profits are not meaningful if business units use different amounts of resources; clearly, the greater the resources used, the greater should be the profits. Such comparisons are used both to judge how well business unit managers are performing and also as a basis for deciding how resources should be allocated.

> **Example.** Golden Grain, a business unit of Quaker Oats, had very high profitability . . . and appeared to be one of Quaker Oats's best divisions. It was, however, acquired by Quaker Oats at a premium above its book value. Based on the assets employed as measured by this premium, Golden Grain was underperforming.[2]

In general, business unit managers have two performance objectives. First, they should generate adequate profits from the resources at their disposal (subject, of course, to legal and ethical considerations). Second, they should invest in additional resources only when such an investment will produce an adequate return. Conversely, they should disinvest if the expected annual profits of any resource, discounted at the company's required earnings rate, is less than the cash that could be realized from its sale. The purpose of relating profits to investments is to motivate business unit managers to accomplish these objectives. As

---

[2]Brian McWilliams, "Creating Value," an interview with William Smithburg, Chairman. Quaker Oats, *Enterprise,* April, 1993.

Exhibit 7–1   Business Unit Financial Statements

Balance Sheet
($000s)

Current assets:			Current liabilities:		
Cash	$ 50		Accounts payable	$ 90
Receivables	150		Other current	110
Inventory	200			
Total current assets	400		Total current liabilities	200
Fixed assets:				
Cost . . . . $ 600			**Corporate equity**	500
Depreciation . . . . . −300				
Book value	300			
Total assets	$700		**Total equities**	$700

Income Statement

Revenue		$1,000
Expenses, except depreciation	$850	
Depreciation	50	900
Income before taxes		100
Capital charge ($500 × 10%)		50
Economic value added (EVA)		50

$$\text{Return on investment} = \frac{\$100}{\$500} = 20\%$$

---

we shall see, however, there are significant practical difficulties involved in creating a system that focuses on both profits and assets employed.

Exhibit 7–1 is a hypothetical, simplified set of business unit financial statements that will be used throughout this analysis. (In the interest of simplicity, income taxes have been omitted from this exhibit and generally will be omitted in the discussion in this chapter. Inclusion of income taxes would change the magnitudes in the calculations that follow, but it would not change the conclusions.) The exhibit shows the two ways of relating profits to assets employed; namely, return on investment (ROI) and economic value added (EVA).

Return on investment (ROI) is a ratio. The numerator is income, as reported on the income statement. The denominator is assets employed. In Exhibit 7–1, the denominator is taken as the corporation's equity in the business unit. This amount corresponds to the sum of noncurrent liabilities plus shareholders' equity in the balance sheet of a separate company. It is mathematically equivalent to total assets less current liabilities, and also to noncurrent assets plus working capital. (This statement can easily be checked against the numbers in Exhibit 7–1.)

EXHIBIT 7–2A   Methods Used to Evaluate Investment Centers

	Reece & Cool (1978)	Govindarajan (1994)
Number of usable responses	620	638
Companies with 2 or more investment centers	459 (74%)	500 (78%)
Percentage of companies using Residual Income or EVA (with 2 or more investment centers)	30%*	36%

*Reece & Cool had separately asked for the exclusive use of Residual Income (2%) and the joint use of Residual Income and Return on Investment (28%). Such a breakdown was not available in the Govindarajan survey.

Sources: Reece and Cool, "Measuring Investment Center Performance," pp. 28–49.
Govindarajan, "Profit Center Measurement," p. 2.

Economic value added (EVA) is a dollar amount, rather than a ratio. It is found by subtracting a capital charge from the net operating profit. This capital charge is found by multiplying the amount of assets employed by a rate, which in Exhibit 7–1 is 10 percent. We shall discuss the derivation of this rate in a later section.

> **Examples.** AT&T used the economic value added measure in evaluating business unit managers. For instance, the Long-Distance Group consisted of 40 business units selling such services as 800 numbers, telemarketing, and public telephone calls. All the capital costs, from switching equipment to new product development, were allocated to these 40 business units. Each business unit manager was expected to generate operating earnings that substantially exceeded the cost of capital.
>
> Other companies that used the economic value added measure include Coca-Cola, Briggs & Stratton, Longhorn Steakhouse, Mary Kay Cosmetics, CSX, and Quaker Oats.[3, 4]

Results from the Govindarajan survey[5] indicate that 78 percent of the respondents used investment centers. Of the American companies using investment centers, 36 percent evaluated them on economic value added (or residual income). Exhibit 7–2A summarizes both the Govindarajan and the Reece and Cool surveys.[6] Similar data for companies from Holland and India are given in Exhibit 7–2B.

For reasons to be explained later, EVA is conceptually superior to ROI; and therefore, we shall generally use EVA in our examples. Nevertheless, it is clear from the surveys that ROI is more widely used in business than EVA.

---

[3]Shawn Tully, "The Real Key to Creating Wealth," *Fortune,* September 20, 1993, pp. 38–50.

[4]Joel M. Stern, "The Mathematics of Corporate Finance—or EVA = $NA[RONA-C]," pp. 26–33.

[5]Govindarajan, "Profit Center Measurement," p. 2.

[6]Reece and Cool, "Measuring Investment Center Performance," pp. 28–49.

EXHIBIT 7–2B   Methods Used to Evaluate Investment Centers in Different Countries

	Holland[a]	India[b]
Number of Usable Responses	72	39
Companies with 2 or more investment centers	59 (82%)	27 (70%)
Percentage of companies using Residual Income or EVA (with 2 or more investment centers)	19%	8%

a) Elbert De With, "Performance Measurement and Evaluation in Dutch Companies," Paper presented at the 19th Annual Congress of the European Accounting Association, Bergen, 1996.

b) V. Govindarajan and B. Ramamurthy, "Financial Measurement of Investment Centers: A Descriptive Study," Working paper, Indian Institute of Management, Ahbedabad, India, August 1980.

Measuring Assets Employed

In deciding on the investment base to be used for evaluating managers of investment centers, headquarters asks two questions: (1) What practices will induce business unit managers to use their assets most efficiently and to acquire the proper amount and kind of new assets? Presumably, when their profits are related to assets employed, business unit managers will try to improve their performance as measured in this way, and senior management wants the actions that they take toward this end to be actions that are in the best interest of the whole corporation. (2) What practices best measure the performance of the unit as an economic entity?

Cash

Most companies control cash centrally because central control permits the use of a smaller cash balance than would be the case if each business unit held cash balances sufficient to provide the necessary buffer for the unevenness of its cash inflows and outflows. Business unit cash balances may well be only the "float" between daily receipts and daily disbursements. Consequently, the actual cash balances at the business unit level tend to be much smaller than would be required if the business unit were an independent company. Many companies, therefore, calculate the cash to be included in the investment base by means of a formula. For example, General Motors is reported to use 4.5 percent of annual sales; Du Pont is reported to use two months' costs of sales minus depreciation.

A reason for including cash at a higher amount than the balance normally carried by a business unit is that the higher amount is necessary to permit comparability with outside companies. If only the actual cash were shown, the return shown by internal units would be abnormally high and might be misleading to senior management.

Some companies omit cash from the investment base. These companies reason that the amount of cash approximates the current liabilities; if this is so, the sum of accounts receivable and inventories will approximate the amount of working capital.

Receivables

Business unit managers are able to influence the level of receivables, not only indirectly by their ability to generate sales, but also directly by establishing credit terms, by approving individual credit accounts and credit limits, and by their vigor in collecting overdue amounts. In the interest of simplicity, receivables often are included at the actual end-of-period balances, although the average of intraperiod balances is conceptually a better measure of the amount that should be related to profits.

Whether the accounts receivable should be included at selling prices or at cost of goods sold is also debatable. One could argue that the business unit's real investment in accounts receivable is only the cost of goods sold and that a satisfactory return on this investment is probably enough. On the other hand, it is possible to argue that the business unit has the opportunity to reinvest the money collected from accounts receivable; therefore, accounts receivable should be included at selling prices. The usual practice is to take the simpler alternative—that is, to include receivables at the book amount, which is the selling price less an allowance for bad debts.

If the business unit does not control credits and collections, receivables may be calculated on a formula basis. This formula should be consistent with the normal payment period—for example, 30 days' sales where payment is normally made 30 days after the shipment of goods.

Inventories

Inventories are ordinarily treated in a manner similar to receivables—that is, they are often recorded at end-of-period amounts even though intraperiod averages would be preferable conceptually. If the company uses LIFO (last in, first out) for financial accounting purposes, a different valuation method is ordinarily used for business-unit profit reporting because, in periods of inflation, LIFO inventory balances tend to be unrealistically low. In these circumstances, inventories should be valued at standard or average costs, and these same costs should be used to measure cost-of-sales on the business unit income statement.

If work-in-process inventory is financed by *advance payments* or by *progress payments* from the customer, as is typically the case with goods that require a long manufacturing period, these payments are either subtracted from the gross inventory amounts or reported as liabilities.

> **Example.** With manufacturing periods a year or greater, Boeing receives progress payments for its airplanes and records them as liabilities.[7]

---

[7]*The Boeing Company: 1993 Annual Report.*

Some companies subtract *accounts payable* from inventory on the grounds that the amount of accounts payable represents financing of part of the inventory by vendors, at zero cost to the business unit; the corporate capital required for inventories is only the difference between the gross inventory amount and accounts payable. If the business unit can influence the payment period allowed by vendors, the inclusion of accounts payable in the calculation encourages the manager to seek the most favorable terms. In times of high interest rates or credit stringency, managers might be encouraged to consider the possibility of forgoing the cash discount to have, in effect, additional financing provided by vendors. On the other hand, delaying payments unduly to reduce net current assets may not be in the company's best interest since this may hurt its credit rating.

Working Capital in General

As can be seen from the above, there is considerable variation in how working capital items are treated. At one extreme, companies include all current assets in the investment base with no offset for any current liabilities. This method is sound from a motivational standpoint if the business units have no influence over accounts payable or other current liabilities. It overstates the amount of corporate capital required to finance the business unit, however, because the current liabilities are a source of capital, often at zero interest cost. At the other extreme, all current liabilities may be deducted from current assets, as was done in calculating the investment base in Exhibit 7–1. This method provides a good measure of the capital provided by the corporation, on which it expects the business unit to earn a return. However, it may imply that business unit managers are responsible for certain current liabilities over which they have no control.

> **Example.** Quaker Oats used controllable working capital, which included items such as inventory, but not those over which the unit manager had no control.[8]

Property, Plant, and Equipment

In financial accounting, fixed assets are initially recorded at their acquisition cost, and this cost is written off over the asset's useful life through depreciation. Most companies use a similar approach in measuring profitability of the business unit's asset base. This causes some serious problems in using the system for its intended purposes. In this part of the chapter, we shall examine these problems.

Acquisition of New Equipment.   Suppose a business unit could acquire a new machine at a cost of $100,000. This machine is estimated to produce cash savings of $27,000 a year for five years. If the company has a required return of

---

[8]Brian McWilliams, op. cit.

EXHIBIT 7–3   Incorrect Motivation for Asset Acquisition ($000)

A. Economic calculation

Investment in machine $100

   Life, 5 years

   Cash inflow, $27,000 per year

Present value of cash inflow ($27,000 × 3.791)* ...... <u>102.4</u>

Net present value 2.4

Decision: Acquire the machine.

B. As reflected on business unit income statement

	As in Exhibit 7–1		First Year with Machine
Revenue	$1,000		$1,000
Expenses, except depreciation	$850		$823
Depreciation	<u>50</u>	<u>900</u>	<u>70</u> <u>893</u>
Income before taxes		100	107
Less capital charge at 10%†		<u>50</u>	<u>60</u>
EVA		<u>50</u>	<u>47</u>

Note: Income taxes are not shown separately for simplicity. Assume they are included in the calculation of the cash flow.

*3.791 is the present value of $1 per year for five years at 10 percent.

†Interest on the new machine is calculated at its beginning book value, which for the first year is $100 × 10% = 10. We have used the beginning-of-the-year book value for simplicity. Many companies use the average book value—(100 + 80) ÷ 2 = 90. The results will be similar.

10 percent, such an investment is attractive, as shown by the calculations in section A of Exhibit 7–3. The proposed investment has a net present value of $2,400, and therefore, should be undertaken. However, if the machine is acquired, and if the business unit measures its asset base as shown in Exhibit 7–1, the reported economic value added of the unit in the first year will decrease, rather than increase. The income statement without the machine (as in Exhibit 7–1) and the income statement if the machine is acquired (and in its first year of use) are shown in section B of Exhibit 7–3. Note that with the acquisition of the machine, income before taxes has increased, but this increase is more than offset by the increase in the capital charge. Thus, the economic value added calculation signals that profitability has decreased, whereas the economic facts are that profits have increased. In these circumstances, the business unit manager may be reluctant to purchase this machine.

   (In Exhibit 7–3, depreciation was calculated on the straight-line basis. If it had been calculated on an accelerated basis, which is not uncommon, the discrepancy between the economic facts and the reported results would have been even greater.)

   In later years, the amount of economic value added will increase, as the book value of the machine declines, as shown in Exhibit 7–4; it goes from

---

EXHIBIT 7–4   Effect of Acquisition on Reported Annual Profits ($000)

Year	Book Value at Beginning of Year (a)	Incremental Income* (b)	Capital Charge† (c)	EVA (b − c)	ROI b ÷ a
1	100	7	10	−3	7%
2	80	7	8	−1	9
3	60	7	6	1	12
4	40	7	4	3	18
5	20	7	2	5	35

Note: True return = approximately 11 percent.
*$27,000 cash inflow − $20,000 depreciation = $7,000.
†10 percent of beginning book value.

−$3,000 in year 1 to +$5,000 in year 5. The increase in economic value added each year does not represent real economic change. The increases appear to show constantly improving profitability, whereas the facts are that there has been no real change in profitability after the time the machine was acquired. Generalizing from this example, it is evident that business units that have old, almost fully depreciated, assets will tend to report larger economic value added than units that have newer assets.

If profitability is measured by return on investment, the same inconsistency exists, as shown in the last column of Exhibit 7–4. Although we know from the present value calculation that the true return is about 11 percent, the business unit financial statement reports that it is less than 10 percent in the first year, and that it increases thereafter. Furthermore, the average of the five annual percentages shown is 16 percent, which far exceeds what we know to be the true annual return.

It is evident that if depreciable assets are included in the investment base at net book value, business unit profitability is misstated, and business unit managers may not be motivated to make correct acquisition decisions.

> **Example.** Quaker Oats discovered they were underinvesting because of the low book value of their 100-year-old plants, "We've been in the business for over 100 years. As a result, we have a lot of plants and equipment with a small book value relative to our newer brands. And just because we're lucky enough to inherit a 100-year-old business doesn't mean we are exempt from substantially improving the controllable earnings of that business from year to year."[9]

Gross Book Value.   The fluctuation in economic value added and return on investment from year to year in Exhibit 7–4 can be avoided by including depreciable assets in the investment base at gross book value rather than at net book

---

[9]Brian McWilliams, op. cit.

value. Some companies do this. If this were done, the investment each year would be $100,000 (original cost), and the additional income would be $7,000 ($27,000 cash inflow—$20,000 depreciation). The economic value added, however, would be decreased by $3,000 ($7,000 – $10,000 interest), and return on investment would be 7 percent ($7,000 ÷ $100,000). Both of these numbers indicate that the business unit's profitability has decreased, which, in fact, is not the case. Return on investment calculated on gross book value always understates the true return.

Disposition of Assets.   If a new machine is being considered as a replacement for an existing machine that has some undepreciated book value, we know that the undepreciated book value is irrelevant in the economic analysis of the proposed purchase (except indirectly as it may affect income taxes). Nevertheless, in the calculation of business unit profitability, the removal of the book value of the old machine can have a substantial effect. Gross book value will increase only by the difference between the net book value after year 1 of the new machine and the net book value of the old machine. In either case, the relevant amount of additional investment is understated, and the economic value added is correspondingly overstated. Managers, therefore, are encouraged to replace old equipment with new equipment, even in situations in which such replacement is not economically justified. Furthermore, business units that are able to make the most replacements will show the greatest improvement in profitability.

In short, if assets are included in the investment base at their original cost, then the business unit manager is motivated to get rid of them, even if they have some usefulness, because the business unit's investment base is reduced by the full cost of the asset.

Annuity Depreciation.   If, instead of straight-line depreciation, depreciation is calculated by the annuity method, the business unit profitability calculation will show the correct economic value added and return on investment, as demonstrated in Exhibits 7–5 and 7–6. This is because the annuity depreciation method actually matches the recovery of investment that is implicit in the present value calculation. Annuity depreciation is the opposite of accelerated depreciation in that the annual amount of depreciation is low in the early years when the investment values are high and increases each year as the investment decreases; the rate of return remains constant.

Exhibits 7–5 and 7–6 show the calculations when the cash inflows are level in each year. Equations are available that derive the depreciation for other cash flow patterns, such as a decreasing cash flow as repair costs increase, or an increasing cash flow as a new product gains market acceptance.

Very few managers accept the idea of a depreciation allowance that increases as the asset ages, however. They visualize accounting depreciation as representing physical deterioration or loss in economic value. Therefore, they believe that accelerated or straight-line depreciation is a valid representation

---

EXHIBIT 7–5   Profitability Using Annuity Depreciation—Smoothing EVA ($000)

Year	Beginning Book Value	Cash Inflow	EVA*	Capital Charge†	Depreciation‡
1	$100.0	$ 27.0	$0.6	$10.0	$16.4
2	83.6	27.0	0.6	8.4	18.0
3	65.6	27.0	0.6	6.6	19.8
4	45.8	27.0	0.6	4.6	21.8
5	24.0	27.0	0.6	2.4	24.0
Total		$135.0	$3.0	$32.0	$100.0

*Annuity depreciation makes the EVA the same each year by changing the amount of depreciation charged. Consequently, we must estimate the total EVA earned over the five years. A 10 percent return on $100,000 would require five annual cash inflows of $26,378. The actual cash inflows are $27,000. Therefore, the EVA (the amount in excess of $26,378) is $622 per year.

†This is 10 percent of the balance at the beginning of the year.

‡Depreciation is the amount required to make the EVA (profits after the capital charge and depreciation) equal $622 per year (rounded here to $600). This is calculated as follows:

$$\$27.0 - \text{Capital charge} - \text{Depreciation} = \$0.6$$

therefore,

$$\text{Depreciation} = \$26.4 - \text{Capital charge}$$

EXHIBIT 7–6   Profitability Using Annuity Depreciation—Smoothing Return on Investment ($000)

Year	Beginning Book Balance	Cash Inflow	Net Profit*	Depreciation†	Return on Beginning Investment
1	$100.0	$ 27.0	$11.0	$ 16.0	11%
2	84.0	27.0	9.2	17.8	11
3	66.2	27.0	7.3	19.7	11
4	46.5	27.0	5.1	21.9	11
5	24.6	27.0	2.4	24.6	10‡
Total		$135.0	$35.0	$100.0	10%

*A return of $27,000 a year for five years on an investment of $100,000 provides a return of approximately 11 percent on the beginning of the year investment. Consequently, in order to have a constant 11 percent return each year, the net profit must equal 11 percent of the beginning of the year investment.

†Depreciation is the difference between the cash flow and the net profit.

‡The difference results because the return is not exactly 11 percent.

---

of what is taking place. Consequently, it is difficult to convince management to use the annuity method for business unit profit measurement.

Annuity depreciation also presents some practical problems. For example, the depreciation schedule in Exhibits 7–5 and 7–6 was developed based on an estimated cash flow pattern. If the actual cash flow pattern differs from that assumed, even though the total cash flow might result in the same rate of return, some years would show higher than expected profits and others would show lower. Should the depreciation schedule be changed each year to conform to the actual pattern of cash flow? This probably is not practical. Annuity depreciation would not be desirable for income tax purposes, of course; and although, as a "systematic and rational" method, it clearly is acceptable for financial accounting purposes, companies do not use it in their financial reporting. Indeed, surveys of company practice in measuring their business unit profitability show practically no use of the annuity method.[10]

Other Valuation Methods.   A few companies depart from the use of either gross book value or net book value in calculating the investment base. Some use net book value but set a lower limit, usually 50 percent, as the amount of original cost that can be written off; this lessens the distortions that occur in business units with relatively old assets. A difficulty with this method is that a business unit with fixed assets that have a net book value of less than 50 percent of gross book value can decrease its investment base by scrapping perfectly good assets. Other companies depart entirely from the accounting records and use an approximation of the current value of the asset. They arrive at this amount by a periodic appraisal of assets (say, every five years or when a new business unit manager takes over), by adjusting original cost by an index of changes in equipment prices, or by using insurance values.

A major problem with using nonaccounting values is that they tend to be subjective, as contrasted with accounting values, which appear to be objective and generally not subject to argument. Consequently, accounting data have an aura of reality for operating management. Although the intensity of this sentiment will vary with different managers, the further one departs from accounting numbers in measuring financial performance, the more likely that both business unit managers and senior management will regard the system as playing a game of numbers.

A related problem with using nonaccounting amounts in internal systems is that business unit profitability will be inconsistent with the corporate profitability as reported to the shareholders. Although the management control system need not necessarily be consistent with the external financial reporting, as a practical matter some managers regard net income, as reported on the financial statements, as constituting the "name of the game." Consequently, they do not favor an internal system that uses a different method of keeping score, regardless of its theoretical merits. Another problem with the economic value added approach is deciding how the economic values are to be determined. Conceptually, the economic value of a group of assets is equal to the present value of the cash flows that these assets will generate in the future. As a practical matter, this amount cannot be determined. Although published indexes of

---

[10]For example, Reece and Cool, "Measuring Investment Center Performance," pp. 28–49.

EXHIBIT 7–7   Effect of Leasing Assets—Income Statement ($000)

	As in Exhibit 7–1		If Assets Are Leased	
Revenue		$1,000		$1,000
Expenses other than below $850			$850	
Depreciation 50		900		
Rental expense			60	910
Income before taxes		100		90
Capital charge $500 × 10%		50		
$200 × 10%				20
EVA		50		70

replacement costs of plant and equipment can be used, most price indexes are not entirely relevant because they make no allowance for the impact of changes in technology.

In any case the inclusion of the investment base of fixed assets at other than the amounts derived from the accounting records appears to be used so rarely that it is of little more than academic interest.[11]

Leased Assets

Suppose the business unit whose financial statements are shown in Exhibit 7–1 sold its fixed assets for their book value of $300,000, returned the proceeds of the sale to corporate headquarters, and then leased back the assets at a rental rate of $60,000 per year. As shown in Exhibit 7–7, the business unit's income before taxes would be reduced because the new rental expense would be higher than the depreciation charge that has been eliminated. Nevertheless, economic value added would be increased because the higher cost would be more than offset by the decrease in the capital charge. Because of this tendency, business unit managers are induced to lease assets, rather than own them, under any circumstances in which the interest charge that is built into the rental cost is less than the capital charge that is applied to the business unit's investment base. (Here, as elsewhere, this generalization is an oversimplification, because, in the real world, the impact of income taxes must also be taken into account.)

Many leases are financing arrangements—that is, they provide an alternative way of obtaining the use of assets that otherwise would be acquired by funds obtained from debt and equity financing. Financial leases (i.e., long-term

---

[11]In a 1984 survey of 101 firms from the Fortune 1,000 list, only 1 respondent reported using replacement cost of fixed assets. (Francis J. Walsh, Jr., *Measuring Business Performance,* The Conference Board Research Bulletin, no. 153, p. 8). In a follow-up 1987 study by The Conference Board, this question was not even asked. In the Govindarajan survey, only 1 percent reported the use of replacement cost of fixed assets (see Exhibit 7–8).

leases equivalent to the present value of the cost of the asset) are similar to debt and are so reported on the balance sheet. Financing decisions are usually made by corporate headquarters. For these reasons, restrictions are usually placed on the business unit manager's freedom to lease assets.

Idle Assets

If a business unit has idle assets that can be used by other units, the business unit may be permitted to exclude them from the investment base if it classifies them as available. The purpose of this permission is to encourage business unit managers to release underutilized assets to units that may have better use for them. However, if the fixed assets cannot be used by other units, permitting the business unit manager to remove them from the investment base could result in dysfunctional actions. For example, it could encourage the business unit manager to idle partially utilized assets that are not earning a return equal to the business unit's profit objective. If there is no alternative use for the equipment, *any* contribution from this equipment will improve company profits.

Intangible Assets

Some companies capitalize intangible assets (such as R&D).[12] These intangible assets are then amortized over a selected life. This method has the potential to change how the business unit manager views these expenditures.[13] By changing the accounting for items such as R&D from an immediate expense to a long-term investment, the business unit manager will gain less short-term benefit from reducing R&D. If R&D expenditures are expensed immediately, each dollar of R&D cut would be a dollar increase in pretax profits. On the other hand, if R&D costs are capitalized, each dollar cut will reduce the assets employed by a dollar; the capital charge is thus reduced only by one dollar times the cost of capital, which has a much smaller positive impact on economic value added.

Noncurrent Liabilities

Ordinarily, a business unit receives its permanent capital from the corporate pool of funds. The corporation obtained these funds from debt providers, from equity investors, and from retained earnings. To the business unit, the total amount of these funds is relevant, but the sources from which they were obtained are irrelevant. In unusual situations, however, a business unit's financing may be peculiar to its own situation. For example, a business unit that builds or operates residential housing or office buildings uses a much larger proportion of debt capital than is the case with typical manufacturing and marketing units. Since this capital is obtained through mortgage loans on the

---

[12]Joel M. Stern, "The Mathematics of Corporate Finance—or EVA = $NA[RONA-C]," pp. 26–33.

[13]Shawn Tully, "The Real Key to Creating Wealth," *Fortune*, September 20, 1993, pp. 38–50.

business unit's assets, it may be appropriate to account for the borrowed funds separately and to compute an economic value added based on the assets that were obtained from general corporate sources, rather than on total assets.

The Capital Charge

The rate used to calculate the capital charge is set by corporate headquarters. It should be higher than the corporation's rate for debt financing because the funds involved are a mixture of debt and higher-cost equity. Usually, the rate is set somewhat below the company's estimated cost of capital (assuming that a company can calculate its cost of capital) so that the economic value added of an average business unit will be above zero.

Although conceptually a good argument can be made for using different rates for business units with different risk characteristics, in practice this is rarely done; that is, the same rate is used for all units.

> **Example.** AT&T used a cost of capital between 11 and 14 percent for all of its business units.[14]

Some companies use a lower rate for working capital than for fixed assets. This may represent a judgment that working capital is less risky than fixed assets because the funds are committed for a shorter time period. In other cases the lower rate is a way of compensating for the fact that the company included inventory and receivables in the investment base at their gross amount (i.e., without a deduction for accounts payable); the lower rate is an implicit recognition of the fact that funds obtained from accounts payable have zero interest cost.

Surveys of Practice

Practices in investment center management among U.S. Corporations are summarized in Exhibits 7–8A, 7–9A, and 7–10A. The great majority of companies include fixed assets in their investment base at their net book value. They do this because this is the amount at which the assets are carried in the financial statements and therefore represents, according to the financial statements, the amount of capital that the corporation has employed in the division. Managements recognize the fact that this method gives misleading signals, but they believe it is the responsibility of users of the business unit profit reports to make allowances for these errors in interpreting the reports and that alternative methods of calculating the investment base are so subjective that they are not to be trusted. They reject the annuity depreciation approach on the grounds that it is inconsistent with the way in which depreciation is calculated for financial statement purposes.

---

[14]Alex J. Mandl, CFO and Group Executive, AT&T, *AT&T 1992 Annual Report.*

EXHIBIT 7–8A   Valuation of Plant and Equipment

	Percentage of Respondents Using the Method	
	Reece & Cool (1978) *459 Respondents*	*Govindarajan (1994)* *500 Respondents*
Gross book value	14%	6%
Net book value	84	93
Replacement cost	2	1
	100%	100%

Sources: Reece and Cool, "Measuring Investment Center Performance," pp. 28–49.
Govindarajan, "Profit Center Measurement," p. 2.

EXHIBIT 7–8B   Valuation of Plant and Equipment

	Holland[a)]	*India[b)]*
Gross book value	9%	17%
Net book value	73%	79%
Replacement cost	18%	4%
	100%	100%

a) Elbert De With, "Performance Measurement and Evaluation in Dutch Companies," Paper presented at the 19th Annual Congress of the European Accounting Association, Bergen, 1996.

b) V. Govindarajan and B. Ramamurthy, "Financial Measurement of Investment Centers: A Descriptive Study," Working paper, Indian Institute of Management, Ahbedabad, India, August 1980.

Exhibits 7–8B, 7–9B, and 7–10B show current practices in investment center management in Holland and India. These exhibits indicate practices quite similar to the ones reported in Exhibits 7–8A, 7–9A, and 7–10A for U.S. corporations.

EVA Versus ROI

As shown in Exhibit 7–2, most companies employing investment centers evaluate business units on the basis of ROI rather than EVA. There are three apparent benefits of an ROI measure. First, it is a comprehensive measure in that anything that affects financial statements is reflected in this ratio. Second, ROI is easy to calculate, easy to understand, and meaningful in an absolute sense. For example, an ROI of less than 5 percent is considered low on an absolute scale, and an ROI of over 25 percent is considered high. Finally, it is a common denominator that may be applied to any organizational unit responsible for profitability, no matter what its size or in what business it practices. The performance of different units may be compared directly to each

EXHIBIT 7–9A   Assets Included in Investment Base

	Percentage of Respondents Including the Asset in the Investment Base	
	Reece & Cool (1978) *459 Respondents*	*Govindarajan (1994)* *500 Respondents*
Current assets		
Cash owned by the profit center	63%	47%
Corporate cash allocated to the profit center	n/a	13
External receivables	94	90
Intracompany receivables	n/a	55
Inventory	95	95
Other current assets	76	83
Fixed assets		
Land & buildings used solely by this profit center	94	97
Equipment used solely by this profit center	83	96
A portion of land & buildings used by 2 or more profit centers	45	49
A portion of equipment used by 2 or more profit centers	41	48
An allocation of assets of headquarters central research or similar units	16	19
Other assets		
Investments	n/a	53
Goodwill	n/a	55

Note: n/a denotes "not asked."
Sources: Reece and Cool, "Measuring Investment Center Performance," pp. 28–49.
Govindarajan, "Profit Center Measurement," p. 2.

other. Also, ROI data is available for competitors that can be used as a basis for comparison. The dollar amount of EVA does not provide such a basis for comparison. Nevertheless, the EVA approach has some inherent advantages over ROI.

There are three compelling reasons to use EVA over ROI. First, with EVA all business units have the same profit objective for comparable investments. The ROI approach, on the other hand, provides different incentives for investments across business units. For example, a business unit that currently is achieving a ROI of 30 percent would be most reluctant to expand unless it is able to earn a ROI of 30 percent or more on additional assets; a lesser return would decrease its overall ROI below its current 30 percent level. Thus, this business unit might forgo investment opportunities whose ROI is *above* the cost of capital but *below* 30 percent.

Exhibit 7–9B   Assets Included in Investment Base

	Holland[a]
Current Assets	
Cash	59%
Accounts receivable	94%
Inventory	93%
Other current assets	79%
Fixed Assets	
Land & buildings used solely by this profit center	82%
Allocated land & buildings used by two or more profit centers	47%
Machines & equipment used solely by this profit center	88%
Allocated machines & equipment used by two or more profit centers	46%
Other noncurrent assets	71%
Assets allocated to the center	16%
Other assets	7%

a) Elbert De With, "Performance Measurement and Evaluation in Dutch Companies," Paper presented at the 19th Annual Congress of the European Accounting Association, Bergen, 1996.

Exhibit 7–10A   Liabilities Deducted in Calculating Investment Base

	Percentage of Respondents Deducting the Liability from the Investment Base	
	Reece & Cool (1978) *459 Respondents*	*Govindarajan (1994)* *500 Respondents*
Current external payables	51%	73%
Current intracompany payables	30	46
Other current liabilities	45	68
Deferred taxes	n/a	28
Other noncurrent liabilities	20	47

Note: n/a denotes "not asked."
Sources: Reece and Cool, "Measuring Investment Center Performance," pp. 28–49.
Govindarajan, "Profit Center Measurement," p. 2.

Example. On an ROI basis, Wal-Mart would have chosen to stop expanding since the late 1980s because its ROI on new stores slipped from 25 percent to 20 percent, even though both rates are substantially above its cost of capital.[15]

---

[15]G. Bennett Stewart III, "Reform Your Governance From Within," *Directors and Boards,* Spring 1993, pp. 48–54.

EXHIBIT 7–10B   Liabilities Deducted in Calculating Investment Base

	Holland[a]
Accounts payable	91%
Other external interest-free current debts (e.g., taxes payable)	69%
Intracompany current debts	57%
External interest-bearing current debts	25%
Provisions	48%
Long-term interest bearing debts	25%
Other liabilities	11%

---

a) Elbert De With, "Performance Measurement and Evaluation in Dutch Companies," Paper presented at the 19th Annual Congress of the European Accounting Association, Bergen, 1996.

Similarly, a business unit that currently is achieving a low ROI, say 5 percent, would benefit from anything over 5 percent on additional assets. As a consequence, ROI creates a bias towards little or no expansion in the high-profit business units, while at the same time, the low-profit units are making investments at rates of return well below those rejected by the high-profit units.

Second, decisions that *increase* a center's ROI may *decrease* its overall profits. For instance, in an investment center whose current ROI is 30 percent, the manager can increase its overall ROI by disposing of an asset whose ROI is 25 percent. However, if the cost of capital tied up in the investment center is less than 25 percent, the absolute dollar profit after deducting capital costs will decrease for the center.

The use of EVA as a measure deals with both of the above noted problems of ROI. The problems relate to asset investments whose ROI falls between the cost of capital and the center's current ROI. If an investment center's performance is measured by EVA, investments which produce a profit in excess of the cost of capital will increase EVA and therefore be economically attractive to the manager.

A third advantage of EVA is that different interest rates may be used for different types of assets. For example, a relatively low rate may be used for inventories while a higher rate may be used for investments in fixed assets. Furthermore, different rates may be used for different types of fixed assets to take into account different degrees of risk. In short, the measurement system can be made consistent with the decision rules that affect the acquisition of the assets. It follows that the same type of asset may be required to earn the same return throughout the company, regardless of the profitability of the particular business unit. Thus, business unit managers should act consistently in decisions involving investments in new assets.

Differences between ROI and EVA are shown in Exhibit 7–11. Assume that the company's required rate of return for investing in fixed assets is 10 percent after taxes, and that the companywide cost of money tied up in inventories and

Exhibit 7–11   Difference between ROI and EVA ($000)

ROI Method

Business Unit	*(1)* Cash	*(2)* Receivables	*(3)* Inventories	*(4)* Fixed Assets	*(5)* Total Investment	*(6)* Budgeted Profit	*(7)* ROI Objective (6) ÷ (5)
A	$10	$20	$30	$60	$120	$24.0	20%
B	20	20	30	50	120	14.4	12
C	15	40	40	10	105	10.5	10
D	5	10	20	40	75	3.8	5
E	10	5	10	10	35	(1.8)	(5)

EVA Method

Business Unit	*(1)* Profit Potential	Current Assets *(2)* Amount	*(3)* Rate	*(4)* Required Earnings	Fixed Assets *(5)* Amount	*(6)* Rate	*(7)* Required Earnings	Budgeted EVA (1) – [(4) + (7)]
A	24.0	$60	4%	$2.4	$60	10%	$6.0	$15.6
B	14.4	70	4	2.8	50	10	5.0	6.6
C	10.5	95	4	3.8	10	10	1.0	5.7
D	3.8	35	4	1.4	40	10	4.0	(1.6)
E	(1.8)	25	4	1.0	10	10	1.0	(3.8)

receivables is 4 percent after taxes. The top section of Exhibit 7–11 shows the ROI calculation. Columns 1 through 5 show the amount of investment in assets that has been budgeted by each business unit for the coming year. Column 6 is the amount of budgeted profit. Column 7 is the budgeted profit divided by the budgeted investment. Column 6 shows, therefore, the ROI objectives for the coming year for each of the business units.

In only one business unit (C) is the ROI objective consistent with the companywide cutoff rate, and in no unit is the objective consistent with the companywide 4 percent cost of carrying current assets. Business Unit A would decrease its chances of meeting its profit objective if it did not earn at least 20 percent on added investments in either current or fixed assets, whereas Units D and E would benefit from investments with a much lower return.

EVA corrects these inconsistencies. The investments, multiplied by the appropriate rates (representing the companywide rates), are subtracted from the budgeted profit. The resulting amount is the budgeted EVA. Periodically, the actual EVA is calculated by subtracting from the actual profits the actual investment multiplied by the appropriate rates. The lower section of Exhibit 7–11 shows how the budgeted EVA would be calculated. For example, if Business

Unit A earned $28,000, and employed average current assets of $65,000 and average fixed assets of $65,000, its actual EVA would be calculated as follows:

$$EVA = 28,000 - 0.04(65,000) - 0.10(65,000)$$
$$= 28,000 - 2,600 - 6,500$$
$$= 18,900$$

This is $3,300 ($18,900 − $15,600) better than its objective.

Note that if any business unit earns more than 10 percent on added fixed assets, it will increase its EVA. (In the case of C and D, the additional profit will decrease the amount of negative EVA, which amounts to the same thing.) A similar result occurs for current assets. Inventory decision rules will be based on a cost of 4 percent for financial carrying charges. (There will be, of course, additional costs for physically storing the inventory.) In this way the financial decision rules of the business units will be consistent with those of the company.

EVA solves the problem of differing profit objectives for the same asset in different business units and the same profit objective for different assets in the same unit. EVA makes it possible to incorporate in the measurement system the same decision rules that are used in the planning process: the more sophisticated the planning process, the more complex the EVA calculation can be. For example, assume the capital investment decision rules call for a 10 percent return on general-purpose assets and a 15 percent return on special-purpose assets. Business unit fixed assets can be classified accordingly, and different rates applied when measuring performance. Managers may be reluctant to make new nonprofitable investments that improve working conditions, reduce pollution, or meet other social goals. Investments of this type would be much more acceptable to business unit managers if they are expected to earn a reduced return on them.

The problem of recognizing that business units have differing profit objectives can be mitigated in an ROI measurement system by using different budgeted ROIs; they allow for differences in the expected profitability of business units.

> **Example:** Mitsubishi Corporation, the Japanese multinational with a sales revenue of $176 billion, employs Return on Equity (ROE) as a management control tool. It has divided the company into seven groups and set differential ROE targets across the groups. For instance, the Information Technology Group which is working in the new field of multimedia has a low ROE target. The Food Group has a very high ROE target.[16]

Alternative Approaches to Evaluating Managers

EVA does not solve all the problems of measuring profitability in an investment center. In particular, it does not solve the problem of accounting for fixed assets discussed above unless annuity depreciation is also used, and this is rarely done in practice. If gross book value is used, a business unit can increase its EVA by taking actions contrary to the interests of the company, as shown in Exhibit 7–3. If net book value is used, EVA will increase simply due to the

---

[16]Joel Kurtzman, "An Interview with Minoru Makihara," *Strategy & Business,* Issue 2, Winter 1996, pp. 86–93.

passage of time. Furthermore, EVA will be temporarily depressed by new investments because of the high net book value in the early years. EVA does solve the problem created by differing profit potentials. All business units, regardless of profitability, will be motivated to increase investments if the rate of return from a potential investment exceeds the required rate prescribed by the measurement system.

Moreover, some assets may be undervalued when they are capitalized, and others when they are expensed. Although the purchase cost of fixed assets is ordinarily capitalized, a substantial amount of investment in start-up costs, new product development, dealer organization, and so forth may be written off as expenses, and, therefore, not appear in the investment base. This situation applies especially in marketing units. In these units the investment amount may be limited to inventories, receivables, and office furniture and equipment. When a group of units with varying degrees of marketing responsibility are ranked, the unit with the relatively larger marketing operations will tend to have the highest EVA.

In view of all these problems, some companies have decided to exclude fixed assets from the investment base. These companies make an interest charge for *controllable assets* only, and they control fixed assets by separate devices. Controllable assets are, essentially, receivables and inventory. Business unit management can make day-to-day decisions that affect the level of these assets. If these decisions are wrong, serious consequences can occur—quickly. For example, if inventories are too high, unnecessary capital is tied up, and the risk of obsolescence is increased; whereas, if inventories are too low, production interruptions or lost customer business can result from the stockouts. To focus attention on these important controllable items, some companies, such as Quaker Oats,[17] include a capital charge for the items as an element of cost in the business unit income statement. This acts both to motivate business unit management properly and also to measure the real cost of resources committed to these items.

Investments in fixed assets are controlled by the capital budgeting process before the fact and by postcompletion audits to determine whether the anticipated cash flows, in fact, materialized. This is far from being completely satisfactory because actual savings or revenues from a fixed asset acquisition may not be identifiable. For example, if a new machine produces a variety of products, the cost accounting system usually will not identify the savings attributable to each product.

The argument for evaluating profits and capital investments separately is that this often is consistent with what senior management wants the business unit manager to accomplish; namely, to obtain the maximum long-run cash flow from the capital investments the business unit manager controls and to add capital investments only when they will provide a net return in excess of the

---

[17]Brian McWilliams, "Creating Value," an interview with William Smithburg, Chairman, Quaker Oats, *Enterprise,* April 1993.

company's cost of funding that investment. Investment decisions, then, are controlled at the point where these decisions are made. Consequently, the capital investment analysis procedure is of primary importance in investment control. Once the investment has been made, it is largely a sunk cost and should not influence future decisions. Nevertheless, management wants to know when capital investment decisions have been made incorrectly, not only because some action may be appropriate with respect to the person responsible for the mistakes but also because safeguards to prevent a recurrence may be appropriate.

Management control systems designers disagree about whether it is better to use a single measure, EVA, to control profits and capital investments, or whether it is better to evaluate profit performance and capital investment performance separately. Most seem to feel that it is important to have a single overall measurement of financial performance. For example, if the actual profit was better than the budgeted profit but the capital investment performance was worse, how does management judge overall financial performance? EVA weighs the impact of the poorer investment performance against the improved profit performance and provides a single measure.

Example. Quaker Oats moved to economic value added from a combination of operating income and return on invested capital. As Quaker Oats Chairman William Smithburg noted, " . . . in this dual-measure system, they [managers] were not clear about which was more important. Frankly, division management tended to focus more heavily on operating income than Return on Invested Capital."[18]

A second reason for using a single measure is that it may motivate managers to be more careful about adding capital investments that may not be profitable.

Example. When CSX Corporation's freight volume increased by 25 percent, it could have added more locomotives, containers and railcars. Instead, its one measure helped motivate its management to reduce capital. The result was that CSX went from 18,000 containers and trailers to only 14,000, without sacrificing its quality.[19]

A third reason is that only major capital expenditures are examined carefully by corporate headquarters. Many minor acquisitions (e.g., routine replacements) are, for practical purposes, almost solely decided by the business unit manager, and in total, these can be significant. (One possible approach is to include minor acquisitions as part of controllable assets when calculating EVA. Only major capital expenditures will be controlled separately.)

In view of the disadvantages of ROI, it seems surprising that it is so widely used. Reece and Cool concluded that the disadvantages of ROI are exaggerated and that designers of control systems are aware of the conceptual flaws of the ROI approach, but that the designers do not believe that these flaws are serious. We know from personal experience that the conceptual flaws of ROI for

---

[18]Brian McWilliams, op. cit.

[19]Shawn Tully, "The Real Key to Creating Wealth," *Fortune,* September 20, 1993, pp. 38–50.

performance evaluation are real and do result in dysfunctional conduct on the part of business unit managers. We are unable to determine the extent of this dysfunctional conduct, however, because few managers are likely to admit its existence and many are unaware of it when it *does* exist. The likelihood of dysfunctional conduct seems related to the importance attached to meeting the ROI objective. Some companies calculate ROI but place primary importance on some other financial objective for evaluating performance (e.g., meeting the budgeted profit goal). Other companies, however, *do* place primary emphasis on meeting the ROI objectives, and this latter group is in greater danger of inducing dysfunctional actions on the part of business unit managers.[20]

Evaluating the Economic Performance of the Entity

The discussion to this point has focused on measuring the performance of business unit managers. As pointed out in Chapter 5, reports are also made on economic performance of business units. The two types of reports are quite different. Management reports are prepared monthly or quarterly, whereas economic performance reports are prepared at irregular intervals, usually once every several years. For reasons stated earlier, management reports tend to use historical information on actual cost incurred, whereas economic reports use quite different information. In this section we discuss the purpose and nature of the economic information.

Economic reports are a diagnostic instrument; they indicate whether the current strategies of the business unit are satisfactory, or whether a decision should be made to do something about the business unit—expand it, shrink it, change its direction, or sell it. The economic analysis of an individual business unit may reveal that current plans for new products, new plant and equipment, or other new strategies, when considered as a whole, will not produce a satisfactory future profit, even though each separate decision seemed sound at the time it was made.

Economic reports are also made as a basis for arriving at the value of the company as a whole. Such a value is called the *breakup value*—that is, the estimated amount that shareholders would receive if individual business units were sold separately. (Consulting firms often use the term *shareholder value.*) The breakup value is useful to an outside organization that is considering making a takeover bid for the company, and of course, it is equally useful to company management in appraising the attractiveness of such a bid. The report indicates the relative attractiveness of the several business units, and it may suggest that senior management is misallocating its scarce time—that is, spending an undue amount of time on business units that are unlikely to contribute much to the company's total profitability. If there is a gap between current profitability and shareholder value, there is an indication that changes

---

[20]For a more complete discussion of the above, see John Dearden, "Measuring Profit Center Managers," *Harvard Business Review,* September–October 1987, pp. 85–88.

may need to be made. (Alternatively, current profitability may be depressed by costs that will enhance future profitability, such as new product development and advertising, as mentioned in an earlier section.)

The most important difference between the two types of reports is that economic reports focus on predicting future profitability, rather than what profitability is or has been. The book value of assets and depreciation based on the historical cost of these assets is used in the performance reports of managers, despite their known limitations. This information is irrelevant in reports that estimate the future; in these reports, the emphasis is on replacement costs.

Conceptually, the value of a business unit is the present value of its future earnings stream. This is calculated by estimating cash flows for each future year and discounting each of these annual flows at a required earnings rate. The analysis covers 5, or perhaps 10, future years. Assets on hand at the end of the period covered are assumed to have a certain value, the *terminal value,* which is discounted and added to the value of the annual cash flows. Although these estimates are necessarily rough, they provide a quite different way of looking at the business units from that conveyed in the performance reports.

Summary

Investment centers are encumbered by all of the measurement issues involved in defining expenses and revenues, which were discussed in Chapters 4, 5, and 6. Investment centers raise additional issues regarding how the assets employed should be measured—issues such as which assets to include, how to value fixed assets and current assets, which depreciation method to use for fixed assets, which corporate assets to allocate, which liabilities to subtract, and so on.

An important goal of a business organization is to optimize return on shareholder equity (i.e., the net present value of future cash flows). It is not practical to use such a measure to evaluate the performance of business unit managers on a monthly or quarterly basis. Accounting rate of return is the best surrogate measure of business unit managers' performance. Economic value added is conceptually superior to return on investment in evaluating business unit managers.

While setting the annual profit objectives, in addition to the usual income statement items, there should be an explicit interest charge against the projected balance of controllable working capital items, principally receivables and inventories. There is considerable debate about the right approach to management control over fixed assets. Reporting on the economic performance of an investment center is quite different from reporting on the performance of the manager in charge of that center.

Suggested Additional Readings

Dearden, John. "Measuring Profit Center Managers." *Harvard Business Review,* September–October 1987, pp. 84–88.

Govindarajan, Vijay. "Profit Center Measurement: An Empirical Study." The Amos Tuck School of Business Administration, Dartmouth College, 1994.

Len, Kenneth, and Anil K. Makhija. "EVA & MVA: As Performance Measures and Signals for Strategic Change." *Strategy & Leadership* 24, 3, May–June 1996, pp. 34–38.

Reece, James S., and William A. Cool, "Measuring Investment Center Performance." *Harvard Business Review,* May–June 1978, pp. 28–49.

Solomons, David. *Divisional Performance: Measurement and Control.* Homewood, IL: Richard D. Irwin, 1965.

Stern, Joel. "E.V.A. share options that maximize value." *Corporate Finance,* August 1993, pp. 31–32.

Stewart, G. Bennett, III, "EVA works—But not if you make these common mistakes." *Fortune,* May 1, 1995, pp. 117–18.

Vancil, Richard F. *Decentralization: Management Ambiguity by Design.* Homewood, IL: Dow Jones-Irwin, 1979.

Walsh, Francis J. *Measuring Business–Unit Performance.* Research Bulletin no. 206. New York: The Conference Board, 1987.

Wanner, David L., and Richard W. Leer. "Managing for Shareholder Value—From Top to Bottom." *Harvard Business Review,* November–December 1989, pp. 52–60.

Case 7–1
Investment Center Problems (A)

1. The ABC Company has three divisions—A, B, and C. Division A is exclusively a marketing division, Division B is exclusively a manufacturing division, and Division C is both a manufacturing and marketing division. Exhibit 1 shows financial facts for each of these divisions.

Question

Assume that the ABC Company depreciates fixed assets on a straight-line basis over 10 years. To maintain its markets and productive facilities, it has to invest $100,000 per year in market development in Division A and $50,000 per year in Division C. This is written off as an expense. It also has to replace 10 percent of its productive facilities each year. Under these equilibrium conditions, what are the annual rates of return earned by each of the divisions?

Exhibit 1   Information about Divisions

	Division A	Division B	Division C
Current assets	$100,000	$ 100,000	$100,000
Fixed assets	—	1,000,000	500,000
Total assets	$100,000	$1,100,000	$600,000
Profits before depreciation and market development costs	$200,000	$ 200,000	$200,000

2. The D Division of the DEF Corporation has budgeted aftertax profits of $1 million for 1987.

This case was prepared by Professor John Dearden. Copyright by Osceola Institute. Suggestions by Jim Reece are incorporated.
Note: In solving these problems, ignore taxes. Most of the problems state that savings or earnings are "after taxes." Assume that the amount of income taxes will not be affected by alternative accounting treatment.

It has budgeted assets as of January 1, 1987, of $10 million, consisting of $4 million in current assets and $6 million in fixed assets. Fixed assets are included in the asset base at gross book value. The net book value of these fixed assets is $3 million. All fixed assets are depreciated over a 10-year period on a straight-line basis.

The manager of the D Division has submitted a capital investment project to replace a major group of machines. The financial details of this project are as follows:

New equipment:	
Estimated cost	$2,000,000
Estimated aftertax annual savings*	300,000
Estimated life	10 years
Old equipment to be replaced:	
Original cost	$1,500,000
Original estimate of life	10 years
Present age........................	7 years
Present book value ($1,500,000–$1,050,000)	$450,000
Salvage value	0

*These are cash inflows, disregarding depreciation and capital gains or losses (except for their tax impact).

Questions

The capital investment project was approved, and the new machinery was installed on January 1, 1987. Calculate the rate of return that is earned on the new investment, using the divisional accounting rules, and calculate the revised 1987 and 1988 budgeted rate of return:

(a) Assuming that the investment and savings are exactly as stated in the project.

(b) Assuming that the investment is overrun by $500,000 and the annual savings are only $200,000.

Notes

A. In answering Problem **2**, ignore the time value of money in your calculations. Use composite straight-line depreciation over the 10-year period. The essential differences between "composite" and "unit" depreciation are these: (1) Under "unit" depreciation, each asset is accounted for as an individual entity. One result of this is that assets disposed of for more (or less) than their net book value give rise to an accounting gain (or loss), which is included in the profit calculation. (2) Under "group" or "composite" depreciation, a pool of assets is accounted for by applying an annual depreciation rate to the gross book value (i.e., original cost) of the entire pool. When an individual asset is retired, the gross book value of the pool of assets is reduced by the original cost of the asset, and the accumulated depreciation account for the pool is reduced by the difference between the asset's original cost and scrap value, if any (i.e., a retired asset is assumed to be fully depreciated). Thus, any gains or losses from the disposal of assets are "buried" in the accumulated depreciation account and do not flow through the income statement.

B. Assume everything is as stated in Problem **2**—*except* that the company used *unit* depreciation. Answer the questions in Problem **2** for the years 1987 and 1988.

3. Assume everything is as stated in Problem **2**—except that the fixed assets are included in the divisional assets base at their net book value at the end of the year. Answer the questions in Problem **2** for 1987 and 1988.

Questions

(a) Do Problem **3** using *unit* depreciation.
(b) Do Problem **3** using *composite* depreciation.
(c) Do Problem **3** on the basis that DEF Corporation depreciates the pool of assets on the basis of the sum-of-the-years'-digits method, using composite depreciation. Calculate the rate of return on the new investment for 1987 and 1988 using the divisional accounting rules, assuming that:
   (1) The investment and savings were exactly as stated in the project proposal.
   (2) The investment was overrun by $500,000, and the annual savings were only $200,000.

Incorporate the following numbers to do your calculations:

Sum of digits 1–10 = 55
$2,000 × 10/55 = $364
$2,000 × 9/55 = $327
$2,500 × 10/55 = $455
$2,500 × 9/55 = $409
$1,500 × 3/55 = $82
$1,500 × 2/55 = $55

4. The G Division of the GHI Corporation proposes the following investment in a new product line:

Investment in fixed assets	$100,000
Annual profits before depreciation but after taxes (i.e., annual cash flow)	25,000
Life	5 years

The GHI Corporation used the time-adjusted rate of return, with a cutoff rate of 8 percent in evaluating its capital investment proposals. A $25,000 cash inflow for five years on an investment of $100,000 has a time-adjusted return of 8 percent. Consequently, the proposed investment is acceptable under the company's criterion. Assume that the project is approved and that the investment and profit were the same as estimated. Assets are included in the divisional investment base at the average of the beginning and end of the year's net book value.

Questions

(a) Calculate the rate of return that is earned by the G Division on the new investment for each year and the average rate for the five years, using straight-line depreciation.

(b) Calculate the rate of return that is earned by the G Division on the new investment for each year, and the average for the five years using the sum-of-the-years'-digits depreciation.

5. A proposed investment of $100,000 in fixed assets is expected to yield aftertax cash flows of $16,275 a year for 10 years. Calculate a depreciation schedule, based on annuity-type depreciation, that provides an equal rate of return each year on the investment at the beginning of the year, assuming that the investment and earnings are the same as estimated.

6. The JKL Company used the economic value added method for measuring divisional profit performance. The company charges each division a 5 percent return on its average current assets and a 10 percent return on its average fixed assets. Listed below are some financial statistics for three divisions of the JKL Company.

	Division		
	J	K	L
Budget data ($000s):			
1987 budgeted profit	$ 90	$ 55	$ 50
1987 budgeted current assets	100	200	300
1987 budgeted fixed assets	400	400	500

	Division		
	J	K	L
Actual data ($000s):			
1987 profits	$ 80	$ 60	$ 50
1987 current assets	90	190	350
1987 fixed assets	400	450	550

Questions

(a) Calculate the ROI objective and actual ROI for each division for 1987.

(b) Calculate the EVA objective for each division for 1987.

(c) Calculate the actual EVA for each division for 1987 and calculate the extent that it is above or below objective.

7. Refer to the budgeted profits and assets of the three divisions of the JKL Company provided in Problem **6.** Listed below are four management actions, together with the financial impact of these actions. For each of these situations, calculate the impact on the budgeted ROI and EVA for each division. (Another way of looking at this problem is to calculate the extent to which these actions help or hurt the divisional managers in attaining their profit goals.)

Situation 1. An investment in fixed assets is made. This action increases the average fixed assets by $100,000 and profits by $10,000.

Situation 2. An investment in fixed assets is made. This action increases the average assets by $100,000 and profits by $7,000.

Situation 3. A program to reduce inventories is instituted. As a result inventories are reduced by $50,000. Increased costs and reduced sales resulting from the lower inventory levels reduce profits by $5,000.

Situation 4. A plant is closed down and sold. Fixed assets are reduced by $75,000 and profits (from reduced sales) are decreased by $7,500.

CASE 7–2
INVESTMENT CENTER PROBLEMS (B)

1. The Complete Office Company has three divisions: Layout and Marketing, Office Furniture, and Office Supplies. Layout and Marketing is primarily a consulting and sales group with no fixed assets and minimal current assets. Office Furniture is a manufacturing division with machinery for the production and assembly of desks, chairs, and modular dividers. The Office Supplies Division has light machinery for the packaging and distribution of paper and other office supplies. It has current assets in the form of inventory and receivables, and it has some fixed assets in the form of machinery.

The Complete Office Company depreciates all of its fixed assets over 10 years on a straight-line basis, and it calculates ROA on beginning of year gross book value of assets. The operating expenses for each division (besides depreciation on fixed assets) are $200,000 for Layout and Marketing, $100,000 for Office Furniture, and $150,000 for Office Supplies. The company's assets and gross profits for 1997 are as follows:

	Layout and Marketing	Office Furniture	Office Supplies
Current assets	200,000	200,000	200,000
Fixed assets	—	1,000,000	500,000
Total assets	200,000	1,200,000	700,000
Gross profit from sales	400,000	400,000	400,000

This case was prepared by Professor Ed Barrett, Thunderbird Graduate School of Management, Phoenix, AZ. Copyright by Ed Barrett.

Question

Please compute an ROA figure for each division for 1997.

2. The manager of the Big Spender Division of Growing Industries has received formal approval to buy a specific new machine for his division. Given the following assumed data excerpted from his capital expenditure request, what ROAs (based on gross book value) will his division earn for 1996 and 1997?

Data Excerpted from Capital Expenditure Request:

(1) Budgeted aftertax profits of $3,000,000 per year.

(2) January 1, 1996, budgeted assets of $30,000,000, consisting of $12,000,000 in current assets and $18,000,000 in fixed assets, at gross book value.

(3) Net book value of the existing fixed assets was $9,000,000.

(4) All fixed assets are depreciated over 10 years on a straight-line depreciation method. There are no noncash expenses or revenues other than depreciation, and the same depreciation method is used for tax and books.

(5) Data relevant to the new equipment:

Budgeted cost	$6,000,000
Estimated annual aftertax savings*	900,000
Estimated depreciable life	10 years
Date of expected purchase	1/1/96

*These are cash inflows net of all tax impacts. That is, they are computed so as to disregard depreciation and book gains or losses except for their tax impact.

(6) Data relative to the old equipment to be replaced:

Gross book value	$4,500,000
Depreciable life	10 years
Present age	7 years
Depreciation taken to date	3,150,000
Salvage value	—

3. The manager of the Big Spender Division did install his new machine. What ROA was really earned in 1996 and 1997 if his machine had installation cost overruns of $1,500,000 and produced cost savings of only $600,000 per year? (All other facts are the same as in problem 2.)

4. Assume that instead of calculating ROA on gross book value, all divisions of Growing Industries calculated ROA using end-of-year net book values. How would that change the projected results for the Big Spender Division? (Use the same projections as in problem 2.)

5. Again, assume that Growing Industries calculates ROA on net book values at end of year. The manager of the Big Spender Division finds that he has a $1,500,000 installation cost overrun and only $600,000 savings per year. How will his actual ROA look for 1996 and 1997?

6. Ace Corporation allows the managers of its divisions a good deal of freedom in choosing their method of computing ROA, as long as the method chosen is consistent from year to year so that performance in each of the years can be compared.

    The new manager of the Diamond Division of Ace Corporation wanted the books to show him managing a relatively large amount of assets and showing improved year-to-year results, so for calculating ROA he used *beginning*-of-year book values and straight-line depreciation so that the assets would show the highest net book value. The Diamond Division had just been formed to run a new machine which cost $10,000,000, was expected to have a five-year life, and it was hoped would produce after-tax cash inflows of $2,500,000 per year.

Questions

(a) What will the new manager's ROA on this machine be for the five years of its expected life?

(b) What will be the average ROA?

(c) If the new manager's bonus were calculated as $100 for each percent of ROA, what would his bonus be in each year?

(d) What is the IRR on this project?

7. The more experienced manager of the Spade Division of Ace Corporation also wants to look good. He's also interested, however, in demonstrating that the bonus plan is not well conceived. He chooses to employ *end* of year net book values for calculating his ROA.

Questions

If the Spade Division were to buy the same machine with the same life, depreciation, and expected after-tax cash inflows as shown in problem 6:

(a) Calculate the manager's ROA for the five years of expected life of the machine.

(b) What would be the average ROA?

(c) What would be *his* bonuses if they were also calculated on the basis of $100 for each percent of ROA each year?

(d) What is the IRR on this project?

8. The far older and wiser manager of the Heart Division of Ace Corporation decided to depreciate the $10,000,000 in new assets in his division over five years using the sum-of-the-years' digits method. He also decides to use beginning-of-the-year net book values. His machines also are expected to produce after-tax cash inflows of $2,500,000 per year.

Questions

(a) What would be the manager's ROA each year?

(b) What would be the average ROA?

(c) What would his bonuses be over the five-year period?

(d) What is the IRR?

9. The corporate management of Ace Corporation later decided to try a different type of machine investment. The machine involved in this decision would last 10 years, although it would have after-tax cash inflows of only $1,627,500 per year. The machine cost $10,000,000. The financial staff chose to use an annuity method of depreciation. (In this method, the depreciation *increases* each year as the machine grows older. In concept, the net book value and the return (after depreciation) on the machine *decrease* commensurately, so as to help create a consistent ROA over the life of the machine.)

Questions

(a) Please construct an annuity depreciation schedule that provides an equal ROA (using net book value of assets at the beginning of the year) for each of the expected 10 years' life of the project.

(b) What advantages or disadvantages do you see with this methodology?

10. The Ultima Company employs a return-on-investment (ROI) methodology to measure divisional performance. "Investment" in their calculations consists of a figure representing average annual current assets plus average annual fixed assets. Shown below are both the budgeted and then the actual data for five divisions of Ultima Company for the year 1997 (in thousands of dollars).

Divisions	Budgeted Profits	Budgeted Average Current Assets	Budgeted Average Fixed Assets
A	90	100	400
B	55	200	400
C	50	300	500
D	100	200	800
E	150	400	800

Divisions	Actual Profits	Actual Average Current Assets	Actual Average Fixed Assets
A	80	90	400
B	60	190	450
C	50	350	550
D	105	200	800
E	155	200	800

Questions

(a) Please compute budgeted ROI for each division.

(b) Please compute actual ROI for each division.

(c) Comment on the comparison of the two sets of results.

11. Some new managers at Ultima Company feel that there should be a way to measure divisional performance, taking into account the basic cost of capital. They suggest running the same numbers for Ultima as in problem 10, based on the concept of economic value added, charging 5 percent for the usage of current assets and 10 percent for the usage of fixed assets.

Questions

Using the budgeted and actual figures for Ultima Company from problem 10, and using the charges for capital given above:

(a) Please compute budgeted EVA for each division.

(b) Please compute actual EVA for each division.

(c) Comment on the comparison of the two sets of results, and a comparison with the results of problem 10.

12. The Ultima Company decides to make an investment in fixed assets costing $100,000. This investment is expected to produce profits of $10,000 per year. How would this investment help the managers of each division attain their budgeted ROI and EVA goals if this project were added to their divisions?

Questions

Using the budgeted figures for Ultima Company in problem 10, please find the impact of this project on:

(a) Budgeted ROI goals of each division.

(b) Budgeted EVA goals of each division.

(c) Please analyze the resulting data.

13. If, instead of making an investment in fixed assets, the Ultima Company decides to make an investment in current assets of $100,000 with an expected profit of $7,000 per year, how would that affect its budgets?

Questions

Using the figures given in problem 10, please compute:

(a) Budgeted ROI for 1997.

(b) Budgeted EVA for 1997.

(c) Please analyze the resulting data.

14. If, instead of expanding operations, Ultima Company decides to retrench in a declining market, what would be the effect on budgeted ROI and EVA of reducing inventories by $50,000? It is expected that slightly increased delivery costs and definitely reduced sales will result in profits lowered by $5,000 per year.

Questions

Starting with the figures for Ultima Company given in problem 10, please calculate the effect these changes would have on:

(a) Budgeted ROI in 1997.

(b) Budgeted EVA in 1997.

(c) Your analysis of the resultant data.

15. If, instead of reducing inventories, Ultima Company prefers to handle its retrenchment by selling a plant, it will reduce fixed assets by $75,000. It is expected that this move will also decrease sales by $5,000 per year.

Questions

What will be the effect of this move on the data about Ultima Company given in problem 10?

(a) Please compute the effect this sale will have on ROI in 1997.

(b) Please compute the effect this sale will have on EVA in 1997.

(c) Please analyze and comment upon the resultant data.

Case 7–3
Quality Metal Service Center

In early March 1982, the casewriter met with Edward Brown, president and chief executive officer of Quality Metal Service Center (Quality). Excerpts of their conversation are given below:

> *Brown:* It has been quite a while since we took a hard look at our planning and control systems. Since you have a special interest in this area, I thought you might want to spend some time examining our systems.
> *Casewriter:* Do you perceive any weaknesses in your current systems?
> *Brown:* I'm not sure. Though I am satisfied with our past performance, I believe that we are capable of achieving even higher levels of sales and profits. Considering the market expansion and the state of competition, I feel we might have missed out on some growth opportunities. I don't know if our controls have inhibited managers from pursuing our goals of aggressive growth and above-average return on assets, as compared to the industry, but you might keep that in mind while evaluating our systems.

The Metal Distribution Industry[1]

Service centers bought metals from many of the mills including USS, Bethlehem, Alcoa, Reynolds, and such smaller firms as Crucible, Northwestern, and Youngstown. These suppliers sold their products in large lots, thereby optimizing the efficiencies associated with large production runs. Service centers sold their products to metal users in smaller lots and on a short lead-time basis.

The metal distribution industry was generally regarded as a mature, highly competitive, and fragmented industry. The percentage of industrial steel products shipped through service centers had increased dramatically during 1974–82. In 1982, about 22 million tons were shipped through service centers, accounting for approxi-

mately 33 percent of all steel shipments in the United States, up from 18 percent in 1974. Some industry experts believed that the service center share could climb as high as 40 percent by 1990. There were a number of key trends in the metal industry that were enhancing service centers' growth potential.

Steel Mills' Retrenchment.   In their efforts to become more competitive through increased productivity, most of the major domestic metals producers had been scaling back product lines by dropping low-volume specialty products. Further, they had cut back on service to customers by reducing sales force size and technical support. Full-line service centers, recognizing that many customers preferred to deal with only a few primary suppliers, had profited from this trend by maintaining wide product lines and increasing customer service.

Just-in-Time Inventory Management.   Given the high cost of ownership and maintenance of inventory, most metal users were attempting to reduce their costs by lowering their levels of raw materials inventories ("just-in-time" inventory management). This resulted in smaller order quantities and more frequent deliveries. Metal service centers had a natural advantage over the mills here because inventory was the service center's stock in trade.

While the service center's price was always higher than buying from the mills, customers were increasingly willing to pay the extra charge. They recognized that the savings they generated from lower inventories and handling costs, plus reduced scrap and risk of obsolescence, would lower the total cost of getting the metal into their production system.

This case was prepared by Vijay Govindarajan, The Amos Tuck School of Business Administration, Dartmouth College. Copyright by Osceola Institute.

Productivity Improvement and Quality Enhancement.   Quality and productivity had become overriding issues with metal users. They had implemented major quality and productivity improvement programs aimed at increasing both the reputation of their products and the overall profitability of operations. In their attempt to focus on quality, end users were reducing the number of suppliers with whom they did business and were concentrating their purchases with those that were best able to meet their specific quality, availability, and service requirements. End users found that closer relationships with fewer suppliers resulted in better quality conformance and stronger ties between supplier and customer as each sought to maximize the long-term benefits of the relationship.

Quality Metal's Strategy[1]

Quality Metals had been established a century ago as a local metals distributor. Since then, it had grown into a firm with national distribution, and its sales in 1981 were well over $300 million. Quality's business strategy provided the framework for the development of specific goals and objectives. According to Mr. Brown, three fundamental objectives guided Quality. [1]

Objective 1: To Focus Sales Efforts on Targeted Markets of Specialty Metal Users. During the 1970s, Quality recognized that it could compete much more effectively in specialty product lines of its own selection than in the broader commodity carbon steel markets where price was the primary determining factor. Consequently, Quality decided to diminish its participation in commodity product lines and redeploy those resources into higher-technology metals, such as carbon alloy bars, stainless steel, aluminum, nickel alloys, titanium, copper, and brass,

which offered higher returns and had less-effective competition. More than 60 percent of its revenues were derived from higher-technology metals in 1982, compared with 29 percent in 1972.

Quality had made a long-term commitment to high-technology metal users. The company's recent introduction of titanium, a natural adjunct to the existing product line, was indicative of the company's strategy of bringing new products to the market to meet the needs of existing customers. Previously, titanium was not readily available on the distributor market. Quality planned to continue to diversify into complementary higher-technology products as new customer requirements arose.

Objective 2: To Identify Those Industries and Geographic Markets Where These Metals Were Consumed.   To identify more accurately the major industries and geographies for these products, Quality developed the industry's first metal usage data base in the early 1980s. Mr. Brown believed that this data base, which was continually refined and updated, was the most accurate in the country. Its use enabled Quality to profile product consumption by industry and by geography. It also enabled the company to analyze total market demand on a nationwide basis and to project potential sales on a market-by-market basis. As a result, Quality had a competitive edge in determining where customers were located and what products they were buying. It used this information in selecting locations for opening new service centers.

Objective 3: To Develop Techniques and Marketing Programs That Would Increase Market Share.   To build market share, Quality offered programs that assisted its customers in implementing just-in-time inventory management systems coordinated with their materials requirement planning programs. The company worked with customer representatives in purchasing, manufacturing, and quality assurance to determine their precise requirements for

---

[1]These sections are taken from: Michael Simpson, "Opportunities for innovation in the metals industry," *Journal of Business Strategy,* Summer 1986, pp. 84–87.

product specifications, quantities, and delivery schedules.

Similarly, Quality emphasized value-added business by offering a wide range of processing services for its customers, such as saw cutting to specific sizes, flame cutting into both pattern and nonpattern shapes, flattening, surface grinding, shearing, bending, edge conditioning, polishing, and thermal treatment. Because of Quality's volume, the sophisticated equipment required for these production steps was operated at a lower cost per unit than most customer-owned equipment.

Organizational Structure

Since the Great Depression, Quality had experienced rapid sales growth and geographical expansion. In 1982, Quality operated in 27 locations, situated in markets representing about 75 percent of metal consumption in the United States. Consistent with this growth was the necessity to decentralize line functions. The firm currently had 4 regions, each of which had about 6 districts for a total of 23 districts. There were staff departments in finance, marketing, operations, and human resources. A partial organizational structure is given in Exhibit 1.

Typically, a district manager had under him a warehouse superintendent, a sales manager, a credit manager, a purchasing manager, and an administration manager (Exhibit 1). The decision-making authorities of these managers are described below:

> The Warehouse Superintendent oversees transportation, loading and unloading, storage, and preproduction processing.
>
> The Sales Manager coordinates a staff that includes "inside" salespersons who establish contacts and take orders over the phone, and an "outside" team who make direct customer contacts and close large deals. Sales price and discount terms are generally established by the District Manager; freight adjustments are also made at the district level.
>
> The Credit Manager assesses the risk of new customer accounts, approves customer credit periods within a

range established by corporate headquarters, and enforces customer collections.

The Purchasing Manager acquires inventory from the regional warehouse, other districts, and outside companies. Districts have freedom to purchase from outside suppliers. However, senior management has established Economic Order Quantity guidelines for the purchase of inventory, and metals are stocked in a district warehouse only if local demand is sufficient to justify it. Within this overall constraint, the Purchasing Manager has authority to choose suppliers and negotiate credit terms, although payments to suppliers are handled centrally at the home office.

Capital expenditures in excess of $5,000 and all capital leasing decisions require corporate approval.

Responsibility Allocation and Performance Measurement

District managers were responsible for attaining predetermined return on asset (ROA) levels, which were agreed to at the beginning of the year. The following items were included in the asset base for ROA calculations.

1. Land, warehouse buildings, and equipment were included in the asset base at gross book value.

2. Leased buildings and equipment (except for leased trucks) were included in the asset base at the capitalized lease value. (Leased trucks were not capitalized; rather, lease expenses on trucks were reported as an operating expense.)

3. Average inventory, in units, was calculated. The replacement costs, based on current mill price schedules, were determined for these units and included in the asset base.

4. Average accounts receivable balance for the period was included in the asset base. (Cash was excluded from district's assets; the amounts were trivial.)

5. As a general rule, accounts payable was not deducted from the asset base. However, an adjustment was made if the negotiated credit period was greater than the company standard of 30 days. If this

Exhibit 1

Partial organizational chart

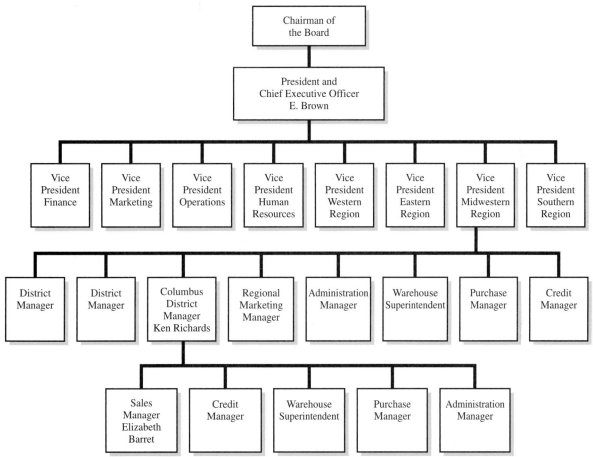

occurred, "deferred inventory," a contra-asset account, was deducted from the amount of the inventory value for the period in excess of the 30-day standard. This was equivalent to a reduction of inventory asset corresponding to the excess credit period. For example, if a district negotiated a credit period of 50 days, then the inventory expenditure was removed from the asset base for 20 days. However, a penalty was not assessed if the negotiated credit period was less than the 30-day company standard.

Income before taxes, for each district, was calculated in accordance with generally accepted accounting principles, except for cost of sales, which was calculated based on current inventory replacement values. Expenses were separated into controllable and noncontrollable categories. Controllable expenses included such items as warehouse labor and sales commissions; rent, utilities, and property taxes are examples of noncontrollable expenses.

No corporate overhead expenses were allocated to the districts. A few years earlier, the company had considered a proposal to allocate

---

Exhibit 2   Incentive Calculation Procedure

Step 1: Measure actual asset base and compare it with targeted asset base.

If actual assets exceed targeted assets, multiply excess by the targeted ROA for the district and charge this amount to profits.

Assets overemployed × District ROA target = Charge to profits

If actual assets are less than targeted assets, multiply difference by the district's ROA target and credit this to profits.

Assets underemployed × District ROA target = Credit to profits

Step 2: Adjusted profits are compared with 90% of the original profit objective.

Adjusted profits − (90% of objective) = Incentive profits

Step 3: Incentive profit ÷ 90% of objective = Payout rate

Step 4: Payout rate × Manager's base salary = Bonus payable

Step 5: Bonuses are awarded on the basis of incentive profits. If incentive profits are less than zero, no bonus is awarded. The bonus increases in proportion to incentive profit, with a maximum bonus of 75 percent of manager's base salary.

---

corporate overheads to the districts. However, the proposal had been rejected on the grounds that the "allocation bases" were arbitrary and that such expenses could not be controlled at the district level.

Performance Evaluation and Incentives

ROA was the sole performance criterion for evaluation of district managers. The incentive bonus for district managers was based on a formula that rigidly tied the bonus to meeting and exceeding 90 percent of their ROA targets. Exhibit 2 contains the detailed procedure used to calculate the incentive bonus. The calculations determine an applicable payout rate, which was then multiplied by the district manager's base salary to yield the amount of the bonus award. Thus, the size of the bonus depended on (1) the amount of the manager's base salary and (2) how far 90 percent of the ROA target was exceeded; there was a maximum bonus amount.

The bonus of a district manager was also affected by his or her region's performance. In 1982, 75 percent of a district manager's bonus was based on district performance, and 25 percent was based on his or her region's perfor-

mance. The bonus of the district manager's staff was based solely on the performance of that district.

Meeting with the Columbus District Manager

A few days after speaking with Mr. Brown, the casewriter visited Ken Richards, the district manager for the Columbus Service Center. Mr. Brown recommended him as one of the company's brightest and most successful district managers. The district had been highly successful in recent years, consistently earning well above 30 percent ROA (pretax).

For 1982, Ken Richards's targeted figure for operating profit was $3.8 million; targeted assets were set at $10 million. He felt that an ROA of 38 percent was reachable, considering historical performance and market opportunities.

As of March 1982, Ken was reviewing a capital investment proposal (for the purchase of new processing equipment), which he had received from his sales manager (Exhibits 3 and 4). Before submitting the proposal to corporate headquarters for approval Ken wanted to make sure that the new investment would have a favorable

---

Exhibit 3   Memorandum

To: Kenneth Richards, District Manager

From: Elizabeth Barret, Sales Manager

Subject: Purchase of Processing Equipment

This district, at present, sells no inventory that has been altered through preproduction processing. Such alterations can be made at other districts with processing capabilities, but many customers in this area complain that, because of transportation time, the lead times are too great to satisfy their needs in acquiring such inventory.

Market research has established that a reasonable demand for processed inventory exists within this district. Therefore, our district should consider obtaining the processing equipment necessary to satisfy this demand.

The economics of this project is summarized in the attached sheet [Exhibit 4]. Let me provide some information as background for these calculations.

We can acquire the equipment for $600,000. Since its expected life is 10 years (negligible salvage value), Quality would benefit from a 10% Investment Tax Credit, making the net investment equal to $540,000.

Sales projections were made by the district's sales department, and costs were based upon the experiences of districts with processing capabilities. Growth in sales and costs include a 7% inflation factor and projected increases in production.

Annual cash flows are calculated by adjusting Earnings after Taxes to account for depreciation, which is expensed by the sum-of-the-years'-digit method, and growth in Working Capital investment, which is calculated using our standard 20% of sales on incremental growth. The resultant end-of-year cash flows, discounted at the cost of capital of 15% (which is the rate head office requires on projects in similar risk classes), yield a positive net present value of $286,000. The payback period for this project is 4.5 years, which is well within the company's criteria of 10 years.

This investment is worth your careful consideration, Ken. This district has the opportunity to expand into a new market and to benefit from favorable earnings and positive sales growth.

I hope you will submit this proposal to the home office for consideration. Please let me know if you have any questions.

Sd/-
Elizabeth Barret

---

effect on his incentive bonus for 1982. Using 1982 profit and asset targets as the benchmark, he compared his incentive bonus for 1982 with and without the new investment. These calculations are shown in Exhibit 5.

Questions

1. Is the capital investment proposal described in Exhibit 3 an attractive one for Quality Metal Service Center?

2. Should Ken Richards send that proposal to home office for approval?

3. Comment on the general usefulness of ROA as the basis of evaluating district managers' performance. Could this performance measure be made more effective?

4. In deciding the investment base for evaluating managers of investment centers, the general question is: What practices will motivate the district managers to use their assets most efficiently and to acquire the proper amount and kind of new assets? Presumably, when his return on assets is being measured, the district manager will try to increase his ROA, and we desire that the action he takes towards this end be actions that are in the best interest of the whole corporation. Given this general line of reasoning, evaluate the way Quality computes the "investment base"

EXHIBIT 4   Columbus District Processing Equipment Proposal

	1982	1983	1984	1985	1986	1987	1988	1989	1990	1991
I. Cash flows (000s)										
Sales *(1)*	$600	1,375	1,510	1,665	1,830	2,010	2,215	2,435	2,680	2,945
Cost of sales	$(560)	(1,145)	(1,236)	(1,355)	(1,490)	(1,660)	(1,845)	(2,051)	(2,290)	(2,545)
Earnings before taxes	40	230	274	310	340	350	370	384	390	400
Tax at 50%	$(20)	(115)	(137)	(155)	(170)	(175)	(185)	(192)	(195)	(200)
Earnings after taxes	20	115	137	155	170	175	185	192	195	200
Depreciation	110	100	85	75	65	55	45	35	20	10
Working capital investment *(2)*	$(120)	(155)	(25)	(35)	(30)	(35)	(45)	(40)	(50)	535
Cash flow	$10	60	197	195	205	195	185	187	165	745

(1) Revenue for 1982 reflects 3-month start-up period

(2) Working capital investment

	1982	1983	1984	1985	1986	1987	1988	1989	1990	1991
20% of sales	$120	275	300	335	365	400	445	485	535	590
Old level	0	120	275	300	335	365	400	445	485	535
Increase in working capital	$(120)	(155)	(25)	(35)	(30)	(35)	(45)	(40)	(50)	(55)
Recovery of working capital										590
Net incremental investment in working capital	$(120)	(155)	(25)	(35)	(30)	(35)	(45)	(40)	(50)	535

II. Project evaluation

A. Payback period: 4.5 years

B. Internal rate of return: 21.8%

C. Net present value (at 15% cost of capital): $286,000

---

for its districts. For each asset category, discuss whether the basis of measurement used by the company is the best for the purpose of measuring district's return on assets. What are the likely motivational problems that could arise in such a system? What can you recommend to overcome such dysfunctional effects?

5. While computing district profits for performance evaluation purposes, should there be a charge for income taxes? Should corporate overheads be allocated to districts? Should profits be computed on the basis of historical costs or on the basis of replacement costs? Evaluate these issues from the standpoint of their motivational impact on the district managers.

6. Evaluate Quality's incentive compensation system. Does the present system motivate district managers to make decisions which are consistent with the strategy of the firm? If not, make specific recommendations to improve the system.

EXHIBIT 5   Incentive Bonus for Columbus District Manager for 1982

A. Incentive Bonus for 1982 without the New Project

	Target for 1982	*Projected Actual for 1982**
Profit	$ 3,800,000	$ 3,800,000
Asset	$10,000,000	$10,000,000

Incentive profit = Actual profit − (90% of targeted profit)

= $3,800,000   − $3,420,000 = $380,000

$$\text{Payout rate} \;=\; \frac{\text{Incentive profit}}{90\% \text{ of targeted profit}}$$

$$\frac{\$380,000}{\$3,420,000} = 11.1\%$$

Therefore, incentive bonus without the new project = 11.1% of base salary.

---

*Assumes that actual results exactly meet the targets in 1982.

B. Incentive Bonus for 1982 with the New Project

	Target for 1982	*Projected Actual for 1982†*
Profit	$ 3,800,000	$ 3,840,000
Asset	$10,000,000	$10,720,000

Step 1: Actual assets − Target assets = Asset overemployed
   $10,720,000   − $10,000,000   = $720,000

Step 2: Asset overemployed × District ROA target = Charge to profits
      $720,000 × 0.38   = $273,600

   Actual profits − Charge to profits = Adjusted profits
      $3,840,000 − $273,600   = $3,566,400

Step 3: Adjusted profits − 90% of targeted profit = Incentive profit
      $3,566,400 − $3,420,000   = $146,400

Step 4: $\dfrac{\text{Incentive profit}}{90\% \text{ of targeted profit}}$ = Payout rate

$$\frac{\$146,400}{\$3,420,000} = 4.28\%$$

Therefore, incentive bonus with the new project = 4.28% of base salary.

---

†Reflects marginal effects of project implementation *only*—that is, an addition of earnings before taxes of $40,000 and an addition to assets of $720,000 (equipment $600,000 plus working capital $120,000). Otherwise, assumes that other district operations meet targets exactly in 1982.

Case 7–4

Industrial Products Corporation

In 1996 the Industrial Products Corporation (IPC) manufactured a variety of industrial products in more than a dozen divisions. Plants were located throughout the country, one or more to a division, and company headquarters was in a large Eastern city. Each division was run by a division manager and had its own balance sheet and income statement. The company made extensive use of long- and short-run planning programs, which included budgets for sales, costs, expenditures, and rate of return on investment. Monthly reports on operating results were sent in by each division and were reviewed by headquarters executives. For many years the principal performance measure for divisions had been their rate of return on investment.

The Baker Division of IPC manufactured and assembled large industrial pumps, most of which sold for more than $5,000. A great variety of models were made to order from the standard parts which the division either bought or manufactured for stock. In addition, components were individually designed and fabricated when pumps were made for special applications. A variety of metalworking machines were used, some large and heavy, and a few designed especially for the division's kind of business.

The division operated three plants, two of which were much smaller than the third and were located in distant parts of the country. Headquarters offices were located in the main plant where more than 1,000 people were employed. They performed design and manufacturing operations and the usual staff and

clerical work. Marketing activities were carried out by sales engineers in the field, who worked closely with customers on design and installation. Reporting to Mr. Brandt, the division manager, were managers in charge of design, sales, manufacturing, purchasing, and budgets.

The division's product line was broken down into five product groups so that the profitability of each could be studied separately. Evaluation was based on the margin above factory cost as a percentage of sales. No attempt was made to allocate investment to the product lines. The budget director said that not only would this be difficult in view of the common facilities, but that such a mathematical computation would not provide any new information since the products had approximately the same turnover of assets. Furthermore, he said, it was difficult enough to allocate common factory costs between products, and that even margin on sales was a disputable figure. "If we were larger," he said, "and had separate facilities for each product line, we might be able to do it. But it wouldn't mean much in this division right now."

Only half a dozen people monitored the division's rate of return; other measures were used in the division's internal control system. The division manager watched volume and timeliness of shipments per week, several measures of quality, and certain cost areas such as overtime payments.

The Division Manager's Control of Assets

During 1996 the total assets of the Baker Division were turned over approximately 1.7 times, and late that year they were made up as follows:

This case was prepared by Professor William Rotch, Johnson and Higgins Professor of Business Administration, University of Virginia. Copyright © by the University of Virginia Darden School Foundation, Charlottesville, VA.

Cash	8%
Accounts receivable	21
Inventory	
Raw material	7
About 3% metal stock	
About 4% purchased parts	
Work in process	9
About 6% manufactured parts	
About 3% floor stocks	
Finished goods	2
Machinery (original cost)	29
Land and buildings (original cost)	24
	100%

Cash (8 percent of total assets)

The Baker Division, like all divisions in IPC, maintained a cash account in a local bank, to which company headquarters transferred funds as they were needed. This local account was used primarily for the plant payroll and for payment of other local bills. Payment of suppliers' invoices as well as collection of accounts receivable was handled by headquarters for Baker as well as for most of the other divisions.

The division's cash account at headquarters was shown on the division's balance sheet as cash and marketable securities. The amount shown as cash had been established by agreement between top management and the division manager, and was considered by both to be about the minimum amount necessary to operate the division. The excess above this amount was shown on the division's balance sheet as marketable securities; it earned interest from headquarters at the rate of 5 percent a year. This account varied with receipts and disbursements, leaving the cash account fixed as long as there was a balance in the securities account. It was possible for the securities account to be wiped out and for cash to decline below the minimum agreed upon, but if this continued for more than a month or two, corrective action was taken. For Baker Division the minimum level was equal to about two weeks' sales, and in recent years cash had seldom gone below this amount.

Whether or not the company as a whole actually owned cash and marketable securities equal to the sum of all the respective divisions' cash and security accounts was the concern of headquarters management. It probably was not necessary to hold this amount of cash and securities since the division accounts had to cover division peak needs and not all the peak needs occurred at the same time.

The size of a division's combined cash and marketable securities accounts was directly affected by all phases of the division's operations which used or produced cash. It also was affected in three other ways. One was the automatic deduction of 40 percent of income for tax purposes. Another was the payment of "dividends" by the division to headquarters. All earnings that the division manager did not wish to keep for future use were transferred to the company's cash account by payment of a dividend. Since a division was expected to retain a sufficient balance to provide for capital expenditures, dividends were generally paid only by the profitable divisions which were not expanding rapidly.

The third action affecting the cash account occurred if cash declined below the minimum, or if extensive capital expenditures had been approved. A division might then "borrow" from headquarters, paying interest as if it were a separate company. At the end of 1996 the Baker Division had no loan and had been able to operate since about 1990 without borrowing from headquarters. Borrowing was not, in fact, currently being considered by the Baker Division.

Except for its part in the establishment of a minimum cash level, top management was not involved in the determination of the division's investment in cash and marketable securities. Mr. Brandt could control the level of this investment by deciding how much was to be paid in dividends. Since only a 5 percent return was received on the marketable securities and since the division earned more than that on its total investment, it was to the division manager's advantage to pay out as much as possible in dividends. When asked how he determined the size of the dividends, Mr. Brandt said that he simply kept what he thought he would need to cover peak demands, capital expenditures, and contingencies. Improving the division's rate of return may have been part of the decision, but he did not mention it.

Accounts Receivable (21 percent of total assets)

All accounts receivable for the Baker Division were collected at company headquarters. Around the 20th of each month a report of balances was prepared and forwarded to the division.

Although in theory Mr. Brandt was allowed to set his own terms for divisional sales, in practice it would have been difficult to change the company's usual terms. Since Baker Division sold to important customers of other divisions, any change from the net 30 terms could disturb a large segment of the corporation's business. Furthermore, industry practice was well established, and the division would hardly try to change it.

The possibility of cash sales in situations in which credit was poor was virtually nonexistent. Credit was investigated for all customers by the headquarters credit department and no sales were made without a prior credit check. For the Baker Division this policy presented no problem, for it sold primarily to well-established customers.

In late 1996 accounts receivable made up 21 percent of total assets. The fact that this corresponded to 45 average days of sales and not to 30 was the result of a higher than average level of shipments the month before, coupled with the normal delay caused by the billing and collection process.

There was almost nothing Mr. Brandt could do directly to control the level of accounts receivable. This asset account varied with sales, lagged behind shipments by a little more than a month, and departed from this relationship only if customers happened to pay early or late.

Inventory: Raw Material Metal Stock (about 3 percent of total investment)

In late 1996 inventory as a whole made up 18 percent of Baker Division's total assets. A subdivision of the various kinds of inventory showed that raw material accounted for 7 percent, work in process 9 percent, and finished goods and miscellaneous supplies 2 percent. Since the Baker Division produced to order, finished goods inventory was normally small, leaving raw material and work in process as the only significant classes of inventory.

The raw material inventory could be further subdivided to separate the raw material inventory from a variety of purchased parts. The raw material inventory was then composed primarily of metals and metal shapes, such as steel sheets or copper tubes. Most of the steel was bought according to a schedule arranged with the steel companies several months ahead of the delivery date. About a month before the steel company was to ship the order, Baker Division would send the rolling instructions by shapes and weights. If the weight on any particular shape was below a minimum set by the steel company, Baker Division would pay an extra charge for processing. Although this method of purchasing accounted for the bulk of steel purchases, smaller amounts were also bought as needed from warehouse stocks and specialty producers.

Copper was bought by headquarters and processed by the company's own mill. The divisions could buy the quantities they needed, but the price paid depended on corporate buying practices and processing costs. The price paid by Baker Division had generally been competitive with outside sources, though it often lagged behind the market both in increases and in reductions in price.

The amounts of copper and steel bought were usually determined by the purchasing agent without recourse to any formal calculations of an economic ordering quantity. The reason for this was that since there was such a large number of uncertain factors that had continually to be estimated, a formal computation would not improve the process of determining how much to buy. Purchases depended on the amounts on hand, expected consumption, and current delivery time and price expectations. If delivery was fast, smaller amounts were usually bought. If a price increase was anticipated, somewhat larger orders often were placed at the current price. Larger amounts of steel had been bought several years earlier, for example, just before expected labor action on the railroads threatened to disrupt deliveries.

The level of investment in raw material varied with the rates of purchase and use. There was a fairly wide range within which Mr. Brandt could control this class of asset, and there were no top management directives governing the size of his raw material inventory.

Inventory: Purchased Parts and Manufactured Parts (about 10 percent of total assets—4 percent in raw material, 6 percent in work in process)

The Baker Division purchased and manufactured parts for stock to be used later in the assembly of pumps. The method used to determine the purchase quantity was the same as that used to determine the length of production run on parts made for work-in-process stocks.

The number of parts bought or manufactured was, with the exception of special adjustments made in two places, based on a series of calculations which led to an economic order quantity (EOQ). Since there were several thousand different items bought and manufactured, these calcu-

lations had been made routine. A computer program had been developed which received data from existing files such as parts usage and price over the past six months, and contained some constants which could be manually changed. The program periodically went through the following steps:

1. Using data on past usage, the program computed a forecast of future usage, using a preset forecasting algorithm.
2. The forecast could then be adjusted by a factor entered to reflect known trends for a specific part or as a constant for all parts. Currently, Mr. Brandt had entered a .9 factor to be used for all parts, in an effort to push inventories down.
3. The program then computed the Economic Order Quantity in dollars and in units, using the following information:
   a. Adjusted forecasted usage rate in dollars from step 2.
   b. For purchased parts the order handling cost, covering paperwork and receiving cost, which Able division's controller had developed using activity-based costing. Currently this was $28.50 per order and was reviewed annually.

   For parts manufactured by the Baker Division, a batch setup cost was used. Again activity-based costing had been used to compute this batch cost which included costs of machine setup, materials handling, first piece inspection, and data reporting. The actual amount used in the EOQ computation depended on the complexity of the setup and currently ranged from $15 to $75.
   c. Inventory carrying cost, which consisted of two components: one was the cost of capital (currently computed to be an annual rate of 12 percent) and the other was a charge for storage,

insurance, taxes, and obsolescence. The current annual rate of 8 percent for those items could be adjusted, if, for example, special storage conditions were required.

The formula used to compute EOQ was as follows:

$$EOQ = \sqrt{\frac{2AS}{I}}$$

where

A = annual usage in dollars
S = either the order handling cost for purchased parts or the setup cost for manufactured parts
I = the inventory carrying cost, expressed as a percent or decimal to be applied to average inventory

For purchased parts, another analysis tested whether supplier quantity discount for purchases above the EOQ would be worthwhile. This adjustment worked as follows:

1. EOQ × unit price times expected orders per year = Material cost (A).
2. Order quantity required for discount times price times orders per year = discounted material cost (B).
3. Annual savings on material cost (A – B) or (S).
4. Decreased ordering cost per year because of fewer orders (C).
5. Increase in carrying cost other than cost of capital: Discount quantity times discount price minus EOQ quantity times EOQ price, all divided by 2[D]. This was the increase in average inventory. Then D times the carrying cost other than capital cost gave the annual increased cost due to higher average inventory (E).
6. Computation of return on investment:

$$\frac{S + C - E}{D} = return\ on\ investment$$

Though IPC's cost of capital was computed to be 12 percent, Baker Division usually required a higher return before volume discounts would be taken. The judgment was entirely up to the Baker Division. The inventory control supervisor who made the decision considered general business conditions, the time required to use up the larger order, the specialization of the particular part, and any general directives made by the division manager concerning inventory levels. A return below 15 percent was probably never acceptable—more than 20 percent was required in most instances—and any quantity discount yielding 25–30 percent or more usually was taken, though each case was judged individually.

The final step of the computer program was developing an order review point. With an estimate of expected delivery time, the program signaled when an order should be placed.

The level of purchased and manufactured parts inventory in the Baker Division varied with changes in rate of consumption and purchase. If the rules for calculating economic order quantity were adhered to, inventory levels increased with usage faster than the rate of usage increased up to a certain level (determined by order or setup cost, and carrying cost), and thereafter increased usage resulted in an inventory increase rate that was lower than the usage increase rate. Most parts purchased and made by Baker Division were above that breakpoint which meant that growth in sales generally resulted in increased return on investment. Of course, since there were several opportunities for Baker Division's management to intervene in the purchase quantity computation, the relationship would not necessarily hold true in practice. By setting the forecasting adjustment, for example, Mr. Brandt had tilted the process toward inventory reduction. Furthermore, continued efforts to reduce setup cost and order handling cost had pushed toward the reduction in inventories.

Inventory: Floor Stocks (about 3 percent of total investment)

Floor stock inventory consisted of parts and components which were being worked on and assembled. Items became part of the floor stock inventory when they were requisitioned from the storage areas or when delivered directly to the production floor.

Pumps were worked on individually so that lot size was not a factor to be considered. There was little Mr. Brandt could do to control the level of floor stock inventory except to see that there was not an excess of parts piled around the production area.

Inventory: Finished Goods (2 percent of total investment)

As a rule pumps were made to order and for immediate shipment. Finished goods inventory consisted of those few pumps on which shipment was delayed. Control of this investment was a matter of keeping it low by shipping the pumps as fast as possible.

Land, Buildings, and Machinery (53 percent of total investment)

Since the Baker Division's fixed assets, stated at gross, comprised 53 percent of total assets at the end of 1996, the control of this particular group of assets was extremely important. Changes in the level of these investments depended on retirements and additions, the latter being entirely covered by the capital budgeting program.

Industrial Products Company's capital budgeting procedures were described in a planning manual. The planning sequence was as follows:

1. Headquarters forecasts economic conditions. (March)
2. The divisions plan long-term objectives. (June)
3. Supporting programs are submitted. (September) These are plans for specific

actions, such as sales plans, advertising programs, and cost reduction programs, and include the facilities program which is the capital expenditure request. The planning manual stated under the heading "General Approach in the Development of a Coordinated Supporting Program" this advice:

Formulation and evaluation of a Supporting Program for each product line can generally be improved if projects are classified by purpose. The key objective of all planning is Return-on-Assets, a function of Margin and Turnover. These ratios are in turn determined by the three factors in the business equation—Volume, Costs, and Assets. All projects therefore should be directed primarily at one of the following:

- To increase volume;
- To reduce costs and expenses; and
- To minimize assets.

4. Annual objective submitted. (November 11 by 8:00 AM!)

The annual objective states projected sales, costs, expenses, profits, cash expenditures, and receipts, and shows pro forma balance sheets and income statements.

Mr. Brandt was "responsible for the division's assets and for provision for the growth and expansion of the division." Growth referred to the internal refinements of product design and production methods and to the cost reduction programs. Expansion involved a 5–10-year program including about two years for construction.

In the actual capital expenditure request there were four kinds of facilities proposals:

1. Cost reduction projects, which were self-liquidating investments. Reduction in labor costs was usually the largest source of the savings, which were stated in terms of the payback period and the rate of return.
2. Necessity projects. These included replacement of worn out machinery, quality improvement and technical

changes to meet competition, environmental compliance projects, and facilities for the safety and comfort of the workers.

3. Product redesign projects.
4. Expansion projects.

Justification of the cost reduction proposals was based on a comparison of the estimated rate of return (estimated return before taxes divided by gross investment) with the 20 percent standard as specified by headquarters. If the project was considered desirable, and yet showed a return of less than 20 percent, it had to be justified on other grounds and was included in the necessities category. Cost reduction proposals made up about 60 percent of the 1997 capital expenditure budget, and in earlier years these proposals had accounted for at least 50 percent. Very little of Baker Division's 1997 capital budget had been allocated specifically for product redesign and none for expansion, so that most of the remaining 40 percent was to be used for necessity projects. Thus a little over half of Baker Division's capital expenditures were justified primarily on the estimated rate of return on the investment. The remainder, having advantages which could not be stated in terms of the rate of return, was justified on other grounds.

Mr. Brandt was free to include what he wanted in his capital budgeting request, and for the three years that he had been division manager his requests had always been granted. However, no large expansion projects had been included in the capital budget requests of the last three years. As in the 1997 budget, most of the capital expenditure had been for cost-reduc-

tion projects, and the remainder was for necessities. Annual additions had approximately equaled annual retirements.

Since Mr. Brandt could authorize expenditures of up to $250,000 per project for purposes approved by the board, there was in fact some flexibility in his choice of projects after the budget had been approved by higher management. Not only could he schedule the order of expenditure, but under some circumstances he could substitute unforeseen projects of a similar nature. If top management approved $100,000 for miscellaneous cost reduction projects, Mr. Brandt could spend this on the projects he considered most important, whether or not they were specifically described in his original budget request.

For the corporation as a whole, about one quarter of the capital expenditure was for projects of under $250,000, which could be authorized for expenditure by the division managers. This proportion was considered by top management to be about right; if, however, it rose much above a quarter, the $250,000 dividing line would probably be lowered.

Questions

1. To what extent did Mr. Brandt influence the level of investment in each asset category?

2. Comment on the general usefulness of return-on-investment as a measure of divisional performance. Could it be made a more effective device?

Case 7–5
Marden Company

A typical division of Marden Company had financial statements as shown in Exhibit 1. Accounts receivable were billed by the division, but customers made payments to bank accounts (i.e., lockboxes) maintained in the name of Marden Company and located throughout the country. The debt item on the balance sheet is a proportionate part of the corporate 9 percent bond issue. Interest on this debt was not charged to the division.

Question

Recommend the best way of measuring the performance of the division manager. If you need additional information, make the assumption you believe to be most reasonable.

Exhibit 1   Typical Division Financial Statements

Balance Sheet
End of Year (condensed; $000)

Assets		Equities	
Cash	$ 100	Accounts payable	$ 400
Accounts receivable	800	Total current liabilities	400
Inventory	900		
Total current assets	1,800	Debt	700
Plant and equipment, cost	1,000	Equity	1,300
Depreciation (straight line)	400		2,000
Plant and equipment, net	600		
Total assets	$2,400	Total equities	$2,400

Divisional Income Statement

Sales	$4,000
Costs, other than those listed below	3,200
Depreciation	100
Allocated share of corporate expenses	100
Income before income tax	600

This case was prepared by Professor Robert N. Anthony. Copyright by Osceola Institute.

CASE 7–6
LEMFERT COMPANY

Lemfert Company was a large manufacturing company organized into divisions, each with responsibility for earning a satisfactory return on its investment. Division managers had considerable autonomy in carrying out this responsibility. Some divisions fabricated parts; others— here called "end-item divisions"—assembled these parts, together with purchased parts, into finished products and marketed the finished products. Transfer prices were used in connection with the transfer of parts among the various fabricating divisions and from the fabricating divisions to the end-item divisions. Wherever possible, these transfer prices were the lowest prices charged by outside manufacturers for the same or comparable items, with appropriate adjustments for inbound freight, volume, and similar factors.

Parts that were not similar to those manufactured by outside companies were called "type K items." In most fabricating divisions, these items constituted only 5 to 10 percent of total volume. In Division F, however, approximately 75 percent of total volume was accounted for by type K items. Division F manufactured 10 such items for various end-item divisions; they were less than 5 percent of the total cost of any one of these end-item divisions. The procedure for arriving at the transfer price for type K items is described below.

First, a tentative transfer price was calculated by the value analysis staff of the corporate purchasing department and was submitted to the two divisions involved for their consideration. This price was supposed to be based on the estimated costs of an "efficient producer" plus a profit margin. An efficient producer was considered to be one conducting its purchasing and using modern equipment in a manner that could reasonably be expected of the company's principal competitors.

The material cost portion of the total cost was based on current competitive price levels. Direct labor cost was supposed to reflect efficient processing on modern equipment. Overhead cost represented an amount that could be expected of an efficient producer using modern equipment. Depreciation expense, expenditures on special tooling, and a standard allowance for administrative expense were included in the overhead figure.

The profit margin was equal to the divisional profit objective applied to the cost of the assets employed to produce the product in question. Assets employed was the sum of the following items.

> Cash and receivables—18 percent of the total manufacturing cost.
> Inventories—the value of the optimum inventory size required at standard volume.
> Fixed assets—the depreciated book value (but not less than one-half original cost) of assets used to fabricate the part, including a fair share of buildings and other general assets, but excluding standby and obsolete facilities.

The percentage used for cash and receivables was based on studies of the cash and receivables balances of the principal outside manufacturers of parts similar to those manufactured in the fabricating divisions. The standard volume was an estimate of the volume that the plants should *normally* be expected to produce, which was not necessarily the same as current volume or projected volume for the next year.

For an average division, the budgeted profit objective was 20 percent of assets employed; but there were variations among divisions. The divisional budgeted profit objective multiplied by the

This case was prepared by Professor Robert N. Anthony, Harvard Business School. Copyright by the President and Fellows of Harvard College. Harvard Business School Case 113–116.

assets employed, as calculated above, gave the profit margin for the item. This profit was added to the cost to arrive at the suggested transfer price, which then was submitted to the two divisions. If either the buying or the selling division believed that the price thus determined was unfair, it first attempted to negotiate a mutually satisfactory price. If the parties were unable to agree, they submitted the dispute to the controller for arbitration. Either party might appeal the results of this arbitration to the executive vice president.

Questions

1. Are these the best transfer price practices for the Lemfert Company? If not, how should they be revised?

2. For what types of companies would the revised policy not be best? Why?

3. Do you think the attempt to measure profitability in Division F is worthwhile? If not, how would you measure performance in this division?

II

The Management Control Process

The management control process is primarily behavioral. It involves interactions among and between managers and their subordinates. Managers differ in their technical ability, their leadership style, their interpersonal skills, their experience, their approach to decision making, their attitude toward the entity, their liking for or dislike of numbers, and in many other ways. Because of these differences, the details of the management control process vary among companies and among the responsibility centers within a company.

Nevertheless, the formal management control system is basically the same throughout an organization; the differences relate principally to how the system is used. For example, managers differ in their attitude toward the relative importance of cooperation and competition. As discussed in Chapter 3, a certain amount of each is essential.

The chapters in Part II discuss steps in the management control process in the sequence in which they occur in practice: Chapter 8 describes strategic planning; Chapter 9, budget preparation; Chapter 10, analyzing financial performance reports; Chapter 11, development of the balance scorecard incorporating financial and nonfinancial measures; and Chapter 12 discusses management compensation as it relates to the management control process.

STRATEGIC PLANNING

This is the first of five chapters that describe the management control process. Chapter 8 describes strategic planning, which is the first activity, sequentially, in the process. The first section of Chapter 8 describes the nature of strategic planning. The second part discusses techniques for analyzing and deciding on proposed new programs. The third part describes techniques that are useful in analyzing ongoing programs. The final part describes the several steps in the strategic planning process.

The discussion implicitly assumes a moderately large organization, typically consisting of a headquarters and several decentralized business units. In such an organization, strategic planning takes place both at headquarters and in the business units. If the organization is small, and especially if it does not have business units, the process involves only senior executives and a planning staff. In a very small organization, the process may involve only the chief executive officer, perhaps assisted by the controller.

Nature of Strategic Planning

Most competent managers spend considerable time thinking about the future. The result may be an informal understanding of the future direction the entity is going to take, or it may be a formal statement of plans. The formal statement of plans is here called a *strategic plan*, and the process of preparing and revising this statement is called *strategic planning*; it is also called *long-range planning*, or *programming*. *Strategic planning is the process of deciding on the programs that the organization will undertake and the approximate amount of resources that will be allocated to each program over the next several years.*

Relation to Strategy Formulation

We draw a distinction between two management processes—strategy formulation and strategic planning. Because "strategic" is used in both terms, there is a possibility for confusion. *The distinction is that strategy formulation is the process of deciding on new strategies, whereas strategic planning is the process of deciding how to implement strategies.* The document that describes how strategies are to be implemented is here called a *strategic plan.*

In the strategy formulation process, management decides on the goals of the organization and the main strategies for achieving these goals. The strategic planning process takes these goals and strategies as given and seeks to develop programs that will implement the strategies efficiently and effectively. The decision by an industrial goods manufacturer to diversify into consumer goods is a *strategic decision.* Having made this basic decision, a number of implementation issues have to be resolved: whether to diversify through acquisition or by building a new organization, what product lines to emphasize, whether to make or to buy, what marketing channels to use, and so on.

In practice, there is a considerable amount of overlap between strategy formulation and strategic planning. Studies made during the strategic planning process may indicate the desirability of changing goals or strategies. Conversely, strategy formulation usually includes a preliminary consideration of the programs that will be adopted as a means of achieving the goals.

An important reason for making a separation in practice between strategy formulation and strategic planning is that the latter process tends to become institutionalized, and this tends to put a damper on purely creative activities. Segregating strategy formulation as a separate activity, either organizationally or at least in the thinking of top management, can provide an offset to this tendency. Strategy formulation should be an activity in which creative, innovative thinking is strongly encouraged.

Strategic planning is systematic; there is an annual strategic planning process, with prescribed procedures and timetables. Strategy formulation is unsystematic. Strategies are reexamined in response to a perceived opportunity or threat. A possible strategic initiative may surface at any time and by anyone in the organization. If initially judged to be worth pursuing, it is analyzed immediately, without waiting to be fitted into a prescribed timetable.

In many companies, goals and strategies are not stated explicitly or communicated clearly to the managers who need to use them as a framework within which program decisions are made. Thus, in a formal strategic planning process an important first step often is to write descriptions of these goals and strategies. This may be a difficult task, for, although top management presumably has an intuitive feel for what the goals and strategies are, they may not have been verbalized with the specificity that is necessary if they are to be used in making program decisions.

Evolution of Strategic Planning

Fifty years ago the strategic planning process in most organizations was unsystematic. Management did give some thought to long-range planning, but not in a systematic and coordinated way. (There were exceptions, not often recognized in the strategic planning literature. Utilities projected their plant requirements for

20 years or more; forest product companies made plans over the 40-year cycle of timber growth; any company that built a new plant gave some thought to the likelihood of making profitable use of the new capacity over many future years).

> **Example.** Formal long-range planning in the federal government began with the "five-year defense program" system introduced by Secretary of Defense Robert S. McNamara in 1963. First attempts to use such a system in other government agencies were unsuccessful, but beginning in the late 1980s, the system was formally adopted in many businesses and in the federal government. Proposed government policies are now customarily stated in terms of their effect over a five-year period, and debates are now understood to include the total five-year impact even though these numbers are not specifically identified. In the government "shutdown" in 1995 and 1996, the legislative and executive branches always stated their proposals in terms of their total effect over the seven-year period ending in 2002. It was assumed that the budget should be balanced by 2002.

A few companies started formal strategic planning systems in the late 1950s. Most of the early efforts were failures. They were minor adaptations of existing budget preparation systems; the required data were much more detailed than was appropriate; most of the work was done by staff people, rather than by line management; and participants spent more time filling in forms than thinking deeply about alternatives and selecting the best ones. Lessons were quickly learned, however: the objectives should be to make difficult choices among alternative programs, not to extrapolate numbers in budgetary detail; much time should be spent on analysis and informal discussion, and relatively less time on paperwork; the focus should be on the program itself, rather than on the responsibility centers that were responsible for carrying it out.

Currently, many organizations appreciate the advantages of making a plan for the next three to five years. The practice of stating this plan in a formal document, or model, is widely, but by no means universally, accepted. The amount of detail is usually much less than the strategic plans used in the 1950s.

Benefits and Limitations of Strategic Planning

A formal strategic planning process can yield several potential benefits for the organization: (1) a framework to develop the annual budget; (2) a management development tool; (3) a mechanism to force managers to think long term; (4) help in aligning managers toward the long term direction of the company; and (5) help in thinking explicitly about the short-run actions required to implement the long-term strategies.

Framework for Developing the Budget. A strategic plan provides the framework within which the operating budget is developed. An operating budget involves resource commitments for the next year; it is essential that such resource commitments are made with a clear idea of where the organization is heading over the next several years. *Thus, an important benefit of preparing a strategic plan is that it facilitates the formulation of an effective operating budget.*

EXHIBIT 8–1

A company without a strategic planning process

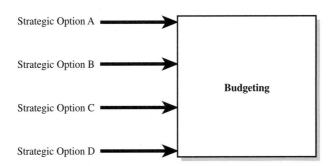

As indicated in Exhibit 8–1, a company without a strategic planning process is forced to consider a large number of strategic issues in the budgeting stage. This might lead to several dysfunctional outcomes: information overload, inadequate consideration of some strategic alternatives, neglect of some choices altogether, and so on. These dysfunctional outcomes could seriously affect the quality of resource allocation decisions. *An important benefit of strategic planning is to facilitate optimal resource allocation decisions in support of key strategic options.* As shown in Exhibit 8–2, the strategic planning process can help to narrow the range of strategic options such that intelligent resource allocation decisions can be made during the budgeting process.

Management Development Tool.   *Formal strategic planning is an excellent management education and training tool; it provides managers with a process to think about strategies and their implementation.* It is not an overstatement to say that in formal strategic planning, the *process* itself is a lot more important than the *output* of the process, which is the *plan document*.

Forces Management to Think Long-Term.   Managers tend to worry more about managing the present, day-to-day tactical issues than thinking about creating future plans. *Formal strategic planning forces managers to make time for important long-term issues.*

Alignment with Corporate Strategies.   *The debates, discussions, and negotiations that take place during the planning process help clarify corporate*

EXHIBIT 8–2

A company with a strategic planning process

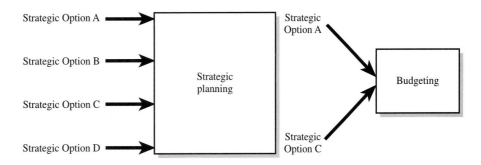

strategies, unify and align managers with such strategies, and show the implications of corporate strategies for individual managers.

Framework for Short-Run Actions.   *The strategic plan shows the implications of programming decisions for action plans in the short term.* As will be described, program decisions are made one at a time, and the strategic plan brings them all together. Preparing the strategic plan may reveal that individual decisions do not add up to a satisfactory whole. Planned new investments may require more funds in certain years than the company can obtain in those years; planned changes in direct programs may require changes in the size of support programs (e.g., research and development, administrative) that were not taken into account when these changes were considered separately. The profit anticipated from individual programs may not add up to satisfactory profit for the whole organization.

> **Example:** Texaco, a large and complex oil and gas producer, has a capital spending and exploration budget of $3.6 billion. Some of its 1996 projects budgeted include " . . . developing offshore projects in the North Sea, Nigeria, Angola, Australia, and Southeast Asia. Continuing to increase production in the neutral zone between Saudi Arabia and Kuwait." With the level of risk associated with the different projects and the amount of resources available, strategic planning and budgeting are a necessity for Texaco, in specific, and all major oil and gas producers, in general.[1]

Limitations.   There are several potential limitations of formal strategic planning. First, *there is a danger that strategic planning could end up becoming a "form-filling," bureaucratic exercise, devoid of strategic thinking.* In order to minimize this risk of bureaucratization, it is useful for organizations to periodically ask, "Are we getting fresh ideas as a result of the strategic planning process?"

A second potential problem could develop if an organization creates a large strategic planning department and delegates the preparation of the strategic plan to that staff department. Strategic planning is a line management function. The staff in strategic planning departments should be kept to a minimum and their role should be one of a catalyst, an educator, and a facilitator of the planning process.

Finally, *strategic planning is time consuming and expensive.* The most significant expense is the time devoted to it by senior management and managers at other levels in the organization. A formal process is not worthwhile in some organizations; the formal planning process in these organizations starts with the preparation of the annual budget, and the decisions that govern the budget are made informally. A formal strategic plan is desirable in organizations that have the following characteristics:

1. Its top management is convinced that strategic planning is important. Otherwise, strategic planning is likely to be a staff exercise that has little impact on actual decision making.

---

[1]"More U.S. companies map 1996 spending plans," *Oil & Gas Journal,* January 29, 1996, p. 39.

2. It is relatively large and complex. In small, simple organizations, an informal understanding of the organization's future directions is adequate for making decisions about resource allocations, which is a principal purpose of preparing a strategic plan.

3. Considerable uncertainty about the future exists, but the organization has the flexibility to adjust to changed circumstances. In a relatively stable organization, a strategic plan is unnecessary; the future is sufficiently like the past, so the strategic plan would be only an exercise in extrapolation. (If a stable organization foresees the need for a change in direction, such as a decline in its markets or drastic changes in the cost of materials, it prepares a contingency plan showing the actions to be taken to meet these new conditions.) If the future is so uncertain that reasonably reliable estimates cannot be made, preparation of a formal strategic plan is a waste of time.

In summary, a formal strategic planning process is not needed in small, relatively stable organizations, and it is not worthwhile in organizations that cannot make reliable estimates about the future or in organizations whose senior management prefers not to manage in this fashion.

Program Structure and Content

In most industrial organizations, programs are products or product families plus research and development, general and administrative activities, planned acquisitions, or other important activities that do not fit into existing product lines. At Procter & Gamble, for example, each product line is a program. By contrast, General Electric structures its programs by profit centers—that is, business units; each business unit is responsible for a specified number of product lines.

In service organizations, programs tend to correspond to the types of services rendered by the entity. The federal government, for example, divides its activities into 10 main programs. In a multi-unit service organization, such as a hotel chain, each unit or each geographical region may constitute a program.

The typical strategic plan covers a period of five future years. Five years is a long enough period to estimate the consequences of program decisions made currently. The consequences of a decision to develop and market a new product or to acquire a major new capital asset may not be fully felt within a short period. The horizon beyond five years may be so murky that attempts to make a program for a longer period are not worthwhile. As mentioned above, some public utilities prepare formal strategic plans that extend as much as 20 years. Many organizations prepare very rough plans that extend beyond five years. In some organizations the strategic plan covers only the next three years.

The dollar amounts for each program show the approximate magnitude of its revenues, expenses, and capital expenditures. Because of the relatively long time horizon, only rough estimates are feasible. Such estimates are satisfactory as a basis for indicating the organization's general direction. If the strategic plan is structured by business units, the "charter," which specifies the boundaries within which the business unit is expected to operate, is also stated.

Organizational Relationships

The strategic planning process involves senior management and the managers of business units or other principal responsibility centers, assisted by their staffs. A primary purpose is to improve the communication between corporate and business unit executives by providing a sequence of scheduled activities through which they can arrive at a mutually agreeable set of objectives and plans. Managers of individual departments usually do not participate in the strategic planning process.

In some organizations, the strategic plan is prepared by the controller organization; in others, there is a separate planning staff. Strategic planning requires analytical skills and a broad outlook that may not exist in the controller organization; the controller organization may be skilled primarily in the detailed analytical techniques that are required in fine-tuning the annual budget and analyzing variances between actual and budgeted amounts.

Even if there is a separate planning staff, the work of disseminating guidelines and assembling the proposed numbers, as described in a later section, is usually done by the controller organization. The numbers in the strategic plan, in the annual budget, and in the accounting system must be consistent with one another, and the best way of assuring this consistency is to assign responsibility for all three to the same staff. Moreover, in some companies, the numbers for all three systems are included in a single computer model.

Headquarters staff members facilitate the strategic planning process, but they should not intervene too strongly. The role of staff members is best conceived of as that of a catalyst; they ensure that the process is properly carried out, but they do not make the program decisions. In particular, if business unit managers perceive that the headquarters staff is overly influential in the decision-making process, these managers will be reluctant to have the frank discussions with staff that are essential in developing sound plans. (Business unit managers, of course, have their own staffs who presumably are loyal to them.)

Top Management Style.   Strategic planning is a management process, and the way in which it is conducted in a given company is heavily dependent on the style of the chief executive officer. Some chief executives prefer to make decisions without the benefit of a formal planning apparatus. If the controller of such a company attempts to introduce a formal system, he or she is likely to be unsuccessful. No system will function effectively unless the chief executive actually uses it; if other managers perceive that the system is not a vital part of the management process, they will give only lip service to it.

In some companies, the chief executive wants some overall plan, for the reasons given earlier but, by temperament, has an aversion to paperwork. In such companies, the system can contain all the elements that will be described in a later section, but with a minimum amount of detail in the written documents and relatively greater emphasis on informal discussion. In other companies, senior management prefers extensive analysis and documentation of plans, and in these companies the formal part of the system is relatively elaborate.

In designing the system, it is important that the style of senior management be correctly diagnosed and that the system be appropriate for that style. This is a difficult task because formal strategic planning has become somewhat of a fad, and some managers think they may be viewed as being old-fashioned if they do not embrace all its trappings. Thus, they may instruct the staff to install an elaborate system, or permit one to be installed, even though they later are uncomfortable in using it.

Analyzing Proposed New Programs

Ideas for new programs can originate anywhere in the organization: with the chief executive, with a headquarters planning staff, or in various parts of the operating organization. For example, in 3M Corporation, the idea for "Post-It" notepads originated down in the organization, not at the initiative of the CEO. Some units are a more likely source than others, for fairly obvious reasons. The R&D organization is expected to generate ideas for new products or processes, the marketing organization for marketing innovations, and the production engineering organization for new equipment and manufacturing methods.

Proposals for programs are essentially either *reactive or proactive*—that is, they arise either as the reaction to a perceived threat such as rumors of the introduction of a new product by a competitor, or they represent an initiative designed to capitalize on a newly perceived opportunity.

Because a company's success depends in part on its ability to find and implement new programs, and because ideas for these can come from a wide variety of sources, it is important that the atmosphere be such that these ideas come to light and that they receive appropriate management attention. A highly structured, formal system may create the wrong atmosphere for this purpose, and therefore it is important that the system be flexible enough and receptive enough so that good new ideas do not get killed off before they come to the attention of the proper decision maker.

It is also important that, wherever possible, the adoption of a new program be viewed not as a single all-or-nothing decision but, rather, as a series of decisions, each one involving a relatively small step in testing and developing the proposed program. Full implementation and its consequent significant investment should be decided upon if, but only if, the tests indicate that the proposal has a good chance of success. Most new programs are not like the Edsel automobile, which involved the commitment of several hundred million dollars in a single decision: rather, they involve many successive decisions: agreement that the initial idea for a product is worth pursuing, then examining its technical feasibility in a laboratory, then examining production problems and cost characteristics in a pilot plant, then testing consumer acceptance in test markets, and only then making a major commitment to full production and marketing. The system must provide for these successive steps, and for a thorough evaluation of the results of each step as a basis for making the decision on the next step.

Capital Investment Analysis

Most proposals require significant amounts of new capital. Techniques for analyzing capital investment proposals attempt either to find (*a*) the net present value of the project—that is, the excess of the present value of the estimated cash inflows over the amount of investment required; or (*b*) the internal rate of return implicit in the relationship between inflows and outflows. An important point is that these techniques, in fact, are used in only about half the situations in which, conceptually, they are applicable.[2] There are at least four reasons for not using present value techniques in analyzing all proposals.

1. The proposal may be so obviously attractive that a calculation of its net present value is unnecessary. A newly developed machine that reduces costs so substantially that it will pay for itself in a year is an example.

2. The estimates involved in the proposal are so uncertain that making present value calculations is believed to be not worth the effort—one can't draw a reliable conclusion from unreliable data. This situation is common when the results are heavily dependent on estimates of sales volume of new products for which no good market data exist. (In these situations, the "payback period" criterion is used frequently.)

3. The rationale for the proposal is something other than increased profitability. The present value approach assumes that the "objective function" is to increase profits in some sense, but many proposed investments are justified on the grounds that they improve employee morale, improve the company's image, or are needed for safety reasons.

4. There is no feasible alternative to adoption of the proposal. An investment that is required to comply with environmental legislation is an example.

The management control system should provide an orderly way of reaching a decision on proposals that cannot be analyzed by quantitative techniques. In particular, the fact that these nonquantifiable proposals exist means that systems that attempt to rank projects in order of profitability are unlikely to be practical; many projects do not fit into a mechanical ranking scheme.

We describe briefly some considerations that are useful in implementing capital expenditure evaluation systems.

Rules.   Companies usually publish rules and procedures for the submission of capital expenditure proposals. These rules specify the approval requirements

---

[2]See the following survey for information on the prevalence of various techniques in practice: Thomas Klammer, Bruce Koch, and Neil Wilmer, *Capital Budgeting Practice: A Survey of Corporate Use*, (Denton, TX: U. of North Texas, 1990).

for proposals of various magnitudes—that is, proposed expenditures to relatively small amounts may be approved by the plant manager, subject to a total specified amount in one year, and larger proposals go successively to business unit managers, to the chief executive officer, and, in the case of very important proposals, to the board of directors.

The rules also contain guidelines for preparing proposals and the general criteria for approving proposals. For example, small cost-saving proposals may require a maximum payback period of two (sometimes three) years. For larger proposals, there is usually a minimum required earnings rate, to be used either in net present value or internal rate of return analysis. The required earnings rate may be the same for all proposals, or there may be different rates for projects with different risk characteristics; also, proposals for additional working capital may use a lower rate than proposals for fixed assets.

Avoiding Manipulation.   Sponsors know that a project with a negative net present value is not likely to be approved. They, nevertheless, may have a "gut feeling" that the project should be undertaken. In some cases, a proposal may be made attractive by adjusting the original estimates so that the project does meet the numerical criteria—perhaps by making more optimistic estimates of sales revenues, perhaps by reducing allowances for contingencies in some of the cost elements. One of the most difficult tasks of the project analyst is to detect such manipulations. The reputation of project sponsors can provide a safeguard; more reliance is placed on numbers from a sponsor who has an excellent track record of past performance. In any event, although all proposals that come up for approval are likely to satisfy the formal criteria, not all of them are truly attractive.

Models.   In addition to the basic capital budgeting model, there are specialized techniques, such as risk analysis, sensitivity analysis, game theory, option pricing models, contingent claims analysis, and decision tree analysis. Some of them have been oversold, but others are of practical value. The planning staff should be acquainted with them and require their use in situations in which the necessary data are available.

Organization for Analysis

A team may be formed to evaluate extremely large and important proposals, and the process may require a year or more. Even for smaller proposals, there is usually considerable discussion between the person who is sponsoring the proposal and the headquarters staff. As many as a dozen functional and line executives may be required to sign off on an important proposal before it is submitted to the chief executive officer. The proposals may be returned by the CEO for further analysis several times before the final decision is made to go ahead with or reject the project. And, as noted earlier, the decision to proceed may require that a succession of development and testing hurdles be crossed prior to full implementation.

Recent work in the rapidly developing field of *expert systems* has found ways of using computer software in the analysis of proposed programs. Software has been developed that permits each participant in the group that is considering a proposal to vote on, and to explicitly rank, each of the criteria used to judge the project. The computer tabulates the results, uncovers inconsistencies or misunderstandings, and raises questions about them. A succession of such votes can lead to a conclusion that expresses the consensus of the group.

There is no set timetable for analyzing investment proposals. Analysis is started as soon after receipt of the proposal as people are available. Approved projects are collected during the year for inclusion in the capital budget. There is a deadline in the sense that the capital budget for next year has a deadline (usually just prior to the beginning of the budget year). If a proposal doesn't make that deadline, its formal approval may wait until the following year, unless there are unusual circumstances. The capital budget contains the authorized capital expenditures for the budget year, and, if additional amounts are approved, cash plans must be revised; there may be problems in financing the additional amount.

Analyzing Ongoing Programs

In addition to developing new programs, many companies have systematic ways of analyzing ongoing programs. Several analytical techniques can aid in this process. This section describes the following analytical tools: value chain analysis and activity-based costing.

Value Chain Analysis

As pointed out in Chapter 2, *the value chain for any firm in any business is the linked set of value-creating activities to produce a product from basic raw material sources for component suppliers to the ultimate end-use product delivered into the final consumers' hands*. Each firm must be understood in the context of the overall chain of value-creating activities of which it is only a part.

From the strategic planning perspective, the value chain concept highlights three potential areas:

1. Linkages with suppliers.
2. Linkages with customers.
3. Process linkages within the value chain of the firm.

Linkages with Suppliers.   As indicated in Exhibit 8–3, the linkage with suppliers should be managed so that both the firm and its supplier can benefit. Such opportunities can be dramatically important in lowering costs, increasing value, or both.

Example. When bulk chocolate began to be delivered in liquid form in tank cars instead of ten-pound molded bars, an industrial chocolate firm (i.e., the supplier)

Exhibit 8–3

Profit improvement opportunities through linkages with suppliers

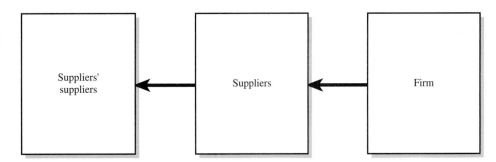

eliminated the cost of molding and packing bars, and a confectionery producer (i.e., the firm) saved the cost of unpacking and melting.[3]

Linkages with Customers.   As indicated in Exhibit 8–4, customer linkages can be just as important as supplier linkages. There are many examples where the linkage between a firm and its customer becomes mutually beneficial.

> **Example.** Some container producers (i.e., the firms) have constructed manufacturing facilities next to beer breweries (i.e., the customers) and deliver the containers through overhead conveyors directly onto the customers' assembly line. This results in significant cost reductions for both the container producers and their customers by expediting the transport of empty containers, which are bulky and heavy.[4]

Process Linkages within the Value Chain of the Firm.   Value chain analysis explicitly recognizes the fact that the individual value activities within a firm are not independent but rather are interdependent (Exhibit 8–5).

> **Example.** At McDonald's, the timing of promotional campaigns (one value activity) significantly influences capacity utilization in production (another value activity). These linked activities must be coordinated if the full effect of the promotion is to be realized.

Exhibit 8–4

Profit improvement opportunities through linkages with customers

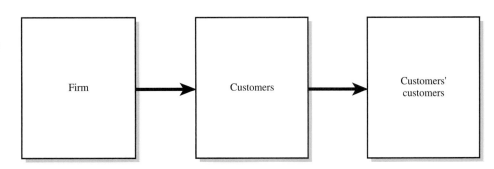

[3]M. Hergert and D. Morris, "Accounting Data for Value Chain Analysis," *Strategic Management Journal*, 10, 1989, 175–88.
[4]Ibid.

EXHIBIT 8–5

*Profit improvement
opportunities
through process
linkages within the
value chain*

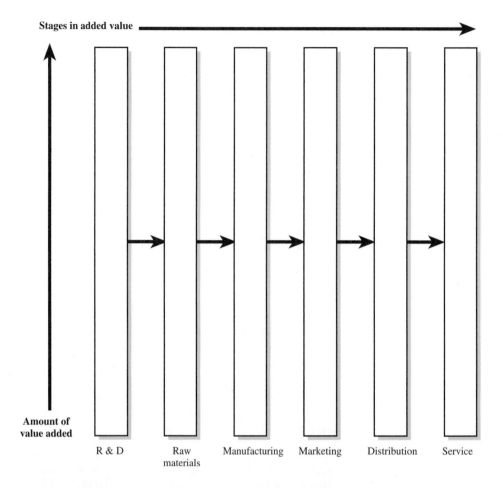

Stages in added value

R & D   Raw materials   Manufacturing   Marketing   Distribution   Service

Amount of
value added

A company might want to analyze the process linkages within the value chain, seeking to improve their efficiency. The overall objective is to move materials from vendors, through production, and to the customer at the lowest cost and in the shortest time.

Efficiency of the design portion of the value chain might be increased by reducing the number of separate parts and increasing their ease of manufacture.

Example. Japanese VCR producers were able to reduce prices from $1,300 in 1977 to $295 in 1984 by emphasizing the impact of an early step in the chain (product design) on a later step (production) by drastically reducing the number of parts in VCRs.[5]

A firm should also work toward improving the efficiency of every activity within the chain through a better understanding of the drivers that regulate costs and value for each activity.

[5]Ibid., p. 320.

Efficiency of the *inward* portion (i.e., the portion that precedes production) might be improved by reducing the number of vendors; by having a computer system place orders automatically; by limiting deliveries to "just-in-time" amounts (which reduces inventories); and by holding vendors responsible for quality, which reduces or eliminates inspection costs.

Efficiency of the *production* portion might be improved by increased automation, perhaps by using robots; by rearranging machines into "cells," each of which performs a series of related production steps; and by better production control systems.

Efficiency of the *outward* portion (i.e., the portion from the factory door to receipt by the customer) might be improved by having customers place orders electronically (which is now common in hospital supply companies and in certain types of retailing); by changing the locations of warehouses; by changing channels of distribution and placing more or less emphasis on distributors and wholesalers; by improving the efficiency of warehouse operations; and by changing the mix between company-operated trucks and transportation furnished by outside agencies.

> **Examples.** Procter & Gamble places order-entry computers in Wal-Mart stores. This eliminates errors that used to occur when Wal-Mart buyers transmitted orders to P&G order-entry clerks, reduces the cost of the operation in both firms, and reduces the time between initiation of an order and shipment of the goods. Levi Strauss has a similar system with its own retail stores.

These efficiency-oriented initiatives usually involve trade-offs. For example, direct orders from customer computers may speed delivery and reduce paperwork but lead to an increase in order-filling costs because of the smaller quantities ordered. Thus, it is important that all related parts of the value chain be analyzed together; otherwise, improvements in one link may be offset by additional costs in another.

Activity-Based Costing

Increased computerization and automation in factories have led to important changes in systems for collecting and using cost information. Fifty years ago, most companies allocated overhead costs to products by means of a plantwide overhead rate based on direct labor hours or dollars. Today, an increasing number of companies collect costs for material-related costs (e.g., transportation, storage) separately from other manufacturing costs; and they collect manufacturing costs for individual departments, individual machines, or individual "cells," which consist of groups of machines that perform a series of related operations on a product. In these cost centers, direct labor costs are combined with other cost elements, giving *conversion cost*—that is, the labor and factory overhead cost of converting raw materials and parts into finished products. In addition to conversion costs, the newer systems also assign R&D, general and administrative, and marketing costs to products. The newer systems also use multiple allocation bases. In these newer systems, the word *activity* is often used instead of *cost center*, and *cost driver* instead of *basis of allocation*; and the cost system is called an *activity-based cost system* (ABC).[5] Exhibit 8–6 indicates differences between traditional and activity-based cost systems.

The basis of allocation, or cost driver, for each of the cost centers reflects the *cause* of cost incurrence—that is, the element that explains why the amount of cost incurred in the cost center, or activity, varies. For example, in procurement, the cost driver may be the number of orders placed; for internal transportation, the number of parts moved; for product design, the number of different parts in the product; and for production control, the number of set-ups. Note that "cause" here refers to the factor causing the costs in the individual cost center, in contrast with the traditional system, in which the cause of cost is taken to be the volume of products as a whole.

> **Examples.** General Motors used ABC analysis to formulate a component make-or-buy strategy. In a single plant, its ABC system had over 5,000 activity cost pools and over 100 different cost drivers (i.e., drivers that traced activity cost pools to products.)[6]
>
> Schrader Bellows, a division of Scovill, Inc., used ABC analysis to re-evaluate marketing and product line strategies. Its ABC analysis had 28 activity cost pools and 16 cost drivers. Its previous system had one cost pool for each of the five production departments and used one cost driver (viz., direct labor) to allocate the cost pools to products.[7]
>
> Stewart Box Company (Case 1–3 in this book) uses ABC analysis to develop price estimates, as described in Exhibit 3 of the case.

Fundamentally, each component of overhead is caused by some activity. In ABC each product is charged for a share of the overhead based on the proportion of that activity which it causes. Production scheduling cost, for example, is generated by the number of production runs to be scheduled. It thus is allocated based on the number of production runs each product generates. Products that generate a large number of relatively short production runs will *always* bear a less than proportionate share of the scheduling cost under *any* volume-based allocation scheme. Scheduling cost is not production volume dependent. It is dependent on how many runs must be scheduled, not how many units the firm produces. Production volume-based allocation methods (labor hours or machine hours) misstates the extent to which the product

---

[5]We use the term *traditional* to refer to systems used by many, but by no means all, companies. As Shank points out, many of the essentials of ABC go back to J. M. Clark's 1923 book, *Studies in the Economics of Overhead Costs*. John K. Shank, "Strategic Cost Management: New Wine or Just New Bottles," *Journal of Management Accounting Research*, Fall 1989, p. 48.

[6]George Beaujon and Vinod Singhal, "Understanding the Activity Costs in an Activity-Based Cost System," *Journal of Cost Management for the Manufacturing Industry*, Spring 1990, pp. 51–72.

[7]Robin Cooper, "Schrader Bellows," Harvard Business School case #186–272.

Exhibit 8–6

Contrast in product costing

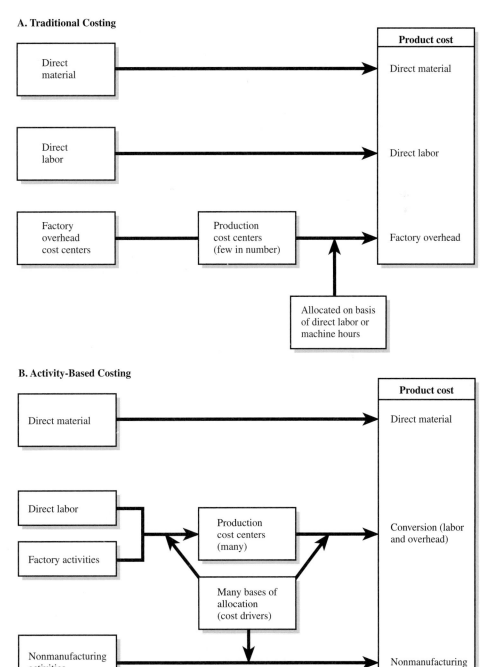

A. Traditional Costing

Direct material → Direct material

Direct labor → Direct labor

Factory overhead cost centers → Production cost centers (few in number) → Factory overhead

Allocated on basis of direct labor or machine hours

Product cost

B. Activity-Based Costing

Direct material → Direct material

Direct labor, Factory activities → Production cost centers (many) → Conversion (labor and overhead)

Many bases of allocation (cost drivers)

Nonmanufacturing activities → Nonmanufacturing

(Design, R & D, G & A, Marketing, Distribution)

Product cost

EXHIBIT 8–7

*ABC versus
traditional cost
system: An example*

	Product A	Product B
Total number of units produced	1,000	1,000
Number of batches	1	10
Inspection time for each batch	2 hours	4 hours
Total direct labor hours	300 hours	120 hours

Traditional cost system uses direct labor hours to allocate inspection costs to products. ABC uses inspection time as the basis of allocation.

	Traditional costing		ABC	
Inspection cost	$4,200		$4,200	
	Product A	Product B	Product A	Product B
Inspection cost	$3,000	$1,200	$200	$4,000
Inspection cost per unit	**$3.00**	**$1.20**	**$0.20**	**$4.00**

with many short runs causes scheduling cost. The basic idea is that transaction volume (number of production runs) is a better proxy for long-run variable cost than is output volume.

The mechanics of ABC contrasted with traditional cost systems are illustrated in Exhibit 8–7. The following example highlights the systematic undercosting of low volume, complex products and the systematic overcosting of high volume, vanilla products under traditional costing systems.

Example. "Imagine a production line in a pen factory in which two kinds of pens are being made, black in high volume and purple in low. Assume that it takes eight hours to program the machinery to shift production from one kind of pen to the other. The total costs include supplies, which are the same for both types of pens, the direct labor of the workers on the line, and factory overhead. The most significant piece of overhead in this instance would be the cost of reprogramming the machinery whenever there's a switch from black to purple or purple to black.

If the company produces 10 times as many black pens as purple pens, 10 times the cost of reprogramming will be allocated to the black as to the purple under any production volume-based allocation scheme. Obviously this understates the cost of producing the low-volume product. The ABC approach comes much closer than traditional costing to showing managers what causes the expenses of manufacture. Once pen manufacturing is broken down into its activities, managers can recognize that the activity of changing pens triggers the cost of retooling. The ABC accountant then calculates an average cost of setting up the machinery and charges it against each batch of pens that requires retooling regardless of the size of the run. Thus, a product carries the cost for only the overhead it actually consumes."[8]

The ABC concept is not particularly subtle or counterintuitive. In fact, it is very much in line with common sense. But, in earlier days, factories tended to produce fewer different products, cost was labor dominated (high labor cost relative to overhead), and products tended to differ less in the amount of support services they consumed. Thus, the activity basis for overhead allocation was not likely to produce product cost results much different from a simple volume-driven basis tied to labor cost.

Today, labor cost in many companies is not only dramatically less important, it is also viewed less and less as a cost to be varied when production volume varies. Indirect cost is now the dominant part of cost in many companies. In the prototypical "flexible factory," raw material is the only production volume-dependent cost and the only cost directly relatable to individual products. Advocates of ABC maintain that a meaningful assessment of full cost today *must* involve assigning overhead in proportion to the activities that generate it in the long run.

Use of ABC Information

Collecting ABC information on a routine basis is not worthwhile in most companies. ABC is a strategic planning tool. If used as part of the strategic planning process, ABC may provide useful insights. For example, it may show that complex products with many separate parts have higher design and production costs than simpler products; that products with low volume have higher unit costs than high-volume products; that products with many setups or many engineering change orders have higher unit costs than other products; and that products with a short life cycle have higher unit costs than other products. Information on the magnitude of these differences may lead to changes in policies relating to full line versus focused product line, product pricing policies, make-or-buy decisions, product mix decisions, policies on adding or deleting products, elimination of nonvalue added activities, and to an emphasis on better factory layouts and simplicity in product design.

> **Examples.** In 1992, Chrysler benefited from ABC analysis in a pilot project that examined the designs for wiring harnesses for the company's popular minivans. The harnesses yoke together bundles of wires. Nine departments, from design to assembly to finance, set out to reckon the optimum number of wiring harnesses. The assembly people favored using just one kind of harness, the design group wanted nine, and so on. When ABC was used to cost out activities across the entire production of the vehicles, everyone saw the optimum number was two.
>
> Hewlett-Packard's successful products, new models of HP 3000 and HP 9000 midrange computers, benefited from better cost information. When ABC showed

---

[8]Terence P. Pare, "A New Tool for Managing Costs," *Fortune*, June 14, 1993, pp. 124–29.

that testing new designs and parts was extremely expensive, engineers changed their plans to favor components that required less testing, thus lowering costs.[9]

Other companies have realized significant cost savings as a result of reducing complexity:

Examples. Procter & Gamble has standardized product formulas and packages. P&G now uses just two basic packages for shampoo in the U.S., saving $25 million a year.[10]

General Motors has reduced the number of U.S. car models from 53 to 44 since 1944 and combined its Pontiac and GMC division to simplify marketing.[11]

The Strategic Planning Process

In a company that operates on a calendar-year basis, the strategic planning process starts in the spring and is completed in the fall, just prior to the preparation of the annual budget. The process involves the following steps:

1. Reviewing and updating the strategic plan from last year.
2. Deciding on assumptions and guidelines.
3. First iteration of the new strategic plan.
4. Analysis.
5. Second iteration of the new strategic plan.
6. Review and approval.

Reviewing and Updating the Strategic Plan

During the past year, decisions were made that changed the strategic plan; management makes decisions whenever there is a need to do so, not in response to a set timetable. Conceptually, the implications of each decision over the next five years should be incorporated in the strategic plan as soon as the decision is made. Otherwise, the formal plan no longer represents the path that the company plans to follow. In particular, the plan may not represent a valid base for testing proposed strategies and programs, which is one of the plan's principal values. As a practical matter, however, very few organizations continuously update their strategic plans. Updating involves more paperwork and computer time than management believes is worthwhile.

The first step in the annual strategic planning process, therefore, is to review and update the strategic plan that was agreed to last year. Actual experience for the first few months of the current year is already reflected in the accounting reports, and these are extrapolated for the current best estimate of the year as a whole. If the computer program is sufficiently flexible, it can extend the impact of current forces to the "out years"—that is, the years beyond

---

[9]Ibid.

[10]Zachary Schiller, "Making It Simple," *Business Week*, September 9, 1996, pp. 96–104.

[11]Ibid.

the current year; if not, rough estimates are made manually. The implications of new program decisions on revenues, expenses, capital expenditures, and cash flow are incorporated. This update is usually made by the planning staff. Management may be involved if there are uncertainties or ambiguities in the program decisions that must be resolved.

Deciding on Assumptions and Guidelines

The updated strategic plan incorporates many assumptions. These include such broad assumptions as the growth in Gross Domestic Product, cyclical movements, labor rates, prices of important raw materials, interest rates, selling prices, market conditions, including the actions of competitors, and the impact of government legislation in each of the countries in which the company operates. These assumptions are reexamined, and, if necessary, they are changed to incorporate the latest information.

The updated strategic plan contains the implications on revenues, expenses, and cash flows of the existing operating facilities and changes in these facilities from opening new plants, expanding existing plants, closing plants, and relocating facilities. It shows the amount of new capital likely to be available from retained earnings and new financing. These conditions are examined to ensure that they are currently valid, and the amounts are extended for another year.

The resulting update is not done in great detail. A rough approximation is adequate as a basis for senior management decisions about objectives that are to be attained in the plan years and about the key guidelines that are to be observed in planning how to attain these objectives. The objectives usually are stated separately for each product line and are expressed as sales revenue, as a profit percentage, or a return on capital employed. The principal guidelines are assumptions on wage and salary increases (including new benefits programs that may affect compensation), new or discontinued product lines, and selling prices. For overhead units, personnel ceilings may be specified. At this stage, they represent senior management's tentative views. In the next stage, business unit managers have an opportunity to present their views.

Management Meetings.   Many companies hold an annual meeting of corporate and business unit managers (often called a "summit conference") to discuss the proposed objectives and guidelines. Such a meeting typically lasts several days and is held away from company facilities to minimize distractions. In addition to the formal agenda, such a meeting provides an opportunity for managers throughout the corporation to get to know one another.

First Iteration of the Strategic Plan

Based on the assumptions, objectives, and guidelines, the business units and other operating units prepare their "first cut" of the strategic plan. It may include different operating plans than those included in the current plan, such as a change in marketing tactics; these are supported by reasons. Much of the analytical work is done by the business unit staffs, but the final judgments are made by business unit managers. Depending on the personal relationships, business unit personnel may seek the advice of the headquarters staff in the development of these plans. Members of the headquarters staff often visit the business units during this process, for the purpose of clarifying the guidelines, assumptions, and instructions, and, in general, to assist in the planning process.

The completed strategic plan consists of income statements; of inventory, accounts receivable, and other key balance sheet items; of number of employees; of quantitative information about sales and production; of expenditures for plant and other capital acquisitions; of any other unusual cash flows; and of a narrative explanation and justification. (The business units need not submit complete balance sheets and cash flow statements; these statements for the whole corporation can be derived from details given in the plan.) The numbers are in considerable detail (although in much less detail than in the annual budget) for the next year and the following year, with only summary information for the later years.

Analysis

When the business unit plans are received at headquarters, they are aggregated into an overall corporate strategic plan, and this plan is analyzed in depth by the planning staff and by the marketing, production, and other functional executives at headquarters. Business Unit X plans a new marketing tactic; is it likely that the resulting sales will be as large as the plan indicates? Business Unit Y plans an increase in general and administrative personnel; are the additional people really needed? Business Unit Z assumes a large increase in productivity; is the supporting justification realistic? Research and development promises important new products; are the business units prepared to manufacture and sell these products? Some business unit managers tend to build *slack* into their estimates, so their objectives are more easily accomplished; can some of this slack be detected and eliminated?

The headquarters people also examine the business unit plans for consistency. If one business unit manufactures for another unit, are the planned shipments from the manufacturing unit equal to the planned sales of the sales unit? In particular, are planned shipments to overseas subsidiaries consistent with the planned sales volume of these subsidiaries?

Some of these questions are resolved by discussions between the headquarters staff and their counterparts in the business units. Others are reported to corporate management, and they are the basis for discussions between corporate managers and business unit managers. This discussion is the heart of the formal planning process. It usually requires several hours and often goes on for a day or more in each business unit.

In many cases, the sum of the business unit plans reveals a *planning gap*— that is, the sum of the individual plans does not add up to attainment of the corporate objectives. There are only three ways to close a planning gap; (1) find opportunities for improvements in the business unit plans, (2) make acquisitions, or (3) review the corporate objectives. Senior management usually focuses on the first.

From the planning numbers, the headquarters staff can develop planned cash requirements for the whole organization. These may indicate the need for additional financing or, alternatively, the possibility of increasing dividends.[12]

Second Iteration of the Strategic Plan

Analysis of the first submission may lead only to a revision of the plans of certain business units, but it may also lead to a change in the assumptions and guidelines that affect all business units. For example, the aggregation of all plans may indicate that the cash drain from increasing inventories and capital expenditures is more than the company can safely tolerate; if so, there may be a requirement for postponing expenditures throughout the organization. These decisions lead to a revision of the plan. Technically, the revision is much simpler to prepare than the original submission, because it requires changes in only a few numbers; but organizationally, it is the most painful part of the process, because difficult decisions must be made.

Some companies do not require a formal revision from the business units. The changes are negotiated informally, and the results are entered into the plan at headquarters.

Final Review and Approval

The revised plan usually is discussed at length in a meeting of senior corporate officials. It also may be presented at a meeting of the board of directors. Final approval comes from the chief executive officer. The approval should come prior to the beginning of the budget preparation process, because the strategic plan is an important input to that process.

Summary

A strategic plan shows the financial and other implications, over the next several years, of implementing the company's strategies.

In the period since the current strategic plan was prepared, the organization has made capital investment decisions. The process of approving proposed capital investments does not follow a set timetable; the decisions are made as soon as the need for them is identified. The implications of these decisions are incorpo-

---

[12]For a discussion of this point, see V. Govindarajan and John K. Shank, "Cash Sufficiency: The Missing Link in Strategy Planning," *Journal of Business Strategy*, Summer 1986, pp. 88–95.

rated in the strategic plan. Assumptions and guidelines about external forces, such as inflation, internal policies, and product pricing, are also incorporated.

Based on this information, the business units and support units prepare proposed strategic plans, and these are discussed in depth with senior management. If the resulting plan does not indicate that profitability will be adequate, there is a planning gap, which is dealt with by a second iteration of the strategic plan.

Several analytical techniques, such as value chain analysis and activity-based costing, can aid in the strategic planning process.

APPENDIX
MERCK'S RESEARCH PLANNING MODEL

Research is the life blood of the pharmaceutical industry; but research by its nature is risky, because management must invest without knowing if that investment is ever going to yield a new drug. Exacerbating this is the trend of increasing R&D costs, which means companies are putting more of their shareholders' money at risk to find that next new drug. To discover one drug, companies must evaluate thousands of compounds, and, even after identifying that one promising drug, there is still only a one in eight chance that it will complete the seven-year-development phase and be approved for sale. Of those drugs that are eventually commercialized, only three in ten ever recover their full cost of discovery and development. A recent study estimated that the cost to discover and develop a new chemical entity was approximately $230 million, including the cost of failures and the time value of money. Consequently, management must actively monitor its research investments to increase the likelihood of returning the company's cost of capital.

To facilitate the R&D management process at Merck & Co., Inc., a comprehensive quantitative planning model, which combines discounted cash flow analysis with probabilistic risk analysis, was developed. This model incorporates monetary and nonmonetary factors affecting an R&D project, and then it applies state-of-the-art financial evaluation techniques to quantify the expected returns and to measure the risks associated with a project or a portfolio of projects.

The Merck model covers a twenty-year time horizon and includes drivers of commercial performance, such as unit volume forecasts, pricing projections, manufacturing costs, manufacturing capital, and exchange and inflation rate projections. To capture the variability and uncertainty that is inherent in projecting these variables, the model uses inputs in the form of frequency distributions, rather than just single point estimates.

As an example of how the inputs are derived, the sales forecast for a product is made by the product manager who takes into consideration the factors that affect the product's performance over the forecast period. These factors include such things as patent life, other competitive products, size of market, and therapeutic or diagnostic profile. For

---

This appendix was written by Judy C. Lewent, Vice President, Finance and Chief Financial Officer of Merck & Co., Inc.

Exhibit 1

Probability of exceeding cost of capital

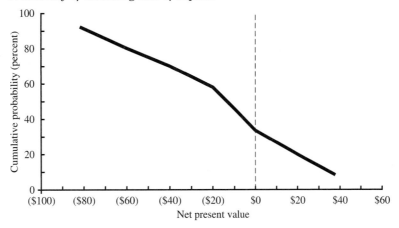

each year, the product manager provides estimates of the optimistic, most likely, and pessimistic forecast levels. These forecasts are then submitted to senior marketing management for approval.

In addition to the financial variables, the model also requires assumptions for key nonmonetary variables, such as dosage, launch date, and most important, the probability of technical success.

The Merck model runs several hundred iterations for each product development candidate, and then statistically describes several critical output variables, including annual nominal and constant dollar sales projections, cash flows, return on investment, and net present value (NPV). Frequency distributions for key variables are created in order to quantify riskiness in terms of dispersion of results, as well as the expected value of the project.

An example of a frequency table for one of the output statistics, net present value, is shown in Exhibit 1. In this case, the project has a 30 percent chance that the NPV will exceed the cost of capital. By selecting points along the x- and y-axis, the probability of a certain NPV being achieved can be determined.

Periodically, forecasts from the Merck model are compared with the actual results for that same period. This process helps test the accuracy and reliability of the model's projections, and highlights areas where assumptions in future forecasts may need to be more closely examined. It also helps to identify areas for future methodological improvements.

This model is used extensively within Merck in three ways: to evaluate business opportunities; to help manage R&D; and to assist in long-range planning. Concerning business opportunities, the model is used in evaluating proposed product licensing candidates, capital expenditures, existing businesses, and acquisition candidates. Regarding management of R&D, it is employed in: making the go/no go investment decisions for product development candidates at various stages of the development process; quantifying the value of back-up compounds; optimizing the portfolio of development projects undertaken; and providing a measure for judging productivity of the R&D organization. Last, the Merck model is used to extend the time horizon of the company's five-year long range operating plan to ten and fifteen-year projections. Such projections can be used to identify strategic issues that face the company, as well as to assess the impact of proposed business alliances on the company's longer-term growth prospects.

Suggested Additional Readings

Banker, Rajiv D., and Holly H. Johnston. "An Empirical Study of Cost Drivers in the U.S. Airline Industry," *The Accounting Review*, 68, 3, July 1993, pp. 576–601.

Brown, James F. "How U.S. Firms Conduct Strategic Planning." *Management Accounting*, February 1986, pp. 38–55.

Cooper, Robin, and Robert Kaplan. "Measure Costs Right: Make the Right Decisions." *Harvard Business Review*, 6, 5, September–October 1988, pp. 96–103.

Govindarajan, Vijay, and John K. Shank. "Strategic Cost Management and the Value Chain," *Journal of Cost Management*, 5, 4, Winter 1992, pp. 5–21.

————. "Strategic Cost Management: The Value Chain Perspective." *Journal of Management Accounting Research*, 4, Fall 1992, pp. 179–97.

Haka, S. F., L. A. Gordan, and G. E. Pinches. "Sophisticated Capital Budgeting Selection Techniques and Firm Performance." *The Accounting Review,* LX4 (October 1985), pp. 651–69.

Hertenstein, Julie H. "Introductory Note on Capital Budgeting Practices." Boston: Harvard Business School, No. 9-188-059, 1988.

Porter, Michael E. *Competitive Advantage*. New York: The Free Press, 1985.

Shank, John K., and Vijay Govindarajan. *Strategic Cost Management*. New York: The Free Press, 1993.

————. "The Perils of Cost Allocation Based on Production Volumes." *Accounting Horizons,* 2, no. 4, (December 1988), pp. 5–16.

Case 8–1
Codman & Shurtleff, Inc.

"This revision combines our results from January to April with the preliminary estimates supplied by each department for the remainder of the year. Of course, there are still a lot of unknown factors to weigh in, but this will give you some idea of our preliminary updated forecast."

As the Board members reviewed the document provided to them by Gus Fleites, vice president of Information and Control at Codman & Shurtleff, Roy Black, president, addressed the six men sitting at the conference table, "This revised forecast leaves us with a big stretch. We are almost two million dollars short of our profit objective for the year. As we discussed last week, we are estimating sales to be $1.1 million above original forecast. This is due in part to the early introduction of the new Chest Drainage Unit. However, three major factors that we didn't foresee last September will affect our profit plan estimates for the remainder of the year.

"First, there's the currency issue: our hedging has partially protected us, but the continued rapid deterioration of the dollar has pushed our costs up on European specialty instruments. Although this has improved Codman's competitive market position in Europe, those profits accrue to the European company and are not reflected in this forecast. Second, we have an unfavorable mix variance; and finally, we will have to absorb inventory variances due to higher than anticipated start-up costs of our recently combined manufacturing operations."

"When do we have to take the figures to Corporate?" asked Chuck Dunn, vice president of Business Development.

"Wednesday of next week," replied Black, "so we have to settle this by Monday. That gives us

only tomorrow and the weekend to wrap up the June budget revision. I know that each of you has worked on these estimates, but I think that the next look will be critical to achieving our profit objective."

"Bob, do you have anything you can give us?"

Bob Dick, vice president of Marketing, shook his head, "I've been working with my people looking at price and mix. At the moment, we can't realistically get more price. Most of the mix variance for the balance of the year will be due to increased sales of products that we are handling under the new distribution agreement. The mix for the remainder of the year may change, but with 2,700 active products in the catalogue, I don't want to move too far from our original projections. My expenses are cut right to the bone. Further cuts will mean letting staff go."

Black nodded his head in agreement. "Chuck, you and I should meet to review our Research and Development priorities. I know that Herb Stolzer will want to spend time reviewing the status of our programs. I think we should be sure that we have cut back to reflect our spending to date. I wouldn't be surprised if we could find another $400,000 without jeopardizing our long-term programs."

"Well, it seems our work is cut out for us. The rest of you keep working on this. Excluding R&D, we need at least another $500,000 before we start drawing down our contingency fund. Let's meet here tomorrow at two o'clock and see where we stand."

Background

Codman & Shurtleff, Inc., a subsidiary of Johnson & Johnson, was established in 1838 in Boston by Thomas Codman to design and fashion surgical instruments. The company developed surgical instrument kits for use in Army field

This case was prepared by Professor Robert Simons. Copyright © by the President and Fellows of Harvard College. HBS 187-081.

hospitals during the Civil War and issued its first catalogue in 1860. After the turn of the century, Codman & Shurtleff specialized in working with orthopaedic surgeons and with pioneers in the field of neurosurgery.

In 1986 Codman & Shurtleff supplied hospitals and surgeons worldwide with over 2,700 products for surgery including instruments, equipment, implants, surgical disposables, fiberoptic light sources and cables, surgical head lamps, surgical microscopes, coagulators, and electronic pain control simulators and electrodes. These products involved advanced technologies from the fields of metallurgy, electronics, and optics.

Codman & Shurtleff operated three manufacturing locations in Randolph, New Bedford, and Southbridge, Massachusetts, and a distribution facility in Avon, Massachusetts. The company employed 800 people in the United States.

In 1964 Codman & Shurtleff was acquired by Johnson & Johnson, Inc., as an addition to its professional products business. Johnson & Johnson operated manufacturing subsidiaries in 46 countries, sold its products in most countries of the world, and employed 75,000 people worldwide. 1985 sales were $6.4 billion with before tax profits of $900 million [Exhibit 1].

Roy Black had been president of Codman & Shurtleff since 1983. In his 25 years with Johnson & Johnson, Black had spent 18 years with Codman, primarily in the Marketing Department. He had also worked at Ethicon and Surgikos. He described his job:

> This is a tough business to manage because it is so complex. We rely heavily on the neurosurgeons for ideas in product generation and for the testing and ultimate acceptance of our products. We have to stay in close contact with the leading neurosurgeons around the world. For example, last week I returned from a tour of the Pacific rim. During the trip, I visited 8 Johnson & Johnson/Codman affiliates and 25 neurosurgeons.
>
> At the same time, we are forced to push technological innovation to reduce costs. This is a matter of survival. In the past, we concentrated on producing superior quality goods, and the market was willing to pay whatever it took

to get the best. But the environment has changed; the shift has been massive. We are trying to adapt to a situation where doctors and hospitals are under severe pressure to be more efficient and cost-effective.

> We compete in 12 major product groups. Since our markets are so competitive, the business is very price sensitive. The only way we can take price is to offer unique products with cost-in-use benefits to the professional user.
>
> Since the introduction of DRG costing[1] by hospitals in 1983, industry volume has been off approximately 20 percent. We have condensed 14 locations to 4 and have reduced staff levels by over 20 percent. There have also been some cuts in R&D, although our goal is to maintain research spending at near double the historical Codman level.

Chuck Dunn, vice president of Business Development, had moved three years earlier from Johnson & Johnson Products to join Codman as vice president for Information and Control. During his 24 years with Johnson & Johnson, he had worked with 4 different marketing divisions as well as the Corporate office. He recalled the process of establishing a new mission statement at Codman:

> When I arrived here, Codman was in the process of defining a more clearly focused mission. Our mission was product oriented, but Johnson & Johnson was oriented by medical specialty. On a matrix, this resulted in missed product opportunities as well as turf problems with other Johnson & Johnson companies.
>
> It took several years of hard work to arrive at a new worldwide mission statement oriented to medical specialty, but this process was very useful in obtaining group consensus. Our worldwide mission is now defined in terms of a primary focus in the neuro-spinal surgery business. This turns out to be a large market and allows better positioning of our products.

---

[1]On October 1, 1983, Medicare reimbursement to hospitals changed from a cost-plus system to a fixed-rate system as called for in the 1983 Social Security refinancing legislation. The new system was called "prospective payment" because rates were set in advance of treatment according to which of 467 "diagnostic-related groups" (or DRGs) a patient was deemed to fall into. This change in reimbursement philosophy caused major cost-control problems for the nation's 5,800 acute-care hospitals which received an average of 36 percent of their revenues from Medicare and Medicaid.

EXHIBIT 1   Johnson & Johnson and Subsidiaries, Consolidated Statement of Earnings and Retained Earnings

Dollars in Millions Except Per Share Figures	*1985*	*1984*	*1983*
Revenues			
Sales to customers	$6,421.3	$6,124.5	$5,972.9
Other revenues			
Interest income	107.3	84.5	82.9
Royalties and miscellaneous	48.1	38.0	49.4
Total revenues	$6,576.7	$6,247.0	$6,105.2
Costs and expenses			
Cost of products sold	$2,594.2	$2,469.4	$2,471.8
Selling, distribution and administrative expenses	2,516.0	2,488.4	2,352.9
Research expense	471.1	421.2	405.1
Interest expense	74.8	86.1	88.3
Interest expense capitalized	(28.9)	(35.0)	(36.9)
Other expenses including nonrecurring charges	50.3	61.8	99.9
Total costs and expenses	$5,677.5	$5,491.9	$5,381.1
Earnings before provision for taxes on income	$ 899.2	$ 755.1	$ 724.1
Provision for taxes on income	285.5	240.6	235.1
Net earnings	$ 613.7	$ 514.5	$ 489.0
Retained earnings at beginning of period	$3,119.1	$2,814.5	$2,540.1
Cash dividends paid (per share: 1985, $2.175; 1984, $1.175; 1983, $1.075)	(233.2)	(219.9)	(204.6)
Retained earnings at end of period	$3,499.6	$3,119.1	$2,824.5
Net earnings per share	$ 3.36	2.75	2.57

In addition to clarifying our planning, we use the mission statement as a screening device. We look carefully at any new R&D project to see if it fits our mission. The same is true for acquisitions.

Reporting Relationships at Johnson & Johnson

In 1985 Johnson & Johnson comprised 155 autonomous subsidiaries operating in 3 health care markets: consumer products, pharmaceutical products, and professional products. **Exhibit 2** provides details of the business operations of the company.

Johnson & Johnson was managed on a decentralized basis as described in the following excerpt from the 1985 Annual Report:

The Company is organized on the principles of decentralized management and conducts its business through operating subsidiaries which are themselves, for the most part, integral, autonomous operations. Direct responsibility for each company lies with its operating management, headed by the president, general manager or managing director who reports directly or through a Company group chairman to a member of the Executive Committee. In line with this policy of decentralization, each internal subsidiary is, with some exceptions, managed by citizens of the country where it is located.

EXHIBIT 1   Johnson & Johnson and Subsidiaries, Consolidated Statement of Earnings and Retained Earnings (continued)

Segments of Business (Dollars in Millions)		1985	1984	1983	Percent Increase (Decreased) 1985 vs. 1984	Percent Increase (Decreased) 1984 vs. 1983
Sales to customers						
Consumer—	Domestic	$1,656.0	$1,588.3	$1,502.5	4.3%	5.7%
	International	1,118.5	1,161.4	1,185.3	(3.7)	(2.0)
	Total	$2,774.5	$1,749.7	$2,687.8	.9%	2.3%
Professional—	Domestic	$1,553.9	1,429.3	1,465.5	8.7	(2.5)
	International	653.1	626.1	620.3	4.3	.9
	Total	$2,207.0	$2,055.4	$2,085.8	7.4	(1.5)
Pharmaceutical—	Domestic	$ 780.0	$ 718.3	$ 642.5	8.6	11.8
	International	659.8	601.1	556.8	9.8	8.0
	Total	$1,439.8	$1,319.4	$1,199.3	9.1	10.0
Worldwide total		$6,421.3	$6,124.5	$5,972.9	4.8%	2.5%
Operating profit						
Consumer		$ 408.7	$ 323.4	$ 422.7	26.4%	(23.5)%
Professional		149.2	118.7	120.0	25.7	(1.1)
Pharmaceutical		461.1	440.4	358.4	4.7	22.9
Segment total		$1,019.0	$ 882.5	$ 901.1	15.5	(2.1)
Expense not allocated to segments		(119.8)	(127.4)	(177.0)	——	——
Earnings before taxes on income		$ 899.2	$ 755.1	$ 724.1	19.1%	4.3%
Identifiable assets at year-end						
Consumer		$1,616.2	$1,560.1	$1,535.9	3.6%	1.6%
Professional		1,876.1	1,717.6	1,673.5	9.2	2.6
Pharmaceutical		1,343.8	1,024.3	996.2	31.2	2.8
Segment total		$4,836.1	$4,302.0	$4,205.6	12.4	2.3
General corporate		259.0	239.4	255.9	——	——
Worldwide total		$5,095.1	$4,541.4	$4,461.5	12.2%	1.8%

Roy Black at Codman & Shurtleff reported directly to Herbert Stolzer at Johnson & Johnson headquarters in New Brunswick, New Jersey. Mr. Stolzer, 59, was a member of the Executive Committee of Johnson & Johnson with responsibility for 16 operating companies in addition to Codman & Shurtleff [Exhibit 3]. Stolzer had worked for Johnson & Johnson for 35 years with engineering, manufacturing, and senior management experience in Johnson & Johnson Products and at the Corporate office.

EXHIBIT 2

Chicopee

Chicopee develops and manufactures products for use by other Johnson & Johnson affiliates, in addition to a wide variety of fabrics that are sold to a broad range of commercial and industrial customers. Chicopee's consumer products include disposable diapers for the private-label market segment.

Codman

Codman & Shurtleff, Inc. supplies hospitals and surgeons worldwide with a broad line of products including instruments, equipment, implants, surgical disposables, fiberoptic light sources and cables, surgical head lamps, surgical microscopes and electronic pain control stimulators and electrodes.

Critikon

Critikon, Inc. provides products used in the operating room and other critical care areas of the hospital. Intravenous catheters, infusion pumps, and controllers, I.V. sets, filters and devices for monitoring blood pressure, cardiac output and oxygen are among its products.

Devro

Edible natural protein sausage casings made by Devro companies in the United States, Canada, Scotland and Australia are used by food processors throughout the world to produce pure, uniform, high-quality sausages and meat snacks.

Ethicon

Ethicon, Inc. provides products for precise wound closure, including sutures, ligatures, mechanical wound closure instruments and related products. Ethicon makes its own surgical needles and provides thousands of needle-suture combinations to the surgeon.

Iolab

Iolab Corporation manufactures intraocular lenses for implantation in the eye to replace the natural lens after cataract surgery, as well as instruments and other products used in ophthalmic microsurgery.

Janssen Pharmaceutica

Janssen Pharmaceutica Inc. facilitates availability in the U.S. of original research developments of Janssen Pharmaceutica N.V. of Belgium. Its products include SUFENTA, INNOVAR, SUBLIMAZE and INAPSINE, INJECTABLE PRODUCTS USED IN ANESTHESIOLOGY; NIZORAL and MONISTAT i.v. for systemic fungal pathogens; NIZORAL Cream 2% topical antifungal; VERMOX, an anthelmintic, and IMODIUM, an anti-diarrheal.

Johnson & Johnson Baby Products Company

The Johnson & Johnson Baby Products Company produces the familiar line of consumer baby products, including powder, shampoo, oil, wash cloths, lotion and others. Additional products include educational materials and toys to aid in infant development, SUNDOWN Sunscreen and AFFINITY Shampoo and Conditioner.

Johnson & Johnson Cardiovascular

Johnson & Johnson Cardiovascular manufactures and markets cardiovascular products used in open heart surgery that include HANCOCK Heart Valves, Vascular Grafts, MAXIMA Hollow Fiber Oxygenators, INTERSEPT Blood Filters and Cardiotomy Reservoirs.

Johnson & Johnson Dental Products Company

The Dental Products Company serves dental practitioners throughout the world with an extensive line of orthodontic, preventive and restorative products. The company also provides dental laboratories with a broad line of crown and bridge materials, including the high-strength ceramic CERESTORE system.

Johnson & Johnson Hospital Services

Johnson & Johnson Hospital Services Company develops and implements corporate marketing programs on behalf of Johnson & Johnson professional companies. These programs make it easier to do business with Johnson & Johnson and respond to the needs of hospitals, multihospital systems, alternative sites and distributors to reduce costs. Programs include Corporate Contracts and the COACT On-Line Procurement System.

Johnson & Johnson Products Inc.

Johnson & Johnson Products' Health Care Division provides consumers with wound care and oral care products. Its Patient Care Division offers hopitals and physicians a complete line of wound care products. Its Orthopaedic Division markets surgical implants and fracture immobilization products. The company also provides products to the athletic market.

Johnson & Johnson Ultrasound

Johnson & Johnson Ultrasound specializes in ultrasound diagnostic imaging equipment. This equipment is used in a wide range of medical diagnoses, including abdominal, cardiovascular, gynecologic, obstetric, pediatric, surgical, neonatal and veterinary applications.

(Continued)

EXHIBIT 2   (Continued)

McNeil Consumer Products Company

McNeil Consumer Products Company's line of TYLENOL acetaminophen products includes regular and extra-strength tablets, caplets and liquid; children's elixir, chewable tablets, drops and junior strength tablets. Other products include various forms of CoTYLENOL Cold Formula, PEDIACARE cough/cold preparations, SINE-AID, Maximum-Strength TYLENOL Sinus Medication and DELSYM cough relief medicine.

McNeil Pharmaceutical

McNeil Pharmaceutical provides the medical profession with prescription drugs, including analgesics, short and long-acting tranquilizers, an anti-inflammatory agent, a muscle relaxant and a digestive enzyme supplement.

Ortho Diagnostic Systems Inc.

Ortho Diagnostic Systems Inc. provides diagnostic systems for the clinical and research laboratory community. Products include instrument and reagent systems for the blood bank, coagulation and hematology laboratories as well as immunology systems and infectious disease testing kits.

Ortho Pharmaceutical Corporation

Ortho Pharmaceutical Corporation's prescription products for family planning are oral contraceptives and diaphragms. Other products include vaginal antibacterial and anti-fungal agents. The Advanced Care Products Division markets non-prescription vaginal spermicides for fertility control, in-home pregnancy and ovulation test kits and an athlete's foot remedy. The Dermatological Division provides dermatologists with products for professional skin treatment.

Personal Products

Products for feminine hygiene—STAYFREE Thin Maxi's, Maxi-Pads and Mini-Pads, STAYFREE SILHOUETTES BODY-SHAPE MAXI's, ASSURE & NATURAL Breathable Panty Liners, CAREFREE PANTY SHIELDS, SURE & NATURAL MAXISHIELDS, MODESS Sanitary Napkins, 'o.b.' Tampons and related products—are the specialty of Personal Products Company. Other consumer products include COETS Cosmetic Squares, TAKE-OFF Make-up Remover Cloths and SHOWER TO SHOWER Body Powder.

Pitman-Moore

Pitman-Moore, Inc. manufactures and sells an extensive line of biological, diagnostic, and pharmaceutical products for use by veterinarians in treating various disease entities in the pet animal segment of the animal health market. Most notable is IMRAB, the only rabies vaccine approved for use in five animal species. Pitman-Moore also supplies vaccines and pharmaceuticals for use in food-producing animals and it markets surgical products of Johnson & Johnson affiliates applicable to animal health.

Surgikos

Surgikos, Inc. markets an extensive line of BARRIER Disposable Surgical Packs and Gowns and surgical specialty products for use in major operative procedures. Other major products include CIDEX Sterilizing and Disinfecting Solutions for medical equipment, SURGINE Face Masks and Head Coverings, MICRO-TOUCH Latex Surgical Gloves and NEUTRALON Brown Surgical Gloves for sensitive skin.

Technicare

Technicare Corporation offers physicians products in four of the most important diagnostic imaging fields—computed tomography (CT) scanning, nuclear medicine systems, digital X-ray and the new field of magnetic resonance (MR).

Vistakon

Vistakon, Inc. develops, manufactures and distributes soft contact lenses. The company provides contact lens dispensing professionals with daily wear and extended wear lenses for nearsighted and farsighted persons. It also is a major supplier of specialty toric lenses for the correction of astigmatism.

Xanar

Xanar, Inc. specializes in products for laser surgery. Laser surgical devices can be used in general surgery and other surgical specialties to provide an effective, less invasive alternative to traditional techniques. Xanar's products include surgical lasers for gynecology, otolaryngology, dermatology and podiatry.

Exhibit 3

Johnson & Johnson partial organization chart

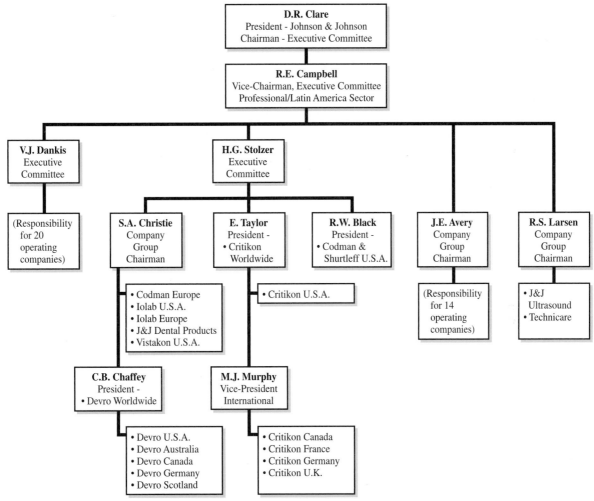

The senior policy and decision-making group at Johnson & Johnson was the Executive Committee comprising the chairman, president, chief financial officer, vice president of administration, and eight Executive Committee members with responsibilities for company sectors. The 155 business units of the Company were organized in sectors based primarily on products (e.g., consumer, pharmaceutical, professional) and secondarily on geographic markets.

Five- and Ten-Year Plans at Johnson & Johnson

Each operating company within Johnson & Johnson was responsible for preparing its own plans and strategies. David Clare, president of Johnson & Johnson, believed that this was one of the key elements in their success. "Our success is due to three basic tenets: a basic belief in decentralized management, a sense of responsibility

EXHIBIT 4

Board of directors

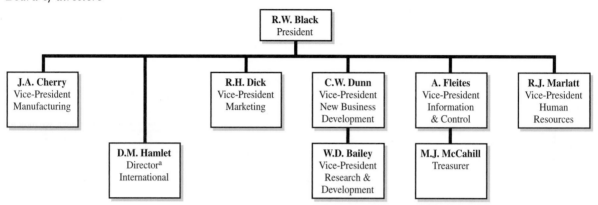

[a]Not a board member

to our key constituents, and a desire to manage for the long term. We have no corporate strategic planning function nor one strategic plan. Our strategic plan is the sum of the strategic plans to each of our 155 business units."

Each operating company prepared annually a five- and ten-year plan. Financial estimates in these plans were limited to only four numbers: estimated unit sales volume, estimated sales revenue, estimated net income, and estimated return on investment. Accompanying these financial estimates was a narrative description of how these targets would be achieved.

To ensure that managers were committed to the plan that they developed, Johnson & Johnson required that the planning horizon focus on two years only and remain fixed over a five-year period. Thus, in 1983 a budget and second-year forecast was developed for 1984 and 1985 and a strategic plan was developed for the years 1990 and 1995. In each of the years 1984 through 1987, the five- and ten-year plan was redrawn in respect of only years 1990 and 1995. Only in year 1988 would the strategic planning horizon shift five years forward to cover years 1995 and 2000. These two years will then remain the focus of subsequent five-

and ten-year plans for the succeeding four years, and so on.

At Codman & Shurtleff, work on the annual five- and ten-year plan commenced each January and took approximately six months to complete. Based on the mission statement, a business plan was developed for each significant segment of the business. For each competitor, the marketing plan included an estimated *pro forma* income statement (volume, sales, profit) as well as a one-page narrative description of their strategy.

Based on the tentative marketing plan, draft plans were prepared by the other departments including research and development, production, finance, and personnel. The tentative plan was assembled in a binder with sections describing mission, strategies, opportunities and threats, environment, and financial forecasts. This plan was debated, adjusted, and approved over the course of several meetings in May by the Codman Board of Directors [see Exhibit 4], comprising the president and seven key subordinates.

In June Herb Stolzer traveled to Boston to preside over the annual review of the five- and ten-year plan. Codman executives considered this a key meeting that could last up to three days. During the meeting Stolzer reviewed the plan, aired his concerns, and challenged the Codman Board on assumptions, strategies, and forecasts. A recurring question during the session was, "If your new projection for 1990 is below what you predicted last year, how do you intend to make up the shortfall?"

After this meeting, Roy Black summarized the plan that had been approved by Stolzer in a two-page memorandum that he sent directly to Jim Burke, chairman and chief executive officer of Johnson & Johnson.

Based on the two-page "Burke letters," the five- and ten-year plans for all operating companies were presented by Executive Committee members and debated and approved at the September meeting of the Executive Committee in New Brunswick. Company presidents, including Roy Black, were often invited to prepare formal presentations. The discussion in these meetings was described by those in attendance as, "very frank," "extremely challenging," and "grilling."

Financial Planning at Johnson & Johnson

Financial planning at Johnson & Johnson comprised annual budgets (i.e., profit plans) for the upcoming operating year and a second-year forecast. Budgets were detailed financial documents prepared down to the expense center level for each operating company. The second-year forecast was in a similar format but contained less detail than the budget for the upcoming year.

Revenues and expenses were budgeted by month. Selected balance sheet items, e.g., accounts receivable and inventory, were also budgeted to reflect year-end targets.

Profit plan targets were developed on a bottom-up basis by each operating company by reference to two documents: (1) the approved five- and ten-year plan and (2) the second-year forecast prepared the previous year.

Chuck Dunn described the budgeting process at Codman & Shurtleff:

> We wrote the initial draft of our 1987 profit plan in the Summer of 1986 based on the revision of our five- and ten-year plan. By August, the profit plan is starting to crystallize; we have brought in the support areas such as accounting, quality assurance, R&D, and engineering, to ensure that they "buy in" to the new 1987 profit and marketing plans.
>
> The first year of the strategic plan is used as a basis for the departments to prepare their own one-year plans for both capital and expense items. The production budget is based on standard costs and nonstandard costs such as development programs and plant consolidations. As for the R&D budget, the project list is always too long, so we are forced to rank the projects. For each project, we look at returns, costs, time expended, sales projections, expected profit, and gross profit percentages as well as support to be supplied to the plants.
>
> The individual budgets are then consolidated by the Information and Control Department. We look very carefully at how this budget compares with our previous forecasts. For example, the first consolidation of the 1986 profit plan revealed a $2.4 million profit shortfall against the second-year forecast that was developed in 1984 and updated in June 1985. To reconcile this, it was necessary to put on special budget presentations by each department to remove all slack and ensure that our earlier target could be met if possible. The commitment to this process is very strong.
>
> We are paying more and more attention to our second-year forecast since it forces us to re-examine strategic plans. The second-year forecast is also used as a benchmark for next year's profit plan and, as such, it is used as hindsight to evaluate the forecasting ability and performance of managers.

The procedure for approving the annual profit plan and second-year forecast followed closely the procedures described above for the review of the five- and ten-year plans. During the early fall, Herbert Stolzer reviewed the proposed budget with Roy Black and the Codman & Shurtleff Board of Directors. Changes in profit commitments from previous forecasts and the overall profitability and tactics of the Company were discussed in detail.

After all anticipated revenues and expenses were budgeted, a separate contingency expense line item was added to the budget; the amount of the contingency changed from year to year and was negotiated between Stolzer and Black based on the perceived uncertainty in achieving budget targets. In 1986 the Codman & Shurtleff contingency was set at $1.1 million.

Stolzer presented the budget for approval at the November meeting of the Johnson & Johnson Executive Committee.

Budget Revisions and Reviews

During the year, budget performance was monitored closely. Each week, sales revenue performance figures were sent to Herb Stolzer. In addition, Roy Black sent a monthly management report to Stolzer that included income statement highlights and a summary of key balance sheet figures and ratios. All information was provided with reference to (1) position last month, (2) position this month, and (3) budgeted position. All variances that Black considered significant were explained in a narrative summary.

The accuracy of budget projections was also monitored during the year and formally revised on three occasions. The first of these occasions occurred at the March meeting of the Executive Committee. Going around the table, each Executive Committee member was asked to update the Committee on his most recent estimates of sales and profits for each operating company for the current year. Herb Stolzer relied on Roy Black to provide this information for Stolzer's review prior to the March meeting.

The "June Revision" referred to the revised budget for the current year that was presented to the Executive Committee in June. The preparation of this revised budget required managers at Codman & Shurtleff and all other Johnson & Johnson companies to rebudget in May for the remainder of the fiscal year. This revision involved rechecking all budget estimates starting with the lowest level expense center as well as revising the second-year forecast when necessary.

The third review of budget projections was the "November update" which was presented to the Executive Committee at the November meeting concurrently with their consideration of the budget and second-year forecast for the upcoming budget year. The November update focused on results for the 10 months just completed and re-

vised projections for the remaining 2 months. At Codman & Shurtleff, preparation of the November update involved performance estimates from all departments but was not conducted to the same level of detail as the June revision.

Corporate View of the Planning and Control Process

David Clare, president of Johnson & Johnson:

> The sales and profit forecasts are always optimistic in the five- and ten-year plans, but this is O.K. We want people to stretch their imagination and think expansively. In these plans we don't anticipate failure; they are a device to open up thinking. There is no penalty for inaccuracies.
>
> The profit plan and second-year forecast are used to run the business and evaluate managers on planning, forecasts, and achievements.
>
> We ask our managers to always include in their plans an account of how and why their estimates have changed over time. That is why we use the five- and ten-year planning concept rather than a moving planning horizon. This allows us to revise our thinking over time and allows for retrospective learning.
>
> If a manager insists on a course of action and we (the Executive Committee) have misgivings, nine times out of ten we will let him go ahead. If we say, 'No,' and the answer should have been, 'Yes,' we say, 'Don't blame us, it was your job to sell us on the idea and you didn't do that.'
>
> Johnson & Johnson is extremely decentralized, but that does not mean that managers are free from challenge as to what they are doing. In the final analysis, managing conflict is what management is all about. Healthy conflict is about *what* is right, not *who* is right.
>
> Our Company philosophy is to manage for the long term. We do not use short term bonus plans. Salary and bonus reviews are entirely subjective and qualitative and are intended to reward effort and give special recognition to those who have performed uniquely. The Executive Committee reviews salary recommendations for all managers above a certain salary level, but Company presidents, such as Roy Black, have full discretion as to how they remunerate their employees.

Herbert Stolzer, Executive Committee member:

> The planning and control systems used in Johnson & Johnson provide real benefits. These systems allow us to find problems and run the business. This is true not only for us at Corporate, but also at the operating companies where they are a tremendous tool. Once a year, managers are forced to review their businesses in depth for costs, trends,

manufacturing efficiency, marketing plans, and their competitive situation. Programs and action plans result.

You have to force busy people to do this. Otherwise, they will be caught up in day-to-day activities—account visits, riding with salesmen, standing on the manufacturing floor.

Our long-term plans are not meant to be a financial forecast; rather, they are meant to be an objective way of setting aspirations. We never make those numbers—who can forecast sales five or ten years out with unforeseen markets, products, and competitors? Even the accuracy of our two-year forecast is bad. The inaccuracy is an indication of how fast our markets are changing. Our businesses are so diverse, with so many competitors, that it is difficult to forecast out two years.

I visit at least twice a year with each operating company board. We usually spend the better part of a week going over results, planning issues, strategic plans, and short and long term problems. The Executive Committee, to the best of my knowledge, never issues quantitative performance targets before the bottom-up process begins.

At the Executive Committee meetings, a lot of argument takes place around strategic planning issues. How fast can we get a business up to higher returns? Are the returns in some businesses too high? Are we moving too fast? However, the outcome is never to go back to the operating company and say we need 8 percent rather than 6 percent. The challenge has already taken place between the Executive Committee member and the Company Board. If the EC member is satisfied with the answers provided by the Board, that's the end of it.

It happens very rarely that the consolidated budget is unacceptable. Occasionally, we might say, 'We really could use some more money.' However, in the second review, this may not turn up any extra. If so, that's O.K.

Our systems are not used to punish. They are used to try and find and correct problems. Bonuses are not tied to achieving budget targets. They are subjectively determined, although we use whatever objective indicators are available—for example, sales and new product introductions for a marketing vice president.

The key to our whole system is the operating Company presidents. We are so decentralized that they define their own destiny. A successful Company president needs to be able to stand up to pressure from above. He needs to have the courage to say, 'I have spent hours and hours on that forecast and for the long term health of the Company, we have to spend that budget.'

Clark Johnson, corporate controller:

At the Executive Committee review meetings, we always review the past five years before starting on the forecast. We look at volume growth rates—sales growth adjusted for inflation—and discuss problems. Then, we compare growth rate against GNP growth. We keep currency translation out of it. We evaluate foreign subsidiaries in their own currency and compare growth against country-specific GNP. We are looking for market share by country. On almost any topic, we start with forecast versus past track record.

The Committee never dictates or changes proposals—only challenges ideas. If it becomes clear to the individual presenting that the forecast is not good enough, only that person decides whether a revision is necessary. These discussions can be very frank and sometimes acrimonious. The result of the review may be agreement to present a revision at the next meeting, specific action items to be addressed, or personal feedback to David Clare.

This process cascades down the organization. Executive Committee members review and challenge the proposals of Company presidents. Company presidents review and challenge the proposals of their vice presidents.

Thursday, May 8, 1986—8:00 P.M. Following the Codman & Shurtleff Board meeting to discuss the June budget revision on the afternoon of Thursday, May 8 (described at the beginning of the case), Roy Black, Chuck Dunn, Bob Dick, and Gus Fleites worked into the evening going over the list of active R&D projects. Their review focused on R&D projects that had been included in the original 1986 budget. They searched for projects that could be eliminated due to changed market conditions or deferred to 1987 because of unplanned slowdowns. After discussing the progress and priority of each major project, Roy Black asked Chuck Dunn to have his staff work the next morning to go over the 40 active projects in detail and look for any savings that could be reflected in the June revision of the budget.

Friday, May 9, 1986—7:45 A.M. In addition to Chuck Dunn, four people were seated around the table in the small conference room. Bob Sullivan and Gino Lombardo were program managers who reported to Bill Bailey, vice president of Research. John Smith was manager, Technical Development, of the research facility in Southbridge that specialized in microscopes, fiberoptics, and light scopes. Gordon Thompson was the research accountant representing the Finance Department.

After coffee was delivered, Chuck closed the door and turned to the others:

> Here's the situation. We are approximately two million short of the June Revision pretax profit target. As you know, our sales volume this year has been good—better than budget, in fact—but a few recent unpredictable events, including unfavorable product mix, and that large variance in the cost of specialty European products, are hurting our profit projection.
>
> This morning, I want the four of you to look at our original spending projections to see where we stand. For example, we know that R&D underspent $200,000 in the first quarter. Therefore, I think we should take it as a starting point that R&D has $200,000 to give up from its 1986 budget. I know that you can argue that this is just a timing difference, but you know as well as I do that, given the record of the R&D department, this money will probably not be spent this year.
>
> It's time to get the hopes and dreams out of the R&D list. If we roll up our sleeves, we can probably find $400,000 without sacrificing either our 1986 objectives or our long-term growth.
>
> We worked late last night looking at the project list and I think it can be done. I have to meet again today at 2:00 with the Board and I want to be able to tell them that we can do it. That leaves it up to you to sift through these projects and find that money. We're looking for projects that have stalled and can be put on hold, and some belt-tightening on ongoing work.

After Chuck Dunn had left the group to its work, Gordon led the group through the list of projects. For each project, the group discussed spending to date, problems with the project, and spending needed for the remainder of the year. For each project, Gordon asked if anything could be cut and occasionally asked for points of clarification. On a separate sheet of paper, he kept track of the cuts to which the R&D managers had agreed. He turned to Project 23:

> How about 23? You were planning on a pilot run of 100 prototypes this year. Should that still be included in the schedule?
>
> Yes, the project is on track and looks promising. I suppose we could cut the run to 50 without sacrificing our objective. Would anyone have a problem with that?
>
> It's a bad idea. That item has a very high material component and we have a devil of a time getting it at a reasonable price, even for a run of 100. If we cut the volume any more, the unit material cost will double.
>
> O.K., we'll stick with 100. How about the salesmen's samples? Is there anything there?
>
> If we reduced the number of samples by a third, we could save $20,000. I suppose I could live with that, but I don't know how that will impact the marketing plan. Let me call Bob Dick and see what he thinks.

Gordon kept a running total of the expense reductions as the morning progressed. Dunn stopped in approximately once an hour to ask how the work was coming.

Friday, May 9—2:00 P.M.   Roy Black opened the meeting, "Gus, do you have the revised budget with the changes we've made? What does it look like?"

As Gus Fleites distributed copies of the budget document to the Codman & Shurtleff Board, Chuck Dunn interjected, "Roy, at the moment, we have found $300,000 in R&D. That reflects adjusting our priority list for the rest of the year and cutting the fat out of ongoing projects. As for the last $100,000, we are still working on recasting the numbers to reflect what I call our 'project experience factor.' In other words, I think we can find that $100,000 by recognizing that our projects always take longer than originally planned. My people say that we've cut right to the bone on ongoing programs. The next round of cuts will have to be programs themselves, and we know we don't want to do that."

"We've discussed this before," responded Black, "and I think we all agree on the answer. In the past, we have authorized more projects than we can handle and have drawn the work out over too long a time. The way to go is fewer projects, sooner. It's the only thing that makes sense. Our mission is more focused now and should result in fewer projects. It's unfortunate that Bill Bailey is unavailable this week, but we are going to have to go ahead and make those decisions."

As Fleites briefed the Board on the revised budget, Roy Black turned to Bob Dick to discuss inventory carrying costs. "Bob, don't you think that our inventory level is too high on some of our low turnover products? Wouldn't we be better to cut our inventory position and take a higher back order level? With 2,700 products, does it make sense to carry such a large inventory?"

Bob Dick nodded his head in agreement, "You're right, of course, our stocking charges are substantial and we could recover part of our shortfall if we could cut those expenses. But our first concern has to be our level of service to customers."

"Agreed. But perhaps there is room here to provide fast turnaround on a core of critical products and risk back orders on the high-specialty items. The 80/20 rule applies to most of our business. For example, say we offered top service for all our disposables and implants and flagged setup products for new hospital construction in our catalogue as '90 day delivery' or 'made to order.' We could then concentrate on the fastest possible turnaround for products where that is important and a slower delivery for products that are usually ordered well in advance in any case."

"I think that may be a good tactic. It won't help us for the June revision, but I'll have our market research people look at it and report back next month."

"Good," responded Black, "that just leaves our commercial expenses. We need some donations from each of you. What I am suggesting is that each of you go back to your departments and think in terms of giving up two percent of your commercial expenses. If everyone gives up two percent, this will give us $500,000. In my opinion, we have to bring the shortfall down to $900,000 before we can draw down part of our contingency fund. We're a long way from the end of the year and it's too early to start drawing down a major portion of the contingency."

Black turned to Bob Marlatt, vice president of Human Resources. "Bob, where do we stand on headcount projections?"

"The early retirement program is set to clear our Corporate Compensation Department next month. That should yield 14 headcount reductions. Otherwise, no changes have been made in our projections through the end of the year. I think that we could all benefit from thinking about opportunities to reduce staff and pay overtime on an as-needed basis to compensate."

Black summed up the discussion:

Well, I think we all know what is needed. Chuck, keep working on that last $100,000. All of you should think in terms of giving up 2 percent on commercial expenses and reducing noncritical headcount. That means that you will have to rank your activities and see what you can lose at the bottom end. Bob, I think that we should go back and look at our marketing plan again to see if we can make any changes to boost revenues.

We need to take a revised budget to Stolzer that is short by no more than $250,000. If necessary, I think we can live with drawing down the contingency to make up the difference.

So, your work is cut out for you. See you back here on Monday. Have a nice weekend! (*Laughter all around.*)

After the meeting, Roy Black reflected on what had transpired, and his role as an operating manager in Johnson & Johnson.

These meetings are very important. We should always be thinking about such issues, but it is tough when you are constantly fighting fires. The Johnson & Johnson system forces us to stop and really look at where we have been and where we are going.

We know where the problems are. We face them every day. But these meetings force us to think about how we should respond and to look at both the upside and downside of changes in the business. They really get our creative juices flowing.

Some of our managers complain. They say that we are planning and budgeting all the time and that every little change means that they have to go back and rebudget the year and the second-year forecasts. There is also some concern that the financial focus may make us less innovative. But we try to manage this business for the long term. We avoid at all costs actions that will hurt us long term. I believe that Herb Stolzer is in complete agreement on that issue.

It is important to understand what decentralized management is all about. It is unequivocal accountability for what you do. And the Johnson & Johnson system provides that very well.

Questions

1. Evaluate the planning and control system in use at Johnson & Johnson. Who gets involved, when, and in what way? What are its strengths and weaknesses?

2. Over the last several years, *Fortune* magazine has polled the CEOs of the 250 largest U.S. companies to gather data on the management quality of major U.S. corporations. CEOs responding to the survey have repeatedly ranked Johnson & Johnson as one of the most innovative and well-managed firms in its industry. What role, if any, do you believe that J&J's management planning and control systems play in achieving (or hindering) innovation?

3. From information provided in the case, suggest how you would design a reward/incentive system for Roy Black and the Codman & Shurtleff board to capture maximum benefit from planning and control procedures. How would you deal with relating pay to performance in rapidly changing environments?

4. Roy Black states that decentralized management is "unequivocal accountability for what you do" (last paragraph). Do you agree with his statement?

CASE 8–2
COPLEY MANUFACTURING COMPANY

Copley Manufacturing Company had begun formal corporatewide planning in 1981. Its planning system was modified in 1982 and modified again in 1983. Company executives reviewed the experiences of these three years to see what lessons could be learned that would lead to an improved planning system.

Copley had grown fairly steadily in size and profitability since its founding in 1919; its growth was particularly rapid in the late 1960s and the 1970s. For most of its history, it was primarily a manufacturer of a wide line of cutting tools and related parts and supplies, and the Cutting Tool Division in 1983 was the largest division. In 1983, there were eight other operating divisions, each making and selling a line of industrial products. Some of these divisions were the outgrowth of acquisitions; others had their origin in products developed by the corporate research department. Divisions had considerable autonomy. Sales volume in 1983 was $700 million, net income was $42 million, and there were 17,000 employees.

Introduction to Formal Planning

The formal planning effort at the corporate level was an outgrowth of work initiated by Russell A. Wilde, in mid-1977. Mr. Wilde had been head of the Precipitator Division's commercial development department and, as such, had been deeply involved in the division's efforts beginning early in 1977 to "plan ahead." Mr. Wilde's effort at the corporate level actually began as a search for companies to acquire, since Copley's top management saw the key question to be: "How should we diversify?" Within six months, Mr. Wilde was arguing that the crucial questions to

be asked really were: "What are our objectives?" and "What is our potential?"

Our result of the dialogue that followed was a request by Stanley Burton, president of Copley, for the divisions to look 10 years ahead and to predict sales, profit, cash flow, and return on investment. Mr. Wilde composed the actual questions asked of the divisions and co-ordinated collection of the data. The resulting consolidated growth projection was not ideal in the eyes of top management, but no imminent crisis was seen.

The 10-year look indicated that many of Copley's markets were mature, that its profits were indeed sensitive to cyclical swings, and that a large cash flow could be expected in the coming years. Before the end of 1978, Charles N. Sagan was appointed director of corporate development, reporting to Mr. Burton. Mr. Sagan was to be mainly concerned with growth through acquisition and merger.

Late in 1980, Mr. Sagan began reporting to Mr. Albert, executive vice president. The two easily agreed that regular formal planning should become part of management's way of life at Copley. They were encouraged to work toward this end when Samuel K. Savage, chairman of board, suggested that Copley should do some five-year sales forecasting.

The 1981 Effort

A corporate planning committee was set up in February 1981 by Mr. Albert to guide the move toward a regular formal planning process. The planning committee comprised the vice president for research, the controller, the corporate economist, Mr. Albert, and Mr. Sagan. The latter was named chief coordinator of the committee.

The planning committee met almost weekly for the next few months and attacked two major questions.

This case was prepared by Robert N. Anthony, Harvard Business School. Copyright © by the President and Fellows of Harvard College. Harvard Business School case 176–189.

1. By what process should formalized planning be ingrained into life at Copley?
2. What are appropriate corporate goals for Copley?

A year later, in early 1982, no answer had yet been given to the second question, but decisions were made concerning the first.

A March 21, 1981, memorandum from Mr. Albert to division general managers cited a need for regular formal planning and outlined a plan and schedule for starting such an effort. The basic idea was to survey divisional planning history and attitudes and, after discussions, to issue guidelines for the preparation of divisional "provisional plans."

Visits by Corporate Groups

The concept of formal planning activities was introduced by the organization through a series of visits to the divisions by corporate groups beginning June 6. The composition of the groups varied somewhat but always included Mr. Albert and Mr. Sagan. In these introductory meetings, Mr. Albert explained the importance of the planning effort, and Mr. Sagan explained the details. Divisions were asked to produce a five-year plan by October 1, 1981. It was left to the divisions to decide exactly who would do what in the process and in what format the final plans would be presented. Corporate staff groups were also instructed to submit plans.

The controller described the financial data to be submitted in the five-year plan in a memorandum dated July 19, 1981, as follows:

> *Sales*—Please state past and future sales at 1981 prices and also in actual dollars, in total, by major product group, and by market group (e.g., domestic customers, export customers, intercompany).
>
> *Profit before Taxes*—Analyze projected dollar profit in terms of variance from projected 1981 dollar profit. The four significant areas of variance should be:
>
> *Price Realization*—The change in profit due to prices being higher or lower than 1981.
>
> *Volume and Product Mix*—The change in profit contribution due to changes in physical volume and

product mix. This is calculated by applying 1981 contribution ratios to the change in physical volume, by product line.

> *Cost Variances*—Changes in unit variable costs or aggregate fixed costs should be stated. These aggregated changes should be separated into *price* (wage and material rates) variances and *efficiency* (all other) variances.
>
> *Profit after Taxes*—Translate pretax to aftertax profit dollars for future years at the 1981 tax rate. Show income taxes and investment credit separately.
>
> *Cash Flow*—The following should be drawn by years in total and by product line where a determination can be made. *Full* product line data is not required, but some indication of cash flow, say inventories and capital expenditures, by product line will be helpful.
>
> Profit after taxes.
> Depreciation.
> Accounts receivable.
> Inventories.
> Capital expenditures.
> Other working capital items:
>   Cash (working balance only).
>   Prepaid expense.
>   Accounts payable and accruals.
>   Etc.
> All other.
> Total Cash Flow.

Planning Review Meetings

Meetings to review divisional plans were held in November and December. As was expected, the format of the divisional plans and presentations varied widely. Attendance at the planning reviews varied, also. The planning committee always attended, as did the head of the division being reviewed. In addition, members of the executive committee attended on occasion. Divisions were free to bring whomever they wished to their planning review. Representatives of other divisions than the one being reviewed on a given day were not invited to attend.

Planning Response Meetings

A second series of meetings was started December 28, 1981. In these meetings, the planning committee commented on the divisional presentation to the division general managers. The divisions had been expecting some reaction by corporate management ever since the planning reviews, and these planning responses were designed to meet this expectation. Typical of these meetings was that of the Cutting Tool Division, whose general manager, Mr. Tyler, had recently become a member of the planning committee. The Cutting Tool Division discussion lasted three hours, with Mr. Tyler and the rest of the committee openly evaluating the Cutting Tool Division's plans and its planning review.

Mr. Albert sent a memorandum to the general manager of each division after its "planning response" meeting. Each memorandum summarized the major points agreed upon in the meeting, thanked the participants for their effort in 1981, and expressed the desire for continued progress in making planning a way of life for the Copley manager.

The results of the first planning cycle were judged as mixed by Mr. Sagan and by members of top management. It was generally felt that the divisions had made a good beginning, but that they had only begun to dent the planning task. Divisional plans were seen generally to be optimistic extrapolations of past operating trends. Some members of management criticized the effort as having been a numbers game. Others countered that these results were a necessary first step. Most agreed that the plans had been helpful in providing information that would aid top management in understanding better the various business activities of the corporation.

1982 Organizational Changes

In 1982 a number of organizational changes affected planning in major ways. Chief among these was the elevation of Mr. Albert to president in March. The corporate planning function moved up with Mr. Albert, continuing to report directly to him.

Several other important organizational changes followed shortly after. Two corporate staff functions were created, one for marketing and the other for research/development. Operating re-

sponsibility was further delegated: the International Division was to report to the new executive vice president, John A. Tyler, the former general manager of the Cutting Tool Division. The Cutting Tool Division was divided along product lines to become two separate divisions.

Two group vice presidents were named, each responsible for three divisions, with the remaining four divisions reporting directly to Mr. Tyler.

Beginning of the 1982 Planning Activities

In contrast with the "numbers" orientation of the 1981 planning efforts, Mr. Sagan recommended an increased emphasis on strategic concepts in 1982. After some discussion, the planning committee decided to separate the formal planning cycle into three phases. The first phase, to be held in the spring, was termed the *Strategy Development* phase. The second, or *Quantitative*, phase would summarize, during the fall, the financial and manpower implications of the strategies selected in the first phase. The final, or *Action*, phase would aim to translate the results of planning into specific programs for action.

In mid-March, the new president, Mr. Albert, sent a letter to each division manager outlining the planning cycle for 1982 and the objectives for the planning efforts that had been agreed to by the planning committee.

The division's strategic plans were presented to corporate management by each division in a review meeting and subsequently evaluated in a response meeting. Unlike 1981, when they were held a month apart, these meetings in 1982 followed each other on the same day.

Further Developments in 1982

Several developments were to impede progress of the planning efforts in 1982. As already mentioned, there was a new president, who introduced seven persons into new corporate executive positions. These changes in top management were temporarily disruptive to the planning effort.

Also, considerable management effort was required in assimilating a recently acquired large company and in working out the split-up of the old Cutting Tool Division into the two new divisions.

In 1981, the company had reported its highest sales and earnings ever. The annual report stated that prospects were for a strong 1982. But the machine tool industry was to suffer from depressed market conditions. Sales were down 1.6 percent from 1981; earnings per share declined 35.8 percent. Efforts to counter the unfavorable business conditions became a dominant preoccupation for key line executives.

On July 11, after completion of the strategy development phase of the beginning cycle, the planning committee met to consider the planning efforts for the remainder of 1982. In view of the developments noted above, it decided against proceeding with the quantitative phase originally scheduled for the fall. It did, however, recommend that staff departments begin the planning process by analyzing past results and identifying resources, strengths, weaknesses, major problems, and major opportunities of their divisions. Mr. Albert approved the recommendations. The Corporate Goals Committee also lessened its efforts to prepare a statement of corporate goals.

In view of the disruption of formal planning at Copley, top management made special efforts to declare that long-range planning was there to stay. In a letter to division managers dated October 24, Mr. Albert explained the decision to curtail formal planning and emphasized that nothing would be allowed to stand in the way of doing the complete planning job in 1983. He reaffirmed his intention to emphasize planning at Copley in his president's statement in the 1982 annual report: "Long-range planning will become a way of life at our Company. By this medium we will set specific goals, allocate resources of talent and money, and measure our progress. There will be increased emphasis on the delegation of responsibility and in the measurement of performance against predetermined goals."

Situation in 1983

The Copley Company recovered financially in 1983 with a 6.2 percent improvement in net sales and a 58 cent gain in earnings per share.

The corporate goals committee held several informal dinner meetings during the first half of 1982 to discuss a framework developed by Mr. Sagan for arriving at corporate goals. Although a definite statement of corporate goals was not drawn up, the members generally felt that much progress had been made and that it had been a useful and educational experience for all who had participated. The committee as originally constituted was inactive in late 1982 and early 1983, but Mr. Sagan continued to work independently with Mr. Albert on that task. In line with these activities, Mr. Albert was quoted in the business press as stating corporate expectations to include a minimum annual profit growth of 10 percent and a return on equity of 12.5 percent.

In 1983, the planning process in large part came to be influenced and administered by Mr. Tyler, executive vice president. Mr. Tyler, who had moved up from head of the Cutting Tool Division when Mr. Albert assumed the presidency of Copley, enjoyed the reputation among his colleagues as a hard-driving, no-nonsense line manager who had little patience for elaborate staff support.

In Mr. Tyler's opinion, division managers had been planning in previous years largely to satisfy the requirements set by the planning staff and had failed to become committed to the plans. He saw voluminous documentation required in 1982 to present a divisional strategy and financial plan as one reason for this failure to identify with the planning output. Thus, in 1983, division managers were asked to present each product group strategy in a statement of two pages or less and the related financial five-year plan on only one page.

The divisional strategy statements were to cover information on such items as industry trends, market size, competition, and major opportunities or threats, as well as a description of the proposed strategic response. For the financial plan, divisions were required to submit figures for only the first, second, and fifth years of the five-year plan. The purpose of this abbreviation was to reduce the time spent on the numbers, thereby allowing divisional management more time for strategic considerations.

The management review process was also altered. Divisional presentations before the planning committee were replaced by two other meetings. The first of these was a one-hour "premeeting" attended by Mr. Albert, Mr. Tyler, the division general manager, and the responsible group vice president. In this premeeting, Albert and Tyler explained Copley's strategy and acquisition policy and reviewed the findings and conclusions of the Product Line Study. During the remainder of the hour, the division manager had to explain and to defend the division's strategy for the coming year. At the end of the one-hour meeting the president gave his decision on the division's plans. This review was immediately followed by a three-hour meeting in which the division manager and his staff presented their plans for the first time to the remaining members of the Executive Committee and to selected members of the corporate staff.

Mr. Sagan, director of corporate development, became visibly disturbed by the recent turn of events in planning. He felt himself increasingly limited to corporate merger and acquisition studies. He was fearful that the company would revert to a short-term orientation if it continued along the present path. In voicing these objectives to Mr. Albert, he realized that the formal planning system that he had worked so hard to develop was at stake. As a result of these discussions, he felt that he still had the full confidence and support of the chief executive. At the same time, Mr. Albert publicly acknowledged the benefits of getting increased line involvement in planning.

Recent Developments

In an interview in late 1984, Mr. Tyler described recent developments:

As was John Albert's desire, we believe planning is now a way of life at Copley. There just does not appear to be as much need today for a structured management of the process with a planning department per se at the corporate level. This is not to say that all line managers develop plans and strategies to the same degree of effectiveness. But the actual responsibility for planning has been placed directly on the line—that is, the executive vice president, the group vice presidents, and, in turn, their various division managers.

For various reasons, Charlie Sagan left the company earlier this year. Fred Fisher has been appointed director of corporate development, but his job description was rewritten to put the emphasis on the planning and execution of growth through acquisition.

The planning process in 1983 followed pretty well the steps we had laid out.

In January 1984, we changed the format for the divisional planning presentations. My letter of January 30 [Exhibit 1] describes our current system of informing all key managers within the company of each division's long-range plans and broad strategies.

This technique of communicating divisional plans was preceded in December of 1983 by a two-day conference in Bermuda, with essentially the same group in attendance. At that conference, we reviewed all of the divisional plans up until that point and announced the broad corporate goals and strategies.

In the same interview Mr. Tyler furnished a copy of a recent talk in which he stated his personal belief about management.

I believe that corporate planning is *the* major responsibility of top management. It involves the direction of the whole company (not the parts) in deciding specifically what businesses the company wants to be in, in determining what rate of growth is desirable, in determining what method of growth is intended (research, acquisition, merger). I am a believer in decentralization; in delegating a great deal of authority; giving people their head; permitting some experiments and some mistakes; but sink or swim is the theory.

I do not believe in too many specialized staff functions to clutter up an organization. I avoid "assistant to's" and "administrative assistants" except for short-term projects or as training spots in someone's career.

I believe a good manager by definition must put out the daily fires, improve the current quarter's earnings,

Exhibit 1   Letter Announcing a Series of Executive Meetings (excerpts)

January 30, 1984

It is always difficult to draw lines across an organization, but those to whom this letter is addressed are either managing profit centers or are directing broad staff functions vital to Copley's operations and to its future growth.

We believe it is important to provide the means for keeping each person in this group better informed of the plans and progress of each division and each staff function as well as the total corporate programs.

The method selected to provide better communications will be tested over the next 12 months and will involve a series of 9 meetings; the time and place of each are listed on the attached schedule. Each meeting will start at 1:30 P.M. on the first Monday of the month. They will end at 5:00 P.M. A different division will host each meeting on a rotating basis.

An agenda is planned as follows. From 1:30 to 2:00 P.M. five or six prepared talks of five minutes' duration will be given on subjects of current and general interest selected by the chairman in consultation with others. The following half hour (2:00–2:30) will be devoted to announcements from both the floor and the chairman.

At 2:30, the division manager serving as host will take charge of the meeting. He will have a total of two and one half hours, during which he is asked to present his long-range plans, allow time for questions and comments, and complete a plant tour of some portion of his facilities.

The group of key executives in attendance does not make up a decision-making committee or a review board in the general sense. They are, however, encouraged to ask questions for interpretation and better understanding. The long-range plans presented by the division manager will previously have been approved by the president, executive and group vice presidents. The division managers are asked to present their plans in simply written reports using an expanded outline technique. Copies will be reproduced by the division manager following the meeting on a request basis.

This test period will last through February 1985 meeting. If it is felt these meetings cannot be made to serve their original intention, they will be discontinued.

/s/John A. Tyler
Executive Vice President

---

and at the same time be a long-range planner. If a manager cannot do both, I do not believe the solution lies in shoring him up via a corporate planning department. I *do* believe it lies in using the talent of both line and specific staff personnel who surround him.

I believe in using the talents already present in marketing, finance, research, and manufacturing—and the head of each of these areas must be a planner himself or *he* will fail. I am opposed to separating the division managers from the top management by allowing any staff group to represent or speak for them—or to take their cues from them.

I believe that America's greatest companies succeeded because one man or group of individuals with strong convictions made things happen. They had vision and used intuition in varying degrees but they did their own planning and monitoring of results. I may be overgeneralizing, but normally a company has its best all-around talent in top line positions. They are there because they have a good balance of talents and experience. For that reason, their judgment should have the greatest influence in strategy formation as well as final decision making. By

this, I do not mean to imply that line personnel think more strategically than staff personnel. The opposite may, in fact, be true. There are often individuals way down the organization in both line and staff who are thinking persons.

Finally, I strongly believe there is a great tendency in American business to overmanage, overplan, overstaff, and overorganize, which is contributing in a major way to our declining ability to compete in world markets. Our fixed costs in staff and management are often a larger factor than factory labor in making us noncompetitive.

Questions

1. How do you appraise for formal planning efforts at the Copley Company?

2. What do you predict will occur with respect to formal planning at Copley?

3. How would *you* handle formal planning at Copley?

CASE 8–3
ALLIED STATIONERY PRODUCTS

Background

Allied Stationery Products was founded in 1866 in Denver, Colorado as a one-man operation producing note paper and cards for sale in general stores in Denver. By 1992 it had grown to a corporation with annual sales of $900 million.

One division of the company produced specialty paper products, such as writing paper, envelopes, note cards, and greeting cards. Another division manufactured and printed business forms. By 1988, this division was one of the top 6 firms in the U.S. business forms industry.

That year the company expanded into business forms inventory management services. This was an area where Allied believed it could offer value-added management services to differentiate the firm from other business forms manufacturers. The forms manufacturing business was mature by 1988 and all competitors were seeking ways to generate sales growth. Allied embarked on a campaign to enrol its corporate clients in a program which it called "Total Forms Control" (TFC). Allied considered TFC to be a key to future success.

By 1992 sales from TFC were about $60 million and Allied had established a separate company within the business forms division to handle these accounts. The services provided under TFC included warehousing and distribution of forms (including inventory financing) as well as inventory control and forms usage reporting. Allied used a sophisticated computer systems network which enabled them to monitor a client's forms inventory, forms usage, and ordering activities. They provided this information to

their clients via comprehensive yet simple to read management reports.

As part of its distribution services, Allied also offered "pick pack" service where trained and experienced workers actually opened full cartons to pick the exact number of forms requested by the clients. Allied's philosophy was that a well run warehousing and distribution network is vital to any forms management program—"we know what you need . . . the *right* product at the *right* place at the *right* time."

For a small number of clients Allied also offered "desk top delivery," where Allied personnel would distribute the forms to individual offices within the company (forms were usually delivered only to the loading dock). As a comprehensive forms management provider, Allied's product line also had to be comprehensive. Their product line included everything from stock computer printout paper and fax paper to custom designed forms tailored by Allied's team of forms design consultants to meet the exact business needs of the client.

Allied also had the ability to custom design its forms management services to meet the needs of each of its clients. Allied clients ranged from small businesses which desired only basic inventory control, to those who had comprehensive forms management programs. Pricing was handled individually for each account based on what the sales department thought it could charge.

Current Cost Accounting System

Allied operated its forms manufacturing and TFC activities as separate profit centers. The transfer of product to TFC was at arm's length with the transfer price set at fair market value.

Allied manufactured business forms in 13 locations. Although the company encouraged internal sourcing for customer orders, TFC

This case is adapted by Professor John Shank of the Amos Tuck School, by permission, from earlier versions prepared by Professor Vijay Govindarajan and Jay Weiss (T'93) of the Amos Tuck School, and copyright by Osceola Institute.

salespeople had the option of outsourcing product. The sales force then marked up the cost of product and services by 20 percent, an average.

Clients who participated in the forms management program kept an inventory of forms at one of Allied's 10 distribution centers. The forms were distributed to the client as they were needed. The client was charged a service fee to cover the cost of warehousing and distribution based on a percentage of the cost of sales of the product for that month, regardless of the specific level of service provided to that client. The standard charges were as follows:

- Warehousing/Distribution, 20.5 percent of product cost
- Inventory financing, 4.7 percent of product cost
- Freight to the customer, 7 percent of product cost

If a TFC client made use of any of the distribution services, they were supposed to be charged a price for the forms which was high enough to allow for an additional 20.5 percent of product cost to cover warehousing and distribution expenses (everything from storage and requisition handling up to and including desk top delivery), plus 4.7 percent to cover the cost of capital tied up in inventory, and 7 percent to cover freight expenses. These percentages were determined based on actual 1990 financial data so that on an aggregate basis, in total, all expenses were covered (see Exhibit 1).

Understanding Customer Profitability

With TFC profitability suffering in October 1992, General Manager John Malone began to question the appropriateness of the distribution charges.

"The Business Forms Division used to earn a 20 percent Return on Investment (ROI). But returns have been dropping for several years. TFC is projected to earn an ROI of only 6 percent for 1992. Something tells me that we are not managing this business very well! It seems to me that the charge for services needs closer scrutiny. I believe the

---

EXHIBIT 1   Calculation of Service Fee Charges
(Current Method) ($000)

1990 Product Sales at Cost	$24,059
1990 Warehousing/Distribution Expense	$4,932
. . . % of Product Cost	20.5%
1990 Average Inventory Balance	$10,873
1990 Average Cost of Capital	10.4%
Total Cost of Inventory Financing	$1,131
. . . % Product Cost	4.7%
1990 Total Freight Charges	$1,684
. . . % Product Cost	7.0%

---

charges should have nothing to do with the cost of the product. We should just charge our clients for the services they use. It doesn't seem fair that if two clients buy the same amount of product from us, but one keeps a lot of inventory at our distribution center and is constantly requesting small shipments and the other hardly bothers us at all, that they should pay the same service fees."

John looked through his records and found two accounts of similar size, accounts A and B, which were handled by different salespeople. Accounts A and B both had annual sales of $79,320 with the cost of the product being $50,000. Under the current system, these accounts carried the same service charges, but John noticed that these accounts were similar only in the value of the product being sold; they were very different on the level of service they required from Allied.

In the past year, customer A had submitted 364 requisitions for product with a total of 910 lines[1] (all of them "pick-pack") while customer B had submitted 790 requisitions with a total of 2500 lines (all "pick-pack"). Customer A kept an average of 350 cartons of inventory at the distri-

---

[1]Whenever a customer requires forms, they submit a requisition for all the different products they need. Each separate product request is a "line." If the request is for whole cartons, it is considered a "carton line." For quantities less than a whole carton, it is considered a "pick-pack line."

Exhibit 2   Actual Service Fee Charges
(Current Method)

	Customer A	Customer B
Product Cost	$50,000	$50,000
Warehousing/Distribution (20.5%)	$10,250	$10,250
Inventory Financing (4.7%)	$ 2,350	$ 2,350
Freight Out (7%)	$ 3,500	$ 3,500
Total Service Fees	$16,100	$16,100
Mark-up (20%)	$13,220	$13,220
Net Sales	$79,320	$79,320

Table 1   Distribution Center Expense
($000)

Rent	$1,424
Depreciation	$ 208
Utilities	$ 187
Salaried payroll	$ 745
Fringe benefits-salaried	$ 164
Telephone	$ 96
Security	$ 3
Taxes/Insurance	$ 104
Travel/Entertainment	$ 40
Postage	$ 56
Hourly payroll-admin	$ 259
Fringes-hourly admin	$ 57
Temporary help	$ 17
Variable warehouse payroll	$1,399
Warehouse fringes	$ 336
Data processing	$ 612
Total	$5,707

bution center while customer B kept 700 on average. Customer B's average monthly inventory balance was $50,000 ($7,000 of which had been sitting around for a whole year) while that of customer A was only $15,000. Because of the greater activity on customer B's account, a shipment went out three times a week at an annual freight cost of $7,500 while Customer A required only one shipment a week at an annual freight cost of $2,250. In addition, customer B had requested desk top delivery 26 times during the past year, while customer A did not request desk top delivery at all. John Malone double-checked his records and confirmed that the two accounts had indeed generated identical sales revenues (see Exhibit 2).

With corporate breathing down his neck, John Malone turned to TFC Controller Melissa Dunhill and Director of Operations Tim Cunningham for help. As a first step, they were able to provide John with the total expenses for the distribution centers in 1992 (Table 1).

John said, "How am I going to use this information to solve my problem?" "Well," Tim said, "if we can figure out, without going overboard of course, what exactly goes on in the distribution centers, maybe we can take these financial numbers and assign them to the activities. If we can do that, we'll have a much better idea of what it costs to serve our various clients." Tim knew that two pri-

mary activities took place in the distribution centers—the warehousing of forms and the distribution of those forms in response to a customer requisition. He decided to talk to some people in the field to get more specific information.

Distribution Center: Activity Analysis

John and Tim visited Allied's Kansas City, MO distribution facility. Site manager Wilbur Smith confirmed, "All we do is store the cartons and process the requisitions. I'll tell you, the amount of warehouse space we need just depends on the number of cartons. It seems like we've got a lot of cartons that just sit here forever. If we got into some flexible lease programs and changed aisle configurations, we could probably adjust our space requirements if the number of cartons we stored was to change. The other thing that really bothers me is that we've got some inventory that's been sitting here forever. What's it to the client? They don't pay for it until they requisition it. Isn't there a way we can make them get this stuff out of here?"

"As far as the administration of the operation goes, everything depends on the number of requisitions. And, on a given requisition, the customer can request as many different items as they like."

The team then interviewed warehouse supervisor, Rick Fosmire, "I don't care if I get a hundred requisitions with one line each or one requisition with a hundred lines on it, my guys still have to go pick a hundred items off the shelves. And those damn "pick-pack" requests. Almost everything is "pick-pack" nowadays. No one seems to order a whole carton of 500 items anymore. Do you know how much more labor it requires to pick through those cartons? And on top of that, this desk top delivery is a real pain for my guys. Sure, we offer the service, but you figure the clients who use it should have to pay something extra. It's not like my guys don't have enough to do."

John and Tim were starting to get a pretty good idea of what goes on in the distribution centers, but there was still one person to talk to. They knew that a lot of money was spent on data processing, mostly labor. They needed to know how those people spent their time.

Hazel Nutley had been a data entry operator at Allied for 17 years. "All I do is key in those requisitions, line by line by line. I've gotten to the point where I know the customers so well that all the order information is easy. The only thing that really matters is how many lines I have to enter."

John and Tim returned to Denver with a better idea of what happens in a distribution center. From what they observed, they broke the distribution center down into 6 primary value-added activities—storage, requisition handling, basic warehouse stock selection, "pick-pack" activity, data entry and desk top delivery. With Melissa's help, they assigned costs to these activities as indicated in Table 2. (See Exhibit 3 for calculations.)

Tim then estimated the following for 1992 based upon historical information and current trends:

TABLE 2   Activity-Based Cost Assignment
($000)

Storage	$1,550
Requisition Handling	$1,801
Basic Warehouse Stock Selection	$ 761
"Pick-Pack" Activity	$ 734
Data Entry	$ 612
Desk top delivery	$ 250
Total	$5,708

- On average, the 10 distribution centers scattered across the country will have combined inventories of approximately 350,000 cartons (most cartons were of fairly standard size).
- TFC will process about 310,000 requisitions for 1992.
- Each requisition will average 2.5 lines.
- About 90 percent of the lines will require "pick-pack" activity (as opposed to shipping an entire carton).

They were still uncomfortable with the way inventory financing and freight were charged out. John checked with the finance department and learned that Allied obtained financing at the prime rate plus 1 percent. He thought they could just pass that along.

"Wait a second," Melissa said, "you're probably only going to adjust the charges every 6 months or every year. We better protect ourselves in case our rate changes. Why don't we make it prime + 3.5 percent?"

"Good thinking."

"Our new computer system is coming on line soon which will track individual freight charges," said Tim, "so, we can just charge the client for what it actually costs us." They all agreed that this sounded fair.

Some things that were said at the distribution center still stuck in Tim's mind. "Don't you think we should do something to get that old inventory

EXHIBIT 3   **Breakdown of Expenses by Activity**
($000)

	Total Expense	Share of Expense*
Rent	$1,424 × 85%	$1,211
Depreciation	$ 208 × 85%	$ 177
Utilities	$ 187 × 85%	$ 159
Security	$ 3	$ 3
Total Storage Expense		**$1,550**
Rent	$1,424 × 15%	$ 214
Depreciation	$ 208 × 15%	$ 31
Utilities	$ 187 × 15%	$ 28
Salaries + Fringes	$ 909	$ 909
Telephone	$ 96	$ 96
Taxes/Insurance	$ 104	$ 104
Travel/Entertainment	$ 40 × 75%	$ 30
Postage	$ 56	$ 56
Hourly Payroll + Fringes	$ 316	$ 316
Temp Help	$ 17	$ 17
Total Requisition Handling Expense		**$1,801**
Variable Warehouse Pay + Fringes	$1,735	$1,735
Travel & Entertainment (25%)	$ 40 × 25%	$ 10
Total Warehouse Activity		$1,745
Basic Warehouse Stock Selection (44%)		**$ 761**
"Pick-Pack" Activity (42%)		**$ 734**
Desk Top Delivery (14%)		**$ 250**
Total Warehouse Activity		$1,745
Data Processing Expense	**$ 612**	**$ 612**

*Some expense items were allocated between activities

moving? What about charging something extra, say 1.5 percent per month, for anything that's been there over 9 months?"

"Great idea," Melissa said, "this will also help protect us against the loss we often take on old inventory when the clients end up changing their forms. You know we just eat that and never charge them for it."

They were almost finished. "What about desk top delivery?" Tim said. "I think we should charge extra for it, but I don't want this to get too complicated."

John said, "How much extra time does it take your guys on average to run around the client company?"

"I'd say about an hour and a half to two hours."

"Alright. At $15 per hour, that's about $30 each time. Sound fair?"

"Sounds OK to me. Also, that ties pretty well to the $250,000 overall assignment, since we will process somewhere around 8,500 'desk top' requests this year."

"Wait just one second," Melissa said, "There's something I don't quite understand. We are able to provide a great deal of information to our clients, but some require only a minimal amount while others want more sophisticated reporting. We haven't discussed differentiating the charges for that at all."

"That's a good point," John replied, "but you know that generating these reports really doesn't cost us very much extra and that we need to offer these services as a marketing tool in order to win clients. Let's say we still provide a monthly inventory status report free of charge, and we charge $15/month for anyone who wants the other more sophisticated reports."

"I guess that makes sense," Melissa said.

The entire management team, including Doug Kingsley, Chief Financial Officer of the Business Forms Division, felt that there had to be a better way of charging out distribution services and that the solution would help TFC become more profitable. They now had a much better understanding of the drivers of costs involved in distribution services. As the four headed off in Doug's Sedan de Ville for the Bronco's first home game, they tried to figure out how to use this information to find a workable alternative.

Services Based Pricing (SBP)

"It wouldn't be easy, getting the sales force on board with an activity-based pricing program," John said. "Some of them get pretty stuck in their ways and don't like change. Some accounts would see increases because of the additional distribution charges under a Services Based Pricing (SBP) scheme. These salespeople wouldn't be very happy. On the other hand, some salespeople may see their margins increase." Overcoming these organizational problems would be only the tip of the iceberg.

Doug Kingsley, as well as many of the senior managers at corporate, continued to be very concerned with TFC profitability. While everyone thought TFC was making great strides in understanding their cost drivers, they were not convinced that overall profitability would improve without significant changes in the marketing strategy. They were still wondering how to use their new activity based costing (ABC) analysis to improve the profitability of TFC. So they decided to do additional analysis on their customer base.

The accounting department had maintained a database which showed all activity against individual accounts and calculated a contribution from that account. However, they had not yet been able to use this information effectively. TFC management took their data and began to analyze it.

Although TFC maintained 1100 separate accounts, a large portion of the business came from very few accounts. The top 40 accounts represented 48 percent of the company's net sales (see Exhibit 4).

As a way of understanding customer profitability, TFC management reworked the information in the database as if the accounts had been charged service fees based on actual usage, leaving net sales and product cost the same as before. They recalculated contribution based on these figures. They ranked the accounts according to profit contribution. Exhibit 5 shows the top 20

Exhibit 4   TFC Net Sales, 1991

Annual Sales/Account	No. of Accounts	% of TFC Net Sales
>$300,000	40	48%
>$150,000	53	19%
>$75,000	86	15%
>$30,000	143	11%
>$0	778	7%
Total	1100	100%

accounts for the month of August and Exhibit 6 shows the bottom 20.

The team looked at all accounts where the revised contribution was below 20 percent and determined that if all of these accounts were managed to a 20 percent contribution, the profit improvement would be $4.3 million annually. The top 40 accounts (ranked by the contribution opportunity if improved to a 20 percent contribution) represented 70 percent of the $4.3 million opportunity. Another way of summarizing the range of profitability across the 1,100 customers is shown in Exhibit 7. This was a new way of looking at account management which combined the effects of both volume and contribution margin. Since such a large piece of the opportunity rested with these few accounts, management determined that it might be possible to significantly improve profitability by concentrating on individual account management. The team felt they were on the right track for improving account profitability and wondered what should be the next step. They also wondered what other issues might be important for improving the overall profitability of TFC.

Management called the ABC based pricing system SBP and was seriously considering adopting it for all TFC customers.

EXHIBIT 5   Top 20 TFC Accounts for August, 1992
(Ranked by Contribution $)

Account	Actual Net Sales	Product Cost	ABC Based Service Costs	Revised Contribution
1	76,904	49,620	2,862	24,422
2	130,582	74,396	34,578	21,608
3	72,956	48,216	3,456	21,284
4	64,903	37,981	6,574	20,348
5	45,088	26,098	1,309	17,681
6	104,689	62,340	25,356	16,993
7	52,890	32,083	4,386	16,421
8	38,902	23,087	1,245	14,570
9	87,130	54,923	17,685	14,522
10	67,935	42,012	12,290	13,633
11	58,290	32,074	12,834	13,382
12	84,589	54,023	17,528	13,038
13	36,587	22,657	1,345	12,585
14	47,890	32,545	3,657	11,688
15	56,294	27,801	16,923	11,570
16	61,056	38,924	11,034	11,098
17	56,902	32,789	13,904	10,209
18	45,893	29,570	6,904	9,419
19	62,954	41,034	13,746	8,174
20	26,699	16,830	2,236	7,633
Total	1,279,133	779,003	209,852	290,278

Questions

1. Using the information in the text and in Exhibit 3, calculate "ABC" based services costs for the TFC business.

2. Using your new costing system, calculate distribution services costs for "Customer A" and "Customer B."

3. What inference do you draw about the profitability of these two customers?

4. Should TFC implement the SBP pricing system?

5. What managerial advice do you have for Allied about the Total Forms Control (TFC) business?

EXHIBIT 6   Bottom 20 TFC Accounts for August, 1992
(Ranked by Contribution $)

Account	Actual Net Sales	Product Cost	ABC Based Service Costs	Contribution
1081	3,657	2,356	2,325	− 1,024
1082	38,467	26,301	13,740	− 1,574
1083	5,926	3,840	4,214	− 2,128
1084	163	89	2,390	− 2,316
1085	3,256	2,006	3,590	− 2,340
1086	82,086	61,224	23,756	− 2,894
1087	29,320	20,647	11,843	− 3,170
1088	467	302	4,086	−3,921
1089	17,935	11,087	10,872	−4,024
1090	17,649	12,903	8,903	−4,157
1091	638	420	5,109	−4,891
1092	16,104	9,102	12,134	−5,132
1093	289	178	5,698	−5,587
1094	23,965	17,345	16,523	−9,903
1095	38,065	23,391	27,623	−12,949
1096	32,898	23,054	22,985	−13,141
1097	129,367	73,128	69,527	−13,288
1098	74,569	50,745	45,698	−21,874
1099	88,345	64,930	53,867	−30,452
1100	113,976	82,987	72,589	−41,600
Total	717,142	486,035	417,472	−186,365

EXHIBIT 7   Current Operating Profit for 1992

1. The most profitable 5% of customers (55) contribute 80%.
2. The next most profitable 45% of customers (145) contribute 220%.

*Profit could be 300% of the current level **if we dropped the remaining 50%** of customers (550)!*

3. 48% of customers (528) reduce profit by 140%.
4. 2% of customers (22) reduce profit by 60%.

CASE 8–4
EMERSON ELECTRIC COMPANY

Emerson Electric Company was founded in 1890 as a manufacturer of motors and fans. In 1993, Emerson marked its thirty-sixth consecutive year of improved earnings per share. On $8.2 billion sales, the diversified St. Louis based company reported a 1993 profit of $708 million. In addition, the company had $2 billion in unconsolidated sales in international joint ventures. It manufactures a broad range of electric, electromechanical, and electronic products for industry and consumers. Brand names include Fisher Control Valves, Skil, Dremel, and Craftsman power tools, In-Sink-Erator waste disposals, Copeland compressors, Rosemount instruments, Automatic Switch valves, and U.S. Electric Motors in the power transmission market. Since 1956, Emerson's annual return to shareholders averaged 18 percent. Sales, earnings per share, and dividends per share grew at a compound rate of 9 percent, 8 percent, and 7 percent, respectively, over the 1983–93 period. International sales have grown to 40 percent of total sales and present a growth area for the company.

Emerson is a major domestic electrical manufacturer. Its U.S. based competitors include companies such as General Electric, Westinghouse, and Honeywell. Its foreign competitors include companies such as Siemens and Hitachi. Emerson has had the narrowest focus as a broadly diversified manufacturing company among its primary competitors. Other manufacturers, such as GE and Westinghouse, are diversified into financial services, broadcasting, aircraft engines, plastics, furniture, etc. Emerson follows a growth-through-acquisition strategy, but no one acquisition has been very large. There are periodic divestitures as management seeks the appropriate or complementary mix of products.

In 1973, Charles F. Knight was elected Chief Executive Officer, after joining the company the prior year. Under Knight's leadership, Emerson analyzed historical records as well as data on a set of "peer companies" the investment community valued highly over time. From this analysis, top management concluded that Emerson needed to achieve growth and strong financial results on a consistent basis reflecting constant improvements. The company set growth rate targets based on revenue growth above and beyond economy-driven expectations.

During the 1980s, the company maintained a very conservative balance sheet rather than using leverage. Top management felt that this was a competitive weapon because it permitted flexibility to borrow when an attractive business investment became available. In the economic downtown of the 1990s, Emerson, unlike a number of companies, was not burdened by heavy debt and interest payments.

Organization

Historically, Emerson was organized into 40 decentralized divisions consisting of separate product lines. Each division was run by a president. The goal was to be number one or two in the market for each product line. The company resisted forming groups, sectors, or other combinations of divisions as found in other large companies until 1990, when Emerson organized its divisions into eight business segments: fractional horsepower electric motors; industrial motors; tools; industrial machinery and components; components for heating and air conditioning; process control equipment; appliance components; and electronics and computer support products and systems. This new structure exploits common distribution channels, organizational capabilities, and technologies.

Management of the company is directed by the Office of the Chief Executive (OCE), which consists of the Chief Executive Officer, the President, two Vice Chairmen, seven business leaders, and three other corporate officers. The OCE meets 10 to 12 times a year to review division performance and discuss issues facing individual divisions or the corporation as a whole.

Each division also has a board of directors which consists of a member of the OCE who serves as chairman, the division president, and the division's key managers. The division boards meet monthly to review and monitor performance.

Corporate staff in 1993 consisted of 311 people, the same number as in 1975, when the company was one-sixth its current size in terms of sales. Staff is kept to a minimum because top management believes that a large staff creates more work for the divisions. To encourage open communication and interaction among all levels of employees, Emerson does not publish an organization chart.

Best Cost Producer Strategy

In the early 1980s, the company was not globally competitive in all of its major product lines, and recognized that its quality levels in some product areas did not match levels available from some non-U.S. competitors, particularly the Japanese. Therefore, top management changed its twenty-year strategy of being the "low cost producer" to being the "best cost producer." There were six elements to this strategy:

1. Commitment to total quality and customer satisfaction.
2. Knowledge of the competition and the basis on which they compete.
3. Focused manufacturing strategy, competing on process as well as product design.
4. Effective employee communications and involvement.
5. Formalized cost-reduction programs, in good times and bad.

6. Commitment to support the strategy through capital expenditures.

Since the 1950s, the low cost producer strategy required the divisions to set cost-reduction goals at every level and required plant personnel to identify specific actions to achieve those goals. Improvements of 6 percent to 7 percent a year, in terms of cost of goods sold, were targeted. With the best cost producer strategy, Emerson now aims for higher levels of cost reduction through its planning process. For example, machine tools were used to streamline a process to save labor costs, and design changes saved five ounces of aluminum per unit. Sometimes a competitor's products were disassembled and studied for cost improvements. Products and cost structures of competitors were used to assess Emerson's performance. Factors such as regional labor rates and freight costs were also included in the analyses. For example, before investing millions of dollars in a new plant to make circular saws, top management wanted to know what competitors, domestic and global, were planning.

In the period 1983 to 1993, capital investments of $1.8 billion were made to improve process technology, increase productivity, gain product leadership, and achieve critical mass in support of the best cost producer strategy. Division and plant management report every quarter on progress against detailed cost reduction targets.

Quality was an important factor in Emerson's best cost producer strategy. Improvements were such that Emerson was counting defects in parts per million. For example, in one electric motor line, employees consistently reached less than 100 rejects per one million motors.

Planning Process

The following comments on Emerson's planning process were made by CEO Knight:

> Once we fix our goals, we do not consider it acceptable to miss them. These targets drive our strategy and determine what we have to do: the kinds of businesses we're in,

how we organize and manage them, and how we pay management. At Emerson this means planning. In the process of planning, we focus on specific opportunities that will meet our criteria for growth and returns and create value for our stockholders. In other words, we "identify business investment opportunities."[1]

Emerson's fiscal year starts October 1. To initiate the planning process, top management sets sales growth and return on total capital targets for the divisions. Each fiscal year, from November to July, the CEO and several corporate officers meet with the management of each division at a one or two day division planning conference. Knight spends 60 percent of his time at these division planning conferences. The meetings are designed to be confrontational in order to challenge assumptions and conventional thinking. Top management wants the division to stretch to reach its goals. It also wants to review the detailed actions that division management believes will lead to improved results.

Prior to its division planning conference, the division president submits four standard exhibits to top management. Developing these four exhibits requires months of teamwork and discipline among each division's operating managers.

The "Value Measurement Chart" compares the division's actual performance five years ago (1989), the current year's expected results (1994), and the long-range forecast for the fifth-year (1999). See Exhibit 1 (Note: the numbers in all exhibits are disguised). The Value Measurement Chart contains the type, amount, and growth rates of capital investment, net operating profit after tax (NOPAT), return on average operating capital, and "economic profit" (NOPAT less a capital charge based on the cost of capital). To create shareholder value, the goal is to determine the extent to which a division's return on total capital (ROTC) exceeds Emerson's cost of

capital. Use of the cost of capital rate (Line 3000 on Exhibit 1) is required in all division plans.

The next two exhibits contain sales data. The "Sales Gap Chart" and "Sales Gap Line Chart" show the current year's expected sales (1994) and five-year sales projections (1995–1999). See Exhibits 2 and 3. These are based on an analysis of sources of growth, the market's natural growth rate, market penetration, price changes, new products, product line extensions, and international growth. The "gap" represents the difference between the division's long range sales forecast and top management's target rate for sales growth (Line 19 in Exhibit 2). Exhibit 2 shows the five-year sources of sales growth in Column H. These are illustrated in the Sales Gap Line Chart in Exhibit 3 for one of the divisions for the 1995–99 period. The division president must explain what specific steps are being taken to close the gap.

The "5-Back by 5-Forward P&L" in Exhibit 4 contrasts detailed division data for the current year (1994) with five prior years of historical data and five years of forecast data (1995–99). This comprises 11 years of profit statements including sales; cost of sales; selling, general and administrative expenses; interest; taxes; and return on total capital (ROTC). This statement is used to detect trends. Division management must be prepared with actions to reverse unfavorable movements or trends.

Beyond the review and discussion of the four required exhibits, the division planning conference belongs to the division president. Top management listens to division management's view of customers, markets, plans for new products, analyses of competition, and reviews of cost reductions, quality, capacity, productivity, inventory levels, and compensation. Any resulting changes in the division plan must be submitted for approval by top management. The logic and underlying assumptions of the plan are challenged so that managers who are confident of their strategies can defend their proposals. CEO Knight views the test of a good planning conference is

---

[1]Knight, C. F., "Emerson Electric: Consistent Profits, Consistently," *Harvard Business Review*, January–February 1992, p. 59.

EXHIBIT 1 The Value Measurement Chart Assesses Value Creation at a Glance*

Growth Rate and Capital Requirements	Line No.	5th Prior Year Actual FY 1989 Amt. (A)	% Sales (B)	Current Year Expected FY 1994 Amt. (C)	% Sales (D)	5th Year Forecast FY 1999 Amt. (E)	% Sales (F)	5-Year Increment Historical CY vs 5th PY Amt. (G)	% Sales (H)	5-Year Increment Forecast 5th Yr vs. CY Amt. (I)	% Sales (J)	10-Year Increment 5th Yr vs. 5th PY Amt. (K)	% Sales (L)
Working capital operating-Y/E	1127	117.1	29.8%	120.2	21.8%	153.3	18.5%	3.1	1.9%	33.1	12.0%	36.2	8.3%
Net noncurrent assets-Y/E	1128	92.9	23.6%	150.0	27.2%	221.6	26.8%	57.1	35.9%	71.6	26.0%	128.7	29.6%
Total operating capital-Y/E	1129	210.0	53.4%	270.2	48.9%	374.9	45.3%	60.2	37.9%	104.7	38.0%	164.9	37.9%
Average operating capital	1130	201.1	51.1%	267.1	48.4%	370.4	44.7%						
Incremental investment	1584							66.0		103.3		169.3	
Net oper. prof. aft. tax (NOPAT)	1119	33.4		49.5		79.0		16.1		29.5		45.6	
Return on incremental investment								24.4%		28.6%		26.9%	
NOPAT growth rate								8.2%		9.8%		9.0%	
Capital growth rate								5.8%		6.8%		6.3%	
Rate of Return													
Return on total capital = NOPAT / Avg. oper. cap.		16.6%		18.5%		21.3%							
Net sales	0001	393.2		552.2		827.9		159.0		275.7		434.7	
Sales growth rate								7.0%		8.4%		7.7%	
NOPAT margin		8.5%		9.0%		9.5%		10.1%		10.7%		10.5%	
Operating capital turnover (T/O)		1.96		2.07		2.24		2.41		2.67		2.57	
Cost of capital	3000	12.0%		12.0%		12.0%							
Capital charge (L1130 X L3000)	3001	24.1		32.1		44.4		8.0		12.3		20.3	
Economic profit (L1119-L3001)		9.3		17.4		34.6		8.1		17.2		25.3	

*In millions of dollars (all numbers in the exhibit are disguised).

Source: Charles F. Knight, "Emerson Electric: Consistent Profits, Consistently," *Harvard Business Review*, January–February 1992, p. 63. Used with permission of the Emerson Electric Company. All numbers are disguised.

whether it results in manager actions that significantly impact the business. According to Knight:

> Since operating managers carry out the planning, we effectively establish ownership and eliminate the artificial distinction between strategic and operating decisions. Managers on the line do not—and must never—delegate the understanding of the business. To develop a plan, operating managers work together for months. They often tell me that the greatest value of the planning cycle lies in the teamwork and discipline that the preparation phase requires.[2]

Late in the fiscal year, the division president and appropriate division staff meet with top management to present a detailed forecast for the coming year and conduct a financial review of the current year's actual performance versus forecast. The forecast is expected to match the data in the plan resulting from the division planning conference, but top management also requests contingency plans for several lower levels of activity. A thorough set of actions to protect profitability at lower sales levels is presented. These are known as contingency plans. Changes to the division's forecast are not likely unless significant changes occurred in the environment or in the underlying assumptions. Changes in the forecast must be approved by top management. It is not Emerson's practice to aggregate financial reports for planning and controlling profits between the division and corporation as a whole.

In August, the information generated for and during the division planning conferences and financial reviews is consolidated and reviewed at corporate headquarters by top management. The objective is to examine the total data and prepare for a corporatewide planning conference.

In September, before the start of the next fiscal year, an annual corporate planning conference is attended by top management and top officers of each division. At this meeting, top management presents the corporate and division forecasts for the next year as well as the strategic plan for the next five years. The conference is viewed as a vehicle for communication. There is open and frank discussion of success stories, missed opportunities, and future challenges.

Reporting

At its meetings the OCE uses the President's Operating Report (POR) to review division performance. Each division president submits the POR (see Exhibit 5), on a monthly basis. This reporting system is different from budget reports found in other companies.

First, the POR contains three columns of data for the "current year." The third column of data (Forecast) reflects the plan agreed to by the division president and top corporate management at the beginning of the fiscal year. The forecast data is not changed during the fiscal year and the division president's performance is measured using the fiscal year's forecast. The first column reports the actual results for completed quarters or expected amounts for the current and future quarters. The division president may update expected quarterly results each month. The second column reports the "prior expected" results so that each month's updated expectations can be compared with data submitted in the prior month's POR. Updated expectations are also compared with the forecast data.

Second, in addition to current year data, the POR lists the prior year's actual results. This permits a comparison with the current year's actual results for completed quarters (or expected results for subsequent quarters) and over (O) or under (U) percentages are reported. Midway through the fiscal year, expected data for the first quarter of the next fiscal year is added to the POR.

Corporate top management meets quarterly with each division president and his or her chief financial officer to review the most recent POR and monitor overall division performance. The

---

[2]Knight, p. 63.

Exhibit 2 The Sales Gap Chart Forecasts Five-Year Plans*

	Line No.	Prior Year Actual FY 93 / A	Current Year Expected FY 94 / B	FY 95 / C	FY 96 / D	FY 97 / E	FY 98 / F	FY 99 / G	5-Year Source of Growth (%) / H	5-Year Company Annual Growth (%) / I
Domestic Excluding Exports										
Current year domestic sales base @ 10/1 prices	1		305.7	305.7	305.7	305.7	305.7	305.7		3.6%
Served industry-growth/(decline)	2			3.0	24.6	39.0	49.6	58.3	21.1%	
Penetration-increase/(decrease) (Including-new line extension/buyouts)	3			6.3	14.1	21.0	29.8	37.6	13.6	2.0
Price increases-current year through 5th year	4		3.3	7.6	14.7	21.6	29.5	38.0	12.6	1.7
Incremental new products:										
Prior 5 year introduction	5		16.1	16.4	17.7	17.4	17.5	19.0	1.1	
Current year through 5th year	6		1.4	5.6	11.6	18.5	25.9	34.2	11.9	
Other	7		3.1	1.4	1.6	2.3	2.5	2.8	-0.1	
Total Domestic	8	363.7	329.6	346.0	390.0	425.5	460.5	495.6		8.5
International Excluding Sales to U.S.										
Current year international sales base @ 10/1 prices	9		202.9	202.9	202.9	202.9	202.9	202.9		3.3
Served industry-growth/(decline)	10			(0.1)	8.8	17.0	24.8	35.4	12.9	
Penetration-increase/(decrease) (Including-new line extensions/buyouts)	11			(0.5)	18.8	27.2	36.2	45.1	16.4	3.6
Price increases-current year through 5th year	12		2.0	4.9	8.5	12.5	16.9	21.7	7.1	1.4
Incremental new products:										
Prior 5 year introduction	13		6.9	7.1	6.7	7.1	8.0	9.2	0.8	
Current year through 5th year	14		1.1	4.5	6.3	10.1	14.3	16.9	5.7	

EXHIBIT 2 The Sales Gap Chart Forecasts Five-Year Plans* (continued)

	Line No.	Prior Year Actual FY 93 (A)	Current Year Expected FY 94 (B)	FY 95 (C)	FY 96 (D)	FY 97 (E)	FY 98 (F)	FY 99 (G)	5-Year Source of Growth (%) (H)	5-Year Company Annual Growth (%) (I)
						Forecast				
Currency	15		9.3	–	–	–	–	–	– 3.4	
Other	16		0.4	0.8	0.7	0.9	1.0	1.1	0.3	
Total international	17	204.3	222.6	219.6	252.7	277.7	304.1	332.3		8.3
Total consolidated	18	568.0	552.2	565.6	642.7	703.2	764.6	827.9	100.0	8.4
Annual growth %—nominal	18		–2.8%	2.4%	13.6%	9.4%	8.7%	8.3%		
Gap:										
15% Target—nominal	19			635.0	730.2	839.8	965.7	1,110.6		15.0
Sales gap—over(under)	20			(69.4)	(87.5)	(136.6)	(201.1)	(282.7)		
U.S. exports (excluding to foreign subsidiaries)	21	35.3	31.3	33.7	35.9	39.9	43.9	47.6		8.7
Foreign subsidiaries (excluding sales to U.S.)	22	169.1	191.4	185.8	216.8	237.8	260.3	284.7		8.3

*In millions of dollars (all numbers in the exhibit are disguised).
Source: Charles F. Knight, "Emerson Electric: Consistent Profits, Consistently," *Harvard Business Review*, January–February 1992, p. 64. Used with permission of the Emerson Electric Company.

EXHIBIT 3

The sales gap line chart projects sales growth against other targets

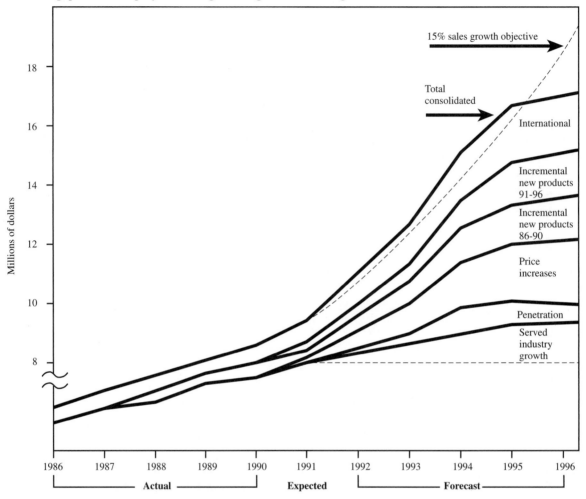

Note: All numbers in the exhibit are disguised.

Source: Charles F. Knight, "Emerson Electric: Consistent Profits, Consistently," *Harvard Business Review*, January–February 1992, p. 65. Used with permission of the Emerson Electric Company.

meetings are taken very seriously by all concerned and any deviations from forecast get close attention. When a division's reported results and expectations are weak, a shift to contingency plans is sometimes ordered by top management. Emerson does not allocate corporate overhead to the divisions but does allocate interest and taxes to divisions at the end of the fiscal year.

Compensation

During the year, each division assesses all department heads and higher level managers against specific performance criteria. Those with high potential are offered a series of assignments to develop their skills. Human resources are identified as part of the strategy implementation. In addition, personnel charts on every management team are kept at corporate headquarters. The charts include each manager's photo, function, experience, and career path. About 85 percent of promotions involve internal managers.

Each executive in a division earns a base salary and is eligible for "extra salary," based on division performance according to measurable objectives (primarily sales, profits, and return on capital). An extra salary amount, established at the beginning of the year, is multiplied by "1" if the division hits targeted performance. The multiplier ranges from .35 to 2.0. Doing better than target increases the multiplier. In recent years, sales and profit margin, as identified in the POR forecast column, have had a 50 percent weighting in computing compensation targets. Other factors include inventory turnover, international sales, new product introductions, and an accounts receivable factor. In addition, stock options and a five-year performance share plan are available to top executives.

Communication

Top management strongly encourages open communication. Division presidents and plant managers meet regularly with all employees to discuss the specifics of the business and the competition. As a measure of communication, top management feels that each employee should be able to answer four essential questions about his or her job:

1. What cost reduction are you currently working on?
2. Who is the competition?
3. Have you met with your management in the past six months?
4. Do you understand the economics of your job?

The company also conducts opinion surveys of every employee. The analysis uncovers trends. Some plants have survey data for the prior twenty years. The CEO receives a summary of every opinion survey from every plant.

Recent Events

As a result of a $2 billion investment in technology during the past 10 years, new products as a percent of sales increased from 13 percent in 1983 to 24 percent in 1993. A new product is defined as a product introduced within the past five years. About 87 percent of total U.S. sales are generated from products that are either first or second in domestic position. Still, some in the investment community do not view Emerson as a technology leader, but as a very efficient world-class manufacturer. Although internally generated new products are part of the planning process, Emerson is sometimes a late entrant in the marketplace. For example, in 1989, a competitor introduced a low-cost, hand-held ultra-sonic gauge. Within 72 days, Emerson introduced its own version at 20 percent less cost than its competitor's gauge. Emerson's gauge was also easier to use and more reliable. It was a bestseller within a year.

To some Wall Street observers, it seems that Emerson is attempting to reduce its dependence on supplying commodity-type products, such as motors and valves, to U.S. based appliance and other consumer-durables manufacturers by moving into faster growing global markets, such as process controls. As the economy recovers, Emerson is likely to continue its acquisition strategy, with an emphasis on foreign acquisitions, and international joint ventures.

The impact of the recent business segment organization structure on the planning and control process is not clear. The added layer of management between the division managers and top management might change the previous relationship between them.

EXHIBIT 4 The 5-Back-by-5-Forward Chart Provides 11 Years of P&L Measures*

	Line No.	Actual/Restated					Current Year	Forecast				
		5th PY FY 89 A	4th PY FY 90 B	3rd PY FY 91 C	2nd PY FY 92 D	Prior Year FY 93 E	Expected FY 94 F	Next Yr FY 95 G	2nd Yr FY 96 H	3rd Yr FY 97 I	4th Yr FY 98 J	5th Yr FY 99 K
Order entries	1143	71,363	77,057	92,716	100,164	126,591	128,247	142,612	157,972	173,743	189,856	207,133
Sales backlog (year end)	1144	13,310	14,051	17,098	16,534	29,334	29,842	31,509	33,082	34,805	36,591	38,363
Net sales	0001	71,163	76,316	89,669	100,728	113,791	127,739	140,945	156,399	172,020	188,070	205,361
Annual growth %-nominal			7.2%	17.5%	12.3%	13.0%	12.3%	10.3%	11.0%	10.0%	9.3%	9.2%
-real							11.3%	7.8%	8.4%	6.7%	6.8%	6.1%
Cost of sales	0009	36,802	39,382	46,487	51,593	60,003	67,651	74,432	82,109	89,966	98,173	106,997
% to sales		51.7%	51.6%	51.8%	51.2%	52.7%	53.0%	52.8%	52.5%	52.3%	52.2%	52.1%
Gross profit	0010	34,361	36,934	43,182	49,135	53,788	60,088	66,513	74,290	82,054	89,897	98,364
% to sales		48.3%	48.4%	48.2%	48.8%	47.3%	47.0%	47.2%	47.5%	47.7%	47.8%	47.9%
SG&A expenses	0011	21,773	22,558	26,246	29,941	32,163	36,150	40,169	44,887	49,714	54,366	59,555
% to sales		30.6%	29.6%	29.3%	29.7%	28.3%	28.3%	28.5%	28.7%	28.9%	28.9%	29.0%
Operating profit	0012	12,588	14,376	16,936	19,194	21,625	23,938	26,344	29,403	32,340	35,531	38,809
% to sales		17.7%	18.8%	18.9%	19.1%	19.0%	18.7%	18.7%	18.8%	18.8%	18.9%	18.9%
Other (inc.)/ded. (excl. int.)	0235	423	1,090	1,395	1,232	1,488	1,764	1,766	1,794	1,530	1,438	1,423
Earnings before interest & taxes	0240	12,165	13,286	15,541	17,962	20,137	22,174	24,578	27,609	30,810	34,093	37,386
% to sales		17.1%	17.4%	17.3%	17.8%	17.7%	17.4%	17.4%	17.7%	17.9%	18.1%	18.2%

	Line No.	Actual/Restated					Current Year	Forecast				
		5th PY FY 89	4th PY FY 90	3rd PY FY 91	2nd PY FY 92	Prior Year FY 93	Expected FY 94	Next Yr FY 95	2nd Yr FY 96	3rd Yr FY 97	4th Yr FY 98	5th Yr FY 99
		A	B	C	D	E	F	G	H	I	J	K
Interest (income)/ expense, net	0230	(771)	(1,041)	(1,127)	(1,326)	(1,781)	(2,224)	(2,330)	(2,576)	(2,734)	(2,903)	(3,070)
Pretax earnings	0015	12,936	14,327	16,668	19,288	21,918	24,398	26,908	30,185	33,544	36,996	40,456
% to sales		18.2%	18.8%	18.6%	19.1%	19.3%	19.1%	19.1%	19.3%	19.5%	19.7%	19.7%
Income taxes	0016	5,445	6,785	7,788	8,447	9,668	10,551	11,753	13,101	14,497	15,948	17,387
Effective tax rate		42.1%	47.4%	46.7%	43.8%	44.1%	43.2%	43.7%	43.4%	43.2%	43.1%	43.0%
Net earnings	0017	7,491	7,542	8,880	10,841	12,250	13,847	15,155	17,084	19,047	21,048	23,069
% to sales		10.5%	9.9%	9.9%	10.8%	10.8%	10.8%	10.8%	10.9%	11.1%	11.2%	11.2%
Return on total capital	1324	20.4%	19.7%	20.3%	23.6%	23.8%	25.1%	26.1%	28.0%	30.1%	32.0%	33.9%
ROTC excluding goodwill	1323	27.3%	28.0%	27.2%	30.6%	31.5%	32.5%	32.9%	34.7%	36.6%	38.3%	40.2%

*In thousands of dollars (all numbers in the exhibit are disguised).

Source: Charles F. Knight, "Emerson Electric: Consistent Profits, Consistently," *Harvard Business Review*, January–February 1992, p. 66. Used with permission of the Emerson Electric Company.

EXHIBIT 5 President's Operating Report Division—Fiscal Year by Quarters/Actual and Expected

(Thousands of Dollars)

Line No.		Current Year						Prior Year		% Act / Exp O/(U) PY
		Actual/ Expected	% Sales	Prior Expected	% Sales	Forecast	% Sales	Actual	% Sales	
1st Quarter Ending December 31										
1	Intercompany Sales	36		36		34		37		-2.7%
2	Net Sales	29,613		29,613		29,463		25,932		14.2%
3	Gross Profit	14,065	47.5%	14,065	47.5%	13,790	46.8%	12,384	47.8%	13.6%
4	SG&A Expenses	8,312	28.1%	8,312	28.1%	8,281	28.1%	7,650	29.5%	8.7%
5	Operating Profit	5,753	19.4%	5,753	19.4%	5,509	18.7%	4,734	18.3%	21.5%
6	Earnings Before Interest & Tax	5,280	17.8%	5,280	17.8%	5,048	17.1%	4,343	16.7%	21.6%
2nd Quarter Ending March 31										
7	Intercompany Sales	5		5		9		56		-91.1%
8	Net Sales	33,324		33,324		31,765		22,661		25.0%
9	Gross Profit	15,283	45.9%	15,283	45.9%	14,812	46.6%	12,518	47.0%	22.1%
10	SG&A Expenses	9,301	27.9%	9,301	27.9%	8,937	28.1%	7,395	27.8%	25.8%
11	Operating Profit	5,982	18.0%	5,982	18.0%	5,875	18.5%	5,123	19.2%	16.8%
12	Earnings Before Interest & Tax	5,785	17.4%	5,785	17.4%	5,612	17.7%	4,918	18.4%	17.6%
3rd Quarter Ending June 30										
13	Intercompany Sales	25		25		39		146		-82.9%
14	Net Sales	32,845		32,845		33,424		30,678		7.1%
15	Gross Profit	15,353	46.7%	15,353	46.7%	15,664	46.9%	14,310	46.6%	7.3%
16	SG&A Expenses	8,916	27.1%	8,916	27.1%	9,399	28.2%	8,424	27.4%	5.8%
17	Operating Profit	6,437	19.6%	6,437	19.6%	6,265	18.7%	5,886	19.2%	9.4%
18	Earnings Before Interest & Tax	6,126	18.7%	6,126	18.7%	5,645	16.9%	5,378	17.5%	13.9%
4th Quarter Ending September 30										
19	Intercompany Sales	94		94		94		25		276.0%
20	Net Sales	36,611		36,611		35,722		30,521		20.0%
21	Gross Profit	17,109	46.7%	17,109	46.7%	16,832	47.1%	14,576	47.8%	17.4%

EXHIBIT 5 President's Operating Report Division—Fiscal Year by Quarters/Actual and Expected (continued)

(Thousands of Dollars)

Line No.		Current Year						Prior Year		% Act / Exp O /(U) PY
		Actual / Expected	% Sales	Prior Expected	% Sales	Forecast	% Sales	Actual	% Sales	
22	SG&A Expenses	10,537	28.7%	10,537	28.7%	10,029	28.1%	8,695	28.5%	21.2%
23	Operating Profit	6,572	18.0%	6,572	18.0%	6,803	19.0%	5,881	19.3%	11.7%
24	Earnings Before Interest & Tax	6,122	16.7%	6,122	16.7%	8,146	22.8%	5,498	18.0%	11.3%
Fiscal Year Ending September 30										
25	Intercompany Sales	160		160		176		264		−39.4%
26	Net Sales	132,393		132,393		130,374		113,792		16.3%
27	Gross Profit	61,810	46.7%	61,810	46.7%	61,098	46.9%	53,788	47.3%	14.9%
28	SG&A Expenses	37,066	28.0%	37,066	28.0%	36,646	28.1%	32,164	28.3%	15.2%
29	Operating Profit	24,744	18.7%	24,744	18.7%	24,452	18.8%	21,624	19.0%	14.4%
30	Earnings Before Interest & Tax	23,313	17.6%	23,313	17.6%	24,451	18.8%	20,137	17.7%	15.8%
31	Pre-Tax Earnings	25,154	19.0%	25,154	19.0%	24,771	19.0%	21,918	19.3%	14.8%
32	Net Earnings	14,361	10.8%	14,361	10.8%	14,024	10.8%	12,250	10.8%	17.2%
Expected First Quarter Next Fiscal Year										
33	Intercompany Sales	67		65				36		86.1%
34	Net Sales	32,830		32,311				29,613		10.9%
35	Gross Profit	15,142	46.1%	15,143	46.9%			14,065	47.5%	7.7%
36	SG&A Expenses	9,179	27.9%	9,217	28.6%			8,312	28.1%	10.4%
37	Operating Profit	5,963	18.2%	5,925	18.3%			5,753	19.4%	3.7%
38	Earnings Before Interest & Tax	5,628	17.1%	5,619	17.4%			5,280	17.8%	6.6%

Used with permission of the Emerson Electric Company. All numbers are disguised.

Questions

1. Evaluate Chief Executive Officer Knight's strategy for the Emerson Electric Company. In view of the strategy, evaluate the planning and control system described in the case. What are its strong and weak points?

2. What changes, if any, would you recommend to the CEO?

3. What role should the eight business segment managers have in Emerson's planning and control system?

BUDGET PREPARATION

This and the following two chapters focus on management control of operations in the current year. Chapter 9 describes the process of budget preparation that takes place *before* the year begins. Chapter 10 describes the appraisal of financial performance *after* its occurrence. Chapter 11 focuses on performance measurement using evaluation of both financial and nonfinancial information.

    Chapter 9 starts by describing the purposes of a budget, and distinguishing a budget from a strategic plan and from a forecast. The next section describes several types of budgets and lists some of the details given in a typical operating budget. The following section describes the steps in preparing an operating budget. Finally, there is a discussion of the behavioral implications of the budget preparation process.

Nature of a Budget

Budgets are an important tool for effective short-term planning and control in organizations. *An operating budget usually covers one year and states the revenues and expenses planned for that year.* It has these characteristics:

- It estimates the profit potential of the business unit.
- It is stated in monetary terms, although the monetary amounts may be backed up by nonmonetary amounts (e.g., units sold or produced).
- It generally covers a period of one year.[1]
- It is a management commitment; managers agree to accept responsibility for attaining the budgeted objectives.
- The budget proposal is reviewed and approved by an authority higher than the budgetee.

---

[1] In businesses that are strongly influenced by seasonal factors, there may be two budgets per year—for example, apparel companies typically have a fall budget and a spring budget.

- Once approved, the budget can be changed only under specified conditions.
- Periodically, actual financial performance is compared to budget, and variances are analyzed and explained.

The process of preparing a budget should be distinguished from (*a*) strategic planning and (*b*) forecasting.

Relation to Strategic Planning

Strategic planning, as we discussed in Chapter 8, is the process of deciding on the nature and size of the several programs that are to be undertaken in implementing an organization's strategies. Both strategic planning and budget preparation involve planning, but the types of planning activities are different in the two processes. The budgeting process focuses on a single year, whereas strategic planning focuses on activities that extend over a period of several years. Strategic planning precedes budgeting and provides the framework within which the annual budget is developed. A budget is, in a sense, a one-year slice of the organization's strategic plan, although, for reasons discussed later in this chapter, the budgeting process involves more than simply carving out a slice.

Another difference between a strategic plan and a budget is that the former is essentially structured by product lines or other programs, while the latter is structured by responsibility centers. This rearrangement of the program—so it corresponds to the responsibility centers charged with executing it—is necessary, because the budget will be used to influence a manager's performance before the fact and to appraise performance after the fact.

Contrast with Forecasting

A budget differs in several respects from a forecast. A *budget* is a management plan, with the implicit assumption that positive steps will be taken by the budgetee—the manager who prepares the budget—to make actual events correspond to the plan; a *forecast* is merely a prediction of what will most likely happen, carrying no implication that the forecaster will attempt to so shape events that the forecast will be realized. As contrasted with a budget, a forecast has the following characteristics:

- It may or may not be stated in monetary terms.
- It can be for any time period.
- The forecaster does not accept responsibility for meeting the forecasted results.
- Forecasts are not usually approved by higher authority.
- A forecast is updated as soon as new information indicates there is a change in conditions.

- Variances from forecast are not analyzed formally or periodically. (The forecaster does some analysis, but the purpose of this is to improve the ability to forecast.)

An example of a financial forecast is one that is made by the treasurer's office to help in cash planning. Such a forecast includes estimates of revenues, expenses, and other items that affect cash flows. The treasurer, however, has no responsibility for making the actual sales, expenses, or other items conform to the forecast. The cash forecast is not cleared with top management; it may change weekly or even daily, without approval from higher authority; and usually the variances between actual and forecast are not systematically analyzed.

From management's point of view, a financial forecast is exclusively a planning tool, whereas a budget is both a planning tool and a control tool. All budgets include elements of forecasting, in that budgetees cannot be held responsible for certain events that affect their ability to meet budgeted objectives. If, however, a budgetee can change a so-called budget each quarter without formal approval (or, if the formal approval is perfunctory), such a budget is essentially a forecast, rather than a true budget. It cannot be used for evaluation and control because, by the end of the year, actual results will always equal the revised budget.

Uses of a Budget

Preparation of an operating budget has four principal purposes: (1) to fine tune the strategic plan; (2) to help coordinate the activities of the several parts of the organization; (3) to assign responsibility to managers, to authorize the amounts they are permitted to spend, and to inform them of the performance that is expected of them; and (4) to obtain a commitment that is a basis for evaluating a manager's actual performance.

Fine Tuning the Strategic Plan.   As discussed in Chapter 8, the strategic plan has the following characteristics: it is prepared early in the year, it is developed on the basis of the best information available at that time, its preparation involves relatively few managers, and it is stated in fairly broad terms. The budget, which is completed just prior to the beginning of the budget year, provides an opportunity to use the latest available information and is based on the judgment of managers at all levels throughout the organization. The "first cut" at the budget may reveal that the overall performance of the organization, or of a business unit within the organization, would not be satisfactory. If so, budget preparation provides an opportunity to make decisions that will improve performance before a commitment is made to a specific way of operating during the year.

Coordination.   Every responsibility center manager in the organization participates in the preparation of the budget. When the pieces are assembled into an overall plan by the staff, inconsistencies may be detected. The most common is the possibility that the plans of the production organization are not consistent with the planned sales volume, in total, or in certain product lines. Within the production organization, plans for shipments of finished products may be inconsistent with the plans of plants or departments within plants to provide components for these products. As another example, line organizations may be assuming a higher level of service from support organizations than those organizations plan to provide. During the budget preparation process, these inconsistencies are identified and resolved.

Assign Responsibility. The approved budget should make clear what each manager is responsible for. The budget also authorizes responsibility center managers to spend specified amounts of money for certain designated purposes without seeking the approval of higher authority.

Basis for Performance Evaluation. The budget represents a commitment by the budgetee to his or her superior. It, therefore, represents a benchmark against which actual performance can be judged. The commitment is subject to change if the assumptions on which it is based change, but it nevertheless is an excellent starting point for performance appraisal. Responsibility is assigned for each responsibility center in the organization. At the top level, the budget summary assigns responsibility to individual profit centers; within profit centers, the budget assigns responsibility to functional areas (such as marketing); and within functional areas, the budget assigns responsibility to individual responsibility centers (such as regional sales offices in the marketing organization).

> **Examples.** Nicolas G. Hayek, the chief executive officer of SMH (makers of Swatch and Omega watches), has been credited with both a dramatic turnaround of SMH as well as the revitalization of the Swiss watch industry itself. Nicolas Hayek used the budgets as part of his broader set of tools in this revitalization process. Hayek remarked: "We are big believers in decentralization. This company has 211 profit centers. We set tough, demanding budgets for them. I personally participate in detailed budget reviews for our major profit centers. Then we track performance closely. We get monthly sales figures for all profit centers on the sixth day of the following month. We get Profit and Loss statements about 10 or 15 days later. The moment anything looks strange, we react very quickly, very decisively, very directly."[2]
>
> As part of turning around Tenneco during 1991–93, Mike Walsh used budgets as a planning and control tool. He required that executives meet budget targets despite outside economic forces. Progress against plan was reviewed weekly and monthly.[3]

Content of an Operating Budget

Exhibit 9–1 shows the content of a typical operating budget and contrasts the operating budget with other types of planning documents: the strategic plan (which was described in Chapter 8); and the capital budget, the cash budget, and the budgeted balance sheet (which will be described in a later subsection). The

---

[2]William Taylor, "Message and Muscle: An Interview with Swatch Titan Nicolas Hayek," *Harvard Business Review*, March–April 1993, p. 110.

[3]"Tenneco CEO Mike Walsh's Fight of His Life," *Business Week*, September 20, 1993, p. 62.

EXHIBIT 9–1

Types of plans and their contents

Strategic Plan	Operating Budget	Capital Budget
Revenue and expense for each major program	For organization as a whole and for each business unit	Each major capital project listed separately
Not necessarily by responsibility centers	Classified by responsibility centers	
Not as much detail as operating budget	Typically includes: revenues production cost and cost of sales marketing expense logistics expense (sometimes) general and administrative research and development income taxes (sometimes) net income	
More expenses are variable	Expenses may be: flexible discretionary committed	
For several years	For one year divided into months or quarters	
Total reconciles to operating budget	Total reconciles to strategic plan (unless revised)	Total project expenditures by quarters

Cash Forecast
Budgeted Balance Sheet

amounts are the planned dollar amounts for the year, together with quantitative amounts, such as head counts (i.e., number of employees) and sales in units.

Operating Budget Categories

In a relatively small organization, especially one that has no business units, the whole budget may fit on one page. In larger organizations, there is a summary page and other pages contain the details for individual business units, plus research and development, and general administrative expenses. The revenue item is listed first, both because it is the first item on an income statement and also because the amount of budgeted revenues influences the amount of many of the other items.

Revenue Budgets.   A revenue budget consists of unit sales projection multiplied by expected selling prices. Of all the elements of a profit budget, the revenue budget is the most critical, but it is also the element that is subject to the greatest uncertainty. The degree of uncertainty differs among companies, and within the same company the degree of uncertainty is different at different times. Companies with large backlogs or companies whose sales volumes are constrained by production capacity will have more certainty in sales projections than companies whose sales volumes are subject to the uncertainties of the marketplace. The revenue budget usually is based on forecasts of some conditions for which the sales manager cannot be held responsible. For example, the state of the economy must be anticipated in preparing a revenue budget, but the marketing manager obviously has no control over it. Nevertheless, effective advertising, good service, good quality, and well-trained salespeople influence the sales volume, and the marketing manager does control these factors.

Budgeted Production Cost and Cost of Sales.   Although textbook illustrations typically show that direct material cost and direct labor cost are developed from the product volumes contained in the sales budget, this often is not feasible in practice because these details depend on the actual mix of products that are to be manufactured. Instead, the standard material and labor costs of the planned volume level of a *standard mix of products* are shown in the budget. Production managers make plans for obtaining quantities of material and labor, and they may prepare procurement budgets for long-lead-time items. They also develop production schedules to ensure that resources needed to produce the budgeted quantities will be available.

The budgeted cost developed by the production managers may not be for the same quantities of products as those shown in the sales budget; the difference represents additions to or subtractions from finished goods inventory. Nevertheless, the cost of sales reported in the summary budget is the standard cost of the products budgeted to be sold. Similarly, the budgeted cost of sales in wholesale and retail establishments is not necessarily the cost of the goods that will be purchased in the budget year. Control over the amounts that may be purchased is obtained by detailed "open to buy" authorizations made during the year, rather than by the amounts shown in the budget. As is the case with manufacturing companies, the difference represents additions to or decreases in inventory.

Marketing Expenses.   Marketing expenses are expenses incurred to obtain sales. A considerable fraction of the amounts included in the budget may have been committed before the year begins. If the budget contemplates a selling organization of a specified number of sales offices with specified personnel, then plans for opening or closing offices and for hiring and training new personnel (or for laying off personnel) must be well underway before the year begins. Advertising must be prepared months in advance of its release, and contracts with media also are placed months in advance. As a practical matter, therefore, commitments for many marketing expenses are agreed to, and implementation is started, well before the beginning of the year.

Logistics expenses usually are reported separately from order getting expenses. They include order entry, transportation from the factory to the consumer, warehousing and order picking, and collection of accounts receivable. Conceptually, they behave more like production costs than marketing costs; that is, many of them are engineered costs. Nevertheless, many companies include them in the marketing budget, because they tend to be the responsibility of the marketing organization.

General and Administrative Expenses.   These are G&A expenses of staff units, both at headquarters and at business units. Overall, they are discretionary expenses, although some parts (such as bookkeeping costs in the accounting department) are engineered expenses. In budget preparation, much attention is given to these categories; because they are discretionary, the appropriate amount to authorize is subject to much debate.

Research and Development Expenses.   Either of two approaches, or a combination of both, may be used in developing the R&D budget. In one approach, the focus is on the total amount. This may be the current level of spending, adjusted for inflation; it may be a larger amount if an increase in sales revenue is planned in the belief that the company can afford to spend more in good times; or it may be a larger amount if there is a good chance of developing a significantly new product or process. The other approach is to obtain the total by aggregating the planned spending on each approved project, plus an allowance for work that is likely to be undertaken even though it is not currently identified. Many companies decide to spend a specified percentage of sales revenue on R&D, but this percentage is based on a long-run average—that is, R&D spending is not geared to short-run changes in sales volume. To permit it to do so could have undesirable effects on the R&D organization; hiring and organizing researchers is a difficult task, and, if spending fluctuates in the short run, inefficiencies are likely.

Income Taxes.   Although the bottom line is income after income taxes, some companies do not take income taxes into account in preparing the budgets for business units. This is because income tax policies are determined at corporate headquarters.

Other Budgets

Although our attention is focused primarily on the preparation of the operating budget, the complete budget also consists of a capital budget, a budgeted balance sheet, and a budgeted cash flow statement. Some companies also prepare a statement of nonfinancial objectives.

Capital Budget

The capital budget states the approved capital projects, plus a lump-sum amount for small projects that do not require high-level approval. It usually is prepared separately from the operating budget and by different people. During the year, proposals for capital expenditures are considered at various levels within the organization, and some are finally approved. This is part of the strategic planning process.

At budget time, the approved projects are assembled into an overall package and examined in total. It may turn out that this total exceeds the amount that the company is willing to spend on capital projects; if so, some are deleted, others are reduced in size, and others are deferred. For the projects that remain, an estimate of the cash that will be spent each quarter is prepared. This is necessary in order to prepare the cash flow statement.

Budgeted Balance Sheet

The budgeted balance sheet shows the balance sheet implications of decisions included in the operating budget and the capital budget. Overall, it is not a management control device, but some parts of it are useful for control. Operating managers who can influence the level of inventories, accounts receivable, or accounts payable often are held responsible for the level of those items.

Budgeted Cash Flow Statement

The budgeted cash flow statement shows how much of the cash needs during the year will be supplied by retained earnings and how much, if any, must be obtained by borrowing or other outside sources. It is, of course, important for financial planning. As its title indicates, the cash flow statement shows the inflows and outflows of cash during the year, usually by quarters. In addition, the treasurer needs an estimate of cash requirements for monthly (or even shorter) intervals as a basis for planning lines of credit and short-term borrowing.

Management by Objectives

The financial objectives that managers are responsible for attaining during the budget year are set forth in the budgets described above. Implicit in the budget amounts are also certain specific objectives: open new sales offices, introduce a new product line, retrain employees, install a new computer system, and so on. Some companies make these objectives explicit. The process of doing so is called *management by objectives* in the literature. The objectives of each responsibility center are set forth in quantitative terms wherever possible, and, as is the case with the budgeted amounts, are accepted by the responsible manager. If nonfinancial objectives can be stated in concrete terms, they may serve a useful purpose in motivating managers and in appraising their performance.

Unfortunately, some management by objectives (MBO) systems are separated from the budget preparation process. In part, this is because MBO was initially advocated by authors of personnel texts and articles, whereas the financial budget is the province of management accounting texts. MBO and budgeting should be two parts of the same planning process.

Companies that do not have an MBO system believe that the effort is not worthwhile. For many responsibility centers, the objectives are implicit in the budget. For others, especially staff and support units, the objectives are versions of "keep on doing what we are now doing as best as we can." In part, the decision to adopt an MBO system depends on senior management's attitude toward the delegation of authority. Many senior managers believe that the way in which a responsibility center accomplishes its financial objectives is up to its manager. That is to say, they hold the manager responsible for the "ends" (i.e., the bottom line), but they leave the "means" (i.e., the decision and actions that lead to the bottom line) up to the manager.

The Budget Preparation Process

Organization

The Budget Department.   The information flow of a budgetary control system is usually administered by the budget department, which normally (but not always) reports to the corporate controller. It performs the following functions:

- It publishes procedures and forms for the preparation of the budget.
- It coordinates and publishes each year the basic corporatewide assumptions that are to be the basis for the budgets (e.g., assumptions about the economy).
- It makes sure that information is properly communicated between interrelated organization units (e.g., sales and production).
- It provides assistance to budgetees in the preparation of their budgets.
- It analyzes proposed budgets and makes recommendations, first to the budgetee and subsequently to senior management.
- It administers the process of making budget revisions during the year.
- It coordinates the work of budget departments in lower echelons (e.g., business unit budget departments).
- It analyzes reported performance against budget, interprets the results, and prepares summary reports for senior management.

The Budget Committee.   The budget committee consists of members of senior management, such as the chief executive officer, chief operating officer, and the chief financial officer. In some companies, the chief executive officer decides without a committee. Regardless of its composition, the budget committee performs a vital role. This committee reviews and either approves or adjusts each of the budgets. In a large diversified company, the budget committee might meet only with the senior operating executives to review the budgets for a business unit or group of business units. In some companies, however, each business unit manager meets with the budget committee and presents his or her budget proposals. Usually, the budget committee must approve major budget revisions made during the year.

Issuance of Guidelines

If a company has a strategic planning process, the first year of the strategic plan, which is usually approved in the summer, is the beginning of the budget preparation process. If the company has no strategic plan, management needs to think about the future in the manner suggested in Chapter 8 as a basis for budget preparation.

Unlike budget preparation, development of the strategic plan usually does not involve lower-level responsibility center managers. Thus, whether or not there is a strategic plan, the first step in the budget preparation process is to develop guidelines that govern the preparation of the budget, for dissemination to all managers. These guidelines are those that are implicit in the strategic plan, modified by developments that have occurred since its approval, especially the company's performance for the year to date and its current outlook. Some of these guidelines are to be followed by all responsibility centers; examples are assumed inflation, in general, and for specific items such as wages; corporate policies on how many persons can be promoted; compensation at each wage and salary level, including employee benefits; and a possible hiring freeze. Others are specific to certain responsibility centers.

These guidelines are developed by the budget staff and approved by senior management. In some cases they may be discussed with lower-level managers before being approved. A timetable for the steps in the budget preparation process also is developed. This material is then disseminated throughout the organization.

Initial Budget Proposal

Based on the guidelines, responsibility center managers, assisted by their staffs, develop a budget request. Because most responsibility centers will start the budget year with the same facilities, personnel, and other resources that they have currently, this budget is based on the existing levels, which are then modified in accordance with the guidelines.[4] Changes from the current level of performance can be classified as (a) changes in external forces and (b) changes in internal policies and practices. They include, but are not limited to, the following:

Changes in External Forces.

- Changes in the general level of economic activity as it affects the volume of sales (e.g., expected growth in the demand for a product line).

---

[4]In the 1970s, there was a proposal for "zero-base budgeting," which involved analyzing each responsibility center's expenses from scratch. Some economists also criticize starting with the current spending levels; they disparage this as "incremental budgeting." Experience has shown that starting from zero is not practical in the time available for budget formulation, nor is it necessary in view of the ongoing nature of most activities.

- Expected changes in the price of purchased materials and services.
- Expected changes in labor rates.
- Expected changes in the cost of discretionary activities (e.g., marketing, R&D, and administration).
- Changes in selling prices. These often are equal to the sum of the changes in the related costs, which assumes that changes in costs can be recovered in selling prices because similar changes will be experienced by competitors.

Changes in Internal Policies and Practices.

- Changes in production costs, reflecting new equipment and methods.
- Changes in discretionary costs, based on anticipated changes in workload.
- Changes in market share and product mix.

Some companies require that specific changes from the current level of spending be classified to such causes as the above. Although this involves extra work, it provides a useful tool for analyzing the validity of proposed changes.

Negotiation

The budgetee discusses the proposed budget with his or her superior. This is the heart of the process. The superior attempts to judge the validity of each of the adjustments. Ordinarily, a governing consideration is that performance in the budget year should be an improvement over performance in the current year. The superior recognizes that he or she will become the budgetee at the next level of the budget process and, therefore, must be prepared to defend the budget that is finally agreed to.

Slack.   Many budgetees tend to budget revenues somewhat lower, and expenses somewhat higher, than their best estimates of these amounts. The resulting budget, therefore, is an easier target for them to achieve. The difference between the budget amount and the best estimate is called "slack." Superiors who examine the budget attempt to discover and eliminate slack, but this is a difficult task. Beginning about 1970, some Russian industries attempted to offset this tendency by developing bonus formulas that attempted to counteract slack. In these formulas, the bonus was proportionally greater for a manager whose actual performance exceeded the budget by a small amount than for a manager who exceeded the budget by a large amount. Although these formulas have been discussed in the literature, they have had practically no acceptance in practice, either in Russia or elsewhere.[5]

---

[5]For a description of the formulas, see Gary J. Mann, "Reducing Budget Slack," *Journal of Accountancy*, August 1988, pp. 118–22.

Review and Approval

The proposed budgets go up through successive levels in the organization. When they reach the top of a business unit, the pieces are put together and the total is examined. In part, the analyst studies consistency—for example, is the production budget consistent with planned sales volume? Are service and support centers planning for the services that are being requested of them? In part, the examination asks whether the budget will produce a satisfactory profit. If not, it often is sent back for reworking. The same type of analysis takes place at corporate headquarters.

Final approval is recommended by the budget committee to the chief executive officer. The CEO also submits the approved budget to the board of directors for ratification. This happens in December, just prior to the beginning of the budget year.

Budget Revisions

One of the principal considerations in budget administration is the procedure for revising a budget after it has been approved. Clearly, if it can be revised at will by the budgetee, there would be no point in reviewing and approving the budget in the first instance. On the other hand, if the budget assumptions turn out to be so unrealistic that the comparisons of actual against budget are meaningless, budget revisions may be desirable.

There are two general types of budget revisions:

1. Procedures that provide for a systematic (say, quarterly) updating of the budgets.
2. Procedures that allow revisions under special circumstances.

Systematic updating obviously requires extra work. Nevertheless, large Japanese companies believe this is worthwhile. They prepare a budget for the whole year, but only the first six months of this budget is formally approved by senior management. The budget for the second six months is revised and approved shortly before the period begins.[6]

If budget revisions are limited only to unusual circumstances, such revision should be adequately reviewed. In general, permission to make revisions should be difficult to obtain. Budget revisions should be limited to those circumstances where the approved budget is so unrealistic that it no longer provides a useful control device. That is to say, *budget revisions must be justified on the basis of significantly changed conditions from those existing when the original budget was approved.*

> **Example:** In 1995, postal rates increased, apparel demand dropped, and paper prices doubled. Lands' End, a $1 billion catalog sales company, chose to cut back mailings to lower costs instead of continuing with the budgeted number of mailings.

---

[6]John F. Rechfield, "What Working for a Japanese Company Taught Me," *Harvard Business Review*, November–December 1990, pp. 168–69.

The dramatic changes in business conditions required Lands' End to change its plans.[7]

An important consideration is that managers should not be required to adhere to plans that subsequent events prove to be suboptimum. This can be a serious problem in budgeting. Because of the time required for budget preparation and review, budgets may provide for actions that are planned months ahead of the time they take place. It is important, therefore, that management actions be based on the latest information available. Consequently, managers should be encouraged to act according to the most recent information. Performance continues to be measured against the original budget, but explanations for reasonable variances are acceptable.

Behavioral Aspects

One of the purposes of a management control system is to encourage the manager to be effective and efficient in attaining the goals of the organization. Some motivational considerations in the preparation of operating budgets are described below.[8]

Participation in the Budgetary Process

Budget processes are either "top down" or "bottom up." With top down budgeting, senior management sets the budget for the lower levels. With bottom up budgeting, lower-level managers participate in setting the budget targets. The top down approach rarely works, however. It leads to a lack of commitment on the part of budgetees; this endangers the plan's success. Bottom up budgeting is most likely to generate commitment to meeting the budgeted objectives; however, unless carefully controlled, it may result in objectives that are too easy or in objectives that may not match the company's over-all objectives.

Actually, an effective budget preparation process blends the two approaches. Budgetees prepare the first draft of the budget for their area of responsibility, which is "bottom up"; but they do so within guidelines established at higher levels, which is "top down." Senior managers review and critique these proposed budgets. A hardheaded approval process helps to ensure that budgetees do not "play games" with the budgeting system. The review process, nevertheless, should be perceived as being fair; if a superior changes the budgeted amounts, he or she should try to convince the budgetee that such a change is reasonable.

Research has shown that budget participation (i.e., a process in which the budgetee is both *involved* in and has *influence* over the setting of budget amounts) has positive effects on managerial motivation for two reasons:

---

[7]Susan Chandler, "Lands' End Looks for Terra Firma," *Business Week,* July 8, 1996, pp. 130–31.

[8]For a description of the behavioral problems associated with budget systems, see G. H. Hofstede, *The Game of Budget Control* (New York: Barnes & Noble, 1968).

1. There is likely to be greater acceptance of budget goals if they are perceived as being under personal control, rather than being imposed externally. This leads to higher personal commitment to achieve the goals.

2. Participative budgeting results in effective information exchanges. The approved budget amounts benefit from the expertise and personal knowledge of the budgetees, who are closest to the product/market environment. Further, budgetees have a clearer understanding of their jobs through interactions with superiors during the review and approval phase.

Participative budgeting is especially beneficial for responsibility centers operating in uncertain environments because managers in charge of such responsibility centers are likely to have the best information regarding the variables that affect their revenues and expenses.

Degree of Budget Target Difficulty

The ideal budget is one that is challenging but attainable. In operational terms, this may be interpreted as meaning that a manager who performs reasonably well has at least a 50 percent chance of achieving the budget amount. We shall refer to such a budget as "achievable." Merchant and Manzoni, in a field study of business unit managers, concluded that business unit budget achievability in practice is usually considerably higher than 50 percent.[9] There are several reasons why senior management approves achievable budgets for business units:

- If the budgeted target is too difficult, managers are motivated to take short-term actions that may not be in the long-term interests of the company. Attainable profit targets are a way of minimizing these dysfunctional actions.
- Achievable budget targets reduce the motivation for managers to engage in data manipulation (e.g., inadequate provision for warranty claims, bad debts, inventory obsolescence, and the like) to meet the budget.
- If business unit profit budgets represent achievable targets, senior management can, in turn, divulge a profit target to security analysts, shareholders, and other external constituencies with a reasonable expectation of being correct.
- A profit budget that is very difficult to attain usually implies an overly optimistic sales target. This may lead to an overcommitment of resources to gear up for the higher sales activity. It is administratively and politically awkward to downsize operations if the actual sales levels do not reach the optimistic targets.

[9] K. A. Merchant and J. Manzoni, "The Achievability of Budget Targets in Profit Centers: A Field Study," *The Accounting Review,* LXIV, no. 3 (July 1989), pp. 539–58.

- When business unit managers are able to meet and exceed their targets, there is a "winning" atmosphere and positive attitude within the company.

One limitation of an achievable target is the possibility that business unit managers will not put forth satisfactory effort once the budget is met. This limitation can be overcome by providing bonus payments for actual performance that exceeds the budget.

If a business unit manager achieves more than the budgeted profit, senior management should not automatically increase the profit budget for the following year. If this happens, business unit managers may not perform up to their maximum capacity in order to avoid showing too large a favorable variance.

Senior Management Involvement

Senior management involvement is necessary for any budget system to be effective in motivating budgetees. Management must participate in the review and approval of the budgets, and the approval should not be a rubber stamp. Without their active participation in the approval process, there will be a great temptation for the budgetee to "play games" with the system—that is, some managers will submit easily attained budgets or budgets that contain excessive allowances for possible contingencies.

Management also must follow up on budget results. If there is no top management feedback, with respect to budget results, the budget system will not be effective in motivating the budgetee.

The Budget Department

The budget department has a particularly difficult behavioral problem. It must analyze the budgets in detail, and it must be certain that budgets are prepared properly and that the information is accurate. To accomplish these tasks, the budget department sometimes must act in ways that line managers perceive as threatening or hostile. For example, the budget department tries to ensure that the budget does not contain excessive allowances (or "water"). In other cases, the explanation of budget variances provided by the budgetee may hide or minimize a potentially serious situation; and when the budget department discloses the facts, the line manager is placed in an uncomfortable position. The budget department must walk a fine line between helping the line manager and ensuring the integrity of the system.

To perform their function effectively, the members of the budget department must have a reputation for impartiality and fairness. If they do not have this reputation, it becomes difficult, if not impossible, for them to perform the tasks necessary to maintain an effective budgetary control system. The members of the budget department should, of course, also have the personal skills required to deal effectively with people.

Quantitative Techniques

There have been many articles on the use of mathematical techniques in the budget preparation process. Although mathematical techniques and computers improve the budgetary process, they do not solve the critical problems of budgetary control. The critical problems in budgeting tend to be in the behavioral area.

Simulation

Simulation is a method that constructs a model of a real situation and then manipulates this model in such a way as to draw some conclusions about the real situation. The preparation and review of a budget is a simulation process. With a computer simulation, senior management can ask what the effect of different types of changes would be and receive almost instantaneous answers. This gives senior management a chance to participate more fully in the budgetary process.

Several computer software packages are available. Some are specific to certain industries, others are general purpose. Most require adaptation to the company's own way of doing things; and this process may require a year, or several years, of intensive effort on the part of company employees or consultants. In some cases, the resulting program has proved to be more complicated than managers will tolerate. If the needs of managers, both budgetees and senior management, are properly taken into account, however, the resulting program can have great benefits.

Probability Estimates

Each number in a budget is a point estimate—that is, it is the single "most likely" amount. For example, sales estimates are stated in terms of the specific number of units of each type of product to be sold. Point estimates are necessary for control purposes. For planning purposes, however, a range of probable outcomes may be more helpful. After a budget has been tentatively approved, it may be possible with a computer model to substitute a probability distribution for each major point estimate. The model then is run a number of times, and a probability distribution of the expected profits can be calculated and used for planning purposes. This is called a *Monte Carlo* process.

Some have proposed that budgets be prepared initially using probability distributions instead of point estimates—that is, the budget committee would approve a number of probability distributions, rather than specific amounts. Subsequent variance analysis would be based on these probability distributions. The work involved in making these estimates is considerable, however. Also, if the procedure is to ask for three numbers—pessimistic, most likely, and optimistic—the result is likely to be a normal curve, with an expected value equal to the most likely number. This is no better than estimating the most likely number in the first instance, except that, theoretically, a measure of dispersion is reported. In any event, probabilistic budgets are rarely found in practice.

Contingency Budgets

Some companies routinely prepare contingency budgets that identify management actions to be taken if there is a significant decrease in the sales volume from what was anticipated at the time of developing the budget (e.g., a contingency budget might determine actions to be taken based on a decrease of 20 percent from the best estimate of sales volume). The contingency budget provides a way of quickly adjusting to changed conditions if the situation arises. If sales volume declines by 20 percent, business unit managers can determine for themselves, according to the predetermined contingency budget, actions to be taken.

> **Examples.** A large diversified firm required contingency budgets from its business units. The budget for business units closed with a series of comparative financial statements, which depicted the estimated item-by-item effect if sales fell to 60 percent or 80 percent of forecast or increased to 120 percent of forecast. For each of these levels of possible sales, costs were divided into three categories: fixed costs, unavoidable variable costs, and management discretionary costs. Business unit managers described the specific actions they would take to control employment, total assets, and capital expenditures in cases of a reduction in sales, and when these actions would be put into effect.[10]
>
> Emerson Electric executives budget for bad news by writing three different plans for varying contingencies.[11]

Summary

A budget is related to a one-year slice of the strategic plan. It is prepared in more detail than the strategic plan, and its preparation involves managers at all levels in the organization. An operating budget shows the details of revenues and expenses for the budget year, for each responsibility center, and for the organization as a whole. It is so structured that amounts are identified with specific responsibility centers. The process starts with the dissemination of guidelines approved by senior management. Based on these guidelines, each responsibility center manager prepares a proposed budget. This is reviewed with his or her superior, and an agreed position is negotiated. When these individual pieces reach the top of the business unit, or of the whole organization, they are reviewed for consistency and adherence to overall corporate goals. The whole process is primarily behavioral. Responsibility center managers must participate in the process, but they do so within constraints decided on by senior management.

---

[10]Galvor Company, Case 10–3 in this book.

[11]Thomas A. Stewart, "Why Budgets Are Bad for Business," *Fortune*, June 4, 1990, pp. 179–87.

Suggested Additional Readings

Brownell, P. "Participation in the Budgeting Process: When It Works and When It Doesn't." *Journal of Accounting Literature*, no. 1 (1982), pp. 124–53.

Chow, C. W., J. C. Cooper, and W. S. Waller. "Participative Budgeting: Effects of a Truth-Inducing Pay Scheme and Information Asymmetry on Slack and Performance." *The Accounting Review*, LXIII, no. 1 (January 1988), pp. 111–22.

Collins F., P. Munter, and D. W. Finn. "The Budgeting Games People Play." *The Accounting Review*, LXII, no. 1 (January 1987), pp. 29–49.

Dunk, Alan S. "The Effect of Budget Emphasis and Information Asymmetry on the Relation between Budgetary Participation and Slack." *The Accounting Review*, LXVIII, 2 (April 1993), pp. 400–410.

Frucot, Veronique, and Winston T. Shearon. "Budgetary Participation, Locus of Control, and Mexican Managerial Performance and Job Satisfaction." *The Accounting Review*, LXVI (January 1991), pp. 80–99.

Govindarajan, Vijay. "Impact of Participation in the Budgetary Process on Managerial Attitudes and Performance; Universalistic and Contingency Perspectives." *Decision Sciences,* 17, no. 4 (Fall 1986), pp. 496–516.

Hirst, Mark K. "The Effects of Setting Budget Goals and Task Uncertainty on Performance: A Theoretical Analysis." *The Accounting Review*, October 1987, pp. 774–84.

Penne, Mark. "Accounting Systems, Participation in Budgeting, and Performance Evaluation." *The Accounting Review*, LXV, no. 2 (April 1990), pp. 303–14.

Case 9–1
Sound Dynamics, Inc.

In April 1990, the manufacturing director of the Reichard subsidiary of Sound Dynamics, Inc. submitted a memorandum (Appendix A) to the managing director of the subsidiary that asked for a supplemental budget for the production control department and explained why increased personnel and funds were needed. In accordance with the company's standard procedure, the request was passed to the subsidiary's financial controller, Ms. Martha Larson, for review. Ms. Larson, after studying the matter, decided the supplemental budget was not justified and wrote a memorandum (Appendix B) to the manufacturing office explaining her position. The manufacturing office, in the latter part of July, sent a memorandum (Appendix C) to Ms. Larson outlining its disagreement with her conclusions and supporting analysis. Now, early in August, Ms. Larson was considering what action she should take on this matter.

Sound Dynamics was a U.S.-based international manufacturer of audio recording equipment, including consumer and commercial lines. Annual sales volume was approximately $1 billion (U.S.) and total employment had passed the 10,000 mark. Sound Dynamics was organized in three sectors, commercial, consumer, and international. In the commercial sector, based out of Atlanta, there were two divisions. One division designed, produced, and sold custom components for recording studios in the U.S. The other division provided services and supplies for those systems. The consumer sector, based in Charlotte, had three divisions, which manufactured audio components and supplies (tapes, cleaners, etc.). The international sector was composed of subsidiaries in 20 countries that distributed

Sound Dynamics products throughout the world. Several of the larger subsidiaries also manufactured some parts of the product line under license agreements with the parent company.

Reichard Produkten, GmbH, located in Munich was one of the larger subsidiaries in the sector. It produced commercial components and supplies for distribution throughout western Europe.

During the last quarter of 1989, the Reichard subsidiary had absorbed the commercial products manufacturing and related activities of the company's Italian affiliate, San Remo, which was located in the German speaking region of Northern Italy, near the Austrian border. The San Remo factory was converted from commercial component manufacturing to consumer components for all of the EC market. Overall responsibility for product planning and marketing of San Remo and Reichard components, however, remained with the international sector sales vice president.

A major reason for the consolidation of manufacturing activities was to achieve scale economies wherever possible. There had been an anticipated annual saving in Reichard's production control department, for example, of $184,000 from a reduction in the number of salaried personnel by 12 through eliminating duplicate jobs. There also had been an expected saving from computerization of production scheduling and control.

Prior to consolidation, the San Remo subsidiary had been using a computerized scheduling and control system, whereas Reichard had been using a manual system. In December 1989, a study was made to determine which system of control would best serve the consolidated commercial manufacturing operation. This study indicated that annual savings of about $138,000 in salary and related expenses, associated with the anticipated elimination of 11 positions, could be

---

This case was adapted by Professor John Shank from an earlier case written by Professor Robert Anthony. The industry described in the case is disguised.

realized from computerization. The manufacturing office of Reichard had concurred with the findings of this study, and the decision was made to computerize production control for the consolidated manufacturing operation.

Strong budgetary control was exercised throughout the Sound Dynamics organization. In the fall of each year, every department manager throughout the worldwide organization developed a proposed budget for the next year. The first step in this annual budget review was the establishment of a realistic timetable and the development of budget assumptions by the budget section of the corporate controller's office. Individual business units tended to base their budget proposals on different assumptions unless instructed otherwise. Within these assumptions, the next step was to establish realistic budget objectives (forecasts) for next year's administrative expenditures based on known assumptions. To develop objectives, the budget section of the corporate controller's office normally began with the current budget, including all supplemental budgets that are of a continuing nature, and then adjusted for any known changes, such as projected cost reductions, or increases based on new programs. The objectives were then reviewed and approved by corporate and sector management, who in turn informed the subsidiaries and divisions that this was to be the basis for their budget planning. These objectives became the primary benchmark against which business unit's proposals were reviewed. Each proposed budget then entered an extensive process of analysis, revision, consolidation, review, and approval by higher levels of management, first within a division or subsidiary and then at sector and corporate levels. At each management level, budgets for subordinate units were consolidated prior to submission to the next higher management level. Financial controllers at each level participated closely in this process. In each business unit a budget analyst reviewed all budgets personally with top management to make certain that they were understood. The budget review process does not save money, but it does apply a

"back pressure" on line and staff managers to make sure they are "cost conscious." Therefore, a close working relationship with division or subsidiary management and a good selling job by the personnel of the budget section are essential.

Once formal approval had been given to a budget, it became a firm commitment for the responsible manager. To exceed this budget required submitting and obtaining approval of a supplemental budget. A supplemental budget was prepared and processed in essentially the same way as the original budget. Policy prescribed that a *supplemental budget could only be justified on the basis of changes in conditions after the original budget was approved.*

Although administrative expense budgets were treated as "fixed" budgets without automatic volume adjustments, years of reviewing these budgets had shown that workload standards, quite similar to those employed in "variable" budgets, could be established for many functions. For instance, in the general manufacturing office, workload in the plant management staff can be measured in part by the number of component lines and sub-assemblies, and in the production scheduling department, workload can be measured by the number of unique parts and the number of separate production runs.

Since the 1990 budgets had been approved prior to the consolidation of commercial manufacturing for Reichard and San Remo, there was a separate budget for each subsidiary, including the production control departments. The approved budgets for 1990 for these two production control departments are summarized in Exhibit 1, together with the estimated savings resulting from consolidation and computerization. The supplemental budget requested by the manufacturing office is also shown for purposes of comparison.

As Ms. Larson reviewed the situation, she saw three possible courses of action: (1) to concur with the manufacturing director's position, in which case the request would very likely receive the necessary approval of the managing director; (2) to continue her opposition, in which case her

**EXHIBIT 1   Budgets and Approved Changes for 1990 Production Control Department—
Consolidated Operations in Germany**

	Reichard		San Remo		Total	
	Number of Salaried Personnel	*Dollars (000)*	*Number of Salaried Personnel*	*Dollars (000)*	*Number of Salaried Personnel*	*Dollars (000)*
Approved budget (before consolidation)	38	$722	27	$668	65	$1,390
Savings from consolidation			(12)	(184)	(12)	(184)
Savings from computerization*	(11)	(138)			(11)	(138)
Budget for the consolidated operations as of 1st January 1990	27	$584	15	$484	42	$1,068
Proposed increase to budget (supplemental budget request)					12	390
Total					54	$1,458

*Based on the study completed in December 1989, concurred in by the manufacturing director of the Reichard Subsidiary.

views and those of the manufacturing office would be placed before the managing director, who would then decide all matters at issue; and (3) to reply with a further analysis, in the hope that the manufacturing office would become convinced of the soundness of her position.

Questions

1. Try to reconcile the numbers in the various positions reflected in the memos in Appendixes A, B, and C. Prepare a *brief* summary that reconciles the differences. Of the disputed differences, how many people and how much money are attributable to alleged workload increase? To salary mix change? To unanticipated one-time computerization implementation costs?[1]

2. Having struggled with Question 1 for a while, what do you think is really going on in the memos?

3. Based on your analysis of the situation, what is a "reasonable" budget for the department for 1990?

4. What should Ms. Larson do now?

5. What lessons for effective controllership should we draw from this case?

[1]The basic question here is, What should the controller do next? The contest is one of a "tight" control system, where budgets have teeth in them and cost control is not just a nice phrase—it is a way of life.

You should first try to reconcile the difference that is floating around. What factors account for the difference, in managerial terms, and what is the dollar impact of each factor you identify? Push this idea far enough so you get a handle on the real "agendas" here. This is an involved case, and you will find it difficult to make much progress without doing some analysis of the conflicting presentations.

Based on this analysis, what seems to be a "reasonable" budget allowance for the production control department for 1990? Why is the number you propose for dollars and people the most "reasonable" one?

Once you have developed a viewpoint on what constitutes a "reasonable" solution, how do you propose that the controller respond to the manufacturing office?

Finally, take a few steps backward from the problems and ask yourself what approach to management is at work here and what you see as the strengths and weaknesses of this approach.

Appendix A:
Memorandum

To: Managing Director—Reichard GmbH.
From: Manufacturing Office
Date: April 6, 1990
Subject: Supplemental Budget for 1990

An increase of 12 in the personnel ceiling for our production control department is requested for the fiscal year 1990. This increase is necessitated by the increased workload of the newly consolidated department.

The proposed personnel ceilings for the consolidated department, broken down by section, are summarized in Table A–1. The approved San Remo personnel ceiling as of December 31, 1989, is shown first, followed by the expected savings in personnel from the consolidation. The reduced personnel requirements for San Remo, plus the Reichard requirements, equal the total personnel requirements for the department.

The consolidated system of production control will have about the same operating characteristics as the computerized system employed earlier by San Remo. Therefore, the workload relationships used to develop the proposed personnel requirements for the consolidated department were derived from last year's workload and authorized personnel levels for San Remo.

Our justification for the proposed personnel ceiling for each of our sections is outlined in the remainder of this memorandum.

Parts Design Control Section (12 people)

Last year, 7 employees were approved in the parts design section at San Remo: 5 processed design change orders, and 2 were clerical and supervisory.

Workload for the design changes activity is determined by the number of product or component changes that have to be processed. Last year, the 5 analysts in the San Remo section processed 2,964 change orders, for an average of 592 change orders per person. In Reichard, 3,680 design change orders were processed.

Design change orders, in turn, are influenced by the number of unique parts. An analysis of both San Remo and Reichard data indicate that there is a definite relationship between the number of design changes processed and the number of unique parts. The nature of this relationship is summarized in Table A–2.

For 1990, the number of unique model parts required for Reichard and San Remo components is estimated at 11,600 and 4,800, respectively. The reason for these large changes from 1990 is that Reichard had added a new line of control boards, and San Remo had dropped a line of components. On the basis of these estimates, we have calculated that 10 design change order personnel are required to handle the workload for 1990, as shown in Table A–3.

Table A–1   Proposed Personnel Ceilings—Production Control Department, 1990

San Remo Commitment Section	Consolidation 12/31/89	Proposed Levels			
		Savings	San Remo	Reichard	Total
Parts design control	7	3	4	8	12
Production control	15	6	9	24	33
Production planning	3	1	2	5	7
Manager's office	2	2	—	2	2
Total	27	12	15	39	54

TABLE A–2   Relationship of Number of Unique New Parts to Design Change Orders

Division	Unique Parts for 1989	Number of Design Change Orders	Design Change Orders per Unique Part
Reichard*	8,810	3,680	0.42
San Remo*	6,584	2,964	0.45
Total	15,394	6,644	0.43

*Although Reichard and San Remo have been consolidated, they are shown separately in this memorandum for calculating purposes.

TABLE A–3   Estimated Personnel Requirements for Parts Design Control Section

A. Equivalent Personnel

Business Unit	Estimated Number of Unique Parts	×	Design Change Orders per Unique Part	÷	Actual Output per Worker	=	Equivalent Personnel
Reichard	11,600		0.42		592		8.2
San Remo	4,800		0.45		592		3.6
Total	16,400						11.8

B. Personnel

Business Unit	Equivalent Personnel	–	Planned Efficiency* (Approx. 10%)	–	Planned Overtime (Approx. 5%)	=	Personnel Ceiling Required
Reichard	8.2		0.8		0.4		7
San Remo	3.6		0.4		0.2		3
Total	11.8		1.2		0.6		10

C. Support Positions

Unit Supervisor	1
Clerk Typist	1
Total	2

D. Total Request

10 + 2 = 12 personnel

*"Planned Efficiency" reduces the calculated personnel requirements to a level approximately consistent with the lowest workload level anticipated during the coming year. In order to handle periodic workload increases during a year, the department is forced to improve its efficiency and, if necessary, to use overtime or temporary clerical help from outside agencies.

TABLE A–4   Estimated Number of Production Controllers Required, 1990

A. Business Unit	Estimated Number of Unique Parts	+	Actual Output Per Person	=	Equivalent Personnel	–	Planned Efficiency (Approx. 5%)	–	Planned Overtime (Approx. 5%)	=	Personnel Ceiling Required
Reichard	11,600		506		22.9		1.2		1.2		20.5
San Remo	4,800		506		9.5		0.5		0.5		8.5
Total	16,400				32.4		1.7		1.7		29.0

B. Position	Total
Section Supervisor	1
Unit Supervisor	2
Clerk Typist	1
Total	4

C. Total Request

29 + 4 = 33 personnel

Production Control Section (33 people)

In this section, the number of unique parts to be processed is the key determinant of the workload. In 1989, 13 production controllers were required at San Remo to handle 6,584 unique parts, for an average of 506 parts per coordinator. On the basis of 11,600 unique parts for the Reichard Division and 4,800 for the San Remo subsidiary, 29 production controllers are required for 1990, as shown in Table A–4.

Production Planning Section (7 people)

In this section, the principal indicator of overall workload is the number of unique parts handled. The relationship between the number of unique parts handled and the number of people fulfilling the functions of this section are summarized in Table A–5. All figures are actual data from the San Remo system for 1989.

On the basis of these relationships and the number of unique parts estimated for 1990, we have estimated that 6 programming personnel are required. The supporting calculations are summarized in Table A–6.

In addition to these 6 people, a section supervisor is required for the planning section. Therefore, the total requirement for operating this section is 7 people.

Manager's Office (2 people)

Two people are required, the manager of the Production Control Department and a secretary.

Estimated Dollar Requirements.   We estimate that a total of $1,458,000 will be needed to operate the consolidated Production Control Department for 1990. This figure is broken down as follows:

Personnel	$1,160,000
Material and supplies	45,000
Computer services	245,000
Miscellaneous	8,000
Total	$1,458,000

Personnel expenses.   This estimate was arrived at by applying to each position in the requested personnel ceiling the actual salary for that position, plus approved fringe benefits.

Materials and supplies expense.   This estimate is about $10,000 greater than the 1989 San Remo actual; this represents an increase of only about 30 percent.

TABLE A–5   **Relationship of Number of Unique Parts to Personnel Production Planning Section**

Position	San Remo Personnel	Number of Unique Parts for San Remo	Output per Worker (Unique Parts)
Computer Programming	1.75	6,584	3,762
Programming Timing and Coordination	1.25	6,584	5,267
	3.00		

TABLE A–6   **Estimated Number of Programming Personnel Required— Planning and Control Section, 1990**

Position	Number of Unique Parts, 1990		Output per Worker	Estimated Equivalent Personnel	Efficiency Savings (10%)	Overtime Allowance (10%)	Ceiling Requested
	Reichard	San Remo	+ Worker =	–	–	=	
Programming Computer	11,600	4,800	3,762	4.4	.45	.45	3.5
Programming Timing and Coordination	11,600	4,800	5,267	3.1	.30	.30	2.5
Total				7.5	.75	.75	6.0

However, the job to be accomplished by the consolidated operation in 1990 is about 2 1/2 times as great as the job accomplished by San Remo in 1989. The small increase in the materials and supplies expense is thus the result of efficiencies in programming and reporting which, in turn, will mean savings in materials and supplies.

Computer services.   In 1989 the San Remo subsidiary spent $190,000 for computer services. For 1990, we have proposed $245,000; included in this amount is $34,000 for start-up costs associated with the conversion of the manual Reichard system to a computerized system. Therefore, the real cost for computer services in the consolidated division is $211,000 or only about 10% more than the 1989 San Remo actual. Yet the job to be done in the consolidated operation in 1990 is 2 1/2 times as great as the job performed by San Remo in 1989. This great increase in output for a nominal increase in expense is the result of efficiencies in programming and reporting.

APPENDIX B:
MEMORANDUM

To: Manufacturing Office—Reichard GmbH.
From: Financial Controller
Date: May 16, 1990
Subject: Supplemental Budget Request dated 6 April, 1990
cc: Managing Director

The manufacturing office has proposed a personnel ceiling of 54 people and a budget of $1,458,000 for the consolidated production control department for 1990. This proposed budget should include both the savings from computerization of the Reichard system, and the savings from consolidation of the two separate operations.

The approved 1990 budgets for the separate production control departments are summarized in Table B–1, together with the proposed budget for the consolidated department submitted by the manufacturing office.

Although the proposed budget for 1990 shows a decrease of 11 personnel, total expenses show an increase of $68,000, despite the planned savings from computerization and consolidation. Further analysis of the Reichard and San Remo requirements shows the following:

Reichard requirements. According to Table B–1, the apparent effect of computerization on the approved 1990 Reichard budget, which was based on a manual system, is to *increase* personnel requirements by one person and expenses by $252,000. We are at a loss to understand why these increases should result from computerization. In fact, the manufacturing office committed itself to a *savings* of 11 people and $138,000 in the Reichard department when its proposal for a computerized system was approved. Thus, the proposed budget is actually 12 people and $390,000 *over* the committed levels. For this reason, we feel that the proposed levels are completely inappropriate.

San Remo requirements. The proposed San Remo requirements reflect savings of 12 people and $184,000.

TABLE B–1   Budget Comparison for Production Control Department (000 omitted for $ figures)

Budget Status	Reichard		San Remo		Total	
	Number	*Dollars*	*Number*	*Dollars*	*Number*	*Dollars*
Budget before consolidation	38	$ 722	27	$ 668	65	$1,390
Proposed	39	974	15	484	54	1,458
Net change	1	$ 252	(12)	$(184)	11	$ 68
Explanation of Changes						
Savings from computerization of Reichard system	(11)*	$(138)*	—	—	(11)	$ (138)
Savings from consolidation	—	—	(12)	$(184)	(12)	(184)
Proposed increase to Reichard budget	12	390	—	—	12	390
Net change	1	$ 252	(12)	$(184)	(11)	$ 68

*Based on study of December 1989; concurred in by manufacturing office.

This reduction is the result of (a) a reduction of supervisory and clerical personnel, which is directly due to the consolidation, and (b) a reduction in the 1990 unique parts count. This savings of 12 people and $184,000, therefore, had nothing to do with computerization and would have occurred in the San Remo budget either under a computerized or a manual system.

Consequently, we believe that the revised budget under a *combined,* computerized system should be as summarized in Table B–2 below.

In this calculation the Reichard personnel ceiling of 27 is based on the precomputerization figure (38) minus the savings agreed to by the manufacturing office as a result of computerization (11). Reichard's budget dollars are based on the same sort of analysis: $722,000 minus $138,000. Similarly, the San Remo personnel ceiling of 15 is based on the preconsolidation figure (27) minus the savings from consolidation and reduced parts count (12), and the budget dollars are the result of $668,000 minus $184,000. Thus, the total budget figures for the consolidated department should be 42 people and $1,068,000.

The main reason for computerizing Reichard's system of production control was financial savings. In view of this analysis, we feel that the manufacturing office should hold to its 1990 consolidated budget for the production control department. If the manufacturing office wishes to continue with their computerized system, reductions in personnel and related expenses in the nature of those summarized in Table B–3 will be required in order to contain the 1990 budget within these recommended levels, based on what a combined manual system would have cost at current workloads.

TABLE B–2   Proposed 1990 Budget (000 omitted for $ figures)

	Reichard	San Remo	Total
Number of personnel	27	15	42
Budget dollars	$584	$484	$1,068

TABLE B–3   Reductions Required to Meet Recommended Maximum 1990 Budget (000 omitted for $ figures)

Proposals	*Personnel*	*Reichard Dollars*	*Personnel*	*San Remo Dollars*	*Personnel*	*Combined Dollars*
Manufacturing office's request	39	$974	15	$484	54	$1,458
Controller's recommended reductions:						
Salary mix	—	(85)	—	—	—	(85)
Overtime	—	(27)	—	(21)	—	(48)
Required personnel (to meet financial objective)	(12)	(197)	—	—	(12)	(197)
Total recommended reductions	(12)	$(309)	—	$ (21)	(12)	$ (330)
Total recommended level	27	$ 665	15	$463	42	$1,128

APPENDIX C:
MEMORANDUM

To: Financial Controller—Reichard GmbH.
From: Manufacturing Office
Date: July 29, 1990
Subject: Supplemental Budget Request dated 6
             April, 1990

In our supplemental budget request of April 6, we requested that the personnel ceiling for our production control department be set at 54, and that the department's budget be revised upward to $1,458,000 for 1990. In your memorandum of May 16, you have recommended that we reduce these proposed 1990 levels by 12 people and $330,000. We cannot agree to these recommended reductions.

We do agree that, generally speaking, a computerized production control system should not be any more costly than a manual system. However, we disagree with your recommendations, since your analysis did not take into account a number of important factors. We feel that the following elements, omitted from your analysis, must be considered:

A. Workload content and volume adjustments.
B. Unavoidable increases in salary mix.
C. Association with integrated data processing plan.
D. Nonrecurring cost penalties.
E. Functional improvements and advantages.

A. Workload content and volume adjustments

Our proposed budget includes additional people to handle an increased workload over the estimated levels that were used in developing the original 1990 Reichard budget for a manual system. There has been an increase of 1,400 new parts for Reichard over the original estimates. In addition, the entire workload for San Remo has been taken on. The parts counts estimates used in developing the original 1990 budget for Reichard (manual system) and the proposed budget for the consolidated department (computerized system) are summarized in Table C–1.

This increased parts count would have resulted in a requirement for at least 5 more people under the manual system, at a cost of about $90,000, plus an estimated $4,000 for operating expenses.

B. Unavoidable increases in salary mix

As a result of the consolidation, and the resulting personnel changes, the average salary per employee retained in the production control department has increased significantly. This increase has resulted from the retention of employees on the basis of seniority. The approved budget for 1990 provided for an average annual salary of $14,218. Our proposed consolidated budget, based on actual salaries, provides for an average annual salary in excess of $15,900. Therefore, if average salaries had remained unchanged after the consolidation, our budget proposal would have been $91,560 less, as shown in Table C–2.

C. Association with integrated data processing plan

By implementing the computerized production control system, we have taken an important step forward in the company's integrated data processing plan, which provides for eventual establishment of a completely computerized master manufacturing system. This step will make it possible to reduce significantly the original expense estimates associated with setting up this master system.

The original proposal for providing a master manufacturing control system, which was submitted prior to the consolidation of the two production control departments, included cost estimates of $94,887 for 1990, and $104,672 for each year thereafter. Had we gone to an all-manual system in the consolidated production control department, the cost estimates for installing the integrated data processing plan would have increased to $111,872 and $159,241, respectively. As a direct result of implementing the computerized production control system, however, we should be able to reduce these costs by $103,000 during 1990,

TABLE C–1   Estimates of Number of Unique Parts

Busines Unit	1990 Original Budget Estimates	Current Known Conditions
Reichard	10,200	11,600
San Remo	—	4,800
Total	10,200	16,400

TABLE C–2   Budget Increase Due to Salary Mix

Salary Base	Proposed Personnel Ceiling ×	Average Annual Salary =	Total Annual Salaries
At approved budget rates	54	$14,218	$ 767,796
At proposed budget rates	54	$15,914	859,356
Difference			$ (91,560)

and $98,000 for each year thereafter. The figures supporting these savings estimates are summarized in Table C–3.

D. Nonrecurring cost penalties

Our proposed budget includes a first-year cost penalty of $112,305. This one-time penalty results from changes in our organization and procedures, and is composed of $72,305 in salaries and wages, and $40,000 in computer expenses. If the volume of work in future years remained unchanged from that in 1990, we would expect our budgets for these years to be lower by this $112,305. The bases for this estimate are summarized in Table C–4.

E. Functional improvements and advantages

In addition the savings outlined above, a computerized production control system offers certain other advantages over a manual system, as follows:

1. It provides a single and better integrated program progress report that reflects the status of engineering, manufacturing, and purchasing actions against schedules on a more timely basis than does a manual system.

TABLE C–3   Effective Cost Decrease of Master Manufacturing Control System Due to Computerization

Revised Cost Factors	1990	1991 Ongoing Level
Original cost estimates based on manual system	$ 94,887	$104,672
Additional cost of consolidation and revised assumptions, based on manual system	16,985	54,569
Total cost estimates to include effect of consolidation based on a manual system	$111,872	$159,241
Revised cost estimates to include effect of consolidation, based on computerized system	(8,700)	(61,010)
Savings directly associated with computerized versus manual system	$103,172	$ 98,231

TABLE C–4   Estimate of Nonrecurring Costs

Budget Items	1990	Future Years	Reductions
Average personnel ceiling	58	54	4
Personnel costs	$1,158,876	$1,086,571	$ 72,305
Computer expense	245,000	205,000	40,000
Other operating costs	54,136	54,136	—
Total	$1,458,012	$1,345,707	$112,305

2. It provides a master file that, once stored in the computer, can be used to produce other useful information.

3. It is compatible with the objective to computerize the issuance of sales confirmation notices which will result in a more efficient method of handling this activity.

While we cannot put a dollar value on these advantages, it is reasonable to expect that they will yield significant cost savings in the future.

Summary

The foregoing adjustments, which we feel are essential to a proper comparison of the costs for a computerized production control system with a manual system, are summarized in Table C–5. On the basis of this analysis, the cost of the computerized system is only $41,000 a year more than that of a manual system, which is more than compensated by the substantial systemwide benefits we will earn. Therefore, our requested budget of $1,458,000 for the combined operations control department is not unreasonable.

TABLE C–5   Summary of Adjustments to Cost Estimates

Costs	**1990 Cost Comparison (000)**	
Unadjusted Costs	*Manual System*	*Computerized System*
Reichard GmbH	$ 722	$ 974
San Remo	406	484
Total unadjusted costs	$1,128*	$1,458**
Increases due to:		
Parts count	94	—
Average salaries	92	—
Cost of implementing computerized operations control system in accordance with company's integrated data processing plan	112	9
Total adjusted costs	$1,426	$1,467

*Estimated by controller's office.
**Proposed by manufacturing office.

Case 9–2
Pasy Company

In 1990 Pasy Company was a diversified packaging company with several major divisions. The Aluminum Can Division was one of the largest manufacturers of aluminum beverage cans in the United States. Each of the product divisions was run by a divisional vice president who reported to Pasy's executive vice president, Charles Kendal. His staff included three financial managers: the controller, chief accountant, and treasurer. The controller, James Yardley, had an assistant controller working with him.

Each division was organized in the same fashion. Reporting to each divisional vice president were two line managers, the general managers of manufacturing and marketing (GMs), and staff members in the customer service and product research functions. The general managers headed all of the division's activities in their respective functional areas. Each GM had a controller and support staff. All of the corporate and divisional management were located in the head office in Springfield. Exhibit 1 shows the organization chart for the Aluminum Can Division.

The Aluminum Can Division's sales were growing slightly faster than industry sales. The division had plants scattered throughout the United States. Plants served customers in their geographic region, often producing different sizes of cans at one location. Customers included both large and small breweries, and soft drink bottlers. Most of the division's customers had two to four suppliers and spread purchases among them. If the division did not meet the customer's cost and quality specifications, or if the division's service was not at a high enough level, another supplier was used. The division had essentially the same technology as other aluminum can producers and there was no difference in product quality between the division and any of its competitors.

Industry Background[1]

Traditionally, containers had been made from one of five materials: aluminum, steel, glass, fiber-foil (paper and metal composite), or plastic. Container manufacturers ranged from small companies supplying few customers to large firms producing many different types of containers. The metal container industry was comprised of over 100 firms producing aluminum and tin-plated steel cans. Metal containers (excluding fiber-foil) accounted for 59 percent of the total containers sold in 1989.

Cans were used for a number of products including beverages, food, paint, and aerosols. Aluminum cans were used for packaging beverages—beer and soft drinks—and tin-plated steel cans were used primarily for food packaging and aerosols. Steel cans accounted for 88 percent of metal can production in 1970. Since that time, aluminum became more widely used, and in 1989 accounted for 71 percent of metal can production. Soft drink bottlers who purchased the containers were, by and large, small independent companies who were franchisees of Coca-Cola and Pepsi Cola; Coca-Cola and Pepsi Cola negotiated the terms with the packaging companies on behalf of their independent bottlers.

Five beverage container manufacturers accounted for 88 percent of the market. These companies typically had plants located within 200 to 300 miles of customers due to the bulk and weight of the cans. The minimum size for a

---

This case was adapted by Anil R. Chitkara (T '94). The case is based (with permission) on an earlier case prepared by Professor David Hawkins. Copyright © Osceola Institute.

[1]The industry background is based on a similar description in Crown Cork and Seal Company case, prepared by Professor Hamermesh.

Exhibit 1

Aluminum can division

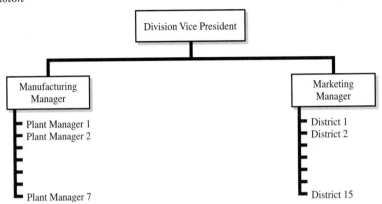

plant was about five lines with a $20 million investment per line in equipment. Raw material prices typically constituted 64 percent of the cost of producing a can. Other costs included labor (15 percent), marketing and general administration (9 percent), transportation (8 percent), depreciation (2 percent), and research and development (2 percent).

For the beer and soft drink companies, each can usually cost more than its contents. The container was approximately 40 percent of the total manufacturing cost for beverage producers. Most producers maintained two or more suppliers. Some customers integrated backward into can manufacture. One large beverage company produced a third of its container requirements and ranked as one of the top five beverage container producers.

The manufacture of cans underwent numerous technological advances from 1970 to 1990. Prior to the early 1970s, cans were produced by rolling a sheet of steel, soldering and cutting it to size, and attaching both the top and the bottom. In 1972 can manufacturing was revolutionized with the perfection of the two-piece process developed by aluminum producers. Cans were manufactured by pushing a flat sheet of metal into a deep cup, then attaching the top. By 1990 manufacturing lines had become even more effi-

cient, producing approximately 2,000 cans per minute.

Aluminum had become more widely used than steel because it offered a number of advantages. It reduced transportation costs due to its lighter weight; it provided more attractive packaging because it was easier to lithograph; it was easier to form; and it reduced the problems of flavoring. Additionally, aluminum was a better metal to recycle than steel; scrap aluminum was nearly three times as valuable per ton as scrap steel. Four global companies supplied aluminum to can producers—Alcoa, Alcan, Reynolds, and Kaiser. Of these suppliers, Alcoa and Reynolds also manufactured aluminum containers.

Budgetary Control System

James Yardley, who had been the corporate controller for Pasy Company for nearly 15 years, described the company's budgetary control system.

> Our management philosophy and budgetary control system go hand in hand. Fundamentally, divisions are structured to encompass broad product categories. The divisional activities are coordinated by the executive vice president with the corporate office providing the policy and review functions. We give the divisional vice presidents full control of their businesses with the exception of two activities, capital raising and labor relations. This structure has allowed us to decentralize the decision making which is

specific to each of the divisions. We use the budget as the primary tool to direct each of the divisions' efforts towards our common corporate objectives. Our budget is a far more critical tool than a simple financial report.

Sales Budget

Each May, the corporate management requests preliminary reports from each divisional vice president outlining their outlook for sales, income, and capital requirements for the following budget year. Divisional vice presidents are also required to submit an evaluation of the expected trends in these items for the two years following the coming budget year. These reports are not in great detail. They are usually not too difficult to pull together since all divisions were required to plan capital expenditures five years out and make predictions of this year's market conditions as part of the strategic planning process.

Once the divisional vice presidents submit their opinions, the market research staff begins to develop a more formal market assessment. The staff examines the coming budget year in great detail and the following two years in more general terms. A sales forecast is then developed for each division and rolled up into a company forecast. In developing the division forecasts, we consider the general economic conditions and their impact on our customers, and our share in each market. We must make fundamental assumptions as to price, new products, changes in particular accounts, new plants, inventory carryovers, forward buying, packaging trends, industry growth trends, weather conditions, and alternative packaging. Each product line, regardless of size, is reviewed in the same manner.

These forecasts are developed at head office for two main reasons: to insure uniformity on basic assumptions and to assure ourselves that the overall corporate sales forecasts are reasonable and achievable. Once the forecasts are compiled, they are forwarded to the divisions for review, criticism, and fine tuning.

Each divisional vice president then compiles a sales forecast from the bottom up. They ask their district managers to estimate sales for the coming budget year. The district managers can request help from the head office or the divisional staff. In the end they must take full responsibility for the sales forecasts they developed.

When all district sales forecasts are submitted, they are consolidated at the division level and then reviewed by the division's general manager of marketing. No changes are made to a district's sales forecast without the agreement of that district manager. Once the budget is approved, nobody is relieved of his or her responsibility until top management approves it. Any changes must also be approved by all people responsible for that budget.

The review and approval process is then repeated at the corporate level. When all the responsible parties are satisfied with the sales budget, the figures become fixed objectives. Each department takes responsibility for its portion of the budget. We conduct the review and approval process for four reasons:

1. To assess each division's competitive position and identify action plans to improve upon that position.
2. To evaluate actions taken to increase market share or respond to competitors' activities.
3. To consider capital expenditures or plant alterations to improve existing products or introduce new products.
4. To develop plans to improve cost efficiency, product quality, delivery methods, and service.

Manufacturing Budget

When final approval is given at the divisional and corporate levels, the overall sales budget is translated into sales budgets for each plant. The breakdown is based on the plants from where the finished goods will be shipped. At the plant level, the sales budget is then categorized by price, volume, and end use.

Plant managers are responsible to the pretax profit line. Once the sales numbers are estimated, each plant budgets gross profit, fixed expenses, and pretax income. Plant managers calculate plant profit as sales budget less budgeted variable costs at standard (which include direct material, direct labor, and variable manufacturing overhead) and the fixed overhead budget. *If actual sales fall below budgeted sales, the plant manager is still responsible for the budgeted profit number.*

With the sales budget handed down from the divisional managers, the plant manager is then required to determine the necessary fixed overhead and variable costs at standard. I believe one of the most important parts of the entire budgeting process is to allow plant managers to develop their own plans. The plant manager does this by breaking down the plant budget into the various departments. Each department plans according to material usage, then costs out their expected physical requirements (e.g., aluminum).

Developing cost standards and cost reduction targets is done by the plant industrial engineering department. The engineering department develops budget performance standards for each department, operation, and cost center within the plant and includes budgeted cost reductions, budgeted unfavorable variances from standards, and budgeted fixed costs in the manufacturing area such as maintenance labor.

One of the most important tasks we do at head office is to visit each plant before plant budgets have been submitted. In the Aluminum Can Division, I visit each plant in the division with my assistant controller and the division's manufacturing staff. We make it clear that these visits are in no way to be viewed as evaluations. One reason for the visits is to become familiar with the reasoning behind the figures. This is essential because when we present the budgets to corporate management, we will be able to answer their questions.

The other reason for the visits is to have us provide guidance as to whether their budgeted profits are in line with corporate goals. However, when we conduct our visits, we do not yet have consolidated figures for the entire division. We must explain that their budgets seem sound, but that once the figures are consolidated, we can better determine what, if anything, needs to be done at the plant level. These final decisions may lead us to drop certain spending programs at plants. We make it clear that it is not because of the lack of merit of any program, but instead, because of the lack of funds.

These visits are extremely important because they give plant managers opportunities to explain their situations and they break the notion that the headquarters staff is not in touch with the plant. Each visit is usually about half a day; the entire process takes three weeks. The plant managers can bring any of their supervisors to the meetings. Most of the plant visit is spent reviewing the budget; however, it is important to walk through the plant and see how the employees are doing. We also take this time to review property replacement and maintenance with the plant manager.

By September 1 the plant budgets are submitted and they are consolidated at the head office. The divisional vice presidents review their budgets and compare them to the corporate objectives. If the budgets are not quite in line with management's expectations, they will ask the plant managers to look for additional savings. When the divisional vice presidents and Charles Kendal are satisfied with the budgets, we will send them up to Hank O'Keefe, the president. He will review them and either approve the budgets or ask for certain modifications by plant managers. The final budget is approved at our Board of Directors meeting in December.

Performance Measurement and Evaluation

On the sixth business day following the close of each month, every plant faxes certain operating variances which we combine into a "variance analysis sheet." These sheets are compiled and distributed the following morning to interested management. They report on variances in critical areas. Plant managers must not wait until the monthly statements are prepared to recognize unfavorable variances; they must be on top of these items and take corrective action on a daily basis.

When corporate receives the actual results, we review the variances for figures that are higher than budget. In this way plant managers need not explain everything

they do, but only when they don't meet budgeted costs. We focus on net sales including price and mix changes, gross margin, and standard manufacturing costs. The budgeted and actual information is summarized in Exhibit 2. Supplemental information is provided in supporting documents which are listed in Exhibit 3. Eight business days after the close of every month, each plant submits the report as per Exhibit 2. This report, along with reports indicated in Exhibit 3, are consolidated for each division and for the entire company. These consolidated reports are distributed on the following business day.

The fixed costs are examined to see if the plants carried out their various programs, if those programs met budgeted costs, and if the results were in line with expectations.

If we sense a problem at the plant level or if a plant manager calls us with his concerns, we may request a daily report to be sent to divisional management. Divisional management may also send a staff specialist, such as a quality control expert, to the plant to help out. Divisional staff will provide recommendations, but it is up to the plant manager to accept or reject these. It is widely known that we expect plant managers to accept the help of our staff and specialists from the division and headquarters.

Once the budget has been approved, it is difficult to make changes. When a problem arises between sales and production at a given plant, it is expected that the problem will be resolved by people in the field. For example, if a customer calls with a rush order that will disrupt production, production can recommend courses of action, but it is the sales manager's responsibility to get the product to the customer. If he or she determines that it is essential to ship the product right away, it will be done. The customer is always our primary concern.

The sales department has the sole responsibility for the price, sales mix, and delivery schedules. The plant manager has responsibility for the operations at the plant, and plant profits.

We motivate plant managers to meet their profit goals in a number of ways. First, only capable managers are promoted. Performance is an important factor when considering candidates for a new position. Second, we have monetary incentives that tie plant managers' compensation packages to achieving their profit budgets. Third, each month we compile a chart which shows manufacturing efficiency[2] by plant and division. This measures variable manufacturing costs for which we believe every plant manager is 100 percent responsible. After all, plant man-

---

[2]Manufacturing Efficiency $= \dfrac{\text{Total actual variable manufacturing costs}}{\text{Total standard variable manufacturing costs}} \times 100$

Exhibit 2   Performance Evaluation Report for a Plant for the Month of November

	Month		Year-to-Date Variances $
Items	*Actual $*	*Variance $*	
Total Sales			
Variances Due To			
Sales Price			
Sales Mix			
Sales Volume			
Total Variable Cost of Sales			
Variances Due To			
Material			
Labor			
Variable Overhead			
Total Fixed Manufacturing Cost			
Variances in Fixed Cost			
Net Profit			
Capital Employed			
Return on Capital Employed			

agers approve all manufacturing standards in the budgeting process.

Most plant managers give a great deal of publicity to the efficiency charts even though the measure may be unfair to certain managers because different products are manufactured at different plants. One plant may have high setup times which will have a greater impact on the plant than a facility with lower setup. Some plants run competitions between production lines and departments to reduce certain cost items. Department heads and foremen are rewarded for their accomplishments. Plant managers, supervisors, and employees take great pride in their plants. In general, the measure is a good gauge of the effectiveness of the plant manager and his staff.

Currently plant managers are focusing on quality as their number one concern. The competitive situation is such that we must meet price and exceed market quality to make sales. Quality not only includes the material quality of a product; it also includes delivery and customer service.

Questions

1. Outline the strengths and weaknesses of the planning and control system of Pasy Company.

2. Trace through the profit budgeting process at Pasy, starting in May and ending with the Board of Directors meeting in December. Be prepared to describe the sorts of activities at each step of the process and the rationale for them.

3. Should the plant managers be held responsible for profits? Why? Why not?

4. How do you assess the performance evaluation system contained in Exhibits 2 and 3?

5. On balance, would you redesign the management control structure at Pasy Company? If so, how and why?

EXHIBIT 3   **Supplemental Reports**

Individual Plant Level Reports

Report	*Content*
Analysis of sales by customer groups	Detailed analysis of sales volume, sales dollars, profit dollars, and profit margin by end use customers (e.g., beer companies, aerosol companies, soft drinks companies)
Analysis of sales	More detailed backup analysis to Exhibit 2 regarding variances due to sales price, sales mix, and sales volume
Analysis of costs	More detailed backup analysis to Exhibit 2 regarding variances due to variable costs and fixed costs of manufacturing

Division Level Reports

Report	*Content*
Comparative analysis of profit performance	Comparison of sales and profits across plants
Comparative analysis of manufacturing efficiency	Comparison of efficiencies in variable and fixed costs across plants

CASE 9–3
BOSTON CREAMERY, INC.

Frank Roberts, Vice-president for Sales and Marketing of the Ice Cream Division of Boston Creamery, was pleased when he saw the final earnings statement for the division for 1973 (see Exhibits 1 and 3). He knew that it had been a good year for ice cream, but he hadn't expected the results to be quite this good.

Only the year before the company had installed a new financial planning and control system. This was the first year that figures comparing budgeted and actual results were available. Jim Peterson, president of the division, had asked Frank to make a short presentation at the next management meeting commenting on the major reasons for the favorable operating income variance of $71,700. Peterson asked him to draft his presentation in the next few days so that the two of them could go over it before the meeting. Peterson said he wanted to illustrate to the management group how an analysis of the profit variance could highlight those areas needing corrective attention as well as those deserving a pat on the back.

The Profit Plan for 1973

Following the four-step approach (Appendix), the management group of the Ice Cream Division prepared a profit plan for 1973 (Table 1).

Based on an anticipated overall ice cream market of about 11,440,000 gallons in their marketing area and a market share of 50 percent, forecasted overall gallon sales were 5,720,329 for 1973. Actually, this forecast was the same as the latest estimate of 1972 actual gallon sales. Since the 1973 budget was being done in October of 1972, final figures for 1972 were not yet available. The latest

revised estimate of actual gallon volume for 1972 was thus used. Rather than trying to get too sophisticated on the first attempt at budgeting, Mr. Peterson had decided just to go with 1972's estimated volume as 1973's goal or forecast. He felt that there was plenty of time in later years to refine the system by bringing in more formal sales forecasting techniques and concepts.

This same general approach was also followed for variable product standard costs and for fixed costs. Budgeted costs for 1973 were just expected 1972 results, adjusted for a few items which were clearly out of line in 1972.

Actual Results for 1973

By the spring of 1973 it had become clear that sales volume for 1973 was going to be higher than forecasted. In fact, actual sales for the year totaled over 5,968,000 gallons, an increase of about 248,000 gallons over budget. Market research data indicated that the total ice cream market in their marketing area was 12,180,000 gallons for the year as opposed to the budgeted figure of about 11,440,000 gallons.

A revised profit plan for the year at the actual volume level is given in Table 2.

The fixed costs in the revised profit plan are the same as in the original plan, $1,945,900. The variable costs, however, have been adjusted to reflect the actual volume level of 5,968,000 gallons instead of the forecasted volume of 5,720,000 gallons, thereby eliminating all cost variances due strictly to the difference between planned volume and actual volume.

For costs which are highly volume dependent, variances should be based on a budget which reflects the volume of operation actually attained. Since the level of fixed costs is independent of volume anyway, it is not necessary to adjust the budget for these items for volume differences.

This case was prepared by Professor John Shank of the Amos Tuck School from an earlier version he wrote at Harvard Business School with the assistance of William J. Rauwerdink, Research Assistant.

TABLE 1

Original Profit Plan for 1973

	Standard Contribution Margin / Gallon	*Forecasted Gallon Sales*	*Forecasted Standard Contribution Margin*
Vanilla	$.4329	2,409,854	$1,043,200
Chocolate	.4535	2,009,061	911,100
Walnut	.5713	48,883	28,000
Buttercrunch	.4771	262,185	125,000
Cherry Swirl	.5153	204,774	105,500
Strawberry	.4683	628,560	294,400
Pecan Chip	.5359	157,012	84,100
Total	$.4530	5,720,329	$2,591,300

Breakdown of Budgeted Total Expenses

	Variable Costs	*Fixed Costs*	*Total*
Manufacturing	$5,888,100	$ 612,800	$6,500,900
Delivery	187,300	516,300	703,600
Advertising	553,200	—	553,200
Selling	—	368,800	368,800
Administrative	—	448,000	448,000
Total	$6,628,600	$1,945,900	$8,574,500

Recap

Sales	$9,219,900
Variable Cost of Sales	6,628,600
Contribution Margin	2,591,300
Fixed Costs	1,945,900
Income from Operations	$ 645,400

The original budget for fixed-cost items is still appropriate.

Assume, for example, that cartons are budgeted at $.04 per gallon. If we forecast volume of 10,000 gallons, the budget allowance for cartons is $400. If we actually sell only 8,000 gallons but use $350 worth of cartons, it is misleading to say that there is a favorable variance of $50 ($350–$400). The variance is clearly unfavorable by $30 ($350–$320). This only shows up if we adjust the budget to the actual volume level:

Carton Allowance	= $.04 per gallon
Forecast Volume	= 10,000 gallons
Carton Budget	= $400
Actual Volume	= 8,000 gallons
Actual Carton Expense	= $350
Variance (Based on Forecast Volume)	= $400 – $350 = $50F
Variance (Based on Actual Volume)	= $320 – $350 = $30U

TABLE 2

Revised Profit Plan for 1973
(Budgeted Profit at Actual Volume)

	Standard Contribution Margin / Gallon	Actual Gallon Sales	Standard Contribution Margin
Vanilla	$.4329	2,458,212	$1,064,200
Chocolate	.4535	2,018,525	915,400
Walnut	.5713	50,124	28,600
Buttercrunch	.4771	268,839	128,300
Cherry Swirl	.5153	261,240	134,600
Strawberry	.4683	747,049	349,800
Pecan Chip	.5359	164,377	88,100
Total	$.4539	5,968,366	$2,709,000

Breakdown of Budgeted Total Expenses

	Variable Costs	Fixed Costs	Total
Manufacturing	$6,113,100	$ 612,800	$6,725,900
Delivery	244,500	516,300	760,800
Advertising	578,700	—	578,700
Selling	—	368,800	368,800
Administrative	—	448,000	448,000
Total	$6,936,300	$1,945,900	$8,882,200

Recap

Sales	$9,645,300
Variable Cost of Sales	6,936,300
Contribution Margin	2,709,000
Fixed Costs	1,945,900
Income from Operations	$ 763,100

Analysis of the 1973 Profit Variance

Exhibit 1 is the earnings statement for the division for the year. The figures for the month of December have been excluded for purposes of this case. Exhibit 2 is the detailed expense breakdown for the manufacturing department. The detailed expense breakdowns for the other departments have been excluded for purposes of this case.

Three days after Jim Peterson asked Frank Roberts to pull together a presentation for the management committee analyzing the profit variance for 1973, Frank came into Jim's office to review his first draft. He showed Jim the schedule shown in Table 3.

Frank said that he planned to give each member of the management committee a copy of this schedule and then to comment briefly on each of the items. Jim Peterson said he thought the schedule was okay as far as it went, but that it just didn't highlight things in a manner which indicated what corrective actions should be

Exhibit 1   ICE CREAM DIVISION
Earnings Statement
December 31, 1973

Month			Year-to-Date	
Actual	*Flexible Budget*		*Actual*	*Flexible Budget*
		Sales—Net	$9,657,300	$9,645,300
		Manufacturing Cost (Schedule A-2)[a]	6,824,900*	6,725,900
		Delivery (Schedule A-3)	706,800	760,800
		Advertising (Schedule A-4)[Note]	607,700	578,700
		Selling (Schedule A-5)	362,800	368,800
		Administrative (Schedule A-6)	438,000	448,000
		Total Expenses	$8,940,200	$8,882,200
		Income from Operations	$ 717,100	$ 763,100
		Variance Analysis in Exhibit 3.		

[a]Schedules A-3 through A-6 have not been included in this case. Schedule A-2 is reproduced as Exhibit 2.
*See Exhibit 3.
Note—In 1973 the company changed from an advertising "budget" of $.06 per gallon sold to a "budget" of 6% of Sales.

taken in 1974 or indicated the real causes for the favorable overall variance. Which elements were uncontrollable, for example? He suggested that Frank try to break down the sales volume variance into the part attributable to sales mix, the

Table 3   Variance Analysis

Favorable Variance Due to Sales:		
Volume	$117,700F	
Price[a]	12,000F	$129,700F
Unfavorable Variance Due to Operations:		
Manufacturing	$99,000U	
Delivery	54,000F	
Advertising	29,000U	
Selling	6,000F	
Administration	10,000F	58,000U
Net Variance—Favorable		$ 71,700F

[a]This price variance is the difference between the actual sales value of the gallons actually sold and the standard sales value ($9,657,300 − $9,645,300).

part attributable to market share shifts, and the part actually attributable to overall volume changes. He also suggested breaking down the unfavorable manufacturing variance to indicate what main corrective actions are called for in 1974. For example, he said, how much of the total was due to price differences versus quantity differences? Since the division was a pure "price taker" for commodities like milk and sugar, he wondered how to best treat the price variances. Finally, he suggested that Frank call on John Vance, the corporate controller, if he needed some help in the mechanics of breaking out these different variances.

As Frank Roberts returned to his office, he considered Jim Peterson's suggestion of getting John Vance involved in revising the variance report. Frank did not want to consult John Vance unless it was absolutely necessary because he thought Vance always went overboard on the technical aspects of any accounting problem. Frank couldn't imagine a quicker way to put people to sleep than to throw one of Vance's

Exhibit 2   **ICE CREAM DIVISION**
Schedule A-2
Manufacturing Cost of Goods Sold
December 31, 1973

	Month			Year-to-Date	
Actual	*Flexible Budget*			*Actual*	*Flexible Budget*
		Variable Costs			
		Dairy Ingredients		$3,679,900	$3,648,500
		Milk Price Variance		57,300	—
		Sugar		599,900	596,800
		Sugar Price Variance		23,400	—
		Flavoring (Including Fruits and Nuts)		946,800	982,100
		Cartons		567,200	566,900
		Plastic Wrap		28,700	29,800
		Additives		235,000	251,000
		Supplies		31,000	35,000
		Miscellaneous		3,000	3,000
		Subtotal		$6,172,200	$6,113,100
		Fixed Costs			
		Labor—Cartonizing and Freezing**		$ 425,200	$ 390,800
		Labor—Other		41,800	46,000
		Repairs		32,200	25,000
		Depreciation		81,000	81,000
		Electricity and Water		41,500	40,000
		Spoilage		31,000	30,000
		Subtotal		$ 652,700	$ 612,800
		Total		$6,824,900	$6,725,900

**The primary reason for the increase in labor for cartonizing and freezing and decrease in delivery cost was a change during the year to a new daily truck loading system.

Before: Every morning, each route sales delivery driver loads the truck from inventory, based on today's sales orders, before leaving the plant. Drivers spend up to 2 hours each day loading the truck before they can begin their sales route.

After: Carton handling workers sort daily production each day onto pallets grouped by delivery truck, based on tomorrow's sales orders. This substitutes lower cost factory labor for higher cost driver labor for loading the trucks and also frees up some driver time each day for more customer contact and point of sale merchandising.

number-filled six-page memos at them. Jim Peterson specifically wants a nontechnical presentation, Frank thought to himself, and that rules out John Vance. Besides, he thought, you don't have to be a CPA to focus on the key variance areas from a general management viewpoint.

A telephone call to John Vance asking about any written materials dealing with mix variances and volume variances produced, in the following day's mail, the document shown here as the Appendix. Vance said to see Exhibit A for the variance analysis breakdown. Armed with this document and his common sense, Frank Roberts dug in again to the task of preparing a nontechnical breakdown of the profit variance for the year.

EXHIBIT 3   Analysis of Variance from Forecasted Operating Income

	Month	Year to Date
(1) Actual Income from Operations	$717,100	
(2) Budgeted Income at Forecasted Volume		645,400
(3) Budgeted Income at Actual Volume		763,100
Variance Due to Sales Volume and Mix [(3) minus (2)]		117,700F
Variance Due to Operations [(1) minus (3)]		46,000U
Total Variance [(1) minus (2)]		$ 71,700F

The next day Frank Roberts learned that his counterpart, John Parker, Vice President for Manufacturing and Operations, had seen the draft variance report and was very unhappy about it. Roberts and Parker were the only two vice presidents in the division. Parker had apparently told Jim Peterson that he felt Roberts was "playing games" with the numbers to make himself look good at Parker's expense. Organizationally, Sales, Marketing and Advertising reported to Roberts, and Manufacturing, Delivery and Administration to Parker.

Questions

1. What changes, if any, would you make in the variance analysis schedule proposed by Frank Roberts? Can the suggestions offered by Jim Peterson be incorporated without making the schedule "too technical"?

2. Can you speculate about how John Parker might structure the variance analysis report? For example, Parker felt it was Marketing's responsibility to set prices so as to recover all commodity cost increases.

3. Indicate the corrective actions you would recommend for 1974, based on the profit variance analysis. Also indicate those areas which deserve commendation for 1973 performance.

4. The approach to "profit planning and control" described in the case is still very common in the 1990s. Many people still consider this approach to be "bread and butter" management theory. What do you see as the main weakness in this approach to management? What is your overall assessment of this "management tool," from a contemporary perspective?

APPENDIX
BOSTON CREAMERY, INC.[1]

The Financial Planning and Control System for the Ice Cream Division

The beginning point in making a profit plan is separating cost into fixed and variable categories. Pure variable costs require an additional amount with each

---

[1]This description of the financial planning and control system is taken from a company operating manual.

increase in volume. The manager has little control over this type of cost other than to avoid waste. The accountant can easily determine the variable manufacturing cost per unit for any given product or package by using current prices and yields. Variable marketing cost per unit is based on the allowable rate (for example, $.06 per gallon for advertising). Costs that are not pure variable are classified as fixed, but they, too, will vary if significant changes in volume occur. There will be varying degrees of sensitivity to volume changes among these costs, ranging from a point just short of pure variable to an extremely fixed type of expense which has no relationship to volume.

The reason for differentiating between fixed and variable so emphatically is because variable cost spending requires no decision; it is dictated by volume. Fixed costs, on the other hand, require a management judgment and decision to increase or decrease the spending. Sugar is an example of a pure variable cost. Each change in volume will automatically bring a change in the sugar cost; only the yield can be controlled. Route salesmen's salaries would be an example of a fixed cost that is fairly sensitive to volume, but not pure variable. As volume changes, pressure will be felt to increase or decrease this expense, but management must make the decision; the change in cost level is not automatic. Depreciation charges for plant would be an example of a relatively extreme fixed cost. Very large increases in volume can usually be realized before this type of cost is pressured to change.

In both cases of fixed cost, a decision from management is required to increase or decrease the cost. It is this dilemma that management is constantly facing: to withstand the pressure to increase or be ready to decrease when the situation demands it. It would be a mistake to set a standard variable cost for items like route salesmen's salaries or depreciation, based on past performance, because they must constantly be evaluated for better and more efficient methods of doing the task.

Advertising is the only cost element not fitting the explanation of a variable cost given in the first paragraph. Advertising costs are set by management decision rather than being an "automatic" cost item like sugar or packaging. In this sense, advertising is like route salesmen's expense. For our company, however, management has decided that the allowance for advertising expense is equal to $.06 per gallon for the actual number of gallons sold. This management decision, therefore, has transformed advertising into an expense which is treated as variable for profit planning purposes.

Following is an example of the four-step approach to one-year profit planning.

The *first step* in planning is to develop a unit standard cost for each element of variable cost, by product and package size. Examples of two different packages for one product are shown below. As already pointed out, the accountant can do this by using current prices and yields for material costs and current allowance rates for marketing costs. After the total unit variable

---

STEP 1
VANILLA ICE CREAM

Item	Regular 1-Gallon Paper Container	Premium 1-Gallon Plastic Container
Dairy Ingredients	$ .53	$ .79
Sugar	.15	.15
Flavor	.10	.12
Production	.10	.16
Warehouse	.06	.08
Transportation	.02	.025
Total Manufacturing	.96	1.325
Advertising	.06	.06
Delivery	.04	.04
Total Marketing	.10	.10
Packaging	.10	.25
Total Variable	1.16	1.675
Selling Price	1.50	2.40
Marginal Contribution per Gallon	.34	.725

STEP 2
VANILLA ICE CREAM SALES FORECAST IN GALLONS

	January	. . .	December	Total
1 Gallon, Paper	100,000		100,000	1,200,000
1 Gallon, Plastic	50,000		50,000	600,000
2 Gallons, Paper	225,000		225,000	2,700,000
1 Gallon, Premium	120,000		120,000	1,440,000
Total	495,000	. . .	495,000	5,940,000

cost has been developed, this amount is subtracted from the selling price to arrive at a standard marginal contribution per unit, by product and package type.

Step 2 is perhaps the most critical in making a profit plan, because all plans derive from the anticipated level of sales activity. Much thought should be given in forecasting a realistic sales level and product mix. Consideration should be given to the number of days in a given period, as well as to the number of Fridays and Mondays, as these are two of the heaviest days and will make a difference in the sales forecast. Other factors that should be considered are:

1 General economic condition of the marketing area
2 Weather
3 Anticipated promotions
4 Competition

Step 3 involves setting fixed-cost budgets based on management's judgment as to the need, in light of the sales forecast. It is here that good planning makes for a profitable operation. The number of routes needed for both winter and summer volume is planned. The level of manufacturing payroll is set. Because this system is based on a one-year time frame, manufacturing labor is considered to be a fixed cost. The level of the manufacturing work force is not really variable until a time frame longer than one year is adopted. Insurance and taxes are budgeted, and so on. After Step 4 has been performed, it may be necessary to return to Step 3 and make adjustments to some of the costs that are discretionary in nature.

Step 4 is the profit plan itself. By combining our marginal contribution developed in Step 1 with our sales forecast from Step 2, we arrive at a total mar-

ginal contribution by month. Subtracting the fixed cost budgeted in Step 3, we have an operating profit by month. If this profit figure is not sufficient, a new evaluation should be made for Steps 1, 2 and/or 3.

Once the plan is completed and the year begins, profit variance is calculated monthly as a "management control" tool. To illustrate the control system, we will take the month of January and assume the level of sales activity for the month to be 520,000 gallons, as shown below. Looking back to our sales forecast (Step 2), we see that 495,000 gallons had been forecasted. When we apply our marginal contribution per unit for each product and package, we find that the 520,000 gallons have produced $6,125 less standard contribution than the 495,000 gallons would have produced at the forecasted mix. So even though there has been a nice increase in sales volume, the mix has been unfavorable. The $6,125 represents the difference between standard profit contribution at forecasted volume and standard profit contribution at actual volume. It is thus due to differences in volume and to differences in average mix. The impact of each of these two factors is also shown in Exhibit A.

Exhibit B shows a typical departmental budget sheet for the month of January comparing actual costs with budget. A sheet is issued for each department, so the person responsible for a particular area of the business can see the items that are in line and those that need attention. In our example, there is an unfavorable operating variance of $22,750 ($570,537–$593,287). You should note that the budget for variable cost items has been adjusted to reflect actual volume, thereby eliminating cost variances due strictly to the difference between planned and actual volume.

Since the level of fixed costs is independent of volume anyway, it is not necessary to adjust the budget

STEP 3
BUDGET FOR FIXED EXPENSES

	January	. . .	December	Total
Manufacturing Expense				
Labor	$ 7,280	. . .	$ 7,920	$ 88,000
Equipment repair	3,332	. . .	3,348	40,000
Depreciation	6,668	. . .	6,652	80,000
Taxes	3,332		3,348	40,000
Total	$20,612	. . .	$21,268	$248,000
Delivery Expense				
Salaries—General	$10,000	. . .	$10,000	$120,000
Salaries—Drivers	10,668	. . .	10,652	128,000
Helpers	10,668	. . .	10,652	128,000
Supplies	668	. . .	652	8,000
Total	$32,004	. . .	$31,956	$384,000
Administrative Expense				
Salaries	$ 5,167	. . .	$ 5,163	$ 62,000
Insurance	1,667	. . .	1,663	20,000
Taxes	1,667	. . .	1,663	20,000
Depreciation	833	. . .	837	10,000
Total	$ 9,334	. . .	$ 9,326	$112,000
Selling Expense				
Repairs	$ 2,667	. . .	$ 2,663	$ 32,000
Gasoline	5,000	. . .	5,000	60,000
Salaries	5,000	. . .	5,000	60,000
Total	$12,667	. . .	$12,663	$152,000

for these items for volume differences. The original budget for fixed-cost items is still appropriate. The totals for each department are carried forward to an earnings statement, Exhibit C. We have assumed all other departments' actual and budget are in line, so the only operating variance is the one for manufacturing. This variance, added to the sales volume and mix variance of $6,125U, results in an overall variance from the original plan of $28,875U.

STEP 4
THE PROFIT PLAN

	Standard Marginal Contribution	January Gallons	$	. . .	Total Year
1 Gallon, Paper	$.340	100,000	$ 34,000		$ 408,000
1 Gallon, Plastic	.305	50,000	15,250		183,000
2 Gallons, Paper	.265	225,000	59,625		715,500
1 Gallon, Premium	.725	120,000	87,000		1,044,000
Total Marginal Contribution	$.3957	495,000	$195,875		$2,350,500
Fixed Cost (See Step 3)					
Manufacturing Expense			$ 20,612		$ 248,000
Delivery Expense			32,004		384,000
Administrative Expense			9,334		112,000
Selling Expense			12,667		152,000
Total Fixed			$ 74,617		$ 896,000
Operating Profit			$121,258		$1,454,500

EXHIBIT A
JANUARY

	Actual Gallon Sales	Standard Contribution Per Gallon	Total Standard Contribution
1 Gallon, Paper	90,000	$.340	$ 30,600
1 Gallon, Plastic	95,000	.305	28,975
2 Gallons, Paper	245,000	.265	64,925
1 Gallon, Premium	90,000	.725	65,250
Total	520,000	$.3649	$189,750
Forecasted Standard Contribution (at 495,000 Gallons)			195,875
Variance			6,125U

	Planned	Actual	Difference
Gallons	495,000	520,000	25,000F
Contribution	$195,875	$189,750	$6,125U
Average Std. Contribution	$ .3957	$ .3649	$.0308U

F, favorable; U, unfavorable.

Variance due to Volume
25,000 gallonsF × $.3957 = $9,892F

Variance due to Mix
$.0308U × 520,000 gallons = $16,017U

Total variance = $6,125U

EXHIBIT B
MANUFACTURING COST
January

Month			Year-to-Date	
Actual	*Flexible Budget*		*Actual*	*Flexible Budget*
$312,744	$299,000	Dairy Ingredients		
82,304	78,000	Sugar		
56,290	55,025	Flavorings		
38,770	37,350	Warehouse		
70,300	69,225	Production		
11,514	11,325	Transportation		
$571,922	$549,925	Subtotal—Variable		
7,300	7,280	Labor		
4,065	3,332	Equipment Repair		
6,668	6,668	Depreciation		
3,332	3,332	Taxes		
$ 21,365	$ 20,612	Subtotal—Fixed		
$593,287	$570,537	Total		

EXHIBIT C
EARNINGS STATEMENT
January

	Month		Year-to-Date	
Actual	*Flexible Budget*		*Actual*	*Flexible Budget*
$867,750	$867,750	Total Ice Cream Sales		
$593,287	$570,537	Manufacturing Cost of Goods Sold		
52,804	52,804	Delivery Expense		
31,200	31,200	Advertising Expense		
76,075	76,075	Packaging Expense		
12,667	12,667	Selling Expense		
9,334	9,334	Administrative Expense		
$775,367	$752,617	Total Expense		
$ 92,383	$115,133	Operating Profit		

Variance Recap

Actual Profit Before Taxes	92,383	(1)
Original Profit Plan	121,258	(2)
Revised Profit Plan, Based on Actual Volume	115,133	(3)
Variance Due to Volume and Mix (3-2)	= 115,133 − 121,258 =	6,125U
Variance Due to Operations (1-3)	= 92,383 − 115,133 =	22,750U
Total Variance (1-2)	= 121,258 − 92,383 =	28,875U

10

ANALYZING FINANCIAL PERFORMANCE REPORTS

This chapter focuses on analyzing financial performance measures. The first part describes how variances between actual and budgeted data are calculated for business units. Since expense and revenue budgets are part of the budgets for business units, the discussion can be extended to cover expense and revenue centers as well. The second part describes how reports of these variances are used by senior management to evaluate business unit performance. In the next chapter, we describe how nonfinancial performance measures can be incorporated into the management control process.

Calculating Variances

Although the focus of this section is on comparing actual performance with the budget, competent operating managers nevertheless adopt a continuous improvement or *Kaizen* mentality; they do not assume that optimal performance is being "on budget." Most companies make a monthly analysis of the differences between actual and budgeted revenues and expenses for each business unit and for the whole organization (some do this quarterly). Some companies merely report the amount of these variances, as in Exhibit 10–1. This statement shows that the actual profit was $52,000 higher than budget, and that the principal reason for this was that revenues were higher than budget. It doesn't illustrate why the revenues were higher or whether there were significant offsetting differences in the variances of the expense items that were netted out in the overall numbers.

A more thorough analysis identifies the causes of the variances and the organization unit responsible. Effective systems identify variances down to the lowest level of management. Variances are hierarchical. As shown in Exhibit 10–2, they begin with the total business unit performance, which is divided into revenue variances and expense variances. Revenue variances are further divided into volume and price variances for the total business unit and for each

---

EXHIBIT 10–1   Performance Report, January (000s)

	Actual	Budget	Actual Better (Worse) Than Budget
Sales	$875	$600	$275
Variable costs of sales	583	370	(213)
Contribution	292	230	62
Fixed overhead	75	75	—
Gross profit	217	155	62
Selling expense	55	50	(5)
Administration expense	30	25	(5)
Profit before taxes	$132	$ 80	$ 52

---

marketing responsibility center within the unit. They can be further divided by sales area and sales district. Expense variances can be divided between manufacturing expenses and other expenses. Manufacturing expenses can be further subdivided by factories and departments within factories. Therefore, it is possible to identify each variance with the individual manager who is responsible for it. This type of analysis is a powerful tool, without which the efficacy of profit budgets would be limited.

The profit budget has embedded in it certain expectations about the state of the total industry and about the company's market share, its selling prices, and its cost structure. Results from variance computations are more "actionable" if changes in actual results are analyzed against each of these expectations. The analytical framework we use to conduct variance analysis incorporates the following ideas:

- Identify the key causal factors that affect profits.
- Break down the overall profit variances by these key causal factors.
- Focus on the profit impact of variation in each causal factor.
- Try to calculate the specific, separable impact of each causal factor by varying only that factor while holding all other factors constant ("spinning only one dial at a time").
- Add complexity sequentially, one layer at a time, beginning at a very basic "commonsense" level ("peel the onion").
- Stop the process when the added complexity at a newly created level is not justified by added useful insights into the causal factors underlying the overall profit variance.

Exhibit 10–3 provides details of the budget of the business unit whose performance is reported in Exhibit 10–1.

Exhibit 10–2

Variance analysis disaggregation

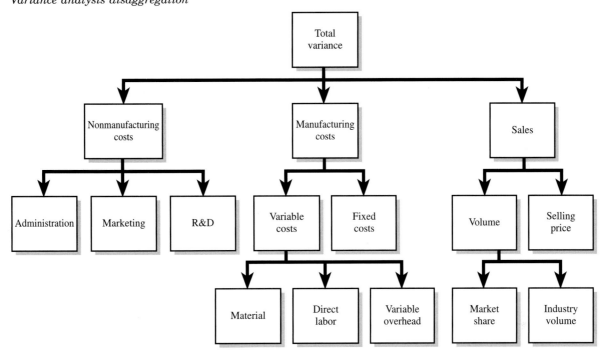

Revenue Variances

In this section, we describe how to calculate selling price, volume, and mix variances. The calculation is made for each product line, and the product line results are then aggregated to calculate the total variance. A positive variance is favorable, because it indicates the actual profit exceeded budgeted profit, and a negative variance is unfavorable.

Selling Price Variance.   The selling price variance is calculated by multiplying the difference between the actual price and the standard price by the actual volume. The calculation is shown in Exhibit 10–4. It shows that the price variance is $75,000, unfavorable.

Mix and Volume Variance.   Often the mix and volume variances are not separated. The equation for the combined mix and volume variance is:

$$\text{Mix and volume variance} = (\text{Actual volume} - \text{Budgeted volume})* \\ (\text{Budgeted unit contribution})$$

The calculation of mix and volume variance is shown in Exhibit 10–5; it is $150,000 favorable.

EXHIBIT 10–3   Budget for January ($000s)

	Product A 100*		Product B 100*		Product C 100*		Total Budget
	Unit	Total	Unit	Total	Unit	Total	
Sales	$1.00	$100	$2.00	$200	$3.00	$300	$600
Standard variable cost:							
Material	0.50	50	0.70	70	1.50	150	270
Labor	0.10	10	0.15	15	0.10	10	35
Variable overhead	0.20	20	0.25	25	0.20	20	65
Total variable cost	0.80	80	1.10	110	1.80	180	370
Contribution	$0.20	20	$0.90	90	$1.20	120	230
Fixed costs:							
Fixed overhead		25		25		25	75
Selling expense		17		17		17	50
Administrative expense		8		8		8	25
Total fixed costs		50		50		50	150
Profit before taxes		$ (30)		$ 40		$ 70	$ 80

*Standard volume (units).

EXHIBIT 10–4   Selling Price Variations, January (000s)

	Product			
	A	B	C	Total
Actual volume (units)	100	200	150	
Actual price per unit	$ 0.90	$ 2.05	$ 2.50	
Budget price per unit	1.00	2.00	3.00	
Actual over/(under) budget per unit	(0.10)	0.05	(0.50)	
Favorable/(unfavorable) price variance	(10)	10	(75)	(75)

The volume variance results from selling more units than budgeted. The mix variance results from selling a different proportion of products from that assumed in the budget. Because products earn different *contributions* per unit, the sale of different proportions of products from those budgeted will result in a variance. If the business unit has a "richer" mix (i.e., a higher proportion of products with a higher contribution margin), the actual profit will be higher than budgeted; and if it has a "leaner" mix, the profit will be lower. Since the

---

EXHIBIT 10–5   Sales Mix and Volume Variance, January ($000s)

(1) Product	(2) Actual Volume	(3) Budgeted Volume	(4) Difference (2) – (3)	(5) Unit Contribution	(6) Variance (4) × (5)
A	100	100	—	—	—
B	200	100	100	$0.90	$ 90
C	150	100	50	1.20	60
Total	450	300			$150

EXHIBIT 10–6   Mix Variance, January ($000s)

(1) Product	(2) Budgeted Proportion	(3) Budgeted Mix at Actual Volume	(4) Actual Sales	(5) Difference (4) – (3)	(6) Unit Contribution	Variance (5) × (6)
A	⅓	150†	100	(50)	$0.20	$(10)
B	⅓	150	200	50	$0.90	45
C	⅓	150	150	—	—	—
Total		450	450			$ 35

†⅓ * 450.

volume and mix variances are joint, techniques for separating them are somewhat arbitrary. One such technique is described below.

Mix Variance.   The mix variance for each product is found from the following equation:

> Mix variance = [(Total actual volume of sales * Budgeted Proportion) – (Actual volume of sales)] * Budgeted unit contribution

The calculation of the mix variance is shown in Exhibit 10–6. It shows that a higher proportion of product B and a lower proportion of product A were sold. Since product B has a higher unit contribution than product A, the mix variance is favorable, by $35,000.

Volume Variance.   The volume variance can be calculated by subtracting the mix variance from the combined mix and volume variance. This is $150,000 minus $35,000, or $115,000. It can also be calculated for each product as follows:

EXHIBIT 10–7   Sales Volume Variance, January ($000s)

(1) Product	(2) Budgeted Mix at Actual Volume	(3) Budgeted Volume	(4) Difference (2) – (3)	(5) Unit Contribution	(6) Volume Variance
A	150	100	50	$0.20	$ 10
B	150	100	50	0.90	45
C	150	100	50	1.20	60
Total	450	300	150		$115

EXHIBIT 10–8   Revenue Variances by Product, January ($000s)

	Product			
	A	B	C	Total
Price variance	$(10)	$ 10	$(75)	$(75)
Mix variance	(10)	45	—	35
Volume variance	10	45	60	115
Total	$(10)	$100	$(15)	$ 75

Volume variance = [(Total actual volume of sales) * (Budgeted percentage)]
    – [(Budgeted sales) * (Budgeted unit contribution)]

The calculation of the volume variance is shown in Exhibit 10–7.

Other Revenue Analyses.   Revenue variances may be further subdivided. In our example, Exhibits 10–4, 10–6, and 10–7 provide the information to classify them by product. Such a classification is shown in Exhibit 10–8.

Market Penetration and Industry Volume.   One extension of revenue analysis is to separate the mix and volume variance into the amount caused by differences in market share and the amount caused by differences in industry volume. The principle is that the business unit managers are responsible for market share, but they are not responsible for the industry volume because that is largely influenced by the state of the economy. To make this calculation, industry sales data must be available. This calculation is given in Exhibit 10–9.

Section A of Exhibit 10–9 provides the assumptions that were made in the original budget shown in Exhibit 10–1, and Section B provides details on actual industry volume and market share for the month of January.

The following equation is used to separate the effect of market penetration from industry volume on the mix and volume variance:

EXHIBIT 10–9 Industry Volume and Market Share Variances, January ($000s)

A. Budgeted Sales Volume

	Product			
	A	B	C	Total
Estimated industry volume (units)	833	500	1,667	3,000
Budgeted market share	12%	20%	6%	10%
Budgeted volume (units)	100	100	100	300

B. Actual Market Share

	Product			
	A	B	C	Total
Actual industry volume, units	1,000	1,000	1,000	3,000
Actual sales (units)	100	200	150	450
Actual market share	10%	20%	15%	15%

C. Variance Due to Market Share

	Product			
	A	B	C	Total
(1) Actual sales (units)	100	200	150	450
(2) Budgeted shares at actual industry volume	120	200	60	380
(3) Difference (1 − 2)	(20)	—	90	70
(4) Budgeted unit contribution	$0.20	$0.90	$1.20	
(5) Variance due to market share (3 * 4)	(4.00)	—	108	$104

D. Variance Due to Industry Volume

	Product			
	A	B	C	Total
(1) Actual industry volume	1,000	1,000	1,000	3,000
(2) Budgeted industry volume	833	500	1,667	3,000
(3) Difference (1 − 2)	167	500	(667)	—
(4) Budgeted market share	12%	20%	6%	
(5) (3) * (4)	20	100	(40)	
(6) Unit contribution (budget)	$0.20	$0.90	$1.20	
(7) Total (5 * 6)	4.00	90.00	(48.00)	$46

EXHIBIT 10–10   Fixed-Cost Variances, January ($000s)

	Actual	Budget	Favorable/ (Unfavorable) Variances
Fixed overhead	$ 75	$ 75	$ —
Selling expense	55	50	(5)
Administrative expense	30	25	(5)
Total	$160	$150	$(10)

Market share variance = [(Actual sales) – (Industry volume) *
Budgeted market penetration] * Budgeted unit contribution

The market share variance is found for each product separately, and the total variance is the algebraic sum. The calculation is shown in Section C. It shows that $104,000 of the favorable mix and volume variance of $150,000 resulted from the fact that market penetration was better than budget. The remaining $46,000 resulted from the fact that actual industry dollar volume was higher than the amount assumed in the budget.

The $46,000 industry volume variance can also be calculated for each product as follows:

Industry volume variance = (Actual industry volume – Budgeted industry
volume) * Budgeted market penetration * Budgeted unit contribution

This calculation of variance due to industry volume is shown in Section D.

Expense Variances

Fixed Costs. Variances between actual and budgeted fixed costs are obtained simply by subtraction, since these costs are not affected by either the volume of sales or the volume of production. This is shown in Exhibit 10–10.

Variable Costs. Variable costs are costs that vary directly and proportionately with volume. The budgeted variable manufacturing costs must be adjusted to the actual volume of production. Assume that the January production was as follows: product A, 150,000 units; product B, 120,000 units; product C, 200,000 units. Assume also that the variable manufacturing costs incurred in January were as follows: material, $470,000; labor, $65,000; variable manufacturing overhead, $90,000. Exhibit 10–3 shows the standard unit variable costs.

The budgeted manufacturing expense is adjusted to the amount that should have been spent at the actual level of production by multiplying each element of standard cost for each product by the volume of production for that product. This calculation is shown in Exhibit 10–11.

EXHIBIT 10–11   Variable Manufacturing Expense Variances, January ($000s)

| | **Product** | | | | | *Favorable/ (Unfavorable)* |
	A	*B*	*C*	*Total*	*Actual*	*Variances*
Material	$ 75	$ 84	$300	$459	$470	$(11)
Labor	15	18	20	53	65	(12)
Overhead (variable)	30	30	40	100	90	10
Total	$120	$132	$360	$612	$625	$(13)

This exhibit shows that there was an unfavorable variance of $13,000 in January. This is called a *spending* variance because it results from spending $13,000 in excess of the adjusted budget. It consists of unfavorable material and labor variances of $11,000 and $12,000, respectively. These are partially offset by a favorable overhead spending variance of $10,000.

The volume that is used to adjust the budgeted variable manufacturing expenses is the *manufacturing* volume, not the *sales* volume, which was used in finding the revenue variances. In the simple example given here, we assumed that the two volumes were the same—namely, that the quantity of each product manufactured in January was the same as the quantity sold in January. If production volume differed from sales volume, the cost difference would show up in changes in inventory. Depending on the company's inventory costing method, this might or might not result in a production volume variance. Calculation of such a variance is explained in the next section.

In this example, we assumed that all the nonmanufacturing expenses were fixed. If some of them had variable components, the variances should be calculated in the same way as was used for the calculation of manufacturing cost variances.

Summary of Variances

There are several ways in which the variances can be summarized in a report for management. One possibility is shown in Exhibit 10–12. It was used primarily because the amounts can be traced easily to the earlier exhibits. Another form of presentation is to show the actual amounts, as well as the variances. This gives an indication of the relative importance of each variance as a fraction of the total revenue or expense item to which it relates.

Variations in Practice

The example given above, although complicated, is a relatively straightforward way of identifying the variances that caused actual profit in a business unit to be different from the budgeted profitability. Some variations from this approach are described in this section.

EXHIBIT 10–12   Summary Performance Report, January ($000s)

Actual profit (Exhibit 10–1)	$132
Budgeted profit (Exhibit 10–1)	80
Variance	$ 52
Analysis of Variance—Favorable/(Unfavorable)	
Revenue variances:	
Price (Exhibit 10–4)	$ (75)
Mix (Exhibit 10–6)	35
Volume (Exhibit 10–7)	115
Net revenue variances	$ 75
Variable-cost variances (Exhibit 10–11):	
Material	$ (11)
Labor	(12)
Variable overhead	10
Net variable-cost variances	$ (13)
Fixed-cost variances (Exhibit 10–10):	
Selling expense	$ (5)
Administrative expense	(5)
Net fixed-cost variances	$ (10)
Variance	$ 52

Time Period of the Comparison

The example compared January's budget with January's actuals. Some companies use performance for the year to date as the basis for comparison. To illustrate, for the period ended June 30, they would use budgeted and actual amounts for the six months ending on June 30, rather than the amounts for June. Other companies compare the budget for the whole year with the current estimate of actual performance for the year. The *actual* amounts for the report prepared as of June 30 would consist of actual numbers for the first six months plus the best current estimate of revenues and expenses for the second six months.

A comparison for the year to date is not as much influenced by temporary aberrations that may be peculiar to the current month and, therefore, that need not be of as much concern to management. On the other hand, it may mask the emergence of an important factor that is not temporary.

A comparison of the annual budget with current expectation of actual performance for the whole year shows how closely the business unit manager expects to meet the annual profit target. If performance for the year to date is worse than the budget for the year to date, it is possible that the deficit will be overcome in the remaining months. On the other hand, forces that caused actual performance to be below budget for the year to date may be expected to continue for the remainder of the year, which will make the final numbers significantly different from the budgeted amounts. Senior management needs a realistic estimate of the profit for the whole year, both because it may suggest the need to change the dividend policy, to obtain additional cash, or to change levels of discretionary spending, and also because a current estimate of the year's performance is often provided to financial analysts and other outside parties.

Obtaining a realistic estimate is difficult. Business unit managers tend to be optimistic about their ability to perform in the remaining months because, if they are pessimistic, this casts doubt on their ability to manage. To some extent, this tendency can be overcome by placing the burden of proof on business unit managers to show that the current trends in volume, margins, and costs are not going to continue. Nevertheless, an estimate of the whole year is *soft*, whereas actual performance is a matter of record. An alternative that lessens this problem is to report performance both for the year to date and for the year as a whole.

Focus on Gross Margin

In the example, we assumed that selling prices were budgeted to remain constant throughout the year. In many companies, changes in costs or other factors are expected to lead to changes in selling prices, and the task of the marketing manager is to obtain a budgeted gross margin—that is, a constant spread between costs and selling prices. Such a policy is especially important in periods of inflation. A variance analysis in such a system would not have a selling price variance. Instead, there would be a gross margin variance. *Unit gross margin is the difference between selling prices and manufacturing costs.*

The variance analysis is done by substituting "gross margin" for "selling price" in the revenue equations. Gross margin is the difference between actual selling prices and the *standard* manufacturing cost. The current standard manufacturing cost should take into account changes in manufacturing costs that are caused by changes in wage rates and in material prices (and, in some companies, significant changes in other input factors, such as electricity in aluminum manufacturing). The standard, rather than the actual, cost is used so that manufacturing inefficiencies do not affect the performance of the marketing organization.

Evaluation Standards

In management control systems, the formal standards used in the evaluation of reports on actual activities are of three types: (1) predetermined standards or budgets, (2) historical standards, or (3) external standards.

Predetermined Standards or Budgets.   If carefully prepared and coordinated, these are excellent standards. They are the basis against which actual performance is compared in many companies. If the budget numbers are collected in a haphazard manner, they obviously will not provide a reliable basis for comparison.

Historical Standards.   These are records of past actual performance. Results for the current month may be compared with the results for last month, or with results for the same month a year ago. This type of standard has two serious weaknesses: (1) conditions may have changed between the two periods in a way that invalidates the comparison, and (2) the prior period's performance may not have been acceptable. A supervisor whose spoilage cost is $500 a month, month after month, is consistent; but we do not know, without other evidence, whether the performance was consistently good or consistently poor. Despite these inherent weaknesses, historical standards are used in some companies, often because valid predetermined standards are not available.

External Standards.   These are standards derived from the performance of other responsibility centers or of other companies in the same industry. The performance of one branch sales office may be compared with the performance of other branch sales offices. If conditions in these responsibility centers are similar, such a comparison may provide an acceptable basis for evaluating performance.

Some companies identify the company that they believe to be the best managed in the industry and use numbers from that company—either with the cooperation of that company or from published material—as a basis of comparison. This process is called *benchmarking*.

Limitations on Standards.   A variance between actual and standard performance is meaningful only if it is derived from a valid standard. Although it is convenient to refer to *favorable* and *unfavorable* variances, these words imply that the standard is a reliable measure of what performance should have been. Even a standard cost may not be an accurate estimate of what costs should have been under the circumstances. This situation can arise for either or both of two reasons: (1) the standard was not set properly; or (2) although set properly in light of conditions existing at the time, changed conditions have made the standard obsolete. An essential first step in the analysis of a variance is an examination of the validity of the standard.

Full-Cost Systems

If the company has a full-cost system, both variable and fixed overhead costs are included in the inventory at the standard cost per unit. If the ending inventory is higher than the beginning inventory, some of the fixed overhead costs incurred in the period remain in inventory rather than flowing through to cost of sales. Conversely, if the inventory balance decreased during the period, more fixed overhead costs were released to cost of sales than the amount actually incurred in the period. Our example assumed that the inventory level did not change. Thus, the problem of treating the variance associated with fixed overhead costs did not arise.

If inventory levels change, and if actual production volume is different from budgeted sales volume, part of the production volume variance is included in inventory. Nevertheless, the full amount of the production volume variance should be calculated and reported. This variance is the difference between budgeted fixed production costs at the actual volume (as stated in the flexible budget) and standard fixed production costs at that volume.

If the company has a variable-cost system, fixed production costs are not included in inventory, so there is no production volume variance. The fixed production expense variance is simply the difference between the budgeted amount and the actual amount.

The important point is that production variances are associated with *production* volume, not sales volume.

Amount of Detail

In the example, we analyzed revenue variances at several levels: first, in total; then by volume, mix, and price; then by analyzing the volume and mix variance by industry volume and market share. At each of these levels, we analyzed the variances by individual products. The process of going from one level to another is often referred to as "peeling the onion"—that is, successive layers are peeled off, and the process continues as long as the additional detail is judged to be worthwhile. Some companies do not develop as many layers as shown in our example; others develop more. It is possible, and in some cases worthwhile, to develop additional sales and marketing variances, such as the following: by sales territories, and even by individual salesperson; by sales to individual countries or regions; by sales to key customers, principal types of customers, or customers in certain industries; by sales originating from direct mail, from customer calls, or from other sources. Additional detail for manufacturing costs can be developed by calculating variances for lower-level responsibility centers and by identifying variances with specific input factors, such as wage rates and material prices.

These layers correspond to the hierarchy of responsibility centers. Taking action based on the reported variances is not possible unless they can be associated with the managers responsible for them.

With modern information technology, about any level of detail can be supplied quickly and at reasonable cost. The problem is to decide how much is worthwhile. In part, the answer depends on the information requested by individual managers—some are numbers-oriented, others are not. In the ideal situation, the basic data exist to make any conceivable type of analysis, but only a small fraction of these data are reported routinely.

Engineered and Discretionary Costs

As we pointed out in Chapter 4, variances in engineered costs are viewed in a fundamentally different way from variances in discretionary costs.

A "favorable" variance in engineered costs is usually an indication of good performance; that is, the lower the cost the better the performance. This is subject to the qualification that quality and on-time delivery are judged to be satisfactory.

By contrast, the performance of a discretionary expense center is usually judged to be satisfactory if actual expenses are about equal to the budgeted amount, neither higher nor lower. This is because a favorable variance may indicate that the responsibility center did not perform adequately the functions that it had agreed to perform. Because some elements in a discretionary expense center are in fact engineered (e.g., the bookkeeping functions in the controller organization), a favorable variance is usually truly favorable for these elements.

Limitations of Variance Analysis

Although variance analysis is a powerful tool, it does have limitations. The most important limitation is that, although it identifies where a variance occurs, it does not tell *why* the variance occurred or what is being done about it. For example, the report may show there was a significant unfavorable variance in marketing expenses, and it may identify this variance with high sales promotion expenses. It does not, however, explain why the sales promotion expenses were high and what, if any, actions were being taken. A narrative explanation, accompanying the performance report, should provide such an explanation.

A second problem in variance analysis is to decide whether a variance is significant. Statistical techniques can be used to determine whether there is a significant difference between actual and standard performance for certain processes; these techniques are usually referred to as *statistical quality control*. However, they are applicable only when the process is repeated at frequent intervals, such as the operation of a machine tool on a production line. The literature contains a few articles suggesting that statistical quality control be used to determine whether a budget variance is significant; but this suggestion has little practical relevance at the business unit level because the necessary number of repetitive actions is not present. Conceptually, a variance should be investigated only when the benefit expected from correcting the problem exceeds the cost of the investigation; but a model based on this premise has so many uncertainties that it is only of academic interest. Managers, therefore, rely on judgment in deciding what variances are significant. Moreover, if a variance is significant but is uncontrollable (such as unexpected inflation), there may be no point in investigating it.

A third limitation of variance analysis is that, as the performance reports become more highly aggregated, offsetting variances might mislead the reader.

For example, a manager looking at business unit manufacturing cost performance might notice that it was on budget. However, this might have resulted from good performance at one plant being offset by poor performance at another. Similarly, when different product lines at different stages of development are combined, the combination may obscure the actual results of each product line.

Also, as variances become more highly aggregated, managers become more dependent on the accompanying explanations and forecasts. Plant managers know what is happening in their plant and can easily explain causes of variances. Business unit managers and everyone above them, however, usually must depend on the explanations that accompany the variance report of the plant.

Finally, the reports show only what has happened. They do not show the future effects of actions that the manager has taken. For example, reducing the amount spent for employee training increases current profitability, but it may have adverse consequences in the future. Also, the report shows only those events that are recorded in the accounts, and many important events are not reflected in current accounting transactions. The accounts don't show the state of morale, for instance.

Management Action

There is one cardinal principle in analyzing formal financial reports: *The monthly profit report should contain no major surprises.* Significant information should be communicated quickly by telephone, fax, electronic mail, or personal meetings as soon as it becomes known. The formal report confirms the general impression that the senior manager has learned from these sources. Based on this information, he or she may have acted prior to the receipt of the formal report.

The formal report is nevertheless important. *One of the most important benefits of formal reporting is that it provides the desirable pressure on subordinate managers to take corrective actions on their own initiative.* Further, the information from informal sources may be incomplete or misunderstood; the numbers in the formal report provide more accurate information, and the report may confirm or cast doubts on the information received from informal sources. Also, the formal report provides a basis for analysis because information from the informal sources often is general and imprecise.

Usually, there is a discussion between the business unit manager and his or her superior, in which the business unit manager explains the reasons for significant variances, the action being taken to correct unfavorable situations, and the expected timing of each corrective action. These explanations are necessarily subjective, and they may be biased. Operating managers, like most people, don't like to admit that unfavorable variances were caused by their errors. A senior manager has an opinion, based on experience, as to the likelihood that a business unit manager will be frank and forthcoming, and he or she judges the report accordingly.

Profit reports are worthless unless they lead to action. The action may consist of praise for a job well done, suggestions for doing things differently, "chewing out," or more drastic personnel actions. However, these actions are by no means taken for every business unit every month. As long as business is going well, praise is the most that may be necessary, and most people don't even expect praise routinely.

Behavioral Considerations in Performance Evaluation

Most companies use similar techniques for preparing and reviewing the profit budget and in the subsequent reporting against the approved budget; that is to say, the *technical aspects* of the budgeting system—the forms used to prepare the budget, the format in which actual performance is compared with the budget, frequency of performance reports, and the like—are similar in many companies. However, companies differ widely in the way they *use* the information generated by the budgeting system. Profit budget systems differ widely in the way they are administered, particularly in the degree to which the profit budget is used to monitor business unit activity.

Individual managers have quite different approaches to the exercise of control. If senior management frequently monitors the activities of business units, we say it is exercising "tight control." On the other hand, if senior management does only limited monitoring of the business unit's activity during the year, we say it is exercising "loose control." The distinction between tight control and loose control refers to the extent of monitoring, not to the degree of delegation. Although tight control is often accompanied by more limited delegation than loose control, this is not always the case.

Tight Control

Tight control is based on the management philosophy that subordinate managers work most effectively when they are required to meet specific short-term goals, typically one-year goals, and that senior management can assist subordinates in solving many day-to-day problems. Put another way, subordinates make better day-to-day decisions if senior management participates in the decision-making process.

Under tight control, the profit goal of a business unit manager is considered to be a firm commitment against which he or she will be measured and, to a considerable extent, evaluated. Each month, performance to date is compared with the expected performance, detailed variances are identified and discussed, and courses of corrective action are considered if it appears that the budgeted objectives are not being met. Thus, a tight control system is one in which a manager's performance is evaluated primarily on his or her ability to attain budgetary objectives during each reporting period.

Examples. Interpublic, a successful multinational advertising agency, used tight financial controls over its business units while giving them considerable autonomy. Interpublic owns McCann-Erickson, Lintas, Dailey & Associates and the Lowe Group. Essentially, the parent monitored the financial numbers and let the agencies do what they would so long as they attained the desired numbers. Each of these four agencies was allowed to compete with the others for new clients. For instance, McCann-Erickson won the $30 million Goodyear account in 1992 in a race that included Lintas. While each agency had autonomy, all had to toe the line financially.[1]

T. J. Rodgers, chief executive of Cypress Semiconductor Corporation, used tight controls over the various company functions that were set up as profit centers. The company had revenues of $300 million in 1992. Rodgers designed software programs to help manage everything from sniffing out minor production glitches to keeping people within deadlines. Every Wednesday, he combed through a dozen printouts on the status of his pet projects, noting the names of managers whose goals were more than five weeks overdue. The offending manager was likely to get a handwritten memo from Rodgers.[2]

Loose Control

Loose control is based on the management philosophy that is illustrated by the statement: "I hire good people, and I leave them alone to do their jobs." Under loose control, the budget is used essentially as a communication and a planning tool. Annually, budgets are prepared, reviewed by senior management, adjusted where management deems appropriate, and approved. Monthly, or quarterly, actual results are compared to the budget, and differences are analyzed and explained. The budget is not considered a management commitment, however. Rather, it is assumed to be the manager's best estimate of profitability as of the time that it was prepared. Subsequently, as conditions change, these are communicated to senior management in the form of revised estimates, which are compared to the original budget and differences explained. The fact that the original objective has not been met does not necessarily indicate poor performance. Further, the causes of variances, the corrective actions being taken, and the timing of these actions are not reviewed in detail during the year by senior management, unless something is clearly amiss.

In recent years, the tendency in the literature has been in the direction of endorsing loose control. Delegating increasing responsibility and authority to lower levels in the organization is called *empowerment*.

Example. Enron, a pipeline and power company, used a loose control structure that empowered its employees to make large decisions without upper-management approval. Traders at Enron Capital, Enron's trading division, structured deals valued at up to $5 million without upper-management approval.[3]

---

[1]"Sibling Rivalry," *Forbes,* February 15, 1993, pp. 119–20.

[2]"The Bad Boy of Silicon Valley," *Business Week,* December 9, 1991, pp. 64–70; "Tough New CEOs," *Fortune,* October 18, 1993, p. 44.

[3]Harry Hurt III, "Power Plays," *Fortune,* August 5, 1996, pp. 94–97.

Behavioral Effects of Tight and Loose Controls

It is useful to place the management control system of a company at some point along a continuum between entirely tight control and entirely loose control. *A company's position on this tight/loose continuum depends on the amount of emphasis senior management places on meeting or exceeding budgetary objectives in the short run.*

A tight control system has two important benefits over a loose control system. First, tight control tends to prevent managers from becoming wasteful or inefficient. It motivates managers to be profit-conscious. Second, consistent pressure motivates the manager to search for better ways to perform existing operations and to initiate new activities to meet the profit budget.

Tight controls, however, can produce several dysfunctional effects.[4] First, short-term actions that are not in the long-term interests of the company may be encouraged. The more pressure that is applied to meet current profit levels, the more likely the business unit manager will take short-term actions that may well be wrong in the long run. If, in addition to tight controls, the manager is given considerable discretion, there is the danger of encouraging uneconomic short-term actions. To illustrate, the manager may deliver inferior-quality products to customers to meet the sales targets, and this will adversely affect customer goodwill and future sales. These are errors of *commission*.

> **Example.** Some divisional presidents in Bausch & Lomb, under pressure to meet bottomline results, began using tactics that were costly for the company in the long term but which maximized their short-term bonuses. One favorite was extending unusually long credit terms to customers in exchange for big orders.[5]

Second, to obtain short-term profits, business unit managers might not undertake useful long-term actions. For instance, managers might be motivated not to undertake investments that promise benefits in the long term but that hurt short-term financial results. A common example is investing inadequate dollars in research and development because such investments must be expensed in the year in which they are incurred, but their benefits will show up only in the future. Also, managers might not propose risky investments—investments where there is a great deal of uncertainty about future cash flows—because cash flow uncertainty translates into a greater probability that budgets will not be met. In other words, managers might propose "safe" investments (which are quite likely to produce adequate future cash flows) as opposed to high-risk projects, even though the high-risk projects may produce high returns. These are errors of *omission*.

---

[4]Curran, "Companies That Rob the Future," *Fortune,* July 4, 1988, pp. 84–89; "More Than Ever, It's Management for the Short-Term," *Business Week,* November 24, 1986, pp. 92–93; P. Wang, "Claiming Tomorrow's Profits Today," *Forbes,* October 17, 1988, p. 78.

[5]Joyce Barnathan, "Blind Ambition," *Business Week,* October 23, 1995, pp. 78–92.

Third, the use of budgeted profit as the sole objective can distort communication between a business unit manager and senior management. If business unit managers are evaluated based on their profit budget, they may try to set profit targets that are easily met. This leads to erroneous planning data for the whole company because the budgeted profit may be lower than the amount that could really be achieved. Also, business unit managers may be reluctant to admit, during the year, that they are likely to miss their profit budget until it is evident that they cannot possibly attain it. This would delay corrective action.

Fourth, tight financial control may motivate managers to engage in data manipulation. This can take several forms. At one level, managers may choose accounting methods that borrow from future earnings to meet current period targets (examples: inadequate provision for bad debts, inventory shrinkage, warranty claims, and so on). At another level, managers may falsify data (i.e., deliberately provide inaccurate information).

> **Examples.** Such companies as Chrysler, Firestone, Heinz, and Union Carbide have been found to use "liberal" accounting policies to boost earnings: one primary factor for their actions being their incentive plans.[6]
>
> An example of data manipulation occurred in the Grocery Products Division of McCormick & Company. Employees improperly postponed recording payments as expenses, front-loaded revenues, distorted invoices, and engaged in other activities to meet profit targets.[7]
>
> Tight financial controls led to data manipulation at Bausch & Lomb, according to *Business Week*: "Under pressure to beat sales targets in 1993, contact lens managers shipped products that doctors never ordered and forced distributors to take up two years of unwanted inventories . . . , while assuring many [distributors] they wouldn't have to pay until they sold the lenses."[8]

In an empirical study, Hopwood found that tight controls led to: (*a*) greater job-related tension, (*b*) poor relations with superiors, (*c*) poor relations with peers, and (*d*) extensive manipulation of the accounting reports.[9] Hopwood also found the opposite effects under loose controls. However, Otley's subsequent empirical examination of the impact of the tightness of control on organizational performance was inconsistent with Hopwood's findings.[10] In his sample, Otley found that greater emphasis on meeting the budget did not lead to high levels of job-related tension. More important, tight control was associated with

---

[6]George Getschow, "Slick Accounting Ploys Help Many Companies Improve Their Income," *The Wall Street Journal,* May 27, 1982, p. 1.

[7]Betsy Morris, "McCormick & Co. Division Is Found to Use Dubious Accounting Methods to Boost Net," *The Wall Street Journal,* June 1, 1982, p. 10.

[8]Joyce Barnathan, "Blind Ambition," *Business Week,* October 23, 1995, pp. 78–92.

[9]A. Hopwood, "An Empirical Study of the Role of Accounting Data in Performance Evaluation," *Journal of Accounting Research,* 10 (1972), pp. 156–82.

[10]D. T. Otley, "Budget Use and Managerial Performance," *Journal of Accounting Research,* Spring 1978, pp. 122–49.

higher performance, a result that is opposite to that of Hopwood's. These conflicting findings suggest that the effectiveness of tight controls is dependent upon situational factors. In the next section, we discuss the situations where a tight control might be appropriate.

Factors Affecting the Choice of Tight versus Loose Controls

The ability of a business unit to set equitable profit goals and to perform so as to attain these goals depends on four factors:

1. The amount of discretion that the business unit manager can exercise.
2. The degree to which the critical performance variables can be influenced by the business unit manager.
3. The relative uncertainty inherent in the operation.
4. The time span of the impact of the manager's decision.

Amount of Discretion.   The amount of discretion that a manager can exercise depends on the nature of the job and the degree of delegation. The more complex the job, the greater the discretion required to manage it effectively. The greater the amount of delegation, the greater the discretion that the business unit manager can exercise.

If managers have much discretion, setting precise objectives is difficult. They have many alternative courses of action, and one cannot determine ahead of time which particular actions are best and what the financial impact of these actions will be. Conversely, if a plant manager has relatively little discretion in deciding what will be produced, how it will be produced, and how much the labor force will be paid, arriving at a reasonable financial objective may be a relatively simple task. By contrast, a business unit manager who is responsible for product development, marketing, production, procurement, and development of personnel has a much larger number of variables to control; the optimal financial objective, therefore, is much less certain.

Degree of Influence.   The greater the influence that a manager can exercise over critical performance variables, the easier it is to develop an effective management control system. The difficulty in measuring a manager's performance is directly related to the number and type of noncontrollable or semicontrollable performance variables that exist. In general, external marketing variables are much more difficult to influence than internal production variables, because a marketing manager has very little control over the actions of competitors or the general state of the economy. Thus, it is much easier to set a profit objective and to judge performance against this objective for a business unit in which sales are limited by production capacity (i.e., everything that can be produced can be sold) than for a business unit that sells in a highly competitive or volatile market and has ample production capacity.

Relative Uncertainty. A business unit manager may face uncertainties both in the external environment and in the internal environment. The external environment consists of four major sectors: (1) customers, (2) suppliers, (3) competitors, and (4) regulators. The internal environment consists of factors inside the firm (e.g., degree of interdependence with other business units). By uncertainty, we mean the unpredictability in the actions of both the external agencies and the internal forces. The greater the uncertainty, the more difficult it is to use the profit budget as a basis for performance appraisal.[11]

There are several reasons for this. First, performance evaluation presupposes establishment of accurate profit targets. To arrive at targets that can serve as valid standards for subsequent performance appraisal, one must be able to predict the conditions that will exist during the coming year. If these predictions are incorrect, the profit objective will also be incorrect. Obviously, these conditions can be predicted more accurately under stable conditions than under changing conditions. The basic effect of uncertainty is to limit the ability of managers to plan or make decisions about activities in advance of their occurrence. Thus, the greater the uncertainty, the more difficult it is to prepare satisfactory targets that could then become the basis for performance evaluation.

Second, because efficiency refers to the amount of output per unit of input, an evaluation of a manager's efficiency depends on a detailed knowledge of the outcomes associated with given management actions—that is, knowledge about cause/effect relationships. Better knowledge about cause/effect relationships exists under stable conditions than under uncertain conditions. Therefore, judgments about efficiency are more difficult under uncertain conditions.

Third, the emphasis of financial performance indicators is on outcomes rather than on processes. Managers control their own actions, but they cannot control the states of nature that combine with their actions to produce outcomes. In a situation with high uncertainty, therefore, financial information does not adequately reflect managerial performance.

Time Span. If a management control system is to provide an adequate basis for judging performance, the comparison of actual with budgeted amounts must measure the actual accomplishments of the manager during the period under review. This is unlikely to happen if the decisions that a manager makes today are not reflected in profitability until some future period, or, conversely, if current profitability reflects the impact of decisions made in some past period. The more these two conditions are present, the less desirable it is to use the budget as a tool to evaluate business unit managers.

---

[11]See V. Govindarajan, "Appropriateness of Accounting Data in Performance Evaluation: An Empirical Evaluation of Environmental Uncertainty as an Intervening Variable," *Accounting, Organizations and Society,* IX, no. 2 (1984), pp. 125–35.

Summary

Business unit managers report their financial performance to senior management regularly, usually monthly. The formal report consists of a comparison of actual revenues and costs with budgeted amounts. The differences, or variances, between these two amounts can be analyzed at several levels of detail. This analysis identifies the causes of the variance from budgeted profit and the amount attributable to each cause.

Companies differ in the emphasis they place on meeting budgetary objectives in the short run. The appropriateness of tight financial controls depends upon situational factors.

Suggested Additional Readings

Brownell, Peter, and Mark Hirst. "Reliance on Accounting Information, Budgetary Participation, and Task Uncertainty: Tests of a Three-Way Interaction." *Journal of Accounting Research,* XXIV, no. 2 (Autumn, 1986), pp. 241–49.

Brownell, Peter, and Morris McInnes. "Budgetary Participation, Motivation, and Management Performance." *The Accounting Review,* October 1986, pp. 587–600.

Chenhall, R. H., and D. Morris. "The Impact of Structure, Environment, and Interdependence on the Perceived Usefulness of Management Accounting Systems." *The Accounting Review,* LXI, no. I (January 1986), pp. 16–35.

Dearden, John. "Measuring Profit Center Managers." *Harvard Business Review,* September–October 1987, pp. 84–86.

Dunk, Alan S. "Reliance on Budgetary Control for Manufacturing Process Automation and Production Subunit Performance." *Accounting, Organizations and Society,* XVII, 4 (April–May 1992), pp. 195–204.

Govindarajan, Vijay. "Appropriateness of Accounting Data in Performance Evaluation: An Empirical Examination of Environment Uncertainty as an Intervening Variable." *Accounting, Organizations and Society,* IX, no. 2 (1984), pp. 125–35.

———, and John K. Shank. "Profit Variance Analysis: A Strategic Focus." *Issues in Accounting Education* 4, no. 2 (Fall 1989), pp. 396–410.

Institute of Management Accountants. "Fundamentals of Reporting Information to Managers." *Statement on Management Accounting,* Supplement 5–6. Montvale, N.J., 1992.

Merchant, Kenneth A. *Control in Business Organizations.* Marshfield, Mass.: Putnam, 1985.

Shillinglaw, Gordon. *Managerial Cost Accounting.* 5th ed. Homewood, Ill.: Richard D. Irwin, 1982, Chap. 27.

Umpathy, Srinivasan. *Current Budgeting Practices in U.S. Industry: The State of the Art.* Westport, Conn.: Quorum, 1987.

CASE 10–1
VARIANCE ANALYSIS PROBLEMS

I. In this case you are asked to analyze the February and March financial performance of the Temple Division of the ABC Company as compared with its budget, which is shown in Exhibit 10–3 of the text.

Part A—February 1988

Below are the data describing the actual financial results of the Temple Division for the month of February 1988.

Sales	$781
Variable cost of sales	552
Contribution	229
Fixed manufacturing costs	80
Gross profit	149
Selling expense	57
Administrative expense	33
Net profit	$ 59

Sales

Product	Unit Sales	Price	Dollar Sales
A	120	$0.95	$114
B	130	1.90	247
C	150	2.80	420
Total	400		781

Production

		Manufacturing Cost			
Product	Units Produced	Material	Labor	Variable Overhead	Total
A	150	$ 80	$20	$ 40	$140
B	130	91	21	35	147
C	120	190	15	30	235
Total	400	361	56	105	522

This case was prepared by John Dearden. Copyright Osceola Institute.

Questions

1. Prepare an analysis of variance from profit budget assuming that the Temple Division employed a variable standard cost accounting system.
2. Prepare an analysis of variance from profit budget assuming that the Temple Division used a full standard cost accounting system. Under this assumption, the actual cost of sales amount would be $632,000. (Can you derive this figure?)
3. Industry volume figures are presented below. Separate the mix and volume variance into the variance resulting from differences in market penetration and variance resulting from differences in industry volume. Make the calculation for the variable cost system only.

Industry volume, February 1988:

	Units (000)
Product A	600
Product B	650
Product C	1,500

Part B—March 1988

Below are the data describing the actual financial results for the Temple Division for the month of March 1988.

Income Statement	
Sales	$498
Variable cost of sales	278
Contribution	220
Fixed manufacturing costs	70
Gross profit	150
Selling expense	45
Administrative expense	20
Net profit	$ 85

Sales

Product	Unit Sales	Price	Dollar Sales
A	90	$1.10	$ 99
B	70	2.10	147
C	80	3.15	252
Total	240		498

Production

Manufacturing costs

Product	Units Produced	Material	Labor	Variable Overhead	Total
A	90	$ 40	$ 8	$17	$ 65
B	80	55	10	18	83
C	100	150	8	19	177
Total	270	245	26	54	325

Question

Answer the same questions included in Part A. The actual cost of sales using full standard costing would be $340,500 in March. Industry volume for March was:

	Units (000)
Product A	500
Product B	600
Product C	1,000

II. The profit budget for the Crocker Company for January 1988 was as follows:

		($000)
Sales		$2,500
Standard cost of sales		1,620
Gross profit		880
Selling expense	$250	
Research and development expense	300	
Administrative expense	120	
Total expense		670
Net profit before taxes		$ 210

The product information used in developing the budget was as follows:

	E	F	G	H
Sales—units (000)	1,000	2,000	3,000	4,000
Price per unit	$0.15	$0.20	$0.25	$0.30
Standard cost per unit:				
Material	0.04	0.05	0.06	0.08
Direct labor	0.02	0.02	0.03	0.04
Variable overhead	0.02	0.03	0.03	0.05
Total variable cost	0.08	0.10	0.12	0.17
Fixed overhead ($000)	20	60	60	160
Total standard cost per unit	0.10	0.13	0.14	0.21

The actual revenues and costs for January 1988 were as follows:

	($000)
Sales	$2,160
Standard cost of sales	1,420
Net standard cost of variances	160
Actual cost of sales	1,580
Gross profit	580
Selling expense	$290
Research and development expense	250
Administrative expenses	110
Total expense	650
Net loss	$ (70)

Operating statistics for January 1988 were as follows:

	E	F	G	H
Sales (units)	1,000	1,000	4,000	3,000
Sales price	$0.13	$0.22	$0.22	$0.31
Production	1,000	1,000	2,000	2,000
Actual manufacturing costs (000):				
Material	$360			
Labor	200			
Overhead	530			

Question

Prepare an analysis of variance between actual profits and budgeted profits for January 1988.

CASE 10–2
SOLARTRONICS, INC.

John Holden, president and general manager of Solartronics, Inc., was confused. Lisa Blocker, the firm's recently hired controller and financial manager, had recently instituted the preparation of a new, summarized income statement. This statement was to be issued on a monthly basis. Mr. Holden had just received a copy of the statement for January 1984 (see Exhibit 1).

Solartronics, Inc., a small, Texas-based manufacturer of solar energy panels, had been in business since mid 1977. By the end of 1983, it had survived some bad years and positioned itself as a reasonably good-sized firm within the industry. As part of a conscious effort to "professionalize" the firm, Mr. Holden had added Ms. Blocker to the staff in the autumn of 1983. Previous to that

time, Solartronics had employed the services of a full time, full charge bookkeeper.

Mr. Holden's confusion arose from the fact that he had not expected the firm to report a loss for the month of January. While he knew that sales had been down, primarily due to the normal seasonal downturn, and that production had been scaled back to help reduce the level of inventory, he was still surprised. He wondered if this first month's results were a bad omen in terms of the likelihood of meeting the budgeted results for the year (see Exhibit 2). Even though the 1984 budget represented only a 10 percent increase in sales volume over 1983, he was concerned that such a poor start to the year might make it difficult to get "back on stream."

EXHIBIT 1

SOLARTRONICS, INC. (B)
Summarized Income Statement
January 1984

Sales			$165,000
Less: Cost of goods sold (at standard)			108,900
Gross margin			$ 56,100
Less: Selling expenses		$26,500	
General corporate overhead		18,000	
Operating variances:			
Direct labor	$ (3,500)		
Direct material	500		
Variable factory overhead	(1,500)		
Fixed factory overhead—spending	2,000		
Fixed factory overhead—volume	(17,500)	20,000	64,500
Profit before tax			$ (8,400)

This case was written by Professor M. Edgar Barrett. Copyright © by M. Edgar Barrett.

EXHIBIT 2

SOLARTRONICS, INC. (B)
Budgeted Income Statement
Calendar Year 1984

Sales.		$3,000,000[3]
Less: Cost of goods sold (at standard)[1]		1,980,000
Gross margin		$1,020,000
Less: Selling expenses[2]	$420,000	
General corporate overhead	240,000	660,000
Profit before tax		$ 360,000

Notes

[1]The standard cost of goods sold consisted of: $420,000 direct labor; $780,000 direct material; $360,000 variable factory overhead; and $420,000 fixed factory overhead. Ms. Blocker treated direct labor and direct materials as variable costs.

[2]Of this amount, $120,000 was considered to be fixed. The remaining $300,000 represented the 10 percent commission paid on sales.

[3]The expected sales volume for the year was 5,000 equivalent units. An "equivalent unit" represented the most popular model sold by Solartronics.

Questions

1. Why are the reported results for January so poor, particularly in light of the expected, average monthly profit of $30,000?

2. What additional data would be useful in analyzing the firm's January performance? Why?

CASE 10–3
GALVOR COMPANY

When M. Barsac replaced M. Chambertin as Galvor's controller in April of 1974, at the age of 31, he became the first of a new group of senior managers resulting from the acquisition by Universal Electric. It was an accepted fact that, in the large and sprawling Universal organization, the controller's department represented a key function. M. Barsac, who was a skilled accountant, had had 10 years' experience in a large French subsidiary of Universal.

He recalled his early days with Galvor vividly and admitted they were, to say the least, hectic.

> I arrived at Galvor in early April 1974, a few days after M. Chambertin had left. I was the first Universal man here in Bordeaux and I became quickly immersed in all the problems surrounding the change of ownership. For example, there were no really workable financial statements for the previous two years. This made preparation of the Business Plan, which Mr. Hennessy and I began in June, extremely difficult. This plan covers every aspect of the business, but the great secrecy which had always been maintained at Galvor about the company's financial affairs made it almost impossible for anyone to help us.

M. Barsac's duties could be roughly divided into two major areas: first, the preparation of numerous reports required by Universal, and, second, supervision of Galvor's internal accounting function. While these two areas were closely related, it is useful to separate them in describing the accounting and control function as it developed after Universal's acquisition of Galvor.

To control its operating units, Universal relied primarily on an extensive system of financial reporting. Universal attributed much of its success in recent years to this system. The system was viewed by Universal's European controller, M. Boudry, as much more than a device to "check up" on the operating units.

> In addition to measuring our progress in the conventional sense of sales, earnings, and return on investment, we believe the reporting system causes our operating people

to focus their attention on critical areas which might not otherwise receive their major attention. An example would be the level of investment in inventory. The system also forces people to think about the future and to commit themselves to specific future goals. Most operating people are understandably involved in today's problems. We believe some device is required to force them to look beyond the problems at hand and to consider longer-range objectives and strategy. You could say we view the reporting system as an effective training and educational device.

Background

The Galvor Company had been founded in 1946 by M. Georges Latour, who continued as its owner and president until 1974. Throughout its history, the company had acted as a fabricator, buying parts and assembling them into high-quality, moderate-cost electric and electronic measuring and test equipment. In its own sector of the electronics industry—measuring instruments—Galvor was one of the major French firms; however, there were many electronics firms in the more sophisticated sectors of the industry that were vastly larger than Galvor.

Galvor's period of greatest growth began around 1960. Between 1960 and 1971, sales grew from 2.2 million 1971 new francs to 12 million, and after-tax profits from 120,000 1971 new francs to 1,062,000. Assets as of December 31, 1971, totaled 8.8 million new francs. (One 1971 new franc = $0.20.) The firm's prosperity resulted in a number of offers to purchase equity in the firm, but M. Latour had remained steadfast in his belief that only if he had complete ownership of Galvor could he direct its affairs with a free hand. As owner/president, Latour had continued over the years to be personally involved in every detail

---

This case is copyrighted by International Institute for Management Development (IMD), Lausanne, Switzerland.

of the firm's operations, including signing of all of the company's important checks.

As of early 1972, M. Latour was concerned about the development of adequate successor management for Galvor. In January 1972 Latour hired a "technical director" as his special assistant, but this person resigned in November 1972. Following the 1973 unionization of Galvor's work force, which Latour had opposed, Latour (then 54 years old) began to entertain seriously the idea of selling the firm and devoting himself "to family, philanthropic, and general social interests." On April 1, 1974, Galvor was sold to Universal Electric Company for $4.5 million worth of UE's stock. M. Latour became chairman of the board of Galvor, and David Hennessy was appointed as Galvor's managing director. Hennessy at that time was 38 years old and had been with Universal Electric for nine years.

The Business Plan

The heart of Universal's reporting and control system was an extremely comprehensive document—the Business Plan—which was prepared annually by each of the operating units. The Business Plan was the primary standard for evaluating the performance of unit managers, and everything possible was done by Universal's top management to give authority to the plan.

Each January, the Geneva headquarters of Universal set tentative objectives for the following two years for each of its European operating units. This was a "first look"—an attempt to provide a broad statement of objectives that would permit the operating units to develop their detailed Business Plans. For operating units that produced more than a single product line, objectives were established for both the unit as a whole and for each product line. Primary responsibility for establishing these tentative objectives rested with eight product-line managers located in Geneva, each of whom was responsible for a group of product lines. On the basis of his knowledge of the product lines and his best judgment of their market potential, each product-line manager set the tentative objectives for his lines.

For reporting purposes, Universal considered that Galvor represented a single product line, even though Galvor's own executives viewed the company's products as falling into three distinct lines—multimeters, panel meters, and electronic instruments.

For each of over 300 Universal product lines in Europe, objectives were established for five key measures.

1. Sales.
2. Net income.
3. Total assets.
4. Total employees.
5. Capital expenditures.

From January to April, these tentative objectives were "negotiated" between Geneva headquarters and the operating managements. Formal meetings were held in Geneva to resolve differences between the operating unit managers and product-line managers or other headquarters personnel.

Negotiations also took place at the same time on products to be discontinued. Mr. Hennessy described this process as a "sophisticated exercise which includes a careful analysis of the effect on overhead costs of discontinuing a product and also recognizes the cost of holding an item in stock. It is a good analysis and one method Universal uses to keep the squeeze on us."

During May, the negotiated objectives were reviewed and approved by Universal's European headquarters in Geneva and by corporate headquarters in the United States. These final reviews focused primarily on the five key measures noted above. In 1976, the objectives for total capital expenditures and for the total number of employees received particularly close surveillance. The approved objectives provided the foundation for preparation of Business Plans.

In June and July, Galvor prepared its Business Plan. The plan, containing up to 100 pages, described in detail how Galvor intended to achieve its objectives for the following two years. The plan also contained a forecast, in less detail, for the fifth year hence (e.g., for 1981 in the case of the plan prepared in 1976).

Summary Reports

The broad scope of the Business Plan can best be understood by a description of the type of information it contained. It began with a brief one-page financial and operating summary containing comparative data for:

> Preceding year (actual data).
> Current year (budget).
> Next year (forecast).
> Two years hence (forecast).
> Five years hence (forecast).

This one-page summary contained condensed data dealing with the following measures for each of the five years:

> Net income.
> Sales.
> Total assets.
> Total capital employed (sum of long-term debt and net worth).
> Receivables.
> Inventories.
> Plant, property, and equipment.
> Capital expenditures.
> Provision for depreciation.
> Percent return on sales.
> Percent return on total assets.
> Percent return on total capital employed.
> Percent total assets to sales.
> Percent receivables to sales.
> Percent inventories to sales.
> Orders received.
> Orders on hand.
> Average number of full-time employees.
> Total cost of employee compensation.

> Sales per employee.
> Net income per employee.
> Sales per $1,000 of employee compensation.
> Net income per $1,000 of employee compensation.
> Sales per thousand square feet of floor space.
> Net income per thousand square feet of floor space.

Anticipated changes in net income for the current year and for each of the next two years were summarized according to their cause, as follows:

> Volume of sales.
> Product mix.
> Sales prices.
> Raw material purchase prices.
> Cost reduction programs.
> Accounting changes and all other causes.

This analysis of the causes of changes in net income forced operating managements to appraise carefully the profit implications of all management actions affecting prices, costs, volume, or product mix.

Financial Statements

These condensed summary reports were followed by a complete set of projected financial statements—income statement, balance sheet, and a statement of cash flow—for the current year and for each of the next two years. Each major item on these financial statements was then analyzed in detail in separate reports, which covered such matters as transactions with headquarters, proposed outside financing, investment in receivables and inventory, number of employees and employee compensation, capital expenditures, and nonrecurring write-offs of assets.

Management Actions

The Business Plan contained a description of the major management actions planned for the next two years, with an estimate of the favorable or

unfavorable effect each action would have on total sales, net income, and total assets. Among
some of the major management actions described in Galvor's 1976 Business Plan (prepared in mid-1975) were the following:

Implement standard cost system.

Revise prices.

Cut oldest low-margin items from line.

Standardize and simplify product design.

Create forward research and development
plan.

Implement product planning.

Separate plans were presented for each of
the functional areas—marketing, manufacturing, research and development, financial control,
and personnel and employee relations. These
functional plans began with a statement of the
function's mission, an analysis of its present
problems and opportunities, and a statement of
the specific actions it intended to take in the next
two years. Among the objectives set for the control area in the 1976 Business Plan, M. Barsac
stated that he hoped to:

Better distribute tasks.

Make more intensive use of IBM equipment.

Replace nonqualified employees with better-
trained and more dynamic people.

The Business Plan closed with a series of comparative financial statements which depicted the
estimated item-by-item effect if sales fell to 60
percent or to 80 percent of forecast or increased to
120 percent of forecast. For each of these levels of
possible sales, costs were divided into three categories: fixed costs, unavoidable variable costs, and
management discretionary costs. Management
described the specific actions it would take to control employment, total assets, and capital expenditures in case of a reduction in sales, and when
these actions would be put into effect. In its 1976
Business Plan, Galvor indicated that its program
for contraction would be put into effect if incoming

orders dropped below 60 percent of budget for two
weeks, 75 percent for four weeks, or 85 percent for
eight weeks. It noted that assets would be cut only
80 percent in a 60 percent year and to 90 percent
in an 80 percent year, "because remodernization of
our business is too essential for survival to slow
down much more."

Approval of Plan

By midsummer, the completed Business Plan was
submitted to Universal headquarters; and beginning in the early fall, meetings were held in Geneva to review each company's Business Plan.
Each plan had to be justified and defended at
these meetings, which were attended by senior
executives from both Universal's European and
American headquarters and by the general managers and functional managers of many of the operating units. Universal viewed these meetings
as an important element in its constant effort to
encourage operating managements to share their
experiences in resolving common problems.

Before final approval of a company's Business
Plan at the Geneva review meeting, changes were
often proposed by Universal's top management.
For example, in September 1976, the 1977 forecasts of sales and net income in Galvor's Business
Plan were accepted; but the year-end forecasts of
total employees and total assets were reduced
about 9 percent and 1 percent, respectively.
Galvor's proposed capital expenditures for the
year were cut 34 percent, a reduction primarily
attributable to limitations imposed by Universal
on all operating units throughout the corporation.

The approved Business Plan became the foundation of the budget for the following year, which
was due in Geneva by mid-November. The general
design of the budget resembled that of the Business Plan, except that the various dollar amounts,
which were presented in the Business Plan on an
annual basis, were broken down by months. Minor changes between the overall key results forecast in the Business Plan and those reflected in
greater detail in the budget were not permitted.

Requests for major changes had to be submitted to Geneva no later than mid-October.

Reporting to Universal

Every Universal unit in Europe had to submit periodic reports to Geneva according to a fixed schedule of dates. All units in Universal, whether based in the United States or elsewhere, adhered to essentially the same reporting system. Identical forms and account numbers were used throughout the Universal organization. Since the reporting system made no distinction between units of different size, Galvor submitted the same reports as a unit with many times its sales. Computer processing of these reports facilitated combining the results of Universal's European operations for prompt review in Geneva and transmission to corporate headquarters in the United States.

The main focus in most of the reports submitted to Universal was on the variance between actual results and budgeted results. Sales and expense data were presented for both the latest month and for the year to date. Differences between the current year and the prior year also were reported, because these were the figures submitted quarterly to Universal's shareholders and to newspapers and other financial reporting services.

Description of Reports

Thirteen different reports were submitted by the controller on a monthly basis, ranging from a statement of preliminary net income, which was due during the first week following the close of each month, to a report on the status of capital projects due on the last day of each month. The monthly reports included:

Statement of preliminary net income.
Statement of income.
Balance sheet.
Statement of changes in retained earnings.
Statement of cash flow.
Employment statistics.

Status of orders received, canceled, and outstanding.
Statement of intercompany transactions.
Statement of transactions with headquarters.
Analysis of inventories.
Analysis of receivables.
Status of capital projects.
Controller's monthly operating and financial review.

The final item, the controller's monthly operating and financial review, often ran to 20 pages or more. It contained an explanation of the significant variances from budget, as well as a general commentary on the financial affairs of the unit.

In addition to the reports submitted on a monthly basis, approximately 12 other reports were required less often, either quarterly, semiannually, or annually.

Cost of the System

The control and reporting system, including preparation of the annual Business Plan, imposed a heavy burden in both time and money on the management of an operating unit. M. Barsac commented on this aspect of the system in the section of Galvor's 1976 Business Plan dealing with the control functional area.

Galvor's previous administrative manager [controller], who was a tax specialist above all, had to prepare a balance sheet and statement of income once a year. Cost accounting, perpetual inventory valuation, inventory control, production control, customer accounts receivable control, budgeting, et cetera did not exist. No information was given to other department heads concerning sales results, costs, and expenses. The change to a formal monthly reporting system has been very difficult to realize. Due to the low level of employee training, many tasks, such as consolidation, monthly and quarterly reports, budgets, the Business Plan, implementation of the new cost system, various analyses, restatement of prior years' accounts, et cetera must be fully performed by the controller and chief accountant, thus spending 80 percent of their full time in spite of working 55–60 hours per week. The number of employees in the controller's department in subsequent years will not depend on Galvor's volume of activity, but rather on Universal's requirements.

Implementation of the complete Universal Cost and Production Control System in a company where nothing existed before is an enormous task, which involves establishing 8,000 machining and 3,000 assembly standard times and codifying 15,000 piece parts.

When interviewed early in 1977, M. Barsac stated:

Getting the data to Universal on time continues to be a problem. We simply don't have the necessary people who understand the reporting system and its purpose. The reports are all in English and few of my people are conversant in English. Also, American accounting methods are different from procedures used in France. Another less serious problem concerns the need to convert all of our internal records, which are kept in francs, to dollars when reporting to Universal.

I am especially concerned that few of the reports we prepare for Universal are useful to our operating people here in Bordeaux. Mr. Hennessy, of course, uses the reports, as do one or two others. I am doing all that I can to encourage greater use of these reports. My job is not only to provide facts but to help the managers understand and utilize the figures available. We have recently started issuing monthly cost and expense reports for each department showing the variances from budget. These have been well received.

Mr. Hennessy also commented on meeting the demands imposed by Universal's reporting system.

Without the need to report to Universal, we would do some things in a less formal way or at different times. Universal decides that the entire organization must move to a certain basis by a specified date. There are extra costs involved in meeting these deadlines. It should be noted, also, that demands made on the controller's department are passed on to other areas, such as marketing, engineering, and production.

M. Boudry, Universal's European controller, acknowledged that the cost of the planning and reporting system was high, especially for smaller units.

The system is designed for a large business. We think that the absolute minimum annual sales volume for an individual unit to support the system is about $15 million; however, we would prefer at least $30 million. By this standard, Galvor is barely acceptable. We really don't know if the cost of the system is unnecessarily burdensome in the sense that it requires information which is

not worth its cost. A reasonable estimate might be that about 50 percent of the information would be required in any smartly managed independent business of comparable size, another 25 percent is required for Universal's particular needs, and 25 percent is probably "dead underbrush" which should be cleaned out. Ideally, every five years we should throw the system out the window and start again with the essentials.

As an indication of some of his department's routine activity, M. Barsac noted that at the end of 1976 Galvor was preparing each working day about 200 invoices. At that time the company had approximately 12,000 active customers.

Early in 1977, 42 people were employed in the controller's department. The organization of the department is described in Exhibit 1.

Headquarters Performance Review

Galvor's periodic financial reports were forwarded to M. Boudry in Geneva. The reports were first reviewed by an assistant to M. Boudry, one of four financial analysts who together reviewed all reports received from Universal's operating units in Europe.

In early 1977, M. Boudry described the purpose of these reviews:

The reviews focus on a comparison of performance against budget for the key measures—sales, net income, total assets, total employees, and capital expenditures. These are stated as unambiguous numbers. We try to detect any trouble spots or trends which seem to be developing. Of course, the written portions of the reports are also carefully reviewed, particularly the explanations of variances from budget. If everything is moving as planned, we do nothing.

The reports may contain a month-by-month revision of forecasts to year end; but if the planning objectives for the year are not to be met, we consider the situation as serious.

If a unit manager has a problem and calls for help, then it becomes a matter of common concern. He can probably expect a bad day in explaining how it happened, but he can expect help, too. Depending on the nature of the problem, either Mr. Forrester, Galvor's product-line manager, or one of our staff specialists would go down to Bordeaux. In addition to the financial analysts, one of whom closely follows Galvor's reports, we have specialists on cost systems and analysis, inventory control, credit, and industrial engineering.

Exhibit 1

Organization of controller's department (January 1977)*

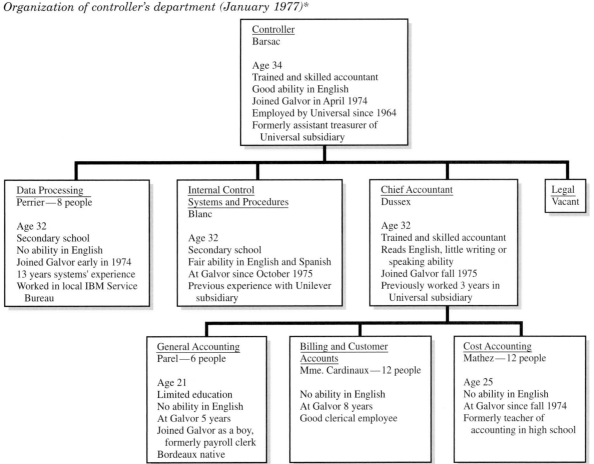

*Immediately prior to Galvor's takeover by Universal Electric, there had been fewer than 20 people in the controller's department.

We have not given Galvor the help it needs and deserves in data processing, but we have a limited staff here in Geneva and we cannot meet all needs. We hope to increase this staff during 1977.

With reference to Galvor's recent performance, M. Boudry states:

Galvor is small and we don't give it much time or help unless its variances appear to be off. This happened in the second half of 1976, when we became increasingly concerned about the level of Galvor's inventories. A series of telexes on this matter between Mr. Hennessy and M.

Poulet, our director of manufacturing here in Geneva, illustrate how the reports are used. [See Exhibits 2 through 5.]

We feel the situation is under control and the outlook for Galvor is OK despite the flat performance between 1973–75 and the downturn in 1976. The company has been turned about and 1977 looks promising.

Although the comprehensive reporting and control system made it appear that Universal was a highly centralized organization, the managements of the various operating units had considerable autonomy. For example, Mr. Hennessy, who was judged only on Galvor's performance,

Exhibit 2   Telex from Poulet to Hennessy, Concerning Level of Inventory

TO: HENNESSY—GALVOR
FROM: POULET—UE
DATE: SEPTEMBER 26, 1976

FOLLOWING ARE THE JULY AND AUGUST INVENTORY AND SALES FIGURES WITH THEIR RESPECTIVE VARIANCES FROM BUDGET ($000s).

	ACTUAL	JULY BUDGET	VARIANCE	ACTUAL	AUGUST BUDGET	VARIANCE
INVENTORY	2,010	1,580	(430)	2,060	1,600	(460)
SALES TO DATE	3,850	3,900	(50)	4,090	4,150	(60)

LATEST AUGUST SALES FORECAST REFLECTS DECREASE IN YEAR-END SALES OF 227 VERSUS INCREASE OF 168 IN YEAR-END INVENTORIES OVER BUDGET.

REQUEST TELEX LATEST MONTH-BY-MONTH INVENTORY AND SALES FORECAST FROM SEPTEMBER TO DECEMBER, EXPLANATION OF VARIANCE IN INVENTORY FROM BUDGET AND CORRECTIVE ACTION YOU PLAN IN ORDER TO ACHIEVE YEAR-END GOAL. INCLUDE PERSONNEL REDUCTIONS, PURCHASE MATERIAL CANCELLATIONS, ETC.

POULET

---

was free to purchase components from other Universal units or from outside sources. There were no preferred "in-house" prices. A slight incentive was offered by Universal to encourage such transactions by not levying certain headquarters fees, amounting to about 2 percent of sales, against the selling unit.

Similarly, Universal made no attempt to shift its taxable income to low-tax countries. Each unit was viewed as though it were an independent company subject to local taxation and regulation. Universal believed that this goal of maximizing profits for the individual units would in turn maximize Universal's profits. Forcing every unit to maximize its profits precluded the use of arbitrary transfer prices for "in-house" transactions.

Recent Developments at Galvor

A standard cost system, which included development and tooling costs as well as manufacturing and assembly, had been in effect since March 1976.

According to Mr. Hennessy:

We had hoped to start in January, but we were delayed. On the basis of our experience in 1976, all standards were reviewed and, where necessary, they were revised in December. We now have a history of development and tooling experience, which we have been accumulating since 1975. This has proved extremely useful in setting cost standards. Simultaneously, we have integrated market and sales forecasts more effectively into our pricing decisions.

Before Universal acquired Galvor, a single companywide rate was used to allocate factory overhead to the costs of products. For many years this rate was 310 percent of direct labor. In a discussion of his pricing policies in 1972, Mr. Latour said: "I have been using this 310 percent for many years and it seems to work out pretty well, so I see no reason to change it."

M. Chambertin had long argued that the less-complex products were being unfairly burdened by the use of a single overhead rate, while electronic products should bear more.

Mr. Latour's response to this argument was:

Exhibit 3   Telex from Hennessy to Poulet Concerning Level of Inventory

---

TO: POULET—UE
FROM: HENNESSY—GALVOR
DATE: SEPTEMBER 27, 1976
YOUR 26.9.76
MONTHLY INVENTORY FORECAST SEPTEMBER TO DECEMBER BY CATEGORY AS FOLLOWS ($000s):

	SEPT. 30	*OCT. 31*	*NOV. 30*	*DEC. 31*
RAW MATERIALS	53	51	50	50
PURCHASED PARTS	180	185	190	195
MANUFACTURED PARTS	95	93	93	91
WORK-IN-PROCESS	838	725	709	599
FINISHED GOODS	632	694	683	705
OTHER INVENTORIES	84	84	82	80
ENGINEERING IN PROCESS	55	58	48	44
RESERVE	(14)	(14)	(14)	(20)
INDICA	50	52	55	55
TOTAL	1,973	1,928	1,896	1,799

THE MAIN EXPLANATIONS OF PRESENT VARIANCE ARE THREE POLICIES ADOPTED END OF 1975 AND DISCUSSED IN MONTHLY LETTERS BUT WHICH LEFT DECEMBER 1976 BUDGET OPTIMISTICALLY LOW. FIRST WAS TO HAVE REASONABLE AMOUNTS OF SELLING MODELS IN STOCK WITHOUT WHICH WE COULD NOT HAVE ACHIEVED 19 PERCENT INCREASE IN SALES WE ARE MAKING WITH OUTMODED PRODUCT.

SECOND POLICY WAS TO MANUFACTURE LONGER SERIES OF EACH MODEL BY DOUBLE WHEREVER SALES WOULD ABSORB IT, OTHERWISE MANY OF OUR COST REDUCTIONS WERE NEARLY ZERO. THIS MEANS OUR MANUFACTURING PROGRAM ANY MONTH MAY CONTAIN FIVE MONTHS' WORTH OF 15 MODELS INSTEAD OF 10 WEEKS' WORTH OF 30 MODELS (OUT OF 70). THIRD WAS NEW POLICY OF REDUCING NUMBER OF PURCHASE ORDERS BY MAINTAINING A MINIMUM STOCK OF MANY THOUSANDS OF LOW-VALUE ITEMS WHICH YOU AGREED WOULD AND DID INCREASE STOCK UPON FIRST PROCUREMENT BUT WE ARE ALREADY GETTING SLIGHT REDUCTION. CORRECTIVE ACTIONS NUMEROUS INCLUDING RUNNING 55 PEOPLE UNDER BUDGET AND ABOUT 63 BY YEAR END PLUS REVIEWING ALL PURCHASE ORDERS MYSELF PLUS SLIDING A FEW SERIES OF MODELS WHICH WOULD HAVE GIVEN SMALL BILLING IN 1976 INTO 1977 PLUS THOSE POSTPONED BY CUSTOMERS. THIS WILL NOT HAVE DRAMATIC EFFECT AS NEARLY ALL THESE SERIES ARE PROCURED AND HAVE TO BE MADE FOR RELATIVELY SURE MARKETS BUT SOME CAN BE HELD IN PIECEPARTS UNTIL JANUARY. WE ARE WATCHING CAREFULLY STOCKS OF SLOW MOVING MODELS AND HAVE MUCH CLEANER FINISHED STOCK THAN END 1975.

FINAL AND GRAVE CONCERN IS ACCURACY OF PARTS, WORK-IN-PROCESS, AND FINISHED GOODS-VALUATION SINCE WE BEGAN STANDARD COST SYSTEM. INTERIM INVENTORY COUNT PLUS VARIANCES VALUED ON PUNCH CARDS STILL DOESN'T CHECK WITH MONTHLY BALANCE USING CONSERVATIVE GROSS MARGINS, BUT NEARLY ALL GAPS OCCURRED FIRST FOUR MONTHS OF SYSTEM WHEN ERRORS NUMEROUS AND LAST 4 MONTHS NEARLY CHECK AS WE CONTINUE REFINING. EXTENSIVE RECHECKS UNDERWAY IN PARTS, WORK-IN-PROCESS, AND FINISHED GOODS AND CORRECTIONS BEING FOUND DAILY.

YOUR INVENTORY STAFF SPECIALISTS ARE AWARE OF PROBLEM AND PROMISED TO HELP WHEN OTHER PRIORITIES PERMIT. WILL KEEP THEM INFORMED OF EXPOSURE WHICH STARTED WITH RECORDING ALL PARTS AND BEGINNING NEW BALANCES WITH NEW STANDARDS AND APPEARS CLOSELY RELATED TO ERRORS IN THESE OPERATIONS. WE CAN ONLY PURGE PROGRESSIVELY WITHOUT HIRING SUBSTANTIAL INDIRECT WORKERS.

HENNESSY

EXHIBIT 4   Telex from Poulet to Hennessy Concerning Level of Inventory

TO: HENNESSY—GALVOR

FROM: POULET—UE

DATE: NOV. 10, 1976

SEPTEMBER INVENTORY INCREASED AGAIN BY 64,000 COMPARED TO AUGUST WHILE SEPTEMBER SALES WERE 145,000 UNDER BUDGET REFERRING TO YOUR LATEST TELEX OF SEPTEMBER 27 IN WHICH YOU HAVE A BREAKDOWN OF THE SEPTEMBER FORECAST. REQUEST DETAILED EXPLANATION FOR NOT MEETING THIS FORECAST IN SPITE OF YOUR CURRENT CORRECTIVE ACTIONS.

SEPTEMBER	*YOUR FORECAST*	*ACTUAL*	*VARIANCE*
RAW MATERIALS	53	96	(43)
PURCHASED PARTS	180	155	25
MANUFACTURED PARTS	95	108	(13)
WORK-IN-PROCESS	838	917	(79)
FINISHED GOODS	632	723	(91)
OTHER INVENTORIES	84	87	(3)
ENGINEERING IN PROCESS	55	52	3
RESERVE	(14)	(14)	—
INDICA	50	51	(1)
TOTAL NET	1,973	2,175	(202)

IN ORDER TO MEET YOUR DECEMBER FORECAST OF 1,799 YOUR WORK-IN-PROCESS HAS TO BE REDUCED BY 318. THIS MEANS A REDUCTION OF ABOUT 100 PER MONTH FROM SEPTEMBER 30 TO DECEMBER 31. THEREFORE, I ALSO WOULD LIKE ACTUAL ACHIEVEMENTS AND FURTHER REDUCTION PLANS DURING OCTOBER, NOVEMBER, AND DECEMBER CONCERNING THE POINTS MENTIONED IN YOUR SAME TELEX OF SEPTEMBER 27. CONSIDER AGGRESSIVE ACTIONS IN THE FOLLOWING SPECIFIC AREAS:

1. REALISTIC MASTER PRODUCTION SCHEDULES.
2. SHORT-TERM PHYSICAL SHORTAGE CONTROL TO ENSURE SHIPMENTS.
3. WORK-IN-PROCESS ANALYSIS OF ALL ORDERS TO ACHIEVE MAXIMUM SALABLE OUTPUT.
4. MANPOWER REDUCTION.
5. ELIMINATION OF ALL UNSCHEDULED VENDOR RECEIPTS. HAVE YOU ADVISED OTHER UNIVERSAL HOUSES NOT TO SHIP IN ADVANCE OF YOUR SCHEDULE UNLESS AUTHORIZED?
6. ADVISE FULL DETAILS ON ALL CURRENT SHORTAGES FROM OTHER UNIVERSAL HOUSES WHICH ARE RESPONSIBLE FOR INVENTORY BUILD-UP.

POULET

I have suspected that our electric products are too high priced, and our electronic products are too low priced. So what does this mean? Why should we lower our prices for multimeters and galvanos? At our current prices, we can easily sell our entire production of electric products.

M. Chambertin remained convinced that eventually Galvor would be forced by competitive pressures to allocate its costs more realistically.

In 1976, as part of the new standard cost system, Galvor did indeed refine the procedure for allocating overhead costs to products. Fifteen different cost centers were established, each with a separate burden rate. These rates, which combined direct labor cost and overhead, ranged from 13.19 francs to 38.62 francs per direct labor hour.

EXHIBIT 5   Telex from Hennessy to Poulet Concerning Level of Inventory

---

TO: POULET—UE
FROM: HENNESSY—GALVOR
DATE: NOV. 15, 1976
      YOUR 10.11.76

WE NOW HAVE OCTOBER 31 FIGURES. OUR ACTUAL ACHIEVEMENTS FOLLOW: RAW MATERIALS 54 VARIANCE PLUS 3, PURCHASED PARTS 173 VARIANCE MINUS 12, MANUFACTURED PARTS 110 VARIANCE PLUS 17, WORK-IN-PROCESS 949 VARIANCE PLUS 224, FINISHED GOODS 712 VARIANCE PLUS 18, OTHER 82 VARIANCE MINUS 2, ENGINEERING 54 VARIANCE MINUS 4, RESERVE MINUS 14 VARIANCE NIL, INDICA 55 VARIANCE PLUS 3, TOTAL 2,175 VARIANCE PLUS 247. EACH ITEM BEING CONTROLLED AND THE ONLY SIGNIFICANT VARIANCES 224 WORK-IN-PROCESS AND 18 FINISHED GOODS ARE MY DECISION UPON SALES DECLINE OF SEPTEMBER AND OCTOBER OF 311 TO DELAY COMPLETION OF SEVERAL SERIES IN MANUFACTURE IN FAVOR OF ANOTHER GROUP OF SERIES, MOSTLY GOVERNMENT, WHICH ARE LARGELY BILLABLE IN 1976 IN ORDER TO PARTLY REGAIN SALES. LAST EIGHT DAYS' ORDERS AND THEREFORE SALES ARE SHARPLY UP AND NONE OF THIS WORK-IN-PROCESS WILL BE ON HAND MORE THAN 3 TO 6 WEEKS LONGER THAN WE PLANNED.

NEVERTHELESS YOU SHOULD BE AWARE WE MANUFACTURE 4 TO 8 MONTHS WORTH OF MANY LOW-VOLUME MODELS. AN EXAMPLE OF HOW WE DETERMINE ECONOMIC SERIES WAS FURNISHED YOUR STAFF SPECIALIST THIS WEEK. WE CANNOT MAKE SIGNIFICANT COST REDUCTIONS IN A BUSINESS WHERE AT LEAST 70 OF 200 MODELS HAVE TO BE ON SHELF TO SELL AND TYPICAL MODEL SELLS 15 UNITS MONTHLY. REGARDING YOUR 5 SUGGESTIONS AND TWO QUESTIONS ARE CARRYING OUT ALL 5 POINTS AGGRESSIVELY AND HAVE NO INTERHOUSE SHORTAGES OR OVERSHIPMENTS.

                                  HENNESSY

Concluding his comments about recent developments, Mr. Hennessy said:

> A formal inventory control system went into effect in January 1977. This, together with the standard cost system, allows us for the first time to really determine the relative profitability of various products, and to place a proper valuation on our inventory.
>
> We are installing a new computer in February, which we will use initially for customer billing and for marketing analysis. We hope this will reduce the number of people required in our customer billing and accounts receivable operations from 12 to 6 or 7.

Questions

1. What is your overall assessment of the effectiveness of Universal Electric's (UE's) planning system as it is applied to Galvor?

2. Identify, in as much detail as possible, all of the new management systems and techniques that UE has required Galvor to establish. In particular, trace the various steps Galvor goes through in preparing its long-range as well as annual plans.

3. What is your evaluation of the effectiveness of the working relationships between Hennessy and the UE executives in Geneva? What do you infer from the telexes about Hennessy's autonomy as a managing director? (Note: You might want to give the telexes a careful and critical reading.)

4. Look at the system from Galvor's viewpoint. Suppose Galvor were an independent company (i.e., not part of Universal Electric). If you were a consultant to Galvor, how would the management planning and control practices you would recommend for the company differ from those that have been imposed by UE? (Please answer this as

completely and specifically as you can, going beyond the response "they would be less detailed and less formal," for example).

5. Look at the system from UE's viewpoint. How (if at all) can UE's imposing planning and control practices different from those required by an independent Galvor be justified? (Again, please try to be specific.)

6. To what extent should a large international organization, such as UE, rely on a comprehensive system of financial reporting and control to achieve its strategic objectives?

7. What specific changes, if any, would you make in UE's planning systems? In its other management systems? If the management processes need improving, how would you change them?

PERFORMANCE MEASUREMENT

In Chapter 10 we described a report that measures actual financial performance compared with budgeted financial performance. This is one type of performance measurement. But financial performance, although important, is only one aspect of what an organization's performance was. In this chapter we describe other aspects.

In the first part of the chapter, we describe the nature of the several types of information managers receive: informal information, task control information, budget reports, and nonfinancial information. In the second part we discuss *performance measurement systems*, especially the balanced scorecard, which blend financial information with nonfinancial information. The objective of performance measurement systems is to aid in strategy implementation. In the final part we discuss *interactive control*—the use of a subset of management control information in developing new strategies.

Informa-tion Used in Control

As pointed out in Chapter 3, managers, when they are acting as managers, do not personally do the work. Their function is to ensure that the work gets done efficiently and effectively. Managers literally do not "control costs." What managers do—or at least attempt to do—is to influence the actions of the people who are responsible for incurring the costs.

Thus, in management control the manager works through others in the following ways:

- selecting employees,
- making sure the employees are adequately trained,
- deciding where the employees fit best in the organization,
- empowering employees,
- providing advice and suggestions,
- solving problems,

- ensuring that the work environment is satisfactory,
- disciplining,
- resolving disputes within the responsibility center,
- approving proposed actions that employees are not authorized to take,
- interacting with other managers to obtain their cooperation and to resolve problems when their activities impede the work of the responsibility center,
- seeking to create a climate that induces employees to work efficiently and effectively.

To carry on these activities, managers need information. In the following paragraphs we describe the nature of the several types of information that are useful in the control process. *Information* is used here in the broad sense of anything that reduces the user's uncertainty.

Informal Information

Much of the information that managers use is informal—that is, the manager receives it through observation, face-to-face conversations, telephone conversations, memoranda, and meetings, as contrasted with information obtained from formal reports. Recently the term *management by walking around* has come to signify the importance of this information. Because it is informal, this information is difficult to describe and categorize. We shall say simply that most managers find informal information more important than any formal report. (A manager who relies principally on the formal reports is the exception.)

Task Control Information

Most of the formal information that flows through an organization in its day-to-day operations is task control information. A production control system provides information that schedules the flow of material, labor, and other resources, so that the correct products in the correct quantities emerge at the end of the process. Systems also control procurement, payroll, storage, and other activities. Management control information is primarily a summary of this task control information. Because of the increasing speed of computers and their low cost per transaction, the principal problem of obtaining useful management information has become one of deciding what small fraction of the available information is worthwhile for the use of managers. Texts on cost accounting and on production and operations management are the best sources for the details of task control systems.

Budget Reports

The approved budget is the principal financial device for controlling the activities of responsibility centers, and a report that compares actual revenues and expenses with budgeted amounts is the principal financial report. Chapters 9 and 10 dealt with budget preparation and reporting relative to budgets. Although an important guide to the responsibility center manager, the budget is only a guide. If the manager discovers a better way of achieving objectives, or if conditions change from those assumed in the budget, the manager should depart from the budget. Nevertheless, there is a presumption that the manager will operate in accordance with the budget unless there is good reason to do otherwise. (Certain departures, such as spending significantly more than the budget amount, require the approval of the manager's superior.) The manager's job is to achieve objectives; conformance with the budget is not desirable if the plan assumed in the budget turns out not to be the best way of achieving objectives. Adherence to the budget is not necessarily good, and departure from it is not necessarily bad.

Budget Signals.   Operating managers should understand which budget amounts are expected amounts, which are ceilings, and which are floors. Some items are ceilings (e.g., entertainment expense, dues and subscriptions, advertising); they signal the manager to spend *no more than* the budget amount without obtaining specific approval. Others are floors (e.g., training); they signal the manager to spend *at least* the budget amount. Still others are general guides in the sense that spending is expected to be approximately, but not exactly, the amount stated. These distinctions may not be explicitly stated in the budget; nevertheless, managers should be aware of them. For items that are guides, managers should be aware of the permissible variation from the amount stated.

Moreover, achieving the bottom line is usually considered to be more important than performance with respect to individual revenue and expense items on the income statement.

Nonfinancial Information

Certain nonfinancial information are key indicators of how well the chosen strategy is being implemented. These are referred to in several ways: *key variables, strategic factors, key success factors, critical success factors, pulse points, or key performance indicators*. In the next section we describe how such nonfinancial information can be blended together with financial information in designing a performance measurement system.

Performance Measurement Systems

Performance Measurement Systems (PMS) have the goal of strategy implementation. In setting up a PMS, senior management selects a series of measures that best represent the company's strategy. These measures can be seen as current and future critical success factors. If these factors are improved, then the company has implemented its strategy. The success of the strategy depends on the strategy itself. A PMS is simply a mechanism for improving the likelihood of the organization successfully implementing a strategy.

Financial measures of corporate success, profit and revenue, show the results of past decisions the company has taken. Because businesses have been using profit and revenue measures for a long time, these measures have become quite sophisticated. Over the past few years, though, there has been an increasing demand for measuring nonfinancial results with the same level of sophistication. As a result many companies, such as FMC, Analog Devices, Cigna P&C, Eastman Chemical, Rockwater, Whirlpool, and PepsiCo, are turning to PMS as a way to link strategy to action. A recent study by the Institute of Management Accountants indicated that new performance measurement systems are being implemented in about 64% of U.S. companies.[1]

Even in the past, companies had used financial and nonfinancial measures. However, companies tended to use nonfinancial measures usually at lower levels in the organization for task control, and used financial measures at higher organizational levels for management control. Under PMS, a blend of financial and nonfinancial measurements are used at all levels in the organization. It is important for senior executives to not only track financial measures, which indicate the results of past decisions, but also nonfinancial measures, which are leading indicators of future performance. Similarly, employees at lower levels need to understand the financial impact of their operating decisions. A well designed PMS must provide proper alignment of the performance measures at all levels in the organization.

An example of a performance measurement system is the *balanced scorecard* approach. After some initial discussion of PMS in general, the discussion of the balanced scorecard will be divided into four parts:[2]

- The balanced scorecard defined.
- Balanced scorecard implementation.
- Common failings with balanced scorecard.
- Current measurement practices.

Performance Measurement Systems in General

When describing performance measurement systems, managers typically compare them to an instrument panel or a dashboard. Both analogies provide important insights into why a mix of financial and nonfinancial measures are needed in a management control system. The most important insight is that a complex system cannot be controlled by just a single measure, and that too many critical measures make the system uncontrollably complex. Expanding the analogy will help make this clearer.

A PMS, like a dashboard, has a series of measures that provide information about the operation of many different processes. Some of these measures tell

---

[1] Joel Kurtzman, "Is Your Company Off Course?" *Fortune*, Feb 17, 1997, pp. 128–30.

[2] This discussion draws on the research of Robert S. Kaplan and David P. Norton, *Balanced Scorecard* (Harvard Business School Press, 1996).

the driver (or the manager) what has happened, say the odometer that reads 40,000 miles (or assets that currently stand at $5 billion). Other measures tell the driver (or the manager) what is going to happen, such as the tachometer at 6000 RPM (or an on-time-delivery percentage of 70). These measures have implicit interactions, and changes in one often reflect changes in another: reducing RPMs will change MPG (or improving on-time delivery will change customer satisfaction).

Interestingly, there are usually multiple ways to change one measure, such as RPM, that may or may not improve the other measure, MPG. A dashboard provides a driver with a series of measures so that he or she can make the necessary trade-offs, such as running the car at 6500 RPM in second gear instead of shifting to fifth gear because shifting would take extra time. By making the trade-offs, a manager can select between behavior that is good for the short- or long-term success of the organization.

The Balanced Scorecard

The balanced scorecard is an example of a performance measurement system. It fosters a balance between otherwise disparate strategic measures in an effort to achieve goal congruence, thus encouraging employees to act in the best interest of the organization. Augmenting the goal-congruence function, the balanced scorecard is a tool for focusing the organization, improving communication, setting organizational objectives, and providing feedback on strategy.

Every measure on a balanced scorecard addresses an aspect of a company's strategy. In creating the balanced scorecard, executives must choose a set of measurements that 1) accurately reflect the critical factors that will determine the success of the company's strategy; 2) show the relationships among the individual measures in a cause–effect manner, indicating how nonfinancial measures affect long-term financial results; and 3) provide a broad-based view of the current status of the company.

The balanced scorecard endeavors to create a blend of strategic measures: outcome and driver measures, financial and nonfinancial measures, and internal and external measures.

Outcome and Driver Measures.   *Outcome* measurements indicate the result of a strategy (e.g., increased revenue or improved quality). The amount by which revenue increased is the result of the successful implementation of the organization's strategy. These measures are typically "lagging indicators," they tell management what has happened. By contrast, *driver* measures are "leading indicators," showing the progress of key areas in implementing a strategy. An example of a driver is cycle time. Outcome measures can only indicate the final result. Driver measures can be taken at a more granular level and indicate incremental changes that will ultimately affect the outcome.

By focusing management attention on key aspects of the business, driver measures affect behavior in the organization. If an element of the strategy is to improve time-to-market, focusing on cycle time allows management to closely track how well this goal is being achieved. This additional focus on cycle time in turn encourages employees to improve this particular measure.

Outcome and driver measures are inextricably linked. If the outcome measures indicate that there is a problem, yet the driver measures indicate that the strategy is being implemented well, then there is a high chance that the strategy needs to be changed.

Financial and Nonfinancial Measures.   Organizations have developed very sophisticated systems to measure financial performance. Unfortunately, as many U.S. companies discovered during the 1980s, industries were being driven by changes in nonfinancial areas, such as quality and customer satisfaction, that eventually impacted the company's financial performance.

> **Example.** By every financial measure during the 1970s, Pan Am Airlines, US Steel, Xerox, and IBM dominated their markets. Yet, by the mid-1980s, they had all been displaced as the market leaders. They had been displaced by competitors who achieved higher quality, higher customer satisfaction, higher levels of innovation, and better business models. These could not be measured by financial means until it was too late.

While recognizing their importance, many organizations have failed to incorporate nonfinancial measures into the executive level performance reviews of the company because these measures tend to be much less sophisticated than financial measures and senior management is less adept with their use.

Internal and External Measures.   Companies must strike a balance between external measures, such as customer satisfaction, and measures of internal business processes, such as manufacturing yields. The reason for this is that companies often sacrifice internal development for external results or ignore external results, under the mistaken belief that good internal measures were sufficient.

> **Example.** One of the early adopters of the balanced scorecard found that while all of their internal measures indicated that the company's performance had dramatically improved (defects were reduced by tenfold and on-time delivery had jumped from the 50 percent range into the 90 percent range), yet its financial and stock performance was stagnant. Rather than acting on both signals, the company chose to continue to act on the internal measures alone for almost four years. During this entire time, their external measures were indicating that their strategy was not working, yet they continued. Their financial results finally turned around after they changed strategies in response to the prolonged poor external measures.

Four Perspectives.   Exhibit 11–1 contains a balanced scorecard developed by Rockwater, an underwater construction and engineering company, with measures categorized under four perspectives viewing the company from financial, customer, internal business process, and learning and innovation perspectives.

EXHIBIT 11-1

Rockwater's balanced scorecard

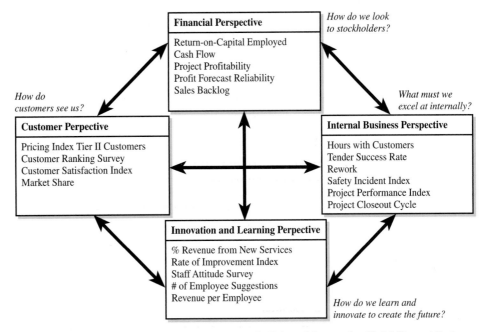

How do we look to stockholders?

Financial Perspective

Return-on-Capital Employed
Cash Flow
Project Profitability
Profit Forecast Reliability
Sales Backlog

How do customers see us?

What must we excel at internally?

Customer Perpective

Pricing Index Tier II Customers
Customer Ranking Survey
Customer Satisfaction Index
Market Share

Internal Business Perspective

Hours with Customers
Tender Success Rate
Rework
Safety Incident Index
Project Performance Index
Project Closeout Cycle

Innovation and Learning Perpective

% Revenue from New Services
Rate of Improvement Index
Staff Attitude Survey
# of Employee Suggestions
Revenue per Employee

How do we learn and innovate to create the future?

Source: Robert S. Kaplan and David P. Norton, "Putting the Balanced Scorecard to Work," *Harvard Business Review*, September–October 1993, p. 136. Reprinted with permission.

Dividing measures into these categories provides explicit balance between the needs of a select series of stakeholders of the organization. Every measure on Rockwater's scorecard relates specifically to Rockwater's strategy to be the preferred provider in the underwater construction and engineering industry.[3] The four perspectives provide a stakeholder balance. The choice of measures varies between outcome measures, such as return-on-capital employed, and driver measures, such as hours with customers on new work or staff attitude survey. The measures also relate to financial dimension (e.g., project profitability) and nonfinancial dimension (e.g., number of employee suggestions). Finally, some measures are external (e.g., market share), while others are internal (e.g., safety incident index). Together they form a focused picture of what Rockwater feels it needs to improve in order to successfully implement its strategy.

Recent examples of companies that have implemented the balanced scorecard approach include FMC, Cigna P&C, and Eastman Chemical.[4]

Measurements Drive Change.   The most important aspect of the balanced scorecard is its ability to measure outcomes and drivers in such a way as to cause the organization to act in accordance with its strategies. The organization

---

[3]Robert S. Kaplan and David P. Norton, "Putting the Balanced Scorecard to Work," *Harvard Business Review*, September–October 1993, pp. 134–43.

[4]Bill Birchard, "Closing the Strategy Gap," *CFO*, October 1996, pp. 26–30.

achieves goal congruence by linking the overall financial and strategic objectives with lower level objectives that can be observed and affected at the different levels of the organization. With these measures every employee can understand how their actions impact the company's strategies.

Because these measures are explicitly tied to an organization's strategies, the measures in the balanced scorecard must be strategy-specific and, therefore, organization-specific. While there is a generic balanced scorecard framework, there is no such thing as a generic scorecard.

The balanced scorecard measures are linked from the top to the bottom and tied to specific targets throughout the entire organization. Objectives can provide an additional level of clarification to a strategy so that the organization knows both what they need to do and how much of it needs to get done.

Finally, the balanced scorecard emphasizes the idea of cause and effect relationships between measures. By explicitly presenting the cause and effect relationship, an organization will understand how nonfinancial measures, such as product quality, drive financial measures, such as revenue. Exhibit 11–2 presents an example of how the measures in the four perspectives link with each other in a cause–effect relationship. Better selection, training, and development of manufacturing employees (measured in terms of "manufacturing skills") lead to better product quality (measured in terms of "first-pass yields") and better on-time delivery (measured in terms of "order cycle time"). In turn, these improvements lead to improved customer loyalty (measured through "customer satisfaction surveys"), finally leading to enhanced sales (measured in terms of "sales growth").

It is critical that the scorecard not simply be a "laundry list" of measures. Rather, the individual measures and the four perspectives in the scorecard must be linked together explicitly in a cause–effect way, as a tool to translate strategy into action.

The better understood these relationships, the more readily each individual in the organization will be able to directly and clearly contribute to the success of the organization's strategies.

Implementing a Balanced Scorecard

We can summarize the implementation of a balanced scorecard in four general steps:

1. Define strategy.
2. Define measures of strategy.
3. Integrate measures into the management system.
4. Review measures and results frequently.

Each of these steps is iterative, requiring the participation of senior executives and employees throughout the organization. Though the controller may be given the duty of overseeing its development, it is a task for the entire management team.

Exhibit 11–2

Cause–effect relationships among measures

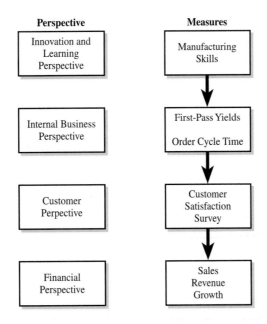

Perspective	Measures
Innovation and Learning Perspective	Manufacturing Skills
Internal Business Perspective	First-Pass Yields / Order Cycle Time
Customer Perpective	Customer Satisfaction Survey
Financial Perspective	Sales Revenue Growth

Define Strategy. The balanced scorecard builds a link between strategy and operational action. As a result it is necessary to begin the process of defining a balanced scorecard by defining the organization's strategy. At this phase it is important that the organization's goals are explicit and that targets have been developed.

For a single industry firm (e.g., Analog Devices, Maytag, Wrigley, Perdue Farms), the scorecard should be developed at the corporate level and then cascaded down to functional levels and below. However, for a multibusiness firm (e.g., General Electric, DuPont, Corning Glass Works) the business unit should be the starting point for developing the scorecard. It is important that functional departments within a business unit have their own scorecards, and there should be alignment between the business unit scorecard and the scorecards below that level. As a final step, for a multibusiness unit organization, a corporatewide scorecard needs to be developed to address, among other things, synergies across business units.

Define Measures of Strategy. The next step is to develop measures in support of the articulated strategy. It is imperative that the organization focuses on a few critical measures at this point, otherwise management will be overloaded with measures. Also, it is important that the individual measures be linked with each other in a cause–effect manner, as was illustrated in Exhibit 11–2.

Integrate Measures into the Management System. The balanced scorecard must be integrated with the organization's formal and informal structures, its culture, and its human resource practices. While the balanced scorecard gives some means for balancing measures, the measures can still become unbalanced by other systems in the organization, such as compensation policies that compensate managers strictly based on financial performance.

Review Measures and Results Frequently.   Once the balanced scorecard is up and running, it must be consistently reviewed by senior management. The organization should be looking for the following:

- How do the outcome measures say the organization is doing?
- How do the driver measures say the organization is doing?
- How has the organization's strategy changed since the last review?
- How have the scorecard measures changed?

The most important aspects of these reviews are as follows:

- They tell management whether the strategy is being implemented correctly and how successfully the strategy is working.
- They show that management is serious about the importance of these measures.
- They maintain alignment of measures to ever changing strategies.
- They improve measurement.

These review sessions will complete the four steps and provide the impetus to start the cycle again.

Pitfalls of the Balanced Scorecard

The following problems, unless suitably dealt with, could limit the usefulness of the balanced scorecard approach:

- Poor correlation between nonfinancial measures and results.
- Fixation on financial results.
- No mechanism for improvement.
- Measures are not updated.
- Measurement overload.
- Difficulty in establishing trade-offs.

Poor Correlation between Nonfinancial Measures and Results.   Simply put, there is no guarantee that future profitability will follow target achievements in any nonfinancial area. This is probably the biggest problem with the balanced scorecard because there is an inherent assumption that future profitability does follow from achieving the scorecard measures. Identifying the cause–effect relationships among the different measures (as illustrated in Exhibit 11–2) is easier said than done.

This will be a problem with any system that is trying to develop proxy measures for future performance. While this does not mean that the balanced scorecard should be abandoned, it is important that companies adopting such a system understand that the links between nonfinancial measures and financial performance are still poorly understood.

> **Example.** Whirlpool announced in its 1991 annual report that it had established objectives and measures to track progress towards performance goals in four areas where it felt it must perform well in order to create an ROE of 18 percent a year. Between 1991 and 1995, Whirlpool did not achieve an ROE above 13.9 percent, averaging only 11.9 percent, which was less than their average ROE of 12.1 percent for the previous five years from 1986 to 1990.

Fixation on Financial Results.   As previously discussed, not only are most senior managers well-trained and very adept with financial measures, but they also most keenly feel pressure regarding the financial performance of their companies. Shareholders are vocal and the Board of Directors often applies pressure on the stakeholders' behalf. This pressure often overwhelms the long-term, uncertain payback of the nonfinancial measures.

Additional pressure results from the balanced scorecard being poorly tied to an incentive program. Instead, senior managers are most often compensated for financial performance. This can disrupt goal congruence, causing managers to be more concerned about the financials than any of the other measures. Even those who have made an effort to tie rewards to balanced scorecard measures use a disproportionate bias toward financial performance.

> **Example.** Cigna Insurance Company's Property and Casualty Division ties its scorecard to bonuses. Of the four categories in the scorecard, financials has the largest impact on the bonus, counting for a full one-half of the bonus.[5]

No Mechanism for Improvement.   One of the most overlooked pitfalls of the balanced scorecard is that a company cannot achieve "stretch goals" if the company has no mechanism for improvement. In order to achieve "stretch goal," an organization must *stretch*, or innovate better business processes. Often, the senior executives will examine a few scenarios, decide on what is considered feasible, and then develop a series of measures that they feel will cause the company to reach that scenario. Unfortunately, achieving many of these goals requires complete shifts in the way that business is done, yet the company often does not have mechanisms to make those shifts. The mechanisms available take additional resources and require a change in the company culture. These changes do not happen overnight, nor do they respond automatically to a new stretch target. Inertia often works against the company: employees are accustomed to a self-limiting cycle of setting targets, missing those targets, and readjusting the targets to reflect what was actually achieved. Without a method for making improvements, improvements are unlikely to consistently happen, no matter how good the stretch goal sounds.

---

[5]Brian McWilliams, "The Measure of Success," *Across the Board*, February 1996, pp. 16–20.

EXHIBIT 11–3   Current Measurement Practices

Measure of	Highly Valued Information	Quality of Information	Clear Measures	Measures Regularly Updated	Linked to Compensation
Financial Performance	82%	61%	92%	88%	94%
Operating Efficiency	79%	41%	68%	69%	54%
Customer Satisfaction	85%	29%	48%	48%	37%
Employee Performance	67%	16%	17%	27%	20%
Innovation/ change	52%	16%	13%	23%	12%

Source: Adapted from John H. Lingle, William A. Schiemann, "From Balanced Scorecard to Strategic Gauges: Is Measurement Worth It," *Management Review*, American Management Association, March 1996, pp. 56–61.

Measures Are Not Updated.   Many companies don't have a formal mechanism for updating the measures to align with changes and shifts in strategy. The result is that the company is still producing measures based on yesterday's strategy. Additionally, measures often build up inertia, particularly as people get comfortable using them.

Measurement Overload.   How many critical measures can one manager track at one time without losing focus? Unfortunately, there is no right answer to this question, except it is more than 1 and less than 50. If it's too few, then the manager is ignoring measures that are critical to creating success. If it's too many, then the manager may risk losing focus and trying to do too many things at once.

Difficulty in Establishing Trade-offs.   Some companies combine financial and nonfinancial measures into a single report, and give weights to the individual measures. But most balanced scorecards do not assign explicit weights across measures. In the absence of such weights, it becomes difficult to establish trade-offs between financial and nonfinancial measures.

Current Measurement Practices

The results of the Lingle and Schiemann study (Exhibit 11–3) provide useful insights into what companies are actually measuring, the perceived quality of these measures, and what measures are being linked to compensation.

Types of Measures.   The Lingle and Schiemann study, published in 1996, found that 76 percent of the responding companies included financial, operating, and customer satisfaction measures in regular management reviews. In

EXHIBIT 11–4

Control system as a strategy implementation tool

contrast, only 33 percent of the companies indicated that measures of innovation and change were included in regular management reviews.

Quality of Measures.   Exhibit 11–3 shows that financial performance measures were the only measures that were considered high quality, current, and tied to compensation. Most companies not only had operating and customer satisfaction measures, over 79 percent of the responding companies considered this information to be highly valuable. Unfortunately, there is often a large difference between the perceived value of these measures and the quality of the information that these measures produce.

There is no doubt from the results in Exhibit 11–3 that the measures of employee performance and innovation and change have generally been thought to be poorly defined and of poor quality. Ironically, the majority of companies in this study considered information about the company's performance in these areas to be highly valuable.

Relationship of Measures to Compensation.   Most current management systems link financial measures to compensation. As Exhibit 11–3 points out, about one third of the companies surveyed used customer satisfaction and well less than one-quarter of the companies used innovation and change measures to drive compensation decisions.

Interactive Control[6]

The primary role of management controls is to help in the execution of strategies. Under this view (Exhibit 11–4), the chosen strategy defines the critical success factors which become the focal point for the design and operation of control systems. The end result is the successful implementation of the chosen strategy. In industries which are subject to very rapid environmental changes, management control information can also provide the basis for thinking about

---

[6]This section is based on the research of Robert Simons, *Levers of Control*, Boston, Mass: Harvard Business School Press, 1995.

Exhibit 11–5

Interactive control

new strategies. This is illustrated in Exhibit 11–5. Simons refers to this as *interactive control.*[7]

In a rapidly changing and dynamic environment, creating a *learning organization* is fundamental to corporate survival. By a *learning organization*, we refer to the capacity of the employees of an organization to learn to cope with changes in the environment on an on-going basis. An effective learning organization is one where employees at all levels of the organization continuously scan the environment, identify potential problems and opportunities, exchange environmental information candidly and openly, and conduct experiments of alternate business models in order to successfully adapt to the emerging environment. *The main objective of interactive control is to facilitate the creation of a learning organization.*

While *critical success factors* are important in the design of control systems to implement the chosen strategy, *strategic uncertainties* guide the use of a subset of management control information interactively in developing new strategies. *Strategic uncertainties* refer to fundamental environmental shifts (changes in customer preferences, technologies, competitors, lifestyles, substitute products, etc.) that could potentially disrupt the rules by which an organization is playing today. Interactive control alerts management of strategic uncertainties—either troubles (e.g., loss of market share; customer complaints) or opportunities (e.g., opening a new market because certain governmental regulations have been removed)—that become the basis for managers to adapt to a rapidly changing environment by thinking about new strategies (Exhibit 11–6). Interactive control has the following characteristics:

1. A subset of the management control information that has a bearing on the strategic uncertainties facing the business becomes the focal point.
2. Senior executives take such information seriously.
3. Managers at all levels of the organization focus attention on the information produced by the system.
4. Superiors, subordinates, and peers meet face to face to interpret and discuss the implications of the information for future strategic initiatives.

---

[7]Ibid, pp. 91–124.

Exhibit 11–6

Control system as a strategy formation tool

5. The face-to-face meetings take the form of debate and challenge of the underlying data, assumptions, and appropriate actions.

Interactive controls are not a *separate* system; they are an integral part of the management control system. Some management control information helps managers think about new strategies; interactive control information usually, but not exclusively, tends to be nonfinancial. Since strategic uncertainties differ from business to business, senior executives in different companies might choose different parts of their management control system to use interactively, as is illustrated by the following examples.

Examples. A business in the hospital supply industry competes as the low-cost producer of intravenous drug delivery products. This business manufactures and sells large quantities of standardized, disposable products such as syringes, wipes, tubing, and plasma containers. Critical performance variables for this low-cost, high-volume strategy relate to product quality and manufacturing and distribution efficiencies . . . These factors are not the strategic uncertainties perceived by senior managers. Instead, the strategic uncertainties they perceive relate to fundamental changes in drug delivery technology, which could undermine the ability of the business to deliver products valued by the market. What if advances in technology lead to ways of delivering drugs orally, or through skin patches, or through some other, as yet uncontemplated, technology? What if the nature of drug technology changes? Could the business adapt?[8] . . . Senior managers use a project management system (one element of their management control system) interactively to focus organizational attention on a dozen or so emerging technological issues. Senior managers meet monthly for several days to debate the impact of technologies—introduced by competitors or in related industries, or developed in-house—on their business . . . From this dialogue, new strategies emerge.[9]

---

[8]Robert Simons. *Levers of Control.* Harvard Business School Press, 1995, pp. 94–95.

[9]Robert Simons, "Control in an Age of Empowerment," *Harvard Business Review*, March–April 1995, p. 87.

Pepsi used the market share data released by Nielsen every week as an interactive control system.[10] Some of the key strategic uncertainties confronting Pepsi included substitution of soft drinks by other drinks, customer response to pricing, promotion, and advertising moves of Coke, and customer preference for diet drinks. These strategic uncertainties affected market share. Hence Pepsi used market share information to debate future strategic actions. According to John Sculley, Pepsi's former CEO: "Pepsi's top managers would carry in their wallets little charts with the latest Nielsen figures . . . We would pore over the data, using it to search for Coke's vulnerable points where an assault could successfully be launched, or to explore why Pepsi slipped a fraction of a percentage point in the game . . . The Nielsens defined the ground rules of competition for everyone at Pepsi."[11]

Summary

For effective management control, managers need information. They receive such information from various sources. Much important information is informal, obtained by "walking around." Formal sources include summaries of task control reports, financial information in budgets and reports comparing actual performance with budget, and nonfinancial information.

The balanced scorecard provides a mechanism for linking strategy to action. It, like all performance measurement systems, operates under the assumption that financial measures alone are insufficient to operate an organization and that special attention must be placed on developing sophisticated nonfinancial measures. The balanced scorecard uses a variety of different types of measures. These measures include both outcome and driver measures, financial and nonfinancial measures, and internal and external measures. Additionally, the balanced scorecard emphasizes the stakeholder model of the organization with its explicit use of the four perspectives of the organization: financial, customer, internal processes, and innovation and learning. The key belief behind the balanced scorecard is that measurement will drive change as the organization conforms to what is being measured. There are many pitfalls that a company can encounter when trying to implement a balanced scorecard: poor correlation between driver and outcome measures, fixation on financial results, no mechanism for making improvements, failure to update the measures, and too many measures.

The primary role of management controls is to help in the execution of chosen strategies. In industries that are subject to very rapid environmental changes, management control information can also provide managers with a tool for thinking about new strategies; this is called interactive control. Interactive controls are not a *separate* system, but are an integral part of the management control system; interactive control information tends to be nonfinancial.

---

[10]Ibid, p. 86.

[11]Sculley, J. *Odyssey: Pepsi to Apple . . . A Journey of Adventure, Ideas, and The Future.* New York: Harper & Row, 1987.

Suggested Additional Readings

Dixon, J. R., A. J. Nanni, and T. E. Vollmann. *The New Performance Challenge: Measuring Operations for World-Class Competition.* Homewood, Ill.: Dow Jones-Irwin, 1990.

Eccles, Robert G. "The Performance Measurement Manifesto." *Harvard Business Review*, January–February 1991, pp. 131–37.

———— and Philip J. Pyburn. "Creating a Comprehensive System to Measure Performance." *Management Accounting*, October 1992, pp. 41–44.

Kaplan, Robert S., and David P. Norton. "Putting the Balanced Scorecard to Work." *Harvard Business Review*, September–October 1993, pp. 134–43.

————. *The Balanced Scorecard: Translating Strategy into Action.* Boston: Harvard Business School Press, 1996.

Kawada, Makoto, and Daniel F. Johnson. "Strategic Management Accounting—Why and How." *Management Accounting*, August 1993, pp. 32–38.

Keating, Patrick J., and Stephen F. Jablonsky. *Changing Roles of Financial Management.* Morristown, N.J.: Financial Executives Research Foundation, 1990.

Lee, John Y. *Managerial Accounting Changes for the 1990s.* Reading, Mass.: Addison-Wesley, 1987.

Lingle, John H., and William A. Schiemann. "From Balanced Scorecard to Strategic Gauges: Is Measurement Worth It?" *Management Review*, March 1996, pp. 56–61.

McKinnon, Sharon, and William Bruns. *The Information Mosaic.* Harvard Business School Press, 1992.

McWilliams, Brian. "The Measure of Success." *Across the Board*, February 1996, pp. 16–20.

Sieger, Joseph M. "Manage Your Numbers to Match Your Strategy." *Management Review*, February 1992, pp. 46–48.

Shank, John K., and Vijay Govindarajan. *Strategic Cost Management.* New York, NY: The Free Press, 1993.

Simons, Robert. *Levers of Control.* Boston: Harvard Business School Press, 1995.

————. "Control in an Age of Empowerment." *Harvard Business Review*, March–April 1995, pp. 80–88.

Vitale, Mike R., and Sarah C. Mavrinac. "How Effective Is Your Performance Measurement System?" *Management Accounting*, August 1995, pp. 43–47.

————, and Mark Hauser. "New Process/Financial Scorecard: A Strategic Performance Measurement System." *Planning Review*, July/August 1994, pp. 12–17.

CASE 11–1
ANALOG DEVICES, INC.

Analog Devices, Inc. (ADI), is a producer of analog and digital semiconductors and electronic components. From 1981 through 1996, ADI experienced periods of growth and stagnation, achieving both record profits and sales while also experiencing its first loss ever. To meet the needs of the changing market, management at ADI introduced a number of different management tools to implement change. One such tool was ADI's *corporate scorecard*. ADI's corporate scorecard has been recognized as a management best practice in a survey conducted by the Nolan-Norton Group in 1991. While seen as a best practice in 1991, ADI's management was wondering in 1996 how to change the scorecard to best fit the needs of management: how fast should they change it, and how best to use it to focus management's attention in the future?

Early History

Analog Devices was founded in 1965 in Cambridge, Massachusetts, by Ray Stata and Matthew Lorber. Ray Stata had a B.S.E.E. and an M.S.E.E., both from MIT. Since its inception, ADI has produced electronic components. Analog Integrated Circuits, also known as linear ICs, is one of ADI's major product lines. These semiconductors and the other products in ADI's wide product line are used in a variety of applications in computers, test equipment, avionics, communications, medical devices, automotive, and consumer electronics.

ADI's first products were modular operational amplifiers, used in instruments and control systems. With worldwide demand for their "op amps," ADI established sales subsidiaries throughout the world. Its domestic sales were handled through a direct sales force and manufacturers' representatives.[1]

In 1969 ADI acquired Pastoriza Electronics and expanded its product line to include analog-to-digital and digital-to-analog converters, which are used in automated processing, linking computers to control systems and sensing devices. That same year ADI went public, trading over the counter. By 1970 ADI had sales subsidiaries in England, West Germany, France, and Japan. In 1971 sales exceeded $12 million and international sales accounted for 41 percent of total volume. ADI continued to add technological capability by acquiring Nova Devices, which had been founded by Stata two years earlier. Nova Devices with its IC manufacturing capability became ADI's semiconductor division. The semiconductor division became responsible for 50 percent of all sales within 10 years.

Throughout the 70s, ADI continued to introduce new products developed in-house and to selectively acquire and take major positions in many new technologies. These new technologies included hybrid ICs and high-speed and video components. ADI established a subsidiary in Limerick, Ireland, in 1976 to design and manufacture CMOS ICs. By the end of the decade, ADI had reached annual sales in excess of $100 million.

Total Quality at ADI—1983 to 1986

In 1983 Ray Stata recognized that ADI was having problems with the quality of its production.

This case was prepared by Kirk Hendrickson [Tuck '97] under the supervision of Professor Vijay Govindarajan. Copyright © Osceola Institute.

[1]Information for this history can be found in "Analog Devices, Inc. In Brief," published by Analog Devices Employee Communications, October 1995, and "Analog Devices, Inc.," *International Directory of Company Histories* (Chicago: St. James Press, 1988), Volume 10, pp. 85–87.

Its on-time delivery record was under 60 percent. Its process yields were in some cases as low as 10 percent.[2] ADI's customers were complaining about quality and ADI's competitors had on-time delivery records and yields well above ADI's level. At this time Stata attended Philip Crosby's Quality School. This was ADI's first introduction to the concepts of Total Quality Management (TQM).

Interested in implementing TQM but not wanting to add additional staff to create a quality improvement function, Stata put Human Resources in charge of establishing a TQM program at ADI. Goodloe Suttler, who was Product Line Director in charge of BiPolar Converter ICs in 1983, indicated that the first TQM effort never got beyond managers trying to become TQM gurus on their own by reading books and going to seminars. As Suttler put it, "I was focused on growing the business, not on TQM."[3]

By the end of 1984, ADI's sales had reached $313 million. During Fiscal Year 1984 revenue had grown by 46 percent, profits by 105 percent, and the orders booked promised another record year in 1985. ADI management felt it was right in the center of some of the fastest growing segments in the economy and many in the company were starting to talk about ADI becoming a $1 billion company by 1988.

Unfortunately, between the end of 1984 and the end of 1986, sales had only grown 6.7 percent, and profits had fallen by 38 percent. As Stata stated:

> . . . for the first time, between 1982 and 1987, we missed our five-year goals—and by a country mile. True enough, like other semiconductor companies we were affected by the malaise in the U.S. electronics industry and by the strong dollar. But the external environment was only part

of the problem: something was also wrong internally, and it had to be fixed.[4]

The factory was missing over 40 percent of its committed delivery dates. When 20 executives with regular customer contact were asked, "The phone rings. It is an angry customer. What did he say?" The executives responded, "The customer said, 'Where's my order!?' "[5]

The defect level of product that reached the customer was over 20,000 parts per million (PPM). Competitors such as Motorola were achieving results under 1,000 PPM. Additionally, the poor quality was responsible for a substantial amount of waste at ADI, such as front-to-back IC yields of less than 15 percent, meaning that only 15 out of every 100 ICs that ADI started made it through the process. These yields were well below industry yields.

While 1985 had seen analog IC sales decline by about 5 percent, 1986 industry-wide analog IC sales grew by 25 percent. The analog circuits industry had returned to growth, yet ADI's revenues were stagnant and its profitability was declining.

The Quality Specialist

In 1986 ADI hired Art Schneiderman as Vice President of Quality and Productivity Improvement. Schneiderman had been a consultant with Bain & Co. where he had been directly involved in establishing many quality improvement programs. Schneiderman was seen as someone who could link ADI to the, " . . . mainstream of experience and knowledge that is rapidly accumulating in this field [TQM] . . . " and be a teacher who could " . . . help our [ADI's] managers

[2]Shank Howell and Fisher Soucy, *Cost Management for Tomorrow*, Financial Executives Research Foundation, 1992, p. 128.

[3]Goodloe Suttler, *Analog Devices Inc.*, presentation on Balanced Scorecard, Amos Tuck School of Business Administration, April 1996.

[4]Ray Stata, "Organizational Learning—The Key to Management Innovation," *Sloan Management Review*, Spring 1989, p. 63.

[5]Goodloe Suttler, *Analog Devices Inc.*, presentation on Balanced Scorecard, Amos Tuck School of Business Administration, April 1996.

become more expert practitioners."[6] Stata wanted Quality Improvement Process (QIP), as ADI called its total quality program, to become a way of life at ADI.

Many of the general managers at ADI were very skeptical of this new quality program, having been through the unsuccessful program during the era of the quality novices. Adding to their skepticism, managers at ADI perceived a conflict between the quality goals and the financial goals of the company. Their perception was reinforced by the fact that both the incentive system and performance measurement system at ADI were financially based.

Half-Life.   Schneiderman believed that " . . . any defect level, subjected to legitimate QIP, decreases at a constant rate, so that when plotted on semi-log paper against time, it falls on a straight line."[7] The result is that every process can experience a 50 percent reduction in defects at a consistent time interval. Schneiderman called this the Half-Life of the improvement process.

Schneiderman had collected data on improvement activities. Exhibit 1 shows three examples of the data that he collected. To capture the full effect of the Half-Life concept, these examples are shown on log-linear graphs. By plotting the improvements this way, it becomes easy for someone to see the line that indicates the rate of improvement. As Exhibit 1 illustrates, each process has its own unique rate that can be found by finding the slope of the line fit to the data. This unique rate is the process's Half-Life.

Using the 1987 Five Year Plan as a tool, Schneiderman introduced goals for a series of quality measures (Exhibit 2) that corresponded to what he considered to be the critical success factors for ADI: having innovative, high quality products and being a reliable, responsive supplier. The goals were determined by combining the demands of the customers with realistic expectations of the Half-Life of each measure.

With proposed reductions such as Process Defect Levels dropping from 5000 PPM in 1987 to fewer than 10 PPM by 1992, many managers just laughed at him. Stata's recollection:

> The first reaction of our organization was to recoil from what looked like unrealistic objectives. But we reminded our managers that if a company really gets its quality improvement act together, there is no fundamental reason why these goals cannot be achieved.[8]

Schneiderman put together a single page that showed three categories of measures—financial, new products, and QIP (Exhibit 3). Within these categories, there were measures that provided indicators of how well ADI was moving towards its goals. Schneiderman called this simple, one-page report the "Scorecard" because it provided a series of financial and nonfinancial measures of the company that did not favor one critical success factor over any other.

ADI's Scorecard

ADI considered the scorecard to be a breakthrough because it condensed pages of reports into a simple single report (Exhibit 3). This scorecard had measurements to support each critical success factor along with the critical measures of financial performance.

Schneiderman added to the corporate scorecard the half-life and target for each of the measurements for the next few periods. Schneiderman did this to provide a link between the short-term results and the long-term plans of ADI, such as improvement in on-time deliveries to 99.8 percent by 1992.

According to Suttler, Schneiderman's first scorecard was a strawman proposal. Senior

---

[6]Ray Stata, "Organizational Learning—The Key to Management Innovation," *Sloan Management Review,* Spring 1989, pp. 63–74.

[7]Arthur M. Schneiderman, "Setting Quality Goals," *Quality Progress,* April 1988, p. 53.

[8]Ray Stata, "Organizational Learning—The Key to Management Innovation," *Sloan Management Review,* Spring 1989, p. 70.

Exhibit 1

Three examples of Half Life*

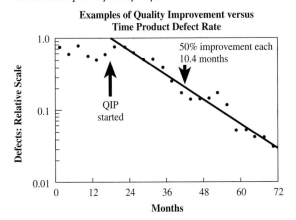

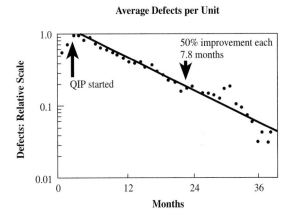

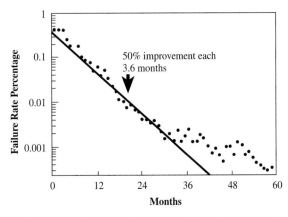

*Ray Stata, "Organizational Learning—The Key to Management Innovation," *Sloan Management Review*, Spring 1989, pp. 63–74. Reprinted by permission.

managers were not convinced that the goals were necessary, nor realistic, and that a scorecard was necessary. They pointed out that the goals that Schneiderman had set for them were from interviews with customers that Schneiderman had done, not from benchmarking competitors. The customers may want these levels, argued the managers, but how does the company know that any of the competitors are performing at anywhere near the levels that Schneiderman targeted? While disagreeing with the target levels, the senior managers did agree with the approach, and they adopted the scorecard.

Making the Scorecard Work

Schneiderman developed a series of rules about how the scorecard would be constructed:

- The entire scorecard had to fit on one 8½ by 11 sheet of paper,
- The font size had to be 12 pica or bigger,

EXHIBIT 2   Analog Devices Quality Improvement Goals*

Measurement	1987	Half Life (in months)	1992
External			
On-Time Delivery	85%	9	> 99.8%
Outgoing Defect Level	500 PPM	9	< 10 PPM
Lead Time	10 weeks	9	< 3 weeks
Internal			
Manufacturing Cycle Time	15 weeks	9	4–5 weeks
Process Defect Level	5000 PPM	6	< 10 PPM
Yield	20%	9	> 50%
Time to Market	36 months	24	6 months

*ibid, p. 70.

 • There were to be six times as many nonfinancial measures as financial measures.

In addition to the scorecard and QIP, Schneiderman helped change ADI from doing five-year planning every five years to doing five-year planning every year.

Then Schneiderman helped create divisional scorecards. The measures for most divisions overlapped; all could be tied directly to the overall scorecard for ADI. The way ADI approached this allowed each division to use the same scorecard if they desired, or a unique one. By tailoring scorecards to each division, Schneiderman gave the divisions the wherewithal to negotiate their goals and determine the appropriate half-lives for their measures.

In 1988 Schneiderman began to roll the balanced scorecard out to the entire company. Slowly, each division developed its own scorecard and had each successive level develop its scorecard. As with the overall division scorecards, the lower levels of management were not required to have unique scorecards. Typically, the lower-level managers' scorecards put very little emphasis on financial measures and more on the nonfinancial measures that they could impact.

Additionally, each division was required to share the quarterly scorecard results with every employee in the division.

Division results for each scorecard measures were compared. Exhibit 4 shows how the different divisions were compared by their on-time customer service performance results. Each division was shown together, and the slope, or half-life, of the improvement was shown. In addition to distributing reports like Exhibit 4, Schneiderman would compare the scorecard performance results with the target results during the executive council meetings. On an overhead he would circle any large favorable variations in green and any large unfavorable variations in red; he would then have the divisions' general managers explain what caused the variations.

According to Goodloe Suttler, Vice President and General Manager of the Semiconductor Division, ADI was using the Balanced Scorecard as a communication tool. To the employees it said:

- Measurement is the key to determining success.
- You cannot know how well you are doing unless you have measures.
- Here is what is happening in your division/plant.

EXHIBIT 3   Example Corporate Scorecard for FY 1988

		1Q88		2Q88		3Q88		4Q88		FY88	
		BMP	*Actual*	*BMP*	*Actual*	*BMP*	*Actual*	*BMP*	*Actual*	*BMP*	*Actual*
Financial											
Revenue	$M										
Revenue Growth	%										
Profit	$M										
ROA	%										
New Products											
NP Introductions	#										
NP Bookings	$M										
NP Break-even	#										
NP Peak Revenue	$M										
Time to Market	Months										
QIP											
On-Time Delivery	%										
Cycle Time	Weeks										
Yield	%										
Outgoing Defects	PPM										
Cost	$M										
Employee Productivity	%										
Turnover	%										

To management, it said:

- These scorecard items are the metrics of success.
- Focus on the items critical to success.
- You are accountable for the success of your division/plant.
- You must meet objectives measured in the scorecard.

By 1991 it was being used aggressively on a day-to-day basis throughout the organization.

Financial Performance

During the late 1980s and early 1990s, ADI continued to experience slow growth (as shown in Exhibit 5 and Exhibit 6) even though their score-card measures had improved. The market had reacted to this slow growth during 1988–91 by driving the stock price (ADI—NYSE) from a high of $24.75 per share to a price of around $9.00 per share by 1991. Analog Devices had suffered its first loss ever in 1990. It missed its profitability goals for 1991 by 50 percent, and laid off 600 employees, 10 percent of its workforce. ADI had only a small presence in many of the new growing markets, such as consumer electronics and automotive; furthermore, its systems were not designed for the delivery demands of these industries. Ray Stata indicated that the results would have been far worse without TQM.[9]

---

[9]Shlomo Maital, "Zen and the Art of Total Quality," *Across the Board*, March 1992, pp. 50–51.

EXHIBIT 4

On-time customer service performance monthly data (August 1987–July 1988)*

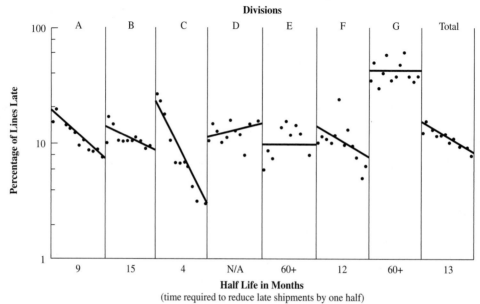

*Ray Stata, "Organizational Learning—The Key to Management Innovation," Sloan Management Review,
Spring 1989, pp. 63–74. Reprinted by permission.

At this same time, ADI's management directly under Stata experienced considerable change. ADI promoted Jerry Fishman to President. It promoted eight new vice presidents, including five from outside of ADI, while a number of long-time vice presidents retired. ADI was attempting to infuse a different culture. As one of the new vice presidents from the outside said, "Analog had a product orientation, not a customer orientation. The financial dip helped bring dramatic changes."[10]

ADI used its corporate scorecard to maintain focus on its critical success factors. ADI had been focusing on new products ever since 1987 and the balanced scorecard kept track of the progress of new product introduction. As a result, by the end

of 1991, products that had been introduced within the last five years accounted for 40 percent of ADI's orders.[11]

Changing Roles

In 1990 Stata decided to become more active in ADI's QIP program. Stata began chairing ADI Quality Council and began sponsoring ADI's quality improvement festival. Also, Stata became a founding member of the Center for Quality Management.

As Stata had already begun doing, the entire senior management team stepped up to the role of quality leaders to demonstrate that improvement is a part of everyone's job. Schneiderman had been ADI's torch bearer during the Era of

---

[10]Interview with Frank Weigold, Vice President and General Manager Transportation and Industrial Products Division, Analog Devices, July 2, 1996.

[11]*Status 1992—A Report On The Integrated Circuit Industry*, Integrated Circuit Engineering Corporation, 1992, pp. 2–12.

Exhibit 5 Consolidated Statement of Income, 1986 to 1995

(Dollars in millions except per share data)	1995	1994	1993	1992	1991	1990	1989	1988	1987	1986
Net Sales	941	773	663	567	538	485	453	439	370	334
Cost of Sales	464	394	351	302	272	244	215	201	172	151
Gross Margin	476	379	315	266	265	241	238	238	199	183
Research and Development expense	134	107	94	88	89	80	69	60	56	45
Selling, marketing, general and administrative expense	184	170	159	151	152	136	126	122	108	97
Total operating expenses	319	277	253	239	248	235	194	183	164	143
Operating Income	157	102	63	26	17	6	44	55	34	40
Total non-operating expenses (income)	(2)	5	7	7	8	20	7	4	9	8
Income before income taxes	159	97	56	19	9	(14)	36	52	26	32
Net income	119	74	44	15	8	(13)	28	38	19	23
Net income per share	1.00	.64	.39	.14	.08	(.28)	.58	.80	.40	.51

Source: Annual Reports

Exhibit 6   Consolidated Balance Sheet, 1986 to 1995

(Dollars in millions)	1995	1994	1993	1992	1991	1990	1989	1988	1987	1986
Assets										
Current Assets:										
Cash, cash equivalents, short-term investments	151	182	81	18	17	8	30	23	6	6
Accounts receivable, net	181	162	146	112	95	98	82	88	76	66
Inventories	144	131	150	142	117	108	98	97	84	79
Total Current Assets	526	505	403	297	249	232	223	221	176	162
Property, Plant and equipment, net	432	282	248	237	224	224	209	201	186	173
Intangible assets, deferred charges and other assets	44	29	27	27	30	31	21	27	35	34
	1,002	816	678	562	503	487	453	449	397	369
Liabilities and Stockholders' Equity										
Current Liabilities:										
Short-term borrowings, current portion of long-term debt and capital lease obligations	2	23	2	3	6	11	9	7	7	10
Accounts payable and accrued liabilities	174	135	99	82	77	93	51	55	46	37
Deferred income on shipments to domestic distributors	28	19	16	13	9	0	0	0	0	0
Income taxes payable	50	29	15	2	5	2	4	11	5	14
Total current liabilities	254	206	133	100	97	106	63	73	58	60
Long-term debt and capital lease obligations	80	80	100	71	37	24	12	23	30	29
Other non-current liabilities	44	8	13	17	15	14	14	13	12	10
Stockholders' equity	656	522	432	375	354	343	363	341	298	270
	1,002	816	678	562	503	487	453	449	397	369

Source: Annual Reports

the Quality Specialist, now it was time to begin the Era of Senior Management. In mid-1992, Art Schneiderman resigned from ADI and passed the torch to the new management team.

QIP Off-Track

Because QIP focused primarily on cost reduction, many managers felt there was little cost reduction left to be done by the early 1990s. Also, the investment necessary to continue the QIP program and to continuously improve were seen as greater than the advantages of continuing. The end result was increased pressure to abandon QIP.

In addition, as Stata pointed out, "There is some closeted cynicism about quality [programs] in the company. Among the engineers, it isn't even closeted. They think it's crap."[12] While many successes had occurred that made QIP appear to be very successful, the cynicism ran deep.

By the mid-1990s, ADI was bouncing back financially and management felt that QIP had improved ADI's profitability by reducing waste, but because it was primarily a cost reduction tool, it could not be credited with ADI's growth. In fact, although ADI was experiencing high growth and profitability, many of the measures of quality were declining. QIP appeared to be at a standstill at ADI. According to Suttler,

> We got off-track on QIP. We hit the stops on capacity and everything was thrown for a loop. This has distracted management for the last two years and caused a disruption in continuous improvement.[13]

ADI still recognized the values of QIP, but felt that it was insufficient to address the new problems that they faced.

---

[12]Rahul Jacob, "QIP, More Than a Dying Fad?" *Fortune*, October 18, 1993, pp. 66–72.

[13]Unless otherwise indicated, the statements in this case attributed to Ray Stata, CEO and Chairman, Goodloe Suttler, Vice President, Strategic Planning, Quality Improvement, and Corporate Marketing, and Frank Weigold, Vice President, Transportation and Industrial Products, all of Analog Devices are from interviews conducted with these individuals on July 2, 1996.

Changing Systems

After Schneiderman left, many of the systems that he had put in place changed or withered away. According to Suttler,

> The Red/Green System died. Art used to take the view that everything had a half-life. Now, we talk about half-life, but we don't push it in setting the scorecard. We don't use it actively in setting objectives. As for the scorecard, its role has changed. It is now a means for communication rather than a means of changing thinking.

Unlike Schneiderman, Suttler had come up through the management ranks at ADI after graduating from the Amos Tuck School of Business Administration, Dartmouth College, in 1976. When ADI started its first venture into QIP back in 1983, Suttler was a Product Line Director. In 1988 he was promoted to General Manager of the Semiconductor Division. He was promoted to Vice President of Strategic Planning, Quality Improvement, and Corporate Marketing in 1992. While originally a QIP skeptic, Suttler became a convert after he had the opportunity to put the QIP to work for him, dramatically improving the quality of his product line.

In Suttler's opinion, there was a "performance paradox." Borrowing ideas from Professor Marshall Meyer at University of Pennsylvania's Wharton School of Management, Suttler believed that all performance measures would eventually degrade. Performance would improve and variability would be reduced to the point where further improvements were of little value. Additionally, people would game the system. As a result, new performance measures must constantly be introduced. Finally, with the new performance measures driving faster change, Meyer states, "accelerated learning rates suggest we will cycle through measures with greater rapidity."[14] Simply put, the better your measure is able to help you improve, the sooner that measure will lose its value. The result of all of this led

---

[14]Goodloe Suttler, Presentation at the Amos Tuck School of Business Administration, April 1996.

EXHIBIT 7

Dynamic complexity of processes

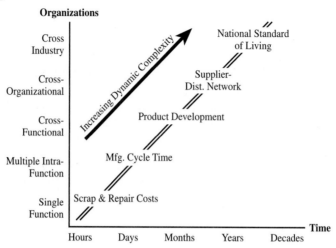

Stata to say, "We are now recognizing as we get more sophisticated, it is harder to get numbers that are meaningful."

ADI began to look for new tools that could make the numbers more meaningful, particularly numbers that were leading indicators of value growth. As Suttler said, "The big problem with QIP is that it has little to say about business strategy. QIP works well at stopping wealth-reducing activities, but wealth creation doesn't naturally come from QIP."

Suttler noted that ADI had been successful in QIP, pointing to a number of dramatic improvements, such as reducing outgoing electrical defectives from over 20,000 PPM in 1987 to less than 50 PPM in 1994 and improving front-to-back IC yields from fewer than 15 percent to more than 60 percent in the same time. On the other hand, Suttler also noted that ADI had started QIP at a point where the cost of waste was 25 percent to 35 percent of sales; ADI had reduced that to under 15 percent in seven years. ADI felt that to reduce the cost due to waste to 3 percent would take another seven years. While management considered cost reduction still important, they stressed that it was not as impor-

tant as trying to discover ways to grow revenues. Using a model of dynamic complexity (see Exhibit 7), ADI's management concluded that growing revenue was a more difficult process than reducing cost, and would take longer to implement.

Hoshin

Feeling that QIP could not work for wealth creation, ADI went in search of new methodologies. Ray Stata learned about a technique called "Hoshin Kanri" as part of his participation in the Center for Quality Management. For Stata, Hoshin was an extension of the QIP effort at ADI and a realistic approach to focusing the energies of the company toward wealth creation. The central idea of Hoshin is to focus the improvement on the one or two breakthrough objectives for the company.

Suttler described Hoshin:

Hoshin literally means "policy deployment and control." Another translation that I have heard the Japanese use is "bright shiny metal compass." So Hoshin tells us to focus on the most important objectives. Analog Devices has two: Delivery and New Products.

Everything you do in Hoshin is based on data collection and PDCA [Plan-Do-Check-Act Cycle]. As a result, we have a much higher degree of confidence that something that is fixed will stay fixed.

Hoshin also leveraged many of the techniques that ADI learned in its QIP program. While already experienced with PDCA, ADI found that implementing Hoshin required more effort than they expected.

Hoshin was believed to provide a mechanism for growth, so Hoshin assumed a prominent place in the ADI scorecard. The Computer Products Division has placed its Hoshin measures at the top of its 1996 Division Scorecard. Throughout ADI the Hoshin measures also took a prominent position on the scorecard. The 1996 Hoshin goals for ADI were 98 percent On-Time Delivery to Platinum Accounts, and 25 percent Sales from New Products (products introduced within the last six quarters).

Key Success Factors

Complementing ADI's scorecard were measurements called "key success factors," which measured milestones related to ADI's business plan. They were monitor points for the tactical plans of ADI's strategy. These factors came from ADI's five-year plan, which it updated yearly, and, in some cases, quarterly because of the speed at which their market was changing. ADI believed that the key success factors were more closely related to wealth creation than those of the scorecard.

One of the differences between the key success factors and the existing scorecard measures is that the key success factors are discrete events. As Suttler states, "The key success factors do not lend themselves to quarterly monitoring. On the other hand, the measures on the balanced scorecard are intrinsically limited, failing to capture key milestones in each business strategy that also need periodic review." The key success factors were either met or not; they did not continue from quarter to quarter. The balanced scorecard

measures, such as on-time delivery, continued to be tracked every quarter.

In 1994 Stata charged Suttler with integrating QIP and planning. As a result Suttler introduced several new tools, such as the 10-step planning methodology adapted from Hewlett-Packard, to try to understand wealth creation in a way that they felt QIP could not. These techniques were used during the five-year planning exercise and to develop tactical plans for ADI. The key success factors were developed with these tools.

One aspect of the new planning system was that the planning was done by teams within the organization, rather than by a centralized planning group. These teams included individual contributors, line managers, and mid-level managers; the people who would be responsible for implementing the plans that they developed.

For 1997, 60 teams have been set loose on topics such as business plans and competitor analysis. ADI management believed that by having the teams develop their business plans themselves, the teams will likely have a high level of commitment to them. For Suttler the most difficult part of this process has been letting go of the strategic strings. Suttler defers to an article by Gary Hamel in the *Harvard Business Review* to make his point:

> Despite years of imploring people to bring their brains to work, to get involved in quality circles, process reengineering, and the like, senior managers have seldom urged them to participate in the process of strategy creation. But if senior managers can't address the challenges of operational improvements by themselves . . . why would they be able to take on the challenge of industry revolution?[15]

In Suttler's opinion, because they result from employee involvement, these business plans have become far more important to ADI than the scorecard.

---

[15]Gary Hamel, "Strategy as Revolution," *Harvard Business Review*, July–August 1996, pp. 75–76.

EXHIBIT 8

The four business drivers for 1996*

Customer Satisfaction	New Product Development
95% on-time delivery by year-end	$300 million in new product sales at 45% gross margin
107,000 6-inch CMOS wafers from external foundries	90% success rate from first silicon with customer samples
13,000 6-inch CMOS wafers from Limerick	6 months to first silicon
3,500 6-inch wafers from Wilmington Mod D	15 months time to market
2,000 6-inch wafers from Sunnyvale	1.5 tapeouts per new product
Organizational Capabilities	**Financial Expectations**
1000 new employees	$1.2 billion in revenue for 25% growth
150 new college graduates	50% gross margin, including new fabs
Employee turnover less than 7%	$175 million in net research and development spending
90% of new employees on board within less than 90 days of requisitions	$200 million in Sales, Marketing, General and Administrative (SMG&A) spending or 16% of sales
Voice-of-the-Employee baseline score established	$225 million in operating profit before taxes or 19% of sales

*Vision 2000: Leadership for the 21st Century, Analog Devices, Inc., 1996.

Vision 2000

Now is the time to set a new vision for the future that builds on the accomplishments of the past; fully exploits our leadership in signal processing; captures new opportunities in rapidly emerging markets; and catapults ADI to a multi-billion dollar enterprise.[16]

As part of its 1995 planning process, ADI developed what it called *Vision 2000* which set forth 3 major objectives:

- Building leadership positions in seven critical areas of signal processing.
- Increasing its growth rate for sales and profits to greater than 20 percent.
- Growing its organization and developing the skills and competencies of all employees.[17]

---

[16]*Vision 2000: Leadership for the 21st Century*, Analog Devices, Inc., 1996.

[17]Ibid.

Through the Hoshin process, these goals have been translated into specific and measurable objectives for every function of ADI.

Vision 2000 also included a plan for 1996 which divided the critical measures into four business drivers (see Exhibit 8).

Each business driver was supported by underlying objectives. For example, the objective of 95 percent on-time delivery by year-end supported the customer satisfaction business driver. The objectives for the four business drivers for 1996 were clear and measurable. Some of these objectives, such as on-time delivery, were also part of the scorecard. Other objectives, such as achieving $175 million in net research and development spending, appeared as key success factors.

ADI was using Hoshin, QIP, the corporate scorecard, and key success factors to create, deploy, and implement strategy. While the systems were in place, the questions still remained: How should Stata and ADI implement needed change? How important is ADI's corporate scorecard in creating change? How must these systems evolve for ADI to achieve its objectives for Vision 2000?

> Much remains to be done. We face unprecedented opportunities and we are poised for extraordinary growth. It is up to all of us to seize these opportunities and to create the future for Analog Devices.

> Ray Stata
> *Vision 2000*

Questions

Time Frame: 1988

1. Critically evaluate the "half-life" concept, in light of Analog Devices' strategy during the second half of the 1980s. What are the potential and limitations of the half-life concept? How would a company develop the half-life for different processes?

2. Identify the conflicts which exist between the QIP measures and the measures reported by the financial system. Which numbers should we believe? Can they be reconciled?

3. Critically assess the usefulness of the information contained in the corporate scorecard in Exhibit 3 as a way to implement Analog Devices' strategy as of 1988. What role does each set of measures play? What should be the relative importance of financial versus nonfinancial measures? What additional information would you like to see included in the scorecard?

Time Frame: 1988–1996

4. Evaluate the evolution of the corporate scorecard and related management planning and control systems at Analog Devices during 1988–95.

5. Describe Analog Devices' strategy as of 1996. How should the corporate scorecard, and other management systems, change in 1996 to best fit the strategic needs of the company?

CASE 11–2
WARREN INSURANCE COMPANY

Joseph Allen was assistant to the controller of Warren Insurance, a large insurance company. Emily Scott, the controller, handed him an article, "Your Company's Most Valuable Asset: Intellectual Capital,"[1] and asked Allen to look into the topic discussed therein and recommend what, if any action, Scott should take. The article contained a number of examples of companies that were making efforts to measure and manage intellectual capital. They are summarized in Exhibit 1.

Skandia Navigator

Allen was intrigued by the practices of Skandia, an international insurance and financial services corporation based in Sweden, referred to in the article. Allen wrote to the company, and received its 1994 and 1995 annual reports together with "supplements" to these reports describing Skandia's views on intellectual capital. Excerpts from these supplements are given in Exhibit 2.

According to its annual reports, Skandia is a dominant provider of life and nonlife insurance and financial services in Sweden, with a marketshare of over 40 percent in life insurance. Skandia also has strong operations in other Nordic countries and competitive operations worldwide. In addition, Skandia is the world leader in a few specialized areas of insurance, such as aviation insurance. Eighty-five percent of Skandia's premiums are generated outside of Sweden.

In 1995 Skandia's premiums were 52,521 million Swedish Kronor (8,097 million USD[2]). Fifty percent of Skandia's premium revenue came from its worldwide life reassurance business. Since 1991 Skandia has seen its profitability vary from a loss of 2,369 MSEK (365 MUSD) in 1992 to a gain of 1,384 MSEK (213 MUSD) in 1993.

With the article and the Skandia supplements, Allen needed to decide if measuring intellectual capital was worth further investigation and consideration by Warren Insurance.

Questions

1. What is your evaluation of Skandia's approach to measuring intellectual capital? How about other companies included in Exhibit 1?
2. What advice do you have for Allen in terms of measuring intellectual capital for Warren Insurance?

This case was prepared by Kirk Hendrickson (Tuck '97) under the supervision of Professor Vijay Govindarajan. The case is mostly based on materials furnished by Skandia. Copyright by Osceola Institute.

[1]Thomas A. Stewart, *Fortune*, July 8, 1994, pp. 68–74.

[2]The exchange rate is an estimate computed based on 6.49 Swedish Kronor (SEK) to 1.00 U.S. dollar (USD).

Exhibit 1   **Examples of Measuring and Managing Intellectual Capital**

Canadian Imperial Bank of Commerce

CIBC has changed its lending strategy to lend based on intellectual, "soft" assets instead of tangible, "hard" assets. CIBC believes that hard assets can devalue more rapidly than soft assets, so companies based on intellectual assets are at a lower risk of default than those based on tangible assets.

CIBC defines intellectual capital in three ways: human capital, structural capital, and customer capital. Human capital comes from each employee's ability to provide value to the customer. Structural capital is assets such as brands, databases, and work methodologies that leverage employee skills to satisfy customers' demands. Customer capital is the base of customers that interact with the company and their attitudes and actions towards the company.

CIBC has a goal of being able to compare all investment opportunities in a direct fashion so that managers can trade-off between investments in hard and soft assets. To do this, CIBC uses a series of measures for the different types of intellectual capital. For example, human capital is measured by such measurements as the speed of learning in a department, weaknesses in competencies within a department, and the number of new ideas implemented. Customer capital is measured by the level of customer satisfaction, the speed of solving customer complaints, the length of a customer relationship, and the level of price sensitivity.

One major area of change as a result of its intellectual capital perspective is that CIBC established a set of competencies that each employee needs to develop. The level to which all employees have developed these competencies measures the level of human capital at CIBC. Different positions require different competencies at varying levels. Each employee is responsible for developing the skills necessary for his/her current job. As a result, CIBC has eliminated its formal training program, which was costing the company $30 million per year, replacing it with a variety of self-paced learning tools and learning centers.

Dow Chemical

Gordon Petrash, Dow Chemical's Director of Intellectual Asset Management, wants to make managing patents as easy as managing tangible assets. Petrash is responsible for actively managing Dow's portfolio of patents, of which Dow has about 29,000 in-force.*

The Intellectual Asset Management group builds and prunes Dow's patent portfolio by managing patents that were frequently ignored. These patents were not being commercialized or licensed and no one was responsible for doing this, even though each patent could cost up to $250,000 per year to keep in-force. Additionally, the group seeks out new opportunities for applying and enhancing the patents.

Petrash developed a six-step approach to managing intellectual assets that assesses, analyzes, and evaluates, or applies value to, various assets; the result of his approach is the formation of a new intellectual assets portfolio.

Dow Chemical credits this six-step process with a number of successes in reducing costs, increasing patent enforceability, and discovering new products.

---

*Petrash believes that patents are the best of the intellectual assets to start managing.

EXHIBIT 1   Examples of Measuring and Managing Intellectual Capital (*Continued*)

Hughes Space & Communications Division

A division of Hughes Aircraft and a designer of communication satellites, Hughes Space & Communications Division is involved in trying to create what it calls its "knowledge highway." The "knowledge highway" is an attempt to turn contextual knowledge into usable tools for its engineers.

Arian Ward, head of business engineering at HSCD, believes that there are two types of knowledge, rules based and contextual.* Rules-based knowledge relies on following a set of rules to get a correct answer. Contextual knowledge uses wisdom, stories, and experience that change meaning depending on the context in which they are applied. Ward feels that HSCD is losing contextual knowledge created when it develops a satellite. The result is that knowledge is often reinvented, consuming many other resources to recreate the intellectual assets.

Ward is implementing "lessons-learned" databases and "knowledge maps" to prevent the loss of intellectual capital. The lessons-learned databases are for improving access to past decisions, designs, and problems, by recording design decisions and how they were made in a format that is more accessible to current engineers. The knowledge maps are for locating where the knowledge is in the company, in what systems and in whose heads. Rather than just being an index of experts, these maps provide paths to the knowledge, leading through the different individuals who possess the intellectual assets. Both systems will improve the contextual knowledge because Ward feels that "people think in terms of stories, not facts." He believes these systems will preserve the stories, not just the facts.

From: Thomas Stewart, "Your Company's Most Valuable Asset: Intellectual Capital," *Fortune*, July 8, 1994, pp. 68–74. © 1994 Time Inc. All rights reserved.

*While Ward did not directly use the word *contextual*, it summarizes the variety of terms with which he described this second type of knowledge.

Exhibit 2   Excerpts from Skandia Annual Reports

A: Visualizing Intellectual Capital in Skandia*

Auditors, analysts, and accounting people have long lacked instruments and generally accepted norms for accurately evaluating service companies and their 'intellectual capital.' . . . At Skandia we have always maintained that our intellectual capital is at least as important as our financial capital in providing truly sustainable earnings. . . . Back in 1991 we instituted a function in our AFS unit to develop a method for describing Skandia's human capital, structural capital, and customer capital. Leif Edvinsson was appointed the world's first director of intellectual capital (according to Tom Stewart, *Fortune*, October 1994). The intention was to try to devise adequate valuation indicators that could at the same time serve as management tools for a service company. . . . As we now extend this information to cover additional Skandia units, we do so under the name *Skandia Navigator*, to underscore the fact that it is an instrument to help us navigate into the future . . .

Hidden Assets in the Company

The aggregate sum of these intangible values [in knowledge-intensive operations] can be called Intellectual Capital, which comprises both human capital and structural capital.

Human capital represents the knowledge, skill, and capability of the individual employees to provide solutions to the customer. Structural capital consists of everything that remains when the employees go home: databases, customer files, software, manuals, trademarks, organizational structures, and so on—in other words, organizational capability. Customer capital, i.e., the relationships built up with the customers, is a significant part of structural capital. Structural capital can be owned, which is not the case with human capital.

Human capital and structural capital are an indication of a company's future value and ability to generate financial results.

Early Indicators

Although substantial investments are made today in intellectual capital, the payoff and value will not be visible in the financial accounting until some time later on. Through systematic accounting of developments in various areas—such as customer base, staff competence, and processes—an earlier indication of the company's future performance can be obtained.

Skandia Navigator

Skandia's new reporting model, the Skandia Navigator [see Figure 1] is designed to provide a balanced picture of the financial and intellectual capital. The focus on financial results, capital, and monetary flows is complemented by a description of intellectual capital and its development. . . . At Skandia the intellectual capital ratios are grouped into major focus areas: the Customer focus, the Process focus, the Human focus, and the Renewal & Development focus.

---

*Supplement to Skandia's 1994 Annual Report.

EXHIBIT 2   Excerpts from Skandia Annual Reports (*Continued*)

FIGURE 1

The Skandia Navigator

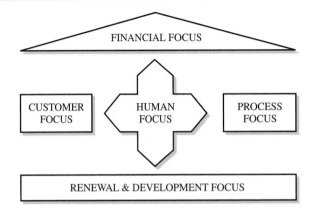

This broadened, balanced type of accounting and reporting results in a more systematic description of the company's ability and potential to transform intellectual capital into financial capital. The specific ratios compiled from the measurements will then become leading indicators.

B: Intellectual Capital: Value-Creating Processes[†]

The Supplement to Skandia's 1995 Annual Report includes Skandia Navigator results for nine selected divisions throughout Skandia's worldwide operations. Each division selected different measures within the five focus areas that they felt best reflected their business situation. The measures and results for three of these divisions are shown below.

Skandia International, Mexico (Table 1)

Twenty-five people work in Mexico with nonlife reinsurance, mainly of fire risks. . . . Due to the risk exposure, it is crucial that Skandia sets the right rate level and keeps its total risk exposure controlled.

TABLE 1   Skandia International, Mexico

Financial Focus	*1995*	*1994*	*1993*
Insurance result, net (MSEK)	66	56	35
Claims ratio, net	48%	37%	63%
Premium income, net (MSEK)	222	185	121
Customer Focus			
Number of visits/underwriter & year	65	65	65
Number of alliances	130	130	130

†Supplement to Skandia's 1995 Annual Report.

Exhibit 2 Excerpts from Skandia Annual Reports (*Continued*)

Table 1 (*Continued*)

Human Focus

Number of employees	25	24	24
Insurance result/employee (MSEK)	2.6	2.3	1.5

Process Focus

Number of offers and endorsements handled	6,550	n.a.	4,320
Adm. costs/premium income, net	3%	n.a.	9%

Renewal & Development Focus

Repeat ratio	98%	98%	98%
(# of renewed contracts in relation to total number of contracts)			
Increase in net premium	20%	53%	38%

One way of measuring the value of regular contacts with customers is to analyse the number of contracts renewed by the office. Coupled with information on profitability, it is possible to calculate the value of the customer portfolio. The renewal rate also affects internal efficiency, since a customer who returns year after year requires less work from the second year onwards.

Customer loyalty and the quality of customer relationships are shown in the contract renewal rate. During the past five years this has been very high, amounting to approximately 90 per cent, with average duration of customers at 4.5 years.

SkandiaLink (Table 2)

. . . SkandiaLink provides unit linked assurance with a focus on the Swedish market.

Table 2 SkandiaLink

Financial Focus	1995	1994	1993
Premium income, gross (MSEK)	2,087	1,874	1,145
Management operating result (MSEK)	176	132	136.5
Funds Managed (MSEK)	6,641	4,257	n.a.
Customer Focus			
Number of contracts	153,104	114,919	74,253
Surrender rate	1.1%	1.0%	n.a.
Human Focus			
Number of employees	48	51	52
Empowerment index (max. value = 1,000)	464	534	n.a.
Process Focus			
Admin. expense/premium income, gross	5.0%	4.5%	5.7%
IT expense/administrative expense	29.7%	28.0%	26.0%
Renewal & Development Focus			
Number of contracts/employee	3,180	2,253	1,439
Fund switches through Telelink	40%	22%	n.a.

EXHIBIT 2   Excerpts from Skandia Annual Reports (*Continued*)

To establish a 'continuous improvement' culture, a control model has been introduced which uses operational indicators that are coupled to the daily work performed by the customer service organization. These indicators measure the parameters that customers—according to surveys—consider to be essential for meeting their quality standards. In addition, through changed work methods, customers should also be able to directly impact these indicators. The responsible departmental heads regularly monitor changes in the indicators through an information system. This enables the company to take corrective measures at an early stage.

Skandia Life UK Group (Table 3)

Skandia Life provides a range of unit linked assurance products, from strictly savings-oriented products, to contracts with varying degrees of insurance protection. The group's products are sold primarily to customers in the UK . . .

TABLE 3   Skandia Life UK Group

Financial Focus	1995	1994	1993
Return on net asset value	22.5%	33.2%	21.8%
Management operating result (MGBP)	36.8	41.5	22.5
Funds managed (MGBP)	3,675	2,942	2,249
Customer Focus			
Number of contracts	250,807	228,397	189,076
Savings/contract (GBP 000s)	15.0	12.8	11.9
Service Awards (max. value = 5)	5	5	5
Human Focus			
Number of employees (full-time)	797	720	566
Process Focus			
Number of contracts/employee	315	317	334
Renewal & Development Focus			
Increase in net premium, new sales	− 34%	95%	92%
Pension products, share of new sales	23%	13%	24%
Increase in funds managed	25%	31%	58%

. . . Skandia Life started a companywide programme in 1993, entitled "Clearly First." This programme continues to yield superb results by focusing the minds of all staff on the prime objective in order to meet the needs of their customers, internal as well as external. The company is striving to be "clearly the first choice provider for the IFA [Independent Financial Advisors] market."

EXHIBIT 2   Excerpts from Skandia Annual Reports (*Continued*)

C: Organizational Capital Summary[‡]

In addition to the Skandia Navigator, Skandia has also included a summary of each division's value-creating processes. Each division focuses on the value-creating processes, developing methods for capturing the intellectual capital. These methods are described in the organization capital column, as they are what creates organizational capital. The third column contains Skandia's description of the effect that these value-creating processes and the ability to create organizational capital have on the division's business performance.

Creating Organizational Capital (Table 4)

Systematic management of intellectual capital creates growth in shareholder value. This is accomplished, among other things, through the continuous recycling and creative utilization of shared knowledge and experience. This, in turn, requires the structuring and packaging of competencies with the help of technology, process descriptions, manuals, networks, and so on, to ensure that the competence will remain with the company when the employees go home.

Based on Skandia's model for development of indicators, critical value-creating work processes can be identified. Once packaged, these become a part of the company's structural capital—or more precisely, its organizational capital.

TABLE 4   Value-Creating Work Processes by Business Unit

Business Unit	Value-Creating Processes	Organizational Capital	Business Effects
Vesta Processes for profitable customer relationships	• Systematized risk assessment and selection • Development of distribution channels to extend the duration • Development of IT-based support systems	• Database with overview of customer categories, so-called observation risks, no-risk, authorization system • Routine manuals & systems for sales, customer care, customer renewal, operations, claims handling • Offer handling & analysis system	• Risk level (claims ratio) better than average • Improved distribution effectiveness • Growing market share • Increasing customer loyalty • Decreasing overhead ratio • Growing sales via alliances
Mexico Processes for risk management	• Risk assessment, management and selection • Relationship development, customer care • Competence cooperation	• Guidelines, manuals for risk management • Work procedures for relationship development and customer care • Packaged, communicated strategy	• Greater customer loyalty • Higher contract renewal rate • Greater number of offers handled • Falling administrative expense ratio

---

[‡]Supplement to Skandia's 1995 Annual Report.

Exhibit 2   Excerpts from Skandia Annual Reports (*Continued*)

Table 4 (*Continued*)

SkandiaLink Learning processes	• Automated fund switching • Transaction processing & telephone accessibility • Staff reward system • Augmentation of customer care	• SkandiaLink Investment Analysis (SIA) • Value development process • Automatic fund-switching service, Telelink • FLINK Index (administrative routines for business handling) • Routine handbook for transaction processing • Customer Centres • Customer Care groups	• Shorter processing times • Decreasing expense ratio • Growing volume of assignments/ representatives • Increased number of automatic fund switches • Greater staff commitment
Skandia Life UK Group Commitment to service - "Clearly First"	• Market referencing • Weekly measurement of administrative processes • Staff programme - "Clearly First"	• Quality processes • Fund management concept • "Investment Department" with 6,000 specialists	• Service Awards • Investment Performance Awards • Growth in market share
American Skandia From process focus to core competence	• Streamlined processes and work routines • Model for identifying value-creating processes - process knowledge • Knowledge from fund managers and IT department	• Process inventory and imaging system/workflow system • Process measurement system • On-line product and rule library (Lotus SmarText) • Sales support & electronic package (ASSESS)	• Streamlining of paperwork flows through image-processing techniques • Structured processes in customer service unit • Assessment of company's IT literacy • Process Hierarchy inventory

---

Source: *Intellectual Capital Value-Creating Processes: Supplement to Skandia's 1995 Annual Report*

Glossary[§]

Contract:	Insurance contract (policy) between Skandia and a policyholder.
Empowerment index:	From a recurring SIFO (the Swedish Institute of Public Opinion Research) survey, an index is created to measure employee motivation, support in the organization, sensitivity to quality demands, matching of responsibility and authority, and competence. The scale is from 0 to 1,000.
Intellectual capital:	The gap between stock market value and book value, also called Tobin's Q, as well as the sum of human capital plus structural capital.
Managed assets:	The amount at a given point in time that is managed on behalf of investors in funds.

[§]Supplement to Skandia's 1995 Annual Report.

Exhibit 2   Excerpts from Skandia Annual Reports (*Continued*)

Organizational capital:	Systematized and packaged competence, plus systems for leveraging the company's innovative strength and value-creating organizational capability.
Surrender ratio:	Surrenders (during the year) in relation to the average mathematical reserve (net).
Unit linked assurance:	A form of life assurance in which the policyholder can choose from a number of investment alternatives offered by the insurance company for the savings portion of paid-in-premiums.
Value creating processes:	Term describing various related activities that create value which customers are cognizant of and are willing to pay for.

CASE 11–3
GENERAL ELECTRIC COMPANY (B)

The General Electric Company is a large multilocation corporation engaged in the manufacture and marketing of a wide variety of electrical and allied products. In 1964, there were almost 400 separate product lines and over three million catalog items. Sales volume in that year totaled $4,941 million, and net income was $237 million. Total employment was about 262,000.

Early in the 1950s, General Electric initiated an extensive decentralization of authority and responsibility for the operations of the company. The basic unit of organization became the product department. As of 1964, there were over 100 of these departments.

The company recognized that if this decentralization was to be fully effective it would need an improved system of management control. It also recognized that any improved system of control would require better measures of performance. To meet this need, the company established a measurements project and created a special organizational unit to carry out this project. This case summarizes the main features of this project, with particular emphasis on measuring performance of the operating (i.e., product) departments.

The Measurements Project

The measurements project was established in 1952. Responsibility for the project was assigned to accounting services, one of the corporate functional services divisions. A permanent organizational unit, initially called measurement service, was set up to carry out this project.

An early step in the measurements project was the development of a set of principles by which the project was to be governed. Five such principles were formulated:

1. Measurements were to be designed to measure the performance of *organizational components*, rather than of *managers*.
2. Measurements were to involve common *indexes* of performance, but not common *standards* of performance. (For example, rate of return on investment might be the index of performance common to all product departments, but the standard in terms of this index might be 12 percent for one department and 25 percent for another.)
3. Measurements were to be designed as aids to judgment in appraisal of performance, and not to supplant judgment.
4. Measurements were to give proper weight to future performance as well as current performance, in order to facilitate the maintenance of a balance between the long run and the near term.
5. Measurements were to be selected so as to facilitate constructive action, not to restrict such action.

The overall measurements project was divided into three major subprojects:

1. Operational measurements of the results of a product department.
2. Functional measurements of the work of engineering, manufacturing, marketing and finance, employee and plant community relations, and legal components of the organization.
3. Measurements of the work of managing as such—planning, organizing, integrating, and measuring itself.

The first step in the subproject on operational measurements was to develop an answer to the following question:

What are the specific areas for which measurements should be designed, bearing in mind that sound measurements of overall performance require a proper balance among the various functions and among the aspects (planning, organizing, for example) of managing?[1]

This case was prepared by R. H. Caplan/R. N. Anthony, Harvard Business School. Copyright © by the President and Fellows of Harvard College Harvard Business School case 113–121.

[1]Lewis, "Measuring, Reporting and Appraising Results of Operations," p. 30.

In seeking an answer to this question, the organization made a careful analysis of the nature and purposes of the basic kinds of work performed by each functional unit with the purpose of singling out those functional objectives that were of sufficient importance to the welfare of the business[2] as a whole, to be termed "key result areas."

The Key Result Areas

In order to determine whether an area tentatively identified according to the preceding analytical framework was sufficiently basic to qualify as a key result area, the organization established a criterion in the form of the following test question.

> Will continued failure in this area prevent the attainment of management's responsibility for advancing General Electric as a leader in a strong, competitive economy, even though results in all other key areas are good?[3]

As an outcome of analysis and application of this test, eight key result areas were decided on. These were as follows:

1. Profitability.
2. Market position.
3. Productivity.
4. Product leadership.
5. Personnel development.
6. Employee attitudes.
7. Public responsibility.
8. Balance between short-range and long-range goals.

Each of these key result areas is described below.

Profitability.　　The key index used by General Electric to measure profitability was "dollars of residual income." Residual income was defined as net profit after taxes, less a capital charge.

The capital charge was a certain percentage (say, 6 percent) of the net assets assigned to the department; it corresponded to an imputed interest charge. The criteria formulated to guide the development of a satisfactory measure of profitability were expressed as follows:

1. An index that recognized the contribution of capital investment to profits.
2. An index that recognized what human work and effort contribute to profits.
3. An index that recognized the "corporate facts of life" (e.g., one consistent with General Electric's needs and organizational objectives).
4. An index that served to make the operating decisions of individual managers in the company's best interests.

In the process of selecting and developing a measure of profitability, the measurements organization considered several more conventional indexes, including rate of return on investment, ratio of profit to sales, and ratio of profit to value added. A weakness of these ratios or indices was stated in this way:

> . . . the acid test of an index should be its effectiveness in guiding decentralized management to make decisions in the best interests of the company overall, since operating managers' efforts naturally will be to improve the performance of their businesses in terms of the index used for evaluation. This test points up the particular weakness of rate of return and of other ratio indexes, such as percent profit to sales. This weakness is the tendency to encourage concentration on improvement of the *ratios* rather than on improvement in *dollar* profits. Specifically, the business with the better results in terms of the ratios will tend to make decisions based on the effect the decisions will have on the particular business's current *ratio* without consideration of the *dollar* profits involved. This tends to retard incentive to growth and expansion because it dampens the incentive of the more profitable businesses to grow.[4]

Market Position.　　Performance in this key result area was measured in terms of the share of

---

[2]The word *business* is used here to refer to a product department, not to the whole company.

[3]Lewis, "Measuring, Reporting and Appraising Results of Operations," p. 30.

[4]Ibid., p. 32.

the market obtained during a given measurement period. The measurement was expressed as a percentage of available business in the market. Market, as used in this sense, was expressed in dollars or units, kilowatt-ampere, or other meaningful terms.

The first major consideration in designing market position measurements is a determination of what constitutes a product line and what constitutes the market for each product line of a business. A product line may be defined as a grouping of products in accordance with the purposes they serve or the essential wants they satisfy. The definition is somewhat misleading in that a product line may be a broad classification, such as clocks, or it may be a narrow classification, such as alarm clocks, kitchen clocks, or mantel clocks. In addition, product lines may overlap so that a particular product could be included in several product lines. Hence, the actual grouping of products by product lines must be accurately identified.

There may be wide variations in the interpretation of what constitutes the market for a given product line. Therefore, it is important that for each of their lines, our product departments identify such things as:

1. Whether the market includes not only directly competing products but also indirectly competing products (electric ranges versus electric ranges; electric ranges versus all types of ranges—electric, gas, oil, and others).

2. Whether the market includes sales by all domestic competitors or only those reporting to trade associations.

3. Whether the market includes imports, if foreign sellers are competing in the domestic market.

4. Whether the market includes export sales.

5. Whether the market includes captive sales.

6. Whether the market is considered to be represented by sales to distributors, or to retailers, or to ultimate users.

In other words, in establishing measurements of market position there should be a clear understanding of precisely what comprises the product line and what comprises the market. The purpose of having sharp definitions of these two items is, of course, to avoid being misled into thinking we are doing better than we actually are simply because of failure to identify the nature and extent of our competition.[5]

Productivity.   Although the concept of productivity is a relatively simple one—a relationship of output of goods and services to the resources consumed in their production—this concept proved a difficult one to make operational as a measure of performance. For the national economy as a whole, it has been the practice to look at productivity simply in terms of the amount of output per unit of labor input. In any given firm, however, labor is only one of the factors contributing to output. Therefore, the company sought to develop an index that would accomplish two things: (1) broaden the input base so as to recognize that capital as well as labor contributed to improvements in productivity, and (2) eliminate from the measure those improvements contributed by suppliers of materials.

On the output side of the productivity ratio, the company considered several refinements of sales billed. One such refinement was the use of value added (e.g., sales billed less the cost of goods or services acquired outside the company). On the input side, the company considered payroll dollars plus depreciation dollars. Payroll dollars were included in the variable, rather than labor hours, so as to give effect to differences in the labor skills employed. The inclusion of depreciation charges constituted an attempt to include the consumption of capital resources. All factors were to be readjusted for changes in the price level, so that changes in the resulting ratio would more nearly reflect real changes in productivity.

Product Leadership.   Product leadership was defined as "the ability of a business to lead its industry in originating or applying the most advanced scientific and technical knowledge in the engineering, manufacturing and marketing fields to the development of new products and to improvements in the quality or value of existing products."[6] To make this definition operational, procedures were established for appraising periodically the products of each department. These

---

[5]Ibid., p. 33.

[6]Ibid., pp. 35–36.

appraisals were directed at providing answers to the following questions.

1. How did each product compare with competition and with company standards?

2. Where within the company was the research conducted upon which the product was based?

3. Who first introduced the basic product and subsequent improvements, General Electric or a competitor?

The appraisal procedures were based largely on qualitative rather than quantitative considerations. Appraisals were made by appropriate experts from the areas of engineering, marketing, accounting, and manufacturing. In general, these experts were located within the product department for which the appraisal was to be made. Standard forms were employed so as to facilitate as high a degree of consistency as possible. The trends revealed by these appraisals over a period of time were considered to be as significant as the specific information revealed by an appraisal for a particular period.

Personnel Development. For the purposes of measurement, personnel development was defined as "the systematic training of managers and specialists to fill present and future needs of the company, to provide for further individual growth and retirements and to facilitate corporate growth and expansion."[7] Management of General Electric defined personnel development as including "programs in each field of functional endeavor, such as engineering, manufacturing, marketing and finance, and broad programs aimed at developing an understanding of the principles of managing. Such programs must be designed to provide a continuous flow of potentially promotable employees in sufficient numbers to permit proper selection and development of individuals for each position. And, at the same time, these programs must encourage competition and initiative for further individual growth."[8]

Three steps were involved in the measurement of performance in this key result area. (1) The basic soundness of the various programs or techniques being sponsored by a product depart-

ment for the development of its employees was appraised. (2) An inventory was taken of the available supply of trained men, as well as their qualifications, for the key positions that must eventually be filled within the department. (3) The effectiveness with which the department executed its personnel development programs was evaluated.

The first step consisted of judgments regarding the adequacy of the following elements in the development process:

Recruitment. How good a job was being done in the selection of candidates for the development process?

On-the-job training. What programs were available for training candidates, for providing information and knowledge about both general company matters and job particulars, and for advanced training for those who had been on the job for a while?

Review and counsel. Was there any provision for periodically reviewing the performance of the men, for discussing with an individual the caliber of his work, for providing help and consultation, and for identifying especially promising talent?

Placement. What was being done to see that recruits were placed in jobs commensurate with their interests and abilities, that the more promising were rotated, and that promotions came to those who merited them?

The second step was accomplished with the aid of manning tables and related inventorying procedures. These procedures were directed primarily at determining the training background of each employee in the inventory; that is, graduates of company-sponsored programs, those hired from outside the company, and those who attained their positions without the benefit of a company-sponsored program.

The investigating group used two statistical measures in carrying out the third step. The first of these was the ratio of the number of employees promoted (both within department and through transfer to another department) in a given period (usually a year) to the total number of employees regarded as "promotable" during the same period. The second measure was tied in with the personnel rating procedure employed throughout the company. At the conclusion of

---

[7]Ibid., p. 37.
[8]Ibid.

each performance review cycle, the rating forms for a particular department were analyzed to determine the proportions of employees whose performance was considered to be (a) improving, (b) unchanged, and (c) deteriorating.

Employee Attitudes.   For purposes of developing measurements of performance in this key area, the group defined an attitude as "a generalized point of view toward objects, events, or persons which might serve to influence future behavior." It used two basic approaches to the measurement of attitudes. The first involved the use of statistical indicators, such as turnover rate, absenteeism, number of grievances, lateness, and accident experience. The second approach involved a periodic survey of employees through questionnaires.

Several shortcomings were recognized in the first approach. (1) The statistical indicators provided little or no information about underlying causes. (2) In general, the indicators told of trouble only after the harm had been done. (3) Because these indicators were traditionally associated with the personnel functions, managers tended to minimize their importance or else place responsibility for improvement on the personnel function. (4) Unfavorable trends in certain of these indicators might be due to external factors (e.g., short labor supply) rather than to some shortcomings of management.

The attitude survey made use of a standardized questionnaire designed to reveal the attitudes of employees in a number of broad areas. The survey was administered at intervals of about 18 months. Results for each attitude area were tabulated in terms of proportion of responses that were favorable. Tabulations were made by work groups and not by individual employees; this practice helped protect the anonymity of responses, and thus the validity of the surveys.

Public Responsibility.   This key result area evolved from General Electric's recognition of its obligation to conduct itself as a good citizen within society, complying faithfully with the laws and ethics governing business conduct. The company believed its progress required not only an active recognition of the broad public interest, but also a responsiveness to certain special publics who had a stake in the success of the business—namely, shareowners, customers, employees, vendors, dealers and distributors, the plant community, educational institutions, and government.

While the responsibility to certain publics such as shareowners, educational institutions, and the federal government could best be measured from an overall company viewpoint rather than departmentally, nevertheless, the actions taken by a product department (including the individual acts of employees of that department) could have an important impact on the whole company's reputation as a good corporate citizen. Accordingly, the company attempted to assure wholehearted observance of the legal and ethical standards of business by insisting that all managerial and professional employees at least once a year conduct periodical surveys of the activities of those who reported to them with respect to antitrust compliance, conflict of interest, and other areas of business practice. These matters were discussed with each individual, who then signed a statement affirming his understanding and compliance.

Other measurements related to the effectiveness of department action in strengthening the company's reputation and business relationships. With respect to fulfilling obligations to customers, it was determined that the previously mentioned product leadership and market position areas were the best indicators. For the remaining publics, the following measures were recommended.

Shareowners.   The total shares of General Electric Company stock were to be "allocated" to the various operating components that were assigned responsibility for preserving and enhancing "their portion" of the shareowners' investment in the company.

Vendors, dealers, and distributors.   Suppliers of raw materials and parts were to be surveyed periodically to determine their appraisal of the department's practices in conducting its business as compared with the practices of others who bought from them. Dealers and distributors were likewise to be interviewed from time to time to measure whether these important relationships were being responsibly maintained.

Plant community.   Again, comprehensive reaction surveys were to be used, aimed at identifying the impact of the actions of a product department on the individuals who made up the community. These reactions disclosed by the opinion surveys were to be supplemented by use of trends developed from various types of data such as community wage rates, number of employment applications received, volume of purchases made locally, contributions to local charities, and participation in civic, church, and business organizations.

Balance between Short-Range and Long-Range Goals.   This factor was set out separately as a key result area in order to emphasize the importance of the long-term survival and growth of the company. Short-range goals and performance had to be balanced against the need for satisfactory performance 5, 10, 15 years in the future, since undue pressure for current profits could, in effect, borrow from the future.

Various means were employed to experiment with suggested measures in this key result area. However, it is important to note that when the eight key result areas were established, each of the first seven had both short-range and long-range dimensions. The eighth area, balance between short-range and long-range goals, had been specifically identified to make sure that the long-range health of the company would not be sacrificed for short-term gains. The plans, goals, and actions in each of the other areas were, therefore, to be appraised in terms of both their short-term and their long-term implications.

Initial Implementation

During the period after the measurements project was established in 1952, deep research work was carried on to establish the specific measurements in each of the eight key result areas. Before communicating these measures to the product departments, the investigators reviewed the recommendations in each area with operating personnel and with officers, for their comments, suggestions, and final approval.

The company's business planning, budgeting, and forecasting program incorporated the use of selected key result areas in (1) reviewing the recent history and current status, (2) setting standards for each department, (3) planning to achieve the standards, and (4) periodic reporting and measurement of accomplishment. Since the first four key result areas lent themselves readily to numerical evaluations, they were a part of the planning, budgeting, forecasting, reporting, and measuring system. Building on this experience in using the key result areas to plan and measure performance, management at the General Electric Company made the search for effective business measurements a continuing, evolutionary process.

Questions

1. For the purpose described, how should profitability be defined? The definition should be specific enough so that a quantitative measure can be constructed from it.

2. What, if anything, do the factors other than profitability add to the proposed measurement system? Isn't the impact of the other factors reflected in the profitability measure if it is properly constructed?

Case 11–4
Enager Industries, Inc.

I don't get it. I've got a nifty new product proposal that can't help but make money, and top management turns thumbs down. No matter how we price this new item, we expect to make $390,000 on it pretax. That would contribute over 15 cents per share to our earnings after taxes, which is more than the 10 cent earnings-per-share increase in 1993 that the president made such a big thing about in the shareholders' annual report. It just doesn't make sense for the president to be touting e.p.s. while his subordinates are rejecting profitable projects like this one.

The frustrated speaker was Sarah McNeil, product development manager of the Consumer Products Division of Enager Industries, Inc. Enager was a relatively young company, which had grown rapidly to its 1993 sales level of over $222 million. (See Exhibits 1 and 2 for financial data for 1992 and 1993.)

Enager had three divisions—Consumer Products, Industrial Products, and Professional Services—each of which accounted for about one-third of Enager's total sales. Consumer Products, the oldest of the three divisions, designed, manufactured, and marketed a line of houseware items, primarily for use in the kitchen. The Industrial Products Division built one-of-a-kind machine tools to customer specifications (i.e., it was a large "job shop"), with a typical job taking several months to complete. The Professional Services Division, the newest of the three, had been added to Enager by acquiring a large firm that provided land planning, landscape architecture, structural architecture, and consulting engineering services. This division has grown rapidly, in part because of its capability to perform "environmental impact" studies, as required by law on many new land development projects.

This case was updated by Professor Vijay Govindarajan and Anil Chitkara (T '94) based on an earlier case prepared by James S. Reece, University of Michigan. Copyrighted by the University of Michigan.

Exhibit 1

**Income Statements
For 1992 and 1993
($000s, except earnings-per-share figures)**

	Year Ended December 31	
	1992	*1993*
Sales	$212,193	$222,675
Cost of goods sold	162,327	168,771
Gross margin	49,866	53,904
Other expenses:		
Development	12,096	12,024
Selling and general	19,521	20,538
Interest	1,728	2,928
Total	33,345	35,490
Income before taxes	16,521	18,414
Income tax expense	5,617	6,261
Net income	$ 10,904	$ 12,153
Earnings-per-share (1,500,000 and 1,650,000 shares outstanding in 1992 and 1993, respectively)	$ 7.27	$ 7.37

Because of the differing nature of their activities, each division was treated as an essentially independent company. There were only a few corporate-level managers and staff people, whose job was to coordinate the activities of the three divisions. One aspect of this coordination was that all new project proposals requiring investment in excess of $1,500,000 had to be reviewed by the chief financial officer, Henry Hubbard. It was Hubbard who had recently rejected McNeil's new product proposal, the essentials of which are shown in Exhibit 3.

Performance Evaluation

Prior to 1992, each division had been treated as a profit center, with annual division profit budgets

EXHIBIT 2

**Balance Sheets
For 1992 and 1993
($000s)**

	As of December 31	
	1992	*1993*
Assets		
Cash and temporary investments . .	$ 4,212	$ 4,407
Accounts receivable	41,064	46,821
Inventories	66,486	76,401
Total current assets	111,762	127,629
Plant and equipment:		
Original cost	111,978	137,208
Accumulated depreciation	38,073	47,937
Net	73,905	89,271
Investments and other assets	6,429	9,357
Total assets	$192,096	$226,257
Liabilities and Owners' Equity		
Accounts payable	$ 29,160	$ 36,858
Taxes payable	3,630	3,135
Current portion of long-term debt	0	4,902
Total current liabilities	32,790	44,895
Deferred income taxes	1,677	2,955
Long-term debt	37,866	46,344
Total liabilities	72,333	94,194
Common stock	52,104	58,536
Retained earnings	67,659	73,527
Total owners' equity	119,763	132,063
Total liabilities and owners' equity	$192,096	$226,257

EXHIBIT 3   Financial Data from New Product Proposal

1. Projected asset investment*

Cash	$ 150,000
Accounts receivable	450,000
Inventories	900,000
Plant and equipment†	1,500,000
Total	$3,000,000

2. Cost Data:

Variable cost per unit	$	9
Differential fixed costs (per year)‡	$	510,000

3. Price/market estimates (per year):

Unit Price	Unit Sales	Break-Even Volume
$18	100,000 units	56,667 units
21	75,000	42,500
24	60,000	34,000

*Assumes 100,000 units sales.
†Annual capacity of 120,000 units.
‡Includes straight-line depreciation on new plant and equipment.

negotiated between the president and the respective division general managers. At the urging of Henry Hubbard, Enager's president, Carl Randall, had decided to begin treating each division as an investment center, so as to be able to relate each division's profit to the assets the division used to generate its profits.

Starting in 1992, each division was measured as based on its return on assets, which was defined to be the division's net income divided by its total assets. Net income for a division was calculated by taking the division's "direct income before taxes," then subtracting the division's share of corporate administrative expenses (allocated on the basis of divisional revenues) and its share of income tax expense (the tax rate applied to the division's "direct income before taxes" after subtraction of the allocated corporate administrative expenses). Although Hubbard realized there were other ways to define a division's income, he and the president preferred this method since "it made the sum of the [divisional] parts equal to the [corporate] whole."

Similarly, Enager's total assets were subdivided among three divisions. Since each division operated in physically separate facilities, it was easy to attribute most assets, including receivables, to specific divisions. The corporate-office assets, including the centrally controlled cash account, were allocated to the divisions on the basis of divisional revenues. All fixed assets were recorded at their balance sheet values—that is, original cost less accumulated straight-line depreciation. Thus, the sum of the divisional assets was equal to the amount shown on the corporate balance sheet ($226,257 as of December 31, 1993).

In 1991, Enager had as its return on year-end assets (net income divided by total assets) a rate of 5.2 percent. According to Hubbard, this corresponded to a "gross return" of 9.3 percent; he defined gross return as equal to earnings *before* interest and taxes ("EBIT") divided by assets. Hubbard felt that a company like Enager should have a gross (EBIT) return on assets of at least 12 percent, especially given the interest rates the corporation had had to pay on its recent borrowing. He, therefore, instructed each division manager that the division was to try to earn a gross return of 12 percent in 1992 and 1993. In order to help pull the return up to this level, Hubbard decided that new investment proposals would have to show a return of at least 15 percent in order to be approved.

1992–93 Results

Hubbard and Randall were moderately pleased with 1992 results. The year was a particularly difficult one for some of Enager's competitors, yet Enager had managed to increase its return on assets from 5.2 percent to 5.7 percent, and its gross return from 9.3 percent to 9.5 percent.

At the end of 1992, the president put pressure on the general manager of the Industrial Products Division to improve its return on investment, suggesting that this division was not "carrying its share of the load." The division manager had bristled at this comment, saying the division could get a higher return "if we had a lot of old machines the way Consumer Products does." The president had responded that he did not understand the relevance of the division manager's remark, adding, "I don't see why the return on an old asset should be higher than that on a new asset, just because the old one cost less."

The 1993 results both disappointed and puzzled Carl Randall. Return on assets fell from 5.7 percent to 5.4 percent, and gross return dropped

EXHIBIT 4   Calculation of Gross Return on Assets, 1993

| | **Specific Assets** | | | | | | |
Division	Sales	EBIT	W/C	Fxd.	Alloc.	Total	Gross ROA
Consumer	74.3	10.8	60.8	34.6	4.6	100.0	10.8
Industrial	74.2	7.2	44.4	54.6	4.6	103.6	6.9
Professional Services	74.2	3.3	18.0	0.0	4.6	22.6	14.6
Total		21.3	123.2	89.2	13.8	226.2	9.4

from 9.5 percent to 9.4 percent. At the same time, return on sales (net income divided by sales) rose from 5.1 percent to 5.5 percent, and return on owners' equity also increased, from 9.1 percent to 9.2 percent. The Professional Services Division easily exceeded the 12 percent gross return target; Consumer Products' gross return on assets was 10.8 percent; but Industrial Products' return was only 6.9 percent (see Exhibit 4). These results prompted Randall to say to Hubbard:

> You know, Henry, I've been a marketer most of my career, but, until recently, I thought I understood the notion of return on investment. Now I see in 1993 our profit margin was up and our earnings-per-share were up; yet two of your return on investment figures were down; return on invested capital went down, and return on owners' equity went up. I just don't understand these discrepancies.
>
> Moreover, there seems to be a lot more tension among our managers the last two years. The general manager of Professional Services seems to be doing a good job, and she's happy as a lark about the praise I've given her. But the general manager of Industrial Products looks daggers at me every time we meet. And last week, when I was eating lunch with the division manager at Consumer Products, the product development manager came over to our table and really burned my ears over a new product proposal of hers I rejected the other day.
>
> I'm wondering if I should follow up on the idea that Karen Kraus in Personnel brought back from the two-day organization development workshop she attended over at the university. She thinks we ought to have a one-day off-site retreat of all the corporate and divisional managers to talk over this entire return on investment matter.

Questions

1. Why was McNeil's new product proposal rejected? Should it have been? Explain.

2. What inferences do you draw from a cash flow statement for 1993? Is a breakdown by divisions useful?

3. What inferences do you draw from the comparative balance sheets and income statements for 1992 and 1993?

4. Evaluate the manner in which Randall and Hubbard have implemented their investment center concept. What pitfalls did they apparently not anticipate?

5. What, if anything, should Randall do now about his investment center approach?

6. Design a balanced scorecard for Consumer, Industrial, and Professional Products Divisions of Enager Industries. Be *specific* for *each* division.

7. What other advice do you have for Randall and Hubbard?

MANAGEMENT COMPENSATION

Incentive compensation is an important mechanism that encourages and motivates managers to achieve organizational objectives. Managers typically put forth a great deal of effort on activities that are rewarded and less on activities that are not rewarded. Numerous examples exist of compensation systems that do not reward the behaviors leading to organizational goals or do reward the behaviors countering the goals. In this chapter, we discuss the design of incentive compensation plans for general managers so as to avoid the "folly of rewarding A while hoping for B."

We first discuss some research findings on organizational incentives. We then describe the nature of compensation plans, which we classify into two types: short-term incentive plans and long-term incentive plans. These plans must be approved by the shareholders. Next, we describe how the compensation of individual managers is decided, first at the corporate level and then at the business-unit level. These decisions typically are made by the board of directors, based on recommendations of the chief executive officer. Finally, we describe agency theory, which is an approach for deciding on the best type of incentive compensation plan.

Research Findings on Organizational Incentives

The solution to the management problem of motivating people to behave in a way that furthers the goals of the organization relies on the relationship of organization incentives to personal goals. Individuals are influenced both by positive and negative incentives. A positive incentive, or "reward," is an outcome that results in increased satisfaction of individual needs. A negative incentive, or "punishment," is an outcome that results in a decrease in the satisfaction of personal needs. Reward incentives are inducements to satisfy those needs that individuals cannot obtain without joining the organization. Organizations provide rewards to participants who perform in agreed-upon ways. Research on incentives tends to support the following:

- Individuals tend to be more strongly motivated by the potential of earning rewards than by the fear of punishment, which suggests that management control systems should be reward-oriented.

- A personal reward is situational. Monetary compensation is an important means of satisfying certain needs; but beyond a satisfaction level, the amount of compensation is not necessarily as important as nonmonetary rewards.

- If senior management signals by its actions that it regards the management control system as important, operating managers will also so regard it. If senior management pays little attention to the system, operating managers are likely to pay little attention.

- Individuals are highly motivated when they receive reports (feedback) about their performance. Without such feedback, people are unlikely to obtain a feeling of achievement or self-realization or to sense corrective actions that are needed to meet their objectives.

- An incentive rapidly becomes less effective as the period between an action and the report of it increases. At lower levels in the organization, the optimal frequency of feedback between the action and the feedback may be only hours; for senior management, it may be months.

- Motivation is weakest when the person perceives an incentive as being either unattainable or too easily attainable. Motivation is strong when the objective can be obtained with some effort and when the individual regards its attainment as important in relation to personal needs.

- The incentive provided by a budget or other statement of objective is strongest when managers participate actively with their superiors in the process of arriving at the budgeted amounts. Objectives, goals, or standards are likely to provide strong incentives only if the manager perceives them as fair and feels committed to attaining them. The commitment is strongest when it is a matter of public record—that is, when the manager has explicitly agreed that the budgeted amounts are attainable.

Characteristics of Incentive Compensation Plans

A manager's total compensation package consists of three components: (1) salary, (2) benefits (principally pension and health benefits, but also perquisites of various types), and (3) incentive compensation. The compensation of managers in large companies tends to be higher than compensation in smaller companies,[1] and compensation in one company tends to be competitive with that of other companies in the industry, but few other generalizations can be made about the level of management compensation.

---

[1] See Luis R. Gomez-Jejia, Henry Tosi, and Timothy Hinkin, "Managerial Control, Performance, and Executive Compensation," *Academy of Management Journal*, March 1987, pp. 31–70.

The three components are interdependent, but the third is specifically related to the management control function; this chapter, therefore, discusses primarily the incentive compensation component. A study of the pay and bonuses received by 14,000 managers over the period 1981–85 (70,284 observations from 219 organizations) found that, on average, bonuses were 20 percent of base pay, but that there were substantial differences among organizations, even those in the same industry. These differences in the proportion of bonus payments were greater than differences in base pay. There was a tendency for organizations with higher ratios of bonuses to have better subsequent financial performance than other organizations.[2]

Most corporate bylaws and securities regulations require that incentive compensation plans and revisions of existing plans be approved by the shareholders. (By contrast, shareholders do *not* approve salaries, nor does the annual proxy statement give information about compensation, except for each of the five most highly paid officers and the total for all officers and directors.) It follows that the plan must be approved by the board of directors before it is voted on at the annual meeting. Before submitting a plan for approval, senior management devotes much attention to devising the best plan for its environment, often hiring outside consultants to assist in this effort. The compensation committee of the board of directors usually is heavily involved in discussions of the proposed plan.

Incentive compensation plans can be divided into (1) short-term incentive plans, which are based on performance in the current year, and (2) long-term incentive plans, which relate compensation to the longer-term accomplishments. Long-term plans usually are related to the price of the company's common stock. A manager may earn a bonus under both plans. The bonus in a short-term plan usually is paid in cash, and the bonus in a long-term plan is usually an option to buy the company's common stock.

Short-Term Incentive Plans

The Total Bonus Pool.   In a short-term incentive plan, shareholders vote on the formula to be used in arriving at the total amount of bonus that can be paid to a qualified group of employees in a given year, which is called the "bonus pool." This formula usually is related to the overall company profitability in the current year (in a few companies, the current quarter). In deciding on the size of this pool, the overriding issue is to make the total compensation paid to executives competitive.

Several methods of establishing the bonus pool are described below.

The simplest method is to make the bonus equal to a set percentage of the profits. For example, if profits of $50 million represents an average profitable

---

[2]Barry Gerhart and George T. Milkovich, "Organizational Differences in Managerial Compensation and Financial Performance," *Academy of Management Journal*, December 1990, pp. 663–91.

year, and if a $1 million bonus fund is required to make the executive compensation package competitive, the bonus formula then could be set up to pay 2 percent of net income in bonuses.

Many companies find this method undesirable because it means paying a bonus even at low levels of profitability. Moreover, it fails to reflect additional investments; thus, profits and, consequently, bonuses can increase simply as a result of new investments, although the performance of the company may be static or even deteriorating. Many companies, therefore, use formulas that pay bonuses only after a specified return has been earned on capital. There are several ways of accomplishing this.

One method is to base the bonus on a percentage of earnings per share after a predetermined level of earnings per share has been attained. Using our earlier example, assume the following situation:

1. Estimated level of satisfactory profitability: $50 million.
2. Desired amount of bonus at the above level of profitability: $1 million.
3. Number of shares outstanding: 10 million.
4. Minimum earnings per share before bonus payments: $2.50.
5. Bonus formula: 4 percent of profits after subtracting $2.50 per share.

This method, however, does not take into account increases in investment from reinvested earnings. The objection can be overcome by increasing the minimum earnings per share each year by a percentage of the annual increase in retained earnings. In the example above, assume that the estimated profits for the year are $50 million before bonuses and that dividends are $30 million. The plan might provide that a 6 percent return must be earned on additional investments before any additional bonuses are paid. The $2.50 minimum earnings per share thus would be adjusted for the coming year in the following manner.

Increase in retained earnings:

$$\$50,000,000 \text{ (profit)} - \$500,000 \text{ (bonus after taxes)}$$
$$- \$30,000,000 \text{ (dividends)} = \$19,500,000$$

Increase in required earnings before bonus:

$$\text{Total} = \$19,500,000 * 0.06 = \$1,170,000$$
$$\text{Per share} = \$1,170,000 \div 10,000,000 = \$0.117$$

Adjusted minimum earnings per share:

$$\$2.50 + \$0.12 = \$2.62$$

Note that no reductions in the required earnings per share are normally made when the company experiences a loss; however, the required earnings would not be increased until retained earnings has exceeded its preloss level.

Another method of relating profits to capital employed is to define capital as shareholder equity plus long-term liabilities. The bonus is equal to a percent of the profits before taxes and interest on long-term debt minus a capital charge on the total of shareholder equity plus long-term debt. (This is similar to the economic value added concept discussed in Chapter 7.) Companies using this method reason that managerial performance should be based on employing corporate net assets profitably, and since the proportion of long-term debt to total capital is determined by financial policy, rather than by operating managers, this proportion should not influence the judgment about operating performance. Companies using Economic Value Added (EVA) in annual bonus calculations include Briggs & Stratton Corp., Cincinnati Milacron, Clark Equipment, and Ball Corp.[3]

Another method is to define capital as equal to shareholder equity. A difficulty with both this and the preceding method is that a loss year reduces shareholder equity and, thereby, increases the amount of bonus to be paid in profitable years. This might tempt management to take a "big bath" in a year with otherwise low profits so as to make earning future bonuses easier.

A few companies base the bonus on increases in profitability over the preceding year. This not only rewards a mediocre year that follows a poor one but also fails to reward a good year if it happens to follow an excellent one. This problem can be partially corrected by basing the bonus on an improvement in the current year that is above a moving average of the profits in a number of past years.

Another method bases bonuses on company profitability relative to industry profitability. Obtaining comparable industry data may be difficult, however, because few companies have the same product mix or employ identical accounting systems. This method also could result in a high bonus in a mediocre year, because one or more of the industry competitors had a poor year.

In calculating both the profit and the capital components of these formulas, adjustments may be made in the reported amount of net income and in the reported amount of shareholder equity. Certain types of extraordinary gains and losses, and gains and losses from discontinued operations may be excluded. Goodwill resulting from acquisition of other companies may be excluded even though it is included in the published financial statements.

Carryovers.   Instead of paying the total amount in the bonus pool, the plan may provide for an annual carryover of a part of the amount determined by the bonus formula. Each year a committee of the board of directors decides how much to add to the carryover, or how much of the accumulated carryover to use if the bonuses would otherwise be too low. This method has two advantages: (1) it offers more flexibility, since payment is not determined automatically by a formula, and the board of directors can exercise its judgment; (2) it can reduce the magnitude of the swings that occur when the bonus payment is based strictly on the formula amount calculated each year. Thus, in an exceptionally good year, the committee may decide to pay out only a portion of the bonus.

---

[3]Jim Fisher, "How Effective Executive Compensation Plans Work," *CMA Magazine*, June 1995, pp. 36–39.

Conversely, in a relatively poor year, the committee may decide to pay out more than the amount justified by current year performance by drawing from the carryover bonus amount. The disadvantage of this method is that the bonus relates less directly to current performance.

Deferred Compensation.   Although the amount of the bonus is calculated annually, payments to recipients may be spread out over a period of years, usually five. Under this system, executives receive only one-fifth of their bonus in the year in which it was earned. The remaining four-fifths are paid out equally over the next four years. Thus, after the manager has been working under the plan for five years, the bonus consists of one-fifth of the bonus for the current year plus one-fifth of each of the bonuses for the preceding four years. In some companies, the deferred period is three years. This deferred payment method offers a number of advantages:

- Managers can estimate, with reasonable accuracy, their cash income for the coming year.
- Deferred payments smooth the manager's receipt of cash, because the effects of cyclical swings in profits are averaged in the cash payments.
- A manager who retires will continue to receive payments for a number of years; this not only augments retirement income but also usually provides a tax advantage, because income tax rates after retirement may be lower than rates during working life.
- The deferred time frame encourages longer-term thinking with regard to decision making.

Deferred bonus plans have the disadvantage of not making the deferred amount available to the executive in the year earned. (The deferred amount may earn interest for the manager and offset this disadvantage.) Because bonus payments in a year are not related to performance in that year, they may have a lesser impact as an incentive.

When bonus payments are deferred, the deferred amount may or may not vest. In some instances, a manager will not receive the deferred bonus if he or she leaves the company before it is paid (excluding disability, death, or being laid off). This arrangement is called a *golden handcuff*, because the manager who leaves voluntarily sacrifices the deferred amount and, therefore, is less willing to leave.

Long-Term Incentive Plans

A basic premise of many long-term incentive plans is that growth in the value of the company's common stock reflects the company's long-run performance. There are several types of such plans. The popularity of specific types of plans changes with, among other factors, changes in the income tax law, changes in accounting treatment, and the state of the stock market. Consequently, different plans are popular at different times.

Stock Options.   A stock option is a right to buy a number of shares of stock at or after a given date in the future (the *exercise date*), at a price agreed upon at the time the option is granted (usually, the current market price or 95 percent of the current market price). The major motivational benefit of stock option plans is that they direct managers' energies toward the long-term, as well as the short-term, performance of the company. The motivational impact of such plans is dampened to the extent that factors beyond the control of managers affect stock prices.

> **Example.** Wendy's was having trouble with high turnover, 300 percent per year among crew members. After introducing a stock-option plan for crew managers, Wendy's first reduced turnover among crew managers which in turn reduced turnover among assistant managers from 60 percent to 38 percent. This contributed to a reduction in turnover among crew members to about 150 percent per year.[4]

The manager gains if he or she later sells the stock at a price that exceeds the price paid for it. Unlike some of the alternatives mentioned below, the outright purchase of stock under a stock option plan gives managers equity that they can retain, even if they leave the company, and a gain that they can obtain whenever they decide to sell the stock. However, many stock options are for *restricted stock*. Managers are not permitted to sell this stock for a specified period after it was acquired.

> **Example.** Most of Microsoft's employees are entitled to stock options; the value of those options amounted to $570 million in 1995. Such options were beneficial to Microsoft. First, employees become motivated to enhance Microsoft's profits to help improve the stock price which, in turn, will benefit the employees. Second, Microsoft can pay lower salaries and bonuses to employees because of the stock option program. Third, the value of stock options does not reduce the bottom line, but the salaries and bonuses paid to employees do.[5]

Phantom Shares.   A phantom stock plan awards managers a number of shares for bookkeeping purposes only. At the end of a specified period (say, five years) the executive is entitled to receive an award equal to the *appreciation* in the market value of the stock since the date of award. This award may be in cash, in shares of stock, or in both. Unlike a stock option, a phantom stock plan has no transaction costs. Some stock option plans require that the manager hold the stock for a certain period after it was purchased, and this involves a risk of a decrease in the market price and the interest costs associated with holding the stock. This risk and cost are not involved in a phantom stock plan.

Stock Appreciation Rights.   A stock appreciation right is a right to receive cash payments based on the increase in the value of stock from the time of the award until a specified future date. Both phantom shares and stock appreciation rights are a form of deferred cash bonus, in which the amount of bonus is a function of the market price of the company's stock. Both these plans have the

---

[4]Kerry Cappell, "Options for Everyone," *Business Week*, July 22, 1996, pp. 80–84.
[5]Sloan, "Games with Numbers 101," *Newsweek*, October 21, 1996, p. 48.

advantages of a stock option plan. As contrasted with a cash bonus paid currently, they involve uncertainty, in both directions, about the ultimate amount paid.

> **Example.** Avis Inc., the rental car company who "tries harder," agreed to sell the company to HFS Inc., a hotel franchiser, for $763 million, including $85 million in phantom stock and stock appreciation rights for Avis Inc.'s management.[6]

Performance Shares.   A performance share plan awards a specified number of shares of stock to a manager when specific long-term goals have been met. Usually, the goals are to achieve a certain percentage growth in earnings per share over a three-to-five year period; therefore, they are not influenced by the price of the stock. This plan has advantages over either the stock option or the phantom stock plan in that the award is based on performance that can be controlled, at least partially, by the executive. Also, the award is not dependent on an increase in stock prices, although the increase in earnings is likely to result in an increase in stock prices. This plan suffers from the limitation of basing the bonus on accounting measures of performance; actions that corporate executives take to improve earnings per share could, under some conditions, not contribute to the economic worth of the firm.

Performance Units.   In a performance unit plan, a cash bonus is paid on the attainment of specific long-term targets. This plan, thus, combines aspects of stock appreciation rights and performance shares. This plan is especially useful in companies with little or no publicly traded stock. Success of this plan depends upon the careful establishment of the long-term targets.

Incentives for Corporate Officers

In the preceding section, we described how the total bonus pool is calculated. In this section and the next, we describe how the total is divided among the corporate officers and among the business-unit managers, respectively.

Each corporate officer, except the chief executive officer, is responsible in part, but only in part, for the company's overall performance. These corporate officers are entitled to, and are motivated by a bonus for good performance. However, the part of performance that each of them generated cannot be measured. For example, how can one measure the contribution to profits made by the chief financial officer? The human resources vice president? The chief counsel?

To induce the desired motivation, the chief executive officer, who recommends such awards to the compensation committee of the board of directors, usually bases them on the assessment of each person's performance. Such an assessment is necessarily subjective. In some companies it is aided by a management by objectives system (MBO) in which specific objectives are agreed upon at the beginning of the year, and attainment of these objectives is assessed by the chief executive officer.

---

[6]Aaron Bernstein, "Should Avis Try Harder—For Its Employees?" *Business Week*, August 12, 1996, pp. 68–69.

CEO Compensation

The chief executive officer's compensation usually is discussed by the compensation committee of the board of directors *after* the CEO has presented recommendations for compensation for his or her subordinates. From this presentation, the CEO's general attitude toward the appropriate percentage of incentive compensation in a given year is fairly obvious. In ordinary circumstances, the committee simply may apply the same percentage to the CEO's compensation. However, the committee may signal a different appraisal of the CEO's performance by deciding on a higher or lower percentage. This, perhaps more than any other expression of the board's opinion, is an important signal about how the board regards the CEO's performance. It should be accompanied by a frank explanation of the reasons for the choice.

Some people believe that the compensation of chief executives in the United States (and also of some professional athletes and performing artists) is too high and is not related to company performance.[7] They cite instances of what they regard as excess compensation: *golden parachutes* (i.e., incentive packages for an incumbent CEO as insurance against takeovers), extraordinary bonuses, lavish perquisites, and bonuses unrelated to profits. Directors who are responsible for deciding on compensation respond that the compensation of excellent CEOs is a tiny fraction of the profits that result from their decisions, and that they must set their CEO's compensation at a level comparable with that in competing companies.

Forbes magazine publishes annually a list of the compensation of hundreds of CEOs, compared with the profits for which they are presumably responsible. Although the details of its analysis are subject to criticism, the general message is that, in some situations, compensation is indeed high relative to performance, but this is not the general pattern. Moreover, there are considerable differences in compensation in different industries. In any event, given their unique skills and capabilities, assessing true "market prices" for chief executives is nearly impossible.

Incentives for Business-Unit Managers

A wide array of options exist in developing an incentive compensation package for business-unit managers (Exhibit 12–1).

Types of Incentives

Some incentives are financial, others are psychological and social. Financial incentives include salary increases, bonuses, benefits, and perquisites (automobiles, vacation trips, club memberships, and so on). Psychological and social incentives include promotion possibilities, increased responsibilities, increased

---

[7]The literature has many discussions about the allegedly excessive pay of executives. See especially the books by Graef S. Crystal and Eric Bok listed in the Suggested Readings.

Exhibit 12–1   Incentive Compensation Design Options for Business-Unit Managers

A. Types of Incentives
  1. Financial Rewards
      a. Salary increase
      b. Bonuses
      c. Benefits
      d. Perquisites
  2. Psychological and Social Rewards
      a. Promotion possibilities
      b. Increased responsibilities
      c. Increased autonomy
      d. Better geographical location
      e. Recognition

B. Size of Bonus Relative to Salary
  1. Upper Cutoffs
  2. Lower Cutoffs

C. Bonus Based on
  1. Business-Unit Profits
  2. Company Profits
  3. Combination of the Two

D. Performance Criteria
  1. Financial Criteria
      a. Contribution margin
      b. Direct business-unit profit
      c. Controllable business-unit profit
      d. Income before taxes
      e. Net income
      f. Return on investment
      g. Economic value added

  2. Time Period
      a. Annual financial performance
      b. Multiyear financial performance
  3. Nonfinancial Criteria
      a. Sales growth
      b. Market share
      c. Customer satisfaction
      d. Quality
      e. New product development
      f. Personnel development
      g. Public responsibility
  4. Relative Weights Assigned to Financial and Nonfinancial Criteria
  5. Benchmarks for Comparison
      a. Profit budget
      b. Past performance
      c. Competitor's performance

E. Bonus Determination Approach
  1. Formula-based
  2. Subjective
  3. Combination of the Two

F. Form of Bonus Payment
  1. Cash
  2. Stock
  3. Stock Options
  4. Phantom Shares
  5. Performance Shares

autonomy, a better geographical location, and recognition (trophy, participation in executive development programs, and the like). In this part of the chapter, we discuss the *financial* incentives for business-unit managers recognizing, however, that the motivation of managers is influenced by both financial and nonfinancial incentives.

> **Example.** In addition to commissions based on the sales revenue generated by the sales force they supervised, directors (i.e., supervisors) of Mary Kay Cosmetics received a dozen pink roses, a plaque, and a custom-designed suit at an award ceremony; and (if they maintained a certain level of performance) they were given the use of a pink Buick or Cadillac for two years.[8]

---

[8]From *Mary Kay Cosmetics*, Case 12–5.

EXHIBIT 12–2

Two philosophies on incentive compensation

Fixed pay

Recruit good people

Pay them well

Expect good performance

Performance-based pay

Recruit good people

Expect good performance

Pay them well *if* performance is actually good

Size of Bonus Relative to Salary

There are two basic philosophies on the issue of the mix between fixed (salary and fringe benefits) and variable (incentive bonus) portions in the managers' total compensation. One school states that we recruit good people, pay them well, and then expect good performance (Exhibit 12–2). Companies subscribing to this school emphasize salary, not incentive bonus; this is called a *fixed pay* system. Compensation is not linked to performance and is, therefore, not at risk. This raises the issue: What happens if the person does not perform well?

Another school states that we recruit good people, expect them to perform well, and pay them well *if* performance is actually good (Exhibit 12–2). Companies subscribing to this philosophy practice *performance-based pay*; they emphasize incentive bonus, not salary.

The fundamental difference between the two philosophies arises from the fact that, under fixed pay, compensation comes first and performance comes later; under performance-based pay, performance comes first and compensation comes later. The two philosophies have different motivational implications for managers. Since salary is an assured income, an emphasis on salary may lead to conservatism and complacency. An emphasis on incentive bonus tends to encourage managers to put forth maximum effort. For this reason, many companies tend to emphasize incentive bonuses for business-unit managers.

Examples. Mead Corporation's Containers Division, for instance, had implemented a bonus program that gives general managers with superior performance tens of thousands of dollars more than their counterparts at other companies while cutting the compensation of lesser lights—in effect, driving the latter out.[9]

Cutoff Levels. A bonus plan may be constrained at either end: (1) the level of performance at which a maximum bonus is reached (*upper* cutoffs); and (2) the level below which no bonus awards will be made (*lower* cutoffs). Both upper and lower cutoffs may produce undesirable side effects. When business-unit managers recognize that either the maximum bonus has been attained or that there will be no bonus at all, the motivational effect of the bonus system may be contrary to corporate goals. Instead of attempting to optimize profits in the current period, managers may be motivated to decrease profitability in one year (by overspendng on discretionary expenses, such as advertising and research and development) to create an opportunity for a high bonus in the next year. Although this would affect only the timing of expenses, such action usually is undesirable.

One way to mitigate such dysfunctional actions is to carry over the excess or deficiency into the following year—that is, the bonus available for distribution in a given year would be the amount of bonus earned during that year plus any excess, or minus any deficiency, from the previous year.

Bonus Basis

A business-unit manager's incentive bonus could be based solely on total corporate profits or solely on business-unit profits, or on some mix of the two. The manager's decisions and actions have a more direct impact on the performance of his or her own unit than that of other business units; this would argue for linking incentive bonus to business-unit performance. However, such an approach could build walls between business units—that is, put significant barriers against interunit cooperation.

> **Example.** Quantum Corporation created a team called "Lethal" to design, make, and deliver a 2.5-inch disk drive (the company made 3.5-inch disk drives at that time) in 14 months (in the past the company had taken 24 months for such new products). Lethal was a cross-functional team consisting of members from engineering, manufacturing, marketing, finance, and human resources. Instead of setting up performance measures for each function, Lethal set up team-based performance measures which helped the team introduce its new product.[10]

In a single industry firm, whose business units are highly interdependent, the manager's bonus is tied primarily to corporate performance, since interunit cooperation is critical. For example, Alfred Sloan instituted a bonus plan in

---

[9]"Executive Compensation: Looking to the Long Term Again," *Business Week*, May 9, 1983, pp. 80–83; "Here Come Richer, Riskier Pay Plans," *Fortune*, December 19, 1988, pp. 51–58; "More Employers Link Incentives to Unit Results," *The Wall Street Journal*, April 10, 1987.

[10]Christopher Meyer, "How the Right Measures Help the Team Excel," *Harvard Business Review*, May–June 1994, pp. 98–99.

General Motors that rewarded business-unit managers based on overall corporate performance to foster cooperation.[11]

In a conglomerate, on the other hand, the business units are usually autonomous. In such a context, it would be counterproductive to base business-unit managers' bonuses primarily on company profits, since this would weaken the link between performance and rewards. Such a system creates *free-rider* problems. Some managers might relax and still get a bonus based on the efforts of other more diligent managers. Alternatively, in a poor profit year for the company, a unit that turns in an outstanding performance will not be adequately rewarded. In a conglomerate, therefore, it is desirable to reward business-unit managers primarily based on business-unit performance and so foster the entrepreneurial spirit.

For related diversified firms, it might be desirable to base part of the business-unit managers' bonus on business-unit profits and part on company profits, to provide the right mixture of incentives—namely, to optimize unit results while, at the same time, cooperating with other units to optimize company performance.

Performance Criteria

A difficult problem in the incentive bonus plan for business-unit managers is to decide the criteria used as the basis for deciding the bonus.

Financial Criteria.   If the business unit is a profit center, the choice of financial criteria include: contribution margin, direct business-unit profit, controllable business-unit profit, income before taxes, and net income. If the unit is an investment center, decisions need to be made in three areas: (1) definition of profit, (2) definition of investment, and (3) choice between return on investment and EVA. We discussed the considerations involved in the choice of the performance criteria for profit centers and investment centers in Chapters 5 and 7, respectively. If the responsibility center is a revenue center, the financial criteria would be sales volume or sales dollars.

> **Example.** Avon, a global cosmetics company, has about 445,000 sales representatives in the United States who call on customers to make sales and who are rewarded on the basis of sales volume. This reward system for its salesforce might be even more critical as Avon enters developing countries like India. In developing countries, retailing outlets are not sophisticated, so direct sales to the end-use customer become very important. Also, women in most developing countries want to work a flexible, part-time schedule, as a way to supplement family income.[12]

Adjustments for Uncontrollable Factors.   In addition to selecting the financial criteria, decisions must be made on which adjustments, if any, will be

---

[11]This General Motors bonus plan is described in chapter 22 of Alfred Sloan, *My Years with General Motors* (New York: Doubleday, 1964).

[12]"Scents and Sensibility," *The Economist*, July 13, 1996, pp. 57–58.

made for uncontrollable factors. Typically, companies make adjustments for two types of uncontrollable influences. One type of adjustment removes expenses that are the result of decisions made by executives above the business-unit level.

> **Example.** A major consumer products company reported, "A few years ago we decided to close a factory in Germany that was working at 30 percent of capacity. The expenses were deducted at the corporate level. It was not the decision of the manager in Germany, so we couldn't penalize him."[13]

Another type of adjustment is to eliminate the effects of losses due to "acts of nature" (fires, earthquakes, floods) and accidents not caused by the negligence of the manager.

> **Example.** The comments by an executive in a distribution company, who was asked if he would make an adjustment if a fire occurred in a warehouse, is typical: "I would start with the assumption that this couldn't be foreseen. Then I would look at the causes. Was the fire caused by a breach of security or a lackadaisical attitude toward safety? If the fire was outside the manager's control, I would make the adjustment."[14]

Benefits and Shortcomings of Short-Term Financial Targets.   Linking business-unit managers' bonus to achieving annual financial targets (after making allowances for uncontrollable events) is desirable. It induces managers to search for ways to perform existing operations in different ways and initiate new activities to meet the financial targets.

However, *sole* reliance on financial criteria could cause several dysfunctional effects.[15] First, short-term actions that are not in the long-term interests of the company (e.g., under-maintenance of equipment) may be encouraged. Second, managers might not undertake investments that promise benefits in the long-term but hurt short-term financial results. Third, managers may be motivated to engage in data manipulation to meet current period targets.

> **Example.** Sunrise Medical, Inc., a medical products company, decentralized its operations and linked the bonus of division managers on the division's own bottom line. If a division did not make suitable profits, its general manager did not receive a bonus, even if the company as a whole was profitable. On January 4, 1996, Sunrise's directors disclosed that one of its divisions, Sunrise Bio Clinic, had falsified its accounting records to show higher than actual profits. Some argue that the bonus system is partly to blame for Bio Clinic's falsified accounts.[16]

---

[13]Kenneth A. Merchant, *Rewarding Results: Motivating Profit Center Managers* (Boston: Harvard Business School Press, 1989), p. 121.

[14]Ibid., pp. 125–26.

[15]J. J. Curran, "Companies That Rob the Future" *Fortune*, July 4, 1988, pp. 84–89; "More Than Ever, It's Management for the Short Term," *Business Week*, November 24, 1986, pp. 92–93.

[16]Tom Petruno, "Bonuses Can Have a Darker Side," *Valley News*, February 4, 1996, p. E3.

Mechanisms to Overcome Short-Term Bias.   If financial criteria are *supplemented* with additional incentive mechanisms, this may overcome the short-term orientation of annual financial goals. One possibility is to base part of the managers' bonus on *multiyear performance* (i.e., performance over a three- to five-year period). Although it has the obvious advantage of extending the time horizon of managers, this approach has certain weaknesses. First, managers have difficulty in seeing the connection between their efforts and rewards in a multiyear award scheme; this lessens the motivational effect of such awards. Second, a manager might retire or be transferred during the multiyear period, thereby greatly adding to the complexity in implementing such a plan. Third, there is more likelihood that factors beyond the control of the manager will influence the achievement of long-range targets.

> **Example.** In investment banking and brokerage houses, it is not uncommon to give bonuses to traders based on profits for each deal they make. This creates incentives for the traders to take big risks in the hope of big paychecks. However, this could potentially lead to serious financial problems for the organization, as is evident in the collapse of Barings, an investment bank in the United Kingdom. In order to mitigate this problem, Salomon Brothers has altered its bonus scheme. Employees at Salomon are entitled to a bonus on a deal only if the company achieves predetermined return on equity. Further, a portion of the bonus is decided based on multiyear performance to be sure that Salomon's future profits are not sacrificed by short-term actions.[17]

Another method to correct for the inherent inadequacies of financial criteria is to develop a *balanced scorecard* including one or more nonfinancial criteria such as sales growth, market share, customer satisfaction, product quality, new product development, personnel development, and public responsibility. Each of these factors will affect long-run profits. Senior management can create the desired long-term versus short-term profit orientation on the part of business-unit managers and allow for factors that are not reflected in the financial measure by a judicious choice of financial and nonfinancial criteria and appropriate weights among these criteria.

> **Examples.** A study of incentive compensation in 1,400 companies by William M. Mercer, Inc., found that 33 percent used customer satisfaction, and 33 percent used rate of on-time delivery of products or services in addition to financial measures.[18]
>
> McDonald's evaluated its store managers on product quality, service, cleanliness, sales volume, personnel training, and cost control.[19]
>
> When General Electric decentralized in the 1950s, it identified multiple measures of divisional performance: profitability, market position, productivity, product leadership, personnel development, employee attitudes, and public responsibility.[20]

---

[17]"Pay and Performance: Bonus Points," *The Economist*, April 15, 1995, pp. 71–72.

[18]*Journal of Accountancy*, "Incentive Pay Plans Emphasize Non-Financial Performance," May 1993, p. 17.

[19]E. W. Sasser and S. H. Pettway, "Case of Big Mac's Pay Plans," *Harvard Business Review*, July–August 1974.

[20]Ralph J. Cordiner, *New Frontiers for Professional Managers* (New York: McGraw-Hill, 1956).

When John Martin, CEO of PepsiCo's fast-food restaurant chain, Taco Bell, embarked on his transformation program in 1988, he pushed decision making away from the company's headquarters to restaurant managers, and increased each manager's responsibility from 5 to 20 restaurants.

This empowerment was supported by a fundamental change in the reward system. Both managerial and hourly compensation had increased significantly, as a result of bonus scheme, linked to customer service levels, profit targets, and sales. If they perform, Taco Bell managers earned more than three times the fast-food industry average. This, coupled with bonuses based on length of service, made hopping from one fast-food chain to the next in search of higher pay—which was always thought to be an endemic practice among fast-food restaurant managers—far less appealing. As a result, Taco Bell reduced restaurant manager turnover by more than 50 percent and the turnover of hourly employees by 30 percent.

These changes in the roles and rewards of restaurant managers contributed significantly to the dramatic improvement in Taco Bell's performance since 1988. Between 1988 and 1993, the company opened more than 2,000 new restaurants, increased worldwide sales from $1.5 billion to nearly $4 billion, and more than tripled net income to over $250 million. Over the same period, customer satisfaction, as measured by value-for-money perceptions, improved sharply, while that of competitors declined.[21]

Another mechanism to correct for the short-term bias is to base part of the business-unit managers' bonus on *long-term incentive plans*, such as stock options, phantom shares, and performance shares. These plans focus the business-unit managers (*a*) on companywide performance and (*b*) on long-term performance. Advantages and limitations of these plans were discussed earlier.

Examples. Interpublic, which runs four advertising agencies (McCann-Erickson, Lintas, Dailey & Associates, and the Lowe Group), designed incentive systems for its business units to make sure they focus on profitability and growth. The compensation for managers was based on long-term performance: four years' performance but awarded every two years. This helped keep managers from jumping ship, an ever-present agency business threat. Employees were rewarded with stock and bonuses, not only for exceeding their numbers but also for qualitative results, such as setting up succession plans and servicing clients.[22]

Since its inception 27 years ago, Science Applications International Corp., a $2 billion research and engineering company, has used employee stock ownership as the key motivational tool. The company believes that its growth in sales and profits over the years has been significantly influenced by its stock ownership program.[23]

Benchmarks for Comparison.   The performance of a business-unit manager can be appraised by comparing actual results with the profit budget, with past performance, or with competitors' performance. The typical practice is to

---

[21]"Renewal at Taco Bell," *Transformation*, Gemini Consulting, 6, Spring 1995, p. 8.

[22]"Sibling Rivalry," *Forbes*, February 15, 1993, pp. 119–20.

[23]Larry Armstrong, "Happy Fallout Down at the Nuke Lab," *Business Week*, October 7, 1996, p. 42.

evaluate the business-unit manager against the profit budget. As discussed in Chapter 9, the following considerations are important when using the profit budget as a motivational tool: (*a*) the business-unit manager participates in the development of the profit budget, and (*b*) the budget is challenging but attainable.

Bonus Determination Approach

A bonus award for a business-unit manager can be determined on the basis of either a strict formula, such as a percentage of the business unit's operating profit, or a purely subjective assessment by the manager's superior, or by some combination of the two. This dichotomy of formula-based versus subjective bonus determination is similar to Ouchi's concepts of output control and behavior control. According to Ouchi, in controlling people's work, only two aspects of that work can be observed and monitored: behavior (leading to "behavior control"), or the outputs that result from behavior (leading to "output control").[24] Behavior control tends to be subjective; a superior using behavior control would base the amount of the business-unit manager's bonus on a subjective judgment of the effectiveness of the decisions and actions taken by the manager. Since output control is amenable to quantitative measurement (e.g., operating profit), it tends to be formula based.

> **Example.** In 1992, though the employees of FormPac worked hard, they did not receive bonuses because the company was not making profits. The employees did not know why they hadn't received bonuses because the bonuses were strictly based on the discretion of a noncommunicative CEO. This led to employee demotivation and distrust. In order to regain credibility in the bonus system, William Duff, CEO of FormPac, published the monthly- and year-to-date sales and profit figures on a display board and linked employees' bonuses to published sales growth and profit figures. By 1996 employees in FormPac seemed to have more faith in the bonus system.[25]

Exclusive reliance on objective formulas (i.e., output control) has some clear merits: reward systems can be specified with precision, there is little uncertainty or ambiguity about performance standards, and superiors cannot exercise any bias or favoritism in assessing the performance of subordinate managers. However, a major limitation of objective formulas is that they are likely to induce managers to pay less attention to the performance of their business units along dimensions that are important, although difficult to quantify (e.g., research and development, and human resource management). Some subjectivity in determining bonuses, therefore, is desirable in most units. A subjective approach is especially desirable when a manager's personal control over a unit's performance is low. In such situations, numerical indicators of the unit's performance have

---

[24]See, for instance, in Suggested Additional Readings at the end of this chapter, Ouchi (1977).

[25]Donna Fenn, "Bonuses That Make Sense," *Inc*, March 1996, p. 95.

little validity as measures of the performance of the manager. This type of situation is likely to happen under the following circumstances:

- When the business-unit manager inherits problems created by a predecessor.
- When the business unit is highly interdependent with other units and, therefore, its performance is influenced by the decisions and actions of outside individuals.
- When the strategy requires much greater attention to longer-term concerns (as is the case in a business unit aggressively building market share).

Agency Theory

Agency theory explores how contracts and incentives can be written to motivate individuals to achieve goal congruence.[26] It attempts to describe the major factors that should be considered in designing incentive contracts. An incentive contract, as used in agency theory, is the same as the incentive compensation arrangements discussed in this chapter. Agency theory attempts to state these relationships in mathematical models. This introduction describes the general ideas of agency theory without giving actual models.

Concepts

An agency relationship exists whenever one party (the principal) hires another party (the agent) to perform some service and, in so doing, delegates decision-making authority to the agent. In a corporation, shareholders are principals, and the chief executive officer is their agent. The shareholders hire the CEO and expect that the CEO will act in their interest. At a lower level, the CEO is the principal, and the business-unit managers are the agents. The challenge becomes how to motivate agents so that they will be as productive as they would be if they were the owners.

One of the key elements of agency theory is that principals and agents have divergent preferences or objectives. The divergent preferences can be reduced through incentive contracts.

Divergent Objectives of Principals and Agents.   Agency theory assumes that all individuals act in their own self-interest. Agents are assumed to receive satisfaction not only from financial compensation but also from the perquisites

---

[26]The term *agency* suggests that the topic is related to agency law, but this is not the case. Agency law defines the obligations of an agent to a principal and the obligations of a principal to the agent, but these legal obligations do not govern or adequately explain the behaviors of superior managers and subordinate managers to one another. "Commitments" and "understandings" between superiors and subordinates are not legal contracts; subordinates rarely are sued for breach of contract.

involved in an agency relationship. The perquisites can take the form of generous amounts of leisure time, attractive working conditions, country club memberships, and flexibility in working hours. For example, some agents may prefer leisure to hard work (effort). Leisure is assumed to be the opposite of effort. Managers' effort increases the value of the firm, while leisure does not. The preference of the agent for leisure over effort is referred to as *work aversion*. The deliberate withholding of agent effort is termed *shirking*. On the other hand, the principals (i.e., shareholders) are assumed to be interested only in the financial returns that accrue from their investment in the firm.

Another divergence between the preferences of principals and agents is *risk preferences*. Agency theory assumes that managers prefer more wealth to less, but that the marginal utility, or satisfaction, decreases as more wealth is accumulated. Agents typically have much of their wealth tied up in the fortunes of the firm. This wealth consists both of their financial wealth and also of their human capital. Human capital is the value of the manager as perceived by the market; it is influenced by the firm's performance. Because of the decreasing utility for wealth and the large amount of agent capital that is dependent on the company, agents are assumed to be *risk averse*: they value increases from a risky investment at less than the expected (actuarial) value of the investment.

On the other hand, the shares of stock of the company are held by many owners, who reduce their risk by diversifying their wealth and becoming owners in many companies. Therefore, owners are interested in the expected value of their investment and are *risk neutral*. Managers cannot as easily diversify away this risk, which is why they are risk averse.

Nonobservability of Agents' Actions.   The divergence in preferences associated with compensation and perquisites arises whenever the principal cannot easily monitor the agent's actions. Shareholders are not in a position to monitor daily the activities of the CEO to ensure that he or she is working in their best interest. Likewise, the CEO is not in a position to monitor daily the activities of business-unit managers.

The principal has inadequate information about the performance of the agent; therefore the principal can never be certain how the agent's effort contributed to actual firm results. This situation is referred to as *information asymmetry*. These asymmetries can take on several forms. Without monitoring, only the agent knows whether he or she is working in the principal's best interest. Moreover, the agent may know more about the task than the principal. The added information that the agent may have about the task is referred to as *private information*.

Because of both the divergence of preferences between the principal and agent and also the private information of the agent, the agent may misrepresent information to the principal. This misrepresentation is of such a general nature that the name *moral hazard* has been given to the situation where an agent being controlled is motivated to misrepresent private information by the nature of the control system.

Control Mechanisms

Agency theorists state there are two major ways of dealing with the problems of divergent objectives and information asymmetry: monitoring and incentives.

Monitoring.   The first control mechanism is monitoring. The principal can design control systems that monitor the actions of the agent. The principal designs these systems to limit actions that increase the agent's welfare at the expense of principal's interest. An example of a monitoring system is the audited financial statements. Financial reports are generated about company performance, they are audited by a third party, and they are then sent to the owners.

Agency theory has attempted to explain why different agency relationships entail different levels of monitoring. For example, the effectiveness of monitoring is increased if the task to be performed by the agent is well defined and the information, or "signal," used in monitoring is accurate. If the task is not well defined or easily monitored, then incentive contracting becomes more appealing as a control device. These alternatives—monitoring and incentives—are not mutually exclusive. For instance, in most firms, the CEO has an incentive contract along with audited financial statements that act as a monitoring device.

Incentive Contracting.   The other mechanism that can align the interests of the principal with those of the agent is incentives. The principal attempts to limit divergent preferences by establishing appropriate incentive contracts that do this. The more an agent's reward depends on a performance measure, the more incentive there is for the agent to improve that measure. Therefore, the principal should so define the performance measure that it furthers his or her interest. The ability to accomplish this is referred to as *goal congruence*, the concept we discussed in Chapter 1. When the contract given to the agent motivates the agent to work in the prinicipal's best interest, the contract is considered goal congruent.

A compensation scheme that does not incorporate an incentive contract poses a serious agency problem. For example, if CEOs were paid a straight salary, they might not be motivated to work as diligently as when compensation consisted of a salary plus bonus. In the latter case, the CEO would be motivated to work harder to increase profits; this would increase the CEO's compensation, and the increased profits would benefit the principal. Contracts, therefore, are written that align the interests between the two parties by incorporating an incentive feature—that is, the principal writes a contract permitting management to share in the wealth when firm value is increased.

> **Example.** To protect against its CEO's possible risk aversion, CBS included a protection clause in CEO Les Moonves's contract that would pay him $5 million in the event of a sale of CBS to another company. A few months after coming to CBS, Westinghouse purchased CBS and the clause was activated.[27]

---

[27]Marc Gunther, "Turnaround time for CBS," *Fortune*, August 19, 1996, pp. 65–68.

A challenge facing the principal is identifying signals that are correlated both with agent effort and firm value. The agent's effort, along with outside factors (e.g., the general economy, natural disasters), combine to determine performance. The more closely an outcome measure reflects the effort of the manager, the more valuable the measure is in an incentive contract. If the measure of performance is not closely correlated with the agent's effort, there is little incentive for the agent to increase the measure.

None of the incentive arrangements can ensure complete goal congruence. This is because of the difference in risk preferences between the two parties, the asymmetry of information, and the costs of monitoring. These differences cause additional costs. Even an efficient system of incentive alignments will still result in some divergence of preferences. This divergence is named the *residual loss*. The addition of the costs of incentive compensation, the costs of monitoring, and the residual loss are formally titled *agency costs*.

CEO Compensation and Stock Ownership Plans.   As an example of the agency costs inherent in incentive compensation, consider a company that pays its CEO a bonus in the form of stock options. One cost is the risk-preference differences between the owners and CEO. The agent, already risk averse, incurs additional risks when his or her pay is based on stock price performance. To compensate the CEO for taking on this risk, the contract will have to increase the amount of expected pay. In addition, to minimize the possible downside potential, the agent may not take on high risk/high return projects that the principal may find desirable.

A second problem with a stock ownership bonus plan is the lack of direct causal relationship between the agent's effort and the change in stock price. Stock prices are affected by factors outside the control of the agent (e.g., general economic conditions, government intervention). If the stock price rises because of factors beyond the control of the agent, then the agent receives increased pay at the expense of the owners without any increased effort. On the other hand, the stock price may decrease even if the agent exerts high effort.

In spite of these two problems, the stock ownership incentive contract is preferred to a contract that does not have an incentive feature. As pointed out earlier, a flat salary has larger agency costs associated with it.

Business-Unit Managers and Accounting-Based Incentives.   The relationship between a business-unit manager's effort and the stock price is more remote than the tie between CEO effort and stock price. Isolating the contributions made by individual business units to increases in the firm's stock price is difficult. Given the remote causal tie between the manager's effort and stock price, the business-unit manager's bonus might be based on business unit net income. However, this incentive contract still has agency costs similar to those discussed in the CEO stock ownership plan. To illustrate, market demand for a product may fall because of a new substitute product, but the manager may still perform well within the new smaller market. However, if the bonus is based strictly on net income, the agent's compensation will decrease. In addition, the agent may inflate net income through accounting manipulations that do not affect firm value. An example of this behavior is the sale of fixed assets that have a market value in excess of book value. While a contract based on business-unit net income may have lower agency costs than straight salary, these costs do not go to zero.

A Critique

Agency theory was invented in the 1960s, but, unlike other developments described in this book (e.g., strategy matrices, just-in-time, quality control, capital investment models, decision support systems), the theory has had no discernible practical influence on the management control process. Although the subject of many articles in academic journals,[28] there has been no real-world payoff from agency theory. By "payoff" we mean that a manager used the results of agency theory to make a better compensation decision. Many managers are not even aware of agency theory.

Agency theory implies that managers in nonprofit and governmental organizations, who cannot receive incentive compensation, inherently lack the motivation necessary for goal congruence; many people do not accept this implication.

Some of those who have studied agency theory state that the models are no more than statements of obvious facts expressed in mathematical symbols. Others state that the elements in the models can't be quantified (what is the "cost of information asymmetry"?), and that the model is a vast oversimplification of the real-world relationship between superiors and subordinates. The models incorporate only a few elements; and they disregard other factors that affect this relationship, such as the personality of the participants, agents who are by no means risk averse, motives other than financial, the principal's trust in the agent, the agent's ability on the present assignment, the agent's potential for future assignments, and on and on.

We describe the theory in the hope that students will find it useful in thinking about the influence of incentive compensation in motivation of managers, but we caution about its usefulness in solving actual compensation problems.

Summary

The incentive compensation system is a key management control device. Incentive compensation plans can be roughly divided into two types: those that relate compensation to profits currently earned by the company, called "short-term incentive plans"; and those that relate compensation to longer-term performance,

---

[28]*Academy of Management Review* 15, no. 3 (1990), contains six articles on aspects of agency theory.

called "long-term incentive plans." Several considerations need to be taken into account in allocating the total bonus pool to corporate executives and business-unit managers. An incentive system that explicitly incorporates the following factors has a much better chance of success:

- The needs, values, and beliefs of the general managers who are rewarded.
- The culture of the organization.
- External factors, such as industry characteristics, competitors' compensation practices, managerial labor markets, and tax and legal issues.
- Organization's strategies.

Suggested Additional Readings

Baker, G. P.; M. C. Jensen; and K. J. Murphy. "Compensation and Incentives: Practice vs. Theory." *Journal of Finance*, July 1988, pp. 593–616.

Bok, Derek. *The Cost of Talent.* New York: The Free Press, 1993.

Bruns, William J., Jr. *Performance Measurement, Evaluation and Incentives.* Boston: Harvard Business School Press, 1991.

Butler, Stephen A., and Michael W. Maher. *Management Incentive Compensation Plans.* Montvale, N.J.: National Association of Accountants, 1986.

Crystal, Graef S. *In Search of Excess: The Overcompensation of the American Executive.* New York: W. W. Norton & Co., 1992.

Donaldson, Gordon. *Managing Corporate Wealth.* New York: Praeger, 1984, Chapter 12.

Finkelstein, Sydney, and Donald C. Hambrick. *Strategic Leadership: Top Executives and Their Effects on Organizations.* St. Paul, MN: West Publishing, 1996.

Fisher, Joseph, and Vijay Govindarajan. "Profit Center Manager Compensation: Impact of Market, Political, and Human Capital Factors." *Strategic Management Journal*, March 1992, pp. 25–27.

Griner, Emmett H., "Stock Option Compensation, CEO Pay, and Corporate Performance: A Board-Level Perspective." *Journal of Managerial Issues*, 8, 2, Summer 1996, pp. 143–53.

Hambrick, Donald C., and Charles C. Snow. "Strategic Reward Systems." In *Strategy, Organization Design, and Human Resource Management*, ed. C. C. Snow. New York: JAI Press, 1989, pp. 333–68.

Henderson, Andrew D., and James W. Fredrickson. "Information-Processing Demands as a Determinant of CEO Compensation," *Academy of Management Journal*, 39, 3, June 1996, pp. 575–606.

Henderson, Richard I. *Compensation Management: Rewarding Performance.* 5th ed. Englewood Cliffs, N.J.: Prentice Hall, 1989.

Lederer, Jack L., and Carl R. Weinberg. "Are CEOs Paid Too Much?" *Chief Executive*, 113, May 1996, pp. 26–31.

Merchant, K. A. *Rewarding Results: Motivating Profit Center Managers*. Boston: Harvard Business School Press, 1989.

Milkovich, George T., and Jerry M. Newman. *Compensation*. 3rd ed. Homewood, Ill.: BPI/Irwin, 1990.

Ouchi, William. "The Relationship Between Organizational Structure and Organizational Control." *Administrative Science Quarterly* 22, 1977, pp. 95–112.

Reibstein, Larry. "More Employers Link Incentives to Unit Results." *The Wall Street Journal*, April 10, 1987.

Schwesinger, Edmund. "Where Do the Executive Bucks Stop Now?" *Coopers & Lybrand Executive Briefing*, April 1987.

Stern, Joel M. "One Way to Build Value in Your Firm, à la Executive Compensation." *Financial Executive*, November–December 1990, pp. 51–54.

Weisenfeld, Leslie W., and Larry N. Killough. "A Review and Extension of Using Performance Reports: A Field Study Based on Path-Goal Theory." *Journal of Management Accounting Research*, Fall 1992, pp. 209–25. (Has an extensive bibliography.)

CASE 12–1
LINCOLN ELECTRIC COMPANY (A)

People are our most valuable asset. They must feel secure, important, challenged, in control of their destiny, confident in their leadership, be responsive to common goals, believe they are being treated fairly, have easy access to authority and open lines of communication in all possible directions. Perhaps the most important task Lincoln employees face today is that of establishing an example for others in the Lincoln organization in other parts of the world. We need to maximize the benefits of cooperation and teamwork, fusing high technology with human talent, so that we here in the USA and all of our subsidiary and joint venture operations will be in a position to realize our full potential.

George Willis, CEO, The Lincoln Electric Company

The Lincoln Electric Company was the world's largest manufacturer of arc-welding products and a leading producer of industrial electric motors. The firm employed 2400 workers in two U.S. factories near Cleveland and an equal number in eleven factories located in other countries. This did not include the field sales force of more than 200. The company's U.S. market share (for arc-welding products) was estimated at more than 40 percent.

The Lincoln incentive management plan had been well known for many years. Many college management texts referred to the Lincoln plan as a model for achieving higher worker productivity. Certainly, the firm was successful according to the usual measures.

When James F. Lincoln died in 1965, there had been some concern, even among employees,

that the management system would fall into disarray, that profits would decline, and that year-end bonuses might be discontinued. Quite the contrary, 24 years after Lincoln's death, the company appeared to be as strong as ever. Each year, except the recession years 1982 and 1983, saw high profits and bonuses. Employee morale and productivity remained very good. Employee turnover was almost nonexistent except for retirements. Lincoln's market share was stable. The historically high stock dividends continued.

A Historical Sketch

In 1895, after being "frozen out" of the depression-ravaged Elliott-Lincoln Company, a maker of Lincoln-designed electric motors, John C. Lincoln, took out his second patent and began to manufacture his improved motor. He opened his new business, unincorporated, with $200 he had earned redesigning a motor for young Herbert Henry Dow, who later founded the Dow Chemical Company.

Started during an economic depression and cursed by a major fire after only 1 year in business, the company grew, but hardly prospered, through its first quarter-century. In 1906, John C. Lincoln incorporated the business and moved from his one-room, fourth-floor factory to a new three-story building he erected in east Cleveland. He expanded his work force to thirty and sales grew to over $50,000 a year. John preferred being an engineer and inventor rather than a manager, though, and it was to be left to another Lincoln to manage the company through its years of success.

In 1907, after a bout with typhoid fever forced him to leave Ohio State University in his senior year, James F. Lincoln, John's younger brother, joined the fledgling company. In 1914 he became active head of the firm, with the titles General

This case was prepared by Arthur D. Sharplin, McNeese State University. Copyright © by the *Case Research Journal* and Arthur D. Sharplin.

Manager and Vice President. John remained President of the company for some years but became more involved in other business ventures and in his work as an inventor.

One of James Lincoln's early actions was to ask the employees to elect representatives to a committee (called the "Advisory Board") which would advise him on company operations. The Advisory Board met with the Chief Executive Officer every 2 weeks. This was only the first of a series of innovative personnel policies which, over the years, distinguished Lincoln Electric from its contemporaries.

The first year the Advisory Board was in existence, working hours were reduced from 55 per week, then standard, to 50 hours a week. In 1915, the company gave each employee a paid-up life insurance policy. A welding school, which continues today, was begun in 1917. In 1918, an employee bonus plan was attempted. It was not continued, but the idea was to resurface later.

The Lincoln Electric Employees' Association was formed in 1919 to provide health benefits and social activities. Over the years, it assumed several additional functions. In 1923, a piecework pay system was in effect, employees got 2 weeks paid vacation each year, and wages were adjusted for changes in the Consumer Price Index. Approximately 30 percent of the common stock was set aside for key employees in 1914. A stock purchase plan for all employees was begun in 1925.

The Board of Directors voted to start a suggestion system in 1929. Cash awards, a part of the early program, were discontinued in the mid-1980s. Suggestions were rewarded by additional "points," which affected year-end bonuses.

The legendary Lincoln bonus plan was proposed by the Advisory Board and accepted on a trial basis in 1934. The first annual bonus amounted to about 25 percent of wages. There was a bonus every year after that. The bonus plan became a cornerstone of the Lincoln management system, and recent bonuses approximated annual wages.

By 1944, Lincoln employees enjoyed a pension plan, a policy of promotion from within, and continuous employment. Base pay rates were determined by formal job evaluation, and a merit rating system was in effect.

In the prologue of James F. Lincoln's last book, Charles G. Herbruck wrote regarding the foregoing personnel innovations:

> They were not to buy good behavior. They were not efforts to increase profits. They were not antidotes to labor difficulties. They did not constitute a "do-gooder" program. They were expressions of mutual respect for each person's importance to the job to be done. All of them reflect the leadership of James Lincoln, under whom they were nurtured and propagated.

During World War II, Lincoln prospered as never before. By the start of the war, the company was the world's largest manufacturer of arc-welding products. Sales of about $4 million in 1934 grew to $24 million by 1941. Productivity per employee more than doubled during the same period. The Navy's Price Review Board challenged the high profits. The Internal Revenue Service questioned the tax deductibility of employee bonuses, arguing they were not "ordinary and necessary" costs of doing business, but the forceful and articulate James Lincoln was able to overcome the objections.

Certainly after 1935 and probably for several years before that, Lincoln productivity was well above the average for similar companies. The company claimed levels of productivity more than twice those for other manufacturers from 1945 onward. Information available from outside sources tended to support these claims.

Company Philosophy

James F. Lincoln was the son of a Congregational minister, and Christian principles were at the center of his business philosophy. The confidence that he had in the efficacy of Christ's teachings was illustrated by the following remark taken from one of his books:

> The Christian ethic should control our acts. If it did control our acts, the savings in cost of distribution would be

tremendous. Advertising would be a contact of the expert consultant with the customer, in order to give the customer the best product available when all of the customer's needs are considered. Competition then would be in improving the quality of products and increasing efficiency in producing and distributing them; not in deception, as is now too customary. Pricing would reflect efficiency of production; it would not be a selling dodge that the customer may well be sorry he accepted. It would be proper for all concerned and rewarding for the ability used in producing the product.

There was no indication that Lincoln attempted to evangelize his employees or customers—or the general public, for that matter. Neither the Chairman of the Board and Chief Executive, George Willis, nor the President, Donald F. Hastings, mentioned the Christian gospel in speeches and interviews. The company motto, "The actual is limited, the possible is immense," was prominently displayed, but there was no display of religious slogans and no company chapel.

Attitude toward the Customer.   James Lincoln saw the customer's needs as the raison d'etre for every company. "When any company has achieved success so that it is attractive as an investment," he wrote, "all money usually needed for expansion is supplied by the customer in retained earnings. It is obvious that the customer's interests, not the stockholder's, should come first." In 1947 he said, "Care should be taken . . . not to rivet attention on profit. Between 'How much do I get?' and 'How do I make this better, cheaper, more useful?,' the difference is fundamental and decisive." Willis, too, ranked the customer as management's most important constituency. This was reflected in Lincoln's policy to "at all times price on the basis of cost and at all times keep pressure on our cost." Lincoln's goal, often stated, was "to build a better and better product at a lower and lower price." "It is obvious," James Lincoln said, "that the customer's interests should be the first goal of industry."

Attitude toward Stockholders.   Stockholders were given last priority at Lincoln. This was a continuation of James Lincoln's philosophy: "The last group to be considered is the stockholders who own stock because they think it will be more profitable than investing money in any other way." Concerning division of the largess produced by incentive management, he wrote, "The absentee stockholder also will get his share, even if undeserved, out of the greatly increased profit that the efficiency produces."

Attitude toward Unionism.   There was never a serious effort to organize Lincoln employees. While James Lincoln criticized the labor movement for "selfishly attempting to better its position at the expense of the people it must serve," he still had kind words for union members. He excused abuses of union power as "the natural reactions of human beings to the abuses to which management has subjected them." Lincoln's idea of the correct relationship between workers and managers was shown by this comment: "Labor and management are properly not warring camps; they are parts of one organization in which they must and should cooperate fully and happily."

Beliefs and Assumptions about Employees. If fulfilling customer needs was the desired goal of business, then employee performance and productivity were the means by which this goal could best be achieved. It was the Lincoln attitude toward employees, reflected in the following comments by James Lincoln, which was credited by many with creating the success the company experienced:

> The greatest fear of the worker, which is the same as the greatest fear of the industrialist in operating a company, is the lack of income. . . . The industrial manager is very conscious of his company's need for uninterrupted income. He is completely oblivious, evidently, of the fact that the worker has the same need.
>
> [The worker] is just as eager as any manager is to be part of a team that is properly organized and working for the advancement of our economy. . . . He has no desire to

make profits for those who do not hold up their end in production, as is true of absentee stockholders and inactive people in the company.

If money is to be used as an incentive, the program must provide that what is paid to the worker is what he has earned. The earnings of each must be in accordance with accomplishment.

Status is of great importance in all human relationships. The greatest incentive that money has, usually, is that it is a symbol of success. . . . The resulting status is the real incentive. . . . Money alone can be an incentive to the miser only.

There must be complete honesty and understanding between the hourly worker and management if high efficiency is to be obtained.

Lincoln's Business

Arc welding had been the standing joining method in shipbuilding for decades. It was the predominant way of connecting steel in the construction industry. Most industrial plants had their own welding shops for maintenance and construction. Manufacturers of tractors and all kinds of heavy equipment used arc welding extensively in the manufacturing process. Many hobbyists had their own welding machines and used them for making metal items such as patio furniture and barbecue pits. The popularity of welded sculpture as an art form was growing.

While advances in welding technology were frequent, arc-welding products, in the main, hardly changed. Lincoln's Innershield process was a notable exception. This process, described later, lowered welding cost and improved quality and speed in many applications. The most widely used Lincoln electrode, the Fleetweld 5P, was virtually the same from the 1930s to 1989. For at least four decades, the most popular engine-driven welder in the world, the Lincoln SA-200, had been a gray-colored assembly, including a four-cylinder Continental "Red Seal" engine and a 200-ampere direct-current generator with two current-control knobs. A 1989 model SA-200 even weighed almost the same as the 1950 model, and it certainly was little changed in appearance.

The company's share of the U.S. arc-welding products market appeared to have been about 40 percent for many years. The welding products market had grown somewhat faster than the level of industry in general. The market was highly price-competitive, with variations in prices of standard items normally amounting to only 1 or 2 percent. Lincoln's products were sold directly by its engineering-oriented sales force and indirectly through its distributor organization. Advertising expenditures amounted to less than 0.75 percent of sales. Research and development expenditures typically ranged from $10 million to $12 million, considerably more than competitors spent.

The other major welding process, flame welding, had not been competitive with arc welding since the 1930s. However, plasma arc welding, a relatively new process which used a conducting stream of superheated gas (plasma) to confine the welding current to a small area, had made some inroads, especially in metal tubing manufacturing, in recent years. Major advances in technology which would produce an alternative superior to arc welding within the next decade or so appeared unlikely. Also, it seemed likely that changes in the machines and techniques used in arc welding would be evolutionary rather than revolutionary.

Products. The company was primarily engaged in the manufacture and sale of arc-welding products—electric welding machines and metal electrodes. Lincoln also produced electric motors ranging from 0.5 to 200 horsepower. Motors constituted about 8 to 10 percent of total sales. Several million dollars had recently been invested in automated equipment that would double Lincoln's manufacturing capacity for 0.5- to 20-horsepower electric motors.

The electric welding machines, some consisting of a transformer or motor and generator arrangement powered by commercial electricity and others consisting of an internal combustion engine and generator, were designed to produce 30 to

1500 amperes of electrical power. This electrical current was used to melt a consumable metal electrode, with the molten metal being transferred in superhot spray to the metal joint being welded. Very high temperatures and hot sparks were produced, and operators usually had to wear special eye and face protection and leather gloves, often along with leather aprons and sleeves.

Lincoln and its competitors marketed a wide range of general-purpose and specialty electrodes for welding mild steel, aluminum, cast iron, and stainless and special steels. Most of these electrodes were designed to meet the standards of the American Welding Society, a trade association. They were thus essentially the same as to size and composition from one manufacturer to another. Every electrode manufacturer had a limited number of unique products, but these typically constituted only a small percentage of total sales.

Welding electrodes were of two basic types:

1. Coated "stick" electrodes, usually 14 inches long and smaller than a pencil in diameter, were held in a special insulated holder by the operator, who had to manipulate the electrode in order to maintain a proper arc width and pattern of deposition of the metal being transferred. Stick electrodes were packaged in 6- to 50-pound boxes.

2. Coiled wire, ranging in diameter from 0.035 to 0.219 inch, was designed to be fed continuously to the welding arc through a "gun" held by the operator or positioned by automatic positioning equipment. The wire was packaged in coils, reels, and drums weighing from 14 to 1000 pounds and could be solid or flux-cored.

Manufacturing Processes.   The main plant was in Euclid, Ohio, a suburb on Cleveland's east side. There were no warehouses. Materials flowed from the ½-mile-long dock on the north side of the plant through the production lines to a very limited storage and loading area on the south side. Materials used on each workstation were stored as close as possible to the workstation. The administrative offices, near the center of the factory, were entirely functional. A corridor below the main level provided access to the factory floor from the main entrance near the center of the plant. *Fortune* magazine declared the Euclid facility one of America's ten best-managed factories,[1] and compared it with a General Electric plant also on the list:

> Stepping into GE's spanking new dishwasher plant, an awed supplier said, is like stepping "into the Hyatt Regency." By comparison, stepping into Lincoln Electric's 33-year-old, cavernous, dimly lit factory is like stumbling into a dingy big-city YMCA. It's only when one starts looking at how these factories do things that similarities become apparent. They have found ways to merge design with manufacturing, build in quality, make wise choices about automation, get close to customers, and handle their work forces.

A new Lincoln plant, in Mentor, Ohio, housed some of the electrode production operations, which had been moved from the main plant.

Electrode manufacturing was highly capital-intensive. Metal rods purchased from steel producers were drawn down to smaller diameters, cut to length, coated with pressed-powder "flux" for stick electrodes or plated with copper (for conductivity), and put into coils or spools for wire. Lincoln's Innershield wire was hollow and filled with a material similar to that used to coat stick electrodes. As mentioned earlier, this represented a major innovation in welding technology when it was introduced. The company was highly secretive about its electrode production processes, and outsiders were not given access to the details of those processes.

Lincoln welding machines and electric motors were made on a series of assembly lines. Gasoline and diesel engines were purchased partially assembled, but practically all other components were

---

[1]Bylinsky, Gene. "America's Best-Managed Factories." *Fortune*, May 28, 1984, p. 16.

made from basic industrial products (e.g., steel bars and sheets and bar copper conductor wire).

Individual components, such as gasoline tanks for engine-driven welders and steel shafts for motors and generators, were made by numerous small "factories within a factory." The shaft for a certain generator, for example, was made from raw steel bar by one operator who used five large machines, all running continuously. A saw cut the bar to length, a digital lathe machined different sections to varying diameters, a special milling machine cut a slot for the keyway, and so forth, until a finished shaft was produced. The operator moved the shafts from machine to machine and made necessary adjustments.

Another operator punched, shaped, and painted sheet-metal cowling parts. One assembled steel laminations onto a rotor shaft, then wound, insulated, and tested the rotors. Finished components were moved by crane operators to the nearby assembly lines.

Worker Performance and Attitudes.   Exceptional worker performance at Lincoln was a matter of record. The typical Lincoln employee earned about twice as much as other factory workers in the Cleveland area. Yet the company's labor cost per sales dollar in 1989, 26 cents, was well below the industry average. Worker turnover was practically nonexistent except for retirements and departures by new employees.

Sales per Lincoln factory employee exceeded $150,000. An observer at the factory quickly saw why this figure was so high. Each worker was proceeding busily and thoughtfully about the task at hand. There was no idle chatter. Most workers took no coffee breaks. Many operated several machines and made a substantial component unaided. The supervisors were busy with planning and record-keeping duties and hardly glanced at the people they "supervised." The manufacturing procedures appeared to be efficient—no unnecessary steps, no wasted motions, no wasted materials. Finished components moved smoothly to subsequent work stations.

The Appendix gives summaries of interviews with employees.

Organizational Structure

Lincoln never allowed development of a formal organization chart. The objective of this policy was to ensure maximum flexibility. An open-door policy was practiced throughout the company, and personnel were encouraged to take problems to the persons most capable of resolving them. Once, Harvard Business School researchers prepared an organization chart reflecting the implied relationships at Lincoln. The chart became available within the company, and management felt that the chart had a disruptive effect. Therefore, no organization chart appears in this case.

Perhaps because of the quality and enthusiasm of the Lincoln work force, routine supervision was almost nonexistent. A typical production foreman, for example, supervised as many as 100 workers, a span of control which did not allow more than infrequent worker-supervisor interaction.

Position titles and traditional flows of authority did imply something of an organizational structure, however. For example, the Vice-President, Sales, and the Vice-President, Electrode Division, reported to the President, as did various staff assistants such as the Personnel Director and the Director of Purchasing. Using such implied relationships, it was determined that production workers had two or, at most three, levels of supervision between themselves and the President.

Personnel Policies

As mentioned earlier, Lincoln's remarkable personnel practices were credited by many with the company's success.

Recruitment and Selection.   Every job opening was advertised internally on company bulletin boards, and any employee could apply for any job so advertised. External hiring was permitted only for entry-level positions. Selection for these jobs was done on the basis of personal interviews; there was no aptitude or psychological testing. Not even a high school diploma was required—except for engineering and sales positions, which were filled by graduate engineers. A committee consisting of vice presidents and supervisors interviewed candidates initially cleared by the Personnel Department. Final selection was made by the supervisor who had a job opening. Out of over 3500 applicants interviewed by the Personnel Department during one period, fewer than 300 were hired.

Job Security.   In 1958 Lincoln formalized its guaranteed continuous employment policy, which had already been in effect for many years. There had been no layoffs since World War II. Since 1958, every worker with over 2 years' longevity had been guaranteed at least 30 hours per week, 49 weeks per year.

The policy was never so severely tested as during the 1981–1983 recession. As a manufacturer of capital goods, Lincoln had business that was highly cyclical. In previous recessions the company had been able to avoid major sales declines. However, sales plummeted 32 percent in 1982 and another 16 percent the next year. Few companies could withstand such a revenue collapse and remain profitable. Yet, not only did Lincoln earn profits, but no employee was laid off and year-end incentive bonuses continued. To weather the storm, management cut most of the nonsalaried workers back to 30 hours a week for varying periods of time. Many employees were reassigned, and the total work force was slightly reduced through normal attrition and restricted hiring. Many employees grumbled at their unexpected misfortune, probably to the surprise and dismay of some Lincoln managers. However, sales and profits—and employee bonuses—soon rebounded, and all was well again.

Performance Evaluations.   Each supervisor formally evaluated subordinates twice a year using the cards shown in Exhibit 1. The employee performance criteria—"quality," "dependability," "ideas and cooperation," and "output"—were considered to be independent of each other. Marks on the cards were converted to numerical scores which were forced to average 100 for each evaluating supervisor. Individual merit rating scores normally ranged from 80 to 110. Any score over 110 required a special letter to top management. These scores (over 110) were not considered in computing the required 100-point average for each evaluating supervisor. Suggestions for improvements often resulted in recommendations for exceptionally high performance scores. Supervisors discussed individual performance marks with the employees concerned. Each warranty claim was traced to the individual employee whose work caused the defect. When that happened, the employee's performance score might be reduced, or the worker might be required to repay the cost of servicing the warranty claim by working without pay.

Compensation.   Basic wage levels for jobs at Lincoln were determined by a wage survey of similar jobs in the Cleveland area. These rates were adjusted quarterly in accordance with changes in the Cleveland area wage index. Insofar as possible, base wage rates were translated into piece rates. Practically all production workers and many others—for example, some forklift operators—were paid by piece rate. Once established, piece rates were never changed unless a substantive change in the way a job was done resulted from a source other than the worker doing the job.

In December of each year, a portion of annual profits was distributed to employees as bonuses. Incentive bonuses since 1934 had averaged about 90 percent of annual wages and somewhat more than after-tax profits. The average bonus for 1988 was $21,258. Even for the recession years 1982 and 1983, bonuses averaged $13,998 and $8,557, respectively. Individual bonuses were proportional to merit rating scores. For

EXHIBIT 1

Merit rating cards

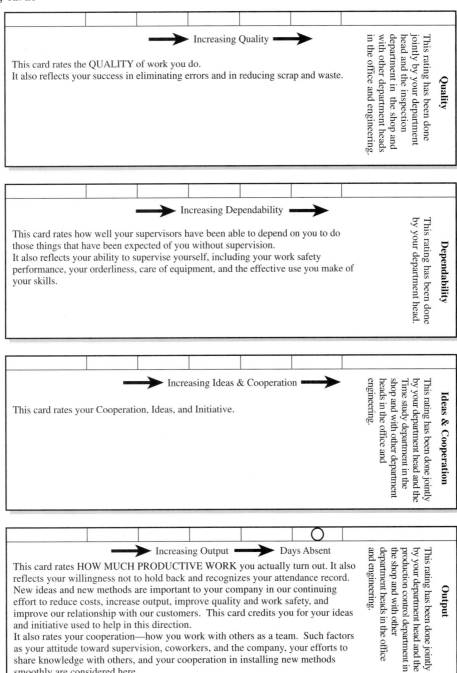

> **Quality**
>
> This rating has been done jointly by your department head and the inspection department in the shop and with other department heads in the office and engineering.

Increasing Quality ➡

This card rates the QUALITY of work you do.
It also reflects your success in eliminating errors and in reducing scrap and waste.

> **Dependability**
>
> This rating has been done by your department head.

Increasing Dependability ➡

This card rates how well your supervisors have been able to depend on you to do those things that have been expected of you without supervision.
It also reflects your ability to supervise yourself, including your work safety performance, your orderliness, care of equipment, and the effective use you make of your skills.

> **Ideas & Cooperation**
>
> This rating has been done jointly by your department head and the Time study department in the shop and with other department heads in the office and engineering.

Increasing Ideas & Cooperation ➡

This card rates your Cooperation, Ideas, and Initiative.

> **Output**
>
> This rating has been done jointly by your department head and the production control department in the shop and with other department heads in the office and engineering.

Increasing Output ➡ Days Absent

This card rates HOW MUCH PRODUCTIVE WORK you actually turn out. It also reflects your willingness not to hold back and recognizes your attendance record. New ideas and new methods are important to your company in our continuing effort to reduce costs, increase output, improve quality and work safety, and improve our relationship with our customers. This card credits you for your ideas and initiative used to help in this direction.
It also rates your cooperation—how you work with others as a team. Such factors as your attitude toward supervision, coworkers, and the company, your efforts to share knowledge with others, and your cooperation in installing new methods smoothly are considered here.

example, assume the amount set aside for bonuses was 80 percent of total wages paid to eligible employees. A person whose performance score was 95 would receive a bonus of 76 percent (0.80×0.95) of annual wages.

Vacations.   The company was shut down for 2 weeks in August and 2 weeks during the Christmas season. Vacations were taken during these periods. For employees with over 25 years of service, a fifth week of vacation could be taken at a time acceptable to superiors.

Work Assignment.   Management had authority to transfer workers and to switch between overtime and short time as required. Supervisors had undisputed authority to assign specific parts to individual workers, who might have their own preferences due to variations in piece rates. During the 1982–1983 recession, fifty factory workers volunteered to join sales teams and fanned out across the country to sell a new welder designed for automobile body shops and small machine shops. The result—$10 million in sales and a hot new product.

Employee Participation in Decision Making.   Thinking of participative management usually evokes a vision of a relaxed, nonauthoritarian atmosphere. This was not the case at Lincoln. Formal authority was quite strong. "We're very authoritarian around here," said Willis. James F. Lincoln placed a good deal of stress on protecting management's authority. "Management in all successful departments of industry must have complete power," he said. "Management is the coach who must be obeyed. The workers, however, are the players who alone can win the game." Despite this attitude, there were several ways in which employees participated in management at Lincoln.

Richard Sabo, Assistant to the Chief Executive Officer, related job enlargement/enrichment to participation. He said, "The most important participative technique that we use is giving

more responsibility to employees. We give a high school graduate more responsibility than other companies give their foremen." Management put limits on the degree of participation which was allowed, however. In Sabo's words:

> When you use "participation," put quotes around it. Because we believe that each person should participate only in those decisions he is most knowledgeable about. I don't think production employees should control the decisions of the chairman. They don't know as much as he does about the decisions he is involved in.

The Advisory Board, elected by the workers, met with the Chairman and the President every 2 weeks to discuss ways of improving operations. As noted earlier, this board had been in existence since 1914 and had contributed to many innovations. The incentive bonuses, for example, were first recommended by this committee. Every employee had access to Advisory Board members, and answers to all Advisory Board suggestions were promised by the following meeting. Both Willis and Hastings were quick to point out, though, that the Advisory Board only recommended actions. "They do not have direct authority," Willis said, "and when they bring up something that management thinks is not to the benefit of the company, it will be rejected."

Under the early suggestion program, employees were awarded one-half of the first year's savings attributable to their suggestions. Later, however, the value of suggestions was reflected in performance evaluation scores, which determined individual incentive bonus amounts.

Training and Education.   Production workers were given a short period of on-the-job training and then placed on a piecework pay system. Lincoln did not pay for off-site education, unless very specific company needs were identified. The idea behind this policy, according to Sabo, was that not everyone could take advantage of such a program, and it was unfair to expend company funds for an advantage to which there was unequal access. Recruits for sales jobs, already college graduates, were given on-the-job training in the plant, followed by a period of work and training at one of the regional sales offices.

Fringe Benefits and Executive Perquisites.
A medical plan and a company-paid retirement program had been in effect for many years. A plant cafeteria, operated on a break-even basis, served meals at about 60 percent of usual costs. The Employee Association, to which the company did not contribute, provided disability insurance and social and athletic activities. The employee stock ownership program resulted in employee ownership of about 50 percent of the common stock. Under this program, each employee with more than 2 years of service could purchase stock in the corporation. The price of the shares was established at book value. Stock purchased through this plan could be held by employees only.

Dividends and voting rights were the same as for stock which was owned outside the plan. Approximately 75 percent of the employees owned Lincoln stock.

As to executive perquisites, there were none. Executives had crowded, austere offices; no executive washrooms or lunchrooms; and no reserved parking spaces. Even the top executives paid for their own meals and ate in the employee cafeteria. On one recent day, Willis arrived at work late due to a breakfast speaking engagement and had to park far away from the factory entrance.

Financial Policies

James F. Lincoln felt strongly that financing for company growth should come from within the company—through initial cash investment by the founders, through retention of earnings, and through stock purchases by those who worked in the business. He saw the following advantages to this approach:

1. Ownership of stock by employees strengthened team spirit. "If they are mutually anxious to make it succeed, the future of the company is bright."

2. Ownership of stock provided individual incentive because employees felt that they would benefit from company profitability.

3. "Ownership is educational." Owner-employees "will know how profits are made and lost; how success is won and lost. . . . There are few socialists in the list of stockholders of the nation's industries."

4. "Capital available from within controls expansion." Unwarranted expansion would not occur, Lincoln believed, under his financing plan.

5. "The greatest advantage would be the development of the individual worker. Under the incentive of ownership, he would become a greater man."

6. "Stock ownership is one of the steps that can be taken that will make the worker feel that there is less of a gulf between him and the boss. . . . Stock ownership will help the worker to recognize his [or her] responsibility in the game and the importance of victory."

Until 1980, Lincoln Electric borrowed no money. The company's liabilities consisted mainly of accounts payable and short-term accruals.

The unusual pricing policy at Lincoln was succinctly stated by Willis: "At all times price on the basis of cost, and all times keep pressure on our cost." This policy resulted in the price for the most popular welding electrode going from 16 cents a pound in 1929 to 4.7 cents in 1938. More recently, the SA-200 welder, Lincoln's largest-selling portable machine, had decreased in price from 1958 through 1965. According to Dr. C. Jackson Grayson of the American Productivity Center in Houston, Texas, Lincoln's prices had increased only one-fifth as fast as the Consumer Price Index from 1934 to about 1970. This resulted in a welding products market in which Lincoln became the undisputed price leader for the products it manufactured. Not even the

Exhibit 2   Lincoln Electric's Financial History

	1974	1979	1980	1981	1982	1983	1987	1988	1989
Sales (in millions of dollars)	$233	$385	$401	$469	$329	$277	$377	$478	$582
Return on Equity*	25%	19%	16%	19%	9%	9%	15%	16%	12%
Debt to equity ratio†	0%	0%	0%	0%	0%	0%	2%	7%	11%
Segment Data:									
Arc-welding products (% of total sales)						91%	91%	91%	91%
Other products (% of total sales)						9%	9%	9%	9%

*Return on equity = $\dfrac{\text{Profit after tax}}{\text{Stockholders' equity}}$

†Debt to equity ratio = $\dfrac{\text{Long-term debt}}{\text{Long-Term debt + Stockholders' equity}}$

major Japanese manufacturers, such as Nippon Steel for welding electrodes and Osaka Transformer for welding machines, were able to penetrate this market.

Substantial cash balances were accumulated each year preparatory to paying the year-end bonuses. The bonuses totaled $54 million for 1988. The money was invested in short-term U.S. government securities and certificates of deposit (CDs) until needed. The company's financial history is shown in Exhibit 2.

How Well Did Lincoln Serve Its Stakeholders?

Lincoln Electric differed from most other companies in the importance it assigned to each of the groups it served. Willis identified these groups, in the order of priority ascribed to them, as (1) customers, (2) employees, and (3) stockholders.

Certainly the firm's customers had fared well over the years. Lincoln prices for welding machines and welding electrodes were acknowledged to be the lowest in the marketplace. Quality was consistently high. The cost of field failures for Lincoln products had recently been determined to be a remarkable 0.04 percent of revenues. The "Fleetweld" electrodes and SA-200 welders had been the standard in the pipe-

line and refinery construction industry, where price was hardly a criterion, for decades. A Lincoln distributor in Monroe, Louisiana, said that he had sold several hundred of the popular AC-225 welders, which were warranted for 1 year, but never handled a warranty claim.

Perhaps best-served of all management constituencies were the employees. Not the least of their benefits, of course, were the year-end bonuses, which effectively doubled an already average compensation level. The foregoing description of the personnel program and the comments in the Appendix further illustrate the desirability of a Lincoln job.

While stockholders were relegated to an inferior status by James F. Lincoln, they did very well indeed. Recent dividends had exceeded $11 a share, and earnings per share approached $30. In January 1980, the price of restricted stock, committed to employees, had been $117 a share. By 1989, the stated value at which the company would repurchase the stock if tendered was $201. A check with the New York office of Merrill Lynch, Pierce, Fenner and Smith at that time revealed an estimated price on Lincoln stock of $270 a share, with none being offered for sale. Technically, this price applied only to the unrestricted stock owned by the Lincoln family, a few other major holders, and employees who purchased it on the open market. Risk associated with Lincoln stock, a major determinant of stock value, was minimal because of the small amount of debt in the capital structure, because of an extremely stable earnings record, and because of Lincoln's practice of purchasing the restricted stock whenever employees offered it for sale.

A Concluding Comment

It was easy to believe that the reason for Lincoln's success was the excellent attitude of the employees and their willingness to work harder, faster, and more intelligently than other industrial workers. However, Sabo suggested that appropriate recognition be given to Lincoln executives, whom he credited with carrying out the following policies:

1. Management limited research, development, and manufacturing to a standard product line designed to meet the major needs of the welding industry.
2. New products had to be reviewed by manufacturing and all producing costs verified before the products were approved by management.
3. Purchasing was challenged not only to procure materials at the lowest cost but also to work closely with engineering and manufacturing to ensure that the latest innovations were implemented.
4. Manufacturing supervision and all personnel were held accountable for reduction of scrap, energy conservation, and maintenance of product quality.
5. Production control, material handling, and methods engineering were closely supervised by top management.
6. Management made cost reduction a way of life at Lincoln, and definite programs were established in many areas, including traffic and shipping, where tremendous savings could result.
7. Management established a sales department that was technically trained to reduce customer welding costs. This sales approach and other real customer services eliminated nonessential frills and resulted in long-term benefits to all concerned.
8. Management encouraged education, technical publishing, and long-range programs that resulted in industry growth, thereby assuring market potential for the Lincoln Electric Company.

Sabo wrote, "It is in a very real sense a personal and group experience in faith—a belief that together we can achieve results which alone would not be possible. It is not a perfect system, and it is not easy. It requires tremendous dedication and hard work. However, it does work, and the results are worth the effort."

APPENDIX
EMPLOYEE INTERVIEWS

Typical questions and answers from employee interviews are presented below. The employees' names have been changed to protect their privacy.

Interview 1

Ed Sanderson, a 23-year-old high school graduate who had been with Lincoln 4 years and who was a machine operator in the Electrode Division at the time of the interview.

Q: How did you happen to get this job?
A: My wife was pregnant, and I was making three bucks an hour and one day I came here and applied. That was it. I kept calling to let them know I was still interested.
Q: Roughly what were your earnings last year including your bonus?
A: $45,000.
Q: What have you done with your money since you have been here?
A: Well, we've lived pretty well, and we bought a condominium.
Q: Have you paid for the condominium?
A: No, but I could.
Q: Have you bought your Lincoln stock this year?
A: No, I haven't bought any Lincoln stock yet.
Q: Do you get the feeling that the executives here are pretty well thought of?
A: I think they are. To get where they are today, they had to really work.
Q: Wouldn't that be true anywhere?
A: I think more so here because seniority really doesn't mean anything. If you work with a guy who has 20 years here, and you have 2 months and you're doing a better job, you will get advanced before he will.
Q: Are you paid on a piece-rate basis?
A: My gang does. There are nine of us who make the bare electrode, and the whole group gets paid based on how many electrodes we make.
Q: Do you think you work harder than workers in other factories in the Cleveland area?

A: Yes, I would say I probably work harder.
Q: Do you think it hurts anybody?
A: No, a little hard work never hurts anybody.
Q: If you could choose, do you think you would be as happy earning a little less money and being able to slow down a little?
A: No, it doesn't bother me. If it bothered me, I wouldn't do it.
Q: Why do you think Lincoln employees produce more than workers in other plants?
A: That's the way the company is set up. The more you put out, the more you're going to make.
Q: Do you think it's the piece rate and bonus together?
A: I don't think people would work here if they didn't know that they would be rewarded at the end of the year.
Q: Do you think Lincoln employees will ever join a union?
A: No.
Q: What are the major advantages of working for Lincoln?
A: Money.
Q: Are there any other advantages?
A: Yes, we don't have a union shop. I don't think I could work in a union shop.
Q: Do you think you are a career man with Lincoln at this time?
A: Yes.

Interview 2

Roger Lewis, a 23-year-old Purdue graduate in mechanical engineering who had been in the Lincoln sales program for 15 months and who was working in the Cleveland sales office at the time of the interview.

Q: How did you get your job at Lincoln?
A: I saw that Lincoln was interviewing on campus at Purdue, and I went by. I later came to Cleveland for a plant tour and was offered a job.
Q: Do you know any of the senior executives? Would they know you by name?

A: Yes, I know all of them—Mr. Hastings, Mr. Willis, Mr. Sabo.

Q: Do you think Lincoln salespeople work harder than those in other companies?

A: Yes. I don't think there are many salespeople for other companies who are putting in 50- to 60-hour weeks. Everybody here works harder. You can go out in the plant, or you can go upstairs, and there's nobody sitting around.

Q: Do you see any real disadvantage to working at Lincoln?

A: I don't know if it's a disadvantage, but Lincoln is a spartan company, a very thrifty company. I like that. The sales offices are functional, not fancy.

Q: Why do you think Lincoln employees have such high productivity?

A: Piecework has a lot to do with it. Lincoln is smaller than many plants, too; you can stand in one place and see the materials come in one side and the product go out the other. You feel a part of the company. The chance to get ahead is important, too. They have a strict policy of promoting from within, so you know you have a chance. I think in a lot of other places you may not get as fair a shake as you do here. The sales offices are on a smaller scale, too. I like that. I tell someone that we have two people in the Baltimore office, and they say, "You've got to be kidding." It's smaller and more personal. Pay is the most important thing. I have heard that this is the highest-paying factory in the world.

Interview 3

Joe Trahan, a 58-year-old high school graduate who had been with Lincoln 39 years and who was employed as a working supervisor in the tool room at the time of the interview.

Q: Roughly what was your pay last year?

A: Over $56,000; salary, bonus, stock dividends.

Q: How much was your bonus?

A: About $26,000.

Q: Have you ever gotten a special award of any kind?

A: Not really.

Q: What have you done with your money?

A: My house is paid for—and my two cars. I also have some bonds and the Lincoln stock.

Q: What do you think of the executives at Lincoln?

A: They're really top-notch.

Q: What is the major disadvantage of working at Lincoln Electric?

A: I don't know of any disadvantage at all.

Q: Do you think you produce more than most people in similar jobs with other companies?

A: I do believe that.

Q: Why is that? Why do you believe that?

A: We are on the incentive system. Everything we do, we try to improve to make a better product with a minimum of outlay. We try to improve the bonus.

Q: Would you be just as happy making a little less money and not working quite so hard?

A: I don't think so.

Q: Do you think Lincoln employees would ever join a union?

A: I don't think they would ever consider it.

Q: What is the most important advantage of working at Lincoln?

A: Compensation.

Q: Tell me something about Mr. James Lincoln, who died in 1965.

A: You are talking about Jimmy, Sr. He always strolled through the shop in his shirt sleeves. Big fellow. Always looked distinguished. Gray hair. Friendly sort of guy. I was a member of the Advisory Board one year. He was there each time.

Q: Did he strike you as really caring?

A: I think he always cared for people.

Q: Did you get any sensation of a religious nature from him?

A: No, not really.

Q: And religion is not part of the program now?

A: No.

Q: Do you think Mr. Lincoln was a very intelligent man, or was he just a nice guy?

A: I would say he was pretty well educated. A great talker—always right off the top of his head. He knew what he was talking about all the time.

Q: When were bonuses for beneficial suggestions done away with?

A: About 18 years ago.

Q: Did that hurt very much?

A: I don't think so, because suggestions are still rewarded through the merit rating system.

Q: Is there anything you would like to add?

A: It's a good place to work. The union kind of ties other places down. At other places, electricians only do electrical work, carpenters only do carpenter work. At Lincoln Electric we all pitch in and do whatever needs to be done.

Q: So a major advantage is not having a union?

A: That's right.

Questions

1. How would you characterize Lincoln Electric's strategy? In this context, what is the nature of Lincoln's business and upon what bases does this company compete?

2. What are the most important elements of Lincoln's overall approach to organization and control that help explain why this company is so successful? How well do Lincoln's organization and control mechanisms fit the company's strategic requirements?

3. What is the corporate culture like at Lincoln Electric? What type of employees would be happy working at Lincoln Electric?

4. What is the applicability of Lincoln's approach to organization and control to other companies? Why don't more companies operate like Lincoln?

5. What could cause Lincoln's strategy implementation approach to break down? What are the threats to Lincoln's continued success?

6. Would you like to work in an environment like that at Lincoln Electric?

Case 12–2
Lincoln Electric Company (B)

Mr. Willis took over the position of CEO in 1986 upon the death of Mr. Irrgang, who had ruled the company under its Lincoln-inspired conservatism since 1972. Don Hastings became the president. Since that time, the NIH (Not Invented Here) syndrome that Lincoln had labored under had begun to crack. As Mr. Hastings observed, "If we didn't develop it, we didn't want to make it. But today that feeling is gone."

Under the leadership of Willis and Hastings, the company broadened its geographical scope of operations. "Today we must be global, with worldwide manufacturing capabilities. We can't just produce in the U.S. and export abroad," Mr. Hastings noted. Lincoln had added plants in Canada, Australia, Brazil, and Mexico, undertaken a joint venture in Venezuela, and was building a new plant in Japan. As the industry moved toward consolidation, Lincoln also had merged its European operation into a strategic alliance with (and eventual purchase of) a Nor-wegian company, Norweld, to establish a manufacturing base to tap the potential of a unified Common Market.

In 1990, Lincoln acquired Harris Calorific, a Gainesville, Georgia, manufacturer and worldwide distributor of plasma and gas cutting and welding products. Emerson Electric, Harris's former parent, also had a very strong corporate culture, placing a great deal of pressure on its divisions to perform and employing a low cost strategy.

This case was prepared by Stephen Elliot (T '92) under the direction of Professors Vijay Govindarajan and Anil K. Gupta, the Amos Tuck School of Business Administration, Dartmouth College. Copyright by Osceola Institute.

Questions

1. How difficult would it be for Lincoln Electric to implement its unique control systems in the manufacturing plants it has opened abroad, as a result of the company's aggressive overseas expansion strategy?

2. Does Lincoln Electric have the organizational capability to integrate its way of operating with the cultures of the acquired companies?

CASE 12–3
ANITA'S APPAREL

For 88 years Nordstrom has been guided by its founder's philosophy: offer the customer the best service, selection, quality and value.

Nordstrom Philosophy

Anita Lamont, founder and CEO of Anita's Apparel, a retailer of high-end women's business apparel, had just opened her fourth retail store in the Midwest. While Lamont was pleased with the company's progress, she was concerned by the growing number of customer complaints and the low sales per square foot compared to some of her better known competitors.

When it was just one store that she individually owned and operated, she was able to control most of the details of the business. While she worked with a few employees, she always knew what they were doing. As the number of stores and the size of the stores increased, the number of employees grew more than proportionately. When she was running the single store, she rarely heard a customer complaint, her pilferage costs were very low, and her sales per square foot was $250, compared with $220 today. This concerned Lamont greatly as her expansion plans for Anita's Apparel had slowed down because the stores were not producing the returns that she expected.

When she opened the second store, she added a store manager at each location. While both managers seemed to be doing well, the number of customer complaints increased. Lamont assumed that this would happen when she had more stores and more customers. By the time that she had opened the fourth store, the number of customer complaints had grown by eightfold from when there was only one store.

This case was prepared by Kirk Hendrickson [Tuck '97] under the supervision of Professor Vijay Govindarajan. Copyright © Osceola Institute. Many of the examples and statistics in this case are from *The Nordstrom Way* by Robert Spector and Patrick D. McCarthy, 1995.

The store managers were also complaining to Lamont because of the high training costs of bringing on new employees. The turnover rate seemed to be very high and Lamont could not understand why. She was paying one of the highest wages in the area to the sales clerks and store managers, yet they were leaving to go work elsewhere. The customers were also complaining about the lack of helpfulness of the sales clerks. Even after extensive employee retraining, Lamont was still hearing many complaints.

Lamont knew that there had to be a better way. Many of her competitors were well known for customer service and high sales per square foot. One of her best-known competitors that had appeared to have solved these problems was Nordstrom, Inc. In a visit to Seattle, Lamont had the opportunity to shop at a Nordstrom and she was impressed by the level of service provided by the cheerful and helpful sales clerks. Lamont could tell that there was a large difference between the level of service that she had received at Nordstrom and the level of service that sales clerks were providing at Anita's Apparel stores.

A few days later, Lamont received in the mail a handwritten thank-you letter from the Nordstrom sales clerk who had helped her in Seattle. Lamont decided right then that she had to find out more about what Nordstrom was doing that was so different from Anita's Apparel. She began by getting a copy of Nordstrom's 1995 Annual Report. Next she read *The Nordstrom Way* by Robert Spector and Patrick McCarthy. Then she found a few magazine articles that discussed Nordstrom and its success. The following is some of what she discovered about Nordstrom and the secrets of its success.

History

Nordstrom was founded in 1901 as Wallin & Nordstrom shoe store by Carl F. Wallin and John

---

EXHIBIT 1   Selected Financial Statements 1992 to 1996

Dollars in thousands except square footage and per share amounts
Year ended January 31.

	1996	1995	1994	1993	1992
Financial Position					
Customer Accounts Receivable, Net	874,103	655,715	565,151	584,379	585,490
Merchandise Inventories	626,303	627,930	585,602	536,739	506,632
Current Assets	1,612,776	1,397,713	1,314,914	1,219,844	1,177,638
Current Liabilities	832,313	690,454	627,485	511,196	553,903
Working Capital	780,463	707,259	687,429	708,648	623,735
Property, Buildings and Equipment, Net	1,103,298	984,195	845,596	824,142	856,404
Long-Term Debt	439,943	373,910	438,574	481,945	511,000
Shareholders' Equity	1,422,972	1,343,800	1,166,504	1,052,031	939,231
Total Assets	2,732,619	2,396,783	2,177,481	2,053,170	2,041,875
Operations					
Net Sales	4,113,517	3,894,478	3,589,938	3,421,979	3,179,820
Cost and Expenses:					
Cost of sales and Related Buying and Occupancy	2,806,250	2,599,553	2,469,304	2,339,107	2,169,437
Selling, General and Administrative	1,120,790	1,023,347	940,579	902,083	831,505
Interest, Net	39,295	30,664	37,646	44,810	49,106
Service Charge Income and Other	(125,130)	(94,644)	(88,509)	(81,140)	(87,443)
Total Costs and Expenses	3,841,205	3,588,920	3,359,020	3,199,860	2,962,605
Earnings Before Income Taxes	272,312	335,558	230,918	222,119	217,215
Income Taxes	107,200	132,600	90,500	85,500	81,400
Net Earnings	165,112	202,958	140,418	136,619	135,815
Dividends per Share	.50	.385	.34	.32	.31
Sales per square foot for Company-Operated Stores	382	395	383	381	388

Source: Robert Spector, Patrick D. McCarthy, *The Nordstrom Way* (New York: John Wiley and Sons, 1995), p. 98.

W. Nordstrom. On their opening day, their total sales were $12.50. In fiscal year 1995, Nordstrom had sales of $4.1 billion (see Exhibit 1 for financial information going back five years). During the intervening 94 years, Nordstrom has become the largest independently owned fashion specialty retailer in the United States, offering a wide variety of fine quality apparel, shoes, and accessories for men, women, and children.

In 1995 the third generation of the Nordstrom family stepped down from the day-to-day management of Nordstrom. Six members of the fourth generation were promoted to co-presidents. The fourth generation has inherited one of the 50 largest retailing chains in the U.S. and one of the seven largest department stores.

Nordstrom operates 93 stores in 15 states, and is expanding into other states. Its 1996 plans call for new stores in Philadelphia and Dallas. Beyond 1996 Nordstrom plans to open stores in Detroit, Denver, Cleveland, and Atlanta.

Nordstrom stores have consistently performed well, often at the expense of its competitors. Nordstrom captured one-third of the

Southern California market in 10 years. The Tyson Corner, Virginia Nordstrom is credited with driving Garfinckels into bankruptcy.[1] Nordstrom stores average sales of $382 per square foot compared with Federated's $190 and May Department's $183.[2] Nordstrom has one of the lowest shrinkage costs in the industry at 1.5 percent versus the 3.0 percent average.

Creating a customer service environment

Nordstrom has developed a number of specific systems that are designed to create the Nordstrom customer service environment:

- Inverted pyramid management
- Commissions
- Unconditional returns
- Rewards
- Recognition
- Heroics

Inverted Pyramid Management.   Nordstrom draws its organizational chart as an inverted pyramid. The inverted pyramid shows the customers on top and the salespeople as the top level of the company. Each level below is responsible for supporting the salespeople and the customers. As co-chairman Raymond Johnson stated, "The only thing we have going for us is the way we take care of our customers and the people who take care of the customers are on the floor."[3]

As part of the pyramid, Nordstrom promotes strictly from within. Every manager and buyer started as a salesperson, including the current six co-presidents who are all Nordstrom family members. As James F. Nordstrom, former co-chairman stated, "One of the reasons our system has continued to work is that all of us, including the family, have served at every level from stock person to buyer. We've all been salespeople for a long time."[4]

Commissions.   Since the 1950s, Nordstrom salespeople have been paid on commission. 1995 standard commission rates ranged from 6.75 percent for apparel to 13 percent for children's shoes.[5] Each salesperson receives a draw against his or her commissions up to $11.00 per hour. Nordstrom monitors sales per hour: if an employee's draw rate is $10 per hour and if the employee is selling women's shoes at a 10 percent commission, then the employee would need to sell $100 per hour to cover his or her draw. Before computing sales per hour, any returns are subtracted from an employee's total sales.

At Nordstrom each department has a minimum hourly sales target. Salespeople who consistently fail to meet the sales per hour quotas receive coaching from their department managers. Salespeople are let go if they miss quota for three consecutive months.[6]

The commission system enables Nordstrom sales associates to earn almost twice what they would be able to make at a competitor's store. As a result, Nordstrom's selling expense is one of the highest in the industry.

Unconditional Returns.   At Nordstrom a customer can return any item for any reason and receive his or her money back. Former co-chairman Bruce Nordstrom explains the return policy to sales people as follows: "If a customer came into the store with a pair of five-year-old shoes and complained that the shoes were worn out and wanted her money back, you have the

---

[1]Dori Jones Yang and Laura Zinn. "Will 'The Nordstrom Way' Travel Well?" *Business Week*, September 3, 1990, pp. 82–83.

[2]Seth Lubove. "Don't listen to the boss, listen to the customer." *Forbes*, December 4, 1995, pp. 45–46.

[3]Robert Spector and Patrick D. McCarthy. *The Nordstrom Way.* (New York: John Wiley and Sons, 1995), p. 99.

---

[4]Ibid.

[5]Ibid., pp. 113–114.

[6]"Nordstrom: Respond to Unreasonable Customer Requests!" *Planning Review*, May/June 1994, pp. 17–18.

right to use your best judgment to give my money away. As a matter of fact, I order you to give my money away."[7] Nordstrom returns are legendary: shoplifted items and a set of tires (Nordstrom does not even sell tires) have been taken back, no questions asked.

Rewards. Nordstrom's general manager of its Southern California region, Jammie Baugh, states that at Nordstrom, "We tend to manage by contest. When we have something we want to improve on, then we have a contest."[8] These contests include monthly "Make Nordstrom Special" contests which reward good suggestions; daily sales contests which reward top sellers for the day; and fourth quarter 1993's "$250,000 Super Service Challenge" which awarded individual and team prizes for the best customer service.

Recognition. Nordstrom uses a number of different methods to recognize the accomplishments of its employees. Nordstrom management acknowledges employee "Pacesetters" and "Customer Service All-Stars"; morning announcements and monthly meetings are opportunities for managers to praise the sales and customer service efforts of the salespeople. The Pacesetter program recognizes the top 8 to 12 percent of each division's sales force based on exceeding a yearly sales target goal (targets which now top $350,000). Pacesetters receive certificates, increased store discounts, events, and trips. The Customer Service All-Stars are selected according to sales volume, customer service, and service to co-workers. The Customer Service All-Stars are selected monthly by store managers. The winners are given increased Nordstrom discounts and priority for selecting work shifts. Every morning, the store manager also praises departments and individuals during the pre-opening announcements for customer service

and sales. At the monthly meetings, managers read letters from customers and employees celebrate sales achievements.

Heroics. An additional piece of employee recognition is the stories of customer service "heroics." Salespeople who consistently perform customer service heroics are recognized by their department and store. They are often selected "Employee of the Month" and have their deeds printed up in a weekly collection of heroics by the sales associates. The following is one example of a heroic deed:

> A Nordstrom's sales associate discovered that a customer had left her airline tickets at the counter. After calling the service representative for the airline who refused to help, the sales associate took a cab out to the airport, found the customer and gave her the tickets.[9]

Union Dispute

In November of 1989, Locals 1001 and 367 of the United Food and Commercial Workers Union (UFCW), which represented about 1600 Nordstrom sales associates in the Seattle-Tacoma area, filed a complaint with the Washington State Department of Labor and Industries Employment Standards Section (ESAC). The complaint charged that Nordstrom required or encouraged employees to attend meetings, perform stock work, and attend to customer service activities, such as hand-carrying items to customers or writing thank-you notes, outside of normal business hours without compensation. UFCW felt that the policy of ranking employees and managers on sales per selling hour caused managers to encourage or coerce employees into under reporting their hours worked.

On February 15, 1990, ESAC concluded that Nordstrom's work practices violated the state's Minimum Wage Act and that Nordstrom had to change these policies and retroactively compensate employees for time worked. Joe Peterson,

---

[7]Robert Spector, Patrick D. McCarthy, *The Nordstrom Way* (New York: John Wiley and Sons, 1995), p. 100.

[8]Ibid., p. 119.

[9]Ibid., p. 125.

the president of Local 1001, suggested that claims could be as high as $40 million in Washington State and $300 million in California. Based on this news, poor revenue projections, and the threat of a class-action lawsuit being filed by Peterson covering Nordstrom employees nationwide, Nordstrom's stock price fell by almost 10 percent in one day.

On February 20, 1990, *The Wall Street Journal* printed a front page article describing horrendous working conditions.[10] The story opens with a discussion of a former Nordstrom employee alleging that he was unlawfully discharged when Nordstrom discovered that he had AIDS. It follows with employment counselor Alice Synder who describes how she regularly receives visits from Nordstrom employees, "suffering from ulcers, colitis, hives and hand tremors," due to the stress of working at Nordstrom. A series of former employees were interviewed for the article. Patty Bemis, former Nordstrom employee, discussed how "The managers were these little tin gods, always grilling you about your sales. You felt like your job was constantly in jeopardy."

Over the next week, Nordstrom announced that it would change its time-keeping procedures and established a $15 million reserve for back-pay claims. Joe Peterson called the reserve, "Wholly inadequate. It won't even cover claims of employees in Washington state."[11] After that the union filed more unfair labor practice lawsuits. The AIDS Coalition to Unleash Power (ACT UP) protested at Nordstrom's downtown San Francisco store. A class action lawsuit was also filed on behalf of shareholders.

As the dispute grew, *60 Minutes* did a segment on Nordstrom which changed some minds. As

Marti Galovic Palmer, producer for *60 Minutes*, stated, "A lot of what I was looking for in terms of hard complaints turned out to be from people who just wanted a job that didn't demand a whole lot."[12]

Bruce Nordstrom gave Nordstrom's perspective on the conflict:

> Freedom is the issue, not just freedom to belong or not belong to a union, but freedom to wait on customers in the best way, freedom to go the extra mile, freedom to pursue a career in sales or in management, freedom to make customer service decisions right there on the sales floor without a lot of silly rules and interference, and freedom from being called "clock-punchers" as they have been by this union's management.[13]

In his comment about the freedom not to belong to the union, Bruce Nordstrom was referring to a request that had been made to Nordstrom by employees to have the union become an open shop where employees could choose to belong to the union or not. Nordstrom had a closed shop in the Seattle area stores where all employees had to be members of the union.

Nordstrom made this request in the 1987 contract negotiation and again in the 1989 contract negotiations. In 1989 Nordstrom would not remove it from the proposed contract. In addition to the contract negotiations, a group called Nordstrom Employees Opposed to Union Representation (NEOUR) began a campaign to have local 1001 decertified. The NLRB disallowed NEOUR's first petition for decertification because of the outstanding charges of labor practice violations by the union. In July of 1990, however, the union was decertified by over a five to two margin.

In the end, the class-action lawsuit by the union was settled out of court. Employee claims from the settlement totaled about $5 million, far less than the $300 million that Peterson pre-

[10]Susan Faludi. "Sales Job: At Nordstrom Stores, Service Comes First—But at What Price." *The Wall Street Journal*, February 20, 1990, p. A1, A16.

[11]George Tibbits. "Earnings Fall 34 percent in 4th Quarter; $15 million Charge For Back Pay." Seattle Priority: Rush, February 26, 1990, Associated Press.

[12]Robert Spector, Patrick D. McCarthy, *The Nordstrom Way* (New York: John Wiley & Sons, 1995), p. 175.

[13]Ibid., p. 176.

dicted for California. The union reportedly received $6.6 million in the settlement.

Anita's Decision

As Anita Lamont considered what she had learned about Nordstrom, she focused on the fact that while she paid her employees good wages, they were still paid by the hour. Anita's Apparel had few incentive plans for the sales clerks and a very strict return policy. Also, about the only heroics that she had ever heard come out of Anita's Apparel were from her days when she started. Many of these heroics became the basis for some of the current policies.

While she recognized the many merits to the Nordstrom approach of commission compensation and incentive pay, Lamont was concerned that the costs and risks associated with Nordstrom's commission based compensation system would be greater than any benefits that Anita's Apparel might derive. In addition, if she did decide to change her compensation system, what else would need to be changed at Anita's Apparel in order to really improve the level of customer satisfaction and the sales per square foot?

Questions

1. How do you evaluate Nordstrom's compensation and other systems in support of its strategy?
2. How would you advise Anita Lamont about compensating her employees?

CASE 12–4
WAYSIDE INNS, INC.

It was May 11, 1992 and Kevin Gray was conducting a routine quarterly inspection of the Memphis Airport Wayside Inn. The property was one of those that fell under his jurisdiction as regional general manager for Wayside Inns, Inc. During his inspection tour Gray was called aside by the Inn's manager, Layne Rembert, who indicated some concern about a proposed expansion of his motel.

"I'm a little worried, Kevin, about that plan to bring 40 more rooms on stream by the end of the next fiscal year."

"Why all the concern, Layne? You're turning away a significant number of customers and, by all indications, the market will be growing considerably."

"Well, I've just spoken with Ed Keider. He's certain that the 80-room expansion at the central Toledo property has lowered his return on investment. I'd really like to chat with you about what effects the planned expansion will have on my incentive compensation and how my income for the year would be affected."

The Company

Wayside Inns, Inc., located in Kansas City, Missouri, was formed in 1980 as the successor corporation to United Motel Enterprises, a company that operated several franchised motels under licensing agreements from two national motel chains. Due to the complicated and restrictive contract covenants, United was unable to expand the scope of either of their two motel operations through geographical dispersion.

The successor corporation was formed to own, operate, and license a chain of motels under the name Wayside Inns, as well as to continue to operate the present franchises held by United. Management felt that the strategy of developing their own motel chain would afford them greater flexibility and would allow them to more easily attain the long-term growth strategies. Another major reason for the move was that the new corporate strategy would allow management to pursue the implementation of a comprehensive marketing plan which they had been slowly developing over the last seven years.

The company's fundamental strategy was to cater to those business travelers who were generally not interested in elaborate settings. There were no common areas such as lobbies, convention rooms, bars, or restaurants. The chain emphasized instead clean rooms, dependable service, and rates that generally were 15 to 20 percent lower than other national motel chains. A free-standing restaurant was always located on the motel's property—in some cases it was operated by Wayside. In general, however, concessionary leases were granted to regional restaurant chains.

Wayside's management made it a point to locate their properties near interstate highways or major arteries convenient to commercial districts, airports, and industrial or shopping facilities. In a given city, one would often find Wayside Inns at various strategic locations. This strategy was founded on the belief that it was preferable to have a total of 600 rooms in five or six locations within one city rather than have one large hotel with 600 rooms. This strategy resulted in the clustering of hotels in those cities that could support the market. Once several hotels had been built in a particular city, management would seek new properties in regions commercially linked to that city.

Wayside was well aware that their aggressive strategy was successful only to the extent that unit managers followed corporate policies to the letter. In order to insure an aggressive spirit

This case was prepared by Charles T. Sharpless, research assistant, under the supervision of Professor M. Edgar Barrett. Copyright © by M. Edgar Barrett.

among the unit managers a multifaceted compensation plan was developed. The plan was composed of four elements, but was basically tied to profitability. A base salary was calculated which was loosely tied to years of service, dollar volume of sales, and adherence to corporate goals. An incentive bonus was calculated on sales volume increases. An additional incentive bonus was calculated using the Inn's return on investment. Fringe benefits were the final element and were a significant factor in the package. (See Exhibit 1.) Generally, base salaries ranged from $16,000 to $21,000 and total compensation was in the neighborhood of $24,000 to $30,000. The unit manager always lived on the premises and his wife usually played a role in managing the Inn. As a result, the average couple were in their late 40s or beyond. Many did not have previous motel experience.

The firm had grown substantially since its inception and the prospects for future growth were favorable. The company's expansion strategy had evolved into a three-tiered attack. Most importantly, management actively pursued the construction of new motels seeking an ever-widening geographical distribution. Second, 76 and 116 room properties were expanded if analysis demonstrated that they were operating near or at full capacity. Third, old properties that became a financial burden or did not contribute the required rate of return were sold. Wayside Inns were usually constructed in one of three sizes—76 rooms, 116 rooms, or 156 rooms.

Wayside Inns was a public corporation listed on the American Stock Exchange. It had 1,542,850 shares outstanding, with an average float of 400,000 shares. The common stock price had appreciated considerably and analysts felt that investor interest was due to a number of factors but was primarily linked to their innovative marketing strategy. Wayside's average occupancy rate on established properties was 10 to 20 percent higher than competitive motels. Their specifically targeted market segment (the business traveler) was generally unaffected by seasonal or environmental factors. Additional company strengths, considered significant by service industry analysts, were an aggressive management, reduction of construction costs and completion times due to standardization, and efficient quality control of present properties.

The Memphis Airport Wayside Inn

The Wayside Inn at Memphis Airport was one of the mid-sized units in the chain—one of the original 116 room properties. It was located at the intersection of Brooks Road and Airways Road, approximately five miles from the center of the city. The motel opened on February 9, 1984 and had developed a very good following in the succeeding years. While the occupancy rate had averaged near 43 percent for the first year, it had increased steadily over the years. By 1991, it operated at near full capacity for five nights a week. The Inn depended on salesmen and commercial travelers for approximately 80 percent of its revenue.

The property had been originally purchased in 1982 for $225,675. Construction costs for the motel had amounted to approximately $923,020, and furnishings, hardware, software and office equipment had been purchased for $265,500.

Wayside Inns had contributed an initial equity capitalization of $75,000. The parent had also loaned $275,000 to the subsidiary which was secured by promissory notes. A national insurance company granted a mortgage of $950,000 on the land and physical plant. Finally, $405,000 had been received from Memphis Interstate Bank to finance equipment and supply purchases and to provide the necessary working capital. (See Exhibits 2 and 3 for operating data and Exhibits 4 and 5 for financial statements.)

There were approximately 10 competitive motels, which were franchises of the major national chains, within a two-mile radius of the Memphis Airport Inn. There also existed a number of independent motels within the area. However, they were generally of the budget type and did not offer the quality on which Wayside based their

---

EXHIBIT 1   Unit Managers' Compensation Package

Base salary

Base salary ranges are calculated on the basis of years of service and relative sales volume for a particular inn. Salaries are subject to annual review and the amount of adjustment will largely depend upon the recommendation of the regional general manager. Every attempt will be made to keep salary levels consistent with competitive chains.

Sales volume incentive

Every unit manager, having earned a profit before taxes, will receive a bonus equal to 1 percent of any revenue increase over the previous year's level. In the event of a revenue decrease, there will be no bonus and the following year's bonus will be calculated using the revenue of the year preceding the decline as a base figure.

Return on investment bonus

Investment will be defined as current assets, fixed assets, other assets, and any deferred expenses. Return is defined as profit before interest expense and taxes.

The formula for the bonus calculation will be:

$$\text{ROI} \times \text{PF} = \text{ROI bonus}$$

where:

$$\text{ROI} = \frac{\text{EBIT}}{\text{Investment}} \text{ and PF = Performance factor}$$

The performance factor is used to differentiate between the larger and smaller investments and to offset the inherent complexities of managing the larger properties.

Size of Investment ($)	Value of Performance Factor ($)*
0 – 600,000	$15,000
600,000 – 1,200,000	$25,000
1,200,000 – 1,800,000	$36,000
1,800,000 – 2,500,000	$45,000
2,500,000 – up	$50,000

*The regional general manager has the discretion to reduce or increase the value of the performance factor for a particular property upon central headquarter's approval.

Fringe benefits

Each unit manager shall receive an apartment (two bedrooms, full kitchen, and den) on the premises, a company car for sales calls, laundry service, and local phone service at no expense.

Exhibit 2   Selected Operating Statistics *(for the Periods January 1 to December 31)*

	1991	*1990*	*1989*	*1988*	*1987*
Occupancy report					
Room nights available	41,975	41,975	41,975	41,975	41,975
Occupied room nights	36,634	35,595	33,454	32,613	31,522
Occupancy rate (%)	87.3	84.8	79.7	77.7	75.1
Room revenue ($)	998,277	857,839	680,789	577,250	510,656
Average room rate ($)	27.25	24.10	20.35	17.70	16.20
Weekly occupancy (%)					
Monday	99	99	95	94	92
Tuesday	99	99	94	92	91
Wednesday	99	98	96	94	89
Thursday	99	97	92	87	86
Friday	91	87	72	70	65
Saturday	61	55	51	50	48
Sunday...........................	63	59	58	57	55
Turnaway tally*					
Monday	26.1	22.8	15.1	10.1	11.5
Tuesday	27.7	21.0	19.3	16.0	12.1
Wednesday	38.2	33.2	26.9	19.5	13.3
Thursday	43.9	36.3	31.4	20.4	16.6
Friday	22.6	15.8	10.9	5.2	2.4
Saturday	9.6	5.7	2.8	0.2	0.6
Sunday...........................	8.5	6.4	3.0	1.3	0.5

*A turnaway is considered a customer who either calls the motel, requests a room in person, or calls central reservation service and is told there are no vacancies. See Exhibit 3 for further data.

Exhibit 3   Daily "Turnaway" Statistics for 1991

Week	*Sun.*	*Mon.*	*Tues.*	*Wed.*	*Thurs.*	*Fri.*	*Sat.*
1	0	25	26	36	45	0	0
2	0	23	21	24	25	0	0
3	0	10	11	17	23	3	0
4	0	20	21	16	46	5	0
5	0	16	17	25	38	0	0
6	0	20	15	38	43	7	0
7	0	25	32	45	25	0	0
8	0	10	12	42	46	10	0
9	0	21	14	40	71	12	0
10	0	23	28	39	23	15	0
11	0	19	25	41	45	16	0

EXHIBIT 3 Selected Operating Statistics (*continued*)

Week	Sun.	Mon.	Tues.	Wed.	Thurs.	Fri.	Sat.
12	0	25	30	43	39	20	0
13	0	46	42	24	45	21	0
14	0	28	25	58	40	30	0
15	0	35	14	61	63	32	0
16	0	24	22	25	45	43	4
17	0	13	46	26	49	15	11
18	0	25	29	13	45	12	2
19	0	43	40	61	71	10	15
20	0	22	55	62	68	45	23
21	20	42	36	67	55	46	36
22	22	39	35	50	47	39	33
23	23	22	33	38	35	38	32
24	24	28	25	25	41	17	0
25	10	29	24	15	41	25	10
26	0	24	20	39	35	18	6
27	0	30	18	25	24	42	38
28	25	29	15	35	35	45	27
29	29	26	66	41	82	11	12
30	15	25	50	62	65	18	9
31	13	42	43	47	48	16	5
32	17	31	25	35	50	17	15
33	18	32	16	28	32	18	12
34	12	15	22	23	28	20	14
35	10	14	25	27	26	21	23
36	6	17	24	61	67	15	12
37	19	56	27	43	40	15	16
38	18	55	71	39	42	20	18
39	14	16	35	46	41	23	17
40	5	12	20	48	47	27	6
41	16	23	15	45	53	29	5
42	7	25	18	42	43	31	4
43	0	18	20	41	39	43	4
44	0	19	21	48	53	46	11
45	0	29	23	19	47	47	4
46	0	31	24	25	29	41	16
47	0	20	26	31	33	52	12
48	10	22	16	49	52	26	10
49	15	24	18	40	38	20	8
50	16	21	19	31	41	10	4
51	43	37	45	47	37	15	2
52	35	31	40	38	42	6	20
Total	442	1,357	1,440	1,986	2,283	1,175	498

Exhibit 4   Memphis Airport Wayside Inn

Income Statement
For the Years Ended December 31

	1990	1991
Revenues:		
Room revenue	$857,839	$ 998,277
Restaurant rental	29,148	32,304
Other	15,798	19,148
Total revenues	902,785	$1,049,729
Operating costs and expenses:		
Room	194,620	229,520
Selling and administrative	204,767	217,020
Depreciation and amortization	48,118	58,320
Utilities	41,610	45,473
Maintenance and repairs	46,672	48,498
Management and reservations fees	46,372	53,394
Operating income:	320,626	397,504
Interest expense	159,617	168,610
Profit before taxes:	161,009	228,894
Federal taxes	55,746	83,406
Net earnings	$105,263	$ 145,488

reputation. Recent surveys conducted by the Memphis Chamber of Commerce indicated that average occupancy rates hovered near 72 percent and that the average room sold for $29.00. Expansion plans by the major chains were expected to account for an additional 800 rooms across the whole city in the following 18 months.

The Proposed Expansion.   Wayside's Project Development staff had arrived at a projected schedule of costs that would be associated with the completion of a 40-room expansion. Cost adjustments would be necessary depending on the particular city and conditions. However, variances were not expected to be significant.

Engineering and legal fees were expected to be somewhere in the neighborhood of $18,000. Environmental Impact Studies to comply with federal regulations and the local building permits were estimated to cost $12,000. Construction costs for the expansion and adjoining parking facility were

expected to be near $1,050,000. Such an expansion was expected to generate additional annual, nondirect operating costs of $46,000 (largely for personnel, utilities, and maintenance). Direct room expenses were expected to remain at an average of 23 percent of room revenue. Management and reservation fees paid to the parent were based on a formula of 5 percent of room revenue plus $30 per room per year.

Performance Evaluation

After dinner that evening, Kevin Gray decided to review his file on Layne Rembert's compensation package and on his related performance evaluation. He checked his records to determine what the Rembert's total compensation had been for 1991. He then performed a rough calculation of what it would be for 1992 if the additional 40 rooms were to have been available during all of this time period (See Exhibit 6).

EXHIBIT 5   **Memphis Airport Wayside Inn**

Balance Sheet

	1990	1991
Assets		
Current assets:		
Cash	$ 19,050	$ 18,800
Trade receivables	86,825	101,620
Merchandise	22,817	25,312
Prepaid expenses:		
Insurance	4,622	4,110
Mortgage interest	8,524	8,022
Linens	2,320	2,480
Total current assets	144,158	160,344
Fixed assets:		
Land	225,675	225,675
Building, equipment, furniture, and fixtures	1,327,740	1,370,515
Less: Accumulated depreciation	(268,375)	(326,695)
Total fixed assets	1,285,040	1,269,495
Other assets:		
Franchise	12,000	10,500
Supplies	28,540	28,450
Total other assets	40,540	38,950
Total assets	$1,469,738	$1,468,789
Liabilities		
Current liabilities:		
Accounts payable	$ 68,671	$ 53,066
Taxes payable	23,240	27,212
Accrued expenses	59,915	52,611
Total current liabilities	151,826	132,889
Long-term liabilities:		
Mortgage payable	684,000	646,000
Notes payable	302,500	248,000
Notes payable to parent	140,000	105,000
Total long-term liabilities	1,126,500	999,000
Net worth:		
Capital stock	75,000	75,000
Retained earnings	116,412	261,900
Total net worth	191,412	336,900
Total liabilities	$1,469,738	$1,468,789

EXHIBIT 6   Effect of Proposed Expansion on Rembert's Income

Total Compensation for 1991		*Projected Compensation after Expansion*	
Base salary	$18,500	Base salary	$18,500
Sales volume incentive		Sales volume incentive	
$(1,049,729 - 902,785) \times .01$		$(1,485,859 - 1,049,729) \times .01$	
$146,944 \times .01 =$	1,469	$436,130 \times .01 =$	4,361
Return on investment bonus		Return on investment bonus	
$\dfrac{397,504}{1,468,789} \times 36,000$		$\dfrac{624,235}{2,573,789} \times 45,000$	
$.2706 \times 36,000 =$	9,743	$.2425 \times 45,000 =$	10,914
Total compensation	$29,712	Total compensation	$33,775

Projected income statement (as calculated by Gray)

Revenue:

Room revenue	$1,420,238
Restaurant rental	40,571
Other	25,050
Total revenues	1,485,859

Operating costs and expenses:

Room	326,700
Operating expenses	376,832
Depreciation and amortization	82,400
Management and reservation fees	75,692
Operating income	$ 624,235

Remarks: Room revenue projected as 47,184 occupied room nights at an average price of $30.10. This figure is attributed slightly to annual growth but largely to turnaways accommodated.

Investment is figured loosely and may vary in actuality, but variance will not significantly affect ROI.

Over the past few years, Gray had also developed a 20-point performance evaluation report which he used to base his decisions on salary increases (See Exhibit 7). This system was derived from one he had witnessed when he had been previously employed by a national food service organization. While the report had been developed primarily for his own use in helping to determine who should receive merit increases in salary, Gray placed a great deal of weight on his report. In fact, he was entertaining the notion of recommending that it be instituted companywide. He made no bones about letting unit managers know that he looked for other things than pure return on investment. He felt that there were a number of variables that could seriously affect profitability over which the unit manager had no control. In addition, he believed an efficient operation was to a large extent contingent on customer satisfaction.

Questions

1. Is the proposed investment likely to be a good one for Wayside Inns, Inc.?

2. Is Layne Rembert's concern justified?

3. Is the current compensation package for inn managers an appropriate one? If not, what would be?

Exhibit 7

	Performance Evaluation Report			
	(1) *Poor*	*(2)* *Average*	*(3)* *Good*	*(4)* *Superior*	
Motel environment					
Exterior appearance	_____	_____	_____	_____ × .2 = _____
Interior appearance	_____	_____	_____	_____ × .5 = _____
Maintenance work	_____	_____	_____	_____ × .3 = _____
Room spot check	_____	_____	_____	_____ × .5 = _____
Personnel attitude	_____	_____	_____	_____ × .3 = _____
Managerial factors					
Accurate reports	_____	_____	_____	_____ × .3 = _____
Reservation control	_____	_____	_____	_____ × .2 = _____
Accounts receivable	_____	_____	_____	_____ × .2 = _____
Payroll	_____	_____	_____	_____ × .3 = _____
Controllable costs	_____	_____	_____	_____ × .5 = _____
Occupancy rate	_____	_____	_____	_____ × .5 = _____
Other factors					
Cooperation with RGM	_____	_____	_____	_____ × .3 = _____
Sales calls	_____	_____	_____	_____ × .3 = _____
Personnel turnover	_____	_____	_____	_____ × .3 = _____
Complaints	_____	_____	_____	_____ × .3 = _____
Total	_____	_____	_____	_____ _____

	Ranking
20.0–17.8	Excellent
17.7–15.0	Good
14.9–11.0	Must improve
10.0–5.0	Very poor

4. Should the performance measurement system for a regional general manager be focused upon the same factors that are used by Kevin Gray and Wayside Inns to evaluate and compensate an inn manager. (An RGM has responsibility for a geographical area containing anywhere from 10 to 15 motels).

Case 12–5
Mary Kay Cosmetics, Inc.

In spring 1983 Mary Kay Cosmetics, Inc. (MKC), the second-largest direct-sales distributor of skin care products in the United States, encountered its first big slowdown in recruiting women to function as Mary Kay beauty consultants and market the Mary Kay cosmetic lines. As of April, MKC's sales force of about 195,000 beauty consultants was increasing at only a 13 percent annual rate, down from a 65 percent rate of increase in 1980. The dropoff in the percentage of new recruits jeopardized MKC's ability to sustain its reputation as a fast-growing company. MKC's strategy was predicated on getting even larger numbers of beauty consultants to arrange skin care classes at the home of a hostess and her three to five guests; at the classes consultants demonstrated the Mary Kay Cosmetics line and usually sold anywhere from $50 to $200 worth of Mary Kay Cosmetics. MKC's historically successful efforts to build up the size of its force of beauty consultants had given the company reliable access to a growing number of showings annually.

The Direct-Sales Industry

In 1984 Avon was the acknowledged leader among the handful of companies that chose to market cosmetics to U.S. consumers using direct-sales techniques; Avon, with its door-to-door sales force of 400,000 representatives, had worldwide sales of about $2 billion. Mary Kay Cosmetics was the second-leading firm. Other well-known companies whose salespeople went either door-to-door with their product or else held "parties" in the homes of prospective customers included Amway Corp. (home cleaning products), Shaklee Corp. (vitamins and health foods), Encyclopedia Britannica,

Tupperware (plastic dishes and food containers), Consolidated Foods' Electrolux division (vacuum cleaners), and StanHome (parent of Fuller Brush). The direct-sales industry also included scores of lesser-known firms selling about every product imaginable—clothing, houseplants, toys, and financial services. Although Stanley Home Products invented the idea, Mary Kay and Tupperware were the best-known national companies using the "party plan" approach to direct selling.

The success enjoyed by Avon and Mary Kay was heavily dependent upon constantly replenishing and expanding their sales forces. New salespeople not only placed large initial orders for products but they also recruited new people into the organization. Revenues and revenue growth thus were a function of the number of representatives as well as the sales productivity of each salesperson. Market size was not seen as a limiting factor for growth because direct-sales companies typically reached fewer than half the potential customer base.

Direct selling was grounded in capitalizing on networking relationships. Salespeople usually got their starts by selling first to relatives, friends, and neighbors, all the while looking for leads to new prospects. Direct-sales specialists often believed that party-plan selling was most successful among working class, ethnic, and small-town population groups where relationships were closer knit and where the social lives of women had a high carryover effect with work and high school. However, industry analysts saw several trends working against the networking approach and party plan type of direct selling—rising divorce rates, the scattering of relatives and families across wider geographic areas, weakening ties to ethnic neighborhoods, declines in the number and strength of the "old girls" networks in many towns and neighborhoods,

This case was prepared by Robin Romblad and Arthur A. Thompson, University of Alabama. Copyright © Arthur A. Thompson, Jr.

increased social mobility, the growing popularity of apartment and condominium living where acquaintances and relationships were more transient, and the springing up of bedroom communities and subdivisions populated by commuters and/or by families that stayed only a few years.

As of 1984, virtually every company in the direct-sales industry was critically evaluating the extent to which changes in the economy and in employment demographics would affect the success of direct selling. Many firms, including Avon and Mary Kay, were reviewing their incentive programs and sales organization methods.

Mary Kay Ash

Before she reached the age of 10, Mary Kay had the responsibility of cleaning, cooking, and caring for her invalid father while her mother worked to support the family. During these years, Mary Kay's mother encouraged her daughter to excel. Years later, Mary Kay noted on many occasions, "The confidence my mother instilled in me has been a tremendous help."[1]

Deserted by her husband of 11 years during the Great Depression, Mary Kay found herself with the responsibility of raising and supporting three children under the age of eight. Needing a job with flexible hours, she opted to try a career in direct sales with Stanley Home Products, a home-party housewares firm. After 13 years with Stanley, Mary Kay joined World Gift, a direct-sales company involved in decorative accessories.

By the time she retired from World Gift, she had remarried and lived in a comfortable Dallas neighborhood. She got so bored with retirement she decided to write a book on her direct-sales experiences. The more she wrote, the more she came to realize just how many problems women faced in the business world. Writing on a yellow legal pad at her kitchen table, Mary Kay listed everything she thought was wrong with male-run companies; on a second sheet she detailed how these wrongs could be righted, how a company could operate in ways that were responsive to the problems of working women and especially working mothers, and how women could reach their top potential in the business world. She decided to do something about what she had written on the yellow pad.

In 1963, using $5,000 in savings as working capital, she proceeded to organize a beauty products company that integrated skin care instruction into its direct-sales approach. The company was named Beauty by Mary Kay; the plan was for Mary Kay to take responsibility for the sales part of the company and for her second husband to serve as chief administrator. One month before operations were to start, he died from a heart attack. Her children persuaded her to go ahead with her plans, and Mary Kay's 20-year-old son, Richard Rogers, agreed to take on the job of administration of the new company.

All of Mary Kay's lifelong philosophies and experiences were incorporated into how the company operated. The importance of encouragement became deeply ingrained in what was said and done. "You Can Do It" was expanded from a technique used by her mother to a daily theme at MKC. Mary Kay's style was to "praise people to success."

The second important philosophy Mary Kay stressed concerned personal priorities: "Over the years, I have found that if you have your life in the proper perspective, with God first, your family second, and your career third, everything seems to work out."[2] Mary Kay particularly stressed giving beauty consultants enough control over how their selling efforts were scheduled so that problems with family matters and sick children were not incompatible with a Mary Kay career. A structure based on no sales quotas, few rules, and flexible hours was essential, Mary Kay believed,

---

[1]Mary Kay Ash, *Mary Kay* (New York: Harper & Row, 1981), p. 3.

[2]Ibid., p. 56.

because working mothers from time to time needed the freedom to let work demands take a backseat to pressing problems at home.

Fairness and personal ethics were put in the forefront, too. The Golden Rule (treating others as you would have them treat you) was high on Mary Kay's list of management guidelines.

To discourage interpersonal rivalry and jealousy, all rewards and incentives were pegged to reaching plateaus of achievements; everybody who reached the target level of performance became a winner. Sales contests based on declaring first place, second place, and third place winners were avoided.

In 1968 the company name was changed to Mary Kay Cosmetics, Inc. Richard Rogers, president, gave two basic reasons for the success of MKC:

> We were filling a void in the industry when we began to teach skin care and makeup artistry and we're still doing that today. And second, our marketing system, through which proficient customers achieve success by recruiting and building their own sales organization, was a stroke of genius because the by-product has been management. In other words, we didn't buy a full management team, they've been trained one by one.[3]

One of the biggest challenges MKC had to tackle during the 1970s was how to adapt its strategy to deal with the influx of women into the labor force. Full- and part-time jobs interfered with attending beauty shows during normal working hours, and many working women with children at home had a hard time fitting beauty shows on weeknights and weekends into their schedules. To make the beauty show sales approach more appealing to working women, the company began to supplement its standard "try before you buy" and "on-the-spot delivery" sales pitch themes. Consultants were trained to tout the ease with which MKC's scientifically formulated skin care system could be followed, the value of investing in good makeup and attractive

appearance, the up-to-date glamour and wide selection associated with MKC's product line, the flexibility of deciding what and when to buy, and the time-saving convenience of having refills and "specials" delivered to one's door instead of having to go out shopping. Mary Kay consultants quickly picked up on the growing popularity of having beauty shows on Tuesday, Wednesday, and Thursday nights; a lesser proportion of weekday hours were used for morning and afternoon showings, and a greater proportion came to be used for seeking and delivering reorders from ongoing users.

MKC's corporate sales goal was to reach $500 million in revenues by 1990. As of 1984, about 65 percent of total sales were made to customers at beauty shows. However, it was expected that as the size of the company's customer base grew, the percentage of orders from repeat buyers would rise well above the present 35 percent level. MKC estimated that the average client spent over $200 a year on cosmetics. The company saw its target clientele as middle-class women in the 18 to 34 age group primarily and in the 35 to 44 age group secondarily and believed that a big percentage of its customers consisted of suburban housewives and white-collar clerical workers. The company's literature always pictured upscale women, dressed in a classy and elegant yet understated way, in either the role of a Mary Kay beauty consultant or the role of a user of Mary Kay cosmetics. As company figurehead, Mary Kay Ash personally made a point of being fashionably and expensively dressed, with perfect makeup and hairstyle—a walking showcase for the company's products and a symbol of the professionally successful businesswoman.

Manufacturing. In 1969, MKC built a 300,000-square-foot facility adjacent to corporate headquarters. Packaging, warehousing, purchasing, and research labs were all housed in this location. Also included was a printing setup that created Mary Kay labels in English, Spanish, and French. Many of the operations were automated.

---

[3]Mary Kay Cosmetics, Inc., "A Company and a Way of Life," company literature.

The company's scientific research approach to skin care was supported by a staff of laboratory technicians skilled in cosmetic chemistry, dermatology, physiology, microbiology, and package engineering. Ongoing tests were conducted to refine existing items and to develop new products. Laboratory staffs were provided with the comments and reactions about the products that came in from the beauty consultants and their customers. Consultants were strongly encouraged to report on their experiences with items and to relay any problems directly to the laboratory staff. About 80 percent of the R&D budget was earmarked for improving existing products.

MKC believed that it was an industry leader in researching the properties of the skin (as concerned skin elasticity and moisture) and the anatomy of skin structure. Much of the research at MKC was performed in cooperation with academic institutions, particularly the University of Pennsylvania and the University of Texas Health Science Center.

Product-Line and Distribution Policies.
As of 1984, the Mary Kay product line consisted of the basic skin care program for various skin types, the glamour collection, the body care products line, and a line of men's products called Mr. K. Most of the women's products were packaged in pink boxes and jars. Mr. K, the men's line, was introduced in the 1960s in response to a number of confessions from men who used their wives' Mary Kay products. A rich chocolate brown package accented with silver was chosen for Mr. K. The men's line included a basic skin care program as well as lotions and colognes. The majority of Mr. K purchases were made by women for their husbands and boyfriends.

Consultants bought their supplies of products directly from MKC at wholesale prices and sold them at a 100 percent markup over wholesale. To make it more feasible for consultants to keep an adequate inventory on hand, the product line at MKC was kept streamlined to about 50 products. Mary Kay consultants were encouraged to carry enough products in their personal inventories that orders could be filled on the spot at the beauty shows. As an incentive to support this practice, MKC offered special awards and prizes when consultants placed orders of $1,500 or more.

A consultant could order as many or as few of the company's products as she chose to inventory. Most consultants stockpiled those items that sold especially well with their own individual clientele, and consultants also had the freedom to offer special promotions or discounts to customers. Nearly 50 percent of sales were for the skin care products that had evolved from the hide tanner's discovery. Consultants were required to pay for all orders with cashier's checks or money orders prior to delivery. MKC dealt only on a cash basis to minimize accounts receivables problems. In 1984, the average initial order of new consultants for inventory was about $1,000 ($2,000 in retail value). Consultants who decided to get out of the business could resell their inventories to MKC at 90 percent of cost.

During the company's early years, consultants were supplied only with an inventory of items to sell; shipments arrived in plain boxes. There were no sales kits and no instruction manuals to assist in sales presentations. However, by the 1970s, each new recruit received training in skin care techniques and was furnished with a number of sales aids. Later, new consultants were required to buy a beauty showcase containing everything needed to conduct a beauty show (samples, pink mirrors, pink trays used to distribute the samples, and a step-by-step sales manual that included suggested dialogue). In 1984 the showcase was sold to new consultants for $85. Along with the showcase came a supply of beauty profile forms to use at showings; guests filled out the form at the beginning of the show, and from the information supplied, a consultant could readily prescribe which of the several product formulas was best suited for the individual's skin type.

In addition to the income earned from product sales, consultants earned bonuses or commissions on the sales made by all the recruits they brought in. MKC paid consultants with one to four recruits a bonus commission equal to 4 percent on the wholesale orders of the recruits. A consultant with five or more recruits earned an 8 percent commission on the orders placed by recruits, or 12 percent if she also placed $600 a month in wholesale orders herself. MKC consultants who were entitled to a 12 percent commission and who had as many as 24 recruits were averaging about $950 monthly in bonuses and recruitment commissions as of 1984.

MKC's Sales Organization.   The basic field organization unit for MKC's 195,000-person force of beauty consultants was the sales unit. Each sales unit was headed by a sales director who provided leadership and training for her group of beauty consultants. The top-performing sales directors were designated as national sales directors, a title that signified the ultimate achievement in the Mary Kay career sales ladder. A corporate staff of seven national sales administrators oversaw the activities of the sales directors in the field and their units of beauty consultants.

The sales units were not organized along strict geographical lines and sales directors were free to recruit consultants anywhere; Mary Kay explained the logic for this approach:

> One of the first things I wanted my dream company to eliminate was assigned territories. I had worked for several direct-sales organizations in the past, and I knew how unfairly I had been treated when I had to move from Houston to St. Louis because of my husband's new job. I had been making $1,000 a month in commissions from the Houston sales unit that I had built over a period of eight years and I lost it all when I moved. I felt that it wasn't fair for someone else to inherit those Houston salespeople whom I had worked so hard to recruit and train.
>
> Because we don't have territories at Mary Kay Cosmetics, a director who lives in Chicago can be vacationing in Florida or visiting a friend in Pittsburgh and recruit someone while there. It doesn't matter where she lives in the United States; she will always draw a commission from the company on the wholesale purchases made by that recruit as long as they both remain with the company. The director in Pittsburgh will take the visiting di-

rector's new recruit under her wing and train her; the recruit will attend the Pittsburgh sales meetings and participate in the local sales contests. Although the Pittsburgh director will devote a lot of time and effort to the new recruit, the Chicago director will be paid the commissions. We call this our "adoptee" program.

> The Pittsburgh recruit may go on to recruit new people on her own. No matter where she lives, she becomes the nucleus for bringing in additional people for the director who brought her into the business. As long as they're both active in the company, she will receive commissions from the company on her recruit's sales activity.
>
> Today we have more than 5,000 sales directors, and most of them train and motivate people in their units who live outside their home states. Some have beauty consultants in a dozen or more states. Outsiders look at our company and say, "Your adoptee program can't possibly work!" But it does work. Each director reaps the benefits from her recruits in other cities and helps other recruits in return.[4]

The Beauty Consultant

Nearly all of MKC's beauty consultants had their first contact with the company as a guest at a beauty show. A discussion of career opportunities with Mary Kay was a standard part of the presentation at each beauty show. As many as 10 percent of the attendees at beauty shows were serious prospects as new recruits.

All beauty consultants were self-employed and worked on a commission basis. Everyone in the entire MKC sales organization started at the consultant level. The progression of each consultant up the "ladder of success" within the MKC sales organization was tightly linked to (1) the amount of wholesale orders the consultant placed with MKC, (2) her abilities to bring in new sales recruits, and (3) the size of the wholesale orders placed by these recruits. There were five rungs on the ladder of success for consultants, with qualifications and rewards as follows:

1. *New beauty consultant* (member of Perfect Start Club).

   Perfect Start Club qualifications:

[4]Ash, *Mary Kay on People Management*, pp. 2–3.

Study and complete perfect start workbook.

Observe three beauty shows.

Book a minimum of eight shows within two weeks of receiving beauty showcase.

Awards and recognition:

Receives perfect start pin.

Earns 50 percent commission on retail sales (less any discounts given to customers on special promotions).

Becomes eligible for a 4 percent recruiting commission on wholesale orders placed by active personal recruits (to be considered active, a consultant had to place at least a $600 minimum wholesale order during the current quarter).

2. *Star consultant.*

Qualifications:

Must have three active recruits.

Be an active beauty consultant (place a minimum wholesale order of $600 within the current calendar quarter).

Awards and recognition:

Earns a red blazer.

Earns a star pin.

Earns Ladder of Success status by placing $1,800 in wholesale orders in a three-month period.

Earns 50 percent commission on personal sales at beauty shows.

Earns 4 percent recruiting commissions on wholesale orders placed by active personal recruits.

Is eligible for special prizes and awards offered during quarterly contest.

Receives a Star of Excellence ladder pin by qualifying as a star consultant for 8 quarters (or a Double Star of Excellence pin for 16 quarters).

3. *Team leader.*

Qualifications:

Must have five or more active recruits.

Be an active beauty consultant.

Awards and recognition:

Earns 50 percent commission on sales at own beauty shows.

Earns a Tender Loving Care emblem for red blazer.

Earns an 8 percent personal recruiting commission on wholesale orders of active personal recruits.

Earns a 12 percent personal recruiting commission if (a) five or more active personal recruits place minimum $600 wholesale orders during the current month and (b) the team leader herself places a $600 wholesale order during the current month.

Receives team leader pin in ladder of success program.

Is eligible for quarterly contest prizes and bonuses.

4. *VIP (Very important performer).*

Qualifications:

Must have obtained team leader status.

Must place wholesale orders of at least $600 for three consecutive months.

Team must place wholesale orders of at least $3,000 each month for three consecutive months.

Awards and recognition:

Earns the use of an Oldsmobile Firenza.

Earns 50 percent commission on sales at own beauty shows.

Earns a 12 percent personal recruiting commission.

Receives VIP pin in ladder of success program.

Is eligible for quarterly contest prizes and bonuses.

5. *Future director.*

Qualifications:

Must have qualified for team leader status.

Must have 12 active recruits at time of application.

Must make a commitment to Mary Kay to become a sales director by actually giving her letter of intent date.

Awards and recognition:

Earns a future director crest for red jacket.

Plus all the benefits accorded team leaders and VIPs, as appropriate, for monthly and quarterly sales and recruiting performance.

New recruits were required to submit a signed beauty consultant agreement, observe three beauty shows conducted by an experienced consultant, book a minimum of eight beauty shows, and hold at least five beauty shows within their first two weeks. Each consultant was asked to appear in attractive dress and makeup when in public and to project an image of knowledge and confidence about herself and the MKC product line.

Consultants spent most of their work hours scheduling and giving beauty shows. A showing took about two hours (plus about an hour for travel time), and many times the hostess and one or more of the guests turned out to be prospective recruits. New consultants were coached to start off by booking showings with friends, neighbors, and relatives and then network these into showings for friends of friends and relatives of relatives.

Consultants were instructed to follow up each beauty show by scheduling a second facial for each guest at the showing. Many times a customer would invite friends to her second facial and the result would be another beauty show.

After the follow-up facial, consultants would call customers periodically to check on whether the customer was satisfied, to see if refills were needed, and to let the customer know about new products and special promotions. Under MKC's "dovetailing" plan, a consultant with an unexpected emergency at home could sell her prearranged beauty show to another consultant and the two would split the commissions generated by the show.

The Sales Director

Consultants who had climbed to the fifth rung of the consultants' ladder of success were eligible to become sales directors and head up a sales unit. In addition to conducting her own beauty shows, a sales director's responsibilities included training new recruits, leading weekly sales meetings, and providing assistance and advice to the members of her unit. Sales directors, besides receiving the commission on sales made at their own showings, were paid a commission on the total sales of the unit they headed and a commission on the number of new sales recruits. In June 1984, the top 100 recruiting commissions paid to sales directors ranged from approximately $660 to $1,900. It was not uncommon for sales directors to have total annual earnings in the $50,000 to $100,000 range; in 1983, the average income of the 4,500 sales directors was between $25,000 and $30,000.

There were six achievement categories for sales directors, with qualifications and awards as shown below:

1. *Director in qualification (DIQ).*

Qualifications:

Must have 15 active personal recruits.

Submits a letter of intent to obtain directorship.

Gets the director of her sales unit to submit a letter of recommendation.

Within three consecutive months:

- Must recruit an additional 15 consultants for a total of 30 personal active recruits.
- The unit of 30 personal active recruits must place combined wholesale orders of $4,000, $4,500, and $5,000 for months one, two, and three, respectively.

Awards and recognition:

Earns personal sales and personal recruiting commissions (as per schedules for at least team leader status).

Eligible for prizes and bonuses in quarterly contests.

2. *Sales director.*

Qualifications:

Sales unit must maintain a minimum of $4,000 in wholesale orders each month for the sales director to remain as head of her unit.

Awards and recognition:

Receives commissions of 9 percent to 13 percent on unit's wholesale orders.

Receives monthly sales production bonuses.

- A $300 monthly bonus if unit places monthly wholesale orders of $3,000–$4,999.
- A $500 monthly bonus if unit places monthly wholesale orders of $5,000 and up.

Receives a monthly recruiting bonus (for personal recruits or for recruits of other consultants in the sales unit).

- $100 bonus if three to four new recruits come into unit.
- $200 bonus if five to seven new recruits come into unit.
- $300 bonus if 8 to 11 new recruits come into unit.
- $400 bonus for 12 or more recruits.

Is given a designer director suit.

Is entitled to all commission schedules and incentives of future sales directors.

3. *Regal director.*

Qualifications:

Members of sales unit must place wholesale orders of at least $24,000 for two consecutive quarters.

Must qualify every two years.

Awards and recognition:

Earns the use of a pink Buick Regal.

Is entitled to all the commission percentages, bonuses, and other incentives of a sales director.

4. *Cadillac director.*

Qualifications:

Sales unit members must place at least $36,000 in wholesale orders for two consecutive quarters.

Must qualify every two years.

Awards and recognition:

Earns the use of a pink Cadillac.

Is entitled to all the commission percentages, bonuses, and other incentives of a sales director.

5. *Senior sales director.*

Qualifications:

One to four sales directors emerge from her unit.

Awards and recognition:

Earns a 4 percent commission on offspring directors' consultants.

Is entitled to all the commission percentages, bonuses, and other incentives of at least a sales director.

6. *Future national director.*

Qualifications:

Five or more active directors emerge from her unit.

Awards and recognition:

Is entitled to all the commission percentages, bonuses, and other incentives of a senior sales director.

As of late 1983, the company had about 700 Regal directors and about 700 Cadillac directors; in one recent quarter, 81 sales directors had met the qualifications for driving a new pink Cadillac.

The National Sales Director. Top-performing sales directors became eligible for designation as a national sales director, the highest recognition bestowed on field sales personnel. NSDs were inspirational leaders and managers of a group of sales directors and received commissions on the total dollar sales of the group of sales units they headed. In 1984, MKC's 50 national sales directors had total sales incomes averaging over $150,000 per year. A 1985 *Fortune* article featured Helen McVoy, an MKC national sales director since 1971, as one of the most successful salespeople in the United States; in 1984 she earned $375,000.

Training

Before holding a beauty show, a new consultant had to observe three beauty shows, attend orientation classes conducted by a sales director, and complete a self-study set of MKC training materials. This training covered the fundamentals of conducting skin care shows, booking future beauty shows, recruiting new Mary Kay consultants, personal appearance, and managing a small business. Active consultants were strongly encouraged to continue to improve their sales skills and product knowledge. In addition to weekly sales meetings and frequent one-on-one contact with other consultants and sales directors, each salesperson had access to a variety of company-prepared support materials—videotapes, films, slide shows, and brochures.

Motivation and Incentives. New sales contests were introduced every three months. Prizes and recognition awards were always tied to achievement plateaus rather than declaring first-, second-, and third-place winners. Top performers were spotlighted in the company's full-color monthly magazine, *Applause* (which had a circulation of several hundred thousand).

Seminar

MKC staged an annual "Seminar" as a salute to the company and to the salespeople who contributed to its success. By 1984, the seminar had grown into a three-day spectacular repeated four consecutive times with a budget of $4 million and attended by 24,000 beauty consultants and sales directors who paid their own way to attend the event. The setting, the Convention Center in Dallas, was decorated in red, white, and blue in order to emphasize the theme, "Share the Spirit." The climactic highlight of the seminar was Awards Night, when the biggest prizes were awarded to the people with the biggest sales. The company went to elaborate efforts to ensure the awards night was charged with excitement and emotion; as one observer of the 1984 Awards Night in Dallas described it, "The atmosphere there is electric, a cross between a Las Vegas revue and a revival meeting. Hands reach up to touch Mary Kay; a pink Cadillac revolves on a mist-shrouded pedestal; a 50-piece band plays; and women sob."

Mary Kay Ash customarily made personal appearances throughout the seminar period. In addition to awards night, the seminar featured sessions consisting of informational and training workshops, motivational presentations by leading sales directors, and star entertainment (Paul Anka performed in 1984, and in previous years there had been performances by Tennessee Ernie Ford, John Davidson, and Johnny Mathis). Over the three days, Cadillacs, diamonds, mink coats, a $5,000 shopping spree at Neiman-Marcus for any director whose team sold $1 million worth of Mary Kay products, and lesser assorted prizes were awarded to the outstanding achievers of the past year. Gold-and-diamond bumblebee pins, each containing 21 diamonds and retailing for over $3,600, were presented to the Queen of Sales on Pageant Night: these pins were the company's ultimate badge of success.

Corporate Environment

The company's eight-story, gold-glass corporate headquarters building in Dallas was occupied solely by Mary Kay executives. An open-door philosophy was present at MKC. Everyone from the mailroom clerk to the chairman of the board was treated with respect. The door to Mary Kay Ash's office was rarely closed. Often people touring the building peeked in her office to get a glimpse of the pink-and-white decor. Mary Kay and all other corporate managers took the time to talk with any employee.

First names were always used at MKC. Mary Kay herself insisted on being addressed as Mary Kay; she felt people who called her Mrs. Ash were either angry at her or didn't know her. In keeping with this informal atmosphere, offices didn't have titles on the doors, executive restrooms didn't exist, and the company cafeteria was used by the executives (there was no executive dining room).

To further enhance the informal atmosphere and enthusiasm at MKC, all sales functions began with a group sing-along.

The company sent Christmas cards, birthday cards, and anniversary cards to every single employee each year. Mary Kay personally designed the birthday cards for consultants. In addition, all the sales directors received Christmas and birthday presents from the company.

The People Management Philosophy at MKC

Mary Kay Ash had some very definite ideas about how people ought to be managed, and she willingly shared them with employees and, through her books, with the public at large. Some excerpts from her book *Mary Kay on People*

Management reveal the approach taken at Mary Kay Cosmetics:

> People come first at Mary Kay Cosmetics—our beauty consultants, sales directors, and employees, our customers, and our suppliers. We pride ourselves as a "company known for the people it keeps." Our belief in caring for people, however, does not conflict with our need as a corporation to generate a profit. Yes, we keep our eye on the bottom line, but it's not an overriding obsession.[5]

> Every person is special! I sincerely believe this. Each of us wants to feel good about himself or herself, but to me it is just as important to make others feel the same way. Whenever I meet someone, I try to imagine him wearing an invisible sign that says: MAKE ME FEEL IMPORTANT! I respond to this sign immediately and it works wonders.[6]

> At Mary Kay Cosmetics we believe in putting our beauty consultants and sales directors on a pedestal. Of all people, I most identify with them because I spent many years as a salesperson. My attitude of appreciation for them permeates the company. When our salespeople visit the home office, for example, we go out of our way to give them the red carpet treatment. Every person in the company treats them royally.[7]

> We go first class across the board, and although it's expensive, it's worth it because our people are made to feel important. For example, each year we take our top sales directors and their spouses on deluxe trips to Hong Kong, Bangkok, London, Paris, Geneva, and Athens to mention a few. We spare no expense, and although it costs a lot extra per person to fly the Concorde, cruise on the Love Boat, or book suites at the elegant Georges V in Paris, it is our way of telling them how important they are to our company.[8]

Questions

1. What is the strategy of Mary Kay Cosmetics to compete effectively in the cosmetics industry?
2. How has the company's compensation system supported its strategy?
3. What is the applicability of Mary Kay's compensation system to other companies?

---

[5]Ibid., p. xix.
[6]Ibid., p. 15.
[7]Ibid., p. 19.
[8]Ibid., p. 20.

III

VARIATIONS IN MANAGEMENT CONTROL

Chapters 8 through 12 described the management control process in what we believe to be fairly typical situations. In this part of the book, we describe factors that lead to modifications of these typical practices and suggest the nature of these modifications. The essentials of the control system are similar, but the environment results in differences in the details. In Chapter 13 we discuss how to differentiate controls in accordance with differentiated corporate and business unit strategies. In Chapter 14 we discuss new developments in manufacturing and their implications for management control. In Chapters 15 through 17, we discuss the modifications that are needed in management control practices as applied to certain types of organizations. These types are service organizations (Chapter 15), financial service organizations (Chapter 16), and multinational organizations (Chapter 17). Characteristics of these organizations and their implications for management control are considered in these chapters. In Chapter 18, we discuss the management control of projects, which is somewhat different from management control of ongoing operations that has been the focus hitherto.

CONTROLS FOR DIFFERENTIATED STRATEGIES

Many factors jointly influence the organization structure and the management control process in a company. Researchers have attempted to examine these factors by applying what is called *contingency theory*; the name simply means that structure and process are contingent on various external and internal factors. Research studies have identified important factors that influence the design of control systems, some of them being size, environment, technology, interdependence, and strategies.[1]

Given the overall framework of this book—namely, that the purpose of a management control system is primarily to help to implement strategies—we suggest in this chapter how different strategies influence the management control process. Two general observations are important. First, the suggestions made in this chapter are tendencies, not hard-and-fast principles. Second, system designers need to take into consideration the influence of other external and internal factors (environment, technology, size, culture, geographical location, management style) when designing control systems.

In the first part of the chapter, we discuss the implications of different corporate strategies—single industry, related diversification, and unrelated diversification—on the design of control systems. Next, we discuss the relationship between different business-level strategies—different missions (build, hold, harvest) and different competitive advantages (low cost, differentiation)—and the form and structure of control systems. We then discuss additional considerations involved in tailoring controls of strategies. Finally, we discuss the implications of management style on the design and operation of control systems.

---

[1]For example, a 1987 study identified certain factors that were statistically significant, but these factors explained less than 10 percent of the differences among the organizations included in the study. (Keith Duncan and Ken Moores, "Residual Analysis: A Better Methodology for Contingency Studies in Management Accounting," *Journal of Management Accounting Research*, Fall 1989, pp. 89–102. This article has an excellent bibliography on contingency theory.)

Corporate Strategy

The logic for linking controls to strategy is based on the following line of thinking:

- Different organizations generally operate in different strategic contexts.
- For effective execution, different strategies require different task priorities, different key success factors, and different skills, perspectives, and behaviors.
- Control systems are measurement systems that influence the behavior of those people whose activities are being measured.
- Thus, a continuing concern in the design of control system should be whether the behavior induced by the system is consistent with the strategy.

As we noted in Chapter 2, corporate strategy is a continuum with "single industry" strategy at one end and "unrelated diversification" at the other end. A firm's location on the continuum depends on the extent and type of its diversification. Different corporate strategies imply different organization structures and, in turn, different controls. The organization structure implications of different corporate strategies are given in Exhibit 13–1.

At the single industry end, the company tends to be functionally organized, with senior managers responsible for developing the company's overall strategy to compete in its chosen industry as well as its functional strategies in such areas as research and development, manufacturing, and marketing. However, not all single industry firms are functionally organized. For instance, chains such as fast foods, hotels, supermarkets, and drug stores are "single industry" firms, but they are organized by business units—they have both production and marketing functions at many locations. In contrast, *every* unrelated diversified company (conglomerate) is organized into relatively autonomous business units. Given the large and diverse set of businesses, the senior managers in such firms tend to focus on portfolio management (i.e., selection of businesses in which to engage and allocation of financial resources to the various business units), and they delegate the development of product/market strategy to the general managers of business units. Thus, at the single industry end, senior managers are likely to have a good deal of familiarity with the industry in which the firm competes and many of them tend to have expertise in research and development, manufacturing, and marketing. In contrast, at the unrelated diversified end, primary expertise of many senior managers tends to be in finance.

As a firm moves from the single industry end to the unrelated diversified end, the autonomy of the business unit manager tends to increase for two reasons. First, unlike a single industry firm, senior managers of unrelated diversified firms may lack the knowledge and expertise to make strategic and operating decisions for a group of disparate business units. Second, there is very little interdependence across business units in a conglomerate, whereas there may be a great deal of interdependence among business units in single

EXHIBIT 13–1   **Different Corporate Strategies: Organizational Structure Implications**

	Single Industry	*Related Diversified*	*Unrelated Diversified*
Organizational structure	Functional	Business units	Holding company
Industry familiarity of corporate management	High	⟶	Low
Functional background of corporate management	Relevant operating experience (mfg, mktg, R&D)	⟶	Mainly finance
Decision-making authority	More centralized	⟶	More decentralized
Size of corporate staff	High	⟶	Low
Reliance on internal promotions	High	⟶	Low
Use of lateral transfers	High	⟶	Low
Corporate culture	Strong	⟶	Weak

industry and related diversified firms; greater interdependence calls for greater top management intervention.

Given the lower degree of involvement of corporate level managers in the operations of business units, the size of corporate staff in a conglomerate—compared with a single industry firm of the same size—tends to be low. Given the unrelated nature of its varied business units, a conglomerate—in contrast to a single industry firm—is less likely to benefit from promoting from within or in lateral transfer of executives from one business unit to another. Also, a conglomerate may not have the single, cohesive, strong corporate culture that a single industry firm often has.

Implications for Management Control

Any organization—however well-aligned its structure is to the chosen strategy—cannot effectively implement its strategy without a consistent management control system. While organization structure defines the reporting relationships and the responsibilities and authorities of different managers, its effective functioning depends on the design of an appropriate control system. In this part of the chapter, we discuss the planning and control requirements of different corporate strategies.

Different corporate strategies imply the following differences in the context in which control systems need to be designed:

- As firms become more diversified, corporate-level managers may not have significant knowledge and experience in the activities of the company's various business units. If so, corporate-level managers for highly diversified firms, cannot expect to control the different businesses based on intimate knowledge of their activities, and performance evaluation tends to be carried out at arm's length.
- Single industry and related diversified firms possess *corporatewide core competencies* (wireless technology in the case of Motorola) on which the strategies of most of the business units are based; channels of communication and transfer of competencies across business units, therefore, are critical in such firms. In contrast, in the case of unrelated diversified firms, there are low levels of interdependence among business units. This implies that, as firms become more diversified, it may be desirable to change the balance in control systems from an emphasis on fostering cooperation to an emphasis on encouraging entrepreneurial spirit.

Specific tendencies in the design of control systems corresponding to variations in corporate strategies are given in Exhibit 13–2.

Strategic Planning. Given the low level of interdependencies, conglomerates tend to use vertical strategic planning systems—that is, business units prepare strategic plans and submit them to senior management for review and approval. Given the high level of interdependencies, strategic planning systems for related diversified and single industry firms tend to be both vertical and horizontal. The horizontal dimension might be incorporated into the strategic planning process in a number of different ways. First, a group executive might be given responsibility for developing a strategic plan for the group as a whole that explicitly identifies synergies across individual business units within the group. Second, strategic plans of individual business units could have an interdependence section, in which the general manager of the business unit identifies the focal linkages with other business units and how those linkages will be exploited. Third, the corporate office could require joint strategic plans from interdependent business units. Finally, strategic plans of individual business units could be circulated to managers of similar business units for critique and review.

These ways of incorporating a horizontal dimension to strategic planning are not mutually exclusive. In fact, several of them could be fruitfully pursued simultaneously.

Example. NEC Corporation (a related diversified firm) adopted two planning systems. In addition to a normal business unit planning system, it established the

EXHIBIT 13–2   **Different Corporate Strategies: Management Control Implications**

	Single Industry	*Related Diversified*	*Unrelated Diversified*
Strategic Planning	Vertical-cum-horizontal	———————▶	Vertical only
Budgeting: Relative control of business unit manager over budget formulation	Low	———————▶	High
Importance attached to meeting the budget	Low	———————▶	High
Transfer pricing: Importance of transfer pricing	High	———————▶	Low
Sourcing flexibility	Constrained	———————▶	Arm's-length market pricing
Incentive compensation: Bonus criteria	Financial and nonfinancial criteria	———————▶	Primarily financial criteria
Bonus determination approach	Primarily subjective	———————▶	Primarily formula-based
Bonus basis	Based both on business unit and corporate performance	———————▶	Based primarily on business unit performance

CBP (corporate business plan) system, in which strategic plans were prepared for important programs that cut across business units. The system forced interdependent business unit managers to agree on a strategic plan for exploiting such linkages. In effect, the system required a special plan for important horizontal issues.[2]

Budgeting.   In a single industry firm, the chief executive officer may have intimate knowledge of the firm's operations, and corporate and business unit managers tend to have more frequent contact. Thus, chief executives of single industry firms may be able to control the operations of subordinates through

---

[2]Michael E. Porter, *Competitive Advantage* (New York: Free Press, 1985), p. 403.

informal and personally oriented mechanisms, such as frequent personal interactions. If so, this lessens the need to rely as heavily on the budgeting system as the tool of control.[3]

On the other hand, in a conglomerate, it is nearly impossible for the chief executive to rely on informal interpersonal interactions as a tool of control; much of the communication and control has to be achieved through the formal budgeting system. This implies the following budgeting system characteristics in a conglomerate:

- Business unit managers have somewhat greater influence in developing their budgets since they (not the corporate office) possess most of the information about their respective product/market environments.
- Greater emphasis is often placed on meeting the budget since the chief executive does not have other informal controls available.

Transfer Pricing.   Transfers of goods and services between business units are more frequent in single industry and related diversified firms than between business units in conglomerates.[4] In a conglomerate, the usual transfer pricing policy is to give sourcing flexibility to business units and to use arm's-length market prices. However, in a single industry or a related diversified firm, synergies may be important, and business units may not be given the freedom to make sourcing decisions. In Chapter 6 we discussed the implications of constraints on sourcing on the appropriate transfer pricing policies.

Incentive Compensation.   The incentive compensation policy tends to differ across corporate strategies in the following ways:

Use of formulas. Conglomerates, in general, tend to make more use of formulas in the determination of the business unit managers' bonus—that is, they may base a larger portion of the bonus on quantitative, financial measures such as X percent bonus on actual economic value added (EVA) in excess of budgeted EVA. Formula-based bonus plans tend to be used in conglomerates because of the inevitable lack of familiarity on the part of senior management with what goes on in a variety of disparate businesses.

Senior management of single industry and related diversified firms tend to determine a larger fraction of the business unit managers' bonus on the basis of subjective factors. Greater degrees of interrelationships in many firms of the latter group imply that the performance of a given unit can be affected by the

---

[3]Empirical support for this conclusion is reported in Kenneth A. Merchant, "The Design of Corporate Budgeting System: Influences on Managerial Behavior and Performance," *The Accounting Review*, no. 4 (1981), pp. 813–28.

[4]In an empirical study, Gupta and Govindarajan found examples of interunit transfers even in conglomerates. A. K. Gupta and V. Govindarajan, "Resource Sharing among SBUs: Strategic Antecedents and Administrative Implications," *Academy of Management Journal* 29, no. 4 (1986), pp. 695–714.

decisions and actions of other units. Therefore, for companies with highly interdependent business units, formula-based plans that are tied strictly to financial performance criteria could be counterproductive.

Profitability measures. The incentive bonus of the business unit managers tends to be determined primarily by the profitability of that unit—rather than the profitability of the firm—in the case of unrelated diversified firms. Its purpose is to motivate managers to act as though the business unit were their own company.

In contrast, single industry and related diversified firms tend to base the incentive bonus of a business unit manager both on the performance of that unit and also on the performance of a larger organizational unit (such as the product group to which the business unit belongs or perhaps even the overall corporation). When business units are interdependent, the more the incentive bonus of general managers emphasizes the separate performance of each unit, the more the possibility of interunit conflict. On the other hand, basing the bonus of general managers more on the overall corporate performance is likely to foster greater interunit cooperation, thereby increasing the managers' motivation to exploit interdependencies, instead of encouraging them to concentrate on their individual results.

> **Example.** In Textron (a conglomerate), the most important measure of performance in allocating bonus awards to business unit managers was return on investment of their respective business units. Thus, the incentive bonus system was formula-based tied to a financial criterion, and the bonus depended on the performance of the business unit.[5]

Business Unit Strategy

So far we have discussed variations in control systems across firms, taking the whole firm as our unit of observation. In this section, we consider *intrafirm* differences in control systems. Diversified corporations segment themselves into business units and typically assign different strategies to the individual business units. Many chief executive officers of multibusiness organizations do not adopt a standardized, uniform approach to controlling their business units; rather, they tailor the approach to the strategy of each business unit.

As we stated in Chapter 2, business unit strategy consists of two interrelated aspects: mission and competitive advantage. We first discuss the control implications of these two dimensions separately. Considering the two dimensions together poses some specific problems, which will be discussed in the next section.

Mission

The mission for existing business units could be either build, hold, or harvest. These missions constitute a continuum, with "pure build" at one end and "pure harvest" at the other end. For effective implementation, there should be

---

[5]Malcolm S. Salter, "Tailor Incentive Compensation to Strategy," *Harvard Business Review*, March–April 1973, pp. 94–102.

congruence between the mission chosen and the types of controls used. We develop the control-mission "fit" using the following line of reasoning:[6]

- The mission of the business unit influences the uncertainties that general managers face and the short-term versus long-term trade-offs that they make.
- Management control systems can be systematically varied to help motivate the manager to cope effectively with uncertainty and make appropriate short-term versus long-term trade-offs.
- Thus, different missions often require systematically different management control systems.

Mission and Uncertainty.   "Build" units tend to face greater environmental uncertainty than "harvest" units for several reasons:

- Build strategies typically are undertaken in the growth stage of the product life cycle, whereas harvest strategies typically are undertaken in the mature/decline stage of the product life cycle. Such factors as manufacturing process, product technology, market demand, relations with suppliers, buyers, and distribution channels, number of competitors, and competitive structure change more rapidly and are more unpredictable in the growth than in the mature/decline stage of the product life cycle.
- An objective of a build business unit is to increase market share. Since the total market share of all firms in an industry is 100 percent, the battle for market share is a zero-sum game; thus, a build strategy pits a business unit into greater conflict with its competitors than does a harvest strategy. Competitors' actions are likely to be unpredictable, and this contributes to the uncertainty faced by build business units.
- Both on the input side and on the output side, build managers tend to experience greater dependencies on external individuals and organizations than do harvest managers. For instance, a build mission signifies additional capital investment (greater dependence on capital markets), expansion of capacity (greater dependence on the technological environment), increase in market share (greater dependence on customers and competitors), increase in production volume (greater dependence on raw material suppliers and labor markets), and so on. The greater the external dependencies that the business unit faces, the greater the uncertainty it confronts.
- Since build business units are often in new and evolving industries, the experience of build managers in their industries is likely to be less. This also

---

[6]This section draws from an extensive body of research that has focused on strategy implementation issues at the business unit level. Some of the key references are: Govindarajan (1988, 1989); Govindarajan and Fisher (1989, 1990, 1991); Govindarajan and Gupta (1985); Gupta and Govindarajan (1984); Shank and Govindarajan (1993).

contributes to the greater uncertainty faced by managers of build units in dealing with external constituencies.

Mission and Time Span.   The choice of build versus harvest strategies has implications for short-term versus long-term profit trade-offs. The share-building strategy includes (*a*) price cutting, (*b*) major R&D expenditures (to introduce new products), and (*c*) major market development expenditures. These actions are aimed at establishing market leadership, but they depress short-term profits. Thus, many decisions that the manager of a build unit makes today may not result in profits until some future period. A harvest strategy, on the other hand, demands attention to tasks with a view to maximize short-term profits.

We now discuss how the form and structure of control systems might differ across business units with different missions.

Strategic Planning.   While designing a strategic planning process, several design issues need to be considered. There are not single answers on these design choices; rather, the answers tend to depend upon the mission being pursued by the business unit (Exhibit 13–3).

When the environment is uncertain, the strategic planning process is especially important. Management needs to give much thought to how to cope with the uncertainties, and this usually requires a longer-range view of planning than is possible in the annual budget. If the environment is stable, there may be no strategic planning process at all, or only a broad-brush strategic plan. Thus, the strategic planning process is more critical and more important for build, as compared with harvest, business units. Nevertheless, some strategic planning for the harvest business units may be necessary because the company's overall strategic plan must encompass all of its businesses to effectively balance cash flows.

In screening capital investments and allocating resources, the system may be more quantitative and financial for harvest units. A harvest business unit operates in a mature industry and does not offer tremendous new investment possibilities. Hence, the required earnings rate for such a business unit may be relatively high to motivate the manager to search for projects with truly exceptional returns. Since harvest units tend to experience stable environments (with predictable products, technologies, competitors, and customers), discounted cash flow (DCF) analysis often can be used with more confidence. The required information used to evaluate investments from harvest units is primarily financial. A build unit, however, is positioned on the growth stage of the product life cycle. The corporate office wants to take advantage of the opportunities in a growing market, and senior management, therefore, may set a relatively low discount rate, thereby motivating build managers to forward more investment ideas to corporate office. Given the product/market uncertainties, financial analysis of some projects from build units may be unreliable. For such projects, nonfinancial data are more important.

EXHIBIT 13–3   Different Strategic Missions: Implications for Strategic Planning Process

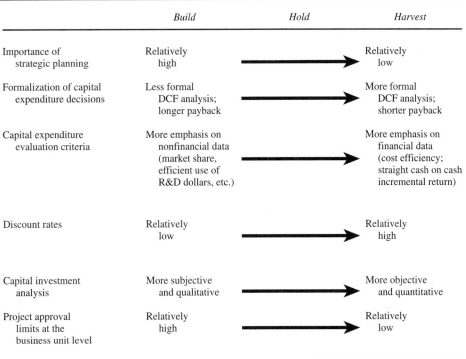

	Build	*Hold*	*Harvest*
Importance of strategic planning	Relatively high	→	Relatively low
Formalization of capital expenditure decisions	Less formal DCF analysis; longer payback	→	More formal DCF analysis; shorter payback
Capital expenditure evaluation criteria	More emphasis on nonfinancial data (market share, efficient use of R&D dollars, etc.)	→	More emphasis on financial data (cost efficiency; straight cash on cash incremental return)
Discount rates	Relatively low	→	Relatively high
Capital investment analysis	More subjective and qualitative	→	More objective and quantitative
Project approval limits at the business unit level	Relatively high	→	Relatively low

Budgeting.   Implications for designing budgeting systems to support varied missions are contained in Exhibit 13–4. The calculational aspects of variance analysis comparing actual results with the budget identify variances as either favorable or unfavorable. However, a favorable variance does not necessarily imply favorable performance; similarly, an unfavorable variance does not necessarily imply unfavorable performance. The link between a favorable or unfavorable variance, on the one hand, and favorable or unfavorable performance, on the other hand, depends upon the strategic context of the business unit under evaluation.

> **Example.** An industrial measuring instruments manufacturer disaggregated the overall profit variance by key causal factors for its two business units: Electric Meters (a "harvest" business) and Electronic Instruments (a "build" business). Senior management interpreted market share, selling price, and manufacturing cost variances very differently while evaluating the performance of managers in charge of the harvest and build businesses.[7]

---

[7]John K. Shank and Vijay Govindarajan, *Strategic Cost Analysis* (Homewood, Ill.: Richard D. Irwin, 1989), pp. 95–113.

Exhibit 13–4   Different Strategic Missions: Implications for Budgeting

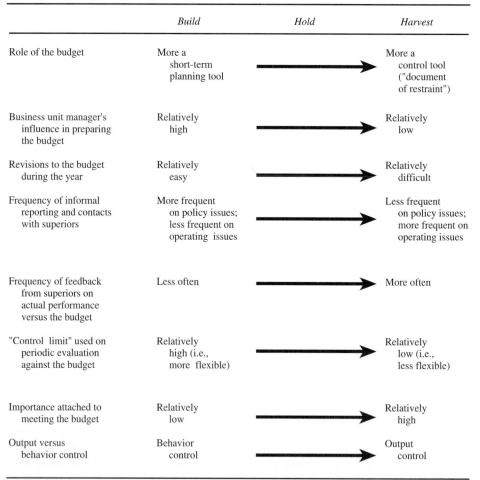

	Build	Hold	Harvest
Role of the budget	More a short-term planning tool	→	More a control tool ("document of restraint")
Business unit manager's influence in preparing the budget	Relatively high	→	Relatively low
Revisions to the budget during the year	Relatively easy	→	Relatively difficult
Frequency of informal reporting and contacts with superiors	More frequent on policy issues; less frequent on operating issues	→	Less frequent on policy issues; more frequent on operating issues
Frequency of feedback from superiors on actual performance versus the budget	Less often	→	More often
"Control limit" used on periodic evaluation against the budget	Relatively high (i.e., more flexible)	→	Relatively low (i.e., less flexible)
Importance attached to meeting the budget	Relatively low	→	Relatively high
Output versus behavior control	Behavior control	→	Output control

---

A related issue is how much importance should be attached to meeting the budget while evaluating the business unit manager's performance. We pointed out in Chapter 10 that the greater the uncertainty, the more difficult it is for superiors to regard subordinates' budget targets as firm commitments and to consider unfavorable budget variances as clear indicators of poor performance. For this reason, less reliance usually is placed on budgets in build units than in harvest units.

Example. The SCM Corporation adopted a two-dimensional yardstick to evaluate business units: bottom-line performance against budget was one dimension, and performance against specific objectives was another. The ratios of the two were made to vary according to the mission of the business unit. For instance, "pure harvest" units were evaluated 100 percent on budget performance; "pure hold," 50 percent on budget and 50 percent on completion of objectives; "pure build," 100 percent on completion of objectives.[8]

The following additional differences in the budget process are likely to exist between build and harvest units:

- In contrast to harvest units, budget revisions are likely to be more frequent for build units because of the more frequent changes in their product/market environment.
- Build unit managers may have relatively greater input and influence in the formulation of the budget than harvest unit managers. This is so because "build" managers operate in rapidly changing environments and have better knowledge of these changes than does senior management. For harvest units with stable environments, the knowledge of the manager is less important.

Incentive Compensation System.   In designing an incentive compensation package for business unit managers, the following are some of the questions that need to be resolved:

1. What should be the size of incentive bonus payments relative to the general manager's base salary? Should the incentive bonus payments have upper limits?
2. What measures of performance (e.g., profit, EVA, sales volume, market share, product development) should be employed as the basis for deciding the general manager's incentive bonus awards? If multiple performance measures are employed, how should they be weighted?
3. How much reliance should be placed on subjective judgments in deciding on the bonus amount?
4. With what frequency (semiannual, annual, biennial, and so on) should incentive awards be made?

Decisions on these design variables are influenced by the mission of the business unit (Exhibit 13–5). As for the first question, many firms use the principle that the riskier the strategy, the greater the proportion of the general manager's compensation in bonus compared to salary (the "risk/return" principle). They maintain that, since managers in charge of more uncertain task situations should be willing to take greater risks, they should have a higher percentage of their remuneration in the form of an incentive bonus. Thus, reliance on bonus is likely to be higher for "build" managers than for "harvest" managers.

---

[8]George E. Hall, "Reflections on Running a Diversified Company," *Harvard Business Review*, January–February 1987, pp. 88–89.

EXHIBIT 13–5   **Different Strategic Missions: Implications for Incentive Compensation**

	Build	*Hold*	*Harvest*
Percent compensation as bonus	Relatively high	⟶	Relatively low
Bonus criteria	More emphasis on nonfinancial criteria	⟶	More emphasis on financial criteria
Bonus determination approach	More subjective	⟶	More formula-based
Frequency of bonus payment	Less frequent	⟶	More frequent

As for the second question, when an individual's rewards are tied to performance according to certain criteria, his or her behaviors are influenced by the desire to optimize performance with respect to those criteria. Some performance criteria (cost control, operating profits, and cash flow from operations) focus more on the short-term performance, whereas other performance criteria (market share, new product development, market development, and people development) focus on long-term profitability. Thus, linking incentive bonus to the former set of criteria tends to promote a short-term focus on the part of the general manager, whereas linking incentive bonus to the latter set of performance criteria is likely to promote a long-term focus. Given the relative differences in time horizons of build and harvest managers, it may be inappropriate to use a single, uniform financial criterion (such as operating profits) to evaluate the performance of every business unit; rather, it may be desirable to use multiple performance criteria, with differential weights for each criterion depending on the mission of the business unit.

Examples. Analog Devices, General Electric Company, and Westinghouse Electric Corporation tailor compensation packages to the different missions of their individual businesses.

Analog Devices designed a bonus system for its business units (SBUs) based on each SBU's potential for growth and profit. For instance, a business unit in the test-instrument market faced considerably different conditions and competition than a business unit in the microprocessor market. While some SBUs might have little growth potential, they might have the ability to deliver high Return on Assets (ROA); other SBUs would be able to generate very high growth but deliver lower ROA. For SBUs pursuing a "harvest" strategy, greater weight was placed on ROA and lower weight on sales growth in determining the SBU manager's bonus. On the other hand, for "build" SBUs, greater weight was placed on sales growth and lower weight on ROA in determining the SBU manager's bonus.[9]

Both GE and Westinghouse have mature as well as young businesses. In the mature businesses, short-term incentives might dominate the compensation packages of managers who were charged with maximizing cash flow, achieving high profit margins, and retaining market share. In the younger businesses, where developing products and establishing marketing strategies are most important, nonfinancial measures geared to the execution of long-term performance might dictate the major portion of managers' remuneration.[10]

As for the third question, in addition to varying the importance of different criteria, superiors must also decide on the approach to take in determining a specific bonus amount. At one extreme, a manager's bonus might be a strict formula-based plan, with the bonus tied to performance on quantifiable criteria (e.g., x percent bonus on actual profits in excess of budgeted profits); at the other extreme, a manager's incentive bonus amounts might be based solely on the superior's subjective judgment or discretion. Alternatively, incentive bonus amounts might also be based on a combination of formula-based and subjective (non-formula) approaches. Performance on most long-term criteria (market development, new product development, and people development) is clearly less amenable to objective measurement than is performance along most short-run criteria (operating profits, cash flow from operations, and return on investment). Since, as already noted, build managers—in contrast with harvest managers—should focus more on the long-run rather than the short run, build managers are typically evaluated more subjectively than harvest managers.

Finally, frequency of bonus awards influence the time horizon of managers. More frequent bonus awards encourage concentration on short-term performance since they have the effect of motivating managers to focus on those facets of the business that they can affect in the short run. Less frequent calculation and payment of bonus encourages the manager to take a long-term perspective. Thus, build managers tend to receive bonus awards less frequently than harvest managers.

> **Example.** Premark International (formed in 1986 in a spin-off from Dart & Kraft, Inc.) used a similar logic in designing the incentive bonus for the general manager of its Tupperware Division, whose mission was to build market share: "[If you award the bonus annually,] Tupperware could reduce advertising and promotional activities and you can look good in profits that year. Then, the franchise starts to go to hell. If you're shooting for an award after three years, there's less tendency to do things short term."[11]

---

[9]Ray Stata and Modesto A. Maidique, "Bonus System for Balanced Strategy," *Harvard Business Review*, November–December 1980, pp. 156–163.

[10]"Executive Compensation: Looking to the Long Term Again," *Business Week*, May 9, 1983, p. 81.

[11]I. Reibstein, "Firms trim annual pay increase and focus on long term: More employers link incentives to unit results," *The Wall Street Journal*, April 10, 1987, p. 25.

Competitive Advantage

A business unit can choose to compete either as a differentiated player or as a low-cost player. The choice of a differentiation approach, rather than a low-cost approach, increases uncertainty in a business unit's task environment for three reasons.

First, product innovation is more critical for differentiation business units than for low-cost business units. This is partly because a low-cost business unit, with its primary emphasis on cost reduction, typically prefers to keep its product offerings stable over time; a differentiation business unit, with its primary focus on uniqueness and exclusivity, is likely to engage in greater product innovation. A business unit with greater emphasis on new product activities tends to face greater uncertainty, since the business unit is betting on unproven products.

Second, low-cost business units typically tend to have narrow product lines to minimize inventory carry costs as well as to benefit from scale economies. Differentiation business units, on the other hand, tend to have a broader set of products to create uniqueness. Product breadth creates high environmental complexity, and consequently, higher uncertainty.

Third, low-cost business units typically produce no-frill commodity products, and these products succeed primarily because they have lower prices than competing products. However, products of differentiation business units succeed if customers perceive that the products have advantages over competing products. Since customer perception is difficult to learn about, and since customer loyalty is subject to change resulting from actions of competitors or other reasons, the demand for differentiated products is typically more difficult to predict than the demand for commodities.

The specifics of the control systems for low-cost and differentiation business units are similar to the ones described earlier for harvest and build business units. This is so because the uncertainty facing low-cost and differentiation business units is similar to the uncertainty facing harvest and build business units.

> **Examples.** Digital Equipment Corporation (DEC) followed a differentiation strategy, whereas Data General followed a low-cost strategy. The control systems in these companies differed accordingly. DEC's product managers were primarily evaluated on the basis of the quality of their interaction with their customers (a subjective measure), whereas Data General's product managers were evaluated on the basis of results, or profits. DEC's sales representatives were on straight salary, but Data General's salesforce received 50 percent of their pay on a commission basis. Salaried compensation indicates behavior control and commission compensation, outcome control.[12]
>
> A broad-based chemicals manufacturer used differentiated management control, focusing on the differing key success factors for its yellow dye unit (which followed a

[12]B. Uttal, "The Gentlemen and the Upstarts Meet in a Great Mini-Battle," *Fortune*, April 23, 1979, pp. 98–108.

cost leadership strategy) and its red dye unit (which followed a differentiation strategy). The manager in charge of yellow dye was tightly held against *theoretical* standard costs rather than currently achievable standard costs. The results of these tight financial controls were remarkable: within a period of two years, actual cost for yellow dye decreased from $5.72 per lb. to $3.84 per lb.—giving the yellow dye unit a major cost advantage. The key strategic issue for red dye was product differentiation, not cost leadership. The management control reports for the red dye unit, therefore, focused on product leadership variables (e.g., milestone reporting on the development project for hot spray dyeing) rather than cost control variables.[13]

Senior managers at one large, high-tech manufacturer took direct responsibility for adding customer satisfaction, quality, market share, and human resources to their formal measurement system. The impetus was their realization that the company's existing system, which was largely financial, undercut its strategy, which focused on differentiation through customer service.[14]

Additional Considerations

Although differentiating controls *within* the same firm has a sound logic, control systems designers need to be cognizant of several problems involved in doing so.

First, a business unit's external environment inevitably changes over time, and a change might imply the need for a shift in strategy. This raises an interesting issue. Success at any task requires commitment. The strategy-control "fit" is expected to foster such a commitment to the current strategy. However, if the control system is too closely related to the current strategy, it could result in overcommitment, thereby inhibiting the manager from shifting to a new strategy when he/she should. There are many examples of declining industries that have transformed into growth industries (examples: the major growth of Arm & Hammer baking soda, which was once in the decline stage of the product life cycle; the 1980s surge in demand for the fountain pen, which was once considered an obsolete product). The following examples in the radio, musical instrument, and motorcycle industries illustrate the problems of overcommitment when there is a close fit between strategy and controls.

> **Examples.** Financially oriented U.S. manufacturers once treated the radio as essentially a dot on the product portfolio matrix. Convinced that every product has a life cycle, they viewed the radio as having passed its peak and was a prime candidate for "milking." Starved for investment funds and resources and being subject to tight financial controls, the radio died in a self-fulfilling prophecy. On the other hand, Japanese radio manufacturers, such as Matsushita (Panasonic) and Sony—ignoring or unaware of product life cycle and portfolio theories—obstinately believed in their product's value. The division heads of these firms had no option but to

---

[13]Shank and Govindarajan, *Strategic Cost Analysis*, Homewood, IL: Richard D. Irwin, 1991, pp. 114–30.

[14]Robert G. Eccles, "The Performance Measurement Manifesto," *Harvard Business Review*, January–February 1991, pp. 131–37.

Exhibit 13–6

Fits and misfits in control system design

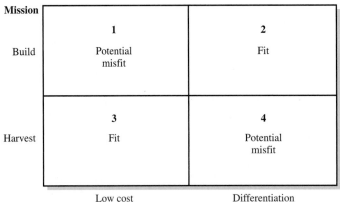

	Mission	
Build	**1** Potential misfit	**2** Fit
Harvest	**3** Fit	**4** Potential misfit
	Low cost	Differentiation

Competitive advantage

extend the life of the product, since to do otherwise would mean dissolving their divisions, which was an untenable option. So they pressed their engineers, component manufacturers, and marketing people for new ideas. . . . Today the portable radio-cassette and Sony Walkman stories are part of business folklore.[15]

Yamaha in the musical instrument market in the United States and Honda, Kawasaki, Suzuki, and Yamaha in the motorcycle market in the United States and in Europe have successfully destroyed the dominance of incumbent manufacturers who concentrated on "milking" their products for profit in a stagnant market.[16]

Thus, there is an ongoing dilemma: how to design control systems that can *simultaneously* maintain a high degree of commitment as well as a healthy skepticism for current strategies.

Second, we have discussed mission and competitive advantage as separate characteristics. However, business units have both a mission and a competitive advantage, which, in some combinations, may result in a conflict regarding the type of controls to be used. As Exhibit 13–6 demonstrates, the ordinal classification of mission and competitive advantage yields four distinct combinations. There is an unconflicting design in cells 2 and 3. Both of these cells have a similar level of uncertainty, and this suggests a similar control system design. Cells 1 and 4, however, have conflicting demands, and designing a control system that fits both is difficult. Several possibilities exist. It might be possible to so change the mission or the competitive advantage that they do not conflict from the standpoint of systems design (i.e., move the business unit to cell 2 or cell 3). If this is not feasible, it might be that either mission or competitive advantage is more critical for implementation and, therefore, would dominate

---

[15]K. Ohmae, "The Long and Short of Japanese Planning," *The Wall Street Journal*, January 18, 1982, p. 28.

[16]B. G. James, "Strategic Planning under Fire," *Sloan Management Review*, Summer 1984, pp. 57–61.

the choice of the appropriate type of control. If mission and competitive advantage are equally important, control system design becomes especially difficult. Here, control systems cannot be designed for the mission or competitive advantage in isolation without incurring costs.

Third, explicitly differentiated controls across business units might create administrative awkwardness and potential dysfunctional effects, especially for managers in charge of harvest units. Many harvest managers believe that their career prospects within the company are somewhat limited. While corporate managers in most diversified firms may find it rational to harvest one or more of their businesses, every company wants to grow at the overall firm level. Thus, as one goes higher in the corporate hierarchy, skills at successfully executing a build strategy become more important than those of successfully executing a harvest strategy. From a career perspective, this likelihood tends to favor managers currently in charge of build businesses.

> **Example.** The following speculation regarding who might succeed Walter Wriston as the next CEO of Citicorp appeared in *The Wall Street Journal* nearly three years *before* the actual announcement of his successor: "Ironically, Mr. Theobald may not get to the top precisely because he runs a division that has always been a big money-maker for Citicorp, its institutional division. Unlike his two competitors, who are charting new courses for Citicorp, Mr. Theobald is simply carrying forward a tradition of profiting handsomely from making loans to corporations and governments, domestically and abroad."[17] Subsequent events confirmed these speculations.

Given these possibilities, harvest managers may perceive their roles as being less important. Explicitly designing tight controls over harvest strategies compounds this problem.

System designers might consider two possibilities to mitigate this problem. First, as part of the planning process, they might consider not using such harshly graphic and negative terms as *cash cow, dog, question mark,* and *star* but, instead, use such terms as *build, hold,* and *harvest.* The former are "static" terms that do not, in any case, indicate missions as well as "dynamic" action-oriented terms, such as *build, hold,* and *harvest* do. Second, to the extent possible, a harvest manager should be given one or more products with high growth potential. This would prevent the possibility of a manager getting typecast solely as a harvester. Corning Glass Works followed this policy of assigning a growth-oriented product to a manager in charge of a harvest business.[18]

Finally, strategy is only one variable, albeit an important one, in influencing the choice of controls. Top management style also has a profound impact on the design and operation of control systems—a topic we turn to next.

---

[17]J. Salamon, "Challenges Lie Ahead for Dynamic Citicorp after the Wriston Era," *The Wall Street Journal,* December 18, 1981, p. 1.

[18]Richard F. Vancil, "Corning Glass Works: Tom MacAvoy," in R. F. Vancil, *Implementing Strategy* (Boston: Division of Research, Harvard Business School, 1982), pp. 21–36.

Top Management Style

The management control function in an organization is influenced by the style of senior management. The style of the chief executive officer affects the management control process in the entire organization. Jack Welch at General Electric, Harold Geneen at ITT, and Percy Barnevik at ABB are well-publicized examples. Similarly, the style of the business unit manager affects the management control process within the unit, and the style of functional department managers affects the management control process within their functional areas. If feasible, designers should consider management style in designing and operating control systems. (If chief executive officers actively participate in system design, as should be the case, the system will reflect their preferences.)

Differences in Management Styles

Managers differ in their styles. Some managers rely heavily on reports and certain formal documents; others prefer conversations and informal contacts. Some think in concrete terms; others think abstractly. Some are analytical; others use heuristics. Some are risk-takers; others are risk-averse. Some are process-oriented; others are results-oriented. Some are people-oriented; others are task-oriented. Some are friendly; others are aloof. Some are long-term-oriented; others are short-term-oriented. Some are "Theory X" (they dominate decision making); others are "Theory Y" (they encourage organization participation in decision making). Some place great emphasis on monetary rewards; others place emphasis on a broader set of rewards.

Management style is influenced by the manager's (1) background, and (2) personality. Background includes things like the manager's age, formal education, and the manager's experience in a given function such as manufacturing, technology, marketing, or finance. Personality characteristics include such variables as the manager's willingness to take risks and his/her tolerance for ambiguity.

Implications for Management Control

The various dimensions of management style significantly influence the operation of the control systems. Even if the same set of reports with the same set of data goes with the same frequency to the CEO, two CEOs would use these reports very differently to manage the business units if their styles are different. The dramatic shift in the control process within General Electric when Jack Welch succeeded Reginald Jones as the CEO, as described in Chapter 3, vividly illustrates this point.

Style affects the management control process—how the CEO prefers to use the information, how the CEO conducts performance review meetings, and so on—which, in turn, affects the actual operation of the control system, even if the formal structure does not change under a new CEO. In fact, when CEOs change, subordinates typically infer what the new CEO really wants based on how the new CEO interacts during the management control process (e.g., how much attention he or she actually gives to performance reports, rather than from speeches or directives.)

Personal versus Impersonal Controls.   Presence of personal versus impersonal controls in organizations is an aspect of managerial style. Managers differ on the relative importance that they attach to formal budgets and reports, contrasted with informal conversations and other personal contacts. Some managers are "numbers-oriented"; they want a large flow of quantitative information, and they spend much time analyzing this information and deriving tentative conclusions from it. Other managers are "people-oriented"; they look at a few numbers, but they usually arrive at their conclusions by talking with people, and they judge the relevance and importance of what they learn partly on their appraisal of the other person. They spend much time visiting various locations and talking with both management people and hourly employees to obtain a feel for how well things are going.

Management's attitude toward formal reports affects the amount of detail they desire, the frequency of these reports, and even such matters as their preference for graphs, rather than tables of numbers, or for supplementing numerical reports with written comments. Designers of management control systems need to identify these preferences and accommodate them.

Tight versus Loose Controls.   As pointed out in Chapter 10 a manager's style affects the *degree* of tight versus loose control in any situation. The manager of a routine production responsibility center can be controlled either relatively tightly or relatively loosely, and the actual control reflects the style of the manager's superior. Thus, the degree of tightness or looseness often is not revealed by the content of the forms or aspects of the formal control documents, rules, or procedures. It depends on how these formal devices are used.

The degree of looseness tends to increase at successively higher levels in the organization hierarchy: higher-level managers typically tend to pay less attention to details and more to overall results (the bottom line, rather than on the details of how the results are obtained) than lower-level managers. However, this generalization might not apply if a given CEO has a different style.

> **Examples.** The classic illustration of this point is ITT under Harold Geneen. One could argue that ITT, being a conglomerate, should be managed based on monitoring the business unit bottom line and not through a detailed evaluation of every aspect of the business unit operations. This is so since, in a conglomerate, the CEO typically has "capacity limitations" in understanding the nuts and bolts of the operations of various business units. In such a context, it was Harold Geneen's personal style that explains the detailed evaluations he made of business unit managers.[19]
>
> When Rand Araskog succeeded Harold Geneen at ITT, he altered the detailed and tight control system since, among other things, Araskog's personal style was not oriented toward exercising tight controls.[20]

The style of the CEO has a profound impact on management control. If a new senior manager with a different style takes over, the system tends to

---

[19]"The Case for Managing by the Numbers," *Fortune*, October 1, 1984, pp. 78–81.
[20]"ITT: Groping for a New Strategy," *Business Week*, December 15, 1980, pp. 66–80.

change correspondingly. It might happen that the manager's style is not a good fit with the management control requirements of the organization. If the manager recognizes this incongruity and adapts his or her style accordingly, the problem disappears. If, however, the manager is unwilling or unable to change his/her style, the organization will experience performance problems. The solution in this case might be to change the manager.

Summary

Designers of management control systems should take explicit notice of the strategic context in which the controls are being applied. The strategies that a firm selects can be arrayed along a continuum, with single industry firms at one extreme and unrelated diversified firms (conglomerates) at the other. The management control process differs according to the firm's strategy in this dimension.

Business units have missions that can be classified as "build," "hold," or "harvest," and their managers can also decide to build competitive advantage based on low cost or differentiation. The appropriate management control process is influenced by which of these strategies is selected for a given business unit.

The discussion in this chapter on linking controls to strategies should not be used in a mechanistic manner; the suggestions made here are tendencies, not universal truths. In fact, control systems should be designed in the context of each organization's *unique* external environment, technology, strategy, organization structure, culture, and top management style.

Suggested Additional Readings

Fisher, Joseph, and Vijay Govindarajan. "Incentive Compensation Design, Strategic Business Unit Mission, and Competitive Strategy." *Journal of Management Accounting Research,* 5, Fall 1993, pp. 129–44.

Galbraith, Jay. *Designing Organizations*. San Francisco: Jossey-Bass Publishers, 1995.

Govindarajan, Vijay. "A Contingency Approach to Strategy Implementation at the Business Unit Level: Integrating Administrative Mechanisms with Strategy." *Academy of Management Journal*, 31, no. 4 (1988), pp. 828–53.

———. "Implementing Competitive Strategies at the Business Unit Level: Implications of Matching Managers with Strategies." *Strategic Management Journal*, 10 (1989), pp. 251–69.

Govindarajan, Vijay, and Joseph Fisher. "Impact of Output versus Behavior Controls and Resource Sharing on Performance: Strategy as a Mediating Variable." *Academy of Management Journal*, June 1990, pp. 259–85.

————. "Incentive Compensation, Strategic Business Unit Mission, and Competitive Strategy." Working paper. The Amos Tuck School of Business Administration, Dartmouth College, 1991.

Govindarajan, Vijay, and Anil K. Gupta. "Linking Control Systems to Business Unit Strategy: Impact on Performance." *Accounting, Organizations, and Society*, 1985, pp. 51–66.

Govindarajan, Vijay, and John K. Shank. "Strategic Cost Management: Tailoring Controls to Strategies." *Journal of Cost Management*, 6, 3, Fall 1992, pp. 14–25.

Gupta, Anil K., and Vijay Govindarajan. "Build, Hold, Harvest: Converting Strategic Intentions into Reality." *Journal of Business Strategy*, 4, no. 3 (1984), pp. 34–47.

Hope, Tony, and Jeremy Hope. *Transforming The Bottom Line: Managing Performance With Real Numbers*. Boston, Mass.: Harvard Business School Press, 1996.

Ross, Gerald H. "Revolution in Management Control." *Management Accounting*, November 1990, pp. 23–27.

Shank, John K., and Vijay Govindarajan. *Strategic Cost Management*. New York: The Free Press, 1993.

CASE 13–1
UNITED INSTRUMENTS, INC.

Steve Park, president and principal stockholder of United Instruments, Inc., sat at his desk reflecting on the 1987 results (Exhibit 1). For the second year in succession, the company had exceeded profit budget. Steve Park was obviously very happy with the 1987 results. All the same, he wanted to get a better feel for the relative contributions of the R&D, manufacturing, and marketing departments in this overall success. With this in mind, he called his assistant, a recent graduate of a well-known business school, into his office.

"Amy," he began, "as you can see from our recent financial results, we have exceeded our profit targets by $622,000. Can you prepare an analysis showing how much R&D, manufacturing, and marketing contributed to this overall favorable profit variance?"

Amy Shultz, with all the fervor of a recent convert to professional management, set to her task immediately. She collected the data (Exhibit 2) and was wondering what her next step should be.

United Instrument's products can be grouped into two main lines of business: electric meters (EM) and electronic instruments (EI). Both EM and EI are industrial measuring instruments and perform similar functions. However, these products differ in their manufacturing technology and their end-use characteristics. EM is based on mechanical and electrical technology, whereas EI is based on microchip technology.

EM and EI are substitute products in the same sense that a mechanical watch and a digital watch are substitutes.

United Instruments uses a variable costing system for internal reporting purposes.

Questions

1. Prepare the report that you feel Amy Shultz should present to Mr. Park.

2. Put yourself in the position of the following six managers: general manager (EM); marketing manager (EM); manufacturing manager (EM); general manager (EI); marketing manager (EI); manufacturing manager (EI). These six managers compete for a share in the company's bonus pool. For each of the six, how would you make a case for your obtaining a share of the bonus pool?

3. As Mr. Park, how would you feel about the 1987 performance of each of the six managers who are competing for a share of the bonus pool? (*Note*: Consider the strategy of EM and EI business units in your performance assessment.)

This case was prepared by Vijay Govindarajan and John K. Shank, The Amos Tuck School of Business Administration, Dartmouth College. Copyright by Osceola Institute.

Exhibit 1   Income Statement for the Year 1987

		Budget (000s)		Actual (000s)
Sales		$16,872		$17,061
Cost of goods sold		9,668		9,865
Gross margin		$ 7,204		$ 7,196
Less: Other operating expenses:				
Marketing	$1,856		$1,440	
R&D	1,480		932	
Administration	1,340	4,676	1,674	4,046
Profit before taxes		$ 2,528		$ 3,150

Exhibit 2   Additional Information

	Electric Meters (EM)	Electronic Instruments (EI)
Selling prices per unit:		
Average standard price	$40.00	$180.00
Average actual prices, 1987	30.00	206.00
Variable product costs per unit:		
Average standard manufacturing cost	20.00	50.00
Average actual manufacturing cost	21.00	54.00
Volume information:		
Units produced and sold—actual	141,770	62,172
Units produced and sold—planned	124,800	66,000
Total industry sales, 1987—actual	$44 million	$76 million
Total industry variable product costs, 1987—actual	$16 million	$32 million
United's share of the market (percent of physical units):		
Planned	10%	15%
Actual	16%	9%

	Planned	Actual
Firm-wide fixed expenses (000s):		
Fixed manufacturing expenses	$3,872	$3,530
Fixed marketing expenses	1,856	1,440
Fixed administrative expenses	1,340	1,674
Fixed R&D expenses (exclusively for electronic instruments)	1,480	932

CASE 13–2
NUCOR CORPORATION

We are a cyclical business . . . Basically when you are at the peak of the cycle—times are good, interest rates are low, people are building—our margins increase. When we go to the trough, of course, the margins are squeezed. But over the last 25 years Nucor has never had a losing quarter. Not only a losing quarter, we have never had a losing month or a losing week . . . [1]

In 1996 Nucor Corporation had sales of $3.6 billion in steel and steel-related products. Nucor is a *Fortune 500* company with 6,800 employees. The company's chairman is F. Kenneth Iverson who has headed the company for over 30 years. During his tenure, the steel industry faced a number of problems such as substitution from other materials, foreign competition, strained labor relations, and slowing of steel demand. Despite these industry problems, Nucor's sales during the past 30 years grew at an annual compound rate of about 17 percent p.a. Summary financial data on Nucor is shown in Exhibit 1 and selected comparative data are shown in Exhibit 2.

History

Nucor traces its origins to auto manufacturer Ransom E. Olds, who founded Oldsmobile and then Reo Motor Cars. Through a series of transactions, the company Olds founded eventually became the Nuclear Corporation of America, a company involved in the nuclear instrument and electronics business in the 1950s and early 1960s.

Nucor suffered through several money-losing years, and when facing bankruptcy in 1965, installed Ken Iverson, a 40-year-old metallurgical engineer, as President. This change in management led to a restructuring and a decision to

rebuild Nucor around its major profitable operations, making steel joists in Florence, South Carolina, and Norfolk, Nebraska.

The company moved its headquarters from Phoenix, Arizona, to Charlotte, North Carolina, in 1966, and in 1972 adopted the Nucor name. Management then directed its energies toward two basic businesses: the steel joist business, operated as Vulcraft; and the steel business, operated as Nucor Steel. Today Vulcraft is the nation's largest producer of steel joists and steel girders, standard building components in non-residential construction. Nucor Steel has become well-recognized for its modern steel making techniques that enable it to compete effectively in worldwide markets.

Operations

Nucor has deliberately committed to locating its diverse facilities in rural locations across America. As a result, Nucor has been able to establish strong ties to its local communities and its work force. The ability to become a leading employer and pay a leading wage has been key to attracting hard-working, dedicated employees. This ability has also enabled Nucor to choose among states more committed to maintaining a climate conducive to business growth through reasonable tax structures, and hospitable to Nucor's commitment to remain union-free. In 1996 Nucor and its subsidiaries consisted of 10 businesses, with 25 mills serving specific target markets.

Nucor Steel

Products: Steel sheet, bars, angles, light
   structural carbon and alloy steels.
Plants: Darlington, SC; Norfolk, NE; Jewett,
   TX; Plymouth, UT; Crawfordsville, IN;
   Hickman, AR; Mt. Pleasant, SC.

This case was prepared by Vijay Govindarajan from materials furnished by F. Kenneth Iverson, Chairman, Nucor Corporation. Copyright © Osceola Institute.

[1]Richard Franklin, "An Interview with John D. Correnti, President and CEO, Nucor Corporation," *The Wall Street Corporate Reporter*, September 9–15, 1996, pp. 19–20.

EXHIBIT 1   Nucor Corporation Financial Data 1985–1995

	1985	1986	1987	1988	1989	1990	1991	1992	1993	1994	1995
Net Sales ($ in millions)	$758	$755	$851	$1,061	$1,269	$1,482	$1,466	$1,619	$2,254	$2,976	$3,462
Net Profit ($ in millions)	59	46	51	109	58	75	65	79	124	227	275
Net Earnings Per Share	$0.68	$0.54	$0.60	$1.29	$0.68	$0.88	$0.75	$0.92	$1.42	$2.60	$3.14
Dividends Declared Per Share	$.07	$.08	$.09	$.10	$.11	$.12	$.13	$.14	$.16	$.18	$.28
Profit Margin %	7.7%	6.1%	5.9%	6.7%	4.6%	5.1%	4.4%	4.9%	5.5%	7.6%	7.9%
Return on Stockholder's Equity	18%	13%	13%	16%	11%	12%	10%	11%	15%	23%	22%
Sales Per Employee	$197,011	$181,983	$189,116	$218,838	$241,716	$271,859	$264,046	$283,455	$384,105	$502,507	$570,353
Current Ratio	2.8	2.5	1.6	1.1	1.4	1.5	1.5	1.4	1.3	1.7	1.9
Stockholders' Equity Per Share	4.16	4.54	5.05	6.25	6.83	7.59	8.23	9.04	10.36	12.85	15.78
Shares Outstanding	85,890,032	84,525,192	84,784,352	85,150,764	85,598,480	85,950,696	86,417,804	86,736,700	87,073,478	87,333,313	87,598,517
Stockholders	22,000	22,000	27,000	28,000	25,000	27,000	27,000	29,000	33,000	38,000	39,000
Employees	3,900	4,400	4,600	5,100	5,400	5,500	5,600	5,800	5,900	5,900	6,200

Source: 1995 Annual Report

EXHIBT 2   **Selected Financial Data**
1992–1996

	Sales 1996 ($ in billions)	Return on Equity (5-year average) 1992–1996	Debt/Capital % 1996	5-year Sales Growth % 1992–96
Nucor	$3.6	17%	7%	21%
Texas Industries* (parent of Chaparral Steel)	$1.0	10%	22%	9%
National Steel**	$2.9	5%	44%	4%
USX-US Steel**	$6.4	6%	38%	3%
Bethlehem Steel**	$4.7	Deficit	29%	NM
LTV**	$4.1	NA	9%	2%
Northwestern Steel*	$ .7	11%	64%	8%
Industry Median	$1.2	8%	34%	6%

*Minimills
**Integrated steel producers.
NA = Not Available
NM = Not Meaningful
Source: *Forbes*, January 13, 1997, pp. 174–75.

Nucor-Yamato Steel Company
Products: Wide flange steel beams, pilings, heavy structural steel products.
Plant: Blytheville, AR.

Vulcraft
Products: Steel joists, joist girders and steel deck for building construction.
Plants: Florence, SC; Norfolk, NE; Fort Payne, AL; Grapeland, TX; Saint Joe, IN; Brigham City, UT.

Nucor Cold Finish
Products: cold finished steel products for shafting, precision machined parts.
Plants: Norfolk, NE; Darlington, SC; Brigham City, UT.

Nucor Fastener
Products: Standard steel hexhead cap screws, hex bolts, socket head cap screws.
Plants: Saint Joe, IN; Conway, AR.

Nucor Bearing Products, Inc.
Products: Unground, semi-ground, automotive steel bearings, machined steel parts.
Plant: Wilson, NC.

Nucor Building Systems
Products: Metal buildings, metal building components.
Plants: Waterloo, IN; Swansea, SC.

Nucor Grinding Balls
Products: Steel grinding balls, used by the mining industry to process ores.
Plant: Brigham City, UT.

Nucor Wire
Products: Stainless steel wire.
Plant: Lancaster, SC.

Nucor Iron Carbide
Products: Electric Arc Furnace Feedstocks.
Location: Trinidad, West Indies.

Strategy

Nucor's strategy was built around two of its competencies—to build steel manufacturing facilities economically and to operate them productively. Nucor emphasized continuous innovation, modern equipment, dedication to each and every customer on each and every order, and commitment to producing high quality steel and steel products at competitive prices. Nucor was the first company to introduce several new products: thin-slab cast steel, direct casting of stainless wire, iron carbide, to name a few.

Nucor produced a greater variety of steel products than any other steel company in the United States. The company participated in the very low end steel products (example: reinforcing bar) as well as very high end (examples: motor lamination steel used in dishwashers, washers, and dryers; stainless steel used in automotive catalytic converter and exhaust systems).

Nucor's customer segments were four: construction industry (60 percent); automotive and appliance (15 percent); oil and gas (15 percent); and miscellaneous (10 percent). Nucor distributed 50 percent of its products through steel service centers; all the low end steel products were distributed this way. Nucor sold the other 50 percent—the high end products—directly to either an OEM, a fabricator, or an end customer.

Nucor's financial policy was that debt to total capital should not exceed 30 percent. In 1996 the debt to total capital was at 7 percent. Nucor did not believe in acquisitions or mergers. Instead, the company was committed to internally generated growth. The company had no plans to diversify outside of steel and steel-related products.

Nucor was, by and large, a U.S. company. The company did, however, have an iron carbide plant in Trinidad, West Indies. Further, in May 1996 the company signed a letter of intent with a steel company in Thailand, Nakornthai Strip Mill Public Co., Ltd. (NSM), to provide management assistance for NSM's new compact strip mill. NSM's new mill will use the same thin-slab casting technology successfully developed by Nucor in its sheet steel mills in Crawfordsville, Indiana, and Hickman, Arkansas. Nucor will provide start-up and management assistance to NSM, and train NSM employees at Nucor's facilities.

Organization

The organizational structure of Nucor was decentralized, consisting of only four management layers as follows:

Chairman/Vice Chairman/President
Vice President/General Manager
Department Manager
Supervisory/Professional
Hourly Employee

The typical *Fortune 500* company tended to have 10 or more layers of management. John Correnti: "We have a very flat organization structure. The standard joke in the company is if you are a janitor and you get five promotions, you have Correnti's job. If you take a typical organization chart, it is the typical pyramid. You take our company, you turn the pyramid upside down; 6800 people do not work for me, I work for 6800 people."[2]

Though a *Fortune 500* company, Nucor had only 22 people (including secretaries) working at the corporate head office. The head office was located in an unassuming office building across the street from a shopping mall.

In 1996 the Board of Directors consisted of the current chairman, president, and chief financial officer of Nucor and two retired Nucor executives.

The general manager at each Nucor facility was given a great deal of autonomy in operating the facility as an independent business. With the day-to-day decisions made at the operating facilities, Nucor was able to solve problems quickly without waiting for decisions from headquarters. Nucor kept the lines of communication open to employees in an informal, efficient manner.

---

[2] Ibid, p. 20.

Employee relations at Nucor were based on four clear-cut principles:

1. Management is obligated to manage Nucor in such a way that employees will have the opportunity to earn according to their productivity.
2. Employees should feel confident that if they do their jobs properly, they will have a job tomorrow.
3. Employees have the right to be treated fairly and must believe that they will be.
4. Employees must have an avenue of appeal when they believe they are being treated unfairly.

As part of its commitment to fairness, Nucor had a grievance procedure that allowed any employee to ask for a review of a grievance if he or she felt the supervisor had not provided a fair hearing. The procedure let the grievance move up to the general manager level, and if the employee was still not satisfied, the grievance can be submitted to headquarters management for final appeal.

Nucor's labor force was not unionized. An employee at Nucor Steel, Hickman, Arkansas, put it this way: "Why is Nucor nonunion? I see two main reasons. First, it's just not needed. Nucor takes very good care of its employees. Its pay and benefits package is top-notch. No one has been capriciously fired. There are no layoffs. Nucor listens to its employees through monthly crew meetings, shop dinners, and employee surveys. We just don't need union mediators . . . The second reason is that we all work together. We don't need divisiveness. We don't need adversaries. We can talk among ourselves and work out our own problems."[3] Iverson's perspective on this issue was: "People like to work here. For example, the last time we had a union organizer in Darlington

we had to send management out to protect the union guy passing out the pamphlets."[4]

Compensation

Nucor was very selective in recruiting employees. The company usually had a large pool of applicants to choose from. To quote Iverson: "Darlington needed eight people, and we put a little ad in the county weekly newspaper that said, 'Nucor Steel will take some applications on Saturday morning at 8:30 for new employees.' When we went out there for the interviewing, there were 1,200 people lined up in that plant. We couldn't even get into the plant to get to the personnel department . . . Finally, we called the state police and said, 'you've got to do something. We've got a traffic jam out here.' And the cop on duty said, 'We can't do it, because we've got three people out there applying for jobs ourselves!' "[5]

Nucor provided employees with a performance-related compensation system that rewarded goal-oriented employees. All employees were covered under one of four basic compensation plans, each featuring incentives related to meeting specific goals and targets.

1. Production Incentive Plan. Employees involved directly in manufacturing were paid weekly bonuses on the basis of the production of their work groups, which ranged from 20 to 40 workers each. Most Nucor employees were covered under this system. The bonus was given not on the basis of an individual's output but on the basis of the group's output. Bonus was paid on "good" output. Bonus was based upon anticipated production time or tonnage produced, depending upon the type of facility. The formulas for determining the bonus were nondiscretionary. Once the standard output was determined, the standard was not revised unless a significant change in the way the production process

[3]Claude Riggin, "Freedom and a Hell of a Lot More at Nucor," Newsfront column. *New Steel*, July 1996.

[4]"Steel Man Ken Iverson," *Inc.*, April 1986, pp. 41–42.
[5]Ibid, p. 42.

was performed resulted from a difference source other than from the workers in the bonus group. The bonus plan created pressure for each individual to perform well and was tied to attendance and tardiness standards. Bonus was paid every week. Even if one worker's tardiness or attendance problems caused the group to miss its weekly output target, every member of the group was denied bonus for that week. No bonus was paid if equipment was not operating. Maintenance personnel were assigned to each shift, and they participated in the bonus along with the other bonus groups. Production supervisors were also a part of the bonus group and received the same bonus as the employees they supervised. Weekly output by each production group and bonuses received by each production group were visibly displayed at the front entrance to the factory. In general, the Production Incentive Bonus averaged 80–150 percent of the base wage.

Iverson remarked: "Now in the case of the lowest level, it's the production-incentive compensation that is probably the most important of all. Everything is arranged in groups of 25 to 40 people who are doing some complete task. For example, in the steel mills, there are nine bonus groups: three in melting and casting, three in rolling, and three in finishing and shipping. Take melting and coating, for example. We start with a base of 12 tons of good billets per hour: above that, the people in the group get a 4 percent bonus for every ton per hour. So if they have a week in which they run, say, 32 tons per hour—and that would be low—that's an 80 percent bonus. Take the regular pay, the overtime pay, everything, multiply it by an additional 80 percent—and we give them that check along with their regular check the next week . . . This bonus system is very tough. If you are late, even only five minutes, you lose your bonus for the day. If you are thirty minutes late or you are absent for sickness or anything else, you lose your bonus for the week. Now, we have four forgiveness days per year when you might need to

close on a house or your wife is having a baby, but only four."[6]

2. Department Manager Incentive Plan. Nucor department managers earned annual incentive bonuses based primarily upon the return on assets of their facility. Nucor paid no discretionary bonuses. Each facility had a common and clear goal since department manager bonuses were based upon written plans that were easy to understand. These bonuses averaged 82 percent of base salary.

3. Non-Production and Non-Department Manager Incentive Plan. This bonus was paid to all employees not on the Production Incentive Plan or the Department Manager Incentive Plan. Its participants included accountants, engineers, secretaries, clerks, receptionists, or any one of a broad number of different employee classifications. The bonus was based primarily upon each facility's return on assets. As with all Nucor incentive compensation bonus plans, there were no discretionary bonuses paid to participants. The bonus was based on a written plan that was clear, easy to understand, and accessible to employees. Every month each operation received a report showing on a year-to-date basis their return on assets. This chart was posted in the employee cafeteria or break area together with the chart showing the bonus payout. The chart kept employees apprised of their expected bonus levels throughout the year. This bonus could total over 25 percent of salary.

4. Senior Officers Incentive Plan. Nucor senior officers did not have employment contracts. They received no profit sharing, pension, discretionary bonuses, nor retirement plans. Their base salaries were set at less than what executives received in comparable companies. Senior officers had only one compensation system. A significant part of each senior officer's compensation was based upon Nucor's return on stockholders'

---

[6]Ibid, pp. 44–45.

equity, above certain minimum earnings. Plant general managers, who were officers of the company, were compensated based on Nucor's return on equity. A portion of pretax earnings was placed into a pool that was divided among the officers in bonuses that were about 60 percent stock and 40 percent cash. If Nucor did well, the officer's compensation was well above average, as much as several times base salary. If Nucor did poorly, the officer's compensation was only base salary and, therefore, significantly below the average pay for this type of responsibility.

During a slack period in the 1980s, Iverson was named the *Fortune 500* CEO with the lowest compensation. To Iverson, this was something to be proud of: "When I walked through a plant during that period of time when we had to cut back to a four-day work week, or even three and a half days, I never heard an employee who complained. His pay may have been cut 25 percent, but he knew that his department head was cut even more and that the officers were cut, percentage-wise, even more than that. I call it our 'share-the-pain' program. . . . Management should take the biggest drop in pay because they have the most responsibility."[7]

In addition to these established bonus plans, Nucor periodically issued an extraordinary bonus to all employees, except officers, during times when Nucor was enjoying a particularly strong performance. This bonus has been as high as $700 for each employee.

Benefits

Nucor took an egalitarian approach in providing benefits to its employees. Senior executives did not enjoy traditional perquisites such as company cars, corporate jets, executive dining rooms, or executive parking places. In fact, certain benefits such as Nucor's Profit Sharing, Scholarship Program, Employee Stock Purchase Plan, Extraordinary Bonus, and Service Awards Program were

not available to Nucor's officers. All employees had the same holidays, vacation schedules, and insurance programs. All the employees wore green color hard hats; CEO's hat was not gold plated! (Typically, in other manufacturing companies, people wore different color hats in accordance with status, authority, or seniority.) In annual reports every employee's name was listed alphabetically on the front cover.

Nucor maintained a Profit Sharing Plan for employees below the officer level. Employees made no contributions to this plan. A minimum of 10 percent of Nucor's pretax earnings was contributed to the Profit Sharing Plan each year. Of this amount, approximately 15 to 20 percent was paid to employees in March of the following year as cash profit sharing. The remainder was placed in trust and allocated to employees based upon their earnings as a percent of the total earnings paid throughout Nucor. Employees became fully vested in their portion of the Profit Sharing Trust after seven full years of service. Profit Sharing Trust funds were paid to employees when they retired, or terminated employment with Nucor. A number of employees had over $300,000 in the Profit Sharing Trust.

Nucor also offered employees a chance to invest in their future with a Monthly Stock Purchase Plan featuring a 10 percent Nucor matching contribution; and a 401(k) Retirement Savings Plan which included a matching contribution ranging from 5 to 25 percent of the employee's contribution based upon Nucor's return on shareholders' equity. Nucor provided its employees with standard types of medical, dental, disability and life insurance programs, as well as standard vacation and holiday packages.

Nucor's Service Award Plan granted employees an award of five shares of Nucor common stock for each five years of continuous service.

Nucor was strongly committed to on-the-job training for its employees; they were trained to do multiple functions.

A unique aspect of Nucor's benefit program was its commitment to education for children of

---

[7]Ibid, p. 44.

Nucor employees. The Nucor Scholarship Program provided four-year scholarships for children of Nucor employees pursuing higher education or vocational training past high school. The program paid up to $2,200 annually for each qualified student for up to four years of college. To quote John Correnti: "It [the Nucor Scholarship Program] costs Nucor about $1.3 million a year and we have over 600 children of our employees in about 200 different learning institutions. This gets Nucor around the dinner table at night. It creates loyalty among our employees. . . . Our turnover is so minuscule we do not even measure it."[8]

Teamwork

Teamwork was a cornerstone of Nucor's employee relations program. The annual employee dinners held at each facility were a reinforcement of the teamwork spirit.

General managers were charged to hold annual dinners with every employee in groups of 25 to 100 at one time. These meetings gave employees a chance to discuss problems relating to scheduling, equipment, organization, and production. The ground rules for these meetings were simple: all comments were to remain business-related and not involve personalities, and all criticism was to be taken under advisement by management for decisive action. Like New England town meetings of old, the format was free and open. Topics could vary widely from year to year. Sessions lasted well beyond midnight in some instances.

In a similar manner, all the plant general managers met as a group with headquarters management three times a year—in February, May, and November—to review each facility's performance and to plan for the months and years ahead. In addition, detailed performance data on each mill were distributed to all plant

managers on a regular basis. It was also quite common in Nucor for plant general managers and machine operators to visit each other's mills.

Technology

Nucor was committed to provide the work force with the best technology available to get the job done right in a safe working environment. As evidence of that commitment, Nucor aggressively pursued the latest advancements in steel making around the world to determine what technology it can adapt to its facilities.

Nucor did not do any R&D. Rather, it relied on equipment suppliers and other companies to do the R&D. Nucor then adopted these new technological advancements—whether it be in steel or iron making, or in fabrication.

Nucor successfully adopted the "minimill" concept—first developed in Europe and Japan—in the plant it built in Darlington, South Carolina, in 1969. Minimills used scrap steel as the raw material and employed smaller scale electric furnaces to convert scrap steel into finished steel. For nonflat, commodity segment of the steel industry (reinforcing bar for construction; rods for pipe, rail, and screws), minimills had a cost advantage vis-à-vis integrated steel producers. Minimills eventually drove the integrated steel producers out of the low end of the steel industry.

Until the mid-80s, minimills could not produce the high end, flat steel products serving the needs of automotive and appliance customers. The flat steel market was the monopoly of the integrated steel producers. Nucor made history in 1987 by building the first minimill in Crawfordsville, Indiana, that could make flat steel. This mill enabled Nucor to enter the premium segment of the steel industry. In the Crawfordsville plant, Nucor gambled on the thin-slab casting technology developed by SMS Schloemann-Siemag, a West German company. The West German company had used this technology in a small pilot plant but had not proven this technology commercially. Technical staff from over 100 steel companies

---

[8]Richard Franklin, "An Interview with John D. Correnti," *The Wall Street Corporate Reporter*, September 9–15, 1996, p. 19.

visited SMS to explore the technology but it was Nucor who first adopted the thin-slab casting technology. Nucor obtained the technology from SMS by signing a non-exclusive contract with an additional technology flow-back clause. The investment in Crawfordsville plant represented approximately five times the net earnings of Nucor in 1987 and was about equal to stockholder's equity of Nucor in 1987! By 1996 Nucor had built two more minimills (Hickman, Arkansas; Charleston, South Carolina) using the thin-slab casting process that produced flat-rolled sheet steel. The first competitive continuous thin-slab-cast flat-rolled steel-making facility appeared in 1995—eight years after Nucor's pioneering effort.

This pursuit of technical excellence had led to the development in 1987 of Nucor-Yamato Steel Company, a facility jointly owned by Nucor and Yamato Kogyo of Japan, which operated a structural steel mill in the United States employing Yamato's continuous casting technology.

Nucor was concerned that, due to the start-ups of minimills by several companies, scrap steel could either become unavailable or its prices could go up significantly in the future. In order to protect against that possibility, Nucor started an iron carbide plant in Trinidad, West Indies, in 1994. This plant has successfully adopted a commercially unproven technology to make iron carbide, a substitute for scrap steel. The Trinidad plant supplied iron carbide to the flat-rolled plant in Crawfordsville. As of 1996 the Trinidad facility was the only facility in the world making iron carbide.

Nucor was committed to continuously modernizing its plants. Nucor's philosophy was to build or rebuild one or more mills every year. Nucor's policy was to rebuild the entire mill rather than just put "new pipes in parts of the old mill." The company did not rely on outside contractors for building or rebuilding mills. Instead, a small group of engineers was selected from existing Nucor mills and given the responsibility to design and manage the construction of a new mill. The actual construction was done by workers hired from the local area; these workers were subsequently recruited to operate the mills.

Future

Eliminating the distinctions between management and hourly employees as much as possible served Nucor well. Nucor's employees responded positively to Nucor's production incentives. In return, Nucor remained strongly committed to not laying off or furloughing employees in periods when business was down. During the past twenty years, Nucor had not laid off a single worker due to lack of work. A former employee of an integrated steel company said, "At Nucor, the cold-mill manager says that almost all of the improvements have come from operators and operating supervisors. At my plant, operators are reluctant to suggest improvements for fear of reducing or eliminating another worker's job."[9]

The expansion program started in the mid-1980s assures that Nucor was well-positioned to develop fresh markets for steel products far into the twenty-first century.

Reflecting on the future, John Correnti commented: "The only thing I lose sleep over at night is even though we are a $3.6 billion company I want this company to look like, smell like, feel like a $300 million company. I want to make sure we still have the same hands-on management style. The same good culture, the same good relationships with our employees and with our customers. Granted, as you become larger, that becomes a little more difficult to do. In doing that you still have to grow. You are like a flower: if you stop growing you die. The goal of the company is to maintain that 15–20 percent growth momentum throughout the next decade."[10]

---

[9]Anthony Edwards, "How Efficient Are Our Work Practices," *New Steel*, July 1996, p. 31.

[10]Richard Franklin, "An Interview with John D. Correnti," *The Wall Street Corporate Reporter*, September 9–15, 1996, p. 20.

Questions

1. Why has Nucor performed so well?
   A. Is Nucor's industry the answer?
   B. Is it a "minimill" effect?
   C. Is it Nucor's home-base (United States)?
   D. Is it market power (scale economies)?
   E. Is it a distribution channel advantage?
   F. Is it a raw material advantage?
   G. Is it a technology advantage?
   H. Is it a location advantage?
   I. Is it entrenched brand name?
   J. Is it Nucor's choice of a unique strategy?
   K. Is it Nucor's ability to execute its strategy?

2. What are the most important elements of Nucor's overall approach to organization and control that help explain why this company is so successful? How well do Nucor's organization and control mechanisms fit the company's strategic requirements?

3. Nucor's success crucially depends on its ability to mobilize two types of knowledge—plant construction and start up know-how, and manufacturing process know-how. What mechanisms does Nucor employ to effectively manage knowledge?
   A. What mechanisms help the company to accumulate these two types of knowledge in individual plants?
   B. What mechanisms exist within the company to facilitate sharing of such knowledge across its 25 plants?
   C. How does Nucor transfer knowledge to a greenfield, start-up operation?

4. Nucor has repeatedly demonstrated an ability to be a successful first mover in technology adoption. How does the company's organization and control contribute to this first mover advantage in technology?

5. Would you like to work for Nucor?

6. What is the applicability of Nucor's approach to organization and control to other companies?

Case 13–3
3M Corporation

> Innovation is important to most companies, but it is our lifeblood at 3M.[1]
>
> Ronald A. Mitsch
> Vice Chairman and Executive Vice President

The Minnesota Mining & Manufacturing Corporation (3M) is a diversified manufacturer of commercial, industrial, consumer, and healthcare products. Its business is divided into three major segments:

- Industrial & Consumer
- Information, Imaging & Electronic
- Life Sciences

Founded in 1902 as a corundum mining operation, 3M had to change directions quickly as the mine was completely unsuccessful, reportedly selling only one ton of ore.[2] Since that time, 3M has grown to achieve an annual world wide revenue of over $15 billion by 1996 (see Exhibit 1).

Currently, 3M makes more than 60,000 products; they also produce 900 varieties of adhesive tapes alone as diverse as reflective material for highway safety and home cleaning sponges. As a result, 3M is a recognized leader in innovation. Additionally, in 1995 3M was awarded the National Medal of Technology®, the U.S. government's top award for innovation.

Early on in 3M's history, William L. McKnight, former Chairman and CEO of 3M and long considered to be "spiritual founder" of 3M, introduced policies and philosophies that are considered to be responsible for 3M's ability to consistently innovate (see Exhibit 2). As articulated in 3M's 1995 Annual Report, current management still embraces these policies and philosophies, seeing innovation as the cornerstone of 3M's future success:

> We believe that 3M will be even more successful in the future. . . . The first reason is technology and new products. . . . Our businesses will concentrate all of their efforts on using this strong technology base to create innovative solutions to customer needs all over the world.[3]
>
> L. D. DeSimone
> Chairman and CEO

This case was written by Kirk Hendrickson, Tuck '97, under the supervision of Professor Vijay Govindarajan. Copyright © Osceola Institute.

[1] Ronald A. Mitsch, "Three Roads to Innovation," *The Journal of Business Strategy*, September/October 1990, p. 18.

[2] James C. Collins and Jerry I. Porras, *Built to Last: Successful Habits of Visionary Companies* (New York: HarperBusiness, 1995), p. 238.

Question

Evaluate the policies and philosophies of 3M from the standpoint of helping 3M implement its strategy rooted in innovation.

---

[3] L. D. DeSimone, *3M Annual Report*, 1995, p. 4.

EXHIBIT 1   Selected Financial Results from 1986 through 1995†
(Year End Dec. 31) (Million $)

Income Statement	1995	1994	1993	1992	1991	1990	1989	1988	1987	1986
Net Sales	13,460	15,079	14,020	13,883	13,340	13,021	11,990	10,581	9,429	8,602
Operating Expenses‡										
Cost of Goods Sold	7,720	8,995	8,529	8,346	8,058	7,656	6,946	6,105	5,513	5,074
Selling, General, & Administrative*	3,440	3,833	3,535	3,557	3,323	3,174	2,894	2,593	2,338	2,118
Total	11,239	12,828	12,064	11,889	11,381	10,830	9,840	8,698	7,851	7,192
Operating Income	2,221	2,251	1,956	1,994	1,959	2,191	2,150	1,883	1,578	1,410
Other Income and Expenses	53	97	(46)	47	82	56	51	1	13	62
Income Taxes	785	771	707	687	691	798	825	728	647	569
Minority Interest	77	61	32	24	32	29	30	0	0	0
Net Income*	976	1,322	1,263	1,233	1,154	1,308	1,244	1,154	918	779

†In 1996 3M spun-off its data storage and imaging systems divisions and discontinued its audio and video tape business. In its 1995 Annual Report, 3M chose to only show its continuing operations, presenting its 1995 financial statements without the effect of the businesses to be spun-off or discontinued.
‡Total Operating Expenses include a restructuring charge in 1995 and legal settlements and special charges in 1992.
*1995 Net Income includes a $373 million loss on disposal of discontinued businesses.
Source: 3M Annual Reports.

EXHIBIT 1   (Continued)
(Year End Dec. 31) (Million $)

Balance Sheet	1995	1994	1993	1992	1991	1990	1989	1988	1987	1986
Assets										
Current Assets										
Cash§	772	491	656	722	502	591	887	897	594	545
Accounts Receivable—Net	2,398	2,948	2,610	2,394	2,362	2,367	2,075	1,727	1,615	
Inventories	2,206	2,763	2,401	2,315	2,292	2,355	2,120	1,831	1,770	
Total Current Assets*	6,395	6,928	6,363	6,209	5,585	5,729	5,382	4,741	4,229	3,961
Property, Plant & Equipment—net	4,638	5,054	4,830	4,792	4,666	4,389	3,707	3,073	2,932	
Total†	14,183	13,496	12,197	11,955	11,083	11,079	9,776	8,922	8,031	7,348
Liabilities and Shareholders' Equity										
Current Liabilities										
Accounts Payable	762	996	878	836	809	811	724	572	586	
Short-term debt	822	917	697	739	709	736	455	347	264	
Total Current Liabilities‡	3,724	3,605	3,282	3,241	3,236	3,339	2,721	2,371	1,931	1,823
Other Liabilities	2,372	2,126	1,607	1,428	752	710	592	367	315	
Long-Term Debt	1,203	1,031	796	687	764	760	885	406	435	436
Stockholders' Equity	6,884	6,734	6,521	6,599	6,293	6,110	5,378	5,514	5,060	4,463
Total	14,183	13,496	12,197	11,955	11,083	11,079	9,776	8,922	8,031	7,348

§Cash includes cash equivalents and other securities.
*Total Current Assets includes Other Current Assets.
†Total Assets includes Investments, Other Assets, and Net Assets of discontinued operations.
‡Total Current Liabilities includes Payroll, Income Taxes, and Other Current Liabilities.

Exhibit 2   Selected Policies and Philosophies of 3M[4]

---

15 percent option:	Many employees have the option to spend up to 15 percent of their work week pursuing individual projects of their own choice.
30 percent rule:	Thirty percent of business unit revenues must come from products introduced in the last four years. Business unit bonuses are based on how successfully each manager achieves this goal.
Dual-ladder career path:	There are two career ladders, a technical career ladder and a management career ladder. Both allow advancement while allowing employees to stay focused on their research and professional interests.
Genesis Grants:	Provides awards up to $50,000 to employees to conduct independent research, product development, and test marketing in areas of emerging technology. About 90 such awards are given each year.
Carlton Award:	This technical honor society honors 3M technical employees who have made large contributions to 3M through fundamental technical innovation.
Golden Step program:	Awards cross-functional teams within 3M who successfully launch new business ventures.
3 tiered research:	*Business Unit Laboratories*: Focuses on specific markets, with near-term products. *Sector Laboratories*: Focuses on applications with a 3 to 10 year time horizon for product viability. *Corporate Laboratories*: Focuses on basic research with a time horizon of as much as 20 years.
Knowledge Sharing:	3M supports formal and informal forums for sharing knowledge throughout the company. Includes extensive e-mail directories, sharing of new products introduced by a business unit, and awards for successful sharing of new technology between business units.
Customer contact:	Scientists are regularly sent into the field to meet with customers and see how the customers are using 3M's products. Also, customers are frequently invited to participate in generating product ideas with 3M scientists.
Intrapreneurs:	Product inventors recruit action teams to develop the product. This team is allowed to champion the product, grow its business, and develop line extensions. As the product achieves certain revenue goals, the team members receive raises and promotions. Those on the management track become project managers, department managers, and then division managers as the product line revenues grow.
Tolerance for Failure:	Company culture emphasizes that a failure can turn into a success. There is no punishment for a product failing in the market. 3M has developed a series of legends around famous failures that have made good, such as the weak adhesive that became the adhesive for Post-It Notes.
Small Business Units:	Business units are split up after they reach a size of approximately $200 to $300 million. It is required that the business unit managers know the names of everyone who works for them.
Profit Sharing:	Almost all of 3M employees are entitled to the profit sharing plan.
R&D Spending:	3M spends approximately 6.5 percent to 7 percent of sales on research and development, and has consistently increased R&D spending over the last two decades.

---

[4]These policies and philosophies are summarized in the following sources: James C. Collins and Jerry I. Porras, *Built to Last: Successful Habits of Visionary Companies* (New York: HarperBusiness, 1995), pp. 156–58; Ronald A. Mitsch, "Three Roads to Innovation," *The Journal of Business Strategy*, September/October 1990, pp. 18–21.

Case 13–4
Texas Instruments and Hewlett-Packard

Texas Instruments (TI) and Hewlett-Packard (HP) developed, manufactured, and sold high technology electric and electronic products. Texas Instruments had three main lines of business in 1984: *components*, which included semiconductor integrated circuits, semiconductor subassemblies, and electronic control devices; *digital products*: which included minicomputers, personal computers, scientific instruments, and calculators; and *government electronics*, which included radar systems, missile guidance and control systems, and infrared surveillance systems. The three businesses generated 46 percent, 19 percent, and 24 percent, respectively, of TI's sales in 1984. Hewlett-Packard operated in two main lines of business: *computer products*, which included factory automation computers, engineering workstations, data terminals, personal computers, and calculators; and *electronic test and measurement systems*, which included instruments that were used to evaluate the operation of electrical equipment against standards, instruments that would measure and display electronic signals, voltmeters, and oscilloscopes. These businesses generated 53 percent and 37 percent, respectively, of HP's 1984 sales. Summary financial information for each company is presented in Exhibit 1.

Though Texas Instruments and Hewlett-Packard competed in similar industries, the strategies chosen by these two firms were very different. Five major concepts related to the content of strategy are summarized for both Texas Instruments and Hewlett-Packard. Perhaps the most significant distinction between TI and HP

Reprinted by permission of Steven C. Wheelright, "Strategy, Management, and Strategic Planning Approaches," *Interfaces*, January–February 1984, pp. 19–33. Copyright 1984 by the Operations Research Society of America and The Institute of Management Sciences, 290 Westminster Street, Providence, Rhode Island 02903, USA.

Exhibit 1   Summary Financial Information
($ in millions)

Texas Instruments

	1980	1981	1982	1983	1984
Assets	$2,414	$2,311	$2,631	$2,713	$3,423
Equity	1,165	1,260	1,361	1,203	1,541
Sales	4,075	4,206	4,327	4,580	5,742
Operating profit	379	253	236	(288)	526
ROI	32.5%	20.1%	17.3%	n.a.	34.1%

Hewlett-Packard

	1980	1981	1982	1983	1984
Assets	$2,337	$2,782	$3,470	$4,161	$5,153
Equity	1,547	1,890	2,349	2,887	3,545
Sales	3,099	3,578	4,254	4,710	6,044
Operating profit	523	567	676	728	860
ROI	33.8%	30.1%	28.8%	25.2%	24.2%

was their generic business and functional strategies (Exhibit 2). They pursued very different approaches. TI preferred to pursue competitive advantage based on larger, more standard markets and a long-term, low-cost position. HP, on the other hand, sought competitive advantage in selected smaller markets based on unique, high-value, high-feature products. The functional strategies used to support those desired competitive advantages also differed.

With regard to the product life cycle (Exhibit 3), TI favored early entry, followed by expansion and consolidation of its position, resulting in a dominant market share when the product matured. HP, on the other hand, tended to create new markets, but then exited (or introduced other new products) as cost-driven competitors entered and the market matured. It is not surprising that

EXHIBIT 2   **Contrasting Strategies of TI and HP**

Texas Instruments		Hewlett-Packard
Business Strategy		
Competitive advantage for large, standard markets based on long-run cost position		Competitive advantage for selected small markets based on unique, high value/high features products
Functional Strategy		
Marketing:	High volume/low price	High value/high price
	Rapid growth	Controlled growth
	Standard Products	Custom features
Manufacturing:	Scale economies and learning curve	Delivery and quality driven
	Vertical integration	Limited vertical integration
	Large, low-cost locations	Small, attractive locations
R&D:	Process and product	Product only
	Cost driven	Features and quality driven
	Design to cost	Design to performance
Financial:	Aggressive	Conservative
	Higher debt	No debt
	Tight ship	Margin of safety (slack)

the two firms viewed prices and costs, the third area, differently. TI emphasized continual price cuts to parallel cost reduction in order to build volume and take advantage of shared experience and learning. HP, on the other hand, put less em-phasis on manufacturing cost reductions and held prices longer so that profit margins expanded during the initial periods. The early returns generated allowed early exit from the market with good returns on investment and provided funds for further product research and development.

A fourth concept that highlights their differences in strategy is the product process matrix, which matches the product life cycle with its production counterpart, the process life cycle. HP concentrated on more flexible production processes (such as job shop and batch operations) to meet the needs of its custom and low-volume markets, while TI concentrated on more capital intensive and cost-effective production processes (assembly lines and continuous flow operations) to supply its more standard, high-volume markets.

A fifth concept, portfolio analysis, further highlights differences in the firms' strategies. TI looked for a portfolio that included low-growth businesses with dominant market shares to provide cash for a select group of high-growth businesses with lower market shares but with the prospect of becoming dominant, high-growth businesses, and eventually "cash cows." HP, on the other hand, wanted all high growth businesses with dominant market shares, and to re-allocate major resources only to fund new businesses. In fact, the traditional solution to any profit problem at HP had been new products and new businesses.

Question

Given the differences in strategy between the two firms, what would you expect would be the differences between TI and HP in their planning and control systems: strategic planning systems; budgeting systems; reporting systems; performance evaluation systems; and incentive compensation systems?

EXHIBIT 3   Differences in Strategy between Texas Instruments and Hewlett-Packard

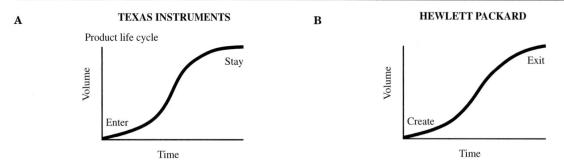

A   TEXAS INSTRUMENTS

B   HEWLETT PACKARD

TI tended to enter early in a product's life cycle, and stayed through maturity. HP tended to create a new product and then replaced it when it matured.

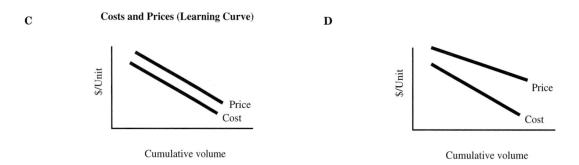

C   Costs and Prices (Learning Curve)

D

TI emphasized aggressive cost improvements, with equally aggressive price cuts. HP desired cost improvements, but sought higher margins and held prices longer.

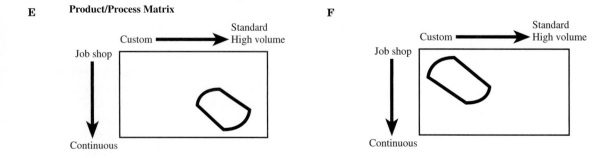

E   Product/Process Matrix

F

TI concentrated on more capital intensive, cost-effective production processes to match high-volume, standard product needs. HP concentrated on flexible production processes to match low-volume, more custom product needs.

Exhibit 3   (Continued)

G   **Portfolio: Positioning and Resource Movement**   H

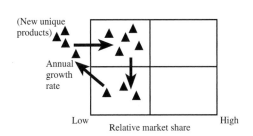

TI sought a balanced portfolio of businesses where mature, large businesses provide resources for young, high-growth businesses. HP sought all high-growth, high-margin businesses that met their own resource needs, largely on an individual basis.

Case 13–5
Texas Instruments

Paul Elmer, vice president-corporate planning at Harvey-Hudson Electronics (HHE), pushed the papers away from him and leaned back in his chair. Mr. Elmer had been reviewing his files on Texas Instruments, Inc. (TI) and its complex and much talked about set of management systems. His hope was that he could learn enough about TI's systems to be able to assess whether a similar system should be considered for use at HHE.

Over the past several weeks, he and several of his immediate subordinates had been poring over various documents, articles, annual reports, and brochures dealing with TI and its management systems. Soon, they would need to pull their thoughts together and come to some conclusions about how well they understood the various systems and about the strengths and weaknesses associated with them.

TI—Some Overview Points

Texas Instruments was a multinational corporation producing a wide variety of products, virtually all of which had a tie of some kind to the electronics industry. In addition to its U.S. plants, TI maintained facilities in Canada, Latin America, Europe, Australia, and the Far East. Around one third of sales came from outside the United States.[1] World wide employment was 85,000.[2]

Since 1946, sales at TI had grown at an average annual rate of 24 percent. Profits had outpaced the sales figure, increasing between 1971 and 1980 at an average annual rate of 34 percent.

The electronics industry was expected to boom in the 1980s, reaching the $280 billion mark by the later part of the decade.[3] TI's sales were expected to increase significantly as a result of lower prices and, therefore, higher volume. The pattern of fast growth in the electronics industry, however, posed a challenge for each firm in the industry—how to balance the amount of relative priority accorded to innovation versus volume. A typical product/price life cycle pattern began with the introduction of a new product into the market at small volume and at high prices. In the presence of sufficient demand, volume quickly expanded resulting in lower unit costs and a corresponding reduction in prices. Given the above situation, the value of inventories could drop dramatically in a matter of months. Such a scenario would require steady write-downs in inventory valuation. Equipment to deal with specialized products posed another problem. Due to rapid technological turnover, a machine had to pay out in a short amount of time or else become unaffordable. Therefore, there was a basic conflict between production and innovation—in other words—expenditures for research versus production. TI's approach to this dilemma was quite succinct. "TI [was] determined to lead in both."[4]

This case was prepared from published sources by Donna Bergstedt, Research Assistant, and Professor M. Edgar Barrett. Copyright © by M. Edgar Barrett.

[1]L. M. Rice Jr., "Texas Instruments Management Philosophies and Growth Experience," remarks to Instituto Panamericano de Alta Direccion de Empresa, Mexico, Texas Instruments, Inc., May 1980, p. 1.

[2]Ibid.

[3]Floyd G. Lawrence, "Could This be America's Best-Managed Company? Part II—Texas Instruments is Determined to Grow and Never to Grow Old," *Today's Manager*, May–June 1977, p. 5.

[4]Ibid.

Company History[5]

Growth at Texas Instruments had been based on innovation as opposed to acquisitions. With the exception of the 1959 merger with Metals and Controls Corporation, TI's growth had come primarily from the sales revenues resulting from the internal development of new products and services. In 1980, sales at TI reached $4.1 billion, and net income was $212 million.

TI had been a technologically based company throughout its history. It originated in 1930 as Geophysical Services Inc. (GSI). The primary activities of GSI focused on the discovery of petroleum reserves throughout the world.

This was accomplished by means of reflection seismology which had been invented by the organization's first president and founder, Dr. J. C. Karcher. The importance of petroleum as a resource helped maintain GSI's growth even during the Depression and eventually led the company into the international arena. By 1946, GSI had 16 geophysical crews operating in different countries throughout the world and billings of $2.25 million.[6] Nearly all of these billings related to the original innovation—seismology.

In 1946, Patrick E. Haggerty joined TI (still GSI). Under his influence the company began to formulate a new objective, the purpose of which was to move the organization beyond geophysical exploration into engineering and manufacturing.

The strategy which was most influential centered around the development of semiconductors. By 1956, work had progressed sufficiently so as to prompt management to begin to play with the idea of producing whole circuits processed on tiny wafers of pure silicon. In 1958, Jack Kilby of TI created the first practical integrated circuit.

Around 1959, management at TI began to believe that a pattern existed in the strategic development of its innovative successes. They further believed that innovation was necessary not only in the creation of improved products but also in the method of developing and marketing such products. This belief eventually led to the development of the "OST System."

By the early 1980s, TI was engaged in activities in four major areas: (1) electronics, (2) geophysical exploration, (3) government electronics, and (4) nonelectronic industry products. In the field of electronics, TI concentrated on three major growth areas which centered around (1) *Semi-Conductor Devices*, (2) *Distributed Computing*, and (3) *Consumer Electronics*. The first area was to be focused upon because it constituted the foundation of the electronics revolution. Distributed computing would place data processing systems within businesses and factories as need required. The last area was thought to offer the potential for lucrative markets in the 1980s.[7]

Corporate Culture

A strong internal culture had developed at Texas Instruments and was considered by top management to be a key factor in the company's success. This culture stressed hard work, loyalty to the corporation, and team spirit. It was sustained in part by its practice of hiring 80 percent of its professional workers directly out of school and socializing them according to the rather rigorous norms of the organization.[8] It was also supported by the company's emphasis on internal growth in contrast to acquisitions. Few executives were brought into the organization at the middle or top management levels. According to one TI vice president, "The TI culture is a religion . . . the climate polarizes

---

[5]Patrick E. Haggerty, "Three Lectures at the Salzburg Seminar on Multinational Enterprise," Texas Instruments, Inc., February 1977. This source has been used extensively as background for this section as well as for much of the remainder of the case.

[6]Haggerty, "Three Lectures," p. 9.

[7]"Texas Instruments Shows U.S. Business," p. 70.

[8]Bro Uttal, "Texas Instruments Wrestles with the Consumer Market," *Fortune*, December 3, 1979, p. 51.

people—either you are incorporated into the culture or rejected."[9]

TI's ability to make the firm's management systems work seemed to stem partly from the atmosphere created by this culture. TI had been compared by some to a Japanese company in terms of management style. This comparison was not viewed unfavorably by TI's senior managers. In the words of J. Fred Bucy, TI's president:

> Japan has a culture and society well suited to achieving increased productivity and the growth that results from it. They are hardworking, dedicated people . . . and are highly motivated, in part, because of a culture that assigns personal responsibility for the quality of work. . . . There is a strong tendency in the Japanese culture to align personal goals with goals set by their companies.[10]

Organizational Structure

Although technological in orientation, TI produced a wide variety of products. By 1980, the firm had divided its line management structure into six groups for the sake of operational flexibility. These groups are illustrated in Exhibit 1 and were arranged in the following manner: (1) Semiconductor Products; (2) Distributed Computing Products; (3) Consumer Electronic Products; (4) Materials and Electrical Products; (5) Government Electronic Products; and (6) Geophysical Exploration Services. In charge of each group was a senior manager who reported directly to the president. These top-level managers were responsible for the worldwide strategic direction of their businesses, as well as for the regular, daily management functions.

Each group was further subdivided into divisions, which were, in turn, broken down into product customer centers (PCCs). A PCC was considered to be a complete business unit responsible for a particular family of products or services targeted at a specific market segment. The PCC manager assumed a profit and loss re-

sponsibility. As of 1980, there were more than 80[11] PCCs within TI. These PCCs were said to be designed in such a way as to allow the firm to have a close relationship with customers. They were also designed to provide entrepreneurial experience for the firm's middle managers.

Objectives, Strategies, and Tactics[12]

The OST System evolved at TI as a system for managing change and innovation. The system, known as the OST System (for objectives, strategies, and tactics) was employed to define the strategies the company intended to follow for further growth and development and to identify the tactics required to successfully implement such strategies. These tactics were set forth in a quantitative manner so that performance could be measured against agreed-upon quantitative goals. The system allowed for a clear separation of strategic and operational activities.

The OST System can be more easily understood if viewed in three stages. The first stage is a presentation of the hierarchy of goals. The second explains the dual responsibility of line management. The third stage discusses the impact of a matrix organization composed of strategic and operating modes.

Hierarchy of Goals.   The Hierarchy of Goals requires that a single statement of quantitative goals be made at the top of the organization and that that statement be supported in a hierarchical or pyramidal fashion by strategies and tactics. This hierarchy is illustrated in Exhibits 2 and 3.

At the top of the structure is the corporate objective. This is an overall statement of what the company hopes to achieve considering its products, markets, and its perception of the

---

[9]"Texas Instruments Shows U.S. Business," p. 68.
[10]Ibid.

[11]Rice, "Texas Instruments Management," p. 11.

[12]Speeches by Mr. Dove of TI at the London School of Business Studies, May 22, 1970, and Patrick E. Haggerty, "Three Lectures at the Salzburg Seminar on Multinational Enterprise," (Texas Instruments Inc., February 1977) were used extensively in the preparation of this section.

Exhibit 1

Organizational structure

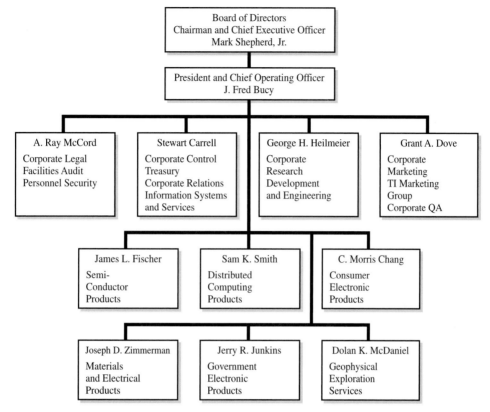

Source: L. M. Rice, Jr., "Texas Instruments Management Philosophies and Growth Experience," remarks to Instituto Panamericano de Alta Direccion de Empresa, Mexico, Texas Instruments Inc., May 1980, p. 2.

expectations of society. It claims to define the financial goals desired by the company in the context of its responsibilities to shareholders, employees, and society as a whole.

At the next level in the hierarchy are business objectives which describe long-range opportunities in different business areas. Each business objective expresses: (1) the goal of the individual business; (2) the boundaries of that business; (3) an appraisal of potential opportunities; (4) a study of the technical and market trends relating to that business; and, (5) an overview of the industry structure and foreseeable trends within the industry.

Performance measures are also established at the business objective level which include such indicators as sales goals, expected profits, return on assets, and market penetration in terms of percentage of served available market. Business objectives relate to 5- and 10-year periods extending into the future. Expectations for the first two years are broken down into quarters, the others remain in annual terms.

Each business objective is reviewed at least once a year in order to adjust the objective for successes or failures of TI or competitors and for changes in the economic environment. Business objectives are also adjusted if they are perceived

EXHIBIT 2

A hierarchy of goals

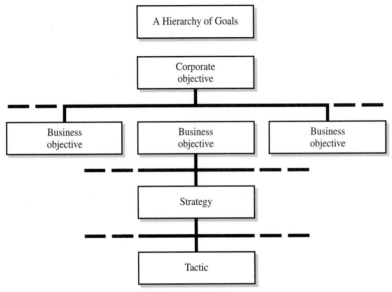

Source: E. W. Helms, "Texas Instruments Objectives, Strategies and Tactics System,"
remarks to Instituto Panamericano de Alta Direccion de Empresa, Mexico, Texas
Instruments, Inc., May 1980, p. 3.

as being not ambitious enough. Mr. Dove expressed this in the following manner.

> We expect the objective to be challenging enough, even shocking enough to force a radical rethinking of the strategies and tactics. For example, any time we have enough well-defined strategies to give us a high confidence level in exceeding the goals stated in a business objective, then that business objective probably is not ambitious enough, and the probability of truly innovative strategic thinking is likely to be low.[13]

The third level in the hierarchy is composed of strategies which support the business objectives. The strategies focus on the economic and opportunity environment and ask one question—what action is necessary in order to ensure the success of the firm's objectives? The process of formulating strategies involves a competitive analysis, a thorough study of market opportunity in order to estimate the potential for market growth, contingency planning for unforeseen events, and an overall review of company resources in order to determine whether the skills, business techniques, and current markets of the firm are sufficient to support the strategy and ensure its success. If not, the innovations and commitments required to do so must be determined.

Major, long-run financial checkpoints are established at the strategy level to help determine if the company is progressing on schedule. The lifetime of a strategy statement extends several years into the future, usually 5 to 10 years.

Tactical Action Programs (TAPs) are found at the bottom level of the hierarchy. Several TAPs support each strategy, and each TAP is under the direction of a program manager. A TAP usually has a relatively short lifetime, from 6 to 18 months.

The TAP document is a detailed description of the quantitative goals set by the program and

---

[13]Grant A. Dove, speech presented at the London School of Business Studies, May 22, 1970.

Exhibit 3

The hierarchy of goals within the OST structure

OST Structure

```
          ┌─────────────────────────┐
          │   Corporate objective   │
          └─────────────────────────┘
          Policy            Goals
          ┌─────────────────────────┐
          │   Business objective    │
          └─────────────────────────┘
     Charter    Opportunity    Goals
          ┌─────────────────────────┐
          │        Strategy         │
          └─────────────────────────┘
       Milestones   Innovations required
          ┌─────────────────────────┐
          │        Tactics          │
          └─────────────────────────┘
```

Action plans   Specific responsibility   Resource allocation

Source: E. W. Helms, "Texas Instruments Objectives, Strategies and Tactics System," remarks to Instituto Panamericano de Alta Direccion de Empresa, Mexico, Texas Instruments, Inc., May 1980, p. 3.

the resources necessary in terms of manpower and capital. It also delineates responsibility for different parts of the program and establishes a schedule of completion dates to which managers are committed. Overall, a TAP defines the contribution of the program to the strategy.

The level of detail becomes increasingly complex as one moves down the hierarchy. The TAP, which lies at the bottom of the hierarchy, is composed of individual work packages which serve as a base for planning and resource allocation within the OST System.

As of 1980, TI had 9 business objectives, over 60 strategies, and more than 250 TAPs.[14]

Dual Responsibility of Management.   The purpose of the OST System was to provide a method whereby long-range, strategic goals could become the prime motivator of the company, while still allowing the company to deal

[14]E. W. Helms, "Texas Instruments Objectives Strategies and Tactics System," remarks to Instituto Panamericano de Alta Direccion de Empresa, Mexico, Texas Instruments, May 1980, p. 6.

effectively with day-to-day operations. TI's attempt to combine this long-run and short-run orientation is reflected by their method of superimposing the OST System onto the traditional corporate structure. (See Exhibit 4.)

This gives management a responsibility for both a "strategic" and an "operating" mode. In this manner, a manager of a PCC may also have responsibility for a TAP; a division manager may also be a strategy manager; and a group manager may also be in charge of managing the progress of a business objective.

About 75 percent of the managers at TI are responsible for both a strategic mode and an operating mode.[15] TI feels that this gives balance to long-term growth and short-term profitability which often are in conflict. (See Exhibit 5.)

TI's apparent philosophy is that by assigning dual responsibility to managers they will force these managers to apportion their time in such a manner so as not to overlook the long-term innovative needs of the firm. These managers will be "wearing two hats," with goals of both growth and profitability.

In the operating mode, a manager is first concerned with the current operating results within the unit. In other words, the manager is primarily concerned with short-term profitability. Performance is measured according to planned operating profits. In the strategic mode, the manager is concerned with the success of his or her specific strategy. This specific strategy, in turn, is a part of the long-range plan set forth under the OST System. As such, the manager will be measured according to the speed and effectiveness of the utilization of the OST budgeted expenses.

One of the responsibilities of a strategy manager is the identification of the different TAPs necessary for the achievement of the strategy. The manager must pull together from across the company the TAPs necessary in the structuring

[15]Dove, speech at London School of Business Studies.

EXHIBIT 4

Dual responsibility of management

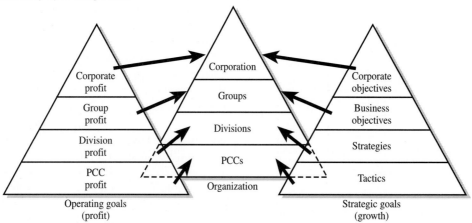

Source: E. W. Helms, "Texas Instruments Objectives, Strategies and Tactics System," remarks to Instituto Panamericano de Alta Direccion de Empresa, Mexico, Texas Instruments, Inc., May 1980, p. 7.

EXHIBIT 5

Conflict between strategic and operating mode

Strategic mode	Operating mode
Long range oriented	Short range oriented
Stable	Flexible
Aligned with corporate objectives	Aligned with operating necessities
Responsible for progress on strategic activities	Responsible for operating profit
Articulates growth viewpoint	Articulates profit viewpoint

←— Conflict —→

Competition for critical resources
Marketing pricing policies
Distribution of operating/strategic cost

Source: E. W. Helms, "Texas Instruments Objectives, Strategies and Tactics System," remarks to Instituto Panamericano de Alta Direccion de Empresa, Mexico, Texas Instruments, Inc., May 1980, p. 10.

of a coordinated strategic plan. In such a case, the "strategic" responsibility of the manager may exceed his or her "operating" authority. The manager may well be required to gain the cooperation of other operating units in order to fully execute the strategic role.

Exhibit 6

Matrix composed of the operating and strategic mode

			OPERATING MODE						
			GROUP 1					GROUP 2	
			Division A			Division B		Division C	
O B J	S T R A T	T A P	PCC 1	PCC 2	PCC 3	PCC 4	PCC 5	PCC 6	PCC 7
STRATEGIC MODE 1	A	1			X				
		2					X		
		3						X	
		4		X					
	B	5					X		
		6				X			
		7	X						
2	C	8	X						
		9							X

Source: E. W. Helms, "Texas Instruments Objectives, Strategies and Tactics System," remarks to Instituto Panamericano de Alta Direccion de Empresa, Mexico, Texas Instruments, Inc., May 1980, p. 7.

Impact of Dual Mode Structure. An easy way to visualize the functioning of this dual system is by comparison to a matrix organization. A traditional matrix organization is arranged so that the project organization overlaps the functional operating structure. Any one project may involve one task in a single operating unit or require the completion of many tasks which cut across several different operating units. The system at TI differs in that the overlap shows the relationship between the strategic and the operating mode. (See Exhibit 6.)

Any one strategy may require TAPs to be completed across several PCCs but within one division and one group, or it may require resources from across several divisions, groups, and the corresponding PCCs. For example, Strategy A requires four TAPs. TAP 1 is to be completed in Group One, Division A, and PCC 3. TAP 3 will find the necessary resources in Group 2, Division C, and PCC 6. The other two TAPs will be channeled to the appropriate operating unit in the same manner. In this way, a strategic program can be implemented without creating a new organizational structure. This is done by identifying the resources necessary for the completion of the strategy and locating the appropriate TAPs in those PCCs that can supply the necessary resources and skills.

Resource Allocation System

The distinction between the operating and strategic mode was also apparent in the resource allocation system at TI. Funding for each of the two functions responded to the profitability of the firm but was in large part a top-level decision concerning the desired tradeoff between long-term and short-term goals. The result of this

Exhibit 7

Planning cycle

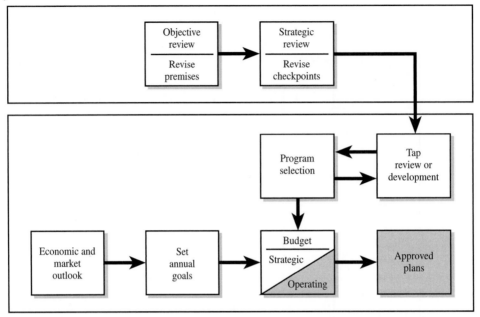

Source: E. W. Helms, "Texas Instruments Objectives, Strategies and Tactics System," remarks to Instituto Panamericano de Alta Direccion de Empresa, Mexico, Texas Instruments, Inc., May 1980, p. 13.

distinction was the preparation of two budgets— one for operating expenses and the other for OST funds. In addition, the internal operating statements showed operating and strategic expense as two separate line items.

Planning Cycle.   In the third quarter of the year, a corporate development committee reached a decision on the amount of OST funding necessary for the forthcoming year. (See Exhibit 7.)

This decision was based on an analysis of the economic and market outlook which was translated into annual goals. Funds assigned to the strategic mode were allocated by a method called "decision package ranking." Funds assigned to the operating mode were distributed according to a technique called zero-based budgeting.

Strategic Funds.   The OST funds were allocated among the business objectives using each

objective's long-term opportunities, momentum, and priorities as decision criteria. TI felt that the continual review of objectives, strategies, and tactics kept the OST System up-to-date as a strategic map of the firm's long-term goals and expectations.

Decision package ranking involved several steps. Tactics, as did objectives and strategies, had to be adjusted for any environmental change or directional change in the company's long-term focus. New TAPs had to be generated to fill in any gaps that may have been discovered leading to the desired long-term goals. These TAPs then were ordered into decision packages. "A decision package is so called because it contains all the resources necessary to implement the innovation.[16] The strategy manager then

---

[16]Haggerty, "Three Lectures," p. 33.

EXHIBIT 8

Decision package ranking

```
┌──────────────────────────────────────────────────┐
│            DECISION PACKAGE RANKING                │
│                                                    │
│   RANK    PROGRAM    COST                          │
│    1         A       $XXX     CUMULATIVE           │
│                               COST CUTOFF          │
│    2         Q        XXX     AT DISCRETIONARY      │
│    3         K        XXX     FUNDING LEVEL         │
│    •                   •                            │
│    •                   •                            │
│    ▼        etc.       ▼                            │
│  ─────────────────────────────────────────         │
│   447        X       $XXX   ┐                      │
│                             │  CREATIVE             │
│   448        Y        XXX   │                       │
│                             │  BACKLOG              │
│   449        Z        XXX   ┘                       │
│              etc.                                  │
└──────────────────────────────────────────────────┘
```

Source: Patrick E. Haggerty, "Three Lectures at the Salzburg
Seminar on Multinational Enterprise," Texas Instruments Inc.,
February 1977, p. 34.

rank ordered these packages by importance. A cut off line was drawn based on the amount of funds made available to the business objectives and individual strategies. Those packages falling above the line received funding while those falling below were put into a "creative backlog." (See Exhibit 8.)

The creative backlog was composed of decision packages which could be funded when additional funds became available or through a direct decision package funding from the corporate level. A small percentage of the OST funds (once cited as being 10 percent) were retained at the corporate level for this purpose and for new opportunities which might arise over time.

The entire procedure was repeated at the objective level in order to adjust the allocation of funds among the objective's strategies. In the same manner as with tactical decision packages, the managers responsible for strategic decision packages had the opportunity to request another review in order to receive special funding in one case that they fell below one cutoff line and were of special potential. TI felt that this allowed them to undertake new ventures which could normally not have been considered.

Operating Funds.   Funds allocated to the operating budget were distributed among projects and departments by means of a technique called zero-based budgeting (ZBB). A company using ZBB requires of each division or section an annual report which justifies their budgeting requirements for the year. ZBB can be compared to the traditional budgeting approach, which is incremental in nature. The traditional approach seeks to identify planned changes from the previous year's expenditure level and then simply adds the additional funds necessary to the previous year's budget. In contrast, managers using ZBB must start from scratch each year in identifying the funds necessary for the smooth operation of the business unit and then must justify this need. TI believed that, while the process required a great deal of effort to implement, it fulfilled the purpose of an increased managerial involvement in the budgeting process. They also felt that it gave visibility to the use and need of

Exhibit 9

Four-loop planning system

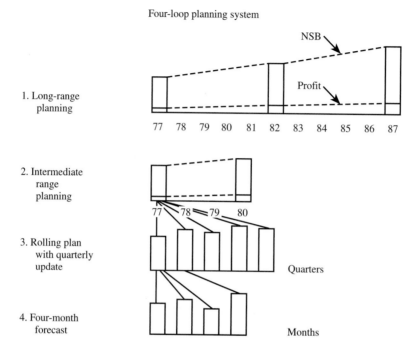

Four-loop planning system

Source: L. M. Rice, Jr., "Texas Instruments Management Philosophies and Growth Experience," remarks to Instituto Panamericano de Alta Direccion de Empresa, Mexico, Texas Instruments Inc., May 1980, p. 13.

funds in an operating unit and, therefore, resulted in an increased efficiency in the resource allocation process.

Timing of Planning Cycle.   TI followed what they called a "four-loop planning system" in order to explain the time base of the planning cycle and for organizing activities within the corporation. (See Exhibit 9.)[17] Mr. L. M. Rice, group vice president at TI, offered an explanation of this system:

The first loop is *long-range planning.* Its focal point is our annual Strategic Planning Conference, where we concentrate on where we are going over the next 10 years. In addi-

tion to setting measurable quantitative goals, this planning emphasizes projections of markets and products and the technology advances required to impact those areas.

The second loop is *intermediate-range planning.* In planning facilities, manufacturing equipment, products, and cost reduction, one year is too short, and 10 years is too long. The intermediate loop fills the gap by concentrating on the current year plus three years ahead. Authorizations for new products, personnel additions, and capital expenditures are based on the intermediate-loop plan. In this second loop, the current year plus one is critical because it ties strategic, intermediate, and rolling planning together.

The third loop is the *"rolling plan,"* a quarterly update of the current year and the coming year. Rolling plans are our prime mechanism for operating in near real time, with quick response to changing business conditions.

The fourth loop is the *four-month forecast* cycle. This is a monthly operational planning effort that originates at the profit center level and consolidates to the corporate

[17]Rice, "Texas Instruments Management," p. 13.

EXHIBIT 10

Separation of strategic and operating expenses on the profit and loss statement

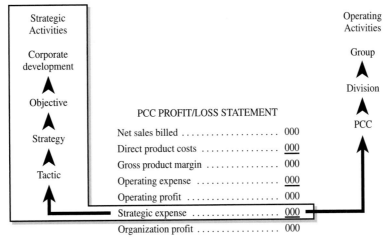

Source: Patrick E. Haggerty, "Three Lectures at the Salzburg Seminar on Multinational Enterprise," Texas Instruments Inc., February 1977, p. 33.

level. It constitutes TI's real-time error detection and control mechanism for near-term profitability.

For each of these loops, financial models and plans are used to forecast and measure performance. The models and plans are supported by computerized management systems to handle the data in as close to real time as possible. With these computerized systems, both the immediate and long-term impact of changes may be quickly evaluated and actions taken as required.[18]

The Reporting System

The Reporting System at TI separated operating expenses from strategic expenses on the income statement as illustrated in Exhibit 10.

Managers assumed responsibility for these differing expenses depending on their role in the organization, that is on whether they were strategy managers, operating managers (e.g., PCC manager), or both.

Progress was reviewed at successively higher levels in the organization in both modes. Accountability passed from the TAP to strategy to objective level in the strategic mode and from the

PCC to division to group level in the operating mode. Monthly status reports of each TAP were distributed at all levels of the OST System, which allowed for a quick appraisal of a TAP's progress relative to several criteria (i.e., budget, scheduling, personnel, facilities).

Managers increasingly tended to assume both responsibilities as they moved up in the organization. It should also be noted that, in contrast to the operating expense, it was most often considered desirable to have spent the full amount of the budgeted strategic expense. To TI, this indicated expenditures in terms of innovative programs.

A difficulty in implementing such a system arose in one definition of what constituted an OST expense. TI attempted to resolve this problem by asking group managers to list those expenses which they viewed as "discretionary." Although the group managers were not in general agreement concerning the matter, TI felt that the approach was valid as long as there was some general consistency in terms of the definition used.

---

[18]Ibid.

Incentive Compensation System

The two formal aspects of the overall incentive compensation system at TI were (1) the Key Personnel Analysis (KPA) system and (2) a stock-option plan.

KPA.[19]   The KPA System, by means of an annual comparative assessment of individual TIers, seeks to identify those managers who have, by their performance, contributed most to the company. The process of identifying those individuals begins at the bottom level of management with the immediate supervisor. Individuals at this level are rank-ordered on the basis of their relative contribution to the firm. The ranks are then combined across the department.

This procedure is repeated at successive levels of the organization until the department level is reached. At this point, the department manager identifies those people whom he judges as having made equal contributions to the firm regardless of their specific function and job level. These "equal" people are called "benchmark" people. The purpose of benchmarking is to allow the various sets of rankings to be merged into a single departmental ranking. From here, each individual is categorized into one of five comparative rating groups. Those in the top 20 percent group are then paired-compared in order to produce a new rank-ordering. These "benchmarking" and "pair-compare" procedures are then repeated at the division and group levels.

Bonuses are awarded to individual TIers in response to their contribution to the firm as reflected by the rankings. Up to 20 percent of the employees receive a bonus in addition to the regular adjustment to their base salary. Even though the majority of bonuses are given to managers at the upper management levels, the KPA System forces an examination of all levels.

------

[19]This section is paraphrased from a speech given by Mr. Dove at the London School of Business Studies, May 22, 1970.

Stock-Option Plan.   TI's second form of incentive compensation is its stock-option plan. Participants in the plan are required to remain with the firm a certain number of years in order to be eligible. The award of a certain number of shares of the firm's stock is further tied to the attainment of a target EPS figure per year.

Several other programs have been installed in an attempt to increase productivity at all levels in the organization.

IDEA.   TI attempts to recognize the fact that good ideas often come from those employees directly engaged in the production of its products. A program dubbed "IDEA" has been introduced in an attempt to draw out as many innovative ideas as possible. Grants up to $25,000[20] are distributed to employees with promising ideas involving a product or process improvement. A well-known result of this program is TI's "Speak and Spell," a talking, learning device for teaching spelling.

Executive Retirement.   Executives at TI are urged to retire at an early age, 55 years. The purpose of this policy is the assurance of competent management succession. The retired officers have the opportunity to use their skill and expertise in an advisory role, that of "Officer of the Board." The early retirement allows younger management more upward mobility, in that top positions are vacated earlier.

Operating Committee.   The Operating Committee dealt with operational as well as strategic issues and defined the OST budget for the forthcoming year. Two corporate-level committees allocated the OST funds. The two committees were: (1) the Corporate Development Committee and (2) the People and Asset Effectiveness Committee. (See Exhibit 11.)

The Corporate Development Committee was responsible for external business analysis and

------

[20]"Texas Instruments Shows U.S. Business," p. 82.

EXHIBIT 11

Corporate committees

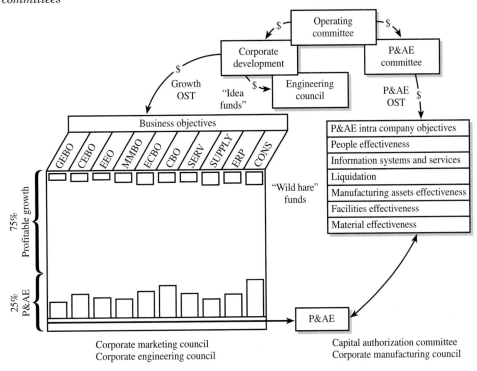

Source: Charles H. Phipps, "The OST System," Texas Instruments Inc., 1979, p. 14.

the initiation of new ventures which lay outside the current scope of business. In addition, it was in charge of a continual review of strategic activities.

The People and Asset Effectiveness Committee was responsible for reviewing potential productivity improvements of the firm based on leveraging the effective utilization of the firm's people and assets. On the "people effectiveness" side, TI had policies, such as educational and training programs, promotion from within, electronic aids for the office, reward based on merit and the posting of new job openings, the purpose of which was to motivate and involve the employees to give their utmost to the firm. Progress in this latter area was measured with an index of "net sales billed/payroll plus bene-

fits." TI believed this program to be a success, and TI management had been quoted as saying:

It is a whole bunch of things acting synergistically. It's the attitudes, team improvement programs, the campus involvement, the open-door management policy, the nonstructural pecking order. It's the unified goal approach—with everyone looking at his own piece of that goal. . . . the key is flexibility. Two things people want in life. They want to achieve, and they want to be loved. And if you provide an atmosphere where these things can occur with a minimum amount of structure in the work flow, you are going to get what you want.[21]

TI believed in the intensive use of assets and remaining at the forefront of asset productivity

---

[21]"How Texas Instruments Turns Its People On," *Business Week*, September 29, 1973, p. 88.

by an aggressive asset renewal cycle. "Asset Effectiveness" was the second aspect of the People and Asset Effectiveness Program. Progress in this area was measured by means of a ratio of "net income (after tax)/average assets."[22]

Conclusion

Mr. Elmer had already called a meeting of his immediate subordinates, those who had been involved in the review of the TI material, for later in that same week in order to reach some resolution as to whether HHE should adopt a similar system. A decision would involve completing their analysis of the OST System and assessing how well the system worked at TI. In addition, an analysis of industry characteristics and/or corporate objectives and policies which would be conducive to the success of such a system would be an important consideration in reaching a decision.

---

[22]Rice, "Texas Instruments Management," p. 14.

Questions

1. Summarize the major features of Texas Instruments' management systems. To what extent, and how, are these systems mutually reinforcing?

2. How does Texas Instruments ensure that its operating managers appropriately allocate their time between short term and long term?

3. Why do you believe the OST System worked so effectively for TI in the '70s? Why is it not working effectively for the company in the mid-to-late '80s?

4. Would systems like these be appropriate in other organizations, such as Harvey-Hudson Electronics? What implementation problems would you foresee?

14

MODERN
CONTROL METHODS

Beginning in the early 1980s, management literature reported significant new developments in management control techniques. (Their actual use in leading companies probably began somewhat earlier.) In part these were consequences of the development of vastly increased computer power. In part they were a reaction in the United States to the realization that many companies in Japan, Germany, Sweden, and other countries were manufacturing products with higher quality and at lower cost than their American counterparts. A flood of books and articles have described the practices in these countries and the consequent changes in American manufacturing environment. U.S. companies that had access to companies in these other countries studied their practices and adopted their manufacturing methods as *benchmarks* that they sought to match. Some of these practices and their implications for management control are described in this chapter.

Just-In-Time (JIT)

In certain industries application of what is called the "just-in-time" (JIT) approach has resulted in significant decreases in setup or procurement costs, and in the recognition that carrying costs per unit are often understated. These developments result in a decrease in the optimum lot size. At the extreme the optimum lot size is one—that is, there is zero inventory, and goods are produced or ordered only when they are needed. Hence the name, *just-in-time*. This extreme case is not common, but the term is a catchy way of stating the direction in which lot size should be headed.

> **Example.** The JIT philosophy is also applicable in nonprofit organizations, as is evidenced by its adoption by the Department of Defense. The DOD has realized impressive gains by adopting JIT—inventories (in 1995 dollars) were reduced from $104 billion in 1990 to $76 billion by 1994.[1]

---

[1]Stan Crock, "The Pentagon Goes to B-School," *Business Week*, December 11, 1995, pp. 98–100.

Cycle Time Analysis

A tool in the analysis of inventory requirements is the equation for *cycle time*:

Cycle time = Processing time + Storage time + Movement time + Inspection time

Only the first element, processing time, adds value to the product. The other three elements do nothing to make the product more valuable. The analysis, therefore, attempts to identify all activities that do not directly add value to the product and to eliminate, or reduce the cost of, these activities. For example, the transportation of in-process work from one workstation to another does not add value, so an effort is made to rearrange the location of workstations to minimize transportation costs.

Just-in-Time Techniques

Reduce Buffer Inventory.   Buffer inventory exists partly because manufacturing workstations break down and partly because they produce defective products. When these events happen, production in following workstations ceases unless there is an inventory on which they can draw—a buffer inventory. Indeed, it is said that the existence of buffer inventory causes workstations to be less concerned about producing good products than they should be. The amount of buffer inventory can be reduced if steps are taken to minimize machine breakdown and improve product quality. The purpose of just-in-time is to ensure that every workstation produces and delivers to the next workstation the right items in the right quantity at the right time; if this purpose were achieved, there would be no need for buffer inventory.

> **Example.** The large amount of assets tied up in buffer inventories was a problem for John Deere. During periods of high demand, John Deere dealers used to buy eight to ten months worth of inventory. When demand decreased, the John Deere dealers sold their equipment at deep discounts. To combat this, John Deere had introduced new controls to help dealers keep no more than four months worth of inventory. As a result, Deere inventories as a percent of cost of goods sold declined from 17 percent in 1988 to 10 percent in 1995. Not only did this free up considerable assets, but it also left John Deere and its dealers with more flexibility for dealing with changes in the business cycle.[2]

Buffer inventory also results from bottlenecks. The "throughput" on a production process is no greater than the output of the slowest workstation. If the output of one workstation slows down, inventory tends to build up in earlier workstations unless steps are taken to stop their work temporarily, which is often expensive because it wastes labor hours. This problem can be mitigated by balancing the output of the several workstations, thus eliminating bottlenecks, and by taking immediate action to stop production when a breakdown or

---

[2]Peter Elstrom, "Heavy equipment gets into gear," *Business Week*, August 5, 1996, p. 29.

other factors cause a bottleneck. Some companies install lights above each workstation that are lit when a worker cannot keep up the pace without making errors or when quality problems are detected.

Decrease Set-up Costs.   With numerically controlled machine tools, setup involves simply inserting a new computer program into a machine. Thus, after the computer program has been created, the cost of setting up for all succeeding lots becomes trivial. The existence of a computer program to control manufacturing machines decreases the cost of providing replacement parts for discontinued models of appliances, automobiles, aircraft, and various other types of machines. For expensive parts with low replacement demand (which are found on ships, aircraft, heavy construction equipment, and weapons), some manufacturers now carry no replacement inventory at all.

With smaller lot sizes, the scrap and rework costs resulting from a defect in a single production run is minimized. With lower inventory, storage space is decreased, permitting plant space to be utilized more efficiently, or obviating the need for plant expansion.

Decrease Procurement Costs.   Traditionally, procurement involved issuing requests for bids from many vendors, analyzing bids, placing an order with the best (usually, the cheapest) vendor, and receiving and inspecting the incoming goods. Some companies now reduce the cost of each of these components by establishing relationships with one to two vendors for each item. Instead of requesting bids for each order, they place orders with no more than notification of how many items are needed on a certain date (or, in some cases, on a certain hour each day). Instead of inspecting the incoming goods, they expect the vendor to inspect them and assure that all items are of acceptable quality. These orders are often transmitted electronically between the vendor and the manufacturer.

Relation with Customers.   The other side of this coin is the practice of establishing relationships with customers for automatic ordering. Some manufacturers have systems in which their salespersons automatically place orders from retailers or other customers on the basis of preset formulas that determine reorder times and quantities; this reduces the customers' ordering costs and also cements a relationship between the customers and the manufacturer. Others provide retailers with bar-coded shelf slips for each item; the route salesperson uses a hand-held scanner to identify the item and enters an order when the supply falls below a preset level. Hospital supply houses provide computer programs to hospitals that permit them to place orders without human intervention. These systems also provide rapid, accurate information to managers.

> **Example.** Using hand-held scanners, 10,000 Frito-Lay salespeople collect information on 100 Frito products in 400,000 stores, and summaries appear on PC computer screens available to all executives in easy-to-read charts. Not only is the information provided more rapidly but also the scanner eliminates a day of paperwork from each salesperson's weekly schedule, according to Michael H. Jordan, president of Frito's

parent. He reported, "Two years ago if I asked how we did in Kansas City on July 4th weekend, I'd get five partial responses three weeks late. Now I get it the next day."[3]

Implications for Management Control

With some just-in-time systems, work-in-process inventory becomes so insignificant that it is disregarded. The only inventories are for raw materials and finished goods; issuances from raw materials inventory are charged directly to finished goods inventory. In effect, a job-cost system is transformed into a process-cost system with only one cost center; this results in a considerable reduction in recordkeeping. Recordkeeping is further reduced by the elimination of the tedious task of calculating "equivalent production," which is necessary to find work-in-process inventory amounts when the inventory in a cost center consists of partially completed products. Products are carried in inventory at standard costs, without tracing actual costs to individual products or batches of a product.

A just-in-time system focuses management attention on *time* in addition to the traditional focus on *cost*. A reduction in cycle time can lead to a reduction in cost. One of the effective ways to monitor progress on just-in-time is to compute the following ratio:

$$\frac{\text{Process time}}{\text{Cycle time}}$$

Ideally, the goal for this ratio should be equal to 1. However, this goal cannot be achieved overnight. The just-in-time system is not a turnkey installation; rather, it is an evolutionary system that seeks to improve the manufacturing process continually. The firm can establish targets for this ratio, monitoring progress against the targets. Best results can be obtained by emphasizing continuous improvements in this ratio toward the ideal number of 1.[4]

Total Quality Management

The Japanese have led the way in greater attention to product quality. Efforts that they initiated and that have been adopted by many American companies are usually described under the rubric *total quality management*.

Consequences of Poor Quality

Product quality can mean either of two things: design quality or conformance quality. *Design quality refers to the inherent value to the customer;* Rolex watches have a higher design quality than Timex watches. *Conformance quality refers to adherence to specifications;* if a product meets specifications, it is a quality product. *Nonconformance means poor quality;* it is measured by the

---

[3]*Business Week*, July 2, 1990, p. 55.

[4]Kaplan, Robert S., and Anthony A. Atkinson, *Advanced Management Accounting*, (Englewood Cliffs, NJ: Prentice Hall, 1989), p. 421.

proportion of defective products. The discussion here is limited to conformance quality.

According to total quality advocates, "zero defects" and "doing it right the first time" should be the firm's quality goals, because anything short of that will result in cost penalties. The earlier a defect is detected, the lower the cost penalty.

> **Example.** Richard W. Anderson, general manager of the Computer Systems Division of Hewlett-Packard, illustrates the damage a 2-cent resistor can do: "If you catch the resistor before it is used and throw it away, you lose 2 cents. If you don't find it until it has been soldered into a computer component, it may cost $10 to repair the part. If you don't catch the component until it is in a computer user's hands, the repair will cost hundreds of dollars. Indeed, if a $5,000 computer has to be repaired in the field, the expenses may exceed the manufacturing costs."[5]

In addition to these measurable quality costs, a defective product hurts the company's reputation significantly.

Total Quality Management Approach

The total quality management approach is summarized below under three headings: responsibility for quality, product design, and relation with suppliers.

Responsibility for Quality.   The traditional view was that quality problems start on the factory floor, that workers were primarily responsible for poor quality, and that the best way to control quality, therefore, was to "inspect quality into the final product." This required a large quality control department. It also set up an adversarial relationship between manufacturing personnel, whose traditional objective was to maximize output, and the quality control staff.

The total quality control view is that responsibility for quality should be shared by everyone in the organization; in fact, most of the quality problems arise before the product even reaches the factory floor. Edward Deming, after whom Japan's Deming Prize for quality is named, states that the production process can be separated into two parts: (1) the system, which is under the control of management; and (2) the workers, who are under their own control. He found that 85 percent of quality problems can be attributed to faulty systems and only 15 percent to the workers.[6]

The system could be faulty for several reasons: designing a product that is difficult to manufacture, procuring inferior raw materials, providing inadequate equipment maintenance, permitting poor working conditions, and applying excessive pressure to maximize output. Since the system is designed by management, quality is primarily a management responsibility, he wrote.

---

[5]Quoted in Jeremy Main, "The Battle for Quality Begins," *Fortune*, December 29, 1990, pp. 28–33.

[6]E. W. Deming, *Quality Productivity, and Competitive Position* (Cambridge, Mass.: MIT Center for Advanced Engineering Study, 1982).

Under total quality management, the philosophy is to "*build* quality into the product," rather than "*inspect* quality of the product." Errors in design, raw material procurement, and so on should be detected at the source. Workers should be held responsible for their own work and should not pass a defective unit on to the next work station; thus, the workers are their own inspectors. Instead of inspecting product quality at the end of production, the quality control staff should monitor the production process and enable workers to "make the product right the first time."

Product Design.   Studies have shown that many quality problems originate with the design of the product. Some designers pay inadequate attention to the "manufacturability" of the product. Others include parts that are unique to the product, whereas parts that are common to several products would be satisfactory and are available at lower cost; or they design more separate parts than are necessary, which gives inadequate recognition to the cost involved in setting up machines for each part. Under total quality control, there has been an effort to have the designers work closely with production engineers who are familiar with the manufacturing problems.

Designing for manufacturability is one aspect of design. The other aspect of design is designing for marketability—that is, the quality of a product should be what the customer wants, not more. Some designers tend to "gold plate" an item—that is, they include features or specifications that do not lead to additional sales in the marketplace. This suggests the need for close cooperation between designers and marketing people.

Relation with Suppliers.   Total quality management involves a change in the traditional relationship with suppliers, as mentioned in the preceding section. Instead of awarding contracts to several suppliers, based primarily on which one bid the lowest price, there are only one or two suppliers for a given item; they are selected on the basis of quality and on-time delivery as well as on price, and long-term relationships are established with them. For example, the average General Motors Corporation assembly plant had 425 suppliers in 1989, compared with 800 in 1986.[7]

Implications for Management Control

Companies collect nonfinancial information about quality, including the number of defective units delivered by each supplier, number and frequency of late deliveries, number of parts in a product, percentage of common versus unique parts in a product, percentage yields, first-pass yields (i.e., percentage of units furnished without rework), scrap, rework, machine breakdowns, number and frequency of times that production and delivery schedules were not met, number of employee suggestions, number of customer complaints, level of customer

---

[7]General Motors 1989 Annual Report, p. 16.

satisfaction (obtained by questionnaire surveys), warranty claims, field service expenses, number and frequency of product returns, and so on.

There are two major advantages with these nonfinancial measures: (1) most of them can be reported almost on a daily basis, and (2) corrective actions can be taken almost immediately. Thus, reporting performance on nonfinancial measures is essential to provide continuous feedback to managers and workers in their pursuit for better quality.

> **Example.** Don Davis, Jr., president of Allen-Bradley Company, wrote, "At Allen-Bradley's Control-Communication Group, we produce solid state devices, such as industrial computers. Their integrity depends on printed circuit boards. We developed a quality-information system (QIS) that automates and organizes quality information. It's an on-line, real-time data collection and measuring system. It's also a huge data base of component, process, and workmanship information, which is generated by incoming inspection, on-line testing, and field repair centers. QIS can tell us which component from which vendor was placed on which board in which location. QIS helps identify problems, redesign the product, and beat down the reject rates on a part-by-part, component-by-component basis. It also helps us select vendors more carefully and choose them on the basis of the best quality instead of the best price."[8]

Computer Integrated Manufacturing (CIM)

In petroleum refineries, chemical processing and similar processing plants, materials and energy enter at the beginning and at various stages of the process, and finished products emerge at the end, all without any hands-on labor and using computer integrated manufacturing (CIM). Human beings maintain the equipment, check the quality of the process, shut it down if it gets out of control, and bring it back into control; that is all. Recent developments have led to production control systems in other industries that are close to those found in process manufacturing. These developments include numerically controlled machine tools, robots, and computers that integrate the work of other computers. These have resulted in decreases in the amount of hands-on labor, improvements in quality, reductions in paperwork, elimination of duplicate recordkeeping, the annoying inconsistencies of data among the formerly separate systems, decreases in inventory, decreases in throughput time, and consequent decreases in production costs.

Complicated, expensive computer systems are now used to link together various stages of production. These go by such names (and acronyms) as Manufacturing Resource Planning II (MRP II),[9] synchronous manufacturing, Flexible Manufacturing System (FMS), Manufacturing Accounting and Production Information Control System (MAPICS II), Manufacturing Resource Planning

---

[8]Don Davis, "Zero-Defects: Cornerstone for Computer Implementation," Working Paper Series 90-3-3, Krannert School of Management, Purdue University, West Lafayette, Indiana, March 1990.

[9]The "II" is used because this system has superseded an earlier system with the same initials; that system was called MRP I.

and Execution System (MRPX), and Computer-Aided Manufacturing-International (CAMI). These systems have the common characteristics that they incorporate into a single system, all, or at least several, of the formerly separate systems for product design, order processing, accounts receivable, payroll, accounts payable, inventory control, bills of materials, capacity planning, product scheduling, and product cost accounting. A computer integrated manufacturing system has some or all of the following components:

- *Computer-aided design* (CAD): use of computers to design new products, replacing the drafting that was traditionally done by hand, and improving the quality of the design effort. The completed designs are converted automatically to detailed instructions for the robots and the computers that control machine tools.
- *Computer-aided manufacturing* (CAM): use of computers to control machine tools and the flow of materials.
- *Numerically controlled machines*: machine tools that are programmed to perform a variety of functions (bore, drill, turn, and the like) on parts with different sizes and shapes.
- *Robots* (Also called "steel-collar workers"): programmable machines with "arms" and "legs" (and, in a few cases, "eyes") that perform a variety of repetitive tasks, such as welding, assembly, and painting.
- *Automated material handling systems*: storage and retrieval systems that locate materials, pick them, and move them from storage bins to the factory floor for processing and to shipping docks for delivery to customers. Also, automated guided vehicles that move materials automatically from one work station to the next.
- *Flexible manufacturing systems*: computer-controlled work stations. Often, the machines used for producing one product or product line are grouped together in a single location, or "cell."[10] They record financial and cost accounting transactions, and they also incorporate the following types of transactions, which were previously handled separately:[11]

1. *Logistical*: order, execute, and confirm material movements.
2. *Balancing*: match supply of material, labor, and machines with demand.
3. *Quality*: validate that production is in conformance with specifications.

---

[10]The General Motors Windsor Trim Plant is divided into nine "focused factories," one for each of the plant's nine product lines. Previously the plant had been divided into four main areas: receiving, cutting, sewing, and shipping. Each focused factory has all these functions in one contiguous location. (Anthony A. Atkinson, "GM's Innovation for Performance," *CMA Magazine* [Canada], June 1990, pp. 10–13.)

[11]Jeffrey G. Miller and Thomas E. Vollman, "The Hidden Factory," *Harvard Business Review*, September-October 1985, pp. 143–46.

4. *Change*: update manufacturing information, engineering change orders, schedules, routings, standards, specifications, and bills of material.

The initial introduction of these systems has been criticized as not taking full advantage of the Japanese approach.

> **Example.** With a few exceptions, the flexible manufacturing systems (FMS) in the United States show an astonishing lack of flexibility. Compared with Japanese systems, those in U.S. plants produce an order-of-magnitude less variety of parts. Further, they cannot run untended for a whole shift, are not integrated with the rest of their factories, and are less reliable.
>
> The average number of parts made by an FMS in the United States was 10 (as reported in 1986); in Japan the average was 93, almost 10 times greater. The U.S. companies used FMS the wrong way for high-volume production of a few parts, rather than for high-variety production of many parts at a low cost per unit.[12]

Additional comparisons from the Jaikumar article are given in Exhibit 14–1.

Implications for Management Control

Increase in Task Control. Fully developed CIM systems convert certain production activities that once required management control into task control. Managers no longer supervise employees; they are required only to handle unusual situations.

Better Information. CIM systems provide information more accurately, more consistently, with more detail, and at much lower cost than previous systems. They provide better information about how costs actually behave. In fact, these systems can provide so much information that systems designers have difficulty deciding on the relatively small fraction of the information that should be reported to managers. This problem is generally solved by providing a relatively small quantity of information routinely, and permitting the manager to access a large data base for other information he or she may wish.

> **Example.** In a manufacturing plant with about 2,000 people, data processing produced 41 reports each month, with 321 copies and 140,000 pages distributed to 63 persons. Interviews with managers showed that 32 of the reports were not used. Eliminating the unnecessary reports and reducing the distribution of other reports resulted in the removal of 300 filing cabinets from the shop floor and other savings amounting to $100,000 a year.[13]

More Prompt Information. Using CIM, information is available shortly after an event occurs, and, in some cases, practically instantaneously.

---

[12]Ramchandran Jaikumar, "Postindustrial Manufacturing," *Harvard Business Review*, November-December 1986, pp. 69–76.

[13]Donald A.J. Byrum, "The Right Way to Control Period Expense," *Management Accounting*, September 1990, p. 56.

Exhibit 14–1   Performance of FMS: Comparison between American and Japanese Machine Tool Companies

	American Companies	Japanese Companies
System development time	2.5–3.0 years	1.25–1.75 years
Number of different parts made	10	93
Average volume per part	1,727	258
Number of parts produced daily	88	120
Number of new parts introduced each year	1	22
Number of systems running untended	0	18
Ratio of actual cutting time to total available	52%	84%
Average cutting time per day	8.3 hours	20.2 hours

Source: R. Jaikumar, "Postindustrial Manufacturing," *Harvard Business Review*, November-December 1986, p. 70.

Summary information is made available daily, instead of several days after the end of the month.

Work Teams.   Some of the CIM systems are built around work teams that are responsible for all the operations, or for some related operations, in the production of products. If work at a certain workstation has broken down, workers at other workstations are expected to help solve the problem. Under the traditional system, a worker's performance was judged by his or her individual output; at the extreme, pay was based on the number of pieces produced. Under the newer systems, performance is no longer based on quantity alone; quality is also important. Also, rewards tend to become group rewards, rather than individual rewards.

Decision Support Systems

We use the term *decision support systems* to apply broadly to systems that aid decision making by providing the answers to a series of "what-if" questions. In this sense they include expert systems, natural language systems, artificial intelligence systems, and knowledge-based systems, although technically there are some differences among these systems.

A decision support system incorporates decision rules that presumably show how an expert in the area would solve a problem, given a certain set of facts; these are "if-then" rules. The decision maker answers a series of questions that provide the relevant information. These questions are asked in plain English—no knowledge of computer programming is required—which is why they are called "natural language" programs. The computer then suggests a course of action. They are called decision *support* systems, because they help the *decision maker* to arrive at a decision; the *decision maker* is free to reject the computer's

---

EXHIBIT 14–2   Examples of Decision Support Rules

IF the part-group for the ordered part = 44
    AND the ordered part has been received
    AND the ordered part was ordered LESS THAN 2 weeks ago
    AND the ordered part HAS BEEN placed in inventory
THEN display on computer screen "inventory status is OK."

IF the part-group number for the ordered part = 44
    AND the ordered part has been received
    AND the ordered part was ordered MORE THAN 2 weeks ago
    AND the ordered part HAS NOT BEEN placed in inventory
THEN display on computer screen "inventory status is NOT OK.
    Call receiving room at extension 29."

IF the part-group number for the ordered part = 44
    AND the ordered part has NOT been received
    AND the ordered part was ordered MORE THAN 2 weeks ago
THEN display on computer screen "Follow up. Phone supplier."

Source: Adapted from Richard W. Kaiser, "Knowledge-Based Systems," *Journal of Accountancy*, January 1990, p. 114.

recommendation, or to modify it. This is not the case with computer programs that govern the actions of machines, that record and summarize accounting transactions, or that calculate ratios or other numbers from these summaries.

> **Example.** A certain decision support system aids the person responsible for order expediting. The system keeps track of hundreds of rules, three of which are shown in Exhibit 14–2. In this case the "part" in question is one of those that are supposed to be delivered and entered in inventory within two weeks from the date the order was placed; all such parts are classified in Group 44. A frequently updated data base provides automatic answers to the "what-if" questions. If the part was ordered more than two weeks ago and has not been added to inventory, a potential problem exists. If the part has been received but not added to inventory, the user is told to follow up with the receiving department. If the part has not been received, the user is told to follow up with the vendor.

Development of a sound set of decision rules is a time-consuming task. A moderately complicated set of rules may require the efforts of a sizable team for many months and involve interviews with experts, which takes more of their time than they are often happy to give. Conflicting opinions from individual experts must be resolved. The initial output is a prototype, which is then practice tested. This test may show that some of the rules are not sensible, and more months are then required to correct them. The effort is worthwhile only when the system will be used frequently by a number of people. Nevertheless, when a sound set of rules is established, the quality and ease of decision making can be improved, and there are usually significant savings in the time required to make decisions without reliance on a decision support system.

In the late 1980s, the basic idea of decision support systems was improved by designing systems that modify the decision rules themselves, based on experience.

> **Example.** Sears Mortgage Corporation is one of the 20 largest mortgage originators in the United States. Prior to the development of what it calls a "neural network system," the average underwriter could make a good loan decision in about 45 minutes. The system requires an input of 30 facts taken from the mortgage application. In one second the neural network then makes a decision for about 65 percent of the loan applications that are routine and refers the others to an underwriter. Underwriters then spend their time on the 35 percent of borderline applications.
>
> Initially, the rules were developed by testing 5,000 previously approved or rejected loan applications. The weight given to each of the 30 variables was modified by trial and error until the program produced results that matched those of the underwriters' decisions. Subsequently, the computer modifies the weights given to the variables according to its actual experience in applying the rules. For example, although "frequency of move" is a criterion, the initial program did not allow for the fact that military personnel moved frequently, and the program penalized their applications unfairly. The computer discovered and allowed for this factor.[14]

Implications for Management Control

Decision support systems may reduce the need for certain types of managers—that is, they may convert management control activities into task control activities. They may also permit managers to spend a larger fraction of their time on other problems.

A decision support system is a double-edged sword insofar as its users are concerned. On the one hand, it can increase the quality of decisions and reduce (or, in some cases, eliminate) the time required to make them. On the other hand, they permit many types of decisions to be made by the computer or by lower-level personnel and, thus, reduce the level of expertise required and, in some cases, eliminate jobs entirely.

Summary

Recent developments in manufacturing methods influence the management control process, and have dramatically restructured organizational activities. They include just-in-time systems, total quality control, computer integrated manufacturing, and decision support systems.

---

[14]Condensed from J. Clarke Smith, executive vice president and chief financial officer of Sears Mortgage Corporation, "A Neural Network—Could It Work for You?" *Financial Executive*, May/June 1990, pp. 26–30.

Suggested Additional Readings

Daniel, S.J., and W.D. Reitsperger. "Linking Quality Strategy with Management Control Systems: Empirical Evidence from Japanese Industry." *Accounting, Organizations, and Society*, 7, 1991, pp. 601–18.

Dean, James W., Jr., and Scott A. Snell. "The Strategic Use of Integrated Manufacturing: An Empirical Examination." *Strategic Management Journal* 17, 6, June 1996, pp. 459–80.

Deming, W. Edwards. *Quality, Productivity, and Competitive Position*. Cambridge, Mass.: MIT Center for Advanced Engineering Study, 1982.

Dixon, J.R., A.J. Nanni, and T.E. Vollmann. *The New Performance Challenge: Measuring Operations for World-Class Competition*. Homewood, Ill: Dow Jones-Irwin, 1990.

Garvin, David A. *Managing Quality: The Strategic and Competitive Edge*. New York: Free Press, 1988.

Govindarajan, Vijay, and John K. Shank. "Cost of Quality Analysis." *Journal of Cost Management*, Fall 1993, pp. 74–86.

Hitomi, Katsundo. "Manufacturing Excellence for 21st Century Production." *Technovation* 16, 1, Jan. 1996, pp. 33–41.

Hunt, V. Daniel. *Quality in America: How to Implement a Competitive Quality Program*. Homewood Ill.: Business One Irwin, 1992.

Kaplan, Robert S., and Anthony A. Atkinson. *Advanced Management Accounting*. Englewood Cliffs, NJ: Prentice Hall, 1989.

Kaplan, Robert S. "Management Accounting for Advanced Technological Environments." *Science*, 25 August 1989, pp. 819–823.

———. *Measures for Manufacturing Excellence*. Boston, Mass.: Harvard Business School, 1990.

Keating, Patrick J., and Stephen F. Jablonsky. *Changing Roles of Financial Management*. Morristown, N.J.: Financial Executives Research Foundation, 1990.

McKinnon, Sharon, and William Bruns. *The Information Mosaic*. Cambridge, Mass.: Harvard Business School Press, 1992.

Nianni, Alfred J., Jr., J. Robb Dixon, and Thomas E. Vollman. "Integrated Performance Measurement: Management Accounting to Support the New Realities." *Journal of Management Accounting Research*, Fall 1992, pp. 1–19.

Schonberger, R.J. *World Class Manufacturing: The Lessons of Simplicity Applied*. New York: The Free Press, 1986.

Stalk, George, and Thomas M. Hout. *Competing Against Time*. New York: The Free Press, 1990.

Turney, Peter B. B., ed. *Performance Excellence in Manufacturing and Service Organizations*. Sarasota, Fla.: American Accounting Association, 1990.

Wilkenson, Adrian, and Hugh Willmott. *Making Quality Critical*. New York, NY: Routledge, 1995.

Womack, James P., Daniel T. Jones, and Daniel Roos. *The Machine That Changed the World*. New York: Rawson Ass., 1990.

CASE 14–1
IRON RIVER PAPER MILL

Mike Lawson:

> While our cost accounting reports don't show it, I would not be surprised if quality costs us about $40 million a year, or about 20 percent of sales.

Lawson, quality assurance department, Iron River Mill, arrived at this estimate of the cost of quality after studying the writings of Deming, Crosby, and Juran and attending a seminar on quality costing presented by Philip Crosby Associates. Lawson elaborated:

> Crosby believes that the average U.S. manufacturing company spends about 20 percent of total sales on quality. According to Crosby, the cost of quality consists of two elements: the Price of Conformance (POC) and the Price of Non-Conformance (PONC). POC refers to what it costs to do things right the first time, while PONC refers to what it costs when you do things wrong. Typically, companies spend far more on nonconformance than on conformance. My experience at the Crosby seminar leads me to believe that we could maintain or even increase the overall quality of our product while spending a lot less money on quality, by worrying more about conformance, instead of spending so much time and money correcting nonconformance. But I can't prove this because we have not yet spent the time necessary to identify all the quality costs in this plant.

In June of 1988, management of the Iron River, Michigan, Paper Mill of Chippewa Paper Company, with the assistance of consultants provided by the corporate office, set out to do a cost of quality analysis (COQA) at the mill.

The Business Setting—"Groundwood Magazine Paper"

The Iron River mill, along with mills in Wisconsin and Maine, was part of the Magazine Papers Division of Chippewa. These mills made papers that were typically used for printing magazines

This case was prepared and copyrighted by Scott Keating and John K. Shank, The Amos Tuck School of Business Administration, Dartmouth College.

(e.g., *Time* or *Newsweek*) and retail catalogs (e.g., the Sears and J. C. Penney catalogs).

Chippewa's magazine paper was used by publishers of magazines and catalogs because it met three important criteria: low cost, light weight, and good print quality. Paper comprised approximately 50 percent of the total cost of producing a magazine or catalog. As a result, it was important to the magazine publishers to keep the cost of paper as low as possible.

Customers.   Iron River's customers fell into two classes, printers and publishers. Printers bought paper for publishers who had not specified the source of the paper to be used (although they probably did specify the weight and type of paper). Often, however, the publisher (especially large-volume publishers) bought the paper to be used and had it shipped directly to the printer.

Most customers, whether printer or publisher, bought paper from multiple sources. This is because most customers had very strict printing deadlines, and multiple sourcing was a form of guarantee that paper will be available when it is needed. In addition, printers wanted to have paper from several sources on hand in case the paper from one of the sources developed printing problems on the printing presses (a common occurrence). In many ways this customer-supplier relationship was still the old-style adversarial game.

Two types of printing processes dominated magazine and catalog printing in 1988—offset printing and rotogravure printing. In offset printing, the image to be printed is etched onto a metal plate, which is wrapped around a steel cylinder (a roll). The ink is picked up on the plate and then transferred from the plate to the "blanket" (another roller). The ink is then transferred from the blanket onto the paper. In rotogravure printing, the ink is transferred directly from an etched impression cylinder onto the paper. Rotogravure printing produces a higher-quality print image but is much more expensive than offset. Rotogravure printing requires very long print runs to amortize the extra costs of the etched rolls. The magazine industry uses mostly offset printers. Although these printers generally prefer coated paper, some magazines, especially magazines for European distribution, now use a super-calendered uncoated sheet. The market for such paper in the United States is about 4 million tons per year.

Paper prices can vary widely. For example, prices for Iron River's paper rose on average by about 20 percent from May of 1987 (a low point in the business cycle) to May of 1988 (a high point). Some individual prices rose more than 50 percent.

For the most part, makers of magazine papers view it as a commodity. They believe that customers choose suppliers largely on the basis of price. Others believe that even though it is a large-volume business, it is nevertheless possible to compete on other bases than price (e.g., quality, flexibility, or service).

Regardless of their overall view, all magazine papers manufacturers recognize that there are important quality and service elements to the business.

Quality.   In this business, quality has two elements: runability and printability. *Runability* describes the degree to which paper will run through a printing press without problems. Problems, when they occur, usually result in breaks or bursts in the roll of paper as it goes through the printing press. When the roll, or "web," breaks, the printer must shut down the press for about 30 minutes to clear out the torn paper, and refeed the roll through the press. Each web break represents printer down-time, which is very expensive. "Zero defects" is not achieved by any paper manufacturer and "web breaks" is a constant problem for printers. Three breaks for every 100 rolls used is a typical industry standard.

Printability, discussed above, describes the degree to which a sheet of paper will provide a good-quality printed page. Printability is typically measured by such specifications as gloss, smoothness, opacity, brightness, and porosity. It is a much more subjective measure than runability.

It was a widely held view in the industry that runability plays a very large role in the selection of a paper by a customer. If a paper runs well on the press, a printer will do almost anything to get it to print well. But if it does not run well—that is, it has a lot of breaks—a printer will reject it no matter how good the print quality.

Service.   For the most part, "service" represented the ability of a supplier to provide timely delivery of paper. Most customers had very strict deadlines to meet. For example, *Time* magazine did not believe it could afford to have its weekly issue arrive on the newsstands even half a day late. As a result, customers put considerable value on a manufacturer's ability to provide on-time delivery of paper to the printer.

Similarly, customers also valued supplier loyalty, even though they wanted loyalty from *several* suppliers. The paper industry was marked by periods of paper shortages. Just as customers could not afford to have paper arrive late, they could not afford to have no paper arrive at all because of a shortage. Customers put considerable value on those suppliers who will guarantee paper availability even in periods of short paper supply.

Iron River Mill.   The paper mill in Iron River, Michigan, was built in 1906 and was originally the Iron River Pulp and Paper Company. The mill was acquired by the Iroquois Paper Company in 1946. Iroquois was acquired by Chippewa in 1980.

The mill had a capacity of 800 tons per day and employed 632 people (511 hourly workers and 121 salaried). In 1987, sales volume at the mill exceeded 290,000 tons, with a total sales value of $220 million.

The mill had three paper machines. Machines #1 and #2 date to 1906, when the mill was first built (although they have been rebuilt on numerous occasions over the past 80 years), and make uncoated paper. Machine #3 was completed in 1982 and makes coated paper.

The mill was organized into 22 departments, each of which reports to one of 12 managers who, in turn, report to the mill manager. Of the 22 departments, 10 are directly involved in the paper-making process; the remaining 12 are support departments (e.g., accounting, engineering, maintenance, and so on).

The mill was a typical paper mill. Timber was purchased, debarked, and cut into small (approximately 1–2 inches) chips. The chips were converted into pulp using a thermo-mechanical process. After various chemicals were added, the pulp went to one of the three paper machines, where it was converted into paper and, on #3 machine, then coated. After the paper machine, the paper went through various finishing processes (e.g., calendering) before it was cut into rolls of specific width to meet customers orders.

Exhibit 1 provides a schematic of the paper-making process at Iron River.

Quality and Cost Accounting at the Mill.
Ken Gibson, the mill manager at Iron River, described the mill's quality position:

> I don't think our quality, or the cost of it, is very much different from the rest of the industry. About four years ago, the mill was the leader in the industry in terms of quality. Since then, our position has slipped a little, not because our quality has declined but because our competitors' quality has increased while ours has not.

Ward Dana, supervisor of the cost accounting department, commented on cost accounting at the mill:

> Our cost accounting system is very conventional. While we have identified some costs at the mill as quality costs,

we certainly do not track quality costs in the depth advocated by the quality gurus like Crosby.

The mill does not have any quality cost reports per se. Quality costs are not routinely tracked and documented. Further, the cost accounting system at the mill does not provide for easy cost of quality analysis. COQ analysis must be done independently of the cost accounting system.

Some of the larger quality costs identified by the mill's cost accounting system include: paper shrinkage (i.e., the difference between the amount of paper made and the amount actually shipped to customers), defective materials, quality-related machine downtime, quality-related capital investments, and the quality assurance department. Dana estimated that the spending in these areas amounted to approximately $20-25 million per year.

Neal Evers, comptroller of the mill, commented on the mill's quality costs:

> I think there are a lot of quality costs out there which we are missing. For example, 60 percent of the daily production meetings, attended by our top 15 or so managers, are consumed by quality-related issues. That's equivalent to about one man-day of top management time every day. I'm sure there are other quality costs like that one that are hard to see, unless you are really looking for them.

A New Approach to Costing Quality

Neal Evers described how the recent quality costing initiative came about:

> Mike Lawson had been arguing for a while that our cost accounting system was not identifying all of the quality costs. Mike believed, from what he had learned at the Crosby quality program, that we might change the way we run the mill if we knew what quality costs we were really incurring. The problem was that we did not have the time to go through the exercise of more accurately measuring quality costs. So when the head office offered us consultants to do the work, we jumped at the opportunity.

Ward Dana described the process which the consultants followed in measuring the quality costs at the mill:

> The consultants weren't experts in the paper industry, so they spent some time understanding how paper was made and how the mill operated. They interviewed the head of the departments at the mill, first to understand

EXHIBIT 1

Iron River paper-making process flow

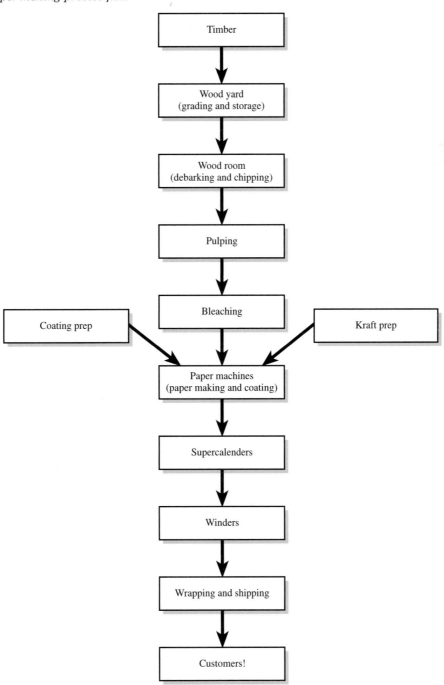

the role which that department played in making the paper, and second, to get an idea of how each department contributed to the quality of our product.

Once they had identified the elements of the total quality cost of the mill, they had to figure out how much each of those elements cost. Each of our departments is followed by a cost analyst in the cost accounting department. The consultants met with the analysts to try to put a dollar figure on each of the quality costs which they had identified. After we agreed on what to include in quality costs, we put a value on it.

This was no easy task. For example, the consultants had reasoned that the cost of the softwood debarker operator in the woodroom is a quality cost since the operator's major responsibility was to look for logs which were not perfectly debarked. They not only wanted to include the wages and benefits of the operators but also the cost of the equipment which is used to accept or reject a log after debarking. To get an accurate estimate of the cost, we had to include not only the cost of the equipment but also a portion of the cost of the building (based on the amount of floor space taken up by the equipment), electricity consumed, and a portion of insurance and other expenses. Our cost accounting system is not designed to provide that information, so it took some time getting it.

Sometimes we had to make estimates. For example, some of the maintenance department's time is devoted to routine maintenance of facilities which is unrelated to quality, while other time is clearly quality related. While we used as much data as we could in accurately apportioning the cost of the department to quality, we invariably had to estimate some of it. Nevertheless, I am confident that the numbers are reasonable, given the purpose of the exercise.

In addition to the departments at the mill, the consultants examined the quality costs incurred at the division headquarters. For example, there is a technical service department which deals with customer complaints. They had to figure out how much of that department's time was spent responding to complaints about Iron River paper.

Neal Evers described the interaction between the consultants and the mill staff during the process of identifying and quantifying quality costs:

We didn't always agree with the costs which the consultants were calling quality costs. For example, they wanted to include all four of the sets of centrifugal cleaners in the pulp mill as quality cost. It is true that these Bauer cleaners are designed to remove impurities from the pulp, and that, if the wood supplied included no impurities, then there would be no need for the cleaners. But, no one in their right mind would build a mill without at least one series of cleaners. We resolved the problem by classifying one set of the cleaners as an inspection cost and the other three as internal failure cost.

Dana described a similar incident:

We also had a lively debate over the maintenance department. Originally, the consultants felt that all of the maintenance department was a quality cost since you have to maintain your equipment in order to make a good quality product. But that isn't the only reason for maintenance. Maintenance also contributes to productivity and efficiency. The consultants ultimately agreed, and we included only those maintenance costs which were directly related to quality.

The study revealed that the total cost of quality at the mill was approximately $43 million. Of that amount, $7.6 million were conformance costs (i.e., prevention and inspection) and $35.3 million were nonconformance costs (i.e., internal and external failure). Exhibits 2 and 3 provide a breakdown, by department, of these costs.

Neal Evers reflected upon the results of the study:

For the most part, the study confirmed what we had been thinking. Forty-three million dollars is a lot to be spending on quality, especially when most of that spending is on bad quality paper.

One of the concerns I have, however, is how useful these numbers are. They would be good if we were building a new mill, because we would have total flexibility in deciding how to do things. But it isn't clear to me how to use them if what we are trying to do is to run an existing mill more effectively.

Nevertheless, the study does provide some valuable insights. For example, more than 80 percent of our quality costs are related to off-quality paper. If we could reduce the amount of off-quality paper we are producing, by concentrating on up-front prevention and inspection, we might be able to significantly reduce the amount of off-quality paper we make. Currently, we don't look at the details behind shrinkage to know where the specific problems are.

We have already had some success, however. Not too long ago, we discovered that the kraft pulp we were using contained a lot of "sieve cells," and that these cells were causing holes in our paper. We were able to reduce the sieve cell content in the pulp, thereby reducing the amount of defective paper. Conservative estimates suggested that we save $500,000 a year as a result of this.

Another area where we've made changes is in process control. There is a real advantage to knowing when you

EXHIBIT 2   Results of Cost of Quality Analysis

Mill Department	Prevention	Inspection	Internal Failure	External Failure	Total COQ	Total Dept.	COQ as percent of Dept.
Wood yard	$ 0	$ 4,930	$ 0	0	$ 4,930	$ 626,123	0.8%
Wood room	0	269,000	594,174	0	863,174	2,589,374	33.3
TMP	0	424,537	419,757	0	844,294	13,088,991	6.5
Bleach plant	0	63,500	0	0	63,500	976,906	6.5
Kraft prep.	0	17,200	0	0	17,200	1,740,904	1.0
Coating prep.	0	206,650	0	0	206,650	1,640,908	12.6
Paper machines	151,460	481,481	1,674,290	0	2,307,231	23,722,355	9.7
Supercalenders and winders	408,600	35,784	294,785	0	739,169	8,691,187	8.5
Salvage winders	0	0	521,804	0	521,804	521,804	100.0
Finishing and shipping	0	134,508	0	0	134,508	2,573,343	5.2
Production control	0	0	0	0	0	363,096	0.0
Utilities	32,772	0	0	0	32,772	13,294,592	0.2
Accounting	0	118,311	0	0	118,311	473,246	25.0
Data processing	0	48,789	0	0	48,789	227,675	21.4
Technical	477,001	2,031,386	0	0	2,508,387	2,508,387	100.0
Quality control	0	99,362	0	0	99,362	99,362	100.0
Engineering	122,855	0	0	0	122,855	491,442	25.0
Human resources	41,379	0	0	0	41,379	897,535	4.6
—Lost work time	251,356	0	0	0	251,356		
General mill	0	0	90,000	0	90,000	4,091,906	2.2
Mill management	132,715	0	0	0	132,715	530,860	25.0
Materials	126,913	0	0	0	126,913	797,268	15.9
Process control	60,000	0	0	0	60,000	60,000	100.0
Accounting for broke	0	0	16,077,423	0	16,077,423		
Downtime	1,632,168	0	4,954,504	0	6,586,672		
Returns and claims	0	0	0	1,276,900	1,276,900		
Goodwill/lost sales	0	0	0	9,000,000	9,000,000		
Raw materials:							
Pulpwood						8,528,078	
Kraft pulp						42,239,000	
Chemicals and other						27,112,000	
Total mill cost	$3,437,219	$3,935,438	$24,626,737	$10,276,294	$42,276,294	$157,886,342	26.8%
Division expenses:							
Timberlands	$ 236,430	$ 1,305	$ 0	$ 0	$ 237,735	$ 358,228	66.4
Customer technical services	0	0	0	250,000	250,000		
Marketing and sales	0	0	0	150,000	150,000		
Total division expenses	236,430	1,305	0	400,000	637,735		
Total cost of quality	$3,673,649	$3,936,743	$24,626,737	$10,676,900	$42,914,029		

Exhibit 3 COQ Analysis Methodology

General Procedure

When any work station or machine was identified as a cost of quality, the COQ figure was obtained by including the direct and indirect costs, including depreciation, insurance, and taxes.

Examples are:

Cost	Type	Amount ($)	Rationale
Wood room:			
Debarker operator	Inspection	$ 159,000	Operator's role is to inspect for proper debarking.
Debarker rework	Internal failure	110,880	Every rejected log must be sent through debarker again.
Chip screens	Inspection	110,000	Checks for proper chip size.
Chip rework	Internal failure	25,848	Oversized chips must be rechipped.
Chip reject	Internal failure	458,246	Undersized chips are rejected. Cost includes cost of rejected chips.
		$ 863,174	
Paper machines:			
Pulp rejection	Internal failure	$ 126,198	Pulp rejected for improper consistency.
Monitoring equipment	Inspection	481,481	Consistency monitor, scanner, hole detector.
Wet end monitoring	Prevention	151,460	Make good paper the first time.
Rejection equipment	Internal failure	1,548,092	Cleaners, save all system, rereelers, broke chest, and broke pulper.
		$2,307,231	
Accounting:			
Cost reporting	Inspection	$ 118,311	Based on portion of department's time spent on quality analysis.
Data processing	Inspection	48,789	Based on portion of department's time (personnel and computer time) spent on quality reporting.
Technical:			
Process engineers	Prevention	477,001	Responsible for maintaining paper quality.
Technical staff	Inspection	2,031,386	Performs lab tests on in-process and finished paper.
Quality control	Inspection	99,362	Liaison between customers and mill for quality problems.
Engineering	Prevention	122,855	Portion of department's time spent on preparing and reviewing quality improvement projects.
Human Resources:			
Training	Prevention	292,735	Portion of training time devoted to quality training. Includes cost of personnel (salaried and hourly) hours spent in quality training.

Goodwill/Lost Sales Cost ($9 million)

An explanation of the calculation of this large, important, and very "soft" number is as follows:

1. We compared the product mix in May '87 (a bad time in the industry) to May '88 (a good time). We asked the question: "What if in May '87 we could have had a product mix like that of May '88? How much different would our profit have been?"
2. To do the analysis, we looked at the profit margins of the different paper grades.

EXHIBIT 3 *(continued)*

	May '87	
Margin	*Percent of Maximum Margin*	*Percent of Total Paper Production*
$195	100%	1%
167	86	3
110	56	66
95	49	6
35	18	<u>24</u>
		<u>100%</u>

	May '88	
Margin	*Percent of Maximum Margin*	*Percent of Total Paper Production*
$237	100%	1%
176	74	4
164	69	93
136	57	<u>2</u>
		<u>100%</u>

3. We then said: "What if in May '87 our production was distributed among the different profit margins like May '88?"

Percent of Maximum Margin (May '88 distribution)	*Percent of Total Production (May '88 distribution)*	*Margin (using May '87 margins)*
100%	1%	$195
74	4	144 (74% of $195)
69	93	135
57	<u>2</u>	111
	<u>100%</u>	

Weighted Average

1% × $194 =	$1.95
4% × 144 =	5.79
93% × 135 =	125.49
2% × 111 =	<u>2.24</u>
	$135.47

4. What would be the profit impact?

Actual avg.		
margin May '87 =	93.66
Theoretical =	135.47
Difference	$41.81 per ton
Production	5,945 tons
Total difference	$248,560 per month
	or $2,982,725 per year for
	PMs 1 and 2

EXHIBIT 3   (continued)

---

5. Similar analysis for PM #3 yields:

Actual margin	=	$61.00
Theoretical	=	$87.80
Difference		$26.84 per ton
Production		17,195 tons
Total difference		461,513 per month
		or $5,538,166 per year

6. Combined total is $3.9 million + $5.5 million, rounded to $9.0 million for the report.

---

are about to make bad paper, versus knowing when you *are making*, or *have just made*, bad paper. By installing on-line sensors, such as color monitors and moisture content monitors at the wet end of the machine, rather than the dry end, we've substantially reduced our quality costs. But there is clearly room for more improvement.

Arnie Pogue, quality assurance manager, commented on potential improvements:

We have a lot of on-line measurement equipment, but we could still use more. For example, we currently measure the acidity in the headbox by taking periodic samples. A lot of time can elapse before we know that the acidity has changed, and acidity changes can result in bad paper. If we had an on-line sensor, we could react a lot sooner to correct the problem, and, as a result, reduce our "broke" [bad paper].

One of the larger costs identified in the study was the external failure cost. On this, Ken Gibson, the mill manager commented:

A lot of people might not agree with the $9 million identified as a cost of sending defective paper to customers, but I suspect it is pretty accurate. In the early 70s, I was at the Searsport [Maine] mill, which was regarded as the best quality producer of magazine papers. When the market for paper went bad, every mill except Searsport had to shut down for some time because there was not enough demand. Searsport operated at 100 percent capacity throughout, largely, I believe, because of the higher quality of their paper. Clearly, quality can really affect your customer goodwill.

A comment from the head buyer of one of Iron River's largest customers confirms Gibson's position. When he heard that the mill was doing a quality cost study, the buyer said, "That's the biggest waste of time and money I've ever heard of. Who cares what it cost to make bad paper? The point is really to make sure you spend the money to make good paper, because without quality you won't have any customers, and without customers, you won't have any sales."

Another of Chippewa's large customers commented on the potential advantage of good quality paper:

Chippewa might not see the benefits of quality immediately, but there would certainly be benefits. For example, if Chippewa were considering building a new mill, and if they were showing a consistent record of good quality paper, then we might consider committing to buy a certain portion of the new mill's output. That sort of commitment would be good enough to take to the bank.

Neal Evers continued:

One of the more intangible benefits of a study like this is that it changes the way we think about quality. The resource allocation process at Chippewa provides a good example of this. One of the classes of applications for capital spending [ARA] is a quality improvement ARA. About one third of the total number of ARAs which we process every year are quality improvement ARAs. Interestingly, a "hurdle rate" is not applied to this type of project. If we are going to start following the cost of quality, then maybe we should start doing investment return analysis on quality-improvement projects. On the other hand, perhaps we should adopt the policy of "quality at any cost," and therefore maintain the status quo.

But the big question is, Where do we go from here? The usefulness of a study like this is that it identifies the problem areas so that we know where to get maximum return for our efforts.

Ken Gibson also commented on the practical applications of the study:

The big point of this study for me is that we have to build quality in our paper in the first place instead of inspecting it after it has been made. To do that, however, you have to give considerable responsibility to the people lower down in the mill who can actually control the quality of the paper as it is being made. Interestingly, we've been recently working on a participative management program at Chippewa, and it makes the exact same point: Give the decision-making power to the people who can most effectively use it to impact the mill's performance.

But we're not ready to do that yet for two reasons. First, many of our workers are not sufficiently trained yet to be able to make effective decisions. Second, our managers are not yet ready to give up some of the decision-making power which has traditionally been theirs. So we have to put some of the possible projects which come out of this study on hold until we get people prepared, and that's going to take time.

A lot of people think that our problem is that we do not understand the paper-making process sufficiently to be able to build in consistently better quality. I disagree. We already know much more about the process than we make use of. True, we still have a lot to learn, but we could make a lot of progress just by using more effectively what we already know. Maybe generating accounting reports that explicitly show quality costs is a good way to help keep our attention focused on this issue.

Questions

1. Be prepared to describe the methodology used by Iron River Mill to quantify cost of quality.
2. How can senior management use Exhibits 2 and 3 to make better decisions?
3. How can senior management use Exhibits 2 and 3 to develop an evaluation system to track performance on quality?
4. "COQ analysis is likely to become an important on-going management control tool in more and more American companies in future years." Comment critically.
5. "COQ analysis is much more a strategic positioning tool than a management control tool." Comment critically.
6. "COQ analysis is quantification futilely searching for a rationale." Comment critically.

Case 14–2
Motorola Inc.

The controller of Motorola's newly formed Application Specific Integrated Circuit (ASIC) Division sensed that he and his staff could play a significant part in determining the success of what promised to be an important new business. Not only was his division competing in a new and dynamic market with unique requirements but it also was radically changing the way in which it delivered its product. These circumstances led the controller to reassess the most basic issues involved in designing a management control system: What should be measured? How should it be measured? Who should measure it? and, For whom should it be measured?

The Company

Founded in 1928, Motorola soon became widely known for its radios and other consumer electrical and electronic products. By the 1960s, it sold semiconductor products, communications equipment, and components to consumers, industrial companies, and the military throughout the world.

Headquartered in Schaumberg, Illinois, in 1984, Motorola achieved over $5.5 billion in sales, employed over 99,000 people, and spent $411 million in research and development. It was one of the few American companies that marketed a wide range of electronic products, from highly sophisticated integrated circuits to consumer electronic products.

Organization

The company was organized along product and technology lines. Each business unit was structured as a sector, group, or division, depending on size.

This case was prepared and copyrighted by Joseph Fisher and Steven Knight, The Amos Tuck School of Business Administration, Dartmouth College.

The Semiconductor Products Sector (SPS) was headquartered in Phoenix, Arizona; sales in 1984 were over $2.2 billion, which was 39 percent of Motorola's net sales. The sector sold its products worldwide to original equipment manufacturers through its own sales force. Semiconductor products were subject to rapid changes in technology. Accordingly, SPS maintained an extensive research and development program in advanced semiconductor technology.

Formation of the ASIC Division

In the early 1980s, the Semiconductor Products Sector produced a large line of both discrete semiconductor components and integrated circuits. Integrated circuits (ICs) can be thought of (at least functionally) as miniature circuit boards. For example, the designer of a video cassette recorder could replace a $12'' \times 12''$ circuit board and all its individual components with a single $1'' \times 1''$ integrated circuit on a silicon chip, saving space and reducing power consumption. By 1985, worldwide sales of integrated circuits reached $20.2 billion.

Among integrated circuit manufacturers, Motorola was widely known for its design and process expertise, and it became a leader in the increasingly popular semicustom integrated circuits.

Semicustom integrated circuits are designed using predetermined functional blocks. In the early 1980s, Motorola produced a version of semicustom ICs called "gate arrays." Each "gate" on a gate array was a transistor that performed a single operation. These were interconnected to produce the desired set of functions. One chip could contain a thousand or more gates. Each was designed to meet the requirements of a specific customer. Gate array customizations were relatively cheap and quick to manufacture, and they were designed by computer-aided design systems.

By 1984, the market for gate arrays had grown to $455 million. Sales in 1985 were expected to be $740 million, and the market was estimated to reach $1.4 billion in sales annually by 1990. The high-performance gate array market totaled $90 million in 1984. Forecasts stated that the market should grow to $600 million by 1990.

Motorola manufactured high-performance gate arrays using two different semiconductor technologies: (1) bipolar and (2) complementary metal-oxide semiconductor (CMOS). Bipolar technology provided increased speeds at which the circuit could perform but at the cost of increased power consumption (and increased difficulty in meeting cooling requirements) when compared to CMOS technology. For this reason, the demand for CMOS gate arrays was expected to grow more rapidly than that for bipolar gate arrays. In 1984, CMOS captured 40 percent of the market. This was expected to increase to 70 percent.

Bipolar gate arrays were produced in Phoenix by the Logic Division of the SPS. Under the Logic Division, Motorola's bipolar gate array business grew rapidly. Motorola achieved a dominant share of this market and became the acknowledged technological leader.

CMOS gate arrays were produced in Austin, Texas, by the Microprocessor Products Group. Since Motorola focused on maintaining its position in the microprocessor market, the CMOS gate arrays did not receive adequate attention in this group. As a result, Motorola had only a small share of the CMOS gate arrays market and faced stiff competition from such companies as LSI, Hitachi, Toshiba, Fujitsu, and NEC.

To exploit fully the growing demand for semicustom integrated circuits, Motorola organized the Application Specific Integrated Circuit (ASIC) Division as part of the Semiconductor Products Sector in 1984. In 1985, the ASIC Division occupied Motorola's Chandler facility, the newest of the company's five Phoenix-area locations. Typically, Motorola worked closely with a customer to design the semicustom integrated circuit. However, several designs were considered standard designs and were kept in stock.

Organization of ASIC Division

The division was organized along functional lines (see Exhibit 1).

Product Engineering Department. Product engineering interacted with the customer and assumed the role of a troubleshooter in dealing with customer complaints. It was responsible for the technical aspects of ongoing product manufacturing. Engineers were assigned to one or more products and served the customers for these products. If a customer had a complaint about an integrated circuit, product engineering responded to the request. Therefore, product engineering was the technical interface between the company and customer for existing products.

Product engineers designed the manufacturing process for existing products, and they typically were responsible for customer-driven capital expenditures. If a customer wanted or required an additional manufacturing process that required a capital expenditure, the process engineering department made a feasibility study. This study divided costs between nonrecurring engineering expenses (NRE) and the per unit cost of production after the initial NRE. In addition, an estimate of revenues was made to estimate product profitability. This report was examined by the marketing department to ensure that the assumptions and estimates made by the product engineers were reasonable.

Part of the start-up cost of a new product was the nonrecurring engineering cost (NRE). This cost included design and software development cost but typically did not include investment in process technologies, unless a very specialized piece of equipment was a unique requirement of the product's manufacture. The NRE was billed to the customer in two stages: 30 percent upon agreement of the development contract and 70 percent upon the shipment of the first prototype units.

Exhibit 1

Organization of ASIC division

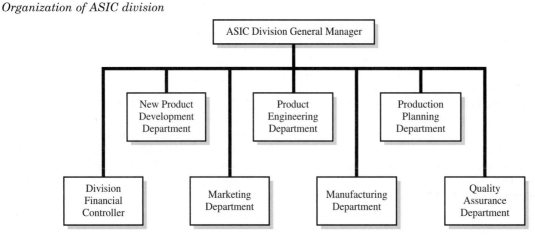

Production Planning Department. The production planning and customer service department scheduled orders from the customer. This department told manufacturing when to start production and when the product run should be finished. Since Motorola did not have a computerized production planning system, this work was done with only standard microcomputer software, such as spreadsheets. Orders had to be tracked manually through the factory floor. When the product was shipped, the department billed the client and reported this information to the financial controller.

Marketing Department. The marketing department was responsible for identifying initial prospects and making sales to them. In addition, the department had certain responsibilities for product pricing and accurate forecasting of market demands.

Once a prospect was identified, the marketing department acted as a liaison to ensure that the requirements of the product were accurately communicated from the prospect to the new products development group. The new products development group then estimated a manufacturing cost, and the marketing department calculated a price, using a target margin of around 60 percent above manufacturing cost. This price was adjusted to take into account the competitive conditions of the market. The marketing department also forecasted the sales volume for the product for the next five years.

New Product Development Department. The new product development group was responsible for the translation of customer product specifications into manufacturable designs and for the production of prototypes. As mentioned above, this group provided an estimate of the manufacturing cost to the marketing group. After the design was completed, the cost estimate was refined; it was included in the product implementation plan, along with yield requirements. Before the product design could be released to the manufacturing department, the product was produced in the development fabrication area with production tooling. At this stage the process had to meet minimum yield specifications. This yield was not the yield estimated in calculating the long-run manufacturing cost of the product, but simply a yield that would be satisfactory as production moved rapidly down a learning curve. The learning curve was estimated to be about 70 percent for most products in the ASIC Division. A 70 percent learning curve implies that unit costs for total production volume will decrease by 30 percent every time the cumulative production volume doubles.

Each month the new products development group provided the financial controller department an updated forecast of future capital expense requirements; this was used in capital planning by the finance department.

Quality Assurance Department. Quality assurance (QA) was responsible for the outgoing quality of the product. After many of the processes on the manufacturing floor, QA inspectors sampled the product for quality. These tests included electrical and visual/mechanical tests. The electrical tests were straightforward (i.e., if the product failed to conduct properly, the product was rejected). The visual/mechanical tests were more subjective. Defects in this area could be misprinting, illegible printing, discolored components, or bent lead wires. Many of these did not affect the viability of the circuit but only its visual appearance. Quality assurance people knew that the Japanese were very sensitive to visual quality and that the product had to be visually perfect if Motorola was to be competitive in the Japanese market. One of the major responsibilities of QA was to convey to manufacturing what constituted a rejection of the product. One manager in QA said that the group should assume the role of a pseudo customer.

QA attempted to take a noncombative role with the other departments; it preferred to function in a preventive role. QA had trainers who discussed with manufacturing operators what constituted a rejection. This program had two benefits: (1) operators became aware that they needed to produce to a certain quality level; and (2) if the product was below acceptable quality at any stage in production, it would be rejected immediately by the operator, thus saving further manufacturing costs. Recently, a procedure was instituted that, if a product was rejected, the

whole line stopped until QA and the production floor could determine the cause(s).

Manufacturing Department. The manufacturing department consisted of hourly workers, supervisors, and a manufacturing engineering staff. The hourly workers were directly involved in operating production machinery and inspecting work-in-process. Manufacturing engineering was charged with sustaining the production processes and methods used in the assembly and test operations. The group's focus was on the manufacturing process, rather than on specific products.

ASIC Market

The managers of the new division realized that the semicustom integrated circuit business had different requirements for success than the commodity-type business from which it grew.

In the semicustom gate arrays market, the customer created a unique design from the "building blocks" provided by Motorola designers. This involvement by the customer in the middle of the development cycle was different from that in the other semiconductor products offered by Motorola. Motorola provided design services to the customer and managed a relatively involved customer relationship. Thus, Motorola's organization focused on its customers, rather than on its products.

The customers of the ASIC division were typically computer manufacturers, such as DEC, Apple Computer, Unisys, Cray, and Prime Computer. These customers competed in markets characterized by rapidly changing technology and rapid introduction of new products. Shortening the product delivery time was a primary concern for them. High quality, quick development time, and the ability to achieve volume production rapidly were paramount in capturing the business of these customers. Compared with these factors, price was of secondary importance.

Some customers, such as Hewlett-Packard, were developing just-in-time (JIT) manufacturing systems and stated their needs for timely deliveries and high-quality incoming components.

Motorola Manufacturing and Accounting Systems

Prior to moving, the ASIC Division was part of another corporate sector. Bipolar production, prior to moving, used Motorola's existing manufacturing and accounting systems. In the plant, machines and workers were organized along functional lines. Each machine was controlled as part of a functional group, and was in close physical proximity with other machines that performed a similar function. This functional design resulted in large physical movements of product over relatively large distances on the factory floor. Each manufactured part had a designated routing through the factory.

In this factory design, there were 29 cost centers, whose inventory was valued at standard cost. The inventory was grouped by stage of completion for costing purposes. The routing of the product through the factory typically included the following steps: (1) piece parts, where the various raw materials were purchased and prepared; (2) wafer fabrication, where the silicon wafers containing the logic arrays were produced; (3) die, where the wafers were tested and cut into individual circuits or chips and mounted to the substrate of the package (permanent chip enclosure); (4) assembly, where lead wires were attached to the chip and the packaging completed; (5) test, where the packaged chip was tested according to customer specifications; and (6) finished goods, where the finished products were packaged for shipping.

This system required extensive recordkeeping. An entry was made every time the product was moved from one cost center to another. A frequent physical audit of inventories was required to track and verify product amounts.

Material, labor, and overhead standards were updated twice a year. Nevertheless, the standards were often obsolete, because of the dynamic environment and the steep learning curves. Overhead was allocated to the product based on direct labor. Direct labor was meticulously tracked in order to cost labor to the product and to provide allocation of overhead to the product. The manufacturing manager estimated that between 8 percent to 12 percent of an employee's productive time was spent in recordkeeping.

Direct labor was paid an hourly wage and a bonus. The bonus was largely determined by comparison of actual direct labor hours to standard labor hours for each employee.

The functional design of the factory caused difficulty in placing responsibility for an individual product. Expediters in the production planning department performed a crucial task in making sure important products were being completed in a timely fashion. Even so, the plant was plagued with slow throughput times. Management felt that turn-around times on the integrated circuits was too slow, compared with competing Japanese firms.

The functional design also resulted in large inventories and large batch sizes. The large batch size resulted in work-in-process (WIP) inventories between functional stations and resulted in large finished goods inventories that were effectively produced but perhaps unwanted by the customer.

Many people felt that, rather than helping managers cope with the complexity of the manufacturing system, the accounting system was actually exacerbating the problem. The division controller noted, "The first important realization of the accounting department is that we were sometimes a barrier to progress. The accounting systems resulted in overall dysfunctional activities and impeded movement to new manufacturing techniques."

The standard cost system was cumbersome and not well understood by factory employees. Factory employees had difficulty in tying a variance to a specific problem. Because a variance did not highlight the actual problem, an appropriate solution to a variance was difficult to determine.

The typical factory worker thought the variance report was irrelevant and, therefore, ignored it.

The timeliness of reports was also a problem. Standard costs were generated monthly. The lack of daily or weekly feedback made it difficult to pinpoint the cause of an unfavorable variance. The monthly variance was an accumulation of many favorable and unfavorable activities, which variance analysis did not specifically identify. Moreover, the variance reports were not timely. The books were closed on the seventh working day after the end of the month. An additional seven working days were required to generate actual costs and the variance report. By the time the reports were received in the factory floor, the manufacturing department was halfway through another accounting period.

Because of the dynamic environment facing a chip manufacturer, the determination of standards was very difficult. New chip designs were constantly flowing through the factory, and the steep learning curve contributed to the rapid obsolescence of standards. The standards were generally perceived as being out of date.

Since the variances were affected by volume, in many cases the way to decrease an individual variance was to keep the employees and machines fully used and produce large lot sizes. This had the undesired result of building up WIP inventory between the work stations and production of products that were not immediately required by a customer. At the same time, products required by a customer might not be produced. This resulted in a buildup of finished goods inventory and out-of-stock orders simultaneously.

In the new plant, there was a dramatic increase in overhead costs and a corresponding decrease in direct labor costs. The allocation of overhead by direct labor no longer seemed relevant.

Opportunities for Change

The manager of the newly formed ASIC Division realized that the opening of a new production facility in Chandler represented an opportunity to introduce substantial changes in the division's manufacturing operations. Accordingly, the new plant's floor layout was designed to be particularly suited to the JIT philosophy and to the specific processes of the plant. One manager at the Chandler site expressed the opinion that reorganizing an existing functional facility to accomplish a JIT plant would have been far more difficult.

The factory was organized around nine cells: (1) assembly preparation; (2) 72-pin assembly; (3) 149-pin assembly; (4) other assembly; (5) sealing, mechanical testing, and marking; (6) heat sink; (7) burn-in; (8) production testing and packing; and (9) warehousing and shipping. (Exhibit 2 is a diagram of the plant layout.) Not all products went through all cells—for example, not all chips required heat sinks. However, all of the chips produced at the Chandler plant were processed in most of the cells.

Products moved from cell to cell in the order shown in Exhibit 2. The wafers (each consisting of a number of chips) were placed in a die cage when they arrived at the plant. From the die cage, the wafers were taken to the die prep cell, where the gate arrays on wafers that had not been tested at the wafer fabrication facility were checked with a probe to determine which arrays were good. Arrays that did not pass inspection were marked, and, when the wafer was cut into individual chips, the marked arrays were thrown away.

Next, the chips were taken to one of the three assembly cells (72-pin, 149-pin, other), depending on the product family and number of connections that needed to be made to the chip. In the assembly cells, the electrical connections to the chip were made. In the sealing, mechanical testing, and marking cell, the chips were sealed in a protective package, tested, and marked for identification. In this cell, some low-volume chips were diverted from the normal product flow into a special option line. This line was for very-low-volume ICs, which were usually built for customers who used them for prototypes and testing. The focus of this option line was fast turnaround time; for new

Exhibit 2

Layout of Chandler plant

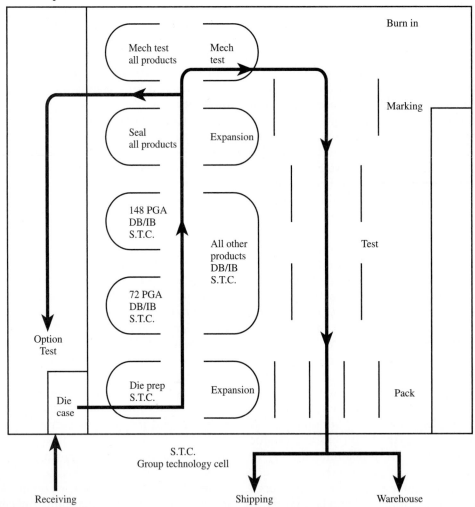

ICs, a dozen or so units could be shipped within three weeks from the time the design was accepted. Higher-volume ICs were routed through the remaining cells. As noted, not all ICs were sent to the heat sink and burn-in cells, but all went through the testing, warehousing, and shipping cells.

Most of the processes were machine-paced, and most of the machinery was complex and ex-pensive. This was particularly true of the assem-bly and test cells. For example, automated test machines at the end of the option line cost over $2 million each.

Each of the cells was run by a production team, which was supervised by a team leader. Work flow was controlled through a pull system, with designated areas where limited inventory was allowed between work stations. (A pull man-

Exhibit 3

Layout of assembly cell

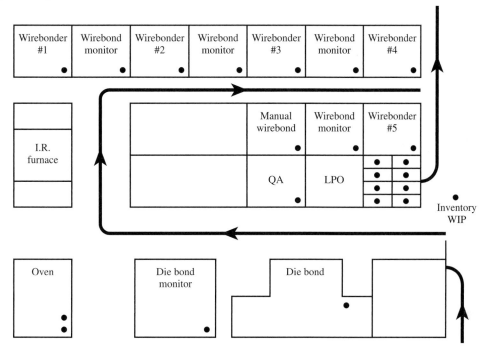

ufacturing system is characterized by triggering production when inventory is removed from finished goods stock.) If the storage area before a work station was full, the preceding station had to remain idle. One of the assembly cells is diagrammed in Exhibit 3. In this cell, chips were attached to the bottom portion of the permanent enclosure (package) in the die bond station, and they moved through the cell as shown by the arrows; the final operation performed in the cell was attaching lead wires in the wirebond stations. The cell was so designed that the product moved in one direction along a U-shaped path.

The Role of the Management Control System

The controller of the ASIC Division was acutely aware of the tendency of outdated and cumbersome control systems to hinder progress in man-

ufacturing operations. He felt strongly that his office should not merely stand aside but should take a positive position in promoting the changes throughout the division. However, he wondered what kind of managerial control system would complement and even guide the progressive changes taking place in the division's operations.

Questions

1. What are the key success factors for Motorola's ASIC Division?

2. Does a traditional standard cost system address these key success factors?

3. What are good measures of these key success factors?

4. How would you control the plant using these measures and the current structure of the plant?

CASE 14–3
RESPONSIBILITY ACCOUNTING VERSUS JIT

When accounting measurement objectives cannot be met because of changing technology, the motivational role of accounting emerges. Managers often estimate costs when accounting systems cannot provide accurate measures. Because a manager's knowledge is often based upon unique expertise, verifying these cost estimates can be difficult. In these circumstances, management accountants should examine the motivational role of accounting systems. Do managers have a vested interest in making truthful estimates? Do these estimates encourage cooperation among managers?

Joint evaluation motivates managers to cooperate for their mutual benefit. Separate, independent evaluation may have an opposite effect. Vested interests, antagonisms, and game playing may bias cost and revenue estimates when the accounting system cannot provide accurate, reliable measurements. These concepts are important when departments can significantly influence each other's efficiency.

A traditional concept in departmental responsibility accounting is controllability. Managers should be held responsible only for costs that they can control. New technologies can make costing systems less accurate and create situations where estimates are more frequent and important.

Conditions can often be created by new technologies where the benefits of cooperation are greater than the costs of violating controllability. When departments significantly influence each other's costs and the accounting system cannot accurately measure these costs, it may actually be preferable to hold managers responsible for costs they cannot control. New technologies have made truly independent departments rare.

The experience of two companies illustrates these points. One, a bathroom fixture manufacturer, uses both separate and joint responsibility accounting for evaluation. The second, a cut-rate auto parts chain, has recently changed from a separate to a joint responsibility system because of the introduction of a just-in-time (JIT) retailing system. The change to shared responsibility was necessary because the introduction of JIT retailing made manufacturing and sales more interdependent.

Auto Parts Chain

The plant manager was angry, really angry. "You just get everything humming along nicely and the big wheels have to change things. I didn't need a sales division before, so why should I pay for it now? Why should I be held responsible for activities I don't control?

This manager ran an operation of about 300 employees who rebuilt carburetors mostly sold by the parent company, a large chain of cut-rate auto part retailers. Originally, the company based this manager's bonus upon the performance of his manufacturing facility alone. He balanced an optimal mix of component prices with work force capacity to maximize the shop's output and his own bonus. By keeping larger stocks of finished product, sales managers were able to meet all customer needs. At the same time, the manufacturing manager had enough scheduling discretion to influence negotiated component costs and smooth production. He was comfortable knowing what to control and how to cope with the uncertainties in this situation. But, this idealistic situation would not last.

Changes have recently been made (see Exhibit 1). Previously, because the plant manager scheduled to minimize his production and purchasing costs, the flow and mix of finished goods

This case was prepared by Associate Professor Jim Mackey, California State University, Sacramento, From *CMA Magazine*, July-August 1989, pp. 22–25. Used with permission.

EXHIBIT 1   Accounting for Bonus Plans

Before		After
Plant	*Sales*	*Plant and Sales*
	Actual sales	Actual sales
Actual costs of manufacture versus budget*	Budgeted costs of manufacture	Actual costs of manufacture
	Gross profit	Gross profit
	Selling expenses	Selling expenses
	Segment profits†	Segment profits*†

----

*Bonus basis for the plant.
†Bonus basis for the sales group.

----

shipped to the stores were often erratic but not a problem. Finished inventories were sufficient for most situations. Now a new JIT merchandising system put pressure on the company to show reductions in inventory levels. The new sales group allowed better coordination of all suppliers with the stores. In essence, a centralized data base cut drastically into the merchandise inventory levels.

These changes adversely affected the production manager, however. Not only did he lose his buffer or extra finished goods stock, which allowed more independent scheduling, but he also had to bear responsibility without any control for the sales activities. He no longer controlled his own destiny. His bonus depended upon the performance of the salespeople as well as his own. He did, however, find some gratification since the sales manager felt the same way—angry. The sales manager's bonus depended as much on manufacturing efficiency as on good sales management. Once their mutual miseries were thoroughly discussed, both managers and their staffs found a clear need for full cooperation in order to maintain bonus levels.

Upper management's hope for motivating cooperation between sales and manufacturing by having bonuses based upon combined performance was fulfilled. This way the carrying costs of inventories, previously a sales responsibility, now affected the compensation of both departments. Under JIT merchandising, the sales department was encouraged to order products only as required without losing sales. At the same time, the plant manager was motivated to cooperate within cost constraints in his scheduling because his bonus was somewhat tied to sales performance.

However successful, this is only one possible solution to a classic agency problem. A better, more detailed cost accounting system could provide an alternative solution but was either unknown or not chosen by this company because of its unique operating conditions.

Sales department conditions contributing to the need for accounting changes were as follows:

1. Sales were difficult to forecast because demand was very uncertain.
2. Sales margins were tight because of significant competition.

The production department, however, was not without its problems:

1. Availability and quality of used carburetors were erratic.
2. Set-up costs and small lot sizes plagued the process.
3. Reconditioning was often more an art than a science.
4. Quality control costs could get out of hand without suitable monitoring.

It was clearly a production environment where standards would be difficult to establish. Large stocks of finished goods became too costly. Production had to be linked more to demand, while uncertainties in both sales and production still existed that could not be measured correctly. Motivation, rather than cost accounting using standards, became a more efficient solution.

An agency problem existed. The sales division, because of its unique knowledge, was in the best position to forecast demand *and* estimate the cost of lost sales. Lost sales were inevitable for any system that minimizes in-stock goods. A lost-sale figure was a difficult number to derive, particularly since one lost sale might cause a customer never to return. Hard data were rarely available; only sales estimates by experienced sales managers were reliable.

Before JIT, the solution was simple—carry large product inventories. Lost sales were rarely a problem. But new technologies brought the cost of carrying inventories to management's attention, and JIT retailing was adopted. Suddenly the company required manufacturing flexibility to meet demand. Prior to JIT, meeting rush orders was rarely an issue for manufacturing. It was merely a benefit from the carrying costs of finished goods. (The carrying costs were borne by sales or the retail outlets.) This was legitimate because all the benefits of meeting rush orders, due to both current and future orders, adhered to sales. Now JIT was like a bandit robbing sales of its least-costly alternative for maintaining satisfied customers.

Rush orders, once satisfied by high inventory levels, collided head-on with JIT. Because of supplier costs, set-ups, and lot-size issues, rush orders could be disruptive and costly. The nature of the production process made standards unreliable and formal planning models often inaccurate. Only an experienced plant manager with intimate knowledge of the company's work force, machinery, and suppliers could give reasonable estimates of rush-order costs.

Under the old system where the manufacturing plant was a cost center, rush orders could be accepted only at a potential cost to the plant manager (see Exhibit 1). They could be a costly way of avoiding lost sales when the plant was already at full capacity. Rush orders were accepted only when the costs were, in the judgment of the plant manager, minimal. Since formal costing systems were imprecise, only the plant manager could judge the ability to meet the cost of a rush order. On the other hand, the benefits of

meeting a single rush order were equally difficult to quantify formally because of the possible influence on future sales. Only an experienced sales staff could come up with a reliable estimate of the value of accepting a rush order. But sales had nothing to lose by accepting all rush orders, and production rarely had anything to gain. A stalemate existed.

A numerical example might be useful here (see Exhibit 2). Consider a last-minute rush order for a $10 part that has a standard cost of $5 per unit. The sales manager expects that meeting this order will generate an additional three sales in the future. The production manager, on the other hand, is evaluated on the basis of his standard manufacturing costs. This rush order will require an additional setup not previously planned. Claiming he just can't do it within the time constraints (when he actually could but at a cost that exceeds his budget), he will reject the rush order.

The new incentive system, merging sales and manufacturing into one profit center, created a system of mutually shared interests. Lost sales now hurt the bonuses of manufacturing as well as those of sales. The incremental production cost and benefits of rush orders impacted on sales as much as manufacturing. Sharing specialized knowledge was motivated because of shared bonuses. The benefits of shared bonuses outweigh the costs of the lost connection between controllability and responsibility. Joint evaluation was made necessary because now technology changed the optimal way of running the business.

Bathroom Fixtures Company

A second company had a similar problem but handled it differently. It produced bathroom fixtures in large quantities. Production involved the use of specialized molds and finishing processes. At the same time maximum capacity varied for different combinations of products passing through from the molding to sanding to kilning to finishing departments. The kilning process, for example, involved using carts that

EXHIBIT 2   Separate Evaluation Accounting (cannot accurately measure rush order costs)

Rush Orders

Manufacturing is in the best position to estimate short-term costs.	Sales is in the best position to estimate long-term benefits.

Book Entries for a Rush Order

	Manufacturing	*Sales*
Selling price		$10
Manufacturing cost	$5*	5
Contribution margin		$ 5†

*Manufacturing bonus base.
†Sales bonus base.

could be loaded only to certain configurations. Often fillers of dummy materials were needed physically to balance the load. If a suitable product mix was scheduled, the dummies were not required, thus increasing overall capacity. Rejects and reworking were also common.

New products were a problem for both production and sales. The following environmental conditions were important for success of new products:

1. Learning curves were relevant for both manufacturing and sales.

2. Consumer tastes could be fickle (small design changes could have a major sales impact).

3. Design changes could greatly influence the cost and quality of production.

4. Compatibility of the new line with the established lines was important for production efficiency.

In addition, established lines were not subject to design changes from sales and were scheduled based upon forecasts of housing starts and GNP. Because of the cyclical nature of new construction, sales had little short-term influence upon

established lines. However, skillful manufacturing management was still required to control costs and meet demand. For established lines, manufacturing had significantly more influence over costs than did sales.

Decentralized Decisions

Manufacturing will reject if costs expected to exceed $5 (e.g., $7).	Meeting rush orders today is expected to generate 3 future sales. Will accept any order > $5. Total benefit: 4 orders × contribution margin = 4 × $5 = $20.

Benefit to the Company as a Whole of Accepting the Rush Order

New sales less (manufacturing costs at standard plus incremental rush order costs)

$$4 \times \$10 - (4 \times 5 + \$2) = 40 - 22 = \underline{\$18}$$

New product lines presented a different set of problems. Small batches were required. Learning both consumer preferences and manufacturing traits took time and was not always successful. At the same time, new lines had to meet consumer preferences within profitability constraints.

As with the previous company, management adopted suitable incentive systems that reflected the differences between established and new product lines. Manufacturing was treated as a cost and bonus center for the established lines. New product lines, on the other hand, used joint bonus systems.

Questions

1. What cost accounting system and transfer price (if any) would you recommend for rebuilt carburetors, and what bonus plan would you recommend for the plant manager and the sales manager?

2. What cost accounting system and transfer price (if any) would you recommend for bathroom fixtures, and what bonus plan would you recommend for the production manager and the sales manager?

3. If your recommendations are different for these two situations, how do you explain the difference?

SERVICE ORGANIZATIONS

Much of the discussion in the previous chapters referred, at least implicitly, to manufacturing organizations—that is, to organizations that produce and market tangible goods. In Chapters 15 and 16, we describe the management control process in service organizations—that is, organizations that produce and market intangible services. In Chapter 15, we discuss the characteristics that distinguish service organizations in general from manufacturing organizations and the special problems that arise in professional, health care, nonprofit, government, and merchandising organizations. Chapter 16 focuses on financial service organizations.

Service Organizations in General

In the 18th and part of the 19th century, the work force in the United States was predominantly in agriculture. Later, it was predominantly in manufacturing. Early in the 20th century, employment in the service sector overtook employment in the manufacturing sector. By 1996, service sector employment grew to more than twice that of manufacturing as illustrated in Exhibit 15–1. Nevertheless, in the previous chapters, we tended to emphasize management control in manufacturing organizations. The reason is that much of the literature, and much of our own experience, is with manufacturing companies. In this and the next chapter we provide insights into management control systems for service organizations.

Characteristics

For several reasons, management control in service industries is somewhat different from the process in manufacturing companies. Some factors that have an impact on most service industries are discussed in this section. Others, which are characteristics of certain service industries, are discussed later. These characteristics also apply to the management control of legal,

---

EXHIBIT 15–1   U.S. Civilian Employment by Industry, 1995

Service Industries	*Number Employed (in 000s)*
Health care	10,588
Education	9,190
Transportation, communication and other public utilities	8,692
Finance, insurance, real estate	8,141
Other professional services*	9,252
Business services†	7,304
Other Services§	6,652
Government (except military)	5,814
Subtotal, services	65,633
Manufacturing, mining, construction	28,319
Wholesale and retail trade	25,699
Agriculture	3,409
Total employment	123,060

*Includes social services and legal services.
†Includes advertising, personnel supply services, services to buildings, consulting, computer and data processing, and protective services.
§Includes hotels and lodging places, private households, entertainment, and recreation.
Source: Statistical Abstract of the United States, 1995; adapted from Table 653.

---

research and development, and other service departments in companies generally.

Absence of Inventory Buffer.   Goods can be held in inventory, which is a buffer that dampens the impact on production activity of fluctuations in sales volume. Services cannot be stored. The airplane seat, hotel room, hospital operating room, or the hours of lawyers, physicians, scientists, and other professionals that are not used today are gone forever. Thus, although a manufacturing company can earn revenue in the future from products that are on hand today, a service company cannot do so. It must try to minimize its unused capacity.

Moreover, the costs of many service organizations are essentially fixed in the short run. In the short run, a hotel cannot reduce its costs substantially by closing off some of its rooms. Accounting firms, law firms, and other professional organizations are reluctant to lay off professional personnel in times of low sales volume because of the effect on morale and the costs of rehiring and training.

A key variable in most service organizations, therefore, is the extent to which current capacity is matched with demand. Organizations attempt this matching in two ways. First, they try to stimulate demand in off-peak periods by marketing efforts and price concessions. Cruise lines and resort hotels offer low rates in off seasons; airlines and hotels offer low rates on weekends; public utilities offer low rates on slack periods during a day. Second, if feasible, they adjust the size of the work force to the anticipated demand, by such measures as scheduling training activities in slack periods and compensating for long hours in busy periods with time off later. The loss from unsold services is so important that occupancy rates, "sold hours," load factors, student enrollment, hospital admissions, and similar indications of success in selling available services are normally key variables in service organizations.

Difficulty in Controlling Quality.   A manufacturing company can inspect its products before they are shipped to the consumer, and their quality can be measured visually or with instruments (tolerances, purity, weight, color, and so on). A service company cannot judge product quality until the moment the service is rendered, and then the judgments are often subjective. Restaurant management can examine the food in the kitchen, but customer satisfaction depends to a considerable extent on the way it is served. The quality of education is so difficult to measure that few educational organizations have a formal quality control system.

> **Example.** In service enterprises, intangible attributes often represent the main value: such attributes are on-time performance of transportation, schedule frequency and match to customer desires, friendliness and helpfulness of people who talk with customers, skill with which the service is carried out, information available at the location and time of customer contact, location of available service, waiting time, and appearance of facilities and people.
>
> When one looks at what it takes to be successful in a competitive service world, such intangibles as these stand out as the key factors of success. These are the important elements of output. In a physical product, such as an automobile, four-way adjustable bucket seats may be important to the customer; however, for purchasers of services, such as airline customers, having ticket counter people who are accessible, friendly, and knowledgeable may be the most important service characteristic. For a management accountant, bucket seats are fairly easy to cost out; the desired attributes of a ticket agent may be recognized as having value for the customer, but measuring the cost of providing that value is a difficult challenge.[1]

Labor Intensive.   Manufacturing companies add equipment and automate production lines that replace labor and reduce costs. Most service companies cannot do this. Hospitals do add expensive equipment; but most of these provide better treatment, and they increase, rather than reduce, costs.

Multi Unit Organizations.   Some service organizations operate many units in different locations, each of which is relatively small. These include fast-food restaurant chains, auto rental companies, gasoline service stations, and many others. Some of the units are owned; others operate under a franchise. The

---

[1]Professor William Rotch, remarks at a symposium on Management Accounting in Service Industries, March 16, 1990.

similarity of these separate units provides a basis for analyzing budgets and evaluating performance that is not present in the usual manufacturing company. The information for each unit can be compared with systemwide or regional averages, and high performers and low performers can be identified.

Because units differ in the mix of services they provide, in the resources that they use, and in other ways, care must be taken in making such comparisons. A technique for adjusting for these differences is called *data envelopment analysis*. It identifies the most efficient units by using statistical methods of allowing for differences. As originally proposed, the technique was overly complicated, but simplifications have made it useful in several industries.[2]

Historical Development

Cost accounting started in manufacturing companies because of the need to value work-in-process and finished goods inventories for financial statement purposes. These systems provided raw data that were easily adapted for use in setting selling prices and for other management purposes. Standard cost systems, separation of fixed and variable costs, and analysis of variances were built on the foundation of cost accounting systems. Until a few decades ago, most texts on cost accounting dealt only with practices in manufacturing companies.

Many service organizations (with the notable exception of railroads and other regulated industries) did not have a similar impetus to develop cost data. Their use of product cost and other management accounting data is fairly recent—mostly since World War II. Their management control systems are rapidly becoming as well developed as those in manufacturing companies.

Professional Organizations

Research and development organizations, law firms, accounting firms, health care organizations, engineering firms, architectural firms, consulting firms, advertising agencies, symphony and other arts organizations, and sports organizations (such as baseball teams) are examples of organizations whose products are professional services.

Special Characteristics

Goals.   As explained in Chapter 3, a dominant goal of a manufacturing company is to earn a satisfactory profit, specifically a satisfactory return on assets employed. A professional organization has relatively few tangible assets; its principal asset is the skill of its professional staff, which doesn't appear on its balance sheet. Return on assets employed, therefore, is essentially meaningless

---

[2]For a description, see H. David Sherman, *Service Organization Productivity Management*, (Hamilton, Ont.: Society of Management Accountants of Canada, 1988), Chapter 3.

in such organizations. Their financial goal is to provide adequate compensation to the professionals.

In many organizations, a related goal is to increase their size. In part, this reflects the natural tendency to associate success with large size. In part, it reflects economies of scale in using the efforts of a central personnel staff and units responsible for keeping the organization up to date. Large public accounting firms need to have enough local offices to enable them to audit clients who have facilities located throughout the world.

Professionals.   Professional organizations are labor intensive, and the labor is of a special type. Many professionals prefer to work independently, rather than as part of a team. Professionals who are also managers tend to work only part time on management activities; senior partners in an accounting firm participate actively in audit engagements; senior partners in law firms have clients. In most professions, education does not include education in management; quite naturally it stresses the importance of the profession, rather than that of management; for this and other reasons, professionals tend to look down on managers. Professionals tend to give inadequate weight to the financial implications of their decisions; they want to do the best job they can, regardless of its cost. This attitude tends to affect the attitude of support staffs and non-professionals in the organization; it leads to inadequate cost control.

Because professionals are the organization's most important resource, some authors have advocated that the value of these professionals should be counted as assets. The system that does this is called *human resource accounting*. In the 1970s, many books and articles were written on this subject, but few companies actually installed such a system, and we do not know of any that use one currently.[3] The problem of measuring the value of human assets is intractable.

Output and Input Measurement.   The output of a professional organization cannot be measured in physical terms, such as units, tons, or gallons. We can measure the number of hours a lawyer spends on a case, but this is a measure of input, not output. Output is the effectiveness of the lawyer's work, and this is not measured by the number of pages in a brief or the number of hours in the courtroom. We can measure the number of patients a physician treats in a day, and even classify these visits by type of complaint; but this is by no means equivalent to measuring the amount or quality of service the physician provided. At most, this measures the physician's efficiency in treating patients, which is of some use in identifying slackers and hard workers. Revenues earned is one measure of output in some professional organizations; but these monetary amounts, at most, relate to the quantity of services rendered, not to their quality (although poor quality is reflected in reduced revenues in the long run).

---

[3]See, for example, Eric G. Flamholtz, *Human Resources Accounting* (Encino, Calif.: Dickerson Publishing Company, 1974).

Example. There are more than 1,300 articles and books dealing with research on student ratings of teachers. They describe as many as 22 dimensions of teaching performance (e.g., "explains clearly," "uses class time well") and 20 variables that affect the ratings (e.g., size of course, time of day, gender, level of course). The best of these rating systems can identify very good teachers and very poor teachers, but none do a satisfactory job of ranking the 70 or 80 percent of teachers who are not at these extremes.[4]

Furthermore, the work done by many professionals is nonrepetitive. No two consulting jobs or research and development projects are quite the same. This makes it difficult to plan the time required for a task, to set reasonable standards for task performance, and to judge how satisfactory the performance was. Some tasks are essentially repetitive: the drafting of simple wills, deeds, sales contracts, and similar documents; the taking of a physical inventory by an auditor; and certain medical and surgical procedures are examples. The development of standards for such tasks may be worthwhile, although, in using these standards, unusual circumstances that affect a specific job must be taken into account.

Some professionals, notably scientists, engineers, and professors, are reluctant to keep track of how they spend their time, and this complicates the task of measuring performance. This reluctance seems to have its roots in tradition; usually, it can be overcome if senior management is willing to put appropriate emphasis on the necessity for accurate time reporting. Nevertheless, difficult problems arise in deciding how time should be charged to clients. If the normal work week is 40 hours, should a job be charged for ¹⁄₄₀th of a week's compensation for each hour spent on it? If so, how should work done on evenings and weekends be counted? (Professionals are "exempt" employees—that is, they are not subject to the government requirements for overtime payments.) How to account for time spent reading literature, going to meetings, and otherwise keeping up to date?

Small Size.   With a few exceptions, such as some law firms and accounting firms, professional organizations are relatively small and operate at a single location. Senior management in such organizations can personally observe what is going on and personally motivate employees. Thus, there is less need for a sophisticated management control system, with profit centers and formal performance reports. Nevertheless, even a small organization needs a budget, a regular comparison of performance against budget, and a way of relating compensation to performance.

Marketing.   In a manufacturing company there is a clear dividing line between marketing activities and production activities; only senior management is concerned with both. Such a clean separation does not exist in most

---

[4]Based on William E. Cashin, "Reliability, Validity, and Generalizability of Student Ratings of Instruction," *IDEA Paper no. 20*, Center for Faculty Evaluation and Development, Kansas State University, September 1988.

professional organizations, however. In some, such as law, medicine, and accounting, the profession's ethical code limits the amount and character of overt marketing efforts by professionals (although these restrictions have been relaxed in recent years). Marketing is an essential activity in almost all organizations, however. If it can't be conducted openly, it takes the form of personal contacts, speeches, articles, golf, and similar activities. These marketing activities are conducted by professionals, usually by professionals who spend much of their time in production work—that is, working for clients.

In such a situation, it is difficult to assign appropriate credit to the person responsible for "selling" a new customer. In a consulting firm, for example, a new engagement may result from a conversation between a member of the firm and an acquaintance in a company, or from the reputation of one of the firm's professionals as an outgrowth of speeches or articles. Moreover, the professional who is responsible for obtaining the engagement may not be personally involved in carrying it out. Until fairly recently, these marketing contributions were rewarded subjectively—that is, they were taken into account in promotion and compensation decisions. Some organizations now give explicit credit, perhaps as a percentage of the project's revenue, if the person who "sold" the project can be identified.

Management Control Systems

Pricing.   The selling price of work is set in a traditional way in many professional firms. If the profession is one in which members are accustomed to keeping track of their time, fees generally are related to professional time spent on the engagement. The hourly billing rate typically is based on the compensation of the grade of the professional (rather than the compensation of the specific person), plus a loading for overhead costs and profit. In other professions, such as investment banking, the fee typically is based on the monetary size of the security issue. In still others, there is a fixed price for the project. Prices vary widely among professions; they are relatively low for research scientists and relatively high for accountants and physicians.

In manufacturing companies, the profit component of the selling price is normally set so as to obtain, on average, a satisfactory return on assets employed. As noted above, the principal "asset" of a professional organization is the skill of its professionals, which is not measurable. Actually, the total value of the whole organization is greater than the sum of what the value of the individuals would be if they worked separately. This is because the firm already has incurred the cost of acquiring and training these individuals, has organized them according to their personality "fit" and other considerations, and has developed policies and procedures for assuring that the work is done efficiently and effectively. In this manner, the firm accepts responsibility for producing a satisfactory product, including the risk of loss if the work is not well done, and absorbs the cost of personnel who are not working on revenue-producing work.

These considerations implicitly affect the size of the "profit" component that is included in the fee.

Profit Centers and Transfer Pricing.   Although this would seem to be a contradiction of terms, nonprofit organizations make extensive use of profit centers. Support units, such as maintenance, information processing, transportation, telecommunication, printing, and procurement of material and services, charge consuming units for their services. The principles for transfer pricing are those described in Chapter 5.

The General Services Administration in the United States and Supply and Services Canada (SSC) are responsible for billions of dollars of such services. In Canada, SSC provides for the acquisition of all items costing more than $500. It operates a financial accounting and reporting system that cost $600 million in 1988, which any agency can use (although this is not required); and its Audit Services Bureau provides audit services similar to those provided by accounting firms (and it competes with these firms).[5]

Strategic Planning and Budgeting.   In general, formal strategic planning systems are not as well developed in professional organizations as in manufacturing companies of similar size. Part of the explanation is that professional organizations have no great need for such a system. In manufacturing companies, many program decisions involve commitments to procure plant and equipment; they have a predictable effect on both capacity and on costs for several future years, and, once made, they are essentially irreversible. In a professional organization, the principal assets are people; and, although short-run fluctuations in personnel levels are avoided, changes in the size and composition of the staff are easier to make and are more easily reversed than changes in the capacity of a physical plant. The strategic plan of a professional organization typically consists primarily of a long-range staffing plan, rather than a full-blown plan for all aspects of the firm's operation.

The budgeting process in professional organizations is similar to that described in Chapter 9.

> **Example.** An interesting variation in the approach to budget preparation is illustrated in Exhibit 15–2, which shows a budget for a relatively small accounting firm. The starting point in preparing this budget was the desired income of $100,000; this was calculated as a percentage of the estimated market value of the firm—that is, what the firm could be sold for. Salaries were estimated at the anticipated rates in the firm's locality in the budget year. Expenses were then estimated. The sum of desired income and expenses is the revenue that must be generated from billings, $1,106,000. Various combinations of billing rates and chargeable hours were calculated until a feasible combination that produces the desired income was found. (The amount in Exhibit 15–2 labeled "special billings" was a reduction in gross revenue for work that was billed at less than standard rates.)

[5]Haru Johri, Phil Charko, and Glyden Headley, "Transfer Pricing in the Federal Government," *CMA Magazine*, July-August 1990, pp. 12–16.

Exhibit 15-2 Budget for a CPA Firm

	Estimated Actual Year				Budget Year			
	Billed Hours	Standard Rate	Gross Revenue	Salary	Billed Hours	Standard Rate	Gross Revenue	Salary
Gross revenue:								
Armstrong	1,200	$150	$ 180,000	$120,000	1,200	$150	$ 180,000	$120,000
Baker	1,500	110	165,000	80,000	1,500	120	180,000	80,000
Colwell	1,500	110	165,000	80,000	1,500	110	165,000	80,000
(Additional)	—	—	—	—	800	100	80,000	40,000
Staff #1	1,800	60	108,000	50,000	1,800	60	108,000	54,000
Staff #2	1,600	60	96,000	40,000	1,800	60	108,000	43,000
Staff #3	1,800	50	90,000	40,000	1,800	55	99,000	43,000
Staff #4	1,700	50	85,000	30,000	1,800	55	99,000	32,000
Staff #5	—	—	—	—	900	50	45,000	25,000
Secretaries (2)	1,000	25	25,000	30,000	1,000	30	30,000	33,000
Clerks (2)	3,000	30	60,000	28,000	3,000	25	75,000	31,000
Total (at standard)	15,100		974,000	$498,000	17,100		1,169,000	$581,000
Special billings			(46,000)				(58,000)	
Net revenue			928,000				1,111,000	
Expenses:								
Salaries (as above)			498,000				581,000	
Benefits			124,000				145,000	
Controllable costs			164,000				150,000	
Fixed costs			120,000				130,000	
Total			$ 906,000				$1,006,000	
Income			$ 22,000				$ 105,000	

Control of Operations.   Much attention is, or should be, given to scheduling the time of professionals. The *billed time ratio*, which is the ratio of hours billed to total professional hours available, is watched closely. If, to use otherwise idle time or for marketing or public service reasons, some engagements are billed at lower than normal rates, the resulting price variance warrants close attention.

The inability to set standards for task performance, the desirability of carrying out work by teams, the consequent problems of managing a matrix organization, and the behavioral characteristics of professionals—all complicate the planning and control of the day-to-day operations in a professional organization. When the work is done by project teams, control is focused on projects. A written plan for each project is needed, and timely reports should be prepared that compare actual performance with planned performance in terms of cost, schedule, and quality, as described in Chapter 18.

Performance Measurement and Appraisal.   As noted above, at the extremes, the performance of professionals is easy to judge. Appraisal of the large percentage of professionals who are within either extreme is much more difficult. In some situations, objective measures of performance are available: the recommendations of an investment analyst can be compared with actual market behavior of the securities; the accuracy of a surgeon's diagnosis can be verified by an examination of the tissue that was removed; and skill can be measured by the success ratio of operation. These measures are, of course, subject to appropriate qualifications. In most circumstances, however, the assessment of performance is a matter of human judgment. These judgments may be made by superiors, peers, self, subordinates, or clients.

Most common are judgments made by superiors. Professional organizations increasingly use formal systems to collect performance appraisals as a basis for personnel decisions and for discussion with the professional. Some systems require numerical ratings of specified attributes of performance and provide for a weighted average of these ratings. Compensation may be tied, in part, to these numerical ratings. In a matrix organization, performance is judged both by the person's project leader and by the head of the functional unit that is his or her organizational "home."

Appraisals by a professional's peers, or by subordinates, are sometimes part of a formal control system. In some organizations, individuals may be asked to make a self-appraisal. Expressions of satisfaction or dissatisfaction from clients are also an important basis for judging performance, although such expressions may not be forthcoming in many engagements.

> **Example.** One firm that sells investment advice to institutional clients keeps a record of letters of commendation and criticism received from these clients, classifies these according to the analysts who made the relevant recommendations, and uses this information as part of its performance evaluation system.

The budget can be used as the basis for measuring cost performance, and the actual time taken can be compared with the planned time. Budgeting and control of discretionary expenses is as important in a professional firm as in a manufacturing company. Such financial measures are relatively unimportant in assessing a professional's contribution to the firm's profitability, however. The major contribution is related to the quantity and quality of the work, and its appraisal must be largely subjective. Furthermore, the appraisal must be made currently; it cannot wait until one learns whether a new building is well designed, a new control system actually works well, or a bond indenture has a flaw.

In some professions, internal audit procedures are used to control quality. In many accounting firms, the report of an audit is reviewed by a partner other than the one who is responsible for it, and the work of the whole firm is "peer reviewed" by another firm. The proposed design of a building may be reviewed by architects who are not actively involved in the project.

Health Care Organizations

Health care organizations consist of hospitals, clinics, and similar physicians' organizations; health maintenance organizations; retirement and nursing homes; home care organizations; and medical laboratories, among others. They constitute the largest industry in the United States: 14 percent of the gross national product, which is about the same percentage as the *total* of all durable goods manufacturers.[6] Although they have most of the characteristics of non-profit organizations, which are discussed in the next section, many of them are profit-oriented companies.

Special Characteristics

Difficult Social Problem.   Society is gradually coming to grips with the fact that the present health care delivery system is unworkable. Although physicians are bound by the Hippocratic oath to provide adequate health care to their patients, the system cannot do this. On the one hand, the cost per treatment is inevitably increasing with the development of new equipment and new drugs; hospital expenses increased from $28.0 billion in 1970 to over $300 billion by 1996. (Contrast this trend with the typical experience of manufacturing companies, in which new equipment usually reduces unit costs.) On the other hand, the number of ill persons is increasing because medical advances prolong the lives of elderly people, who are the most likely to require treatment. Society cannot pay for the predictable increases if the present rate of increase in cost continues much longer. Health care providers are aware of this problem; but they don't know how society, especially the Congress, will deal with it. It is

---

[6]Data in this section are taken from the following tables in the *Statistical Abstract of the United States*, 1995; No. 136 (overall expenditures); No. 166 (hospitals); and No. 629 (employment). For more detailed data, see the following annual publications: U.S. National Center for Health Statistics, *Health, United States*; U.S. Health Care Financing Administration, *Health Care Financing Review*; American Hospital Association, *Hospital Statistics*.

clear, however, that health care delivery will change drastically. Health care organizations must be alert to these changes.

Change in Mix of Providers.   Within the overall increase in health care cost, significant changes have occurred in the way in which health care is delivered and, hence, in the viability of certain types of providers. Many services that traditionally were provided in hospitals on an inpatient basis are now provided in outpatient clinics or in patients' homes. Entrepreneurs have entered the industry to provide these new services. There also has been a shift from small local hospitals to larger regional or medical center hospitals. The number of hospital beds decreased by 30 percent from 1970 to 1995. To remain viable, hospitals must have the flexibility to adapt to these changes, either by providing more outpatient services themselves or by eliminating inpatient services that are no longer profitable.

Third-Party Payers.   Of the more than $800 billion total expenditures for health care in 1996, 43 percent was financed by the government, 35 percent by insurance companies, and only 22 percent by individual patients. An estimated 37 million people in the United States have no health insurance; their costs are met by Medicaid, absorbed by health care providers, or paid for by the patient directly. The largest government program is Medicare, a federal program that provides support for persons age 65 and up and for younger persons with certain disabilities. The Medicaid program pays for services provided to low-income people; it is financed by the states within general guidelines set by the federal government.

Until 1983, Medicare reimbursed on the basis of "reasonable" costs incurred, which gave health care providers little incentive to control costs. Currently, Medicare reimburses hospitals on the basis of Diagnostic Related Groups (DRGs). Medical and surgical procedures are classified into one of about 500 DRGs, each DRG is priced annually at a set dollar amount, and hospitals are reimbursed for these amounts, regardless of the actual length of stay or the actual costs incurred for individual patients. Other third-party payers have moved toward a similar system of reimbursement.

The DRG system, and the increase in hospital costs per patient, has motivated hospitals to install sophisticated cost accounting systems, usually systems that they purchase from an outside computer software organization and then adapt to their own needs. Some hospitals provide information processing services to other hospitals on a contract basis. These systems provide information on individual patients (similar to job-cost systems in automobile repair shops), and they report actual costs compared with standard costs for each DRG; costs are classified by departments and even by attending physicians within departments.

This information is in addition to information traditionally collected in hospitals; it focuses on outputs (patient care), as well as on inputs (cost per laboratory test).

Increasingly, health maintenance organizations (HMOs) reimburse physicians, hospitals, and other providers. They contract with companies to provide medical services to employees at a fixed cost per person covered. In turn, the HMO contracts with hospitals and other providers, in some cases at a specified amount per DRG. The HMO therefore has the difficult task of controlling its payments so that they do not exceed the fees earned, but nevertheless seeing to it that adequate health care is provided.

Professionals.   The health care industry employed 3,225,000 professionals (physicians, dentists, registered nurses, and therapists), which was more than any other industry except education. The management control implications of professionals are the same as those discussed in the preceding section. Their primary loyalty is to the profession, rather than to the organization. Departmental managers typically are professionals whose management function is only part-time; the chief of surgery does surgery. Historically, physicians have tended to give relatively little emphasis to cost control. In particular, there has been an impression that they prescribe more than the optimum number of tests, partly because of the danger of malpractice suits if they don't detect all the patient's symptoms.

Importance of Quality Control.   The health care industry deals with human lives, so the quality of the service it provides is of paramount importance. There are tissue reviews of surgical procedures, peer review of individual physicians, and, in recent years, outside review agencies mandated by the federal government.

Management Control Process

Subject to the characteristics described above, the management control process in the health care industry is similar to that described in Chapters 8 through 12. Because of the shift in the product mix and because of the increase in the quantity and cost of new equipment, the strategic planning process in hospitals is becoming of increasing importance. The annual budget preparation process is conventional. Huge quantities of information are available quickly for the control of operating activities. Financial performance is analyzed by comparing actual revenues and expenses with budgets, identifying important variances, and taking appropriate actions on them.

Nonprofit Organizations

A nonprofit organization, as defined in law, is an organization that cannot distribute assets or income to, or for the benefit of, its members, officers, or directors. The organization can, of course, compensate its employees, including officers and members, for services rendered and for goods supplied. This definition does not prohibit an organization from *earning* a profit; it prohibits only the *distribution* of profits. A nonprofit organization needs to earn a modest profit, on average, to provide funds for working capital and for possible "rainy days."

Nonprofit organizations that meet the criteria of Section 501(c) of the Internal Revenue Code are exempt from income taxes (except on their "unrelated business income"); about 1.2 million organizations satisfy these criteria in the U.S. If they are religious, charitable, or educational organizations as defined in Section 501(c) (3) of the code, contributions made to them are tax deductible by the contributor; they are called "501(c) (3) organizations." Most such organizations are exempt from property taxes and from certain types of sales taxes.

In many industry groups, there are both nonprofit and profit-oriented (i.e., business) organizations. There are nonprofit and for-profit hospitals, nonprofit and for-profit ("proprietary") schools and colleges, and even for-profit religious organizations. SRI International is a nonprofit research organization that competes with Arthur D. Little, Inc., a for-profit research organization.

Special Characteristics

Absence of the Profit Measure.   A dominant goal of most businesses is to earn a satisfactory profit; net income measures performance toward this goal. No such measure of performance exists in nonprofit organizations. Many of them have several goals, and an organization's effectiveness in attaining its goals rarely can be measured by quantitative amounts. The absence of a satisfactory, quantitative, overall measure of performance is the most serious management control problem in a nonprofit organization.

The income statement is the most useful financial statement in a nonprofit organization, just as it is in a business. The net income number is interpreted differently in the two types of organizations, however. In a business, as a general rule, the larger the income, the better the performance. In a nonprofit organization, net income should average only a small amount above zero. A large net income signals that the organization is not providing the services that those who supplied resources had a right to expect; a string of net losses will lead to bankruptcy, just as in a business. Although financial performance is not the dominant goal in a nonprofit organization, it is a necessary goal because the organization cannot survive if its revenues on average are less than its expenses.

Contributed Capital.   There is only one major difference between the accounting transactions in a business and those in a nonprofit organization; it relates to the equity section of the balance sheet. A business corporation has transactions with its shareholders—issuance of stock and the payment of dividends—that a nonprofit organization doesn't have. A nonprofit organization receives contributed capital, which few businesses have. (In both businesses and nonprofit organizations, equity is increased by earning income.)

There are two principal categories of contributed capital: plant and endowment. Plant includes contributions of buildings and equipment, or contributions of funds to acquire these assets; works of art and other museum objects. Endowment consists of gifts whose donors intend that the principal amount will remain intact indefinitely (or at least for many years); only the income on this principal will be used to finance current operations.

The receipt (or pledge) of a contributed capital asset is not revenue—that is, neither contributions of plant nor of endowment are available to finance the operating activities of the period in which the contribution is received. Endowment assets must be kept separate from operating assets. This is a legal requirement for a "true" endowment, and it is sound policy for a "board-designated" endowment—that is, funds that the trustees have decided to treat as endowment, even though there is no legal requirement that they do so. It follows that capital contributions should be reported separately from operating contributions, that is, from revenues from annual fund drives, grants, and other gifts intended to finance current operations.

Thus, a nonprofit organization has two sets of financial statements. One set relates to operating activities; it includes an operating statement, a balance sheet, and a statement of cash flows that are the same as those found in business. The second set relates to contributed capital; it has a statement of inflows and outflows of contributed capital during a period and a balance sheet that reports contributed capital assets and the related liabilities and equity. Inflows of contributed capital are capital contributions received in the period and gains on the endowment portfolio; outflows are the endowment income that is reported as operating revenue, losses on the endowment portfolio, and write-offs of plant.

Fund Accounting.   Many nonprofit organizations use an accounting system that is called "fund accounting." Accounts are kept separately for several funds, each of which is self-balancing (i.e., the sum of the debit balances equals the sum of the credit balances). Most organizations have (1) a *general fund or operating fund*, which corresponds closely to the set of operating accounts mentioned above; (2) a *plant fund* and an *endowment fund*, which account for contributed capital assets and equities mentioned above; and (3) a variety of other funds for special purposes. Some of these other funds, such as the pension fund, are also found in business, although in business they are reported in the notes to the financial statements, rather than in the financial statements themselves. Others are useful for internal control purposes. For management control purposes, the primary focus is on the general fund.

Financial Accounting.   The Financial Accounting Standards Board (FASB) has issued four standards on nonprofit organizations: *Statement No. 93* on depreciation (1987), *Statement No. 116* on contributions (1993), *Statement No. 117* on financial statements (1993), and *Statement No. 124* on investments (1995). These pronouncements govern financial statements prepared for external purposes; their requirements are fundamentally different from those described in the preceding paragraphs. In reports for management and the governing board, many nonprofit organizations continue to use the practices described above. The basic difference is that the management system makes a basic distinction between operating and nonoperating transactions, whereas the FASB system makes a basic distinction between transactions restricted by contributors and other transactions.

Governance. Nonprofit organizations are governed by boards of trustees. Trustees usually are not paid, and many of them are unfamiliar with business management. Therefore, they generally exercise less control than the directors of a business corporation. Moreover, because performance is more difficult to measure in a nonprofit organization than in a business, the board is less able to identify actual or incipient problems.

The need for a strong governing board in a nonprofit organization is greater than that in a business, because the vigilance of the governing board may be the only effective way of detecting when the organization is in difficulty. In a profit-oriented organization, a decrease in profits provides this danger signal automatically.

Management Control Systems

Product Pricing. Many nonprofit organizations give inadequate attention to their pricing policies. Pricing of services at their full cost is desirable.

A "full-cost" price is the sum of direct costs, indirect costs, and, perhaps, a small allowance for increasing the organization's equity. This principle applies to services that are directly related to the organization's objectives. Pricing for peripheral activities should be market-based. Thus, a nonprofit hospital should price its health care services at full cost, but prices in its gift shop should be market-based.

In general, the smaller and more specific the unit of service that is priced, the better the basis for decisions about the allocation of resources. For example, a comprehensive daily rate for hospital care, which was common practice a few decades ago, masks the revenues for the mix of services actually provided. Beyond a certain point, of course, the cost of the paperwork associated with pricing units of service outweighs the benefits.

As a general rule, management control is facilitated when prices are established prior to the performance of the service. If an organization is able to recover its incurred costs, management is not motivated to worry about cost control.

Strategic Planning and Budget Preparation. In nonprofit organizations that must decide how best to allocate limited resources to worthwhile activities, strategic planning is a more important and more time-consuming process than in the typical business. The process is similar to that described in Chapter 8, except that the absence of a profit measure makes program decisions more subjective.

The budget preparation process is similar to that described in Chapter 9. Colleges and universities, welfare organizations, and organizations in certain other nonprofit industries know, before the budget year begins, the approximate amount of their revenues. They do not have the option of increasing revenues during the year by increasing their marketing efforts. They budget expenses so the organization will at least break even at the estimated amount of revenue. They require that managers of responsibility centers limit spending close to the budget amounts. The budget is, therefore, the most important management control tool, at least with respect to financial activities.

Operation and Evaluation.   In most nonprofit organizations, there is no way of knowing what the optimum operating costs are. Responsibility center managers, therefore, tend to spend whatever is allowed in the budget, even though the budgeted amount may be higher than is necessary. Conversely, they may refrain from making expenditures that have an excellent payoff simply because the expenditure was not included in the budget.

Although nonprofit organizations had a reputation for operating inefficiently, this perception has been changing in recent years, for good reasons. Many organizations have had increasing difficulty in raising funds, especially from government sources. This has led to belt-tightening and to increased attention to management control. As mentioned above, the most dramatic change has been in hospital costs, with the introduction of reimbursement on the basis of standard prices for diagnostic-related groups.

Government Organizations

Government organizations are service organizations and, except for businesslike activities, they are nonprofit organizations. Thus, the characteristics described above for these organizations apply to government. Their businesslike activities, such as electric and water utilities, operate like their private-sector counterparts.

Special Characteristics

Political Influences.   In government organizations, decisions result from multiple and often conflicting pressures. In part, these political pressures are an inevitable—and up to a point are a desirable—substitute for the forces of the marketplace. Elected officials cannot function if they are not reelected; and to be reelected, they must—up to a point—advocate the perceived needs of their constituents, even though these needs may not be in the best interests of society as a whole. These conflicting pressures result in less than optimum decisions. Elected officials may inhibit managers from making sound business decisions; they may be required to favor certain suppliers or to hire political supporters. Strict procurement policies and civil service regulations attempt to lessen these pressures, with some success.

Public Information.   In a democratic society the press and public believe that they have a right to know everything there is to know about a government organization. In the federal government and in some states, this feeling is recognized by *freedom of information* statutes. Channels for distributing this information may be biased. Some media stories that describe mismanagement tend to be exaggerated and to give inadequate recognition to the fact that mistakes are inevitable in any organization. To reduce opportunities for unfavorable media stories, government managers take steps to limit the amount of sensitive, controversial information that flows through the formal management control system. This lessens the effectiveness of the system.

Attitude toward Clients.   For-profit companies and many nonprofit organizations are *client supported*—that is, they obtain their revenues from clients. Additional clients mean additional revenues, so these organizations welcome actual and potential clients and treat them well. Most government organizations are *public supported*; they obtain their revenues from the general public. To them, additional clients are a burden, to be accepted with misgivings, because they create an additional demand for a fixed amount of service capacity. Although this tendency may be mitigated by the professional's desire to do a good job, it nevertheless exists and results in well-known complaints about poor service and the surly attitude of "bureaucrats." Managers recognize this and do their best to persuade employees to provide satisfactory service. The revenue sources of public-supported organizations are legislative bodies and granting agencies; legislators and grantors are given even more consideration than are clients in client-supported organizations.

Red Tape.   The government, especially the federal government, has promulgated huge and increasing numbers of rules and regulations. Some of these are necessary; every Internal Revenue Service examiner should use the same rules in resolving income tax issues. Others are reactions to minor misdeeds that become highly publicized.

> **Example.** In 1993, responding to a few instances in which contractors "ripped off" the Agency, the Environmental Protection Agency (EPA) adopted new rules that involved filling out many new forms; research scientists in EPA laboratories were required to monitor adherence to these rules. Consequently, EPA scientists diverted substantial amounts of their time from research work to compliance work, and the time required to approve contracts increased from 16 months to 26 months.[7]

Under the direction of Vice President Al Gore, the government in 1993 initiated the latest of many efforts to reduce the amount of this red tape.

Management Compensation.   Managers and other professionals in government organizations tend to be less well compensated than their counterparts in business. This results from a populist perception on the part of the general

---

[7]*Science*, October 1993, p. 647.

public—a feeling that "one person is as good as another"—which, in turn, influences legislators. Consequently, the best managers do not go into public service (unless they have acquired wealth from other sources). There are exceptions to this generalization; some government organizations pay competitive compensation to school administrators, university faculty, and certain types of scientists and engineers. At lower levels, compensation tends to be higher than that prevailing in the private sector. This results in "salary compression," which complicates the problem of rewarding good performance.

Financial Accounting.   Accounting standards for state and local governments and other nonfederal organizations are established by the Governmental Accounting Standards Board. Accounting standards for the federal government are established by the Federal Accounting Standards Advisory Board; its first complete set of standards was published in 1996.

Management Control Systems

Strategic Planning and Budget Preparation.   Strategic planning is especially important in government organizations. Managers and legislators must make difficult decisions about the allocation of resources. Some of these decisions reflect political pressures. Others, however, are the results of sophisticated analyses. Especially in the federal government, benefit/cost techniques are more highly developed and more skillfully applied than in most business organizations. Until the 1960s, the process was informal; but, with the development of the Planning-Programming-Budgeting System (PPBS) in the federal government, it has become increasingly formalized. The annual budget process is an extremely important control device in government, as it is in other nonprofit organizations.

Performance Measurement.   Income is the difference between revenues and expenses. Expenses can be measured approximately as accurately in government organizations as in business (although currently the accounting systems in most government organizations do not do a good job of this). Revenue is not a measure of output in government organizations, however. In the absence of this monetary measure, governments have developed nonmonetary indicators. These measures can be classified in various ways. One classification based on what they purport to measure is (1) results measures, (2) process measures, and (3) social indicators.

A *results measure* (also known as *outcomes measure*) is a measure of output that is supposedly related to the organization's objectives. Number of students graduating from high school, number of miles of roads completed, number of on-time arrivals at airports, are examples. These measures are rarely an exact measure of output; the number of graduates says nothing about how well the students were educated. Nevertheless, the measures may be a satisfactory *surrogate*.

A *process measure* is related to an activity carried on by the organization. Examples are the number of livestock inspected in a week, the number of purchase orders issued in a day, or the number of lines entered into a computer in an hour. Process measures are useful in measuring current, short-run performance. They are easier to interpret than results measures, because usually there is a close causal relationship between inputs (i.e., costs) and the process measure. Process measures relate to efficiency, not to effectiveness—that is, they measure what was done, not whether what was done helped achieve the organization's objectives. They are "means-oriented," as contrasted with results measures, which are "ends-oriented."

A *social indicator* is a broad measure of output that reflects the result of the work of the organization. Since social indicators are affected by external forces, they are at best only a rough indication of the accomplishments of the organization itself. Life expectancy is an indication of the effectiveness of a country's health care system; but it is also affected by the standard of living, dietary and smoking habits, and other causes. Social indicators are useful principally in long-range analyses of strategic problems. They are so nebulous, so difficult to obtain on a current basis, so little affected by current efforts, and so much affected by external influences that they are of limited usefulness in day-to-day management.

Merchandising Organizations

Retailers, distributors, wholesalers, and similar organizations usually are not classified as service organizations; however, they obviously are not manufacturing organizations either. To avoid omitting them entirely, they are discussed briefly in this section.

Unlike service organizations, inventory is important in merchandising organizations. Indeed, department heads in these organizations usually are called "buyers," rather than "managers," which indicates the importance of the procurement function. A principal control device is *open to buy*, which is the maximum amount that the buyer can have in inventory *and on order* at any time.

Control of working capital is especially important in merchandising companies. Many companies reduce inventories by systems that automatically place orders with vendors when an item reaches a reorder point. Receivables have greatly decreased in size because credit sales are now handled largely by credit-card companies.

For retailers, sales (or gross margin) per foot of shelf space or per square foot of showroom space is an important control device. Similar products from different manufacturers must compete with one another for scarce space.

Merchandising industries have well-developed management control systems. Although we have tended to emphasize techniques in manufacturing companies, similar techniques have been used for many years in merchandising companies. Furthermore, trade associations and private organizations have developed systems for collecting information on revenues, costs, and other elements, which are useful in comparing one company's performance with averages in the industry.

Summary

Management control in service organizations is different from that in manufacturing organizations, primarily because of the absence of an inventory buffer between production and sales, because of the difficulty of measuring quality, and because the organizations are labor-intensive. Professional organizations do not have the dominant goal of return on assets employed; professionals have their own behavioral characteristics, output measurements are subjective, and there is no clear line between marketing and production activities. Health care organizations must adjust to the fact that the current system is unworkable. Nonprofit organizations lack the advantages that the profit measure provides, and they must account for contributed capital that rarely occurs in a business. Government organizations have the well-known problems associated with political influences and the bureaucracy. In merchandising organizations, inventory and working capital management are especially important.

Nevertheless, the essentials of the management control systems in service organizations are the same as those described in earlier chapters.

Suggested Additional Readings

Albrecht, Karl, and Ron Zemke. *Service America: Doing Business in the New Economy*. Homewood, Ill.: Dow Jones-Irwin, 1985.

Anthony, Robert N., and David W. Young. *Management Control in Nonprofit Organizations*, 5th edition. Homewood, Ill.: Richard D. Irwin, 1994.

Barton, Thomas L., and Robert J. Fox. "Evolution at American Transtech." *Management Accounting*, April 1988, pp. 49–52.

Collier, David A. *Service Management*. Reston, Va.: Reston Publishing, 1985.

Douglas, Patricia P. *Governmental and Nonprofit Accounting*. Orlando, Fla.: Harcourt Brace Jovanovich, 1991.

Hay, Leon E. *Accounting for Governmental and Nonprofit Entities*. 7th ed. Homewood, Ill.: Richard D. Irwin, 1985.

Henke, Emerson O. *Introduction to Nonprofit Organization Accounting*. 2nd ed. Belmont, Calif.: Wadsworth, 1985.

Herbert, Leo A., Harry N. Killough, and Alan Walter Steiss. *Accounting and Control for Governmental and Other Nonbusiness Organizations*. New York: McGraw-Hill, 1987.

Heskitt, James L. *Managing in the Service Economy*. Boston: Harvard Business School Press, 1984.

McGregor, Calvert C., Jr., Larry N. Killough, and Robert M. Brown. "An Investigation of Organization-Professional Conflict in Management Accounting." *Journal of Management Accounting Research*, Fall 1989, pp. 104–18.

Prince, Thomas R. *Financial Reporting and Cost Control for Health Care Entities*. Health Administration Press, 1992.

Quinn, J. B. *Intelligent Enterprise*. New York: The Free Press, 1993, Chapter 1.

Sherman, H. David. *Service Organization Productivity Management*. Hamilton, Ontario: Society of Management Accountants of Canada, 1988.

U.S. General Accounting Office. "Budget Issues: Human Resource Programs Warranting Consideration as Human Capital." Washington, D.C.: 1990, GAO/AFMd-90-52.

————. Program Evaluation and Methodology Division. *Designing Evaluations: A Workbook*. Washington, D.C.: February 1986, U.S. GAO.

CASE 15–1
COOKIE, INC.

The advertising industry was experiencing a shakeout, which compelled Cookie's management to consider the profitability of its client accounts.

Background

In 1990 Cookie Associates, Inc., was one of the largest advertising agencies in America. Advertising billings for the industry were over $260 billion on a worldwide basis in 1988, compared to $125 billion in 1982. The 20 largest firms accounted for nearly 35 percent of worldwide billings in 1990. Of the top 20 agencies, 14 were independent agency networks and six were advertising groups (firms with more than one agency network). The majority of these firms were based in the United States or United Kingdom. The proliferation of extensive advertising groups was due to the need to provide services around the globe as their clients entered new markets.

Advertising agencies were retained by large and small companies to develop marketing plans, create advertising strategies and campaigns, and execute the advertising plans. Agencies ranged from those strictly providing traditional advertising services to those with extensive market research and consulting capabilities. The most successful partnerships between advertisers and agencies were those that lasted for years. To best serve a client, an agency had to be extremely knowledgeable about its clients' products and strategies. Cookie had worked with many of its clients for more than 20 years.

Advertising agencies were compensated by their clients in one of two ways. First, the ad agency would receive a 15 percent commission on advertising placed in television, radio, or print. The client would be billed the full amount, and 15 percent would be "kicked back" to the agency from the medium. Creative work and development of the campaign would not be charged to the client (except out-of-pocket expenditures). This had been the traditional compensation structure.

With the increased use of nonadvertising services, a fee based system was introduced. These services included design, graphics, market research, sales promotion, direct mail campaigns, merchandising, event planning, and public relations. For the use of these non-traditional services, clients were charged for billable hours plus expenditures (similar to the compensation arrangement for law firms). For production of the campaign (actually producing material or copy), the client was billed on a cost plus 15 percent arrangement. This fee structure was necessary because the kickback scheme was no longer feasible with the new services and different media.

Cookie was organized into six divisions, as indicated below:

Account management: The account executive and his/her staff were responsible for the overall client contact. This group handled development of the marketing plan and strategy and coordination of other divisions within the advertising firm.

Creative management: The creative division conceived, created, and developed the advertising copy and artwork for the advertisements.

Information management: The information division's primary responsibility was planning and conducting market research. The division recommended promotion strategies and merchandising

This case was adapted by Anil Chitkara (T'94). This case is based (with permission) on an earlier case prepared by J. M. McInnes under the supervision of J. R. Yeager.

programs. A library and training group was maintained for client sales training.

Media management: The media division developed the media strategy and purchased media space and time in various media.

Administrative management: This division managed the advertising agency itself including the human resource, finance, and support functions.

Production management: In the past, agencies hired producers, booked studios, and produced television and radio copy externally. As Cookie grew, it established a production department that employed a staff of producers, directors, and production personnel; it owned some production and editing equipment. This group worked closely with the creative and account management teams.

The account executive was responsible for the overall management of the client account. The executive coordinated the client work within the agency including the creative, marketing, and media strategies. A new account executive was typically given one account; as the account executive developed, additional accounts would be transferred to him or her. The frequent turnover required the executives to learn new businesses each time an account was transferred to them. The learning was an expensive undertaking, but Cookie felt that it brought fresh thinking to the client's products.

New Client Decisions

One of the most critical roles of the agency's senior management was to decide which new clients to accept. Potential clients with products that competed with an existing client's products could not even be considered. With this exception, Cookie would consider any new client that met the following criteria: the client must have a solid business reputation and be in good standing in the community, and the client's product must meet a consumer need.

Cookie used its past experience to assess the profit potential of new accounts. The agency served approximately 50 clients and over 250 products, covering a wide range of product categories. Using cost data from these current accounts, an estimate of the servicing cost would be calculated for new accounts. Additionally, an estimate would be made of the spending necessary to build up a product to the desired market share. Typically a product's cost included an allowance for advertising costs. If the advertising allowance could cover the expected cost of building market share and maintaining the product, that would constitute prima facie evidence for accepting the assignment.

New Product Introduction

Launching new products generated a host of problems when estimating the costs of introduction. First the information management division would conduct marketing studies and use focus groups to determine if there was a consumer need. If a need existed, the consumer benefit would be identified. This did not constitute limited introduction, but instead it was considered test marketing to gauge consumer acceptance. Cookie maintained a research panel of several thousand consumers around the country to conduct test marketing.

If a consumer need was identified, a creative strategy, based primarily on the consumer benefit, was developed. Test marketing would continue to determine the effectiveness of the execution of the creative strategy. If this test marketing was unsuccessful, it was assumed that the selling message was not conveyed effectively and changes would be made to the execution. The creative strategy would not be challenged; this would be time consuming for both the client and the agency.

After concluding the test marketing phase, the agency would make recommendations to the client regarding the probable outcome of a full-scale product launch. Only after the client decided to proceed and advertising spending had grown would the agency generate any significant revenue from the assignment. This revenue had to cover all expenses up to that time; management's early assessment of the product's chances of success was critical to the profitability of Cookie.

Existing Product Support

Advertising strategy related to existing products was quite different from that of new products. Market acceptance of existing products was better known, although product obsolescence was a constant concern. The reason for advertising support of an existing product was to maintain consumer awareness of the product's attributes. The client's marketing group worked closely with the agency to develop new plans to increase the product's market share.

A new campaign for an existing product would begin when the previous campaign's run period had concluded. The decision to develop a new campaign required both the client and the agency's judgment. A drop in a product's market share was a definite sign that a new campaign should be considered. Additionally, meeting competitive threats was a critical part of the maintenance of a product.

New campaigns would be managed within the agency by the account executive. First the creative department would develop a strategy. The account executive and his or her staff would review the strategy with the client's sales team. An advertising strategy and marketing plan would be agreed upon and the necessary advertisements, commercials, and other promotional material would be prepared. The media department would then arrange for the execution of the plan through the various media.

Account Profitability

Another critical responsibility of the agency's top management was to assess the profitability of various accounts. The most profitable accounts were those which advertised frequently with the same copy. The agency's major expenses were incurred up to and including the preparation of advertising copy. After that time, the agency simply executed the advertising plan through the purchase of media time and space. A client that required constant development of new copy was far less profitable than one that used the same copy numerous times. Constant development meant additional creative strategy and copy development, which were expensive undertakings.

A client's size frequently had an impact on its profitability. In large client organizations, the advertising plan had to be cleared at numerous levels, which involved a great deal of time and effort on the agency's behalf. Additional revisions to the plan and numerous conferences might deem a large client's account unprofitable.

There were more compelling reasons to keep a client account other than its profitability. If a particular product account was unprofitable, it might be retained because the agency held accounts for additional client products that were profitable. Additionally, the client may choose to continue a marginally profitable product line for competitive reasons. In this case, little advertising was in order. The agency would continue to handle such an account, albeit minimally.

Personnel Costs

A large part of the costs associated with servicing an account was personnel. Payroll accounted for 60 to 65 percent of the gross revenues of Cookie. In a typical agency, other expenses accounted for 20 to 25 percent of revenues; the remaining 10-20 percent was pretax profit.

All employees except administrative staff filed time sheets that accounted for all of their working time and the client associated with each fraction thereof. Administrative personnel who could allocate their time to a specific client did so. Approximately 85 percent of the payroll was accountable to individual clients. Since 65 percent of revenues covered payroll and 85 percent of payroll was accountable, 55 percent of revenues were direct personnel expenses. The rule-of-thumb was developed that if direct payroll associated with an account was less than 55 percent of revenues, the account was profitable.

Of the nonpayroll expenses, approximately 20 percent (4 to 5 percent of revenues) could be allocated to a client. This included travel, entertainment, rough copy costs, research, and copy pretesting. Indirect expenses included rent, telephone, and utilities. These expenses were allocated based on direct payroll.

Cookie was extremely secretive about the profitability of its accounts. The agency differed from others in the industry in that account profitability was known to only three people: Cookie's chairman, president, and treasurer. This policy was created so that the team on an account provided the highest level of service to a client, without knowledge of the account's profitability. The agency's management believed that employees would have less enthusiasm when working on unprofitable accounts and the quality of work would be poor. It was top management's job to decide on account retention, and the rest of the firm would be responsible for serving the clients.

T&D Corporation Account

T&D Corporation was a large manufacturer of tools and dies that were sold to industrial customers. The corporation had numerous autonomous divisions each of which conducted its own business, except when the overall corporate image was involved—this included advertising. The corporation's divisions used both Cookie and other advertising agencies.

Until a recent review, each of T&D's divisions that used Cookie were thought to be profitable to the agency. However, a recent review of T&D's International Division account questioned its profitability. A profit and loss worksheet for the T&D International Division account is provided in Exhibit 1.

The International Division was not an advertiser in the mass media. Additionally, it undertook its own artwork in-house. Cookie's main responsibilities were to provide advertising copy and buy media space. To best serve the client, the account executive on T&D International had spent considerable time and energy learning the client's business and understanding T&D Corporation's objectives. This was done to create an advertising plan that would be supported by the client's corporate management. The account executive spent considerable time ensuring that the copywriters were thoroughly familiar with the company as well so that the copy would be in line with T&D's corporate policies.

Miles Brush, a member of Cookie's staff at headquarters, had been told to prepare a report for the agency's top management review of the T&D International account. The report was to cover all relevant issues, set forth alternative courses of action, estimate the consequences of each, and articulate Brush's recommendation.

Questions

1. What management control system would you recommend for Cookie, Inc.?
2. What would you include in the report described at the end of the case?

EXHIBIT 1   Income Statement for T&D International Division

Customer = T&D International Division
Product = Professional Prod.
Period = Year to 12/31/89

Billing	$870,000
Commissions and fees	$154,500
Direct payroll:	
Account management	45,000
Copy	55,000
Art	25,000
Media	7,500
Administrative	3,750
	136,250
Other direct expenses:	
Unbillable costs	1,500
Travel	500
Entertainment	1,500
	3,500
Indirect expenses:	
Occupancy	20,000
Employee benefits	8,000
Telephone	5,250
Indirect service departments	36,500
Other indirect	17,000
	86,750
Total expense	226,500
Profit (loss) before taxes	($ 72,000)

CASE 15–2
WILLIAMSON AND OLIVER

In early 1984, the policy board of Williamson and Oliver approved the suggestion of Ted Johnson, national managing partner, to institute an incentive compensation plan applicable to all the partners in the firm. (The plan is described in Exhibit 1.) One senior partner in the firm observed:

> In my opinion, this incentive plan is a step in the right direction. We want our partners to improve current profits; but, at the same time, we cannot lose sight of the longer-term development of our firm. I think the incentive plan explicitly considers the multidimensional nature of the partner's tasks. I am sure, though, that the plan needs to be fine-tuned as we gain more experience.

In 1984 Williamson and Oliver was one of the largest and fastest-growing public accounting firms in the United States. It had offices in more than 50 major cities and had over 500 partners. A major part of the firm's growth came from bases established through acquisition of local and regional CPA practices. Each office engaged in auditing, management advisory services, and taxation services. The practice offices were grouped into five areas, each headed by an area director. Reporting to the area directors were partners-in-charge (PIC), who managed the individual offices. Each area director was also the partner-in-charge for one of the offices in the area. About 15 partners and the related supporting staff constituted the executive office of the firm. The executive partners, including the national managing partner, reported to the policy board, which was a rotating group elected by the partners.

This case was prepared by Vijay Govindarajan and John K. Shank, The Amos Tuck School of Business Administration, Dartmouth College. Copyright by Osceola Institute.

The Public Accounting Profession

Although there are literally thousands of CPA firms in this country, the profession is dominated by a small set of about 10 international firms. These firms account for perhaps 90 percent of the annual audits of publicly traded companies. For each of these 10 firms, auditing accounts for somewhere between 60 and 75 percent of gross billings. Taxation advisory services and management consulting services make up the remainder of the billings. The percentage of total billings from auditing has been falling for all the firms over the past 15 years. Each of the major firms maintains offices in most major cities across the country and offers a full range of client services in each office. No one firm is dominant in any region. In fact, it is extremely rare for any one firm to have even a 20 percent share of market in any one city or state.

The canons of professional ethics prohibit the corporate legal form, but the major firms all operate much like closely held professional service corporations, anyway, in terms of governance, management succession, and distribution of profits. The accounting business has been an excellent one over the past 40 years in terms of growth and profitability. In the 10 top firms, compound growth rates over the years have been in excess of 10 percent per year, and partner income averaged more than $100,000 per year in 1984.

Auditing has been the traditional "major profit machine" for all the firms. In recent years, however, the auditing business has shown many signs of maturity, such as slowed growth, declining margins, fierce price competition, and declining client loyalty. Although many people believe the annual audit is becoming a "commodity," this business was still highly profitable, on average, in 1984.

Different firms are responding to the changes in the auditing environment in different ways, including ignoring it while hoping it will go away, emphasizing product differentiation to justify a price premium, trying to develop low-cost leader- ship to make possible aggressive pricing, and trying to shift the product mix toward nonaudit services, which are still highly differentiated and, thus, less price sensitive.

Exhibit 1   Office Evaluation System

The Policy Board has approved 15 percent of distributable earnings as variable compensation for fiscal year 1984, 10 percent to be distributed based on partner performance against goals set forth in accountability statements, and 5 percent to be allocated to offices based upon an office evaluation system.*

The system is designed to produce improvement in critical areas of office practice management and to reward offices that improve or maintain existing high standards. The measurement criteria can be changed to emphasize areas where management feels the partners' attention should be focused. Thus, emphasis can be varied from net income to chargeable hours, or from performance versus last year to performance versus standard, simply by changing the allocation percentages. It also will provide peer pressure to achieve improvement since each office will be rated and the listing will be circulated.

The system will measure the four key responsibility areas: Practice Management, Practice Development, Human Resources, and Client Service.

Within these key responsibility areas, six specific factors on which to evaluate the office will be considered. They are:

- Net income.
- Collections (outstanding days).
- Chargeable-hours growth.
- Client service.
- Human resources development.
- One-firm commitment.

The system will be fully implemented over the next few years. In fiscal 1984, evaluation would be based on performance in net income, collections, and chargeable hours. The remaining three factors will be added as soon as possible.

Weighting

As can be seen from the attached **Schedule A**, each of the three factors has been assigned a percentage, under the column heading "*Weight*," namely, 60 percent, 15 percent, and 25 percent for all practice offices in fiscal 1984.

Schedule A also shows the three criteria used to measure each factor.

Performance versus budget.

Performance versus last year.

Performance versus "ideal" or standard.

These, too, have been assigned a percentage, under the column heading "*Composite Weight*," which places emphasis where management considers it most appropriate, namely, 50 percent, 20 percent, and 30 percent, respectively.

Grading

The "basic score" shown on **Schedule A** is the level at which a practice office is rated, as follows:

5 Excellent.

4 Above average.

3 Average.

2 Below average.

1 Unsatisfactory.

To determine where an office is to be rated, the following criteria were developed:

Net Income

1. Percent of net income versus budget.
2. Percent of net income versus last year.
3. Percent of net income versus ideal target of 20 percent.

Outstanding Days (Collections)

4. Percent of outstanding days versus budget.
5. Percent of outstanding days versus last year.
6. Percent of outstanding days versus standard (105 days).

Chargeable-Hours Growth

7. Percent of chargeable hours growth versus budget.
8. Percent of chargeable hours growth versus last year.
— (Percent of chargeable hours growth versus standard, which is 5 percent, is not used because it would duplicate performance versus last year, since the firm achieved the 5 percent goal last year.)

Offices are then separated into two groups based on their budgeted net billings.

— Over $2.2 million.

— Under $2.2 million.

Offices are ranked within their group in each of the eight criteria and given a rate (5 to 1) using the bell curve theory as follows:

Top	10%—5	
	20%—4	
	40%—3	
	20%—2	
Bottom	10%—1	

In measuring performance against budget for 1984, budget will be the amount agreed upon by the Area Director, Deputy Director, and PIC as a reasonable level of attainment by that office. This will enable us to continue to improve our budgeting procedures in 1984. *This plan contemplates that budgets are at reasonable levels of attainment for each office.*

Exceptions

- Offices with an operating loss at year end are excluded from bonus pool allocation, unless a development loss is budgeted and approved by the National Director-Operations. Their grade will show as zero in all eight criteria, disregarding what results could have been obtained in collections and chargeable hours.
- Offices with net income as a percent of net fees under 10 percent for last year are adjusted to 10 percent for grading purposes. This is done to prevent offices with a loss or low net income the year before from getting a high grade when compared to this year's results, illustrated as follows:

	Actual 1983	Actual 1984	Percent of '84 over '83
Office A:			
Net fees	1,000	1,050	
Net income	20	40	100%
Office B:			
Net fees	1,000	1,200	
Net income	300	400	33%

Without the rule, Office A would rank considerably higher than Office B, which is not logical. After adjusting Office A net income to 10 percent of its net fees in 1983, the result would be:

	1983	1984	Percent '84/'83
Net income	100	40	(60%)

- Mergers in current year or last year or both will be deducted from actual results in both years to make the comparison valid.
- New offices (which do not have "last year" results) will be weighted as follows:

Performance versus budget 70%

Performance versus standard 30%

After applying all of the foregoing, the mathematical result will be determined (**Schedule B**) and offices listed in decreasing order according to their final weighted score. Then a final grade is given, using the bell curve theory. The bonus pool is allocated based on the following table:

Percent Applied to Base Compensation

Rank	Average	Highest	Lowest
5	10.0%	11.25%	8.80%
4	7.5	8.75	6.30
3	5.0	6.25	3.80
2	2.5	3.75	1.25
1	0.0	—	—

Distribution of the 5 percent incentive pool will be based on the grading shown and will be the percentage of base compensation in each office as shown above.

The incentive pool award will be allocated to the individual partners in an office based on performance relative to accountability statement goals. This allocation is subject to the approval of both Area and Deputy Directors.

Final Comments

It is very important to realize the only component of the office evaluation system that does not change from year to year is its philosophy. The others might and likely will change according to the firm's needs.

Office Evaluation Summary FY 1984   **Schedule A**

Office_____

	Composite Weight	Basic Score	Adjusted Score	Weight	Total
Net Income					
Percent of income versus budget	50%				
Percent of net income versus last year	20%		—		
Performance versus standard	30%				
Total	100%			60%	—

Outstanding Days (collections)

Percent of outstanding days versus budget	50%			
Percent of outstanding days versus last year	20%		—	
Performance versus standard	30%			
Total	100%		15%	—

Chargeable-Hours Growth

Percent growth in chargeable hours versus budget	50%			
Percent growth in chargeable hours versus last year	50%			
Total	100%	—	25%	—
				—
Total			100%	—

Office Evaluation Summary FY 1984   **Schedule B**
Office   Hypothetical

	Composite Weight	Basic Score	Adjusted Score	Weight	Total
Net Income					
Percent of income versus budget	50%	3	1.5		
Percent of net income versus last year	20%	5	1.0		
Performance versus standard	30%	4	1.2		
Total	100%		3.7	60%	2.22
Outstanding Days (collections)					
Percent of outstanding days versus budget	50%	4	2.0		
Percent of outstanding days versus last year	20%	5	1.0		
Performance versus standard	30%	3	0.9		
Total	100%		3.9	15%	0.59
Chargeable-Hours Growth					
Percent growth in chargeable hours versus budget	50%	3	1.5		
Percent growth in chargeable hours versus last year	50%	4	2.0		
Total	100%		3.5	25%	0.89
Total				100%	3.70

*Case note: The pool of funds to be distributed through the office evaluation system, 5 percent of partner earnings, could be about $2 million in a normal year. Individual awards could range from $15,000 to zero.

Competitive position for an accounting firm or an individual office within a firm can be looked at in terms of the two-dimensional grid on the following page, with service mix on one dimension and mix of client size on the other dimension (see Exhibit 2).

Although each of the major firms probably generates some billings each year from each of the 12 niches, no two firms are comparable in terms of aggregate positioning within the grid. Since all the firms are constrained by their ability to attract and retain first-class professional staff, careful delineation of where, within the grid, to place particular emphasis is a major element in strategic planning for a firm.

Because the only productive resource for a CPA firm is people, successful management of the people resource is critically important to the continued prosperity of all such firms. High turnover (both voluntary and forced) has always been part of the structure of the business—of every 10 staff accountants hired, no more than 4 will stay beyond four years and no more than 1 or 2 will become partners. There are no career professionals below the partner level. The rule is "up or out." Admission to the partnership typically comes somewhere between 8 and 15 years. In the major firms, the ratio of partners to staff accountants ranges from a low of 1 to 5 to a high of 1 to 12. Apparently, the partner/staff ratio is a strategic variable.

Traditionally, 40 percent of billings go to pay the professional staff (each staff member should generate billings of 2.5 times salary), 40 percent go to pay overhead (much of which is salary for support personnel), and 20 percent go to the partners as profit. This 40-40-20 economic model has been amazingly durable across firms and over the years.

EXHIBIT 2   An Accounting Practice

	Mix of Services			
			Consulting	
Size of Clients	*Opinion Audits*	*Taxation Advisory Services*	*Project Consulting*	*General Advisory Services*
Large (Fortune 1,000 companies)	(1)	(4)	(7)	(10)
Medium (publicly traded, but not huge)	(2)	(5)	(8)	(11)
Small (Privately held, not large enough to have professional financial management)	(3)	(6)	(9)	(12)

The following comments relate to these individual practice niches:

(1) This is a very-low-growth business. There is erosion from expansion of corporate internal auditing. There is rising price sensitivity among clients, resulting in efforts to "manage the audit fee," and growing price competition among accounting firms. Many people believe that the basic legally mandated opinion audit is very much a "commodity" now. A "Big Eight" image is critical to be a participant in this niche.

(2) Almost all real growth in the audit business is here. Accounting firms can use nonaudit work as a way to gain audit clients here. This niche is also price sensitive; but there is still much room to push differentiation, based on high-quality personal service to the client. As client companies grow, they usually reach a point where they switch to a major auditing firm, even if they did not start out with a major firm.

(3) This is a very minor niche, because small firms typically do not have annual audits unless required by a bank or other lender.

(4) This is a limited niche, because major companies tend to have their own tax planning and tax advisory personnel.

(5), (6) These are large, growing, and very profitable niches. They represent an excellent example of a niche that represents very-low price sensitivity coupled with very-high perceived product differentiation.

(7), (8), (9) These are all profitable niches with relatively low price sensitivity and relatively high differentiation. The clear competitive advantage and the perceived areas of expertise for CPA firms lie in projects related to financial controls, computer-based financial systems, and financial planning. The major accounting firms differ substantially in the breadth of projects they are willing to undertake, ranging all the way to virtually a full-range management consulting practice.

(10),(11) These are very small niches, because the relevant expertise is as likely to exist in the company as in the accounting firm.

(12) This is a significant and profitable niche that is exploited very aggressively by some of the accounting firms but not by all.

The Firm of Williamson and Oliver

The name Williamson and Oliver (WO) is an amalgam of parts of the names of predecessor firms dating back more than 50 years. Through a long series of more than 40 mergers of local and regional CPA practices, the current firm gradually emerged. In fact, although the current name was less than 10 years old, Messrs. Williamson and Oliver had both been dead for more than 20 years.

The current firm comprised more than 2,500 professionals in addition to the more than 500 partners. Billings in 1983 were more than $200 million, with 20 offices doing more than $5 million. In about half of the top 50 market areas, the firm is one of the top six in size. It is the largest firm in about 10 of those 50 markets. Counting its international affiliates around the world, Williamson and Oliver is one of the top few firms in terms of billable hours. Its major client strength is in "medium-sized" companies. The firm's situation is comparable to the other major firms in terms of history, size, services mix, and management challenge. One distinguishing characteristic of WO is that, for about two-thirds of its offices, it is not one of the six largest firms in town. It, thus, has a particularly severe marketing challenge in a great many of its offices.

The Job of an Office PIC

Essentially, the PIC for an office is the general manager of a moderately autonomous profit center. Each office is part of the WO network and, thus, does part of its work for local affiliates of WO clients from other offices. Also, each office farms out some work on its clients to other WO offices. But a major share of the work in each office is done for clients of that office. The PICs are responsible for managing businesses ranging in size from about $1 million in annual billings to over $30 million and serving markets as diverse as Manhattan or Muncie, Indiana.

The career path for virtually every PIC is the same—college graduate in accounting, entry-level staff accountant (technical professional in a work team), senior-level accountant (supervising the work team on individual jobs), managing accountant (supervising several work teams while also maintaining a heavy client load), client service partner (managing the overall relationship for several clients while still carrying a heavy load of chargeable hours), then promotion to running an office. The person may have come from audit, tax, or consulting and may or may not have had a staff assignment somewhere along the line; but the overall theme is the same—progression up the technical ladder of the firm.

This career path raises some important issues in considering the job of the PIC and the role of an incentive compensation system in that job context. First, virtually no PICs have had any general management experience until they arrive at the PIC job—their experience is as technical professionals. Second, the set of skills associated with success up the career ladder to the PIC job is not necessarily highly correlated with the set of skills required of a successful general manager—"managing" is different from "doing." Third, while it is the dream of every newly hired staff accountant to someday become a PIC, having *become* one, many persons don't seem to like *being* one. The things they enjoyed while becoming a PIC included task-oriented project work, providing technical service to clients, the status associated with having your expertise valued by clients, heavy involvement with work teams, and success in managing a work schedule paced by defined projects with deadlines. These things have very little to do with the job of *being* a successful PIC. In fact, although many PICs try to maintain some involvement in the work of the office (because they enjoy it), the policy of the firm is that a PIC should not have any chargeable hours at all—100 percent of each PIC's time should be devoted to managing the business. It is not necessarily surprising that the kind of person who enters the accounting profession and then is successful in a large CPA firm may not really want to be a general manager and may not be very good at it. What is surprising is that the dramatic change from being a client service partner to a PIC comes as such an unpleasant surprise to so many of the newly minted PICs.

Ted Johnson's View of the Incentive Program

Ted Johnson was in the middle of his first five-year term as national managing partner of WO. He could serve additional terms if he were willing and if the policy board reelected him. He had come up through the ranks in one of the predecessor firms that merged into WO. He had run one of the largest WO offices for 10 years and been an area director before becoming national managing partner. He saw his task as helping to improve the profitability of the firm while also ensuring that the right strategic decisions were made to keep the firm prosperous over the longer term. The concept of strategic planning was embryonic at WO, and at the other large CPA firms as well. Johnson was grasping for a way to identify the critical strategic issues and to coalesce the management of the firm around an appropriate strategic thrust. But, at the same time, on the day-to-day front he was "hip deep in alligators."

One major problem was inexperience. One third of the PICs had less than four years' tenure in the job. About 10 had less than two years' tenure. Thus, in a substantial number of offices, a critical issue was just getting the PIC to "think like a general manager," rather than like a client service professional. Also, in many offices, profits were not as good as the partnership felt they should be. This was not only true for offices with an inexperienced PIC. Tough-minded, day-to-day business management skills seemed to be lacking too often. This was particularly troublesome to Ted Johnson, because his election to the top job had been based in large part on a consensus view that he could lead the firm to a better realization of its profit potential. His predecessor's retirement had been somewhat "early" because of widespread concern that the firm was not being managed aggressively enough.

Another problem for Ted Johnson was that many of the PICs just wanted to be left alone by senior management. They were content running a self-contained business. They were willing to pay an "overhead assessment" to the executive office in exchange for use of the national name and for access to national technical expertise. However, they had not made the psychological transition from a local firm to a local office of a national firm. They had to be convinced, somehow, that their local prosperity was significantly related to the prosperity of the national firm.

Finally, Johnson was convinced that managing primarily for short-run profits would hurt the business in the long run. Thus, in addition to getting the PICs oriented to profit and committed to profit growth, he had to try to make them think longer term and beyond their local offices. To top off this challenge, Johnson was not totally sure that the growth theme being pushed in the firm ("We must prove that WO is a firm of comparable stature to the other major firms") was appropriate to bring about the profit growth upon which his future and that of the firm depended. Overall, Ted Johnson believed that the new incentive system would help "calibrate" the partners' actions appropriately for the success of the firm.

The casewriters obtained the following comments from partners in the firm about the new incentive plan.

The Partner-in-Charge of a Large Office in a Fast-Growing Urban Area.   The real focus of this plan is on short-term profits. Net income, collections, and chargeable hours all relate directly to the bottom line. But it is just as important for me to build new clients in this high-growth area. That depends on my efforts to project a favorable image with prospective clients. That means I have to give speeches, be seen and liked around the country club, participate in community activities, and participate in business leadership activities like Rotary and Chamber of Commerce. In addition, I have to develop people internally to manage the future growth in our business. That means paying high salaries, allowing heavy training time, and programming in heavy supervision and "mentoring" time. All these activities are negative in terms of their impact on current billings and short-run profit. In fact, all of these activities take my time away from billable work and from collection efforts. Also, if I am successful in developing talented young people in this office, the chances are very good that those people will get "exported" to other offices because of the firmwide need for good managers. So, I wind up with a thank you and the chance to start all over again spending extra people-related dollars, which hurts current profits. As I see it, I am not personally rewarded for developing the firm, just for being profitable.

An Area Director. Profit is the name of the game in this firm. It ought to be, because that is what matters most in the ultimate analysis. This is a business and the way businesses keep score is the bottom line. Sure it's tough to balance growth goals and intangible factors as well as profitability, but we pay our partners very well to do exactly that. Profit without growth or growth without profit is pretty easy—the trick is getting both. Outstanding partners are the ones who can give you both. I think the incentive plan's focus on short-run profits, with some attention to longer-run issues, is right on track.

The Partner-in-Charge of a Major Office. The system says that by 1985 we will include "client service," "human resource development," and "one firm commitment" as additional factors on which a partner's compensation will depend.

Let me raise a few issues. What do we mean by "client service?" by "human resource development?" by "one firm commitment?" How do we measure performance on these factors on a monthly or even annual basis? When there are six factors in the equation, what weights are we going to assign to them? Would these weights be the same or different across the practice offices? Who would decide the weights? I think we have to resolve some fundamental questions before we can be sure that our incentive plan would motivate our partners to do the things that senior management wants them to do.

Questions

1. Is Williamson and Oliver committing the "fallacy of hoping for A while rewarding B"?
2. Can you expect PICs to worry a lot about factors not in the formal reward system?
3. Can the "soft," future-oriented performance areas be sufficiently quantified to permit inclusion in the reward system?
4. Given the management task at hand, how would you structure the set of measurements for an office of WO? (What measures and what weights across the set of measures?) Would your answer vary across offices?
5. Given your understanding of the industry situation, WO's position within the industry, and Ted Johnson's sense of mission for WO, is the new incentive plan a positive or a negative factor in the management of the firm?

CASE 15–3
HARLAN FOUNDATION

Harlan Foundation was created in 1953 under the terms of the will of Martin Harlan, a wealthy Minneapolis benefactor. His bequest was approximately $3 million and its purpose was broadly stated: Income from the funds was to be used for the benefit of the people of Minneapolis and nearby communities.

In the next 35 years, the trustees developed a wide variety of services. These included three infant clinics, a center for the education of special needs children, three family counseling centers, a drug abuse program, a visiting nurses program, and a large rehabilitation facility. These services were provided from nine facilities, located in Minneapolis and surrounding cities. Harlan Foundation was affiliated with several national associations whose members provided similar services.

The foundation operated essentially on a break-even basis. A relatively small fraction of its revenue came from income earned on the principal of the Harlan bequest. Major sources of revenue were fees from clients, contributions, and grants from city, state, and federal governments.

Exhibit 1 is the most recent operating statement. Program expenses included all the expenses associated with individual programs. Administration expenses included the costs of the central office, except for fund-raising expenses. Seventy percent of administration costs were for personnel costs. The staff members (excluding two senior officers) earned an average of $18,000 per year in salaries and fringe benefits.

In 1987, the foundation decided to undertake two additional activities. One was a summer camp, whose clients would be children with physical disabilities. The other was a seminar intended

for managers in social service organizations. For both of these ventures, it was necessary to establish the fee that should be charged.

Camp Harlan

The camp, which was renamed Camp Harlan, was donated to the foundation in 1986 by the person who had owned it for many years and who decided to retire. The property consisted of 30 acres, with considerable frontage on a lake, and buildings that would house and feed some 60 campers at a time. The plan was to operate the camp for eight weeks in the summer and to enroll campers for either one or two weeks. The policy was to charge each camper a fee sufficient to cover the cost of operating the camp. Many campers would be unable to pay this fee, and financial aid would be provided for them. The financial aid would cover a part, or in some cases all, of the fee and would come from the general funds of the foundation or, it was hoped, from a government grant.

As a basis for arriving at the fee, Henry Coolidge, financial vice president of the foundation, obtained information on costs from the American Camping Association and from two camps in the vicinity. Although the camp could accommodate at least 60 children, he decided to plan on only 50 at a time in the first year, a total of 400 camperweeks for the season. With assured financial aid, he believed there would be no difficulty in enrolling this number. His budget prepared on this basis is shown in Exhibit 2.

Coolidge discussed this budget with Sally Harris, president of the foundation. Harris agreed that it was appropriate to plan for 400 camper-weeks and also agreed that the budget estimates were reasonable. During this discussion, questions were raised about several items that were not in the budget.

This case was prepared by Robert N. Anthony, Harvard Business School. Copyright © by Osceola Institute.

EXHIBIT 1   Operating Statement for the Year Ended June 30, 1986

Revenues:

Fees from clients	$ 917,862
Grants from government agencies	1,792,968
Contributions	683,702
Investment income	426,300
Other	24,553
Total revenues	3,845,385

Expenses:

Program expenses:

Rehabilitation	1,556,242
Counseling	157,621
Infant clinics	312,007
Education	426,234
Drug abuse	345,821
Visiting nurses	267,910
Other	23,280
Total program expenses	3,089,115

Support:

Administration	480,326
Dues to national associations	24,603
Fund-raising	182,523
Other	47,862
Total support	735,314
Total expenses	3,824,429
Net income	$ 20,956

The central office of the foundation would continue to plan the camp, do the necessary publicity, screen applications and make decisions on financial aid, pay bills, and do other bookkeeping and accounting work. There was no good way of estimating how many resources this work would require. Ten staff members worked in administration, and as a rough guess about half a person-year might be involved in these activities.

There were no plans to hire an additional employee in the central office. The work load associated with other activities usually tapered off somewhat during the summer, and it was believed that the staff could absorb the extra work.

At the camp itself, approximately four volunteers per week would help the paid staff. They would receive meals and lodging, but no pay. No allowance for the value of their services was included in the budget.

The budget did not include an amount for depreciation of the plant facilities. Lakefront property was valuable, and, if the camp and its buildings were sold to a developer, perhaps as much as $500,000 could be realized.

EXHIBIT 2   **Budget for Camp Harlan**

Staff salaries and benefits	$ 90,000
Food	19,000
Operating supplies	4,000
Telephone and utilities	9,000
Insurance	15,100
Rental of equipment	7,000
Contingency and miscellaneous (5%)	7,200
Total	$151,300

The Seminar

The foundation planned to hold a one-day seminar in the fall of 1987 to discuss the effect on social service organizations of the income tax act passed in 1986 and other recent regulatory developments. (Although these organizations were exempt from income taxes, except on unrelated business income, recent legislation and regulations were expected to have an impact on contributions, investment policy, and personnel policies, among other things.) The purposes of the seminar were partly to generate income and partly to provide a service for smaller welfare organizations.

In the spring of 1987, Harris approved the plans for this seminar. The following information is extracted from a memorandum prepared by Coolidge at that time.

It is estimated that there will be 30 participants in the seminar.

The seminar will be held at a local hotel, and the hotel will charge $200 for rental of the room and $20 per person for meals and refreshments.

Audiovisual equipment will be rented at a cost of $100.

There will be two instructors, and each will be paid a fee of $500.

Printing and mailing of promotional material will cost $900.

Each participant will be given a notebook containing relevant material. Each notebook will cost $10 to prepare, and 60 copies of the notebook will be printed.

Coolidge will preside, and one Harlan staff member will be present at the seminar. The hotel will charge for their meals and for the meals of the two instructors.

Other incidental out-of-pocket expenses are estimated to be $200.

Fees charged for one-day seminars in the area range from $50 to $495. The $50 fee excluded meals and was charged by a brokerage firm that probably viewed the seminar as generating customer goodwill. The $495 fee was charged by several national organizations that run hundreds of seminars annually throughout the United States. A number of one-day seminars are offered in the Minneapolis area at a fee in the range of $150 to $250, including a meal.

Except for the number of participants, the above estimates were based on reliable information and were accepted by Harris.

Questions

1. What weekly fee should be charged for campers?

2. Assuming a fee of $100, what is the break-even point of the seminar?

3. What fee should be charged for the seminar?

Case 15–4
Piedmont University

When Hugh Scott was inaugurated as the 12th President of Piedmont University in 1984, the university was experiencing a financial crisis. For several years enrollments had been declining and costs had been increasing. The resulting deficit has been made up by using the principal of "quasi-endowment" funds. (For true endowment funds, only the income could be used for operating purposes; the principal legally could not be used. Quasi-endowment funds had been accumulated out of earlier years' surpluses with the intention that only the income on these funds would be used for operating purposes; however, there was no legal prohibition on the use of the principal.) The quasi-endowment funds were nearly exhausted.

Scott immediately instituted measures to turn the financial situation around. He raised tuition, froze faculty and staff hirings, and curtailed operating costs. Although he had come from another university and, therefore, was viewed with some skepticism by the Piedmont faculty, Scott was a persuasive person, and the faculty and trustees generally agreed with his actions. In the year ended June 30, 1986, there was a small operating surplus.

In 1986, Scott was approached by Neil Malcolm, a Piedmont alumnus and partner of a local management consulting firm, who volunteered to examine the situation and make recommendations for permanent measures to maintain the university's financial health. Scott accepted this offer.

Malcolm spent about half time at Piedmont for the next several months and had many conversations with Scott, other administrative officers, and trustees. Early in 1987, he submitted

This case was prepared by Robert N. Anthony, Harvard Business School. Copyright by Osceola Institute.

his report. It recommended increased recruiting and fund-raising activities, but its most important and controversial recommendation was that the university be reorganized into a set of profit centers.

At that time the principal means of financial control was an annual expenditure budget submitted by the deans of each of the schools and the administrative heads of support departments. After discussion with the president and financial vice president, and usually with minor modifications, these budgets were approved. There was a general understanding that each school would live within the faculty size and salary numbers in its approved budget, but not much stress was placed on adhering to the other items.

Malcolm proposed that in future the deans and other administrators would submit budgets covering both the revenues and the expenditures for their activities. The proposal also involved some shift in responsibilities and new procedures for crediting revenues to the profit centers that earned them and charging expenditures to the profit centers responsible for them. He made rough estimates of the resulting revenues and expenditures of each profit center using 1986 numbers; these are given in Exhibit 1.

A series of discussions about the proposal were held in the University Council, which consisted of the president, academic deans, provost, and financial vice president. Although there was support for the general ideas, there was disagreement on some of the specifics, as described below.

Central Administrative Costs

Currently, no universitywide administrative costs were charged to academic departments. The proposal was that these costs would be allocated to profit centers in proportion to the rela-

EXHIBIT 1   Piedmont University: Rough Estimates of 1986 Impact of the Proposals ($ millions)

Profit Center:	Revenue	Expenditures
Undergraduate liberal arts school	$30.0	$29.2
Graduate liberal arts school	5.6	11.5
Business school	15.3	12.3
Engineering school	17.0	17.3
Law school	6.7	6.5
Theological school	1.2	3.4
Unallocated revenue*	5.0	
Total, academic	80.8	80.2
Other:		
Central administration	10.1	10.1
Athletic	2.6	2.6
Computer	3.4	3.4
Central maintenance	5.7	5.7
Library	3.4	3.4

*Unrestricted gifts and endowment revenue, to be allocated by the president.

tive costs of each. The graduate school deans regarded this as unfair. Many costs incurred by the administration were in fact closely related to the undergraduate school. Furthermore, they did not like the idea of being held responsible for an allocated cost that they could not control.

Gifts and Endowment

The revenue from annual gifts would be reduced by the cost of fund-raising activities. The net amount of annual gifts plus endowment income (except gifts and income from endowment designated for a specific school) would be allocated by the president, according to his decision on the needs of each school, subject to the approval of the board of trustees. The deans thought this was giving the president too much authority. They did not have a specific alternative but thought that some way of reducing the president's discretionary powers should be developed.

Athletics

Piedmont's athletic teams did not generate enough revenue to cover the cost of operating the athletic department. The proposal was to make this department self-sufficient by charging fees to students who participated in intramural sports or who used the swimming pool, tennis courts, gymnasium, and other facilities as individuals. Although there was no strong opposition, some felt that this would involve student dissatisfaction, as well as much new paperwork.

Maintenance

Each school had a maintenance department that was responsible for housekeeping in its section of the campus and for minor maintenance jobs. Sizable jobs were performed at the school's request by a central maintenance department. The proposal was that in future the central maintenance department would charge schools and other profit centers for the work they did at the actual cost of this work, including both direct and overhead costs. The dean of the business school said that this would be acceptable provided that profit centers were authorized to have maintenance work done by an outside contractor if its price was lower than that charged by the maintenance department. Malcolm explained that he had discussed this possibility with the head of maintenance, who opposed it on the grounds that outside contractors could not be held accountable for the high-quality standards that Piedmont required.

Computer

Currently, the principal mainframe computers and related equipment were located in and supervised by the engineering school. Students and faculty members could use them as they wished, subject to an informal check on overuse by people in the computer rooms. About one quarter of the capacity of these computers was used for administrative work. A few departmental mainframe computers and hundreds of microcomputers and word processors were located throughout the university, but there was no central record of how many there were.

The proposal was that each user of the engineering school computers would be charged a fee based on usage. The fee would recover the full cost of the equipment, including overhead. Each school would be responsible for regulating the amount of cost that could be incurred by its faculty and students so the total cost did not exceed the approved item in the school's budget. (The computers had software that easily attributed the cost to each user.) Several deans objected to this plan. They pointed out that neither students nor faculty understood the potential value of computers, and they wanted to encourage computer usage as a significant part of the educational and research experience. A charge would have the opposite effect, they maintained.

Library

The university library was the main repository of books and other material, and there were small libraries in each of the schools. The proposal was that each student and faculty member who used the university library would be charged a fee, either on an annual basis or on some basis related to the time spent in the library or the number of books withdrawn. (The library had a secure entrance at which a guard was stationed, so a record of who used it could be obtained without too much difficulty.) There was some dissatisfaction with the amount of paperwork that such a plan would require, but it was not regarded as being as important as some of the other items.

Cross Registration

Currently, students enrolled at one school could take courses at another school without charge. The proposal was that the school at which a course was taken would reimburse the school in which the student was enrolled. The amount charged would be the total semester tuition of the school at which the course was taken, divided by the number of courses that a student normally would take in a semester, with adjustments for variations in credit hours.

Questions

1. How should each of the issues described above be resolved?
2. Do you see other problems with the introduction of profit centers? If so, how would you deal with them?
3. What are the alternatives of a profit center approach?
4. Assuming that most of the issues could be resolved to your satisfaction, would you recommend that the profit center idea be adopted, rather than an alternative?

Case 15–5
Riverview

In April 1994, Jerry Johnson, financial vice-president of Montvale Corporation, made a three-day visit to Riverview, its newest retirement community. From time to time thereafter, he pondered how he should respond to a suggestion for a new approach to financial planning that had been discussed at one of the meetings there. Was it worth serious exploration? Or was it a well-intentioned but impractical idea from a novice in the retirement home industry?

Montvale Corporation and Riverview

Montvale Corporation was a nonprofit corporation, organized and controlled by the headquarters office of a religious denomination. It supervised the operation of several continuing care retirement communities (CCRC) located throughout the United States. The first was established in 1970. All had operated consistently "in the black." Riverview was the newest. Plans for another retirement community were being discussed.

Construction of Riverview began in 1990, the first residents entered in July 1992, and the first full year of operation was fiscal year 1993 (ended September 30, 1993). Riverview consisted of 199 apartments, ranging in size from a studio to two bedrooms plus a den. Most were located in four connected frame buildings, each three stories high. A few of the larger apartments were in single story, separate buildings. The total population at capacity would be 356 persons, some of whom would be couples and the remainder single persons. In addition, there was a separate, but connected, health center with 70 beds.

Riverview had a dining room for apartment residents; another dining room for health center residents; a coffee shop; a general room for concerts, lectures, and social events, seating 200; several rooms for arts and crafts; a library; a small gift shop; a branch bank; a hair-styling shop; an exercise room; and an indoor swimming pool. The buildings were set on 40 acres of land.

In January 1994, occupancy reached 95 percent of capacity, which was a criterion for accreditation by the CCRC accrediting association. By April 1994, occupancy was 99 percent. Several hundred persons and couples were on a waiting list that extended to 2004; each had made a deposit of $1,100, $1,000 of which was refundable.

Pricing Policy

As was the case with many retirement communities, Riverview charged an entrance fee. Each resident also was charged a monthly fee, covering meals, health care costs, electricity, cable TV, heating and air conditioning, and housekeeping—that is, almost everything except telephone. In 1994 the entrance fee averaged $186,000 per apartment, and the monthly fee averaged $2,100 for one person, plus $770 for a second person. Both the entrance fee and the monthly fee varied, depending primarily on the size of the apartment. The monthly fee was reduced if the resident had only one or two meals a day, and also if the resident was away for at least one month at a time. Part of the entrance fee was refunded if the occupant died or moved out; the refund decreased by two percent a month for each month of occupancy. As of April 1994, only one person had moved out and obtained a refund.

Montvale's policy was that the fees should be fair, both to the residents and to the organization. This meant that fees for a year should cover the costs relevant to occupancy in that year, plus

This case was written by Professor Robert N. Anthony with the assistance of Peter T. Magee (Tuck 1994). Copyright by Osceola Institute.

a modest allowance that was to provide for working capital and for contingencies. It was planned that this amount would eventually equal several months' cash costs. (The amount had not yet been decided.)

Johnson, the financial vice-president, said that he did not know of a logical way of dividing the total amount of revenue needed in a year between the entrance fee and the monthly fee. Practice varied widely in the industry. At one extreme, some retirement communities charged only a small entrance fee (or charged a fee that, although large, permitted the occupant's estate to sell the apartment to another party after the occupant's death) and charged correspondingly higher fees for apartment rental, meals, and various services. Montvale's policy of a large entrance fee and a correspondingly lower monthly fee was near the other extreme.

In the accounting system, entrance fees were recognized as annual revenues on a straight-line basis, spread over the years of expected life of each resident, obtained from standard mortality tables.

The April Meeting

One long meeting during Johnson's April visit dealt with financial matters. At that meeting, he met with Walter Heaney, Riverview administrator, and Jeanne Mills, Riverview controller.

Heaney, age 40, had been the Riverview administrator from the beginning of construction. He had 15 years of experience in the retirement home industry before coming to Riverview.

Mills, age 30, joined the organization as controller in 1990. She had worked in the controller's department of a medium-sized city for nine years and had been controller for the last three years. She left that job because there was no likelihood of further promotion in her municipality.

The first topic of the April meeting was a review of financial performance of the current year. Since actuals were close to budgeted amounts, this review went quickly.

The discussion then focused on the strategic financial plan, which was part of a larger project to decide on the goals and objectives of the Montvale organization. Development of such a plan had just been started at all Montvale communities. It was to cover operating activities for the fiscal years 1995 through 1999 and capital requirements for 1995 through 2014.

Heaney and Mills presented a first draft of this plan at the April meeting. Mills had prepared this draft based primarily on data obtained from Montvale. As was the case in each of its retirement communities, Montvale prepared an estimate, covering 20 future years, as a basis for judging the feasibility of a proposed community, for estimating the financing required, and for demonstrating credit worthiness to prospective lenders. Mills used the general format of this plan, which was similar to that in the annual budget, and also used many of the assumptions in the Riverview 20-year plan. The most important Riverview assumptions were:

For inflation:	
Monthly fee	4.5% (1995 and 1996)
	5.0% (other years)
Entrance fee	4.0%
Wages	4.0%
Benefits	5.0%
Utilities	8.0%
New entrants per year:	11 in 1985, increasing to 33 in 1999
Health care residents:	38 in 1995, increasing to 70 in 1999
Employees:	124 in 1995, increasing to 150 in 1999

The Proposal

Following this discussion, Heaney turned the meeting over to Jeanne Mills, who described a new approach to strategic planning that Mills had developed and that Heaney supported. Mills made two main proposals: (1) a different format and (2) a different treatment of fixed assets. A summary of Mills's explanation of each point follows.

Format

The Montvale format focuses on a bottom line that results from certain assumed revenue increases. My suggestion is that we should focus on the amount of monthly fees needed to cover our estimated expenses (including a contingency allowance). The monthly fee revenue, therefore, becomes the bottom line; it shows how much revenue needs to be increased, if at all, in order to obtain the desired financial result.

This is the way many municipalities budget. The governing concept is called *interperiod equity*, which means that in a given year taxpayers should provide the revenues that would be needed to meet the expenses associated with the services that the municipality provides in that year. This amount, divided by the assessed valuation, determines the tax rate for the year. A higher tax rate than this amount means that taxpayers will be paying more than the municipality needs for that period, and a lower rate means that the resulting deficit will burden taxpayers in future periods.

Fixed Assets

My approach eliminates the depreciation number. Depreciation is a useless number for planning purposes. It is determined by past decisions, and no current or future decisions can change it. It has no cash flow implications.

I suggest that instead of depreciation, we use three other numbers in our strategic plan: (1) debt-service principal, (2) minor capital expenditures, and (3) a provision for renewal. Each of these numbers affects future cash flows, and, except for debt-service principal, each can be changed by management decision.

Debt-service principal is easily calculated.

We currently capitalize and depreciate all fixed asset acquisitions costing more than $1,000 each. Excluding a few major items, our planned asset acquisitions total approximately $125,000 a year. I suggest that we count the planned amount of these minor capital acquisitions, as shown in the capital budget, as an expense in each of the years 1995–1999.

I suggest that we establish a fund to provide for major renewals planned over the next 20 years. We now list six such projects, as shown on Exhibit 3. For some of them, actual expenditures will be made over three years, and I have used the middle year of the three in the calculation. Annual charges to this fund, plus interest earned on the fund, will pay for the renewals in the year in which expenditures for them are made. For the next several years, this charge would be $70,000 annually, calculated as the present value of these expenditures, using a 4 percent interest rate.

In addition to these renewals, we plan to expand the health-care unit in the year 2000 at a cost of $840,000 (in 1994 dollars). This is not a renewal, and I assume that it will be paid for by new borrowing made at that time.

Construction costs at Riverview were $900,000 for land, $1,900,000 for land improvements, and $40,200,000 for other depreciable assets—a total of $43,000,000. These costs were financed by a 30-year, 8-percent bond issue in the amount of $43,000,000. Level semiannual payments, consisting of principal payments and interest, were required for these bonds. Mills explained that the principal component of these payments added up to the cost of the borrowing—$43,000,000. The $43,000,000 exceeded the cost of depreciable assets because land is not depreciated.

To illustrate her proposal, Mills passed out two exhibits. Both were based on the current draft of Riverview's five-year strategic plan. In both exhibits, the bottom line was the amount of fee revenue needed to meet the annual expenses. They therefore differed from the current format in which fee revenue, calculated at the assumed annual rate of interest was one of the revenue items at the top of the exhibit.

Exhibit 1 was based on the current method of planning, and the numbers for 1995–1999 were taken from that plan. The numbers for the later years used the same assumptions as those used to develop the current strategic plan.

Exhibit 2 eliminated depreciation, included the new amounts described in her proposal, and also included a small contingency fund. In all other respects, the numbers in Exhibit 2 were the same as those in Exhibit 1.

Discussion of the Proposal

Johnson first pointed out that the proposal to eliminate depreciation would not be consistent with generally accepted accounting principles. Mills replied that these numbers would be used only for internal purposes, and the published financial statements would continue to include depreciation. Johnson said that Montvale's audit committee usually did not look favorably on

EXHIBIT 1   Riverview Current Strategic Plan ($000s)

	Budget FY 1994	Plan FY 1995	Plan FY 1996	Plan FY 1997	Plan FY 1998
Revenues					
Medicare & other ins..............	461	477	493	511	529
Entrance fees earned	3,160	3,287	3,418	1,490	1,981
Interest income	1,269	897	940	952	999
Other program services	168	166	174	183	192
Other revenue	18	19	19	20	21
Total revenues (except residential fees)	5,076	4,846	5,044	3,156	3,722
Expenses					
Administration					
Personnel.....................	440	464	486	511	540
Insurance & other	375	392	409	428	447
Management fee...............	492	500	513	541	572
Housekeeping					
Personnel.....................	509	572	621	649	693
Other	57	78	87	96	103
Maintenance					
Personnel.....................	427	483	506	558	586
Other	192	219	232	246	263
Food service					
Personnel.....................	958	991	1,099	1,160	1,266
Raw food	305	328	359	398	423
Other	164	176	193	215	311
Health services					
Personnel.....................	1,303	1,428	1,635	1,822	2,047
Other	345	380	413	446	478
Utilities	601	650	701	758	818
Real estate taxes	547	674	603	633	665
Amortization (Start-up Costs)	115	115	115	115	115
Other expenses	87	91	95	98	102
Interest expense	4,036	3,998	3,956	3,911	3,862
Depreciation	1,155	1,167	1,182	1,199	1,211
Total Expenses	12,108	12,706	13,205	13,784	14,502
Income (before fees)	(7,032)	(7,860)	(8,161)	(10,628)	(10,780)
Residential fees	7,069	9,100	9,700	12,500	13,000

EXHIBIT 2   Riverview Proposed Strategic Plan ($000s)

	Budget FY 1994	Plan FY 1995	Plan FY 1996	Plan FY 1997	Plan FY 1998
Revenues					
Medicare & other ins.	461	477	493	511	529
Entrance fees earned	3,160	3,287	3,418	1,490	1,981
Interest income	1,269	897	940	952	999
Other program services	168	166	174	183	192
Other revenue	18	19	19	20	21
Total revenues (except residential fees)	5,076	4,846	5,044	3,156	3,722
Expenses					
Administration					
Personnel	440	464	486	511	540
Insurance & other	375	392	409	428	447
Management fee	492	500	513	541	572
Housekeeping					
Personnel	509	572	621	649	693
Other	57	78	87	96	103
Maintenance					
Personnel	427	483	506	558	586
Other	192	219	232	246	263
Food service					
Personnel	958	991	1,099	1,160	1,266
Raw food	305	328	359	398	423
Other	164	176	193	215	311
Health services					
Personnel	1,303	1,428	1,635	1,822	2,047
Other	345	380	413	446	478
Utilities	601	650	701	758	818
Real estate taxes	547	674	603	633	665
Amortization (Start-up costs)	115	115	115	115	115
Other expenses	87	91	95	98	102
Interest expense	4,036	3,998	3,956	3,911	3,862
Debt-service principal	473	512	554	599	648
Minor capital expenditures	419	116	151	169	123
Provision for renewal	70	70	70	70	70
Contingency fund	152	145	151	95	112
Total Expenses	12,067	12,382	12,949	13,563	14,244
Income (before fees)	(6,991)	(7,536)	(7,905)	(10,407)	(10,522)
Residential fees	7,069	8,800	9,200	11,700	11,800

EXHIBIT 3   Major Item, 1995 Provision

	Amount	First Year of Contribution	Year of Expenditure*	Years of Contribution	Annual Charge†
Paving	113,000	1995	2006	12	$ 7,520
Fire alarm system	200,000	1995	2009	15	$ 9,988
Lighting fixtures	258,000	1995	2005	11	$19,130
Emergency generator	90,000	1995	2012	18	$ 3,509
Roofing	200,000	1995	2013	19	$ 7,228
Elevators	495,000	1995	2011	17	$20,888

*Middle year of expenditure.
†Annual charge at 4% needed to cumulate to amount needed in future year.

---

internal accounting practices that were inconsistent with those in the published statements.

There was considerable discussion of how the policy of fairness applied to this situation. With conventional depreciation, residents would pay their share of the actual cost of the fixed assets they used each year. Under the proposal, they would not pay for depreciation as such, but they would help pay for the cost of future renewals that would not benefit them. Mills argued that their current usage of the assets was the ultimate cause of the need for renewal, and that having current residents pay for this cost was fair. Johnson wondered how this argument would apply to technological improvements that were unknown but likely, especially in the case of medical equipment in the health care facility.

Johnson asked why the discount rate on the proposed fund for renewals was the low rate of 4 percent. Mills replied that with this rate, inflation need not be taken into account because the renewal fund should earn 4 percent plus inflation and the excess over 4 percent would offset the error of including renewal costs at 1994 prices.

In the course of the discussion, the issue of a possible tennis court was raised. A recent survey showed that about 40 couples wanted to play tennis on the premises. (The nearest tennis courts were about a five-minute drive.) If two tennis courts were built (at a total cost of approximately $50,000), should all residents, in effect, pay for them via their monthly fees? Or should they be financed by a levy on users and/or a fee for using the facility, as was the case when residents used a nearby golf course?

Next Steps

Jerry Johnson knew that if he decided to back the proposal, he would need the support of Montvale's president. He would also need the consent of the audit committee and the budget committee of the board of trustees. If he decided not to proceed, he was obligated to explain his reasons to Charlie Anderson and Jeanne Mills.

Questions

1. What should Johnson do?
2. What are the implications of your conclusion on the concept of "fairness" in arriving at prices and fees in nonprofit organizations?
3. Suggest a way of deciding how the proportion of total revenue from residents should be divided between entrance fees and monthly fees.
4. Who should pay for the tennis court if it is built?

FINANCIAL SERVICE ORGANIZATIONS

Financial services companies are in the business, primarily, of managing money. Some act as intermediaries; that is, they obtain money from depositors and lend it to individuals or companies. Others act as risk shifters; that is, they obtain money in the form of premiums, invest these premiums, and accept the risk of the occurrence of specific events, such as death or damages to property. Still others are traders; that is, they buy and sell securities, either for their own account or for customers. Financial service companies have management control problems that are in some respects different from those of the service companies discussed in Chapter 15.

In the first section of this chapter we describe the general characteristics of these organizations that are relevant for management control. In the other sections, we discuss three types of organizations: commercial banks and thrift institutions, securities firms, and insurance companies.

Financial Service Organizations in General

The Financial Services Sector

In 1996, financial services firms accounted for $250 billion, or 5 percent, of the gross domestic product, but their importance in the overall performance of the economy is considerably greater than this percentage indicates.

The period since the 1980s was one of great turbulence in the industry. Many commercial banks and thrift institutions failed and many others merged. The number of banks decreased from 15,500 in 1985 to 11,500 in 1992 (although it is generally agreed that there are still more banks than the country needs). Several large financial service firms and individual executives in these firms were convicted of serious illegal acts. Most notable failure among financial services firms was the collapse of Barings, Britain's oldest merchant bank, in 1995. Deficient controls partly contributed to Barings' debacle.[1]

---

[1]Thomas Sheridan, "The Barings Debacle," *Management Accounting*, May 1995, pp. 6–7.

During the 1990s, new forms of financial instruments (such as derivatives) designed by financial service firms sometimes resulted in millions of dollars of losses for their clients. In 1994 Gibson Greetings sued Bankers Trust for $23 million, as a result of losses on interest-rate derivative transactions. In December 1994 Orange County lost $1.7 billion in leveraged interest-rate products. In April 1994 Procter & Gamble sued Bankers Trust since it lost over $100 million on interest-rate swaps designed by Bankers Trust. In July 1994 Glaxo made losses of $180 million on derivatives and asset-based bonds.[2]

New types of businesses were created that took substantial amounts of business away from banks and other conventional firms. Mutual funds and pension funds accounted for an increasing percentage of financial transactions.

General Characteristics

Monetary Assets.   Most of the assets of financial service firms are monetary. The current value of monetary assets is much more easily measured than the value of plant and other physical assets, or patents and other intangible assets. Currency is the extreme example of a fungible commodity. At any moment in time, dollars held by all companies have the same value; each dollar is worth a dollar, valued at both its face amount and its purchasing power. Its purchasing power changes with time, but at any given future time, all dollars have equal value. This means that everyone's dollar has the same quality at a given moment in time. In the financial services industry, quality refers to the quality of services rendered and to the quality of financial instruments other than money; there is no need for quality control safeguards for money.

Financial assets also can be transferred from one owner to another easily and quickly. In an electronic funds transfer, money moves almost instantaneously. In other transactions, it moves in a few days at most. Its portability is tempting to thieves and forgers. For this reason, firms that handle financial assets, especially money, must take strong measures to protect them. These involve not only physical measures to safeguard currency and documents, but also measures designed to maintain the integrity of the system for transferring money from one party to another.

Time Period for Transactions.   The ultimate financial success or failure of a bond issue, a mortgage loan to an individual, or a life insurance policy may not be known for 30 years or more. During this period, the soundness of the loan or policy may change, and the purchasing power of money will certainly change. This means that the ultimate performance of those involved in authorizing and structuring the loan, or in selling and pricing the insurance policy, cannot be measured at the time the initial decision is made. It also means that control requires that there be a means of continued surveillance of the soundness of the

---

[2]"Corporate Risk Management: A New Nightmare in the Boardroom," *The Economist*, February 10, 1996, pp. 3–22.

transaction during its life, including periodic audits of all outstanding loans. (Failure to identify "troubled loans" at an early stage is one important reason for the recent rash of failures of banks and thrift institutions.)

At the other extreme, some transactions are completed quickly. Many trades are made on the basis of information that the trader has acquired in the previous few minutes, or even seconds. For currency transactions and for listed securities, new information may become available almost instantaneously in markets throughout the world. Traders either buy or sell securities based on the information they have. If they buy securities, future changes in prices will change the value of the securities held. Therefore, there is a need for a system to report securities held and assess the risk to the organization if prices move against the trader's securities. This means that the firm must have an accurate, prompt system for obtaining this information, for summarizing it, for estimating the risk of the securities held (if applicable), and for making this information available to traders; a computer model ("expert system") evaluates the information and in some cases acts without human intervention.

Risk and Reward.   Many financial services firms are in the business of accepting risks in return for rewards. Most business decisions involve a trade-off between risks and rewards. The greater the risk, the greater should be the anticipated reward. In financial services firms, this trade-off is more explicit than in business investments, such as those involving the purchase of a machine or the introduction of a new product. Interest rates on loans and premiums on insurance policies are based on assumptions about risk that may, or may not, turn out to be accurate.

Regulation.   Financial services firms are heavily regulated. Banks and securities dealers are regulated by federal and state agencies. Insurance firms are regulated by individual states. Although regulation is necessary, some of these regulations inhibit sound business practices and others specify accounting rules that are different from generally accepted accounting principles (GAAP). For certain decisions, the effect on both GAAP accounting and regulatory accounting must be considered.

Technology.   Technology has revolutionized the financial services industry. Financial service firms have used information technology as a way to offer innovative services. Automated teller machines of banks are just one example. Insurance and mutual funds have developed electronic marketplaces. Financial service firms, via their web site on the Internet, market their products electronically to consumers. Investment banks, using concepts from quantum physics and high-level mathematics formulas, have designed new forms of financial instruments. Banks have become "virtual" by offering cyber-payment systems.[3]

---

[3]"Technology In Finance," *The Economist*, October 26, 1996, pp. 3–22.

Commercial Banks and Thrift Institutions

General Characteristics

This section describes management control problems and practices in commercial banks, savings banks, thrift institutions (i.e., savings and loan associations and credit unions), and finance companies. Until about 1980, the distinction among these types of organizations was clear-cut. The typical commercial bank obtained money from depositors, at essentially zero interest cost for demand deposits and 5 percent (a government-imposed ceiling) for savings deposits; it made medium-term loans (about five years or less) to businesses and individuals; it made fixed-rate loans, secured by mortgages on business property or homes, with maturities of 20 to 30 years at fixed rates of interest; and it managed trust accounts and provided other financial services. A savings bank or similar thrift institution obtained funds from savings deposits and loaned them to homeowners on mortgages, or it made other secured loans. Both commercial banks and thrift institutions were heavily regulated, either by the federal government, by the states, or by both. Most deposits were insured by the federal government. Finance companies (e.g., Beneficial, Household Finance, General Electric Credit Corporation) made loans that were secured by automobiles or other personal property.

Beginning in 1980, the means of obtaining and lending money became much more complicated. Government regulation was greatly relaxed (but by no means eliminated) by the Depository Institutions Deregulation and Monetary Control Act of 1980. Savings and loan associations were permitted to lend to businesses. Banks were permitted to pay interest on demand deposits, and the 5 percent ceiling on savings deposits was, for all practical purposes, eliminated. Dozens of new financial instruments were developed—money market funds, certificates of deposit, variable-rate mortgages, credit cards, debit cards, interest-rate futures, bond options, interest-rate swaps.[4] These provided new sources of funds, and they were ways of adjusting a bank's exposure to various levels of risk. One unfortunate consequence of deregulation (although deregulation was not the only cause) was that many savings and loan associations and some commercial banks made unwise loans and failed; the federal government was required to compensate their depositors. By hindsight, we know that the government's decision to deregulate (and at the same time decrease the number of bank examiners), while continuing to protect depositors, will ultimately result in a cost to taxpayers of at least $400 billion; it was the most expensive decision in American history, except for the decisions to fight wars.[5]

Nevertheless, the fundamentals of commercial banking remain unchanged. Banks earn income primarily by lending and investing money. The interest on

---

[4]A recent glossary lists 250 terms, many of which were developed since 1970. Institute of Management Accountants, "Evaluating Financial Instruments," *Statement of Management Accounting Practices No. 4n*, Montvale, N.J., 1990. For descriptions of new securities, see this publication and also Henry A. Davis, *Financial Products for Medium-Sized Companies,* (Morristown, N.J.: Financial Executives Research Foundation, 1989).

[5]By "government" we mean both the executive branch and the Congress.

this money is their revenue.[6] They obtain the money by attracting deposits. The interest they pay on these deposits corresponds approximately to cost of sales in a manufacturing company. Thus, net interest income, which is the difference between interest revenue and interest expense, is a key number for bank management to watch; it corresponds to gross margin in a manufacturing company.

Regulatory Capital. A bank's ability to lend or invest money is restricted by the federal requirement that its equity must equal at least a specified percentage of its assets. This percentage varies from zero for short-term U.S. government bonds, through 5 percent for consumer high-quality first mortgages, to 8 percent for other consumer and corporate loans. Nevertheless, banks are highly leveraged; a debt-to-equity ratio of 20 to 1 is typical, contrasted with the ratio of 1 to 1 in many industrial and commercial companies.

New Products. Until fairly recently, commercial banks' activities were mostly in deposit and lending activities, with relatively small amounts of income being generated by fees charged for managing trust funds and safeguarding customer assets. Banks provided various minor services for customers without charge, or with indirect charges resulting from requiring companies to maintain specified minimum balances (*compensating balances*) on which zero interest was paid.

Banks now provide many services, and earn substantial fees for doing so. Examples are credit card fees from both cardholders and merchants, receiving and accounting for accounts receivable payments made to companies (*lock boxes*), calculating payroll and depositing payroll checks to employees, handling foreign exchange and letter-of-credit transactions, making regular payments on behalf of depositors (*electronic fund transfers*), writing insurance (under certain circumstances), and even making travel arrangements.

When net interest income is low because of the small spread between deposit and lending rates and restrictions imposed by the regulatory capital requirement, a bank may nevertheless be highly profitable because of this fee revenue.

Risks. Banks are exposed to three types of risk: (1) *credit risk*, which is the risk that a loan will not be repaid; (2) *interest rate risk*, which is the risk that interest rates—especially the spread between rates paid on deposits and rates earned on loans and investments—will change in unforeseen ways; and (3) *transaction risk*, which is the risk of errors or theft in the processing of transactions.

Minimizing (or, more accurately, optimizing) credit risk requires that a careful evaluation be made before a loan is made and that the condition of the borrower be closely monitored during the life of the loan. Interest rate risk is discussed in the next section. Minimizing transaction risk requires a well-designed control system and a continuing audit of this system.

---

[6]Unlike manufacturing companies, bankers refer to this amount as "income," rather than "revenue," which can cause confusion.

Automation.   In all banks the customer deposit and withdrawal functions are highly automated. A large and increasing number of transactions are made through Automated Teller Machines (ATM). Many lending decisions are also automated, especially, but by no means exclusively, for consumer mortgage loans. Indeed, these functions have become so highly automated that many experts believe that in the near future the only function of employees in branch banks will be to keep customers satisfied (for example, by assisting in preparing loan applications, as contrasted with making lending decisions) and to obtain new accounts.

Management Control Implications

If branches are treated as profit centers, the following issues need attention: (1) the relationship of the rates and maturities of deposits to the rates and maturities of loans,[7] (2) deposit volume, (3) loan losses, (4) expenses, (5) joint revenues, and (6) transfer prices. We discuss these issues in this section. In addition, we discuss the control system considerations if the branches are evaluated as expense centers rather than as profit centers.

Interest Rates.   In a banker's utopia, deposits would be obtained at, say, 4 percent, loans would earn 7 percent, and the spread would cover expenses (including loan losses) and leave a satisfactory profit. More generally, if the interest revenue in each month was 2 or 3 percentage points higher than the interest expense, and if volume was satisfactory, the constant spread, whatever the actual rates, would generate a satisfactory profit. In the early 1980s, however, many thrift institutions and commercial banks made loans at a fixed rate of interest; but they needed to pay a relatively high rate to attract and retain deposits, so the spread between interest revenue and interest expense became inadequate.

Thus, the relationship between interest revenue and interest expense is a key variable. Banks regularly calculate the amount of interest-sensitive assets, interest-sensitive liabilities, and the *gap*, which is the difference between them. The monetary amount of this gap is the bank's interest-rate exposure; both prudent management and rules of regulatory bodies require that it be kept within certain bounds.

Traditionally, interest-rate exposure was kept within satisfactory limits by buying or selling securities or by increasing or decreasing the amount of new loans. The increasing use of new types of financial transactions, such as futures, options, caps, floors, and swaps, has greatly complicated the process, has made the net effect of a manager's actions more difficult to understand, and, therefore, has increased the difficulty of management control. Moreover, actions taken to keep interest-rate exposure within satisfactory bounds should be

---

[7]For brevity, we shall use "loans" to include both funds lent directly to borrowers and investments in bonds, stocks, and similar securities. For many purposes, loans are treated differently from investments.

separated from actions taken simply to earn short-term gains on appreciated securities, and such a separation is difficult to detect.

Conceptually, the higher the risk of a loan, the higher the interest rate that the bank will charge. Banks refer to the elements of credit risk as the "four Cs": the borrower's general *character*, its *capability* to repay the loan from earnings or other sources, its *capital*, or net assets, and the *collateral* pledged for the specific loan. For accepting greater risks, the bank expects a greater reward. This risk/reward trade-off governs the lender's decision to make a loan and the interest rate to be charged.

In a bank of even moderate size, many officers are involved in making loans and investments. Senior management has the task of setting the rates on loans of various risks and maturities, of setting corresponding rates for deposits, and of assuring that the actions of individual managers add up to a satisfactory interest-rate exposure for the bank as a whole. Because one bank's money has the same "quality" as the money of competing banks (there are no brand names or other quality differentials), the rates are strongly influenced by the actions of competitors. The management control system must ensure that its rates are communicated throughout the organization and that they are adhered to. Factors affecting these rates can change daily.

In addition to the rates charged, lending and investment managers are also limited with respect to the amount of loans and investments, in total, by various types of instruments, and with respect to maturities. They shouldn't make more loans than there are funds available. This balance between loans and deposits is obtained by establishing quotas to be observed by the individuals or committees who authorize the loans.

Large banks attempt to obtain a specified mix of "stable" accounts (e.g., individual checking and saving accounts, certificates of deposit) and "volatile" accounts (corporate deposits); often the target proportion is 50-50. Daily they also check the balance between maturities of loans and deposits at various time intervals: 30-day, 60-day, 90-day, and so on. The difference at each time interval is referred to as the *net interest balance*. If the balance is unsatisfactory, they hedge; that is, they buy or sell various instruments to arrive at the desired balance.

Currently, there is a strong tendency to centralize loan decisions in large banks. Branches help customers to fill out the loan application, and this is forwarded to a central office that makes the decision. As noted above, decisions on consumer mortgages and similar loans may be made by a computer. This mitigates the problem of communicating and enforcing rules for making loans throughout the organization.

Volume.   Most expenses are fixed in the short run. Therefore, if a bank can increase its volume of deposits, other things being equal, it will be able to make more loans, and the increased interest margin will increase its profits. Banks use various marketing devices to do this (except in times when the demand for new loans temporarily has dried up).

Loan Losses. The principal cause of the savings and loan debacle in the late 1980s was that many loans turned sour. In part, this was a consequence of a cyclical decline in real estate prices and businesses generally, in certain sections of the country. In part, it reflected incompetent or unethical management. To some extent, it was the result of fraud. The government has imposed strict limits for "nonperforming loans" (i.e., loans whose payments are delinquent). Committees, internal auditors, bank examiners, and external auditors watch the quality of the loan portfolio, but they can't undo damage that was done when the loan was made.

Expenses. Most of the expenses in a bank are personnel-related. The "back office" expenses—recording and proving transactions—are subject to budgeting and controls that are similar to the controls in a manufacturing company. Cost accounting is a fairly recent development in banks, however. Banks have a problem of allocating common costs that is similar to the problem in manufacturing companies. Accounting and check processing usually are done centrally, and the costs of such work must be equitably assessed to the branches. The Automated Teller Machine system is a fairly expensive operation that is managed centrally but that benefits the branch in which the deposit account is maintained.

Nevertheless, as is the case with many organizations that are dominated by professionals, less attention tends to be given to efficiency than to the more glamorous tasks of making loans, handling trusts, and dealing with customers in other ways.[8]

Joint Revenues. A depositor whose account is maintained in one branch may do business at another branch, or may be persuaded to use the central trust department and other services provided centrally. Branch managers want to be rewarded for the revenues that they generate by such activities, and for services that they furnish to customers of other branches. If branches are organized as profit centers, the allocation of joint revenues can have a significant effect on profits.

Moreover, if branch managers do not receive proper credit for new business that they generate but that actually results in deposits or other revenue-generating transactions at another unit, they are unlikely to spend much time seeking such business. Similarly, if a branch does work for a depositor whose deposit is maintained at another branch, but receives no revenue for doing so, the branch is unlikely to spend much effort on such work. Satisfied customers are the bank's principal asset, and, unless the customer receives proper service by everyone in the bank, the whole bank suffers. Some banks urge employees to

---

[8]In a 1989 survey of members of the Controllers Council of the Institute of Management Accountants, only 19 percent of the respondents in the financial services industry rated their cost accounting systems as "good," and half rated them as less than adequate or unreliable. (Montvale, N.J.: Institute of Management Accountants), *Controllers Update*, May 1990, p. 1.

accept the premise that the principal success factor in the long run is managing customer relationships.

Transfer Prices.   Many commercial banks set up profit centers for their branches, or for their individual headquarters activities, or for both. They then must solve the difficult problem of arriving at the transfer price for money. This price is an expense (analogous to cost of sales) to activities that make loans and investments, and it is revenue to activities that generate deposits. Some branches are *loan heavy* (i.e., their loans exceed their deposits), and others are *deposit heavy*; profitability will not be measured correctly unless the transfer price is fair to each type. If the transfer price for the cost of money is set too low, the profitability of the loan-heavy branches will be overstated; whereas if it is set too high, the profitability of deposit-heavy branches will be overstated.

Measurement of the cost of money is also important in assessing the profitability of loans with different maturities, loans with different risk characteristics (e.g., consumer installment loans compared with high-grade corporate loans), and loans to different markets (local, national, and transnational). The Federal Reserve System has facilitated such analyses in its Functional Analysis Program, which collects costs by functions from member banks, computes averages, and makes these available to banks.

Money is obtained by borrowing from other financial institutions, from customers who make savings account deposits (*time deposits*), from customers who purchase certificates of deposit, and from customers who have checking accounts (*demand deposits*). The interest cost of borrowed funds, of time deposits, and of certificates of deposits is readily determined.

Interest cost on demand deposits is more difficult. In addition to the cost of servicing an account, a bank may provide free services to customers who maintain a checking account balance of a prescribed amount (although this practice is becoming less common); the cost of providing these services is a cost of obtaining the funds. Moreover, government regulations require that a certain fraction of deposits be held in reserves on which low interest rates are earned. These reserves must be taken into account in calculating the cost of the money that is available for lending.

To summarize, the cost of obtaining funds from different sources varies widely. If a bank obtains $1,000 from one source at an annual interest of 5 percent, its cost is $50; if it obtains $1,000 from another source at annual interest of 10 percent, its cost is $100. The second source costs twice as much as (i.e., 200 percent of) the first—*not* 5 percent. Large differences in the cost of funds from various sources are common in banking. This is in contrast with differences in the cost of a given raw material that was purchased from several vendors by a manufacturing company, which ordinarily are only a few percent. The transfer price of funds must take account of these differences. One alternative is to compute some sort of average. Another is to define "pools" of funds obtained at similar rates and establish transfer prices for each pool. The former is simple, but rough. The latter is complicated.

Expense Centers.   Arguments about transfer prices are common among bank managers. Some banks have decided that the topic is so controversial that they decide not to develop transfer prices.[9] They, therefore, control branches and other units as expense centers, and they measure performance by such indicators as unit or dollar output per staff member, dollars of revenue and market share by product type, expenses per dollars of revenue compared with budget, and quality indicators. Some use a management-by-objectives (MBO) system, in which a principal objective is obtaining a specified number of additional customers. They make special analyses of profitability as a basis for setting selling prices and for making decisions about opening and closing branches and about adding or discontinuing services.

In comparing the performance of the several branches, measurement of volume is a problem. Computers can easily report the volume of each type of transaction; but aggregating these individual totals into an overall measure of volume can be misleading, unless differences in the effort required for the various types are taken into account. Recording a deposit in a savings account requires much less effort than issuing a U.S. savings bond, for example. And the effort involved in processing a loan application may vary substantially from one applicant to another. A few banks have developed explicit weights for each of the main types of transactions; but most assume that the overall mix is sufficiently similar at various times and among the main types of branches so overall measures of volume are adequate.

Accounting System.   Banks collect vast quantities of information. They are required to "balance out" (i.e., prove the accuracy of transactions) daily and in detail. The regulatory agencies require periodic reports. Unfortunately, these reports tend to be in a form that is not useful for management purposes, so the bank must set up additional accounts to collect data for management purposes. Because most of the raw data flows through computers, this is an easy task once the system has been developed. Computer programs are available that usually can be adapted to the situation in a given bank without too much difficulty.

Securities Firms

In this section, we discuss firms that have the general characteristic of dealing in securities. They include investment bankers, securities traders, securities brokers and dealers, managers of funds (investment, mutual, and pension funds), and investment advisors.

Until the 1930s, long-term financing of corporations (i.e., the issuance of stocks and bonds) was generally arranged by commercial banks and by a small elite group of partnerships and individuals called *investment bankers*; J. P. Morgan, Morgan Stanley, Salomon Brothers, and Goldman Sachs are the best known

---

[9]Nevertheless, 80 percent of the respondents to a 1984 survey of large banks reported that they favored profit centers. (Mona J. Gardner and Lucille E. Lammers, "Cost Accounting in Large Banks," *Management Accounting*, April 1988, pp. 1–36.)

examples. The management of the investment portfolio of individuals and companies was handled by bank trust departments. In 1933, the Glass-Steagall Act prohibited commercial banks from engaging in investment banking, including selling and trading in securities. (This prohibition was considerably weakened by the Federal Reserve Board in 1989; the Fed permitted large banks to establish securities affiliates.) The role of bank trust departments decreased partly because their attitude toward fiduciary responsibility resulted in an overemphasis on "safe" investments, which kept their returns low. Between 1975 and 1985, commercial banks lost one-third of their trust business.[10]

Many traditional investment bankers expanded their services to include all forms of securities underwriting, trading, and investment counseling; several set up a network of branches to service individual investors, including relatively small investors. Firms that specialized in providing investment advice were established. In the 1970s, mutual funds of all types proliferated, and pension funds absorbed an increasing fraction of securities issues. These developments led to increased competition and to reduced profit margins among securities firms.

Moreover, financing became more complicated. In addition to the "plain vanilla" issues of long-term debt, preferred stock, and common stock, a variety of issues with different risk/reward characteristics were invented. Foreign investors became an increasingly important source of funds. Computer programs made possible the execution of complicated decision rules for buying and selling huge quantities of securities in a matter of minutes (in some cases, seconds).

All these developments have complicated the management control issues in securities firms.

Management Control Implications

The characteristics of securities firms that are relevant to management control are quite different from those of the organizations discussed in earlier chapters. They include: (1) the importance of customer relationships, (2) stars and teamwork, (3) the need for rapid information flow, and (4) a focus on short-term performance. These are discussed in the following sections, and there is also a discussion of the measurement of financial performance and compensation.

Customer Relationships.[11]   The products of securities firms are intangible, and their quality is difficult to measure. The principal ingredient of quality is the skill of the firm's professionals. At one time, firms could count on a group of loyal customers who stayed with the firm for a generation; but currently customers are more sophisticated and change firms whenever they decide that

---

[10]Lawrence K. Fish, in Eileen M. Friars and Robert N. Gogel, eds. *The Financial Services Handbook* (New York: John Wiley & Sons, 1987), p. 173.

[11]The information in this section is based primarily on Robert G. Eccles and Dwight B. Crane, *Doing Deals: Investment Banks at Work* (Boston: Harvard Business School Press, 1988). Reading Tom Wolfe's 1988 novel, *Bonfire of the Vanities*, is an excellent way of learning about the behavior of professionals in a securities firm.

another firm can offer a similar quality at a better price. The attitude of customers toward a firm is influenced primarily by their judgments about the professionals with whom they have contact.

Management, therefore, goes to great lengths to find out what customers' opinions are and how well (and also how often) a professional interacts with a customer or potential customer. At the lowest level of detail, most firms require that personnel fill out *call reports* for every customer contact; these at least measure the quantity of employee efforts.

There are two principal external sources of information. First, Greenwich Associates has representatives who interview members of the financial staff of at least 1,500 businesses and then report on both the quantity and the perceived quality of the securities firm's calling efforts. A firm can compare the number of its calls with those of its competitors, and it can also learn the customers' judgment about the effectiveness of the presentations. Greenwich Associates also surveys 500 institutional investors, 1,800 institutional buyers, and 1,200 security analysts for their opinions on firms' research and sales forces. Second, the magazine *Institutional Investor* annually surveys institutional investors to rank analysts in each industry; it reports an "All American Research Team" in its October issue. With a few exceptions (e.g., advertising and broadcasting), other service industries do not have comparable information about customer reaction.

In addition, senior managers have informal contacts with clients (including prospective clients and lost clients) that influence their judgments about the performance of their professionals. Some firms make formal surveys of their clients for this purpose.

Stars and Teamwork.   Some professionals in securities firms make decisions about buying or selling securities, or recommendations for corporate financing, that involve tremendous amounts of money. Buy and sell transactions may be executed in a space of a minute or so, as relevant information becomes available. Execution of a merger (or protection of a company against a takeover), a project that is started and finished within a few months, may involve hundreds of millions of dollars in securities and millions in fees to the securities firms. The best professionals—its stars—are, of course, the firm's most valuable asset.

> **Example.** In August 1988, Nomura Securities announced the purchase for $20 million of a 20 percent equity in the firm of Wasserstein, Perella & Company. Bruce Wasserstein and Joseph Perella had organized the firm early in 1988 after a spectacularly successful career with another securities firm; they were the firm's principal assets. The purchase of a 20 percent equity for $20 million indicates that Nomura Securities, the largest and most profitable securities company in the world, judged that these two stars were worth $100 million.[12]

---

[12]Based on Samuel L. Hayes III and Philip M. Hubbard, *Investment Banking: A Tale of Three Cities* (Boston: Harvard Business School Press, 1990), pp. 288–89.

Because of the dominance of star performers, the organization structure of securities firms has relatively few levels, and the relationships between superiors and subordinates are typically unstructured and informal. Hayes and Hubbard describe securities firms as follows:

> Wall Street is practically a caricature of American frontier values, strangely transported through time and space to the canyons of Manhattan. Its youthful gunslinger traders and investment bankers brashly confront each other across the deal table, confident of success and rewards that push the limits of common sense. Personal allegiance is to one's craft, not to a firm.[13]

In such an environment, loose control is appropriate. Firms that have acquired such organizations (e.g., the American Express acquisition of E. F. Hutton and the General Electric acquisition of Kidder Peabody) have difficulty in adapting their management control systems.

The stars who trade in securities or service customers are supported by other professionals, some of whom also are stars. For an important task, such as a major financing or assisting a company in an acquisition, the lead professional may assemble a team that works on the project, sometimes full time but more often part time. Securities traders rely heavily on the advice of research people and others who may know about a given company. An expert in one type of security or industry may ask the advice of colleagues who are knowledgeable about other types of securities or industries, often over the telephone, sometimes in a brief meeting. These informal, but important, relationships contrast with the relationships between production departments and support departments in a manufacturing company. Production supervisors who want the maintenance departments to do some work fill out a work request and wait their turn for the work to be done. In a securities firm there is little paperwork, and the response to the request is often instantaneous.

Need for Rapid Information.   Many securities and commodities are listed on exchanges in London, Tokyo, and New York, which are in three different time zones. A large securities firm, therefore, conducts trading business 24 hours a day, passing responsibility from London to New York to Tokyo when each market closes. Each trader has a *book* showing the firm's position in each security for which he or she is responsible and in the buy and sell orders that are to be executed. Each also has computer screens giving information on worldwide developments that might affect prices. Important developments affect security and commodity market prices within a few minutes of when they occurred. Investment bankers also need current and complete information on all topics that bear on deals in which they are, or may become, involved.

The information systems must signal "flash" news separately from routine flows, they must transform mountains of detail into meaningful summaries, they must develop comparable data from raw data that may not have been comparable,

---

[13]Ibid., pp. 290–91.

and the data, of course, must be accurate. The development and maintenance of information systems in securities firms are important functions.

Focus on Short Run.   A growth stock purchased today may produce satisfactory results three years from now, or it may never pay off. A securities firm's profit on a leveraged buyout is easily measured, and all parties may judge, today, that this deal was a good deal; however, it may result in bankruptcy a few years down the road. In short, the real soundness of investment decisions made currently may not be observable until some considerable time in the future.

Nevertheless, with some important exceptions, securities firms tend to focus on short-run performance, and by "short-run" they mean the current quarter. This short-run emphasis may seem strange; pension fund managers are the largest single class of investors, and they should have little interest in current performance, because their objective is to provide the funds for payments to be made over the lifetime of the pensioners. The short-run focus exists partly because no one knows what the long-run future will be, but primarily because this short-run emphasis has become traditional.

Investors tend to rely on information about current performance, and performance in the recent past, of the securities firms that they hire to manage their funds. Because performance of a securities firm is heavily influenced by the decisions of the firm's stars, who probably were not with the firm for many past years, data on performance over five or ten years may provide an invalid basis for judging the performance of a firm or of a specific fund that the firm manages.[14] For similar reasons, senior managers of security firms tend to rely on short-run performance in judging personnel. Japanese firms tend to pay more attention to the long run. Many people are convinced that the American emphasis on short-run performance has serious adverse economic consequences, but no one seems to be able to change this emphasis.

Measuring Financial Performance.   The financial performance of securities firms and of managers, account executives, and others within the firm who trade or deal with customers tends to be measured primarily in terms of revenue, and, secondarily, in terms of gross profit (the difference between revenue and direct expenses). Little effort is made to measure the net income of various activities or individuals. Commissions to account executives are based on the revenue or gross profit of transactions with their customers. Investment banking professionals are compensated primarily by bonuses that in part are based on the firm's fee for the work and in part on the judgment of senior management.

---

[14]The performance of Peter Lynch is a well-publicized exception to this generalization. Lynch became manager of the Fidelity Magellan Fund in 1977, when its assets were a few million dollars. When he left in May 1990, its assets were $13 billion. Over the 13-year period, the total return of the Magellan Fund was 2,461 percent, compared with 508 percent for the Standard and Poor's stock index. The majority of equities mutual funds earned less than the S&P index.

Securities firms tend not to make much use of the profit center idea, nor do they do much detailed cost accounting.[15]

Part of the reason for the absence of profit centers and detailed cost accounting is that, unlike law or accounting firms, which typically bill customers according to the actual hours spent on the assignment, securities firms typically charge a fee that is a percentage of the amount involved in the deal. They, therefore, have less need to collect costs by assignments than do other firms. Another reason is the informal exchange of advice and other assistance that occurs in securities firms. The cost of this assistance to the recipient is much more difficult to measure than the cost of a maintenance work order in a factory. A third reason is that expenses are relatively unimportant. The direct expense (i.e., the transaction cost) of a securities trade is small relative to the gross margin. The direct cost of a deal that generates many millions of dollars in fees may be only a few hundred thousand dollars. Nevertheless, although the relative amount may not be large, every dollar of expense that legitimately can be saved increases net income by the same pretax amount.

Insurance Companies

There are two types of insurance companies: life and casualty.

A life insurance company collects premiums from policyholders (or from someone else), invests these premiums, and pays a specified amount to a beneficiary when the policyholder dies. Term insurance provides coverage for a specified number of years; whole life provides coverage for the insured person until death. Whole life insurance contracts usually include an investment feature—that is, part of the premium goes to building up the policy's cash value. In the annuity version of such a policy, cash is paid out regularly over a specified period. In the 1980s, the universal life policy became popular. Instead of paying a fixed payment in return for a fixed stream of premium payments, the payout or the premiums, or both, change with changes in interest rates.

A casualty company collects premiums, invests them, and makes payment to policyholders for specified losses. These may be losses to property by fire, theft, accidents, or other causes; or they may be losses to individuals arising from negligence, malpractice, accidents, illness, and similar causes. Nearly half the casualty policies, measured by the dollar amount of premiums, are for automobile insurance. Casualty policies provide coverage for only a short period,

---

[15]As an exception, Lawrence K. Fish, a leading banker, suggests that it would be relatively easy to develop profit by customers. He suggests that, as a rule of thumb, 50 percent of the cost of producing revenue includes designing, implementing, and communicating portfolio decisions to customers, and this can be allocated on a per-account basis with some adjustment for size; 10 percent is account administration, which can be allocated on a per-account basis; 20 percent is support, including research and trading, which can be allocated by the type of service and number of trades; and 20 percent is custody and recordkeeping services which can be allocated according to the activity level of the account. See Lawrence K. Fish, in *The Financial Services Handbook*, Eileen M. Friars and Robert N. Gogel, eds. (New York: John Wiley & Sons, 1987), pp. 173–75.

usually not more than three years. Some policies pay for claims made during this period; others pay for losses incurred during the period, even though claims are made in a later period. The billions of dollars of claims against the asbestos industry for losses incurred decades earlier is the most dramatic example of the uncertainties associated with loss occurrence policies.

Insurance usually is sold by agents. Some agents are independent entities who sell the policies of a number of companies. Others are franchised by a single company. For both, their revenue is a specified percentage of premium revenue from the policies they sell. Insurance companies exercise some control over the activities of agents through branch offices.

Insurance companies are regulated by each of the 50 states. The regulatory authorities require an accounting system that differs in significant respects from generally accepted accounting principles (GAAP). The most important difference is that the regulatory authorities require companies to set up substantial reserves when a new policy is written, and these reserves are released if a policy lapses. As a consequence, writing a new life insurance policy typically results in a regulatory accounting loss in the first year, whereas it results in GAAP income. A lapsed policy can increase regulatory accounting income in the year of lapse, whereas it can decrease GAAP income.

Management Control Implications

The central management control problem in insurance companies, especially life insurance companies, is that they do not know the profits from current policy sales until years later. They set premiums based on their best estimate of the inflows and outflows associated with the policy, but these estimates may turn out to have been wide of the mark. Although profitability cannot be known until the final payment has been made, management cannot wait that long to make control decisions; it needs information currently. Unlike investment bankers, insurance managers give much attention to expense control.

Product Pricing.   A typical insurance company has dozens of products, and the price (i.e., the policy premium) charged for a given product varies among different customers in many respects. For example, the premium for a whole life policy, per thousand dollars of coverage, varies with the age of the insured person (and, hence, his or her life expectancy), health, smoking habits, and, in some cases, gender. Actuaries calculate a tentative premium, and the final premium reflects the marketing people's judgment about the attractiveness of the policy and premiums charged by competitors. The actuary's calculation considers the following factors:

- Acquisition cost: the commission paid to sales agents and the costs associated with the selling organization.
- Servicing cost: the cost of collecting premiums and accounting for them, plus an allocation of corporate overhead.

- Profit: the return desired by the company.
  (Acquisition cost, servicing cost, and profit are referred to collectively as *loading*.)
- Lapse probability: the probability that the policy will be canceled, because the policyholder does not make payments.
- Investment income: the income that will be earned on the investment of premiums until the policy is paid.
- Probability of payment: for life policies, this depends on the age of the insured, with the probability of death determined from mortality tables; adjusted for health and other characteristics mentioned above. For casualty policies, it depends on data about the likelihood of occurrence of the events insured against, together with the probable amount of payments for these events; these estimates are much less certain than those for life insurance policies.
- Income taxes: income tax regulations for the insurance industry are considerably different from those for other industries.
- Required earnings rate: the rate at which the above flows are discounted to arrive at their present value.

The annual premium arrived at in the actuarial calculation is set so that the present value of the stream of premium payments is equal to the present value of the other cash flows.

As is the case in any profession, some actuaries are better than others. Because of the crucial importance of the premium calculation, senior management observes closely the performance of each actuary and the accuracy and promptness of the huge data collection activity that furnishes current information to the actuaries. Is the calculated premium out of line with those of competitors? If so, why? Is the actuary using the very latest information?[16] Is the calculation overly conservative or overly liberal?

Sales Performance   The actual profitability of various types of insurance policies varies widely, in part because of adjustments made to the actuarial calculation when the premium was set and in part because subsequent developments made the assumptions included in the actuarial calculation unrealistic. Management wants the sales organization to emphasize those products that actually are the most profitable. However, calculating the current profitability of various policies is a difficult task, and communicating this information to the sales organization is also difficult. The tendency, therefore, is to focus on sales volume, rather than on profitability. Commissions are based on first-year or early-year premiums, or on the face amount of policies written. Similar rough

---

[16]For example, in the 1980s, claims for malpractice in various professions and awards for malpractice suits fluctuated widely. They increased rapidly from one year to the next in the early years of the decade and increased at a slower rate in the later years.

measures typically are used in appraising the performance of branches. Computer programs that help agents compute the actual profitability of various types of policies are becoming increasingly used.

Expense Control.   Expenses are controlled through programs and budgets as in industrial companies. Productivity measures are widely used in the control of clerical and other repetitive operations. Although judgments about their performance are somewhat subjective, the activities of claims adjustors are carefully monitored.

Control of Investing.   As is the case with other financial services organizations, the management of the investment function is important. Traditionally, insurance companies followed rather conservative investment policies, partly because of the influence of regulatory agencies. In recent years they have diversified into direct placement of loans and in investments in real estate and other commercial ventures. This shift requires a different approach to investing and involves increasing risk. Control is similar to that exercised by other financial services organizations.

Summary

Financial services organizations differ in two fundamental respects from industrial companies. First, their "raw material" is money. At a given moment of time, the value of each unit of money in inventory is the same for all organizations, but the cost of using money obtained from various sources varies considerably. Second, the profitability of many transactions cannot be measured until years after the commitment has been made. In particular, the company is profitable only if the future revenues obtained from current loans, investments, and insurance premiums exceed the cost of the funds associated with these revenues (which is analogous to cost of sales in a manufacturing company) by an amount that is sufficient to cover operating expenses and losses.

The management control problem is complicated in investment banking, securities trading, and some other organizations by the fact that huge profits or losses can be generated in a single transaction. The "stars" who make such transactions are only loosely controlled.

Suggested Additional Readings

Aspinwall, Richard C., and Robert A. Eisenbeis, eds. *Handbook for Banking Strategy*. New York: John Wiley & Sons, 1985.

Association of Management Accountants. "Use and Control of Financial Instruments." *Statement on Management Accounting 4Q*, 1993.

Baughn, William A., Thomas I. Storrs, and Charles E. Walker, eds. *The Bankers' Handbook*. 3rd ed. Homewood, Ill.: Dow Jones-Irwin, 1988. (See especially Part 5.)

Bettinger, Cass. *High Performance in the 90s*. Homewood, IL.: Richard D. Irwin, 1991.

Bollenbacher, George M. *The New Business of Banking*. Chicago: Bankers Publishing Company, 1992.

Davenport, Thomas O., and H. David Sherman. "Measuring Branch Profitability." *The Bankers Magazine*, September–October 1987, pp. 34–38.

Eccles, Robert G., and Dwight B. Crane. *Doing Deals: Investment Banks at Work*. Boston: Harvard Business School Press, 1988.

Friars, Eileen M., and Robert N. Gogel, eds. *The Financial Services Handbook*. New York: John Wiley & Sons, 1987.

Hayes, Samuel L., ed. *Financial Services: Perspectives and Challenges*. Boston: Harvard Business School Press, 1993.

Hayes, Samuel L. III, and Philip M. Hubbard. *Investment Banking: A Tale of Three Cities*. Boston: Harvard Business School Press, 1990.

Quinn, J. B. *Intelligent Enterprise*. New York: The Free Press, 1993.

Rappaport, Stephen P. *Management on Wall Street: Making Securities Firms Work*. Homewood, Ill.: Dow Jones-Irwin, 1988.

Rose, Peter S., and Donald R. Fraser. *Financial Institutions*. 3rd ed. Homewood, Ill.: Business Publications, Inc., 1988.

Sandretto, Michael J. "Controlling Financial Instruments." *Management Accounting*, May 1993, pp. 55–61.

CASE 16–1
CHEMICAL BANK

Chemical Bank, with deposits averaging well over $1 billion, was one of the largest banks in the United States in 1960. Its banking operations were conducted in a main office and in several dozen branch offices located throughout the New York metropolitan area. A partial organization chart is shown in Exhibit 1.

Branch offices operated as if they were independent banks. They served individual, commercial, and industrial customers by accepting demand, savings, and time deposits, by extending various types of loans, and by performing other services normally expected of a bank. The sizes and operating characteristics of the branches varied over a wide range. Average deposits outstanding ranged from $1 million to over $100 million; average loans outstanding, from no loans to over $100 million. Moreover, the ratio of deposits to loans varied considerably from one branch to another; most branches had more deposits than loans, but a few had more loans than deposits. In brief, both the magnitude and composition of assets and liabilities were significantly different among the different branches. Inasmuch as these differences were related to the geographical location of the branches, the difficulty of evaluating and comparing the performance of branches for the purpose of overall planning and control was inherent in the situation. The design and operation of a planning and control system for this purpose was the responsibility of the control division.

Among various reports reaching top management, the quarterly comparative earnings statement (see Exhibits 2 and 3) played a central role in the evaluation of branch performance. The report was designed to show the extent to which branches attained three important goals: (1)

branches should operate within their budgets, (2) branches should grow in deposits and loans, and (3) branches should earn satisfactory profits. Accordingly, the statement showed for each branch the budgeted and actual amounts of deposits and loans outstanding, and income, expenses, and earnings for the current quarter, the year to date, and the year to date for the preceding year.

Budget

In early November, each branch prepared a budget for the following year for submission to headquarters of the banking division and to top management. The branches were furnished a booklet containing sample forms, 24 pages of detailed instructions, and a brief set of policy guides from top management to facilitate the preparation of their budgets. The instructions gave the procedures to be followed in arriving at the budget amounts for specific items. It was, for instance, specified that the starting point for forecasting was to be the prior year's figures on the quarterly basis, that the income item of interest on loans was to be derived from the projected volume of loans and loan rates, that painting cost should not be included in the item for building maintenance expense, and so on.

Since salaries were the biggest single expense item, and the hiring and releasing of employees involved considerable cost, utmost care was required in budgeting this item. Branches were instructed to arrive at staffing requirements for the next year after a thorough examination of anticipated increases in productivity arising from computerization or otherwise improved operating procedures, of anticipated changes in the volume of activity, and of advantages and disadvantages of using overtime or temporary or part-time help. If the number of the required staff of a

---

This case was prepared by R. N. Anthony, Harvard Business School. Copyright by the President and Fellows of Harvard College. Harvard Business School case 172–228.

Exhibit 1

Partial organization chart

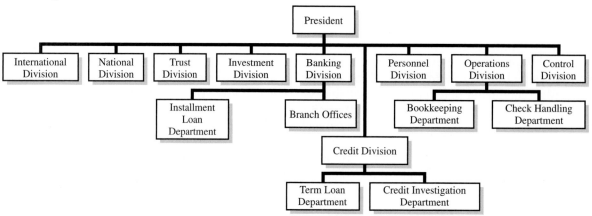

branch thus determined exceeded the number previously authorized by top management, the reason for the difference had to be thoroughly documented and substantiated to banking division headquarters and the budget committee. Top management was extremely critical of subsequent requests by the branches for staff increases that had not been reflected in the budgets.

In general, there were two types of income and expense items—those directly identifiable with a particular branch, and those not directly identifiable with a particular branch. Branches were instructed to budget only those direct expenses under their control. Indirect expenses were allocated to branches by the control division. In addition, the budgeting of certain direct expenses, such as depreciation of fixtures, employee benefits, and deferred compensation, was done by the control division because the branches had only secondary control over these expenses.

Earnings Statement

The control division had encountered a number of serious problems in trying to produce an earnings statement that would be most useful for the branches and for the management of the bank-

ing division. The control division resolved some of these problems in the following ways.

Installment Loans.   Recordkeeping, issuance of coupon books, and part of collection work for installment loans generated by all branches were handled centrally by the installment loan department; and income earned from installment loans, therefore, was credited initially to this department. This income was in large part attributable to the branches that generated the loans and, therefore, was redistributed to them. The current procedure was to distribute gross operating income less the direct cost of "borrowed" funds and operating expenses of the department on the basis of the total indirect installment loans generated by the branch during a revolving annual cycle.

An alternative basis that had been considered was to apportion the net income of the installment department according to the number of payments received by branches, since this measure of activity reflected the clerical time spent for coupon handling. This alternative was not adopted, on the grounds that it did not give branches enough motivation to seek more new installment loans, particularly since customers could make their installment payments at any

EXHIBIT 2   Comparative Statement of Earnings, 1960 (Branch A)

3rd Quarter			January 1 through September 30	
Actual	*Budget*		*Actual*	*Budget*
		Income:		
$ 13,177	$ 12,600	Interest on loans	$ 33,748	$ 35,200
6,373	4,800	Service chgs.—regular A/C's	14,572	14,100
3,816	3,600	Service chgs.—special ck	11,114	10,700
1,168	1,300	Safe deposit rentals	4,317	4,500
2,237	2,154	Installment loans (net)	5,126	5,406
—	—	Special loans (net)	—	—
1,010	1,200	Fees, comm., other income	3,321	3,300
27,781	25,654	Total direct income	72,198	73,206
104,260	102,128	Interest on excess (borr.) funds	324,434	306,166
$ 132,041	$ 127,802	Gross income	$ 396,632	$ 379,372
		Expenses:		
$ 32,363	$ 32,617	Salaries	$ 96,151	$ 97,164
2,995	2,995	Deferred compensation	8,865	8,865
5,232	4,689	Employee benefits	14,925	14,067
11,485	11,489	Rent and occupancy	34,398	33,947
6,824	7,560	Interest on deposits	20,455	21,780
9,458	8,090	Other direct	25,688	23,930
3,128	3,097	Office administration	9,676	9,725
19,183	17,642	Service departments	57,059	52,399
6,415	5,061	Indirect and overhead	14,964	14,273
97,043	93,200	Gross expenses	282,181	276,150
34,998	34,602	Net earnings before taxes	114,451	103,222
18,955	18,741	Income tax prov. (credit)	61,978	55,906
$ 16,043	$ 15,861	Net earnings after taxes	$ 52,464	$ 47,316
$12,655,000	$12,550,000	Average deposits—Demand	$13,134,000	$12,650,000
979,000	1,100,000	Savings	986,000	1,057,000
55,000	55,000	Time	40,000	43,000
233,000	190,000	U.S.	213,000	183,000
$13,922,000	$13,895,000	Total	$14,373,000	$ 33,000
900,000	870,000	Average loans	775,000	827,000
5.82	5.76	Average loan rate	5.82	5.69
		Earnings rate on:		
4.08	3.95	Excess (borr.) funds	4.05	3.95
6.50	6.40	Savings deposits	6.46	6.40
26.5%	27.1%	Net earnings ratio (before taxes)	28.9%	27.2%
		Memo:		
—	—	Losses—before taxes	—	—
—	—	Recoveries—before taxes	—	—

EXHIBIT 3   Comparative Statement of Earnings, 1960 (Branch B)

3rd Quarter			January 1 through September 30	
Actual	*Budget*		*1960 Actual*	*1960 Budget*
		Income:		
$ 951,617	$ 833,300	Interest on loans	$ 2,646,813	$ 2,202,750
7,015	7,400	Service chgs.—regular A/C's	24,020	21,900
8,211	7,600	Service chgs.—special ck	23,284	22,600
2,049	2,100	Safe deposit rentals	6,712	7,100
9,202	9,478	Installment loans (net)	21,402	23,790
—	212	Special loans (net)	85	556
8,081	3,100	Fees, comm., other income	22,517	12,800
986,175	863,190	Total direct income	2,744,933	2,291,496
(191,650)	(121,960)	Interest on excess (borr.) funds	(430,444)	(121,493)
$ 794,525	$ 741,230	Gross income	$ 2,314,489	$ 2,170,003
		Expenses:		
$ 69,308	$ 62,633	Salaries	$ 197,572	$ 185,634
5,646	5,646	Deferred compensation	16,938	16,938
9,180	7,989	Employee benefits	25,833	23,967
27,674	27,775	Rent and occupancy	82,726	83,375
15,878	18,230	Interest on deposits	47,589	52,650
25,637	23,660	Other direct	86,112	71,400
17,232	17,072	Office administration	53,321	53,606
89,724	95,719	Service departments	290,082	283,531
22,406	18,001	Indirect and overhead	53,643	51,166
282,685	276,725	Gross expenses	853,816	822,267
511,840	464,505	Net earnings before taxes	1,460,673	1,347,736
277,212	251,576	Income Tax prov. (credit)	791,100	729,934
$ 234,628	$ 212,929	Net earnings after taxes	$ 669,573	$ 617,802
$67,901,000	$70,000,000	Average deposits—Demand	$69,425,000	$72,667,000
2,354,000	2,700,000	Savings	2,328,000	2,600,000
74,000	90,000	Time	52,000	66,000
5,194,000	1,900,000	U.S.	4,086,000	1,733,000
$75,523,000	$74,690,000	Total	$75,891,000	$77,066,000
72,129,000	65,500,000	Average loans	67,446,000	57,666,000
5.25	5.10	Average loan rate	5.24	5.10
		Earnings rate on:		
4.08	3.95	Excess (borr.) funds	4.05	3.95
6.50	6.40	Savings deposits	6.46	6.40
64.4%	62.7%	Net earnings ratio (before taxes)	63.1%	62.1%
		Memo:		
—	—	Losses—before taxes	5,559	—
—	66	Recoveries—before taxes	798	—

EXHIBIT 4   Calculation of interest income on Excess Funds, Branch A (first three quarters of 1960)

Calculation of Excess Funds

	(000s)	
Total demand deposits	$13,134	
Less: reciprocal bank balances; float	(727)	
Plus: treasury tax and loan a/c	221	
Adjusted demand deposits	12,628	
Less: reserve at 18%	(2,273)	
Net demand deposits		$10,355
Savings deposits	1,026	
Less: reserve at 5%	$ (51)	
Net savings deposits		975
Net deposits available for investment		11,330
Less: loans, cash, other assets		(1,229)
Net excess funds		$10,101

Calculation of Interest Income on Excess Funds	Principal	Annual Rate	Three Quarters	Interest
In special investment pool (63%)	$614,000 ×	7.88% ×	¾	= $ 36,270
In regular investment pool (37%)	361,000 ×	4.05% ×	¾	= 10,962
Savings deposits (100%)	975,000 ×	6.46% ×	¾	= 47,232
In regular investment pool—demand deposits	9,126,000 ×	4.05% ×	¾	= 277,202
Net excess funds	$10,101,000			
Interest on excess funds				$324,434

---

branch they chose. An alternative basis considered was the amount of average loans outstanding. The controller thought this might be more equitable than the currently used basis, but he was of the opinion that the gain to be obtained from the adoption of the new basis was not large enough to offset the additional necessary record-keeping.

Interest on Excess (or Borrowed) Funds.
Branches and other operating units, with funds available for investment in excess of their own requirements for loans, cash, and other assets, shared in the net earnings of the investment division; branches and other operating units

whose asset requirements exceeded their available funds were charged for funds "borrowed." There was a wide variation in the ratio of deposits to loans among branches, and some branches were credited with the interest on excess funds in an amount higher than their direct income. An example of the calculation of this important income or charge item is shown in Exhibit 4.

As shown in the top section of Exhibit 4, the first step was to compute the amount of excess (or borrowed) funds for the branch. Funds were divided into two pools: (1) special pool—earnings from special long-term, high-yield municipal securities, which were considered as an investment of part of the savings and time deposits; and

(2) regular pool-earnings from other portfolio securities investments, interest on certain loans, and sundry earnings. As a result, the special-pool investments yielded a higher rate of return than the regular-pool investments.

Third, branches with savings deposits were credited at the interest rate of the special pool on the basis of their pro rata share of savings deposits. Net savings deposits in excess of the principal of investment in the special pool, together with excess funds other than savings deposits, received pro rata credit from the earnings of the regular investment pool. Branches that borrowed funds were charged at the regular-pool rate. In summary, the two rates from the two pools were as follows:

Special-pool rate: Net earnings of special pool/ special pool securities principal (part of total savings deposits)

Regular-pool rate: Net earnings from regular pool ÷ excess funds less borrowed funds less special securities principal.

For the first three quarters of 1960, the budgeted regular pool rate and special pool rate were 3.95 percent and 7.81 percent; the actual rates were 4.05 percent and 7.88 percent, respectively. Thus, for Branch A the interest on excess funds for the first three quarters was calculated as shown in the lower section of Exhibit 4.

Rent and Occupancy Cost. Some branches operated in leased space, whereas others operated in bank-owned buildings. The first group was charged with the actual rent paid; but the second was charged with the "fair rental value," which was determined by outside real estate appraisers. The practice was thought to put the two groups on the same footing. The fair rental value charges were internal bookkeeping entries offset by credits to real estate accounts and, therefore, indicated the profitability of each building. The determination of the fair rental value was not difficult, and there had been no significant controversies involving its calculation.

Advertising. General or institutional advertising was charged to other indirect expenses. (See below for the allocation of other indirect expenses.) Advertising related to a specific branch was charged directly to that branch, except that, when advertising was placed in mass media, such as radio, television, and newspapers with general circulation, 33 percent of the expense was allocated to other indirect expenses and 67 percent was allocated to the specific branches involved. The theory of the exception was that, when mass media were used, the whole bank benefited to a certain extent.

Banking Division Headquarters and General Administration. All expenses of the banking division headquarters, including the salaries of officers in the division headquarters, were allocated to branches on the basis of their prior year's average gross deposits. The figure for average gross deposits was considered as the best single measure of branch activity.

The salaries of general administrative officers of the bank were first allocated among divisions on the basis of the time spent on problems of each division as estimated by each officer. The amount of general administrative salaries thus allocated to the banking division was, in turn, allocated among branches on the basis of gross deposits in the prior year. All other general administrative expenses were charged on the same basis.

Bookkeeping Department. Much of the bookkeeping work was centralized for the whole bank. However, since the central department had been established only in 1959, several offices continued to do their own bookkeeping in 1960. The expenses of the central bookkeeping department, therefore, were allocated only to the branches it serviced. There were eight functional cost centers in the bookkeeping department, and each cost center had its own basis of allocation. The bases of four of the cost centers are given below.

1. *Regular Bookkeeping Cost Center*. In the bookkeeping department, a permanent clerical staff was assigned to process the accounts of each branch. Allocations to branches were based on the salaries of this assigned staff, plus fringe benefits and related overhead cost.

2. *Bank Ledgers Cost Center*. Allocation was on the basis of debit and credit activity as determined by an analysis made from time to time. Inasmuch as the main activity of this cost center was the posting of transactions to ledger sheets, the number of debit and credit entries was preferred to any other basis (e.g., number of accounts). A new survey of debit and credit statistics was made by the analysis department whenever it was believed that there had been a material change from the prior survey period and, in any event, at least once a year.

3. *Special Checking Cost Center*. Same as 2.

4. *Special Statement Section*. Allocation was on the basis of a number of accounts handled. The activity of the section was to send out special statements on customers' special requests.

Before adoption of the current method based on the cost center concept, weight of statements mailed out had been the basis of allocation for the expenses of the entire department. The current practice was regarded as more accurate, because there were very few temporary movements of staff and machine services from one cost center to another and because there was a significant variation in the activity measures of the cost centers.

According to the controller, the main controversy involving the expenses of the bookkeeping department was not with respect to the basis of allocation but, rather, with respect to the absolute level of expenses of the department. Complaints were heard from those branches serviced by the department to the effect that they were handicapped relative to branches that did their own bookkeeping, because the cost charged by the central bookkeeping department was considerably higher than the cost that would be incurred if the branch did its own bookkeeping. The controller thought branches that had this opinion failed to recognize that the bookkeeping expenses shown in the earnings statements of the branches with their own bookkeeping were only part of the true bookkeeping cost, because an appropriate portion of supervisory salaries,

occupancy costs, supplies, etc., was not included in the item. When the bookkeeping was centralized for a branch, the benefit gained from relieving the supervisors of supervising bookkeeping activity usually appeared as increased loans and deposits, and better management generally.

Check Clearance Department. The total cost of this department was divided among 12 functional cost centers, based on the number of employees assigned to each and the volume of its work. The cost of each cost center was, in turn, charged to branches. Examples of the basis of allocation are given below.

1. *IBM proof machine operation—exchanges*: allocated on the basis of number of checks handled.

2. *IBM proof machine operation—deposits*: allocated on the basis of the number of deposit items.

3. *Check desk*: allocated on the basis of the number of checks handled.

4. *Transit clerical*: allocated on the basis of number of deposit items.

5. *Supervision*: allocated to the various check clearance department cost centers in ratio to labor costs.

As was the case with the bookkeeping centers, the measures of activity (checks handled and number of deposit items) were based on periodic surveys and remained unchanged until significant changes in the relative activity of branches indicated the need for a new survey. Every cost center's activity was reviewed at least once a year for this purpose.

There were two important sources of trouble in allocation of the expenses of the check clearance department. One was that branches cashed checks issued by other branches; the other was that branches received deposits for customers whose accounts were in other branches. In the periodic activity analyses made to determine the basis of allocating cost, the "number of checks cashed" was the number of checks actually cashed in the branch, whether or not the account was located in the branch. Similarly, the "number of deposit items" was the number of deposits made in the branch. Although it had been believed that the effect of these interbranch services largely offset one another, a recent study by the control division indicated that they, in fact, resulted in distortions with respect to certain branches. The control division was currently working on a method of allocation by which the charge would be made to the branch that benefited most—that is, the branch in which the account was located.

Credit Investigation Department.   Although most branches had their own credit analysis staffs, they often asked the central credit department to make investigations. The expenses of the central credit investigation department, therefore, were allocated to the branches that requested its service. The basis of allocation was the number of requests for credit investigation weighted by the typical time required for the analyses performed. The weight for the various types of investigation was determined by the analysis department on the basis of an actual time study.

Term Loan Department.   Income from term loans was credited to the branches that generated the loans. Officers of the term loan department actively counseled the branches in negotiating terms with customers, in drawing up loan contracts, and in reviewing existing loans. It was necessary, therefore, that the expenses of the term loan department be allocated to the branches that used its service. The basis of allocation was the number of loans considered, the number of loans outstanding, and the number of amendments to existing loans, weighted by the unit handling time of each of three classes. To determine the weight, the analysis department asked the staff of the term loan department to estimate the time spent on each class.

Personnel Division.   The expenses of this division were allocated to all operating units in the ratio of the number of employees in each operating unit to the total.

Other Indirect Expenses.   Items of a general overhead nature, such as expenses of the operations division (except the direct cost of examining a branch, which was charged directly), cost of the senior training program, general institutional advertising, contributions, etc., were included under this heading. The basis of allocation of these expenses among branches was the ratio of annual operating expenses (excluding other indirect expenses and interest on deposits) of each branch to the total operating expenses of all branches.

Deposits and Loans.   In the lower part of the comparative statement were shown the budgeted and actual loans and deposits outstanding. Both top management and branch managers exercised a close watch over these primary indicators of the level of the branch's operation. The controller, however, believed that the ultimate test of the office performance should not rest with these items but, rather, with earnings. He maintained that the effect of changes in deposits and loans should and would be reflected in the earnings statement.

Controller's Views on Allocations

The controller believed that some arbitrariness was inevitable in the allocation of the income and expense items described above. With dozens of branches, each with its own operating characteristics, it was impossible to have a "perfect" or "right" system for all of them. What was more important, according to the controller, was agreement on the part of the branch managers that the system was generally equitable. If managers agreed on the fairness of the system, he believed, it was likely to be a success. The controller, therefore, let it be known to branch managers that the system was always open for revision, and he encouraged them to make known any criticisms they had. After the control division had done its best to find a workable system, the initiative for suggesting changes was with the branch managers. The controller said that several changes had been made as a result of branch managers' suggestions.

He warned them, however, against a blind and apathetic acceptance; the acceptance should be positive and constructive. On acceptance of the system, branch managers should be concerned with the reported result and make necessary efforts to improve it. Thus, he said, branch managers were told clearly that the earnings statement was used to evaluate their performance. This, he thought, attached sufficient importance to the matter to prevent any possible indifference.

Attitudes of Branch Managers on Allocations. The managers of two offices, A and B, held different opinions about the system. The operating characteristics of these branches were different, as indicated by their comparative statements of earnings for the third quarter of 1960, reproduced in Exhibits 2 and 3. Branch A was relatively small and deposit-heavy, did its own bookkeeping, and operated in a leased space, whereas Branch B was larger, loan-heavy, used the centralized bookkeeping department, and operated in a bank-owned building.

Comment by Manager of Branch A. The statement is useful because I like to see, at least quickly, whether I am within the budget and what caused the deviations from it, if any.

The earnings of our branch are relatively low, because the volume of business is limited by the location. We have more deposits than our loan requirements; consequently, we get credit for the excess funds. In fact, as you see, for the first three quarters of 1960, interest on excess funds was more than four times the total direct income. The 4.05 percent rate on the excess funds seems fair enough, but we try always to increase our loans in order to increase our earnings. However, the location of our office is a limiting factor.

Since rent and occupancy is the actual rent paid to the owner of the building, we can't have any quarrel about that, but the service department charges are certainly too high. We don't have any control over these costs; yet we are charged for them. I am not complaining that this is unfair; on the contrary, I believe branches should share the burden. My only misgiving is whether those service departments are doing enough to cut down on their costs.

About one-half of the service department expenses charged to our branch is for check clearing service. Although I don't know the basis of allocation, I don't doubt that it is fair. Besides, even if I should have some questions about the basis, probably it wouldn't reach up there; the communication channel from here to the top is long and tedious.

At present, we do our own bookkeeping, but soon this will be centralized. I have heard some managers complain that the cost charged to them for the centralized bookkeeping is higher than the cost when they did their own bookkeeping. However, such intangible gains as prestige and customer relations may justify a little higher cost. At any rate, we wouldn't have any choice if top management decides to centralize our bookkeeping. It may be better in the long run.

Although I don't know exactly what items are included in other direct and indirect and overhead expenses, I don't think they are excessive. The control division is trying to be fair.

In summary, I think the statement is useful, but there are many factors you should consider in interpreting it.

Comment by Manager of Branch B. The statement is a fair measure of how branches are doing. It is true that the location of a branch has a lot to do with its operation; in evaluating a particular branch, the location is an important element to be taken into account. To take the extreme case, you don't need a branch in a desert. If a branch can't show earnings after being charged with its fair share of all costs, perhaps the purpose of its existence is lost.

High volume and efficient operation have contributed to our high level of earnings. Our branch has more loans than can be sustained by our own deposits; thus, we are charged with interest on borrowed funds on the theory that we would have to pay the interest if we borrowed from outside. Of course, by increasing deposits we could meet the loan requirements and add to our earnings a good part of the interest on borrowed funds; indeed, we have been trying to lure more deposits to our branch. Quite apart from this special effort, however, we do not neglect to seek more loan opportunities, for loans increase earnings even after the interest charge.

Our office is in a bank-owned building; but, instead of controversial depreciation and maintenance charges, we are charged with the fair rental value. We are satisfied with this practice.

The bookkeeping of our branch is centralized. I believe we could do it for less money if we did our own bookkeeping; but competing banks have centralized bookkeeping departments, and we have to go along. I suspect there are some intangible benefits being gained, too.

If I really sat down and thoroughly examined all the allocation bases, I might find some things that could be improved. But the fact of life is that we must draw a line somewhere; some arbitrariness will always be there. Furthermore, why should our branch raise questions? We are content with the way things are.

Comments by Banking Division Headquarters. We call this report [Exhibits 2 and 3] our Bible, and, like the actual Bible, it must be interpreted carefully. Many factors affect the performance of a branch that do not show up on the report. For example, in an area that is going downhill the manager of a branch has to work terribly hard just to keep his deposits from declining, whereas in a growing area, the manager can read the *New York Times* all day and still show an impressive increase in deposits. The location of the branch in the neighborhood, its outward appearance, its decor, the layout of its facilities—all can affect its volume of business. Changes in the level of interest rates, which are noncontrollable, also have a significant effect on income. At headquarters, we are aware of these factors and take them into account when we read the reports. The unfortunate fact is that some managers—for example, those in declining areas—may not believe that we take them into account. Such a manager may worry about his apparently poor performance as shown on the report, and this has a bad psychological effect on him.

One other difficulty with the report is that it may encourage the manager to be interested too much in his own branch at the expense of the bank as a whole. When a customer moves to another part of town, the manager may try to persuade him to leave his account at the same branch, even though the customer can be served better by a branch near his new location. We even hear of two branches competing for the same customer, which certainly doesn't add to the reputation of the bank. Or, to take another kind of problem, a manager may be reluctant to add another teller because of the increased expense, even though he actually needs one to give proper service to his customers.

Of course, the earnings report is just one factor in judging the performance of a bank manager. Among the others are the growth of deposits compared with the potential for the area; the number of calls he makes soliciting new business (we get a monthly report on this); the loans that get into difficulty; complaint letters from customers; the annual audit of operations made by the control division; and, most important, personnel turnover, or any other indications of how well he is developing his personnel. Some of these factors are indicated in these statistics [see Exhibit 5], which are prepared at banking division headquarters.

Questions

This case deals with the use of the profit center concept as a management control device for branch offices in a service industry. A particular problem in banking is how to set the transfer price for money.

Discuss the adequacy of the following structural components of Chemical's control systems.

1. **Cost allocation** of headquarter's expense. Should these costs be allocated? Are these methods of allocation appropriate?

2. **Noncontrollable costs** included in performance reports. Should noncontrollable costs be omitted from the earnings statement? If so, what items would be affected?

3. **Performance evaluation** of dissimilar branches. Does this reporting system provide enough information? Too much? Should Exhibit 5 be discontinued?

4. **Profit center** organization of branches. Do you believe branches should be evaluated as "profit centers"? What factors are critical to the success of a branch bank? To what extent are these factors controllable by a branch manager?

5. **Transfer pricing** system used. If you believe the profit center system should be continued as a control device, discuss the appropriateness of the data developed in Exhibit 4 for transfer pricing purposes. Can you suggest better ways to price the transfer of funds between branches? Bank of America, one of the largest banks in the United States, charges its profit centers for the use of money at current interest rates for obtaining funds of like maturities and risk. For example, if a branch makes a 90-day loan, it would be charged at the current rate that the bank pays on 90-day certificates of deposit. Should Chemical Bank adopt this practice?

Exhibit 5 Branch Office Report

All Dollar Amounts in Thousands Unless Otherwise Stated	JAN.	FEB.	MAR.	APRIL	MAY	JUNE	JULY	AUG.	SEPT.	OCT.	NOV.	DEC.	YEAR AVERAGE
DEPOSITS—AVERAGE													
1 Demand—(Ind., Part., Corp.) $	14,038	13,473	12,330	12,919	13,108	12,911	12,596	11,907	12,746	12,202			
2 Demand—Banks $	50	50	—	—	—	—	—	—	—	—			
3 Special Checking $	221	218	220	251	235	216	237	244	236	219			
4 Treas. Tax & Loan Account $	118	149	238	124	270	321	232	202	265	196			
5 Savings $	987	974	1,001	990	976	1,012	972	978	986	1,013			
6 Christmas Club $	15	23	30	35	41	46	51	55	60	63			
7 Time $	—	—	—	—	—	—	—	—	—	—			
8 Total $	15,429	14,887	13,819	14,319	14,630	14,506	14,088	13,386	14,293	13,693			
NUMBER OF ACCOUNTS													
9 Demand—(Ind., Part., Corp.)	1,515	1,513	1,507	1,503	1,516	1,511	1,514	1,497	1,478	1,473			
10 Demand—Banks	1	—	—	—	—	—	—	—	—	—			
11 Special Checking	868	865	884	892	894	900	903	911	939	948			
12 Savings	585	587	593	589	587	591	593	587	621	645			
13 Christmas Club	540	536	534	538	533	530	526	519	516	511			
14 Time	—	—	—	—	—	—	—	—	—	—			
15 Total	3,509	3,501	3,518	3,522	3,530	3,532	3,536	3,514	3,554	3,577			
LOANS													
16 Total Loans—Average $	723	755	720	627	672	773	841	889	971	961			
17 Installment Loan—Volume $	20	24	36	31	35	22	25	34	27	39			
18 Spec. Loan Dept.—Month End $	—	—	—	—	—	—	—	—	—	—			
NUMBER OF BORROWERS													
19 Total Loans	48	58	50	49	51	54	55	60	62	63			
20 Installment Loan—Made	24	37	46	50	32	30	28	45	44	39			
21 Special Loan Dept.	—	—	—	—	—	—	—	—	—	—			
22 Staff—Number of Officers	4	4	4	4	4	4	4	4	3	3			
23 No. of Employees—Auth Budget	25	25	25	25	25	25	25	25	25	25			
24 Total	29	29	29	29	29	29	29	29	28	28			
25 Overtime & Supper Money Payments (To nearest dollar) $	276	135	273	93	496	123	536	370	350	220			
SERVICE CHARGES (To nearest dollar)													
26 Regular Checking Accounts $	1,543	1,578	1,445	225	2,550	858	2,378	1,998	1,997	1,833			
27 Special Checking Accounts $	1,017	1,119	220	397	223	322	313	237	266	340			
28 Total $	2,560	2,697	2,665	622	773	180	691	235	263	173			

Income and Expense By Quarters And Cumulative

To Nearest Dollar	1st Quarter	2nd Quarter	Jan. thru June	3rd Quarter	Jan. thru Sept.	4th Quarter	Jan. thru Dec.
Gross Income $	133,060	131,531	264,591	132,041	396,632		
Gross Expenses $	92,050	93,088	185,138	97,043	282,181		
Net Before Taxes $	41,010	38,443	79,453	34,998	114,451		
Net After Taxes $	18,799	17,622	36,421	16,043	52,464		
Average Loan Rate	5.80	5.83	5.81	5.82	5.82		
Earn. Rate—Excess Funds	4.02	4.06	4.04	4.08	4.05		
Earn. Rate—Savings Deposits	6.52	6.55	6.54	6.59	6.55		

EXHIBIT 5 (continued) Branch Office Report—Supplement

1960

Location and Office No.   A

All Dollar Amounts in Thousands

	JAN.	FEB.	MAR.	APRIL	MAY	JUNE	JULY	AUG.	SEPT.	OCT.	NOV.	DEC.	YEAR TOTALS	
Regular Checking Accounts—Number														
Opened—New	26	17	7	15	16	17	10	9	14	11				1
Opened—A/C Trans. within Office	—	1	1	1	4	—	1	—	—	—				2
Opened—A/C Trans. from other Off.	—	1	1	—	3	—	2	—	1	—				3
Total Number Opened	26	19	9	16	23	17	13	9	15	11				4
Close	24	17	12	17	6	19	9	17	24	14				5
Closed—A/C Trans. within Office	—	2	1	2	2	—	—	8	6	1				6
Closed—A/C Trans. to other Offices	4	3	2	1	2	3	1	1	4	1				7
Total Number Closed	28	22	15	20	10	22	10	26	34	16				8
Net Opened or Closed	-2	-3	-6	-4	+13	-5	+3	-17	-19	-5				9
Regular Checking Accounts Average Deposits Closed—Monthly														
Closed $	16	7	3	15	7	14	4	11	18	7				10
Closed—Trans. within Office $	—	19	2	4	2	—	—	6	4	1				11
Closed—Trans. to other Offices $	5	6	2	—	1	3	1	1	2	2				12
Total Average—Closed Accts. $	21	32	7	19	10	17	5	18	24	10				13
Accounts Since Jan. 1st—Cumulated*														
*No. Opened (Line 1)	26	43	50	65	81	98	108	117	131	142				14
No. Closed (Line 5)	24	41	53	70	76	95	104	121	145	159				15
*Opened—Current Mo. Avg. (Line 14) $	83	191	162	143	120	102	120	109	114	127				16
Closed—Total Avg. Bal. (Line 10) $	16	23	26	41	48	62	66	77	95	102				17
Business Development														
No. of calls—Customers	3	8	7	4	10	8	6	9	5	5				18
No. of calls—Prospects	3	4	4	4	1	4	2	6	5	5				19
Total	6	12	11	8	11	12	8	15	10	10				20
Spec. Checking Accts.—Opened	26	21	31	21	19	22	15	33	37	29				21
Spec. Checking Accts.—Closed	13	24	12	13	17	16	12	25	9	20				22
Spec. Checking Accts.—Net	+13	-3	+19	+8	+2	+6	+3	+8	+28	+9				23
Savings Accounts—Opened	17	9	22	9	15	24	15	9	52	39				24
Savings Accounts—Closed	21	7	16	13	17	20	13	15	18	15				25
Savings Accounts—Net	-4	+2	+6	-4	-2	+4	+2	-6	+34	+24				26
S. D. Boxes—New Rentals	9	6	3	9	3	6	5	6	4	—				27
S. D. Boxes—Surrendered	9	4	9	11	12	10	6	7	7	3				28
S. D. Boxes—Net	—	+2	-6	-2	-9	-4	-1	-1	-3	-3				29
No. of Personal Money Orders Sold	523	543	583	643	421	467	447	419	452	367				30

CASE 16–2
METROPOLITAN BANK

Fred Marple, senior vice president of Metropolitan Bank, studied the Chemical Bank case as a participant in a senior management development program during August 1993. The instructor informed the class that this case was originally written in the early 1960s. Mr. Marple told the case writer how and why Metropolitan's system differed from the system described in that case.

Background

With deregulation of consumer banking in the early 1970s, commercial banking became a highly profitable business. Banks earned an interest rate spread (the difference between the rate generated on loans and the rate paid out to depositors) that provided a profitable margin over expenses. Loan growth and expense control increased profitability. The 1980s brought unprofitable times to the banking industry as ill-fated loans to less developed countries went into default and huge loan losses drained earnings. Also in the late 1980s and early 1990s, losses on real estate loans and leveraged transactions were large. Banking became intensely competitive with nonbank competitors such as brokerage houses entering the business with money market accounts. Consequently, commercial banks examined individual areas to identify profitable lines of business and look for downsizing opportunities.

The bank was divided into two operating units: Global Bank and Regional Bank. Global Bank provided sophisticated lending, corporate finance, and treasury services to Fortune 1000 companies, foreign multinationals, and public sector clients. Regional Bank was responsible for retail banking, middle-market commercial banking, and private banking for high net-worth individuals.

This case was prepared by Anil R. Chitkara (T '94) under the supervision of Professor Robert N. Anthony. Copyright by Osceola Institute.

This case describes the Retail Banking Group that was a component of Regional Bank. In 1992, Regional Bank generated approximately 32 percent of the revenues and net income of Metropolitan Bank and constituted 28 percent of Metropolitan's assets.

In 1991, in order to analyze its retail banking business, Metropolitan Bank decided that it needed a better assessment of the profitability of its customers and products. A team was assembled for this purpose. The team developed a new organization structure and management control system.

The team recognized that the entire organization had to be mobilized in a coherent and focused direction. To that end they developed the following mission, strategy, and business synergies/linkages.

Retail Bank Mission

"Our mission is to achieve superior customer focus and responsiveness. We view our customers as our most important corporate asset. We believe that the best way to create value for the corporation is to create value for our customers. Value is the experience of conducting business with Metropolitan. It is the combination of product, price, convenience, and service. By providing the best value for our customers, Metropolitan will be recognized as the leader in retail financial services within our chosen markets."

Retail Bank Strategy

The Retail Bank strategy is to grow its franchise by creating superior customer value.

1. Creating superior customer value engenders the following four principles:
   a. Understanding and anticipating customer needs.
   b. Developing products and services to meet important needs.

c. Delivering conveniently with high quality service.

d. Pricing competitively.

2. Continuation of this strategy will drive revenue growth and strengthen the franchise by:

a. Acquiring new customers through aggressive pursuit of new value propositions.

b. Expanding and strengthening relationships with existing and new customers.

The Retail Bank is moving aggressively to implement a strategic platform to grow the franchise by generating superior customer value. Execution of this platform involves a broad range of business unit and cross organization initiatives.

Business Synergies and Linkages

Understand the Market: Identify performance opportunities where significant market segments are currently under or over served and *we* could more appropriately meet their needs—set the benefit and pricing parameters for the value proposition.

Develop and Communicate the Value Proposition: Translate our improved market understanding into a profitable, unique service proposition and communicate this proposition to our target audience—define the cost, capability and service level objectives for the delivery system.

Adapt the Delivery System: Ensure that the value proposition is being delivered to maximize profitability and build required capabilities—finalize the quantitative business models (e.g., market and supply) to support rigorous performance management.

Upgrade the Performance Management Systems: Ensure that the goal-setting, planning, performance measurement, and reward systems stimulate behavior at all organization levels which optimizes operating performance—identify requirements to upgrade the business

models or develop market understanding, value proposition or delivery system. See Exhibit 1.

Retail Banking Group

The Retail Banking Group (RBG) served three classes of customers: regional consumers, commercial and professional businesses, and consumers on a national basis. The RBG previously had been organized around the branch banking network. Under the new organizational structure, RBG was organized around three major business lines: Local Markets, Retail Card Services, and National Consumer Business Group. Local Markets Group works with branch dependent customers for deposits, insurance, investments, and small business lending; Retail Card Services Group handles payment systems and revolving credit on a nationwide basis; and National Consumer Business Group consists of nonpayment system related lending, including mortgages, home equity, education, recreational vehicles, and automobiles (see Exhibit 2).

Organization of the Local Markets Group

Local Market Development.   The Market Development Group was responsible for understanding the market. The objective of the Market Development Group was to identify significant performance opportunities where current value propositions poorly or unprofitably serve significant segments. Key steps in this process included understanding needs segmentation and the value of current service offerings, estimating economic opportunity from redesigned offerings, evaluating current competitive position, and conducting environmental scans (i.e., regulation, technology, economy, demographics). Major groups of customers were separated into various segments, each indicating similar characteristics such as demographic, behavioral, and psychographic profile. The segments were tracked based on use of products, services, and distribution channels. The objective of monitoring customer segments was to assess profitability dynamics, value propositions,

Exhibit 1

The performance improvement wheel is a systematic discipline to identify and prioritize all significant performance opportunities and embed a continuous improvement system.

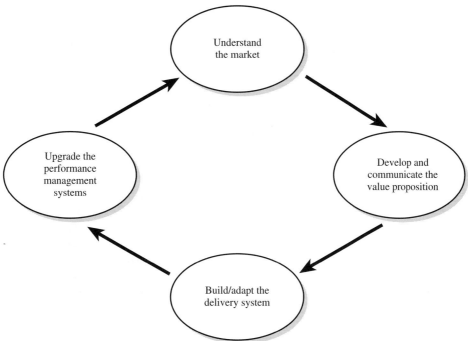

and examine processes whereby nonvalue processes would be eliminated via reengineering. The performance of the Market Development Group was measured on major market segment profitability, its progress in developing new market segment programs, and effective management of the overall Local Markets marketing budget.

This group also served as the catalyst to develop new business lines. As competition intensified, the need to expand business offerings was essential; therefore major business line strategies surrounding insurance, investments, and electronic banking (i.e., Debit Cards, Home Banking) were employed.

Product Management. The Product Management Group was responsible for working with the Market Development Group to ensure

product offerings were aligned with customer needs, included the appropriate value functions, and were priced profitably. The overall objective was to develop a service offering which uniquely meets segment needs/values at profitable prices and communicates the value proposition to target segments. The key steps included designing the new value proposition by adding/eliminating features on the basis of willingness to pay and establishing pricing levels/structure, functionality, service levels, and access. Communicating the new value proposition included message development, channel selection, and brand management. Every week the Product Management Group prepared a report detailing the changes in volume for the products and listed Metropolitan's prices and its competitor's prices (obtained both internally and from an outside data-gathering organization). These findings,

Exhibit 2

Partial organization chart

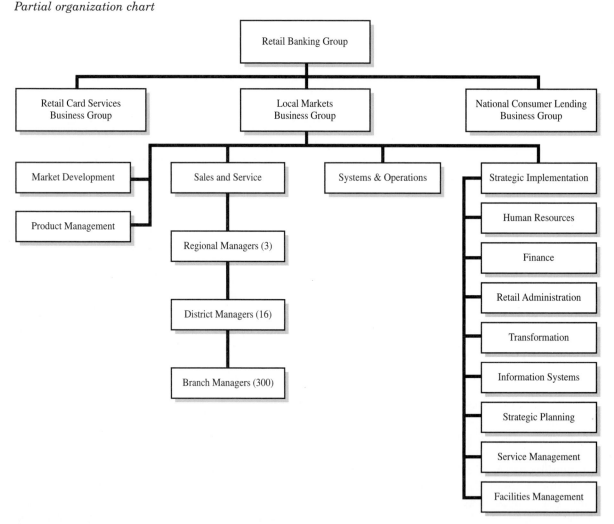

together with recommendations for product feature enhancements, new products, and pricing, were presented at a pricing committee meeting that included members of each group within Local Markets. The performance of the Product Management Group was measured on major product grouping's profitability.

Sales & Service.   The Sales and Service Group (S & S) supervised the local distribution channel of

the bank, including branches, automated teller machines (ATMs), and customer telephone service lines. This group was responsible for executing the product management and market development strategies. The overall objective of S & S was to build/adapt the delivery system to ensure that the value proposition is delivered to maximize profitability and build required capabilities. Key steps in the process included assessing the gap between actual and target activity performance measures

EXHIBIT 3   **Weighting of Evaluation Criteria for Bonus Incentive Plan**

Deposit growth		
Personal transactions	12	
Personal investments	8	
Business investments and transactions	15	
Subtotal		35
Asset growth:		
Mortgage loans	3	
Home equity and quick loans	7	
Direct installment loans	3	
Revolving credit	5	
Business lending	6	
Subtotal		24
Revenue:		
Nonbank investments	12	
Fees	9	
Subtotal		21
Customer satisfaction		20
Total		100

(i.e., cost, customer satisfaction, service levels, revenue, product delivered), assuring value created by all activities, and performing internal and external surveys via benchmarking and best practice comparisons (i.e., scale, service levels, technology). The performance of S & S was measured against key performance measures designed to reflect the goals of the strategies and growth targets.

Branch managers were within the S & S group, and their performance was measured by the Bonus Incentive Plan (BIP) linked directly to the strategies and growth targets of the market segments and product groupings. The BIP set forth 11 specific criteria (see Exhibit 3). Each criterion had a point weighting and a band around which the point weighting fluctuated. Each branch was given specific goals for each of the 11 criteria. If the goal was met, the branch received the points assigned to it. If the goal was exceeded, additional points within the band were earned; if performance was below goal, fewer points were earned. Compensa-

tion of district managers, branch managers, and key personnel was affected by the Bonus Incentive Plan. These measures differed markedly from the profit center system described in the Chemical Bank case.

Support Functions.   Centralized support groups such as Human Resources, Finance, Strategic Planning, Service Management, Systems, Back Office Operations, Retail Facilities and Transformation,[1] were treated as expense centers, and their financial performance was measured against their budgets, the group's financial performance including specific Key Performance Measures, and implementation of appropriate tactics to support the Market Product and Sales & Service groups.

Organization of the National Business Groups

The Retail Card Services and National Consumer Business Groups served Metropolitan's national consumer base. The groups were responsible for asset originations, credit approval, customer service, quality control, and remittance processing of the national customer business base. The performance of the groups was measured on their own profitability.

Retail Card Services Business Group

Mission.   Retail Card Services Business Group will take advantage of its national customer base and direct communications channel to help shape a competitively advantaged national purchase and payment system, based on fundamental, "real value" propositions to the customer. These propositions would be used to build durable, meaningful relationships with customers over the course of their lives, using the credit product as a "wedge."

---

[1]Transformation consists of reengineering the retail bank and includes productivity enhancements and operations and service workflow redesigning (i.e., balance retention programs, quality, and customer focus).

Beyond repositioning its card products, Retail Card Services Business Group was defining a vision for the future that will allow Metropolitan to fully realize its potential in the new world as well as serve as a beacon for "Evolving Card Business Developments."

The strategic functions were redefined as follows:

1. Primary role is to provide strategic blueprints that will bring together and give direction to marketing, operations, product development, product management, etc.

2. Ensure that the organization does not get focused solely on deals and transactions, but creates a context and framework for these efforts. Dedicated attention to the big picture helps the entire organization develop the ability to adapt to change.

3. Expand to a broader view of Purchase/Payment System products and services in order to competitively position the Metropolitan franchise and grow the earnings base.

4. Provide increased project management and implementation support.

National Consumer Business Group

Mission.   The mission was to establish a multi-channel, broad-based, and cost-effective origination capability that generated assets with attractive risk-adjusted returns.

1. Leveraging risk-management capabilities to offer competitive products at competitive pricing to a broader customer base, while providing a level of service that resulted in high customer satisfaction.

2. Becoming a top-tier player in the home secured market. Home Equity products provided a strong base on which to build because of the size and depth of the market, the profitability of the product for

lenders, and the attractive demographics of home-secured borrowers. Metropolitan Bank had an established expertise to take advantage of the existing fragmentation within the market.

3. Continuing to offer consumer loans where our leadership position in these products resulted in superior economic returns and/or opportunities to attract new customers.

The National Consumer Business Group was composed of four major business lines, each with strong competitive positions:

1. Metropolitan had created a Mortgage franchise with enormous value. The mortgage industry was undergoing rapid consolidation and Metropolitan had become a top tier player in both originations and servicing. Scale economics, effective risk management, and technological enhancements in new origination, servicing, and secondary marketing systems were major challenges.

    Servicing represented the store of economic value to be harvested over the life of a mortgage loan. Efficiency was the key. The new systems and technology (automated workflow/imaging) being implemented will enhance our position.

2. Metropolitan had also become one of the largest Guaranteed Student Loan providers. In a consolidating industry, it was one of the few vertically integrated processors. The guaranteed nature of Student Loans produced a stable earnings stream with very low equity requirements. The challenge was to continue to achieve growth while reducing operating risk.

3. National Consumer Finance was a profitable consumer finance business operating through a national network of 12 regional offices. Their national distribution system will continue to be

leveraged to expand the origination of home equity loans through correspondents.

4. Consumer Asset Group was a high margin, high ROE business focused in the local area. Metropolitan had a dominant market share of total consumer loan households, representing a strong second position.

Transfer Pricing

Metropolitan Bank used transfer prices for funds and services provided by one bank unit to another. The Retail Banking Group generated funds in the form of deposits and these funds were used to finance loans and investment activities throughout the Bank. All funds received were transferred into Metropolitan's Treasury Group, a corporate function. The Treasury Group's primary responsibility was to remove interest rate risk in the business unit's results, thereby minimizing the impact of profits or losses associated with the mismatching of asset and liability terms.

The Treasury Group calculated interest rates, or "pool rates," for different products[2] with differing maturities. Pool rates were based on an average of a "core rate" and the current (or slightly lagged) LIBID[3] rate. The core rate was the historical average interest rate earned by the Bank. It was applied to a specified fraction of the total amount of money in the pool. For other products, the interest rate was based entirely on the LIBID, and for still others it was related to the interest on wholesale borrowings of the same maturity. Some rates were modified to take account of rates charged by competing banks, based on information obtained by the Product Management Group and supplied by an outside data-gathering organization.

---

[2]Demand deposits, NOW accounts, savings accounts, 91-day certificates of deposit, and 6-month certificates of deposit are examples of products.

[3]LIBID is an acronym for "London Inter Bank Interest Rate on Deposits," a commonly used short-term interest rate.

Sales and Service (branches and telephone service) also provided a wide array of services to other major areas of the corporation that housed the large corporate, middle market, and private banking customers. Compensation (payment for services provided) was set for approximately 75 different services including deposits, checks cashed, account maintenance, automatic teller machine transactions, and payroll preparation. Individual charges were set at the beginning of the year by estimating the quantity of the services to be provided and the total expenses associated with each service. Transaction cost per unit of service was calculated by multiplying the rate agreed to by the actual volume.

Profit Planning Process

The Retail Bank Group budget preparation process had four phases. First, the Market Development Group set gross revenue targets for each major customer segment. Next, the Product Management Group developed specific product functions and pricing to support the marketing programs and gross revenue projections. Third, the Sales and Service and support groups developed the expense levels and appropriate compensation goals based on key performance measures needed to meet the market and product groups' plans. The final phase was consolidation of the three previous phases and development of a coherent plan for the entire Retail Banking Group. The planning process required five months, beginning in early July.

Questions

1. Compare the Retail Banking Group in Metropolitan Bank with the corresponding organization in Chemical Bank.

2. Do you think the organizational structure and control systems are consistent with the bank's strategies?

3. What changes to the organization structure and control systems would you recommend for Metropolitan Bank?

CASE 16–3
CITIBANK INDONESIA

In November 1983 Mehli Mistri, Citibank's country manager for Indonesia, was faced with a difficult situation. He had just received a memorandum from his immediate superior, David Gibson, the division head for Southeast Asia, informing him that during their just-completed review of the operating budgets, Citibank managers at corporate had raised the SE-Asia division's 1984 aftertax profit goal by $4 million. Mr. Gibson, in turn, had decided that Indonesia's share of this increased goal should be between $500,000 and $1,000,000. Mr. Mistri was concerned because he knew that the budget he had submitted was already very aggressive; it included some growth in revenues and only a slight drop in profits, even though the short-term outlook for the Indonesian economy, which was highly dependent on oil revenues, was pessimistic.

Mr. Mistri knew that, to have any realistic expectation of producing profits for 1984 higher than those already included in the budget, he would probably have to take one or more actions that he had wanted to avoid. One possibility was to eliminate (or reduce) Citibank's participation in loans to prime government or private enterprises, as these loans provided much lower returns than was earned on the rest of the portfolio. However, Citibank was the largest foreign bank operating in Indonesia, and failing to participate in these loans could have significant costs in terms of relations with the government and prime customers in Indonesia and elsewhere. The other possibility was to increase the total amount of money lent in Indonesia, with all of the increase going to commercial enterprises. But with the deteriorating conditions in the Indonesian economy, Mr. Mistri knew that it was

---

This case was prepared by Associate Professor Kenneth A. Merchant, Harvard Business School. Copyright by the President and Fellows of Harvard College. Harvard Business School case 185-061.

probably not a good time for Citibank to increase its exposure. Also, the government did not want significant increases in offshore loans to the private sector at this time because of their adverse impact on the country's balance of payments and services account.

So, Mr. Mistri was contemplating what he should do at an upcoming meeting with Mr. Gibson. Should he agree to take one or both of the actions described above to increase 1984 profits? Should he accept the profit increase and hope that the economy turned around and/or that he was able to develop some new, hitherto unidentified sources of income? Or should he resist including any of the division's required profit increase in his budget?

Citibank

Citibank, the principal operating subsidiary of Citicorp, is one of the leading financial institutions in the world. The bank was founded in 1812 as a small commercial in New York City, and over the years it had grown to a large global financial services intermediary. In 1983, the bank had revenues of almost $5.9 billion and employed over 63,000 people in almost 2,600 locations in 95 countries.

Citibank's activities were organized into three principal business units: institutional banking, individual banking, and the capital markets group. The institutional banking units provided commercial loans and other financial services, such as electronic banking, asset-based financing, and foreign exchange, to corporations and governmental agencies around the world. The individual banking units, which operated in the United States and 18 other countries, provided transactional, savings, and lending services to consumers. The capital markets group served as an intermediary in flows of funds from providers

EXHIBIT 1   Selected Citicorp Financial Data—1983 (dollars in millions)

	Citicorp Consolidated	Institutional Bank	Individual Bank	Capital Markets Group
Revenues	$5,883	$2,896	$2,380	$587
Net income	860	758	202	128
Return on shareholders' equity	16.5%	22.0%	17.7%	32.2%
Return on assets	0.64%	0.87%	0.69%	1.26%

Source: 1983 Citicorp *Annual Report.*

to users. With a staff of 3,500, this group was one of the largest investment banks in the world. (Exhibit 1 shows the relative size of these activities, and Exhibit 2 shows a summary corporate organization chart.)

Mehli Mistri

Mehli Mistri, Citibank's country corporate officer for Indonesia, joined Citibank as a management trainee in the Bombay office in 1960, just after finishing a B.A. degree in economics from the University of Bombay. Between 1960 and 1964, Mehli gained experience in a number of assignments in the Bombay office, and in 1965 he transferred to New York to work in the credit analysis division. He returned to Bombay in 1966, and then became manager of Citibank branches in Madras (1968), Calcutta (1969–71), New Delhi (1972), and Beirut (1973). In 1974, he was promoted to regional manager with responsibility for five countries in the Middle East (Turkey, Syria, Iraq, Jordan, Lebanon), and he held that position until 1979, when he was appointed the country head of Indonesia. He remained in that position up until the time of this case. In 1982, Mehli attended the Advanced Management Program at the Harvard Business School.

Control of International Branches

Citibank managers used two formal management processes to direct and control the activities of the corporation's international branches: reviews of sovereign risk limits for each location and reviews of operating budgets and accomplishments.

Sovereign Risk Limits.   Each year Citibank management set sovereign risk limits for its international branches based on country risk analyses. The term *sovereign risk* actually refers to a wide spectrum of concerns that would impair the bank's ability to recapture the capital it invested in foreign countries. These included macroeconomic risk—foreign exchange controls that the government of the host country might employ that would make it difficult for clients to pay their obligations, or, in the extreme, expropriation of assets. Once Citibank had opened a given branch, however, it intended to keep it open, so the reviews of sovereign risk were concerned only with setting limits of the amount of money a branch could lend in foreign currency.

The sovereign risk review process started in midyear with the country manager proposing a sovereign risk limit. This limit was discussed with division and group managers and was finally approved, on a staggered time schedule, by a senior international specialist on the corporate staff. The foreign currency lending limit for Indonesia had grown substantially as the branch had grown.

The sovereign risk limit set during these reviews was an upper guideline. When the economic conditions in a country changed in the period between sovereign risk reviews, country

Exhibit 2

Citibank Indonesia partial organization chart

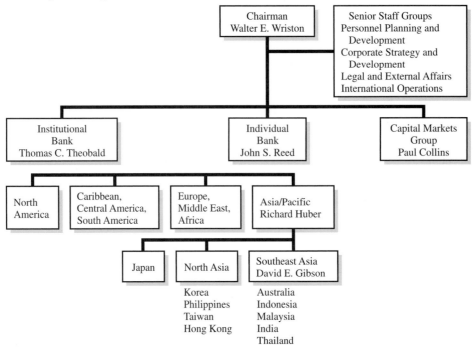

managers sometimes chose to operate their branches with self-imposed sovereign risk limits that were below the limits set by management in New York. Corporate managers encouraged this behavior because they knew that the managers on site often had a better appreciation of the risks in the local environment.

Budgeting.   Budgeting at Citibank was a bottom up process, which started in July when headquarters sent out instructions to the operating units describing the timing and format of the submissions and the issues that needed to be addressed. The instructions did not include specific targets to be included in the budget, although it was widely recognized that the corporation's combined long-term goals were approximately as follows:

Growth: 12–15% per annum.

Return on assets: 1.25% (125 basis points).

Return on equity: 20%.

The above norms were established for Citibank as a whole, but a number of international branches, including Indonesia, traditionally exceeded these norms, and these entities often established their own targets at higher levels.

At the time the operating managers received the budget instructions, they would have the results for half the year (through the end of June); and, in the period from July until the end of September, they would prepare a forecast for the remainder of the current year and a budget for the following year. The starting point for the preparation of the budget was projections about each of the major account relationships, and discussions continued until the summation of the account relationship projections could be reconciled with the desired profit center bottom line.

EXHIBIT 3   **Line Items on Budget Submission Form**

Revenue/expense	*Profit center earnings*
Local currency NRFF	Equity adjustments—translations
Foreign currency NRFF	Placements (average)
Allocated equity NRFF	Total staff (EOP)
Bad debt reserve earnings	Total nonperforming loans—EOP
Net revenue from funds	Total nonperforming loans—EOP
Exchange	Rev./nonperforming loans
Translation gains/losses	Average total assets—local currency
Trading account profits	Average total assets—foreign currency
Trade financing fees	Allocated equity
Securities gains/losses	*Local currency—average volume*
Fees, commissions, and other revenue	Loans
Affiliate earnings	Sources—noninterest bearing
Gross write-offs	Sources—interest bearing
Gross recoveries	*Foreign currency—average volume*
Loan provision excess	Loans
Direct staff expenses	Sources—noninterest bearing
Direct charges	Sources—interest bearing
Other direct expenses	*End of period (EOP)*
Allocated processing costs	Past due obligations
Minority interest	Interest earned not collected
Other allocated costs	Loans
Matrix earnings	Assets
EBIT	
Foreign taxes	
U.S. taxes	

Then costs were considered. The budget submission form included all the line items shown in Exhibit 3. In some past years, the bank had prepared two- and five-year projections, but the numbers were seen to be very soft and not very useful.

Formal reviews of the annual budgets were held according to the following schedule:

Level of Review	*Timing*
Division	end of September
Group	mid-October
Institutional bank	end of September

If the sovereign risk review for a particular entity had not yet been held, the budgets were submitted with the assumption that the risk limits would be approved as submitted. If this assumption proved to be incorrect, the budget had to be revised before it was incorporated in the corporate consolidated budget.

Performance was monitored and compared against budget each month during the year. Every quarter a new forecast for the remainder of the year was made. Whether these were reviewed formally by division managers varied widely, depending on the division manager's style. Some managers held relatively formal on-site reviews of performance and budget revisions, and others communicated only by mail or by telephone.

Mr. Mistri was very comfortable with the review processes.

Every level of management has a role to play, and there is a lot of horse trading and give and take in the budget review processes. Usually there is more revision of the numbers at lower management levels, but revisions do not necessarily mean increased profit goals. I have seen cases where the division head thought the country level was being too aggressive and he asked for the budget to be lowered. The managers sitting further away are more objective, and the review processes are consultative, collegial, and constructive.

Budgets were taken very seriously at Citibank, not only because they were thought to include the most important measures of success, but also because incentive compensation for managers at Citibank was linked to budget-related performance. For a country manager, incentive compensation could range up to approximately 70 percent of base salary, although awards of 30–35 percent were more typical. Assignment of bonuses was based approximately 30 percent on corporate performance and 70 percent on individual performance, primarily performance related to forecast. The key measures for assessing both corporate and international-branch performance were growth, profits, return on assets, and return on equity. However, in the analyses of individual performance for the purposes of assigning incentive compensation, considerable care was taken to differentiate base earnings from extraordinary earnings (or losses) for which the manager should not be held accountable.

Citibank in Indonesia

Indonesia was a relatively young country; it achieved independence only in 1949 after many years of being a Dutch colony. Citibank had operated in Indonesia only since 1968, when President Suharto allowed eight foreign banks to set up operations in Jakarta. From the point of view of the Indonesian government, the role of the foreign banks was to help develop a young economy by transferring capital into the country, establishing a modern banking infrastructure, attracting foreign investment, and developing trained people.

The foreign banking community operated in Indonesia with some important restrictions. The most serious constraints were that foreign banks were not allowed to open branches outside the Jakarta city limits, and local currency loans could be made only to corporations with headquarters and principal operations within the Jakarta city limits. But, on the other hand, the Indonesian government did not require any local ownership of equity, it set no lending quotas for the banks (e.g., requirements to lend certain amounts of money to certain types of businesses at favorable rates), and it valued and maintained a free foreign exchange system.

In explaining the goals of the government with respect to the foreign banks, Mr. Mistri commented:

> We consider ourselves privileged to be in Indonesia. We realize that the country wants to develop economically, and we know that the government sees us in the role of a development and change agent, attracting and developing not only capital but also new financial products, services, and techniques, and trained managers and professionals for the financial services industry. The government also expects us and other international banks to participate in extensions of credit to both the public and private sectors.

Citibank and the other foreign banks were interested in operating in Indonesia for several reasons: (1) to serve their international and local customers, (2) to assist in the economic development of the country, and (3) to share in the potential for profits and growth the Indonesian economy offered. The Indonesian economy had tremendous potential: the country was the fifth largest in the world in terms of population, and the economy had shown excellent growth for many years, as the figures shown in Exhibit 4 illustrate. The country was rich in raw materials, particularly oil and tin, and the Indonesian government was very interested in developing the country's industrial activities.

In 1983, Citibank's Indonesian operation included activities in each of the three major lines of business—institutional, individual, and capital markets. Mehli Mistri was the country corporate officer, and, as such, he was the primary spokesman for all of Citibank's activities in Indonesia.

EXHIBIT 4   **Indonesia Gross Domestic Product (billions of rupiahs)**

Year	Gross Domestic Product	Gross Domestic Product (1980 prices)
1968	2,097	18,493
1969	2,718	20,188
1970	3,340	21,499
1971	3,672	22,561
1972	4,564	24,686
1973	6,753	27,479
1974	10,708	29,576
1975	12,643	31,049
1976	15,467	33,187
1977	19,011	36,094
1978	22,746	38,925
1979	32,025	41,359
1980	45,446	45,446
1981	54,027	49,048
1982	59,633	50,150
1983	72,111	52,674

Source: *International Statistics Yearbook*, 1984.

His prime line responsibility, however, was the institutional banking activity, which provided by far the greatest proportion of revenues and profits. Other individuals headed the individual banking and capital markets activities in Indonesia, and they reported through separate management channels (see Exhibit 5).

Since its inception, Citibank's Indonesian operation had been very successful. Its growth paralleled that of the Indonesian economy.

The Situation in 1983

In 1983, Mr. Mistri was concerned about the risk/return ratio in his branch. He felt comfortable with Indonesia's long-term prospects, but the country, which was highly dependent on oil revenues, had slipped into a recession when oil prices decreased significantly. His concern was whether the government would take strong enough steps to correct its balance-of-payments problem.

Inside the bank, Mr. Mistri was faced with a problem of high staff turnover. High turnover had been a problem for Citibank for many years, because the bank provided its people with training that was recognized as probably the best in Indonesia, and local financial institutions had lured many Citibank people away with generous offers. This had happened so often that Citibank had been given labels, such as "Citi-university" and "Harvard-on-wheels," and the government often held Citibank up as an example of how foreign banks could (and should) supply trained professionals to the country. To attempt to retain more of its trained people, Citibank had recently increased its compensation levels; but some people in the branch felt that the bank could not compete on the basis of salary because of its desire to be profitable, its limited domestic branch network, and significant career opportunities elsewhere.

The year 1983 was particularly difficult from a staff turnover standpoint, as the losses included Mr. Mistri's chief of staff and two senior officers. In mid-1983, the average account manager experience was under two years, and there

Exhibit 5

Partial organization chart

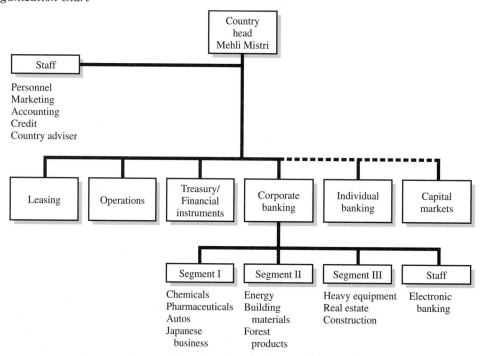

Country
head
Mehli Mistri

Staff

Personnel
Marketing
Accounting
Credit
Country adviser

Leasing

Operations

Treasury/
Financial
instruments

Corporate
banking

Individual
banking

Capital
markets

Segment I

Segment II

Segment III

Staff

Chemicals
Pharmaceuticals
Autos
Japanese
  business

Energy
Building
  materials
Forest
  products

Heavy equipment
Real estate
Construction

Electronic
  banking

were three unfilled slots at management levels. Mr. Mistri knew that the inexperience and people shortages in the branch were also serious constraints to growth.

Given these significant problems, Mr. Mistri thought that the budget he submitted, which projected modest growth, should be considered as aggressive. He wanted to submit an aggressive budget because "we are an aggressive organization. We like to stretch because we feel the culture of our corporation and the will and desire of our people to succeed and excel can make up the difference."

In reflection of the fast-changing uncertainties in the economy and the personnel problems, however, Mr. Mistri decided to operate with a self-imposed sovereign risk limit that was somewhat lower than what had been formally approved by management in New York. He knew that his responsibility was as much to manage risk as to generate profits.

In late October 1983, however, the budget for the whole Institutional Bank was reviewed at headquarters, and the consolidated set of numbers did not show the growth that top management desired. This led management to suggest some budget increases, and these increases presented Mr. Mistri with the dilemma described in the introduction to this case.

Questions

1. What should Mehli Mistri do about the budget issue described in the first three paragraphs of the case? (*Note:* You can assume that the amount by which Mehli is asked to increase his budget is about 10 percent of the original budget).

2. Should Mehli Mistri be evaluated against a budget prepared in U.S. dollars?

MULTINATIONAL ORGANIZATIONS

In this chapter we describe management control problems and practices in multinational (also called *transnational*) organizations. Most of the practices for controlling foreign operations are similar to those for controlling domestic operations, and these are discussed only briefly. There are, however, two problems that are unique to foreign operations: transfer pricing and exchange rates. Most of this chapter is devoted to these two problems. Although our discussion is stated in terms of a U.S. corporation and its foreign subsidiaries, the same general problems exist with respect to the parent company in any country and its foreign subsidiaries.

General Considerations

In general, foreign operations may be organized as expense centers, revenue centers, profit centers, or investment centers, and the considerations that govern the choice of a particular type of responsibility center are, in most respects, similar to those for domestic operations. One important difference, however, is that, even if a foreign operation is an expense center or a revenue center for control purposes, it is often a profit center for accounting purposes. Many foreign operations are legal entities, incorporated in the host country, and, therefore, they must maintain a complete set of accounting records for legal and tax reasons.

Cultural Differences

The planning and control processes that we described in Chapters 8 through 12—strategic planning, budget preparation, operating, variance analysis and reporting, performance evaluation, and management compensation—generally are applicable to multinational organizations. Although these processes are similar, they need to be tailored to the context of multinational organizations.

Countries, and even regions within countries, have different cultures. These differences may not affect the design of the management control system, but they can have a great effect on how information from the system is used.

Hofstede has made a systematic analysis of these differences, based on a questionnaire that was answered by approximately 80,000 employees of IBM located in 64 countries.[1] He classified the characteristics of control in a given country in four dimensions: *collectivism*, which refers to the degree to which employees place the collective interests of their firm ahead of their personal interests; *uncertainty avoidance*, the degree to which employees feel uncomfortable with uncertainty and ambiguity; *power distance*, the degree to which employees accept centralized decisions; and *masculinity versus femininity*, the relative importance that employees place on achievement and material success versus the quality of life.

Although most of the recent literature on this topic focuses on the difference between American and Japanese cultures, managers may make serious mistakes if they do not recognize the cultural aspects of whatever country they are involved in.

Differences in financial and other institutions among countries need to be considered also.

> **Example.** A British author, Charles Handy, writes: "To keep punters [i.e., speculators] happy we have to pay them. UK dividends are nearly twice as high as German dividends and three times as high as Japanese. This raises the effective cost of capital. . . . So it is that British companies currently look for a return of 25 percent on new projects, German companies 15 percent or so, and Japanese ones 8 percent. Guess which countries invest most in long-term manufacturing plant and which go for the less capital-intensive industries."[2]

Many special rules and regulations affect transnational transactions in addition to those summarized here. For example, beginning in 1993, all companies that export products to the European Community are required to comply with International Organization of Standardization (ISO) 9000. They must certify that their products and quality control systems meet ISO 9000 minimum quality standards.

Transfer Pricing

Criteria

Transfer pricing for goods, services, and technology represents one of the major differences between management control of domestic and foreign operations. In domestic operations, the criteria for the transfer price system almost exclusively are those described in Chapter 6. In foreign operations, however, several

---

[1]Geert Hofstede, *Culture's Consequences: International Differences in Work Related Values*, 3d Edition (Beverly Hills, Calif., SAGE Publications, 1986). See also Geert Hofstede, "Cultural Constraints in Management Theories," *Academy of Management Executive*, Vol. 7 No. 1, 1993; Shirley J. Daniel and Wolf D. Reitsperger, "Management Control Systems for Quality: An Empirical Comparison of the U.S. and Japanese Electronics Industries," *Journal of Management Accounting Research*, Fall 1992; and Chee W. Choi, Yutaka Kato, and Kenneth A. Merchant, "The Use of Organizational Controls and Their Effect on Data Manipulation and Management Myopia: A U.S. vs. Japan Comparison," *Accounting, Organizations and Society*, 21, 3, Feb./April 1996, 175–192.

[2]Charles Handy, "What Is a Company For?" Michael Shanks Memorial Lecture, London, December 5, 1990, p. 4.

other considerations are important in arriving at the transfer price. They include taxation, government regulations, tariffs, foreign exchange controls, funds accumulation, and joint ventures.

Taxation.   Effective income tax rates can differ considerably among foreign countries. A transfer price system that results in assigning profits to low-tax countries can reduce total worldwide income taxes.

Government Regulations.   In the absence of government regulations, the firm would set transfer prices to minimize taxable income in the countries with high income tax rates. However, government tax authorities are aware of such possibilities, and governments have passed regulations that affect the way in which transfer prices can be calculated.

Tariffs.   Tariffs are often levied as a percentage of the import value of a product. The lower the price, the lower will be the tariff. The incidence of tariffs is usually opposite to the incidence of income taxes in transfer pricing. Although tariffs for goods shipped to a given country will be low if the transfer price is low, the profit recorded in that country—and hence the local income tax on the profit—will be correspondingly high. Thus, the net effect of these factors must be calculated in deciding on the appropriate transfer price. Because income taxes are typically a larger amount than tariffs, international transfer pricing is usually driven more by income tax than by tariff considerations.

Foreign Exchange Controls.   Some countries limit the amount of foreign exchange available to import certain commodities. Under these conditions, a lower transfer price allows the subsidiary to bring in a greater quantity of these commodities.

Funds Accumulation.   A company may wish to accumulate its funds in one country, rather than in another. Transfer prices are a way of shifting funds into or out of a particular country.

Joint Ventures.   Joint ventures create additional complications in transfer pricing. Suppose a U.S. firm has a joint venture operation in Japan with a local Japanese firm. If the U.S. parent charges a higher price for a component transferred to Japan, the Japanese joint venture partner is likely to resist that price since it lowers the profits of the Japanese operation and, consequently, the share of the profits for the Japanese joint venture partner. Ford Motor Company, partly to avoid transfer pricing disputes, purchased the large British minority interest in Ford, Ltd. in 1961. For similar reasons, General Motors has not used joint ventures until its arrangement with Toyota in the late 1980s.

Use of Transfer Pricing Methods

Exhibit 17–1 shows the transfer pricing methods used by a sample of multinational companies headquartered in Canada, Japan, United Kingdom, and United States for their cross-border transfer of goods.

EXHIBIT 17–1   Transfer Pricing Methods Used by Multinational Companies

Pricing Method	Canada[a]	Japan[b]	United Kingdom[c]	United States[d]
Cost-based methods:				
Variable cost—actual or standard	5%	3%	5%	1%
Full cost—actual	—	—	—	4
Full cost—standard	26	38	28	7
Variable cost plus markup	—	—	—	1
Full cost plus markup	2	—	5	28
	33%	41%	38%	41%
Market-based methods:				
Market price	—	—	—	26
Market price less selling expense	—	—	—	12
Other	—	—	—	8
	37%	37%	31%	46%
Negotiated price	26%	22%	20%	13%
Other	4%	—	11%	—
	100%	100%	100%	100%

Source: *a)* Tang, R., "Canadian Transfer Pricing in the 1990s," *Management Accounting*, February 1992.

    b) Tang, R., C. Walter, and R. Raymond, "Transfer Pricing—Japanese vs. American Style," *Management Accounting*, January 1979, pp. 12–16.

    c) Mostafa, A., J. Sharp, and K. Howard, "Transfer Pricing—A Survey Using Discriminant Analysis," *Omega*, 12, 5, 1984.

    d) Roger, Y., and W. Tang, "Transfer Pricing in the 1990s," *Management Accounting*, February 1992, pp. 22–26.

Legal Considerations

Almost all countries place some constraints on the flexibility of companies to set transfer prices for transactions with foreign subsidiaries. The reason is to prevent the multinational company from avoiding the host country's income taxes. An article in *The Wall Street Journal*[3] highlights this point:

> A House subcommittee investigation of 36 foreign-owned U.S. companies has found that more than half paid little or no U.S. income tax over a 10-year period.
>
> Largely by inflating the prices they paid their foreign parents for goods, services, and technology, a number of the U.S. subsidiaries were able to reduce their taxable income to almost nothing.
>
> Among the cases the investigators cited were these:
>
> - A foreign parent sold television sets to its U.S. subsidiary at $250 each but charged only $150 to an unrelated distributor.
> - A foreign auto manufacturer sold cars to its U.S. subsidiary at an average of $800 more than it charged its Canadian subsidiary for identical cars.

---

[3]Hilary Stout, "Foreign Firms Pay Little U.S. Tax, House Panel Says," *The Wall Street Journal*, July 11, 1994 p. 1.

- A foreign company shipping trucks to a U.S. subsidiary and an unrelated distributor in the United States charged almost $200 more per truck in shipping costs to the related company.

Regulations for the United States are basically set forth in Section 482 of the Internal Revenue Code. In general, Section 482 tries to ensure that financial transactions between the units of a *controlled taxpayer* (a company that can control transactions between domestic and foreign profit centers) are conducted as if the units were *uncontrolled taxpayers* (independent entities dealing with one another at arm's length). In case of a dispute, Section 482 permits the Internal Revenue Service to calculate what it believes to be the most appropriate transfer price, and the burden of proof is then on the company to show that this price is unreasonable. This is in contrast with most provisions of the Internal Revenue Code, which permit the company to select whatever permissible alternative it wishes and place the burden of proof on the Internal Revenue Service to show that the company's method is unacceptable.

Section 482 provides rules for determining the transfer price on sales between members of the controlled group. Acceptable intercompany pricing methods, listed in descending order of priority, are as follows:

1. *Comparable uncontrolled price method*. An arm's-length price is ascertained from comparable sales of goods or services between the multinational firm and unrelated customers, or between two unrelated firms. Comparability is based on the similarity of the controlled and uncontrolled sale with respect to the physical properties and factual circumstances underlying the transactions. An uncontrolled sale will be considered comparable if the differences are such that they can be reflected by an adjustment of the selling price (e.g., where the difference is accounted for by a variance in shipping terms). However, a sale will not be considered comparable if it represents an occasional or marginal transaction or is a sale at an unrealistically low price.

Circumstances that may affect the price include the quality of the product, terms of sale, market level, and geographical area in which the item is sold; but quantity discounts, promotional allowances, and special losses due to currency exchange and credit differentials are excluded.

Lower prices, and even sales at a price below full cost, are permitted in certain instances, such as during the penetration of a new market or in maintaining an existing market in a particular area.

2. *Resale price method*. If comparable sales are not available, the next preferred method is the resale price method. Under this method, the taxpayer works back from the final selling price at which property purchased from an affiliate is resold in an uncontrolled sale. This *resale price* is reduced by an appropriate markup percentage based on uncontrolled sales by the same affiliate or by other resellers selling similar property in a comparable market. Markup percentages of competitors and industry averages are also helpful.

The regulations require that this method be used (1) if there are no comparable uncontrolled sales, (2) the resales are made within a reasonable time before or after the intercompany purchase, (3) the reseller has not added significant value to the property by physically altering it, other than packaging, labeling, and so forth, or by the use or application of intangible property.

3. *Cost-plus method.* Under this method, which is the lowest priority of the three prescribed methods, the starting point for determining an arm's-length price is the cost of producing the product, computed in accordance with sound accounting practices. To this is added an appropriate gross profit expressed as a percentage of cost and based on similar uncontrolled sales made by the seller, by other sellers, or the rate prevalent in the industry.

A schematic representation of these three methods is as follows:

1. *Comparable uncontrolled price method*:

Transfer price = Price paid in comparable uncontrolled sales ± Adjustments

In a controlled sale, the transaction is between two members of a controlled group. In an uncontrolled sale, one of the two parties is not a member of the controlled group.

2. *Resale price method*:

Transfer price = Applicable resale price – Appropriate markup ± Adjustments

Applicable resale price is the price at which property purchased in a controlled sale is resold by the buyer in an uncontrolled sale.

Appropriate markup = Applicable resale price * Appropriate markup percentage

Appropriate markup percentage = Percent of gross profit

(expressed as a percent of sales) earned by the buyer (reseller) or by another party in an uncontrolled purchase and resale similar to controlled resale.

3. *Cost-plus method*:

Transfer price = Costs + Appropriate markup ± Adjustments

Appropriate markup = Costs * Appropriate gross profit percent

Appropriate gross profit percent = Gross profit percent

(expressed as a percent of cost) earned by seller or another party on uncontrolled sale similar to controlled sale.

The organization for Economic Cooperation and Development (OECD) Committee on Fiscal Affairs recommends these three methods in European countries.[4]

---

[4]"Transfer Pricing and Multinational Enterprises," Report of the Organization for Economic Cooperation and Development Committee on Fiscal Affairs (Paris: OECD, 1979).

Implications of Section 482

From a management control point of view, there are two important implications of Section 482, each of which is discussed below:

1. Although there are legal restrictions on a company's flexibility in transfer pricing, there is considerable latitude within these restrictions.
2. In some instances, the legal constraints may dictate the type of transfer prices that must be employed.

Latitude in Transfer Prices.   In many multinational companies there is a difference between the transfer prices that management would use purely for control purposes and the legally allowable transfer prices that minimize the sum of the tax and tariff impacts. Since a certain amount of subjectivity is involved in applying Section 482 to many goods and services, there may be a considerable range in the permissible transfer price for a particular item. Management can minimize the sum of income taxes and tariffs by maintaining transfer prices as far as possible at the appropriate end of the range. For example, if a U.S. parent company sells a product to a subsidiary in a country with materially lower income tax rates than those in the United States, profits can be shifted to the foreign subsidiary by keeping the transfer price as low as is legally allowable. This practice, however, may cause a management control problem because profits in a foreign subsidiary would be reported as being higher, and profits in the American parent would be reported as being lower, than would be the case if the transaction took place between independent entities.

There are two extremes of policy in dealing with this problem. Some companies permit subsidiaries to deal with each other at arm's length and let the impact of taxes and tariffs fall where it may. With this policy, there is no question about the legality of transfer prices because the subsidiaries are trying to do exactly what the regulations say they should do—deal at arm's length. Under this policy, foreign transfer pricing policies will be essentially the same as domestic transfer pricing. Consequently, the transfer price system supports the management control system. On the other hand, this policy could result in higher total costs.

At the other extreme, foreign transfer prices may be controlled almost entirely by corporate headquarters, for the purpose of minimizing total corporate costs, maximizing dollar cash flow, or obtaining the optimum mix of currency positions. Such a policy can severely restrict the usefulness of the control system, however, because, in some instances, the transfer prices may bear little relationship to the prices that would prevail if the buying and selling units were independent. If this policy is followed, the question arises of what to do about the control system.

One possibility is to adjust profits for internal evaluation purposes to reflect competitive market prices. For example, the total differences between the prices actually charged and those that would have been in effect had taxation not been a consideration could be added to the selling subsidiary's revenue and the buying subsidiary's costs when profit budget reports are analyzed. This is a questionable practice, however, and few companies use it. If asked, a company would be required to disclose these adjustments to the Internal Revenue Service, and their existence could raise questions concerning the validity of the transfer prices being used for tax purposes.

Many companies that price to minimize taxes and tariffs use the same transfer prices for profit budget preparation and reporting as are used for accounting and tax purposes. The approved budget reflects any inequities arising from the transfer prices. To illustrate, a subsidiary that sells for lower than normal prices might have a budgeted loss. If reports of actual performance show that the subsidiary loses less than budget, its performance is considered to be satisfactory, other things being equal. In short, the transfer prices are considered both in preparing the budget and in analyzing results.

If profit budgets and reports reflect uneconomic transfer prices, care must be taken to make certain that subsidiary managers make decisions that are in the best interests of the company. For example, suppose that Subsidiary A purchases a line of products from Subsidiary B at a price that gives B most of the profit. In these circumstances, Subsidiary A can improve its reported profit performance by not selling B's products aggressively and by concentrating its marketing effort on products that add more to its reported profits. Such a practice could be contrary to the best interests of the company as a whole. If uneconomic transfer prices are used in budgeting, therefore, it is important to guard against such situations. It may be necessary to use other measures of performance than profitability or, at least, other measures *in addition* to profitability, such as sales volume or market share.

Legal Constraints on Transfer Pricing Systems.   In some instances, legal constraints may require that a particular transfer pricing system be used, or that a preferred transfer system not be used. For example, the two-step transfer price system described in Chapter 6 might be questioned by the tax authorities simply because it is not mentioned in Section 482 and is not widely known abroad.

In other instances, the "full cost" approach implicit in Section 482 may limit a company's ability to transfer some products at less than full costs. For example, the marketing department may want to introduce a new product in a market at a price that is lower than its normal price, perhaps not even high enough to cover its full costs. This may be a sound marketing tactic, but the IRS may not recognize it as a valid basis for arriving at the transfer price.

If Section 482 requires the use of transfer prices different from the ones that would be used for control purposes, a company is in the same position as the company that used one set of transfer prices for taxation and another for control, except that such a company can safely adjust subsidiary revenues and costs for differences between the Section 482 transfer price and the preferred transfer price in most cases. Since the company presumably would have no objection to using the preferred transfer price for tax purposes, no harm comes from, in effect, keeping two sets of books.

Foreign Sales Corporations

To encourage U.S. companies to develop increased amounts of foreign trade, the Congress has authorized the use of foreign sales corporations (FSCs). An FSC is a separate subsidiary corporation that buys goods from its U.S. parent corporation and sells such goods abroad. It is to the advantage of a parent company to charge the lowest price possible to the FSC, since the FSC receives favorable tax treatment. Consequently, the transfer price to the FSC is of interest both to management and to the Internal Revenue Service.

Congress has limited the transfer price options by requiring companies to choose from one of the following methods for setting the transfer price between the parent company and the FSC:

1. Using an arm's-length price as prescribed under Section 482.
2. The overall profit on a transaction is calculated by, first, considering the parent and the FSC as a single entity. Then, the total profit is allocated to the parent company and the FSC in the proportion of 77 percent and 23 percent, respectively.
3. The profit allocated to the FSC is determined by multiplying FSC's sales revenues from outside customers by 1.83 percent.

The second and third options are referred to as *administrative pricing methods*. To be eligible for the use of these pricing methods, the FSC must perform the following eight activities outside the United States: advertise and promote export sales, solicit business, negotiate terms, close sales, process orders, deliver the goods to foreign customers, send the invoice and receive payment, and assume the credit risk on the export sale.

Three potential benefits derive from using one of the administrative pricing methods. First, as compared to the arm's-length price, the administrative price typically allocates more profits to the FSC. Second, an administrative price results in a lower tax on this profit. The FSC is exempt on $15/23$ of its foreign trade income if administrative pricing rules are used. However, the FSC is exempt on only 30 percent of its foreign trade income under the arm's-length price. Third, the IRS will not contest the profit arrived at under an administrative method, while it might contest an arm's-length price.

Whether the third option is better than the second option can easily be determined by calculating the aftertax profit under each method.

Minority Interests

Whenever minority interests are involved, top management's flexibility in distributing profits between subsidiaries can be severely restricted because the minority parties have a legal right to a fair share of the corporation's profit. In this event, subsidiaries must deal with each other at arm's length, to the extent possible.

Exchange Rates

The cash flows of a domestic company are denominated in dollars, and at a given moment each dollar has the same value as every other dollar. By contrast, the cash flows of a multinational enterprise (MNE) are denominated in several currencies, and the value of each currency relative to the value of the dollar is different at different times. These variations complicate the problem of measuring the performance of subsidiaries and subsidiary managers. Specifically, MNEs face *translation, transaction*, and *economic* exposure to changes in exchange rates. We first discuss exchange rates briefly, and then we define the three types of exchange rate exposure and their implications for the design of management control systems.

Exchange Rates

An exchange rate is the price of one currency in terms of another currency. It can be expressed either as the number of units of the home currency that are needed to buy one unit of foreign currency (called the *direct quote*), or the number of units of the foreign currency that are needed to buy one unit of the home currency (called the *indirect quote*). For example, if the U.S. dollar ($) is the home currency and the French franc (FF) is the foreign currency, then to express the exchange rate as $0.20/FF is the direct quote, and to express it as FF5/$ is the indirect quote. In the markets for foreign exchange, both types of quotes are used, but traders usually use one or the other type for particular currencies. Exhibit 17–2 provides examples of both, for exchange rates prevailing on August 7, 1996, for the most heavily traded currencies.

Exchange rates that are usually quoted (such as those above) are called *nominal* exchange rates. The *spot* exchange rate is the nominal exchange rate that prevails on a given day. The *real* exchange rate is the spot exchange rate *after* adjusting for inflation differentials between the two countries in question. There are also *forward* exchange rates, which are exchange rates known today at which transactions can be entered into for completion at some future point in time.

EXHIBIT 17–2   Exchange Rates for Various Foreign Currencies on August 7, 1996

Country	Monetary Unit	*Dollar per Unit Foreign Currency (direct quote)*	*Foreign Currency Units per Dollar (indirect quote)*
United Kingdom	pound	1.54	0.65
France	franc	0.20	5.06
Japan	yen	0.009	107.93
Switzerland	franc	0.83	1.21
Germany	mark	0.67	1.48

Using the direct quote, if the number of dollars required to buy a unit of foreign currency rises, then the dollar is said to have undergone a *depreciation* relative to the foreign currency; the reverse is true for an appreciation. Suppose, for example, that one year ago the spot U.S./U.K. exchange rate was $1/£, and today's spot rate is $1.20/£. These rates are "nominal" exchange rates that prevailed one year ago and are prevailing today, respectively. In nominal terms, we would then say that the U.S. dollar depreciated 20 percent against the pound sterling, since it takes 20 percent more dollars to buy the same number of pounds sterling today, compared to a year ago.

However, suppose that the inflation during this period was 10 percent in the United States and 5 percent in the United Kingdom. Then, according to *purchasing power parity* (PPP), these inflation rates would predict that the U.S. dollar should have depreciated against the U.K. pound sterling by about 5 percent, or to the approximate extent of the inflation differential between the two countries, and not by 20 percent. Thus, under PPP, we would have expected the exchange rate today to be $1.05/£. At the spot rate of $1.20/£, the nominal value of the U.S. dollar depreciated by 14.3 percent *more* than PPP would predict. This additional depreciation of 14.3 percent in currency values in excess of the inflation differential between the two countries is the *real depreciation* of the U.S. dollar; analogous arguments apply in the case of appreciation. The real exchange rate is the exchange rate after adjusting for inflation differentials between the United States and the United Kingdom and, in our example, it is $1.143/£.

Ever since the evolution of the floating exchange rate system in the early 1970s, there have been substantial swings in real exchange rates. In the broadest terms, real exchange rate changes create changes in the cost competitiveness of a domestic manufacturer against its foreign competitors: if all else remained equal and U.S. real exchange rates depreciated by 10 percent against the Japanese yen, then U.S. firms are likely to have become 10 percent more cost competitive, compared to their Japanese competitors. The explanation is as follows: a 10 percent real depreciation of the U.S. dollar must mean that goods priced in U.S. dollars have become 10 percent cheaper *over and above* the price adjustments that should have normally resulted from inflation in both the United States and in Japan.

Different Types of Exchange Rate Exposure

Translation exposure to exchange rates is the income statement and balance sheet exposure of MNEs to changes in nominal exchange rates. It results from the fact that MNEs must consolidate their accounts in a single (usually home country) currency although their cash flows are denominated in multiple currencies. Understanding translation exposure in MNEs comes down to understanding the answer to the following question: Given that the cash flows of the firm are denominated in multiple currencies and given that there have been nominal changes in currency values during the year, how should revenues, expenses, assets, and liabilities be consolidated into one currency at a point in time?

Transaction exposure is the exchange rate exposure that the firm has in its cross-border transactions when such transactions are entered into today, but payments to settle the transaction are made at some future time. During the period that payment or receipt commitments are outstanding, nominal exchange rates could change and put the value of transactions at risk. Examples of such transactions include receivables and payables, and debt or interest payments outstanding, in foreign currencies.

Economic exposure is the exchange rate exposure of the firm's cash flows to real exchange rate changes. Economic exposure is also referred to as *operating exposure* or *competitive exposure* to exchange rates.

Choice of Metric in Performance Evaluation

In a survey of MNEs, Choi and Czechowicz found almost all the respondents had performance evaluation systems that compared actuals against budgets in assessing subsidiary performance.[5] There are basically three possibilities for choice of metric in setting and tracking budgets: the exchange rate prevailing at the time budgets are set (the *initial* exchange rate), the exchange rates projected at the time budgets are set (the *projected* exchange rate), or the actual exchange rates prevailing at the time budgets are tracked ("ending" exchange rate). There are, then, nine possible combinations of metrics in setting and tracking budgets, as shown in Exhibit 17–3.[6]

Not all nine cells are feasible, however; only the five underlined ones are. The obviously feasible ones consist of the three where the budget is set and

EXHIBIT 17–3

Choice of metric in performance evaluation

		Tracking Budget		
		Initial	Projected	Ending
	Initial	1	2	3
Setting Budget	Projected	4	5	6
	Ending	7	8	9

[5]F. D. S. Choi and I. J. Czechowicz, "Assessing Foreign Subsidiary Performance: A Multinational Comparison," *Management International Review* 4 (1983), pp. 14–25.

[6]These possibilities were originally discussed in D. Lessard and P. Lorange, "Currency Changes and Management Control: Resolving the Centralization/Decentralization Dilemma," *Accounting Review*, July 1977, pp. 628–37.

tracked using the same metric (initial–initial, cell 1, projected–projected, cell 5; ending–ending, cell 9[7]); similarly, it is feasible to set the budget using an "initial" rate and track it using an "ending" rate (cell 3), as well as to set at a "projected" rate and track at the "ending" exchange rate (cell 6). It is illogical, however, to set the budget at the "ending" exchange rate and then to track actuals using initial or projected exchange rates (thus ruling out 7 and 8). Similarly, to project an exchange rate in setting the budget and then to track it at the rate that initially prevailed also seems illogical (thus ruling out cell 4).

Control System Design Issues

From the point of view of performance evaluation, these are the important questions in control systems design:

- Should subsidiary managers be held responsible for the impact of exchange rate fluctuations on their bottom line?
- Should the parent company use the home country currency or should it use the local currency in performance evaluation? Further, should it use the initial exchange rate, the projected exchange rate, or the ending exchange rate in setting and tracking budgets?
- Should the parent company distinguish between the effects of different types of exchange rate exposure while evaluating the performance of the subsidiary manager? If yes, how?
- How should different types of exchange rate exposure affect the evaluation of the economic performance of the subsidiary, as distinct from the evaluation of the manager in charge of the subsidiary?

Translation Effects

Consider an example of a U.S. company with a subsidiary in France. Exhibit 17–4 describes the budget and the actuals for this subsidiary. Suppose that the initial exchange rate was FF10/$ and the ending exchange rate was FF11/$ (that is, the French franc depreciated in both real and nominal terms by 10 percent relative to the dollar, so that the French inflation rate did not change). The subsidiary was given a volume target, based on which the budgeted profit at the initial exchange rate was $1, or FF10. Further, assume that the French subsidiary incurs all its costs in France and sells entirely in France; it does not engage in any *cross-border* transactions. Such a subsidiary is called a *balanced unit*. Assume that the subsidiary met all its volume targets, but the exchange rate changed to FF11/$. Under the new exchange rate, the dollar profits generated by the subsidiary would only be $0.91—or an unfavorable

---

[7]To set the budget at the "ending" rate means that, at the time performance is being evaluated, the original budget is recast using the exchange rate prevailing at the end-of-period.

EXHIBIT 17–4   **Budget and Actuals for Balanced Subsidiary (initial exchange rate: FF10/\$; ending exchange rate: FF11/\$)**

	Budget		Actual	
	FF	*\$*	*FF*	*\$*
Revenue	100	10	100	9.09
Profit	10	1	10	0.91

budget variance of about 10 percent in dollar terms—even though it met its volume objectives.

Should the manager of the French subsidiary be held accountable for exchange rate fluctuations even though the actual performance was exactly as budgeted? The French subsidiary is self-contained (i.e., it does not engage in cross-border transactions). Therefore, the manager of that subsidiary need not be concerned with strategic and operating decisions (such as pricing and sourcing) in response to exchange rate changes. In addition, changes in exchange rates are completely beyond the control of the subsidiary manager. It seems fair, therefore, that subsidiary managers not be held responsible for translation effects. The simplest way to achieve this objective is to set and track budgets using the same metric (cells 1, 5, or 9 in Exhibit 17–3).

This example presumed that the exchange rate was both real and nominal. However, if the change was purely nominal, then it must mean that French inflation was 10 percent higher compared to the U.S., and there is purely an inflation effect on the subsidiary's cash flows. In this case, the subsidiary may be able to raise its FF prices 10 percent and costs would also presumably go up by 10 percent. Consequently, the U.S. dollar target is met. Even in this case, the suggestion is as follows: set and track the budget using the same metric, but isolate the variance that is due to the pure inflation effect. That is, the subsidiary manager is held responsible for appropriate inflation-related pricing and sourcing strategies, but is not held responsible for exchange rate effects.

In the example in Exhibit 17–4, if the budget was tracked using the same metric as that on which the budget was set (FF10/\$), then the subsidiary would have been shown to have generated \$1. Alternatively, if the budget at the end of the year was reset to the ending exchange rate of FF11/\$, the subsidiary would have been only *expected* to generate \$0.91 in profits. Thus, if the same metric is used to set and track the budget, then the choice of metric (whether local or foreign currency; whether initial, projected, or ending exchange rate) is not relevant; the resulting performance reflects the operating performance of the manager, independent of translation effects.

However, the parent company suffered a "translation" loss at the end of the year. Parent companies can do little to control such exchange rate shifts. If they use translation gains or losses in evaluating the subsidiary managers' performance, this could lead to several problems: (1) it would make the subsidiary managers responsible for factors that are beyond their control; (2) it does not get rid of the translation gain or loss; (3) it will not account for other types of exchange rate exposure that subsidiaries face (see next section); and (4) it will confound the performance of the manager and the subsidiary (see next section).

When companies report to stockholders, they have to consolidate the accounting numbers of foreign subsidiaries with the accounting numbers of the parent. Translation gains and losses arising out of converting the income statement and the balance sheet of the foreign subsidiary into the monetary unit of the parent company should *not* affect the performance evaluation of the subsidiary manager. The required method of calculating translation gains and losses for financial reporting purposes is described in the Appendix at the end of this chapter.

Economic Exposure

In the balanced unit that we considered above, exchange rates led only to translation effects. However, when subsidiaries have cross-border transactions, they also are subject to economic exposure. A control system that effectively deals with economic exposure differs in a fundamental way from the one that we have described for translation exposure. Under economic exposure, it would be appropriate for the control system to evaluate the subsidiary manager on decisions that would have enabled the subsidiary to respond to real exchange rate changes. We explain how this can be done by considering two generic types of subsidiaries in MNEs: "net importers" and "net exporters."

A *net importer* is a subsidiary that sells most of its products in its own country, but imports most of its inputs from outside that country (either from sister subsidiaries or from outside companies); a *net exporter* is a subsidiary that sells most of its products outside its own country (either to sister subsidiaries or to outside companies), but purchases most of its inputs within that country. As the following example shows, given an exchange rate shift, such subsidiaries will not only face translation effects but also "dependence" effects resulting from real exchange rate changes.

To keep the example simple, we will consider subsidiaries that have transactions only between the home country and the host country. The conclusions from this example can be generalized to any subsidiary that has cross-border transactions with sister subsidiaries or other companies outside the host country. Also, we will include the balanced unit in the analysis for purposes of comparison. Suppose a U.S. MNE has three subsidiaries, A, B, and C in France. Subsidiary A is the balanced unit, the one considered in the preceding section. B is a net importer; it obtains its inputs from its parent in the United States and sells all its output in France. C is a net exporter, it sources entirely in France and sells all its outputs in the United States. The initial exchange rate is $1 = 10FF, and the budgets have been set as indicated in Exhibit 17–5.

Now, as before, suppose that the United States dollar appreciated against the French franc by 10 percent in *real* terms, with the new exchange rate being

---

Exhibit 17–5 **Budgets for A, B, and C (initial exchange rate: 10FF/$)**

	A: Balanced		B: Net Importer		C: Net Exporter	
	FF	*US$*	*FF*	*US$*	*FF*	*US$*
Sales	100	10	100	10	100	10
Costs	90	9	90	9	90	9
Profit (value)	10	1	10	1	10	1
Profit (margin)	10%	10%	10%	10%	10%	10%

Exhibit 17–6 **Performance of A, B, and C (current exchange rate: 11FF/$)**

	A: Balanced		B: Net Importer		C: Net Exporter	
	FF	*US$*	*FF*	*US$*	*FF*	*US$*
Sales	100	9.09	103	9.36	109	9.91
Costs	90	8.18	95	8.63	95	8.63
Profit (value)	10	0.91	8	0.73	14	1.28
Profit (margin)	10%	10%	7.9%	7.9%	12.9%	12.9%

$1 = FF11 by the time the budget was tracked.[8] Suppose the parent company set the budget at the initial rate (FF10/$) and tracked it at the ending rate (FF11/$). Let us suppose that, at the end of the year, the performance of the three subsidiaries looked like Exhibit 17–6 from the perspective of the parent company.

The net exporter outperformed the budget (in both $ and FF, both profit value and margin), the balanced unit performed approximately at budgeted levels (met the profit objective in FF, but a bit below in $; met the margin objectives in both currencies) and the net importer underperformed the budget (in both $ and FF, profit value and margin).

Now let us examine the exchange rate effects a bit more closely. Note that, under the new real exchange rates scenario, the net exporter should have been able to achieve FF110, without any extra efforts. In fact, given the nature of its demand and cost structure, it may have been able to achieve much higher levels of sales than even FF110. Thus, its sales of FF109 represent *under*achievement relative to what should have been expected, given the real exchange rate shift.

---

[8]We could have made the example somewhat more realistic by including nominal exchange rate changes as well—that is, we could assume that part of the exchange rate change was nominal and that we take out the purchasing power parity effect to only include real exchange rate changes. In this example, we simply assume that all of the exchange rate change is real. Conclusions are not altered by this assumption.

Further, its underperformance on the sales front was exacerbated by underperformance on the cost front (since it incurred local costs of FF95, although it was budgeted for FF90).

Now, consider the net importer. Under the new exchange rate scenario, Firm B became *less* cost competitive against its competitors that did not have similar exchange rate exposure in relation to inputs. Against B's cost of $8.63, competitors that were sourcing entirely locally (as, for example, the balanced subsidiary was doing) were incurring a cost of only $8.18. They could easily have (and perhaps did) undercut B in prices to gain both profits and market share. Yet, the net importer not only exceeded his FF sales target but, in the process, did so at a lower local input cost than originally budgeted.

This example not only underscores the point that setting and tracking budgets using different metrics can be unfair; it also highlights the problems of measuring management performance and subsidiary performance. In addition, such a situation confounds translation and dependence effects. If only the translation effect was considered, manager B would have been criticized and manager C rewarded. If the dependence effect was isolated from the translation effect, manager B would have been rewarded and manager C criticized. To illustrate, manager C would have been told that, given the real appreciation of the U.S. dollar, his or her sales performance of FF109 represents inadequate performance; if he or she expected to be rewarded for above budget performance, the subsidiary should have done more.

For subsidiaries like B and C (which have cross-border transactions), real exchange rate changes require important strategic and operating decisions. For example, if the US$ depreciated against the foreign currencies, this implies that goods priced in US$ have become cheaper in real terms, compared to those priced in foreign currencies. For a subsidiary that imports from the United States, this provides major strategic opportunities—for example, it can now afford to costlessly pursue a market share strategy by dropping its local currency prices, thereby increasing demand and market share. Still, they would not suffer in terms of US$ profitability. Or the subsidiary could pursue a skimming strategy where it retains local currency prices at predepreciation levels, and simply pockets the extra US$ profits without losing market share.[9]

While on the one hand we have shown that it is not fair to reward or penalize subsidiary managers for exchange rate changes per se, on the other hand it is important to evaluate the performance of the managers in terms of the quality of

---

[9]The appropriate choice of pricing strategies, given a real currency movement, is dealt with in A. Sundaram and V. Mishra, "Currency Movements and Corporate Pricing Strategies," in *Recent Developments in International Banking and Finance*, vol. IV, North-Holland, 1990. Given the 35 percent real depreciation of the US$ between 1985 and 1987, many U.S. firms pursued skimming, rather than market share, pricing strategies abroad. For example, articles in *The Wall Street Journal* (May 15, 1987), and *Business Week* (August 27, 1987) pointed out that the norm for U.S. firms operating in Japan was to go for " . . . profits rather than market share." There have been many reports of exactly the reverse pricing behavior on the part of Japanese firms operating in the United States, when the US$ appreciated between 1981 and 1984.

their decisions, when changes in real exchange rates create strategic opportunities of the type described here. As in the case of the translation effect, the unfair reward or penalty can be avoided by setting and tracking the budget using the same metric. However, additional mechanisms need to be developed to evaluate the quality of managerial decisions given the real exchange rate changes. One such mechanism is *contingent budgeting*.[10] This works as follows:

1. Set and track budgets using the same metric; don't worry about the appropriate metric, and simply use the one that is most convenient. Isolate nominal exchange rate effects (which are purely inflation-related) through variance analysis. This recommendation is identical to the one proposed as a way of dealing with translation exposure. However, to deal with economic exposure, additional steps are needed.

2. Prepare the budget based on the "most likely" exchange rate scenario. At the end of the year, only one of three outcomes is possible with respect to the real exchange rate contingency; it was roughly equal to the initial projection, it depreciated relative to the initial projection, or it appreciated relative to the initial projection.

3. At the time of budget *preparation*, discuss with subsidiary managers their anticipated responses, given possible real exchange rate shifts. This discussion would deal with what the subsidiary manager would do about revenues (production and pricing strategies) and costs (sourcing strategy), given a real appreciation or given a real depreciation. To illustrate, the net exporter in our example above would have been told that, for every 1 percent real depreciation of the FF, it would have been expected to generate at least 1 percent in extra sales. Thus, only sales generation above that level would be considered as "above average" performance.

4. At the time of budget *tracking*, when exchange rates are known, revise the original budget for the decisions the manager is expected to make *given* the exchange rates that were actually realized. The subsidiary manager's performance then would be compared against the revised budget.

Clearly, developing and implementing such a system is not easy. But the very process of preparing such a contingent budget, and advance discussions that identify the subsidiary manager's responses to exchange rate contingencies, will go a long way toward making the subsidiary manager sensitive to real exchange rate changes.

Transaction Effects

The basic approach to dealing with transaction exposure is by appropriate foreign exchange hedging strategies. *Hedging* is any transaction by which risk associated with future cash flows is reduced. In the process, the company that

---

[10]This idea was originally proposed by D. Lessard and D. Sharp, "Measuring the Performance of Operations Subject to Fluctuating Exchange Rates," *Midland Corporate Finance Journal* 2 (Fall 1984), pp. 18–30.

buys the hedge shifts risk to the entity selling the hedge—typically a commercial bank in the case of foreign exchange markets. Naturally, such hedging services come at a price.

Hedging is commonly practiced by most firms—for example, whenever a company purchases insurance, it is, in effect, undertaking a hedge transaction. Hedging is particularly common among companies engaged in international transactions, and it is used as a means of counteracting the effects of transaction exposure.[11] There are many ways of hedging transaction exposure. To illustrate the simplest: if an American company sells products to a French company at a price that is stated in French francs, it can simultaneously buy the right to purchase French francs at the same price as of the future date that the account receivable is due. If it has a transaction loss on the sale, it will have an equal gain on the hedge. Other hedging techniques include making use of the option market and matching assets/liabilities and revenues/expenses in the same currency. The commonly used techniques of hedging use forward and future markets, as well as foreign currency options markets.[12] From the perspective of performance evaluation, the key question is whether subsidiary managers be held responsible for hedging transaction exposure.

Hedging transactions are probably best done at the parent company level, rather than permitting individual subsidiaries to make them. There are a number of reasons for this. First, in most MNEs, there are payables and receivables in different parts of the overall firm that may naturally hedge each other if information on all such transactions is collected and dealt with at one central location. This reduces transaction costs associated with hedging. Second, the parent company probably has better access to a wider (and perhaps more sophisticated) range of hedging instruments, across a greater range of maturities, than a subsidiary typically has. Third, there is no reason to presume that the manager of a subsidiary can forecast exchange rates any better than the corporate treasurer; in fact, parent companies may not want managers of subsidiaries to hedge, since this runs the risk of making subsidiary managers exchange rate speculators.

Thus, from the perspective of performance evaluation, it is unnecessary to make subsidiary managers responsible for transaction effects.

Performance of the Subsidiary

We have thus far suggested that it is important to distinguish between the economic performance of the subsidiary and the performance of its manager, and the guidelines discussed above primarily have dealt with isolating the impact of exchange rates on the performance of the subsidiary manager. It is

---

[11]One study suggests that 84 percent of treasurers at companies engaged in international trade hedge foreign transaction exposure; see Scott Flicker and Dennis Bline, "Managing Foreign Currency Exchange Risk," *Journal of Accountancy*, August 1990, pp. 128–30.

[12]See, for example, D. Eiteman and A. Stonehill, *Multinational Business Finance* (Reading, Mass.: Addison-Wesley, 1989) or A. Shapiro, *Multinational Financial Management* (Boston: Allyn & Bacon, 1990).

important to recognize that the economic performance of the subsidiary itself should reflect the negative or positive consequences of translation, transaction, and economic exposures.

If the long-term economic performance of the subsidiary (after incorporating exchange rate effects) continues to be poor, even though the performance of the manager is excellent, then the parent company should address a more basic question: Does it make continued economic sense for the MNE to carry on operations in that country, or should it take its business elsewhere? The answer to this question comes down to a business location decision, rather than a performance evaluation decision; these should be independent decisions.

Management Considerations

In designing performance evaluation systems of MNE subsidiaries, companies could use the following guidelines:

• Subsidiary managers should not be held responsible for translation effects. The simplest way to achieve this objective is to compare budgets and actual results using the same metric and isolate inflation-related effects through variance analysis. It is pointless for managers to worry about the appropriate metric. The MNE should choose whatever metric is more convenient.

• Transaction effects are best handled through centralized coordination of the MNE's overall hedging needs. This is likely to be cheaper and simpler, and it prevents the subsidiary manager from becoming a foreign exchange rate forecaster and speculator.

• The subsidiary manager should be held responsible for the dependence effects of exchange rates resulting from economic exposure. One approach is to use a contingent budgeting system, which would revise the budget standard to reflect the exchange rate contingency, on the assumption that responses to such contingencies were explicitly dealt with at the time of budget preparation. However, such a system is complicated.

• Evaluation of the subsidiary as a basis for a decision to locate operations in a country or to relocate operations from a country should reflect the consequences of translation, transaction, and economic exposures.

In a 1982 survey, Sapy-Mazella et al. found that, in evaluating the subsidiary managers' performance, 79 percent of the respondents used different metrics to prepare budgets and report performance; 66 percent used some forecast of exchange rates to prepare the budget and used the actual end-of-period exchange rate to report the subsidiary's performance relative to the budget, and 13 percent used the initial exchange rate to prepare the budget and the end-of-period actual to report performance.[13] These findings are inconsistent with the guidelines we have developed above.

---

[13]Jean-Pierre Sapy-Mazella, R. Woo, and J. Czechowicz, "New Directions in Managing Currency Risk: Changing Corporate Strategies and Systems under FAS No. 52," *Business International Corporation*, New York, 1982.

There are two possible explanations for this inconsistency. First, most of these control systems were developed in the 1950s and 60s, when exchange rates were fixed; given the recent vintage of flexible exchange rates, MNEs may not have tailored their performance evaluation system to the new reality. Second, many companies may not distinguish between the financial performance of the manager and the financial performance of the subsidiary.

Whatever the reason, it is important to recognize that an MNE that chooses to use different metrics to prepare subsidiary budgets and report actual performance runs the various types of risks we have discussed.

Summary

From the standpoint of management control, two problems are unique to MNEs: transfer pricing and exchange rates. In addition to goal congruence, other considerations are important in arriving at transfer prices in MNEs: taxation, government regulations, tariffs, foreign exchange controls, funds accumulation, and joint ventures.

An evaluation of the economic performance of the subsidiary should incorporate the negative or positive consequences of translation, transaction, and economic exposures. However, while evaluating the performance of the manager in charge of the subsidiary, effects of translation and transaction exposures should be removed; even so, the subsidiary manager should be held responsible for the dependence effects of exchange rates resulting from economic exposure.

Suggested Additional Readings

Bartlett, Christopher A., and Sumantra Ghoshal. *Managing across Borders*. Boston: Harvard Business School Press, 1989.

Demirag, I. S. "Assessing Foreign Subsidiary Performance: The Currency Choice of U.K. MNCs." *Journal of International Business Studies*, Summer 1988, pp. 257–75.

Glaister, Keith W. "Dimensions of Control in UK International Joint Ventures." *British Journal of Management* 6, 2, June 1995, pp. 77–96.

Gupta, A. K., and V. Govindarajan. "Knowledge Flows and the Structure of Controls within Multinational Organizations." *Academy of Management Review*, October 1991, pp. 768–92.

Gupta, Anil K., and Vijay Govindarajan. "Coordination and Control within Multinationals." In Bala Chakravarthy and Peter Lorange (eds.). *Research on Strategy Process*. Cambridge, MA: Basil Blackwell Ltd., 1993.

Halperin, R., and B. Srinidhi. "The Effects of U.S. Income Tax Regulations' Transfer Pricing Rules on Allocating Efficiency." *The Accounting Review*, October 1987, pp. 686–706.

International Transfer Pricing. New York: Business International Corporation and Ernst & Young, 1993.

Jones, C. J. "Financial Planning and Control Practices in U.K. Companies: A Longitudinal Study." *Journal of Business Finance and Accounting*, Summer 1986, pp. 161–86.

Lessard, D. R., and D. Sharp. "Measuring the Performance of Operations Subject to Fluctuating Exchange Rates." *Midland Corporate Finance Journal*, Fall 1984, pp. 18–30.

Rogman, A. M., and L. Eden (eds.). *Multinationals and Transfer Pricing*. New York: St. Martin's Press, 1985.

Scapens, R. W., and J. T. Sales. "An International Study of Accounting Practices in Divisionalized Companies and Their Associations with Organizational Variables." *The Accounting Review* LX, no. 2 (April 1985), pp. 231–47.

Shapiro, A. C. "The Evaluation and Control of Foreign Affiliates." *Midland Corporate Finance Journal*, Spring 1984, pp. 13–25.

Yunker, P. J. *Transfer Pricing and Performance Evaluation in Multinational Corporations*. New York: Praeger, 1982.

Appendix
SFAS No. 52: Foreign Currency Translation

Statement of Financial Accounting Standards No. 52 requires the all-current method for translating the balance sheet. Under this method all balance sheet items are translated at the rate of exchange in effect on the balance sheet date.[14] Conversion or translation gains and losses are reported as direct credits or charges to shareholders' equity; they do not affect net income for the year. This practice is similar to that used in the United Kingdom. Income statement items are translated at the exchange rate in effect on the date when the income or expense items are recognized, except that companies can use a weighted-average exchange rate if using the actual rates is too complicated.

An example of these exchange translations follows.

Assume that a United States corporation had a Swiss subsidiary with the following financial statements, expressed in Swiss francs (Sfr):

Beginning Balance Sheet
December 31, 1989

Assets	Sfr 100,000
Liabilities	Sfr 60,000
Capital stock	20,000
Retained earnings	20,000
	Sfr 100,000

---

[14]The name *all current* is used to contrast with the *current/noncurrent* method that the Financial Accounting Standards Board considered and rejected. Under the current/noncurrent method, only current assets and current liabilities are translated at current rates.

During 1990, the subsidiary had the following two transactions.
1) Borrowed Sfr 10,000 from a local bank:

1990 Transactions

Assets	Sfr 10,000	
Liabilities		Sfr 10,000

(2) Earned Sfr 5,000 from operations:

Revenues	Sfr 15,000
Expenses	10,000
Profit	Sfr 5,000

The impact of (2) is to increase assets by Sfr 5,000 and retained earnings by Sfr 5,000.

Ending Balance Sheet
December 31, 1990

Assets	Sfr 115,000
Liabilities	Sfr 70,000
Capital stock	20,000
Retained earnings	25,000
	Sfr 115,000

Assume that the Swiss franc was worth $.60 on December 31, 1989, and $50 on December 31, 1990. The average value during 1990 was $.55.

Under *SFAS No. 52*, the subsidiary results would be consolidated with the parent company's financial statement as shown below.

Beginning Balance Sheet
December 31, 1989

Assets (Sfr 100,000 × .6)	$60,000
Liabilities (Sfr 60,000 × .6)	$36,000
Capital stock (Sfr 20,000 × .6)	12,000
Retained earnings (Sfr 20,000 × .6)	12,000
	$60,000

Income Statement

Revenues (Sfr 15,000 × .55)	$8,250
Expenses (Sfr 10,000 × .55)	5,500
Profit	$2,750

Ending Balance Sheet
December 31, 1990

Assets (Sfr 115,000 × .5)	$57,500
Liabilities (Sfr 70,000 × .5)	$35,000
Capital stock (Sfr 20,000 × .5)	10,000
Retained earnings (Sfr 25,000 × .5)	12,500
	$57,500
Reconciliation of retained earnings in dollars:	
Beginning balance	$12,000
Profit	2,750
Indicate ending balance	14,750
Actual ending balance	12,500
Translation loss	$ 2,250

The United States corporation would include profit of $2,750 in its consolidated income statement and a reduction of $2,250 in a segregated part of retained earnings. This represents the financial effect of the fall in the Swiss franc; put another way, the rise in value of the dollar.

CASE 17–1
AB THORSTEN

"You will see from my report that the XL–4 project shows an excellent rate of return on the Skr 700,000 investment and is also a logical extension of our product development and growth strategy here in Sweden. My management and I strongly recommend this project."

> Anders Ekstrom, *Managing Director*
> AB Thorsten, Stockholm (100 percent owned subsidiary of Roget S.A.)

"Any extra XL–4 which Ekstrom might sell in Sweden can be produced in our existing plant in Gent for no additional investment. Ekstrom is not only very optimistic about the sales potential, he is also underestimating the manufacturing problems and costs he will face. I recommend that you inform Ekstrom that it is in Roget's best interest for him to import from Belgium any XL–4 he can sell in Sweden."

> Pierre Lambert, *Vice President for Domestic and Export Sales and Manufacturing, Industrial Products Group, Roget S.A. Brussels*

Roget S.A.

Roget S.A.[1] was one of the largest industrial companies in Belgium. The company was incorporated in 1928 by merging three smaller firms that all produced industrial chemicals for sale in Belgium. By 1981 Roget had expanded to produce 208 basic and specialty chemical products in 21 factories, for sale throughout Europe.

Mr. André Juvet, Director General of Roget, explained its organization:

> Until five years ago, we were organized with one large manufacturing division here in Belgium, and one large

sales division. One department of the sales division was devoted to export sales. However, exports grew so fast, and domestic markets became so complex, that we created three main product divisions (Food, Industrial, and Textile), each with its own manufacturing plants and sales organization. In addition, we have created foreign subsidiaries to take over the businesses in certain areas. For example, in Industrial Chemicals we have two subsidiaries—one in the United Kingdom and one in Sweden (Thorsten), which serves all of Scandinavia. At the same time, the Domestic Department of the Industrial Chemicals Division exports to the rest of Europe. The United Kingdom and Sweden account for 9 percent and 5 percent, respectively, of sales in that Division.

Another thing we achieve in the new organization is individual profit responsibility of all executives at all levels. Mr. Gillot (see Exhibit 1) is responsible for profits from all industrial chemicals, Mr. Lambert is responsible for profits from domestic operations (manufacturing and sales of industrial chemicals) and export sales to countries where we do not have subsidiaries or factories, and Mr. Ekstrom is responsible for profits in Scandinavia. We also utilize a rather liberal bonus system to reward executives at each level, based on the profits of their divisions.

This, together with a policy of promotion from within, helps stimulate managers in Roget to a degree not enjoyed by some of our competitors. It also helps us to retain key people in an industry where experience is of great importance. Many of our executives have been in the starch chemicals business all of their business lives. It is a complex business, and we feel that it takes many years to learn it.

We have developed certain policies—rules of the game—which govern relationships with our subsidiary companies. These policies are intended to maintain the efficiency of the whole Roget complex, while at the same time giving subsidiary managers autonomy to run their own businesses. For example, a subsidiary manager can determine what existing Roget products to sell in the local market. Export sales will quote the same price as they quote agents in all countries. Of course, all prices are subject to bargaining on both sides. Second, we encourage subsidiaries to propose to division management in Brussels the development of new products. If these are judged feasible, we manufacture them in Belgium for supply to world-markets. Third, the subsidiary managing director can build manufacturing plants if we can justify the investment in the local market.

This case is adapted from AB Thorsten (A), (B), and (C) cases which are copyrighted by the Institute for Management Development in Lausanne, Switzerland.

[1]"AB" and "S.A." are abbreviations used in Sweden and Belgium that are similar to "Corp." or "Inc." in the United States.

EXHIBIT 1

Roget S.A. organizational chart

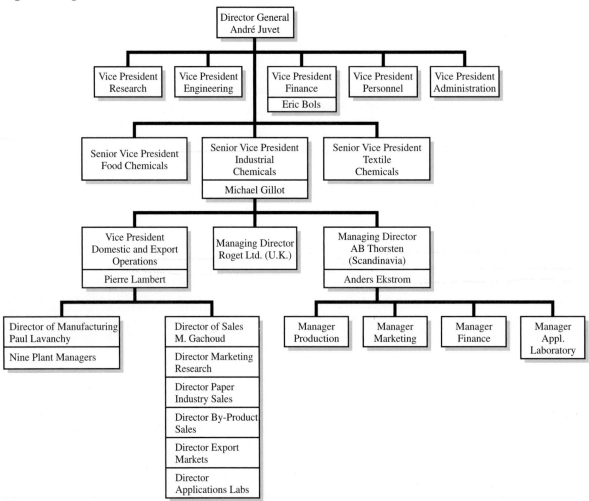

AB Thorsten

AB Thorsten was purchased by Roget S.A. in 1972. Since that time, Thorsten's board of directors had consisted of four persons: Mr. Michel Gillot, senior vice president in charge of Roget's industrial chemicals division; Mr. Ingve Norgren, a Swedish banker; Mr. Ove Svensen, a Stockholm industrialist; and the managing director. Swedish law required any company incorporated in Sweden to have at least two outside Swedish directors, and the Roget management felt fortunate in finding two men as prominent as Norgren and Svensen to serve on the Thorsten board.

During the first four years of Roget's ownership, Thorsten's sales fluctuated between Skr. 5

and 7 million, but hit a low in 1976.[2] The Board decided at that time that the company was in serious trouble, and that the only alternative to selling the company was to hire a totally different management group to overhaul and streamline company operations.

On the advice of the Swedish directors, Mr. Anders Ekstrom, a 38-year-old graduate of the Royal Institute of Technology, was hired as managing director. He had 16 years of experience as a production engineer for a large paper machinery company, as marketing manager of a British subsidiary in Sweden, and as division manager responsible for profits in a large paper company.

Ekstrom joined AB Thorsten in January of 1977. Since that time, sales had increased to Skr. 20 million and profits had reached levels that Roget's management found highly satisfactory.

Ekstrom said that at the time he joined Thorsten, he knew it was a risk.

> I liked the challenge of building a company. If I did a good job here I would have the confidence of Norgren and Svensen as well as of the Roget management in Brussels. I felt that succeeding in this situation would teach me things that would make me more competent as a top executive. So I chose this job even though I had at the time (and still have) offers from other companies.

Initial Proposal for Manufacture of XL–4

In September of 1980, Ekstrom had informed the Thorsten board of directors that he proposed to study the feasibility of constructing a factory in Sweden for the manufacture of XL–4, a starch-based adhesive chemical used in drying paper. He explained that he and his customer engineers had discovered a new way of helping paper mills adapt the dryer sections of their huge paper machines at very low cost so that they could use XL–4 instead of competitors' products. Large paper mills would realize dramatic savings in material handling and storage costs and also shorten drying time substantially. Shortened

---

[2]Most monetary amounts in this case are stated in Swedish kronor (Skr).

drying time increases the effective capacity of a paper machine. It was Ekstrom's judgment that his innovation would allow him to develop a market in Sweden almost as big as Roget's present worldwide market for XL–4. This product was currently being produced in Roget's Domestic Department at the rate of 600 tons per year, with none going to Sweden. Ekstrom stated:

> At that meeting, Mr. Gillot and the other directors seemed enthusiastic. Gillot said, "Of course—go ahead with your study and when you have a complete proposal, with the estimated return on investment, send it in and we will consider it thoroughly."
>
> During the next six months, we did the analysis. My marketing director used modern market research techniques to estimate the total potential in Sweden at 800 tons of XL–4 per year, using the custom engineered approach we were proposing. We interviewed important customers and conducted trials in the mills of three big companies which proved that with the introduction of our machine designs, the large cost savings and capacity expansion would indeed materialize. We determined that if we could sell the product for Skr. 1,850 per ton, we could capture at least one-half of the market within a three-year period, or 400 tons a year.
>
> At the same time, I called the head of the corporate engineering division in Belgium and asked for his help in designing a plant to produce 400 tons of XL–4 per year and in estimating the cost of the investment. This is a routine thing. The central staff divisions are advisory and always comply with requests for help. He assigned a project manager and four other engineers to work on the design of factory and machinery and to estimate the cost. At the same time I assigned three men from my staff to work on the project. In three months this joint task group reported that the necessary plant could be built for about Skr 700,000.
>
> All of this we summarized in a pro forma calculation [Exhibit 2]. This calculation, together with a complete written explanation, was mailed to Mr. Gillot in early April 1981. I felt rather excited, as did most of my staff. We all know that introduction of new products is one of the keys to our continued growth and profitability. The yield on this investment was well above the minimum 8 percent established as a guideline for new investment by the Roget vice president of finance. We also knew that it was a good analysis, using modern tools of management. In the cover letter, I asked that it be put on the agenda for the next Thorsten board meeting.

The minutes of the next board meeting held in Stockholm on April 28, 1981 quoted Ekstrom's

EXHIBIT 2 XL–4: The Swedish Proposal (in Skr.)

	1	2	3	4	5	6	7	8	9	10
End of Year	Plant	Working Capital	Sales Price/Ton	Variable Cost/Ton	Contribution/Ton (col. 3 − 4)	Number of Tons	Total Contribution (col. 5 × 6)	Promotion Costs	Taxes†	Net Cash Flows (1 + 2 + 7 − 8 − 9)
0	−700,000	−56,000*								−756,000
1		−2,000*	2,000	1,000	1,000	200	200,000	130,000	(35,000)	103,000
2		−7,000*	1,850	1,000	850	300	255,000	75,000	20,000	153,000
3			1,850	1,000	850	400	340,000	50,000	75,000	215,000
4			1,850	1,000	850	400	340,000	50,000	75,000	215,000
5			1,850	1,000	850	400	340,000	50,000	75,000	215,000
6			1,850	1,000	850	400	340,000	50,000	145,000	145,000
7	+150,000‡	+65,000*	1,850	1,000	850	400	340,000	50,000	145,000	360,000

*These working capital investment amounts are net of tax credits.

†Taxes are calculated after depreciating Skr. 700,000 over a 5-year period on straight-line basis.

‡Sales value, net of appropriate taxes, assuming plant will be closed at end of seven years.

remarks as he explained the proposal to other directors.

> You will see from the summary table [Exhibit 2] that this project is profitable. Gentlemen, it seems clear from these figures that we can justify this investment in Sweden on the basis of sales to the Swedish market. The group vice president for finance has laid down the policy that any new investment should yield at least an 8 percent return. This particular proposal exceeds that substantially, using a very conservative seven-year life. My management and I strongly recommend this project.

Ekstrom later recalled Gillot's reactions in his role as chairman of the Thorsten board.

> Gillot said that it seemed to him to be a clear case. He asked positive questions, mainly about the longer-term likelihood that we could sell more than 400 tons a year, and about how we would finance any further expansion. I explained that we in Sweden were very firm in our judgment that we would reach 400 tons a year even before one year, but felt constrained to show a conservative estimate of a three-year transition period. We also showed him how we could finance any further expansion by borrowing in Sweden. That is, if Roget would furnish the initial capital, and if the 400 tons goal were reached quickly, any further expansion would easily be financed by local banks. The two Swedish directors confirmed this. The board voted unanimously to construct the plant.

Disagreement about the XL–4 Proposal

About a week later, Gillot telephoned Ekstrom.

> I have been through some additional discussions with the production and marketing people here in the Domestic Department. They think the engineering design and plant cost is accurate, but that you are too optimistic on your sales forecast. It looks like you will have to justify this more.

Ekstrom said:

> I pushed him to set up a meeting the following week. This was attended by myself and my marketing and production directors from Sweden, and four people from Belgium—Gillot, Lavanchy [director of manufacturing], Gachoud [director of sales], and Lambert [vice president for domestic and export].
>
> That was one of the worst meetings of my life. It lasted all day. Gachoud said that they had sales experience from other countries and that in his judgment the market potential and our share were too optimistic. I told him over and over how we arrived at this figure based on our cus-

tom engineered approach, but he just kept repeating the over-optimism argument. Then Lavanchy said that the production of this product is complicated, and that he had difficulties producing it in Belgium, even with trained workers who had long experience. I told him I only needed five trained production workers and that he could send me two men for two months if he liked, to train Swedes to do the job. I impressed on him that they could oversee manufacturing for us in Sweden until we learn, if they did not have confidence in Swedish technology. He repeated that the difficulties in manufacturing were enormous.

> Lavanchy then said that since the whole world market for Roget was only 600 tons a year, it was inconceivable that Sweden alone could make 400 tons.

> Gillot ended the meeting without a decision, and said that he hoped all concerned would do more investigation of this subject. He indicated that he would think about it himself and let us know when another meeting would be held.

Ekstrom returned to Stockholm and reported the meeting to his own staff, and to the two Swedish members of his board.

> They, like I, were really disgusted. Here we were, operating with initiative and with excellent financial techniques. Roget management had often made speeches in which they emphasized the necessity for decentralized profit responsibility, and for authority and initiative on the part of foreign subsidiaries. One of my men said that they seem to talk decentralization and act like tin gods at the same time.

Mr. Norgren, the Swedish banker on Thorsten's board, expressed surprise.

> I considered this carefully. It is sound business for AB Thorsten, and XL–4 will help to build one more growth company in the Swedish economy. Somehow, the management in Brussels has failed to understand this. I dictated a letter to Mr. Gillot telling him that I didn't know why the project was rejected, that Roget has a right to its own reasons, but that I was prepared to resign as a director. It is not that I am angry, or that I have a right to dictate decisions for the whole worldwide Roget organization. It is simply that if I spend my time studying policy decisions, which are not appreciated by parent company management, then it is a waste of my time to continue.

Finally, Ekstrom stated,

> While I certainly wouldn't bring these matters out in a public meeting, I think those Belgian production and sales people simply want to build their empire and make

EXHIBIT 3 XL–4: The BELGIAN Proposal (in Skr.)

End of Year	1 Plant	2 Working Capital	3 Sales Price/Ton	4 Variable Cost/Ton†	5 Contribution/Ton (col. 3 − 4)	6 Number of Tons	7 Total Contribution (col. 5 × 6)	8 Promotion Costs	9 Taxes	10 Net Cash Flows (1 + 2 + 7 − 8 − 9)
0	0	−54,000*								−54,000
1		−10,000*	2,000	1,380	620	200	124,000	130,000	(3,000)	−13,000
2		−10,000*	1,850	1,380	470	300	141,000	75,000	33,000	23,000
3			1,850	1,380	470	400	188,000	50,000	69,000	69,000
4			1,850	1,380	470	400	188,000	50,000	69,000	69,000
5			1,850	1,380	470	400	188,000	50,000	69,000	69,000
6			1,850	1,380	470	400	188,000	50,000	69,000	69,000
7		+74,000	1,850	1,380	470	400	188,000	50,000	69,000	143,000

*Working capital amounts are net of tax credits.
†Variable cost per ton   = SKr. 1,380
Manufacturing   =   930
Shipping from Belgium to Sweden =   50
Swedish import duty   =   400
Total variable cost   1,380

the money in Belgium. They don't care about Thorsten and Sweden. We have the ideas and initiative, and they take them and get the payoff.

Further Study

Mr. Gillot received Norgren's letter in late May 1981. He then contacted Messrs. Lavanchy, Gachoud, and Bols (V.P. finance, Roget) and told them that the Swedish XL–4 project had become a matter of key importance for the whole Roget Group, because of its implications for company profits, and for the morale and autonomy of subsidiary management. He asked them to study the matter very carefully and report their recommendations in one month. Meanwhile, he wrote Ekstrom, "Various members of the Corporate Headquarters are studying the proposal very seriously. You will hear from me within about six weeks regarding my final decision."

Lavanchy's Response

A month after he was asked to study the XL–4 project more closely, Lavanchy gave Gillot a memorandum explaining his reasons for opposing the proposal:

> At your request, I have reexamined thoroughly all of the cost figures that bear on the XL–4 proposal. I find that manufacture of this product in Sweden would be highly uneconomical, for two reasons: (1) overhead costs would be higher; and (2) variable costs would be greater.
>
> As to the first, we can produce XL–4 in Gent in our existing plant with less overhead cost. Suppose that Thorsten does sell 400 tons a year so that our total worldwide sales rise to 1,000 tons. We can produce the whole 1,000 tons in Belgium with essentially the same capital investment we have now. If we produce 1,000 tons, our fixed costs will decrease by Skr. 120 a ton.[3] That means Skr. 72,000 in savings on production for domestic and export to countries other than Sweden (600 tons a year), and Skr. 120,000 for worldwide production including Sweden (1,000 tons).

---

[3]Total fixed cost in the Gent factory was the equivalent of Skr. 180,000 a year. Divided by 600, this equals Skr. 300 a ton. If it were spread over 1,000 tons, the average fixed cost would be Skr. 180.

Second we could also save on variable costs. If we were to produce the extra 400 tons in Belgium, the total production of 1,000 tons a year would give us longer production runs, lower average set-up costs, and larger raw material purchases, thus allowing mass purchasing and material handling and lower purchase prices. My accounting department has studied this and concludes that our average variable costs will decrease from Skr. 950 a ton to Skr. 930. This Skr. 20 per ton difference means a savings of Skr. 12,000 on Belgian domestic production and a saving of Skr. 20,000 for total worldwide production, assuming that Sweden takes 400 tons a year.

Taxes on these added profits are about the same in Belgium and Sweden—about 50 percent of taxable income.

In conclusion, a new plant should not be built. Ekstrom is a bright young man, but he does not know the adhesives business. He would be caught up in costly production mistakes from the very beginning. I recommend that you inform the Thorsten management that it is in the Company's interest that they must buy from Belgium.

Bols's Response

The same week, Gillot received the following memorandum from Eric Bols, Roget's financial vice president:

> I am sending you herewith estimates of the working capital requirements if Roget increases its production of XL–4 in our Belgian plant from 600 to 1,000 tons a year [Exhibit 3]. Initially, we will need Skr. 54,000, for additional inventories and accounts receivable. By the end of the second year, this will have increased to Skr. 74,000. The working capital amounts shown in this exhibit are based on the applicable law which permits businesses to deduct 60 percent of incremental inventory costs from taxable income.
>
> I have also looked at Lavanchy's calculations for the fixed and variable manufacturing costs, and am in full agreement with them. . . .
>
> In conclusion, I see no reason to spend Skr 700,000 to build a factory in Sweden when we have excess capacity in our Belgian plant which can produce the incremental tons at lower cost and with lower manufacturing risk.

Gillot's Response

In early July 1981, Gillot sent a letter to Ekstrom indicating that the XL–4 proposal was turning out to be more of a problem than he had anticipated. He included copies of the memos from Lavanchy and Bols. He said he was not yet in a position to give final approval. He said he would let Ekstrom know his decision as soon as possible.

Ekstrom's Thoughts

Ekstrom expressed some impatience with the way things were going.

> I have other projects that need developing for Thorsten, and this kind of long-range planning takes much time and energy. Also, just keeping on top of the normal operating problems of the business we already have takes up a lot of my time. Sometimes I feel like telling them to go and sell XL–4 themselves.

Questions

1. Using the numbers from Exhibit 2, what is your estimate of the NPV (at 8 percent) for the Swedish proposal. Also, what is the 6 year IRR?

2. What is the NPV (at 8 percent) and IRR of the Belgian proposal in Exhibit 3?

3. What are the most important elements of Thorsten's proposed investment as presented by Ekstrom? as presented by the Belgian management team? What are the key arguments for and against the alternatives presented by the contending parties from Belgium and Sweden?

4. Is everything that is being expressed by Ekstrom and the Belgium management above board? What are the respective hidden agendas that can be anticipated for each party and in what way do they coincide? In what way can they be expected to diverge?

5. If you were in Gillot's shoes, would you support the Swedish or the Belgian proposal? Why?

6. Ignoring your answer to question 5, if the plant were not built and the product were shipped from Belgium to Sweden, what transfer price would be appropriate?

7. What are the competitive advantages of Roget S.A.? What is Roget's strategy in the industrial chemicals business? Are the management control systems designed to support this strategy?

8. How has the organization structure of Roget been changing over the last five years? Why? How does this affect your decision in the Thorsten situation?

9. What changes in the management control systems would you recommend to Gillot?

CASE 17–2
VICK INTERNATIONAL DIVISION: TOM MCGUIRE

Sitting at breakfast, Tom McGuire was going over in his mind the key issues that were likely to come up during the day. Across the top of the menu propped in the holder at the next table was the date: Thursday, August 10, 1978.

Throughout the week, management personnel from headquarters and field offices of Vick International, Latin America/Far East Division (LA/FE), had been attending the mid-August quarterly review meeting. As division president, McGuire had scheduled for that day individual agreement sessions with six of his overseas directors. There would be much ground to cover. It was essential that important questions not be lost in a myriad of details. Tom also wanted to be sure that he assumed the appropriate role with regard to each critical issue, and that he was clear in his mind on the roles of others.

Of particular concern was a program in Mexico to develop and launch Alpha, a new nutritional product. The Alpha situation required special attention, because it touched on the way in which the division's formal management system was working.

"It's ironic," McGuire mused. "Our management system calls for the explicit assignment of work roles to the various managers within the division who must contribute to the attainment of a certain objective. Yet, with regard to Alpha, there seems to be some misunderstanding about who is responsible for each role, and what that means in terms of managing the project."

Background

McGuire had been president of Vick International, Latin America/Far East, since 1969. A na-

tive of New York, he had studied chemistry at Notre Dame before working for Union Carbide. In 1956, at 29, he joined Richardson-Merrell, Inc., a diversified company engaged in the development, manufacturing, and marketing of proprietary medicines and toiletries, ethical pharmaceuticals, veterinary products, laboratory and diagnostic chemicals and equipment, and plastics packaging.

McGuire

As one of RMI's nine operating divisions, we are given considerable independence in running our business, so long as we contribute to the company's goals of stable growth, improving profitability, and product excellence. Richardson-Merrell's original business, starting in 1905, was built around Vick's VapoRub and subsequently other proprietary drugs in the cold remedy area. But in order to achieve more stability and growth, the company began to diversify in the 1930s. As a result, a number of other products have been added to RMI's lines; but the Vick divisions, which handle proprietary health and personal care products, continue to be the mainstay of the business.

When I became division general manager in 1969, Vick International, LA/FE was having difficulty sustaining adequate growth and profitability. During the previous two years we had missed our budgets by wide margins. My initial analysis of the situation was that the division had an inadequate budget system, ineffective tracking and control mechanisms, and a lack of action-oriented reporting. So we instituted a budget manual, undertook improvements in the data base for planning, initiated a program to improve communications, and overhauled our reporting system. As a result, it was extremely frustrating when we didn't make our budgets the next two years, either.

I had not experienced this type of failure before, and it led me to a far-ranging examination of what the division's business was and how we went about accomplishing it. Dick Waters, my executive vice president, had expressed his concern. I told him I would like to initiate some fundamental changes. He promised me his support and wished me success. The pressure to deliver was now really on my back.

Our business strategy was based on running with products already developed by other divisions within the company. In essence, it was an extension of our highly

This case was abridged with permission by Professors Robert N. Anthony and Vijay Govindarajan from Harvard Business School case 179–068, written under the direction of Professor Richard F. Vancil. Copyright © by the President and Fellows of Harvard College.

successful export business of the 40s and 50s, but it no longer fit the requirements of our expanding and changing markets. During the 60s we had set up manufacturing and distribution operations in a large number of countries, and, as a result, the management emphasis had been on sales generation to cover the rather substantial overhead.

My challenge was to refocus the division's resources and energies into more productive and successful patterns. I became convinced that we should stop running and pushing products in favor of returning to a more comprehensive marketing stance. We had to put major emphasis on analyzing consumer needs, to identify or develop products to satisfy those needs. We had to improve communications to the consumer that the product was available and superior in meeting his needs. Measurement of our success would then shift from sales volume shipped to distributors and focus on consumer awareness and retail take-off.

I also decided the division should concentrate on fewer products with higher profitability potential and higher volume potential across the countries. This meant encouraging our overseas operating units to reduce the number of low-volume and low-margin items in their product line, to shift away from price-controlled categories, and to consider introducing products that were highly successful in other markets. It has become something of a slogan that "we can't afford one-market products or one-product markets." This required that we become proficient in the transfer of strategy and expertise among the markets.

To bring about these changes, we had to introduce significant improvements in our organization and management practices.

Clearly, we needed to delegate more responsibility for key managerial decisions, especially in marketing, to our operating units, but we lacked the focus, discipline, and procedural mechanisms to assure that such delegation would produce positive results.

John Steiner joined the division as finance director shortly thereafter and went to work on improving and systematizing our financial reporting and planning practices. Even before that, I had started working on ways to bring more rigor and discipline to our marketing activities in line with the new view of our business strategy. I set up the headquarters marketing departments to help me manage this new approach. The essence of the approach is reflected in a memo I issued in 1976, which formalized a classification of our products into three categories, each of which we had found to require different management approaches. The first, which we call "development products," are those that are not currently being sold in commercial volume in any of our markets but promise to be winners. The main job of the HQ marketing directors is to assure that enough of these products

are successfully introduced and spread throughout the division to provide us growth in future years. In the jargon of our management system, the development product program is "prime moved" by our HQ marketing directors.

Commercial products are those currently marketed successfully in several regions. They provide the bulk of our current business, but we have to watch their product life cycle and be especially wary of declining profitability in price-controlled markets under the pressure of cost inflation. Our HQ staff plays only a supporting role in the management of these products, with the Prime Movers being in the overseas operating units.

Nondivisional products are those associated with only one market, with unknown or no potential for expansion to other (our insecticide line in Australia is a good example). We want our people overseas who handle these products to make them fully self-supportive while meeting our policies and standards. If they can't, we must divest the products. Generally, they cannot rely on division resources and support for these products. Further, the overseas units must not divert their own resources or attention from the expansion of profitable commercial products and the introduction of promising development products.

Given the diversity of our markets and of the local personnel working in each of them (see Exhibit 1 for LA/FE organization chart) as well as the inherent difficulties in obtaining timely information flows that would allow markets to learn from each other and HQ staff to provide adequate support, we have developed a set of elaborate, formalized and rather standardized management procedures. Through them we have been trying to professionalize our management and clarify the relationship between the various country operations and the headquarters' departments.

Vick International, LA/FE's CP-R Management System

Vick International, LA/FE employed an extensive formalized system of planning and control to direct and coordinate its widely scattered operating units. The system, known affectionately as CP-R (continuous planning and review), was not put in place all at once. McGuire built up the division's management capacity piece by piece over a period of several years. He moved management personnel around to make better use of talent. He brought in additional help, especially in the marketing management area. He worked closely with his headquarters staff to develop an all-encompassing marketing methodology, which

EXHIBIT 1

Division organization structure

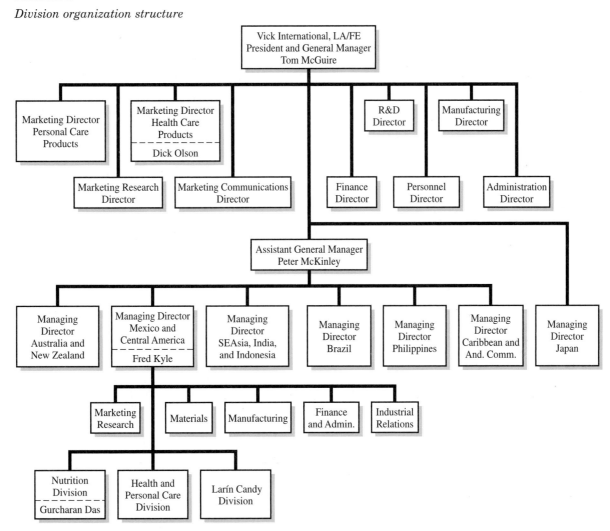

Source: Reproduction of original company document.

could be applied consistently throughout the division and serve as a link for coordination with other functions. He worked individually with each manager reporting directly to him to develop a mutual understanding about the nature of managers' responsibilities. He knew that, as the division grew, effective delegation of decision making to the appropriate levels would be indis-

pensable. To assist in making this possible and to improve coordination, he established a work-role assignment process. And to energize the division, he instituted a series of periodic management meetings tied to a detailed planning and review system that looked backward 12 months and forward three years, with a complete update every quarter.

Over the years, the division gained substantial experience with the various components of this process. Eventually, much of it became formalized in a series of manuals: the Product Marketing Guides, the Managers' Guides, and the Planning and Review Guides.

McGuire

The key to our management process is its thoroughness, combined with its flexibility. Take the Marketing Guides, for example. For each of our major products we develop a guide, which includes eight separate documents. The first two, the Product Profile Statement (PMG-1) and the Product Marketing Policy (PMG-2), are developed by one of the marketing directors and his staff at division headquarters as a standardized blueprint for the product across the division. They serve as a basis for planning the expansion or introduction of the product in a market.

The Product Data Book (PMG-3) and Product Marketing Assessment Statement (PMG-4) are developed by each regional or country unit handling or interested in introducing the product, to assess its appropriateness and potential in the local market. The regional market managing director is assigned the Approver role for the PMG-3; but, because of its strategic importance, the PMG-4 is approved by the division president. The assessment in these two documents includes the discussion of reasons for deviations from the policies or standards set for the products in PMGs 1 and 2, if any are deemed necessary.

The remaining PMG documents, covering specific aspects of marketing, advertising, promotion, and sales and distribution strategy in a given market, are put together to refine the assessment of the feasibility of the product in that market, and then to serve as the basis for the management of the product once it is introduced.

The elaboration of each PMG document must be preceded by extensive research work. This might involve analysis of market conditions, product development, consumer attitude surveys, packaging design and testing, and so forth. Once the PMG package has been completed for a given product in a given market, however, all the pertinent results of this work are brought together in one place and are available for assessment and reference by managers throughout the division.

As one of our product managers at HQ, who has had substantial field experience, likes to say, "The PMG system doesn't let you take anything for granted. We are forced to go through all the steps and, as a result, we don't make those mistakes that used to slip by when we tried to finesse a difficult part of the marketing planning process." But, at the same time, each overseas operating unit is free to adapt the product policy to its own circumstances, giv-

ing us substantial built-in flexibility. And each exception to standard practice is thus made explicit.

The marketing management process is embedded within a wider planning and review process, through which we obtain agreement on business financial objectives and functional operational objectives for each regional or country market, and between those markets and the division headquarters. These objectives in turn are tied to explicitly formulated strategic objectives for each unit and the division as a whole.

The process also provides procedures for the continuing review, analysis, testing, and reporting of performance and progress toward achieving division and market objectives and standards. We have found it necessary to break with RMI's traditional annual planning and budgeting cycle. It isn't dynamic enough for our markets, nor does it take a systematic enough look at the prospects for three, four, and five years out. So we have opted for our own system, which calls for quarterly updates and includes the prior year, the current year, and the next three years. (See Exhibit 2 for graphic representation of the CP-R planning cycle.)

Once operational objectives are set, we use succinct but explicit Work Programs following a standard format. These serve to draw together from all involved parts of the organization the information required so that we can view each program as a whole. This lets us test and evaluate the risk/cost/benefit relationship of the operational objective and the Work Program for its achievement. We can also assure efficient use and timing of resources and identify conflicts between the demands of various Work Programs for limited resources.

The Work Programs, of course, quickly multiply. They can cover objectives related to development products and commercial products within various markets. They can touch on issues of personnel development, improving inventory management, building new facilities, managing an acquisition or divestment, and so on and so forth. The roles our managers are called upon to play will vary from one Work Program to another. As a result, we have found it indispensable to devise a mechanism for keeping our wires untangled. We assign all concerned parties a specific role in each Work Program, Action Plan, or other formal CP-R scheduling document. The four roles are: Approver, Prime Mover, Concurrer, and Contributor. The terms are all positive by design. We want to get things done, not get them hung up.

The Prime Mover, as the name implies, is the manager with the action. Quite frequently he will be a third or fourth level in our hierarchy. This allows us to get around the rigidity of a chain of command and recognize the important and indispensable contribution to be made by those who actually push the work to its completion.

The Approver is a higher-level manager than the Prime Mover—frequently, but not always, his immediate

Exhibit 2

CP-R planning cycle

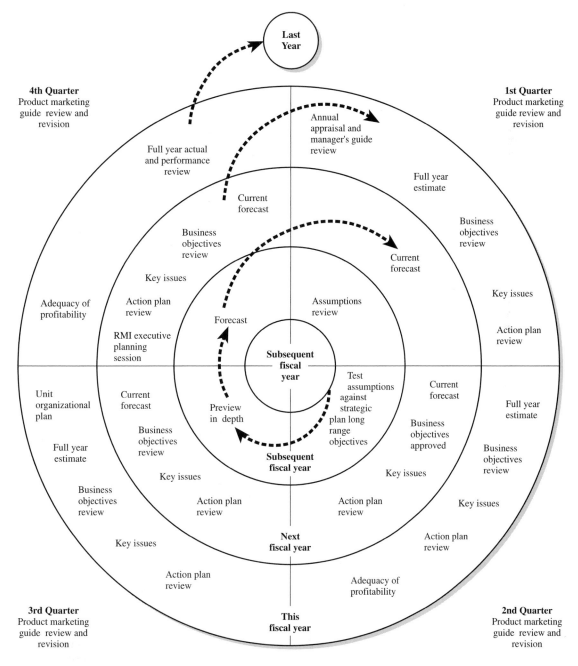

Source: Reproduction of original company document.

superior. His job is to assure that the measures taken by the Prime Mover are in line with division policies and overall objectives. And especially in the case of relatively inexperienced Prime Movers, the Approver will take care to see that serious mistakes, which might damage the division or the subordinate's career, are avoided.

Concurrers, of which there can be more than one on any given job, supply technical or specialized judgment to the Prime Mover. Their agreement is necessary prior to the implementation of any decision involving their area of expertise, although unresolvable disagreements can be referred to higher management. This perhaps is the one area where we still have to learn to do a better job. There is at times a tendency for concurrers to behave as vetoers rather than as positive collaborators. But by making the roles explicit, we find that such behavior becomes visible and can be dealt with.

I personally find the work-role assignment process very valuable. By nature I am inclined to get involved in the details of every task. But now that the roles are formally specified, it has become commonplace for some of my directors to remind me to stay off their turf when I start getting too involved. There are days when I will be with one of them in two successive meetings in which our formally assigned roles change. It really helps us change gears.

Dick Olson also found the CP-R management system of much help. As marketing director for Health Care Products, he had several hats to wear and many markets to work with. Olson had been with RMI for 15 years since receiving his MBA from Cornell. Most of his career so far had been within the marketing function with the Vicks Domestic Health Care Division. He had been in his present job for the last three years.

Olson

I have enjoyed this job very much. While some people might find it difficult to move from the less formally structured management process in a domestic division to LA/FE with its CP-R system, I have found it invigorating. Tom is a great guy to work for. He is bright, competent, and has a very professional approach to management. He has involved me deeply in the development and refinement of the division's marketing management approach and the techniques and procedures needed to carry it out. These are brought together in the PMG process.

Working with Tom on the elaboration of my Manager's Guide has made it possible to see where I can concentrate my efforts most productively for the division. It also has helped me see where my actions and those of my department affect the outcomes of other units and in what ways we are dependent on them. (Exhibit 3 shows one page from Olson's Managers Guide.)

As I see it, I have three main responsibilities. First, as part of Tom's management team, I help him as he feels the need on a broad set of general issues along with the other division headquarters directors. Then, more specifically, I assist him in the development of the marketing function throughout the division in the Health Care area.

Second, I am responsible for the adequate functioning of the division's activities aimed at business development in the health care field, including, more recently, nutritional products. My staff and I look for new ideas or products both from our people abroad and from outside the division or even outside the company. We undertake projects on our own to translate some of these ideas into physical products backed by a marketing strategy and marketing materials that can be tested in a trial market. Then we get the cooperation of one of our overseas units to test and launch it.

For example, just over a year ago the Australian Board of Health relaxed limitations on the advertisement of liquid cold remedies. Australia saw this as an opportunity for itself, and we saw it as a good opportunity for the division, especially as we had indications that similar policy changes were in the making in some other countries in our half of the world. At division headquarters we pooled information worldwide on RMI's capabilities in this area. Working with our Australian marketing staff, we did some consumer survey work. Out of this we concluded that NyQuil, which was being sold successfully in the United States and Europe, had promising potential. We then drew up a plan that would allow us to launch the product successfully in Australia within nine months. Members of my department and I, as well as other HQ staff members, traveled to Sydney several times during the subsequent months working very closely with, and providing assistance to, our local people out there. It required a concentrated joint effort, but we were successful in launching the product, which we call "MediNite" in that market, within the time period specified. We beat the competition into the market by several weeks. We used the PMG process very successfully as an aid in getting all the pieces together, and the CP-R process helped get all the actors collaborating in a timely fashion. Manufacturing and marketing MediNite in Australia is now primarily the responsibility of our people out there, although in our third role as a resource department on marketing we will continue to be available to assist our people in Australia if and when they need it.

Back to the issue of business development: when our overseas units have a substantial nondivision business segment, which warrants product development as part of its long-term strategy, we allow them to develop such

Exhibit 3   Excerpt from Olson's Managers' Guide

Key Result Area:

Tomorrow's Products

KEY TASK #1 Position: Div. Marketing Dir.

    Page:
    Date:
    Revised: December 6, 1976

KEY TASK # 1

As Prime Mover to ensure that sufficient viable ideas for *Development Products* are being identified and acted upon at least to meet future Division growth needs.

STANDARDS OF PERFORMANCE

a. When there is an approved plan, consistent with Division objectives and strategy, for Long-Term Business development of the field of activity, including product development, acquisition and licensing.

b. When there is an ongoing program to track and screen, against Division criteria and objectives for the category, new product activity within the Vick Divisions.

c. When there is an ongoing program to test objectives and screening criteria and to identify or generate ideas for prospective Development Products.

d. When all ideas which pass the screening against Divisional criteria are promptly referred to R & D for exploratory feasibility.

e. When 80% of the recommendations of the Active Development Slate are approved and allocated the necessary resources on the basis of reasonable or supportable quantified statements of costs and potential benefits/risks.

f. When the marketing checkpoints included in assigned Active Development Projects are adequate to validate continuance, to select an alternative course or to terminate, and when appropriate action is taken when each checkpoint is reached.

g. When no assigned Active Development Project is significantly delayed, has its cost increased, or fails because of inadequate or delayed marketing information or because of failure to provide, promptly, requested and agreed upon HQ Marketing support or resources.

h. When, at all times, there is at least one Development Product of the assigned category on the Active Development Slate or under negotiation for license/acquisition *and* at least one other undergoing testing (including Test Marketing) each with a first sustaining year national contribution *total* for *major* markets in excess of $1 million, at a Contribution ratio, growth rate, investment level and ROAE equal to or better than criteria for the category; and whose resource requirements are within the capabilities of the Division and the major markets.

EVIDENCE OF ACHIEVEMENT

a. GM Approval of HQ Marketing Preview in Depth (PID) for the category

b. Individual Performing Reviews against Action Plans Minutes of Meetings within the Program

c. Individual Performance Reviews against Action Plans Minutes of Meetings within the Program

d. R & D Approved Projects

e. GM Approvals of not less than 80% of submitted Project Guides

f. GM Approval of Action Plan Individual Performance Reviews against Action Plans

g. Individual Performance Reviews against Action Plans

h. Project Guides and Action Plans

Source: Reproduction of original company document.

products, within our policies, procedures, and standards, and try to support them in every way we can. The PMG system provides us with regular feedback reports, and through it we are assured that a thorough review is made of all aspects of the product that could make it successful or cause it to flounder. Several of our units, especially Australia, Mexico, and India, are strong in new product development, but they still each have some shortcomings. We try to capitalize on their strengths by letting them take a lot of initiative and operate quite independently, while we remain available to help whenever it's needed.

This job allows me to act both as a marketing staff director and as an operating director for the new product development program. This is challenging and personally satisfying. I know that my counterpart for Personal Care Products feels the same way. It is what attracted him to come to RMI. It would be nearly impossible to carry out this dual role without the work-role assignment approach of the CP-R system. Since it started being used regularly in the division, the amount of wasted time and effort has dropped considerably. Delays in communication between the field and headquarters have also been reduced substantially.

Fred Kyle, managing director in Mexico since 1974, while committed to the CP-R system, was less enthusiastic about it. Of his 20 years with RMI, he had spent about half in manufacturing and marketing management, first with Vicks domestic and then with International. For the last 10 years, he had held various field management positions in Latin America.

Kyle

CP-R certainly has a lot going for it, but it does cause us some problems. The quarterly management review meetings are tremendously helpful. We get a lot of problems resolved and are able to adjust our objectives often enough to keep an even keel in a very volatile political and economic environment. But there is an overload of paper work. My financial director has to keep records for me under the CP-R system; but since we also service the Mexican office of Merrell International, he has to follow a different set-up for them.

And then there is the language barrier. Most of our Mexican management people have a working knowledge of English; but we conduct our business in Spanish and, as a result, they find it hard to tune into the CP-R system, which is all in English. Some of the terminology can't even be translated. Then of course there is a cultural barrier in almost all LA/FE overseas locations. Some are not comfortable with such explicitly assigned responsibilities—

with everyone's performance open to the general view, especially if they are accustomed to use a more personalized form of supervision.

We are trying to apply the CP-R system to our operations, but so far it has been more difficult than we anticipated. However, I feel it will be worth all the effort.

Some of our managers feel CP-R is really an extension of Tom McGuire, that he makes it work by pure willpower, and they're sure we are all the better for it. The division's performance certainly has improved. In part it's a big advantage, but in part it may be a drawback, that Tom knows so much about our market and our operations. He has a tendency to get too involved from time to time in the details of running our business. Maybe Mexico is a special case. He spent 18 months here in 1964–65 as director.

Return on equity for Vick International during 1973–78 was as follows: 1973, 13.5 percent; 1974, 15.4 percent; 1975, 18.5 percent; 1976, 24.2 percent; 1977, 28.5 percent; 1978, 27.3 percent.

Project Alpha

Mexico was the largest operating entity within LA/FE and had concentrated traditionally on proprietary drugs. In 1964, it entered the nutrition field with acquisition of ChocoMilk, a well-established brand of powdered milk supplement with an existing distribution network. Consisting mainly of powdered milk, chocolate, and sugar, ChocoMilk provided nutritional reinforcement as well as flavoring. It took several years to modernize the production facilities, improve the formula to suit changing tastes and meet several competitive entries, and develop the management capacity to deal with this new market. One of the main stumbling blocks was the absence of a reliable source of supply for high-quality chocolate that would make it possible to upgrade the product. This was achieved in 1966 with the acquisition of the Larín Candy Company, one of Vick's major chocolate suppliers. Now local management faced a new set of challenges. Not only did it have to proceed with the upgrading and expansion of ChocoMilk, but it also had to learn to manage the specialty candy business into which it had entered. It took several more years for both tasks to be accomplished.

When Fred Kyle became managing director in Mexico in 1974, one of his early concerns was to strengthen the ChocoMilk segment of the business. It seemed risky to have such an important segment relying on only one product, which already dominated its market with a 50 percent market share, and which was under considerable competitive pressure. Secondly, the traditional proprietary drug business continued to be price controlled, offering negative prospects for improved profitability. Additional entries into the nutrition field appeared to be worth serious consideration.

After consultation with division headquarters, Kyle commissioned a study of potential entries for the Mexican nutritional product market. The study was carried out by the marketing research department in Mexico with assistance from a New York consulting firm in 1975–1976. The study took an exhaustive look at food items sold in grocery stores in Mexico, the United States, and Canada, to identify categories of consumer needs for which solutions were sought through processed foods sold in food stores. Then surveys were carried out with panels of Mexican housewives to learn their underlying concerns regarding each class of needs. Out of this emerged a slate of product concepts for development and testing. These were screened for feasibility as products for Vick Mexico.

At a divisional management meeting in August of 1976, the results of the study were presented, along with a final slate of potential new products for development and market testing. The slate was approved, as was an overall new product development program. A target was set to test market at least one new product from the slate each year. Product Alpha was the first new item on the slate.

Gurcharan Das was assigned in October of 1976 to become director of Vick Mexico's newly established Nutrition Division, responsible for the ongoing ChocoMilk business and the new nutritional product development program. He already had a track record of successful development and introduction of new products with Vick International's Indian subsidiary.

A philosophy major at Harvard College, Das had decided after graduation to look for opportunities in business management that would allow him to return to India, use his creative energies, and still have time for personal development as a thinker and writer. He found the opportunity with RMI, which he joined in 1963. In 1976, Das was offered the choice of joining the division's Health Care Products marketing department to work on new product development, or to take the job in Mexico.

Das

I decided to go to Mexico because I wanted to be close to the market, where the action is. I wanted to have responsibility for all the facets of product development, testing, and launching. I like to have control over my piece of the business and to be judged by the results I achieve. It allows me to exercise my creative energies. I guess I have an entrepreneurial spirit.

Alpha was Das's first challenge in this new position. The product was aimed at a felt need of the Mexican mother for a quick, easy, yet nourishing beverage for use on hectic school days. Over the next 18 months Das worked intensively with a technical group in the ChocoMilk plant to develop a suitable product. He also enlisted the help of the marketing research department to carry out extensive product concept research with potential users. During this period there was little interaction with headquarters staff, other than routine communication of progress and occasional inputs from the division research and development director on issues of product quality.

No formal Work Program was drawn up. Nonetheless, Vick Mexico did have extensive internal plans and schedules, including a PERT-type plan for Alpha. Since it was a totally new product with which the HQ staff had no familiarity, there were no PMG-1 and PMG-2. Kyle and Das considered Alpha a nondivisional product like ChocoMilk, for which they were responsible.

In January of 1978, Das contracted with a Mexico City advertising agency to start developing material for use in the first market tests later that year. He had another contractor develop an innovative container for Alpha.

With the time approaching to make initial commitments for market testing, it was necessary to obtain overall division management approval of the project's current status and direction. A meeting for this purpose was planned for early May. In preparation for this meeting, the PMGs 3, 4, 5, 6, 7, and 8 were completed in late April and sent to headquarters personnel for their review.

By separating the PMG into various documents, the CP-R system made it possible to assign different work roles to various individuals for each piece. While PMGs 1 and 2 were primarily the work of headquarters staff, the remaining parts required substantial collaboration between headquarters and field. The Approver role for the PMG 2 and 3 was assigned to the regional managing director, with the Prime Mover, Concurrers, and Contributors coming from the local staff. The PMGs 4 and 5, which were key strategy documents, required the approval of the division president and the concurrence of several headquarters directors, as well as overseas unit functional managers. PMGs 6, 7, and 8, which usually were prepared after 4 and 5 had been approved, usually could be approved by the division assistant general manager with concurrence only from the headquarters director with specific functional expertise in each case.

With the Alpha PMG, however, because all six parts arrived at the same time, the package was reviewed as a unit by all the potential Concurrers and Approvers. Dick Olson, as Prime Mover for the overall Development Product program, became the focal point for the review at HQ.

In studying the PMG documents on Product Alpha, Olson was surprised to see it classified as a nondivisional product. Nonetheless he felt that an excellent job had been done in the area of product concept research, product development

in the lab, and assessment of market potential. Reactions from other headquarters departments were similarly supportive, with a few technical suggestions for improvement. The material on marketing strategy and advertising, however, was very spotty and failed to take full advantage of this marketing research.

During the next several weeks Das made three trips to division headquarters in the hope of getting the necessary approvals to proceed with a test market launch of Alpha. After the first meeting in May, Tom McGuire approved the Alpha program and the PMG-4 in principle. It was agreed that Mexico would undertake several technical improvements having to do with packaging, labeling, and product quality, as well as obtain some additional information on potential users. McGuire also asked Das to review PMGs 5 through 8 with Olson after the meeting, since extensive comment had been made about their adequacy. At this point a Work Program was prepared (see Exhibit 4).

For the first time, Das became aware that an MC-1 (a CP-R document designed to provide an advertising agency with guidance for developing advertising materials) would be required, and that for Development Products the MC-1 had to be approved by the division president and concurred with by assistant general manager Peter McKinley, Dick Olson, and the marketing communications director.

In June, Das returned with a draft MC-1 and a package of advertising material that he wished to use in the test launch. He needed various concurrences and approval from headquarters management in order to proceed. Dick Olson and the marketing communications director had previously reviewed the material and made some suggestions for improvement. When Das met with Tom McGuire for approval, he found that Tom thought basic changes in the market positioning of Alpha, implicit in the advertising copy, would be necessary. He suggested that Das return to Mexico and revise the PMG-5, PMG-6, and MC-1, in line with their discussion. He

<hr>

Exhibit 4   Alpha Work Program

<hr>

OBJECTIVE/STANDARD:

Test Market and evaluate Alpha leading to a
decision to introduce nationally.

MAJOR STEPS	PERSON OR UNIT	OUTPUTS	START DATE	END DATE	*	COMMENTS
1. Wilton approval of project	GCD	1. Minutes of May 8 meeting		05/78	*	1. Completed.
2. Order packaging molds, raw and packaging materials.	RB	2. a. Approval of preliminary molds. b. Receipt of all materials necessary for initial production.	R7/78 R8/78	R9/78 R10/78	*	2. A. Tassin will be required to approve preliminary molds.
3. Obtain advertising approval.	GCD AQ	3. Approved commercials for air. a) MC-1 approval b) Storyboard approval c) Pretesting/SSA d) Approval to produce	R6/78	R2/79 R7/78 R8/78 R10/78 R10/78	*	
4. Manufacturing booklet	SH/WRG	4. Red Book issued	R8/78	R9/78	*	4. W.R. Gillap to issue.
5. Product ready	APS	5. Pipeline stock plus first 2 mos. expected consumer takeoff of finished stock in warehouse	Rt-135	Rt-15	*	5. Contingent on approval of MO-2 (test market proposal) or separate approval to buy material and packaging inventories.
6. Production of marketing communication materials	GCD	6. Commercials in can Promotion/display materials in warehouse	Rt-75 Rt-60	Rt-15 Rt-15	*	
		Media space booked Sales force briefing/training	RT-30 Rt-5	Rt-30 Rt-1	*	
7. Test market distribution		7. Pipeline horizontal and vertical distribution objectives and promotion/display objectives achieved or surpassed	Rt	Rt+21 Rt+56	*	(Note: In the date columns O stands for originals and R stands for revised) GCD = Das
8. Month x evaluation of test market	GCD	8. Implement month x reaction program	O 1/w R 1/x	O 30/w R 30/x	*	RB = Mexico Materials Mgr. AQ = Mexico Nutritional Dn. Prod. Mgr.
9. Month y evaluation of test market	GCD FWK	9. Month y reaction program. Order balance of equipment.	O 1/x R 1/y	O 30/x R 30/y	*	WGR = Division Manuf. Director
10. Month z evaluation of test market	GCD FWK	10. TMM approval to go national, expand test market, or recycle.	O 1/y R 1/z	O 30/y R 1/z	*	APS = Mexico Manuf. Director HB = Mexico Nutritional Dir. Sales Mgr. t = Test market starting date - disguised for competitive reasons

CORP/COUNTRY MEXICO	WORK PROGRAM	PRIME MOVER GCDas	BUSINESS SEGMENT OR DEPARTMENT	ALPHA PROJECT	DATE INITIATED 5/78	CP-R WP	PAGE
		APPROVER FWKyle	NUTRITIONAL		LAST REVISION 8/78		

March 78

(In preparation for mid-Aug. Inventory Review Meeting.)

<hr>

should then submit the MC-1 to headquarters for approval which, Tom promised, would be forthcoming within 48 hours. To assure a quick turnaround, he delegated the Approver role jointly to McKinley and Olson.

Das was crushed. He told McGuire that he felt let down by the whole system. How could it be that, after getting professional inputs from the agency in Mexico, approval in principle of the PMG, and comments about the advertising copy from headquarters staff that had been incorporated into the material, a major flaw should come out in a meeting with the division president? And with every passing day the project was falling further behind schedule.

Upon returning to Mexico, Das revised the MC-1 and sent it to division HQ in early July. A week later he received a request from Olson to come to the United States for a meeting to get the MC-1 approved. In late July that meeting took place. The PMG-5, PMG-6 and MC-1 were jointly rewritten. Then all Concurrers and the Approvers initialed the MC-1 document. Das returned to Mexico to have the agency prepare storyboards for TV ads. He had instructions to return to headquarters with these for approval in late August.

Prior to his departure for the mid-August quarterly review meeting, Fred Kyle, who had been away for six weeks at a management education program, had a long discussion with Gucharan about the Alpha project.

Kyle

Gucharan was very unhappy. He had worked for a year and a half getting Alpha off the ground. He had been successful in getting our Mexican R & D, marketing research, manufacturing, and other departments involved and excited. They were all committed to a tightly programmed project schedule and had produced truly innovative top-quality results. We were convinced that we had identified a project with very significant potential.

After moving along so well, however, we are now running into trouble. While the difficulties focus on Alpha, it is really the entire nutritional new product program that is at stake. The establishment of such a program had been attempted without success ever since the acquisition of ChocoMilk in 1964. I had taken a different approach from my predecessors and, after four years with the entire Mexican organization and with the full knowledge of division management, appeared to be achieving results.

To succeed, however, our people need to be free to take risks, to move quickly, to be entrepreneurial, and to feel that they will be judged on their results. The way the CP-R process is being applied is making this extremely difficult.

I hope at the quarterly meeting we can work out some way of maintaining our present momentum and of providing the freedom and flexibility we need to ensure the continued progress of our whole nutritional new product program.

Questions

1. What strategy is McGuire pursuing for his division? What are the key success factors in this business? What critical tasks must be accomplished to achieve success?

2. What is your appraisal of the role Olson played in the introduction of MediNite in Australia?

3. Identify the major elements of the planning and control systems that McGuire has established. Why has he installed these systems? What is your evaluation of the effectiveness of this approach?

4. Who is to blame for the delay in introducing Alpha? Why did McGuire punish Das in this situation?

5. Under what circumstances would the systems used by McGuire be particularly useful?

6. What are the limitations of such systems?

CASE 17–3
NESTLÉ S.A.

In February 1980, Mr. G. Smith, a zone director in the Nestlé headquarters in Vevay was reviewing the status of the company's subsidiaries in Argentina. The political and economic situation in that country was unsettled, and these conditions impacted on the subsidiaries' performance. Mr. Smith was considering what, if any, actions he should take in view of this situation, the subsidiaries' recent performance, and their proposed budget for 1980, which had just arrived in Vevey.

The Company

Nestlé S.A. was the largest food company in the world. It was founded in 1867 in Vevey, Switzerland, and its headquarters, referred to as "Centre," was still in Vevey in 1980. It is the largest company in Switzerland, although only some 2.5 percent of its sales are made in Switzerland. In 1984, it had 138,000 employees, 292 factories located in 58 countries, and marketing organizations in almost every country in the world. In 1984, 44 percent of its employees were in Europe, 19 percent in North America, 22 percent in Latin America, 5 percent in Africa, 8 percent in Asia, and 2 percent in Australasia.

Nestlé's operating units were referred to as "markets." Each market was a profit center. Typically, a market consisted of all Nestlé activities, both production and marketing, in one country. Each profit center manager (referred to as "head of the market") reported to the managing director through a zone director whose office was in the Centre in Vevey. In 1980, there were five zone directors, each responsible for Nestlé activi-

ties in one part of the world, and each assisted by a staff of around 20 persons.

At the Centre also were staff units for: production (called "technical"), including engineering, quality control, and purchasing; marketing, including advertising, market research, and recipes; finance and control, including treasury, internal control, audit, financial accounting, cost accounting, pensions, and planning; administration; legal; and personnel.

Argentina: Background

From 1966 through 1974, Argentina was governed by a military junta, most recently headed by General Juan Peron. Following Peron's death in 1974, there was a period of turbulence that left the economy in shambles. By early 1976, the economic growth rate was negative, the inflation rate was 650 percent, the trade balance was negative, capital was fleeing the country, and it appeared that Argentina might have to default on its international debts.

In March 1976, there was a coup, and a new military government took over. It immediately took measures to curb inflation, reduce imports, increase exports, reduce the budget deficit, and shift the economy away from state-owned entities to more private enterprise. These measures were successful in avoiding default on debt payments and they had some success in reducing the rate of inflation. However, inflation remained at a rate of 160 percent in 1977.

In 1978, the recovery drive had a sharp setback. After five successive quarters of growth, the gross domestic product decreased by 4.2 percent for the year as a whole. The decline resulted from the imposition of strict economic controls, a sharp reduction in the budget deficit, and an increase in interest rates. Inflation remained at 160 percent.

This case was prepared by F. Voegtli. This condensed version was prepared by Professor Robert N. Anthony, Harvard Business School. Names of most persons are fictitious. Copyright Nestec S.A., Vevay, Switzerland.

In 1978 and 1979, the government took additional measures. Foreigners were encouraged to invest in all types of enterprises, import tariffs were reduced, and the program to shift from state-owned enterprises to private business was accelerated. The tariff reduction aimed at an average tariff of 15 percent in 1984, compared with an average of 60 percent in 1976. Restrictions of the flow of capital were eased, although there was a requirement that foreign loans had to have a maturity of at least one year, to discourage short-term capital movements for speculative purposes.

These changes in financial regulations had a rapid and significant impact. Since banks and companies could obtain one-year funds from foreign banks at a monthly cost of 5.5 percent, compared with 7.0 percent locally, they tended to switch to foreign funding. In 1979, Argentine liabilities to foreign banks grew by over 50 percent. The result was a pressure to reduce local interest rates; they became about 2 percent lower than the rates of inflation. This led to increased domestic investment and a growth of 13 percent in industrial production in the first nine months. A record harvest and an increase in the world price of export commodities (beef, wheat, and corn) also aided the economy. Nevertheless, inflation for the first three quarters of 1979 remained at an annual rate of 170 percent.

In the last quarter of 1979, there was an important boom of unprecedented proportions. Imports were up 53 percent, compared with the last quarter of 1978. Since exports increased by only 30 percent, there was a negative trade balance, which wiped out the positive impact of capital inflows. A consequence of the flood of imports was that many domestic plants were operating at low volumes.

Nestlé Argentina: Background

S.A. Nestlé de Productos Alimenticios (hereafter SANPA) opened an office in Buenos Aires in 1931 and built a large chocolate factory in a suburb of that city in the same year. In 1935, it built a milk factory and, as was its usual practice, devoted considerable resources to helping farmers improve their techniques to provide an adequate supply of milk. Between 1944 and 1959, three additional milk factories were built. In 1971, milk intake at all factories was 127 million kilograms (kg.); it reached a peak of 234 million kg. in 1976, was 196 million kg. in 1977, and 203 million kg. in 1978.

In the 1930s, regional distribution offices were established throughout the country, and the distribution network was gradually expanded thereafter. A large distribution center was established near Buenos Aires in 1968; in 1979, it handled almost half the domestic sales volume.

In 1978, Nestlé acquired Fruticon S.A., a manufacturer of canned tomato and fruit products with a staff of some 300 persons. Fruticon was operated as a separate company.

Although SANPA's sales volume grew rapidly, its profits did not keep pace. In addition to heavy start-up costs and marketing investments for new lines, such as ice-cream, as well as strong competitive pressure, Nestlé suffered from the consequences of the government's economic programme.

Business was certainly not easy under the economic conditions prevailing in 1978, and SANPA's 1978 annual report stated:

> Interest rates remained at a high level, which forced us to intensify the controls over our working capital with a view to keeping the financing costs within an acceptable range. On the other hand, we had to maintain sufficient stocks of raw materials and finished products in line with the turnover (i.e., sales) growth objectives.

The Centre was satisfied that the end-1978 level of working capital was acceptable.

In June 1978, Mr. L. Gonzales, head of market, wrote to the zone director at the Centre that the government policy would eliminate much competition that had managed to maintain itself only because of the industrial protection of the last 20 years. Healthy companies would gain in strength. Under these circumstances, he said, SANPA should "move away from the traditional policy of profitability maximization which had restrained volume growth" and during the next two years should "make up the lost ground with heavy marketing support." The Centre agreed with this strategy in a letter of September 1978.

Events of 1979

January to June. SANPA's budget request for 1979 had been based on the new strategy and on a predicted gradual improvement in the economic situation; it forecasted a turnover increase of 150 percent, to pesos 303.7 billion. Considering the generally expected moderations of inflation in 1979, the budget appeared to be reasonably conservative and had been accepted by the Centre.

Actual sales of SANPA during the first six months of 1979 followed no regular patterns. Sales varied between 67 percent and 113 percent of the respective monthly budgets for the first five months and were approximately on budget in June.

SANPA sent a revised budget to the Centre in early April, showing considerably increased turnover forecasts; 1979 sales were now budgeted at pesos 410.8 billion, some 35 percent above the original budget and 239 percent above actual 1978 sales. This revision did not provoke any unusual reaction at the Centre.

SANPA's debt collection performance in the first half of the year was, similar to the one of sales, not always in line with expectations; but the monthly report of June was optimistic: "the debtors situation will improve in subsequent months; thanks to the planned reorganization of the sales force and a series of measures we shall try to reach the standard of 40 days."

July to September. Inflation continued unabated in July (7.2 percent for the month) and August (11.5 percent), before coming down in September (6.8 percent), a month coinciding with the introductions of governmental wage increase limits.

Actual SANPA sales for this quarter fell short of revised budget figures by pesos 35.3 billion, or some 32 percent. For July, invoicing problems during the first 10 days of the month were cited as the main responsible factor. These were said to be due to changes in the marketing set-up.

September saw another very poor performance of SANPA. Sales revenues for most product groups fell considerably behind budget. SANPA commented on the September sales results as follows:

> . . . continuous price increases of the products forming the household shopping basket and the rate of adjustments for services (electricity, etc.) had led to a marked reduction of consumer demand. The trade is faced with a slow stock rotation, high financing costs, as well as debt collection pressure by suppliers, which do not represent incentives to quickly replace stock sold; the trade works at minimum stock levels and tries to purchase only during special offers.

October. On October 2, Mr. Smith, the zone director, sent a letter to Luis Gonzalez, the head of the Argentine market, reminding him "once more of the importance of maintaining working capital and especially the trade debtors at reasonable levels in view of the high financing costs and the increasing difficulties encountered in obtaining sufficient credit." The letter concluded: " . . . it would be a pity to jeopardize the achievements made with respect to product profitability by offering too generous selling conditions to the trade."

In October, SANPA reported record sales of close to pesos 70 billion, which was some 45 percent above the revised budget and nearly as much as total sales in the preceding three months. Some promotions, offering discounts of up to 20 percent, helped to smooth the impact of selling price increases. These increases ranged from 10 percent to 24 percent and were made to recover increases in production and operating costs. Collections reached only 61 percent of the forecasted amount, leaving SANPA debtors at 78

Exhibit 1   SANPA Excess Working Capital

Month 1979	Month-End Stock Value Finished Goods (1)	Value of Stocks above Standard (3 months) (2)	Month-End Debtors Value (3)	Value of Debtors above Standard (40 days) (4)	Resulting Excess Working Capital (5) = (2) + (4)
January	24,678	4,577	24,440	12,665	17,242
February	28,339	5,931	23,960	9,971	15,902
March	30,660	5,326	32,775	7,779	13,105
April	32,786	3,498	34,707	13,002	16,500
May	32,753	354	37,734	12,850	13,204
June	31,270	—	45,240	14,333	14,333
July	29,769	—	59,953	28,471	28,471
August	33,372	1,096	58,986	21,281	22,377
September	39,201	177	62,334	29,447	29,624
October	32,829	1,145	107,303	16,811*	17,956
November	31,715	213	135,574	57,279	57,492
December	41,538	12,343	151,720	68,773	81,116

*Incorrect reporting: actual figures should have been some 11,000 higher.

days and "causing our financial position to continuously deteriorate, a situation which is not expected to change during the remainder of the year."

The technical section of the monthly report stated that the production programmes were exceeded by 20 percent for milk powders and by 11 percent for chocolates. Chocolate stocks still stood at four months, and the value of the total excess stock was indicated as pesos 1.1 billion (see Exhibit 1).

The end-September budget revision for SANPA contained the following forecasts of the 1979 results: total turnover pesos 368.86 billion, net operating loss pesos 6.00 billion, net loss pesos 3.00 billion. Debtors were expected to drop to 50 days by year end.

The revision reflected optimism for the whole of 1979, despite the dismal actual performance in the first nine months of the year. Given the high rate of inflation, the fact that the fourth quarter had often been buoyant in the past, and the possibility of cutting certain expenses, especially in the marketing area, the Centre did not question this optimism. According to a letter from Mr. Gonzalez, the new estimate had been made with the knowledge of the actual results for the first eight months of 1979; a net operating loss of pesos 17 billion, equivalent to 10.3 percent of turnover for SANPA. He went on to say: "higher prices will not only boost turnover but also help the net operating profit to reach its budgeted level." The letter of Mr. Gonzalez concluded: "You can be assured that we shall do the impossible to reach our budgeted sales for 1979." (Mr. Smith had urged this in a letter dated October 2.)

November. On November 28, the zone director wrote to Mr. Gonzalez, reminding him of the contents of the letter sent on October 2 and mentioning that "with a certain preoccupation I have taken note of the deterioration that has occurred in your trade debtors position. . . . While acknowledging the existence of considerable economical difficulties, with high inflation and a slow recovery pace, I insist once more on the crucial importance of paying special attention to this problem."

The monthly report for November, received at the Centre on December 21, again contained predominantly good news: inflation was down to a monthly rate of 5.1 percent, the government published inflation estimates of 45 percent to 48 percent for 1980, interest rates had come down as a result of a more liquid financial market, and SANPA sales were pesos 66 billion, "exceeding the objectives of the month." Successful promotional activities, particularly in instant drinks and chocolates (20 percent discount for certain items), were given credit for the excellent performance, despite selling price increases of 11 percent to 16 percent for most products (none for chocolates). Ice-cream sales were reportedly once more the victim of bad weather, remaining below budget and 10 percent below the November 1978 volume. "With view to making up for turnover shortfall due to lost volume," the Frigor Division modified its pricing policy, which had not planned for any adjustments before year end, and increased its selling prices by an average of 14.1 percent on November 26.

On the financial side, poor-debtors collection further increased SANPA's bank indebtedness, but it was hoped that this situation would improve by February 1980. There were no special comments concerning production.

December.   Ernst Keller, zone controller, paid a visit to the Argentine market from December 4 to 7. He summarized his impressions in a note to the vice president controlling, the finance director, and the zone director on December 20, as follows:

> Inflation estimated at 140 percent for 1979 and 70 percent for 1980; peso devaluation will be 60/70 percent in 1979 and 30 percent in 1980 according to optimistic forecasts. During my visit to our major distribution centre on December 5, I came across an anomaly in the delivery of ordered goods; there was a delivery on that day of an order invoiced on November 11. The manager of the distribution center admitted he had several such undelivered invoices; the goods had not been shipped because they were physically not available.

Ernst Keller went on to say that the invoices were for big customers, that the goods had been sold at the promotional discounts, and that exceptionally favorable payment terms of 90 days had been granted. If these goods could not be delivered by year end, Mr. Keller concluded, a reinvoicing would become necessary in January, at November 1979 prices and conditions. He also found that considerable quantities of goods were being stored on behalf of customers, even though they had already been recorded as sales.

The zone director immediately called the market head when he learned of this situation, asking him to take the necessary corrective actions at once.

On January 24, 1980, the monthly report of December reached the Centre. It stated that the government had reiterated its intention to stick to the planned devaluation scheme in 1980. It further stated that "positive real interest rates of up to 2 percent per month occurred in December despite a further reduction in nominal rates. In the capital goods sector, the softening of demand observed in November has continued, and there was a general increase in bankruptcies in the country."

Sales for December were disappointing. SANPA explained this by the "heavy sales of the preceding two months, which had not only reduced the demand due to oversaturation but also led to out-of-stock situations for several product lines." Unavailability of stocks was cited for important products, such as the instant drinks Nescafé and Nesquik. Selling prices had been increased for most products, ranging from 5 percent to 21 percent.

In the financial area, SANPA reported low debtors collections and an increase by US$5.5 million in its foreign currency loans.

Actual Results for 1979

The overall results for the whole year, reaching the Centre in early February 1980, showed a combined net profit of around pesos 1 billion. SANPA net profit was pesos 4.15 billion on sales of pesos 363.00 billion. However, the net profit was primarily due to exceptional items of pesos 3.90 billion (mainly revaluation of fixed assets); the net operating profit (NOP), was only pesos 0.29 billion, or less than 0.1 percent of turnover. Of the nonproduct-related fixed expenses of pesos 101.2 billion incurred by SANPA in 1979, interest was the major cost item, reaching pesos 52.8 billion, or 14.5 percent of turnover, which was considerably more than in previous years.

Balance sheet data are given in Exhibit 2 and monthly sales in Exhibit 3.

Budget 1980

On January 10, 1980, the Argentine market sent a telex to the Centre, indicating the key figures of the budgets of SANPA and Fruticon S.A. for the year 1980 (figures in pesos billions):

	SANPA	Fruticon
Sales	880.35	38.78
Net operating profit/(loss)	32.32	(6.45)
Net profit/(loss)	36.57	(6.95)

On February 4, the hardcopy of the budget was received at the Centre, confirming the telexed key data. Under the economic heading, the report made reference to the government's free market policy and stated: "the increasing flow of imports, as a consequence of an overvalued peso, will probably lead to a negative trade balance, a fall in the gross domestic product (GDP), and to increasing difficulties for companies not able to obtain foreign financing, as well as for those confronted with improved competitive products." SANPA expected for 1980 an inflation of 69.4 percent p.a. (with monthly rates ranging from 7 percent in January to 3 percent in December), average local interest rates of 75 percent (reaching 50 percent by year end), and a devaluation of the peso of 31.6 percent. The optimism with re-

spect to inflation was based on the government's budget with predicted deficit reduction to 2 percent of GDP and a limitation of public investments to 8 percent of GDP.

SANPA's objectives were to consolidate the market positions achieved in 1979 through constant and aggressive marketing activity and to increase selling prices in line with cost increases. A softening demand was expected for dietetic products and chocolates ("falling consumer purchasing power, strong competitive activity, and heavy pressure from cheap imports").

Regarding sales volumes, SANPA expected the following tonnage increases over 1979: milk products, 4 percent; dietetics, 15 percent; instant drinks, 7 percent; chocolates, 13 percent; catering products, 33 percent; culinary, 22 percent; Frigor ice-cream, 4 percent; total SANPA, 7.6 percent.

SANPA planned to add 452 new persons to its payroll in 1980, bringing the total personnel at the end of 1980 to 4,556; the largest increases by function were for production (309 persons, or 12 percent), sales (63 persons, or 11 percent), and general management/administration at head office (53 persons, or 11 percent). Data on SANPA staffing are given in Exhibit 4.

Events of Early 1980

After receiving the (delayed) debtors and stocks report for December 1979, the zone controller wrote, for the signature of the zone director, a letter to Mr. Gonzalez on February 12, reminding him of the letters sent on October 2 and November 28, 1979, on the same subject and telling him that "the debtors situation has reached alarming proportions considering the 85 days outstanding at year end and the low collections in January." The zone director asked for immediate explanations and comments on corrective actions taken.

On February 18, 1980, the monthly report for January arrived at the Centre. It stated that the inflation increase was 7.2 percent for the month of January; interest rates, however, continued to

Exhibit 2   SANPA Year-End Balance Sheets (in pesos millions)

	1977		1978		1979 Original Budget		1979 September Revision		1979 Actual		1980 Original Budget	
Assets												
Fixed assets	14,992	38.2	36,165	36.3	87,644	45.9	97,998	35.0	87,239	25.1	193,417	34.0
Raw and packaged materials	6,480	16.5	12,156	12.2	23,423	12.3	36,360	13.0	29,579	8.5	65,131	11.5
Finished products	4,553	11.6	10,761	10.8			35,477	12.7	31,120	9.0	85,155	15.0
Debtors	9,458	24.1	34,115	34.3	79,931	41.8	98,565	35.3	181,875	52.3	199,175	35.0
Sundry	3,741	9.6	6,357	6.4			11,117	4.0	17,771	5.1	25,718	4.5
Total	39,224	100%	99,554	100%	190,998	100%	279,517	100%	347,584	100%	568,596	100%
Liabilities												
Equity	13,038	33.2	37,339	37.5	80,483	42.2	100,287	35.9	91,243	26.3	202,237	36.5
Trade, creditors	2,277	5.8	5,494	5.5	44,198	23.1	75,091	26.9	14,709	4.2	110,000	19.3
Accounts payable	15,026	38.3	22,042	22.2					65,497	18.8		
Bank Credits	8,883	22.7	34,679	34.8	66,317	34.7	104,139	37.2	176,135	50.7	256,359	45.1
Total	39,224	100%	99,554	100%	190,998	100%	279,517	100%	374,584	100%	568,596	100%

EXHIBIT 3   Sales SANPA 1979 (in pesos millions)

Month	Original Budget	Budget 1st Revision (March)	Actual Sales	Deviation from 1st Revision
1979:				
January	11,909	11,909	8,004	(3,905)
February	15,728	15,728	13,231	(2,497)
March	21,342	21,342	24,026	2,684
April	22,577	21,942	17,602	(4,340)
May	23,664	26,531	23,452	(3,079)
June	26,278	25,301	26,678	1,377
July	28,904	32,623	20,797	(11,826)
August	29,536	35,467	30,761	(4,706)
September	31,372	42,514	23,711	(18,803)
October	30,805	48,227	69,794	21,567
November	30,669	65,747	66,031	284
December	30,953	63,438	36,396*	(27,042)
Total 1979	303,737	410,769	360,483	(50,286)

*Result of canceled sales due to negative stock figures.

EXHIBIT 4   Selected Operating Data

	1976	1977	1978	1979
Sales (pesos millions)	15,160	45,523	121,237	363,001
Net operating profit (percent of sales)	19.3%	9.9%	5.9%	0.1%
Interest (pesos millions)	825	4,762	13,250	52,786
Employees:				
Head office	427	469	462	489
Marketing	514	646	616	695
Production	2,369	2,525	2,573	2,655
Total employees	3,310	3,640	3,650	3,839

slide, reflecting a liquid situation of the local financial market. Demand for consumer goods had slowed further.

Sales were pesos 10.77 billion. SANPA debtors collections were only 60 percent of forecasts, which was said to be "due to holiday season," an explanation also used with respect to the poor sales, together with "the effects of our heavy efforts made in the last months of 1979 to achieve the budgeted volumes." Only dietetic products and chocolates exceeded budgeted sales, despite a selling price increase of 10 percent for the latter. The low debtors collections had an adverse impact on the financial situation.

In the production area, most programmes reportedly had been carried out at 87 percent to

110 percent of the planned tonnages, except for items with supply or technical problems.

The debtors and stocks report for end-January showed the following data: total accounts receivable, pesos 135.89 billion (104 days) representing an excess working capital of pesos 111.07 billion; total finished products stock, pesos 67.04 billion, with milk powders 1.5 months above the standard cover of 4.0 months ("due to advanced production"), resulting in an excess stock value of pesos 20.09 billion.

Upon receipt of this monthly report, the assistant to the zone manager immediately telephoned Mr. Gonzalez asking for clarification concerning the low level of January sales and the debtors situation. Mr. Gonzalez explained that the disappointing sales and collections were due rather to seasonal (holidays) and temporary factors than to fundamental changes in the business outlook. A letter was sent to Mr. Gonzalez on February 20, confirming the telephone conversation.

Questions

1. In a country with high inflation and unstable government actions, what should be Nestlé's policies? Consider such aspects as selling prices, accounts receivable terms, accounts payable, inventory levels, and billing in advance of shipment.

2. How can the Centre learn whether these policies have been adhered to?

3. What should Mr. Smith, the zone director, do on the basis of the information available as of the middle of February 1980?

Case 17–4
Xerox Corporation (B)

"There is no real process difference between our international and domestic transfer pricing systems. The breadth of the issues, however, is far greater for the international. Transfer pricing and currency translation are not a problem for us. I manage the process and resolve potential conflicts very quickly as we operate under clear and simple guidelines."

Raghunandan "Sach" Sachdev, *corporate controller*

Sach was explaining the process by which Xerox takes the sting and frustration out of two very volatile topics for many global corporations—multinational transfer pricing and currency trading. He further illustrated the specifics of the system.

Transfer Pricing

As Sach described the transfer pricing policy, purely domestic transfers utilized a full standard cost price method while foreign transfers used an arm's-length market price method. This was the general rule, but, the system was quite flexible, which enabled a quick response to changing market conditions. The document processing industry was extremely competitive, and Xerox management realized that they must respond to various global market pressures and competitive challenges. A manager from the Xerox Brazilian operation asserted the following: "The transfer pricing system is designed to attack the market place. We drive the products in the market place, and Xerox knows the source of the revenue is the customer."

The domestic transfer pricing was less complicated than the international situation. The controller for the U.S. customer operations explained.

We purchase copiers from one of the Webster, New York, factories, part of the Office Documents Products division. Normally, the transfer is made on a full standard cost

basis, which includes a small percentage for administration. If we need to respond to a competitive pricing threat, we are unable to renegotiate. The manufacturing unit cannot sell below cost as they are structured to, at a minimum, cover their costs. In this case, the respective unit controllers would discuss possibilities of cost savings and the volume implications if pricing erodes unit sales. The corporate controller would step in, as appropriate, to help facilitate a solution. The aggressive business targets and the fierce competition made for some very heated and hard meetings. We were both under the same legal entity with the effects of transfer pricing balanced at consolidation. The primary concern was the influence of transfer pricing on achieving unit performance targets.

In the past, this (transfer pricing) would have been a big problem. We were totally focused on our individual business units given the tight unit performance targets. Today, we know the value of market share and the need to respond to competition. We learned that the performance comes from sales to external customers. Besides with TQL [total quality leadership] the factory has become very sensitive to their costs.

Transfer pricing between foreign units was a little more complicated due to a greater breadth of issues. There were different legal entities, two different sets of regulatory authorities (for tax, duty, etc.), and two different currencies. In this situation Xerox used a market based transfer price (market price less a discount). This method conformed to the U.S. tax laws and to the rules of most of the other taxing authorities. In addition, market price followed the OECD guidelines. The transfer price denomination (currency) varied based on the product value added (explained in the next section). The market based transfer price provided a margin to the selling unit as well as sufficient margin to the buying unit. This enabled the buying unit to be competitive in their local market.

The buying unit was responsible for duty and regulatory compliance. The geographic sales offices cooperated with the factories and kept them well apprised of their country regulations and routinely communicated changing requirements

Prepared by Lawrence P. Carr, Associate Professor, Babson College. Copyright by Lawrence P. Carr.

to the factories. They also ensured that production facilities were aware of the competitive pressures. Xerox sales units constantly encouraged quality and price improvements (part of the TQL program).

The new Xerox culture enhanced the awareness of the customer. The selling unit knew that they must respond to their internal customer (the buying unit). At the same time, they understood that the source of successful business was the satisfaction of the outside customer.

The financial impact of transfer pricing on performance plans concerned managers from both the buying and selling units. External factors such as a change in duty rates or country regulations (i.e., quotas, etc.) may have an adverse effect on performance. The pressure eased somewhat with the recent incorporation of more operating statistics to evaluate unit and manager performance. Sach points out:

> We know what is going on and do not just manage by the financial numbers. Our regular controller conversations permit an open discussion of potential problems and offer a vehicle to explore alternative solutions. This is where the financial manager can help the line manager understand the full range of the business implications of their decisions. We also avoid surprises at corporate.

The arm's-length market price preserved the independence of the legal entity, but, at the same time, required managers to more closely consider the economic variables. A unit manager from South America said the following:

> The financial measures are fair. Sometimes, however, there are events beyond our control, like a devaluation or unanticipated local inflation or an uncertain regulatory environment, which can alter our performance. I feel it is unfair that management sometimes does not take this into account. We need financial measures which have a longer time horizon [greater than one year].

As with the domestic transfer pricing, multinational transfer prices were negotiated if there were changes in the current competitive situation or changes in the economic variables such as currency, tax, duty, and country regulations. In this case, they employed a market based transfer price as a reference point for negotiation. The corporate controller resolved conflicts or impasses between entities.

Currency exposure can create major swings in the economics of transfer pricing and was critical in the consolidation of foreign operations. Sach explains the Xerox policy as follows:

> All units are responsible for their transaction currency exposure. There are no exceptions. The managers must manage. For product sourced through our manufacturing units the rule is simple. If manufacturing adds more than one-third of the product value, then the manufacturing unit is responsible for managing the currency hedging. Note that the transfer price uses the buyer's currency to calculate the price. If the manufacturing units add less than one-third of the product value, then the buying unit is responsible for the currency hedging. Note that the transfer price uses the seller's currency to calculate the price. In this case, the value passes through the marketing organization for recovery. In essence, we determine the denomination of the transfer price by the value added to the product based on the cost and the final selling price.

Xerox management used both local and U.S. currencies for foreign unit performance measures. The foreign manager, however, realized that the consolidation currency was U.S. dollars, and dollar reporting was the basis of the corporate plan. Foreign unit managers made their commitment in U.S. dollars, and corporate managers expected them to meet that commitment. The pressure to manage local currency changes was clearly on the foreign manager.

Sach explains the translation exposure currency policy as follows:

> Normal changes in the foreign currency, from 3 to 5 percent, are the responsibility of the foreign unit management to cover. We consolidate and report the company's results in dollars, and we expect the managers to deliver their plan. It is up to the local managers to oversee their translation currency exposure. If the currency swings vis-à-vis the dollar is greater than 3 to 5 percent, then the translation exposure becomes a corporate issue. We will peg off the standard (PDR) and coordinate and share the managing of the exposure with the foreign operation. We regularly discuss the currency topic during our weekly informal controller talks.

Sach indicated that if the currency goes in a favorable direction for the foreign operation then corporate discounts the boosted financial results for unit performance measurement purposes. In

Exhibit 1

Venray plant reporting organization

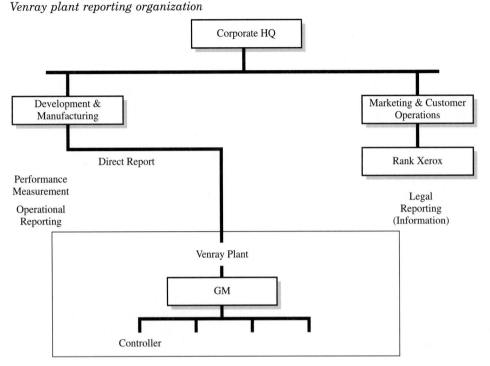

this instance, corporate management may authorize the foreign operation to invest the currency-driven portion of their profits back into their unit, depending on the attractiveness of the proposals.

Sach said, "We regularly discuss the currency and transfer pricing topic at the FEC and on the telephone between controllers. We trust each other and are comfortable discussing the topics. This is how we prevent year-end surprises."

A subunit manager said the following:

> In the Americas Customer Operations [Central and South America], the U.S. dollar is our functional currency.[1] We make all our trades in dollars and our accounting based performance measures are in dollars. We work off a PDR (plan development rate), which is our reference point for all translations. We update the transfer prices on a quarterly basis.

---

[1]The local currency is the functional currency for all other parts of the world.

An example of the complexity of the transfer pricing, currency translation, and performance measurement system is the following.

The Venray, Netherlands, facility regularly sold or transferred copiers to the U.S. marketing unit. The Venray plant was legally part of Rank Xerox, but for performance purposes the general manager reports to Manufacturing Support (MS), a central corporate function. Corporate management explained the following:

> The Venray site director currently reports to MS through the Rank Xerox Manufacturing Operations organization. We are currently working on recommendations on how to align and transition focus factories to report to the business teams/business divisions. The Venray product array does, however, support more than one business division. There will be areas that are not included in the focus factories and that will remain reporting to MS.

Note that within the Venray site (Exhibit 1) there were functions that reported to the Venray site Director as well as to organizations outside Manufacturing Support.

Performance measures were driven by the Manufacturing Support organization with Supplies and the Materials and Supply functions being driven by the respective organizations managing them as indicated on the organization chart. This responsibility will transition to the divisions in line with the reporting structure referenced above with ongoing support from MS, Supplies, Integrated Supply Chain, and Customer Operations organization. In essence, central support organizations provided services for the business divisions and sustained the performance measures as appropriate.

Questions

1. You are the Western regional sales controller, and the sales manager has asked for your help. A major California bank with over 200 branches has chosen to cancel the Xerox copier contract (annual lease revenue of over $1 million per year) due to pricing. The competition with a West coast assembly plant has made an offer 27 percent less than yours. You can make up 5–7 percent of the difference without materially affecting your budget. If the customer is to be preserved, you need pricing help from the factory. You call the U.S. Customer Operations controller because the loss of sales revenue will significantly affect your budget. What are the options for Xerox and how will Sach resolve the issue?

2. The Venray plant transfers copiers to the U.S. Customer Operations for a FOB EC port price. If the U.S. customer price is 100 percent and the Venray transfer price is 60 percent, answer the following:
   a. What currency is used to value the trade?
   b. Who is responsible for hedging?
   c. As the Venray controller, what is your currency exposure?
   d. How does this influence your performance measures?
   e. Does this system seem fair to you? What, if anything would you change?

CHAPTER 18

MANAGEMENT CONTROL OF PROJECTS

In earlier chapters we focused on management control in an organization that tends to carry on similar activities, day after day. Chapter 18 describes the somewhat different process that is used in the management control of projects. After a discussion of the nature of projects and how the management control process for projects differs from the control of ongoing operations, the main sections deal with (*a*) the environment in which project control takes place, and (*b*) the steps in the project control process—namely, project planning, project execution, and project evaluation.

Nature of Projects

A project is a set of activities intended to accomplish a specified end result of sufficient importance to be of interest to management. Projects include construction projects, the production of a sizable unique product (such as a turbine), rearranging a plant, developing and marketing a new product, consulting engagements, audits, acquisitions and divestitures, litigation, financial restructuring, research and development work, development and installation of information systems, and many others.

A project begins when management has approved the general nature of what is to be done and has authorized the approximate amount of resources that are to be spent in doing this work (or, in some cases, the amount to be spent in the first phase of the work). The project ends when its objective has been accomplished, or when it has been canceled. The construction of a building and the renovation of a building are projects; the routine maintenance of a building is not. The production of a television "special" is a project; the production of a nightly television news broadcast is an ongoing operation.

The completion of a project may lead to an ongoing operation, as in the case of a successful development project. The transition from the project

818

organization to the operating organization involves complex management control issues, but these are not discussed here.[1]

Projects vary greatly. At one extreme, a project may involve one or a few persons working for a few days or weeks, performing work similar to that done many times previously—for example, an annual financial audit that is conducted by a public accounting firm. At the other extreme, a project may involve thousands of people working for several years, performing work unlike that ever done before, as was the case with the project to land the first men on the moon. The discussion here will not describe either of these extremes. Rather, it focuses on projects that have a formal control organization and that consume enough resources so that a formal management control system is necessary. Extremely complex first-of-a-kind projects have more complicated control problems than those described here, although the general nature of these problems and of the appropriate management control system are similar.

Contrast with Ongoing Operations

This section describes characteristics of projects that make the management control of projects different from the management control of ongoing activities.

Single Objective. A project usually has a single objective; ongoing operations have multiple objectives. In addition to supervising day-to-day work, the manager of a responsibility center in an ongoing organization must both supervise today's work and also make decisions that affect future operations. Equipment that affects future operations is ordered; marketing campaigns are planned; new procedures are developed and implemented; and employees are trained for new positions. Although the project manager also makes decisions that affect the future, the time horizon is the end of the project. Project performance can be judged in terms of the desired end product; operating performance should be judged in terms of all the results that the manager achieves, some of which will not be known until a year or more later.

Organization Structure. In many cases, the project organization is superimposed on an ongoing operating organization, and its management control system is superimposed on the management control system of that organization. These problems do not exist in an ongoing organization. Satisfactory relationships must be established between the project organization and the ongoing operating organization. Similarly, the management control system for the project must mesh at certain points with the control system of the ongoing organization.

Focus on the Project. Project control focuses on the project, whose objective is to produce a satisfactory product, within a specified time period, and at an

---

[1]For a discussion of this problem, see Paul R. Lawrence and Jay W. Lorsch, *Organization and Environment* (Homewood, Ill.: Richard D. Irwin, 1969).

optimum cost. In contrast, control in ongoing organizations focuses on the activities of a specified time period, such as a month, and on all the products worked on in that period. The primary focus of the management control of operating activities tends to be on cost, with quality and schedule being treated on an exception basis—that is, the formal system emphasizes cost performance, but special reports are prepared if quality and schedule are judged to be less than satisfactory.

Need for Trade-offs.   Projects usually involve trade-offs between scope, schedule, and cost. Costs can be reduced by decreasing the scope of the project. The schedule can be shortened by incurring overtime costs. Similar trade-offs occur in ongoing organizations, but they are not typical of the day-to-day activities in such organizations.

Less-Reliable Standards.   Performance standards tend to be less reliable for projects than for ongoing organizations. Although the specifications of one project and the method of producing it may be similar to those for other projects, the project design literally is used only once.

Nevertheless, standards for repetitive project activities can be developed from past experience or from engineering analyses of the optimum time and costs. To the extent that the activities on a given project are similar to those on other projects, the experience on these projects can be used as a basis for estimating time and costs. If the project is the construction of a house, good historical information exists on the unit costs of building similar houses. (However, changes in materials, in the technology of house building, or in building codes may make this information unreliable as a guide to the cost of building the next house, and site-specific problems may also affect the actual cost of a given house.) Many projects are sufficiently different from prior projects, so that historical information is not of much help, and allowances must be made for their unique characteristics. The cost estimate for constructing a house usually contains a contingency allowance, whereas such an allowance is not customary in calculating the standard cost of producing a product in the factory.

Frequent Changes in Plans.   Plans for projects tend to be changed frequently and drastically. Unforeseen environmental conditions on a construction project or unexpected facts uncovered during a consulting engagement may lead to changes in plans. The results of one phase of the investigation in a research and development project may completely alter the work originally planned for subsequent phases.

Different Rhythm.   The rhythm of a project differs from that of ongoing operations. Most projects start small, build up to a peak activity, and then taper off as completion nears and only cleanup remains to be done. Ongoing activities tend to operate at the same activity level for a considerable time and then to change, in either direction, from that level to another.

Greater Environmental Influence.   Projects tend to be influenced more by the external environment than is the case with operations in a factory. The walls and roof of a factory protect production activities from the environment. Construction projects occur outdoors and are subject to climatic and other geographical conditions. If the project involves excavating, conditions beneath the earth's surface may cause unexpected problems, even for such a simple project as building a house. Consulting projects take place on the client's premises and involve "finding one's way around," both geographically and organizationally.

Resources for many projects are brought to the project site. Workers on a construction project go to the project, and a construction project has other logistical problems that do not ordinarily occur with production operations. Workers on a production line stay in one room.

Exceptions.   These distinctions are not clear-cut. A job shop, such as a printing company, produces dissimilar end products; however, the focus of management control in such an organization is on the totality of its activities during a month or other specified period, not on individual jobs. In some projects, team members are hired for the job; they are not associated with functional departments in an ongoing organization. Projects in a research laboratory are conducted on the premises rather than in outside facilities.

The Control Environment

Project Organization Structure

A project organization is a temporary organization. A team is assembled for conducting the project, and the team is disbanded when the project has been completed. Team members may be employees of the sponsoring organization, they may be hired for the purpose, or some or all of them may be engaged under a contract with an outside organization.

If the project is conducted entirely or partly by an outside contractor, the project sponsor should quickly establish satisfactory working arrangements with the contractor's personnel. These relationships are influenced by the terms of the contract, as will be discussed later. If the project is conducted by the sponsoring organization, some of the work may be assigned to support units within the organization, and similar relationships should be established with them. For example, a central drafting unit in an architectural firm may do drafting for all projects, and management control problems of such arrangements are similar to those involved in contracting with an outside drafting organization.

Matrix Organizations.   If members of the project team are employees of the sponsoring organization, they have two "bosses": the project manager and the manager of the functional department to which they are permanently assigned. Such an arrangement is called a *matrix organization*. In overhauling a ship, craftspeople (e.g., electricians, sheet metal workers, pipe fitters) are drawn from various functional departments in the shipyard, and they work on the project when their skills are needed. However, their basic loyalty is to their functional department. Whether they appear at the work site at the scheduled time depends in part on decisions made by the manager of their functional department, who considers the relative priorities of all projects requiring the resources he or she controls. The project manager, therefore, has less authority over personnel than the manager of a production department, whose employees have an undivided loyalty to that department.

Project managers want full attention given to their projects, while functional responsibility center managers must take into account all the projects on which the employees of that center work. This conflict of interest is inevitable; it creates tension. As Vancil writes, there is "an atmosphere of constructive conflict."[2]

Evolution of Organization Structure.   Different types of management personnel and management methods may be appropriate at different stages of the project. In the planning phase of a construction project, architects, engineers, schedulers, and cost analysts predominate. In the execution of the project, the managers are production managers. In the final stages, the work tapers off, and the principal task may be to obtain the sponsor's acceptance, with marketing skills being a principal requirement (especially in consulting projects).

Contractual Relationships

If the project is conducted by an outside contractor, an additional level of project control is created. In addition to the control exercised by the contractor who does the work, the sponsoring organization has its own control responsibilities. The contractor may bring its own control system to the project, and this system may need to be adapted to provide information that the sponsor needs. (This does not imply that there are duplicate systems; the sponsor's system should use data from the project system.)

The form of the contractual arrangement has an important impact on management control. Contracts are of two general types: fixed price and cost reimbursement, with many variations within each type.

Fixed-Price Contracts.   In a fixed-price contract, the contractor agrees to complete the specified work by a specified date at a specified price. Usually, there are penalties if the work is not completed to specifications or if the scheduled date is not met. It would appear, therefore, that the contractor assumes all the risks and consequently has all the responsibility for management control; however, this is by no means the case. If the sponsor decides to change the scope of the project, or if the contractor encounters conditions not contemplated by

---

[2]Richard F. Vancil, "What Kind of Management Control Do You Need?" *Harvard Business Review*, March–April 1973, p. 75.

the contractual agreement, a *change order* is issued. The parties must agree on the scope, schedule, and cost implications of each change order. To the extent that change orders involve increased costs, these costs are borne by the sponsor. The construction of a conventional house may involve a dozen or so change orders; on some complex projects, there are thousands. In these circumstances, the final price of the work is actually not fixed in advance.

In a fixed-price contract, the sponsor is responsible for auditing the quality and quantity of the work to ensure that it is done as specified. This may be as comprehensive a task as auditing the cost of work under a cost-reimbursement contract.

Cost-Reimbursement Contracts.   In a cost-reimbursement contract, the sponsor agrees to pay reasonable costs plus a profit (often with a "not-to-exceed" upper limit). In such a contract, the sponsor has considerable responsibility for the control of costs and, therefore, needs a management control system and associated control personnel that are comparable to the system and personnel used by the contractor with a fixed-price contract. A cost-reimbursement contract is appropriate when the scope, schedule, and cost of the project cannot be estimated reliably in advance.

Contrasts in Contract Types.   The price for a fixed-price contract is bid by, or proposed by, the contractor. In arriving at this price, a competent contractor includes an allowance for contingencies, and the size of this allowance varies with the degree of uncertainty. Thus, for a project with considerable uncertainty and a correspondingly large contingency allowance, the sponsor may end up paying more under a fixed-price contract than under a cost-reimbursement contract in which there is no such contingency allowance. This extra payment is the contractor's reward for the assumption of additional risk.

Fixed-price contracts are appropriate when the scope of the project can be closely specified in advance and when uncertainties are low. In these circumstances, the contractor cannot significantly increase the price by negotiating change orders and, therefore, is motivated to control costs. If the contractor signs a contract that does not include adequate provisions for adjustments caused by changes in scope or by uncontrollable uncertainties, he will resist the sponsor's requests to make desirable changes, and, in the extreme case, he may be unwilling to complete the project. If the contractor walks away from the project, no one gains: the sponsor doesn't get the product, the contractor doesn't get paid, and both parties may incur legal fees.

In a cost-reimbursement contract, the profit component, or fee, usually should be a fixed monetary amount. If it is a percentage of costs, the contractor is motivated to make the costs high and thereby increase his profit. However, the fixed fee normally is adjusted if the scope or schedule of the project is significantly changed.

Variations.   Within these two general types of contracts are many variations. In an *incentive contract*, completion dates or cost targets, or both, are defined in advance, and the contractor is rewarded for completing the project earlier than the target date or for incurring less than the target cost. This reward is in the form of a completion bonus that is set at an amount per unit of time saved or a cost bonus that is set as a percentage of the costs saved, or both. Such a contract would appear to overcome the inherent weakness of a cost-reimbursement contract, which has no such rewards. However, if the targets are unrealistic, the incentive is ineffective. Thus, an incentive contract is a middle ground; it is appropriate when moderately reliable estimates of completion and cost can be made.

Different contract types may be used for different activities on the project. For example, direct costs may be reimbursed under a cost-reimbursement contract because of the high degree of uncertainty, while the contractor's overhead costs may be covered by a fixed-price contract, either as an amount for the total project or for each month. A fixed-price contract for overhead motivates the contractor to control these costs; avoids the necessity of checking on the reasonableness of individual salary rates, fringe benefits, bonuses, and other amenities; reduces the contractor's tendency to load the overhead payroll with less qualified personnel; and encourages the contractor to complete the work as soon as possible so supervisory personnel will be freed for other projects. However, such a contract may also motivate the contractor to skimp on supervisory personnel, on a good control system, or on other resources that help get the project completed in the most efficient manner.

If unit costs can be estimated reasonably well, but the quantity of work is uncertain, the contract may be for a fixed price per unit applied to the actual number of units provided—for example, in a catering activity, reimbursement is often a stated amount per meal served (plus, perhaps, a fixed monthly amount for overhead).

Information Structure

Work Packages.   In a project control system, information is structured by elements of the project. The smallest element is called a *work package*, and the way in which these work packages are aggregated is called the *work breakdown structure*.

A work package is a measurable increment of work, usually of fairly short duration (a month or so). It should have an unambiguous, identifiable completion point; which is called a *milestone*. Each work package should be the responsibility of a single manager.

If the project has similar work packages (e.g., a separate work package for the electrical work on each floor of an office building), each should be defined in the same way, so that cost and schedule information can be compared with similar work packages. Similarly, if an industry has developed cost or time standards for the performance of certain types of work packages (as is the case in many branches of the construction industry), or if the project organization has developed such standards on the basis of prior work, definitions used in these standards should be followed.

Indirect Cost Accounts.   In addition to work packages for direct project work, cost accounts are established for administrative and support activities. Unlike the work packages, these activities have no defined output. Their estimated costs usually are stated as per unit of time, such as a month, just as the overhead costs of ongoing responsibility centers are stated.

The chart of accounts, the rules for charging costs to projects, and the approval authorities and their specific signing powers also are developed in advance. Which cost items will be charged directly to work packages? What will be the lowest level of monetary cost aggregation? Should cost commitments be recorded, in addition to actual costs incurred? (For many types of projects, this is highly desirable.) How, if at all, will overhead costs and equipment usage be allocated to work packages?

If during the project it turns out that the work breakdown structure or the accounting system is not useful, it must be revised. This may require recasting much information, both information already collected and information describing future plans. Revising the information structure in midstream is a difficult, time-consuming, frustrating task. To avoid this work, the project planners should give considerable attention, before the project starts, to designing and installing a sound management control system.

Project Planning

In the planning phase, the project planning team takes as a starting point the rough estimates that were used as the basis for the decision to undertake the project. It refines these estimates into detailed specifications for the product, detailed schedules, and a cost budget. It also develops a management control system and underlying task control systems (or adapts these from systems used previously), and an organization chart. The boxes on this organization chart gradually are filled with the names of personnel who are to manage the work.

On a project of even moderate complexity, there is a *plan for planning*, that is, a description of each planning task, who is responsible for it, when it should be completed, and the interrelationships among tasks. The planning process is itself a subproject within the overall project. There is also a control system to insure that the planning activities are properly carried out.

Nature of the Project Plan

The final plan consists of three related parts: scope, schedule, and cost.

The **scope** part states the specifications of each work package and the name of the person or organization unit responsible. If the project is one in which specifications are nebulous, as is the case with many consulting and research and development projects, this statement is necessarily brief and general.

The **schedule** part states the estimated time required to complete each work package and the interrelationships among work packages (i.e., which

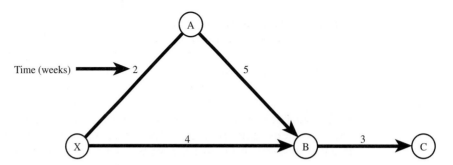

work package(s) must be completed before another can be started). The set of
these relationships is called a *network*. Networks are described in the next
section.

   Costs are stated in the project budget, usually called the *control budget*.
Unless work packages are quite large, monetary costs are shown only for aggre-
gates of several work packages. Resources to be used for individual work packages are stated as nonmonetary amounts, such as person-days or cubic yards of
concrete.

Network Analysis

Several tools are available for constructing the time schedule for the project.
They go by such acronyms as PERT (program evaluation and review technique)
and CPM (critical path method). Each technique has three basic steps: (1) estimating the time required for each work package; (2) identifying the interdependencies among work packages (which work packages must be completed before
a given work package can be started); and (3) calculating the critical path.
Collectively, these are techniques for *network analysis*. A network diagram
consists of (*a*) a number of *nodes* (i.e., *milestones*), each of which is a subgoal
that must be completed to accomplish the project; and (*b*) lines joining these
nodes to one another; these lines represent *activities*. The estimated time to
carry out each activity is shown on the network diagram. An activity connecting two events, say A and B, indicates that the activity leading to B cannot be
started until event A has happened. These activities are work packages. Thus,
a network diagram shows the chronological sequence in which events must be
completed in order to complete the whole project.

Critical Path and Slack.   Computer programs are available for analyzing
project networks. They identify the *critical path*, which is the sequence of
events that has the shortest total time to complete the project. The nature of
the critical path is shown in Exhibit 18–1. To complete event B, event A must
first be completed; this requires two weeks. A–B requires an additional five
weeks. Then B–C, requiring an additional three weeks, is done to complete the
project. This is the critical path, and it is 10 weeks long. Note that, to complete

event B, activity X–B also must be undertaken, with an estimated time of four weeks. However, activity B–C cannot be started until both A–B and X–B have been completed. X–A and A–B require a total of seven weeks; and X–B, which requires only four weeks, can be performed at any time during this seven-week period. Activity X–B is said to have three weeks of *slack*.

There are several management control implications in the concepts of critical path and slack. First, in the control process, special attention must be paid to those activities that are on the critical path, and less attention needs to be paid to slack activities (although time must not be allowed to slip by that eats up the amount of slack; the activity then automatically is on the critical path). Second, in the planning process, attention should be given to possibilities for reducing the time required for critical path activities; if such possibilities exist, the overall time required for the project can be reduced. Third, it may be desirable to reduce critical path times by increasing costs, such as incurring overtime; but additional money should not be spent to reduce the time of slack activities.

Probabilistic PERT.   As PERT was originally conceived, the estimated times required for each activity in the network were arrived at on a probabilistic basis. Three estimates were made for each activity; a most likely time, an optimistic time, and a pessimistic time. The optimistic and pessimistic times were supposed to represent probabilities of approximately 0.01 and 0.99 on a normal probability distribution. It was soon discovered that this approach had serious practical difficulties. Engineers, and others who were asked to make the three estimates, found this to be a most difficult task. It turned out not to be possible, in most cases, to convey what was intended by "optimistic" and "pessimistic" in a way that was interpreted similarly by all the estimators. Although probabilistic PERT is still referred to in the literature and in formal descriptions of the PERT technique, the probabilistic part is not widely used in practice.

Estimating Costs

For practical reasons, cost estimates are often made at a level of aggregation that incorporates several work packages. Resources used on individual work packages are controlled in terms of physical quantities, rather than costs, and costing out each work package would serve no useful purpose.

Cost estimates for most projects tend to be less accurate than those for manufactured goods, because projects are less standardized, and cost information that has been accumulated for similar work is therefore not as valid a basis for comparison. Nevertheless, if a contractor has performed similar work in the past, the costs incurred on these work packages provide a starting point in estimating the costs of the new project. For some work, industry norms, or rules of thumb, have been developed that are useful in estimating costs.

Obviously, no one knows what actually will happen in the future; therefore, no one knows for sure what future costs actually will be. In estimating what costs are likely to be, two types of unknowns must be taken into account. The first are the *known unknowns*. These are estimates of the cost of activities that are known to be going to occur, such as digging the foundation for a house. The nature of the task is known; and the costs, although unknown, often can be estimated within reasonable limits on the basis of past experience. If unexpected rock or other conditions are encountered, however, these estimates may turn out to be far from the mark.

The other unknowns are the *unknown unknowns*. For these activities, the estimator does not know that they are going to occur, and obviously, therefore, has no way of estimating their cost. Work stoppages, destruction caused by storms or floods, delays in receiving materials, accidents, and failure of government inspectors to act in a timely manner, are examples. A fixed-price contract usually states that costs caused by such events are added to the fixed price.

In using cost estimates in the evaluation phase, the impossibility of estimating the cost of unknown unknowns must be recognized. Their actual costs may range from zero up to any amount whatsoever. There is no definable upper limit. If the contract does not provide that all these costs are added to the fixed price, the estimator should include a contingency allowance for them.

Preparing the Control Budget

The control budget is prepared close to the inception of the work, allowing just enough time for approval by decision makers prior to the commitment of costs. For a lengthy project, the initial control budget may be prepared in detail only for the first phase of the project, with fairly rough cost estimates for later phases. Detailed budgets for later phases are prepared just prior to the beginning of work on these phases. Delaying preparation of the control budget until just prior to the start of work ensures that the control budget incorporates current information about scope and schedule, the results of cost analyses, and current data about wage rates, material prices, and other variables. It, therefore, avoids making budget estimates that are based on obsolete information; this is a waste of effort.

The control budget is an important link between planning and the control of performance. It represents both the sponsor's expectations about what the project will cost and also the project manager's commitment to carry out the project at that cost. If, as the project proceeds, it appears there will be a significant budget overrun, the project may no longer be economically justified. In these circumstances the sponsor may reexamine the scope and the schedule, and perhaps modify them.

Other Planning Activities

During the planning phase, other activities are performed: material is ordered, permits are obtained, preliminary interviews are conducted, personnel are selected, and so on. All these activities must be controlled and integrated into the overall effort.

One set of activities involves the selection and organization of personnel. After personnel come on board, they get to know one another, they find out where they fit in the project organization, they learn what to expect and what not to expect from other parts of the organization, and they learn what is expected of them. Information learned and expectations developed during this stage are a part of the control *climate*, and they can have a profound effect on the successful completion of the project.

Project Execution

At the end of the planning process, there exists for most projects a specification of work packages, a schedule, and a budget; also, the manager who is responsible for each work package is identified. The schedule shows the estimated time for each activity, and the budget shows estimated costs of each principal part of the project. This information often is stated in a financial model. If resources to be used in detailed work packages are expressed in nonmonetary terms, such as the number of person-days required, the control budget states monetary costs only for a sizable aggregation of individual work packages. In the control process, data on actual cost, actual time, and actual accomplishment are compared with these estimates. The comparison may be made either when a designated milestone in the project is reached or at specified time intervals, such as weekly or monthly.

Basically, both the sponsor and the project manager are concerned with these questions: (1) Is the project going to be finished by the scheduled completion date? (2) Is the completed work going to meet the stated specifications? (3) Is the work going to be done within the estimated cost? If at any time during the course of the project the answer to one of these questions is "no," the sponsor and the project manager need to know why and they need to know the alternatives for corrective action.

These three questions are not considered separately from one another, for it is sometimes desirable to make trade-offs among time, specifications, and cost, using the financial model and other available information. For example, overtime might be authorized to assure completion on time, even though this would add to costs; or some of the specifications might be relaxed to reduce costs.

Nature of Reports

Managers need three somewhat different types of reports: trouble reports, progress reports, and financial reports.

Trouble reports report both on trouble that has already happened (such as a delay resulting from any of a number of possible causes) and also anticipated future trouble. Critical problems are flagged. It is essential that these reports get to the appropriate manager quickly, so corrective action can be initiated; they often are transmitted by face-to-face conversation, telephone, or facsimile. Precision is sacrificed in the interest of speed; rough numbers often are used—person-hours, rather than labor costs, or numbers of bricks, rather than material cost. If the matter reported on is significant, an oral report later is confirmed by a written document, so as to provide a record.

Progress reports compare actual schedule and costs with planned schedule and costs for the work done, and they contain similar comparisons for overhead activities not directly related to the work. Variances associated with price, schedule delays, and similar factors may be identified and measured quantitatively, using techniques for variance analysis that are similar to those used in the analysis of ongoing operations.

Financial reports are accurate reports of project costs that must be prepared as a basis for progress payments if there is a cost-reimbursement contract; and they usually are necessary as a basis for financial accounting entries for fixed-price contracts. However, these reports are less important for management control purposes than the cost information contained in progress reports. Because the financial reports must be accurate, they are carefully checked, and this process takes time. Approximate information that is available quickly is more important to project management.

Much of the information in management reports comes from detailed records collected in task control systems. These include such documents as work schedules, time sheets, inventory records, purchase orders, requisitions, and equipment records. In designing these task control systems, their use as a source of management control information is one consideration.

Quantity of Reports.   To make certain that all needs for information are satisfied, management accountants sometimes create more than the optimum number of reports. An unnecessary report, or extraneous information in a report, incurs extra costs in assembling and transmitting the information. More important, users may spend unnecessary time reading the report, or they may overlook important information that is buried in the mass of detail. In the course of the project, therefore, a review of the set of reports often is desirable, and this may lead to the elimination of some reports and the simplification of others.

This *paperwork problem* (often referred to in the literature as *information overload*) is not necessarily serious. Competent managers learn which reports, or sections of a report, are likely to be useful to them, and they focus first on these. If, but only if, possible problems are identified from this inspection, they refer to more detailed information.

Percent Complete.   Some work packages will be only partially completed at the reporting date, and the percentage of completion of each such work package must be estimated as a basis for comparing actual time with scheduled time and actual costs with budgeted costs. If accomplishment is measured in physical terms, such as cubic yards of concrete poured, the percentage of completion for a given work package can be measured easily. If no quantitative measure is available, as in the case of many R & D and consulting projects, the percentage of completion is subjective. Some organizations compare actual labor-hours with budgeted labor-hours as a basis for estimating completion; but this assumes that the actual labor effort accomplished all that was planned, which may not have been the case. Narrative reports of progress may be of some help, but these often are difficult to interpret. If the percentage of completion is not ascertainable from quantitative data, the manager relies on personal observation, meetings, and other informal sources as a basis for judging progress.

Summarizing Progress.   In addition to determining the percentage of completion of individual work packages, a summary of progress on the whole project is useful. Progress payments often are made when specified milestones are reached. Thus, the system usually contains some method of aggregating individual work packages, which provides an overall measure of accomplishment. A simple approach is to use the ratio of actual person-hours on work packages completed to date to total person-hours for the project; but this is reliable only if the project is labor-intensive. If the system includes estimated costs for each work package, a weighting based on the planned cost of each work package may be informative.

Punch List.   Close to the end of a construction project, the sponsor prepares a list of items yet to be accomplished, including defects that need to be corrected. This punch list is negotiated with the project manager. Final payment is held up until the agreed-upon work has been done. Progress payments made during the course of the project are somewhat smaller than costs plus profits to date, thus providing a cushion for this purpose.

Use of Reports

Trouble Reports.   Managers spend much time dealing with reports of trouble. The typical project has many such reports, and one of the manager's tasks is to decide which ones have the highest priority. In the limited number of hours in a day, the manager of a large project cannot possibly deal with all the situations that have caused, or that may cause, the project to proceed less than smoothly. The manager, therefore, has to decide which problems will get his or her personal attention, which will be delegated to someone else, and which will be disregarded on the assumption that operating personnel will take the necessary corrective action.

Progress Reports.   Not only do managers try to limit the number of trouble spots to which they give personal attention, they also try to avoid spending so much time solving immediate problems that no time remains for careful analysis of the progress reports. Such an analysis may reveal potential problems that are not apparent in the reports of trouble, and the manager needs to identify these problems and plan how they are to be solved. The temptation is to spend too much time on current problems and not enough time identifying problems

Exhibit 18–2

Interpretation of cost / schedule reports

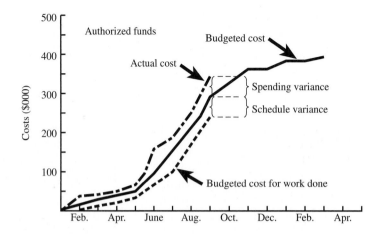

that are not yet apparent. Some managers deliberately set aside a block of time to reflect on what lies ahead.

The approach to analyzing progress reports is the familiar one of "management by exception." If progress in a particular area is satisfactory, no attention needs to be paid to the area (except to congratulate the persons responsible). Attention is focused on those areas in which progress is, or may become, unsatisfactory.

The analyses of reports that show actual time compared to the schedule, and actual cost compared to the budget, are relatively straightforward. In interpreting the time report, the usual presumption is that if a work package was completed in less than the estimated time, the responsible supervisor is to be congratulated; if more than the estimated time was spent, questions are raised. The interpretation of the cost report is somewhat different, for the possibility exists that if actual costs were less than budget, quality may have suffered. For this reason, unless there is some independent way of estimating what costs should have been, good cost performance often is interpreted to mean being on budget, neither higher nor lower.

It is important that actual costs be compared with the budgeted costs of the work done, which is not necessarily the same as the budgeted costs for the time period. The danger of misinterpretation is illustrated in Exhibit 18–2, which shows actual and budgeted costs for a project. As of the end of September, actual costs were $345,000, compared with budgeted costs of $300,000, which indicates a cost overrun of $45,000. However, the budgeted cost of the work actually completed through September was only $260,000, so the true overrun was $85,000.

Reports on indirect costs are prepared separately. These reports measure costs in a different dimension than do reports on the direct costs of project work. In the case of direct costs, actual costs are compared with budgeted costs for the work actually accomplished. In the case of indirect costs, the actual costs for a period, such as a month, are compared with the budgeted costs for that same period.

Cost to Complete.   In their progress reports, some organizations compare actual costs to date with budgeted costs for the work that has been done to date. Others report the current estimate of total costs for the entire project, compared with the budgeted cost for the entire project. The current estimate is obtained by taking the actual cost to date and adding an estimated cost to complete—that is, the additional costs required to complete the project. The latter type of report is a useful way of showing how the project is expected to come out, provided that the estimated cost to complete is properly calculated.

In most circumstances, the current estimate of total cost should be at least equal to the actual cost incurred to date plus the *original* estimates made for the remaining work. If project managers are permitted to use lower amounts, they can hide overruns by making overly optimistic future estimates. In fact, if overruns to date are caused by factors that are likely to persist in the future, such as unanticipated inflation, the current estimates of future costs probably should be higher than the amounts estimated originally.

Informal Sources of Information

Because written reports are tangible, descriptions of management control systems tend to focus on them. In practice, these reports usually are less important than information that the project manager gathers from talking with people who actually do the work, from members of his or her staff, from regularly scheduled or ad hoc meetings, from informal memoranda, and from personal inspection of the status of the work. From these sources, the manager learns of potential problems and of circumstances that may cause actual progress to deviate from the plan. This information also helps the manager to understand the significance of the formal reports because these reports may not describe important events that affected actual performance.

In many cases, a problem may be uncovered and corrective action taken before a formal report is prepared, and the formal report does no more than confirm facts that the manager has already learned from informal sources. This is an illustration of the principle that *formal reports should contain no surprises*. Nevertheless, formal reports are necessary. They document the information that the manager has learned informally, and this documentation is important if questions about the project are raised subsequently, especially if there is a controversy about the results. Also, subordinate managers who read the formal reports may discover that these are not an accurate statement of what has happened, and they take steps to correct the misunderstanding.

Revisions

If a project is complex, or if it is lengthy, there is a good chance that the plan will not be adhered to in one or more of its three aspects: scope, schedule, or cost. A common occurrence is the discovery that there is likely to be a cost overrun— that is, actual costs will exceed budgeted costs. If this happens, the sponsor might decide to accept the overrun and proceed with the project as originally planned, decide to cut back on the scope of the project with the aim of producing an end product that is within the original cost limitation, or decide to replace the project manager if the sponsor concludes that the budget overrun was unwarranted. Whatever the decision, it usually leads to a revised plan. In some cases, the sponsor may judge that the current estimate of benefits is lower than the current cost-to-complete estimate and, therefore, decide to terminate the project. (Costs that have already been incurred are sunk and, therefore, should be disregarded in making this decision.)

If the plan is revised, the following question arises: Is it better to track future progress against the revised plan or to track against the original plan? The revised plan is presumably a better indication of the performance that is currently expected, but there is a danger that a persuasive project manager can negotiate unwarranted increases in budgeted costs or that the revised plan will incorporate, and thus hide, inefficiencies that have accumulated to date. In either case, the revised plan may be a *rubber baseline*—that is, instead of providing a firm benchmark against which performance is measured, it may be stretched to cover up inefficiencies.

This possibility can be minimized by taking a hardheaded attitude toward proposed revisions. Nevertheless, there is a tendency to overlook the fact that a revised plan, by definition, does not show what was expected when the project was initiated. On the other hand, if performance continues to be monitored by comparing it with the original plan, the comparison may not be taken seriously because the original plan is known to be obsolete.

A solution to this problem is to compare actual cost with *both* the original plan and the revised plan. The first section of such a summary report shows the original budget, the revisions that have been authorized to date, and the reasons for making them. Another section shows the current cost estimate and the factors that caused the variance between the revised budget and the current estimate of costs. Exhibit 18–3 is an example of such a report.

Project Auditing

In many projects, the audit of quality must take place as the work is being done. If it is delayed, defective work on individual work packages may be hidden; they are covered up by subsequent work. (For example, the quality of plumbing work on a construction project cannot be checked after walls and ceilings have been finished.) In some projects, the audit of costs also is done as the work progresses; in others, the cost audit is not made until the project has been completed. In general, auditing as the work progresses is preferable; it may uncover potential errors that can be corrected before they become serious. However, project auditors should not take an undue amount of the time of those who are responsible for doing the work.

In recent years internal auditors have expanded their function into what is called *operational auditing*. In addition to examining costs incurred, they call

EXHIBIT 18–3   Project Cost Summary ($000s)

Original budget	$1,000
Authorized revisions to date:	
For inflation	50
For specification changes	200
For time delays	60
For cost savings	(30)
Revised budget	1,280
Current estimate to complete	1,400
Variance	120
Explanation of variance:	
Material cost increases	$ 20
Overtime	60
Spending variances	40
	120

attention to management actions that they believe are substandard. Properly done, operational auditing can be useful. However, there is the great danger that the auditors, who, after all, are not managers, will second-guess the decisions that managers made in the light of all the circumstances—as the managers understood them—at the time that decisions were made.

Project Evaluation

The evaluation of projects has two separate aspects: (1) an evaluation of performance in executing the project, and (2) an evaluation of the results obtained from the project. The former is carried out shortly after the project has been completed; the latter may not be feasible until several years later.

Evaluation of Performance

The evaluation of performance in executing the project has two aspects: (1) an evaluation of project management, and (2) an evaluation of the process of managing the project. The purpose of the former is to assist in decisions regarding project managers, including rewards, promotions, constructive criticism, or reassignment. The purpose of the latter is to discover better ways of conducting future projects. In many cases these evaluations are informal. If the results of the project were unsatisfactory and if the project was important, a formal evaluation is worthwhile. Also, formal evaluation of a highly successful project may identify techniques that will improve performance on future projects.

Because work on a project tends to be less standardized and less susceptible to measurement than work in a factory, evaluation of a project is more subjective than evaluation of production activities. It resembles the evaluation of marketing activities, in that the effect of external factors on performance must be taken into account. A judgment about whether actual accomplishment was satisfactory under the actual circumstances encountered is highly subjective.

Cost Overruns.   When actual costs exceed budgeted costs, there is said to be a cost overrun. To some, this implies that actual costs were too high. An equally plausible conclusion, however, is that the budgeted costs were too low. If the higher costs resulted from changes in the scope of the project or from noncontrollable factors, the explanation is that there was an underestimate of costs, rather than excessive actual costs. Interpretation of the cost reports is complicated by the need to analyze both the budget and the actual costs.

A common error in analyzing costs is to assume that the budget represents what the costs should have been. It does not. At best, the budget estimates what the cost should have been *based on the information that was available at the time it was prepared*. This information rarely is an accurate reflection of conditions that will be encountered on the project; to the extent that it is inaccurate, the budget does not reflect what the costs should be. Moreover, budget numbers are estimates made by human beings, and they are based, in part, on judgments and assumptions. Although reasonable people can differ in their judgments and assumptions, only one set of conclusions is incorporated in the budget.

Hindsight.   In looking back at how well the work on the project was managed, the natural temptation is to rely on information that was not available at the time. With hindsight, one can usually discover instances in which the "right" decision was not made. However, the decision made at the time may have been entirely reasonable. The manager may not have had all the information at that time, the manager may not have addressed a particular problem because other problems had a higher priority, or the manager may have based the decision on personality considerations, trade-offs, or other factors not recorded in written reports.

Nevertheless, some positive indications of poor management may be identified. Diversion of funds or other assets to the personal use of the project manager is one obvious example. If there were major specification changes or cost overruns, these changes should have been authorized, and cash flows should have been recalculated to determine whether the return on the project was still acceptable. Another example of poor management is a manager's failure to tighten a control system that permits others to steal, but this is more difficult to judge because overly tight controls may impede progress on the project. Evidence that the manager regards cost control as much less important than an excellent product that was completed on schedule is another indication of poor management, but it is not conclusive. The sponsor may overlook budget overruns if the product is outstanding and financially successful, as often happens for motion picture projects and investment banking deals.

The evaluation of the process may indicate that reviews conducted during the project were inadequate, or that timely action was not taken on the basis of these reviews. For example, the review may indicate that, on the basis of information available at the time, the project should have been redirected or even discontinued, but this was not done. This may suggest that more frequent or more thorough analyses of progress should have been made; consequently, requirements for such reviews on future projects should be modified.

The evaluation also may lead to changes in rules or procedures. It may identify some rules that impeded efficient conduct of the project. Conversely, it may uncover inadequate controls. As part of the evaluation, suggestions for improving the process should be solicited from project personnel.

Evaluation of Results

The success of a project cannot be evaluated until enough time has elapsed to permit measurement of its actual benefits and costs. This may take years. Unless the impact can be specifically measured, such an evaluation may not be worthwhile. To take extreme examples, the benefits of the introduction of a new product line usually can be measured because the revenues and expenses associated with that line will be known, whereas the benefits of installing a labor-saving machine will not be identifiable if the resulting costs are buried in a variety of product costs and not separately traced to the new machine. Furthermore, there is no point in attempting to evaluate a project unless some action can be taken based on this analysis.

For many projects, evaluation of results is complicated by the fact that the expected benefits were not stated in objective, measurable terms, and the actual benefits also were not measurable. In these cases, a quantitative benefit/cost analysis is not feasible, and reliance must be placed on judgments by knowledgeable people about the project's accomplishments. This is the situation in the majority of projects undertaken by governments and nonprofit organizations, many research and development projects undertaken by staff units, and projects whose objective is to improve safety or eliminate environmental deficiencies.

Part of the evaluation should be a comparison of the actual results with the results that were anticipated when the project was approved. The anticipated results were based on certain assumptions (e.g., for a new product: size of the market, market share, competitor's reactions, inflation), and these assumptions should have been documented during the process of approving the project. Unless the need for such documentation was recognized, the record is likely to be incomplete or vague. The evaluator should foresee the possible future need for this documentation and ensure that the necessary information is collected and preserved. Because of these limitations, the results of relatively few projects are subjected to a formal evaluation (often called a *post-completion audit*).[3] The

---

[3] In a survey using responses from 282 large industrial companies, only 25 percent reported use of what the survey authors described as "adequate post audit procedures," and these were used only for selected projects, usually projects with long-run implications and major resource commitments. (Lawrence A. Gordon and Mary D. Myers, "Postauditing Capital Projects," *Management Accounting*, January 1991, pp. 39–42.)

points made in the preceding paragraph suggest criteria for selecting those that are to be evaluated:

1. The project should be important enough to warrant the considerable expenditure of effort that is involved in a formal evaluation.

2. The results usually should be quantifiable. Specifically, if the project was intended to produce a specified amount of additional profit, the actual profit attributable to the project should be measurable.

3. The effects of unanticipated variables should be known, at least approximately, and they should not swamp the effect of changes in the assumptions on which the project was approved. If the results of a new product introduction were unsatisfactory because the market for the product evaporated, not much worthwhile information can be learned from an evaluation.

4. Results of the evaluation should have a good chance of leading to action. In particular, the analysis may lead to better ways of proposing and deciding on future projects.

Occasionally, projects that do not meet these criteria should be selected for analysis. Deficiencies in the system for controlling relatively unimportant projects may be overlooked if the appraisal is limited only to major projects.

Summary

The most important difference between the management control of ongoing operations and the management control of projects is that the ongoing operations continue indefinitely, whereas a project ends. Exhibit 18–4 illustrates this point. The elements in the management control of operations recur: one leads to the next in a prescribed way and at a prescribed time. Although some operating activities change from one month to the next, many of them continue relatively unchanged, month after month, or even year after year. By contrast, a project starts, moves forward from one milestone to the next, and then stops. During its life, plans are made, they are executed, and the results are evaluated. The evaluations are made at regular intervals, and these may lead to revision of the plan.

Suggested Additional Readings

Barlog, Ramon J., and Dana K. Ginn. "Reduce Project-Cycle Time." *Chemical Engineering* 101, 7, July 1994, pp. 133–35.

Dean, Peter N. "Accounting for Development Projects: The Issues." *Association of Government Accountants Journal*, Summer Quarter 1990, pp. 62–72. Contains an excellent bibliography of international development projects.

Lock, Dennis (ed.). *Project Management Handbook.* Aldershot, Hanks, England: Gower Technical Press, 1987.

EXHIBIT 18–4

Phases of management control

A. In an Operating Organization

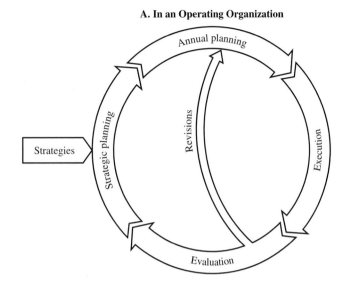

B. In a Project

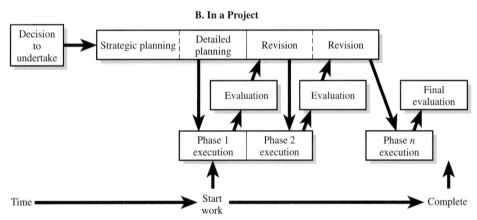

Maciariello, Joseph A. *Project Management Control Systems*. New York: Ronald Press, 1978.

Pillai, A. Sivathanu, and K. Srinivasa Rao. "Performance Monitoring in R & D Projects." *R & D Management* 26, 1, January 1996, pp. 57–60.

Sayles, L. R., and M. K. Chandler. *Managing Large Systems: Organizations for the Future*. New York: Harper & Row, 1971.

Sigurdsen, Arild. "Method for Verifying Project Cost Performance." *Project Management Journal* 25, 4, December 1994, pp. 26–31.

Stuckenbruck, Linn C. *The Implementation of Project Management: The Professional's Handbook*. Reading, Mass.: Addison-Wesley, 1989.

Case 18–1
Northeast Research Laboratory

On a Friday morning in late December 1973, Sam Lacy, head of the Physical Sciences Division of Northeast Research Laboratory (NRL), thought about two letters that lay on his desk. One, which he had received a few weeks before, was a progress report from Robert Kirk, recently assigned project leader of the Exco project, who reported that earlier frictions between the NRL team and the client had lessened considerably, that high-quality research was underway, and that the prospects for retaining the Exco project on a long-term basis appeared fairly good. The other letter, which had just arrived in the morning's mail, came from Gray Kenney, vice president of Exco, and stated that the company wished to terminate the Exco contract effective immediately.

Lacy was puzzled. He remembered how pleased Gray Kenney had been only a few months before when the Exco project produced its second patentable process. On the other hand, he also recalled some of the difficulties the project had encountered within NRL, which had ultimately led to the replacement of project leader Alan North to avoid losing the contract. Lacy decided to call in the participants in an effort to piece together an understanding of what had happened. Some of what he learned is described below. But the problem remained for him to decide what he should report to top management. What should he recommend to avoid the recurrence of such a situation in the future?

Company Background

Northeast Research Laboratory was a multidisciplinary research and development organization employing approximately 1,000 professionals. It was organized into two main

sectors, one for economics and business administration, and the other for the physical and natural sciences. Within the physical and natural sciences sector, the organization was essentially by branches of science. The main units were called "divisions" and the subunits were called "laboratories." A partial organization chart is shown in Exhibit 1.

Most of the company's work was done on the basis of contracts with clients. Each contract was a project. Responsibility for the project was vested in a project leader, and through him up the organizational structure in which his laboratory was located. Typically, some members of the project team were drawn from laboratories other than that in which the project leader worked; it was the ability to put together a team with a variety of technical talents that was one of the principal strengths of a multidisciplinary laboratory. Team members worked under the direction of the project leader during the period in which they were assigned to the project. An individual might be working on more than one project concurrently. The project leader also could draw on the resources of central service organizations, such as model shops, computer services, editorial, and drafting. The project was billed for the services of these units at rates intended to cover their full costs.

Inception of the Exco Project

In October 1972, Gray Kenney, vice president of Exco, had telephoned Mac Davidson of NRL to outline a research project that would examine the effect of microwaves on various ores and minerals. Davidson was associate head of the Physical Sciences Division and had known Kenney for several years. During the conversation, Kenney asserted that NRL ought to be particularly intrigued by the research aspects of the project, and Davidson

This case was prepared by Robert N. Anthony and Richard T. Johnson, Harvard Business School. Copyright by the President and Fellows of Harvard College, Harvard Business School case 175–184.

EXHIBIT 1

Organization chart (simplified)

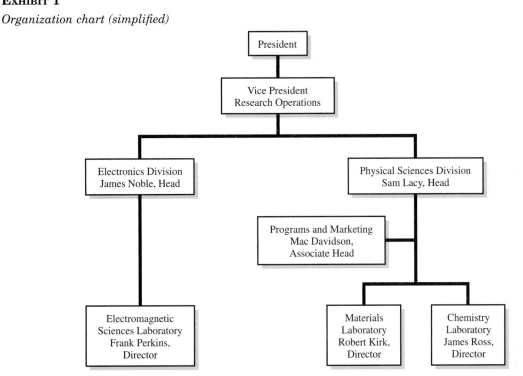

readily agreed. Davidson also was pleased because the Physical Sciences Division was under pressure to generate more revenue, and this potentially long-term project from Exco would make good use of the available workforce. In addition, top management of NRL had recently circulated several memos indicating that more emphasis should be put on commercial, rather than government, work. Davidson was, however, a little concerned that the project did not fall neatly into one laboratory or even one division, but in fact required assistance from the Electronics Division to complement work that would be done in two different physical sciences laboratories (the Chemistry Laboratory and the Materials Laboratory).

A few days later, Davidson organized a joint client–NRL conference to determine what Exco wanted and to plan the proposal. Kenney sent his assistant, Tod Denby, who was to serve as the Exco liaison officer for the project. Representing NRL were Davidson; Sam Lacy; Dr. Robert Kirk, director of the Materials Laboratory (one of the two physical sciences laboratories involved in the project); Dr. Alan North, manager of Chemical Development and Engineering (and associate director of the Chemistry Laboratory); Dr. James Noble, executive director of the Electronics Division; and a few researchers chosen by Kirk and North. Davidson also would like to have invited Dr. James Ross, director of the Chemistry Laboratory, but Ross was out of town and couldn't attend the preproposal meeting.

Denby described the project as a study of the use of microwaves for the conversion of basic ores and minerals to more valuable commercial products. The study was to consist of two parts.

Task A—An experimental program to examine the effect of microwaves on 50 ores and minerals and to select those processes appearing to have the most promise.

Task B—A basic study to obtain an understanding of how and why microwaves interact with certain minerals.

It was agreed that the project would be a joint effort of three laboratories: (1) Materials, (2) Chemistry, and (3) Electromagnetic. The first two laboratories were in the Physical Sciences Division, and the last was in the Electronics Division.

Denby proposed that the contract be open-ended, with a level of effort of around $10,000–$12,000 per month. Agreement was quickly reached on the content of the proposal. Denby emphasized to the group that an early start was essential if Exco were to remain ahead of its competition.

After the meeting Lacy, who was to have overall responsibility for the project, discussed the choice of project leader with Davidson. Davidson proposed Alan North, a 37-year-old chemist who had had experience as a project leader on several projects. North had impressed Davidson at the preproposal meeting and seemed well suited to head the interdisciplinary team. Lacy agreed. Lacy regretted that Dr. Ross (head of the laboratory in which North worked) was unable to participate in the decision of who should head the joint project. In fact, because he was out of town, Ross was neither aware of the Exco project nor of his laboratory's involvement in it.

The following day, Alan North was told of his appointment as project leader. During the next few days, he conferred with Robert Kirk, head of the other physical sciences laboratory involved in the project. Toward the end of October, Denby began to exert pressure on North to finalize the proposal, stating that the substance had been agreed upon at the preproposal conference. North thereupon drafted a five-page letter as a substitute for a formal proposal, describing the nature of the project and outlining the procedures and equipment necessary. At Denby's request, North included a paragraph that authorized members of the client's staff to visit NRL frequently and observe progress of the re-

search program. The proposal's cover sheet contained approval signatures from the laboratories and divisions involved. North signed for his own area and for laboratory director Ross. He telephoned Dr. Noble of the Electronics Division, relayed the client's sense of urgency, and Noble authorized North to sign for him. Davidson signed for the Physical Sciences Division as a whole.

At this stage, North relied principally on the advice of colleagues within his own division. As he did not know personally the individuals in the Electronics Division, they were not called upon at this point. Since North understood informally that the director of the Electromagnetic Sciences Laboratory, Dr. Perkins, was quite busy and often out of town, North did not attempt to discuss the project with Perkins.

After the proposal had been signed and mailed, Dr. Perkins was sent a copy. It listed the engineering equipment that the client wanted purchased for the project and described how it was to be used. Perkins worried that performance characteristics of the power supply (necessary for quantitative measurement) specified in the proposal were inadequate for the task. He asked North about it and North said that the client had made up his mind about the microwave equipment he wanted and how it was to be used. Denby had said he was paying for that equipment and intended to move it to Exco's laboratories after the completion of the NRL contract.

All these events had transpired rather quickly. By the time Dr. Ross, director of the Chemistry Laboratory, returned, the proposal for the Exco project had been signed and accepted. Ross went to see Lacy and said that he had dealt with Denby on a previous project and had serious misgivings about working with him. Lacy assuaged some of Ross's fears by observing that if anyone could succeed in working with Denby it would be North—a flexible man, professionally competent, who could move with the tide and get along with clients of all types.

Conduct of the Project

Thus, the project began. Periodically, when decision arose, North would seek opinions from division management. However, he was somewhat unclear about whom he should talk to. Davidson had been the person who had actually appointed him project leader. Normally, however, North worked for Ross. Although Kirk's laboratory was heavily involved in the project, Kirk was very busy with other Materials Laboratory work. Adding to his uncertainty, North periodically received telephone calls from Perkins of the Electronics Division, whom he didn't know well. Perkins expected to be heavily involved in the project.

Difficulties and delays began to plague the project. The microwave equipment specified by the client was not delivered by the manufacturer on schedule, and there were problems in filtering the power supply of the radio-frequency source. Over the objection of NRL electromagnetic sciences engineers, but at the insistence of the client, one of the chemical engineers tried to improve the power supply filter. Eventually the equipment had to be sent back to the manufacturer for modification. This required several months.

In the spring of 1973, Denby, who had made his presence felt from the outset, began to apply strong pressure. "Listen," he said to North, "top management of Exco is starting to get on my back and we need results. Besides, I'm up for a review in four months and I can't afford to let this project affect my promotion." Denby was constantly at NRL during the next few months. He was often in the labs conferring individually with members of the NRL teams. Denby also visited North's office frequently.

A number of related problems began to surface. North had agreed to do both experimental and theoretical work for this project, but Denby's constant pushing for experimental results began to tilt the emphasis. Theoretical studies began to lapse, and experimental work became the focus of the Exco project. From time to time North argued that the theoretical work should precede or at least accompany the experimental program, but Denby's insistence on concrete results led North to temporarily deemphasize the theoretical work. Symptoms of this shifting emphasis were evident. One day a senior researcher from Kirk's laboratory came to North to complain that people were being "stolen" from his team. "How can we do a balanced project if the theoretical studies are not given enough workforce?" he asked. North explained the client's position and asked the researcher to bear with this temporary realignment of the project's resources.

As the six-month milestone approached, Denby expressed increasing dissatisfaction with the project's progress. To have concrete results to report to Exco management, he directed North a number of times to change the direction of the research. On several occasions, various members of the project team had vigorous discussions with Denby about the risks of changing results without laying a careful foundation. North himself spent a good deal of time talking with Denby on this subject, but Denby seemed to discount its importance. Denby began to avoid North and to spend most of his time with the other team members. Eventually the experimental program, initially dedicated to a careful screening of some 50 materials, deteriorated to a somewhat frantic and erratic pursuit of what appeared to be "promising leads." Lacy and Noble played little or no role in this shift of emphasis.

On June 21, 1973, Denby visited North in his office and severely criticized him for proposing a process (hydrochloric acid pickling) that was economically infeasible. In defense, North asked an NRL economist to check his figures. The economist reported back that North's numbers were sound and that, in fact, a source at U.S. Steel indicated that hydrochloric acid pickling was "generally more economic than the traditional process and was increasingly being adopted." Through this and subsequent encounters, the relationship between Denby and North became increasingly strained.

Denby continued to express concern about the Exco project's payoff. In an effort to save time, he discouraged the NRL team from repeating experiments, a practice that was designed to ensure accuracy. Data received from initial experiments were frequently taken as sufficiently accurate and, after hasty analysis, were adopted for the purposes of the moment. Not surprisingly, Denby periodically discovered errors in these data. He informed NRL of them.

Denby's visits to NRL became more frequent as the summer progressed. Some days he would visit all three laboratories, talking to the researchers involved and asking them about encouraging leads. North occasionally cautioned Denby against too much optimism. Nonetheless, North continued to oblige the client by restructuring the Exco project to allow for more "production line" scheduling of experiments and for less systematic research.

In August, North discovered that vertile could be obtained from iron ore. This discovery was a significant one, and the client applied for a patent. If the reaction could be proved commercially, its potential would be measured in millions of dollars. Soon thereafter, the NRL team discovered that the operation could, in fact, be handled commercially in a rotary kiln. The client was notified and soon began planning a pilot plant that would use the rotary kiln process.

Exco's engineering department, after reviewing the plans for the pilot plant, rejected them. It was argued that the rotary process was infeasible and that a fluid bed process would have to be used instead. Denby returned to NRL and insisted on an experiment to test the fluid bed process. North warned Denby that agglomeration (a sticking together of the material) would probably take place. It did. Denby was highly upset, reported to Gray Kenney that he had not received "timely" warning of the probability of agglomeration taking place, and indicated that he had been misled about the feasibility of the rotary kiln process.[1]

---

[1]Ten months later the client was experimenting with the rotary kiln process for producing vertile from iron ore in his own laboratory.

Work continued, and two other "disclosures of invention" were turned over to the client by the end of September.

Personnel Changes

On September 30, Denby came to North's office to request that Charles Fenton be removed from the Exco project. Denby reported he had been watching Fenton in the Electromagnetic Laboratory, which he visited often, and had observed that Fenton spent relatively little time on the Exco project. North, who did not know Fenton well, agreed to look into it. But Denby insisted that Fenton be removed immediately and threatened to terminate the contract if he were allowed to remain.

North was unable to talk to Fenton before taking action because Fenton was on vacation. He did talk to Fenton as soon as he returned, and the researcher admitted that, due to the pressure of other work, he had not devoted as much time or effort to the Exco work as perhaps he should have.

Three weeks later, Denby called a meeting with Mac Davidson and Sam Lacy. It was their first meeting since the preproposal conference for the Exco project. Denby was brief and to the point.

> *Denby:* I'm here because we have to replace North. He's becoming increasingly difficult to work with and is obstructing the progress of the project.
> *Lacy:* But North is an awfully good man . . .
> *Davidson:* Look, he's come up with some good solid work thus far. What about the process of extracting vertile from iron ore he came up with. And . . .
> *Denby:* I'm sorry, but we have to have a new project leader. I don't mean to be abrupt, but it's either replace North or forget the contract.

Davidson reluctantly appointed Robert Kirk project leader and informed North of the decision. North went to see Davidson a few days

EXHIBIT 2

Weekly project status report

PROJECT/ACCOUNT STATUS REPORT	ORG 325	PROJECT 3273	SUB 000	WAO 000	WEEK ENDING DATE 12-22-73	TYPE PROJ	REV TYPE INDUS	PRICE SCA	CLIENT YD	INT/DOM DOMESTIC	NOTICES	PAGE 1

DIVISION PHYSICAL SCI | DEPARTMENT CHEMISTRY LAB | SUPERVISOR ROBERT KIRK | LEADER ROBERT KIRK | PROJECT TITLE MICROWAVES IN CONVERSION OF BASIC ORES AND MINERALS

INST EXCO | READY DATE 11-06-72 | STOP WORK DATE - - | TERM DATE 11-06-74 | BURDEN % 28.00 | OVERHEAD % 105.00 | FEE % 15.00

COST CATEGORIES	OBJECT CODE	DOLLARS PTD13WK1	DOLLARS TO DATE	LABOR HOURS ESTIMATE	LABOR HOURS TO DATE	LABOR HOURS BALANCE
SUPERVISOR	(11, 12)		560		36	
SENIOR	(13)	192	17986		1348	
PROFESSIONAL	(14)	150	16787		1678	
TECHNICAL	(15)	529	5299		1037	
CLER/SUPP	(16, 17, 18)		301		84	
OTHER	(10), (19)	72	72		12	
LABOR(S. T.)		943	41005		1644	
BURDEN		248	11481			
OVERHEAD		1227	55110			
OVERTIME PREM	(21)	160	1540			
OVS./OTH. PREM	(22-29)	242	476			
TOTAL PERSONNEL COSTS		2820	109612			
TRAVEL	(56-59)		776			
SUBCONTRACT	(36)					
MATERIAL	(41, 42)		3726			
EQUIPMENT	(43)					
COMPUTER	(37, 45)					
COMMUN	(62, 63, 70, 71)	2	507			
CONSULTANT	(74, 75)					
REPORT COST	(44, 47)					
OTHER M&S		54	99			
TOTAL M&S COST		56	5098			
COMMITMENTS			26847	ESTIMATED		BALANCE
TOTAL LESS FEE		2876	141557	250435		108878
FEE (15.00)		158	24376	37565		13189
TOTAL		3031	165933	288000		122067

LAST BILLING: DATE 11-30-73 AMOUNT 11350

ACCOUNT STATUS TO DATE: BILLED 154583 PAID 154583

TIME BALANCE % 39.4 COST BALANCE % 43.5 TIME BALANCE WKS. 41

COMMITMENT STATUS TO DATE

PO NO		OBJ	VENDOR/DESCRIPTION	TOTAL	CHARGES	BALANCE
A61289	11-21-73	41	MINNESOTA MINING	111	61	50
A61313	11-23-73	41	ALDRICH CHEMICAL	348		348
A95209	11-28-73	43	TENNECO CHEMICAL CO	5		5
A95093	11-15-73	41	UNION CARBIDE CORP	23194		23194
B95104	11-19-73	37	SCIENTIFIC PRODUCTS	600		600
B95232	11-25-73	41	VAN WATERS & ROGERS	2500		2500
O18046	12-15-73	57	ROGER MD	300	150	150
					T	26847

TRANSACTIONS RECORDED 12-15-73 - 12-22-73

LABOR

ORG	ID	W/E DATE	T/S NO	OBJ	NAME	HOURS WEEK	HOURS TO DATE
322	02345	12-22-73	363073	13	KIRK	6.0	150
322	02345	12-22-73	363073	22	KIRK	6.0	
322	03212	12-22-73	363082	13	DENSMORE	8.0	25
322	03260	12-22-73	236544	14	COOK	15.0	30
325	12110	12-08-73	C30093	15	HOWARD	15.0	82
325	12110	12-15-73	236548	15	HOWARD	36.0	
325	12110	12-22-73	376147	15	HOWARD	8.0	
325	12357	12-22-73	376149	15	SPELTZ	15.0	68
325	12369	12-22-73	376150	15	GYUIRE	15.0	17
325	12384	12-22-73	R08416	15	DILLON	40.0-	44
325	12397	12-22-73	336527	15	NAGY	31.0	31
325	12397	12-22-73	336527	21	NAGY	15.0	
652	12475	12-22-73	236548	15	KAIN	8.0	20
652	12475	12-22-73	236548	21	KAIN		

	HOURS	DOLLARS
LABOR (STRAIGHT TIME)	117.0	943
PAYROLL BURDEN		248
OVERHEAD RECOVERY		1227
OVERTIME PREMIUM LABOR	30.0	160
OTHER PREMIUM LABOR	6.0	242
TOTAL PERSONNEL COSTS		2820 S

MATERIALS & SERVICES

PO NO	REF NO	OBJ	DESRIPTION	REQUESTOR	
61289	54065	48	438 REA EXPRESS	KIRK	42
17234	87413	48	456 GED SUPPLY CO	COOK	10
	04461	71	448 P. T. & T. 326-6200	NAGY	2
			TOTAL M&S COSTS		56 S
			FEE		158
			TRANSACTIOIN TOTAL		3034 T

later. Davidson told him that, although management did not agree with the client, North had been replaced to save the contract. Later Dr. Lacy told North the same thing. Neither Lacy nor Davidson made an effort to contact Exco senior management on the matter.

Following the change of project leadership, the record became more difficult to reconstruct. It appeared that Kirk made many efforts to get the team together, but morale remained low. Denby continued to make periodic visits to NRL but found that the NRL researchers were not talking as freely with him as they had in the past. Denby became skeptical about the project's value. Weeks slipped by. No further breakthroughs emerged.

Lacy's Problem

Dr. Lacy had received weekly status reports on the project, the latest of which is shown in Exhibit 2. He had had a few informal conversations about the project, principally with North and Kirk. He had not read the reports submitted to Exco. If the project had been placed on NRL's "problem list," which comprised about 10 percent of the projects that seemed to be experiencing the most difficulty. Lacy would have received a written report on its status weekly, but the Exco project was not on that list.

With the background given above, Lacy reread Kenney's letter terminating the Exco contract. It seemed likely that Kenney, too, had not had full knowledge of what went on during the project's existence. In his letter, Kenney mentioned the "glowing reports" that reached his ears in the early stages of the work. These reports, which came to him only from Denby, were later significantly modified, and Denby apparently implied that NRL had been "leading him on." Kenney pointed to the complete lack of economic evaluation of alternative process in the experimentation. He seemed unaware of the fact that at Denby's insistence all economic analysis was supposed to be done by the client. Kenney was most dissatisfied that NRL had not complied with all the provisions of the proposal, particularly those that required full screening of all materials and the completion of the theoretical work.

Lacy wondered why Denby's changes of the proposal had not been documented by the NRL team. Why hadn't he heard more of the problems of the Exco project before? Lacy requested a technical evaluation of the project from Ronald M. Benton, director of the Process Economics Program. Dr. Benton's eight-page report concluded that the approach was technically sound, that the technical conduct of the project was good, that the patent on vertile was a significant accomplishment, and that three other developments, not mentioned in the above narrative, were also significant accomplishments. He pointed out the difficulties of the relationships with Denby. He did say that decisions on the project were not well documented, that the project leader did not convey the importance of some decisions to the client's management, and that there was inadequate coordination between Dr. North and personnel in the Electromagnetic Sciences Laboratory. He discussed each of the nine "claims" given by the client as reasons for terminating the contract made in the letter terminating the contract and found that some were "completely unfounded," others were a matter of interpretation, and still others could not be evaluated one way or the other because of a lack of documentation.

His final conclusion was that this was a high-risk project and that it should have been so identified and treated accordingly early in the project.

Lacy then asked Mac Davidson for his appraisal of the project. Davidson's reply is given in Exhibit 3.

Questions

1. What, if any, additional information did Lacy need to reach his own conclusion about the project?
2. Suggest steps that should be considered to lessen the likelihood that a similar situation would develop in the future.

EXHIBIT 3

MEMORANDUM

January 8, 1974

To: Sam Lacy

From: Mac Davidson

RE: The Exco Project—Conclusions

The decision to undertake this project was made without sufficient consideration of the fact that this was a "high-risk" project.

The proposal was technically sound and within the capabilities of the groups assigned to work on the project.

There was virtually no coordination between the working elements of Physical Sciences and Electronics in the preparation of the proposal.

The technical conduct of this project, with few exceptions, was, considering the handicaps under which the work was carried out, good and at times outstanding. The exceptions were primarily due to lack of attention to detail.

The NRL reports were not well prepared, even considering the circumstances under which they were written.

The client, acting under pressure from his own management, involved himself excessively in the details of experimental work and dictated frequent changes of direction and emphasis. The proposal opened the door to this kind of interference.

There was no documentation by NRL of the decisions made by the client which altered the character, direction, and emphasis of the work.

There was no serious attempt on the part of NRL to convey the nature or consequence of the above actions to the client.

Fewer than half of the major complaints made by the client concerning NRL's performance are valid.

The project team acquiesced too readily in the client's interference and management acquiesced too easily to the client's demands.

Management exercised insufficient supervision and gave inadequate support to the project leader in his relations with the client.

There were no "overruns" either in time or funds.

Case 18–2
Modern Aircraft Company

Modern Aircraft Company (MAC) produced and marketed a very successful six-passenger, single-engine corporate jet (Model 69 C). Market research indicated that there was a need in friendly, less-developed countries for a relatively low-cost subsonic fighter/bomber aircraft for use in small, defensive air forces. The military version of the MAC corporate jet was designated as the F-69 fighter/bomber aircraft. It used "off-shelf" technology to provide a highly reliable and easily maintainable fighter/bomber.

MAC formed an F-69 project group with Nicky St. John as the project manager. The president made it crystal clear that the F-69 is MAC's project and that there should be no delays in the scheduled first flight test. That was crucial for the follow-on production contract of 100 F-69 aircraft at $5 million each.

The F-69 engine would be an existing jet engine model currently used on MAC's fighter/bomber. However, this engine was to be modified to include an afterburner section, which was part of the specifications for the F-69 fighter/bomber. Time estimates were: modification design (six months); engineering of the afterburner section to match the modified engine (four months); fabrication of modified engine and afterburner section (five months); prototype assembly and engine test-cell run (three months).

The airframe would be the MAC Model 69 C corporate jet, with the passenger compartment modified to a bomb bay and the nose baggage compartment modified for 7.62 mm machine-gun installation. Time estimates were: design airframe modification (seven months); engineering and wind tunnel testing (three months); and prototype fabrication and assembly of airframe (six months).

Subsystems, such as the ultrahigh-frequency (UHF) radio, navigation units, autopilot, instruments, and so on would be off-the-shelf components—that is, subsystems in current use with high reliability and ease of maintenance. There would be no radar subsystem because of its complexity. The F-69 fighter/bomber would be a daytime fighter/bomber only. There would be a simple lead computing sight subsystem for gunnery and manual bombing purposes; this subsystem was also off-the-shelf hardware. Time estimates were: request for bids on subsystems (four months); selection of subsystems (two months); award of contracts (two months); delivery of subsystems (six months); and checkout and installation in prototype aircraft (three months).

Upon completion of the prototype F-69 fighter/bomber, there would be a series of powered checks, taxi tests, and the like for one month, followed immediately by the first test flight. If all tests were successful, the F-69 prototype design and the specifications would be used for the production phase.

Questions

1. Using the critical path method (CPM) technique, develop a network for the F-69 pre-production project.
2. What is the time in months for the prototype F-69 to the fully assembled?
3. What is the time in months for the first F-69 test flight?
4. What is the critical path (engine, airframe, subsystem)?
5. If there was a one-month delay in obtaining bomb bay racks for the F-69 bomb bay, should Nicky St. John authorize the use of overtime to make up for this delay?

This case was prepared by John E. Setnicky, Mobile College, Mobile, Alabama. Copyright by John E. Setnicky.

6. If there was a two-week delay in the receipt of an alignment jig for aligning the center axis of the engine with the center axis of the afterburner section, should Nicky St. John authorize the use of overtime to make up for this delay?

7. If there was a strike at one of the subsystem vendors that delayed delivery of the UHF radio by two months, should Nicky St. John authorize the formation of a second shift for the subsystem check-out and installation in the prototype aircraft activity?

Company Index

Topical Index